Anthropology

TWELFTH EDITION

Carol R. Ember
Human Relations Area Files

Melvin Ember
Human Relations Area Files

Peter N. Peregrine
Lawrence University

PEARSON

Prentice
Hall

Upper Saddle River, New Jersey 07458

Library of Congress Cataloging-in-Publication Data
Ember, Carol R.
Anthropology / Carol R. Ember, Melvin Ember, Peter N. Peregrine.—12th ed. p. cm.
ISBN 0-13-227753-0
1. Anthropology. I. Ember, Melvin. II. Peregrine, Peter N. (Peter Neal), 1963- III. Title.
GN25.E45 2007
301—dc22
2006001415

Editorial Director: Leah Jewell
AVP, Publisher: Nancy Roberts
VP, Director of Production and Manufacturing: Barbara Kittle
Director of Marketing: Brandy Dawson
Executive Marketing Manager: Marissa Feliberty
Prepress and Manufacturing Manager: Nick Sklitsis
Prepress and Manufacturing Buyer: Ben Smith
Full-Service Project Management: Jan Pushard, Pine Tree Composition, Inc.
Production Liaison: Cheryl Keenan
Editorial Assistant: Lee Peterson
Marketing Assistant: Anthony DeCosta
Creative Design Director: Leslie Osher
Interior and Cover Design: Ilze Lemesis
Digital Design Assistance: James B. Killmer
Director, Image Resource Center: Melinda Reo
Manager, Rights and Permissions: Zina Arabia
Manager, Visual Research: Beth Brenzel
Manager, Cover Visual Research & Permissions: Karen Sanatar
Cover Art: John Reader/Photo Researchers, Inc.
Image Permission Coordinator: Francis Toepfer
Photo Researcher: Sheila Norman
Supplements Editor: LeeAnn Doherty
Media Editor: Harriet Jackson

This book was set in 10/11.5 Minion by Pine Tree Composition, Inc., and was printed and bound by Quebecor World. The cover was printed by Phoenix Color Corp.

For permission to use copyrighted material, grateful acknowledgment is made to the copyright holders listed on page 632, which is considered an extension of this copyright page.

Pearson Education LTD.
Pearson Education Singapore, Pte. Ltd
Pearson Education, Canada, Ltd
Pearson Education–Japan
Pearson Education Australia PTY, Limited

Pearson Education North Asia Ltd
Pearson Educación de Mexico, S.A. de C.V
Pearson Education Malaysia, Pte. Ltd
Pearson Education, Upper Saddle River, New Jersey

10 9 8 7 6 5 4 3

ISBN: 0-13-227753-0

Brief Contents

Contents

Boxes

MIGRANTS AND IMMIGRANTS

APPLIED ANTHROPOLOGY

CURRENT RESEARCH AND ISSUES

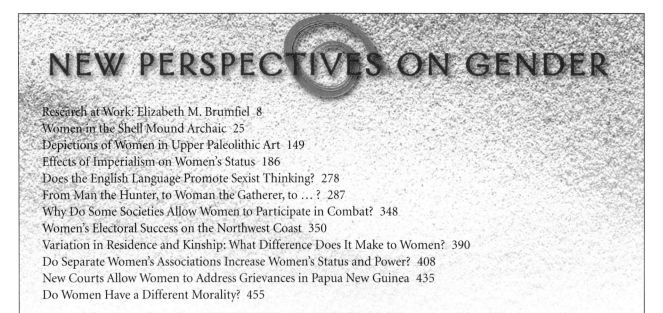

NEW PERSPECTIVES ON GENDER

Preface

The human species may be the most widespread species in the world today. Humans have been moving tremendous distances ever since *Homo Erectus* moved out of Africa. In the last 100 years or so, the number of migrants has grown enormously. For example, between the 1880s and 1920s, 20 million people left China for other parts of Asia, the Americas, and many other places around the world. And the migrations continue today. With jet planes, cell phones, and the internet, people live more and more global lives, and often move back and forth from one country to another. Anthropology is increasingly studying immigrant populations and the flow of people and ideas across the globe. To highlight the importance of these movements, we have prepared a new box feature for this edition which we call "Migrants and Immigrants." About half the chapters now contain a box about some aspect of the movement of people, ranging from prehistory to recent times. Examples include why some immigrant groups retained their "mother tongues" longer than others, the spread of foods in recent times, arranging marriages in the diaspora, and the problem of refugees.

New to this edition is a map feature with text to highlight migration, immigration, and globalization. We have included maps to illustrate human origins in Africa and the spread of earlier hominids. We also illustrate European exploration, the slave trade, and 19th century migrations, among other things about human history. (For more on the maps, see the features section on page xvi.)

In updating the book, we try to go beyond descriptions, as always. We are interested not only in *what* humans are and were like; we are also interested in *why* they got to be that way, in all their variety. When there are alternative explanations, we try to communicate the necessity to evaluate them logically as well as on the basis of the available evidence. Throughout the book, we try to communicate that no idea, including ideas put forward in textbooks, should be accepted even tentatively without supporting tests that could have gone the other way.

Organization of the Text

Part I: Introduction

Chapter 1: What Is Anthropology?

Chapter 1 introduces the student to anthropology. We discuss what we think is distinctive about anthropology in general, and about each of its subfields in particular. We outline how each of the subfields is related to other disciplines such as biology, psychology, and sociology. We direct attention to the increasing importance of applied anthropology and the importance of understanding others in today's more globalized world. There are three boxes on individual anthropologists—an archaeologist, an ethnographer, and an applied anthropologist—and their work.

Chapter 2: How We Discover the Past

This chapter gives an overview of archaeological and paleoanthropological research. We discuss the types of evidence archaeologists and paleoanthropologists use to reconstruct the past, the methods they use to collect the evidence, and how they go about analyzing and interpreting the evidence of the past. We also describe the many techniques used by archaeologists and paleoanthropologists to determine the age of archaeological materials and fossils. For this edition we have revised the section on dating techniques and added a section on ethics in archaeology. There are two boxes, one examining the evidence for unilinear trends in cultural evolution, the other considering how gender is studied by archaeologists.

Part II: Human Evolution: Biological and Cultural

Chapter 3: Genetics and Evolution

This chapter discusses evolutionary theory as it applies to all forms of life, including humans. Following an extensive review of genetics and the processes of evolution, including natural selection and what it means, we discuss how natural selection may operate on behavioral traits and how cultural evolution differs from biological evolution. We consider ethical issues posed by the possibility of genetic engineering. For this edition we have expanded our discussion of creationism and added a section on intelligent design. We also added a discussion of hybridization as a potentially important process of evolution. The first box feature examines the evidence suggesting that evolution proceeds abruptly rather than slowly and steadily. The second box feature discusses whether genetic engineering should be feared.

Chapter 4: The Living Primates

This chapter describes the living nonhuman primates and their variable adaptations as background for understanding the evolution of primates in general and humans in particular. After describing the various kinds of primate, we discuss the distinctive features of humans in comparison with the other primates. The chapter ends with a discussion of some possible explanations of how the primates differ—in body and brain size, size of social group, and female sexuality. The first box feature deals with how and why many primates are endangered and how they might be protected. The second box feature describes a primatologist and some of her work.

Chapter 5: Primate Evolution: From Early Primates To Hominoids

This chapter begins with the emergence of the early primates and ends with what we know or suspect about the Miocene apes, one of whom (known or unknown) was ancestral to bipedal hominids. We link major trends in primate evolution to broader environmental changes that may have caused natural selection to favor new traits. The chapter has been thoroughly updated for this edition, and we have added a section on the evolution of variations in primates. We also added material on the newly discovered *Pierolapithecus* middle Miocene ape. To highlight how theory is generated and revised, the first box deals with how a paleoanthropologist has reexamined his own theory of primate origins. The second box describes a giant ape that lived at the same time as the first humans, and why that ape may have become extinct.

Chapter 6: The First Hominids

This chapter discusses the evolution of bipedal locomotion—the most distinctive feature of the group that includes our genus and those of our direct ancestors, the australopithecines. We discuss the various types of australopithecines and how they might have evolved. This chapter has been extensively revised to include discussions of new species and theories of hominid evolution. It also contains a much expanded discussion of gracile australopithecines. There are two boxes. The first discusses new australopithecine finds and how they appear to fit into our current understanding of human evolution. The second describes the technique of cladistic analysis, widely used by paleoanthropologists to chart evolutionary relationships.

Chapter 7: The Origins of Culture and the Emergence of *Homo*

This chapter examines the first clear evidences of cultural behavior—stone tools—and other clues suggesting that early hominids had begun to develop culture around 2.5 million years ago. We discuss what culture is and how it may have evolved. We then discuss the hominids—the first members of our genus, *Homo*—who are most likely responsible for the early signs of cultural behavior, and then we discuss *Homo erectus,* the first hominid to leave Africa and the first to demonstrate complex cultural behavior. New to this edition is an overview of *Homo floresiensis* and discussions of the genetic evidence for early human movements out of Africa. The first box explains how archaeologists and paleoanthropologists distinguish stone tools from ordinary rocks. The second box, one of the new boxes on "Migrants and Immigrants," discusses research on when hominids first migrated out of Africa.

Part III: Modern Humans

Chapter 8: The Emergence of *Homo Sapiens*

This chapter examines the transition between *Homo erectus* and *Homo sapiens* and the emergence of modern-looking humans. In keeping with our global orientation, we discuss fossil and archaeological evidence from many areas of the world, not just Europe and the Near East. We give special consideration to the Neandertals and the question of their relationship to modern humans. While keeping a balance between the various models of modern human origins, we provide new evidence from genetics and fossils that seems to support the "Out of Africa" model over the "Multiregional" model. One box feature describes how paleoanthropologists and artists work together to reconstruct the faces of early humans. The second box examines patterns of growth and development among Neandertals as a way of evaluating how long their period of infancy was.

Chapter 9: The Upper Paleolithic World

This chapter considers the cultures of modern humans in the period before agriculture developed—roughly 40,000 to 10,000 years ago. We examine their tools, their economies, and their art—the first art made by humans. We also discuss human colonization of North and South America, and the impact of humans on the new environments they encountered. The first box considers how women are depicted in Upper Paleolithic art. The second box, one of the "Migrants and Immigrants" boxes, examines the possible routes humans may have taken in their migration to the Americas.

Chapter 10: Origins of Food Production and Settled Life

This chapter deals with the emergence of broad-spectrum collecting and settled life, and then the domestication of plants and animals, in various parts of the world. Our discussion focuses mainly on the possible causes and consequences of these developments in Mesoamerica and the Near East, the areas best known for these developments, but we also consider southeast Asia, Africa, North and South America, and Europe. For this edition we have expanded our discussion of the genetic evidence showing how and when particular plants first became domesticated. The first box discusses the domestication of dogs and cats. The second box describes how researchers are finding out about ancient diets from chemical analysis of bones and teeth.

Chapter 11: Origins of Cities and States

This chapter deals with the rise of civilizations in various parts of the world and the theories that have been offered to explain the development of state-type political systems. Our focus is on the evolution of cities and states in Mesoamerica and the Near East, the areas archaeologists know best, but we also discuss the rise of cities and states in South America, South Asia, China, and Africa. For this edition we added information on the new discoveries of early states in Peru. We discuss how states affect people living in them and their environments. We conclude with a discussion of the decline and collapse of states. There are two boxes. The first discusses the consequences of ancient imperialism for women's status. The second, one of the "Migrants and Immigrants" boxes, discusses the links between imperialism, colonialism, and the state.

Chapter 12: Human Variation and Adaptation

In this chapter we bring the discussion of human genetics and evolution into the present, dealing with physical variation in living human populations and how physical anthropologists study and explain such variation. We examine how both the physical environment and the cultural environment play important roles in human physical variation. In a section on "race" and racism we discuss why many anthropologists think the concept of "race" as applied to humans is not scientifically useful. We discuss the myths of racism and how "race" is largely a social category in humans. The first box is one of the new "Migrants and Immigrants" box features, and deals with physical differences between native and immigrant populations; the second box deals with differences in average I.Q. scores and what they mean.

Part IV: Cultural Variation

In most of the chapters that follow, we try to convey the range of cultural variation with ethnographic examples from all over the world. Wherever we can, we discuss possible explanations of why societies may be similar or different in regard to some aspect of culture. If anthropologists have no explanation as yet for the variation, we say so. But if we have some idea of the conditions that may be related to a particular kind of variation, even if we do not know yet why they are related, we discuss that too. If we are to train students to go beyond what we know now, we have to tell them what we do not know, as well as what we think we know.

Chapter 13: The Concept of Culture

This chapter introduces the concept of culture and includes an expanded discussion of the concept of society. We first try to convey a feeling for what culture is before dealing more explicitly with the concept and some assumptions about it. A section on cultural relativism puts the concept in its historical context and discusses recent thinking on the subject. We discuss the fact that individual behavior varies in all societies and how such variation may be the beginning of new cultural patterns. The first box is one of the new "Migrants and Immigrants" box features, and discusses the increasing cultural diversity within countries of the world as a result of immigration and migration. The second box, which asks whether Western countries are ethnocentric in their ideas about human rights, incorporates the debate within anthropology about cultural relativism. The third box discusses an applied anthropologist's view of why Bedouin are reluctant to settle down.

Chapter 14: Theoretical Approaches in Cultural Anthropology

New to this edition is a separate chapter on theoretical approaches in cultural anthropology. Although some theoretical approaches were contained in the previous edition in a chapter on theory and evidence in cultural anthropology, we have responded to reviewers' requests for more on theory. The various theoretical orientations or approaches are discussed in more or less historical sequence.

The box uses a research question about the Abelam of New Guinea to illustrate how different theoretical orientations suggest different types of answers.

Chapter 15: Explanation and Evidence

In this chapter we discuss what it means to explain and what kinds of evidence are needed to evaluate an explanation. We end with a discussion of the major types of study in cultural anthropology—ethnography, ethnohistory, within-culture comparisons, regional comparions, and worldwide cross-cultural comparisons. Consistent with our expanded discussion of ethics, we have added a new section on ethics in fieldwork. We have expanded our discussion of cross-cultural research. The first box explores the differences between scientific and humanistic understanding and points out that the different approaches are not really incompatible. In the second box, we have two purposes: One is to give a feeling for the experience of fieldwork; the second is to use the Mead-Freeman controversy to explore the issue of how we can know that an ethnographer is accurate.

Chapter 16: Communication and Language

We begin by discussing communication in humans and other animals. We have expanded our discussion of nonverbal human communication to include kinesics and paralanguage. We describe the debate about the degree of difference between human and nonhuman primate language abilities. We discuss the origins of language and how creoles and children's language acquisition may help us understand the origins. We have added new research on infant understanding of language. We describe the fundamentals of descriptive linguistics and the processes of linguistic divergence. After discussing the interrelationships between language and other aspects of culture, we discuss the ethnography of speaking and the differences in speech by status, gender, and ethnicity. We discuss interethnic or intercultural communication, indicating how linguists can play a role in helping people improve their cross-cultural communication. At the end of the chapter we have added a new section on writing and literacy. The first box discusses language extinction and what some anthropologists are doing about it. To stimulate thinking about the possible impact of language on thought, we ask in the second box whether the English language promotes sexist thinking. The last box, which is part of the new series on "Migrants and Immigrants," discusses why some immigrant groups retain their "mother tongues" longer than others.

Chapter 17: Getting Food

Chapter 17 discusses how societies vary in getting their food, how they have changed over time, and how the variation seems to affect other kinds of cultural variation—including variation in economic systems, social stratification, and political life. We include a discussion of "market foragers" to emphasize that most people in a modern market economy are not in fact producers of food. We have expanded our discussion of complex foragers for this edition. The first box deals with the change from "Man the Hunter" to "Woman the Gatherer," and we raise the question of whether either view is accurate. Although it is commonly thought that industrialization is mainly to blame for negative developments in the environment, our second box deals with the negative effects in preindustrial times of irrigation, animal grazing, and overhunting. Our third box, which is new and part of the "Migrants and Immigrants" set, explores where particular foods came from and how different foods and cuisines spread around the world as people migrated.

Chapter 18: Economic Systems

Chapter 18 discusses how societies vary in the ways they allocate resources (what is "property" and what ownership may mean), convert or transform resources through labor into usable goods, and distribute and perhaps exchange goods and services. We have expanded and updated the discussions of pastoralists, decision-making about work, and Chayonov's rule, and we have added a discussion of experimental evidence on sharing and cooperation. The first box addresses the controversy over whether communal ownership leads to economic disaster. The second box, which is part of the new series on "Migrants and Immigrants," discusses the impact of working abroad and sending money home. The third box illustrates the impact of the world system on local economies, with special reference to the deforestation of the Amazon.

Chapter 19: Social Stratification: Class, Ethnicity, and Racism

This chapter explores the variation in degree of social stratification and how the various forms of social inequality may develop. We discuss how egalitarian societies work hard to prevent dominance, and the controversy about whether pastoral societies with individual ownership of animals are egalitarian. We have added a new section on the recognition of social class and how people in the United States generally deny the existence of class. We have expanded our section on the castelike nature of racism in the northern United States. We end with an extensive discussion of "race," racism, and ethnicity and how they often relate to the inequitable distribution of resources. The first box discusses social stratification on the global level—how the gap between rich and poor countries has been widening, and what may account for that trend. The second box discusses possible reasons for disparities in death by disease between African Americans and European Americans.

Chapter 20: Sex, Gender, and Culture

In the first part of Chapter 20 we open with a new section on culturally varying gender concepts, including cultures that have more than two genders. We discuss how and why sex and gender differences vary cross-culturally. In addition to discussing the gender division of labor in primary and secondary subsistence, we have added a section on how and why females generally work harder. We include material on female hunting and what impact it has on theories about the gender division of labor, and we have revised our discussion of gender roles in warfare. In the second part of the chapter we discuss variation in sexual attitudes and practices. Following revised sections on marital sex and extramarital sex, there is an expanded discussion of homosexuality, including female-female relationships. In the first box, we examine cross-cultural research about why some societies allow women to participate in combat. A second box discusses research on why women's political participation may be increasing in some Coast Salish communities of western Washington State and British Columbia, now that they have elected councils.

Chapter 21: Marriage and the Family

After discussing various theories about why marriage might be universal, we move on to discuss variation in how one marries, restrictions on marriage, whom one should marry, and how many one should marry. We close with a discussion of variation in family form. We introduce recent research on the Hadza that supports one of the theories about marriage. We now discuss the phenomenon of couples choosing to live together, and we have expanded our discussion of behavioral ecological theories about polygyny. Our new box in the "Migrants and Immigrants" series discusses arranged marriage and how it has changed among South Asian immigrants in England and the United States. To introduce topics regarding the husband-wife relationship that are only beginning to be investigated, the second box discusses variation in love, intimacy, and sexual jealousy. The third updated box discusses why one-parent families are on the increase in countries like ours.

Chapter 22: Marital Residence and Kinship

This chapter has been rearranged so that explanations of all types of residence can be found together. We hope the discussion of kinship now flows more smoothly. In addition to explaining the variation that exists in marital residence, kinship structure, and kinship terminology, this chapter emphasizes how understanding residence is important for understanding social life. The first box discusses the possible relationship between neolocality and adolescent rebellion. The second box is on how variation in residence and kinship affects the lives of women. The new third box, on "Migrants and Immigrants," discusses the role that Chinese lineages play in supporting migration and making a living in the diaspora.

Chapter 23: Associations and Interest Groups

We discuss the importance of associations in many parts of the world, particularly the increasing importance of voluntary associations. We have expanded the section on rotating-credit associations, discussing the variety of types of such association We discuss how they work to provide lump sums of money to individuals, how they are especially important to women, and how they become even more important when people move to new places. The first box addresses the question of whether separate women's associations increase women's status and power. The second box discusses why street gangs develop and why they often become violent. The new last box, in the "Migrants and Immigrants" series, discusses the role of ethnic associations in Chinatowns in North America.

Chapter 24: Political Life: Social Order and Disorder

We look at how societies have varied in their levels of political organization, the various ways people become leaders, the degree to which they participate in the political process, and the peaceful and violent methods of resolving conflict. We discuss how colonialization has transformed legal systems and ways of making decisions and we have expanded our discussion of states as empires. The new box in the "Migrants and Immigrants" series discusses the role of migrants in the growth of cities. The second box deals with the cross-national and cross-cultural relationship between economic development and democracy. The third box deals with how new local courts among the Abelam of New Guinea are allowing women to address sexual grievances.

Chapter 25: Psychology and Culture

Chapter 25 discusses some of the universals of psychological development, some psychological differences between societies and what might account for them, how people in different societies conceive of personality differently (e.g., in regard to the concept of self), and how knowledge of psychological processes may help us understand cultural variation. We identify some larger processes that may influence personality, such as the importance of the settings that children are placed in and how native theories ("ethnotheories") about parenting vary by culture. We have updated the section on schooling to show how schooling might increase patience, and we have added a discussion of the inconsistency between U.S. parents' expectations of independence in their children and their encouragement of dependency. The first box refers to a comparison of preschools in Japan, China, and the United States, discussing how schools may consciously and unconsciously teach values. The second box discusses the idea that women may have a different sense of themselves than men have, and therefore a different sense of morality.

Chapter 26: Religion and Magic

After discussing why religion may be culturally universal, we discuss variation in religious belief and practice with extensive examples. We discuss revitalization movements and how humans tend to anthropomorphize in the face of unpredictable events. We have expanded our sections on life after death, divination, and our discussion of why women may predominate in possession trances. The first box discusses research on New England fishermen that suggests how their taboos, or "rituals of avoidance," may be anxiety reducing. The second box, which is part of the new "Migrants and Immigrants" set, discusses the role of colonialism in religious change. The last box discusses the emergence of new religions and points out that nearly all the major churches or religions in the world began as minority sects or cults.

Chapter 27: The Arts

After discussing how art might be defined and the appearance of the earliest art, we discuss variation in the visual arts, music, and folklore, and review how some of those variations might be explained. In regard to how the arts change over time, we discuss the myth that the art of "simpler" peoples is timeless, and how arts have changed as a result of European contact. We address the role of ethnocentrism in studies of art with a section on how Western museums and art critics look at the visual art of less complex cultures. The first box discusses how art varies with different kinds of political systems. The second box, dealing with universal symbolism in art, reviews recent research on the emotions displayed in masks. The last box, which is new and part of the "Migrants and Immigrants" set, discusses the spread of popular music.

Chapter 28: Culture Change and Globalization

After discussing the ultimate sources of culture change—discovery and innovation—we discuss some of what is known about the conditions under which people are likely to accept innovations. We discuss the costs and benefits of innovations, and types of external and internal pressures for culture change. We draw particular attention to processes of change in the modern world including colonialization, commercialization, industrialization, and globalization. We also discuss the rise of new cultures or ethnogenesis. We close with a discussion of the likelihood of cultural diversity in the future. We have added a new section on the rise of fundamentalist movements. We point out that globalization does not always result in similarity and how McDonald's in Japan has become very Japanese. We discuss how worldwide communication can sometimes allow the less powerful to be heard. To convey that culture change often has biological consequences, the first box discusses obesity, hypertension, and diabetes as health consequences of modernization. The second box examines culture change in China—what has changed because of government intervention and what has nevertheless persisted.

Part V: Using Anthropology

Chapter 29: Applied and Practicing Anthropology

This chapter discusses the types of jobs outside of academia, the history and types of applied anthropology in the United States, the ethical issues involved in trying to improve people's lives, the difficulties in evaluating whether a program is beneficial, and ways of implementing planned changes. We point out how applied anthropologists are playing more of a role in planning, rather than serving just as peripheral advisers to change programs already in place. We have expanded our discussion of ethics to include issues in archaeology and physical anthropology, for example the case of "Kennewick Man." The two boxes show how anthropologists have been able to help in business and in reforestation.

Chapter 30: Medical Anthropology

This chapter discusses cultural understandings of health and illness, the treatment of illness (particularly from a biocultural rather than just a biomedical point of view), political and economic influences on health, and more material on the contributions of medical anthropologists to the study of various health conditions and diseases. Those conditions and diseases include AIDS, mental and emotional disorders, the folk illness *susto*, depression, and undernutrition. The first box deals with why an applied medical project didn't work. The second box, which is part of the new set on "Migrants and Immigrants," discusses the spread of leprosy. The third box, now considerably revised on the basis on recent research, deals with eating disorders, biology, and the cultural construction of "beauty."

Chapter 31: Global Social Problems

In this chapter we discuss the relationship between basic and applied research, and how research may suggest possible solutions to various global social problems, including natural disasters and famines, homelessness, crime, family violence, war, and terrorism. The section on family violence has been updated with new research on corporal punishment and the effects of television on children. There are three boxes; the last one is new. One is on global warming and our dependence on oil. The second is on ethnic conflicts and whether or not they are inevitable. The last box, in the new series on "Migrants and Immigrants," describes how the problem of refugees has become a global problem.

Features New to This Edition

Migrant and Immigrant Map Feature

To emphasize this important theme, we have adapted maps originally produced by Dorling Kindersley—a leading publisher of educational maps—to highlight aspects of human migration and globalization.

Map Table of Contents:

Migrants and Immigrants Box Feature

These boxes deal with humans on the move, and how migration and immigra-

tion have impacted recent and contemporary social life. Examples include why some immigrant groups retained their "mother tongues" longer than others, the spread of foods in recent times, arranging marriages in the diaspora, and the problem of refugees.

New Chapter on Theoretical Approaches. We have decided to reintroduce a separate chapter on theoretical approaches in cultural anthropology, which reviewers suggested. This new chapter now complements the separate chapter on "Explanation and Evidence," which has new material on ethics in fieldwork and an expanded discussion of cross-cultural research. Ethical issues are also discussed in various other chapters.

Discovering Anthropology: Researchers at Work. New to this edition, we have compiled a book of case studies that provides students with engaging, up-to-date examples of anthropologists at work. The original articles were commissioned by us to highlight the personal experiences of anthropologists as they conduct research; we have chosen one case study to correspond with every chapter in the textbook. Discussion and homework questions about the case studies can be found at the end of every chapter in the text.

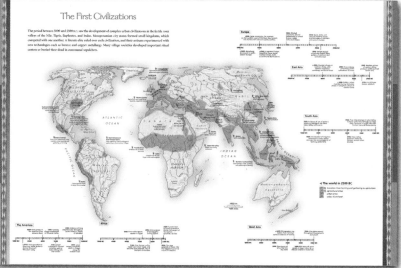

MIGRANTS AND IMMIGRANTS

Why Are "Mother Tongues" Retained, and For How Long?

The longer an immigrant group lives in another country, the more they incorporate the culture of their new home. At some point the original language is no longer even partially understood. Consider people who originally came from Wales, the region west of England in Great Britain. In that region, until about 100 years ago, most people spoke the Welsh language, which belongs to the Celtic subfamily of Indo-European along with Irish and Scottish Gaelic and Breton. (Celtic is a different subfamily from the one English belongs to, which is Germanic.) In 1729, the Welsh in Philadelphia established the Welsh Society, the oldest ethnic organization in the United States. Many of the members, if not all, spoke Welsh in addition to English at that time. But

group lived in tightly knit communities, retained religious rituals from the old country, had separate schools and special festivals, visited their homeland, did not intermarry, or worked with others of their ethnic group.

Schrauf used data on 11 North American ethnic groups drawn from the HRAF Collection of Ethnography. The major advantage of the HRAF materials is that ethnographies written for more general purposes, or for purposes other than linguistic ones, contain a wealth of information concerning sociocultural features of ethnic groups that may be tested for their possible effects on language retention and loss.

We might suspect that all of the factors measured by Schrauf would lead people to retain their native lan-

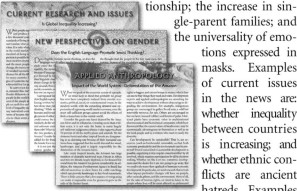

Research Navigator™ Exercises. At the end of every chapter, students are given an exercise that asks them to use Research Navigator™, a powerful database search engine. Students can be encouraged to use the resources found on Research Navigator™ to discover more about the changes that are occurring in the field of anthropology.

Features Retained in This Edition

Current Research and Issues Boxes. These boxes deal with current research, topics students may have heard about in the news, and research controversies in anthropology. Examples of current research are: variation in love, intimacy, and sexual jealousy in the husband-wife relationship; the increase in single-parent families; and the universality of emotions expressed in masks. Examples of current issues in the news are: whether inequality between countries is increasing; and whether ethnic conflicts are ancient hatreds. Examples of topics that are currently the subject of debate in the profession are: science versus humanism; and human rights versus cultural relativity.

New Perspectives on Gender Boxes. These boxes involve issues pertaining to sex and gender, both in anthropology and everyday life (examples: sexism in language; separate women's associations and women's status and power; morality in women versus men).

Applied Anthropology Boxes. These boxes deal with some of the ways anthropologists have studied or applied their knowledge to health and other practical problems (examples: deforestation in the Amazon, preventing the extinction of languages, modernization and obesity.).

Readability. We derive a lot of pleasure from trying to describe research findings, especially complicated ones, in ways that introductory students can understand. Thus, we try to minimize technical jargon, using only those terms students must know to appreciate the achievements of anthropology and to take advanced courses. We think readability is important, not only because it may enhance the reader's understanding of what we write, but also because it should make learning about anthropology more enjoyable! When new terms are introduced, which of course must happen sometimes, they are set off in boldface type and defined in the text (and in the glossary at the end of the book).

Student Friendly Pedagogy

Glossary. At the end of each chapter we list the new terms that have been introduced; these terms were identified by boldface type and defined in the text. We deliberately do not repeat the definitions at the end of the chapter to allow students to ask themselves if they know the terms. However, we do provide page numbers to find the definitions and we also provide all the definitions again in the Glossary at the end of the book.

Summaries. In addition to the outline provided at the beginning of each chapter, there is a detailed summary at the end of each chapter that will help the student review the major concepts and findings discussed.

Critical Questions. We provide three or four questions at the end of each chapter that will stimulate thinking about the implications of the chapter. The questions do not ask for repetition of what is in the text. We want students to imagine, to go beyond what we know or think we know.

End of Book Notes. Because we believe in the importance of documentation, we think it essential to tell our readers, both professionals and students, what our conclusions are based on. Usually the basis is published research. The abbreviated notes in this edition provide information to find the complete citation in the bibliography at the end of the book.

Supplements

This textbook is part of a complete teaching and learning package that has been carefully created to enhance the topics discussed in the text.

Instructor's Resource Manual with Tests: (0-13-227756-5) For each chapter in the text, this valuable resource provides a detailed outline, list of objectives, discussion questions and classroom activities. In addition, test questions in multiple-choice and short answer formats are available for each chapter; the answers to all questions are page-referenced to the text.

TestGEN-EQ: (0-13-227757-3) This computerized software allows instructors to create their own personalized exams, to edit any or all of the existing test questions and to add new questions. Other special features of this program include random generation of test questions, creation of alternate versions of the same test, scrambling question sequence, and test preview before printing.

Prentice Hall Anthropology PowerPoint® Slides: These PowerPoint slides combine graphics and text for each chapter in a colorful format to help you convey anthropological principles in a new and exciting way. For easy access, they are available on the Faculty Resources on CD, within the instructor portion of the OneKey for *Anthropology*, 12/E, or at www.prenhall.com

Faculty Resources on CD-ROM: (0-13-227759-X) Pulling together all of the media assets available to instructors, this CD allows instructors to insert media—PowerPoint® slides of graphs, charts, maps—into their classroom presentations. This CD also offers electronic versions of the Instructor's Manual and Test Item file.

Strategies in Teaching Anthropology, Fourth Edition: (0-13-173371-0) Unique in focus and content, this book focuses on the "how" of teaching Anthropology across all of its sub-fields: Cultural, Social, Biological, Archaeology, and Linguistics to provide a wide array of associated learning outcomes and student activities. It is a valuable single-source compendium of strategies and teaching "tricks of the trade" from a group of seasoned teaching anthropologists—working in a variety of teaching settings—who share their pedagogical techniques, knowledge, and observations. Please see your local Prentice Hall sales representative for more information.

OneKey: This innovative, passcode protected resource pulls together the teaching and learning materials associated with the text and integrates them into a single location. For students, OneKey offers video, animations, interactive exercises, assignments, and an interactive e-book. Instructors can access all student materials, presentation materials, assessment materials, and communication tools tied to *Anthropology, 12/E.* For a preview of OneKey or for more on ordering information, please visit http://www.prenhall.com/onekey or see your local Prentice Hall representative.

Study Guide: (0-13-227754-9) This complete guide helps students to review and reflect on the material presented in *Anthropology.* Each of the chapters in the Study Guide provides an overview of the corresponding chapter in the student text, summarizes its major topics and concepts, offers review exercises, and features end-of-chapter tests with solutions.

Companion Website™: (0-13-227755-7) This online study guide provides unique support to help students with their studies in anthropology. Featuring a variety of interactive learning tools, including online quizzes with immediate feedback, this site is a comprehensive resource organized according to the chapters in *Anthropology, 12/E.* It can be found at www.prenhall.com/ember.

Discovering Anthropology: Researchers at Work: (0-13-227762-X) This collection of case studies provides examples of anthropologists working in a variety of settings. The case studies are correlated with the chapters of *Anthropology, 12/E,* and the end of chapter material in the text contains discussion and homework questions directly tied to the case study.

The New York Times/Prentice Hall eThemes of the Times: The New York Times and Prentice Hall are sponsoring e*Themes of the Times,* a program designed to en-

hance student access to current information relevant to the classroom. Through this program, the core subject matter provided in the text is supplemented by a collection of timely articles downloaded from one of the world's most distinguished newspapers, *The New York Times.* These articles demonstrate the vital, ongoing connection between what is learned in the classroom and what is happening in the world around us. Access to *The New York Times/* Prentice Hall *eThemes of the Times* is available on the *Ember* Companion Website™ or the Ember OneKey Website.

Research Navigator™: Research Navigator™ can help students to complete research assignments efficiently and with confidence by providing three exclusive databases of high-quality, scholarly and popular articles accessed by easy-to-use search engines.

- **EBSCO's ContentSelect™ Academic Journal Database,** organized by subject, contains many of the leading academic journals for anthropology. Instructors and students can search the online journals by keyword, topic, or multiple topics. Articles include abstract and citation information and can be cut, pasted, e-mailed, or saved for later use.

- **The New York Times Search-by-Subject Archive** provides articles specific to anthropology and is searchable by keyword or multiple keywords. Instructors and students can view full-text articles from the world's leading journalists writing for *The New York Times.*

- **Link Library** offers editorially selected "best of the web" sites for anthropology. Link Libraries are continually scanned and kept up to date, providing the most relevant and accurate links for research assignments.

Gain access to Research Navigator™ by using the access code found in the front of the brief guide called *The Prentice Hall Guide to Research Navigator™* or by accessing the OneKey Website. Please contact your Prentice Hall representative for more information.

The Dorling Kindersley/Prentice Hall Atlas of Anthropology: Beautifully illustrated by Dorling Kindersley, with narrative by leading archaeological author Brian M. Fagan, this striking atlas features 30 full-color maps, timelines, and illustrations to offer a highly visual but explanatory geographical overview of topics from all four fields of anthropology. Please contact your Prentice Hall representative for ordering information.

Acknowledgments

We thank the people at Prentice Hall for all their help, and particularly Nancy Roberts, Publisher for the Social Sciences; Jan Pushard for seeing the manuscript through the production process, and Sheila Norman for photo research.

We want to thank the following for reviewing our chapters and making suggestions about them:

Garrett Cook, Baylor University
Daniel R. Maher, University of Arkansas-Fort Smith
Sheperd Jenks, Albuquerque TVI Community College

Thank you all, named and unnamed, who gave us advice.

Carol R. Ember, Melvin Ember, and Peter N. Peregrine

Carol R. Ember started at Antioch College as a chemistry major. She began taking social science courses because some were required, but she soon found herself intrigued. There were lots of questions without answers, and she became excited about the possibility of a research career in social science. She spent a year in graduate school at Cornell studying sociology before continuing on to Harvard, where she studied anthropology primarily with John and Beatrice Whiting.

For her Ph.D. dissertation she worked among the Luo of Kenya. While there she noticed that many boys were assigned "girls' work," such as babysitting and household chores, because their mothers (who did most of the agriculture) did not have enough girls to help out. She decided to study the possible effects of task assignment on the social behavior of boys. Using systematic behavior observations, she compared girls, boys who did a great deal of girls' work, and boys who did little such work. She found that boys assigned girls' work were intermediate in many social behaviors, compared with the other boys and girls. Later, she did cross-cultural research on variation in marriage, family, descent groups, and war and peace, mainly in collaboration with Melvin Ember, whom she married in 1970. All of these cross-cultural studies tested theories on data for worldwide samples of societies.

From 1970 to 1996, she taught at Hunter College of the City University of New York. She has served as president of the Society of Cross-Cultural Research and was one of the directors of the Summer Institutes in Comparative Anthropological Research, which were funded by the National Science Foundation. Since 1996 she has served as executive director of the Human Relations Area Files, Inc., a nonprofit research agency at Yale University.

After graduating from Columbia College, Melvin Ember went to Yale University for his Ph.D. His mentor at Yale was George Peter Murdock, an anthropologist who was instrumental in promoting cross-cultural research and building a full-text database on the cultures of the world to facilitate cross-cultural hypothesis testing. This database came to be known as the Human Relations Area Files (HRAF) because it was originally sponsored by the Institute of Human Relations at Yale. Growing in annual installments and now distributed in electronic format, the HRAF database currently covers more than 385 cultures, past and present, all over the world.

Melvin Ember did fieldwork for his dissertation in American Samoa, where he conducted a comparison of three villages to study the effects of commercialization on political life. In addition, he did research on descent groups and how they changed with the increase of buying and selling. His cross-cultural studies focused originally on variation in marital residence and descent groups. He has also done cross-cultural research on the relationship between economic and political development, the origin and extension of the incest taboo, the causes of polygyny, and how archaeological correlates of social customs can help us draw inferences about the past.

After four years of research at the National Institute of Mental Health, he taught at Antioch College and then Hunter College of the City University of New York. He has served as president of the Society for Cross-Cultural Research. Since 1987 he has been president of the Human Relations Area Files, Inc., a nonprofit research agency at Yale University.

Peter N. Peregrine came to anthropology after completing an undergraduate degree in English. He found anthropology's social scientific approach to understanding humans more appealing than the humanistic approach he had learned as an English major. He undertook an ethnohistorical study of the relationship between Jesuit missionaries and Native American peoples for his master's degree and realized that he needed to study archaeology to understand the cultural interactions experienced by Native Americans prior to contact with the Jesuits.

While working on his Ph.D. at Purdue University, Peter Peregrine did research on the prehistoric Mississippian cultures of the eastern United States. He found that interactions between groups were common and had been shaping Native American cultures for centuries. Native Americans approached contact with the Jesuits simply as another in a long string of intercultural exchanges. He also found that relatively little research had been done on Native American

interactions and decided that comparative research was a good place to begin examining the topic. In 1990 he participated in the Summer Institute in Comparative Anthropological Research, where he met Carol R. Ember and Melvin Ember.

Peter Peregrine taught at Juniata College and is currently professor and chair of the anthropology department at Lawrence University in Appleton, Wisconsin. He serves as research associate for the eHRAF Collection of Archaeology and is co-editor with Melvin Ember of the 9-volume *Encyclopedia of Prehistory*. He continues to do archaeological research, and to teach anthropology and archaeology to undergraduate students.

Carol R. Ember, Melvin Ember, Peter N. Peregrine

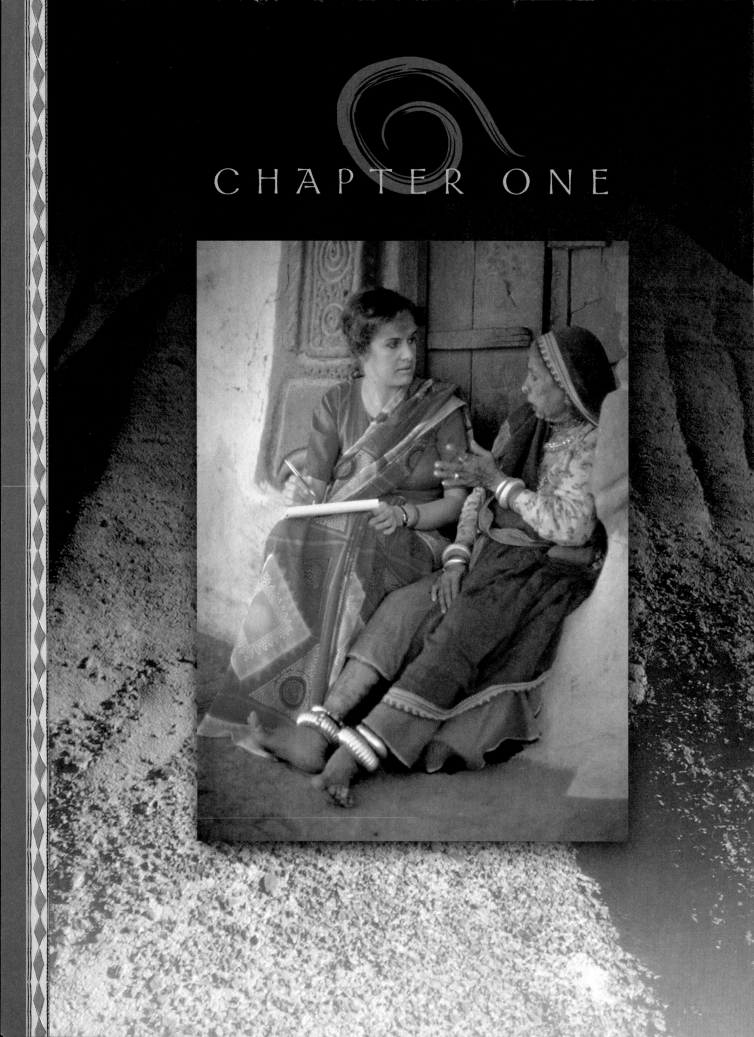

CHAPTER ONE

What Is Anthropology?

Anthropology, by definition, is a discipline of infinite curiosity about human beings. The term comes from the Greek *anthropos* for "man, human" and *logos* for "study." Anthropologists seek answers to an enormous variety of questions about humans. They are interested in discovering when, where, and why humans appeared on the earth, how and why they have changed since then, and how and why modern human populations vary in certain physical features. Anthropologists are also interested in how and why societies in the past and present have varied in their customary ideas and practices. There is a practical side to anthropology too. Applied and practicing anthropologists put anthropological methods, information, and results to use, in efforts to solve practical problems.

But defining anthropology as the study of human beings is not complete, for such a definition would appear to incorporate a whole catalog of disciplines: sociology, psychology, political science, economics, history, human biology, and perhaps even the humanistic disciplines of philosophy and literature. Needless to say, practitioners of the many other disciplines concerned with humans would not be happy to be regarded as being in sub-branches of anthropology. After all, most of those disciplines have existed longer than anthropology, and each is somewhat distinctive. There must, then, be something unique about anthropology—a reason for its having developed as a separate discipline and for its having retained a separate identity over the last 100 years.

The Scope of Anthropology

Anthropologists are generally thought of as individuals who travel to little-known corners of the world to study exotic peoples or who dig deep into the earth to uncover the fossil remains or the tools and pots of people who lived long ago. These views, though clearly stereotyped, do indicate how anthropology differs from other disciplines concerned with humans. Anthropology is broader in scope, both geographically and historically. Anthropology is concerned explicitly and directly with all varieties of people throughout the world, not just those close at hand or within a limited area. It is also interested in people of all periods. Beginning with the immediate ancestors of humans, who lived a few million years ago, anthropology traces the development of humans until the present. Every part of the world that has ever contained a human population is of interest to anthropologists.

Anthropologists have not always been as global and comprehensive in their concerns as they are today. Traditionally, they concentrated on non-Western cultures and left the study of Western civilization and similarly complex societies, with their recorded histories, to other disciplines. In recent years, however, this division of labor among the disciplines has begun to disappear. Now anthropologists work in their own and other complex societies.

What induces anthropologists to choose so broad a subject for study? In part, they are motivated by the belief that any suggested generalization about human beings, any possible explanation of some characteristic of human culture or biology, should be shown to apply to many times and places of human existence. If a generalization or explanation does not prove to apply widely, we are entitled or even obliged to be skeptical about it. The skeptical attitude, in the absence of persuasive evidence, is our best protection against accepting invalid ideas about humans.

For example, when American educators discovered in the 1960s that African American schoolchildren rarely drank milk, they assumed that lack of money or education was the cause. But evidence from anthropology suggested a different explanation. Anthropologists had known for years that in many parts of the world where milking animals are kept, people do not drink fresh milk; rather, they sour it before they drink it, or they make it into cheese. Why they do so is now clear. Many people lack an enzyme, lactase, that is necessary for breaking down lactose, the sugar in milk. When such people drink regular milk, it actually interferes with digestion. Not only is the lactose in milk not digested but other nutrients are less likely to be digested as well; in many cases, drinking milk will cause cramps, stomach gas, diarrhea, and nausea. Studies indicate that milk intolerance is found in many parts of the world.[1] The condition is common in adulthood among Asians, southern Europeans, Arabs and Jews, West Africans, Inuit (Eskimos), and North and South American Indians, as well as African Americans. Because anthropologists are acquainted with human life in an enormous variety of geographic and historical settings, they are often able to correct mistaken beliefs about different groups of people.

The Holistic Approach

In addition to the worldwide as well as historical scope of anthropology, another distinguishing feature of the discipline is its **holistic,** or multifaceted, approach to the study of human beings. Anthropologists study not only all varieties of people but many aspects of human experience as well. For example, when describing a group of people, an anthropologist might discuss the history of the area in which the people live, the physical environment, the organization of family life, the general features of their language, the group's settlement patterns, political and economic systems, religion, and styles of art and dress. While these features might be described separately, most anthropologists try to understand the connections between different aspects of physical and social life.

In the past, individual anthropologists tried to be holistic and cover many subjects. Today, as in many other disciplines, so much information has been accumulated that anthropologists tend to specialize in one topic or area. Thus, one anthropologist may investigate the physical characteristics of some of our prehistoric ancestors. Another may study the biological effect of the environment on a human population over time. Still another will concentrate on many customs of a particular group of people. Despite this specialization, however, the discipline of anthropology retains its holistic orientation in that its many different specialties, taken together, describe many aspects of human existence, both past and present.

The Anthropological Curiosity

Thus far we have described anthropology as being broader in scope, both historically and geographically, and more holistic in approach than other disciplines concerned with human beings. But this statement again implies that anthropology is the all-inclusive human science. How, then, is anthropology really different from those other disciplines? We suggest that anthropology's distinctiveness lies principally in the kind of curiosity it arouses.

In studying a human population anthropologists tend to focus on *typical* characteristics (traits, customs) of that population: People in many societies depend on agriculture. Why? And where, when, and why did people first start to farm? Why do some populations have lighter skin than others? Why do some languages contain more terms for color than others? Why do some societies have more political participation than others? Individuals may provide information to anthropologists, but the anthropological curiosity mostly focuses on the typical characteristics of human groups and how to understand and explain them. For example, whereas economists take a monetary system for granted and study how it operates, anthropologists would ask how frequently monetary systems are found, why they vary, and why only some societies during the last few thousand years used money. In short, anthropologists are curious about the typical characteristics of human groups—how and why populations and their characteristics have varied around the globe and throughout the ages.

Fields of Anthropology

Different anthropologists concentrate on different typical characteristics of societies. Some are concerned primarily with *biological* or *physical characteristics* of human populations; others are interested principally in what we call *cultural characteristics.* Hence, there are two broad classifications of subject matter in anthropology: **biological (physical) anthropology** and **cultural anthropology.** Biological anthropology is one major field of anthropology. Cultural anthropology is divided into three major subfields—

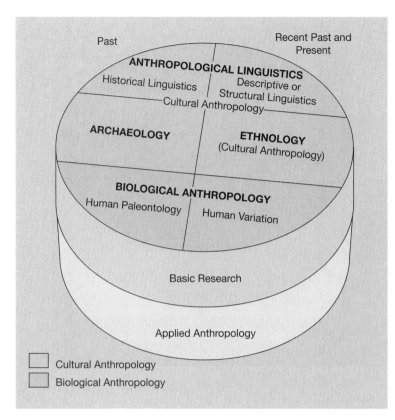

Figure 1–1 The Subdivisions of Anthropology
The four major subdisciplines of anthropology (in bold letters) may be classified according to subject matter (biological or cultural) and according to the period with which each is concerned (distant past vs. recent past and present). There are applications of anthropology in all four subdisciplines.

archaeology, linguistics, and ethnology. Ethnology, the study of recent cultures, is now usually referred to by the parent name, cultural anthropology (see Figure 1–1). Crosscutting these four fields is a fifth, **applied** or **practicing anthropology.**

Biological Anthropology

Biological (physical) anthropology seeks to answer two distinct sets of questions. The first set includes questions about the emergence of humans and their later evolution (this focus is called **human paleontology** or **paleoanthropology**). The second set includes questions about how and why contemporary human populations vary biologically (this focus is called **human variation**).

In order to reconstruct human evolution, human paleontologists search for and study the buried, hardened remains or impressions—known as **fossils**—of humans, prehumans, and related animals. Paleontologists working in East Africa, for instance, have excavated the fossil remains of humanlike beings who lived more than 3 million years ago. These findings have suggested the approximate dates when our ancestors began to develop two-legged walking, very flexible hands, and a larger brain.

In attempting to clarify evolutionary relationships, human paleontologists may use not only the fossil record but also geological information on the succession of climates, environments, and plant and animal populations. Moreover, when reconstructing the past of humans, paleontologists are also interested in the behavior and evolution of our closest relatives among the mammals—the prosimi-

ans, monkeys, and apes, which, like ourselves, are members of the order of **Primates.** Anthropologists, psychologists, and biologists who specialize in the study of primates are called **primatologists.** The various species of primates are observed in the wild and in the laboratory. One especially popular subject of study is the chimpanzee, which bears a close resemblance to humans in behavior and physical appearance, has a similar blood chemistry, and is susceptible to many of the same diseases. It now appears that chimpanzees share 99 percent of their genes with humans.[2]

From primate studies, biological anthropologists try to discover characteristics that are distinctly human, as opposed to those that might be part of the primate heritage. With this information, they may be able to infer what our prehistoric ancestors were like. The inferences from primate studies are checked against the fossil record. The evidence from the earth, collected in bits and pieces, is correlated with scientific observations of our closest living relatives. In short, biological anthropologists piece together bits of information obtained from different sources. They construct theories that explain the changes observed in the fossil record and then attempt to evaluate their theories by checking one kind of evidence against another. Human paleontology thus overlaps disciplines such as geology, general vertebrate (and particularly primate) paleontology, comparative anatomy, and the study of comparative primate behavior.

The second major focus of biological anthropology, the study of human variation, investigates how and why contemporary human populations differ in biological or physical characteristics. All living people belong to one species, **Homo sapiens,** for all can successfully interbreed. Yet there

Birute Galdikas works with two orangutans in Borneo.

is much that varies among human populations. Investigators of human variation ask such questions as: Why are some peoples taller than others? How have human populations adapted physically to their environmental conditions? Are some peoples, such as Inuit (Eskimos), better equipped than other peoples to endure cold? Does darker skin pigmentation offer special protection against the tropical sun?

To understand better the biological variations observable among contemporary human populations, biological anthropologists use the principles, concepts, and techniques of at least three other disciplines: human genetics (the study of human traits that are inherited), population biology (the study of environmental effects on, and interaction with, population characteristics), and epidemiology (the study of how and why diseases affect different populations in different ways). Research on human variation, therefore, overlaps research in other fields. Biological anthropologists, however, are concerned most with human populations and how they vary biologically.

Cultural Anthropology

Cultural anthropology is concerned with universals and variation in culture in the past and present. But what is culture? Because the concept of culture is so central to anthropology, we devote a whole chapter to it. To an anthropologist, the term **culture** refers to the customary ways of thinking and behaving of a particular population or society. The culture of a social group includes many things—its language, religious beliefs, food preferences, music, work habits, gender roles, how they rear their children, how they construct

their houses, and many other learned behaviors and ideas that have come to be widely shared or customary among the group. The three main branches of cultural anthropology are **archaeology** (the study of past cultures, primarily through their material remains), **anthropological linguistics** (the anthropological study of languages), and **ethnology** (the study of existing and recent cultures), now usually referred to by the parent name, cultural anthropology.

ARCHAEOLOGY   The archaeologist seeks not only to reconstruct the daily life and customs of peoples who lived in the past but also to trace cultural changes and to offer possible explanations for those changes. This concern is similar to that of the historian, but the archaeologist reaches much farther back in time. The historian deals only with societies that left written records and is therefore limited to the last 5,000 years of human history. Human societies, however, have existed for more than a million years, and only a small proportion in the last 5,000 years had writing. For all those past societies lacking a written record, the archaeologist serves as historian. Lacking written records for study, archaeologists must try to reconstruct history from the remains of human cultures. Some of these remains are as grand as the Mayan temples discovered at Chichén Itzá in Yucatán, Mexico. More often they are as ordinary as bits of broken pottery, stone tools, and garbage heaps.

Most archaeologists deal with **prehistory,** the time before written records. But there is a specialty within archaeology, called **historical archaeology,** that studies the remains of recent peoples who left written records. This specialty, as its name implies, employs the methods of both archaeologists and historians to study recent societies for which there is both archaeological and historical information.

In trying to understand how and why ways of life have changed through time in different parts of the world, archaeologists collect materials from sites of human occupation. Usually, these sites must be unearthed. On the basis of materials they have excavated and otherwise collected, they then ask various questions: Where, when, and why did the distinctive human characteristic of toolmaking first emerge? Where, when, and why did agriculture first develop? Where, when, and why did people first begin to live in cities?

To collect the data they need in order to suggest answers to these and other questions, archaeologists use techniques and findings borrowed from other disciplines, as well as what they can infer from anthropological studies of recent and contemporary cultures. For example, to guess where to dig for evidence of early toolmaking, archaeologists rely on geology to tell them where sites of early human occupation are likely to be found, because of erosion and uplifting, near the surface of the earth. To infer when agriculture first developed, archaeologists date the relevant excavated materials by a process originally developed by chemists. And to try to understand why cities first emerged, archaeologists may use information from historians, geographers, and others about how recent and contemporary cities are related economically and politically to their hinterlands. If we can discover what recent and contemporary cities have in common, we can speculate on why cities developed originally. Thus, archaeologists use information from the present and recent past in trying to understand the distant past.

ANTHROPOLOGICAL LINGUISTICS Anthropological linguistics is another branch of cultural anthropology. Linguistics, or the study of languages, is a somewhat older discipline than anthropology, but the early linguists concentrated on the study of languages that had been written for a long time—languages such as English that had been written for nearly a thousand years. Anthropological linguists began to do fieldwork in places where the language was not yet written. This meant that anthropologists could not consult a dictionary or grammar to help them learn the language. Instead, they first had to construct a dictionary and grammar. Then they could study the structure and history of the language.

Like biological anthropologists, linguists study changes that have taken place over time, as well as contemporary variation. Some anthropological linguists are concerned with the emergence of language and also with the divergence of languages over thousands of years. The study of how languages change over time and how they may be related is known as **historical linguistics.** Anthropological linguists are also interested in how contemporary languages differ, especially in their construction. This focus of linguistics is generally called **descriptive** or **structural linguistics.** The study of how language is used in social contexts is called **sociolinguistics.**

In contrast with the human paleontologist and archaeologist, who have physical remains to help them reconstruct change over time, the historical linguist deals only with languages—and usually unwritten ones at that. (Remember that writing is only about 5,000 years old, and most languages since then have not been written.) Because an unwritten language must be heard in order to be studied, it does not leave any trace once its speakers have died. Linguists interested in reconstructing the history of unwritten languages must begin in the present, with comparisons of contemporary languages. On the basis of these comparisons, they draw inferences about the kinds of change in language that may have occurred in the past and that may account for similarities and differences observed in the present. The historical linguist typically asks such questions as these: Did two or more contemporary languages diverge from a common ancestral language? If they are related, how far back in time did they begin to differ?

Unlike the historical linguist, the descriptive (or structural) linguist is typically concerned with discovering and recording the principles that determine how sounds and words are put together in speech. For example, a structural description of a particular language might tell us that the sounds *t* and *k* are interchangeable in a word without causing a difference in meaning. In American Samoa, one could say *Tutuila* or *Kukuila* as the name of the largest island, and everyone, except perhaps the newly arrived anthropologist, would understand that the same island was being mentioned.

The sociolinguist is interested in the social aspects of language, including what people speak about and how they interact conversationally, their attitudes toward speakers of other dialects or languages, and how people speak differently in different social contexts. In English, for example, we do not address everyone we meet in the same way. "Hi, Sandy" may be the customary way a person greets a friend. But we would probably feel uncomfortable addressing a doctor by her or his first name; instead, we would probably say, "Good morning, Dr. Brown." Such variations in language use, which are determined by the social status of the persons being addressed, are significant for the sociolinguist.

ETHNOLOGY (CULTURAL ANTHROPOLOGY) Ethnologists seek to understand how and why peoples today and in the recent past differ in their customary ways of thinking and acting. Ethnology—now usually called *cultural anthropology*—is concerned with patterns of thought and behavior, such as marriage customs, kinship organization, political and economic systems, religion, folk art, and music, and with the ways in which these patterns differ in contemporary societies. Ethnologists also study the dynamics of culture—that is, how various cultures develop and change. In addition, they are interested in the relationship between beliefs and practices within a culture. Thus, the aim of ethnologists is largely the same as that of archaeologists. Ethnologists, however, generally use data collected

NEW PERSPECTIVES ON GENDER

Researcher at Work: Elizabeth M. Brumfiel

Now a professor of anthropology at Northwestern University, Elizabeth M. Brumfiel became interested in the origins of social inequality when she was an undergraduate. Archaeologists had known for some time that substantial wealth differences between families developed only recently (archaeologically speaking), that is, only after about 6,000 years ago. The archaeological indicators of inequality are fairly clear—elaborate burials with valuable goods for some families and large differences in houses and possessions. But why the transformation occurred was not so clear. When she was in graduate school at the University of Michigan, Brumfiel says, she didn't accept the then-current explanation, that inequality provided benefits to the society (e.g., the standard of living of most people improved as the leaders got richer). Consequently, for her Ph. D. research in central Mexico, she began to test the "benefit" explanation in an area that had been independent politically at first and then became part of the Aztec Empire. She studied the surface material remains in the area and historical documents written by Europeans and Aztec nobility. Her findings contradicted the benefit explanation of social inequality; she found little improvement in the standard of living of the local people after the Aztec Empire had absorbed them.

Another important part of her research agenda was understanding the lives of women. How were they af-

Elizabeth M. Brumfiel.

fected by the expansion of the Aztec Empire? Did their work change? How were women portrayed in art? In the Aztec capital of Tenochtitlán, images of militarism and masculinity became increasingly important with the growth of the empire, and sculptures showed women in subordinate positions (e.g., kneeling). But the images of women in the area of Brumfiel's fieldwork did not change. For example, most of the sculptures after the Aztecs had taken over still showed women standing, not kneeling.

Like many anthropologists, Brumfiel asked herself how she could contribute to the community in which she did her fieldwork. She decided to design an exhibit to display the successes of the people who had lived in the area for 1,200 years. The exhibit tells the people of Xaltocan what she found out from her studies.

As she continues to explore issues about the origins of inequality and the position of women, Brumfiel is quite comfortable with knowing that someone will think that she has "gotten it wrong, and will set out on a lifetime of archaeological research to find her own answers."

Source: Elizabeth M. Brumfiel, "Origins of Social Inequality," in *Research Frontiers,* in Carol R. Ember, Melvin Ember, and Peter N. Peregrine, eds., *New Directions in Anthropology* (Upper Saddle River, NJ: Prentice Hall, CD-ROM, 2004).

through observation and interviewing of living peoples. Archaeologists, on the other hand, must work with fragmentary remains of past cultures, on the basis of which they can only make inferences about the customs of prehistoric peoples.

One type of ethnologist, the **ethnographer,** usually spends a year or so living with, talking to, and observing the people whose customs he or she is studying. This fieldwork provides the data for a detailed description (an **ethnography**) of customary behavior and thought. Ethnographers vary in the degree to which they strive for completeness in their coverage of cultural and social life. Earlier ethnographers tended to strive for holistic coverage; more re-

cent ethnographers have tended to specialize or focus on narrower realms such as ritual healing or curing, interaction with the environment, effects of modernization or globalization, or gender issues. Ethnographies often go beyond description; they may address current anthropological issues or try to explain some aspect of culture.

Because so many cultures have undergone extensive change in the recent past, it is fortunate that another type of ethnologist, the **ethnohistorian,** is prepared to study how the ways of life of a particular group of people have changed over time. Ethnohistorians investigate written documents (which may or may not have been produced by anthropologists). They may spend many years going through documents, such as missionary accounts, reports by traders and explorers, and government records, to try to establish the cultural changes that have occurred. Unlike ethnographers, who rely mostly on their own observations, ethnohistorians rely on the reports of others. Often, they must attempt to piece together and make sense of widely scattered, and even apparently contradictory, information. Thus, the ethnohistorian's research is very much like that of the historian, except that the ethnohistorian is usually concerned with the history of a people who did not themselves leave written records. The ethnohistorian tries to reconstruct the recent history of a people and may also suggest why certain changes in their way of life took place.

With the data collected and analyzed by the ethnographer and ethnohistorian, the work of a third type of ethnologist, the **cross-cultural researcher,** can be done. The cross-cultural researcher is interested in discovering general patterns about cultural traits—what is universal, what is variable, why traits vary, and what the consequences of the variability might be. Why, for example, is there more gender inequality in some societies than in others? Is family violence related to aggression in other areas of life? What are the effects of living in a very unpredictable environment? In testing possible answers to such questions, cross-cultural researchers use data from samples of cultures to try to arrive at explanations or relationships that hold across cultures. Archaeologists may find the results of cross-cultural research useful for making inferences about the past, particularly if they can discover material indicators of cultural variation.

Because ethnologists may be interested in many aspects of customary behavior and thought—from economic behavior to political behavior to styles of art, music, and religion—ethnology overlaps with disciplines that concentrate on some particular aspect of human existence, such as sociology, psychology, economics, political science, art, music, and comparative religion. But the distinctive feature of cultural anthropology is its interest in how all these aspects of human existence vary from society to society, in all historical periods, and in all parts of the world.

Applied Anthropology

All knowledge may turn out to be useful. In the physical and biological sciences it is well understood that technological breakthroughs like DNA splicing, spacecraft docking in outer space, and the development of miniscule computer chips could not have taken place without an enormous amount of basic research to uncover the laws of nature in the physical and biological worlds. If we did not understand fundamental principles, the technological achievements we are so proud of would not be possible. Researchers are often simply driven by curiosity, with no thought to where the research might lead, which is why such research is sometimes called *basic research.* The same is true of the social sciences. If a researcher finds out that societies with combative sports tend to have more wars, it may lead to other inquiries about the relationships between one kind of aggression and an-

other. The knowledge acquired may ultimately lead to discovering ways to correct social problems, such as family violence and war.

Whereas basic research may ultimately help to solve practical problems, applied research is more explicit in its practical goals. Today about half of all professional anthropologists are applied, or practicing, anthropologists. **Applied** or **practicing anthropology** is explicit in its concern with making anthropological knowledge useful.[3] Applied anthropologists may be trained in any or all of the subfields of anthropology. In contrast to basic researchers, who are almost always employed in colleges, universities, and museums, applied anthropologists are usually employed in settings outside traditional academia, including government agencies, international development agencies, private consulting firms, businesses, public health organizations, medical schools, law offices, community development agencies, and charitable foundations.

Biological anthropologists may be called upon to give forensic evidence in court, or they may work in public health, or design clothes and equipment to fit human anatomy. Archaeologists may be involved in preserving and exhibiting artifacts for museums and in doing contract work to find and preserve cultural sites that might be damaged by construction or excavation. Linguists may work in bilingual educational training programs or may work on ways to improve communication. Ethnologists may work in a wide variety of applied projects ranging from community development, urban planning, health care, and agricultural improvement to personnel and organizational management and assessment of the impact of change programs on people's lives.[4] We discuss applied anthropology more fully in the section "Using Anthropology."

◎ Specialization

As disciplines grow, they tend to develop more and more specialties. This trend is probably inevitable because, as knowledge accumulates and methods become more advanced, there is a limit to what any one person can reasonably keep track of. So, in addition to the general divisions we have outlined already, particular anthropologists tend to identify themselves with a variety of specializations. It is common for anthropologists to have a geographic specialty, which may be as broad as Old World or New World or as narrow as the southwestern United States. And those who study the past (archaeologists or human paleontologists) may also specialize in different time periods. Ethnologists often specialize in more specific subject matters in addition to one or two cultural areas. Just as most of the chapters in this book refer to broad subject specialties, so some ethnologists identify themselves as *economic anthropologists,* or *political anthropologists,* or *psychological anthropologists.* Others may identify themselves by theoretical orientations, such as *cultural ecologists,* who are concerned with the relationship between culture and the physical and social environments.

CURRENT RESEARCH AND ISSUES

Researcher at Work: Terence E. Hays

Books and articles often report research in a straightforward manner: Here's the problem, here's the answer—that kind of thing. But many researchers know from experience that knowledge does not always come in a straightforward manner. Now a professor at Rhode Island College, Terence E. Hays has reflected on the twists and turns in his fieldwork among the Ndumba in the Eastern Highlands Province of Papua New Guinea. He first started studying whether different types of people (e.g., women and men) had different types of plant knowledge and whether they classified plants differently. (The interest in plant and animal classification, *ethnobiology,* is closely connected with linguistic research.) In the course of his first fieldwork, in 1972, he witnessed an initiation ceremony for 10- to 12-year-old males—a dramatic and traumatic rite of passage ceremony that included the physical trauma of nose-bleeding as well as the social traumas of "attacks" by women and seclu-

sion in the forest. The ceremony was full of symbolism of why the sexes needed to avoid each other. And while he collected stories and myths about plants for his research on ethnobiology, he kept uncovering themes in the stories about the danger of men associating with women.

Hays's curiosity was aroused about these ceremonies and myths. How important are myths in perpetuating cultural themes? Do other societies that have separate men's houses have similar myths? He realized when he returned home from the field that many societies have similar stories. Are these stories generally linked to initiation rites and to physical segregation of the sexes? Answering these questions required comparison, so he embarked on collecting myths and folktales from colleagues who worked in other New Guinea Highland societies. In the course of collecting these comparative materials, he realized he didn't have all the ethnographic information he needed, so he went back to the field to get it. As Hays remarked, "As an ethnographer I was continually faced with the question, How do you know it's true? But even when I could reach a (hard-won) conviction that something was true for the Ndumba, the second question awaited: How do you know it's generally true, which you can't know without comparison?"

Terence Hays.

Source: Terence E. Hays, "From Ethnographer to Comparativist and Back Again," in *Research Frontiers,* in Carol R. Ember, Melvin Ember, and Peter N. Peregrine eds., *New Directions in Anthropology* (Upper Saddle River, NJ: Prentice Hall, CD-ROM, 2004).

These specialties are not mutually exclusive, however. A cultural ecologist, for example, might be interested in the effects of the environment on economic behavior, or political behavior, or how people bring up their children.

Does specialization isolate an anthropologist from other kinds of research? Not necessarily. Some specialties have to draw on information from several fields, inside and outside

anthropology. For example, *medical anthropologists* study the cultural and biological contexts of human health and illness. Thus, they need to understand the economy, diet, and patterns of social interaction, as well as attitudes and beliefs regarding illness and health. In addition, they may need to draw on research in human genetics, public health, and medicine.

APPLIED ANTHROPOLOGY

Getting Development Programs to Notice Women's Contributions to Agriculture

When Anita Spring first did fieldwork in Zambia in the 1970s, she was not particularly interested in agriculture. Rather, medical anthropology was her interest. Her work focused on customary healing practices, particularly involving women and children. She was surprised at the end of the year when a delegation of women came to tell her that she didn't understand what it meant to be a woman. "To be a woman is to be a farmer," they said. She admits that it took her a while to pay attention to women as farmers, but then she began to participate in efforts to provide technical assistance to them. Like many others interested in women in development, Spring realized that all too often development agents downplay women's contributions to agriculture.

How does one bring about change in male-centered attitudes and practices? One way is to document how much women actually contribute to agriculture. Beginning with the influential writing of Ester Boserup in *Woman's Role in Economic Development* (1970), scholars began to report that in Africa south of the Sahara, in the Caribbean, and in parts of Southeast Asia, women were the principal farmers or agricultural laborers. Moreover, as agriculture became more complex, it required more work time in the fields, so the women's contribution to agriculture increased. In addition, men increasingly went away to work, so women had to do much of what used to be men's work on the farms.

In the 1980s, Spring designed and directed the Women in Agricultural Development Project in Malawi, funded by the Office of Women in the U.S. Agency for International Development. Rather than focusing just on women, the project aimed to collect data on both women and men agriculturalists and how they were treated by development agents. The project did more than collect information; mini-projects were set up and evaluated so that successful training techniques could be passed on to development agents in other regions. Spring points out that the success of the program was due not just to the design of the project. Much of the success depended on the interest and willingness of Malawi itself to change. And it didn't hurt that the United Nations and other donor organizations increasingly focused attention on women. It takes the efforts of many to bring about change. Increasingly, applied anthropologists like Anita Spring are involved in these efforts from beginning to end, from the design stage to implementation and evaluation.

Source: Anita Spring, *Agricultural Development and Gender Issues in Malawi* (Lanham, MD: University Press of America, 1995).

The Relevance of Anthropology

Anthropology is a comparatively young discipline. It was only in the late 1800s that anthropologists began to go to live with people in faraway places. Compared to our knowledge of the physical laws of nature, we know much less about people, about how and why they behave as they do. That anthropology and other sciences dealing with humans began to develop only relatively recently is not in itself a sufficient reason for our knowing less than in the physical sciences. Why, in our quest for knowledge of all kinds, did we wait so long to study ourselves? Leslie White suggests that those phenomena most remote from us and least significant as determinants of human behavior were the first to be studied. The reason, he surmises, is that humans like to think of themselves as citadels of free will, subject to no laws of nature. Hence, there is no need to see ourselves as objects to be explained.[5]

The idea that it is impossible to account for human behavior scientifically, either because our actions and beliefs are too individualistic and complex or because human beings are understandable only in otherworldly terms, is a self-fulfilling notion. We cannot discover principles explaining human behavior if we neither believe such principles exist nor bother to look for them. The result is assured from the beginning. Persons who do not believe in principles of human behavior will be reinforced by their finding none. If we are to increase our understanding of human beings, we first have to believe it is possible to do so.

If we aim to understand humans, it is essential that we study humans in all times and places. We must study ancient

In urban areas before new construction begins, archaeologists may be called upon to excavate and record information on historical sites, as here in New York City.

humans and modern humans. We must study their cultures and their biology. How else can we understand what is true of humans generally or how they are capable of varying? If we study just our own society, we may come up only with explanations that are culture-bound, not general or applicable to most or all humans. Anthropology is useful, then, to the degree that it contributes to our understanding of human beings everywhere.

In addition, anthropology is relevant because it helps us avoid misunderstandings between peoples. If we can understand why other groups are different from ourselves, we might have less reason to condemn them for behavior that appears strange to us. We may then come to realize that many differences between peoples are products of physical and cultural adaptations to different environ-

A large number of emigrants from the former Soviet Union, particularly from Black Sea cities and towns such as Odessa, live in the Brighton Beach neighborhood of Brooklyn. Migrant and immigrant communities, such as "Little Odessa," are an increasing focus of anthropological study.

ments. For example, someone who first finds out about the !Kung as they lived in the Kalahari Desert of southern Africa in the 1950s might assume that the !Kung were "backward." (The exclamation point in the name !Kung signifies one of the clicking sounds made with the tongue by speakers of the !Kung language.) The !Kung wore little clothing, had few possessions, lived in meager shelters, and enjoyed none of our technological niceties like radio and computers. But let us reflect on how a typical North American community might react if it awoke to find itself in an environment similar to that in which the !Kung lived. The people would find that the arid land makes both agriculture and animal husbandry impossible, and they might have to think about adopting a nomadic existence. They might then discard many of their material possessions so that they could travel easily, in order to take advantage of changing water and food supplies. Because of the extreme heat and the lack of extra water for laundry, they might find it more practical to be almost naked than to wear clothes. They would undoubtedly find it impossible to build elaborate homes. For social security, they might start to share the food brought into the group. Thus, if they survived at all, they might end up looking and acting far more like the !Kung looked than like typical North Americans.

Physical differences, too, may be seen as results of adaptations to the environment. For example, in our society we admire people who are tall and slim. If these same individuals were forced to live above the Arctic Circle, however, they might wish they could trade their tall, slim bodies for short, compact ones, because stocky physiques conserve body heat more effectively and may therefore be more adaptive in cold climates.

Exposure to anthropology might help to alleviate some of the misunderstandings that arise between people of different cultural groups from subtle causes operating below the level of consciousness. For example, different cultures have different conceptions of the gestures and interpersonal distances that are appropriate under various circumstances. Arabs consider it proper to stand close enough to other people to smell them.[6] On the basis of the popularity of deodorants in our culture, we can deduce that Americans prefer to keep the olfactory dimension out of interpersonal relations. We may feel that a person who comes too close is being too intimate. We should remember, however, that this person may only be acting according to a culturally conditioned conception of what is proper in a given situation. If our intolerance for others results in part from a lack of understanding of why peoples vary, then the knowledge accumulated by anthropologists may help lessen that intolerance.

As the world becomes increasingly interconnected or globalized, the importance of understanding and trying to respect cultural and physical differences becomes necessary. Misunderstandings can cause people to go to war, and war with modern weapons of mass destruction can kill more people than ever before. The gap between rich and poor countries has widened and anthropologists have been increasingly concerned with the effects of inequality. Even when the powerful countries want to help others, they often try to impose their ways of life, which they consider superior. But anthropologists may not think that particular ways of life are generally superior. What's good for some may not be good for other people in different circumstances. To find out if some change will be advantageous requires careful study. And there are ethical issues. Is it ethical to try to interfere with other people's lives? Is it ethical not to, if they are suffering or ask for help? Anthropologists often have to wrestle with these questions.

Knowledge of our past may bring both a feeling of humility and a sense of accomplishment. If we are to attempt to deal with the problems of our world, we must be aware of our vulnerability so that we do not think that problems will solve themselves. But we also have to think enough of our accomplishments to believe that we can find solutions to problems. Much of the trouble we get into may be a result of feelings of self-importance and invulnerability—in short, our lack of humility. Knowing something about our evolutionary past may help us to understand and accept our place in the biological world. Just as for any other form of life, there is no guarantee that any particular human population, or even the entire human species, will perpetuate itself indefinitely. The earth changes, the environment changes, and humanity itself changes. What survives and flourishes in the present might not do so in the future.

Yet our vulnerability should not make us feel powerless. There are many reasons to feel confident about the future. Consider what we have accomplished so far. By means of tools and weapons fashioned from sticks and stones, we were able to hunt animals larger and more powerful than ourselves. We discovered how to make fire,

and we learned to use it to keep ourselves warm and to cook our food. As we domesticated plants and animals, we gained greater control over our food supply and were able to establish more permanent settlements. We mined and smelted ores to fashion more durable tools. We built cities and irrigation systems, monuments and ships. We made it possible to travel from one continent to another in a single day. We conquered some illnesses and prolonged human life.

In short, human beings and their cultures have changed considerably over the course of history. Human populations have often been able to adapt to changing circumstances. Let us hope that humans continue to adapt to the challenges of the present and future.

◎ Summary

1. Anthropology is literally the study of human beings. It differs from other disciplines concerned with people in that it is broader in scope. It is concerned with humans in all places of the world (not simply those places close to us), and it traces human evolution and cultural development from millions of years ago to the present day.

2. Another distinguishing feature of anthropology is its holistic approach to the study of human beings. Anthropologists study not only all varieties of people but also all aspects of those peoples' experiences.

3. Anthropologists are concerned with identifying and explaining typical characteristics (traits, customs) of particular human populations.

4. Biological or physical anthropology is one of the major fields of the discipline. Biological anthropology studies the emergence of humans and their later physical evolution (the focus called human paleontology). It also studies how and why contemporary human populations vary biologically (the focus called human variation).

5. Another broad area of concern to anthropology is cultural anthropology. Its three subfields—archaeology, anthropological linguistics, and ethnology (now usually referred to by the parent name, cultural anthropology)—all deal with aspects of human culture, that is, with the customary ways of thinking and behaving of particular societies.

6. Archaeologists seek not only to reconstruct the daily life and customs of prehistoric peoples but also to trace cultural changes and offer possible explanations for those changes. Therefore, archaeologists try to reconstruct history from the remains of human cultures.

7. Anthropological linguists are concerned with the emergence of language and with the divergence of languages

over time (a subject known as historical linguistics). They also study how contemporary languages differ, both in construction (descriptive or structural linguistics) and in actual speech (sociolinguistics).

8. The ethnologist (now often called simply a cultural anthropologist) seeks to understand how and why peoples of today and the recent past differ in their customary ways of thinking and acting. One type of ethnologist, the ethnographer, usually spends a year or so living with and talking to a particular population and observing their customs. Later, she or he may prepare a detailed description (an ethnography) of many or some aspects of cultural and social life. Another type of ethnologist, the ethnohistorian, investigates written documents to determine how the ways of life of a particular group of people have changed over time. A third type of ethnologist, the cross-cultural researcher, studies data collected by ethnographers and ethnohistorians for a sample of cultures and attempts to discover which explanations of particular customs may be generally applicable.

9. In all four major subdisciplines of anthropology, there are applied anthropologists, people who apply anthropological knowledge to achieve more practical goals, usually in the service of an agency outside the traditional academic setting.

10. Anthropology may help people to be more tolerant. Anthropological studies can show us why other people are the way they are, both culturally and physically. Customs or actions that appear improper or offensive to us may be other people's adaptations to particular environmental and social conditions.

11. Anthropology is also valuable in that knowledge of our past may bring us both a feeling of humility and a sense of accomplishment. Like any other form of life, we have no guarantee that any particular human population will perpetuate itself indefinitely. Yet knowledge of our achievements in the past may give us confidence in our ability to solve the problems of the future.

◎ Glossary Terms

anthropological linguistics	6	cross-cultural researcher	9
anthropology	3	cultural anthropology	6
applied (practicing) anthropology	9	culture	6
archaeology	6	descriptive (structural) linguistics	7
biological (physical) anthropology	5	ethnographer	8

ethnography	8	human paleontology	5
ethnohistorian	8	human variation	5
ethnology	6	paleoanthropology	5
fossils	5	prehistory	6
historical archaeology	6	Primates	5
historical linguistics	7	primatologists	5
holistic	4	sociolinguistics	7
Homo sapiens	5		

◎ Critical Questions

1. Why study anthropology? What are its goals and how is it useful?

2. How does anthropology differ from other fields of study you've encountered that deal with humans? (Compare with psychology, sociology, political science, history, or biology, among others.)

3. What do you think about the suggestion that anthropology is the fundamental discipline concerned with humans?

◎ Research Navigator

1. To access the full resources of Research Navigator, please find the access code printed on the inside cover of the *Prentice Hall Guide to Research Navigator*. You may have received this booklet if your instructor recommended this guide be packaged with new textbooks. (If your book did not come with this printed guide, you can purchase one through your college bookstore.) Visit our Research Navigator site at **www.researchnavigator.com**. Once at this site click on REGISTER under New Users and enter your access code to create a personal LOGIN NAME and PASSWORD. (When revisiting the site, use the same Login Name and Password.) Browse the features of the Research Navigator Web site and search the databases of academic journals, newspapers, magazines, and Web links.

2. Go to the Link Library section and search using the "Anthropology" subject in the pull-down menu. Using the letters A–Z search for the various subfields of anthropology (cultural anthropology or ethnology, archaeology, linguistics, and physical or biological anthropology). For each of the subfields find a relevant Web site and describe something new you've learned from the Web site.

Chapter 1 © WHAT IS ANTHROPOLOGY? 15

© Discovering Anthropology: Researchers at Work

Read the chapter by Terence E. Hays, "From Ethnographer to Comparativist and Back Again," in the accompanying *Discovering Anthropology* reader, and answer the following questions:

1. Many researchers find that their interests change when they go to the field. What did Hays start out studying? What did he get more interested in?

2. Explain why Hays thinks that you need both ethnography and comparison.

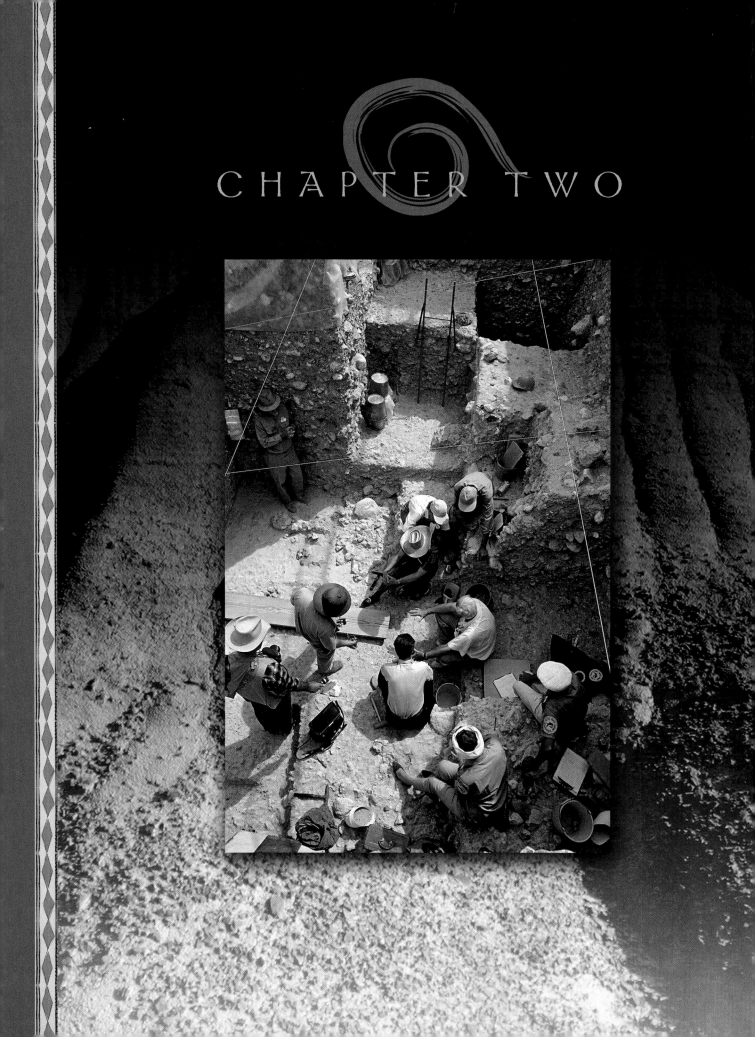

CHAPTER TWO

How We Discover the Past

ow can archaeologists and **paleoanthropologists** (anthropologists who study human evolution) know about what may have happened thousands or even millions of years ago? There are no written records from those periods from which to draw inferences. But we do have other kinds of "record," other kinds of evidence from the past. And we have ways of "reading" this evidence that allow us to know quite a lot about how our human ancestors evolved and how they lived long ago.

The Evidence of the Past

Archaeologists and paleoanthropologists rely on four kinds of evidence to learn about the past: *artifacts, ecofacts, fossils,* and *features.* As we will see, each provides unique information about the past. Together, artifacts, ecofacts, fossils, and features provide a detailed story about human life long ago. However, we need to be trained to "read" this story.

Artifacts

Anything made or modified by humans is an **artifact.** The book you are reading now, the chair you are sitting in, the pen you are taking notes with are all artifacts. In fact, we are surrounded by artifacts, most of which we will lose or throw away. And that is exactly how things enter what we call the "archaeological record." Think about it: How much garbage do you produce in a day? What kinds of things do you throw away? Mostly paper, probably, but also wood (from the ice cream bar you had at lunch), plastic (like the pen that ran out of ink last night), and even metal (the dull blade on your razor). Into the garbage they go and out to the dump or landfill. Under the right conditions many of those items will survive for future archaeologists to find. Most of the artifacts that make up the archaeological record are just this kind of mundane waste—the accumulated garbage of daily life that archaeologists may recover and examine to reconstruct what daily life was like long ago.

By far the most common artifacts from the past are stone tools, which archaeologists call **lithics**. Indeed, lithics are the only kind of artifact available for 99 percent of human history. Humans first started using stone tools more than 2.5 million years ago, and some tools of stone (grinding and polishing stones, for example) are still used today. Stone has been used for almost any purpose you can think of, from cutting tools to oil lamps, although their most common use has probably been as hunting, butchering, and hide-processing tools. Another common kind of artifact is **ceramics** (pots and other items made from baked clay). Humans first started making ceramics about 10,000 years ago, and ceramic objects such as storage and cooking vessels quickly came to be used widely. Because they are both fragile and relatively easy to make, ceramics show up frequently in the garbage that makes up the archaeological record. Wood and bone artifacts are common too, and were used to make hide-working, cooking, hunting, and even butchering tools. Wood and bone tools have been used by humans at least as long as stone tools, but unlike stone tools, they tend not to survive well in the

archaeological record. In some places metals and glass are also common artifacts. These survive well in the archaeological record, and hence they are often found where they were used.

Ecofacts

Ecofacts are natural objects that have been used or affected by humans. A good example is the bone from animals that people have eaten. These bones are somewhat like artifacts, but they haven't been made or modified by humans, just used and discarded by them. Another example is pollen found at archaeological sites. Because humans bring plants back to their houses to use, pollens from many plants are commonly found. These pollens may not have come from the same location. The only reason they are together is that they have been brought together by human use. Other examples are the remains of insect and animal pests that associate with humans, such as cockroaches and mice. Their remains are found in sites because they associate with humans and survive by taking advantage of the conditions that humans create. Their presence is in part caused by the human presence, and thus they are considered ecofacts too.

Fossils

And then there are fossils, which are rare but particularly informative about human biological evolution. A **fossil** may be an impression of an insect or leaf on a muddy surface that now is stone. Or it may consist of the actual hardened remains of an animal's skeletal structure. When an animal dies, the organic matter that made up its body begins to deteriorate. The teeth and skeletal structure are composed largely of inorganic mineral salts, and soon they are all that remains. Under most conditions, these parts eventually deteriorate too. But once in a great while conditions are favorable for preservation—for instance, when volcanic ash, limestone, or highly mineralized groundwater is present to form a high-mineral environment. If the remains are buried under such circumstances, the minerals in the ground may become bound into the structure of the teeth or bone, hard-ening the remains and thus making them less likely to deteriorate.

But we don't have fossil remains of everything that lived in the past, and sometimes we only have fragments from one or a few individuals. So the fossil record is very incomplete. For example, Robert Martin estimates that the earth has probably seen 6,000 primate species; remains of only 3 percent of those species have been found. It is hardly surprising that primate paleontologists cannot identify most of the evolutionary connections between early and later forms. The task is particularly difficult with small mammals, such as the early primates, which are less likely than large animals to be preserved in the fossil record.[1]

Features

Features are a kind of artifact, but archaeologists distinguish them from other artifacts because they cannot be easily removed from an archaeological site. Hearths are good examples. When humans build a fire on bare ground the soil becomes heated and is changed—all the water is driven out of it and its crystalline structure is broken down and reformed. It becomes hard, redder, and even slightly magnetic (as we discuss later). When an archaeologist finds a hearth, what exactly is found? An area of hard, reddish soil, often surrounded by charcoal and ash. Here, then, is an artifact—an object of human manufacture. But it would be very hard, if not impossible, for the archaeologist to pick the hearth up and take it back to the lab for study like a lithic or ceramic. A hearth is really an intrinsic feature of a site—hence the name *feature*.

Hearths are common features, but by far the most common features are called *pits*. Pits are simply holes dug by humans that are later filled with garbage or eroded soil. They are usually fairly easy to distinguish because the garbage or soil they are filled with is often different in color and texture from the soil the pit was dug into. *Living floors* are another common type of feature. These are the places where humans lived and worked. The soils in these locations are often compacted through human activity and are full of minute pieces of garbage—seeds, small stone flakes, beads,

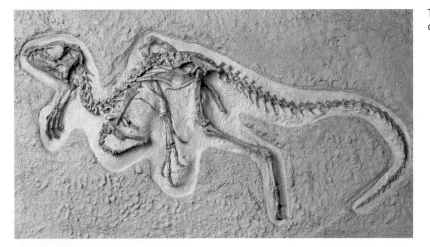

The fossilized skeleton of an Ornithopod dinosaur.

and the like—that became embedded in the floor. A large or very deep area of such debris is called a *midden.* Middens are often the remains of garbage dumps or areas repeatedly used over long periods of time, such as caves. Finally, *buildings* are a common feature on archaeological sites. These can range from the remains of stone rings that once held down the sides of tents to palaces built of stones that had been shaped and fitted together. Even the remains of wooden houses (or parts of them) have been preserved under some conditions. Features are a diverse array of things that can provide lots of information about the past.

Finding the Evidence

Evidence of the past is all around us, but finding it is not always easy or productive. Archaeologists and paleoanthropologists usually restrict their search to what are called *sites.* **Sites** are known or suspected locations of human activity in the past that contain a record of that activity. Sites can range from places where humans camped for perhaps only one night to large ancient cities. Regardless of their size or complexity, sites can reveal many things about life in the past.

How Are Sites Created?

Sites are created when the remnants of human activity are covered or buried by some natural process. The most dramatic one is volcanic activity; the record of human behavior (and even the humans themselves) can be totally buried within seconds. The most impressive example of this must be Pompeii, an entire city that was buried in the eruption of Mount Vesuvius in A.D. 79. Today archaeologists are digging out the city and finding the remains of ancient life just as it was left in the moments before the eruption.[2] Less dramatic means of burying the record of human behavior are the natural processes of dirt accumulation and erosion. Wind- or water-borne soil and debris can cover a site either quickly (as in a flood) or over a long period of time, pre-

serving intact the artifacts, ecofacts, fossils, and features left by humans. Finally, the processes through which soils are built up can also bury artifacts, ecofacts, fossils, and features in a way that allows archaeologists to uncover them later. In forests, for example, falling leaves cover the locations where humans camped. Over time the leaves decay and build up soil, covering the remains of the human encampment slowly but completely over many years.

Since good locations to live and work in are often reused by humans, many sites contain the remains of numerous human occupations. The most valuable sites to archaeologists and paleoanthropologists are those in which the burial processes worked quickly enough that each use of the site is clearly separated from the previous one. Such sites are called **stratified;** each layer, or *stratum,* of human occupation is separate like a layer in a layer cake. Not only do stratified sites allow the archaeologist or paleoanthropologist to distinguish the sequence of site occupations, but the strata themselves provide a way to know the relative ages of the occupations—earlier occupations will always be below later ones.

Taphonomy

It is important to note that the very processes that create sites can often damage or destroy them. The study of the processes of site disturbance and destruction is called **taphonomy.** Some archaeologists and paleoanthropologists argue that natural processes such as wind and water erosion not only bury the materials left by humans but may affect them so significantly that we need to be very cautious when interpreting what is found in an archaeological site. For example, Harold Dibble and his colleagues have argued that the Lower Paleolithic site of Cagny-L'Epinette in France does not actually contain locations where Lower Paleolithic peoples lived and worked, as previous excavators suggested. Rather, Dibble and his colleagues argue that what looks like locations of human activity were created by water running across the site and accumulating artifacts in low-lying places.[3] This doesn't mean that nothing can be learned from such a site, even one that has been subjected to considerable

A site is a location where archaeological materials are found in context. Here Vietnamese archaeologists expose the remains of the ancient citadel of Hanoi, preserved below the modern city.

disturbance, but rather that archaeologists and paleoanthropologists must use caution when interpreting the site. An understanding of site taphonomy can help an archaeologist make an informed and cautious interpretation of the past.[4]

How Are Sites Found?

There is no single method of finding sites, and indeed many sites are found by happenstance—someone digs into the ground and discovers a lot of artifacts or perhaps a feature. But when archaeologists and paleoanthropologists want to go out and find sites, they typically employ one of two basic methods: pedestrian survey and remote sensing.

Pedestrian survey is what the name suggests—walking around and looking for sites. But there are a number of techniques that archaeologists and paleoanthropologists use to enhance the effectiveness of pedestrian survey beyond simply walking around. These include the use of sampling and systematic surveying methods to reduce the area to be covered on foot. Another way archaeologists reduce the area to be examined is by focusing their search on places humans are likely to have occupied. Paleoanthropologists, for example, typically focus only on those locations where there are exposed fossil beds dating to the time period of the early humans or apes they are interested in finding. Pedestrian survey, while very low tech, can be an extremely effective way of finding sites.

Remote sensing is a much more high-tech way of finding sites. With remote sensing techniques, archaeologists and paleoanthropologists find archaeological deposits by sensing their presence from a remote location, usually the current surface of the ground beneath which the archaeological deposits are buried. Most remote sensing techniques are borrowed from exploration geology, and are the same ones geologists use to find mineral or oil deposits. They typically involve the measurement of minute variations in phenomena like the earth's magnetic or gravitational field, or changes in an electric current or pulse of energy directed into the ground. When these subtle changes, called *anomalies,* are located, more detailed exploration can be done to map the extent and depth of the buried archaeological deposits.

One of the most common remote sensing techniques used in archaeology is *geomagnetics.* Geomagnetic sensing is based on the fact that the earth has a strong magnetic field that varies locally depending on what is beneath the ground. Features such as hearths, stone walls, and pits filled with organic material can alter the earth's magnetic field, as can metal and ceramic artifacts. By carefully measuring the earth's magnetic field, an archaeologist can often locate these features and artifacts. The archaeologist uses a highly sensitive instrument called a magnetometer to map the earth's magnetic field over a large area. When the map is complete, areas with anomalously high or low readings point to locations where buried features or artifacts may be present. In many cases, these anomalies form patterns that can be easily interpreted. For example, the remains of a buried house may be "seen."

Geomagnetic sensing is called a "passive" technique because the archaeologist simply measures the existing magnetic field. There are also "active" remote sensing techniques by which the archaeologist sends a pulse of energy into the ground and records how it is affected by whatever is buried. One of the most commonly used active techniques is *soil interface radar* (SIR), sometimes also called *ground penetrating radar* (GPR). This technique is based on the fact that different soils reflect radar energy differently. By sending a radar pulse into the ground and recording how the soils reflect it, the archaeologist can map the various soils below the ground. More importantly, if there are features such as walls and pits below the ground, those can be mapped as well. To conduct a radar survey, the archaeologist pulls an antenna along the ground, the size of which depends on the depth of penetration the archaeologist wants and the features expected. The antenna both sends and receives the radar pulses, and the received radar reflections are recorded on a paper strip or in a computer file. These recordings give the archaeologist a picture of what is below the ground.

How Are Artifacts, Ecofacts, and Features Recovered from Sites?

Whether they are identified by pedestrian survey or remote sensing, once archaeological deposits are found there is only one way to recover them—by excavation. Excavation itself is a complex process with two goals: (1) to find every scrap of evidence (or a statistically representative sample) about the past that a given site holds, and (2) to record the horizontal and vertical location of that evidence with precision. Archaeologists and paleoanthropologists have developed many excavation strategies and techniques to accomplish these goals, but all of them involve the careful removal of the archaeological deposits; the recovery of artifacts, ecofacts, fossils, and features from the soil in which those deposits have been buried; and the detailed recording of where each artifact, ecofact, fossil, and feature was located on the site.

Excavation does not mean simply digging holes, not even neat square ones. But few sites can ever be fully excavated. The cost involved would be tremendous, and most archaeologists feel it is important to leave some archaeological deposits undisturbed for future archaeologists using new techniques. And so archaeological excavations usually use some method of sampling, which allows archaeologists to recover a full range of artifacts, ecofacts, fossils, and features from only a small portion of a site. Sampling, however, requires that the archaeologist carefully plan where excavations will be conducted so that all areas of the site have an equal likelihood of being examined.

To date, no one has figured out a way to recover artifacts, ecofacts, fossils, and features from a site without destroying the site in the process, and this is one of the strange ironies of archaeological research. As we discuss shortly, it is the relationships between and among artifacts, ecofacts, fossils, and features that are of most interest to archaeologists, and it is precisely these relationships that are destroyed when archaeologists remove them from a site. For this reason most excavation by professional archaeologists today is done only when a site is threatened with destruction, and then only by highly

Paleoanthropologists excavating an early human site in northwestern Kenya. The exposed fossils are those of an elephant that may have been butchered by humans.

trained personnel using rigorous techniques. Archaeologists and paleoanthropologists collect data in basically the same ways, with one important difference. Archaeologists are most concerned with recovering intact features, whereas paleoanthropologists are most concerned with recovering intact fossils. This leads to some differences in approaches to collecting data, particularly where to look. So archaeologists tend to seek out undisturbed sites where intact features can be found. In contrast, disturbances are a plus for paleoanthropologists, because disturbed sites may make finding fossils easier—they may be eroding out of the surface of the ground and be easily visible without digging. This doesn't mean archaeologists never excavate disturbed sites, because they do. And paleoanthropologists have sometimes made important discoveries by excavating undisturbed sites.[5]

⊚ Analyzing the Evidence

Once archaeologists and paleoanthropologists have found a site and recovered artifacts and other materials from it, they are ready to begin "reading" what they've found to learn the story of the past. This "reading" of the archaeological record is called *analysis.* Like excavation, archaeological analysis is a varied and sophisticated process that we will touch on only briefly here.

It should be obvious from our discussion of the archaeological record that much of what is lost or discarded by humans never survives. It is also the case that much of what does survive comes to us in fragments and in a fragile, deteriorated state. Before doing analysis, then, archaeologists and paleoanthropologists must first conserve and reconstruct the materials they have found.

Conservation and Reconstruction

Conservation is the process of treating artifacts, ecofacts, and in some cases even features, to stop decay and, if possible, reverse the deterioration process. Some conservation is

very simple, involving only cleaning and drying the item. Some conservation is highly complex, involving long-term chemical treatments and long-term storage under controlled conditions. The so-called "Ice Man," for example, the 5,000-year-old individual found in 1993 in the Italian Alps, is kept in permanently glacial-like conditions after investigators found to their dismay that warming the remains for study induced the growth of mold. The archaeologists removed the mold, but decided that his remains would have to be kept under the same conditions that preserved them in the first place, and so a complex storage facility had to be built to recreate the glacial environment in which he was originally found.[6]

Reconstruction is like building a three-dimensional puzzle where you're not sure which pieces belong and you know not all of the pieces are there. First, materials have to be sorted into similar types. For example, to reconstruct ceramics from a site, all the ceramics have to be sorted into types with similar color, decoration, and shapes. Then the similar pieces are compared to see if any seem to come from the same vessel. Once all the pieces thought to be from the same vessel are located, they can be assembled. Reconstruction is a long, difficult process—in some cases taking years.

What Can We Learn from Artifacts?

Once conservation and reconstruction are complete, the archaeologist or paleoanthropologist can begin to analyze the artifacts they've found. Archaeologists have developed specific and often unique ways to analyze the many different types of artifacts. Stone tools are examined in different ways from ceramics, and both are examined differently from bone. But there are some commonalities in the way artifacts are analyzed, regardless of what they are made of.

First, archaeologists typically examine the *form* or shape of an artifact. For most common artifacts, such as lithics and ceramics, forms are known well enough to be grouped into a **typology** or set of types, which is often the primary

A conservator applying preservative to a decaying Alaskan totem pole.

partial artifacts that might not be classifiable by formal analysis.

Third, archaeologists often attempt to understand how an artifact was made. By examining the material the artifact is made from and how that material was manipulated, archaeologists can learn about the technology, economy, and exchange systems of the peoples who made the artifact. For example, if the material is not locally available, that means the people traded for it. Archaeologists can also study present-day peoples and how they make similar artifacts in order to understand how ancient artifacts were made. Anne Underhill was interested in understanding how ceramics were produced during the Longshan period in China—a time known for its elegant, thin-walled pottery. In addition to studying the Longshan ceramics and the sites they came from, Underhill also visited living potters who make similar vessels today. She found that both full-time and part-time potters produce ceramics today, but was this the case in the past? Underhill measured ceramics being produced by these potters and performed a metric analysis. She found, to her surprise, that both full-time and part-time potters produce high-quality and highly uniform ceramics, difficult to distinguish from one another.[7]

Finally, archaeologists attempt to understand how an artifact was used. Knowing how an artifact was used gives the archaeologist a direct window onto ancient life. A number of sophisticated techniques have been developed to determine use. For stone, bone, and wood tools, there is a technique called *use-wear analysis,* which can determine how a

purpose of *formal analysis.* This is because typologies allow archaeologists to place a particular artifact into context with other artifacts found at the site or at other sites. Typologies often provide a lot of information about an artifact, including its age, the species or culture with which it is affiliated, and in some cases even how it was made, used, or exchanged in the past. Figure 2–1 shows a projectile point typology for a site in Tennessee from the time period between about 7300 and 5000 B.C. Over time the forms of the projectile points changed. The bases of points (*f*) and (*g*) are very different in their form from those of (*c*), (*d*), and (*e*), and all of them are different from (*a*). With this sort of typology, an archaeologist can estimate the age of a projectile point just by looking at the form of its base.

Second, archaeologists often measure artifacts, recording their size in various, often strictly defined, dimensions. Such *metric analysis,* as this activity is called, is used much like formal analysis to group artifacts into a typology. Figure 2–2 shows the standard measurements taken from projectile points. With these measurements one can create a typology similar to that in Figure 2–1. Instead of looking at the form of the projectile points, one looks at their sizes. Clearly, the base widths of points (*a*), (*d*), and (*f*) in Figure 2–1 are going to differ in a manner similar to the way their base forms differ. The value of metric analysis, however, is that the typology created is less subjective than a typology using forms. In addition, many measurements can be taken from broken or

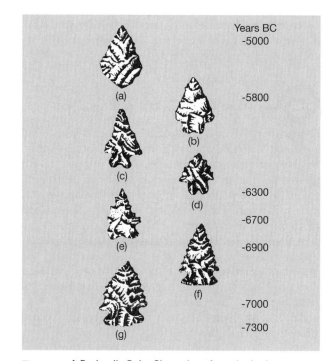

Figure 2–1 A Projectile Point Chronology from the Icehouse Bottom Site in Tennessee

Source: Jefferson Chapman, Tellico Archaeology (Knoxville: Tennessee Valley Authority, 1985), Fig. 1.15.

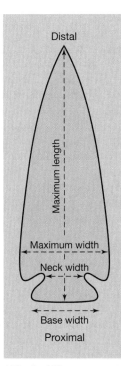

Figure 2–2 Standard Metrical Measurements of Chipped Stone Tools

tool was used through the careful examination of the kind of wear on its edges. We discuss use-wear analysis in more detail in later chapters. For ceramic vessels, techniques have been developed to extract residues trapped in the clay and determine what the vessel held. Archaeologist Patrick McGovern and chemist Rudolf Michel, for example, took samples of a pale yellow residue found in grooves inside ceramic vessels from Grodin Tepe in Turkey. Their analysis determined that the residue was from barley beer, providing the earliest evidence of brewing in the world (the ceramics date from 3500 to 3100 B.C.).[8]

So what can archaeologists learn by placing artifacts in typologies through formal and metric analysis, and by learning how an artifact was manufactured and used? A lot. Typologies allow archaeologists to use relative dating (which we discuss below) to determine the age of an artifact or site by locating it in a sequence involving other artifacts and sites with known ages. Typologies thus allow archaeologists to determine which human groups were related to one another in the distant past, how information was shared among those groups, and in some cases even what social behavior was like (how labor was organized, who traded with whom).

For example, Carla Sinopoli examined the ceramics from the Iron Age site of Vijayanagara, in southern India. Previous excavations had identified distinct residential areas of the site, including a "Noblemen's Quarter," composed of elite residences of high-caste Hindus, the "East Valley," which is thought to contain residences of lower-caste Hindus, and the "Islamic Quarter," which is thought to house Muslim mercenaries. When Sinopoli compared ceramics across the three areas, she found distinct differences: The "Islamic Quarter" had significantly more eating vessels than either of the two other areas, a difference that Sinopoli interpreted as being related to Hindu restrictions on the use of ceramics for holding food (some Hindus will not reuse food containers, so they are often made of disposable materials, such as leaves). So ceramics not only can inform the archaeologist about the social organization of a site, they can also reveal religious beliefs![9] Even gender roles can be revealed archaeologically (see the box "Women in the Shell Mound Archaic").

Knowing how an artifact was made allows the archaeologist to understand the technology and technical abilities of peoples in the past. For example, Thomas Wynn analyzed both the final forms and the methods used by early humans—*Homo erectus*—to make stone tools roughly 300,000 years ago. He found that manufacturing these tools was a multistage process, involving several distinct steps and several distinct stone-working techniques to arrive at the finished product. He then took this information and evaluated it in terms of a measure of human cognitive ability developed by Jean Piaget, and concluded that the people who made these tools probably had organizational abilities similar to those of modern humans.[10]

Longshan thin-walled ceramics of the type studied by Anne Underhill.

Finally, knowing how an artifact was used allows the archaeologist to know something of people's behavior and activities. Lawrence Keeley conducted detailed use-wear analyses on Acheulian hand axes made by *Homo erectus* peoples and found that they had a variety of uses. Some apparently cut meat, others cut wood, and others were used to dig in the ground (probably for edible roots). On some hand axes, one edge was apparently used for one activity and the other for a different activity. Thus hand axes appear to have been multipurpose tools for our *Homo erectus* ancestors—something like a Swiss Army knife that they carried along with them. This knowledge gives us an interesting picture of these people: They used a fairly sophisticated manufacturing technique to make multipurpose tools that they carried with them and used for whatever job was at hand. This is a picture of the behavior of our ancient ancestors that is unavailable from any other source.[11]

What Can We Learn from Ecofacts and Fossils?

Ecofacts are diverse, and what archaeologists and paleoanthropologists can learn from them is highly diverse as well. Here we'll focus on fossils. In a later chapter on the Upper Pa-

An Acheulian hand axe. Lawrence Keeley examined the edge wear on hand axes to determine how they were used.

leolithic world we'll discuss how archaeologists use ecofacts to reconstruct ancient environments. And in a still later chapter on the origins of domesticated plants and animals we'll learn how archaeologists use ecofacts to distinguish wild from domestic plants and animals and to reconstruct how these plants and animals were domesticated.

Paleontologists (studying humans or other species) can tell a great deal about an extinct animal from its fossilized bones or teeth, but that knowledge is based on much more than just the fossil record itself. Paleontologists rely on comparative anatomy to help reconstruct missing skeletal pieces, as well as the soft tissues attached to bone. New techniques, such as electron microscopy, CAT scans, and computer-assisted biomechanical modeling, provide much information about how the organism may have moved about, the microstructure of bone and teeth, and how the organism developed. Chemical analysis of fossilized bone can suggest what the animal typically ate. Paleontologists are also interested in the surroundings of the fossil finds. With methods developed in geology, chemistry, and physics, paleontologists use the surrounding rocks to identify the time period in which the organism died. In addition, the study of associated fauna and flora can suggest what the ancient climate and habitat were like.

Much of the evidence for primate evolution comes from teeth, which are the most common animal parts (along with jaws) to be preserved as fossils. Animals vary in *dentition*—the number and kinds of teeth they have, their size, and their arrangement in the mouth. Dentition provides clues to evolutionary relationships because animals with similar evolutionary histories often have similar teeth. For example, no primate, living or extinct, has more than two incisors in each quarter of the jaw. That feature, along with others, distinguishes the primates from earlier mammals, which had three incisors in each quarter. Dentition also suggests the relative size of an animal and often offers clues about its diet. For example, comparisons of living primates suggest that fruit-eaters have flattened, rounded tooth cusps, unlike leaf- and insect-eaters, which have more pointed cusps.[12] CAT scan methodology has helped paleontologists image the internal parts of teeth, such as the thickness of enamel, which can also suggest the diet (seed- and nut-eaters have thicker enamel). Electron microscopy has revealed different patterns of growth in bones and teeth; different species have different patterns.[13]

Paleontologists can tell much about an animal's posture and locomotion from fragments of its skeleton. Arboreal quadrupeds have front and back limbs of about the same length; because their limbs tend to be short, their center of gravity is close to the branches on which they move. They also tend to have long grasping fingers and toes. Terrestrial quadrupeds are more adapted for speed, so they have longer limbs and shorter fingers and toes. Disproportionate limbs are more characteristic of vertical clingers and leapers and *brachiators* (species that swing through the branches). Vertical clingers and leapers have longer, more powerful hind limbs; brachiators have longer forelimbs.[14] Even though soft tissues are not preserved,

NEW PERSPECTIVES ON GENDER

Women in the Shell Mound Archaic

One of the main issues addressed by archaeologists interested in gender is how we can learn about and understand gender roles in prehistoric cultures. Gender roles might seem impossible to study in archaeological contexts. How is gender preserved in the archaeological record? How can knowledge about gender roles be recovered? Information about gender roles can be recovered if one is aware of how particular kinds of material culture are associated ethnographically with particular gender roles, and changes in them over time. Archaeologists argue that such an awareness leads not only to a better understanding of gender in prehistory but can also lead to a fuller understanding of prehistoric cultures overall.

An example is Cheryl Claassen's work on the Shell Mound Archaic culture of the Tennessee River valley. The Shell Mound Archaic represents the remains of people who lived in Tennessee and Kentucky between about 5,500 and 3,000 years ago. They were hunters and gatherers who lived in small villages, and probably moved seasonally between summer and winter communities. The most distinctive feature of the Shell Mound Archaic is the large mounds of mollusk shells they constructed for burying their dead. Tens of thousands of shells were piled together to create these mounds. Yet, around 3,000 years ago, shellfishing and thus the creation of shell burial mounds stopped abruptly. Claassen wondered why.

Suggested explanations include climate change, overexploitation of shellfish, and the migration of shellfishing peoples from the area. None has proven wholly satisfactory. In contemporary cultures shellfishing is typically done by women and children, and Claassen wondered whether an approach that considered gender roles might be more productive. She decided to approach the problem through the perspective of women's workloads, since it would have been women who would have most likely been the ones shellfishing. The end of shellfishing would have meant that women would have had a lot of free time—free time that could have been put to use in some other way. What might have changed to lead women to stop shellfishing? Did some other activities become more important, so that women's labor was needed more for those other tasks?

Women's labor might have been redirected toward domesticated crops. There is archaeological evidence that about 3,000 years ago several productive crops that required intensive labor came into wide use. For example, *chenopodium*, one of the more plentiful and nutritious of these new crops, has tiny seeds that require considerable labor to harvest, clean, and process. Women were likely the ones burdened with such work. They not only would have harvested these crops but also would have been the ones to process and prepare meals from them. Thus the emergence of agricultural economies would have required women to undertake new labor in food production and processing that may well have forced them to stop engaging in other tasks, like shellfishing, especially if the new tasks produced a larger food supply.

The development of agricultural activities might also have brought about changes in ritual and ceremonialism. The shell burial mounds were clearly central to Shell Mound Archaic death ceremonies. Considerable labor, mostly by women, would have been required to collect the shells and to build these mounds. Later societies in the region buried their dead in earthen mounds. Could this be a reflection of the new importance dirt had in an emerging agricultural economy? If so, what role did women play in ceremonies of death and burial? If they were no longer the providers of the raw materials needed for burial, does that mean their status in society as a whole changed?

We may never know exactly why the Shell Mound Archaic disappeared, or how women's work and women's roles in society changed. But as Claassen points out, taking a gender perspective provides new avenues along which to pursue answers to these questions, and interesting new questions to pursue.

Sources: Cheryl Claassen, "Gender and Archaeology." In P. N. Peregrine, C. R. Ember, and M. Ember, eds., *Archaeology: Original Readings in Method and Practice* (Upper Saddle River, NJ: Prentice Hall, 2002), pp. 210–224, also in Carol R. Ember, Melvin Ember, and Peter N. Peregrine, eds., *Research Frontiers,* in *New Directions in Anthropology* (Upper Saddle River, NJ: Prentice Hall, CD-ROM, 2004); Cheryl Claassen, "Gender, Shellfishing, and the Shell Mound Archaic." In J. Gero and M. Conkey, eds., *Engendering Archaeology: Women and Prehistory* (Oxford: Blackwell, 1991), pp. 276–300.

much can be inferred from the fossils themselves. For example, the form and size of muscles can be estimated by marks found on the bones to which the muscles were attached. And the underside of the cranium may provide information about the proportions of the brain devoted to vision, smell, or memory. The skull also reveals information about characteristics of smell and vision. For example, animals that rely more on smell than on vision tend to have large snouts. Nocturnal animals tend to have large eye sockets.

What Can We Learn from Features?

The analysis of features is a little bit different from the analysis of artifacts, ecofacts, and fossils. Because we cannot remove features to the lab (see our earlier discussion of hearths), we cannot subject them to the same range of analyses as artifacts, ecofacts, and fossils. However, archaeologists have developed a number of powerful tools to analyze features in the field. The primary one is detailed mapping, usually using a surveyor's transit. Extensive records about each feature describe not only what the feature is, but also what archaeological materials were found associated with it. These kinds of information can be combined using a *geographic information system* (GIS). A GIS allows the archaeologist to produce a map of the features on a site and combine that map with information about other archaeological materials found there. Combining these kinds of information can reveal patterns in the archaeological record that tell us about human behaviors in the past.

A good example of how patterns of features can reveal past human behavior comes from the Range Site in west-central Illinois. Humans lived on the Range Site for over a thousand years, and during that time the ways they organized their settlement changed. About 2,300 years ago the people at the Range Site lived in small houses arranged around a circular courtyard. This pattern continued with some elaboration for almost 700 years; the courtyard area was a focus of activity and perhaps ritual. About 1,000 years ago the pattern changed. Houses became more substantial and were arranged linearly, in rows. This change suggests a radical alteration in social organization. From cross-cultural research (comparative studies using ethnographic data), we know that a circular community commonly functions as a single political and economic unit, whereas a community

arranged linearly often consists of more than one political and economic unit. What the changes in the Range Site seem to show is an attenuation or reduction of the basic social and economic unit, from the community to the individual household. This change seems to have occurred because a large, centralized polity developed at Cahokia, only 15 kilometers away. The circular community, and the sociopolitical system it reflected, had persisted at the Range Site for almost a millennium, and then was transformed with the rise of Cahokia.[15]

Putting It All in Context

You might have gained the impression from our discussion that archaeologists and paleoanthropologists analyze artifacts, ecofacts, fossils, and features as individual objects, separate from one another. Nothing could be further from the truth. In fact, the analysis of the Range Site just described is much more like a typical archaeological analysis. It combines information about features across time to come to a generalization about how the social and economic organization of the people living there changed. We call this putting the material in context. **Context** is how and why the artifacts and other materials are related. This is really what archaeology and paleoanthropology are all about. Artifacts, ecofacts, fossils, and features in isolation may be beautiful or interesting by themselves, but it is only when they are placed in context with the other materials found on a site that we are able to "read" and tell the story of the past.

To illustrate this point, let's consider a set of letters that were found separately: A E G I M N N. They are arranged here in alphabetical order, the way a set of beautiful artifacts might be arranged in a museum display in order of size. But do these arrangements tell us anything? No. What if we knew

Archaeologists examining the wall of an excavation at Nippur, Iraq. The thick white line in the wall is the plastered floor of a building. Items found on the floor can all be assumed to date from the same time, while items found below it can be assumed to date from an earlier time. This is a simple example of using stratigraphy for relative dating.

something about the relationships between and among these letters—their context? What if, for example, we knew that the *M* was the first letter found, and that the *A* and *E* were found next to the *M*, but in reverse order, that one *N* was found between the *E* and *I*, and that the other *N* was found between the *I* and the *G*? Knowing in what context the letters were found would tell us that the letters should be arranged like this: *M E A N I N G*. And meaning is exactly what context gives to artifacts, ecofacts, fossils, and features.

Dating the Evidence

An important, indeed vital, part of putting artifacts and other materials into context is putting them in chronological order. To reconstruct the evolutionary history of the primates, for example, one must know how old primate fossils are. For some time, relative dating methods were the only methods available. The last half century has seen important advances in absolute dating, including techniques that allow the dating of the earliest phases of primate evolution. **Relative dating** is used to determine the age of a specimen or deposit relative to another specimen or deposit. **Absolute dating,** or **chronometric dating,** is used to measure how old a specimen or deposit is in years.

Relative Dating Methods

The earliest, and still the most commonly used, method of relative dating is based on **stratigraphy,** the study of how different rock or soil formations are laid down in successive layers or strata (see Figure 2–3). Older layers are generally deeper or lower than more recent layers. Indicator artifacts or ecofacts are used to establish a stratigraphic sequence for the relative dating of new finds. These **indicator artifacts or ecofacts** are items of human manufacture or remains from animals and plants that spread widely over short periods of time, or that disappeared fairly rapidly, or that changed rapidly. Different artifacts and ecofacts are used as indicators of relative age in different areas of the world. In Africa, elephants, pigs, and horses have been particularly important in establishing stratigraphic sequences. Figure 2–3 shows the stratigraphy of Olduvai Gorge, an important site where early human fossils have been found. The stratigraphy here was established in part on the basis of fossil pigs.[16] The various species of pig in the successive strata are different, allowing the archaeologist or paleoanthropologist to differentiate the strata based on the species found within them. Once the stratigraphy of an area is established, the relative ages of two different fossils, or features, in the same or different sites are indicated by the associated indicator artifacts or ecofacts. Major transitions in indicator artifacts or ecofacts define the epochs and larger units of geologic time. The dates of the boundaries between such units are estimated by absolute dating, described in the next section.

If a site has been disturbed, stratigraphy will not be a satisfactory way to determine relative age. As noted earlier, remains from different periods may be washed or blown together by water or wind. Or a landslide may superimpose an earlier layer on a later layer. Still, it may be possible using absolute, or chronometric, dating methods to estimate the relative age of the different fossils found together in a disturbed site.

Absolute, or Chronometric, Dating Methods

Many of the absolute dating methods are based on the decay of a radioactive isotope. Because the rate of decay is known, the age of the specimen can be estimated, within a range of possible error.

RADIOCARBON DATING Radiocarbon, or **carbon-14** (**^{14}C**), **dating** is perhaps the most popularly known method of determining the absolute age of a specimen. It is based on the principle that all living matter possesses a certain amount of a radioactive form of carbon (carbon-14, or ^{14}C). Radioactive carbon, produced when nitrogen-14 is bombarded by cosmic rays, is absorbed from the air by plants and then ingested by animals that eat the plants (see Figure 2–4). After an organism dies, it no longer takes in any of the radioactive carbon. Carbon-14 decays at a slow but steady pace and reverts to nitrogen-14. (By *decays,* we mean that the ^{14}C gives off a certain number of beta radiations per minute.) The rate at which the carbon decays—its **half-life**—is known: ^{14}C has a half-life of 5,730 years. In other words, half of the original amount of ^{14}C in organic matter will have disintegrated 5,730 years after the organism's death; half of the remaining ^{14}C will have disintegrated after another 5,730 years; and so on. After about 50,000 years, the amount of ^{14}C remaining in the organic matter is too small to permit reliable dating.

To discover how long an organism has been dead—that is, to determine how much ^{14}C is left in the organism and therefore how old it is—we either count the number of beta radiations given off per minute per gram of material, or use a particle accelerator to measure the actual amount of ^{14}C in a sample. Modern ^{14}C emits about 15 beta radiations per minute per gram of material, but ^{14}C that is 5,730 years old emits only half that amount (the half-life of ^{14}C) per minute per gram. So if a sample of some organism gives off 7.5 radiations a minute per gram, which is only half the amount given off by modern ^{14}C, the organism must be 5,730 years old. Similarly, because the amount of ^{14}C in a sample slowly declines over time, the atoms in a sample can be sent through a particle accelerator to separate them by weight (the lighter ^{12}C accelerates faster than the heavier ^{14}C) and measure the actual amount of each. This method, called AMS (accelerator mass spectrometry), is more accurate than the beta radiation method, requires only a very small sample of material, and provides a way to date specimens that are up to 80,000 years old.[17]

THERMOLUMINESCENCE DATING Many minerals emit light when they are heated (*thermoluminescence*), even before they become red hot. This cold light comes from

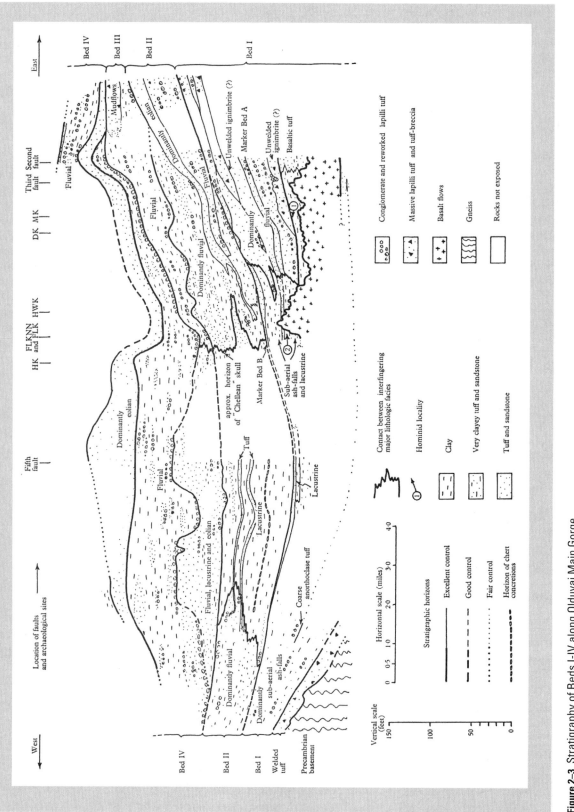

Figure 2-3 Stratigraphy of Beds I–IV along Olduvai Main Gorge

Notice how complex the four stratigraphic layers are—each has numerous layers of soil and rock within them. Index fossils, particularly pigs, along with a series of potassium-argon dates, allowed the researchers to identify the four major strata of the site, which correspond to four major periods of human occupation. Reprinted by permission of Cambridge University Press. Copyright © 1965.

Source: Olduvai Gorge, 1951–61, Volume I, by L. S. B. Leakey.

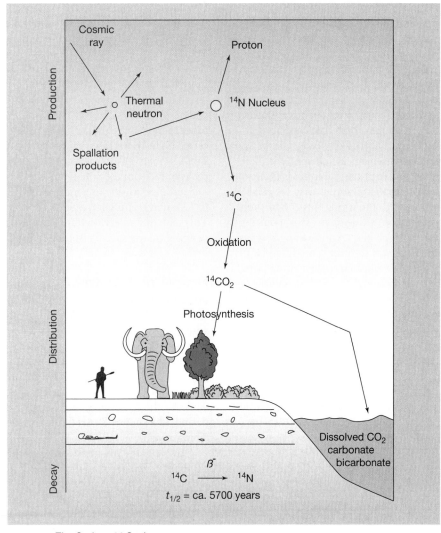

Figure 2–4 The Carbon-14 Cycle

Source: "The Carbon-14 Cycle" from "Radiocarbon Dating" by R. E. Taylor, from *Chronometric Dating in Archaeology* by R. E. Taylor and M. J. Aitken, eds.

the release, under heat, of "outside" electrons trapped in the crystal structure. **Thermoluminescence dating** makes use of the principle that if an object is heated at some point to a high temperature, as when clay is baked to form a pot, it will release all the trapped electrons it held previously. Over time, the object will continue to trap electrons from radioactive elements (potassium, thorium, uranium) around it. The amount of thermoluminescence emitted when the object is heated during testing allows researchers to calculate the age of the object, if it is known what kind of radiation the object has been exposed to in its surroundings (e.g., the surrounding soil in which a clay pot is found).

Thermoluminescence dating is well suited to samples of ancient pottery, brick, tile, terra cotta, and other objects that are made at high temperatures. This method can also be applied to burnt flint tools, hearth stones, lava or lava-covered objects, meteorites, and meteor craters.[18]

ELECTRON SPIN RESONANCE DATING   Electron spin resonance dating is a technique that, like thermoluminescence dating, measures trapped electrons from surrounding radioactive material. But the method in this case is different. The material to be dated is exposed to varying magnetic fields, and a spectrum of the microwaves absorbed by the tested material is obtained. Because no heating is required for this technique, electron spin resonance is especially useful for dating organic material such as bone and shell, which decompose if heated.[19]

PALEOMAGNETIC DATING   When rock of any kind forms, it records the ancient magnetic field of the earth. When this knowledge is put together with the fact that the earth's magnetic field has reversed itself many times, the geomagnetic patterns in rocks can be used to date the fossils within those rocks. **Paleomagnetic dating dates rocks in terms of the sequence of geomagnetic patterns in them.

Strictly speaking, paleomagnetic dating is not an absolute dating method, but geomagnetic time periods have been dated absolutely in conjunction with potassium-argon dating (described below). Paleomagnetic dating has dated primate fossil finds from the Eocene through the Miocene, from 55 million to 5 million years ago.[20]

Not only does the earth's magnetic field reverse itself, but the locations of its poles move constantly (albeit very slowly) over time. The wanderings of the North Pole have been determined for the recent past, and this knowledge allows archaeologists to date some archaeological features. When soil, rock, or metal is heated to a high temperature, it liquifies and its constituent molecules align themselves to the earth's magnetic field. When cooled, the molecules retain their alignment, and thus create something of an arrow pointing to the earth's magnetic poles. When an archaeologist finds a hearth, pottery kiln, metal workshop, or something else in which earth, rock, or metal was heated to its melting point and cooled in place, the archaeologist can take a sample of that material, record its location in terms of the earth's present-day magnetic field, and then measure the material's magnetic field in the laboratory. The difference between the direction of the earth's current magnetic field and that recorded in the material can be used to date when the material melted and cooled.

POTASSIUM–ARGON DATING AND ARGON–ARGON DATING   Potassium-40 (^{40}K), a radioactive form of potassium, decays at an established rate and forms argon-40 (^{40}Ar). The half-life of ^{40}K is a known quantity, so the age of a material containing potassium can be measured by the amount of ^{40}K compared with the amount of ^{40}Ar it contains.[21] Radioactive potassium's (^{40}K's) half-life is very long— 1,330 million years. This means that **potassium–argon (K-Ar) dating** may be used to date samples from 5,000 years up to 3 billion years old.

The K-Ar method is used to date potassium-rich minerals in rock, not the fossils that may be found in the rock. A very high temperature, such as occurs in a volcanic event, drives off any original argon in the material. The amount of argon that accumulates afterward from the decay of radioactive potassium is directly related to the amount of time since the volcanic event. This type of dating has been extremely useful in East Africa, where volcanic events have occurred frequently since the Miocene, which began 24 million years ago. If the material to be dated is not rich in potassium, or the area did not experience any high-temperature events, other methods of absolute dating are required.

One problem with the K-Ar method is that the amounts of potassium and argon must be measured on different rock samples; researchers must assume that the potassium and argon are evenly distributed in all the rock samples from a particular stratum. Researchers got around this problem by developing the **^{40}Ar–^{39}Ar dating** method. After measuring the amount of ^{40}Ar, a nuclear reactor is used to convert another kind of argon, ^{39}Ar, to potassium so that the potassium–argon ratio can be measured from the same sample.[22]

URANIUM-SERIES DATING   The decay of two kinds of uranium, ^{235}U and ^{238}U, into other isotopes (such as ^{230}Th, thorium) has also proved useful for dating sites, particularly in caves where stalagmites and other calcite formations form. Because water that seeps into caves usually contains uranium but not thorium, the calcite formations trap uranium. Uranium starts decaying at a known rate into other isotopes (such as thorium-230, or ^{230}Th), and the ratio of those isotopes to uranium isotopes can be used to estimate the time elapsed. The thorium–uranium ratio is useful for dating cave sites less than 300,000 years old where there are no volcanic rocks suitable for the potassium–argon method. Early *Homo sapiens* (modern-looking humans) from European cave sites in Germany, Hungary, and Wales were dated this way.[23] There are different varieties of **uranium-series dating,** depending on the specific isotope ratios used.

FISSION-TRACK DATING   **Fission-track dating** is another way to determine the absolute age of fossil deposits. Like the K-Ar method, it dates minerals contemporaneous with the deposit in which fossils are found and it also requires the prior occurrence of a high-temperature event, such as a volcanic eruption. But the kinds of samples it can date, such as crystal, glass, and many uranium-rich minerals, include a much wider variety than those that can be dated by the K-Ar method. The age range of fission-track dating, like that of K-Ar dating, is extensive—20 years to 5 billion years.[24]

How does fission-track dating work? This method is basically the simplest of all the methods discussed here. It entails counting the number of paths or tracks etched in the sample by the fission—explosive division—of uranium atoms as they disintegrate. Scientists know that ^{238}U, the most common uranium isotope, decays at a slow, steady rate. This decay takes the form of spontaneous fission, and each separate fission leaves a scar or track on the sample, which can be seen, when chemically treated, through a microscope. To find out how old a sample is, one counts the tracks, then measures their ratio to the uranium content of the sample.

The fission-track method was used to date Bed I at Olduvai Gorge in Tanzania, East Africa, where some early human ancestors were found.[25] It was able to corroborate earlier K-Ar estimates that the site dated back close to 2 million years. That the K-Ar and fission-track methods use different techniques and have different sources of error makes them effective as checks on each other. When the two methods support each other, they provide very reliable evidence.

OTHER TECHNIQUES   The dating techniques outlined above are the most commonly used in archaeology and paleoanthropology, but there are many others, and new techniques are being developed all the time. For example, stone tools made from obsidian can be dated in some cases because a thin layer of stone, called an hydration layer, builds up on the obsidian over time when it is exposed to air. Similarly, rock art is sometimes dated by measuring the buildup of a patina over the art after it has been painted or carved on a piece of stone. Bones can sometimes be dated by measuring the breakdown of DNA, which occurs in a regular manner (similar to radioisotope decay) when heat and humidity are stable. These and many other techniques add a wide range of choices to the tool-kit that archaeologists and paleoanthropologists can use to date their finds.

The Results of Archaeological Research

When archaeologists and paleoanthropologists finish a research project, what is the result? What are the goals of archaeological research?

One goal is the description or reconstruction of what happened in the past. Much of what archaeologists do, and much of what we do in this book, has this goal. Archaeologists attempt to determine how people lived in a particular place at a particular time, and when and how their lifestyles changed. Also of interest, of course, is whether new populations carrying new cultures arrived, or whether people with a particular culture moved out of a given area. Creating histories of cultures and their changes over time is called, simply enough, **culture history.** Doing culture history was the primary goal of archaeology until the 1950s.[26]

A second major goal of archaeological research, and one that has become the primary goal since the 1950s, is testing specific explanations about human evolution and behavior. In part this change in focus results from our increased knowledge about the past—the culture history of many areas is well known today. But this change is also due to changes going on in anthropology as a whole. Until the 1950s a school of thought called historical particularism was dominant in American anthropology. It suggested that variation in human cultures was best explained by considering the specific historical developments of particular cultures. Like the purpose of historical particularism, the purpose of culture history was to trace historical developments.

After the 1950s a variety of new approaches arose in anthropology, most of them sharing the idea that the environment and how humans use it actively shapes cultures and mostly explains cultural variability. Archaeology became a key tool for anthropologists attempting to understand how changes in the ways humans used the environment explained variation in human cultures. One of the results of this focus on hypothesis testing and human use of the environment was research on agricultural origins, which we discuss in the chapter on the origins of food production and settled life. Another was a concern with the rise of cities and states, which radically transformed human use of the environment. We devote a separate chapter also to that subject.

In addition to testing explanations, archaeology has a primary role within anthropology in its attempt to identify and understand general trends and patterns in human biological and cultural evolution. As we discussed in the first chapter, cross-cultural research (comparative ethnography) has this goal as well. But only archaeology is able to look through long stretches of time and directly examine evolutionary trends. In the box "Are There Unilinear Trends in Cultural Evolution?" we consider one way archaeology is able to discover long-term trends. In later chapters in this book we trace the evolution of humans and human cultures from their beginnings. As we shall see, a major emphasis in paleoanthropology is demonstrating long-term trends and patterns in the biological evolution of humans. These trends and patterns help us understand how and why we have come to be the way we are. In this pursuit, both archaeology and paleoanthropology help us answer what may be the fundamental question of anthropology: What does it mean to be human?

Ethics in Archaeological Research

Archaeologists must always be concerned with the ethics of their work when undertaking or reporting the results of their research. Archaeology does not simply describe past cultures; it can also have a profound effect on living peoples. For example, many people find the idea of archaeologists excavating, cleaning, and preserving the remains of ancestors to be offensive. Therefore, archaeologists must be sensitive to the desires and beliefs of the populations that descend from the ones they are researching. In addition, artifacts from some ancient cultures are in great demand by art and antiquities collectors, and archaeological finds can lead to uncontrolled looting if archaeologists are not careful about how and to whom they report their discoveries. Wholesale ransacking of ancient cemeteries in some parts of China, for example, started because new archaeological discoveries led Chinese antiquities to become increasingly popular among collectors, and hence, increasingly valuable to those able to discover them.[27]

While it is the ethical responsibility of archaeologists to consult with descendant populations and to be careful about how archaeological finds are reported, it is also an ethical responsibility of archaeologists to present the results of their work to the general public. Publishing archaeological results increases public awareness about the past and the importance of historic preservation. If people know how much can be learned from the archaeological record, they may be less likely to destroy it or to support those who destroy it for personal gain. Of course, when archaeologists excavate sites, they also destroy some of the context of the artifacts, ecofacts, fossils, and features found in the sites. But if they leave some of the sites unexcavated, they are preserving them (at least partially) for future investigation. To offset their partial destruction, archaeologists are ethically obligated to publish the results of their work. Reporting the results of archaeological research, therefore, plays a central role in both archaeological research and archaeological ethics.

CURRENT RESEARCH AND ISSUES

Are There Unilinear Trends in Cultural Evolution?

Late in the 1800s, in the early days of anthropology, the prevailing view of theorists like Edward Tylor and Lewis Henry Morgan was that culture generally develops or evolves in a uniform or progressive manner. It was thought that most societies pass through similar stages, to arrive ultimately at a common end. The early evolutionists believed that European and European-derived cultures were at the highest stages of evolution. Other cultures were still in the lower stages. The school of historical particularism associated with Franz Boas rejected the idea that there were universal laws governing all human cultures. Instead, the historical particularists proposed that culture traits had to be studied in the context of the society in which they appeared. Boas stressed the need to collect data on as many societies as possible, an activity that became a central part of the anthropological enterprise.

Evolutionism did not die with the early evolutionists, however. For example, in the 1960s, Marshall Sahlins and Elman Service discussed two kinds of evolutionary processes—specific evolution, which refers to the particular changes of a particular society, and general evolution. General evolution refers to the general tendency of "higher" forms to surpass "lower" forms, but it does not insist that every society goes through exactly the same stages or progresses toward the "higher" stages. Nonetheless, anthropologists are not particularly keen on the idea of unilinear (one-directional) evolution, perhaps because the idea is still associated with the assumption of European superiority by the early evolutionists. But looking at the long stretch of human history, we see that some things seem to have changed in a fairly consistent way. For example, human populations have grown, technology has become more sophisticated, and most people on earth have come to live in state societies. Surely there are some unilinear trends in cultural evolution—or are there? How can we tell?

The third author of this textbook (Peter Peregrine) approached the question through cross-cultural research. He decided to test whether overall cultural complexity has increased over time. To do so he needed a measure of cultural complexity, and he needed a group of cultures to measure that represented all the cultures on earth over a long period of time. Happily, both exist. The measure of cultural complexity he used was developed by anthropologist George Peter Murdock to examine variation in cultural complexity among ethnographically known cultures. The measure looks at ten different features of the culture, including its technology, economy, political system, and population density. Peregrine simplified this measure to make it easier to use with archaeologically known cultures, and he limited himself to Old World cultures dating to the last 15,000 years listed in the *Outline of Archaeological Traditions*. He measured cultural complexity for these cultures using the information about them given in the *Encyclopedia of Prehistory*.

Peregrine found strong evidence that cultural complexity has increased in a fairly regular manner over the last 15,000 years. The figure in this box displays this trend graphically. The horizontal scale is the date of the culture, starting with today at the left and going back into the past as you move to the right. The vertical scale is the culture's cultural complexity score. It's clear from the figure that cultural complexity scores have tended to increase over time. Indeed the increase is statistically significant (unlikely to be due to chance). However, it is also clear that the increase is not universal: Some cultures scored low in the past while others scored higher, and some score low today while others score higher. Thus not all cultures have undergone change in the same way. But the figure suggests that human cultures generally have tended to become more complex over time. Why? We offer no answer, but we suggest it is an excellent question to ponder as you read through this book.

Sources: Peter N. Peregrine, *Outline of Archaeological Traditions*, 2nd ed. (New Haven, CT: HRAF, 2006); Peter N. Peregrine and Melvin Ember, eds., *Encyclopedia of Prehistory*, 9 vols. (New York: Kluwer Academic/Plenum, 2001–2002); Peter N. Peregrine, "Cross-Cultural Approaches in Archaeology." *Annual Review of Anthropology* 30 (2001): 1–18.

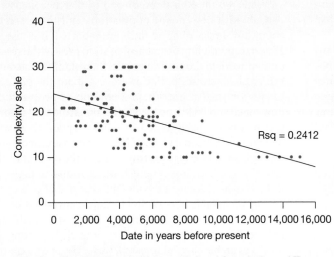

Figure 2–5 The Relationship between Cultural Complexity and Time
In general, cultural complexity has increased over time.

◎ Summary

1. Archaeologists and paleoanthropologists have four basic sources of evidence about the past: artifacts, ecofacts, fossils, and features. Artifacts are any objects made by humans. Ecofacts are natural objects used or modified by humans. Fossils are the preserved remains of ancient plants and animals. And features are artifacts that cannot be removed from archaeological sites.

2. Archaeological sites are locations where the evidence of the past has been buried and preserved. Sites are found through pedestrian survey or remote sensing, and artifacts, ecofacts, fossils, and features are recovered from sites through excavation. Key to excavation is the preservation of context; that is, the relationships between and among artifacts, ecofacts, fossils, and features.

3. Information about the past is obtained by analyzing the evidence recovered from sites. Much information can be gained through the analysis of the forms, sizes, and composition of archaeological materials, but the materials themselves are not the primary focus of analysis. Rather, it is the context between and among artifacts, ecofacts, fossils, and features that allows the archaeologist or paleoanthropologist to gain insights about the past.

4. A key aspect of putting archaeological material into context is being able to date material accurately. Many kinds of dating techniques are used. Relative dating techniques determine the age of archaeological materials relative to other materials of known ages. Absolute dating techniques determine the age of the archaeological deposits or materials themselves.

5. Archaeology allows for cultural histories to be developed and explanations about cultural change to be tested. Its primary goal is to provide insights into human physical and cultural evolution—the central concern of this book.

◎ Glossary Terms

◎ Critical Questions

1. Why is context so important in archaeological research?
2. What kinds of information can be learned from a stone projectile point?
3. What factors have to be considered when choosing a dating technique?

◎ Research Navigator

1. Please go to **www.researchnavigator.com** and enter your LOGIN NAME and PASSWORD. For instructions on registering for the first time, please view the detailed instructions at the end of Chapter 1.

2. Go to the *New York Times* section and search using the "Anthropology/Archeology" subject in the pull-down menu. Find an article focused on the excavation of a site. After reading the article, answer the following questions: What types of artifacts, ecofacts, fossils, and features were discovered? What types of dating techniques were used? What did the excavators learn from their analyses? What ethical issues arose during the excavation?

◎ Discovering Anthropology: Researchers at Work

Read the chapter by Mark J. Lynott titled "Ethics in Archaeology" in the accompanying *Discovering Anthropology* reader. Answer the following questions:

1. Lynott states that stewardship is at the center of archaeological ethics. Explain why he thinks so.

2. Some have argued that stewardship is not a good principle upon which to base archaeological ethics. They suggest service to descendant populations or protecting the rights of the ancient peoples themselves would be more appropriate. What do you think? Is stewardship a good foundational principle for archaeological ethics?

CHAPTER THREE

Genetics and Evolution

Astronomers estimate that the universe has been in existence for some 15 billion years, plus or minus a few billion. To make this awesome history more understandable, Carl Sagan devised a calendar that condenses this span into a single year.[1] Using as a scale 24 days for every billion years and 1 second for every 475 years, Sagan moves from the "Big Bang," or beginning of the universe, on January 1 to the origin of the Milky Way on May 1. September 9 marks the beginning of our solar system, and September 25 the origin of life on earth. At 10:30 in the evening of December 31, the first humanlike primates appear. Sagan's compression of history provides us with a manageable way to compare the short span of human existence with the total time span of the universe. Humanlike beings have been around for only about 90 minutes out of a 12-month period! In this book we are concerned with what has happened in the last few hours of that year.

Some 55 million to 65 million years ago, the first primates appeared. They were ancestral to all living primates, including monkeys, apes, and humans. The early primates may or may not have lived in trees, but they had flexible digits and could grasp things. Later, about 35 million years ago, the first monkeys and apes appeared. About 15 million years ago, some 20 million years after the appearance of monkeys and apes, the immediate apelike ancestors of humans probably emerged. About 4 million years ago the first humanlike beings appeared. Modern-looking humans evolved only about 100,000 years ago.

How do we account for the biological and cultural evolution of humans? The details of the emergence of primates and the evolution of humans and their cultures are covered in subsequent chapters. In this chapter we focus on how the modern theory of evolution developed and how it accounts for change over time.

The Evolution of Evolution

Traditional Western ideas about nature's creatures were very different from Charles Darwin's theory of *evolution,* which suggested that different species developed, one from another, over long periods of time. In the 5th millennium B.C., the Greek philosophers Plato and Aristotle believed that animals and plants form a single, graded continuum going from more perfection to less perfection. Humans, of course, were at the

top of this scale. Later Greek philosophers added the idea that the creator gave life or "radiance" first to humans, but at each subsequent creation some of that essence was lost.[2] Macrobius, summarizing the thinking of Plotinus, used an image that was to persist for centuries, the image of what came to be called the "chain of being": "The attentive observer will discover a connection of parts, from the Supreme God down to the last dregs of things, mutually linked together and without a break. And this is Homer's golden chain, which God, he says, bade hand down from heaven to earth."[3]

Belief in the chain of being was accompanied by the conviction that an animal or plant species could not become extinct. In fact, all things were linked to each other in a chain, and all links were necessary. Moreover, the notion of extinction threatened people's trust in God; it was unthinkable that a whole group of God's creations could simply disappear.

The idea of the chain of being persisted through the years, but it was not discussed extensively by philosophers, scientists, poets, and theologians until the 18th century. Those discussions prepared the way for evolutionary theory. It is ironic that, although the chain of being did not allow for evolution, its idea that there was an order of things in nature encouraged studies of natural history and comparative anatomical studies, which stimulated the development of the idea of evolution. People were also now motivated to look for previously unknown creatures. Moreover, humans were not shocked when naturalists suggested that humans were close to apes. This notion was perfectly consistent with the idea of a chain of being; apes were simply thought to have been created with less perfection.

Early in the 18th century, an influential scientist, Carolus Linnaeus (1707–1778), classified plants and animals in a *systema naturae,* which placed humans in the same order (Primates) as apes and monkeys. Linnaeus did not suggest an evolutionary relationship between humans and apes; he mostly accepted the notion that all species were created by God and fixed in their form. Not surprisingly, then, Linnaeus is often viewed as an anti-evolutionist. But Linnaeus's hierarchical classification scheme, in descending order going from kingdom to class, order, **genus** (a group of related species), and species, provided a framework for the idea that humans, apes, and monkeys had a common ancestor.[4] See Figure 3–1.

Others did not believe that species were fixed in their form. According to Jean Baptiste Lamarck (1744–1829), acquired characteristics could be inherited and therefore species could evolve; individuals who in their lifetime developed characteristics helpful to survival would pass those characteristics on to future generations, thereby changing the physical makeup of the species. For example, Lamarck explained the long neck of the giraffe as the result of successive generations of giraffes stretching their necks to reach the high leaves of trees. The stretched muscles and bones of the necks were somehow transmitted to the offspring of the neck-stretching giraffes, and eventually all giraffes came to have long necks. But because Lamarck and later biologists

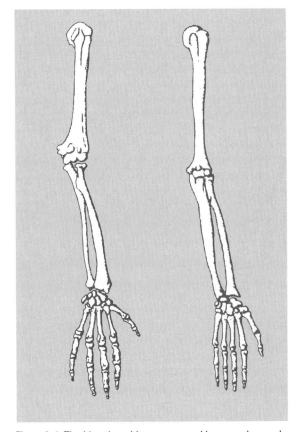

Figure 3–1 The idea that chimpanzees and humans descend from a common ancestor is suggested by anatomical similarities, such as in their forelimbs. Chimpanzee forelimb skeleton (left); human forelimb skeleton (right).

failed to produce evidence to support the hypothesis that acquired characteristics can be inherited, this explanation of evolution is now generally dismissed.[5]

By the 19th century, some thinkers were beginning to accept evolution while others were trying to refute it. For example, Georges Cuvier (1769–1832) was a leading opponent of evolution. Cuvier's theory of catastrophism proposed that a quick series of catastrophes accounted for changes in the earth and the fossil record. Cataclysms and upheavals such as Noah's flood had killed off previous sets of living creatures, which each time were replaced by new creations.

Major changes in geological thinking occurred in the 19th century. Earlier, geologist James Hutton (1726–1797) had questioned catastrophism, but his work was largely ignored. In contrast, Sir Charles Lyell's (1797–1875) volumes of the *Principles of Geology* (1830–1833), which built on Hutton's earlier work, received immediate acclaim. Their concept of *uniformitarianism* suggested that the earth is constantly being shaped and reshaped by natural forces that have operated over a vast stretch of time. Lyell also discussed the formation of geological strata and paleontology. He used fossilized fauna to define different geological epochs. Lyell's works were read avidly by Charles Darwin before and during Darwin's now-famous voyage on the *Beagle.* The two corresponded and subsequently became friends.

Gemalde von John Collier, 1883, "Charles Robert Darwin." Ol auf Leinwand, 125.7 × 96.5 cm. London, National Portrait Gallery / 1024. Bildarchiv Preussischer Kulturbesitz. Photo: Jochen Remmer.

After studying changes in plants, fossil animals, and varieties of domestic and wild pigeons, Charles Darwin (1809–1882) rejected the notion that each species was created at one time in a fixed form. The results of his investigations pointed clearly, he thought, to the evolution of species through the mechanism of natural selection. While Darwin was completing his book on the subject, Alfred Russel Wallace (1823–1913), a naturalist, sent him a manuscript which came to conclusions about the evolution of species that matched Darwin's own.[6] In 1858, the two men presented the astonishing theory of natural selection to their colleagues at a meeting of the Linnaean Society of London.[7]

In 1859, when Darwin published *The Origin of Species by Means of Natural Selection*,[8] he wrote, "I am fully convinced that species are not immutable; but that those belonging to what are called the same genera are lineal descendants of some other and generally extinct species, in the same manner as the acknowledged varieties of any one species."[9] His conclusions outraged those who believed in the biblical account of creation, and the result was bitter controversy that continues to this day.[10]

Until 1871, when his *The Descent of Man* was published, Darwin avoided stating categorically that humans were descended from nonhuman forms, but the implications of his theory were clear. People immediately began to take sides. In June 1860, at the annual meeting of the British Association for the Advancement of Science, Bishop Wilberforce saw an opportunity to attack the Darwinists. Concluding his speech, he faced Thomas Huxley, one of the Darwinists' chief advocates, and inquired, "Was it through his grandfather or his grandmother that he claimed descent from a monkey?" Huxley responded,

> If . . . the question is put to me would I rather have a miserable ape for a grandfather than a man highly endowed by nature and possessing great means and influence and yet who employs those faculties and that influence for the mere purpose of introducing ridicule into a grave scientific discussion—I unhesitatingly affirm my preference for the ape.[11]

While Huxley's retort to Bishop Wilberforce displays both humor and quick wit, it does not answer the Bishop's question very well. A better answer, and one we pursue in the next few chapters, is that Darwinists would claim that we descended from monkeys neither through our grandmother or our grandfather, but that both we and monkeys are descended from a common ancestor who lived long ago. Darwinists would further argue that natural selection was the process through which the physical and genetic form of that common ancestor diverged to become both monkey and human.

Natural selection is a process we can see at work in the world today. It is a process that has been studied in both the laboratory and in nature, and it is a process that most scientists would argue is very well understood. However, as in all scientific endeavors, understanding grows and changes as new information is obtained. The understanding of natural selection we have today is quite different from that originally put forward by Darwin. A century and a half of research has added tremendously to the information Darwin had to work with, and entirely new fields, like population genetics, have emerged. With this new information we know that Darwin was wrong about some things. For example, it seems clear that natural selection is not always a uniform process, but can act in jumps and starts (see the box titled "Is Evolution Slow and Steady or Fast and Abrupt?"). As we will see, different types of natural selection occur—some that make particular traits more common in a population, others that limit overall variation.

The fact that the ideas put forward by Darwin have changed, and are changing as new research is done, does not mean they were wrong. Darwin's ideas were simply incomplete. Each day as we add to our knowledge base we move closer to an even more complete understanding of natural selection. The development and transformation of ideas as new information is discovered is one of the hallmarks of science. Indeed, this is a central facet of science that proponents of "creation science" and "intelligent design theory" ignore. What physical evidence could be put forward to demonstrate that God (or some intelligent force) created the diversity of life on earth? In the absence of objective evidence supporting creationism or intelligent design, scientists conclude that natural selection, which *is* supported by objective evidence, better explains the diversity of life. We discuss creationist ideas further in the section on speciation below.

CURRENT RESEARCH AND ISSUES

Is Evolution Slow and Steady or Fast and Abrupt?

Darwin's evolutionary theory suggested that new species emerge gradually over time. Through the process of natural selection, frequencies of traits would slowly change, and eventually a new species would appear. But Darwin did not explain why so much speciation has occurred. If trait frequencies change only gradually over time, wouldn't descendant populations retain their ability to interbreed and wouldn't they, therefore, continue to belong to the same species?

In the 1930s and 1940s, biologists and geneticists advanced what came to be called the "modern synthesis" in evolutionary theory, adding what was known from genetics about heredity. Mutation and the recombination of genes now provided for genetic variety. The driving force of change was still adaptation to environments through natural selection; gene frequencies of a population presumably changed slowly as adaptive traits (because of existing genes or mutations) increased in prevalence and maladaptive traits de-

creased. As for speciation, the development and divergence of different species, the modern synthesis postulated that it would occur when subpopulations became isolated by geographic barriers or when different subpopulations encountered different climatic conditions or moved into new ecological niches; those environmental isolating processes would eventually result in the development of reproductive isolation and therefore new species.

This gradualist view of evolution was challenged in 1972 by Niles Eldredge and Stephen Jay Gould. Their alternative model of evolution is referred to as "punctuated equilibrium." They still assume that natural selection is the primary mechanism of evolutionary change, but they see the pace of evolution quite differently. In their view, new species evolve quickly; but once a successful species emerges, its characteristics are likely to change very little over long periods of time. Thus, in contrast to the modern synthesis, Eldredge and Gould do not think it is common for the world's species to change gradually into descendant species. Rather, species are born more or less abruptly, they have lifetimes during which they do not change much, and they become extinct. As examples, Eldredge and Gould cite the history of North American trilobites and Bermudan land snails. In both groups of animals, it looks as if the different species did not change for a long period of time—millions of years for some species—but then certain species seem to have been quickly replaced by related species from nearby areas. In short, Eldredge and Gould believe that the succession of one species after another in-

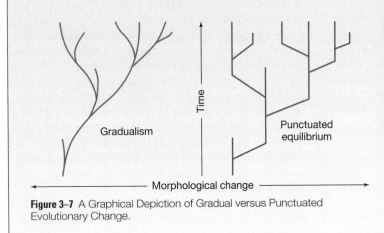

Figure 3–7 A Graphical Depiction of Gradual versus Punctuated Evolutionary Change.

The Principles of Natural Selection

Darwin was not the first person to view the creation of new species in evolutionary terms, but he was the first to provide a comprehensive, well-documented explanation—natural selection—for the way evolution had occurred. **Natural selection** is the main process that increases the frequency of adaptive traits through time. The operation of natural selection involves three conditions or principles.[12] The first is

variation: Every species is composed of a great variety of individuals, some of which are better adapted to their environment than others. The existence of variety is important. Without it, natural selection has nothing on which to operate; without variation, one kind of characteristic could not be favored over another. The second principle of natural selection is *heritability:* Offspring inherit traits from their parents, at least to some degree and in some way. The third principle of natural selection is *differential reproductive success:* Since better adapted individuals generally produce more offspring over the generations than the poorer adapted, the

volves replacement from outside more often than gradual change over time.

Evolution may or may not occur as the model of punctuated equilibrium specifies, but most evolutionists today agree that change could occur relatively quickly. Recent research suggests that some relatively quick climate changes in the earth's history helped bring about massive extinctions of species and families of species and exponential increases in the subsequent number of new families. For example, there is considerable evidence that a large meteorite collided with the earth at the end of the Cretaceous geological period, about 65 million years ago. Louis Alvarez and his colleagues proposed that so much dust was sent into the atmosphere by the collision that the earth was shrouded in darkness for months, if not longer. Some investigators now think that the meteorite impact may have also triggered a great deal of volcanic activity, even on the opposite side of the world, which would also have reduced solar radiation to the earth's surface. Not only the dinosaurs disappeared about 65 million years ago, so also did many sea animals and plants. Afterward, the earth saw the proliferation of many other kinds of animals, such as fish, lizards, birds, and mammals, as well as flowering trees. As we shall see in the chapter on primate evolution, our own biological order, the Primates, is believed to have emerged around that time.

Peter Grant recently studied the same finches on the Galápagos Islands that partially inspired Darwin's theory. But, unlike Darwin, Grant had the chance to see natural selection in action. And it was surprisingly quick. Central to the project was the attachment of colored bands to each individual bird, which allowed each bird to be identified at a distance. In the midst of the project, in 1977, when half the birds had been banded, there was a serious drought. Of the two main species of finch on one island, the cactus finch (*Geospiza scandens*) and the medium ground finch (*Geospiza fortis*), only the cactus finches were able to breed, but they had no surviving offspring. During the next 18 months, 85 percent of the adult medium ground finches disappeared. Those finches that survived tended to be larger and to have larger beaks than the ones that died. Why larger beaks? Both species of finch eat seeds, but small seeds produced by grasses and herbs are scarce in a drought; bigger seeds are more available. So it seems that natural selection under conditions of drought favored finches with bigger beaks, which are better at cracking the husks of large seeds.

If it were not for the fact that wet years, which favor smaller finches, occur between years of drought, we might see the quick evolution of new finch species. It is estimated that 20 drought episodes would be sufficient to produce a new species of finch. Galápagos finches do not really provide an example of punctuated equilibrium (no replacement from outside occurred), but they do suggest that evolutionary change could be a lot quicker than Darwin imagined.

Controversy continues over whether evolution is slow and steady or fast and abrupt. But many scholars, including Gould, point out that there is no need to pit one model against the other. Both may be correct in different instances. In any case much more investigation of evolutionary sequences is needed to help us evaluate the competing theoretical models.

Sources: Ian Tattersall, "Paleoanthropology and Evolutionary Theory." In Peter N. Peregrine, Carol R. Ember, and Melvin Ember, eds., *Physical Anthropology: Original Readings in Method and Practice* (Upper Saddle River, NJ: Prentice Hall, 2002), pp. 29–41, also in Carol R. Ember, Melvin Ember, and Peter N. Peregrine, eds., *New Directions in Anthropology* (Upper Saddle River, NJ: Prentice Hall, CD-ROM, 2004); Charles Devillers and Jean Chaline, *Evolution: An Evolving Theory* (New York: Springer-Verlag, 1993); Peter R. Grant, "Natural Selection and Darwin's Finches," *Scientific American* (October 1991): 82–87; Jonathan Weiner, *Beak of the Finch* (New York: Vintage, 1994).

frequency of adaptive traits gradually increases in subsequent generations. A new species emerges when changes in traits or geographic barriers result in the reproductive isolation of the population.

When we say that certain traits are **adaptive** or advantageous, we mean that they result in greater reproductive success in a particular environment. The phrase "particular environment" is very important. Even though a species may become more adapted to a particular environment over time, we cannot say that one species adapted to its environment is "better" than another species adapted to a different environment. For example, we may like to think of ourselves as "better" than other animals, but humans are clearly less adapted than fish for living under water, than bats for catching flying insects, or than raccoons for living on suburban garbage.

Although the theory of natural selection suggests that disadvantageous or **maladaptive** traits will generally decline in frequency or even disappear eventually, it does not necessarily follow that all such traits will do so. After all, species derive from prior forms that have certain structures. This means that not all changes are possible; it also means that

The giraffe's long neck is adaptive for eating tree leaves high off the ground. When food is scarce, longer-necked giraffes would get more food and reproduce more successfully than shorter-necked giraffes; in this environment, natural selection would favor giraffes with longer necks.

some traits are linked to others that might have advantages that outweigh the disadvantages. Choking may be very maladaptive for any animal, yet all vertebrates are capable of choking because their digestive and respiratory systems cross in the throat. This trait is a genetic legacy, probably from the time when the respiratory system developed from tissue in the digestive system of some ancestral organism. Apparently, the propensity to choke has not been correctable evolutionarily.[13]

Changes in a species can be expected to occur as the environment changes or as some members of the species move into a new environment. With environmental change, different traits become adaptive. The forms of the species that possess the more adaptive traits will become more frequent, whereas those forms whose characteristics make continued existence more difficult or impossible in the modified environment will eventually become extinct.

Consider how the theory of natural selection would explain why giraffes became long-necked. Originally, the necks of giraffes varied in length, as happens with virtually any physical characteristic in a population. During a period when food was scarce, those giraffes with longer necks, who could reach higher tree leaves, might be better able to survive and suckle their offspring, and thus they would leave more offspring than shorter-necked giraffes. Because of heredity, the offspring of long-necked giraffes are more likely to have long

necks. Eventually, the shorter-necked giraffes would diminish in number and the longer-necked giraffes would increase. The resultant population of giraffes would still have variation in neck length but on the average would be longer necked than earlier forms.

Natural selection does not account for all variation in the frequencies of traits. In particular, it does not account for variation in the frequencies of neutral traits—that is, those traits that do not seem to confer any advantages or disadvantages on their carriers. Changes in the frequencies of neutral traits may result rather from random processes that affect gene frequencies in isolated populations—*genetic drift*—or from matings between populations—*gene flow*. We discuss these other processes later in the chapter.

Observed Examples of Natural Selection

Because the process of natural selection may involve nearly imperceptible gradations over generations, it is often difficult to observe directly. Nevertheless, because some life forms reproduce rapidly, some examples of natural selection have been observed over relatively short periods in changing environments.

For example, scientists think they have observed natural selection in action in British moths. In 1850, an almost black moth was spotted for the first time in Manchester. That was quite unusual, for most of the moths were speckled gray. A century later, 95 percent of the moths in industrial parts of Britain were black; only in the rural areas were the moths mostly gray. How is this to be explained? It seems that in the rural areas, the gray-speckled moth is hard to spot by bird predators against the lichen growing on the bark of trees. But in industrial areas, lichen is killed by pollution. The gray-speckled moths, formerly well adapted to blend into their environment, became clearly visible against the darker background of the lichen-free trees and were easier prey for birds. In contrast, the black moths, which previously would have had a disadvantage against the lighter bark, were now better adapted for survival. Their dark color was an advantage, and subsequently the darker moths became the predominant variety in industrial regions.

How can we be sure that natural selection was the mechanism accounting for the change? Consistent evidence comes from a series of experiments performed by H. B. D. Kettlewell. He deliberately released specially marked moths, black and gray, into two areas of England—one urban industrial and one rural—and then set light traps to recapture them subsequently. The proportions of the two kinds of moths recovered tell us about differential survival. Kettlewell found that proportionately more black moths compared with gray moths were recovered in the urban industrial area. Just the reverse happened in the rural area; proportionately more gray-speckled moths were recovered.[14] Questions have been raised recently about whether the Kettlewell experiments were properly conducted.[15] However, the basic conclusion has been replicated by subsequent research.[16] The same transformation—the switch to darker color—has occurred in 70 other species of moth, as well as in a beetle and a millipede. And the transformation did not just occur in Britain;

The changes that occurred in the moth population in different areas of England show natural selection in action. Before industrialization, tree trunks were lighter and light-colored moths predominated. (Rural areas today, with little or no industrial air pollution, show that natural selection in unpolluted areas still favors light-colored moths.) But with industrial pollution and the darkening of tree trunks, light-colored moths became more visible to predators. Darker-colored moths quickly increased in number in the new industrial environment.

it also happened in other highly polluted areas, including the Ruhr area of Germany and the Pittsburgh area of the United States. Moreover, in the Pittsburgh area, antipollution measures in the last 50 years have apparently caused the black moth to dwindle in number once again.[17]

The type of natural selection in the moth example is called **directional selection** because a particular trait seems to be positively favored and the average value shifts over time toward the adaptive trait. But there can also be **normalizing selection.** In this type of selection the average value does not change, but natural selection removes the extremes. An example is the birthweight of babies. Both very low birthweights and very high birthweights are disadvantageous and would be selected against. Directional and normalizing selection both assume that natural selection will either favor or disfavor genes, but there is a third possibility—balancing selection. **Balancing selection** occurs when a *heterozygous* (varied) combination of *alleles* (genes) is positively favored even though a *homozygous* (genes in the pairs are the same) combination is disfavored. In the chapter on human variation, we discuss a trait that apparently involves balancing selection—sickle-cell anemia—which is found in persons of West African ancestry, among other populations.

Another well-known example of observed natural selection is the acquired resistance of houseflies to the insecticide DDT. When DDT was first used to kill insects, beginning in the 1940s, several new, DDT-resistant strains of housefly evolved. In the early DDT environment, many houseflies were killed, but the few that survived were the ones that reproduced, and their resistant characteristics became common to the housefly populations. To the chagrin of medical practitioners, similar resistances develop in bacteria. A particular antibiotic may lose its effectiveness after it comes into wide use because new, resistant bacterial strains emerge. These new strains will become more frequent than the original ones because of natural selection. In the United States now, a few strains are resistant to all antibiotics on the market, a fact that worries medical practitioners. One possible way to deal with the problem is to stop using antibiotics for a few years, so resistance to those antibiotics might not develop or develop only slowly.

The theory of natural selection answered many questions, but it also raised at least one whose answer eluded Darwin and others. The appearance of a beneficial trait may assist the survival of an organism, but what happens when the organism reproduces by mating with members that do not possess this new variation? Will not the new adaptive trait eventually disappear if subsequent generations mate with individuals that lack this trait? Darwin knew variations were transmitted through heredity, but he did not have a clear model of the mode of inheritance. Gregor Mendel's pioneering studies in the science of genetics provided the foundation for such a model, but his discoveries did not become widely known until 1900.

⊚ Heredity

Gregor Mendel's Experiments

Mendel (1822–1884), a monk and amateur botanist who lived in what is now the Czech Republic, bred several varieties of pea plants and made detailed observations of their offspring. He chose as breeding partners plants that differed by only one observable trait. Tall plants were crossed with short ones, and yellow ones with green, for example.

Gregor Mendel.

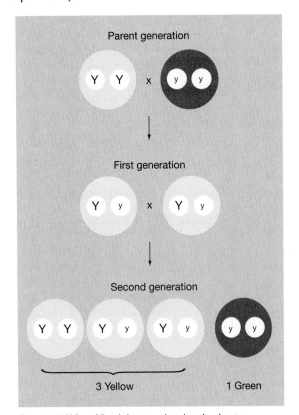

Parent generation

First generation

Second generation

3 Yellow   1 Green

Figure 3–2 When Mendel crossed a plant having two genes for yellow peas (YY) with a plant having two genes for green peas (yy), each offspring pea was yellow but carried one gene for yellow and one gene for green (Yy). The peas were yellow because the gene for yellow is dominant over the - recessive gene for green. Crossing the first generation yielded three yellow pea plants for each green pea plant.

When the pollen from a yellow pea plant was transferred to a green pea plant, Mendel observed a curious phenomenon: All of the first-generation offspring bore yellow peas. It seemed that the green trait had disappeared. But when seeds from this first generation were crossed, they produced both yellow and green pea plants in a ratio of three yellow to one green pea plant (see Figure 3–2). Apparently, Mendel reasoned, the green trait had not been lost or altered; the yellow trait was simply **dominant** and the green trait was

recessive. Mendel observed similar results with other traits. Tallness dominated shortness, and the factor for smooth-skinned peas dominated the factor for wrinkled ones. In each cross, the 3-to-1 ratio appeared in the second generation. Self-fertilization, however, produced different results. Green pea plants always yielded green pea plants, and short plants always produced short plants.

From his numerical results, Mendel concluded that some yellow pea plants were pure (*homozygous*) for that trait, whereas others also possessed a green factor (the plants were *heterozygous*). That is, although two plants might both have yellow peas, one of them might produce offspring with green peas. In such cases, the genetic makeup, the **genotype,** differed from the observable appearance, or **phenotype.**

Genes: The Conveyors of Inherited Traits

Mendel's units of heredity were what we now call **genes.** He concluded that these units occurred in pairs for each trait and that offspring inherited one unit of the pair from each parent. Each member of a gene pair or group is called an **allele.** If the two genes, or alleles, for a trait are the same, the organism is **homozygous** for that trait; if the two genes for a characteristic differ, the organism is **heterozygous** for that trait. A pea plant that contains a pair of genes for yellow is homozygous for the trait. A yellow pea plant with a dominant gene for yellow and a recessive gene for green, although phenotypically yellow, has a heterozygous genotype. As Mendel demonstrated, the recessive green gene can reappear in subsequent generations. But Mendel knew nothing of the composition of genes or the processes that transmit them from parent to offspring. Many years of scientific research have yielded much of the missing information.

The genes of higher organisms (not including bacteria and primitive plants such as green-blue algae) are located on ropelike bodies called **chromosomes** within the nucleus of every one of the organism's cells. Chromosomes, like genes, usually occur in pairs. Each allele for a given trait is carried in the identical position on corresponding chromosomes. The two genes that determined the color of Mendel's peas, for example, were opposite each other on a pair of chromosomes.

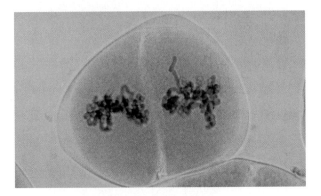
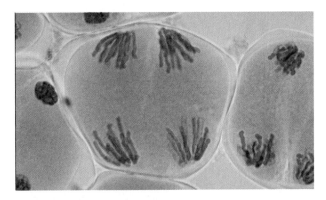

Meiosis in a plant cell. The left image shows the metaphase stage. Note how the chromosomes (stained dark red) lie against and even on top of one another. The right image shows the anaphase stage, when the chromosomes separate and the cell is ready to divide.

MITOSIS AND MEIOSIS   The body cells of every plant or animal carry chromosome pairs in a number appropriate for its species. Humans have 23 pairs, or a total of 46 chromosomes, each carrying many times that number of genes. Each new body cell receives this number of chromosomes during cellular reproduction, or **mitosis,** as each pair of chromosomes duplicates itself.

But what happens when a sperm cell and an egg cell unite to form a new organism? What prevents the human baby from receiving twice the number of chromosomes characteristic of its species—23 pairs from the sperm and 23 pairs from the egg? The process by which the reproductive cells are formed, **meiosis,** ensures that this will not happen (see Figure 3–3). Each reproductive cell contains half the number of chromosomes appropriate for the species. Only one member of each chromosome pair is carried in every egg or sperm. At fertilization, the human embryo normally receives 23 separate chromosomes from its mother and the same number from its father, which add up to the 23 pairs.

DNA   As we have said, genes are located on chromosomes. Each gene carries a set of instructions encoded in its chemical structure. It is from this coded information carried in genes that a cell makes all the rest of its structural parts and chemical machinery. It appears that in most living organisms, heredity is controlled by the same chemical substance, **DNA**—deoxyribonucleic acid. An enormous amount of research has been directed toward understanding DNA—what its structure is, how it duplicates itself in reproduction, and how it conveys or instructs the formation of a complete organism.

One of the most important keys to understanding human development and genetics is the structure and function of DNA. In 1953, American biologist James Watson, with British molecular biologist Francis Crick, proposed that DNA is a long, two-stranded molecule shaped like a double helix (see Figure 3–4). Genetic information is stored in the linear sequences of the bases; different species have different sequences, and every individual is slightly different from

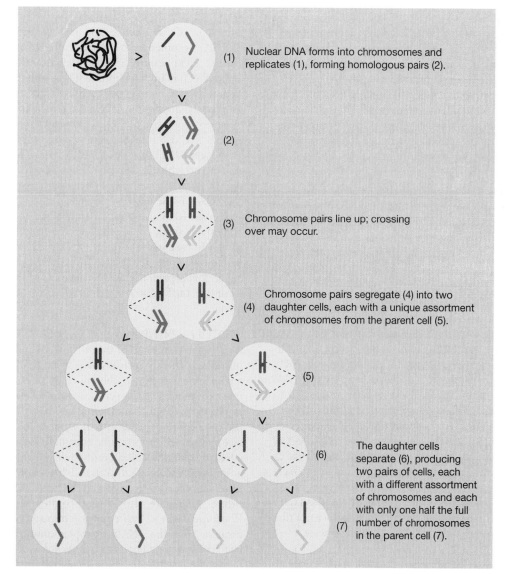

(1) Nuclear DNA forms into chromosomes and replicates (1), forming homologous pairs (2).

(2)

(3) Chromosome pairs line up; crossing over may occur.

(4) Chromosome pairs segregate (4) into two daughter cells, each with a unique assortment of chromosomes from the parent cell (5).

(5)

(6) The daughter cells separate (6), producing two pairs of cells, each with a different assortment of chromosomes and each with only one half the full number of chromosomes in the parent cell (7).

(7)

Figure 3–3 Meiosis (sex cells)

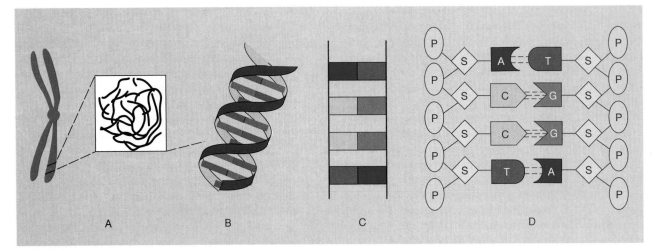

Figure 3–4 DNA
Chromosomes are built of DNA (A), which consists of two spiral sugar-phosphate strands (B) linked by the nitrogenous bases adenine, guanine, thymine, and cytosine (C). When the DNA molecule reproduces, the bases separate and the spiral strands unwind (D). Because adenine can only bond to thymine, and cytosine can only bond to guanine, each original strand serves as a mold along which a new complementary chain is formed.

every other individual. Notice that in the DNA molecule each base always has the same opposite base; adenine and thymine are paired, as are cytosine and guanine. The importance of this pattern is that the two strands carry the same information, so that when the double helix unwinds each strand can form a template for a new strand of complementary bases. Because DNA stores the information required to make up the cells of an organism, it has been called the language of life. As George and Muriel Beadle put it,

> the deciphering of the DNA code has revealed our possession of a language much older than hieroglyphics, a language as old as life itself, a language that is the most living language of all—even if its letters are invisible and its words are buried deep in the cells of our bodies.[18]

Once it was understood that genes are made of DNA, concerted efforts were begun to map DNA sequences and their locations on the chromosomes of different organisms. A project known as the Human Genome Project set out to assemble a complete genetic map for humans. In July 2000, the initial mapping of the human genome was completed.[19] This was a significant achievement and has already led to several breakthroughs in our understanding of how the genetic code functions.[20] For example, researchers recently reported finding two genes that appear to provide partial resistance to malaria, but without the damaging effects of the sickle cell gene. These newly found genes appear to have evolved recently, perhaps only a few thousand years ago. If researchers can discover how these genes help to defend their carriers against malaria, that may help medical science discover how to prevent or treat this devastating disease.[21]

MESSENGER RNA   DNA stores the information to make cells, but it does not directly affect the formation of cells.

One type of ribonucleic acid (RNA), **messenger RNA (mRNA),** is copied from a portion of DNA and moves outside the cell nucleus to direct the formation of proteins. Proteins have so many functions that they are considered to be responsible for most of the characteristics of an organism. They act as catalysts for synthesizing DNA and RNA and for the activities of cells; they also contribute many structural elements that determine the shape and movement of cells. Messenger RNA is like DNA in that it has a linear sequence of bases attached to a sugar-phosphate backbone, but it is slightly different chemically. One difference is that messenger RNA has the base uracil instead of the base thymine. Messenger RNA also has a different sugar-phosphate backbone and is single- rather than double-stranded. Messenger RNA is formed when a double-stranded DNA molecule unwinds and forms a template for the mRNA. After a section of DNA is copied, the mRNA releases from the DNA and leaves the nucleus, and the double helix of the DNA is reformed.

PROTEIN SYNTHESIS   Once the mRNA is released from the DNA, it travels out of the cell nucleus and into the body of the cell. There it attaches to a structure in the cell called a **ribosome,** which uses the information on the mRNA to make proteins. The ribosome essentially "reads" the chemical bases on the mRNA in commands that tell the ribosome the specific amino acids to join together to form a protein (see Figure 3–5). For example, the mRNA sequence adenine, adenine, guanine (AAG) tells the ribosome to place the amino acid lysine in that location, whereas the sequence adenine, adenine, cytosine (AAC) calls for the amino acid histidine. There are also mRNA commands that tell the ribosome when to begin and when to stop constructing a protein. Thus, the DNA code copied onto mRNA provides all the information necessary for ribosomes to build the proteins that make up the structures of organisms and drive the processes of life.

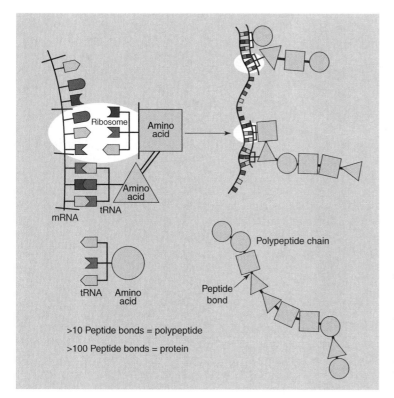

>10 Peptide bonds = polypeptide

>100 Peptide bonds = protein

Figure 3–5 Translation and Protein Synthesis
The mRNA copy of the cellular DNA is "read" by a ribosome that attaches the amino acid with the corresponding transfer RNA (tRNA) to a growing chain of amino acids (called a polypeptide chain because the amino acids are linked together by peptide bonds). A chain more than 100 amino acids long is called a protein.

⦿ Sources of Variability

Natural selection proceeds only when individuals within a population vary. There are two genetic sources of new variation: genetic recombination and mutation. There are also two processes through which variations are shuffled through populations: gene flow and genetic drift. Scholars have recently begun to consider one other potential source of variability: hybridization.

Genetic Recombination

The distribution of traits from parents to children varies from one offspring to another. Brothers and sisters, after all, do not look exactly alike, nor does each child resemble 50 percent of the mother and 50 percent of the father. This variation occurs because when a sperm cell or an egg is formed, the single member of each chromosome pair it receives is a matter of chance. Each reproductive cell, then, carries a random assortment of chromosomes and their respective genes. At fertilization, the egg and sperm that unite are different from every other egg carried by the mother and every other sperm carried by the father. A unique offspring is thus produced by a shuffling of the parents' genes. One cause of this shuffling is the random **segregation,** or sorting, of chromosomes in meiosis. Conceivably, an individual could get any of the possible assortments of the paternal and maternal chromosomes. Another cause of the shuffling of parental genes is **crossing-over,** the exchange of sections of chromosomes between one chromosome and another (Figure 3–6). Thus, after

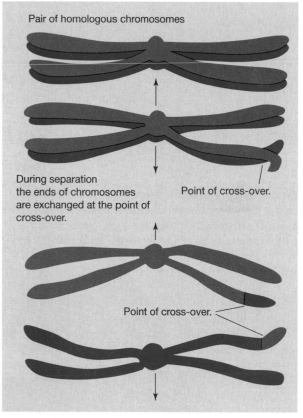

Figure 3–6 Crossing-Over

Source: From Boaz/Almquist, Biological Anthropology.

CURRENT RESEARCH AND ISSUES

Do We Need to Fear Genetic Engineering?

So much is known about molecular genetics that it is now possible to alter individual genes and even whole organisms in very precise ways. The revolution occurred very quickly after the structure of DNA was first identified in 1953 by James Watson and Francis Crick. Particular genetic traits could then be linked to particular sequences of DNA messages. In the 1970s, the development of recombinant DNA techniques allowed researchers to splice pieces of DNA from one organism into the DNA of another, in precise locations. Researchers learned how to make copies by putting these "recombined" strands into host organisms such as bacteria, which reproduce by cloning. The applications of these techniques are potentially enormous. Biotechnology companies are already doing genetic engineering to manufacture medicines (such as insulin and a vaccine against hepatitis B) and to produce more desirable plant and animal products (e.g., a strain of tomato that can be shipped when it's ripe without spoiling). They are also working on how to reintroduce altered cells into organisms to fix genetic defects. As of now, about 4,000 human disorders are known to be caused by defects in a few genes; theoretically, they should be fixable some day by genetic engineering. As more becomes known about the precise location of genes and the DNA sequences that convey particular information, much more engineering will be possible. Already some imagine that genetic therapy will eventually cure various cancers and heart disease.

Might there be risks associated with such interventions? Some fear that recombinant DNA engineering may have disastrous consequences. Could a dangerous runaway strain of bacteria or virus be produced in the lab? Might a kind of "Frankenstein" be produced? Could unscrupulous governments mandate certain kinds of alterations? Do we have reason to entertain such fears?

It is important to remind ourselves that although DNA alteration by recombinant techniques is new, genetic engineering is not new. Humans have genetically altered plants and animals for thousands of years. We usually do not call it genetic engineering—we call it domestication or breeding. To be sure, the mechanism of traditional genetic engineering, selective breeding, is different from DNA splicing, but the effect is genetic alteration nonetheless. By breeding for preferred traits, humans are able to produce breeds of horses, dogs, cattle, varieties of corn and beans, and all of the other animals and plants we depend on for food, fiber, and other materials and chemicals. All of them are different, often very different, from their wild progenitors. Humans have also domesticated microorganisms. An example that goes back thousands of years is the yeast used for brewing beer and baking bread; a more recent example is a particular mold used to produce penicillin. And live vaccines that are deliberately weakened viruses, as, for example, in the vaccine against polio, have already been widely used to prevent illness.

---

meiosis, the egg and sperm do not receive just a random mixture of complete paternal and maternal chromosomes; because of crossing-over they also receive chromosomes in which some of the sections may have been replaced.

The traits displayed by each organism are not simply the result of combinations of dominant and recessive genes, as Mendel had hypothesized. In humans, most traits are influenced by the activity of many genes. Skin color, for example, is the result of several inherited characteristics. A brownish shade results from the presence of a pigment known as *melanin;* the degree of darkness in the hue depends largely on the amount of melanin present and how it is distributed in the layers of the skin. Another factor contributing to the color of all human skin is the blood that flows in blood vessels located in the outer layers of the skin. Humans carry at least five different genes for the manufac-

ture of melanin and many other genes for the other components of skin hue. In fact, almost all physical characteristics in humans are the result of the concerted action of many genes. Some traits are sex-linked. The X chromosome, which together with the presence or absence of a Y chromosome determines sex, may also carry the gene for hemophilia or the gene for color blindness. The expression of these two characteristics depends on the sex of the organism.

Genetic recombination produces variety, which is essential for the operation of natural selection. Ultimately, however, the major source of variability is mutation. This is because mutation replenishes the supply of variability, which is constantly being reduced by the selective elimination of less fit variants. Mutation also produces variety in organisms that reproduce asexually.

So what does our past engineering tell us about the risks of future engineering? In general, the past suggests that no serious harm is attributable to domestication. In fact, domesticated animals and plants are less likely to do well if reintroduced into the wild than their wild cousins. They usually need human help to eat, to get shelter from the elements, and to care for their offspring. So why should genetic engineering be any different? It has basically the same purpose as selective breeding—humans want organisms, large or small or microscopic, to be useful to humans. So far, the available evidence indicates that organisms altered genetically to satisfy human needs are no threat to humans because they are unlikely to survive without human assistance. Needless to say, that does not obviate the need to test for risks. It is reassuring that even though DNA in nature can cross over from one organism to another, such natural genetic alteration is not generally harmful to us.

People may mostly be afraid that a dangerous microbe could be accidentally released from a laboratory and multiply uncontrollably. But, as already noted, any microbe or new genetic form is unlikely to be as hardy as its wild cousins. If a bacterium is mistakenly released, it is not going into an artificially empty environment like a sterile petri dish. The natural environment is already filled with bacteria (most of them beneficial to humans), as well as organisms that attack bacteria. In short, it is not so easy to produce a harmful microbe.

The improbability of making destructive organisms does not mean that humans should not guard against the possibility. That is why we have government agencies to certify new products, along with guidelines for testing procedures and oversight panels. A new product of recombinant DNA research has to be approved before it can be widely used.

Can humans use such technology for eugenic purposes, such as creating superhumans or for biological warfare? Possibly. But recombinant DNA techniques are not the problem. After all, the lack of such technology has not prevented genocide, ethnic cleansing, sterilization, and rape. The absence of recombinant technology did not prevent the use of natural biological weapons (such as smallpox-infected blankets given to Native Americans in the 19th century) or the manufacture and use of poison gas in World War I and since. On the other hand, genetically engineered rice has been demonstrated to provide higher crop yields and lower the use of pesticides among small farm households in China. So while there are dangers to genetic engineering, there are also vast potential benefits.

Sources: Allan M. Campbell, "Microbes: The Laboratory and the Field," Bernard D. Davis, "The Issues: Prospects versus Perceptions" and "Summary and Comments: The Scientific Chapters," and Henry I. Miller, "Regulation." All in Bernard D. Davis, ed., *The Genetic Revolution: Scientific Prospects and Public Perceptions* (Baltimore: Johns Hopkins University Press, 1991), pp. 28–44, 1–8, 239–65, 196–211, respectively; Paul Berg and Maxine Singer, *Dealing with Genes: The Language of Heredity* (Mill Valley, CA: University Science Books, 1992), pp. 221–44; Jikun Huang, Rufia Hu, Scott Rozelle, and Carl Pray, "Insect-Resistant GM Rice in Farmers' Fields," *Science* 308 (April 29, 2005): 688–90.

Mutation

A **mutation** is a change in the DNA sequence. Such a change produces an altered gene. The majority of mutations are thought to occur because of occasional mismating of the chemical bases that make up DNA. Just as a typist will make errors in copying a manuscript, so will DNA, in duplicating itself, occasionally change its code. A mutation will result from such an error. Some mutations have more drastic consequences than others. Suppose the error is in one base on a DNA strand. The effect depends on what that portion of the DNA controls. The effect may be minimal if the product hardly affects the organism. On the other hand, if the change occurs at a place where the DNA regulates the production of many proteins, the effect on the organism can be serious.

Although it is very difficult to estimate the proportions of mutations that are harmful, neutral, or beneficial, there is no doubt that some mutations have lethal consequences. We can discuss the relative merits or disadvantages of a mutant gene only in terms of the physical, cultural, and genetic environment of that gene. Galactosemia, for example, is caused by a recessive mutant gene and usually results in mental retardation and blindness. But it can be prevented by dietary restrictions begun at an early age. In this instance, the intervention of human culture counteracts the mutant gene and allows the afflicted individual to lead a normal life. Thus, some cultural factors can modify the effects of natural selection by helping to perpetuate a harmful mutant gene. People with the galactosemia trait who are enabled to function normally can reproduce and pass on one of the recessive genes to their children. Without cultural interference, natural selection would prevent such reproduction. Usually, natural selection acts to retain only those mutations that aid survival.

Even though most mutations may not be adaptive, those that are will multiply in a population relatively quickly, by natural selection. As Theodosius Dobzhansky has suggested:

> Consistently useful mutants are like needles in a haystack of harmful ones. A needle in a haystack is hard to find, even though one may be sure it is there. But if the needle is valuable, the task of finding it is facilitated by setting the haystack on fire and looking for the needle among the ashes. The role of the fire in this parable is played in biological evolution by natural selection.[22]

The black moth that was spotted in Manchester in 1850 probably resulted from a mutation. If the tree trunks had been light colored, that moth or its offspring probably would have died out. But as industrialization increased and the tree trunks became darker, a trait that was once maladaptive became adaptive.

Genetic recombination and mutation are the sources of new variations, but evolutionary biologists have identified two other processes that are important in distributing those variations through populations: genetic drift and gene flow.

Genetic Drift

The term **genetic drift** refers to various random processes that affect gene frequencies in small, relatively isolated populations. Genetic drift is also known as the *Wright effect,* after geneticist Sewall Wright, who first directed attention to this process. Over time in a small population, genetic drift may result in a neutral or nearly neutral gene becoming more or less frequent just by chance.

One variety of genetic drift, called the *founder effect,* occurs when a small group of organisms recently derived from a larger population migrates to a relatively isolated location. If a particular gene is absent just by chance in the migrant group, the descendants are also likely to lack that gene, assuming that the group remains isolated. Similarly, if all members of the original migrant group just by chance carried a particular gene, their descendants would also be likely to share that gene. Isolation can occur for physical reasons, such as when a group moves to a previously uninhabited place and does not return. The populations that traveled over land when the Bering land bridge connected Asia to North America could not readily return when the sea level rose. This may explain why Native Americans have a higher proportion of individuals with type O blood than other populations—the first migrants may have had, by chance, a predominance of individuals with type O blood.

Or the isolation can occur for social reasons. A religious sect of Dunkers emigrated from Germany to the United States in the early 1700s. The fact that the 50 original families kept to themselves probably explains why some of their gene frequencies differ from what is found in both the German and general U.S. populations.[23]

Gene Flow

Gene flow is the process whereby genes pass from one population to another through mating and reproduction. Unlike the other processes of natural selection and genetic drift, which generally increase the differences between populations in different environments, gene flow tends to work in the opposite direction—it *decreases* differences between populations. Two populations at opposite ends of a region may have different frequencies of a particular gene, but the populations located between them have an intermediate gene frequency because of gene flow between them. The variation in gene frequency from one end of the region to the other is called a **cline.** In Europe, for example, there is a cline in the distribution of blood type B, which gradually diminishes in frequency from east to west.[24]

Most genetically determined characteristics in humans have gradually or clinally varying frequencies as one moves from one area to another. Neighboring regions have more similar gene frequencies than regions widely separated. But these clines do not always coincide, which makes the concept of "race" as applied to humans not very useful for understanding human biological variation.[25] We discuss this in more detail in the chapter on human variation.

Gene flow may occur between distant as well as close populations. Long-range movements of people, to trade or raid or settle, may result in gene flow. But they do not always do so.

Hybridization

A **species** is a population that consists of organisms able to interbreed and produce fertile and viable offspring. In general, individuals from one species do not successfully mate with members of a different species because of genetic and behavioral differences. If members of different species do mate, fertilization usually does not occur and, if it does, the embryo does not survive. In the cases where offspring are born, they are usually infertile. However, recent studies have suggested that **hybridization,** the creation of a viable offspring from two different species, may be more possible than once thought. Hybridization may be an important source of new variation in some populations.

The finches of the Galápagos Islands that Darwin used as evidence for natural selection and that we refer to in the box "Is Evolution Slow and Steady or Fast and Abrupt?" also provide an example of hybridization in action. Many female cactus finches (*Geospiza scandens*) died during a period of severe drought, leaving an abundance of males. High competition for mates led some female ground finches (*Geospiza fortis*) to mate with the abundant male cactus finches, something that would not normally occur. The result was hybrid offspring with unique characteristics. These hybrids, both male and female, went on to mate only with cactus finches, because they imprinted on the male cactus finch song as infants. The end result was a one-time influx of ground finch genes into the cactus finch population, adding new variations upon which natural selection could work.[26]

 The Origin of Species

One of the most controversial aspects of Darwin's theory was the suggestion that one species could, over time, evolve into another. How could one species evolve into another? What is the explanation for this differentiation? How does one group of organisms become so unlike another group with the same ancestry that it forms a totally new species? **Speciation,** or the development of a new species, may occur if one subgroup of a species finds itself in a radically different environment. In adapting to their separate environments, the two populations may undergo enough genetic changes to prevent them from interbreeding, should they renew contact. Numerous factors can prevent the exchange of genes. Two species living in the same area may breed at different times of the year, or their behavior during breeding—their courtship rituals—may be distinct. The difference in body structure of closely related forms may in itself bar interbreeding. Geographic barriers may be the most common barriers to interbreeding.

Do new species diverge quickly or slowly from their ancestors? Paleontologists disagree about the pace of speciation. The traditional view is that evolution occurs very slowly over time; new species emerge gradually. Others who espouse what's called "punctuated equilibrium" believe that species are very stable over long periods of time, but when divergence occurs it is quick (see the box titled "Is Evolution Slow and Steady or Fast and Abrupt?")

Speciation versus Creation

But some people, particularly those who call themselves "scientific creationists," argue that while natural selection can produce variation within species (often referred to as *microevolution*), it cannot produce new species (often referred to as *macroevolution*). Creationists argue that God created all living things, and that evolution has only changed those living things in minor ways and has not created new kinds of living things. The major problem with the creationist view is that there is solid empirical evidence for speciation. For example, William Rice and George Salt demonstrated that if they sorted fruit flies by their environmental preferences (such as light intensity and temperature) and then bred the sorted groups separately, they could produce flies incapable of interbreeding—separate species—in as little as 35 generations.[27] The fossil record contains numerous examples of speciation and even the development of entirely new kinds of creatures. For example, the evolution of birds from terrestrial creatures is clearly evidenced in the fossil record.[28] While many creationists downplay the evidence for speciation, the evidence is plentiful, and can be seen by the public in museums all over the world.

With the abundant evidence for speciation found in both the fossil record and in experimental observations, creationists have recently developed a new argument to discount the role of natural selection in the process of speciation. The new argument is that life in general, and species in particular, are so complex that a random, undirected process like natural selection could never have created them. The complexity of life, these creationists argue, must stem from "intelligent design." This new appeal to intelligent design in the origin of species is actually an old, and widely discredited, one. In his 1802 book *Natural Theology,* William Paley wrote, "Suppose I had found a watch upon the ground, and it should be enquired how the watch happened to be in that place . . . the inference, we think, is inevitable; that the watch must have had a maker. . .".[29] By this Paley implied that if we find a complex mechanism at work in the world, like a watch, we must conclude that a maker exists. Paley extended the argument to the complexity of life, and concluded that life must stem from an intelligent designer—God.

Darwin wrote *On the Origin of Species* in part as a response to Paley, and Darwinists have been responding ever since. But in recent years the "intelligent design" movement, or as proponents call it, the "wedge," has brought Paley's ideas back with force. Indeed the force is an active political one, with the explicit purpose "to reverse the stifling dominance of the materialist world view, and to replace it with a science consonant with Christian and theistic convictions."[30] Intelligent design is, at the core, a political movement.

Does being a political, rather than scientific, movement mean intelligent design ideas have no value in understanding speciation? Of course not. The problem is that intelligent design cannot explain speciation in a scientific way. The central argument made by proponents of intelligent design is simply that what we see in the world is too complex to be accounted for by natural selection, but they offer no alternative natural mechanism. They argue that if natural selection may not account for all cases of speciation, then the only alternative is divine intervention. Clearly this reasoning is flawed. Just because we do not understand something today does not mean we should toss out all we do know. Rather, the scientific approach is to continue to examine unexplained phenomena in order to learn more about them.

Intelligent design proponents also fail to answer critics who point out that natural selection can and has accounted for even the most complex of features—such as wings and eyes—and hence that intelligent design arguments lack a basis in fact. The key facts that intelligent design and other creationist scholars appeal to are Biblical ones. But it is important to point out that most Biblical scholars do not agree with creationist arguments. As theologian Ernan McMullin suggests, the Bible "ought to be understood as conveying fundamental theological truths about dependence of the natural and human worlds on their Creator, rather than explaining how exactly these worlds first took shape."[31] On the other hand, there is nothing in science that can absolutely rule out supernatural intervention in the natural world, because supernatural activities are beyond the realm of scientific explanation. For example, while we now know that people with a condition called hypertrichosis grow hair all over their faces because of a single mutation on the X chromosome, science cannot rule out the possibility that the mutation was caused by the "curse of the werewolf" or a divine punishment for sin.[32] Science cannot rule out such possibilities because they cannot be observed, measured, or experimentally tested. Science and religion should be regarded as different ways of understanding the world, the former relying on evidence, the latter relying on faith.

◎ Natural Selection of Behavioral Traits

Until now we have discussed how natural selection might operate to change a population's physical traits, such as the color of moths or the neck length of giraffes. But natural selection can also operate on the behavioral characteristics of populations. Although this idea is not new, it is now receiving more attention. The approaches called **sociobiology,**[33] **behavioral ecology,**[34] and **evolutionary psychology**[35] involve the application of evolutionary principles to the behavior of animals and humans. Behavioral ecology is interested in how all kinds of behavior related to the environment; sociobiology is particularly interested in social organization and social behavior; and evolutionary psychology is interested in how evolution may have produced lasting variation in the way humans behave, interact, and perceive the world. The typical behaviors of a species are assumed to be adaptive and to have evolved by natural selection. For example, why do related species exhibit different social behaviors even though they derive from a common ancestral species?

Consider the lion, as compared with other cats. Although members of the cat family are normally solitary creatures, lions live in social groups called *prides*. Why? George Schaller has suggested that lion social groups may have evolved primarily because group hunting is a more successful way to catch large mammals in open terrain. He has observed that not only are several lions more successful in catching prey than are solitary lions, but several lions are more likely to catch and kill large and dangerous prey such as giraffes. Then, too, cubs are generally safer from predators when in a social group than when alone with their mothers. Thus, the social behavior of lions may have evolved primarily because it provided selective advantages in the lions' open-country environment.[36]

It is important to remember that natural selection operates on expressed characteristics, or the phenotype, of an individual. In the moth example, the color of the moth is part of its *phenotype,* subject to natural selection. Behavior is also an expressed characteristic. If hunting in groups, a behavioral trait gets you more food, then individuals who hunt in groups will do better. But we must also remember that natural selection requires traits to be heritable. Can the concept of heritability be applied to learned behavior, not just genetically transmitted behavior? And, even more controversially, if the concept of heritability can include learning, can it also include cultural learning? Recent research on domesticated dogs suggests it may. Domesticated dogs appear to inherently understand social cues used by humans, such as pointing, while wolves do not. These findings suggest that some aspects of cultural learning in animals may be heritable.[37]

Early theorizing in sociobiology and behavioral ecology appeared to emphasize the genetic component of behavior. For example, Edward O. Wilson, in his book *Sociobiology,* defined sociobiology as "the systematic study of the biological causes of behavior."[38] But Bobbi Low points out that, although the term *biological* may have been interpreted to mean "genetic," most biologists understand that expressed or observable characteristics are the results of genes, environment, and life history, all interacting. Behavior is a product of all three. If we say that some behavior is heritable, we mean that the child's behavior is more likely to resemble the parents' behavior than the behavior of others.[39] Learning from a parent could be an important part of why the offspring is like the parent. If the child is more like the parent than like others, then the likeness is heritable, even if it is entirely learned from the parent.

The sociobiological approach has aroused considerable controversy in anthropology, probably because of its apparent emphasis on genes, rather than experience and learning,

Prides of lions that live in open country are more successful in catching large animals than are solitary lions. This social behavior may have evolved because it provided selective advantages in the lions' open-country environment.

Mountain lions live in wooded environments and hunt individually. Here we see one chasing down a snowshoe rabbit.

as determinants of human behavior. Anthropologists have argued that the customs of a society may be more or less adaptive because cultural behaviors also have reproductive consequences. It is not just an individual's behavior that may have reproductive consequences. So does natural selection also operate in the evolution of culture? Many biologists think not. They say there are substantial differences between biological and cultural evolution. How do cultural evolution and biological evolution compare? To answer this question, we must remember that the operation of natural selection requires three conditions, as we already noted: variation, heritability or mechanisms that duplicate traits in offspring, and differential reproduction because of heritable differences. Do these three requirements apply to cultural behavior?

In biological evolution, variability comes from genetic recombination and mutation. In cultural evolution, it comes from recombination of learned behaviors and from invention.[40] Cultures are not closed or reproductively isolated, as species are. A species cannot borrow genetic traits from another species, but a culture can borrow new things and behaviors from other cultures. The custom of growing corn, which has spread from the New World to many other areas, is an example of this phenomenon. As for the requirement of heritability, although learned traits obviously are not passed to offspring through purely genetic inheritance, parents who exhibit adaptive behavioral traits are more likely to "reproduce" those traits in their children, who may learn them by imitation or by parental instruction. Children and adults may also copy adaptive traits they see in people outside the family. Finally, as for the requirement of differential reproduction, it does not matter whether the trait in question is genetic or learned or both. As Henry Nissen emphasized, "behavioral incompetence leads to extinction as surely as does morphological disproportion or deficiency in any vital organ. Behavior is subject to selection as much as bodily size or resistance to disease."[41]

Many theorists are comfortable with the idea of applying the theory of natural selection to cultural evolution, but others prefer to use different terminology when dealing with traits that do not depend on purely genetic transmission from one generation to the next. For example, Robert Boyd and Peter Richerson discuss human behavior as involving "dual inheritance." They distinguish cultural transmission, by learning and imitation, from genetic transmission, but they emphasize the importance of understanding both and the interaction between them.[42] William Durham also deals separately with cultural transmission, using the term *meme* (analogous to the term *gene*) for the unit of cultural transmission. He directs our attention to the interaction between genes and culture, calling that interaction "coevolution," and provides examples of how genetic evolution and cultural evolution may lead to changes in each other, how they may enhance each other, and how they may even oppose each other.[43]

So biological and cultural evolution in humans may not be completely separate processes. As we will discuss, some of the most important biological features of humans—such as our relatively large brains—may have been favored by natural selection because our ancestors made tools, a cultural trait. Conversely, the cultural trait of informal and formal education may have been favored by natural selection because humans have a long period of immaturity, a biological trait.

As long as the human species continues to exist and the social and physical environment continues to change, there is reason to think that natural selection of biological and cultural traits will also continue. However, as humans learn more and more about genetic structure they will become more and more capable of curing genetically caused disorders and even altering the way evolution proceeds. Today, genetic researchers are capable of diagnosing genetic defects in developing fetuses, and parents can and do decide often whether to terminate a pregnancy. Soon genetic engineering will probably allow humans to fix defects and even try to "improve" the genetic code of a growing fetus. Whether and to what extent humans should alter genes will undoubtedly be the subject of continuing debate. Whatever the decisions we eventually make about genetic engineering, they will affect the course of human biological and cultural evolution.

◎ Summary

1. If we think of the history of the universe in terms of 12 months, the history of humanlike primates would take up only about one and a half hours. The universe is some 15 billion years old; modern-looking humans have existed for about 100,000 years.

2. Ideas about evolution took a long time to take hold because they contradicted the biblical view of events; species were viewed as fixed in their form by the creator. But in the 18th and early 19th centuries increasing evidence suggested that evolution was a viable theory. In geology, the concept of uniformitarianism suggested that the earth is constantly subject to shaping and reshaping by natural forces working over vast stretches of time. A number of thinkers during this period began to discuss evolution and how it might occur.

3. Charles Darwin and Alfred Wallace proposed the mechanism of natural selection to account for the evolution of species. Basic principles of the theory of natural selection are that (1) every species is composed of a great variety of individuals, some of which are better adapted to their environment than others; (2) offspring inherit traits from their parents at least to some degree and in some way; and (3) since better adapted individuals generally produce more offspring over the generations than the poorer adapted, the frequency of adaptive traits increases in subsequent generations. In this way, natural selection results in increasing proportions of individuals with advantageous traits.

4. Mendel's and subsequent research in genetics and our understanding of the structure and function of DNA and mRNA help us to understand the biological mechanisms by which traits may be passed from one generation to the next.

5. Natural selection depends on variation within a population. The primary sources of biological variation are genetic recombination, mutation, genetic drift, gene flow, and hybridization.

6. Speciation, the development of a new species, may occur if one subgroup becomes separated from other subgroups. In adapting to different environments, these subpopulations may undergo enough genetic changes to prevent interbreeding, even if they reestablish contact. Once species differentiation occurs, it is believed that the evolutionary process cannot be reversed.

7. So-called "creation scientists" and proponents of "intelligent design" theory argue that the origin of species cannot be accounted for through natural selection. This argument ignores the enormous body of evidence—experimental, fossil, and field data—that demonstrates how natural selection works to create new species.

8. Natural selection can also operate on the behavioral characteristics of populations. The approaches called sociobiology and behavioral ecology involve the application of evolutionary principles to the behavior of animals. Much controversy surrounds the degree to which the theory of natural selection can be applied to human behavior, particularly cultural behavior. There is more agreement that biological and cultural evolution in humans may influence each other.

◎ Glossary Terms

adaptive	39	homozygous	42
allele	42	hybridization	48
balancing selection	41	maladaptive	39
behavioral ecology	50	meiosis	43
chromosome	42	messenger RNA (mRNA)	44
cline	48		
crossing-over	45	mitosis	43
directional selection	41	mutation	47
DNA	43	natural selection	38
dominant	42	normalizing selection	41
evolutionary psychology	50	phenotype	42
genes	42	recessive	42
gene flow	48	ribosome	44
genetic drift	48	segregation	45
genotype	42	sociobiology	50
genus	36	speciation	49
heterozygous	42	species	48

◎ Critical Questions

1. Do you think the theory of natural selection is compatible with religious beliefs? Explain your reasoning.
2. How might the discovery of genetic cures and the use of genetic engineering affect the future of evolution?
3. Why do you think humans have remained one species?

◎ Research Navigator

1. Please go to www.researchnavigator.com and enter your LOGIN NAME and PASSWORD. For instructions on registering for the first time, please view the detailed instructions at the end of Chapter 1.
2. Use the link library for Anthropology to find links about evolution. Use these links to create a "museum" of evolution using Web sites as "exhibits." Have a fellow student "walk" though the "museum" by going to each of the Web sites you chose for "exhibits." Explain why you chose each "exhibit" and what lessons the "museum" is intended to teach.

◎ Discovering Anthropology: Researchers at Work

Read the chapter by Jonathan Marks titled "Genes, Bodies, and Species" in the accompanying *Discovering Anthropology* reader. Answer the following questions:

1. Compare Marks's discussion of the "Hardy-Weinberg Law" and Figure 4–2, which displays the distribution of genotypes in pea plants identified by Mendel. Explain how the Hardy-Weinberg Law relates to Mendel's discovery.

2. Marks argues that speciation requires a gene pool to be divided into isolated groups. Explain why this is the case. Given the enormous gene flow in human populations, is it likely (or even possible) that a new species of human will evolve under current conditions?

3. Marks concludes his essay by stating that genetic mutation is more complex than we had previously thought. In what ways does Marks's discussion of mutation and its effects differ from that we present in this text? Does Marks's discussion appear to make the process of mutation more complex than ours?

CHAPTER FOUR

The Living Primates

The goal of **primatology**, the study of primates, is to understand how different primates have adapted anatomically and behaviorally to their environments. The results of such studies may help us to understand the behavior and evolution of the human primate.

But how can living primates such as chimpanzees tell us anything about humans or the primates that were our ancestors? After all, each living primate species has its own history of evolutionary divergence from the earliest primate forms. All living primates, including humans, evolved from earlier primates that are now extinct. Nonetheless, by observing how humans and other primates differ from and resemble each other, we may be able to infer how and why humans diverged from the other primates.

In conjunction with fossil evidence, anatomical and behavioral comparisons of living primates may help us reconstruct what early primates were like. For example, if we know that modern primates that swing through the trees have a particular kind of shoulder bone structure, we can infer that similar fossil bones probably belonged to an animal that also swung through the trees. Differing adaptations of living primates may also suggest why certain divergences occurred in primate evolution. If we know what traits belong to humans, and to humans alone, this knowledge may suggest why the line of primates that led to humans branched away from the line leading to chimpanzees and gorillas.

In this chapter we first examine the common features of the living primates. Next we introduce the different animals that belong to the order Primates, focusing on the distinctive characteristics of each major type. Then we discuss the traits that make humans different from all other primates. We close with a look at possible explanations of some of the varying adaptations exhibited by the different primate species. The purpose of this chapter is to help us understand more about humans. Therefore, we emphasize the features of primate anatomy and behavior that perhaps have the greatest bearing on human evolution.

Common Primate Traits

All primates belong to the class Mammalia, and they share all the common features of mammals. Except for humans, the bodies of primates are covered with dense hair or fur, which provides insulation. Even humans have hair in various places, though perhaps not always for insulation. Mammals are *warm-blooded;* that is, their body temperature is more or less constantly warm and usually higher than that of the air around them. Almost all mammals give birth to live young that develop to a considerable size within the mother and are nourished by suckling from the mother's mammary glands. The young have a relatively long period of dependence on adults after birth. This period is also a time of learning, for a great deal of adult mammal behavior is learned rather than instinctive. Play is a learning technique common to mammal young and is especially important to primates, as we shall see later in this chapter.

The primates have a number of physical and social traits that set them apart from other mammals.

Physical Features

No one of the primates' physical features is unique to primates; animals from other orders share one or more of the characteristics described below. But the complex of all these physical traits is unique to primates.[1]

Many skeletal features of the primates reflect an **arboreal** (tree-living) existence. All primate hind limbs are structured principally to provide support, but the "feet" in most primates can also grasp things (see Figure 4–1). Some primates—orangutans, for instance—can suspend themselves from their hind limbs. The forelimbs are especially flexible, built to withstand both pushing and pulling forces. Each of the hind limbs and forelimbs has one bone in the upper portion and two bones in the lower portion (with the exception of the tarsier). This feature has changed little since the time of the earliest primate ancestors. It has remained in modern primates (although many other mammals have lost it) because the double bones give great mobility for rotating arms and legs.

Another characteristic structure of primates is the clavicle, or collarbone. The clavicle also gives primates great freedom of movement, allowing them to move the shoulders both up and down and back and forth. Although humans obviously do not use this flexibility for arboreal activity, they do use it for other activities. Without a clavicle we could not throw a spear or a ball; no fine tools could be made and no doorknobs turned if we did not have rotatable forearms.

Primates generally are **omnivorous;** that is, they eat all kinds of food, including insects and small animals, as well as fruits, seeds, leaves, and roots. The teeth of primates reflect this omnivorous diet. The chewing teeth—the **molars** and **premolars**—are unspecialized, particularly in comparison with those of other groups of animals, such as the grazers.

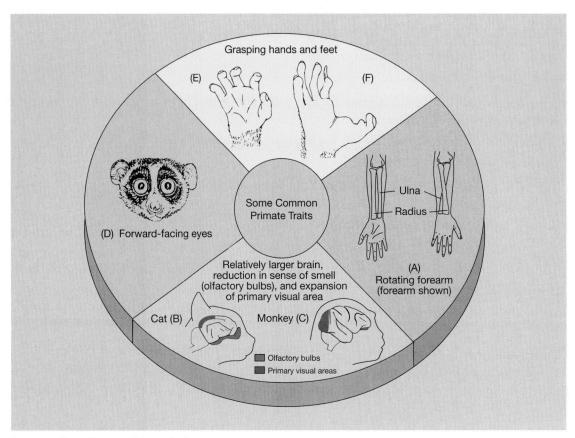

Figure 4–1 Some Common Primate Traits

Source: (A) From Ronald G. Wolff, *Functional Chordate Anatomy* (Lexington, MA: D. C. Heath and Company, 1991), p. 255. Reprinted with permission of D. C. Heath. (B, C) From Terrence Deacon, "Primate Brains and Senses," in Stephen Jones, Robert Martin, and David Pilbeam, eds., *The Cambridge Encyclopedia of Human Evolution* (New York: Cambridge University Press, 1992), p. 110. (D) From Matt Cartmill, "Non-Human Primates," in ibid., p. 25. (E, F) From ibid., p. 24.

The front teeth—the **incisors** and **canines**—are often very specialized, principally in the lower primates. For example, in many prosimians the slender, tightly packed lower incisors and canines form a "dental comb" the animals use in grooming or for scraping hardened tree gum (which is a food for them) from tree trunks.[2]

Primate hands are extremely flexible. All primates have prehensile—grasping—hands, which can be wrapped around an object. Primates have five digits on both hands and feet (in some cases, one digit may be reduced to a stub), and their nails, with few exceptions, are broad and flat, not clawlike. This structure allows them to grip objects; the hairless, sensitive pads on their fingers, toes, heels, and palms also help them to grip. Most primates have **opposable thumbs,** a feature that allows an even more precise and powerful grip.

Vision is very important to primate life. Compared with other mammals, primates have a relatively larger portion of the brain devoted to vision rather than smell. Primates are characterized by stereoscopic, or depth, vision. Their eyes are directed forward rather than sideways, as in other animals—a trait that allows them to focus on an object (insects or other food or a distant branch) with both eyes at once. Most primates also have color vision, perhaps to recognize when plant foods are ready to eat.

Another important primate feature is a large brain relative to body size. That is, primates generally have larger brains than animals of similar size, perhaps because their survival depends on an enormous amount of learning, as we discuss later. In general, animals with large brains seem to mature more slowly and to live longer than animals with small brains.[3] The more slowly an animal matures and the longer it lives, the more it can learn.

Finally, the primate reproductive system sets this order of animals apart from other mammals. Males of most primate species have a pendulous penis that is not attached to the abdomen by skin, a trait shared by a few other animals, including bats and bears. Females of most primate species have two nipples on the chest (a few prosimians have more than two nipples). The uterus is usually constructed to hold a single fetus (only the marmosets and tamarins typically give birth to twins), not a litter, as with most other animals. This reproductive system can be seen as emphasizing quality over quantity—an adaptation possibly related to the dangers of life in the trees, particularly the risk of falls.[4] Primate infants tend to be relatively well developed at birth, although humans, apes, and some monkeys have helpless infants. Most infant primates, except humans, can cling to their mothers from birth. Primates typically take a long time to mature. For example, the rhesus monkey is not sexually mature until about 3 years of age, the chimpanzee not until about age 9.

Social Features

For the most part, primates are social animals. And just as physical traits such as grasping hands and stereoscopic vision may have developed as adaptations to the environment, so may have many patterns of social behavior. For most primates, particularly those that are **diurnal**—that is, active during the day—group life may be crucial to survival, as we will see later in this chapter.

DEPENDENCY AND DEVELOPMENT IN A SOCIAL CONTEXT Social relationships begin with the mother and other adults during the fairly long dependency period of primates. (For the dependency period of primates, the infancy and juvenile phases, see Figure 4–2.) The prolonged dependency of infant monkeys and apes probably offers an evolutionary advantage in that it allows infants more time to observe and learn the complex behaviors essential to survival while enjoying the care and protection of mature adults.

Primates without a warm, social relationship with a mother or another individual do not appear to develop appropriate patterns of social interaction. In a series of classic experiments with rhesus monkeys, Harry Harlow investigated the effects of maternal neglect and isolation on offspring.[5] He found that as a result of either inadequate mothering or isolation from other infants, some monkeys are unable to lead normal social lives. They develop aberrant sexual activities and may even become juvenile delinquents. Harlow mated socially deprived female monkeys with well-adjusted males. When these females gave birth, their behavior was not at all motherly, and they often rejected their babies entirely. Their abnormal behavior was offered as evidence that mothering is more than instinctive. Harlow's experiments underline the importance of maternal care and attention for monkeys and, as a corollary, for humans.

In many primate groups the mother is not the only individual providing care to the dependent young. Among gray langur monkeys, the birth and subsequent rearing of a baby absorb the attention of most female members of the troop.[6]

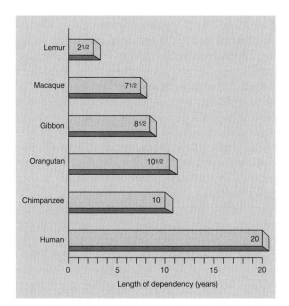

Figure 4–2 A Comparison of the Dependency Periods of Primate Offspring

Source: Data from Alison Jolly, *The Evolution of Primate Behavior,* 2nd ed. (New York: Macmillan, 1985), p. 292.

A baby Macaque clings to its (wire and cloth) "surrogate mother" during the Harry Harlow experiment. Harlow demonstrated that social interaction was necessary for primates to develop normally.

And in some primate species, the father may spend as much time caring for infants as the mother.[7]

PRIMATES AT PLAY   Harlow's investigations have provided other information about social learning in young primates. The experiments that showed the importance of maternal care to baby rhesus monkeys also revealed that play is another crucial ingredient of normal development during the dependency period. Just as monkeys raised without mothers showed abnormal behavior as adults, so did monkeys raised with mothers but with no peers to play with. In fact, when some of the monkeys raised without mothers were allowed a regular playtime with peers, many of them behaved more normally. Subsequent work has supported Harlow's findings.[8]

Play is important for learning.[9] It provides practice for the physical skills necessary or useful in adulthood. For example, young monkeys racing through the trees at top speed are gaining coordination that may save their lives if they are chased by predators later on. Play is also a way of learning social skills, particularly in interacting and communicating with other members of the group. Some dominance relationships seem to be established partly through the rough-and-tumble games that older juveniles play, where winning depends on such factors as size, strength, and agility. These qualities, or the lack of them, may influence the individual's

status throughout adult life. (Other factors also help determine an individual's status. For instance, the mother's status has been shown to be very important in some primates.[10])

LEARNING FROM OTHERS   We know that primates, nonhuman and human alike, learn many things in social groups. Among humans, children often imitate others, and adults often deliberately teach the young. In English we say, "Isn't it cute how Tommy 'apes' his father?" But do apes (and monkeys) imitate others, or do they just learn to do similar things whether or not a model is observed? There is controversy among researchers as to how much imitation versus independent learning occurs in nonhuman primates. Even more arguable is whether deliberate teaching occurs among nonhuman primates.[11]

Some fieldworkers have suggested that chimpanzees may learn by imitation to use tools. For example, Jane Goodall cited an occasion when a female with diarrhea picked up a handful of leaves to wipe her bottom. Her 2-year-old infant watched closely, and then twice picked up leaves to wipe its own, clean behind.[12] Termite "fishing," using a grass stalk to withdraw termites from a termite mound, is probably the best known example of chimpanzee tool use. Immature chimpanzees in the wild have been observed to watch attentively and pick up stalks while others are "fishing." And mothers let their infants hold on to the stalks while the mothers "fish." But some observers do not think these reports provide clear evidence of imitation or teaching. Even though the mother lets the infant hold on to the "fishing" stalk, the infant is doing the activity with her, not watching it and then independently repeating it soon after.[13]

◎ Classification of Primates

Classification provides a useful way to refer to groups of species that are similar in biologically important ways. Sometimes classification schemes vary because the classifiers emphasize somewhat different aspects of similarity and difference. For instance, one type of classification stresses the evolutionary branching that led to the primates of today, another the quantity of shared features. A third approach considers the evolutionary lines as well as similarity and difference of features, but not all features are equally weighted. More "advanced" and specialized features that develop in an evolutionary line are emphasized.[14] Figure 4–3 gives a classification scheme that follows this last approach.[15]

Despite the different ways to classify, there is generally little disagreement about how the various primates should be classified. Most of the disagreement, as we shall see when we discuss the various primates, revolves around the classification of tarsiers and humans.

The order Primates is often divided into two suborders: the *prosimians*—literally, premonkeys—and the *anthro-poids*. The prosimians include lemurs, lorises, and tarsiers. The anthropoid suborder includes New World monkeys, Old World monkeys, the lesser apes (gibbons,

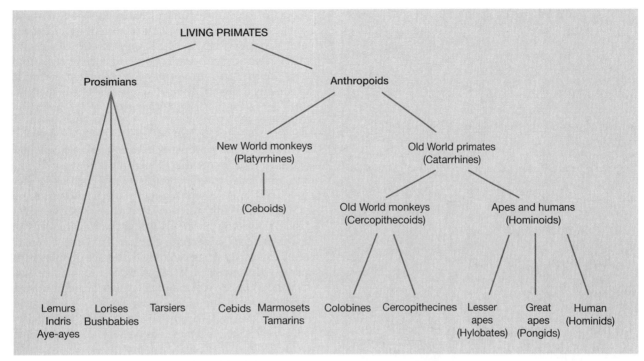

Figure 4–3 A Simplified Classification of the Living Primates

siamangs), the great apes (orangutans, gorillas, chimpanzees), and humans.

The Various Primates

Now that we have discussed their common features, let us focus on some of the ways in which the primates living in the world today vary.

Prosimians

The **prosimians** resemble other mammals more than the anthropoid primates do. For example, the prosimians depend much more on smell for information than do anthropoids. Also in contrast with the anthropoids, they typically have more mobile ears, whiskers, longer snouts, and relatively fixed facial expressions. The prosimians also exhibit many traits shared by all primates, including grasping hands, stereoscopic vision, and enlarged visual centers in the brain.

LEMURLIKE FORMS Lemurs and their relatives, the indris and the aye-ayes, are found only on two island areas off the southeastern coast of Africa, Madagascar and the Comoro Islands. These primates range in size from the mouse lemur to the 4-foot-long indri. Members of the lemur group usually produce single offspring, although twins and even triplets

A ringtailed lemur mother and its baby holding on. Prosimians such as ring-tailed lemurs depend much more on smell than do anthropoids. Prosimians also have more mobile ears, whiskers, longer snouts, and relatively fixed facial expressions.

The bushbaby is a small arboreal prosimian that eats both fruit and insects. It is an energetic nocturnal animal that moves by vertical clinging and leaping.

are common in some species. Many of the species in this group are **quadrupeds**—animals that move on all fours; they walk on all fours in the trees as well as on the ground. Some species, such as the indris, use their hind limbs alone to push off from one vertical position to another in a mode of locomotion called **vertical clinging and leaping.** Lemurs are mostly vegetarians, eating fruit, leaves, bark, and flowers. Lemur species vary greatly in their group size. Many lemur species, particularly those that are **nocturnal** (active during the night), are solitary during their active hours. Others are much more social, living in groups ranging in size from a small family to as many as 60 members.[16] An unusual feature of the lemurlike primates is that females often dominate males, particularly over access to food. In most primates, and in most other mammals, female dominance is rarely observed.[17]

LORISLIKE FORMS   Members of the loris group, found in both Southeast Asia and sub-Saharan Africa, are all nocturnal and arboreal. They eat fruit, tree gum, and insects, and usually give birth to single infants.[18] There are two major subfamilies, the lorises and the bushbabies (galagos), and they show wide behavioral differences. Bushbabies are quick, active animals that hop between branches and tree trunks in the vertical-clinging-and-leaping pattern. On the ground they often resort to a kangaroo-like hop. Lorises are much slower, walking sedately along branches hand over hand in the quadrupedal fashion.

   With the use of searchlights and technical aids such as radio tracking, field researchers have learned a good deal

about these nocturnal primates. For example, we know that among bushbabies, females, particularly mothers and young adult daughters, stay together in small groups, whereas the males disperse. Newborns are born in nests or hollows of trees (which related females may share), and mothers return to nurse them regularly. A few days after birth, a mother may carry her infant in her mouth to nearby trees, "parking" it while she eats.[19]

TARSIERS   The nocturnal, tree-living tarsiers, found now only on the islands of the Philippines and Indonesia, are the only primates that depend completely on animal foods. They are usually insect-eaters, but they sometimes capture and eat other small animals. They are well equipped for night vision, possessing enormous eyes, extraordinary eyesight, and enlarged visual centers in the brain. The tarsiers get their name from their elongated tarsal bones (the bones of the ankle), which give them tremendous leverage for their long jumps. Tarsiers are very skilled at vertical clinging and leaping. They live in family groups composed of a mated pair and their offspring. Like some higher primates, male and female tarsiers sing together each evening to advertise their territories.[20]

   The classification of tarsiers is somewhat controversial. Instead of placing them with the suborder prosimians, as we have done here, some classifiers group tarsiers with anthropoids. In this other classification scheme the suborders of primates are labeled *strepsirhines* (which includes lemurs and lorises) and *haplorhines* (which includes tarsiers and anthropoids). Tarsiers have chromosomes similar to those of other prosimians; they also have claws for grooming on some of their toes, more than two nipples, and a uterus shaped like that of other prosimians (two-horned). Like bushbabies, tarsiers move about through vertical clinging and leaping. In other respects tarsiers are more like the anthropoids. They have a reduced dependence on smell; not only are their noses smaller, but they lack the wet, doglike snout of lemurs. In common with the anthropoids, their eyes are closer together

Nocturnal tree-living tarsiers, like this one in the Philippines, are the only primates that depend completely on animal foods. Their enormous eyes equip them to find insects and other prey in the night. Their elongated ankle bones (tarsals) make them very good at vertical clinging and leaping.

and are protected by bony orbits. Reproductively, the tarsier, like anthropoids, has a placenta that allows contact between the mother's blood and that of the fetus.[21]

Anthropoids

The anthropoid suborder includes humans, apes, and monkeys. Most **anthropoids** share several traits in varying degrees. They have rounded braincases; reduced, nonmobile outer ears; and relatively small, flat faces instead of muzzles. They have highly efficient reproductive systems. They also have highly dextrous hands.[22] The anthropoid order is divided into two main groups: **platyrrhines** and **catarrhines** (see Figure 4–4). These groups take their names from the nose shape of the different anthropoids, but as we shall see they differ in other features as well. Platyrrhines have broad, flat-bridged noses, with nostrils facing outward; these monkeys are found only in the New World, in Central and South America. Catarrhines have narrow noses with nostrils facing downward. Catarrhines include monkeys of the Old World (Africa, Asia, and Europe), as well as apes and humans.

NEW WORLD MONKEYS   Besides the shape of the nose and the position of the nostrils, other anatomical features distinguish the New World monkeys (platyrrhines) from the catarrhine anthropoids. The New World species have three premolars, whereas the Old World species have two. Some New World monkeys have a **prehensile** (grasping) tail; no Old World monkeys do. All the New World monkeys are completely arboreal; they vary a lot in the size of their groups; and their food ranges from insects to nectar and sap to fruits and leaves.[23]

Two main families of New World monkeys have traditionally been defined. One family, the *callitrichids,* contains marmosets and tamarins; the other family, the *cebids,* contains all the other New World monkeys. Although scholars recognize some problems with this division, it is a useful one for gaining a basic understanding of the New World monkeys. The callitrichids are very small, have claws instead of fingernails, and give birth to twins who mature in about two years. Perhaps because twinning is so common and the infants have to be carried, callitrichid mothers cannot take care of them alone. Fathers and older siblings have often been observed carrying infants. Indeed, males may do more carrying than females. Callitrichid groups may contain a mated pair (monogamy) or a female mated to more than one male (polyandry). The callitrichids eat a lot of fruit and tree sap, but like other very small primates, they obtain a large portion of their protein requirements from insects.[24]

Cebids are generally larger than callitrichids, take about twice as long to mature, and tend to bear only one offspring at a time.[25] The cebids vary widely in size, group composition, and diet. For example, squirrel monkeys weigh about 2 pounds, whereas woolly spider monkeys weigh more than 16 pounds. Some cebids have small groups with one

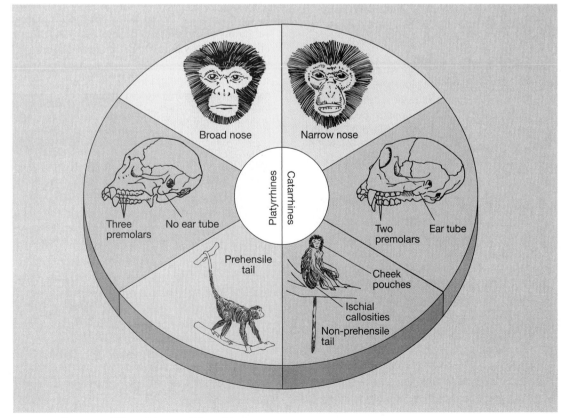

Figure 4–4 Features of Platyrrhines and Catarrhines

Source: Based on Noel T. Boaz and Alan J. Almquist, *Biological Anthropology.*

The squirrel monkey, like all platyrrhines, almost never leaves the trees. It is well suited to an arboreal lifestyle; note how it uses both hands and feet to grasp branches.

male–female pair, others have groups of up to 50 individuals. Some of the smallest cebids have a diet of leaves, insects, flowers, and fruits, whereas others are mostly fruit-eaters with lesser dependence on seeds, leaves, or insects.[26]

OLD WORLD MONKEYS   The Old World monkeys, or **cercopithecoids,** are related more closely to humans than to New World monkeys. They have the same number of teeth as apes and humans. The Old World monkey species are not as diverse as their New World cousins, but they live in a greater variety of habitats. Some live both in trees and on the ground; others, such as the gelada baboon, are com-

pletely **terrestrial,** or ground-living. Macaques are found both in tropical jungles and on snow-covered mountains, and they range from the Rock of Gibraltar to Africa to northern India, Pakistan, and Japan. There are two major subfamilies of Old World monkeys.

Colobine Monkeys   The colobine group includes Asian langurs, the African colobus monkeys, and several other species. These monkeys live mostly in trees, and their diet consists principally of leaves and seeds. Their digestive tracts are equipped to obtain maximum nutrition from a high-cellulose diet; they have pouched stomachs, which provide a large surface area for breaking down plant food, and very large intestinal tracts.

One of the most noticeable features of colobines is the flamboyant color typical of newborns. For example, in one species dusky gray mothers give birth to brilliant orange babies.[27] Observational studies suggest that the colobines are also unusual among the primates (except for humans) in that mothers let other group members take care of their infants shortly after birth. But males who are not members of the group are dangerous for infants; males trying to enter and take over a group have been observed to kill infants. Although this description may suggest that a one-male group is the typical group structure, there does not appear to be a typical pattern for a given species. When more than one site of a species has been studied, both one-male and multiple-male groups have been found.[28]

Cercopithecine Monkeys   The cercopithecine subfamily of monkeys includes more terrestrial species than any other subfamily of Old World monkeys. Many of these species are characterized by a great deal of **sexual dimorphism** (the

This langur, like all catarrhines, has a relatively narrow nose with nostrils that point downward. Langurs are Asian members of the colobine family and are primarily leaf-eaters.

Grooming is an important activity among Old World primates. Here two macaques groom one another.

CURRENT RESEARCH AND ISSUES

Researcher at Work: Katharine Milton

Katharine Milton is a professor in the Department of Environmental Science, Policy and Management at the University of California, Berkeley, and has an avid interest in the scientific study of monkeys. But that is far from how she started out. Born in Alabama, Milton went to Sweet Briar College in Virginia. She was an English major in college and went on to receive her M.A. in that subject at the University of Iowa. It wasn't until later, while she was living in Argentina, that she discovered her great interest in animal behavior and primates in particular.

After receiving her Ph.D. from New York University, with a dissertation on the "economics" of the howler monkeys of Panama, she was fortunate to be able to study the woolly spider monkey—a little-known endangered monkey species living in southeastern Brazil. Because so little was known about them, she started out doing a basic review of their diet and behavior. Woolly spider monkeys look like spider monkeys, so they were assumed also to be fruit-eaters, as are the spider monkeys. But Milton discovered through systematic observation over a year's time that this "commonsense" view was wrong. As she put it: "Apparently no one ever connected the short lifespan of captive woolly spider monkeys with the fact that perhaps, just perhaps, they were being fed the wrong food. Zoos, listen up—if you are ever fortunate enough to obtain a woolly spider monkey or two, be sure to give them leafy matter as their major dietary component, not ripe sugary fruits!"

Much of Milton's research has been devoted to understanding the implications of diet for both nonhuman and human primates. Compared with fruit-eaters, leaf-eating primates are generally larger, require relatively less area to feed in, and have relatively smaller brains. Why? Milton suggested that despite the energy costs of a larger brain, the greater intellectual difficulties of remembering locations of dispersed high-quality food (e.g., fruit, which provides more nutrients by weight than leaves) favored greater mental development in such primates.

Sources: Katharine Milton, "The Evolution of a Physical Anthropologist." In Peter N. Peregrine, Carol R. Ember, and Melvin Ember, eds., *Physical Anthropology: Original Readings in Method and Practice* (Upper Saddle River, NJ: Prentice Hall, 2002), also in Carol R. Ember, Melvin Ember, and Peter N. Peregrine, eds., *New Directions in Anthropology* (Upper Saddle River, NJ: Prentice Hall, CD-ROM, 2004); Katharine Milton, "Foraging Behaviour and the Evolution of Primate Intelligence." In Richard W. Bryne and Andrew Whiten, eds., *Machiavellian Intelligence: Social Expertise and the Evolution of Intellect in Monkeys, Apes, and Humans* (Oxford: Clarendon Press, 1988), pp. 285–305.

sexes look very different); the males are larger, have longer canines, and are more aggressive than the females. Cercopithecines depend more on fruit than do colobines. They are also more capable of surviving in arid and seasonal environments.[29] Pouches inside the cheeks allow cercopithecines to store food for later eating and digestion. An unusual physical feature of these monkeys is the ischial callosities, or callouses, on their bottoms—an adaptation that enables them to sit comfortably in trees or on the ground for long periods of time.[30]

Studies of baboons and macaques suggest that closely related females form the core of a local group, or troop. In large groups, which are common among rhesus monkeys, many social behaviors seem to be determined by degree of biological relatedness. For example, an individual is most likely to sit next to, groom, or help an individual who is closely related maternally.[31] Moreover, a closely related subgroup is likely to stay together when a large troop divides.[32]

The Hominoids: Apes and Humans

The **hominoid** group includes three separate families: the lesser apes, or **hylobates** (gibbons and siamangs); the great apes, or **pongids** (orangutans, gorillas, and chimpanzees); and humans, or **hominids.** Several characteristics distinguish the hominoids from the other primates. Their brains are relatively large, especially the areas of the cerebral cortex associated with the ability to integrate data. All hominoids have fairly long arms, short, broad trunks, and no tails. The wrist, elbow, and shoulder joints of hominoids allow a greater range of movement than in other primates. Hominoid hands are longer and stronger than those of other primates. These skeletal features probably evolved along with the hominoids' unique abilities in suspensory locomotion. Unlike other anthropoids, who move quadrupedally along the ground or along tops of tree branches, hominoids often suspend themselves from below the branches and swing or climb hand over hand from branch to branch.[33] This suspensory posture also translates to locomotion on the ground; all hominoids, at least occasionally, move bipedally, as we discuss in more detail in the chapter on the first hominids.

The dentition of hominoids demonstrates some unique features as well (see Figure 4–5). Hominoid molars are flat and rounded compared to those of other anthropoids, and have what is called a **"Y-5" pattern** on the lower molars—that is, the lower molars have five cusps with a Y-shaped groove opening toward the cheek running between them. Other anthropoids have what is called a **bilophodont**

A troop of baboons in Kenya spends most of its time on the ground.

pattern—their molars have two ridges or "loafs" running perpendicular to the cheeks. All hominoids except for humans also have long canine teeth that project beyond the tops of the other teeth, and a corresponding space on the opposite jaw, called a **diastema,** where the canine sits when the jaws are closed. The contact of the upper canine and the lower third premolar creates a sharp cutting edge, in part due to the premolar being elongated to accommodate the canine.[34] These dental features are related to the hominoids' diets, which often include both fibrous plant materials, which can be efficiently cut with sharp canines against elongated premolars, and soft fruits, which can be efficiently chewed with wide, flat molars.

The skeletal and dental features shared by the hominoids point toward their common ancestry. Their blood proteins show many similarities, too. This blood likeness is particularly strong among chimpanzees, gorillas, and humans. For this reason, primatologists think chimpanzees and gorillas are evolutionarily closer to humans than are the lesser apes and orangutans, which probably branched off at some earlier point. We discuss the fossil evidence that supports an early split for the orangutans in the next chapter.

GIBBONS AND SIAMANGS   The agile gibbons and their close relatives the siamangs are found in the jungles of Southeast Asia. The gibbons are small, weighing only about 11–15 pounds. The siamangs are somewhat larger, but no more than 25 pounds. Both are mostly fruit-eaters, although they also eat leaves and insects. They are spectacular **brachiators;** their long arms and fingers let them swing hand over

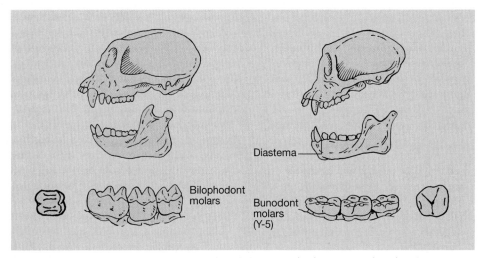

Diastema

Bilophodont molars

Bunodont molars (Y-5)

Figure 4–5 Difference in dentition between an Old World monkey (left) and an ape (right). In Old World monkeys the cusps of the lower molars form two parallel ridges; in apes, the five cusps form a Y-shaped pattern. Apes also have a space between the lower canine and first premolar, called a diastema.

Source: Adapted from Noel T. Boaz and Alan J. Almquist, *Essentials of Biological Anthropology* (Upper Saddle River, NJ: Prentice Hall, 1999), p. 164.

A white-handed gibbon demonstrates its ability as a brachiator.

hand through the trees.[35] A gibbon can move more than 30 feet in a single forward swing.

Gibbons and siamangs live in small family groups consisting of an adult pair, who appear to mate for life, and one or two immature offspring. When the young reach adulthood, they are driven from home by the adults. There is little sexual dimorphism—males and females do not differ in size or appearance—nor is there any clear pattern of dominance by either sex. These lesser apes are also highly territorial; an adult pair advertises their territory by singing and defends it by chasing others away.[36]

ORANGUTANS Orangutans survive only on the islands of Borneo and Sumatra. Unlike gibbons and siamangs, they are clearly recognizable as males or females. Males not only weigh almost twice as much as females (up to 200 pounds), but they also have large cheek pads, throat pouches, beards, and long hair.[37] Like gibbons and siamangs, orangutans are primarily fruit-eaters and arboreal. They are the heaviest of the arboreal primates, and perhaps for this reason they move slowly and laboriously through the trees. Orangutans are unusual among the higher primates in that, except for mothers and their young, adults spend much of their time alone. Some researchers, however, have found evidence of group behavior. One field study of orangutans on Sumatra found that groups of as many as 10 adults fed together in the same tree.[38] And when different researchers pool their information on orangutan behavior, there appear to be regional differences, suggesting the presence of distinct local orangutan

cultures.[39] Cultural differences would not likely arise without different groups.

Different ideas have been proposed about the largely solitary habit of the orangutans that live in the mountainous areas of Borneo. One is that there may be insufficient food in any one tree or home range to support more than a single adult orangutan, a pretty large animal, as animals go. To obtain sufficient food each day without having to travel over a huge area, orangutans thus may live alone rather than in groups.[40] Another idea is that animals live in groups when they are subject to heavy predation; the large size of orangutans may make them immune to attacks from most animals, so living alone may be a viable option.[41] A third idea, which on the face of it seems opposite to the second, is that living alone may be an adaptation to heavy predation by humans. The orangutan's best defense against humans with guns may be to hide alone in the trees.[42]

GORILLAS Gorillas are found in the lowland areas of western equatorial Africa and in the mountain areas of Congo, Uganda, and Rwanda.[43] Unlike the other apes, who are mostly fruit-eaters, gorillas mostly eat other parts of plants—stems, shoots (e.g., bamboo), pith, leaves, roots, and flowers. The amount of fruit eaten varies greatly. In many populations fruit-eating is rare; in some, however, fruit is a common part of the diet.[44]

Gorillas are by far the largest of the surviving apes. In their natural habitats, adult males weigh up to 450 pounds and females up to 250 pounds. To support the weight of massive chests, gorillas travel mostly on the ground on all fours in a form of locomotion known as **knuckle walking:** They walk on the thickly padded middle joints of their fingers. Gorillas' arms and legs, especially those of the young, are well suited for climbing. As adults, their heavier bodies make climbing more precarious.[45] They sleep on the ground or in tub-shaped nests they make from nonfood plants each time they bed down.[46]

Gorillas tend to live in groups consisting of a dominant male, called a silverback, other adult males, adult females, and immature offspring. Both males and females, when mature, seem to leave the groups into which they were born to join other groups. The dominant male is very much the center of attention; he acts as the main protector of the group and the leader in deciding where the group will go next.[47]

CHIMPANZEES Perhaps because they are more sociable and easier to find, chimpanzees have been studied far more than gorillas. Chimpanzees live in the forested areas of Africa, from Sierra Leone in the west to Tanzania in the east.

There are two distinct species of chimpanzee—the common chimpanzee (*Pan troglodytes*) and the bonobo, or pygmy, chimpanzee (*Pan paniscus*). While they share many features in common (indeed, they were not recognized as distinct species until 1929), bonobos tend to be more slender than common chimpanzees, with longer limbs and digits, smaller heads, darker faces, and a distinct part in their hair. Unlike common chimpanzees, bonobos show almost no sexual dimorphism in dentition or skeletal structure. More significant seem to be differences in social behavior.

A young gorilla shows how it knuckle-walks. The back feet are flat on the ground, and only the knuckles of the "hands" touch the ground.

Bonobos are more gregarious than common chimpanzees, and groups tend to be more stable. Groups also tend to be centered around females rather than males.[48]

Although they are primarily fruit-eaters, chimpanzees show many similarities to their close relatives, the gorillas. Both are arboreal and terrestrial. Like gorillas, chimpanzees are good climbers, especially when young, and they spend many hours in the trees. But they move best on the ground, and when they want to cover long distances they come down from the trees and move by knuckle walking. Occasionally, they stand and walk upright, usually when they are traveling through tall grass or are trying to see long distances. Chimpanzees sleep in tree nests that they carefully prepare anew, complete with a bunch of leaves as a pillow, each time they bed down.[49]

Chimpanzees (including bonobos) are less sexually dimorphic than the other great apes. Males weigh a little more than 100 pounds on the average, females somewhat less. But males have longer canines.

For some time it was thought that chimpanzees ate only plant food. Although most of their diet is vegetarian, among common chimpanzees a significant amount comes from meat. After three decades of studies at Gombe Park in Tanzania and elsewhere, researchers have found that common chimpanzees not only eat insects, small lizards, and birds, but they also actively hunt and kill larger animals.[50] They have been observed hunting and eating monkeys, young baboons, and bushbucks in addition to smaller prey. At Gombe, the red colobus monkey is by far the most often hunted animal. So it is not only humans who endanger other primates (see the box "Endangered Primates"); the red colobus monkey population is very small in areas of intense chimpanzee hunting. Hunting appears to be undertaken more often during the dry season when food is scarce.[51] Prey is caught mostly by the males, which hunt either alone or in small groups. It is then shared with—or, perhaps more accurately, begged by—as many as 15 other chimpanzees in friendly social gatherings that may last up to nine hours.[52]

Despite considerable observation, the organization of chimpanzee social groups is still not clear. Groups of common chimpanzees usually are multimale and multifemale, but the size may range considerably from a few to 100 or so members. In Gombe, males typically remain in their natal group throughout life, and females often move to a neighboring group; but males in Guinea do not tend to stay in their natal groups.[53] It appears that chimpanzees come together and drift apart depending on circumstances such as the availability of food and the risk of predation.[54] Scholars have recently compared information from nine long-term studies of chimpanzee social organization and behavior, and have come to the conclusion that there are behaviors specific to particular groups. These behaviors, which include customary tool use, grooming, and mating displays, do not

A bonobo's slender limbs, dark face, and parted hair are some of the traits that distinguish them from common chimpanzees.

Chimpanzees, though they spend much time in the trees, can also move very quickly on the ground.

appear to be determined by the environment, and hence have been interpreted by some scholars as being cultural.[55]

HOMINIDS According to the classification we use here, the hominoids we call hominids include only one living species—modern humans. Humans have many distinctive characteristics that set them apart from other anthropoids and other hominoids, which lead many to place humans in a category separate from the pongids. (These traits are discussed below and also throughout much of the rest of the book.) However, others believe that the differences are not so great as to justify a separate hominid category for humans. For example, humans, chimpanzees, and gorillas are very similar in their proteins and DNA. And it is widely agreed that the lines leading to humans, chimpanzees, and gorillas diverged from a common ancestor perhaps 5–6 million years ago.[56] Whether we stress the similarities or differences between humans and apes does not matter that much; what does matter is that we try to understand the reasons for those similarities and differences.

◎ Distinctive Hominid Traits

We turn now to some of the features that distinguish us— the hominids—from the other primates. Although we like to think of ourselves as unique, many of the traits we discuss here are at the extreme of a continuum that can be traced from the prosimians through the apes.

Physical Traits

Of all the primates, only hominids consistently walk erect on two feet. Gibbons, chimpanzees (particularly bonobos), and gorillas (and some monkeys too) may stand or walk on two feet some of the time, but only for very short periods. All other primates require thick, heavy musculature to hold

their heads erect; this structure is missing in hominids, for our heads are more or less balanced on top of our spinal columns. A dish-shaped pelvis (peculiar to hominids), a lumbar curve in the spine, straight lower limbs, and arched, nonprehensile feet are all related to **bipedalism.** Because hominids are fully bipedal, we can carry objects without impairing our locomotor efficiency.

Although many primates have an opposable thumb, which enables them to grasp and examine objects, the greater length and flexibility of the hominid thumb allow us to handle objects with greater dexterity. We are capable of both a power grip, to hold large or heavy objects firmly, and a precision grip, to hold small or delicate objects without dropping or breaking them. We also have remarkable hand–eye coordination, as well as a remarkably sophisticated brain.

The hominid brain is large and complex, particularly the **cerebral cortex,** the center of speech and other higher mental activities. The brain of the average adult modern human measures more than 1,300 cubic centimeters, compared with 525 cubic centimeters for the gorilla, the primate with the next largest brain. The frontal areas of the hominid brain are also larger than those of other primates, so that hominids have more prominent foreheads than monkeys or gorillas. Hominids have special areas of the brain that are dedicated to speech and language. The large hominid brain requires an enormous amount of blood, and the way blood is carried to and from the brain is also unique.[57] We'll say more about the hominid brain and its evolution in the chapter on the emergence of the genus *Homo.*

Hominid teeth reflect our completely omnivorous diet, and they are not very specialized, which may reflect the fact that we use tools and cooking to prepare our food. As discussed earlier, other hominoids have long canines and a diastema, whereas hominid canines do not usually project beyond the tops of the other teeth. This allows hominids to move their jaws both vertically and horizontally when chewing; horizontal movement would be prevented by the long upper canines of the other hominoids. Hominid molars have thicker enamel than the molars of other hominoids, and both horizontal movement and thickened molars may be related to a dietary emphasis on coarse grains and seeds, something we'll discuss further in the chapter on the first hominids. The hominid jaw is shaped like a parabolic arch, rather than a U-shape, as in the apes, and is composed of relatively thin bones and light muscles. Modern humans have chins; other primates do not.

One other distinctive hominid trait is the sexuality of hominid females, who may engage in intercourse at any time throughout the year; most other primate females engage in sex only periodically, just around the time they can conceive.[58] Hominids are also unusual among the primates in having female–male bonding.[59] Later, in the discussion of the origins of culture, we examine some theories suggesting why male–female bonding, which in modern humans we call "marriage," may have developed. It used to be thought that more or less continuous female sexuality may be related to female–male bonding, but comparative research on mammals and birds contradicts this idea. Those mammals and birds that have more frequent sex are not more likely to have male–female bonding.[60]

APPLIED ANTHROPOLOGY

Endangered Primates

In contrast to many human populations that are too numerous for their resources, many populations of nonhuman primates face extinction because they are not numerous enough. The two trends—human overpopulation and nonhuman primate extinctions—are related. Were it not for human expansion in many parts of the world, the nonhuman primates living in those habitats would not be endangered. Various lemur and other prosimian species of Madagascar, the mountain gorilla and red colobus monkeys of Africa, and the lion tamarin monkeys of Brazil are among the species most at risk.

Many factors are responsible for the difficulties faced by nonhuman primates, but most of them are directly or indirectly the result of human activity. Perhaps the biggest problem is the destruction of tropical rain forest, the habitat of most nonhuman primates, because of encroaching agriculture and cattle ranching and the felling of trees for wood products. The people who live in these areas are partly responsible for the threats to nonhuman primates—population pressure in the human populations increases the likelihood that more forest will be cleared and burned for agriculture, and in some areas nonhuman primates are an important source of hunted food. But world market forces are probably more important. The increasing need for "American" hamburger in fast-food restaurants has accelerated the search for places to raise beef inexpensively. There is also enormous demand for wood products from tropical forests; Japan imports half of all the timber from rain forests to use for plywood, cardboard, paper, and furniture.

Some would argue that it is important to preserve all species. Primatologists remind us that it is especially important to preserve primate diversity. One reason is the scientific one of needing those populations to study and understand how humans are similar and different and how they came to be that way. Another reason is the usefulness of nonhuman primates in biomedical research on human diseases; we share many of our diseases, and many of our genes, with our primate relatives. (As we noted in the first chapter, chimpanzees share 99 percent of their genes with humans.) The film *The Planet of the Apes,* in which the humans are subordinate to the apes, tells us that the primates in zoos could have been us.

So how can nonhuman primates be protected from us? There really are only two major ways: Either human population growth in many places has to be curtailed, or we have to preserve substantial populations of nonhuman primates in protected parks and zoos. Both are difficult but humanly possible.

Sources: Russell A. Mittermeier and Eleanor J. Sterling, "Conservation of Primates." In Steve Jones, Robert Martin, and David Pilbeam, eds., *The Cambridge Encyclopedia of Human Evolution* (Cambridge: Cambridge University Press, 1992), pp. 33–36; Toshisada Nishida, "Introduction to the Conservation Symposium." In Naosuke Itoigawa, Yukimaru Sugiyama, Gene P. Sackett, and Roger K. R. Thompson, *Topics in Primatology,* vol. 2 (Tokyo: University of Tokyo Press, 1992), pp. 303–304.

A golden lion tamarin.

Why, then, does hominid female sexuality differ from that of most other primates? One suggestion is that more or less continuous female sexuality became selectively advantageous in hominids after female–male bonding developed in conjunction with local groups consisting of at least several adult males and adult females.[61] More specifically, the combination of group living and male–female bonding—a combination unique to hominids among the primates—may have favored a switch from the common higher-primate pattern of periodic female sexuality to the pattern of more or less continuous female sexuality. Such a switch may have been favored in hominids because periodic rather than continuous female sexuality would undermine female–male bonding in multimale–multifemale groups.

Field research on nonhuman primates strongly suggests that males usually attempt to mate with any females ready to mate. If the female (or females) a male was bonded to was not interested in sex at certain times, but other females in the group were, it seems likely that the male would try to mate with those other females. Frequent "extramarital affairs" might jeopardize the male–female bond and thereby presumably reduce the reproductive success of both males and females. Hence natural selection may have favored more or less continuous sexuality in hominid females if hominids already had the combination of group living (and the possibility of "extramarital affairs") and marriage. If bonded adults lived alone, as do gibbons, noncontinuous female sexuality would not threaten bonding, because "extramarital" sex would not be likely to occur. Similarly, seasonal breeding would also pose little threat to male–female bonds, because all females would be sexually active at more or less the same time.[62] So the fact that the combination of group living and male–female bonding occurs only in hominids may explain why continuous female sexuality developed in hominids. The bonobo, or pygmy chimpanzee, female does engage in intercourse throughout the year, but bonobos do not have male–female bonding and the females are not interested in sex quite as often as hominid females.[63]

Behavioral Abilities

In comparison with other primates, a much greater proportion of hominid behavior is learned and culturally patterned. As with many physical traits, we can trace a continuum in the learning abilities of all primates. The great apes, including orangutans, gorillas, and chimpanzees, are probably about equal in learning ability.[64] Old and New World monkeys do much less well in learning tests, and, surprisingly, gibbons perform more poorly than most monkeys.

TOOLMAKING   The same kind of continuum is evident in inventiveness and toolmaking. There is no evidence that any nonhuman primates except great apes use tools, although several species of monkeys use "weapons"—branches, stones, or fruit dropped onto predators below them on the ground. Chimpanzees both fashion and use tools in the wild. As we have noted, they strip leaves from sticks and then use the sticks to "fish" termites from their mound-shaped nests. They use leaves to mop up termites, to sponge up water, or to wipe themselves clean. Indeed, tool use varies enough in chimpanzees that primatologist Christophe Boesch has suggested that local chimpanzee groups have cultural differences in terms of the tools they employ.[65]

One example of chimpanzee tool use suggests planning. In Guinea, West Africa, observers watched a number of chimpanzees crack oil palm nuts with two stones. The "platform" stone had a hollow depression; the other stone was used for pounding. The observers assumed that the stones had been brought by the chimpanzees to the palm trees, because no stones like them were nearby and the chimps were observed to leave the pounding stone on top of or near the platform stone when they were finished.[66] Observers in other areas of West Africa have also reported that chimpanzees use stones to crack nuts. In one location in Liberia, an innovative female appeared to have started the practice; it seems to have been imitated within a few months by 13 others who previously showed no interest in the practice.[67]

Chimps in the wild use tools—in this case, a stone to crack palm nuts. As far as we know, though, they don't use tools to make other tools, as humans do.

In captivity, chimpanzees have also been observed to be inventive toolmakers. One mother chimpanzee was seen examining and cleaning her son's teeth, using tools she had fashioned from twigs. She even extracted a baby tooth he was about to lose.[68]

Hominids have usually been considered the only toolmaking animal, but observations such as these call for modification of the definition of toolmaking. If we define toolmaking as adapting a natural object for a specific purpose, then at least some of the great apes are toolmakers too. Perhaps it would be more accurate to say hominids are the only habitual toolmaking animal, just as we say hominids are the only habitual bipedal hominoid, even though the other hominoids all can and do walk bipedally sometimes. As far as we know, though, hominids are unique in their ability to use one tool to make another.

LANGUAGE   Only modern humans have spoken, symbolic language. But, as with toolmaking abilities, the line between modern human language and the communications of other primates is not as sharp as we once thought. In the wild, vervet monkeys make different alarm calls to warn of different predators. Observers playing tape recordings of these calls found that monkeys responded to them differently, depending on the call. If the monkeys heard an "eagle" call, they looked up; if they heard a "leopard" call, they ran high into the trees.[69]

Common chimpanzees are also communicative, using gestures and many vocalizations in the wild. Researchers have used this "natural talent" to teach chimpanzees symbolic language in experimental settings. In their pioneering work, Beatrice T. Gardner and R. Allen Gardner raised a female chimpanzee named Washoe and trained her to communicate with startling effectiveness by means of American Sign Language hand gestures.[70] After a year of training, she was able to associate gestures with specific activities. For example, if thirsty, Washoe would make the signal for "give me" followed by the one for "drink." As she learned, the instructions grew more detailed. If all she wanted was water, she would merely signal for "drink." But if she craved soda pop, as she did more and more, she prefaced the drink signal with the sweet signal—a quick touching of the tongue with her fingers. Later, the Gardners had even more success in training four other common chimpanzees, who were taught by fluent deaf users of American Sign Language.[71]

Bonobos have provided strong evidence that they understand simple grammatical "rules," very much like 2-year-old humans. Pointing to graphic symbols for different particular meanings, a bonobo named Kanzi regularly communicated sequences of types of symbols; for example, he would point to a symbol for a verb ("bite") and then point to a symbol for an object ("ball," "cherry," "food").[72]

OTHER HOMINID TRAITS   Although many primates are omnivores, eating insects and small reptiles in addition to plants—some even hunt small mammals—only hominids hunt very large animals. Also, hominids are one of the few primates that are completely terrestrial. We do not even sleep in trees, as many other ground-living primates do. Perhaps our ancestors lost their perches when the forests receded, or cultural advances such as weapons or fire may have eliminated the need to seek nightly shelter in the trees. In addition, as we have noted, we have the longest dependency period of any of the primates, requiring extensive parental care and support for up to 20 years or so.

Finally, hominids are unlike almost all other primates in having a division of labor by gender in food-getting and food sharing in adulthood. Among nonhuman primates, both females and males forage for themselves after infancy. Hominids have more gender-role specialization, perhaps because men, unencumbered by infants and small children, were freer to hunt and chase large animals.

◎ Primate Adaptations

Thus far we have discussed the common features of primates and introduced the different primates that survive in the world today. Now let us examine possible explanations, suggested by research, of some of the ways in which the living primates (as opposed to fossil primates, which we discuss in the next chapter) have adapted to their varying environments.

Body Size

The living primates vary enormously in body size, ranging from the two or so ounces of the average gray mouse lemur to the 350 pounds of the average male gorilla. What accounts for this sizable variation? Three factors seem to predict body size—the time of day the species is active, where it is active (in the trees or on the ground), and the kinds of food eaten.[73] All the nocturnal primates are small; and among the primates active during the day, the arboreal ones tend to be smaller than the terrestrial ones. Finally, species that eat mostly leaves tend to be larger than species that eat mostly fruits and seeds.

Why do these factors predict size? One important consideration is the general relationship in mammals between body weight and energy needs. Generally, larger animals require more absolute energy, but smaller animals require much more energy for their body weight. That being so, smaller animals (and small primates) need more energy-rich food. Insects, fruits, tree gum, and sap are full of calories and tend to be more important in the diet of small primates. Leaves are relatively low in energy, so leaf-eaters have to consume a lot of food to get enough energy. They also need large stomachs and intestines to extract the nutrients they need, and a bigger gut in turn requires a bigger skeleton and body.[74] Small primates, which eat insects and other rich foods, probably would compete with birds for food. But most very small primates are nocturnal, whereas most forest-living birds are diurnal. So there is little competition between small primates and birds.

Energy requirements may also explain why arboreal primates are usually smaller. Moving about in trees usually requires both vertical and horizontal motion. The energy required to climb vertically is proportional to weight, so larger animals require more energy to climb. But the energy for traveling horizontally, as on the ground, is not proportionate to weight, so larger animals use energy more efficiently on the ground than in the trees.[75] An additional consideration is the amount of weight that can be supported by small tree branches, where foods such as fruits are mostly located. Small animals can go out to small branches more safely than large animals. Also, ground dwellers might be bigger because large size is a protection against predation.[76]

Relative Brain Size

Larger primates usually have larger brains, but larger animals of all types generally have larger brains (see Figure 4–6). Thus primatologists are interested in relative brain size, that is, the ratio of brain size to body size.

Perhaps because hominid primates have the largest brains relatively of any primate, we tend to think a larger brain is "better." However, a large brain does have "costs." From an energy perspective, the development of a large brains requires a great deal of metabolic energy; therefore it should not be favored by natural selection unless the benefits outweigh the costs.[77]

Fruit-eating primates tend to have relatively larger brains than leaf-eating primates do. This difference may be due to natural selection in favor of more capacity for memory, and therefore relatively larger brains, in fruit-eaters. Leaf-eaters may not need as much memory, because they depend on food that is more readily available in time and space, and therefore they may not have to remember where food might be found. In contrast, fruit-eaters may need greater memory and brain capacity because their foods ripen at different times and in separate places that have to be remembered to be found.[78] The brain requires large supplies of oxygen and glucose. Because leaf-eating primates do not have as much glucose in their diets as fruit-eating primates, they may also not have the energy reserves to support relatively large brains.[79]

Group Size

Primate groups vary in size from solitary males and females with young (orangutans) to a few individuals and young (e.g., gibbons) to 100 or more individuals in some Old World monkey troops.[80] What factors might account for such variation?

Nocturnal activity is an important predictor not only of small body size but also of small group size. Nocturnal primates feed either alone or in pairs.[81] John Terborgh has noted that most nocturnal predators hunt by sound, so a nocturnal animal might best avoid attack by being silent.[82] Groups are noisy, and therefore nocturnal animals might be more likely to survive by living alone or in pairs.

On the other hand, a large group might provide advantages in the daytime. The more eyes, ears, and noses a group has, the more quickly a would-be predator might be detected—and perhaps avoided. Also, a larger group would have more teeth and strength to frighten or mob a predator that actually attacked.[83] But this line of reasoning would lead us to expect that all diurnal terrestrial species would have large groups. Yet not all do. Other factors must be operating. One seems to be the amount and density of food. If food resources occur in small amounts and in separate places, only small groups can get enough to eat; but if food occurs in large patches, there will be enough to support large groups.[84] An additional factor may be competition over resources. One suggestion is that substantial but separated patches of resources are likely to be fought over, and therefore individuals living in larger groups might be more likely to obtain access to them.[85]

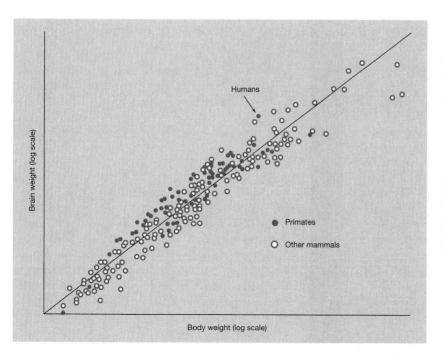

Figure 4–6 As this graph shows, larger animals generally have larger brains. Primates generally have even larger brains than we would expect from their body weight. Note that most of the primates (as indicated by the colored circles) fall above the line showing the relationship between brain weight and body weight. The brains in primates are about twice as heavy as the brains of nonprimate mammals of the same body weight.

Source: From Terrence W. Deacon, "Primate Brains and Senses," in Stephen Jones, Robert Martin, and David Pilbeam, eds., *The Cambridge Encyclopedia of Human Evolution* (New York: Cambridge University Press, 1992), p. 111.

Having examined our distinctive traits, those traits we share with other primates, and some of the possible ways primates might have adapted to different environments, we need to ask what selective forces may have favored the emergence of primates, what forces may have favored the line of divergence leading to the first hominids, and what forces led to the emergence of the genus *Homo*. These questions are the subjects of the next several chapters.

⊚ Summary

1. Although no living primate can be a direct ancestor of humans, we do share a common evolutionary history with the other surviving primates. Studying the behavioral and anatomical features of our closest living relatives may help us make inferences about primate evolution. Studying distinctive human traits may help us understand why the line of primates that led to humans branched away from the line leading to chimpanzees and gorillas.

2. No one trait is unique to primates. However, primates do share the following features: two bones in the lower part of the leg and in the forearm, a collarbone, flexible prehensile (grasping) hands, stereoscopic vision, a relatively large brain, only one (or sometimes two) offspring at a time, long maturation of the young, and a high degree of dependence on social life and learning.

3. The order Primates is divided into two suborders: the prosimians and the anthropoids. Compared with the anthropoids, prosimians depend more on smell for information. They have mobile ears, whiskers, longer snouts typically, and relatively fixed facial expressions. Anthropoids have rounded braincases; reduced, nonmobile outer ears; and relatively small, flat faces instead of muzzles. They have highly dextrous hands.

4. The anthropoid order is divided into two main groups: platyrrhines (monkeys of the New World) and catarrhines. The catarrhines are subdivided into cercopithecoids (Old World monkeys) and hominoids (apes and humans). The anthropoid apes consist of the hylobates, or lesser apes (gibbons and siamangs), and the pongids, or great apes (orangutans, gorillas, and chimpanzees).

5. Along with the gorilla, the chimpanzee has proteins and DNA remarkably similar to those of humans, as well as anatomical and behavioral similarities to humans. Wild chimpanzees have been seen to create and use tools, modifying a natural object to fulfill a specific purpose. High conceptual ability is also demonstrated by both the chimpanzee's and the gorilla's facility in learning sign language.

6. The differences between hominids and the other anthropoids show us what makes humans distinctive as a species. Hominids are totally bipedal; they walk on two legs and do not need the arms for locomotion. The hominid brain, particularly the cerebral cortex, is the largest and most complex. In contrast to females of almost all other primates, hominid females may engage in sexual intercourse at any time throughout the year. Hominid offspring have a proportionately longer dependency stage. And in comparison with other primates, more hominid behavior is learned and culturally patterned. Spoken, symbolic language and the use of tools to make other tools are uniquely modern human behavioral traits. Hominids also generally have a division of labor in food-getting and food sharing in adulthood.

7. Variable aspects of the environment, differences in activity patterns, and variation in diet may explain many of the traits that vary in the primates. Nocturnal primates tend to be small and to live alone or in very small groups. Among diurnal species, the arboreal primates tend to be smaller and to live in smaller social groups than terrestrial primates. Fruit-eaters have relatively larger brains than leaf-eaters.

⊚ Glossary Terms

anthropoids	61	molars	56
arboreal	56	nocturnal	60
bilophodont	63	omnivorous	56
bipedalism	67	opposable thumb	57
brachiators	64	platyrrhines	61
canines	57	pongids	63
catarrhines	61	prehensile	61
cercopithecoids	62	premolars	56
cerebral cortex	67	primatology	55
diastema	64	prosimians	59
diurnal	57	quadrupeds	60
hominids	63	sexual dimorphism	62
hominoids	63	terrestrial	62
hylobates	63	vertical clinging and leaping	60
incisors	57	"Y-5" pattern	63
knuckle walking	65		

⊚ Critical Questions

1. How could you infer that a fossil primate lived in the trees?
2. Under what conditions would the ability to communicate be adaptive?
3. Why are humans immature for so long?

◎ Research Navigator

1. Please go to www.researchnavigator.com and enter your LOGIN NAME and PASSWORD. For instructions on registering for the first time, please view the detailed instructions at the end of Chapter 1.

2. Use Content Select to search the keyword "primates" in the Anthropology and Psychology databases. Select two articles from anthropology journals and two from psychology journals. Try to avoid articles from more general science journals (like *Science News* or *Proceedings of the National Academy of Science*). When you are finished reading these articles, answer the following questions: How does the study of primates by psychologists differ from that of anthropologists? What appears to be the general focus of the psychologist's research? How does the anthropological focus fit better with the general aims and purposes of anthropology?

◎ Discovering Anthropology: Researchers at Work

Read the chapter by Craig B. Stanford titled "Chimpanzee Hunting Behavior and Human Evolution" in the accompanying *Discovering Anthropology* reader. Answer the following questions:

1. How might the study of chimpanzee behavior, and particularly hunting behavior, benefit our understanding of early hominid behavior and of human evolution in general?

2. For many years chimpanzees were thought to be vegetarians. Why did it take so long for chimpanzee hunting to be identified and studied?

3. What do you think is the best answer to the question "Why do chimpanzees hunt"?

CHAPTER FIVE

Primate Evolution: From Early Primates to Hominoids

Primate paleontologists and paleoanthropologists focus on various questions about primate evolution. How far back in time did the primates emerge? What did they look like? What conditions favored them? How did the early primates diverge after that point? What kinds of niches did the different primates occupy? Although our concern as anthropologists is largely with the emergence of humans, and with the primates that are in the ancestral line leading to humans, we must remember that evolution does not proceed with a purpose or to give rise to any particular species; rather, organisms adapt, or fail to adapt, to the environments in which they find themselves. Thus, the primate fossil record is full of diversity; it is also full of apparent extinctions. Probably most of the primate lineages of the past never left any descendants at all.[1]

The reconstruction of primate evolution requires the finding of fossil remains. Although many fossils have been discovered and continue to be discovered, the fossil record is still very incomplete. If geological strata are not uplifted, exposed by erosion, or otherwise accessible in the areas where ancient primates lived, paleoanthropologists cannot recover their fossils. The fossils that are found are usually fragmented or damaged, and judgments about what the organism looked like may be based on one or just a few pieces. As we discussed in the chapter on how we discover the past, piecing together the evolutionary history of the primates requires much more than recovering fossil remains. The knowledge gained from anatomical studies of living species can allow us to make inferences about physical and behavioral traits that are likely to have been associated with the fossil features. Dating techniques developed in geology, chemistry, and physics are used to estimate the age of fossil remains (see Figure 5–1). And studies of ancient plants and animals, geography, and climate help us reconstruct the environments of ancient primates.

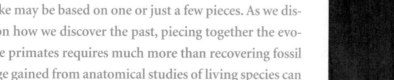

Although much of primate evolution is not yet known or is still controversial, there is a lot we do know. We know that as of the early Eocene epoch, which began about 55 million years ago, primates with some of the features of modern prosimians had already emerged. Primates with monkey- and ape-like features appeared in the Oligocene epoch, beginning about 34 million years ago. The Miocene epoch, beginning about 24 million years ago, saw the appearance of many different kinds of apes. The ancient primates we know from fossils had some of the features of today's primates, but none of the ancient primates looked like the primates of today.

In this and the following chapters we describe the main features of current theory and evidence about primate evolution, from the origin of primates to the origin of modern humans. In this chapter we deal with that part of the story before the emergence of definite bipedal hominids. Our overview in this chapter covers the period from about 65 million years ago to the end of the Miocene, a little over 5 million years ago (see Figure 5–1).

The Emergence of Primates

When did the primates first emerge? This question turns out to be hard to answer with the current fossil record. Some paleoanthropologists have suggested that fossil finds from the **Paleocene** epoch, which began about 65 million years ago, are from archaic primates. These are the *plesiadapiforms.* They have been found in both Europe and North America, which in the Paleocene were one landmass. The most well known of the plesiadipiforms is **Plesiadipis.** This squirrel-like animal had a large snout and large incisors. It also had a large nasal cavity and eye orbits located on the sides of the skull, suggesting a well-developed sense of smell

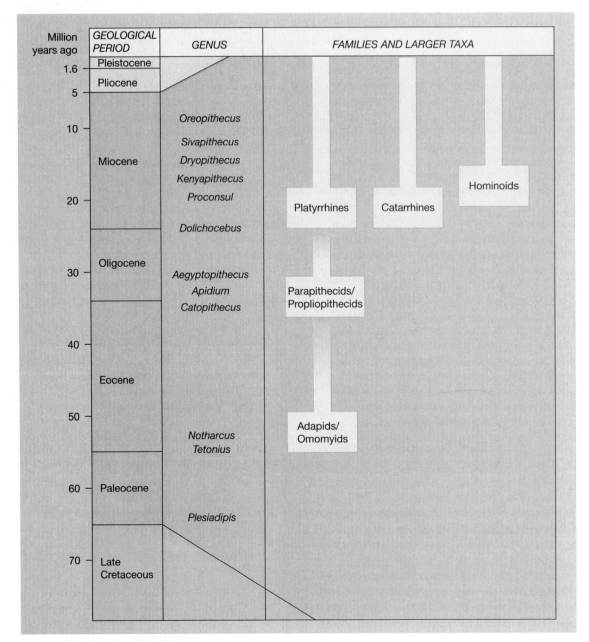

Figure 5–1 The Evolution of the Primates

and little or no stereoscopic vision (depth perception). The fingers of *Plesiadipis* had claws, and its hands and feet did not appear to allow for grasping. These features suggest that *Plesiadipis* was not a primate. However, the elbow and ankle joints suggest great mobility, and despite the large incisors the teeth suggest a primatelike omnivorous diet. The structure of their inner ears also resembled that of modern primates. Because it had these primatelike features, some scholars believe that the plesiadipiforms were archaic primates.[2]

Other paleoanthropologists find so few similarities between the plesiadapiforms and later obvious primates that they do not include the plesiadapiforms in the order Primates.[3] There is no dispute, however, about fossils dating from the early **Eocene,** about 55 million years ago. These oldest definite primates appear in two major groups of prosimians—*adapids* and *omomyids.* Because these two kinds of primate are different from each other in major ways, and because they both appeared rather abruptly at the border of the Paleocene and Eocene, there presumably was an earlier common primate ancestor. One strong candidate for the common primate ancestor is *Carpolestes simpsoni,* a

mouse-sized arboreal creature from Wyoming dating to about 56 million years ago. *Carpolestes* has an interesting mix of primate and nonprimate characteristics. While it lacks stereoscopic vision, *Carpolestes* has nails instead of claws on its big toes, and it has grasping hands and feet.[4] Not all scholars are convinced that *Caropolestes* is the common ancestor of all primates, and in Figure 5–2 the circled P represents where paleontologist Robert D. Martin placed the common ancestor of primates, in the late Cretaceous.

Now we turn to the conditions that may have favored the emergence of the primates.

The Environment

It is generally agreed that the earliest primate may have emerged by the Paleocene, 65 million to 55 million years ago, and perhaps earlier, in the late **Cretaceous.** What was the environment like in those times? The beginning of the Paleocene marked a major geological transition, what geologists call the transition from the Mesozoic to the Cenozoic era. About 75 percent of all animal and plant life that lived in the last part of the Cenozoic (the late Cretaceous)

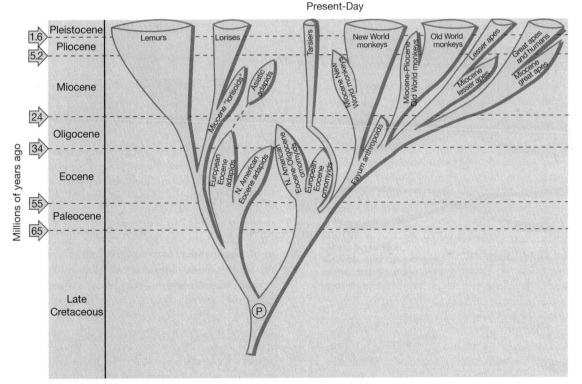

Figure 5–2 A view of the evolutionary relationships between early primates and living primates, adapted from one suggested by R. D. Martin. The primate lineages that do not extend to the present day indicate presumed extinctions. Branching from a common "stalk" suggests divergence from a common ancestor. ℗ represents the unknown common ancestor of all primates.

Source: From Robert D. Martin, *Primate Origins and Evolution: A Phylogenetic Reconstruction* (Princeton, NJ: Princeton University Press, 1990). The dates for the Paleocene, Eocene, Oligocene, and the beginning of the Miocene are from William A. Berggren, Dennis V. Kent, John D. Obradovich, and Carl C. Swisher III, "Toward a Revised Paleogene Geochronology," in Donald R. Prothero and William A. Berggren, eds., *Eocene-Oligocene Climatic and Biotic Evolution* (Princeton, NJ: Princeton University Press, 1992), pp. 29–45. The dates for the end of the Miocene, Pliocene, and Pleistocene are from Steve Jones, Robert Martin, and David Pilbeam, eds., *The Cambridge Encyclopedia of Human Evolution* (New York: Cambridge University Press, 1992).

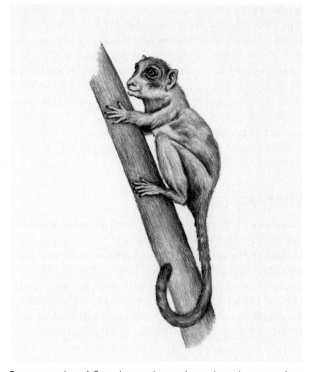

Reconstruction of *Carpolestes simpsoni,* an arboreal creature from the late Paleocene, that may be the common ancestor of the primates.

vanished by the early Paleocene. The extinction of the dinosaurs is the most famous of these disappearances.[5]

The climate of the Cretaceous period was almost uniformly damp and mild, but temperatures began falling at the end of the Cretaceous. Around the beginning of the Paleocene epoch, both seasonal and geographic fluctuations in temperature began to develop. The climate became much drier in many areas, and vast swamplands disappeared. The climate of the Paleocene was generally somewhat cooler than in the late Cretaceous, but by no means cold. Forests and savannas thrived in fairly high latitudes. Subtropical climates existed as far north as latitude 62 in Alaska.[6]

One important reason for the very different climates of the past is **continental drift** (Figure 5–3). In the early Cretaceous (ca. 135 million years ago), the continents were actually clumped into two large landmasses or "supercontinents"—*Laurasia,* which included North America and Eurasia, and *Gondwanaland,* which included Africa, South America, India, Australia, and Antarctica. By the beginning of the Paleocene (ca. 65 million years ago) Gondwanaland had broken apart, with South America drifting west away from Africa, India drifting east, and Australia and Antarctica drifting south. As the continents changed position, they moved into locations with different climatic conditions. More importantly, however, the very movement of the continents affected the climate, sometimes on a global scale.[7]

Large landmasses affect wind and weather patterns differently than smaller landmasses, so weather patterns across Laurasia would have been different from weather in the subsequently separated continents. When continents collide, mountain ranges are formed, and mountains can also have

a profound effect on weather patterns. Clouds drop their moisture as they meet a mountain range, and therefore the side away from the prevailing movement of weather systems is often very dry (a condition called a *rain shadow*), whereas the other side (called the *windward side*) is often wet. When the location of continents prevents the movement of ocean currents from the tropics to the poles, the earth's climate becomes colder. Continental drift and climate change had profound effects on the evolution of the primates.[8]

With changes in climate come changes in vegetation. Although the first deciduous trees (that lose their leaves in winter) and flowering plants (called *angiosperms*) arose during the Cretaceous, it was during the late Paleocene and early Eocene that large trees with large fruits and seeds became common.[9] New species of animals evolved as the climate and environment changed. Although some mammals date from the Cretaceous, the Paleocene saw the evolution and diversification of many different types of mammals, and the expansion and diversification of deciduous trees and flowering plants probably played a large role in mammalian expansion and diversification. Indeed, primate paleontologists think primates evolved from one of these mammalian *radiations*, or extensive diversifications, probably from the **insectivore** order of mammals, including modern shrews and moles, that is adapted to eating insects—insects that would have lived off the new deciduous trees and flowering plants.

To put it simply, the new kinds of plant life opened up sources of food and protection for new animal forms. Of

Squirrels are arboreal, but lack many of the features that characterize primates. Matt Cartmill argued that primate features are adapted to the slender terminal branches of trees, while squirrel features are adapted to the trunks and main branches.

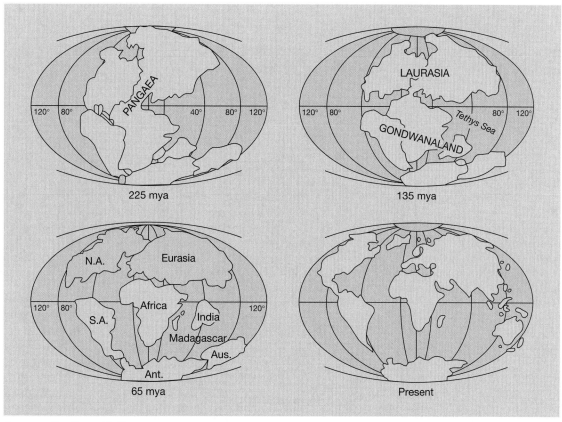

Figure 5–3 Continental Drift
The supercontinent Pangea split into Laurasia and Gondwanaland 135 million years ago (mya). These further divided into the continents as we know them today.

Source: Noel T. Boaz and Alan J. Almquist, *Biological Anthropology* (Upper Saddle River, NJ: Prentice Hall, 1999).

most interest to us is that the new plant life provided an abundant food supply for insects. The result was that insects proliferated in both number and variety, and in turn there was an increase in *insectivores*—the mammals that ate the insects. The insectivores were very adaptable and were able to take advantage of many different habitats—under the ground, in water, on the ground, and above the ground, including the woody habitat of bushes, shrubs, vines, and trees. It was the last kind of adaptation, above the ground, that may have been the most important for primate evolution. The woody habitat had been exploited only partially in earlier periods. But then several different kinds, or taxa, of small animals, one of which may have been the archaic primate, began to take advantage of the woody habitat.

What in Particular May Have Favored the Emergence of Primates?

The traditional explanation of primate origins is called the *arboreal theory*. According to this view, the primates evolved from insectivores that took to the trees. Different paleoanthropologists emphasized different possible adaptations to life in the trees. In 1912, G. Elliot Smith suggested that taking to the trees favored vision over smell. Searching for food by sniffing and feeling with the snout might suit terrestrial insectivores, but vision would be more useful in an animal

that searched for food in the maze of tree branches. With smaller snouts and the declining importance of the sense of smell, the eyes of the early primates would have come to face forward. In 1916, Frederic Wood Jones emphasized changes in the hand and foot. He thought that tree climbing would favor grasping hands and feet, with the hind limbs becoming more specialized for support and propulsion. In 1921, Treacher Collins suggested that the eyes of the early primates came to face forward not just because the snout got smaller. Rather, he thought that three-dimensional binocular vision would be favored because an animal jumping from branch to branch would be more likely to survive if it could accurately judge distances across open space.[10] In 1968, Frederick Szalay suggested that a shift in diet—from insects to seeds, fruits, and leaves—might have been important in the differentiation of primates from insectivores.[11]

Arboreal theory still has some proponents, but Matt Cartmill highlighted some crucial weaknesses in the theory.[12] He argued that tree living is not a good explanation for many of the primate features because there are living mammals that dwell in trees but seem to do very well without primatelike characteristics. One of the best examples, Cartmill says, is the tree squirrel. Its eyes are not front-facing, its sense of smell is not reduced in comparison with other rodents, it has claws rather than nails, and it lacks an opposable thumb. Yet these squirrels are very successful in trees. They can leap

CURRENT RESEARCH AND ISSUES

Matt Cartmill Reexamines His Own Theory of Primate Origins

Matt Cartmill originally conceived his visual predation theory to explain primate origins because he thought that the arboreal theory did not explain enough. Why do other animals, such as tree squirrels, manage very well in the trees, even though they don't have primate traits? Cartmill's theory attracted some criticism. How did he respond?

One criticism, by J. Allman, is that if visual predation is such an important predictor of forward-facing eyes, then why don't some visual predators have such eyes? Cats and owls have forward-facing eyes, but mongooses and robins do not. A second criticism, by Paul Garber, is that if claws were disadvantageous for moving on slender branches, why does at least one small primate—the Panamanian tamarin—feed on insects among small twigs and vines but have claws on four of its five digits? And Robert Sussman pointed out that most small nocturnal prosimians eat more fruit than insects. Sussman suggests that the need for precise finger manipulation to grasp small fruits and flowers at the ends of small branches, while hanging on by the hind feet, might favor both clawless digits and grasping extremities.

Cartmill acknowledged these problems and responded to them by revising his theory. He also suggests how new research could test some of the implications of his revised theory.

In regard to the problem of forward-facing eyes, Cartmill says that Allman's own research suggests a solution: namely, that forward-facing eyes are advantageous for seeing something in front more clearly in dim light. Daytime predators have eye pupils that constrict to see ahead more clearly, so fully forward-facing eyes are not necessary for daytime predation. Nocturnal predators relying on sight are more likely to have forward-facing eyes because constricting pupils would be disadvantageous at night. So Cartmill now believes that the earliest primates were probably nocturnal. And he now thinks that they also probably ate fruit (in addition to insects), as Sussman suggests, just as many contemporary nocturnal prosimians do. If they ate fruit and insects at the ends of small branches and twigs, claws may have been disad-

vantageous. The Panamanian tamarin is not a case to the contrary; it has claws, to be sure, but it also eats tree gum on the tree trunks to which it clings, using its claws as a tree squirrel does.

Cartmill thinks that his modified theory explains the changes in primate vision better than Sussman's theory. For example, how can we explain stereoscopic, forward-facing eyes in the early primates? Sussman says that the early primates were fruit-eaters, but Cartmill points out that, although stereoscopic, forward-facing eyes are not necessary for getting nonmoving fruit. Rather, forward-facing eyes might be essential for catching insects.

Cartmill suggests how future research on other arboreal mammals may help us answer some of the remaining questions about the origins of primates. Arboreal marsupials, for instance, tend to have grasping hind feet with clawless divergent first toes, and many have reduced claws on some other toes and fingers. The eyes of arboreal marsupials are also somewhat convergent (not as much, of course, as the eyes of primates). One genus of marsupial, an opposum in South America (*Caluromys*), has many additional primatelike features, including a relatively large brain, more forward-facing eyes, a short snout, and a small number of offspring at one time. Studies by Tab Rasmussen suggest that *Caluromys* fits both Cartmill's and Sussman's theories because it eats fruit on terminal branches and catches insect prey with its hands. More field research on marsupials and other animals with some primate-like habits or features could tell us a lot more. So would new fossil finds.

Sources: Matt Cartmill, "Explaining Primate Origins." In Peter N. Peregrine, Carol R. Ember, and Melvin Ember, eds., *Physical Anthropology: Original Readings in Method and Practice* (Upper Saddle River, NJ: Prentice Hall, 2002), pp. 42–52, also in Carol R. Ember, Melvin Ember, and Peter N. Peregrine eds., *Research Frontiers in New Directions in Anthropology* (Upper Saddle River, NJ: Prentice Hall, CD-ROM, 2004); Matt Cartmill, "New Views on Primate Origins," *Evolutionary Anthropology,* 1 (1992): 105–11; Robert Sussman, "Primate Origins and the Evolution of Angiosperms," *American Journal of Primatology,* 23 (1991): 209–23; D. Tab Rasmussen, "Primate Origins: Lessons from a Neotropical Marsupial," *American Journal of Primatology,* 22 (1990): 263–77.

accurately from tree to tree, they can walk over or under small branches, they can go up and down vertical surfaces, and they can even hang from their hind legs to get food below them. Furthermore, other animals have some primate traits but do not live in trees or do not move around in trees as primates do. For example, carnivores, such as cats, hawks, and owls, have forward-facing eyes, and the chameleon, a

reptile, and some Australian marsupial mammals that prey on insects in bushes and shrubs have grasping hands and feet.

Cartmill thinks, then, that some factor other than moving about in trees may account for the emergence of the primates. He proposes that the early primates may have been basically insect-eaters, and that three-dimensional vision, grasping hands and feet, and reduced claws may have been selectively advantageous for hunting insects on the slender vines and branches that filled the undergrowth of tropical forests. Three-dimensional vision would allow the insect hunter to gauge the prey's distance accurately. Grasping feet would allow the predator to move quietly up narrow supports to reach the prey, which could then be grabbed with the hands. Claws, Cartmill argues, would make it difficult to grasp very slender branches. And the sense of smell would have become reduced, not so much because it was no longer useful, but because the location of the eyes at the front of the face would leave less room for a snout. (See the box "Matt Cartmill Reexamines His Own Theory of Primate Origins" for a discussion of Cartmill's recent revision in response to criticisms.)

Robert Sussman's theory builds on Cartmill's *visual predation theory* and on Szalay's idea about a dietary shift.[13] Sussman accepts Cartmill's point that the early primates were likely to eat and move about mostly on small branches, not on large trunks and branches (as do squirrels). If they did, grasping hands and feet and nails rather than claws (as squirrels have) would have been advantageous. Sussman also accepts Szalay's point that the early primates probably ate the new types of plant foods (flowers, seeds, and fruits) that were beginning to become abundant, as flowering trees and plants spread throughout the world. But Sussman asks an important question: If the early primates ate mostly plant foods rather than quick-moving insects, why did they become more reliant on vision than on smell? Sussman suggests it was because the early primates were probably nocturnal (as many prosimians still are): If they were to locate and manipulate small food items at the ends of slender branches in dim light, they would need improved vision.

We still have very little fossil evidence of the earliest primates. *Carpolestes* suggests that grasping hands and feet evolved first, sometime in the late Paleocene, and stereoscopic vision evolved somewhat later. When more fossils become available, we may be better able to evaluate the various explanations that have been suggested for the emergence of primates.

The Early Primates: What They Looked Like

The earliest definite (undisputed) primates, dating back to the Eocene epoch, appear abruptly in what is now North America, Europe, and Asia about 55 million years ago. At that time Laurasia, the supercontinent made up of North America and Eurasia linked though Greenland, was still a single landmass, though it would separate by the middle Eocene. Africa was not yet connected to Eurasia, nor was India, but both would make contact with the Eurasian landmass by the end of the Oligocene, initiating dramatic climatic changes that we will discuss later. The beginning of the Eocene was warmer and less seasonal than the Paleocene, and vast tropical forests abounded.[14]

The anatomy of the diverse Eocene primates suggests that they already had many of the features of modern primates—nails rather than claws, a grasping, opposable first toe, and a bony bar around the side of the eye socket.[15] Vertical clinging and leaping was probably a common method of loco-

motion. Eocene prosimians not only moved around the way modern prosimians do; some were similar skeletally to living prosimians.

Early Eocene Primates: Omomyids and Adapids

Two groups of prosimians appear in the early Eocene. One group, called **omomyids,** had many tarsier-like features; the other group, **adapids,** had many lemur-like features. The omomyids were very small, no bigger than squirrels; the adapids were kitten- and cat-sized.

Omomyids are considered tarsier-like because of their large eyes, long tarsal bones, and very small size. The large eyes suggest that they were active at night; the smaller-sized omomyids may have been insect-eaters and the larger ones may have relied more on fruit.[16] Most of the omomyids had dental formulas characteristic of modern prosimians: two incisors and three premolars on each side of the lower jaw rather than the three incisors and four premolars of early mammals.[17] The importance of vision is apparent in a fossilized skull of the Eocene omomyid *Tetonius*. Imprints in the skull show that the brain had large occipital and temporal lobes, the regions associated with perception and the integration of visual memory.[18]

The lemur-like adapids were more active during the day and relied more on leaf and fruit vegetation. In contrast to the omomyids, adapid remains show considerable sexual dimorphism in the canines. And they retain the four premolars characteristic of earlier mammals (although with fewer incisors).[19] One adapid known from its abundant fossil finds is *Notharctus*. It had a small, broad face with full stereoscopic vision and a reduced muzzle. It appears to have lived in the forest and had long, powerful hind legs for leaping from tree to tree.[20]

There was a great deal of diversity among all mammals during the Eocene epoch, and the primates were no exception. Evolution seems to have proceeded rapidly during those years. Both the omomyids and adapids had a few features

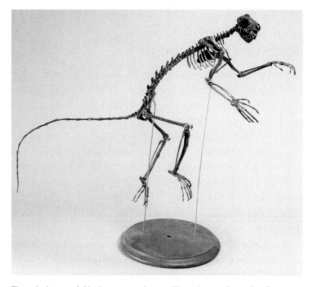

The skeleton of *Notharctus,* a lemur-like primate from the Eocene.

that suggest links between them and the anthropoids that appear later, in the Oligocene, but there is no agreement that either group gave rise to the anthropoids.[21] Although the omomyids had some resemblances to modern tarsiers and the adapids had some resemblances to lemurs and lorises, paleoanthropologists are not sure that either group was ancestral to modern prosimians. But it is generally thought that the populations ancestral to lemurs and lorises as well as tarsiers did emerge in the Eocene or even earlier, in the late Paleocene.[22]

The Emergence of Anthropoids

The anthropoids of today—monkeys, apes, and humans—are the most successful living primates and include well over 150 species. Unfortunately, the fossil record documenting the emergence of the anthropoids is extremely spotty, and there is no clear fossil record of the Old World forms (the catarrhines) in the two areas where they are most abundant today—the rain forests of sub-Saharan Africa and Southeast Asia.[23] Some paleoanthropologists think that recent Eocene primate finds from China, Southeast Asia, and Algeria have anthropoid affinities, but there is no clear agreement on their evolutionary status.[24]

Undisputed remains of early anthropoids date from a somewhat later period, the late Eocene and early Oligocene, about 34 million years ago, in the **Fayum** area, southwest of Cairo, Egypt. One of the earliest fossil primates at Fayum is *Catopithecus*, dating to around 35 million years ago. Several recent finds have made it one of the best-known late Eocene primates. *Catopithecus* was about the size of a modern marmoset or squirrel monkey. Its dentition suggests a mixed diet of fruit and insects. Its eyes were small, suggesting it was active during the day (diurnal). The few skeletal remains of *Catopithecus* suggest it was an agile arboreal quadruped. It may be the best candidate for the earliest anthropoid, though how it was related to other primates is still debated.[25]

Oligocene Anthropoids

The Fayum is an uninviting area of desert badlands, but it has yielded a remarkable array of early anthropoid fossils. During the **Oligocene** epoch, 34 million to 24 million years ago, the Fayum was a tropical rain forest very close to the shores of the Mediterranean Sea. The area had a warm climate, and it contained many rivers and lakes. The Fayum, in fact, was far more inviting than the northern continents then, for the climates of both North America and Eurasia were beginning to cool during the Oligocene. The general cooling seems to have resulted in the virtual disappearance of primates from the northern areas, at least for a time.

Oligocene anthropoids from the Fayum are grouped into two main types: the monkeylike **parapithecids** and the apelike **propliopithecids.** Dating from 35 million to 31 million years ago, the parapithecids and the propliopithecids had

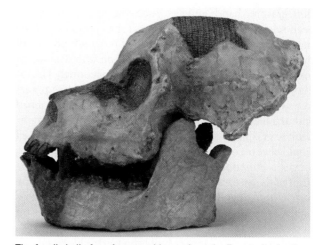

The fossil skull of an *Aegyptopithecus* from the Fayum. Its dentition, its small, bony eye sockets, and its relatively large brain make it an unambiguous ancestor of Old World monkeys and apes.

enough features to be unquestionably classified as anthropoids.

PARAPITHECIDS   The monkeylike parapithecids had three premolars (in each quarter), as do most prosimians and the New World monkeys. They were similar to modern anthropoids, with a bony partition behind the eye sockets, broad incisors, projecting canines, and low, rounded cusps on their molars. But they had prosimianlike premolars and relatively small brains. The parapithecids were small, generally weighing under 3 pounds, and resembled the squirrel monkeys living now in South and Central America.[26] Their relatively small eye sockets suggest that they were not nocturnal. Their teeth suggest that they ate mostly fruits and seeds. Locomotion is best known from one of the parapithecids, *Apidium*, an arboreal quadruped that also did a considerable amount of leaping.[27] The parapithecids are the earliest definite anthropoid group, and although there is still disagreement among paleoanthropologists, most believe that the emergence of the anthropoids preceded the split between the New World monkeys (platyrrhines) and the Old World monkeys (catarrhines).[28]

That parapithecids may be ancestral to New World monkeys (platyrrhines) raises an interesting puzzle in primate evolution: the origin of the New World monkeys. Anthropoidal primates such as *Dolichocebus*, a small fruit-eating monkey similar to the modern squirrel monkey,[29] appear suddenly and without any apparent ancestors in South America around 25 million years ago. Since the parapithecids predate the appearance of anthropoids in South America, and resemble them in many ways, it seems reasonable to view them as part of the population ancestral to the New World monkeys.[30]

But how did anthropoidal primates get from Africa to South America? Although the continents were closer together in the late Oligocene, when primates first appear in South America, at least 3,000 kilometers separated South America and Africa. An extended continental shelf and islands created by lower sea levels in the late Oligocene may have made it possible to "island-hop" from Africa to South America over ocean stretches as short as 200 kilometers, but that is still a long distance for an arboreal primate.

Going from Africa to Europe and North America, which were still joined in the late Oligocene, is not a likely route either. North America and South America were not joined until some 5 million years ago, so even if the ancestors of the New World monkeys made it to North America, they would still have needed to make a long ocean crossing to reach South America. One suggestion is that the ancestors of the New World monkeys "rafted" across the Atlantic on large mats of vegetation. Such "rafts," of matted plants, roots, and soil, break away from the mouths of major rivers today, and they can be quite large. It seems an unlikely scenario, but many scholars believe such drifting vegetation must have been the means of bringing anthropoids to South America.[31]

PROPLIOPITHECIDS   The other type of anthropoid found in the Fayum, the propliopithecids, had the dental formula of modern catarrhines. This trait clearly places the propliopithecids with the catarrhines.[32] In contrast with the parapithecids, which had three premolars (in each quarter of the jaw), the propliopithecids had only two premolars, as do modern apes, humans, and Old World monkeys. Propliopithecids shared with the parapithecids the anthropoid dental characteristics of broad lower incisors, projecting canines, and lower molars with low, rounded cusps. And, like para-

A reconstruction of what two Oligocene primates might have looked like. In the foreground is a group of *Aegyptopithecus;* in the background are two individuals of *Apidium.* Some of the fauna that shared the Fayum region with these early primates are also shown.

pithecids, propliopithecids had a bony partition behind the eye socket.

Aegyptopithecus, the best-known propliopithecid, probably moved around quadrupedally in the trees, and weighed about 13 pounds. Its molars were low with large cusps, and it had relatively large incisors, suggesting that *Aegyptopithecus* ate mostly fruit. Its eyes were relatively small, and thus it was probably active during the day. It had a long muzzle and a relatively small brain. Endocasts of the brain cavity suggest *Aegyptopithecus* had a relatively large area of the brain dedicated to vision and a relatively small area dedicated to smell. The skulls of *Aegyptopithecus* show considerable sexual dimorphism, and individuals also changed dramatically as they aged, developing bony ridges along the top and across the back of the skull, much like modern great apes. Although its teeth, jaws, and some aspects of the skull were ape-like, the rest of *Aegyptopithecus's* skeleton was monkey-like,[33] and they are classified by most scholars as primitive catarrhines. Because the propliopithecids lack the specialized characteristics of living Old World monkeys and apes (catarrhines), but share the dental formula of the catarrhines, some paleoanthropologists think that the propliopithecids included the ancestor of both the Old World monkeys and the hominoids (apes and humans).[34]

◎ The Miocene Anthropoids: Monkeys, Apes, and Hominids (?)

During the **Miocene** epoch, 24 million to 5.2 million years ago, monkeys and apes clearly diverged in appearance, and numerous kinds of apes appeared in Europe, Asia, and Africa. In the early Miocene, the temperatures were considerably warmer than in the Oligocene. From early to late Miocene, conditions became drier, particularly in East Africa. The reasons for this relate again to continental drift. By about 18 million years ago, Africa came into contact with Eurasia, ending the moderating effect that the Tethys Sea, which separated Africa from Eurasia, had on the climates of both continents. The contact of Africa and, more significantly, India with the Eurasian continent also initiated mountain building, changing established weather patterns. The overall effect was that southern Eurasia and eastern Africa became considerably drier than they had been. Once again, these changes appear to have significantly influenced primate evolution.

We can infer that late in the Miocene, between about 8 million and 5 million years ago, the direct ancestor of humans—the first hominid—may have emerged in Africa. The inference about where hominids emerged is based on the fact that undisputed hominids lived in East Africa after about 5 million years ago. The inference about when hominids emerged is based not as much on fossil evidence as it is on comparative molecular and biochemical analyses of modern apes and humans. As we will see in the next chapter, the effect of a drier climate and the creation of more open, grassland environments may have directly influenced the evolution of the hominids.

One of the Miocene apes (known or unknown) was ancestral to hominids, so our discussion here deals mostly with the *proto-apes*—anthropoids with some ape-like characteristics—of the early Miocene and the definite apes of the middle and late Miocene. But before we get to the apes, we should say something about monkeys and prosimians in the Miocene. Unfortunately, monkey fossils from the early Miocene are rare. In the New World, the whole Miocene fossil record is quite small. There are only a few primate fossils found in Colombia and Argentina; they show close affinities with present-day South American monkeys. In the Old World, early Miocene monkey fossils have been found only in northern Africa. The situation is different for the middle and late Miocene: Old World monkey fossils become much more abundant than ape fossils.[35] As for prosimians, fossils from the Miocene are scarce, but we know that at least some adapids survived into the middle Miocene in India and the late Miocene in China.[36] Some loris-like prosimians appear in East Africa, Pakistan, and India during the Miocene.[37]

Early Miocene Proto-Apes

Most of the fossils from the early Miocene are described as proto-apes. They have been found mostly in Africa. The best-known genus is **Proconsul,** found in sites in Kenya and Uganda that are about 20 million years old.[38]

All of the various *Proconsul* species that have been found were much bigger than any of the anthropoids of the Oligocene, ranging from about the size of a gibbon to that of a female gorilla.[39] They lacked a tail. That lack is one of the most definitive features of hominoids, and most paleoanthropologists now agree that *Proconsul* was definitely hominoid, but quite unlike any ape living today. Modern hominoids have many anatomical features of the shoulder, elbow, wrists, and fingers that are adapted for locomotion by

suspension (brachiation). Suspension was apparently not *Proconsul's* method of getting around. Its elbows, wrists, and fingers may have permitted brachiation,[40] but, like the Oligocene anthropoids, *Proconsul* was primarily an arboreal quadruped (see Figure 5–4). Some of the larger forms may have sometimes moved on the ground. Judging by teeth, most *Proconsul* species appear to have been fruit-eaters, but larger species may have also consumed leaves.[41]

If *Proconsul* is the best-known group of the many kinds of primates with some hominoid features from the early Miocene, some recent finds from East Africa suggest that other types of proto-ape were also on the scene. But these other finds are fragmentary and not clearly classifiable. *Proconsul* may or may not have been ancestral to later apes and humans, but given its combination of monkey-like and ape-like features, it may have looked a lot like the common ancestor of apes and humans.

Middle Miocene Apes

The first definitely ape-like finds come from the middle Miocene, 16 million to 10 million years ago. The oldest, dating to about 13 million years ago, is **Pierolapithecus,** and was recently found near Barcelona, Spain.[42] Another hominoid, **Kenyapithecus,** was found on Maboko Island and nearby locations in Kenya.[43]

Both *Pierolapithecus* and *Kenyapithecus* have many of *Proconsul's* features, but have teeth and faces that resemble those of more modern hominoids. And, in contrast to *Proconsul, Kenyapithecus* was probably more terrestrial. It also had very thickly enameled teeth and robust jaws, suggesting a diet of hard, tough foods, or possibly a great deal of grit in the food because *Kenyapithecus* lived mostly on the ground. Whether *Kenyapithecus* is ancestral to the later apes and humans is something of a puzzle because its limbs do not show

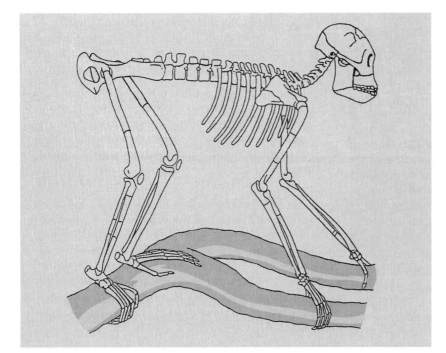

Figure 5–4 The forelimbs and hind limbs of *Proconsul africanus* (dating from about 20 million years ago) are about the same length, suggesting that it moved on all fours on the tops of branches. *Proconsul africanus* was the smallest of the *Proconsul* species, weighing about 22 to 26 pounds.

Source: From *New Interpretation of Ape and Human Ancestry* (Englewood Cliffs, NJ: Prentice Hall, 1994) by R. Ciochon and R. Corruccin, eds.

A reconstruction of what *Heliopithecus,* a close relative of *Kenyapithecus,* may have looked like.

the capacity for brachiation that is characteristic of all the later apes.[44] *Pierolapithecus,* however, has wrists and vertebrae that would have made it capable of brachiation, but also has relatively short fingers like modern monkeys. *Pierolapithecus* probably spent most of its time in trees, walking along larger branches as monkeys do, and also brachiating among smaller branches, as apes do.[45] Thus, *Pierolapithecus* is a good candidate for the ancestor of later forest-dwelling apes.

Late Miocene Apes

From the end of the middle Miocene into the late Miocene, the apes diversified and moved into many areas. Fossils are abundant in Europe and Asia, less so in Africa. This does not mean that apes were more numerous than monkeys. In fact, the fossil record suggests that monkeys in the Old World became more and more numerous than apes toward the end of the Miocene, and this trend continues to the present day. There are many more monkey than ape species now. The climate throughout the Miocene was turning cooler and drier, which probably favored more drought-resistant plants with thicker cell walls. Modern monkeys tend to be more adapted than apes for eating leaves, so monkeys may have had an advantage in the changing environment toward the end of the Miocene, and since.[46]

One well-known late Miocene ape from Europe is *Oreopithecus,* which dates from about 8 million years ago. It is particularly interesting because, despite being well represented by fossils, including nearly complete ones preserved in beds of hard coal, its classification is enigmatic. *Oreopithecus* was clearly adapted to life in thickly forested marshlands. It had extremely long arms and hands and mobile joints, and was likely an agile brachiator. Its dentition suggests it had a diet that consisted mostly of leaves. However, the dentition and skull of *Oreopithecus* also had a num-

ber of unique features that suggest affinity to some Old World monkeys. In short, *Oreopithecus* had an ape-like body and a monkey-like head. Because of its suspensory locomotion and other ape-like features, most scholars today consider it an early, albeit specialized, ape.[47]

Most paleoanthropologists divide the later Miocene apes into at least two main groups: the sivapithecids, represented primarily by the genus *Sivapithecus* and found primarily in western and southern Asia, and the dryopithecids, represented primarily by the genus *Dryopithecus* and found primarily in Europe.

SIVAPITHECIDS   At one time **Sivapithecus,** which dates from roughly 13 million to 8 million years ago, was thought to be ancestral to hominids. It had flat and thickly enameled molars, smaller canines, and less sexual dimorphism than other Miocene apes, and in some reconstructions (now considered faulty) had a parabolic dental arcade—all

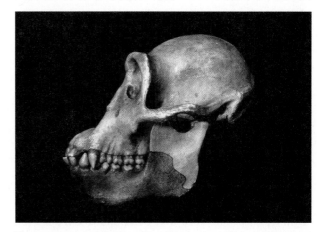

The reconstructed skull of a *Dryopithecus* strongly resembles that of modern African apes.

CURRENT RESEARCH AND ISSUES

What Happened to *Gigantopithecus?*

In studying human evolution we tend to focus on the primate lineages that presumably are ancestral to modern humans and our closest primate cousins. There were, however, other primate lineages that left no apparent descendants but were very successful in the sense that they persisted for millions of years. The first definite primates, the omomyids and the adapids, first appeared early in the Eocene and stayed for more than 20 million years, much longer than bipedal hominids have been around! Why some primates were successful for so long is an important question, so is why they became extinct. To understand evolution, we need to investigate not only why some form may have survived for a while; we need also to investigate why it died out. For example, what happened to the largest primate that ever lived, *Gigantopithecus?*

A paleoanthropologist, Russell Ciochon, and an archaeologist, John Olsen, have searched for clues to understanding the extinction of "Giganto," as they call it, which apparently left no descendants living in the world today. Ciochon and Olsen think that the largest form of *Gigantopithecus, G. blacki,* persisted for at least 5 million years and did not become extinct until about 250,000 years ago. And if you count earlier *Gigantopithecus* forms, the genus may have been around for nearly 10 million years. Ciochon and Olsen think it likely that Giganto and *Homo erectus,* a hominid that looked very much like modern humans from the head down, met up about a quarter of a million years ago in at least two Asian locations—now parts of China and Vietnam. The possible contact with *H. erectus* may have been partly responsible for the demise of Giganto.

What did Giganto look like? Reconstruction requires some guesswork, particularly with Giganto, because the

Gigantopithecus probably lived mostly on bamboo. It is the largest primate known to us. The genus survived for about 10 million years and only became extinct 250,000 years ago. Bill Munns is shown here with the model of Giganto that he and Russell Ciochon reconstructed.

only remains we have are teeth and jaw fragments. But we can reasonably infer some of Giganto's features and measurements from the body proportions of existing apes and the more complete fossil remains of extinct

hominid features. It also lived in a mixed woodland–grassland environment, and the wear on its teeth suggested a diet of coarse grasses and seeds, much like the diet of the later early hominids (although some scholars argue that the *Sivapithecus* diet was focused on fruit with coarse pits rather than on grasses and seeds). However, as more fossil material was uncovered, scholars recognized that *Sivapithecus* was remarkably similar to the modern orangutan in the face, and it is now thought to be ancestral to the orangutan.[48]

The closely related *Gigantopithecus* was similar in its teeth to *Sivapithecus,* but, as its name suggests, it was huge, perhaps 10 feet tall erect. Some paleoanthropologists suggest that *Gigantopithecus* weighed over 600 pounds and got even larger over the nearly 10 million years of its existence.[49] (See the box "What Happened to *Gigantopithecus?*")

Gigantopithecus was restricted to the forests of Southeast Asia, and is thought to have had a diet focused on bamboo.

DRYOPITHECIDS *Dryopithecus,* which appears about 15 million years ago, was a chimpanzee-sized ape that lived in the forests of Eurasia. It was mainly arboreal and apparently omnivorous. *Dryopithecus* had thinner tooth enamel than *Sivapithecus,* lighter jaws, and pointed molar cusps. In the palate, jaw, and midface, *Dryopithecus* looked like the African apes and humans. In contrast to later hominoids, however, *Dryopithecus* had a very short face and a relatively small brow ridge.[50]

The fingers and elbows of *Dryopithecus* and *Sivapithecus* suggest that they were much more capable of suspending themselves than were earlier hominoids. *Sivapithecus* may

apes. Thus, it is estimated that Giganto was 10 feet tall and weighed over 600 pounds.

What did Giganto eat? Ciochon's guess is that Giganto ate mostly bamboo from the then-plentiful bamboo forests. The large size of the jaw, the wear patterns on the teeth, and the fact that large primates eat mostly foods with a lot of cellulose all suggest a diet of bamboo or something like it. Another kind of evidence suggests the same conclusion. A student had suggested to Ciochon that he look for phytoliths on the fossil teeth of Giganto. Phytoliths are microscopic granules of silicon dioxide that enter a plant's cells and take their shape. When the plants decompose, the phytoliths remain. Different plants have phytoliths of different shapes.

So, on the chance that phytoliths were on the fossil teeth from Giganto, the researchers looked microscopically at the teeth. They found phytoliths that belong to a family of grasses as well as phytoliths from a kind of fruit. Bamboo is a kind of grass, so the phytoliths found on the Giganto teeth are consistent with both bamboo- and fruit-eating. The teeth revealed something else too. Many showed pitting of the tooth enamel (hypoplasias), which suggests that Giganto suffered periodically from malnutrition. (Hypoplasias are produced by dietary insufficiencies.)

Bamboo forests are found almost everywhere in China and Southeast Asia, but for reasons not yet understood they dwindle every 20 years or so. If Giganto ate bamboo, it would have had a serious problem every so often, which is consistent with the hypoplasias. Could the extinction of Giganto be linked to something that happened to the bamboo forests? Perhaps. Giant pandas, which are bamboo-eaters almost exclusively, are now at risk of extinction because of the spread of humans throughout China and Southeast Asia. Bamboo is used by humans for shelter, boats, tools, and food (bamboo shoots), and the bamboo forests are now drastically reduced. In their time, *H. erectus* may also have reduced the bamboo forests, thus contributing to the demise of Giganto. It is also possible that *H. erectus* hunted Giganto for food. This possibility is very speculative, but nonhuman primates have been hunted for food by many recent human societies. Like the giant panda, Giganto was probably very slow-moving and easy to hunt, as are most megaherbivores.

Humans in different places tell stories about huge, hairy, humanlike creatures—"Bigfoot" or Sasquatch in northwestern North America, the "Abominable Snowman" or Yeti of the Himalayas. Is it possible that Giganto is still around? Ciochon and Olsen point out that no recent Giganto bones have been found, so it is very unlikely that Giganto is still out there. But perhaps humans continue to believe it because they encountered Giganto in the not-so-distant past. After all, Australian aborigines still tell stories referring to events that happened more than 30,000 years ago.

What we do know is that *Gigantopithecus* persisted for a very long time, until humans came on the scene. Researchers have learned a lot about Giganto from very fragmentary remains. If more fossils are found in the future, we can expect that more will come to be known about the gigantic ape.

Source: Russell Ciochon, John Olsen, and Jamie James, *Other Origins: The Search for the Giant Ape in Human Prehistory* (New York: Bantam, 1990), pp. 99–102.

have moved about more on the ground than *Dryopithecus*, but both were probably mostly arboreal.[51] Indeed, recent finds of *Dryopithecus* hand, arm, shoulder, and leg bones strongly suggest that *Dryopithecus* was highly efficient at suspensory locomotion and probably moved through the trees like modern orangutans do.

It is still very difficult to identify the particular evolutionary lines leading from the Miocene apes to modern apes and humans. Only the orangutans have been linked to a late Miocene ape genus, *Sivapithecus,* so presumably that lineage continued into modern times.[52] *Dryopithecus* disappears from the fossil record after about 10 million years ago, leaving no descendants, perhaps because less rainfall and more seasonality reduced the forests where they lived.[53]

◎ The Divergence of Hominids from the Other Hominoids

The later Miocene apes are best known from Europe and Asia. Until recently there has been an almost complete lack of African fossil hominoids dating between 13.5 million and 5 million years ago.[54] Recently, two species, *Orrorin tugenensis,* from Kenya and dated to about 6 million years ago, and *Sahelanthropus tchadensis,* from Chad and dated to perhaps 7 million years ago, have provided a glimpse of hominoid evolution during this time period, which we discuss in the next chapter. Still, this scarcity of fossils from 13.5 to 5 million years ago is unfortunate for our understanding of human evolution because the earliest unambiguous bipedal primates (hominids) appear in Africa near the beginning of the Pliocene, after 5 million years ago. To understand the evolutionary links between the apes of the Miocene and the hominids of Africa, we need more fossil evidence from late Miocene times in Africa.

However, we do have some idea about the transition to hominids beyond the few fossil remains. The molecular biology of the various modern primates suggests when the last common ancestor of humans and our closest primate relatives, chimpanzees, probably lived.

The Molecular Clock

In 1966, on the basis of biochemical comparisons of blood proteins in the different surviving primates, Vincent Sarich and Allan Wilson estimated that gibbons diverged from the other hominoids about 12 million years ago, orangutans 10 million years ago, and the other apes (gorillas and chimps) from hominids only 4.5 million years ago. These estimates depended on the assumption that the more similar in chemistry the blood proteins of different primates are—for instance, comparing chimpanzees and humans—the closer those primates are in evolutionary time. In other words, the more similar the blood proteins of related species, the more recently they diverged.[55]

But knowing that species are close molecularly does not translate into evolutionary time unless it is assumed that molecular changes occur at a constant rate. After all, a reliable "molecular clock" should not slow down or speed up from one period of time to another. To maximize the likelihood of molecular change at a constant rate, researchers try to examine molecular characteristics that are probably neutral in terms of adaptation. (Natural selection can speed up the rate of molecular change in the case of a characteristic that is very advantageous or very disadvantageous.) The rate of change in a neutral characteristic is calculated from the time of some divergence that is absolutely dated. For example, if we know that two lineages split 20 million years ago, and we know the degree of molecular difference between a contemporary representative of each, we can estimate the rate of change that produced that degree of difference. Given such an estimated rate of change (in a particular characteristic), we can estimate the amount of time that has elapsed since other pairs of related species diverged from each other.[56]

Subsequent comparative studies of the living primates have employed a variety of techniques, including comparisons of amino acid sequences, chromosomal structures, and the degree of matching of DNA strands from different species.[57] These studies have confirmed the probable recency of the hominid divergence from chimpanzees and gorillas. Although the different techniques yield slightly different estimates, the results are not that divergent. Most of the recent comparisons place the split somewhat earlier than the Sarich and Wilson estimates, but not by much. The common ancestor of chimpanzees and hominids is estimated to have lived 5 million to 6 million years ago, the common ancestor of gorillas and hominids a little further back.[58]

So what does the fossil evidence tell us about where and when hominids first emerged? *Sahelanthropus tchadensis* and *Orrorin tugenensis* appear to support the molecular data. Both show mixed hominid and hominoid traits, both are from Africa, and both date to 6–7 million years ago. We turn to the early hominids in the next chapter.

◎ Summary

1. We cannot know with certainty how primates evolved. But fossils, a knowledge of ancient environments, and an understanding of comparative anatomy and behavior give us enough clues to have a tentative idea of when, where, and why primates emerged and diverged.

2. The surviving primates—prosimians, New World monkeys, Old World monkeys, apes, and humans—are thought to be descendants of small, originally terrestrial insectivores (the order, or major grouping, of mammals, including modern shrews and moles, that is adapted to feeding on insects). However, exactly who the common ancestor was and when it emerged are not yet known.

3. Fossils dating from the early Eocene, about 55 million years ago, are definitely primates. They appear to fall into two major groups of prosimians—adapids and omomyids. These two kinds of primates are different from each other in major ways, and they both appeared rather abruptly at the border of the Paleocene and Eocene, so their common ancestor would have had to emerge earlier, probably in the Paleocene.

4. What conditions may have favored the emergence of the primates? The proliferation of insects led to an increase in insectivores—the mammals that ate the insects, some of which lived above ground, in the woody habitat of bushes, shrubs, vines, and trees. Eventually, trees with large flowers and fruits evolved. The exploitation of resources in the woody habitat was probably the key adaptation in the emergence of the primates.

5. The traditional view of primate evolution was that arboreal (tree) life would have favored many of the common primate features, including distinctive dentition, greater reliance on vision over smell, three-dimensional binocular vision, and grasping hands and feet. A second theory proposes that some of the distinctive primate characteristics were selectively advantageous for hunting insects on the slender vines and branches that filled the undergrowth of forests. A third theory suggests that the distinctive features of primates (including reliance more on vision than on smell) were favored because the early primates were nocturnal and ate flowers, fruits, and seeds, which they had to locate on slender branches in dim light.

6. Undisputed remains of early anthropoids unearthed in Egypt date from the early Oligocene (after 34 million years ago). They include the monkey-like parapithecids and the propliopithecids with ape-like teeth.

7. During the Miocene epoch (24 million to 5.2 million years ago), monkeys and apes clearly diverged in appearance, and numerous kinds of apes appeared in Europe, Asia, and Africa. Most of the fossils from the early Miocene are described as proto-apes. From the end of the middle Miocene into the late Miocene, the apes diversified and spread geographically. Most paleoanthropologists divide the later Miocene apes into at least two main groups: dryopithecids, found primarily in Europe, and sivapithecids, found primarily in western and southern Asia.

8. The fossil record does not tell us much about the first hominids, but biochemical and genetic analyses of modern apes and humans suggest that the hominid–ape split occurred during the late Miocene (after about 6 million years ago). Because undisputed hominids lived in East Africa after about 4 million years ago, the first hominid probably emerged in Africa.

◎ Glossary Terms

adapid	81	Miocene	83
Aegyptopithecus	83	Oligocene	82
Carpolestes	77	omomyid	81
continental drift	78	Paleocene	76
Cretaceous	77	parapithecids	82
Dryopithecus	86	*Pierolapithecus*	84
Eocene	77	*Plesiadipis*	76
Fayum	82	*Proconsul*	84
insectivore	78	propliopithecids	82
Kenyapithecus	84	*Sivapithecus*	85

◎ Critical Questions

1. What an animal eats and how it gets its food are suggested by its skeletal anatomy. Discuss possible examples in the evolution of the primates.

2. Why do you suppose there are more monkey than ape species?

3. We like to think of the human lineage as biologically unique, which of course it is (like all evolutionary lineages). But some paleoanthropologists say that humans, chimpanzees, and gorillas are so similar that all three should be grouped as hominids. What do you think, and why do you think so?

◎ Research Navigator

1. Please go to **www.researchnavigator.com** and enter your LOGIN NAME and PASSWORD. For instructions on registering for the first time, please view the detailed instructions at the end of Chapter 1.

2. Use the Link Library for the subject Anthropology to view links about "anthropoids," "hominoids," and "prosimians." Use the linked sites to find at least two taxonomic or evolutionary trees depicting primate evolution. Compare and contrast these two trees and identify any differences you find. What might explain these differences?

◎ Discovering Anthropology: Researchers at Work

Read the chapter by David Begun titled "Miocene Apes" in the accompanying *Discovering Anthropology* reader. Answer the following questions:

1. Begun begins his essay describing the area where he looks for fossils of ancient primates. Why are so many important primate fossil deposits in what are today arid, windswept landscapes like southern Spain and the Fayum Depression in Egypt?

2. Begun suggests that the modern African apes—chimpanzees and gorillas—should be placed in the same taxonomic family as humans, and that the Asian apes—orangutans—should be in a different family. Why does he suggest this? Does the fossil record of Miocene apes support his suggestion?

CHAPTER SIX

The First Hominids

Bipedal locomotion is a defining feature of the hominids. Undisputed bipedal hominids lived in East Africa about 4 million years ago (see Figure 6–1). These hominids, and some others who may have lived later in eastern and southern Africa, are generally classified in the genus *Australopithecus*. In this chapter we discuss what we know or suspect about the transition from hominoids to hominids, the emergence of australopithecines, and their relationship to later hominids, including ourselves.

The Evolution of Bipedal Locomotion

Perhaps the most crucial change in early hominid evolution was the development of *bipedal locomotion,* or walking on two legs. We know from the fossil record that other important physical changes—including the expansion of the brain, modification of the female pelvis to allow bigger-brained babies to be born, and reduction of the face, teeth, and jaws—did not occur until about 2 million years after the emergence of bipedalism. Other human characteristics, such as an extended period of infant and child dependency and increased meat-eating, may also have developed after that time.

We do not know whether bipedalism developed quickly or gradually, because the fossil record for the period between 8 million and 4 million years ago is very skimpy. We do know, on the basis of their skeletal anatomy, that many of the Miocene anthropoids were capable of assuming an upright posture. For example, *brachiation,* swinging by the arms through the trees, puts an animal in an upright position; so does climbing up and down trees with the use of grasping hands and feet. It is also likely that the protohominids were capable of occasional bipedalism, just as many modern monkeys and apes are.[1]

Definitely bipedal hominids emerged in Africa, judging by the available fossil record. The emergence of bipedal hominids coincides with a change from extensive tropical forest cover to more discontinuous patches of forest and open country.[2] About 16 million to 11 million years ago, a drying trend set in that continued into the Pliocene. Gradually, the African rain forests, deprived of intense humidity and rainfall, dwindled in extent; areas of **savanna** (grasslands) and scattered deciduous woodlands became more common. The tree-dwelling primates did not completely lose their customary habitats, because some tropical forests remained in wetter regions, and natural selection continued to favor the better adapted tree dwellers in those forested areas. But the new, more open country probably favored characteristics adapted to ground living in some primates as well as other animals. In the evolutionary line leading to humans, these adaptations included bipedalism.

Theories for the Evolution of Bipedalism

What in particular may have favored the emergence of bipedal hominids? There are several possible explanations for this development. One idea is that bipedalism was adaptive for life amid the tall grasses of the savannas because an erect posture may have

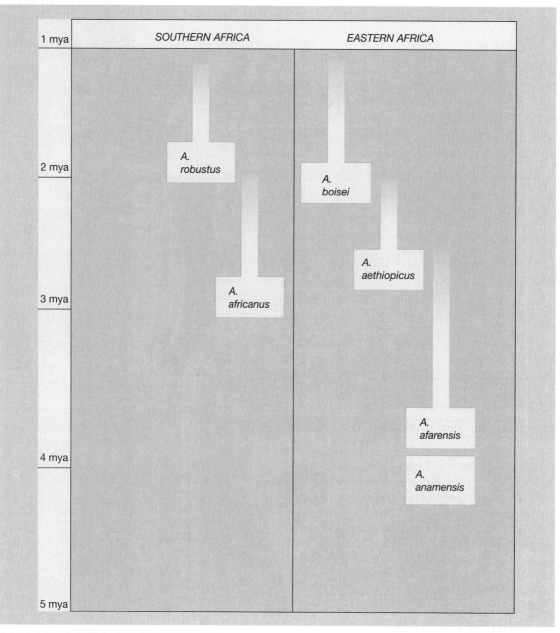

Figure 6–1 The Evolution of the Australopithecines

made it easier to spot ground predators as well as potential prey.[3] This theory does not adequately account for the development of bipedalism, however. Baboons and some other Old World monkeys also live in savanna environments, yet, although they can stand erect and occasionally do so, they have not evolved fully bipedal locomotion. And recent evidence suggests that the area where early hominids lived in East Africa was not predominantly savanna; rather, it seems to have been a mix of woodland and open country.[4]

Other theories stress the importance of freeing the hands. If some hand activity is critical while an animal is moving, selection may favor bipedalism because it frees the hands to perform other activities at the same time. What hand activities might have been so critical?

Gordon Hewes suggested that carrying food in the hands was the critical activity; if it were necessary to carry food from one locale to another, moving about only on the hind limbs would have been adaptive.[5] Hewes emphasized the importance of carrying hunted or scavenged meat, but many paleoanthropologists now question whether early hominids hunted or even scavenged.[6] However, the ability to carry any food to a place safe from predators may have been one of the more important advantages of bipedalism. C. Owen Lovejoy has suggested that food carrying might have been important for another reason. If males provisioned females and their babies by carrying food back to a home base, the females would have been able to conserve energy by not traveling and therefore might have been able to produce and care for more babies.[7] Thus, whatever the advantages of carrying food, the more bipedal a protohominid was, the more it might reproduce.

But carrying food or provisioning families might not have been the only benefit of freeing the hands; feeding itself may have been more efficient. Clifford Jolly has argued that bipedalism would have allowed early hominids to efficiently harvest small seeds and nuts because both hands could be used to pick up food and move it directly to the mouth.[8] Natural selection would not have favored bipedalism just for locomotion, but also for more efficient foraging. In the changing environments of East Africa, where forests were giving way to more open woodlands and savannas, an advantage in foraging for small seeds and nuts might well have proven important for survival, and thus have been favored by natural selection.

Bipedalism might also have been favored by natural selection because the freeing of the hands would allow protohominids to use, and perhaps even make, tools that they could carry with them as they moved about. Consider how advantageous such tool use might have been. Sherwood Washburn noted that some contemporary ground-living primates dig for roots to eat, "and if they could use a stone or a stick they might easily double their food supply."[9] David Pilbeam also suggests why tool use by the more open-country primates may have appreciably increased the number and amount of plant foods they could eat: In order to be eaten, many of the plant foods in the grassy areas probably had to be chopped, crushed, or otherwise prepared with the aid of tools.[10] Tools may also have been used to kill and butcher animals for food. Without tools, primates in general are not well equipped physically for regular hunting or even scavenging. Their teeth and jaws are not sharp and strong enough, and their speed afoot is not fast enough. So the use of tools to kill and butcher game might have enlarged even further their ability to exploit the available food supply.

Finally, tools may have been used as weapons against predators, which would have been a great threat to the relatively defenseless ground-dwelling protohominids. In Milford Wolpoff's opinion, it was the advantage of carrying weapons *continuously* that was responsible for transforming occasional bipedalism to completely bipedal locomotion.[11] In particular, Sue Savage-Rumbaugh has suggested that the ability to abduct or snap the wrist would have permitted early humans "to perfect both throwing and rock-striking skills [for toolmaking] and consequently to develop throwing as a much more effective predator defense system than apes could ever manage."[12]

But some anthropologists question the idea that tool use and toolmaking favored bipedalism. They point out that the first clear evidence of stone tools appears more than 2 million years *after* the emergence of bipedalism. So how could toolmaking be responsible for bipedalism? Wolpoff suggests an answer. Even though bipedalism appears to be at least 2 million years older than stone tools, it is not unlikely that protohominids used tools made of wood and bone, neither of which would be as likely as stone to survive in the archaeological record. Moreover, unmodified stone tools present in the archaeological record might not be recognizable as tools.[13]

Some researchers have taken a closer look at the mechanics of bipedal locomotion to see if it might be a more efficient form of locomotion in the savanna-woodland environment, where resources are likely to be scattered. Compared with the quadrapedal locomotion of primates such as chimpanzees, bipedalism appears to be more efficient for long-distance travel (see Figure 6–2).[14] But why travel long distances? If the ancestors of humans had the manipulative ability and tool-using capability of modern chimpanzees (e.g., using stones to crack nuts), and those ancestors had to move around in a more open environment, then those individuals who could efficiently travel longer distances to exploit those resources might do better.[15]

Finally, bipedalism might have been favored by natural selection as a way of regulating body temperature, particularly in the increasingly hot and dry environments of East Africa at the end of the Miocene and the beginning of the Pliocene. Peter Wheeler has argued that a bipedal posture limits the area of the body directly exposed to the sun, especially when the sun is at its hottest, at midday.[16] Bipedal posture would also facilitate convective heat loss by allowing heat to rise up and away from the body rather than being trapped underneath it. (We radiate a lot of body heat through the head.) Cooling through the evaporation of sweat would also be facilitated by a bipedal posture, as more skin area would be exposed to cooling winds. Thus, natural selection may have favored bipedalism because it reduced heat stress in the warming environments of East Africa.

All theories about the origin of bipedalism are speculative. We do not yet have direct evidence that any of the factors we have discussed were actually responsible for bipedalism. Any or all of the factors may explain the transformation of an occasionally bipedal protohominid to a completely bipedal hominid.

The "Costs" of Bipedalism

We must remember that there are also "costs" to bipedal walking. Bipedalism makes it harder to overcome gravity to supply the brain with sufficient blood,[17] and the weight of the body above the pelvis and lower limbs puts greater stress on the hips, lower back, knees, and feet. As Adrienne Zihlman points out, the stresses on the lower body are even greater for females.[18] Females have to support extra weight during pregnancy, and as mothers they usually are responsible for carrying nursing infants. So whatever the advantages of bipedalism, they must be greater than the disadvantages—or our ancestors never would have become bipedal.

We must also remember that the evolution of bipedalism required some dramatic changes in the ancestral ape skeleton. While apes today can and do walk bipedally, they cannot do so efficiently or for long periods of time. To be habitually bipedal, the ancestral ape skeleton had to be modified, and the major changes that allowed the early hominids to become fully bipedal occurred primarily in the skull, pelvis, knees, and feet.[19] Let's take a look at each of these changes.

In both ancient and modern apes, the spinal column enters the skull toward the back, which makes sense because

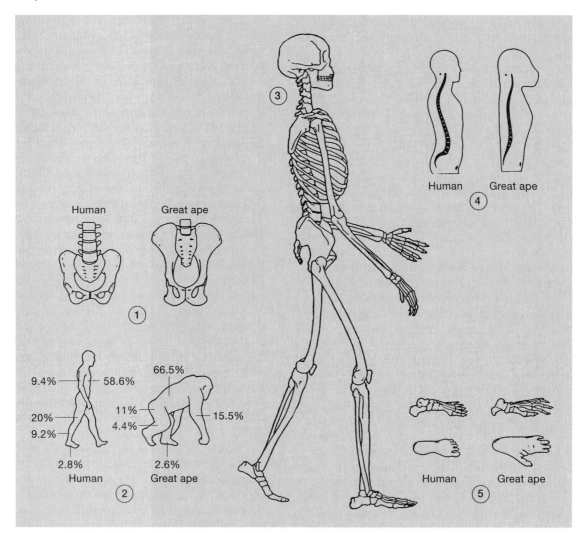

Figure 6–2 Skeletal Evidence of Bipedalism
Because humans move about on their legs only, the human skeleton differs from the skeleton of the great ape. The human head is more or less balanced on the backbone (see the feature marked 3 in the figure). There is no need for powerful muscles at the back of the neck, as in the great ape. The human vertebral column (see 4 in the figure) has a forward curvature in the neck and lower back regions. These two extra curves, along with the curvature in the middle back region, allow the backbone to act more like a spring, which is advantageous given that the legs have to bear all the weight and given the need to balance on one leg with each stride. Bipedal locomotion has favored a human pelvis (see 1 in the figure) that is lower and broader than the ape pelvis. In contrast to the apes, the legs in humans are longer than the arms and represent a larger proportion of the body weight (see 2 in the figure); this change lowers the body's center of gravity and is advantageous with bipedalism. The most obvious adaptation to bipedalism is the human foot (see 5 in the figure). The big toe is not opposed to the other toes, as in the other primates, and the foot can no longer grasp. When we walk, the big toe is the last point of contact with the ground before the leg swings forward, which explains why the big toe has become aligned with the other toes.

Source: From Stephen Jones, Robert Martin, and David Pilbeam, eds., *The Cambridge Encyclopedia of Human Evolution* (New York: Cambridge University Press, 1992), p. 8.

apes generally walk on all fours, with the spine roughly parallel to the ground. In bipedal hominids, the spinal column enters the skull at the bottom, through a hole called the **foramen magnum.** Thus, when hominids became bipedal, the skull ended up on top of the spinal column.

The shape of ancient and modern ape pelvises is considerably different from that of a bipedal hominid. Ape pelvises are long and flat, forming a bony plate in the lower back to which the leg muscles attach. In bipedal hominids the pelvis is bowl-shaped, which supports the internal organs and also lowers the body's center of gravity, allowing better balance on the legs. The hominid pelvis also provides a different set of muscle attachments and shifts the orientation of the femurs (the upper leg bones) from the side of the pelvis to the front. These changes allow hominids to move their legs forward in a bipedal stride (and do things like kick a soccer ball). Apes, in comparison, move their legs forward (when they walk bipedally) by shifting their pelvis from side to side, not by kicking each leg forward alternately as we do.[20]

Another change associated with the hominid ability to kick the leg forward is our "knock-kneed" posture. Ape legs hang straight down from the pelvis. Bipedal hominid legs, on the other hand, angle inward toward one another. This configuration not only helps us move our legs forward but also helps us maintain a center of gravity in the midline of our bodies, so that our center of gravity does not shift from side to side when we walk or run.

Finally, the feet of bipedal hominids have two major changes compared to those of apes. First, hominid feet have an enlarged group of ankle bones forming a robust heel that can withstand the substantial forces placed on them as a result of habitual bipedalism. Second, hominid feet have an arch, which also aids in absorbing the forces endured by the feet during bipedal locomotion. We know this arch is vital to our ability to be habitually bipedal because "flat-footed" people who lack it have chronic problems in their feet, ankles, knees, and back.[21]

When did these changes take place? We don't know for sure, but fossils from East Africa—Ethiopia, Tanzania, and Kenya—clearly show that bipedal hominids lived there between 4 million and 5 million years ago, perhaps even earlier.

⟲ The Transition from Hominoids to Hominids

Western Chad, in north-central Africa, and its windswept deserts do not seem a likely place to find fossil apes or hominids, but paleoanthropologist Michel Brunet thinks it might be.[22] Western Chad was covered by an ancient lake, and for several million years was a location where forest-dwelling mammals, including primates, congregated. Around 7 million years ago a primate called **Sahelanthropus tchadensis** lived on the shores of the lake, where its bones were fossilized and recovered by Brunet and his colleagues in 2001. *Sahelanthropus,* represented by an almost complete skull, has a unique mix of hominid and hominoid traits. While the skull itself is hominoid, with a small brain, large brow ridges, and wide face, the teeth seem more hominid-like, especially the canines, which do not project below the tooth row.[23] Unfortunately, there is no evidence that *Sahelanthropus* was bipedal. For now, we have to wait for additional evidence to know whether *Sahelanthropus* was the first bipedal ape.

There is, however, tantalizing evidence that another possible early hominid, **Orrorin tugenensis,** was bipedal. Discovered in western Kenya by Brigitte Senut and colleagues in 1998, *Orrorin tugenensis* consists of 19 specimens of jaw, teeth, finger, arm, and leg bones, including the top of a femur.[24] The femur in *Orrorin,* according to Senut, shows adaptations to bipedalism, including a long, angled "head" (or top). Other scholars are not convinced. *Orrorin* dates between 5.8 and 6 million years, so if further research supports *Orrorin* bipedalism it may turn out to be the earliest hominid.

In 1992, a team of researchers led by anthropologist Tim White began surveying a 4.4-million-year-old fossil deposit

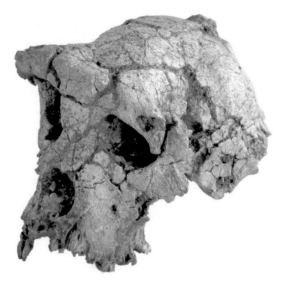

Reconstructed skull of *Sahelanthropus tchadensis,* possibly the earliest hominid, dating to almost seven million years ago.

at Aramis, in the Middle Awash region of Ethiopia. There they discovered 17 fossils of what may be the earliest hominid (more have been found since, including some fragments dating perhaps as early as 5.8 million years ago). Although initially suggested to be a new australopithecine species, White and his colleagues decided that *ramidus,* the species name given to the new fossils, was distinct enough from the australopithecines to warrant a new genus: *Ardipithecus.*[25]

What makes **Ardipithecus ramidus** unique is the combination of apelike dentition along with evidence of bipedal locomotion and an overall hominidlike skeleton. Like apes, *Ardipithecus* has relatively small cheek teeth with thin enamel and relatively large canines. However, its arm bones seem hominid-like, and the base of its skull shows the foramen magnum positioned underneath the skull, just as in definitely bipedal hominids.[26] The feet of *Ardipithecus* also seem adapted to bipedalism.[27] While more evidence is needed to be sure, *Ardipithecus* may be the earliest hominid yet found.

⟲ *Australopithecus:* The First Definite Hominid

Although some doubt remains about the status of *Ardipithecus* as a hominid genus, there is no doubt that the australopithecines (members of the genus **Australopithecus**) were hominids. (Figure 6–3 shows australopithecine sites.) Their teeth share the basic hominid characteristics of small canines, flat and thickly enameled molars, and a parabolic dental arch, and there is unambiguous evidence that even the earliest australopithecines were fully bipedal. Not only do their skeletons reflect bipedal locomotion, but at Laetoli, Tanzania, more than 50 hardened humanlike footprints about 3.6 million years old give striking confirmation that the hominids there were fully bipedal. The bipedalism of the

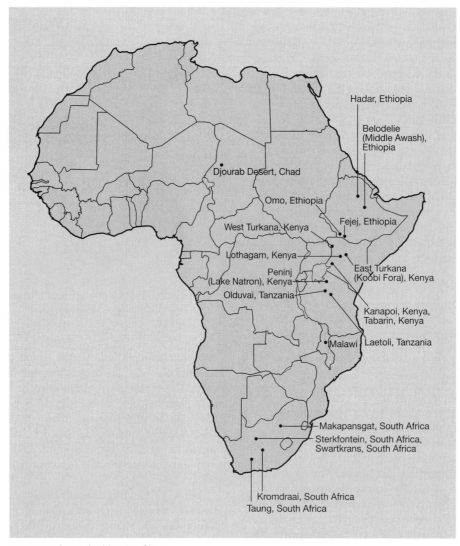

Hadar, Ethiopia

Belodelie
(Middle Awash),
Ethiopia

Djourab Desert, Chad

Omo, Ethiopia

Fejej, Ethiopia

West Turkana, Kenya

Lothagam, Kenya

East Turkana
(Koobi Fora), Kenya

Peninj
(Lake Natron), Kenya

Olduvai, Tanzania

Kanapoi, Kenya,
Tabarin, Kenya

Malawi   Laetoli, Tanzania

Makapansgat, South Africa
Sterkfontein, South Africa,
Swartkrans, South Africa

Kromdraai, South Africa
Taung, South Africa

Figure 6–3 Australopithecine Sites

Source: From Russell L. Ciochon and John G. Fleagle, eds., *The Human Evolution Source Book.* (Englewood Cliffs, NJ: Prentice Hall, 1993).

australopithecines does not mean that these earliest definite hominids were terrestrial all of the time. All of the australopithecines, including the later ones, seem to have been capable of climbing and moving in trees, judging by arm versus leg length and other skeletal features.[28]

Most scholars divide the various australopithecine species into two groups, the "gracile" australopithecines and the "robust" australopithecines.[29]

The **gracile australopithecines** include *A. anamensis, A. afarensis,* and *A. africanus.* All of them have smaller dentition and lighter facial and dental musculature than the robust australopithecines. ***Australopithecus anamensis,*** which may be 4.2 million years old, is the earliest australopithecine, and has been found only in northern Kenya. Other hominids found in East Africa from 4 million to 3 million years ago are classified by most paleoanthropologists as belonging to the species ***Australopithecus afarensis.*** A few paleoanthropologists do not think that these hominids should be placed in a separate species, because they resemble the later hominid

species ***Australopithecus africanus,*** which lived between about 3 million and 2 million years ago, primarily in southern Africa. But the temporal and spatial separation of these forms leads many paleoanthropologists to argue that they were different species.

New fossils from Eastern Africa found in the last decade suggest there may have been other species of gracile australopithecine as well. Two groups of fossils in particular are considered by most scholars to represent new australopithecine species, named ***Australopithecus bahrelghazali*** and ***Australopithecus garhi.*** *A. bahrelghazali* is currently represented by a single, fragmentary jaw, and only a handful of skull and limb fragments represent *A. garhi.* While the finds are intriguing, we will not know how important either species is, or how they may change our understanding of early hominid evolution, until more fossils from them are found.

Australopithecus garhi, found in rock dating to approximately 2.5 million years ago, is particularly interesting, as it is similar to, but is not clearly a member of, any of the other australopithecine species. *A. garhi* has larger molars than *A. afarensis*, yet does not have the huge face and jaws of the robust australopithecines. It also lacks the enlarged brain of early *Homo*. Several limb bones were found in the same rock layers, and these do resemble *A. afarensis*. *A. garhi*, then, looks to be an *afarensis*-like creature but with greatly enlarged molars.[30] It may represent one end of the range of variation in *afarensis*, or it may represent an adaptation to eating tough foods, similar to that made by the robust australopithecines, whom we will discuss shortly.

It is interesting, however, that the remains of butchered animals were found in the same rock layer as the *A. garhi* remains. Several bones found near the *A. garhi* fossils show unambiguous cut marks and signs of having been broken with a stone tool. Unfortunately, no stone tools have been found, but the evidence for butchery suggests they must have been used. And since no other species of hominid have been found in the area, it is reasonable to think that *A. garhi* was the toolmaker and butcher. The fossil's discoverer, Berhane Asfaw, suggests that *A. garhi* is in the right place, at the right time, and has the right physical and behavioral traits to be the direct ancestor of early *Homo*.[31]

Equally intriguing is *Australopithecus bahrelghazali*, not so much because of its physical features, but because it was found further west, in what is now central Chad. *A. bahrelghazali* is the first early hominid to be found outside of the Rift Valley (a long valley in East Africa where the earth is pulling apart, exposing fossils from millions of years ago), and until *A. bahrelghazali* surfaced, few thought early hominids were present anywhere else. *A. bahrelghazali* dates to about 3 million years ago, and is very similar to contemporary *A. afarensis* fossils from the Rift Valley. It differs from *A. afarensis* in some distinct ways (its premolars, for example, have thinner enamel and more well-defined roots), but the important difference is where *A. bahrelghazali* lived. Most

scholars assume the early hominids represent a specific adaptation to the Rift Valley. The discovery of an early australopithecine some 2,500 kilometers west of the Rift Valley calls this assumption into question.[32]

A related hominid genus, **Kenyanthropus platyops,** is thought by some scholars to be yet another australopithecine (and hence should not be regarded as a separate genus). The nearly complete 3.5-million-year-old skull of *Kenyanthropus platyops* from western Kenya shows traits that Meave Leakey and her colleagues suggest separate it from the australopithecines that lived at the same time. Its face is smaller and flatter, and its molars are smaller than those of the australopithecines. Leakey believes *Kenyanthropus* may be a direct link to *Homo*, but others are not so sure. The skull is distorted, and scholars are not convinced that its features lie outside the range of the australopithecines.[33] The debate over the relation of *Kenyanthropus* to *Australopithecus* will continue until more fossils are found.

The **robust australopithecines** have larger dentition than the gracile species, and massive faces and jaws. Some robust individuals had a ridge of bone called a **sagittal crest** on the top of their heads; the ridge anchored the heavy musculature for their large teeth and jaws. The earliest robust species is **Australopithecus aethiopicus,** which lived in eastern Africa between 2.7 and 2.3 million years ago. Most paleoanthropologists think that the later robust australopithecines, who lived between 2.3 and 1 million years ago, consist of two species: the East African species **Australopithecus boisei** and the South African species **Australopithecus robustus.**

The picture that emerges from this brief overview of the australopithecines is one of diversity. There seem to have been many different species of australopithecine, and even within species there seems to be a relatively high level of variation.[34] All shared similar environments in eastern and southern Africa, but those environments were diverse and changing. Forests were giving way to open woodlands and grasslands. Large lakes were formed and then broken apart through uplifting and volcanic activity in the rift valley of eastern Africa. And the climate continued to warm until the end of the **Pliocene,** some 1.6 million years ago. The apparent diversity of the australopithecines may reflect an *adaptive radiation* (a dispersal and divergence) of bipedal hominids to these dynamic environmental conditions.[35] On the other hand, Tim White has suggested that we really do not know enough about the australopithecines to judge how many species there are. He also suggests some variations may be the result of differences in the fossilization process itself.[36] Whatever the cause, diversity seems to be the key word when thinking about the australopithecines. Let's take a closer look at the diverse gracile species of *Australopithecus*, and then the robust species.

Gracile Australopithecines

AUSTRALOPITHECUS ANAMENSIS The earliest australopithecine species is *A. anamensis*, which has been found in several locations in northern Kenya and is dated between 3.9 and 4.2 million years ago.[37] While there is controversy about some of the specimens included in *A. anamensis*, the

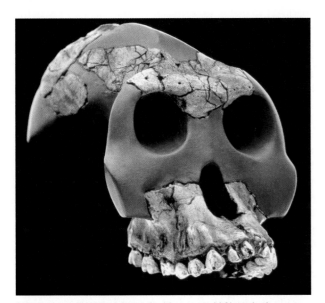

Reconstructed skull of *Australopithecus garhi*. Note the large molars but relatively small face.

general picture is that it was a small bipedal hominid with teeth similar to those of the later *A. afarensis*.[38] The more controversial specimens have long bones, suggesting well-developed bipedalism, but their elbow and knee joints look more like those of the later *Homo* genus than like those of any other species of *Australopithecus*. It has been said that *A. anamensis* is "*afarensis*-like from the neck up and *Homo*-like from the neck down."[39]

AUSTRALOPITHECUS AFARENSIS *A. afarensis* is perhaps the most well-represented australopithecine species. Remains from at least two dozen individuals were unearthed at Laetoli, Tanzania.[40] Although the remains there consisted largely of teeth and jaws, there is no question that the Laetoli hominids were bipedal, because it was at the Laetoli site that the now-famous trail of footprints was found. Two hominids walking erect and side by side left their tracks in the ground 3.6 million years ago. The remains of at least 35 individuals have been found at another site, Hadar, in Ethiopia. The Hadar finds are remarkable for their completeness. Whereas paleoanthropologists often find just parts of the cranium and jaws, many parts of the skeleton were also found at Hadar. For example, paleoanthropologist Donald Johanson found 40 percent of the skeleton of a female hominid he named Lucy, after the Beatles' song "Lucy in the Sky with Diamonds."[41]

Dating of the hominid remains at Laetoli suggests that the hominids there lived between 3.8 million and 3.6 million

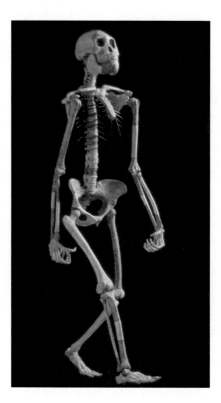

A reconstruction of a female *Australopithecus afarensis* skeleton. Note how long the arms are relative to the legs, and the long fingers. Both suggest *A. afarensis* was at least partially arboreal.

Mary Leakey's expedition discovered a trail about 70 yards long of 3.8-million-year-old fossilized footprints at Laetoli, Tanzania. Shown here is one of the footprints that were left by two adults who were clearly upright walkers. The footprint shows a well-developed arch and forward-facing big toe.

years ago.[42] Although Lucy and the other hominids at Hadar were once thought to be about as old as those at Laetoli, recent dating suggests that they are somewhat younger—less than 3.2 million years old. Lucy probably lived 2.9 million years ago.[43] The environment Lucy lived in was semiarid, upland savanna with rainy and dry seasons.[44]

The existence of such extensive fossil collections has allowed paleoanthropologists such as Donald Johanson and Tim White to develop a portrait of this ancient hominid species. *A. afarensis* was a small hominid, but, like most of the living great apes, was sexually dimorphic. Females weighed perhaps 65 pounds and stood a little more than 3 feet tall; males weighed more than 90 pounds and stood about 5 feet tall.[45]

A. afarensis teeth were large compared to their body size, and they had thick molar enamel. They also had large, ape-like canines, which, on some specimens, projected beyond the adjacent teeth. However, even the longer canines did not rub against the lower teeth or fit into a diastema (a space between the teeth), and thus did not prevent side-to-side movement of the lower jaw.[46] This is important, because side-to-side movement of the lower jaw allowed *A. afarensis* to efficiently chew small seeds and nuts. The thick enamel on the molars and wear patterns on the molar crowns suggest that such small, hard materials made up a significant part of the diet of *A. afarensis*.[47] The cranium of *A. afarensis* reflects its dentition. The face juts forward because of the large teeth and jaws, and the base of the skull flares out to provide attachment areas for large neck muscles to support

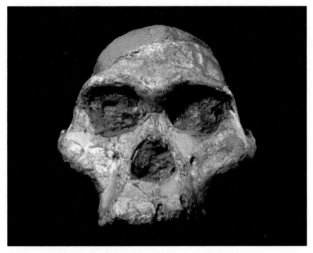

Fossil skull of an *Australopithecus africanus* (STS 5) nicknamed "Mrs. Ples" found by Robert Broom at Sterkfontein cave in 1947.

the heavy face. The brain is small, about 400 cubic centimeters (cc), but relatively large for an animal this size.[48]

The arms and legs of *A. afarensis* were about the same length, and the fingers and toe bones are curved, suggesting they were heavily muscled. Most scholars believe these limb proportions and strong hands and feet point to a partially arboreal lifestyle.[49] In other words, it appears that *A. afarensis* spent a lot of time in the trees, probably feeding, sleeping, and avoiding terrestrial predators. The pelvis and leg bones of *A. afarensis,* however, demonstrate that it moved bipedally when on the ground. The pelvis is wide and flaring, but has the bowl-like shape of all later hominids. The legs angle inward, and the feet have an arch and an ankle much like later hominids.[50] Detailed analyses of the Laetoli footprints suggest that *A. afarensis* may have had a shorter and less efficient stride than modern humans.[51]

While *A. afarensis* is the most well-represented australopithecine species, it was not the first one discovered. That distinction rests with *Australopithecus africanus.*

AUSTRALOPITHECUS AFRICANUS In 1925, Raymond Dart, Professor of Anatomy at the University of Witwatersrand in Johannesburg, South Africa, presented the first evidence that an erect bipedal hominid existed in the Pliocene epoch. As he separated bones from a matrix of material found in the Taung cave on the edge of the Kalahari Desert, Dart realized he was looking at more than the remains of an ape. He described the experience:

> On December 23, [1924,] the rock parted. I could view the face from the front, although the right side was still embedded. The creature that had contained this massive brain was no giant anthropoid such as a gorilla. What emerged was a baby's face, an infant with a full set of milk teeth and its permanent molars just in the process of erupting.[52]

By the teeth Dart identified the fossil as the remains of a 5- to 7-year-old child (although recent analysis by elec-

tron microscope suggests that the child was no more than 3½[53]). He named the specimen *Australopithecus africanus,* which means "southern ape of Africa." Dart was certain the skull was that of a bipedal animal. He based his conclusion on the fact that the foramen magnum faced downward, indicating that the head was carried directly over the spine. Furthermore, the Taung child's incisors and canine teeth were short, and therefore definitely more human- than apelike.

Dart's conclusion met with widespread skepticism and opposition. Not the least of the problems was that scientists at the time believed hominids had originated in Asia. But there were probably other reasons: Dart had found only one fossil; it was an infant rather than an adult; and no other hominid fossils had yet been found in Africa. Other australopithecines were not discovered until the 1930s, when Robert Broom recovered some fossils from the Sterkfontein cave near Johannesburg. Dart's and Broom's conclusions did not begin to be accepted until after 1945, when Wilfred Le Gros Clark, a Professor of Anatomy at Oxford, supported the hominid status of their finds.[54]

Since the Taung child's discovery 80 years ago, the remains of hundreds of other similar australopithecines have been unearthed from caves at Sterkfontein and Makapansgat in South Africa. From this abundant evidence a fairly

A reconstruction of an *Australopithecus africanus* mother and child picking berries in a tree. Like *A. afarensis, A. africanus* probably spent time in trees both feeding and avoiding predators.

CURRENT RESEARCH AND ISSUES

New Finds of Early "Robust" Australopithecines Are Puzzling

Where do the robust australopithecines, with their big jaws and bony skull ridges, fit into the evolution of humans? Paleoanthropologists agree that the robust australopithecines are a side branch of human evolution, but when did they diverge from the *Homo* line? The very early date of some robust australopithecine fossils in East Africa presents a puzzle, according to paleoanthropologist Henry McHenry. These fossils, classified as *Australopithecus aethiopicus*, date apparently from about 2.5 million years ago. If the late robust forms—*A. robustus* and *A. boisei*—descend from *A. aethiopicus*, and if the line leading to *Homo* had already split off from an earlier australopithecine (see Figure 8–4), then why do the late robust australopithecines resemble *Homo erectus* more than they resemble the australopithecines who were their presumed ancestors?

The late robust australopithecines are like *H. erectus* in having a relatively large brain (as compared with *A. africanus*), reduced prognathism (lower face projection), and a deep jaw joint. If they diverged recently from the *Homo* line, similarity to *Homo* would not present a puzzle. But if the robust line diverged earlier, as the 2.7-million-year-old *A. aethiopicus* suggests, the late robust forms should be much more divergent from *Homo*. After all, the further back in time the two lines diverge, the more you would expect the later examples in each to differ.

What could explain some of the similarities between the late robust australopithecines and the *Homo* line? McHenry suggests two possible explanations, both involving convergence. He points out that convergence, the independent appearance of similar structures in different lines of descent, can obscure the issue of how far back there was common ancestry. Bats, birds, and butterflies have wings, but they are not closely related—their common ancestor is way back in evolutionary time. One possible explanation for the similarities between the late robust australopithecines and the *Homo* line is that the late robust forms descend from the early robust forms but resemble *H. erectus* because of convergence. A second possibility is that the late robust forms and *Homo* share a recent, not yet found ancestor; if they do, then the early robust forms were not ancestral to the late robust forms. Convergence, not close common ancestry, might then explain the resemblance between the late and early robust forms.

McHenry prefers the second possibility. On the basis of his analysis of trait similarities, McHenry thinks that the two late robust australopithecine species (*A. robustus* and *A. boisei*) share a common ancestor but that ancestor was not the early robust form, *A. aethiopicus*. In many ways, the late robust forms are not that similar to *A. aethiopicus*. One of the best examples of *A. aethiopicus* is a nearly complete skull (the "Black

complete picture of *A. africanus* can be drawn: "The brain case is rounded with a relatively well-developed forehead. Moderate brow ridges surmount a rather projecting face."[55] The estimated cranial capacity for the various finds from Taung and Sterkfontein is between 428 and 485 cc.[56]

Like *A. afarensis*, *A. africanus* was very small; the adults were 3½ to 4½ feet tall, weighed 60 to 90 pounds, and were sexually dimorphic.[57] The large, chinless jaw of *A. africanus* resembles that of *A. afarensis*, but some of the dental features of *A. africanus* are similar to those of modern humans—broad incisors and small, short canines. And, although the premolars and molars were larger than in modern humans, their form was very similar. Presumably, function and use were also similar.

Dating of the australopithecine finds from the South African limestone caves is somewhat difficult because none of the absolute dating techniques can be applied. But relative dating is possible. Comparisons of the fauna found in the strata with fauna found elsewhere suggest that the South

African *A. africanus* lived between 3 million and 2 million years ago. The climate was probably semiarid, not too different from the climate of today.[58]

Robust Australopithecines

The robust australopithecines lived in eastern Africa and in southern Africa from about 2.7 million to 1 million years ago, and are quite distinct from the gracile australopithecines. Indeed, some paleoanthropologists think these fossils are so different that they deserve to be classified in a different genus, which they call *Paranthropus*, literally, "beside humans." Robust australopithecines were found first in South African caves, in Kromdraai and in Swartkrans, and later in East Africa, in the Omo Basin in Ethiopia, on the east and west sides of Lake Turkana in Kenya, and Olduvai Gorge in Tanzania.[59] Most paleoanthropologists classify the South African robust australopithecines from about 1.8 million to 1 million years ago as *A. robustus* and the East African

Skull"). It is no doubt robust. It has huge premolars and molars and an enormous sagittal crest. But in other ways it resembles *A. afarensis:* protruding muzzle, shallow jaw joint, and small braincase. McHenry thinks that convergent evolution produced the resemblances between the early and late robust australopithecines and the convergence happened because of strong selective pressure for heavy chewing. Features good for heavy chewing have evolved in other primates as well, in evolutionary lines far removed from the human line. *Gigantopithecus,* with its enormous premolars and molars, was one such primate. Thus, although McHenry still considers the late robust australopithecines to constitute a side branch to the *Homo* line, his analysis suggests that *A. robustus* and *A. boisei* were not as far from *Homo* as previously thought.

Timothy Bromage, who has studied fossil facial growth, and Randall Susman, who has studied the hominid thumb, have other suggestions about the robust australopithecines. Bromage has used the scanning electron microscope to study images of fossil faces, particularly to see how the face would have grown from infancy to adulthood. The maturing face changes in shape by a combination of deposition of bone in some locations and resorption of bone in other locations. So, for instance, a jaw becomes more protruding when bone deposits on the forward-facing surfaces and resorbs on the opposite surfaces. Scanning electron microscopy can reveal whether bone is deposited or resorbed. Bromage found differences between the growth patterns of the robust australopithecines and *A. africanus. Australopithecus africanus* and even early *Homo* finds are more apelike in their growth pattern than the later robust australopithecines.

Susman has studied thumb bones and attached musculature to see what traits would be needed to make tools. Modern humans have longer but stouter thumbs than apes, so they can perform the kind of precision grasping needed for toolmaking. Did any early hominids have such precision-grasping ability? Susman thinks that all the australopithecines after about 2.5 million years ago, including the robust ones, had toolmaking hand capabilities. This doesn't mean that they made tools, only that they could have.

The robust australopithecines, with their small foreheads, extremely flat cheeks, and enormous jaws, may have looked very different from the forms in the *Homo* line, but they could be closer to us evolutionarily than we once thought.

Sources: Henry M. McHenry, "'Robust' Australopithecines, Our Family Tree, and Homoplasy," and Timothy G. Bromage, "Paleoanthropology and Life History, and Life History of a Paleoanthropologist," in Peter N. Peregrine, Carol R. Ember, and Melvin Ember, eds., *Physical Anthropology: Original Readings in Method and Practice* (Upper Saddle River, NJ: Prentice Hall, 2002), pp. 254–63, also in Carol R. Ember, Melvin Ember, and Peter N. Peregrine eds., *Research Frontiers* in *New Directions in Anthropology* (Upper Saddle River, NJ: Prentice Hall, CD-ROM, 2004); Randall L. Susman, "Fossil Evidence for Early Hominid Tool Use," *Science* (September 9, 1994): 1570–73.

robust forms from 2.3 million to 1.3 million years ago as *A. boisei.*[60] The third robust species, *A. aethiopicus,* is even earlier, dating back more than 2.5 million years ago, and may have been ancestral to *A. boisei* (see the box "New Finds of Early 'Robust' Australopithecines Are Puzzling").

In contrast to the gracile australopithecines, the robust australopithecines had thicker jaws, with larger molars and premolars but smaller incisors, more massive muscle attachments for chewing, and well-developed sagittal crests and ridges to support heavy chewing.[61] In addition, *A. robustus* and *A. boisei* have somewhat larger cranial capacities (about 490–530 cc) than any of the gracile species.

It used to be thought that the robust australopithecines were substantially bigger than the other australopithecines—hence the term *robust.* But recent calculations suggest that these australopithecines were not substantially different in body weight or height from the other australopithecines. The robustness is primarily in the skull and jaw, most strikingly in the teeth. If the robust forms were larger in body size, their slightly bigger brain capacity would not be surprising, since larger animals generally have larger brains. However, the body of the robust forms is similar to that of *A. africanus,* so the brain of the robust australopithecines was relatively larger than the brain of *A. africanus.*[62]

AUSTRALOPITHECUS AETHIOPICUS *A. aethiopicus* is the earliest and also the least known of the robust australopithecines. *A. aethiopicus* is represented by a small group of fossils found in northern Kenya and southern Ethiopia dating between 2.3 million and 2.7 million years ago, including one spectacular find—a nearly complete skull (known as the "Black Skull" because of its dark color) found in 1985.[63] Even though we have only a few fossils, it seems clear that *A. aethiopicus* was quite different from other australopithecines. They differ from *A. afarensis* specimens from roughly the same region and perhaps even the same time period by having much larger dentition, particularly molars, huge cheekbones, projecting and dish-shaped (round and flat) faces,

CURRENT RESEARCH AND ISSUES

Cladistic Analysis

Traditional models of human evolution take the form of a phylogenetic tree like that shown in Figure 8–4. The models are usually based on several lines of evidence, including the age of the species, their locations, and, most importantly, the characteristics they seem to share with other species. In many ways phylogenetic trees are subjective, since they are often based on those items the designer of the tree thinks are the most important characteristics shared, or not shared, by a group of species. In recent years, many paleoanthropologists have found cladistic analysis to be a more useful way of looking at the relationships between species.

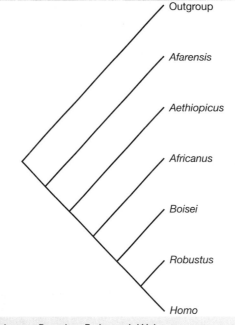

Outgroup

Afarensis

Aethiopicus

Africanus

Boisei

Robustus

Homo

Cladogram Based on Endocranial Volume

Source: From Henry McHenry, " 'Robust' Australopithecines, Our Family Tree, and Homoplasy," in Peregrine, Ember, and Ember, *Physical Anthropology.*

Cladistic analysis focuses exclusively on the derived traits (traits that have changed over time) in a group of species. One lists the changes in a given trait for each species in the analysis, and then orders the various species in terms of their ages. Finally, one diagrams the relationships between species by age and the direction of change in the trait being analyzed. The result is a cladogram, such as that shown first in this box, which illustrates the relationships between species based on changes in a single trait. In this case, the change is in endocranial volume or, to put it more simply, brain size. The "outgroup" here defines the most primitive form. As one moves down the left–right sloping line, one reaches branching points where endocranial volume changes. Here *A. robustus*

---

and large sagittal crests. But they are similar to *A. afarensis* in most other ways. Overall, *A. aethiopicus* resembles *A. afarensis* with a massively "scaled-up" dental apparatus.[64]

AUSTRALOPITHECUS ROBUSTUS In 1936, Robert Broom, then curator of vertebrate paleontology at the Transvaal museum in South Africa, began visiting quarries seeking fossils for the museum, particularly hominids that might support Raymond Dart's earlier discovery of the Taung child. In 1938, a quarry manager gave Broom a hominid jaw that had been found in a nearby cave called Kromdraai. Broom immediately began excavating in the cave, and within days was able to piece together the skull of what would prove to be a new australopithecine species—*Australopithecus robustus.*[65]

While Broom had expected another example of *Australopithecus africanus* (he had found an *A. africanus* skull in 1936), this one was different. It had larger teeth, a massive jaw, and a flatter face than *A. africanus.*[66] Indeed, after further study, Broom decided that the fossil represented an entirely new hominid genus: *Paranthropus.* Broom's genus designation was not widely accepted at the time (scholars thought the specimen represented a species of *Australopithecus*), but as we noted earlier many scholars today believe the robust australopithecines are unique enough to warrant classification in a separate *Paranthropus* genus.

During the 1940s Broom added many new fossils of *A. robustus* and *A. africanus* to the collections of the Transvaal Museum. But his discoveries also raised a problem. How did two strikingly different hominid species evolve in the same environment? In 1954, John T. Robinson proposed that *A. africanus* and *A. robustus* had different dietary adaptations—*A. africanus* being an omnivore (dependent on meat and plants) and *A. robustus* a vegetarian, with a need for heavy chewing. Robinson's view was hotly debated for many years. Evidence from electron microscopy supports Robinson's view that *A. robustus* ate mostly small, hard objects such as seeds, nuts, and tubers. But how different was *A. africanus* in

and early *Homo* are more like one another than any others in the cladogram; early *Homo*, *A. robustus*, and *A. boisei* are more like one another than the others; and so on.

One of the main benefits of this approach is that it is a formal procedure: Assumptions must be made clear, and traits used in the analysis must also be defined precisely. This allows the results of a cladistic analysis to be less affected by an unacknowledged bias or subjective preconception than traditional phylogenetic trees are prone to. Often cladistic analyses lead to quite different pictures of evolutionary relationships, compared with traditional phylogenetic trees.

The second figure in this box represents a cladogram of early hominid species based on 77 traits. It suggests that early *A. robustus* and *A. boisei* are more like one another on these traits than like other species, and thus are likely to share a common ancestor. Early *Homo* shares a common ancestor with *A. robustus* and *A. boisei*. All three share a common ancestor with *A. africanus*. *A. afarensis* is the least like the others, and shares a common ancestor with all the rest. Compare this with Figure 6–4. There are a number of similarities, and yet the close relationship between the robust australopithecines and early *Homo* is not apparent in the traditional phylogeny. Though we will probably never know the true phylogenetic relationships among our ancient ancestors, many scholars believe cladistic analyses provide the best approximations.

Sources: Henry McHenry, "'Robust' Australopithecines, Our Family Tree, and Homoplasy." In Peter N. Peregrine, Carol R. Ember, and Melvin Ember, eds., *Physical Anthropology: Original Readings in Method and Practice* (Upper Saddle River, NJ: Prentice Hall, 2002), pp. 124–39, also in Carol R. Ember, Melvin Ember, and Peter N. Peregrine eds., *Research Frontiers* in *New Directions in Anthropology* (Upper Saddle River, NJ: Prentice Hall, CD-ROM, 2004); Willi Hennig, *Phylogenetic Systematics* (Urbana: University of Illinois Press, 1966).

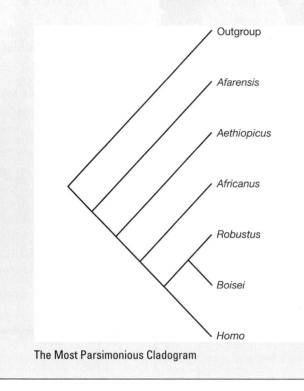

Outgroup

Afarensis

Aethiopicus

Africanus

Robustus

Boisei

Homo

The Most Parsimonious Cladogram

this respect? Recent analyses suggest that *A. africanus* also practiced fairly heavy chewing.[67]

The idea that *A. robustus* was just a vegetarian is also questioned by a relatively new chemical technique that analyzes strontium–calcium ratios in teeth and bones to estimate the proportion of plant versus animal food in the diet. This new kind of analysis suggests that *A. robustus* was an omnivore.[68] Thus *A. robustus* may have needed large teeth and jaws to chew seeds, nuts, and tubers, but that doesn't mean that it didn't eat other things too.

Was *A. robustus* adapted, then, to a drier, more open environment than *A. africanus*? This is a possibility, but the evidence is controversial. At any rate, most paleoanthropologists think that *A. robustus* died out shortly after 1 million years ago[69] and is not ancestral to our own genus, *Homo*.[70]

AUSTRALOPITHECUS BOISEI Legendary paleoanthropologist Louis Leakey began his search for a human ancestor in 1931 at Olduvai Gorge in western Tanzania. It was not until 1959 that his efforts paid off with the discovery of *Australopithecus boisei* (named after a benefactor, Charles Boise). The nearly 30 years that Leakey, his wife, Mary Leakey, and their children (including paleoanthropologist Richard Leakey) worked at Olduvai before finding *A. boisei* were not wasted. The Leakeys assembled a rich collection of nonhominid fossils and established a detailed understanding of the ancient environment of the region.[71] As we discuss in the next chapter, they also amassed a remarkable collection of ancient stone tools. So, on a hot July morning, when Mary Leakey rushed to tell Louis, who was sick in bed, that she had discovered the hominid they had long been searching for, the Leakeys were able immediately to place their find into a rich environmental and perhaps cultural context.

The discovery of *A. boisei* was particularly important because it demonstrated that early hominids were present in East Africa. Until the Leakeys found *A. boisei*, it was thought that South Africa was the homeland of the hominids. Indeed, Leakey initially assigned *A. boisei* to a new genus—

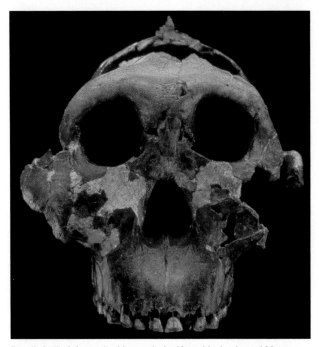

Fossil skull of *Australopithecus boisei* found by Louis and Mary Leakey in 1959. Note its huge face and teeth and its sagittal crest.

Zinjanthropus—to highlight its location (*Zinj* means "East Africa" in Arabic). Today we know that the most ancient fossil hominids are all found in East Africa, but in 1959 simply finding a fossil hominid in East Africa was remarkable.

What did *A. boisei* look like? Compared with *A. robustus*, *A. boisei* had even more extreme features that reflected a huge chewing apparatus—enormous molar teeth and expanded premolars that look like molars; a massive, thick and deep jaw; thick cheekbones; and a more pronounced sagittal crest.[72] Indeed, *A. boisei* has been called a "hyperrobust" australopithecine—a name that definitely captures the species.

A. boisei lived between about 2.3 and 1.3 million years ago. Like *A. robustus*, it seems to have lived in a dry, open environment and ate a lot of coarse seeds, nuts, and roots. And, like *A. robustus*, most paleoanthropologists think *A. boisei* is not ancestral to our genus, *Homo*.[73] We don't know for sure whether *A. boisei* was the maker of the stone tools the Leakeys found at Olduvai for, as we will learn in the next chapter, it lived alongside at least two other hominid species—*Homo habilis* and *Homo erectus*—who are perhaps the more likely toolmakers.

☙ One Model of Human Evolution

At this point you may well be wondering how all these species fit together. Figure 6–4 shows one model entertained by paleoanthropologists about how the known fossils may be related. The main disagreement among paleontologists concerns which species of *Australopithecus* were ancestral to the line

leading to modern humans. For example, the model shown in Figure 8–4 suggests that *A. africanus* is not ancestral to *Homo*, only to one line of robust australopithecines. *Australopithecus afarensis* is viewed as ancestral to both lines of robust australopithecines and to the line leading to modern humans. Those who think that *A. afarensis* was the last common ancestor of all the hominid lines shown in Figure 8–4 think the split to *Homo* occurred over 3 million years ago.[74]

Despite the uncertainty and disagreements about what species was ancestral to the *Homo* line, there is widespread agreement among paleoanthropologists about other aspects of early hominid evolution: (1) There were at least two separate hominid lines between 3 million and 1 million years ago; (2) the robust australopithecines were not ancestral to modern humans but became extinct about 1 million years ago; and (3) *Homo habilis* (and successive *Homo* species) were in the direct ancestral line to modern humans. It is our direct ancestors, the first members of the *Homo* genus, to whom we turn in the next chapter.

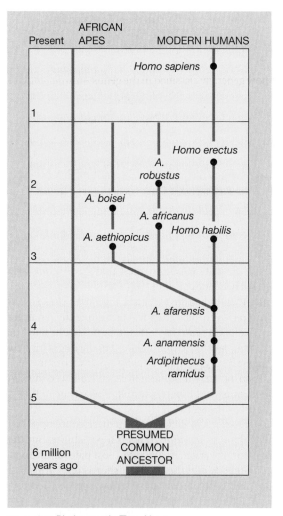

Figure 6–4 Phylogenetic Time Lines

Source: Adapted from *The New York Times,* September 5, 1995, p. C9. Dates changed slightly to reflect recent redating.

⊚ Summary

1. The drying trend in climate that began about 16 million to 11 million years ago diminished the extent of African rain forests and gave rise to areas of savanna (grasslands) and scattered deciduous woodlands. The new, more open country probably favored characteristics adapted to ground living in some primates. In the evolutionary line leading to humans, these adaptations included bipedalism.

2. One of the crucial changes in early hominid evolution was the development of bipedalism. There are several theories for this development: It may have increased the emerging hominid's ability to see predators and potential prey while moving through the tall grasses of the savanna; by freeing the hands for carrying, it may have facilitated transferring food from one place to another; tool use, which requires free hands, may have favored two-legged walking; and bipedalism may have made long-distance traveling more efficient.

3. *Sahelanthropus, Orrorin,* and *Ardipithecus* are likely candidates for the first hominid. They date as early as 6 million years ago, and may have walked bipedally. Undisputed hominids dating before 4 million years ago have been found in East Africa. These definitely bipedal hominids are now generally classified in the genus *Australopithecus.*

4. At least six species of australopithecine have been identified, and these are generally divided into two types: gracile and robust. The gracile australopithecines have relatively smaller teeth and jaws, and include *A. anamensis, A. afarensis,* and *A. africanus.* The robust australopithecines have relatively larger teeth and jaws, and are more muscular than the gracile australopithecines. They include *A. aethiopicus, A. robustus,* and *A. boisei.*

⊚ Glossary Terms

Ardipithecus ramidus	95	*Australopithecus robustus*	97
Australopithecus	95	foramen magnum	94
Australopithecus aethiopicus	97	gracile australopithecines	96
Australopithecus afarensis	96	*Kenyanthropus platyops*	97
Australopithecus africanus	96	*Orrorin tugenensis*	95
Australopithecus anamensis	96	Pliocene	97
Australopithecus bahrelghazali	96	robust australopithecines	97
		sagittal crest	97
Australopithecus boisei	97	*Sahelanthropus tchadensis*	95
Australopithecus garhi	96	savanna	91

⊚ Critical Questions

1. How could there have been more than one species of hominid living in East Africa at the same time?

2. What may have enabled australopithecines to survive in the face of many ground predators?

3. What evolutionary processes can you envision that may have led the genus *Australopithecus* to divide into two major types: gracile and robust?

⊚ Research Navigator

1. Please go to **www.researchnavigator.com** and enter your LOGIN NAME and PASSWORD. For instructions on registering for the first time, please view the detailed instructions at the end of Chapter 1.

2. Go to the *New York Times* section and search using the keyword "hominid" subject in the pull-down menu. Research on early hominids is a dynamic field, and new discoveries are changing our knowledge almost daily. Choose a recent article on early hominids, and after reading it, answer the following questions: What new information about the first hominids did you gain from this article? Has the information in the article changed your understanding of early hominids? Has the information in the article changed any of the information presented in the textbook?

⊚ Discovering Anthropology: Researchers at Work

Read the chapter by Scott Simpson titled "*Australopithecus afarensis* and Human Evolution" in the accompanying *Discovering Anthropology* reader. Answer the following questions:

1. Why is the Afar region of Ethiopia such a rich and important area for finding early hominid fossils?

2. How does Simpson come to the conclusion that only one species, *A. afarensis,* is represented in the collections from Hadar and Laetoli?

CHAPTER SEVEN

The Origins of Culture and The Emergence of *Homo*

I n the last chapter we discussed the origins of bipedalism and how that fundamental hominid means of locomotion first appeared and was refined in the australopithecines. In this chapter we will consider a number of other trends in hominid evolution, including the routine use of patterned or nearly standardized stone tools, which is considered one sign of the emergence of culture. It is assumed, but not known for sure, that patterned stone tools were made by the first members of our own genus, *Homo*, for it is in the genus *Homo* that we first see a number of trends that probably started because of habitual stone toolmaking and use—expansion of the brain, modification of the female pelvis to accommodate bigger-brained babies, and reduction in the teeth, face, and jaws.

Even though stone tools are found at various sites in East Africa before the time early *Homo* appeared, most anthropologists surmise that members of early *Homo* species, rather than the australopithecines, made those tools (see Figure 7–1). After all, early *Homo* had a brain capacity almost one-third larger than the australopithecines'. But the fact is that none of the earliest stone tools is clearly associated with early *Homo*, so it is impossible as yet to know who made them.[1] We turn now to a discussion of those earliest stone tools and what archaeologists and paleoanthropologists infer about the lifestyles of their makers, the hominids (whoever they were) who lived between about 2.5 million and 1.5 million years ago.

Early Hominid Tools

The earliest identifiable stone tools found so far come from various sites in East Africa and date from about 2.5 million years ago,[2] and maybe earlier. The oldest tools, some 3,000 in number, were discovered at Gona, Ethiopia. They range from very small flakes (thumb-size) to cobble or core tools that are fist-size.[3] These early tools were apparently made by striking a stone with another stone, a technique called **percussion flaking.** Both the sharp-edged flakes and the sharp-edged cores (the pieces of stone left after flakes are removed) were probably used as tools.

What were those earliest stone tools used for? What do they tell us about early hominid lifestyles? Unfortunately, little can be inferred about lifestyles from the earliest

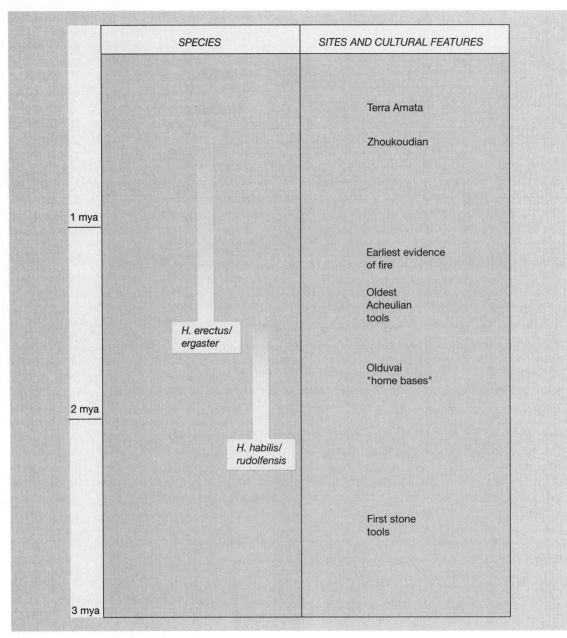

Figure 7–1 Early Evolution of the Genus *Homo*

tool sites because little else was found with the tools. In contrast, finds of later tool assemblages at Olduvai Gorge in Tanzania have yielded a rich harvest of cultural information. The Olduvai site was uncovered accidentally in 1911, when a German entomologist followed a butterfly into the gorge and found fossil remains. As we discussed in the last chapter, Louis and Mary Leakey beginning in the 1930s searched the gorge for clues to the evolution of early humans. Of the Olduvai site, Louis Leakey wrote,

> [It] is a fossil hunter's dream, for it shears 300 feet through stratum after stratum of earth's history as through a gigantic layer cake. Here, within reach, lie countless fossils and artifacts which but for the faulting and erosion would have remained sealed under thick layers of consolidated rock.[4]

The oldest cultural materials from Olduvai (Bed I) date from Lower Pleistocene times (about 1.6 million years ago). The stone artifacts include core tools and sharp-edged flakes. Flake tools predominate. Among the core tools, so-called choppers are common. Choppers are cores that have been partially flaked and have a side that might have been used for chopping. Other core tools, with flaking along one side and a flat edge, are called scrapers. Whenever a stone has facets removed from only one side of the cutting edge, we call it a **unifacial tool.** If the stone has facets removed from both sides, we call it a **bifacial tool.** Although there are some bifacial tools in the early stone tool assemblages, they are not as plentiful or as elaborated as in later tool traditions. The kind of tool assemblage found in Bed I and to some extent in later (higher) layers is referred to as **Oldowan** (see Figure 7–2).[5]

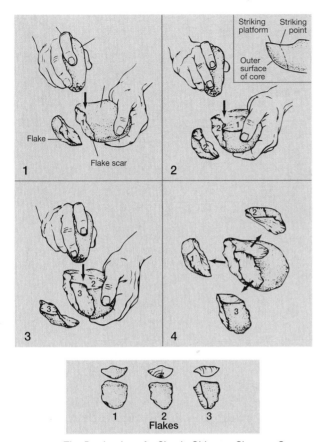

Figure 7–2 The Production of a Simple Oldowan Chopper Core and the Resultant Flakes

Source: From "The First Technology" by R. Freyman in *Scientific American.* Reprinted by permission of the artist, Ed Hanson.

◎ Early Hominid Lifestyles

Archaeologists have speculated about the lifestyles of early hominids from Olduvai and other sites. Some of these speculations come from analysis of what can be done with the tools, microscopic analysis of wear on the tools, and examination of the marks the tools make on bones; other speculations are based on what is found with the tools.

Archaeologists have experimented with what can be done with Oldowan tools. The flakes appear to be very versatile; they can be used for slitting the hides of animals, dismembering animals, and whittling wood into sharp-pointed sticks (wooden spears or digging sticks). The larger stone tools (choppers and scrapers) can be used to hack off branches or cut and chop tough animal joints.[6] Those who have made and tried to use stone tools for various purposes are so impressed by the sharpness and versatility of flakes that they wonder whether most of the core tools were really used as tools. The cores could mainly be what remained after wanted flakes were struck off.[7]

Archaeologists surmise that many early tools were also made of wood and bone, but these do not survive in the archaeological record. Present-day populations use sharp-pointed digging sticks for extracting roots and tubers from

the ground; stone flakes are very effective for sharpening wood to a very fine point.[8]

None of the early flaked stone tools can plausibly be thought of as weapons. So, if the toolmaking hominids were hunting or defending themselves with weapons, they had to have used wooden spears, clubs, or unmodified stones as missiles. Later Oldowan tool assemblages also include stones that were flaked and battered into a rounded shape. The unmodified stones and the shaped stones might have been lethal projectiles.[9]

Experiments may indicate what can be done with tools, but they cannot tell us what was *actually* done with them. Other techniques, such as microscopic analysis of the wear on tools, are more informative. Early studies looked at the microscopic scratches formed when a tool was used in different ways. Scratches parallel to the edge of a tool often occur when a tool is used in a sawing motion; perpendicular scratches suggest whittling or scraping.[10] Lawrence Keeley used high-powered microscopes in his experimental investigations of tools and found that different kinds of "polish" develop on tools when they are used on different materials. The polish on tools used for cutting meat is different from the polish on tools used for woodworking. On the basis of microscopic investigation of the 1.5-million-year-old tools from the eastern side of Lake Turkana, Keeley and his colleagues concluded that at least some of the early tools were probably used for cutting meat, others for cutting or whittling wood, and still others for cutting plant stems.[11]

Olduvai Gorge, Tanzania. Bed I, where evidence of early human culture was found, is at the very bottom of the Gorge.

In the 1950s and 1960s, Olduvai Gorge revealed the presence of both Oldowan tools and the remains of broken bones and teeth from many different animal species. For many years it seemed plausible to assume that hominids were the hunters and the animals their prey. But, as we discussed in the chapter on how we discover the past, archaeologists had to reexamine this assumption with the emergence of the field of *taphonomy,* which studies the processes that can alter and distort an assemblage of bones. So, for example, flowing water can bring bones and artifacts together, which may have happened at Olduvai Gorge about 1.8 million years ago. (The area of what is now the gorge bordered the shores of a shallow lake at that time.) And other animals such as hyenas could have brought carcasses to some of the same places that hominids spent time. Taphonomy requires archaeologists to consider all the possible reasons things may be found together.[12]

But there is little doubt that shortly after 2 million years ago hominids were cutting up animal carcasses for meat. Microscopic analyses show that cut marks on animal bones were unambiguously created by stone flake tools, and microscopic analyses of the polish on stone tools indicate that the polish is consistent with butchering. We still do not know for sure whether the hominids around Olduvai Gorge were just scavenging meat (taking meat from the kills of other animals) or actually hunting the animals.

On the basis of her analysis of cut marks on bone from Bed I in Olduvai Gorge, Pat Shipman suggested that scavenging, not hunting, was the major meat-getting activity of the hominids living there between 2 million and 1.7 million years ago. For example, the cut marks made by the stone tools usually (but not always) overlie teeth marks made by carnivores. This suggests that the hominids were often scavenging the meat of animals killed and partially eaten by non-hominid predators. The fact that the cut marks were sometimes made first, however, suggested to Shipman that the hominids were also sometimes the hunters.[13] On the other hand, prior cut marks may indicate only that the hominids scavenged before carnivores had a chance to consume their prey.

The artifact and animal remains from Bed I and the lower part of Bed II at Olduvai suggest a few other things about the lifestyles of the hominids there. First, it seems that the hominids moved around during the year; most of the sites in what is now the Olduvai Gorge appear to have been used only in the dry season, as indicated by an analysis of the kinds of animal bones found there.[14] Second, whether the early Olduvai hominids were hunters or scavengers, they apparently exploited a wide range of animals. Although most of the bones are from medium-sized antelopes and wild pigs, even large animals such as elephants and giraffes seem to have been eaten.[15] It is clear, then, that the Olduvai hominids scavenged or hunted for meat, but we cannot tell yet how important meat was in their diet.

There is also no consensus about how to characterize the Olduvai sites that contain concentrations of stone tools and animal bones. In the 1970s, there was a tendency to think of them as home bases to which hominids (presumably male)

A replica of an Oldowan stone tool is used to chop into a large bone to extract the nutrient-rich marrow. Few animals have jaws powerful enough to break open the bones of large mammals, but stone tools would have allowed early humans to do so.

brought meat to share with others (presumably nursing mothers and young children). Indeed, Mary Leakey identified two locations where she thought early hominids had built simple structures (Figure 7–3). One was a stone circle that she suggested formed the base of a small brush windbreak. The other was a circular area of dense debris surrounded by an area virtually without debris. Leakey suggested that the area lacking debris may represent the location of a ring of thorny brush with which early hominids surrounded their campsite in order to keep out predators—much like pastoralists living in the region do today.[16] But archaeologists today are not so sure that these sites were home bases. For one thing, carnivores also frequented the sites. Places with meaty bones lying around may not have been so safe for hominids to use as home bases. Second, the animal remains at the sites had not been completely dismembered and butchered. If the sites had been hominid home bases, we would expect more complete processing of carcasses.[17] Third, natural processes as simple as trees growing through a site can create circular areas of debris such as the ones Leakey identified as structures, and without better evidence that early hominids made them, one cannot be sure that the circles of debris were indeed structures.[18]

If these sites were not home bases, what were they? Some archaeologists are beginning to think that these early sites with many animal bones and tools may just have been places where hominids processed food but did not live. Why would the hominids return repeatedly to a particular site? Richard Potts suggests one possible reason—that hominids left caches of stone tools and stones for toolmaking at various locations to facilitate recurrent food-collecting and processing activities.[19] Future research may tell us more about early hominid life. Did they have home bases, or did they just move from one processing site to another? How did they protect themselves from predators? They apparently did not have fire to keep the predators away. Did they climb trees to get away or to sleep?

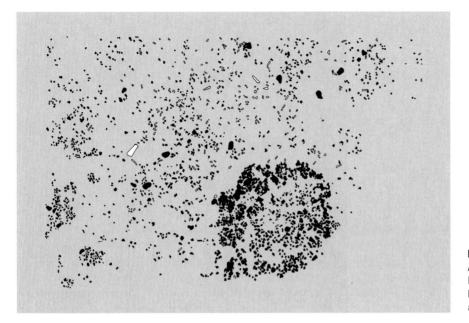

Figure 7–3 Olduvai "Hut"
A ring of stones and bones found in Bed I of Olduvai Gorge that Mary Leakey interpreted as the remains of an ancient hut.

Stone Tools and Culture

Regardless of the answers to these questions, the presence of patterned stone tools means that these early hominids had probably developed **culture**. Archaeologists consider a pattern of behavior, such as a particular way to make a tool that is shared and learned by a group of individuals, to be a sign of cultural behavior. To be sure, toolmaking does not imply that early humans had anything like the complex cultures of humans today. Chimpanzees have patterns of tool use and toolmaking that appear to be shared and learned, but they do not have that much in the way of cultural behavior.

What, exactly, makes human culture so different from other forms of animal behavior? Anthropologists have spent more than a century trying to answer this question, and there is still no widely accepted answer. One thing is clear, however: Culture must be understood as a set of interrelated processes, not as a thing.[20] What are the processes that make up culture? Let's consider some of the more important ones.

First, culture is *learned* as well as *shared*. This is the fundamental difference between culture and most other forms of animal behavior. Culture is not a set of innate behaviors but, rather, a set of learned ones. Culture is something individuals acquire during their lifetimes as they mature and interact with others. Interaction is key here, because not only are cultural behaviors learned, they are learned through interaction with others, through education, and through shared experiences. Culture, then, is a social process, not an individual one. It also includes attitudes, values, and ideals as well as behavior.

Second, culture is generally *adaptive*. What this means is that most of the learned and shared behaviors that make up a culture are thought to have developed and spread through a group of people because they help that group of people survive in a given environment. Thus, cultural behaviors may be favored by natural selection just as genes are. The extent to which human culture is a product of natural selection is hotly debated, but few anthropologists would argue that culture is not a key aspect of human adaptation. What makes culture quite different from the behavioral systems of other animals is that, because culture is learned and shared rather than innate, humans can develop new behaviors quickly and adapt to diverse and changing conditions with relative ease. Adaptation, then, is perhaps the most significant process of culture.

Change is the third major process of culture, for culture is always *changing*. Culture change regularly occurs as new and beneficial means of adaptation are developed and shared. But anthropologists also assume that when new behaviors or ideas are developed they tend to become integrated with existing behaviors or ideas. That is, new items that conflict with established ones may lead to one or the other changing. For example, a group of early humans could not have both scavenged meat and, at the same time, prohibited eating meat that they did not themselves kill. Such a situation would create a contradiction, and something would probably have to change. Working out contradictions between new, highly beneficial behaviors and established but less beneficial ones may be one of the reasons that cultures are so dynamic. (For more on the concept of culture, see the chapter with that title.)

It seems clear that the early hominids, like other primates, were social beings. It also seems clear from the archaeological record that early hominids were making and using stone tools on a regular basis. Tools are frequently found in discrete concentrations, and often in association with animal bones and other debris from human activity. And, as we have already noted, a number of paleoanthropologists have argued that such concentrations of debris may represent campsites

CURRENT RESEARCH AND ISSUES

How Do You Know Something Is a Tool?

When you look at photographs or drawings of early stone tools, do you ever wonder how paleoanthropologists can distinguish them from ordinary rocks? It is not always easy. Paleoanthropologists mainly look for flakes or rocks with flakes removed, but rocks can be flaked by knocking against other rocks in a riverbed or rolling down a craggy hill. To tell that a core tool is not a naturally flaked rock, paleoanthropologists typically look for three distinct features.

First, the tool has to be made of the *right kind of rock*. The rock must be both flakable and durable. You can flake shale, for example, but it is not durable. Many metamorphic rocks are durable, but you cannot flake them because there are too many flaws in the rock. Most stone tools are made from obsidian, quartz, flint, or chert.

Second, paleoanthropologists look for *bilateral flaking*. Bilateral flaking occurs when flakes are struck from two sides of a stone to form a cutting edge. Natural processes may knock a couple of flakes from one side of a stone but will rarely knock them off from opposite sides.

Third, paleoanthropologists look for *retouching*. Retouching occurs when additional flakes are removed from an existing tool in order to resharpen it. Again, natural processes may knock a series of flakes from one side of a rock but will rarely create something resembling a retouched cutting edge.

Paleoanthropologists may also look for a distinct *striking platform* on flakes. A striking platform is the place where the blow landed that knocked the flake from the core. When a flake is struck from a core, it leaves a clean scar that can be used as a striking platform to knock a flake from the opposite side of the core. On flakes made by humans, the striking platform is often

the scar left by a previous flake. Just as bilateral flaking is rare in nature, so too is a flake scar with a clearly prepared striking platform.

With these features, paleoanthropologists can usually distinguish naturally flaked rocks from stone tools. But this is not always the case, and many paleoanthropologists have made mistakes. Indeed, one of the most famous mistakes was made by Louis Leakey, one of the first paleoanthropologists to identify early hominid tools. In the late 1960s, Leakey claimed that a site in California called Calico Hills contained early human tools. This claim was met with disbelief, as no evidence of premodern humans has ever been found in North America, and, as we discuss in the chapter on the Upper Paleolithic world, there is good evidence that modern-looking humans were the continent's first inhabitants. However, because it was Leakey who made the claim, it had to be taken seriously. A group of respected paleoanthropologists met at the site upon Leakey's request to make a determination. Their finding? The alleged stone tools were natural objects, not made by humans.

Calico Hills is an important cautionary tale. How do you know something is a tool? In addition to the tool's physical features, paleoanthropologists must also consider the context in which it is found. When alleged tools are found in the absence of hominids or with no other clear evidence of stone tool use, as in the case of Calico Hills, and the context does not suggest the possibility of tools, paleoanthropologists should question their presence.

Sources: Vance Haynes, "The Calico Site: Artifacts or Geofacts?" *Science,* 181 (1973): 305–10; Leland Patterson, "Criteria for Determining the Attributes of Man-Made Lithics," *Journal of Field Archaeology,* 10 (1983): 297–307.

or even small shelters. Home bases of some sort may have been a part of early hominid culture.

Whether they reflect home bases or not, large numbers of animal bones and tools are found in discrete locations, and these accumulations suggest that the areas were being used by groups of individuals over periods of time. In such a situation sharing of food is very likely. It seems counterintuitive to think that individuals would have purposely brought food to a common location only to keep it to themselves. And although we must move into the realm of pure speculation, it does seem reasonable to think that closely related individuals, like parents, children, and siblings, would be more likely to associate and share food with one another than more distantly related individuals. This speculation is supported by

the fact that when food sharing takes place among chimpanzees it is usually among closely related individuals.[21] Thus, the ancient locations of early hominid social activity may be evidence of family groups. How would such a system of social behavior—the creation of a common meeting, resting, and living place for a group of related individuals to share food—have evolved? Let's consider one model.

One Model for the Evolution of Culture

Early *Homo* had a brain almost one-third larger than that of the australopithecines. As we discuss later in the section on trends in hominid evolution, one of the possible consequences of brain expansion was the lessening of maturity at birth. That babies were born more immature may at least partly explain the lengthening of the period of infant and child dependency in hominids. Compared with other animals, we spend not only a longer proportion of our life span, but also the longest absolute period, in a dependent state. Prolonged infant dependency has probably been of great significance in human cultural evolution. According to Theodosius Dobzhansky,

> it is this helplessness and prolonged dependence on the ministrations of the parents and other persons that favors . . . the socialization and learning process on which the transmission of culture wholly depends. This may have been an overwhelming advantage of the human growth pattern in the process of evolution.[22]

It used to be thought that the australopithecines had a long period of infant dependency, just as modern humans do, but the way their teeth apparently developed suggests that the early australopithecines followed an apelike pattern of development. Thus, prolonged maturation may be relatively recent, but just how recent is not yet known.[23]

Although some use of tools for digging, defense, or scavenging may have influenced the development of bipedalism, full bipedalism may have made possible more efficient toolmaking and consequently more efficient foraging and scavenging. As we have seen, there are archaeological signs that early hominids may have been scavenging (and perhaps even hunting) animals as far back as the late Pliocene. Indeed, we have fairly good evidence that early hominids were butchering and presumably eating big game some 2 million years ago.

Whenever it was that hominids began to scavenge for game and perhaps hunt regularly, the development of scavenging would require individuals to travel long distances frequently in search of suitable carcasses. Among groups of early *Homo*, longer infant and child dependency may have fostered the creation of home bases or at least established meeting places. The demands of childbirth and caring for a newborn might have made it difficult for early *Homo* mothers to travel for some time after the birth. Certainly, it would have been awkward for a mother carrying a nursing child to travel long distances in order to hunt. While carrying an infant might be possible with a sling, successful hunting might not be so likely with a needy and potentially noisy child along. Because early *Homo* males (and perhaps females without young children) would have been freer to roam farther from home, they probably became the scavengers or hunters. Women with young children may have gathered wild plants within a small area that could be covered without traveling far from the home base or meeting place.

The creation of home bases or meeting places among early *Homo* groups may have increased the likelihood of food sharing. If mothers with young children were limited to gathered plant foods in a relatively small area, the only way to ensure that they and their children could obtain a complete diet would have been to share the other foods obtained elsewhere. With whom would such sharing take place? Most likely with close relatives. Sharing with them would have made it more likely that their offspring would survive to have offspring. Thus, if early *Homo* had home bases and families, those characteristics could have encouraged the development of the learned and shared behaviors we call culture.

Obviously this is a "just-so" story—a tale that we may never be able to prove really happened. However, it is a tale that is consistent with the archaeological record. Patterned stone tools do not appear until early *Homo* comes on the scene. And with early *Homo* we see the start of several trends in hominid evolution that appear to reflect the manufacture and use of patterned stone tools—the expansion of the brain, the modification of the female pelvis to accommodate bigger-brained babies, and a general reduction in the size of teeth, face, and jaws.

◎ Trends in Hominid Evolution

Expansion of the Brain

The australopithecines had relatively small cranial capacities, about 380–530 cubic centimeters (cc)—not much larger than that of chimpanzees. But around 2.3 million years ago, close to the time that patterned stone tools first appeared, some hominids show evidence of enlarged brain capacity. These hominids, early *Homo*, had cranial capacities averaging about 630–640 cc, which is about 50 percent of the brain capacity of modern humans (which averages slightly more than 1,300 cc). (See Figure 7–4.) A later member of our genus, *Homo erectus*, which may have first appeared about 1.8 million years ago, had a cranial capacity averaging about 895–1,040 cc, or about 70 percent of the brain capacity of modern humans.[24]

The australopithecines were small, and the earliest *Homo* finds were hardly bigger, so much of the increase in brain size over time might have been a result of later hominids' bigger bodies. When we correct for body size, however, it turns out that brain size increased not only absolutely but also relatively after 2 million years ago. Between about 4 million and 2 million years ago, relative brain size remained just about the same. Only in the last 2 million years has the hominid brain doubled in relative size and tripled in absolute size.[25]

What may have favored the increase in brain size? As we noted earlier, many anthropologists think that the increase is linked to the emergence of stone toolmaking about 2.5 million years ago. The reasoning is that stone toolmaking was important for the survival of our ancestors, and therefore natural selection would have favored bigger-brained individuals because they had motor and conceptual skills that enabled them to be better toolmakers. According to this view, the expansion of the brain and more sophisticated toolmaking would have developed together. Other anthropologists think that the expansion of the brain may have been favored by other factors, such as warfare, hunting, longer life, and language.[26] Whatever the factors favoring bigger brains, they also provided humans with an expanded capacity for culture. Thus, along with bipedalism, the expansion of the brain marks a watershed in human evolution.

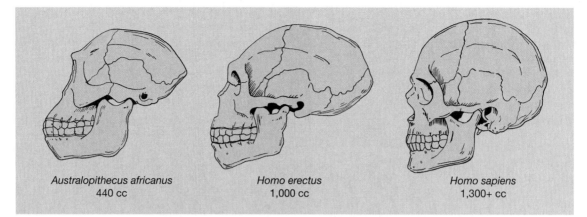

Australopithecus africanus
440 cc

Homo erectus
1,000 cc

Homo sapiens
1,300+ cc

Figure 7–4 Comparison of the estimated cranial capacities of *Australopithecus africanus, Homo erectus,* and *Homo sapiens,* demonstrating the expansion of the brain in hominid evolution.

Source: Estimated cranial capacities from Ian Tattersall, Eric Delson, and John van Couvering, eds., *Encyclopedia of Human Evolution and Prehistory.* Reproduced by permission of Routledge, Inc., part of The Taylor & Francis Group.

As the hominid brain expanded, natural selection also favored the widening of the female pelvis to allow larger-brained babies to be born. But there was probably a limit to how far the pelvis could widen and still be adapted to bipedalism. Something had to give, and that something was the degree of physical development of the human infant at birth—for instance, the human infant is born with cranial bones so plastic that they can overlap. Because birth takes place before the cranial bones have hardened, the human infant with its relatively large brain can pass through the opening in the mother's pelvis. Human infants are born at a relatively early stage of development, and are wholly dependent on their parents for many years. As we have noted, this lengthy period of infant dependency may have been an important factor in the evolution of culture.

Reduction of the Face, Teeth, and Jaws

As in the case of the brain, substantial changes in the face, teeth, and jaws do not appear in hominid evolution until after about 2 million years ago. The australopithecines all have cheek teeth that are very large relative to their estimated body weight, perhaps because the diet of the australopithecines was especially high in plant foods,[27] including small, tough objects such as seeds, nuts, and tubers. The australopithecines have thick jawbones, probably also related

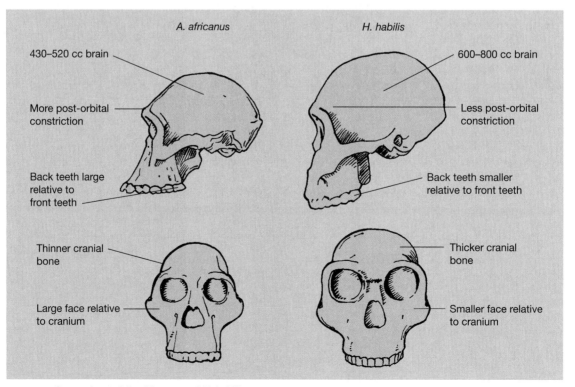

A. africanus

H. habilis

430–520 cc brain

600–800 cc brain

More post-orbital constriction

Less post-orbital constriction

Back teeth large relative to front teeth

Back teeth smaller relative to front teeth

Thinner cranial bone

Thicker cranial bone

Large face relative to cranium

Smaller face relative to cranium

Figure 7–5 Comparison of *A. africanus* and *H. habilis*

to their chewing needs. The australopithecines have relatively large faces that project forward below the eyes. But when we get to the *Homo* forms, we see reduction in the size of the face, cheek teeth, and jaws (see Figure 7–5). It would seem that natural selection in favor of a bigger and stronger chewing apparatus was relaxed. One reason might be that members of the *Homo* genus started to eat foods that were easier to chew. Such foods might have included roots, fruits, and meat. As we discuss later, it may have been the development of habitual tool use and the control of fire that allowed members of the *Homo* genus to change their diet to include easier to chew foods, including meat. If food is cooked and easy to chew, individual humans with smaller jaws and teeth would not be disadvantaged, and therefore the face, cheek teeth, and jaw would get smaller on average over time.[28]

The expansion of the brain and reduction of the face occurred at about the same time, and were probably related. A recent discovery in human genetics appears to provide direct evidence of a connection. Researchers studying muscle diseases in modern humans discovered that humans have a unique myosin gene called MYH16 (myosin is a protein in muscle tissue) that is only present in jaw muscles. Comparing MYH16 to related genes in primates, the researchers determined that MYH16 evolved about 2.4 million years ago—around the time the brain began to enlarge and the face and jaw began to shrink. So, the expansion of the brain appears to have been aided by a mutation in myosin that caused jaw muscles to shrink.[29]

Other Evolved Traits

The fossil evidence, which we discuss below and in the next chapter, suggests when, and in which hominids, changes occurred in brain size and in the face, teeth, and jaws. Other changes in the evolution of hominids cannot yet be confidently dated with regard to time and particular hominid. For example, we know that modern humans are relatively hairless compared with the other surviving primates. But we do not know when hominids became relatively hairless, because fossilized bones do not tell us whether their owners were hairy. On the other hand, we suspect that most of the other characteristically human traits developed after the brain began to increase in size, during the evolution of the genus *Homo*.

What is the evidence that the physical and behavioral changes we have been discussing occurred during the evolution of the *Homo* genus? We shall now consider the earliest *Homo* fossils and how they are associated with brain expansion and the reduction of the face, jaws, and teeth.

 Early *Homo*

Hominids with a brain absolutely and relatively larger than that of the australopithecines appear about 2.3 million years ago. These hominids, classified in our own genus, *Homo,* are generally divided into two species: **Homo habilis** and **Homo rudolfensis.** Both are known primarily from the western parts of Kenya and Tanzania, but remains have been found elsewhere in eastern and southern Africa, including the Omo

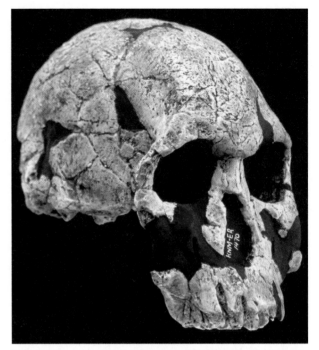

The skull of a Homo habilis/rudolfensis (ER-1470) found by Richard Leakey in 1972. Note its high forehead and large braincase.

Basin of Ethiopia and Sterkfontein cave in South Africa. Both lived in the same place and time as the robust australopithecine, *Australopithecus boisei,* and may later have lived at the same time as *Homo erectus.*

Homo habilis appears to be the earlier of these two species, appearing around 2.3 million years ago. Compared with the australopithecines, *H. habilis* had a significantly larger brain, averaging 630–640 cc,[30] and reduced molars and premolars.[31] The rest of the skeleton is reminiscent of the australopithecines, including the presence of powerful hands and relatively long arms, suggesting that *H. habilis* was at least partially arboreal. *H. habilis* may also have been sexually dimorphic like the australopithecines, as individuals seem to have greatly differed in size.

Homo rudolfensis is roughly contemporary with *Homo habilis,* and shares many of its features. Indeed, many paleoanthropologists make no distinction between the two species, putting *H. rudolfensis* into *H. habilis*. Those who do see them as distinct species point to the larger and more thickly enameled cheek teeth of *H. rudolfensis,* its flatter and broader face, and its more modernlike limb proportions. Even with its larger teeth and broader face, the dentition of *H. rudolfensis* is considerably reduced over the australopithecines and, as in *H. habilis,* its brain is at least a third larger.

We have little postcranial skeletal material for either early *Homo* species, so it is impossible to tell whether the female pelvis had changed. But, with brains averaging a third larger than the australopithecines', it seems likely that some modifications must have developed to allow bigger-brained babies to be born. We do know that changes in the female pelvis to accommodate bigger-brained babies can be seen in *Homo erectus,* and it is this species that we turn to next.

Homo erectus

Homo erectus evolved very shortly after *Homo habilis,* probably about 1.8 million years ago. **Homo erectus** was the first hominid species to be widely distributed in the Old World. Examples of *H. erectus* were found first in Java, later in China, and still later in Africa (see the box "The First Migrants"). Most paleoanthropologists agree that some human ancestor moved from Africa to Asia at some point. Until recently, it was assumed that it was *H. erectus* who moved, because *H. erectus* lived in East Africa about 1.6 million years ago but not until after about 1 million years ago in Asia.[32] Recent redating, however, suggests that *H. erectus* in Java may be somewhat older, dating to perhaps 1.8 million years ago.[33] And new *H. erectus* fossils from Dmanisi, in the southeastern European nation of Georgia, have recently been dated to at least 1.7 million years ago.[34] If this last dating is accurate, early hominids may have moved out of Africa earlier. Indeed, one well-preserved skull found at Dmanisi in 2001 has some features that are reminiscent of *H. habilis*—a brain only about 600 cc, relatively large canines, and a relatively thin browridge.[35] While the excavators classify the skull as *H. erectus,* it does make one wonder whether *H. habilis* or transitional *habilis-erectus* individuals were the first to leave Africa.

There is also the question of whether there is only one species *of H. erectus* or whether *H. erectus* contains several distinct species. Some scholars see enough differences between Asian and African populations of *H. erectus* to argue that they should be separated into two distinct species, *Homo erectus* for the Asian populations and *Homo ergaster* for the African ones. Furthermore, *Homo erectus* (or *Homo ergaster*) fossils are also found in Europe. But some paleoanthropologists think that the finds in Europe typically classified as *H. erectus* are actually early examples of *H. sapiens.*[36] Others think that the European fossils and similar ones found in southern Africa and the Near East should be grouped into a distinct species, *Homo heidelbergensis.* There is also *Homo floresiensis,* a diminutive hominid that appears to be a miniature form of *Homo erectus* that evolved only on the isolated island of Flores, Indonesia. It is all a bit confusing. Later we will try to sort it all out.

The Discovery of *Homo erectus*

In 1891, Eugene Dubois, a Dutch anatomist digging in Java, found what he called *Pithecanthropus erectus,* meaning "erect ape man." (We now refer to this hominid as *Homo erectus.*) The discovery was not the first humanlike fossil found; Neandertals, which we discuss in the next chapter, were known many years earlier. But no one was certain, not even Dubois himself, whether the fossil he found in Java was an ape or a human.

The actual find consisted of a cranium and a thighbone. For many years it was thought that the fragments were not even from the same animal. The skull was too large to be that of a modern ape but was smaller than that of an average human, having a cranial capacity between the average ape's 500 cc and the average modern human's 1,300 cc. The thighbone, however, matched that of a modern human. Did the two fragments in fact belong together? The question was resolved many years later by fluorine analysis. If fossils from the same deposit contain the same amount of fluorine, they are the same age. The skull fragment and thighbone found by Dubois were tested for fluorine content and found to be the same age.

A discovery by G. H. R. von Koenigswald in the mid-1930s, also in Java, not only confirmed Dubois's earlier speculations and extended our knowledge of the physical characteristics of *Homo erectus* but also gave us a better understanding of this early human's place in time. Since then, many more *H. erectus* fossils have been found in Java. These *H. erectus* in Java were thought not to be more than 1 million years old.[37] Now argon–argon dating puts some of the Java specimens back to perhaps 1.8 million years ago.[38]

Between the times of Dubois's and von Koenigswald's discoveries, Davidson Black, a Canadian anatomy professor teaching in Peking (Beijing), China, set out to investigate a large cave at nearby Zhoukoudian where a fossilized tooth had been found. Confident that the tooth came from a hitherto unknown hominid genus, he obtained funds to excavate the area extensively. After two years of excavation, he and his colleagues found a skull in limestone, which they dubbed "Peking Man." Black died in 1934, and his work was carried on by Franz Weidenreich.

It was not until the 1950s that *H. erectus* fossils were uncovered in northern Africa (see Figure 7–6). Many finds since then have come from East Africa, particularly two sites—Olduvai Gorge in Tanzania and the Lake Turkana region of Kenya. An almost complete skeleton of a boy was found at Nariokotome, on the western side of Lake Turkana, dating from about 1.6 million years ago. The Olduvai finds are from about 1.2 million years ago.[39]

Physical Characteristics of *Homo erectus*

The *Homo erectus* skull generally was long, low, and thickly walled, with a flat frontal area and prominent brow ridges. It had a unique pentagonal shape when looked at from the back, formed in part by a rounded ridge, called a **sagittal keel,** running along the crest of the skull. There was also a ridge of bone running horizontally along the back of the skull, called an **occipital torus,** which added to the skull's overall long shape (see Figure 7–7).[40]

Compared with early *Homo, H. erectus* had relatively small teeth. *H. erectus* was the first hominid to have third molars that were smaller than the second or first molars, as in modern humans. The molars also had an enlarged pulp cavity, called **taurodontism,** which may have allowed the teeth to withstand harder use and wear than the teeth of modern humans. But the *H. erectus* jaw was lighter and thinner than in either early *Homo* or the australopithecines, and the face was less **prognathic,** or forward thrusting, in the upper and lower jaw.

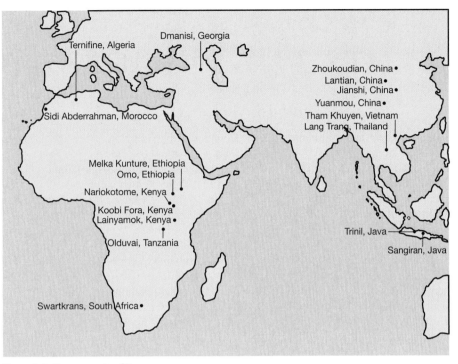

Figure 7–6 *Homo erectus* Sites

Source: From Russell L. Ciochon and John G. Fleagle, eds., *The Human Evolution Source Book.* Copyright © 1993. Reprinted by permission of Pearson Education, Inc., Upper Saddle River, NJ 07458.

The brain, averaging 895–1,040 cc, was larger than that found in any of the australopithecines or early *Homo* species, but smaller than the average brain of a modern human.[41] Endocasts, which provide a picture of the surface of the brain, suggest that it was organized more like the brain of modern humans than like that of australopithecines.

Homo erectus had a prominent, projecting nose, in contrast to the australopithecines' flat, nonprojecting nose.[42]

From the neck down, *H. erectus* was practically indistinguishable from *H. sapiens.* In contrast to the smaller australopithecines and early *Homo* species who lived in East Africa around the same time, *H. erectus* was comparable to modern humans in size. The almost complete skeleton of the boy at Nariokotome suggests that he was about five and a half feet tall and about 11 years of age when he died; researchers estimate that he would have been over six feet tall had he lived to maturity. About 1.6 million years ago, the Nariokotome region was probably open grassland, with trees mostly along rivers.[43] *Homo erectus* in East Africa was similar in size to Africans today who live in a similarly open, dry environment.[44] *H. erectus* was also less sexually dimorphic than either the australopithecines or early *Homo.* The degree of sexual dimorphism in *H. erectus* was comparable to that in modern humans.

Those scholars who group the African populations into a distinct species, *Homo ergaster,* point to several differences between them and other *Homo erectus* populations: The cranial proportions differ in *Homo ergaster;* the brow ridge is thinner and is arched above each of the eye sockets; the eye sockets are more rounded; and the face is oriented more vertically below the skull, among others. On the other hand, some scholars believe that the differences between *Homo erectus* and modern humans are not large enough to be identified as different species, and argue that *Homo erectus* populations should be lumped into *Homo sapiens.*[45] These arguments will not be settled any time soon, and for the purposes of this book we will stick with the single taxon, *Homo erectus.*

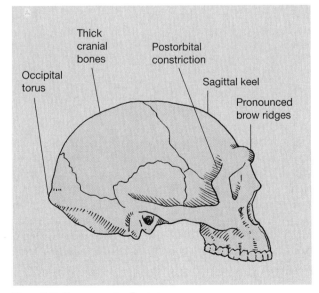

Figure 7–7 *Homo erectus* Features

MIGRANTS AND IMMIGRANTS

The First Migrants

Hominids evolved in Africa, yet today hominids are found on every continent. Who were the first hominids to leave Africa, and when did they first leave? For many years the clear answer was that *Homo erectus* were the first to leave Africa, and they did so perhaps 700,000 to 1 million years ago. In recent years new findings and sources of evidence have led scholars to question this established answer.

The first new information came from geochemist Carl Swisher, who in the mid-1990s redated the Java sites where *Homo erectus* fossils had been found and determined they dated to perhaps 1.8 million years ago. Since the earliest *H. erectus* fossils in Africa share a similar date, this created a problem—how did *H. erectus* appear in Java at about the same time they appeared in Africa? As this question was being pondered, a remarkable set of new *H. erectus* fossils were being uncovered in Dimanisi, Georgia. Dated at 1.7 million years ago, these fossils made it clear that *H. erectus* left Africa almost as soon as they had evolved. The discovery of a *Homo habilis*-like fossil at Dimanisi, and of Oldowan-like tools at Riwat, Pakistan and Loggupo, China, suggested that *H. habilis* may have been the first to leave Africa and *H. erectus* followed a path their predecessors blazed. If they were following an earlier migration, it could explain how *H. erectus* were able to move so quickly across Asia.

A more unusual source of information on when hominids first left Africa comes from the parasites that accompanied them. All hominoids are plagued by lice, but humans host a distinct species, *Pediculus humanus*. Geneticist David Reed and his colleagues found that *P. humanus* diverged from other lice about 5.6 million years ago—about the time the first hominids appeared. More interesting, however, Reed and colleagues discovered that there are two subspecies of *P. humanus* that appear to have diverged about 1.2 million years ago. One subspecies is found worldwide today, the other is restricted to the New World. Reed and colleagues suggest this is evidence that at least some hominid migrants (probably *H. erectus*) became isolated in Asia by at least 1.2 million years ago, where their lice diverged from that of other hominid populations, only to be picked up much later by modern human migrants who ended up colonizing the New World.

So, who were the first hominid migrants? They may have been *H. habilis,* or they may have been very early *H. erectus*. When did the first hominid migrations out of Africa take place? Probably slightly less than 2 million years ago, but once these hominids left, they moved quickly, and they moved long distances. By 1.6 million years ago *H. erectus* was in both western and southern Asia, and by 1.2 million years ago their populations had moved far enough to have become isolated from one another. Whether or not they were the first migrants out of Africa, *H. erectus* migrated fast, far, and for life.

Sources: D. Reed, V. Smith, S. Hammond, A. Rogers, and D. Clayton, "Genetic Analysis of Lice Supports Direct Contact Between Modern and Archaic Humans," *PLoS Biology* 2 (November 2004): 1972–83; I. Tattersall, "Out of Africa Again. . .and Again?" *Scientific American* 276 (April 1997): 60–68.

Homo floresiensis

Whether or not there are distinct African and Asian species of *Homo erectus,* most scholars agree that **Homo floresiensis** is a distinct species that is closely related to *Homo erectus*. *H. floresiensis* has only been found on the Indonesian island of Flores, and only a handful of individuals have been located to date. All are tiny (they stood perhaps three feet tall), and have very small brains, on the order of 380 cc.[46] The structure of the brain, however, seems closely related to that of *H. erectus,* as do the structures of the skull.[47] In other words, *H. floresiensis* appears to be a tiny version of *H. erectus. H. floresiensis* even made tools that look similar to those made by *H. erectus,* and in some cases the tools look even more sophisticated. So, although they were small in stature

and had very small brains, *H. floresiensis* seems to have been culturally and intellectually similar to *H. erectus*.[48]

How might a miniature version of *H. erectus* have evolved? The answer is that both dwarfism and gigantism are common phenomena in isolated populations. Dwarfism appears to be an adaptation that occurs when there are few predators—a species in isolation can become smaller, and have a large population, if there are no predators threatening them. This may be what happened on Flores.[49] It is interesting that the island also hosted a number of dwarf species in addition to *H. floresiensis,* including a dwarf elephant that appears to have been one of the favorite foods of *H. floresiensis*. Perhaps even more interesting is the fact that *H. floresiensis* may have survived until as recently as 12,000 years ago—well into

The skull of the *Homo erectus/ergaster* boy found at Nariokotome, Kenya. Though an adolescent when he died, he already stood five and a half feet tall.

the time period when modern humans were living on in Indonesia. Could modern humans and the tiny *H. foresiensis* have met some time in the distant past? It is an intriguing possibility, but there is no evidence to tell us.

The Evolution of *Homo erectus*

The evolution of *Homo erectus* reflects a continuation of the general evolutionary trends we discussed previously. The brain continued to expand, increasing more than a third over early *Homo* (just as early *Homo* had increased more than a third over the australopithecines). The face, teeth, and jaws continued to shrink, taking on an almost modern form. An increasing use and variety of tools may have led to a further development of the brain. *Homo erectus* was eating and probably cooking meat, and this may have led to further reduction in the teeth and jaws.

One additional change in *Homo erectus* is an apparent reduction in the extent of sexual dimorphism to almost modern levels. Recall that the australopithecines and early *Homo* were quite sexually dimorphic. *Homo erectus* does not appear to be as sexually dimorphic as these earlier hominids. What might have caused this change? In other primates, sexual dimorphism appears to be linked to social systems in which males are at the top of dominance hierarchies and dominant males control sexual access to multiple females. In contrast, lack of sexual dimorphism seems most pronounced in the animals where *pair bonding* exists—that is, where one male and one female form a breeding pair that lasts for a long period of time.[50] Could pair bonding have developed in *Homo erectus?* It seems possible.

Recall that early *Homo* may have established some of the basic elements of human culture, including home bases or meeting places, family groups, and sharing. Another basic element of recent human culture, one that is present in all known cultures, is *marriage.* Marriage is a socially recognized sexual and economic bond between two individuals that is intended to continue throughout the lifetimes of the individuals and to produce socially accepted children. It is a pair bond with a set of behaviors, expectations, and obligations that extend beyond the pair to those individuals'

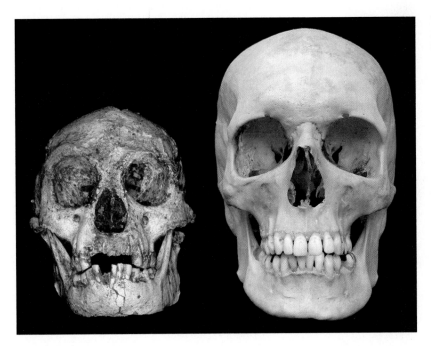

The skull of the dwarf species *Homo floriensis* next to that of a modern human. Note how small it is in comparison.

families. With marriage, then, the competition between males for access to females may have diminished, lessening the importance of sexual dimorphism. But why might marriage have developed in *Homo erectus*?

In animal species where females can feed themselves and their babies after birth, pair bonding is rare. But in species where females cannot feed both themselves and their babies, pair bonding is common. Why? We think it is because a pair bond provides the best solution to the problem of incompatibility between a mother's feeding requirements and tending a newborn baby. A male partner can bring food and/or watch the newborn while the mother gets food.[51] But most primates lack pair bonding. This may be because primate infants are able to cling to their mother's fur soon after birth, so that the mother's hands are free to forage. Human infants demonstrate a residual form of this innate ability to cling during their first few weeks of life. This is called the *Moro reflex*. If a human infant feels it is falling backward, it will automatically stretch out its arms and clench its fists.[52]

We have no way of knowing if *Homo erectus* had fur like other primates, but we think probably not because, as we discuss below, we think they may have worn clothing. The brain in *Homo erectus* may also have already expanded enough that *Homo erectus* infants, like modern human infants, could not adequately support their heads even if they could hold onto their mother's fur. In any case, when early hominids began to depend on scavenging and hunting for

This orangutan mother has no problem traveling with her infant, as it can cling tightly to her fur. *Homo erectus* mothers probably had no fur to hold on to and had to carry their infants.

food (and for skins to be used in clothing), it would have been difficult and hazardous for a parent with a newborn baby to engage in these activities with a baby along. Marriage would have been an effective solution to this problem because each parent could help protect the baby while the other was away getting food. (For further discussion of this theory, see the chapter on marriage.)

Another important aspect of the evolution of *Homo erectus* was the movement of populations out of eastern and southern Africa. As with the lessening of sexual dimorphism, it seems likely that cultural innovations were the key to allowing *Homo erectus* to move into new environments. Why? Because upon entering new environments *Homo erectus* would have been faced with new (and generally colder) climatic conditions, new and different sources of raw material for tools, and new plants and animals to rely on for food. All animals adapt to such changes through natural selection, but natural selection typically takes a relatively long time and requires physical changes in the adapting organisms. *Homo erectus* was able to adapt to new environments very quickly and without apparent physical changes. This suggests that the primary mechanisms of adaptation for *Homo erectus* were cultural rather than biological.

What cultural adaptations might *Homo erectus* have made? Fire might have been the crucial cultural adaptation to colder climates. As we discuss below, there is tantalizing evidence that *Homo erectus* used fire. But fire can only warm people when they are stationary; it doesn't help when people are out collecting food. To be mobile in colder climates, *Homo erectus* may have begun to wear animal furs for warmth. Some *Homo erectus* tools look like the hide-processing tools used by more recent human groups,[53] and it seems unlikely that *Homo erectus* could have survived in the colder locations where they have been found, in eastern Europe and Asia, without some form of clothing. And if *Homo erectus* was wearing furs for warmth, they must have been hunting. *Homo erectus* could not have depended on scavenging to acquire skins—the skin is the first thing predators destroy when they dismember a carcass. *Homo erectus* needing skins would have had to kill fur-bearing animals themselves if they wanted intact skins and furs for clothing.

As we mentioned earlier, fossil remains themselves cannot provide evidence for whether or not *H. erectus* was hairless. But scientists have found that the genes of modern peoples may offer clues to when our ancestors became hairless. For example, one of the primary genes responsible for hair and skin color, called MC1R, demonstrates uniformity among modern dark-skinned African populations, but diversity among non-Africans. Alan Rogers and colleagues have recently argued that the uniformity in this gene among Africans demonstrates recent, powerful selective pressure in favor of darker skin, and that protection against the tropical sun after the loss of body hair is the likely reason. When did this selective pressure start? Rogers and colleagues estimate it was at least 1.2 million years ago.[54]

It is interesting to consider that in eastern Africa *Homo erectus* coexisted with at least one other species of hominid (*A. boisei*), and possibly with as many as three others (*A. boi-*

sei, A. africanus, and *H. habilis/rudolfensis*). Why did *Homo erectus* survive and flourish while these other species went extinct? Again, culture may be the answer. *A. boisei* seems to have been a specialized grasslands species. Their large molars and powerful dental architecture would have allowed them to eat hard grass seeds and other coarse materials that other hominids could not chew. However, they had to compete with the many other grassland animals that also relied on these plants, but reproduced faster and had speed to help them escape from predators. Early *Homo* was apparently a tool user and relied at least in part on scavenging and hunting, but compared to *Homo erectus,* early *Homo* technology was crude and early *Homo* populations may not have been as well organized to scavenge and hunt and to defend themselves against predators. These differences in culture may have provided advantages to *Homo erectus* that drove early *Homo* to extinction.

This scenario, just like the one we suggested for the evolution of early *Homo,* is a "just-so" story that may or may not be true. But it does fit the facts we now have about *Homo erectus* and the area in which it evolved. Regardless of this story's particular details, there seems no doubt that the development of a more complex culture was vital to the evolution of *Homo erectus.*

 ## Lower Paleolithic Cultures

The stone tool traditions of *Homo erectus* are traditionally called **Lower Paleolithic.** These stone tool traditions involve "core" tool techniques, in which a core of stone, rather than a flake, is used as the basic raw material for finished tools (we will talk more about Lower Paleolithic stone tool technology later). Since stone tools are the most common cultural material in the archaeological record of these ancient peoples, the entire culture of *Homo erectus* is often termed *Lower Paleolithic,* a practice we follow here.

The archaeological finds of tools and other cultural artifacts dating from 1.5 million years to about 200,000 years ago are assumed to have been produced by *Homo erectus.* But hominid fossils are not usually associated with these materials. Therefore it is possible that some of the tools during this period were produced by hominids other than *H. erectus,* such as australopithecines earlier and *H. sapiens* later. But the so-called *Acheulian* tool assemblages dating from 1.5 million years ago to more than a million years later are very similar to each other, and *H. erectus* is the only hominid that spans the entire period. Thus it is conventionally assumed that *H. erectus* was responsible for most if not all of the Acheulian tool assemblages we describe below.[55]

The Acheulian Tool Tradition

The stone toolmaking tradition known as the **Acheulian** was named after the site at St. Acheul, France, where the first examples were found. But the oldest Acheulian tools recovered are from East Africa, on the Peninj River, Tanzania, dating back about 1.5 million years.[56] In contrast to Oldowan, Acheulian assemblages have more large tools created according to standardized designs or shapes. Oldowan tools have sharp edges made by a few blows. Acheulian toolmakers shaped the stone by knocking more flakes off most of the edges. Many of these tools were made from very large flakes that had first been struck from very large cores or boulders.

One of the most characteristic and common tools in the Acheulian tool kit is the so-called **hand axe,** which is a teardrop-shaped, bifacially flaked tool with a thinned sharp tip. Other large tools resemble cleavers and picks. There were also many kinds of flake tools, such as scrapers with a wide edge.

Early Acheulian tools appeared to have been made by blows with a hard stone, but later tools are wider and flatter and may have been made with a **soft hammer** of bone or antler.[57] This soft hammer technique of making stone tools was an important innovation. Tools made by a **hard hammer** technique, rock against rock, have limits in terms of their sharpness and form, because only large and thick flakes can be made with a hard hammer technique (unless the flintknapper is very skillful and the stone being used has unique qualities). Flakes created by soft hammer flaking are much thinner and longer than hard hammer flakes, and the flintknapper generally has better control over their size and shape. This means that thinner and sharper tools can be made, as well as tools with complex shapes. Hand axes can be made with either technique, as their shape is simple, but those made using a soft hammer have much thinner and sharper edges.[58]

Were hand axes made for chopping trees, as their name suggests? We cannot be sure what they were used for, but experiments with them suggest that they are not good for cutting trees; they seem more suited for butchering large animals.[59] Lawrence Keeley microscopically examined some Acheulian hand axes, and the wear on them is more consistent with animal butchery. They may also have been used for woodworking, particularly hollowing and shaping wood, and they are also good for digging.[60] William Calvin has even suggested that a hand axe could be used as a projectile thrown like a discus into a herd of animals in the hope of injuring or killing an animal.[61]

Acheulian tools are found widely in Africa, Europe, and western Asia, but bifacial hand axes, cleavers, and picks are not found as commonly in eastern and southeastern Asia.[62] Because *H. erectus* has been found in all areas of the Old World, it is puzzling that the tool traditions seem to differ from west to east. Some archaeologists have suggested that large bifacial tools may be lacking in eastern and southeastern Asia because *H. erectus* in Asia had a better material to make tools out of—bamboo. Bamboo has been used recently in Southeast Asia for many purposes, including incredibly sharp arrows and sticks for digging and cutting. Geoffrey Pope has shown that bamboo is found precisely in those areas of Asia where hand axes and other large bifacial tools are largely missing.[63]

Big-Game Eating

Some of the Acheulian sites have produced evidence of big-game eating. F. Clark Howell, who excavated sites at Torralba and Ambrona, Spain, found a substantial number of elephant remains and unmistakable evidence of human presence in the form of tools. Howell suggests that the humans at those sites used fire to frighten elephants into muddy bogs from which they would be unable to escape.[64] To hunt elephants in this way, the humans would have had to plan and work cooperatively in fairly large groups.

But do these finds of bones of large and medium-sized animals, in association with tools, tell us that the humans definitely were big-game hunters? Some archaeologists who have reanalyzed the evidence from Torralba think that the big game may have been scavenged. Because the Torralba and Ambrona sites are near ancient streams, many of the elephants could have died naturally, their bones accumulating in certain spots because of the flow of water.[65] What seems fairly clear is that the humans did deliberately butcher different kinds of game—different types of tools are found with different types of animals.[66] Thus, whether the humans hunted big game at Torralba and Ambrona is debatable; all we can be sure of, as of now, is that they consumed big game and probably hunted smaller game.

Control of Fire

One way in which *H. erectus* is thought to have hunted is by using *fire drives*—a technique still used by hunting and gathering peoples in recent times. It is highly effective: Animals are driven out of their hiding places and homes by fire and dispatched by hunters positioned downwind of the oncoming flames. Most peoples who use this technique today set fires deliberately, but fires caused by lightning strikes may have also been utilized. Did *H. erectus* set these fires? Because *H. erectus* was the first hominid to be found throughout the Old World and in areas with freezing winters, most anthropologists presume that *H. erectus* had learned to control fire, at least for warmth. There is archaeological evidence of fire in some early sites, but fires can be natural events. Thus, whether fire was under deliberate control by *H. erectus* is not definitely established.[67]

Suggestive but not conclusive evidence of the deliberate use of fire comes from Kenya in East Africa and is over 1.4 million years old.[68] More persuasive evidence of human control of fire, dating from nearly 800,000 years ago, comes from the site of Gesher Benot Ya'aqov in Israel. Here researchers found evidence of burned seeds, wood, and stone, as well as concentrations of burned items suggestive of hearths.[69] Evidence of the deliberate use of fire comes from Europe somewhat later. Unfortunately, the evidence of control of fire at Gesher Benot Ya'aqov and European sites is not associated with *H. erectus* fossils, so the link between deliberate use of fire and *H. erectus* cannot definitely be established yet.[70] The lack of clear evidence does not, of course, mean that *H. erectus* did not use fire. After all, *H. erectus* did move into cold areas of the world, and it is hard to imagine how that could have happened without the deliberate use of fire. Such a move is also hard to imagine if *H. erectus* were relatively hairless and did not get warm skins and furs from hunting.

Clothing, therefore, may have been necessary, but fire might have been even more important, and not only for warmth. Cooking would be possible. The control of fire was a major step in increasing the energy under human control. Cooking would have made all kinds of food (not just meat) more safely digestible and therefore more usable.[71] Fires would also have kept predators away, a not inconsiderable advantage given that there were many.

Campsites

Acheulian sites were usually located close to water sources, lush vegetation, and large stocks of herbivorous animals. Some camps have been found in caves, but most were in open areas surrounded by rudimentary fortifications or windbreaks. Several African sites are marked by stony rubble brought there by *H. erectus,* possibly for the dual purpose of securing the windbreaks and providing ammunition in case of a sudden attack.[72]

Homo erectus ate—and probably hunted—large game animals, and they probably also learned to control fire.

The presumed base campsites display a wide variety of tools, indicating that the camp was the center of many group functions. More specialized sites away from camp have also been found. These are marked by the predominance of a particular type of tool. For example, a butchering site in Tanzania contained dismembered hippopotamus carcasses and rare heavy-duty smashing and cutting tools. Workshops are another kind of specialized site encountered with some regularity. They are characterized by tool debris and are located close to a source of natural stone suitable for toolmaking.[73]

A camp has been excavated at the Terra Amata site near Nice, on the French Riviera. The camp appears to have been occupied in the late spring or early summer, judging by the pollen found in fossilized human feces. The excavator describes stake holes driven into the sand, paralleled by lines of stones, presumably marking the spots where the people constructed huts of roughly 30 by 15 feet (Figure 7–8). A basic feature of each hut was a central hearth that seems to have been protected from drafts by a small wall built just outside the northeast corner of the hearth. The evidence suggests that the Terra Amata occupants gathered seafood such as oysters and mussels, did some fishing, and hunted in the surrounding area. The animal remains suggest that they obtained both small and large animals but mostly got the young of larger animals such as stags, elephants, boars, rhinoceroses, and wild oxen. Some of the huts contain recognizable toolmakers' areas, scattered with tool debris; occasionally, the impression of an animal skin shows where the toolmaker actually sat.[74]

Religion and Ritual

Thus far we have discussed the lifestyles of Lower Paleolithic and, in the last chapter, of late Pliocene peoples, but we have not talked about the less material aspects of life, such as religion and ritual. What beliefs did *Homo erectus* hold about the world around them? Did they take part in rituals? Did *H. erectus* have religion? The data we have to answer these questions are limited, but there are some hints that ritual and religion may have been a part of Lower Paleolithic culture.

Remains of *red ochre* (oxidized clay) have been found on a number of Lower Paleolithic sites.[75] This may be significant because in many later cultures, even modern ones, red ochre has been used in rituals of various types to represent blood or, more generally, life. Ochre seems to be particularly important in burial rituals, and human remains sprinkled with red ochre have been found in many parts of the world and dating as far back as the Middle Paleolithic (about 200,000 years ago). However, there is no evidence that *Homo erectus* buried their dead, nor any evidence that ochre was used in rituals. It may have been used for body decoration, or simply for protection against insects or sunburn.

More significant, and even more controversial, is the suggestion made by the excavators of Zhoukoudian (in northern China) that some of the *H. erectus* remains there showed evidence of ritual cannibalism.[76] The foramen magnum of some specimens had been deliberately enlarged and the facial bones had been deliberately broken away from the

Figure 7–8 A Reconstruction of the Oval Huts Built at Terra Amata
These huts were approximately 30 feet by 15 feet.

Source: Copyright © 1969 by Eric Mose.

cranium on others. A possible reason may have been to remove the brain for ritual consumption. Ritual cannibalism has been widely reported among living peoples, so its presence among ancient peoples is not impossible. But scholars point out that the parts of the skull that seem to have been purposely enlarged (to remove the brain) are those that are also the weakest points on the skull, and may have broken away because of decay or disturbance over the millennia.

At this point, we simply cannot say whether religion and ritual were parts of Lower Paleolithic culture.

◎ Summary

1. The earliest identifiable stone tools found so far come from various sites in East Africa and date from about 2.5 million years ago. Flake tools predominate, but choppers are also common. Choppers are cores that have been partially flaked and have a side that might have been used for chopping. These early stone tools are referred to as Oldowan.

2. Archaeologists have experimented with what can be done with Oldowan tools. The flakes appear to be very versatile; they can be used for slitting the hides of animals, dismembering animals, and whittling wood. The choppers can be used to hack off branches or cut and chop tough animal joints. Hominids shortly after 2 million years ago were cutting up animal carcasses for meat, mostly obtained through scavenging rather than hunting.

3. There are archaeological sites dating as early as 2 million years ago that contain concentrations of stone tools and animal bones. Some scholars think these might have been early hominid home bases, others do not. If these sites were not home bases, what were they? Some archaeologists are beginning to think that these early sites with many animal bones and tools may just have been places where hominids processed food but did not live.

4. The presence of stone tools and perhaps home bases suggests that early hominids had culture. Culture is a dynamic, adaptive process of learned, shared, and integrated behaviors and ideas.

5. Important physical changes in early hominids that led to the evolution of our genus, *Homo,* include the expansion of the brain, the modification of the female pelvis to allow bigger-brained babies to be born, and the reduction of the face, teeth, and jaws. These physical changes are seen in the species *Homo habilis* and *Homo rudolfensis,* both of which date to around 2.3 million years ago. Early *Homo* appears to have used tools and scavenged or possibly hunted meat, so culture, or the evolution of cultural behavior, seems to have played a role in these physical changes as well.

6. *Homo erectus* emerged about 1.8 million to 1.6 million years ago. It had a larger brain capacity than *Homo habilis* and an essentially modern postcranial skeleton. What differentiates *Homo erectus* most from modern humans is the shape of the skull, which is long, low, and has prominent brow ridges.

7. *Homo erectus* was the first hominid species to be widely distributed in the Old World. Some of the locations where *Homo erectus* lived in eastern Europe and Asia were quite cold, and *Homo erectus* was able to adapt to these new and often colder environments through culture. Some scholars reserve *Homo erectus* for those populations living outside of Africa, and call the African populations *Homo ergaster.* Outside of Africa, there was at least one additional species of hominid, *Homo floresiensis.*

8. Lower Paleolithic tools and other cultural artifacts from about 1.6 million to about 200,000 years ago were probably produced by *H. erectus.* Acheulian is the name given to the most well-known tool tradition of this period. Acheulian tools include both small flake tools and large tools, but hand axes and other large bifacial tools are characteristic.

9. Although it is presumed that *H. erectus* had learned to use fire to survive in areas with cold winters, there is no definite evidence of the control of fire by *H. erectus.* There is evidence in some sites of big-game eating, but whether *H. erectus* hunted those animals is debated. There is little evidence of ritual behavior among *H. erectus.*

◎ Glossary Terms

Acheulian	121	Lower Paleolithic	121
bifacial tool	108	occipital torus	116
culture	111	Oldowan	108
hand axe	121	percussion flaking	107
hard hammer	121	prognathic	116
Homo erectus	116	sagittal keel	116
Homo floresiensis	118	soft hammer	121
Homo habilis	115	taurodontism	116
Homo rudolfensis	115	unifacial tool	108

◎ Critical Questions

1. Why might early hominids have begun to make stone tools? How would stone tools have been more useful than wood or bone tools?

2. How do the physical changes that occur in early hominids correlate with the apparent changes in their behavior?

3. How did *Homo erectus* culture differ from the culture of earlier hominids?

4. When compared to earlier hominids, *Homo erectus* is larger, has a larger brain, and smaller teeth. How might these physical changes correlate with apparent behavioral changes in *Homo erectus?*

5. *Homo erectus* lived in many places in the Old World. What may have enabled them to spread so widely?

◎ Research Navigator

1. Please go to www.researchnavigator.com and enter your LOGIN NAME and PASSWORD. For instructions on registering for the first time, please view the detailed instructions at the end of Chapter 1.

2. The discovery of the dwarf hominid species *Homo floresiensis* is one of the most remarkable in the history of physical anthropology. Go to the *New York Times* or Content Select sections and search using the keyword "floresiensis." Choose a recent article on *Homo floresiensis*. What new findings, controversies, or interpretations of these diminutive hominids are being reported?

◎ Discovering Anthropology: Researchers At Work

Read the chapter by Andrew Kramer titled "The Natural History and Evolutionary Fate of *Homo erectus*" in the accompanying *Discovering Anthropology* reader. Answer the following questions:

1. What is the primary question Kramer attempts to answer in his article? Why is this question important?

2. What methods does Kramer use to determine whether different populations of *H. erectus* were different species?

3. Describe the difference between "lumpers" and "splitters." How might this difference affect the way each group of scholars views human evolution?

CHAPTER EIGHT

The Emergence of *Homo Sapiens*

Recent finds in Africa indicate the presence of *Homo sapiens* perhaps 160,000 years ago (Figure 8–1). Completely modern-looking humans, *Homo sapiens sapiens,* appeared by 50,000 years ago. One paleoanthropologist, Christopher Stringer, characterizes the modern human, *Homo sapiens sapiens,* as having "a domed skull, a chin, small eyebrows, brow ridges, and a rather puny skeleton."[1] Some of us might not like to be called puny, but except for our larger brain, most modern humans definitely are puny compared with *Homo erectus* and even with earlier forms of our own species, *H. sapiens.* We are relatively puny in several respects, including our thinner and lighter bones, as well as our smaller teeth and jaws.

In this chapter we discuss the fossil evidence, as well as the controversies, about the transition from *H. erectus* to modern humans, which may have begun 500,000 years ago. We also discuss what we know archaeologically about the Middle Paleolithic cultures between about 300,000 and 40,000 years ago.

The Transition from *Homo erectus* to *Homo sapiens*

Most paleoanthropologists agree that *H. erectus* evolved into *H. sapiens,* but they disagree about how and where the transition occurred. There is also disagreement about how to classify some fossils from about 500,000 to 200,000 years ago that have a mix of *H. erectus* and *H. sapiens* traits.[2] A particular fossil might be called *H. erectus* by some anthropologists and "archaic" *Homo sapiens* by others. And, as we shall see, still other anthropologists see so much continuity between *H. erectus* and *H. sapiens* that they think it is completely arbitrary to call them different species. According to these anthropologists, *H. erectus* and *H. sapiens* may just be earlier and later varieties of the same species and therefore all should be called *H. sapiens.* (*H. erectus* would then be *H. sapiens erectus.*)

Homo Heidelbergensis

In recent years some scholars have suggested that the "transitional" fossils share common traits and may actually represent a separate species—***Homo heidelbergensis,*** named after a jaw found in 1907 in the village of Mauer near Heidelberg, Germany.[3] Other specimens that have been suggested as members of this species have been found in many parts of the world: Bodo, Hopefield, Ndutu, Elandsfontein, and Rabat in Africa; Bilzingsleben, Petralona, Arago, Steinheim, and Swanscombe in Europe; and Dali and Solo in Asia.

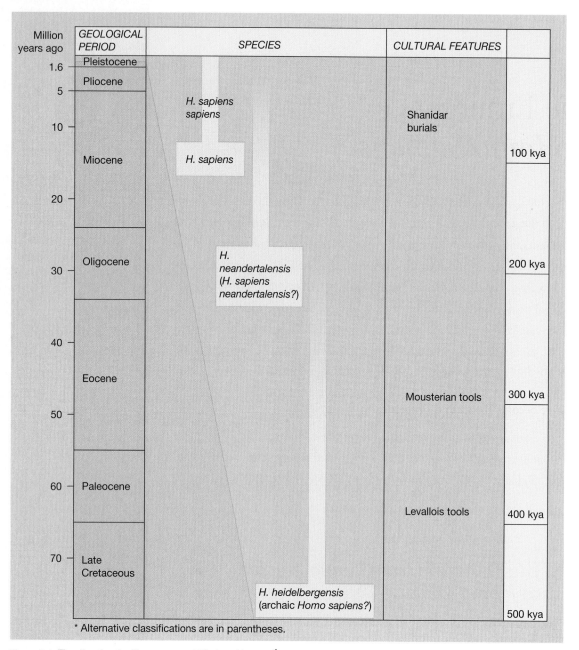

Figure 8–1 Timeline for the Emergence of Modern Humans*

Homo heidelbergensis differs from *Homo erectus* in having smaller teeth and jaws, a much larger brain (on the order of 1,300 cc), a skull that lacks a sagittal keel and occipital torus, a brow ridge that divides into separate arches above each eye, and a more robust skeleton (see Figure 8–2). *Homo heidelbergensis* differs from *Homo sapiens* in retaining a large and prognathic face with relatively large teeth and jaws, a brow ridge, a long, low cranial vault with a sloping forehead, and in its more robust skeleton.[4]

Many scholars question whether *Homo heidelbergensis* represents one or several species of Middle Pleistocene hominid, or whether it is indeed a separate species at all. Many would argue that *Homo heidelbergensis* should be considered an archaic *Homo sapiens*. As noted, some scholars

also argue that *Homo erectus* should be included in the *Homo sapiens* species.

Neandertals: *Homo sapiens* or *Homo neandertalensis?*

There may be disagreement about how to classify the mixed-trait fossils from 500,000 to 200,000 years ago, but recently an outright battle has emerged about many of the fossils that are less than 200,000 years old. Some anthropologists argue that they were definitely *Homo sapiens* and classify them as *Homo sapiens neandertalensis.* Others, that they were part of a distinct species, **Homo neandertalensis,** more commonly referred to as the **Neandertals.** The Neandertals have been

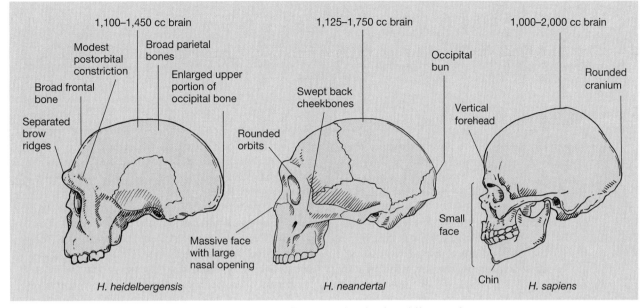

Figure 8–2 Comparison of the crania of *Homo heidelbergensis, Homo neandertalensis,* and *Homo sapiens,* showing important differences.

a confusing hominid fossil group since the first specimen was found in 1856. Somehow through the years, the Neandertals have become the victims of their cartoon image, which usually misrepresents them as burly and more ape than human. Actually, they might go unnoticed in a cross-section of the world's population today. Were they part of our species? For a while the answer seemed to be yes. But recent archaeological and genetic evidence has led most to question the relationship between Neandertals and modern humans, and today the tide seems to have turned against those who would group them together. Let's take a look at some of the history of research on the Neandertals.

In 1856, three years before Darwin's publication of *The Origin of Species,* a skullcap and other fossilized bones were discovered in a cave in the Neander Valley (*tal* is the German word for "valley"), near Düsseldorf, Germany. The fossils in the Neander Valley were the first that scholars could

tentatively consider as an early hominid. (The fossils classified as *Homo erectus* were not found until later in the 19th century, and the fossils belonging to the genus *Australopithecus* not until the 20th century.) After Darwin's revolutionary work was published, the Neandertal find aroused considerable controversy. A few evolutionist scholars, such as Thomas Huxley, thought that the Neandertal was not that different from modern humans. Others dismissed the Neandertal as irrelevant to human evolution; they saw it as a pathological freak, a peculiar, disease-ridden individual. However, similar fossils turned up later in Belgium, Yugoslavia, France, and elsewhere in Europe, which meant that the original Neandertal find could not be dismissed as an oddity.[5]

The predominant reaction to the original and subsequent Neandertal-like finds was that the Neandertals were too "brutish" and "primitive" to have been ancestral to modern

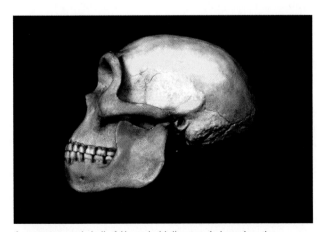

A reconstructed skull of *Homo heidelbergensis,* based on the mandible found at Mauer, Germany. While resembling *Homo erectus, Homo heidelbergensis* has smaller teeth and jaws and a larger brain.

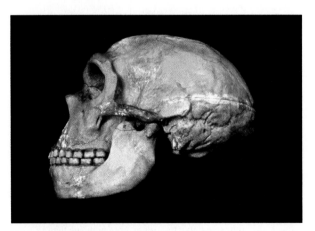

The reconstructed skull of a *Homo neandertalensis* man found at La Chapelle-aux-Saints, France.

CURRENT RESEARCH AND ISSUES

Putting Faces on Fossils

Have you ever wondered how we know what early humans looked like? We have pictures of them throughout this book, but how did the artists determine what to sculpt or draw? The answer lies in the field of forensic anthropology and more particularly in the field of facial reconstruction.

Facial reconstruction is based on knowledge of skull musculature and the thickness of soft tissue, determined over many years (the first such analysis was done in 1895) from cadavers and, more recently, magnetic resonance images of living people. From these measurements, forensic anthropologists have established a standard set of 21 to 34 locations on the skull where the average soft tissue thicknesses are known. The first step in facial reconstruction is to mark these locations on a cast of the skull to be reconstructed, using pegs that are the same length as the thickness of muscle and soft tis-

Boule's reconstruction of a Neandertal as displayed at Chicago's Field Museum in 1929 illustrates how subjective fossil reconstructions can be. It falsely implies that Neandertals could not stand upright or straighten their knees, and that they were more primitive than we know today that they actually were.

sue at that location. Clay is then used to cover the skull cast to the depth of these pegs (the musculature of the face is first modeled in more sophisticated reconstructions, then clay is used to represent the soft tissues, up to the depth of the pegs).

The size and shape of the nose are reconstructed based on the size and shape of the nasal opening. The size and shape of lips and ears are more difficult to determine, and the skull itself can tell the forensic anthropologist almost nothing about hair or eye color, whether the person had facial hair, or how the person's hair was cut. Those aspects of facial reconstruction require some artistic intuition, and it is helpful to know something about the person, such as sex, age, and ethnicity.

But what about ancient humans? The standard measurements used to reconstruct faces from modern human skulls cannot be assumed to work for ancient skulls. For those, the forensic anthropologists have to go back to the basis of facial reconstruction—muscle and soft tissue. When reconstructing the faces of ancient humans, forensic anthropologists begin with a careful reconstruction of skull musculature, often aided by the comparative anatomy of modern great apes. Once the muscles are in place, glands, fatty tissue, and skin are added, and the face begins to take shape. The size and shape of the nose are determined much like that for modern humans, from the size and shape of the nasal opening. Lips, ears, eyes, and hair are, however, subject to almost pure guesswork—we really have no way of knowing how hairy our ancestors were, whether they had full lips like ours or thin lips like other great apes, or whether their ears were large or small.

Though based on study of the likely muscular anatomy in fossils and the comparative anatomy of modern humans and great apes, it is important to realize that the reconstruction of ancient faces is in part an artistic exercise. We can never know for sure what, for example, *Homo erectus* really looked like. We do not know how hairy they were or how they "styled" their hair. We do not know if their ears were like ours. We do not know the color of their eyes or skin. This is why reconstructions vary in the ways they depict ancient humans. We need to keep in mind when we look at reconstructions that they are educated, perhaps biased, guesses, and not necessarily true depictions of ancient people.

Sources: John Prag and Richard Neave, *Making Faces: Using Forensic and Archaeological Evidence* (College Station: Texas A&M University Press, 1997); Stephanie Moser, *Ancestral Images: The Iconography of Human Origins* (Ithaca, NY: Cornell University Press, 1998).

humans. This view prevailed in the scholarly community until well into the 1950s. A major proponent of this view was Marcellin Boule, who claimed between 1908 and 1913 that the Neandertals would not have been capable of complete bipedalism. Boule, however, misinterpreted the bowed legs and bent spine in the Neandertal skeleton he examined—these were not normal in Neandertals, but were the result of disease in this particular individual. It is now universally agreed that the skeletal traits of the Neandertals are completely consistent with bipedalism.

Perhaps more important, when the much more ancient australopithecine and *H. erectus* fossils were accepted as hominids in the 1940s and 1950s, anthropologists realized that the Neandertals did not look that different from modern humans—despite their sloping foreheads, large brow ridges, flattened braincases, large jaws, and nearly absent chins (see Figure 11–2).[6] After all, they did have larger brains (averaging more than 1,450 cc) than modern humans (slightly more than 1,300 cc).[7] Some scholars believe that the large brain capacity of Neandertals suggests that they were capable of the full range of behaviors characteristic of modern humans. Their skeletons did, however, attest to one behavioral trait markedly different from behaviors of most modern humans: Neandertals apparently made very strenuous use of their bodies.[8]

It took almost 100 years for scholars to accept the idea that Neandertals were not that different from modern humans and perhaps should be classified as *Homo sapiens neandertalensis*. But in the last decade there has been a growing debate over whether the Neandertals in western Europe were ancestral to modern-looking people who lived later in western Europe, after about 40,000 years ago. Neandertals lived in other places besides western Europe. A large number of fossils from central Europe strongly resemble those from western Europe, although some features, such as a projecting midface, are less pronounced.[9] Neandertals have also been found in southwestern Asia (Israel, Iraq) and Central Asia (Uzbekistan). One of the largest collections of Neandertal fossils comes from Shanidar cave in the mountains of northeastern Iraq, where Ralph Solecki unearthed the skeletons of nine individuals (see Figure 8–3).[10]

What has changed scholars' opinions of the Neandertals so that they are now most commonly seen as not belonging to the *Homo sapiens* group?

In 1997, a group of researchers from the United States and Germany published findings that forced a reconsideration of the Neandertals and their relationship to modern humans. These scholars reported that they had been able to extract DNA from the original Neandertal specimen found in 1856.[11] The DNA they extracted was not nuclear DNA—

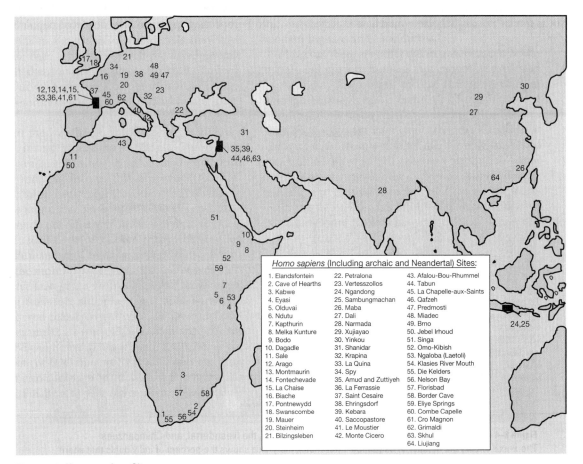

Figure 8–3 *Homo sapiens* Sites

Source: From Russell L. Ciochon and John G. Fleagle, eds., *The Human Evolution Source Book* (Englewood Cliffs, NJ: Prentice Hall, 1993).

Neandertals already living there. Sites with tools thought to be associated with Neandertals disappear throughout Europe as sites with tools thought to be associated with modern humans expand their range.[18] Significantly, the area of Europe (Iberia) last colonized by modern humans contains the very latest Neandertal fossils yet found, dating to some 30,000 years ago.[19]

With all this evidence pointing to Neandertals not being part of the modern human species, why is there an ongoing debate? In part this is because none of the evidence is conclusive, and much of it can be interpreted in alternate ways. There is also evidence suggesting that Neandertals were not all that different physically from modern humans (see the box "Neandertal Growth and Development"). Perhaps more important, however, Neandertal culture, typically referred to as Middle Paleolithic after the predominant tool technology, has some features that make it seem similar to the culture of early modern humans.

◎ Middle Paleolithic Cultures

The period of cultural history associated with the Neandertals is traditionally called the **Middle Paleolithic** in Europe and the Near East and dates from about 300,000 years to about 40,000 years ago.[20] For Africa, the term *Middle Stone Age* is used instead of Middle Paleolithic. The tool assemblages from this period are generally referred to as Mousterian in Europe and the Near East and as *post-Acheulian* in Africa.

Tool Assemblages

THE MOUSTERIAN The Mousterian type of tool complex is named after the tool assemblage found in a rock shelter at Le Moustier in the Dordogne region of southwestern France. Compared with an Acheulian assemblage, a **Mousterian tool assemblage** has a smaller proportion of large core tools such as hand axes and cleavers and a bigger proportion of small flake tools such as scrapers.[21] Although many flakes struck off from a core were used "as is," the Mousterian is also characterized by flakes that were often altered or "retouched" by striking small flakes or chips from one or more edges (see Figure 8–5).[22] Studies of the wear on scrapers suggest that many were used for scraping hides or working wood. The fact that some of the tools, particularly points, were thinned or shaped on one side suggests that they were hafted or attached to a shaft or handle.[23]

Toward the end of the Acheulian period, a technique developed that enabled the toolmaker to produce flake tools of a predetermined size instead of simply chipping flakes away

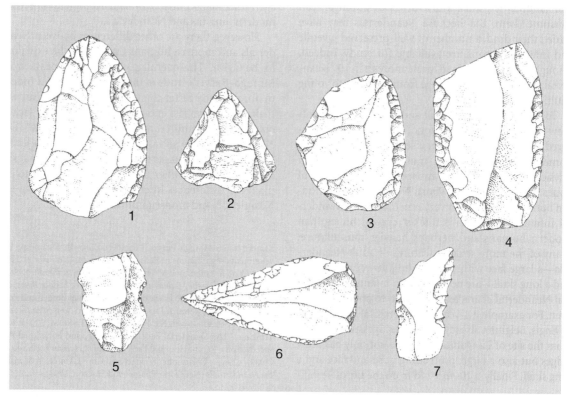

Figure 8–5 A Typical Mousterian Tool Kit
A Mousterian tool kit emphasized sidescrapers (1–4), notches (5), points (6), and saw-toothed denticulates (7). How these stone artifacts were actually used is not known, but the points may have been joined to wood shafts, and denticulates could have been used to work wood. The tools illustrated here are from Mousterian sites in western Europe.

Source: From Richard G. Klein, "*Ice-Age Hunters of the Ukraine.*" *Scientific American*, 1974.

from the core at random. In this **Levalloisian method,** the toolmaker first shaped the core and prepared a "striking platform" at one end. Flakes of predetermined and standard sizes could then be knocked off. Although some Levallois flakes date as far back as 400,000 years ago, they are found more frequently in Mousterian tool kits.[24]

The tool assemblages in particular sites may be characterized as Mousterian, but one site may have more or fewer scrapers, points, and so forth, than another site. A number of archaeologists have suggested possible reasons for this variation. For example, Sally Binford and Lewis Binford suggested that different activities may have occurred in different sites. Some sites may have been used for butchering and other sites may have been base camps; hence the kinds of tools found in different sites should vary.[25] And Paul Fish has suggested that some sites may have more tools produced by the Levalloisian technique because larger pieces of flint were available.[26]

THE POST-ACHEULIAN IN AFRICA Like Mousterian tools, many of the post-Acheulian tools in Africa during the Middle Stone Age were struck off prepared cores in the Levalloisian way. The assemblages consist mostly of various types of flake tools. A well-described sequence of such tools comes from the area around the mouth of the Klasies River on the southern coast of South Africa. This area contains rock shelters and small caves in which early and later *Homo sapiens* lived. The oldest cultural remains in one of the caves may date back 120,000 years.[27] These earliest tools include parallel-sided flake blades (probably used as knives), pointed flakes (possibly spearpoints), burins or gravers (chisel-like tools), and scrapers. Similar tools discovered at Border cave, South Africa, may have been used almost 200,000 years ago.[28]

Homesites

Most of the excavated Middle Paleolithic homesites in Europe and the Near East are located in caves and rock shelters. The same is true for the excavated Middle Stone Age homesites in sub-Saharan Africa. We might conclude, therefore, that Neandertals (as well as many early modern humans) lived mostly in caves or rock shelters. But that conclusion could be incorrect. Caves and rock shelters may be overrepresented in the archaeological record because they are more likely to be found than are sites that originally were in the open but now are hidden by thousands of years, and many feet, of sediment. Sediment is the dust, debris, and decay that accumulate over time; when we dust the furniture and vacuum the floor, we are removing sediment.

Still, we know that many Neandertals lived at least part of the year in caves. This was true, for example, along the Dordogne River in France. The river gouged deep valleys in the limestone of that area. Below the cliffs are rock shelters with overhanging roofs and deep caves, many of which were occupied during the Middle Paleolithic. Even if the inhabitants did not stay all year, the sites do seem to have been occupied year after year.[29] Although there is evidence of some use of fire in earlier cultures, Middle Paleolithic humans seem to

have relied more on fire. There are thick layers of ash in many rock shelters and caves and evidence that hearths were used to increase the efficiency of the fires.[30]

Quite a few Neandertal homesites were in the open. In Africa, open-air sites were located on floodplains, at the edges of lakes, and near springs.[31] Many open-air sites have been found in Europe, particularly eastern Europe. The occupants of the well-known site at Moldova in western Russia lived in river-valley houses framed with wood and covered with animal skins. Bones of mammoths, huge elephants now extinct, surround the remains of hearths and were apparently used to help hold the animal skins in place. Even though the winter climate near the edge of the glacier nearby was cold at that time, there still would have been animals to hunt because the plant food for the game was not buried under deep snow.

The hunters probably moved away in the summer to higher land between the river valleys. In all likelihood, the higher ground was grazing land for the large herds of animals the Moldova hunters depended on for meat. In the winter river valley sites, archaeologists have found skeletons of wolf, arctic fox, and hare with their paws missing. These animals probably were skinned for pelts that were made into clothing.[32]

Getting Food

How Neandertals and early modern humans got their food probably varied with their environment. In Africa, they lived in savanna and semiarid desert. In western and eastern Europe, they had to adapt to cold; during periods of increased glaciation, much of the environment was steppe grassland and tundra.

The European environment during this time was much richer in animal resources than the tundra of northern countries is today. Indeed, the European environment inhabited by Neandertals abounded in game, both big and small. The tundra and alpine animals included reindeer, bison, wild oxen, horses, mammoths, rhinoceroses, and deer, as well as bears, wolves, and foxes.[33] Some European sites have also yielded bird and fish remains. For example, people in a summer camp in northern Germany apparently hunted swans and ducks and fished for perch and pike.[34] Little, however, is known about the particular plant foods the European Neandertals may have consumed; the remains of plants are unlikely to survive thousands of years in a nonarid environment.

In Africa, too, early *Homo sapiens* varied in how they got food. For example, we know that the people living at the mouth of the Klasies River in South Africa ate shellfish as well as meat from small grazers such as antelopes and large grazers such as eland and buffalo.[35] But archaeologists disagree about how the Klasies River people got their meat when they began to occupy the caves in the area.

Richard Klein thinks they hunted both large and small game. Klein speculates that because the remains of eland of all ages have been found in Cave 1 at the Klasies River site, the people there probably hunted the eland by driving them into corrals or other traps, where animals of all ages could

Neandertals appear to have hunted a wide variety of game. In this reconstruction two Neandertals are shown attacking a mastodon they have trapped in a pit.

be killed. Klein thinks that buffalo were hunted differently. Buffalo tend to charge attackers, which would make it difficult to drive them into traps. Klein believes that, because bones from mostly very young and very old buffalo are found in the cave, the hunters were able to stalk and kill only the most vulnerable animals.[36]

Lewis Binford thinks the Klasies River people hunted only small grazers and scavenged the eland and buffalo meat from the kills of large carnivores. He argues that sites should contain all or almost all of the bones from animals that were hunted. According to Binford, since more or less complete skeletons are found only from small animals, the Klasies River people were not, at first, hunting all the animals they used for food.[37]

But new evidence suggests that people were hunting big game as much as 400,000 years ago. Wooden spears that old were recently found in Germany in association with stone tools and the butchered remains of more than ten wild horses. The heavy spears resemble modern aerodynamic javelins, which suggests they would have been thrown at large animals such as horses, not at small animals. This new evidence strongly suggests that hunting, not just scavenging, may be older than archaeologists once thought.[38]

Funeral and Other Rituals?

Some Neandertals appear to have been deliberately buried. At Le Moustier, the skeleton of a boy 15 or 16 years old was found with a beautifully fashioned stone axe near his hand. At La Ferrassie, five children and two adults were apparently interred together in a family plot. These finds, along with several at Shanidar cave in Iraq, have aroused speculation about the possibility of funeral rituals.

The most important evidence at Shanidar consists of pollen around and on top of a man's body. Pollen analysis suggests that the flowers included ancestral forms of modern grape hyacinths, bachelor's buttons, hollyhocks, and yellow flowering groundsels. John Pfeiffer speculated about this find:

> A man with a badly crushed skull was buried deep in the cave with special ceremony. One spring day about 60,000 years ago members of his family went out into the hills, picked masses of wild flowers, and made a bed of them on the ground, a resting place for the deceased. Other flowers were probably laid on top of his grave; still others seem to have been woven together with the branches of a pinelike shrub to form a wreath.[39]

Can we be sure? Not really. All we really know is that there was pollen near and on top of the body. It could have gotten there because humans put flowers in the grave, or it could have gotten there for other, even accidental, reasons. Some scholars have argued that other Shanidar burials are actually the remains of people who were trapped under rockfalls within the cave and killed—they were not deliberately buried at all, but rather buried accidentally.[40]

Neandertals may have taken part in other rituals as well, but, like funeral rituals, the evidence is ambiguous. At Drachenloch cave in the Swiss Alps, for example, a stone-lined pit holding the stacked skulls of seven cave bears was found in association with a Neandertal habitation. Why preserve these skulls? One reason might be for rituals intended to placate or control bears. Cave bears were enormous—some nearly nine feet tall—and competed with Neandertals for prime cave living sites. Perhaps the Neandertals preserved the skulls of bears they killed in the cave as a way of honoring or appeasing either the bears or their spirits. But, as with funeral rituals, the evidence is not completely persuasive. In our own society some may hang a deer or moose head on the wall without any associated ritual. At this point we cannot say for certain whether or not Neandertals engaged in ritual behavior.[41]

The Emergence of Modern Humans

Cro-Magnon humans, who appear in western Europe about 35,000 years ago, were once thought to be the earliest specimens of modern humans, or *Homo sapiens sapiens*. (The Cro-Magnons are named after the rock shelter in France where they were first found, in 1868.[42]) But we now know that modern-looking humans appeared earlier outside of Europe. As of now, the oldest unambiguous fossils classified as *H. sapiens* come from Ethiopia and date to perhaps 160,000 years ago.[43] Additional fossils, discovered in one of the Klasies River mouth caves in South Africa, are possibly as old as 100,000 years.[44] Other *Homo sapiens* fossils of about the same age have been found in Border cave in South Africa.[45] Remains of anatomically modern humans (*Homo sapiens sapiens*) found at two sites in Israel, at Skhul and Qafzeh, which used to be thought to date back 40,000 to 50,000 years, may be 90,000 years old.[46] There are also anatomically modern human finds in Borneo, at Niah, from about 40,000 years ago and in Australia, at Lake Mungo, from about 30,000 years ago.[47]

These modern-looking humans differed from the Neandertals and other early *H. sapiens* in that they had higher, more bulging foreheads, thinner and lighter bones, smaller faces and jaws, chins (the bony protuberances that remain after projecting faces recede), and only slight brow ridges (or no ridges at all; see Figure 8–2).

Theories about the Origins of Modern Humans

Two theories about the origins of modern humans continue to be debated among anthropologists. One, which can be called the *single-origin theory,* suggests that modern humans emerged in just one part of the Old World and then spread to other parts, replacing Neandertals. (Africa is generally thought to be the place of modern humans' origin.) The second theory, which has been called the multiregional theory, suggests that modern humans evolved in various parts of the Old World after *Homo erectus* spread out of Africa.[48]

SINGLE-ORIGIN THEORY   According to the single-origin theory, the Neandertals did not evolve into modern humans. Rather, Neandertals became extinct after 35,000 years ago because they were replaced by modern humans. The presumed place of origin of the first modern humans has varied over the years as new fossils have been discovered. In the 1950s, the source population was presumed to be Neandertals in the Near East, who were referred to as "generalized" or "progressive" Neandertals. Later, when earlier *Homo sapiens* were found in Africa, paleoanthropologists postulated that modern humans emerged first in Africa and then moved to the Near East and from there to Europe and Asia. Single-origin theorists think that the originally small population of *H. sapiens sapiens* had some biological or cultural advantage, or both, that allowed them to spread and replace Neandertals.

The main evidence for the single-origin theory comes from the mtDNA of living peoples. In 1987, Rebecca Cann and her colleagues presented evidence that the mtDNA from people in the United States, New Guinea, Africa, and East Asia showed differences suggesting that their common ancestor lived only 200,000 years ago. Cann and colleagues further claimed that, since the amount of variation among individuals was greatest in African populations, the common ancestor of all lived in Africa.[49] (It is generally the case that people living in a homeland exhibit more variation than any emigrant descendant population.) Thus was born what the media called the "mitochondrial Eve" and the "Eve hypothesis" for the origins of modern humans. Of course, there wasn't just one "Eve"; there must have been more than one of her generation with similar mtDNA.

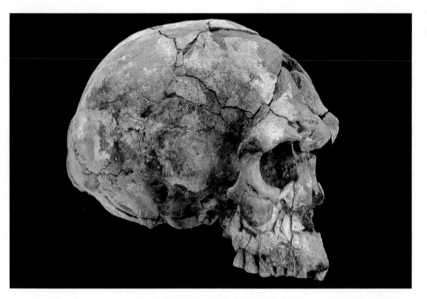

This *Homo sapiens* skull from Ethiopia is the oldest member of our species yet found, dating to 160,000 years ago.

There were many problems with early mtDNA studies, but over the years those problems have been addressed and new and better mtDNA analyses have been performed. Most scholars now agree that the mtDNA of modern humans shows a remarkably small degree of variation (in fact, less than half the variation found in most chimpanzee populations), which strongly suggests that we all share a very recent, common ancestry.[50] More detailed analyses of mtDNA diversity in modern humans have allowed scholars to identify the ancestral roots of contemporary populations around the world, and these analyses also point to modern human origins in East Africa and a subsequent spread out of that region.[51]

Evidence for an East African origin of modern humans and the subsequent expansion also comes from research on variation in the Y chromosome. The Y chromosome is the chromosome that determines whether a person is male. A female inherits an X chromosome from both her mother and father, while a male inherits an X chromosome from his mother and a Y chromosome from his father. Only men have a Y chromosome, and since there is only one copy in any given man, the Y chromosome is the only nuclear chromosome that, like mtDNA, does not undergo recombination. While the Y chromosome can be affected by selection, it is thought that most variation in the Y chromosome, like variation in mtDNA, is caused by random mutations. Variation in the Y chromosome can therefore be analyzed in much the same way as variation in mtDNA.[52]

The results of research on variation in the Y chromosome mirror those on variation in mtDNA to a remarkable extent. Analysis of Y chromosome variation points to Africa as the source of modern humans, and suggests an exodus from Africa of modern humans. One of the major differences between mtDNA studies and those employing the Y chromosome is in the dating of the most recent common ancestor. As noted above, studies of mtDNA suggest the most recent common ancestor lived about 200,000 years ago, while studies of the Y chromosome suggest the most recent ancestor lived only about 100,000 years ago.[53] Additional research, including new research on variation in nuclear DNA, may help to resolve these differences. For now, however, it seems clear that the modern human gene pool has a single, and fairly recent, origin in Africa.[54]

The mtDNA analyses of Neandertals, and the archaeological evidence suggesting that Neandertals and modern humans lived without apparent interaction in Europe and the Near East, also tend to support the single-origin theory. The *Homo sapiens* skeletal material from Ethiopia, Africa, in the 150,000–200,000-year-ago time range further supports the single-origin theory.[55] However, such evidence does not necessarily contradict the validity of the multiregional theory of human origins.

MULTIREGIONAL THEORY   According to the multiregional theory, *Homo erectus* populations in various parts of the Old World gradually evolved into anatomically modern-looking humans. The theorists espousing this view believe that the "transitional" or "archaic" *H. sapiens* and the Neandertals represent phases in the gradual development of more

"modern" anatomical features. Indeed, as we have noted, some of these theorists see so much continuity between *Homo erectus* and modern humans that they classify *Homo erectus* as *Homo sapiens erectus*.

Continuity is the main evidence used by the multiregional theorists to support their position. In several parts of the world there seem to be clear continuities in distinct skeletal features between *Homo erectus* and *Homo sapiens*. For example, *Homo erectus* fossils from China tend to have broader faces with more horizontal cheekbones than specimens from elsewhere in the world, traits that also appear in modern Chinese populations.[56] Southeast Asia provides more compelling evidence, according to multiregional theorists. There, a number of traits—relatively thick cranial bones, a receding forehead, an unbroken brow ridge, facial prognathism, relatively large cheekbones, and relatively large molars—appear to persist from *Homo erectus* through modern populations (see Figure 8–6).[57] But others suggest that these traits cannot be used to establish a unique continuation from *Homo erectus* in Southeast Asia because these traits are found in modern humans all over the world. And still others argue that the traits are not as similar as the multiregional theorists claim.[58]

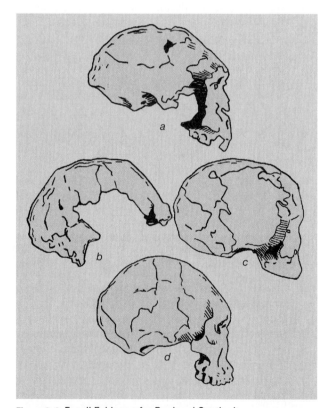

Figure 8–6 Fossil Evidence for Regional Continuity
Continuity in southeast Asian and Australian populations: Skulls of (a) *Homo erectus*, (b) early *Homo sapiens*, and (d) modern *Homo sapiens*, all from southeast Asia and Australia, have similar foreheads, brow ridges, and occipital and facial shapes, while skulls from Africa, represented here by (c), an early *Homo sapiens*, have different forms. The similarity in southeast Asian and Australian populations over more than 500,000 years argues for regional continuity rather than replacement.

In support of their position, multiregional theorists argue that the mtDNA and Y chromosome evidence supports multiregional evolution rather than a single-origin of modern humans, that genetic variation in modern humans may reflect the emigration of *Homo erectus* out of Africa rather than the emigration of *Homo sapiens sapiens.* This interpretation would mean that the accepted rates of mutation in both mtDNA and the Y chromosome are wrong, that both actually mutate much more slowly than currently thought.[59] However, this interpretation is contradicted by established correlations between differences in mtDNA among human groups known to have colonized New Guinea and Australia at particular points in time, which seem to fit the accepted rate of mutation, and with the divergence between humans and apes, the date of which also seems to accord with the accepted faster rate of mtDNA mutation.

To explain why human evolution would proceed gradually and in the same direction in various parts of the Old World, multiregional theorists point to cultural improvements in cutting-tool and cooking technology that occurred all over the Old World. These cultural improvements may have relaxed the prior natural selection for heavy bones and musculature in the skull. The argument is that unless many plant and animal foods were cut into small pieces and thoroughly cooked in hearths or pits that were efficient thermally, they would be hard to chew and digest. Thus people would have needed robust jaws and thick skull bones to support the large muscles that enabled them to cut and chew their food. But robust bone and muscle would no longer be needed after people began to cut and cook more effectively.[60]

INTERMEDIATE THEORIES   The single-origin and multiregional theories are not the only possible interpretations of the available fossil record. There is also the intermediate interpretation that there may have been some replacement of one population by another, some local continuous evolution, and some interbreeding between early modern humans, who spread out of Africa, and populations encountered in North Africa, Europe, and Asia.[61] As biologist Alan Templeton has noted, the debates over a single-origin versus multiregional evolution

> are based on the myth that replacement of one physical feature in a fossil series with another feature can only be created by one population replacing another (by exterminating them, for example), but such fossil patterns could be a reflection of one genotype replacing another through gene flow and natural selection. Morphological replacement should not be equated with population replacement when one is dealing with populations that can interbreed.[62]

Interestingly, data on the genetic diversity of human body lice seems to support an intermediate theory of human origins. As noted in the discussion of hair loss in early humans in a previous chapter, humans are plagued by a single species of hair lice, *Pediculus humanus,* which happens to have two distinct genetic lineages. One is found worldwide, the other

only in the Americas. These two genetic lineages of lice appear to have diverged over one million years ago. If modern humans evolved less than 200,000 years ago (and the worldwide louse lineage suggests it experienced some dramatic changes about 100,000 years ago, which may relate to modern humans leaving Africa), then how did the other lineage continue? One answer is that they were transferred to modern humans from a previously isolated population of *Homo erectus* in Asia.[63] But if that were the case, then very close contact—either body to body or sharing clothing—would had to have taken place between modern and archaic humans.

What Happened to the Neandertals?

Regardless of which theory (single-origin, multiregional, or intermediate) is correct, it seems clear that Neandertals and modern humans (*H. sapiens sapiens*) coexisted in Europe and the Near East for at least 20,000 years, and maybe as long as 60,000 years. What happened to the Neandertals? Three answers have generally been considered. First, they interbred with modern humans and the unique Neandertal characteristics slowly disappeared from the interbreeding population. Second, they were killed off by modern humans. Third, they were driven to extinction due to competition with modern humans. Let's take a look at each of these scenarios.

INTERBREEDING   The interbreeding scenario seems the most probable, yet evidence supporting it is weak. If modern humans and Neandertals interbred, we should be able to find "hybrid" individuals in the fossil record. In fact, a group of scholars has argued that an Upper Paleolithic skeleton from Portugal demonstrates a combination of modern human and Neandertal features.[64] The finding remains controversial, however, because it is a child's skeleton (approximately 4 years old) and its Neandertal-like features have not been corroborated by other scholars. More significantly, if the interbreeding hypothesis is correct, then the mtDNA analysis we have discussed several times in this chapter must be wrong. On the other hand, recent research on Neandertal tools suggests that some Neandertal groups adopted new techniques of tool manufacture that are thought to be uniquely associated with modern humans (we discuss these in more detail in the next chapter).[65] If Neandertals were learning from modern humans, then the idea that they could have interbred and perhaps been absorbed within the modern human population gains credibility.

GENOCIDE   The genocide scenario, that modern humans killed off Neandertals, has appeal as a sensational story, but little evidence. Not a single "murdered" Neandertal has ever been found, and one might wonder, in a fight between the powerful Neandertals and the more gracile modern humans, who might get the better of whom.

EXTINCTION   Finally, the extinction scenario, that Neandertals simply could not compete with modern humans, seems to have the best archaeological support. As we discussed earlier, there appear to be "refugee" populations of Neandertals in Iberia as recently as perhaps 30,000 years ago. The "retreat" of Neandertals from the Near East, eastern Europe, and finally western Europe following the movement of modern humans into the region seems to support the "refugee" interpretation.[66] More importantly, physical anthropologist Erik Trinkaus has argued, based on both physical characteristics of the Neandertal skeleton and their apparent patterns of behavior, that Neandertals were less efficient hunters and gatherers than modern humans.[67] And not only may Neandertals have been less efficient than modern humans in getting food, they may have needed more of it. Steve Churchill has suggested that Neandertals' stocky bodies and great muscle mass might have required 25 percent more calories than modern humans.[68] If this is true, a modern human group would have been able to live and reproduce more easily than a Neandertal group in the same territory, and this would likely drive the Neandertals away. When there were no new territories to run to, the Neandertals would go extinct—precisely what the archaeological record seems to suggest.[69]

But were modern humans and their cultures really that much more efficient than Middle Paleolithic cultures? As we will see in the next chapter, the Upper Paleolithic does seem to mark a watershed in the evolution of human culture, allowing humans to expand their physical horizons throughout the world and their intellectual horizons into the realms of art and ritual.

◎ Summary

1. Most anthropologists agree that *Homo erectus* began to evolve into *Homo sapiens* after about 500,000 years ago. But there is disagreement about how and where the transition occurred. The mixed traits of the transitional fossils include large cranial capacities (well within the range of modern humans), together with low foreheads and large brow ridges, which are characteristic of *H. erectus* specimens. The earliest definite *H. sapiens,* who did not look completely like modern humans, appeared about 160,000 years ago.

2. *Homo sapiens* have been found in many parts of the Old World—in Africa and Asia as well as in Europe. Some of these *H. sapiens* may have lived earlier than the Neandertals of Europe. There is still debate over whether the Neandertals in western Europe became extinct or survived and were ancestral to the modern-looking people who lived in western Europe after about 40,000 years ago.

3. The period of cultural history associated with the Neandertals is traditionally called the Middle Paleolithic in Europe and the Near East and dates from about 300,000 to about 40,000 years ago. For Africa, the term

Middle Stone Age is used. The assemblages of flake tools from this period are generally referred to as Mousterian in Europe and the Near East and as post-Acheulian in Africa. Compared with an Acheulian assemblage, a Mousterian tool assemblage has a smaller proportion of large hand axes and cleavers and a larger proportion of small flake tools such as scrapers. Some Mousterian sites show signs of intentional burial.

4. Fossil remains of fully modern-looking humans, *Homo sapiens sapiens,* have been found in Africa, the Near East, Asia, and Australia, as well as in Europe. The oldest of these fossils have been found in East Africa and may be 160,000 years old.

5. Two theories about the origins of modern humans continue to be debated among anthropologists. One, the *single-origin theory,* suggests that modern humans emerged in just one part of the Old World—the Near East and, more recently, Africa have been the postulated places of origin—and spread to other parts of the Old World, superseding Neandertals. The second theory, the *multiregional theory,* suggests that modern humans emerged in various parts of the Old World, becoming the varieties of humans we see today.

◎ Glossary Terms

Cro-Magnon	137	Middle Paleolithic	134
Homo heidelbergensis	127	Mousterian tool assemblage	134
Homo neandertalensis	128		
Homo sapiens sapiens	127	Neandertal	128
Levalloisian method	135		

◎ Critical Questions

1. If the single-origin or "out-of-Africa" theory were correct, by what mechanisms could *Homo sapiens* have been able to replace *Homo erectus* and *Homo neandertalensis* populations?

2. If modern human traits emerged in *Homo erectus* populations in different areas more or less at the same time, what mechanisms would account for similar traits emerging in different regions?

3. How do Middle Paleolithic cultures differ from Lower Paleolithic cultures?

◎ Research Navigator

1. Please go to **www.researchnavigator.com** and enter your LOGIN NAME and PASSWORD. For instructions

on registering for the first time, please view the detailed instructions at the end of Chapter 1.

2. Use Content Select to search in the Anthropology database with the keyword "mitochondrial DNA." What questions about modern human origins and history are being addressed using mitochondrial DNA evidence? What findings are being made? Are there any controversies surrounding the results of research using mitochondrial DNA?

◎ Discovering Anthropology: Researchers at Work

Read the chapter by David Frayer titled "Testing Theories and Hypotheses about Modern Human Origins" in the accompanying *Discovering Anthropology* reader. Answer the following questions:

1. What does Frayer identify as the key elements of debate between the "Out of Africa" (or, as he calls it, "Noah's Ark") and "Multiregional" models of modern human origins?

2. What problems does Frayer identify with mitochondrial DNA evidence of modern human origins?

3. Frayer is in the minority among physical anthropologists today in supporting the multiregional model of human evolution. What reasons does he give for rejecting the more broadly accepted "Out of Africa" model?

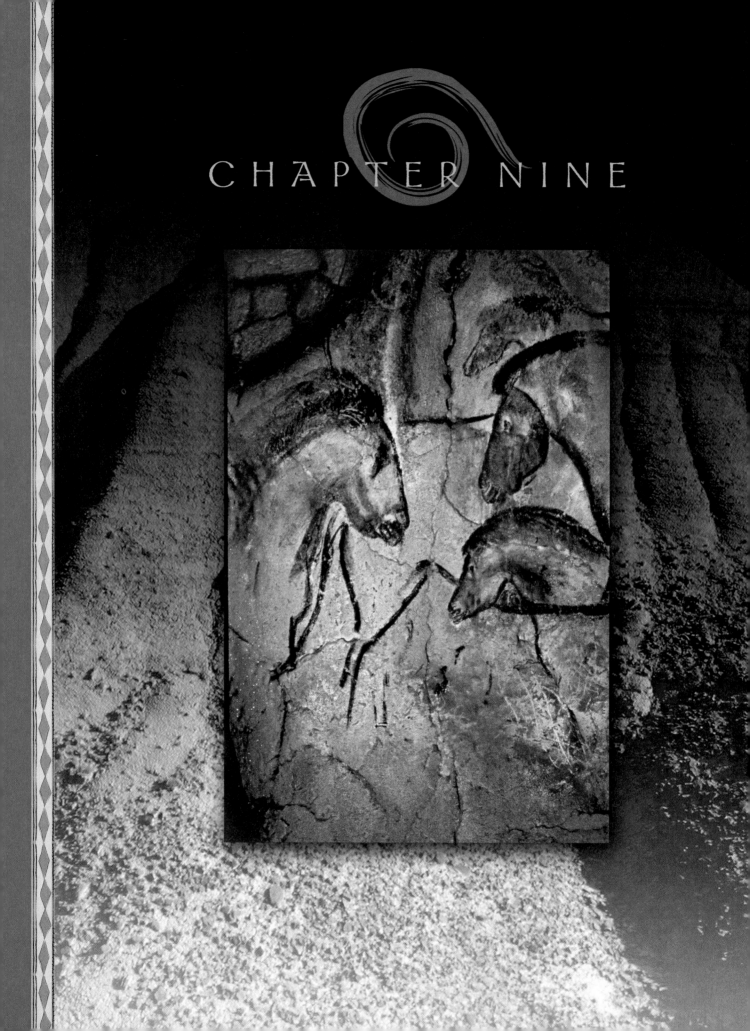

CHAPTER NINE

The Upper Paleolithic World

The period of cultural history in Europe, the Near East, and Asia known as the Upper Paleolithic (see Figure 9–1) dates from about 40,000 years ago to the period known as the *Neolithic* (beginning about 10,000 years ago, depending on the area). In Africa, the cultural period comparable to the Upper Paleolithic is known as the *Later Stone Age* and may have begun much earlier. In North and South America the period begins when humans first entered the New World, some time before 12,000 years ago (these colonizers are typically called *Paleo-Indians*) and continues until what are called *Archaic traditions* emerged some 10,000 years ago. To simplify terminology, we use the term Upper Paleolithic to refer to cultural developments in all areas of the Old World during this period.

In many respects, lifestyles during the Upper Paleolithic were similar to lifestyles before. People were still mainly hunters and gatherers and fishers who probably lived in small mobile bands. They made their camps out in the open in skin-covered huts and in caves and rock shelters. And they continued to produce smaller and smaller stone tools.

But the Upper Paleolithic is also characterized by a variety of new developments. One of the most striking is the emergence of art—painting on cave walls and stone slabs, and carving tools, decorative objects, and personal ornaments out of bone, antler, shell, and stone. (Perhaps for this as well as other purposes, people began to obtain materials from distant sources.) Because more archaeological sites date from the Upper Paleolithic than from any previous period and some Upper Paleolithic sites seem larger than any before, many archaeologists think that the human population increased considerably during the Upper Paleolithic.[1] And new inventions, such as the bow and arrow, the spear-thrower, and tiny replaceable blades that could be fitted into handles, appear for the first time.[2]

The Last Ice Age

The Upper Paleolithic world had an environment very different from today's. The earth was gripped by the last ice age, with glaciers covering Europe as far south as Berlin and Warsaw, and North America as far south as Chicago. To the south of these glacial fronts was a tundra zone extending in Europe to the Alps and in North America to the Ozarks,

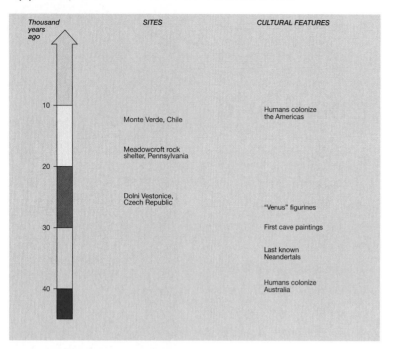

Figure 9–1 Places and Events in the Upper Paleolithic

Appalachians, and well out onto the Great Plains (see Figure 9–2). Environmentally, both Europe and North America probably resembled contemporary Siberia and northern Canada. Elsewhere in the world conditions were not as extreme, but were still different from conditions today.[3]

For one thing, the climate was different. Annual temperatures were as much as 10 degrees Celsius below today's, and changes in ocean currents would have made temperature contrasts (i.e., the differences between summer and winter months) more extreme as well. The changing ocean currents also changed weather patterns, and Europe experienced heavy annual snowfall. Not all the world was cold, however; still, the presence of huge ice sheets in the north changed the climate throughout the world. North Africa, for example, appears to have been much wetter than today, and South Asia was apparently drier. And everywhere the climate seems to have been highly variable.[4]

The plants and animals of the Upper Paleolithic world were adapted to these extreme conditions. Among the most important, and dramatic, were the large game animals collectively known as *Pleistocene megafauna*.[5] These animals, as their name suggests, were huge compared to their contemporary descendants. In North America, for example, giant ground sloths stood some 8–10 feet tall and weighed several thousand pounds. Siberian mammoths were the largest elephants ever to live—some standing more than 14 feet tall. In East Asia, species such as the woolly rhinoceros and giant deer were present.

⑥ Upper Paleolithic Europe

With the vast supplies of meat available from megafauna, it is not surprising that many Upper Paleolithic cultures relied on hunting, and this was particularly true of the Upper Paleolithic peoples of Europe, on whom we focus here. Their way of life represents a common pattern throughout the Old World. But as people began to use more diverse resources in their environments, the use of local resources allowed Upper Paleolithic groups in much of the Old World to become more sedentary than their predecessors. They also began to trade with neighboring groups in order to obtain resources not available in their local territories.[6]

As was the case in the known Middle Paleolithic sites, most of the Upper Paleolithic remains that have been excavated were situated in caves and rock shelters. In southwestern France, some groups seem to have paved parts of the shelter floors with stones. Tentlike structures were built in some caves, apparently to keep out the cold.[7] Some open-air sites have also been excavated.

The site at Dolni Vestonice in what is now the Czech Republic, dated to around 25,000 years ago, is one of the first for which there is an entire settlement plan.[8] The settlement seems to have consisted of four tentlike huts, probably made from animal skins, with a great open hearth in the center. Around the outside were mammoth bones, some rammed into the ground, which suggests that the huts were surrounded by a wall. All told, there were bone heaps from about 100 mammoths. Each hut probably housed a group of related families—about 20–25 people. (One hut was approximately 27 by 45 feet and had five hearths distributed inside it, presumably one for each family.) With 20 to 25 people per hut, and assuming that all four huts were occupied at the same time, the population of the settlement would have been 100–125 people.

Up a hill from the settlement was a fifth and different kind of hut. It was dug into the ground and contained a bake oven and more than 2,300 small, fired fragments of animal figurines. There were also some hollow bones that may have been musical instruments. Another interesting feature of the

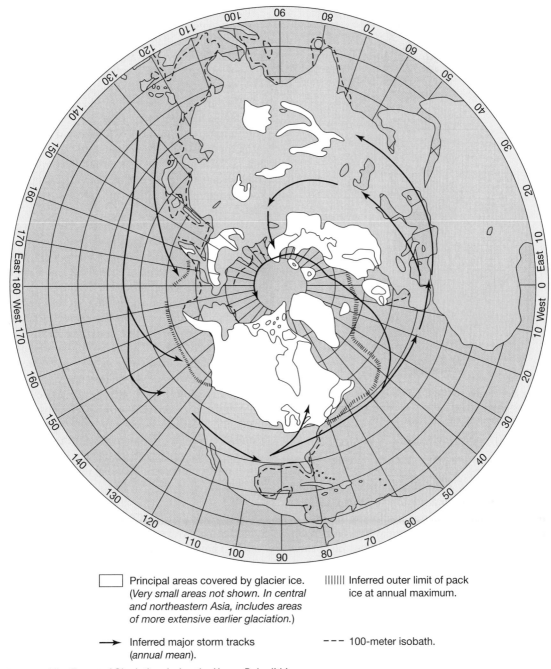

Principal areas covered by glacier ice.
(*Very small areas not shown. In central
and northeastern Asia, includes areas
of more extensive earlier glaciation.*)

||||||| Inferred outer limit of pack
ice at annual maximum.

⟶ Inferred major storm tracks
(*annual mean*).

‐ ‐ ‐ 100-meter isobath.

Figure 9–2 The Extent of Glaciation during the Upper Paleolithic

Source: From *Physical Anthropology,* 7th ed. by P. Stein and B. Rowe. (Boston: McGraw Hill, 2000).

settlement was a burial find, of a woman with a disfigured face. She may have been a particularly important personage; her face was found engraved on an ivory plaque near the central hearth of the settlement.

Upper Paleolithic Tools

Upper Paleolithic toolmaking appears to have had its roots in the Mousterian and post-Acheulian traditions, because flake tools are found in many Upper Paleolithic sites. But the Upper Paleolithic is characterized by a preponderance of blades; there were also burins, bone and antler tools, and microliths. In addition, two new techniques of toolmaking appeared—*indirect percussion* and *pressure flaking.* Blades were found in Middle Paleolithic assemblages, but they were not widely used until the Upper Paleolithic. Although blades can be made in a variety of ways, **indirect percussion** using a hammer-struck punch was common in the Upper Paleolithic. After shaping a core into a pyramidal or cylindrical form, the toolmaker put a punch of antler, wood, or other hard material into position and struck it with a hammer. Because the force is readily directed, the toolmaker was able to strike off consistently shaped **blades,** which are more than twice as long as they are wide[9] (see Figure 9–3).

Figure 9–3 One way to remove blades from a core is to hit them with a punch using indirect percussion. The object being struck is the punch, which is made of bone or horn.

Source: From Brian M. Fagan, *In the Beginning* (Boston: Little, Brown, 1972), p. 195.

The Upper Paleolithic is also noted for the production of large numbers of bone, antler, and ivory tools; needles, awls, and harpoons made of bone appear for the first time.[10] The manufacture of these implements may have been made easier by the development of many varieties of burins. **Burins** are chisel-like stone tools used for carving; bone and antler needles, awls, and projectile points could be produced with them.[11] Burins have been found in Middle and Lower Paleolithic sites but are present in great number and variety only in the Upper Paleolithic.

Pressure flaking also appeared during the Upper Paleolithic. Rather than using percussion to strike off flakes as in previous technologies, pressure flaking works by employing pressure with a bone, wood, or antler tool at the edge of the tool to remove small flakes. Pressure flaking would usually be used in the final stages of retouching a tool.[12]

As time went on, all over the Old World smaller and smaller blade tools were produced. The very tiny ones, called **microliths,** were often hafted or fitted into handles, one blade at a time or several blades together, to serve as spears, adzes, knives, and sickles. The hafting required inventing a way to trim the blade's back edge so that it would be blunt rather than sharp. In this way the blades would not split the handles into which they might be inserted; the blunting would also prevent the users of an unhafted blade from cutting themselves.[13]

Some archaeologists think that the blade technique was adopted because it made for more economical use of flint.

André Leroi-Gourhan of the Musée de l'Homme in Paris calculated that with the old Acheulian technique, a 2-pound lump of flint yielded 16 inches of working edge and produced only two hand axes. If the more advanced Mousterian technique were used, a lump of equal size would yield 2 yards of working edge. The indirect percussion method of the Upper Paleolithic would yield as much as 25 yards of working edge.[14] With the same amount of material, a significantly greater number of tools could be produced. Getting the most out of a valuable resource may have been particularly important in areas lacking large flint deposits. Then again, if the population were increasing, that by itself would require more tools and more working edges to be produced.

Jacques Bordaz suggested that the evolution of toolmaking techniques, which continually increased the amount of usable edge that could be gotten out of a lump of flint, was significant because people could then spend more time in regions where flint was unavailable. Another reason for adopting the blade toolmaking technique may have been that it made for easy repair of tools. For example, the cutting edge of a tool might consist of a line of razorlike microliths set into a piece of wood. The tool would not be usable if just one of the cutting edge's microliths broke off or was chipped. But if the user carried a small prepared core of flint from which an identical-sized microlith could be struck off, the tool could be repaired easily by replacing the lost or broken microlith. A spear whose point was lost could be repaired similarly. Thus, the main purpose of the blade toolmaking technique may not have been to make more economical use of flint but rather to allow easy replacement of damaged blades.[15]

HOW WERE THE TOOLS USED? Ideally, the study of tools should reveal not only how the implements were made but also how they were used. One way of suggesting what a particular tool was used for in the past is to observe the manner in which similar tools are used by members of recent or contemporary societies, preferably societies with subsistence activities and environments similar to those of the ancient toolmakers. This method of study is called reasoning from **ethnographic analogy.** The problem with such reasoning, however, is obvious: We cannot be sure that the original use of a tool was the same as the present use. When selecting recent or contemporary cultures that may provide the most informative and accurate comparisons, we should try to choose those that derive from the ancient culture we are interested in. If the cultures being compared are historically related—prehistoric and recent Pueblo cultures in the southwestern United States, for example—there is a greater likelihood that the two groups used a particular kind of tool in similar ways and for similar purposes.[16]

Another way of suggesting what a particular kind of tool was used for is to compare the visible and microscopic wear marks on the prehistoric tools with the wear marks on similar tools made and experimentally used by contemporary researchers. The idea behind this approach is that different uses leave different wear marks. A pioneer in this research was S. A. Semenov, who recreated prehistoric stone tools and

Upper Paleolithic bone needle and spear or harpoon points. Upper Paleolithic peoples made a much wider variety of tools than their predecessors.

that the Siberian blades were probably also used to cut meat.[17]

The tools made by Upper Paleolithic peoples suggest that they were much more effective hunters and fishers than their predecessors.[18] During the Upper Paleolithic, and probably for the first time, spears were shot from a spear-thrower rather than thrown with the arm. We know this because bone and antler **atlatls** (the Aztec word for "spear-thrower") have been found in some sites. A spear propelled off a grooved board could be sent through the air with increased force, causing it to travel farther and hit harder, and with less effort by the thrower. The bow and arrow was also used in various places during the Upper Paleolithic; and harpoons, used for fishing and perhaps for hunting reindeer, were invented at this time.

These new tools and weapons for more effective hunting and fishing do not rule out the possibility that Upper Paleolithic peoples were still scavenging animal remains. Olga Soffer suggests that Upper Paleolithic peoples may have located their settlements near places where many mammoths died naturally in order to make use of the bones for building (see Figure 9–4). For example, in Moravia the mammoths may have come to lick deposits of calcite and other sources of magnesium and calcium, particularly during the late spring and early summer when resources were short and mortality was high. Consistent with the idea that humans may not have killed so many of the enormous mammoths is the fact that in some places there are few human-made cut marks on mammoth bones. For example, at Dolni Vestonice, where bones of 100 mammoths were found, few bones show cut marks from butchering and few bones were found inside the huts. In contrast, the site is littered with bison, horse, and reindeer bones, suggesting that these other animals were deliberately killed and eaten by humans. If the people had been able to kill all the mammoths we find the remains of, why would they have hunted so many other animals?[19]

used them in a variety of ways to find out which uses left which kinds of wear marks. For example, by cutting into meat with his recreated stone knives, he produced a polish on the edges that was like the polish found on blades from a prehistoric site in Siberia. This finding led Semenov to infer

Figure 9–4 Here we see the type of mammoth-bone shelters constructed about 15,000 years ago on the East European Plain. Often mammoth skulls formed part of the foundation for the tusk, long bone, and wooden frame, covered with hide. As many as 95 mammoth mandibles were arranged around the outside in a herring-bone pattern. Ten men and women could have constructed this elaborate shelter of 258 square feet in six days, using 46,000 pounds of bone.

Paintings in the "Hall of Bulls" at Lascaux in France. Cave paintings like this demonstrate the remarkable skill of Upper Paleolithic artists.

Upper Paleolithic Art

The earliest discovered traces of art are beads and carvings, and then paintings, from Upper Paleolithic sites. We might expect that early artistic efforts were crude, but the cave paintings of Spain and southern France show a marked degree of skill. So do the naturalistic paintings on slabs of stone excavated in southern Africa. Some of those slabs appear to have been painted as much as 28,000 years ago, which suggests that painting in Africa is as old as painting in Europe.[20] But painting may be even older than that. The early Australians may have painted on the walls of rock shelters and cliff faces at least 30,000 years ago and maybe as much as 60,000 years ago.[21] And at Blombos Cave in South Africa engraved pieces of red ochre date back to more than 77,000 years ago.[22]

Peter Ucko and Andrée Rosenfeld identified three principal locations of paintings in the caves of western Europe: (1) in obviously inhabited rock shelters and cave entrances—art as decoration or "art for art's sake"; (2) in "galleries" immediately off the inhabited areas of caves; and (3) in the inner reaches of caves, whose difficulty of access has been interpreted by some as a sign that magical-religious activities were performed there.[23]

The subjects of the paintings are mostly animals. The paintings are on bare walls, with no backdrops or environmental trappings. Perhaps, like many contemporary peoples, Upper Paleolithic men and women believed that the drawing of a human image could cause death or injury. If that were indeed their belief, it might explain why human figures are rarely depicted in cave art. Another explanation for the focus on animals might be that these people sought to improve their luck at hunting. This theory is suggested by evidence of chips in the painted figures, perhaps made by spears thrown at the drawings. But if hunting magic was the chief motivation for the paintings, it is difficult to explain why only a few show signs of having been speared. Perhaps then the paintings were inspired by the need to increase the supply of animals. Cave art seems to have reached a peak toward the end of the Upper Paleolithic period, when the herds of game were decreasing.

The particular symbolic significance of the cave paintings in southwestern France is more explicitly revealed, perhaps, by the results of Patricia Rice and Ann Paterson's statistical study.[24] The data suggest that the animals portrayed in the cave paintings were mostly the ones that the painters preferred for meat and for materials such as hides. For example, wild cattle (bovines) and horses are portrayed more often than we would expect by chance, probably because they were larger and heavier (meatier) than the other animals in the environment. In addition, the paintings mostly portray animals that the painters may have feared the most because of their size, speed, natural weapons such as tusks and horns, and unpredictability of behavior. That is, mammoths, bovines, and horses are portrayed more often than deer and reindeer. Thus, the paintings are consistent with the idea that "the art is related to the importance of hunting in the economy of Upper Paleolithic people."[25] Consistent with this idea, according to the investigators, is the fact that the art of the cultural period that followed the Upper Paleolithic also seems to reflect how people got their food. But in that period, when getting food no longer depended on hunting large game (because they were becoming extinct), the art ceased to focus on portrayals of animals.

Upper Paleolithic art was not confined to cave paintings. Many spear shafts and similar objects were decorated with figures of animals. Alexander Marshack has an interesting interpretation of some of the engravings made during the Upper Paleolithic. He believes that as far back as 30,000 years ago, hunters may have used a system of notation, engraved on bone and stone, to mark the phases of the moon. If this is true, it would mean that Upper Paleolithic people were capable of complex thought and were consciously aware of their environment.[26] In addition, figurines representing the human female in exaggerated form have been found at Upper Paleolithic sites. Called Venuses, these figurines portray women with broad hips and large breasts and abdomens.

What the Venus figurines symbolized is still controversial. Most scholars believe these figurines represented a goddess or fertility symbol, but that belief is not universally held. For

NEW PERSPECTIVES ON GENDER

Depictions of Women in Upper Paleolithic Art

It is a common misperception that depictions of the human form in Upper Paleolithic art are restricted to Venus figurines. To the contrary, there are many other depictions of humans, both female and male, running the whole range of ages from infants to elderly people. For women, figures of obese or pregnant women, like those sometimes depicted in Venus figurines, appear to be only one type in a wide range of images, many of which offer accurate rather than stylized representations.

In a survey of Upper Paleolithic art, Jean-Pierre Duhard found that all shapes and sizes of women as well as all age ranges were present. Indeed, he argued that a range of female body types can be seen. One engraved figure from Gönnersdorf cave on the Rhine River, for example, depicts four women. Three are the same size, but one is smaller and has small breasts—she may be an adolescent. Of the three larger figures, one appears to have a child tied to her back, and she also has large, rounded breasts, as opposed to the flat and pointed breasts of the other two. Duhard argued that this is an

accurate depiction of four women, one with a child she is breast-feeding.

Duhard also argued that while depictions of women are common in Upper Paleolithic art, similar depictions of men and children are comparatively rare. He suggested this disparity may reflect women's status in Upper Paleolithic societies. Most depictions of women show them in some motherhood role—pregnant, in childbirth, or carrying an infant (and perhaps walking with older children). Duhard suggested that women's roles as mothers may have given them a privileged status in Upper Paleolithic life, which may be why that status is the most frequently depicted subject in Upper Paleolithic art.

In a similar way, Patricia Rice has argued that Venus figurines accurately reflect the social importance of women in Upper Paleolithic society. She demonstrated that a range of body types and ages are represented in Venus figurines, and argued that, since the Venuses depict real women of all ages, not just pregnant women, they should be seen as symbols of "womanhood" rather than "motherhood." The wide distribution of Venus figurines and their apparent importance to Upper Paleolithic peoples reflect, according to Rice, the recognized importance of women in Upper Paleolithic society.

Arguing along similar lines, Olga Soffer examined the clothing worn by some Venus figures. Soffer and her colleagues show that woven items are the most frequently depicted, and argue that, since these woven items would have been highly valued in Upper Paleolithic society, their presence on some Venus figurines suggests that some women held positions of high status in Upper Paleolithic society.

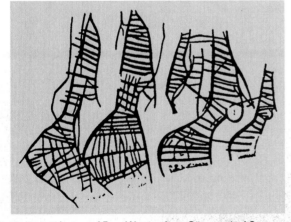

Figure 9–7 Image of Four Women from Gönnersdorf Cave

Source: From Jean-Pierre Duhard, "Upper Paleolithic Figures as a Reflection of Human Morphology and Social Organization," *Antiquity,* 67 (1993): 86.

Sources: Jean-Pierre Duhard, "Upper Paleolithic Figures as a Reflection of Human Morphology and Social Organization," *Antiquity,* 67 (1993): 83–91; Patricia Rice, "Prehistoric Venuses: Symbols of Motherhood or Womanhood?" *Journal of Anthropological Research,* 37 (1981): 402–14; Olga Soffer, J. M. Adovasio, and D. C. Hyland, "The 'Venus' Figurines: Textiles, Basketry, Gender, and Status in the Upper Paleolithic," *Current Anthropology,* 41 (2000): 511–37.

example, LeRoy McDermott has argued that Venus figurines are not symbolic representations at all but rather accurate self-portraits made by pregnant women. Their exaggerated breasts, hips, and stomachs are distortions that can be attributed to the perspective gained by a person looking down at herself, as is the lack of facial details on many of the figurines.[27] Others have argued that the figurines are examples

of early erotica made by males for their sexual gratification or education. Still others suggest they were made by females to instruct young women in pregnancy and childbirth.[28]

The controversies surrounding Venus figurines provide insight into a basic problem in archaeology: There is often little or no evidence available that allows us to accept or reject a particular interpretation (see the box "Depiction of

The Venus of Willendorf, one of the most famous Venus figurines.

Women in Upper Paleolithic Art"). Rather, in most cases we have to balance data and interpretation to come to an informed judgment, recognizing that our judgment will likely change as new data are uncovered.

Upper Paleolithic Cultures in Africa and Asia

Europe was not the only region where Upper Paleolithic peoples thrived. In North Africa, for example, Upper Paleolithic peoples hunted large animals on the grasslands that covered the region during that period. They lived in small communities located within easy access to water and other resources, and moved regularly, probably to follow the animal herds. Trade took place between local groups, particularly for high-quality stone used in making tools.[29] In eastern and southern Africa, a way of life known as the Later Stone Age developed that persisted in some areas until very recently. People lived in small, mobile groups, hunting large animals and collecting a wide variety of plant foods. Interaction was common among these bands. Among their ethnographically known descendants, individuals would regularly switch their membership from one band to another.[30]

In South Asia the Upper Paleolithic saw an increasingly sedentary lifestyle developing along the banks of freshwater streams. The Upper Paleolithic peoples in South Asia combined hunting, fishing, and gathering with seasonal movements to exploit seasonally abundant resources.[31] In East and Southeast Asia ocean resources became vital to coastal-dwelling peoples, while those inland lived primarily in caves,

hunting and collecting broadly in the local environment. Many of these sites appear to have been occupied for long periods of time, suggesting some degree of sedentism. During the Upper Paleolithic, peoples from Asia also populated Australia, New Guinea, and some of the islands of western Melanesia, clearly demonstrating the ability of these peoples to navigate on the sea and to use its resources.[32]

The Earliest Humans and Their Cultures in the New World

So far in this chapter we have dealt only with the Old World—Africa, Europe, and Asia. What about the New World—North and South America? How long have humans lived there, and what were their earliest cultures like?

Because only *Homo sapiens sapiens* fossils have been found in North and South America, migrations of humans to the New World had to have taken place some time after the emergence of *H. sapiens sapiens*. But exactly when these migrations occurred is subject to debate, particularly about when people got to areas south of Alaska. On the basis of similarities in biological traits such as tooth forms and blood types, and on possible linguistic relationships, anthropologists agree that Native Americans originally came from Asia. The traditional assumption is that they came to North America from Siberia, walking across a land bridge (Beringia) that is now under water (the Bering Strait) between Siberia and Alaska. The ice sheets or glaciers that periodically covered most of the high latitudes of the world contained so much of the world's water (the ice sheets were thousands of feet thick in some places) that Beringia was dry land in various periods (see Figure 9–5). For example, there was a land bridge for a while, until the last 10,000 years or so. Since then, the glaciers have mostly melted, and the Bering "bridge" has been completely covered by a higher sea level.

Until recently, the prevailing view was that humans were not present south of Alaska until after 11,500 years ago. Now it appears from an archaeological site called Monte Verde in Chile that modern humans got to southern South America by at least 12,500 years ago, and maybe as much as 33,000 years ago. The Monte Verde site contains more than 700 stone tools, the remains of hide-covered huts, and a child's footprint next to a hearth.[33] The site suggests that there was at least one wave of human migration into the New World before 11,500 years ago, by walking and/or perhaps in boats. Even when the last glaciers were at their fullest extent, there was a small ice-free corridor through which people could have walked. And there were ice-free corridors earlier.

It was geologically possible then for humans to have walked into the New World at various times, and they could have traveled by boat, too (see the box "Alternative Avenues of Migration into the New World"). Parts of the Beringia land bridge were exposed from about 60,000 to 25,000 years ago. It wasn't until between 20,000 and 18,000 years ago that the

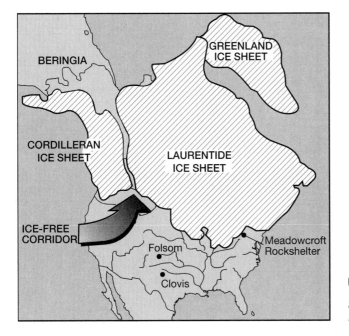

Figure 9–5 Beringia and the Ice Sheets

Source: David K. Meltzer, "Pleistocene Peopling of the Americas," *Evolutionary Anthropology,* Vol. 1, 1993. Copyright © 1993.

land bridge was at its maximum. When did the last land bridge disappear? It used to be widely believed that the land bridge was flooded around 14,000 years ago, but recent evidence suggests that walking across Beringia was still possible until about 10,000 years ago. An ice-free corridor between the Laurentide and Cordilleran ice sheets may have been present after 25,000 years ago, but that corridor is not likely to have supported big game, and permitted humans to hunt enough for sustenance, until after about 14,000 years ago. So some investigators suggest that moving through the ice-free corridor to what is now south of Canada was not likely until after that time.[34]

The people there may or may not have hunted big game, but just a little while later there were people living in the Amazon jungle of what is now Brazil who were definitely not hunters of mammoths and other big game, as the contemporaneous Clovis people of North America were. In other words, it looks like the earliest inhabitants of the New World—in Chile, Brazil, North America—varied in culture. The people in the Amazon lived by collecting fruits and nuts, fishing, and hunting small game. They lived in caves with painted art on the walls and left 30,000 stone chips from making tips of spears, darts, or harpoons.[35]

There is no disagreement that humans were living south of Canada around 11,000 years ago. The Clovis people, as they are called (after an archaeological site near Clovis, New Mexico), left finely shaped spear points in many locations in North

Clovis points, the earliest stone weapons in the Americas, dating to more than 11,000 years ago.

MIGRANTS AND IMMIGRANTS

Alternative Avenues of Migration into the New World

The most widely accepted model for how humans entered the New World is the one presented in the body of this textbook: by walking across Beringia, which joined Asia and North America at the end of the last ice age, when sea levels were lower than today. There is good evidence to support this model, both archaeological and geological. But there are also some problems.

One of the most persistent problems with the Beringia model is the presence of archaeological sites in both North and South America dated to time periods before glacial ice had retreated far enough to allow access to North America. In addition, several of the South American sites appear to be earlier than the earliest North American sites, which seems contradictory to a model based on humans moving into the New World from north to south.

Alternative models for human entry into the New World, which solve some of the problems with the Beringia model, have been proposed. The one with more support suggests that humans came to the New World from Asia by boat. These people would have moved along the sea edge of the glaciers, subsisting on fish and sea mammals. Once past the glaciers, they either would have moved farther down the coast, perhaps all the way to the tip of South America, or proceeded inland into North America. Small groups of people may have made such voyages on many occasions, and it may be that none established communities that lasted more than a few generations.

Some scholars posit that the few very early archaeological sites may be the remnants of these early explorers. The small numbers would leave only a small archaeological record, so it is not surprising that more material has not been found. The fact that early occupations at a number of sites are separated from later occupations by soil showing no signs of human presence may also be evidence that these early explorers were present, but died out. Additional support for the coastal migration model has recently come from archaeological explorations of ancient coastlines now lying deep beneath the Bering Sea. Archaeologists have found stone tools in locations that would have been coastal during the last ice age.

A second, and more controversial, model is that humans may have come to the New World by boat from Europe. Like those who may have boated from Asia, these Europeans would have moved along the glacial ice front, not across the open sea. They would have fished and hunted sea mammals during their voyage, which may have taken many generations. The primary evidence for this model are the Clovis stone tools made by the Paleo-Indians. Archaeologists and stone tool experts Bruce Bradley and Dennis Stanford have argued that the techniques used to manufacture Clovis tools bear little resemblance to techniques used by peoples in eastern Asia, but are identical to those used by the Solutrean peoples of Europe. One major problem with this model is that the Solutrean period ends about 17,000 years ago, and the earliest evidence of Solutrean-like tools in North America does not appear until at least 12,000 years ago.

Both of the alternative models for human entry into the New World have some archaeological support and provide explanations for the presence of very early sites. It still appears that a large migration of humans from Asia began about 12,500 years ago, probably across Beringia, and that it was those people who successfully colonized the New World.

Sources: Thomas Dillehay, *The Settlement of the Americas* (New York: Basic Books, 2000); Lawrence Guy Strauss, "Solutrean Settlement of North America? A View of Reality," *American Antiquity,* 65 (2000): 219–26; Michael Parfit, "Who Were the First Americans?" *National Geographic* (December 2000): 41–67; Eliot Marshall, "Pre-Clovis Sites Fight for Acceptance," *Science,* 291 (2001): 1730–32.

America. And we have human skeletal remains from after 11,000 years ago. Now that the Monte Verde site has been reliably dated, we know that there were people south of Canada before the Clovis people were in New Mexico. And there are other possible sites of pre-Clovis occupation, although many archaeologists do not agree that the presumed tools at these sites were made by humans (these objects could have been made by rockfalls or other natural forces) or that the sites are accurately dated. One site that may be another pre-Clovis site is the Meadowcroft Rockshelter in western Pennsylvania.[36]

In the bottom third of a stratum that seems to date from 19,600 to 8,000 years ago, the Meadowcroft site shows clear signs of human occupation—a small fragment of human bone, a spearpoint, and chipped knives and scrapers. If the dating is accurate, the tools would be about 12,800 years old. William Parry suggests we need to date the human bone found in the site. If the bone turns out to date from before 12,000 years ago, few anthropologists would question the conclusion that humans occupied the Meadowcroft site before the time of the Clovis people.[37]

According to comparative linguists Joseph Greenberg and Merritt Ruhlen, there were three waves of migration into the New World.[38] They compared hundreds of languages in North and South America, grouping them into three different language families. Because each of these language families has a closer relationship to an Asian language family than to the other New World language families, it would appear that three different migrations came out of Asia. The first arrivals spoke a language that diverged over time into most of the languages found in the New World, the Amerind family of languages; the speakers of these related languages came to occupy all of South and Central America as well as most of North America. Next came the ancestors of the people who speak languages belonging to the Na-Dené family, which today includes Navajo and Apache in the southwestern United States and the various Athapaskan languages of northern California, coastal Oregon, northwestern Canada, and Alaska. Finally, perhaps 4,000 years ago, came the ancestors of the Inuit (Eskimo) and Aleut (the latter came to occupy the islands southwest of Alaska and the adjacent mainland), who speak languages belonging to the Inuit-Aleut family.

Christy Turner's study of New World teeth supports the Greenberg and Ruhlen proposal of three separate migra-tions. Turner looked at the proportions of shovel-shaped incisors, a common Asian trait, in New World populations. The varying proportions fall into three distinct groupings, the same three suggested by the linguists[39] (see Figure 9–6). But a recent genetic analysis suggests that Inuit-Aleut may have split from Na-Dené in the New World.[40] The peopling of the New World may have been even more complicated. There could have been four separate migrations from the Old World, from different regions of Asia.[41]

The Paleo-Indians

Archaeological remains of early New World hunters, called *Paleo-Indians,* have been found in the United States, Mexico, and Canada. Just south of the farthest reaches of the last glaciation, the area east of the Rockies known as the High Plains abounded with mammoths, bison, wild camels, and wild horses. The tools found with mammoth kills are known as the *Clovis complex,* which includes the Clovis projectile point as well as stone scrapers and knives and bone tools. The Clovis projectile point is large and leaf-shaped, flaked on both sides. It has a broad groove in the middle, presumably so that the point could be attached to a wooden spear shaft.[42] Because one mammoth was found with eight Clovis points

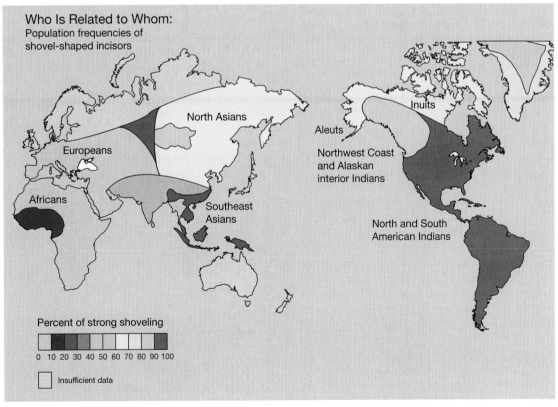

Figure 9–6 Inuit (Eskimos) and Aleuts, speakers of Na-Dené languages, and other Native American language groups differ in the frequency of shovel-shaped incisors. These genetic differences seem to reflect three waves of migration into the New World.

Source: From Christy G. Turner II, "Telltale Teeth," *Natural History,* January 1987, p. 8.

The "river of bones" at the Olsen-Chubbuck site. These are the remains of bison that Paleo-Indian hunters stampeded into an arroyo.

in it, there is little dispute that Clovis people hunted large game.[43] Recent dating places most Clovis sites between 11,200 and 10,900 years ago.[44]

The mammoth disappeared about 10,000 years ago, and the largest game animal became the now-extinct large, straight-horned bison. The hunters of that bison used a projectile point called the *Folsom point*, which was much smaller than the Clovis point. Tools are also found with many other kinds of animal remains, including wolf, turtle, rabbit, horse, fox, deer, and camel, so the bison hunters obviously depended on other animals as well.[45] In the Rio Grande valley, the Folsom toolmakers characteristically established a base camp on low dune ridges overlooking both a large pond and broad, open grazing areas. If we assume that the pond provided water for the grazing herds, the people in the camp would have been in an excellent position to watch the herds.[46]

As the climate of what is now the American Southwest became drier, the animals and the cultural adaptations changed somewhat. About 9,000 years ago the smaller modern bison replaced the earlier straight-horned variety.[47] Base camps began to be located farther from ponds and grazing areas and closer to streams. If the ponds were no longer reliable sources of water during these drier times, the animals probably no longer frequented them, which would explain why the hunters had to change the sites of their base camps. Not much is known about the plant foods these Paleo-Indian people may have exploited, but on the desert fringes plant gathering may have been vital. In Nevada and Utah, archaeologists have found milling stones and other artifacts for processing plant food.[48]

The Olsen-Chubbuck site, a kill site excavated in Colorado, shows the organization that may have been involved in hunting bison.[49] In a dry gulch dated to 6500 B.C. were the remains of 200 bison. At the bottom were complete skeletons and at the top, completely butchered animals. This find clearly suggests that Paleo-Indian hunters deliberately stampeded the animals into a natural trap—an arroyo, or steep-sided dry gully. The animals in front were probably pushed by the ones behind into the arroyo. Joe Ben Wheat estimated that the hunters may have obtained 55,000 pounds of meat from this one kill. If we judge from 19th-century Plains Indians, who could prepare bison meat to last a month, and estimate that each person would eat a pound a day, the kill at the Olsen-Chubbuck site could have fed more than 1,800 people for a month (they probably did not all live together throughout the year). The hunters must have been highly organized not only for the stampede itself but also for butchering. It seems that the enormous carcasses had to be carried to flat ground for that job. In addition, the 55,000 pounds of meat and hides had to be carried back to camp.[50]

Although big game may have been most important on the High Plains, other areas show different adaptations. For example, Paleo-Indian people in woodland regions of what is now the United States seem to have depended more heavily on plant food and smaller game. In some woodland areas, fish and shellfish may have been a vital part of the diet.[51] On the Pacific coast, some Paleo-Indian people developed food-getting strategies more dependent on fish.[52] And in other areas, the lower Illinois River valley being one example, Paleo-Indian people who depended on game and wild vegetable foods managed to get enough food to live in permanent villages of perhaps 100–150 people.[53]

Once humans colonized the Americas, they established a way of life very similar to that of their Upper Paleolithic cousins in the Old World, a life generally based on big-game hunting. As time went on, life became more sedentary, with increasing interaction among local groups.

◎ The End of the Upper Paleolithic

After about 10,000 years ago, the glaciers began to disappear, and with their disappearance came other environmental changes. The melting of the glacial ice caused the oceans to rise, and, as the seas moved inland, the waters inundated some of the richest fodder-producing coastal plains, creating islands, inlets, and bays. Other areas were opened up for human occupation as the glaciers retreated and the temperatures rose.[54] The cold, treeless plains, tundras, and grasslands eventually gave way to dense mixed forests, mostly birch, oak, and pine, and the Pleistocene megafauna became extinct. The warming waterways began to be filled with fish and other aquatic resources.[55]

Archaeologists believe that these environmental changes induced some populations to alter their food-getting strategies. When the tundras and grasslands disappeared, hunters could no longer obtain large quantities of meat simply by remaining close to large migratory herds of animals, as they probably did during Upper Paleolithic times. Even though deer and other game were available, the number of animals per square mile (density) had decreased, and it became difficult to stalk and kill animals sheltered in the thick woods. Thus, in many areas people seemed to have turned from a reliance on big-game hunting to the intensive collecting of wild plants, mollusks, fish, and small game to make up for the extinction of the large game animals they had once relied upon.

The Maglemosian Culture of Northern Europe

Some adaptations to the changing environment can be seen in the cultural remains of the settlers in northern Europe who are called *Maglemosians* by archaeologists. Their name derives from the peat bogs (*magle mose* in Danish means "great bog") where their remains have been found.

To deal with the new, more forested environment, the Maglemosians made stone axes and adzes to chop down trees and form them into various objects. Large timbers appear to have been split for houses; trees were hollowed out for canoes; and smaller pieces of wood were made into paddles. The canoes presumably were built for travel and perhaps for fishing on the lakes and rivers that abounded in the postglacial environment.

We do not know to what extent the Maglemosians relied on wild plant foods, but there were a lot of different kinds available, such as hazelnuts. However, we do know many other things about the Maglemosians' way of life. Although fishing was fairly important, as suggested by the frequent occurrence of bones from pike and other fish, as well as fishhooks, these people apparently depended mainly on hunting for food. Game included elk, wild ox, deer, and wild pig. In addition to many fishing implements and the adzes and axes, the Maglemosians' tool kit included the bow and arrow. Some of their tools were ornamented with finely engraved designs. Ornamentation independent of tools also appears in amber and stone pendants and small figurines representing, for example, the head of an elk.[56]

Like the Maglemosian finds, many of the European post–Upper Paleolithic sites are along lakes, rivers, and oceanfronts. But these sites probably were not inhabited year round; there is evidence that at least some groups moved seasonally from one place of settlement to another, perhaps between the coast and inland areas.[57] Finds such as kitchen

middens (piles of shells) that centuries of post–Upper Paleolithic seafood-eaters had discarded and the remains of fishing equipment, canoes, and boats indicate that these people depended much more heavily on fishing than had their ancestors in Upper Paleolithic times.

The Archaic Cultures of Eastern North America

A related set of adaptations to the changing environment can be seen among the peoples who inhabited eastern North America at the end of the ice age. As the climate became warmer and drier, the flora and fauna of North America changed. Megafauna, as elsewhere in the world, went extinct, and were replaced by smaller mammals, particularly deer. The availability of meat was greatly reduced—hunters could count on coming home with pounds, not tons, of meat. Warmer adapted plants replaced cold adapted plants, and were used for food to replace the meat that was no longer available. Warmer adapted plants had advantages as food resources for humans over cold adapted ones because edible seeds, fruits, and nuts were more common, and often more plentiful and accessible, on the warmer adapted plants. Thus a much greater diversity of plants and animals came to be used by the Archaic peoples.[58]

Some examples of Archaic ground stone woodworking tools from eastern North America (wooden handles are reproductions). Archaic peoples apparently used wood more extensively than the Paleoindians.

The Archaic peoples of North America, like the Maglemosian peoples in Europe, began to follow a more sedentary lifestyle. Two forms of Archaic settlement appear to have been typical. One was a residential base camp, which would have been inhabited seasonally by several, probably related, families. The other was a special-purpose camp, which would have been a short-term habitation near a particular resource or perhaps used by a group of hunters for a short period of time.[59] On the Atlantic coast, for example, individual groups apparently moved seasonally along major river valleys, establishing summer base camps in the piedmont and winter camps near the coast. Special-purpose camps were created year-round as groups went out from the base camp to hunt and collect particular resources, such as stone for making tools.[60]

One of the innovations of the Archaic peoples was the development of ground stone woodworking tools. Axes, adzes, and tools for grinding seeds and nuts become more and more common in the tool kit.[61] This probably reflects the emergence of greater areas of forest following the retreat of the glaciers from North America, but it also demonstrates a greater reliance on forest products and, most likely, a greater use of wood and wood products. Fish and shellfish also came to be relied upon in some areas, and this too reflects the adjustment made by the Archaic peoples to the changing conditions they faced at the end of the last ice age.

The innovation of most lasting importance in both the New and Old Worlds, however, was the development of domesticated plants and animals. In both parts of the world, peoples at the end of the ice age began to experiment with plants. By around 14,000 years ago in the Old World, and 10,000 years ago in the New World, some species had been domesticated. It is this fundamental change in food-getting—the invention of agriculture—to which we turn in the next chapter.

◎ Summary

1. The period of cultural history known as the Upper Paleolithic in Europe, the Near East, and Asia or the Later Stone Age in Africa dates from about 40,000 years ago to about 14,000 to 10,000 years ago. During this time the world was locked in an ice age, with glaciers covering much of northern Europe and North America, and annual temperatures as much as 10 degrees Celsius below today's.

2. The Upper Paleolithic tool kit is characterized by the preponderance of blades; there were also burins, bone and antler tools, and (later) microliths. In many respects, lifestyles were similar to lifestyles before. People were still mainly hunters and gatherers and fishers who probably lived in highly mobile bands. They made their camps out in the open and in caves and rock shelters.

3. The Upper Paleolithic is also characterized by a variety of new developments: new techniques of toolmaking, the emergence of art, population growth, and new inventions such as the bow and arrow, the spear-thrower (atlatl), and the harpoon.

4. Only *Homo sapiens sapiens* remains have been found in the New World. The prevailing opinion is that humans migrated to the New World over a land bridge between Siberia and Alaska in the area of what is now the Bering Strait. Until recently it was thought that humans were not present south of Alaska until after 11,500 years ago. Now it appears from an archaeological site called Monte Verde in Chile that modern humans got to southern South America by at least 12,500 years ago and perhaps as much as 33,000 years ago.

5. At the end of the ice age, around 14,000 years ago, the climate began to become more temperate. Many large animals relied upon by Upper Paleolithic peoples for food went extinct, and at the same time new, warmer-adapted plants provided a rich, new food source. Around the world people began to use more plant foods and a broader range of resources overall. In many parts of the world people began experimenting with domesticating plants and animals.

◎ Glossary Terms

atlatl	147	indirect percussion	145
blade	145	microlith	146
burin	146	pressure flaking	146
ethnographic analogy	146	Upper Paleolithic	143

◎ Critical Questions

1. How do Upper Paleolithic tools differ from Middle Paleolithic tools? What is the significance of these differences in terms of human culture?

2. Upper Paleolithic cave paintings arouse our imaginations. We have described some research that tested ideas about what these paintings might mean. Can you think of other ways to understand the significance of cave art?

3. What factors might have led humans to colonize the New World?

◎ Research Navigator

1. Please go to **www.researchnavigator.com** and enter your LOGIN NAME and PASSWORD. For instructions on registering for the first time, please view the detailed instructions at the end of Chapter 1.

2. Use the Link Library for Art History to browse the links for Paleolithic Cave Painting. Once you have finished, write an essay addressing one of the following questions: How were Upper Paleolithic cave paintings made? What

do Upper Paleolithic cave paintings depict? Why were Upper Paleolithic cave paintings created?

◎ Discovering Anthropology: Researchers at Work

Read the chapter by William Parry titled "When and How Did Humans Populate the New World?" in the accompanying *Discovering Anthropology* reader. Answer the following questions:

1. Why is the issue of when and how humans first colonized the Americas such a vibrant and important topic in archaeology?

2. Parry states that the following is the key question needing to be answered: "Is there any evidence of pre-Clovis people in the Americas, or were the Clovis people the first immigrants?" What is Parry's answer, and why did he have such difficulty developing it?

CHAPTER TEN

Origins of Food Production and Settled Life

Toward the end of the period known as the Upper Paleolithic, people seem to have gotten most of their food from hunting migratory herds of large animals, such as wild cattle, antelope, bison, and mammoths. These hunter-gatherers were probably highly mobile in order to follow the migrations of the animals. Beginning about 14,000 years ago, people in some regions began to depend less on big-game hunting and more on relatively stationary food resources, such as fish, shellfish, small game, and wild plants (see Figure 10–1). In some areas, particularly Europe and the Near East, the exploitation of local, relatively permanent resources may account for an increasingly settled way of life. The cultural period in which these developments took place is usually now called the **Epipaleolithic** in the Near East and the **Mesolithic** in Europe. Other areas of the world show a similar switch to what is called *broad-spectrum* food-collecting, but they do not always show an increasingly settled lifestyle, as, for example, in Mesoamerica where this period is called the **Archaic**.

We see the first clear evidence of a changeover to **food production**—the cultivation and domestication of plants and animals—in the Near East, about 8000 B.C.[1] This shift, called the *Neolithic revolution* by archaeologist V. Gordon Childe, occurred, probably independently, in other areas of the Old and New Worlds within the next few thousand years. In the Old World there were independent centers of domestication in China, Southeast Asia (what is now Malaysia, Thailand, Cambodia, and Vietnam), and Africa around 6000 B.C.[2] In the New World there were centers of cultivation and domestication in the highlands of Mesoamerica (about 7000 B.C.), the central Andes around Peru (about 7000 B.C.), and the Eastern Woodlands of North America (about 2000 B.C., but perhaps earlier).[3] Most of the world's major food plants and animals were domesticated well before 2000 B.C. Also developed by that time were techniques of plowing, fertilizing, fallowing, and irrigation.[4] Figure 10–2 shows the regions of the world that domesticated today's main food crops.

In this chapter we discuss what is believed about the origins of food production and settled life, called **sedentarism**—how and why people in different places may have come to cultivate and domesticate plants and animals and to live in permanent villages. **Agriculture** (which we use here to refer to all types of domestic plant cultivation) and a sedentary life did not necessarily develop together. In some regions of the world, people began to live in permanent villages before they cultivated and domesticated plants and animals, whereas in other places people planted crops without settling down permanently. Much of our discussion focuses on the Near East and Mesoamerica, the areas we know best archaeologically for the developments leading to food production and settled life. As much as we can, however, we try to indicate how data from other areas appear to suggest patterns different from, or similar to, those in the Near East and Mesoamerica.

Preagricultural Developments

The Near East

In the Near East there seems to have been a shift from mobile big-game hunting to the utilization of a broad spectrum of natural resources at the end of the Upper Paleolithic, similar to those changes that happened in Europe, which we discussed at the end of the last chapter.[5] There is evidence that people subsisted on a variety of resources, including fish, mollusks, and other water life; wild deer, sheep, and goats; and wild grains, nuts, and legumes.[6] The increased utilization of stationary food sources such as wild grain may

partly explain why some people in the Near East began to lead more sedentary lives during the Epipaleolithic.

Even today, a traveler passing through the Anatolian highlands of Turkey and other mountainous regions in the Near East may see thick stands of wild wheat and barley growing as densely as if they had been cultivated.[7] Wielding flint sickles, Epipaleolithic people could easily have harvested a bountiful crop from such wild stands. Just how productive these resources can be was demonstrated in a field experiment duplicating prehistoric conditions. Using the kind of flint-blade sickle an Epipaleolithic worker would have used, researchers were able to harvest a little over two pounds of wild grain in an hour. A family of four, working only during the few weeks of the harvest season, probably could have reaped more wheat and barley than they needed for the entire year.[8]

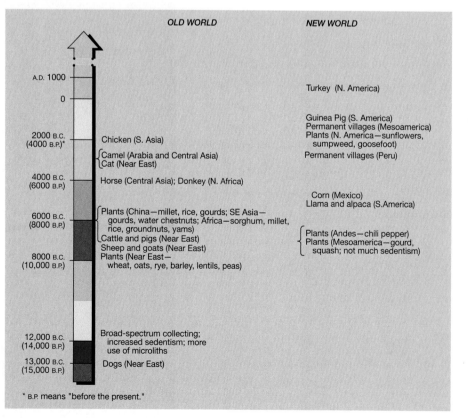

Figure 10–1 The Evolution of Domestication

Source: Dates for animal domestication are from Juliet Clutton-Brock, "Domestication of Animals," in Stephen Jones, Robert Martin, and David Pilbeam, eds., *The Cambridge Encyclopedia of Human Evolution* (New York: Cambridge University Press, 1992), p. 384.

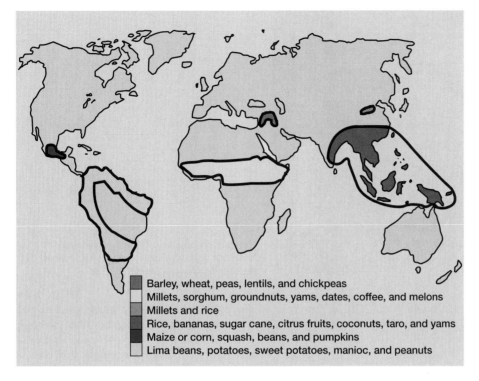

Figure 10–2 Original Locations of the World's Main Food Crops
The world's main food crops were originally domesticated in different regions.

Source: From Frank Hole, "Origins of Agriculture," in Stephen Jones, Robert Martin, and David Pilbeam, eds., *The Cambridge Encyclopedia of Human Evolution* (New York: Cambridge University Press, 1992), p. 376.

The amount of wild wheat harvested in the experiment prompted Kent Flannery to conclude, "Such a harvest would almost necessitate some degree of sedentism—after all, where could they go with an estimated metric ton of clean wheat?"[9] Moreover, the stone equipment used for grinding would have been a clumsy burden to carry. Part of the harvest would probably have been set aside for immediate consumption, ground, and then cooked either by roasting or boiling. The rest of the harvest would have been stored to supply food for the remainder of the year. A grain diet, then, could have been the impetus for the construction of roasters, grinders, and storage pits by some preagricultural people, as well as for the construction of solid, fairly permanent housing. Once a village was built, people may have been reluctant to abandon it. We can visualize the earliest preagricultural settlements clustered around such naturally rich regions, as archaeological evidence indeed suggests they were.

THE NATUFIANS OF THE NEAR EAST Eleven thousand years ago the Natufians, a people living in the area that is now Israel and Jordan, inhabited caves and rock shelters and built villages on the slopes of Mount Carmel in Israel. At the front of their rock shelters they hollowed out basin-shaped depressions in the rock, possibly for storage pits. Examples of Natufian villages are also found at the Eynan site in Israel.

Eynan is a stratified site containing the remains of three villages in sequence, one atop another. Each village consisted of about 50 circular *pit houses*. The floor of each house was sunk a few feet into the ground, so that the walls of the house consisted partly of earth, below ground level, and partly of stone, above ground level. Pit houses had the advantage of retaining heat longer than houses built above the ground. The villages appear to have had stone-paved walks; circular

stone pavements ringed what seem to be permanent hearths; and the dead were interred in village cemeteries.

The tools suggest that the Natufians harvested wild grain intensively. Sickles recovered from their villages have a specific sheen, which experiments have shown to be the effect of flint striking grass stems, as the sickles would have been used in the cutting of grain. The Natufians are the earliest Epipaleolithic people known to have stored surplus crops. Beneath the floors of their stone-walled houses they constructed plastered storage pits. In addition to wild grains, the Natufians exploited a wide range of other resources.[10] The remains of many wild animals are found in Natufian sites; Natufians appear to have concentrated on hunting gazelle, which they would take by surrounding whole herds.[11]

The Natufians, as well as food collectors in other areas at the time, show many differences as compared with food collectors in earlier periods.[12] Not only was Natufian food collection based on a more intensive use of stationary resources such as wild grain, but the archaeological evidence suggests increasing social complexity. Natufian sites on the average were five times larger than those of their predecessors. Communities were occupied for most of the year, if not year-round. Burial patterns suggest more social differences between people. Although the available wild cereal resources appear to have enabled the Natufians to live in relatively permanent villages, their diet seems to have suffered. Their tooth enamel shows signs of nutritional deficiency, and their stature declined over time.[13]

Mesoamerica

A similar shift toward more broad-spectrum hunting and gathering occurred in the New World at the end of the Paleo-Indian period, about 10,000 years ago. Climate change seems

Hayonim, one of the many caves in which the Natufians built relatively permanent settlements. Archaeologists are at work at the site.

to have been vital here too, as it was in the Old World. The retreat of glacial ice from North America and overall warmer and wetter climate brought dramatic changes to plant and animal communities throughout North America and Mesoamerica. Pleistocene megafauna, such as mammoths, mastodon, rhinoceros, giant ground sloth, and others, as well as a variety of smaller game animals, such as the horse, all went extinct in a relatively short period of time.[14] Hunting strategies shifted toward a broader range of game species, particularly deer, antelope, bison, and small mammals. At the same time, deciduous woodlands and grasslands expanded, providing a range of new plants to exploit. Ground stone woodworking tools such as axes and adzes first appeared, as did nut-processing tools such as mortars and pestles. Shellfish began to be exploited in some areas. Throughout North America and Mesoamerica people began to expand the range of plants and animals they relied upon.[15]

THE ARCHAIC PEOPLES OF HIGHLAND MESO-AMERICA   In Highland Mesoamerica, the mountainous regions of central and southern Mexico, we also see a shift from big-game hunting to a broader use of resources, in part due to a change in climate more like today's. Altitude became an important factor in the hunting and collecting regime, as different altitudes have different plant and animal resources. Valleys tend to have scrubby, grassland vegetation, whereas foothills and mountains have "thorn forests" of cactuses and succulents giving way to oak and pine forests at higher altitudes, where there is more moisture. This vertical zonation means that a wide range of plants and animals were available in relatively close proximity—different environments were close by—and the Archaic peoples took advantage of these varied conditions to hunt and collect a broad range of resources.[16]

About 8,000 years ago the Archaic peoples in Mesoamerica appear to have moved seasonally between communities of two different sizes: camps with 15–30 residents (*macrobands*) and camps with only 2–5 residents (*microbands*). Macroband camps were located near seasonally abundant resources, such as acorns or mesquite pods. Several families would have come together when these re-

sources were in season, both to take advantage of them and to work together to harvest them while they were plentiful, perhaps to perform rituals, and simply to socialize. Microband camps were also inhabited seasonally, probably by a single family, when groups were not assembled into macroband camps. Remains of these microband camps are often found in caves or rock shelters from which a variety of environments could be exploited by moving either upslope or downslope from the campsite.[17]

Unlike the Natufians of the Near East, there is no evidence of social differences among the Archaic peoples of Highland Mesoamerica. The largest social unit, the macroband camp, was probably composed of related family groups, and leadership in these groups was probably informal. There is little evidence of ritual behavior beyond the presence of what may have been a ceremonial dance floor at Gheo-Shih, a macroband campsite in the Valley of Oaxaca. In short, lifestyles remained much like the simple and egalitarian ones of the Paleo-Indians, despite the transition to a much broader strategy of food collection.

Other Areas

People in other areas of the world also shifted from hunting big game to collecting many types of food before they began to practice agriculture. The still-sparse archaeological record suggests that such a change occurred in Southeast Asia, which may have been one of the important centers of original plant and animal domestication. The faunal remains in inland sites there indicate that many different sources of food were being exploited from the same base camps. For example, at these base camps we find the remains of animals from high mountain ridges as well as lowland river valleys, birds and primates from nearby forests, bats from caves, and fish from streams. The few coastal sites indicate that many kinds of fish and shellfish were collected and that animals such as deer, wild cattle, and rhinoceros were hunted.[18] The preagricultural developments in Southeast Asia probably were responses to changes in the climate and environment, including a warming trend, more moisture, and a higher sea level.[19]

These young Fulbe-Waila girls in Chad are collecting seeds much like preagricultural peoples did.

In Africa, too, the preagricultural period was marked by a warmer, wetter environment. The now-numerous lakes, rivers, and other bodies of water provided fish, shellfish, and other resources that apparently allowed people to settle more permanently than they had before. For example, there were lakes in what is now the southern and central Sahara Desert, where people fished and hunted hippopotamuses and crocodiles. This pattern of broad-spectrum food-collecting seems also to have been characteristic of the areas both south and north of the Sahara.[20] One area showing increased sedentism is the Dakhleh Oasis in the Western Desert of Egypt. Between 9,000 and 8,500 years ago, the inhabitants lived in circular stone huts on the shores of rivers and lakes. Bone harpoons and pottery are found there and in other areas from the Nile Valley through the central and southern Sahara westward to what is now Mali. Fishing seems to have allowed people to remain along the rivers and lakes for much of the year.[21]

Why Did Broad-Spectrum Collecting Develop?

It is apparent that the preagricultural switch to broad-spectrum collecting was fairly common throughout the world. Climate change was probably at least partly responsible for the exploitation of new sources of food. For example, the worldwide rise in sea level because of glacial melting may have increased the availability of fish and shellfish. Changes in climate may have also been partly responsible for the decline in the availability of big game, particularly the large herd animals. In addition, it has been suggested that another possible cause of that decline was human activity, specifically overkilling of some of these animals.[22] The evidence suggesting overkill is that the extinction in the New World of many of the large Pleistocene animals, such as the mammoth, coincided with the movement of humans from the Bering Strait region into the Americas.[23]

The overkill hypothesis has been questioned on the basis of bird as well as mammal extinctions in the New World.

An enormous number of bird species also became extinct during the last few thousand years of the North American Pleistocene, and it is difficult to argue that human hunters caused all of those extinctions. Because the bird and mammal extinctions occurred simultaneously, it is likely that most or nearly all the extinctions were due to climatic and other environmental changes.[24] Then again, the example of the New Zealand moas, which went extinct soon after humans colonized the islands, may be instructive. Moas had low reproductive rates; computer simulations suggest their population would have been very sensitive to increases in adult mortality. Because many large animals have low reproductive rates like moas, human overhunting may have been responsible for their extinction.[25]

The decreasing availability of big game may have stimulated people to exploit new food resources. But they may have turned to a broader spectrum of resources for another reason—population growth (see Figure 10–3). As Mark Cohen has noted, hunter-gatherers were "filling up" the world, and they may have had to seek new, possibly less desirable sources of food.[26] (We might think of shellfish as more desirable than mammoths, but only because we don't have to do the work to get such food. A lot of shellfish have to be collected, shelled, and cooked to produce the amount of animal protein obtainable from one large animal.) Consistent with the idea that the world was filling up around this time is the fact that not until after 30,000 years ago did hunter-gatherers begin to move into previously uninhabited parts of the world, such as Australia and the New World.[27]

Broad-spectrum collecting may have involved exploitation of new sources of food, but that does not necessarily mean that people were eating better. A decline in stature often indicates a poorer diet. During the preagricultural period, height apparently declined by as much as two inches in many parts of the Old World (Greece, Israel, India, and northern and western Europe).[28] This decline may have been a result of decreasing nutrition, but it could also be that natural selection for greater height was relaxed because leverage

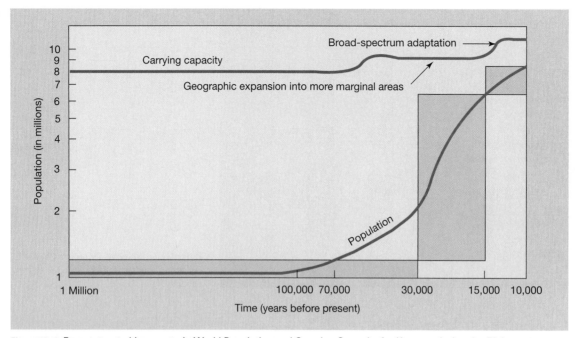

Figure 10–3 Reconstructed Increases in World Population and Carrying Capacity for Humans during the Pleistocene
Estimates of human population suggest that substantial increases preceded the movement of humans into more marginal areas. Further population increase preceded the emergence of broad-spectrum collecting.

Source: Figure adapted from *Demographic Archaeology* by F. A. Hassan. (New York: Academic Press, 1981).

for throwing projectiles such as spears was not so favored after the decline of big-game hunting. (Greater limb-bone length, and therefore greater height, would enable a hunter to throw a spear with more force and farther.[29]) In other areas of the world, such as Australia and what is now the midwestern United States, skeletal evidence also suggests a decline in the general level of health with the rise of broad-spectrum collecting.[30]

Broad-Spectrum Collecting and Sedentarism

Does the switch to broad-spectrum collecting explain the increasingly sedentary way of life we see in various parts of the world in preagricultural times? The answer seems to be both yes and no. In some areas of the world—some sites in Europe, the Near East, Africa, and Peru—settlements became more permanent. In other areas, such as the semiarid highlands of Mesoamerica, the switch to broad-spectrum collecting was not associated with increasing sedentarism. Even after the Highland Mesoamericans began to cultivate plants, they still did not live in permanent villages.[31] Why?

It would seem that it is not simply the switch to broad-spectrum collecting that accounts for increasing sedentarism in many areas. Rather, a comparison of settlements on the Peruvian coast suggests that the more permanent settlements were located nearer, within three and a half miles, to most, if not all, of the diverse food resources exploited during the

year. The community that did not have a year-round settlement seems to have depended on more widely distributed resources. What accounts for sedentarism may thus be the nearness[32] or the high reliability and yield[33] of the broad-spectrum resources, rather than the broad spectrum itself.

Sedentarism and Population Growth

Although some population growth undoubtedly occurred throughout the hunting and gathering phase of world history, some anthropologists have suggested that populations would have increased dramatically when people began to settle down. The evidence for this suggestion comes largely from a comparison of recent nomadic and sedentary !Kung populations.

The settling down of a nomadic group may reduce the typical spacing between births.[34] Nomadic !Kung have children spaced four years apart on the average; in contrast, recently sedentarized !Kung have children about three years apart. Why might birth spacing change with settling down? There are several possibilities.

The spacing of children far apart can occur in a number of ways. One way, if effective contraceptives are not available, is prolonged sexual abstinence after the birth of a child—the postpartum sex taboo—which is common in recent human societies. Another way is abortion or infanticide.[35] Nomadic groups may be motivated to have children farther apart because of the problem of carrying small children. Carrying one small child is difficult enough; carrying

A !Kung group moving camp. When hunters and gatherers move, they have to carry their children and all their possessions with them. Spacing births an average of four years apart helps to ensure that a woman will not have to carry more than two children at a time.

two might be too burdensome. Thus, sedentary populations could have their children spaced more closely because carrying children would not always be necessary.

Although some nomadic groups may have deliberately spaced births by abstinence or infanticide, there is no evidence that such practices explain why four years separate births among nomadic !Kung. There may be another explanation, involving an unintended effect of how babies are fed. Nancy Howell and Richard Lee have suggested that the presence of baby foods other than mother's milk may be responsible for the decreased birth spacing in sedentary agricultural !Kung groups.[36] It is now well established that the longer a mother nurses her baby without supplementary foods, the longer it is likely to be before she starts ovulating again. Nomadic !Kung women have little to give their babies in the way of soft, digestible food, and the babies depend largely on mother's milk for two to three years. But sedentary !Kung mothers can give their babies soft foods such as cereal (made from cultivated grain) and milk from domesticated animals. Such changes in feeding practices may shorten birth spacing by shortening the interval between

birth and the resumption of ovulation. In preagricultural sedentary communities, it is possible that baby foods made from wild grains might have had the same effect. For this reason alone, therefore, populations may have grown even before people started to farm or herd.

Another reason sedentary !Kung women may have more babies than nomadic !Kung women has to do with the ratio of body fat to body weight. Some investigators suspect that a critical minimum of fat in the body may be necessary for ovulation. A sedentary !Kung woman may have more fatty tissue than a nomadic !Kung woman, who walks many miles daily to gather wild plant foods, often carrying a child with her. Thus, sedentary !Kung women might resume ovulating sooner after the birth of a baby and so for that reason alone may be likely to have more closely spaced children. If some critical amount of fat is necessary for ovulation, that would explain why in our own society many women who have little body fat—long-distance runners, gymnasts, and ballet dancers are examples—do not ovulate regularly.[37]

Microlithic Technology

Technologically, these preagricultural cultures did not differ radically from Upper Paleolithic cultures.[38] The trend toward smaller and lighter tools continued. Microliths, small blades half an inch to two inches long, which were made in late Upper Paleolithic times, were now used in quantity. In place of the one-piece flint implement, the preagricultural peoples in Europe, Asia, and Africa equipped themselves with *composite* tools—that is, tools made of more than one material.

A sickle made with microliths.

Microliths, too small to be used one at a time, could be fitted into grooves in bone or wood to form arrows, harpoons, daggers, and sickles. A sickle, for example, was made by inserting several microliths into a groove in a wooden or bone handle. The blades were held in place by resin. A broken microlith could be replaced like a blade in a modern razor. Besides being adaptable for many uses, microliths could be made from many varieties of available stone. Since they did not need the large nodules to make large core and flake tools, people using microliths could work with smaller nodules to make the small blades.[39]

The Domestication of Plants and Animals

Neolithic means "of the new stone age"; the term originally signified the cultural stage in which humans invented pottery and ground-stone tools. We now know, however, that both were present in earlier times, so we cannot define a Neolithic state of culture purely on the basis of the presence of pottery and ground-stone tools. At present, archaeologists generally define the **Neolithic** in terms of the presence of domesticated plants and animals. In this type of culture, people began to produce food rather than merely collect it.

The line between food-collecting and food-producing occurs when people begin to plant crops and to keep and breed animals. How do we know when this transition occurred? In fact, archaeologically we do not see the beginning of food production; we can see signs of it only after plants and animals show differences from their wild varieties. When people plant crops, we refer to the process as cultivation. It is only when the crops cultivated and the animals raised are *modified*—different from wild varieties—that we speak of plant and animal **domestication.**

We know, in a particular site, that domestication occurred if plant remains have characteristics different from those of wild plants of the same types (see Figure 10–4). For example, wild grains of barley and wheat have a fragile **rachis**— the seed-bearing part of the stem—which shatters easily, releasing the seeds. Domesticated grains have a tough rachis, which does not shatter easily. In addition, the grain of wild barley and wheat has a tough shell protecting the seed from premature exposure, whereas domesticated grain has a brittle shell that can be easily separated, which facilitates preparing the seed for grinding into flour.

How did the domesticated plants get to be different from the wild varieties? Artificial or human selection, deliberate or accidental, obviously was required. Consider how the rachis of wheat and barley may have changed. As we said, when wild grain ripens in the field, the rachis shatters easily, scattering the seed. This trait is selectively advantageous under wild conditions; it is nature's method of propagating the species. Plants with a tough rachis, therefore, have only a slight chance of reproducing themselves under natural conditions, but they are more desirable for planting. When humans arrived with sickles and flails to collect the wild stands of grain, the seeds harvested probably contained a

Figure 10–4 Seed Heads of Wild and Domesticated Wheat
Note the larger and more numerous seeds on domesticated wheat.

Source: From *Past in Perspective,* 2nd ed., by K. Feder. (Mountain View, CA: Mayfield, 2000).

high proportion of tough-rachis mutants, because these could best withstand the rough treatment of harvest processing. If planted, the harvested seeds would be likely to produce tough-rachis plants. If in each successive harvest seeds from tough-rachis plants were the least likely to be lost, tough-rachis plants would come to predominate.[40]

Domesticated species of animals also differ from the wild varieties. For example, the horns of wild goats in the Near East are shaped differently from those of domesticated goats.[41] But differences in physical characteristics may not be the only indicators of domestication. Some archaeologists believe that imbalances in the sex and age ratios of animal remains at particular sites also suggest that domestication had occurred. For example, at Zawi Chemi Shanidar in Iraq, the proportion of young to mature sheep remains was much higher than the ratio of young to mature sheep in wild herds. One possible inference to be drawn is that the animals were domesticated, the adult sheep being saved for breeding purposes while the young were eaten. (If mostly young animals were eaten, and only a few animals were allowed to grow old, most of the bones found in a site would be from the young animals that were killed regularly for food.[42])

Domestication in the Near East

For some time most archaeologists have thought that the Fertile Crescent (see Figure 10–5), the arc of land stretching up from Israel and the Jordan Valley through southern Turkey and then downward to the western slopes of the Zagros Mountains in Iran, was one of the earliest centers of plant and animal domestication. We know that several varieties of domesticated wheat were being grown there after about 8000 B.C., as were oats, rye, barley, lentils, peas, and various fruits and nuts (apricots, pears, pomegranates, dates,

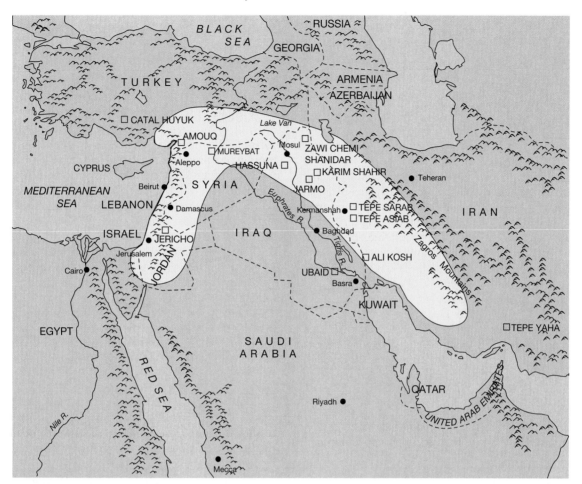

Figure 10–5 Early Agricultural Settlements in the Near East
Modern cities are represented by a dot, early settlements by a square. The yellow color indicates the area known as the Fertile Crescent.

figs, olives, almonds, and pistachios).[43] It appears that animals were first domesticated in the Near East. Dogs were first domesticated before the rise of agriculture, around 13,000 B.C. (see the box "Did Dogs [and Cats] Domesticate Themselves?"), goats and sheep around 7000 B.C., and cattle and pigs around 6000 B.C.[44]

Let us look at two early Neolithic sites in the Near East to see what life there may have been like after people began to depend on domesticated plants and animals for food.

ALI KOSH At the stratified site of Ali Kosh in what is now southwestern Iran (see Figure 10–5), we see the remains of a community that started out about 7500 B.C. living mostly on wild plants and animals. Over the next 2,000 years, until about 5500 B.C., agriculture and herding became increasingly important. After 5500 B.C., we see the appearance of two innovations—irrigation and the use of domesticated cattle—that seem to have stimulated a minor population explosion during the following millennium.

From 7500 to 6750 B.C., the people at Ali Kosh cut little slabs of raw clay out of the ground to build small, multi-room structures. The rooms excavated by archaeologists are seldom more than 7 by 10 feet, and there is no evidence that

the structures were definitely houses where people actually spent time or slept. Instead, they may have been storage rooms. On the other hand, house rooms of even smaller size are known in other areas of the world, so it is possible that the people at Ali Kosh in its earliest phase were actually living in those tiny, unbaked, "brick" houses. There is a bit of evidence that the people at Ali Kosh may have moved for the summer (with their goats) to the grassier mountain valleys nearby, which were just a few days' walk away.

We have a lot of evidence about what the people at Ali Kosh ate. They got some of their food from cultivated emmer wheat and a kind of barley and a considerable amount from domesticated goats. We know the goats were domesticated because wild goats do not seem to have lived in the area. Also, the fact that virtually no bones from elderly goats were found in the site suggests that the goats were domesticated and herded rather than hunted. Moreover, it would seem from the horn cores found in the site that mostly young male goats were eaten, so the females probably were kept for breeding and milking. But with all these signs of deliberate food production, there is an enormous amount of evidence—literally tens of thousands of seeds and bone fragments—that the people at the beginning of Ali Kosh

CURRENT RESEARCH AND ISSUES

Did Dogs (and Cats) Domesticate Themselves?

Early evidence of a close relationship between dogs and people comes from an archaeological site in northern Israel dating to nearly 12,000 years ago. At that site, archaeologists found the grave of an elderly woman, lying on her right side with her legs folded up, with a dog under her left hand. The Embers' dog was always happy to greet them when they came home. She also was a retriever, an alarm system, could follow a scent, and ate everything that dropped on the floor. Do any of these attributes explain why humans all over the world have had domesticated descendants of wolves around the house for the last 10,000–15,000 years?

Dogs were probably the first animals domesticated by humans, probably about 15,000 years ago, and several thousand years before plants, sheep, and goats were domesticated in the Near East. Humans were starting to settle down in semipermanent camps and villages, as they began to depend less on big game (which they would have had to follow over long distances) and more on relatively stationary food resources, such as fish, shellfish, small game, and wild plants rich in carbohydrates, proteins, and oils.

Why would humans have been interested in taming wolves at that time? One theory is that humans were shifting their prey from large animals to small, and they needed dogs for tracking wounded game or for retrieving killed game from bodies of water or under-

brush. Dogs might also have been useful as alarm-givers in case predators came close. Finally, dogs might have helped to keep a camp clean by scavenging garbage.

The Embers think that this last use of dogs suggests an alternative theory of dog domestication. Perhaps it wasn't so much that humans domesticated dogs, but that some wolves domesticated themselves by hanging around human camps. Why would wolves be interested in those humans who were first settling down? It couldn't have been the possibility of a human dinner, because that would have been a possibility for millions of years before. So perhaps something else lured wolves to those early settled camps and villages. What was different about those early settlements? For the first time in human history, people were staying put for considerable periods of time—months at a time, year after year—because they could count on being able to "harvest" and live on the wild resources of the area. If they lived in a place for years, even if only seasonally, they would eventually have a problem with garbage.

The residues of meals, in particular, would have been a problem. They might not only come to stink; they might also attract rodents and bigger threats to health and children. What could the people do about this problem? Well, as any camper nowadays realizes, they could

depended mostly on wild plants (legumes and grasses) and wild animals (including gazelles, wild oxen, and wild pigs). They also collected fish, such as carp and catfish, and shellfish, such as mussels, as well as waterfowl that visited the area during part of the year.

The flint tools used during this earliest phase at Ali Kosh were varied and abundant. Finds from this period include tens of thousands of tiny flint blades, some only a few millimeters wide. About 1 percent of the chipped stone found by archaeologists was **obsidian,** or volcanic glass, which came from what is now eastern Turkey, several hundred miles away. Thus, the people at Ali Kosh during its earliest phase definitely had some kind of contact with people elsewhere. This contact is also suggested by the fact that the emmer wheat they cultivated did not have a wild relative in the area.

From 6750 to 6000 B.C., the people increased their consumption of cultivated food plants; 40 percent of the seed remains in the hearths and refuse areas were now from emmer wheat and barley. The proportion of the diet coming from

wild plants was much reduced, probably because the cultivated plants have the same growing season and grow in the same kind of soil as the wild plants. Grazing by the goats and sheep that were kept may also have contributed to the reduction of wild plant foods in the area and in the diet. The village may or may not have gotten larger, but the multi-room houses definitely had. The rooms were now larger than 10 by 10 feet; the walls were much thicker; and the clay-slab bricks were now held together by a mud mortar. Also, the walls now often had a coat of smooth mud plaster on both sides. The stamped-mud house floors were apparently covered with rush or reed mats (you can see the imprints of them). There were courtyards with domed brick ovens and brick-lined roasting pits. Understandably, considering the summer heat in the area, none of the ovens found was inside a house.

Even though the village probably contained no more than 100 individuals, it participated in an extensive trading network. Seashells were probably obtained from the Persian Gulf, which is some distance to the south; copper may have

have buried the garbage so that its scent would not attract unwelcome visitors. But eventually they would have run out of room for garbage pits in or close to the settlement. Of course, they could have moved the settlement. But maybe they didn't want to. After all, they had spent a lot of time and effort building a permanent house that was warm in the winter and dry in the rains. And they had a lot of things stored there. So what could they do?

Maybe people didn't have to do anything. Maybe those wolves hanging around the neighborhood solved the problem for our ancestors. How? By scavenging, which is something most dogs (particularly larger ones, like the first domesticated dogs) do quite naturally and efficiently. The Embers' dog ate anything (except maybe undressed lettuce). So even a few tame wolves or domesticated dogs could have kept a garbage pit or pile from stinking and growing. And the people "feeding" that pit or pile could stay put in one place for a long time, safe from smells, vermin, and disease. Dogs may have mostly domesticated themselves because it was good for some of them as well as for those preagricultural humans.

A similar theory may explain the domestication of cats. Cats are especially good at catching and killing mice. Masses of mice skeletons (of the house mouse) begin to appear in basements of Near East dwellings after the emergence of agriculture. It is possible that humans purposely tried to domesticate cats to catch mice, but it is more likely that cats would have domesticated themselves by adapting to life near or in a granary or storage cellar. Of course, humans might have

helped the process of domestication a little, by killing the more ferocious wild cats that were attracted to the settlement. The same was probably true for the wolves attracted to garbage. Even if you didn't at first want to "pet" the canids or felids who were hanging around, you wouldn't want them to attack humans. Wolves in the wild have a dominance–submission hierarchy, so they would be preadapted to heeding a "dominant" human; those that were not sufficiently submissive could be killed.

How could these theories of dog and cat domestication be tested? If dogs domesticated themselves as scavengers, archaeologists should find evidence of dog domestication (e.g., changes in anatomy) only in sites that were occupied for a good part of the year over a period of years. Only under those circumstances would garbage be a problem and dogs a solution. Similarly, evidence of cat domestication should be found only in sites that show signs of year-to-year storage of grain. Only then would rodents be a problem and cats a solution. We hope archaeologists will make these tests in the future.

Sources: Juliet Clutton-Brock, "Domestication of Animals," and Frank Hole, "Origins of Agriculture." In Steve Jones, Robert Martin, and David Pilbeam, eds., *The Cambridge Encyclopedia of Human Evolution* (New York: Cambridge University Press, 1992), pp. 380–85, 373–79, respectively; Juliet Clutton-Brock, "Dog," and Roy Robinson, "Cat." In Ian L. Mason, *Evolution of Domesticated Animals* (New York: Longman, 1984), pp. 198–210, 217–25, respectively; Stephen Budiansky, *The Covenant of the Wild: Why Animals Chose Domestication* (New York: Morrow, 1992).

come from what is now central Iran; obsidian was still coming from eastern Turkey; and turquoise somehow made its way from what is now the border between Iran and Afghanistan. Some of these materials were used as ornaments worn by both sexes—or so it seems from the remains of bodies found buried under the floors of houses.

After about 5500 B.C., the area around Ali Kosh begins to show signs of a much larger population, apparently made possible by a more complex agriculture employing irrigation and plows drawn by domesticated cattle. In the next thousand years, by 4500 B.C., the population of the area probably tripled. This population growth was apparently part of the cultural developments that culminated in the rise of urban civilizations in the Near East,[45] as we will see in the next chapter.

Population growth may have occurred in and around Ali Kosh but did not continue in all areas of the Near East after domestication. For example, one of the largest early villages in the Near East, 'Ain Ghazal (on the outskirts of what is now Amman, Jordan), suffered a decline in population and

standard of living over time, perhaps because the environment around 'Ain Ghazal could not permanently support a large village.[46]

CATAL HÜYÜK On a windswept plateau in the rugged, mountainous region of southern Turkey stand the remains of a mud-brick town known as Catal Hüyük (see Figure 10–5). *Hüyük* is the Turkish word for a mound formed by a succession of settlements, one built on top of another.

About 5600 B.C., Catal Hüyük was an adobe town. Some 200 houses have been excavated, and they are interconnected in *pueblo fashion* (each flat-roofed structure housed a number of families). The inhabitants decorated the walls of the houses with imaginative murals, and their shrines with symbolic statuary. The murals depict what seem to be religious scenes and everyday events. Archaeologists peeling away frescoes found layer upon layer of murals, indicating that old murals were plastered over to make way for fresh paintings. Several rooms are believed to have been shrine rooms. They contain many large bull murals and clay bull figurines and

Excavation in one of the pueblo-like structures of Neolithic Catal Hüyük.

have full-sized clay heads of cattle on the walls. Other "shrine-room" murals depict scenes of life and death, painted in red and black, respectively. Clay statuettes of a pregnant woman and of a bearded man seated on a bull have also been found in these rooms.

Farming was well advanced at Catal Hüyük. Lentils, wheat, barley, and peas were grown in quantities that produced a surplus. Archaeologists were astonished at the richly varied handicrafts, including beautifully carved wooden bowls and boxes, that the people of the town produced. These people also had obsidian and flint daggers, spearheads, lance heads, scrapers, awls, and sickle blades. Bowls, spatulas, knives, ladles, and spoons were made from bone. The houses contained belt hooks, toggles, and pins carved from bone. Evidence also suggests that men and women wore jewelry fashioned from bone, shell, and copper and that they used obsidian mirrors.[47]

Because Catal Hüyük is located in a region with few raw materials, the town evidently depended on exchange with other areas to secure the rich variety of materials it used. Shells were procured from the Mediterranean, timber from the hills, obsidian from 50 miles away, and marble from western Turkey.

Domestication in Mesoamerica

A very different pattern of domestication is seen in Mesoamerica. Here the semi-nomadic Archaic hunting and gathering lifestyle persisted long after people first domesticated plants.[48] How can this be? Don't people have to settle near their crops to take care of them? Once they have domesticated plants, don't they stop collecting wild plants? The answer is no. In Mesoamerica, people sowed a variety of plants, but after doing so they went on with their seasonal rounds of hunting and gathering, and came back later to harvest what they had sown. Many of the early domesticates in Mesoamerica were not basic to subsistence, even if they

were highly desirable. Domestication may have been a way for Archaic peoples to make desirable plants more common in their environment. For example, one of the first domesticates was the bottle gourd. These were not eaten but were used to carry water. Joyce Marcus and Kent Flannery hypothesize that the bottle gourd was domesticated by people deliberately planting them in areas where they did not grow naturally, so that as groups moved through those areas they always had access to gourds for carrying water.[49]

Bottle gourds are only one of many early domesticates from Highland Mesoamerica. Others include tomatoes, cotton, a variety of beans and squashes, and, perhaps most importantly, maize. The earliest domesticated form of maize (corn), dating from about 5000 B.C., has been found in Tehuacán, Mexico. Genetic studies of maize show that it was domesticated from teosinte, a tall wild grass that still grows widely in Mexico (see Figure 10–6).[50] Indeed, these genetic studies suggest that changes occured in only two genes, one related to the kernel glumes (outer casing), and one related to the stalk shape.[51] The genes of modern corn were already established 4,000–6,000 years ago.

Teosinte is quite different from maize in several important ways, but small genetic changes led to major phenotypic changes. The genetic malleability of maize may be one reason it has become one of the most important domesticated crops on earth. Teosinte stalks do look a lot like maize, but teosinte has a "spike" to which 7–12 individual seeds are attached in a single row, unlike the maize cob, which has many seeds in many rows. Each teosinte seed has its own brittle shell, whereas the entire maize cob is covered with a tough husk. However, early maize was also considerably different from modern maize. The oldest maize cobs—dating to about 7,000 years ago—are tiny, only about an inch long. They have only a half-dozen rows of seeds, and each seed is tiny. One interesting fact about both ancient and modern maize is that it is almost completely dependent on humans to reproduce—the shift from seeds with brittle coats to cobs

Figure 10–6 Teosinte Plant, Spike, and Seeds and Maize Plant, Cob, and Kernels
Note how much larger the domesticated maize cob and kernels are compared to the teosinte spike and seeds.

Source: From *Past in Perspective* by K. Feder. (Mountain View, CA: Mayfield, 2000).

with a tough husk meant that someone had to open the husk without damaging the seeds in order for them to be dispersed and reproduce.[52]

Like maize and the bottle gourd, beans and squash were probably domesticated by simple manipulation of wild varieties. Runner beans, for example, grow naturally in the soils on the slopes outside of rock shelters and caves. It is not a stretch of the imagination to envision Archaic peoples harvesting these beans (for their roots to begin with—nondomestic runner bean seeds are tiny and probably were not eaten) and selectively planting those with desired qualities, like large seeds. Similarly, only the seeds of wild squashes were likely eaten by Archaic peoples, as the flesh of wild squashes often has an unattractive smell and taste. But they may have selectively planted mutants with good-tasting flesh and larger seeds, eventually producing the domestic varieties over time.[53]

People who lived in Mesoamerica, Mexico and Central America, are often credited with the invention of planting maize, beans, and squash together in the same field. This planting strategy provides some important advantages. Maize takes nitrogen from the soil; beans, like all legumes, put nitrogen back into the soil. The maize stalk provides a natural pole for the bean plant to twine around, and the low-growing squash can grow around the base of the tall maize plant. Beans supply people with the amino acid lysine, which is missing in maize. Thus, maize and beans together provide

all the essential amino acids that humans need to obtain from their food. Teosinte may have provided the model for this unique combination, as wild runner beans and wild squash occur naturally where teosinte grows.[54]

GUILA NAQUITZ The Guila Naquitz cave, excavated in the 1960s by Kent Flannery, provides a good picture of early domestication in Highland Mesoamerica. Here small groups of people, probably only a single family at a time, lived intermittently (and probably seasonally) over a period of 2,000 years (ca. 8900 B.C.–6700 B.C.), the period during which plants were domesticated. The cave itself is located in the thorn forest of the upper piedmont above the floor of the Valley of Oaxaca. The residents of Guila Naquitz hunted deer and peccary (a wild piglike animal) with spears and spear-throwers, and trapped small animals such as rabbits. They also collected plant foods from the surrounding area, particularly prickly pear fruits, cherries, acorns, and piñon nuts from the forests above the cave, along with agave hearts, onions, and various other nuts and fruits from a variety of thorn forest plants.[55]

Also found in Guila Naquitz cave are the remains of domesticated plants, including bottle gourd and several varieties of squashes. How did these come to be in the cave? Were the inhabitants planting fields of squashes? Probably not in the way one thinks of planting a field today. Squashes are common wild plants in Highland Mesoamerica, and thrive in disturbed soils such as those outside of caves. It may be that the inhabitants of the Guila Naquitz cave knew squashes would grow easily near their cave, and so actively planted some with better-tasting flesh or larger seeds than those that might naturally grow there.[56] Domestication and the use of domesticated plants would be rather informal—a supplement to a diet already rich in animal and plant species. This picture seems much different from that at Near Eastern sites such as Ali Kosh and Catal Hüyük. Domestication in Guila Naquitz appears to have been accomplished by hunters and gatherers who supplemented their basic diet with some desired plants (squashes with tasty flesh, for example); there was no "revolution" that enabled the people to rely on domesticated plants.

Domestication Elsewhere in the World

SOUTH AMERICA AND THE EASTERN UNITED STATES

Outside of Mesoamerica, evidence of independent domestication of plants comes from at least two areas in the New World: South America and the eastern United States. The first plants to be domesticated in the New World were members of the cucurbit family, including the bottle gourd and a variety of squashes, all probably domesticated some time after 7500 B.C. In addition to these and other plants domesticated in Mesoamerica, we can trace more than 200 domesticated plants to the Andes in South America, including potatoes, lima beans, peanuts, amaranth, and quinoa. The first clear domesticates were squashes and gourds, which may date back to 8000 B.C., which makes domestication in the Andes as old as in Mesoamerica, and perhaps even older.[57] The origins of the root crops manioc and sweet potato are less certain, but those crops probably originated in lowland tropical forest regions of South America.[58]

Many of the plants grown in North America, such as corn, beans, and squash, were apparently introduced from Mesoamerica. However, at least three seed plants were probably domesticated independently in North America at an earlier time—sunflowers, sumpweed, and goosefoot. Sunflowers and sumpweed contain seeds that are highly nutritious in terms of protein and fat; goosefoot is high in starch and similar to corn in food value.[59] Sumpweed is an unusually good source of calcium, rivaled only by greens, mussels, and bones. It is also a very good source of iron (better than beef liver) and thiamine.[60] These plants may have been cultivated in the area of Kentucky, Tennessee, and southern Illinois beginning around 2000 B.C. (Corn was introduced about A.D. 200.)

All of the pre-corn domesticates are nutritionally superior to corn, so why did North American agriculturalists switch to a reliance on corn in the last 1,000 years?[61] In archaeologist Bruce Smith's words, "With the exception of the sunflower, North American seed crops are not exactly household words."[62] Crop yields of corn would have had to be quite high to surpass the yields of those other crops, so perhaps the crucial factors were the time of harvest and the amount of effort required. Goosefoot, for example, was comparable to corn nutritionally. But harvesting and preparing it for storage took a lot of work and also had to be done dur-

ing the fall, the time of year when deer could be hunted intensively. So perhaps the incompatibility of goosefoot production and deer hunting, and the ease of harvesting corn and preparing it for storage, explain the switch to corn.[63]

On the whole, domestic animals were less important economically in the New World than they were in many parts of the Old World. In North America, dogs and turkeys were the main domesticated animals before the arrival of the Spanish. Dogs in North and South America probably accompanied the first colonizers of the Americas, as all domestic dogs appear to be descended from a common Asian ancestor.[64] Domesticated turkeys from about A.D. 500 have been found in pueblos in the American Southwest.[65] Their feathers were used for arrows, ornaments, and weaving, and their bones for tools; but they do not seem to have been used frequently for food. However, turkeys were an important food in Mexico, where they may have been independently domesticated, and in Central America. When Cortes came to Mexico in 1519, he found domesticated turkeys in great quantities.[66]

The central Andes was the only part of the New World where animals were a significant part of the economy. Used for meat, transportation, and wool, llamas and alpacas (members of the camel family) were domesticated as early as 5000 B.C. in the Andes.[67] Guinea pigs, misnamed because they are neither pigs nor from Guinea, are rodents that were domesticated in the Andes sometime later. They were an important source of food even before domestication.[68] Since they were domesticated, they have been raised in people's dwellings.

Animal domestication in the New World differed from that in the Old World because different wild species were found in the two hemispheres. The Old World plains and forests were the homes for the wild ancestors of the cattle, sheep, goats, pigs, and horses we know today. In the New World, the Pleistocene herds of horses, mastodons, mammoths, and other large animals were long extinct, allowing few opportunities for domestication of large animals.[69]

EAST ASIA

The archaeological record for the domestication of seed crops is better known than for soft-flesh crops because the latter do not preserve well. The earliest clear evidence of cereal cultivation outside the Near East is from China. Late in the 6th millennium B.C. in North China there were sites where foxtail millet was cultivated. Storage pits, storage pots, and large numbers of grinding stones suggest that millet was an enormously important item in the diet. The wild-animal bones and the hunting and fishing tools that have been found suggest that people still depended on hunting and fishing somewhat, even though domesticated pigs (as well as dogs) were present. In South China, from about the same time, archaeologists have found a village by the edge of a small lake where people cultivated rice, bottle gourds, water chestnuts, and the datelike fruit called jujube. The people in South China also raised water buffalo, pigs, and dogs. And, as in the North China sites, some of their food came from hunting and fishing.[70]

Mainland Southeast Asia may have been a place of domestication as early as the Near East was. The dating of

Bananas and taro were domesticated in New Guinea nearly 7000 years ago.

domestication in Southeast Asia is not yet clear; the dates of the oldest site with probable domesticates—Spirit cave in northwest Thailand—range from about 9500 B.C. to 5500 B.C. Some of the plants found at Spirit cave are not clearly distinguishable from wild varieties, but others, such as gourds, betel nut, betel leaf, and water chestnut, were probably domesticates.[71]

Most of the early cultivation in mainland Southeast Asia seems to have occurred in the plains and low terraces around rivers, although the main subsistence foods of early cultivators were probably the fish and shellfish in nearby waters. The first plants to be domesticated probably were not cereal grains, as they were in the Near East. Indeed, some early cultivated crops may not have been used for food at all. In particular, bamboo may have been used to make cutting tools and for a variety of building purposes, and gourds were probably used as containers or bowls. We do not know yet exactly when rice was first domesticated, but there is definite evidence of cultivated rice in Thailand after 4000 B.C.

Bananas and taro may have been first domesticated in New Guinea. Recent analyses of soils from archaeological deposits at Kuk Swamp have identified phytoliths (small silica crystals formed between plant cells that are unique to particular species of plants) from bananas and taro dating from almost 7,000 years ago.[72] Archaeologists have known that agricultural fields with soil mounds and irrigation features have a long history in New Guinea, dating back as far as 10,000 years. The new findings of very early taro and banana cultivation suggest that New Guinea may have been the location where these plants were first domesticated. Other major food plants domesticated in Southeast Asia include yams, breadfruit, and coconuts.[73]

AFRICA   Some plants and animals were domesticated first in Africa. Most of the early domestications probably occurred in the wide, broad belt of woodland-savanna country south of the Sahara and north of the equator. Among the cereal grains, sorghum was probably first domesticated in the central or eastern part of this belt, bulrush millet and a kind of rice (different from Asian rice) in the western part, and finger millet in the east. Groundnuts (peanuts) and yams

were first domesticated in West Africa.[74] We do know that farming became widespread in the northern half of Africa after 6000 B.C.; investigators continue to debate whether the earliest crops grown there were indigenous or borrowed from the Near East. There is little doubt, however, that some of the plant foods were first domesticated in sub-Saharan Africa because the wild varieties occur there.[75] Many of the important domestic animals in Africa today, especially sheep and goats, were first domesticated elsewhere in the Old World, but one form of cattle, as well as donkey and guinea fowl, were probably first domesticated in Africa.[76]

A man harvesting sorghum in Burkina Faso. Sorghum is one of several plant species domesticated in Africa.

Why Did Food Production Develop?

We know that an economic transformation occurred in widely separate areas of the world beginning after about 10,000 years ago, as people began to domesticate plants and animals. But why did domestication occur? And why did it occur independently in many different places within a period of a few thousand years? Considering that people depended only on wild plants and animals for millions of years, the differences in exactly when domestication first occurred in different parts of the world seem small. The spread of domesticated plants seems to have been more rapid in the Old World than in the New World, perhaps because the Old World spread was more along an east–west axis (except for the spread to sub-Saharan Africa), whereas the New World spread was more north–south. Spreading north and south may have required more time to adapt to variation in day lengths, climates, and diseases.[77]

There are many theories of why food production developed; most have tried to explain the origin of domestication in the area of the Fertile Crescent. Gordon Childe's theory, popular in the 1950s, was that a drastic change in climate caused domestication in the Near East.[78] According to Childe, the postglacial period was marked by a decline in summer rainfall in the Near East and northern Africa. As the rains decreased, people were forced to retreat into shrinking pockets, or oases, of food resources surrounded by desert. The lessened availability of wild resources provided an incentive for people to cultivate grains and to domesticate animals, according to Childe.

Robert Braidwood criticized Childe's theory for two reasons. First, Braidwood believed that the climate changes may not have been as dramatic as Childe had assumed, and therefore the "oasis incentive" may not have existed. Second, the climatic changes that occurred in the Near East after the retreat of the last glaciers had probably occurred at earlier interglacial periods too, but there had never been a similar food-producing revolution before. Hence, according to Braidwood, there must be more to the explanation of why people began to produce food than simply changes in climate.[79]

Braidwood and Gordon Willey claimed that people did not undertake domestication until they had learned a great deal about their environment and until their culture had evolved enough for them to handle such an undertaking: "Why did incipient food production not come earlier? Our only answer at the moment is that culture was not ready to achieve it."[80]

But most archaeologists now think we should try to explain why people were not "ready" earlier to achieve domestication. Both Lewis Binford and Kent Flannery suggest that some change in external circumstances must have induced or favored the changeover to food production.[81] As Flannery pointed out, there is no evidence of a great economic incentive for hunter-gatherers to become food producers. In fact, some contemporary hunter-gatherers obtain adequate nutrition with far *less* work than many agriculturalists. So what might push food collectors to become food producers?

Binford and Flannery thought that the incentive to domesticate animals and plants may have been a desire to reproduce what was wildly abundant in the most bountiful or optimum hunting and gathering areas. Because of population growth in the optimum areas, people might have moved to surrounding areas containing fewer wild resources. It would have been in those marginal areas that people might have first turned to food production in order to reproduce what they used to have.

The Binford–Flannery model seems to fit the archaeological record in the Levant, the southwestern part of the Fertile Crescent, where population increase did precede the first signs of domestication.[82] But, as Flannery admitted, in some regions, such as southwestern Iran, the optimum hunting-gathering areas do not show population increase before the emergence of domestication.[83]

The Binford–Flannery model focuses on population pressure in a small area as the incentive to turn to food production. Mark Cohen theorizes it was population pressure on a global scale that explains why so many of the world's peoples adopted agriculture within the span of a few thousand years.[84] He argues that hunter-gatherers all over the world gradually increased in population so that by about 10,000 years ago the world was more or less filled with food collectors. Thus people could no longer relieve population pressure by moving to uninhabited areas. To support their increasing populations, they would have had to exploit a broader range of less desirable wild foods; that is, they would have had to switch to broad-spectrum collecting, or they would have had to increase the yields of the most desirable wild plants by weeding, protecting them from animal pests, and perhaps deliberately planting the most productive among them. Cohen thinks that people might have tried a variety of these strategies but would generally have ended up depending on cultivation because that would have been the most efficient way to allow more people to live in one place.

Recently, some archaeologists have returned to the idea that climatic change (not the extreme variety that Childe envisaged) might have played a role in the emergence of agriculture. It seems clear from the evidence now available that the climate of the Near East about 13,000–12,000 years ago became more seasonal: The summers got hotter and drier than before and the winters became colder. These climatic changes may have favored the emergence of annual species of wild grain, which archaeologically we see proliferating in many areas of the Near East.[85] People such as the Natufians intensively exploited the seasonal grains, developing an elaborate technology for storing and processing the grains and giving up their previous nomadic existence to do so. The transition to agriculture may have occurred when sedentary foraging no longer provided sufficient resources for the population. This could have happened because sedentarization led to population increase and therefore resource scarcity,[86] or because local wild resources became depleted after people settled down in permanent villages.[87] In the area of Israel and Jordan where the Natufians lived, some of the people apparently turned to agriculture, probably to increase the supply of grain, whereas other people returned to nomadic food collection because of the decreasing availability of wild grain.[88]

Change to a more seasonal climate might also have led to a shortage of certain nutrients for food collectors. In the dry seasons certain nutrients would have been less available. For example, grazing animals get lean when grasses are not plentiful, so meat from hunting would have been in short supply in the dry seasons. Although it may seem surprising, some recent hunter-gatherers have starved when they had to rely on lean meat. If somehow they could have increased their carbohydrate or fat intake, they might have been more likely to get through the periods of lean game.[89] So it is possible that some wild-food collectors in the past thought of planting crops to get them through the dry seasons when hunting, fishing, and gathering did not provide enough carbohydrates and fat for them to avoid starvation.

Mesoamerica presents a very different picture, because the early domesticates were not important to subsistence. Theories about population pressure and nutrient shortage don't seem to fit Mesoamerica well. However, there were apparently shortages of desired plants, such as bottle gourds, and domestication may well have occurred as humans actively sowed these desired plants. The difference between this model and the ones described above is that humans in Mesoamerica were apparently not forced into domestication by climate change or population pressure, but actively turned to domestication to obtain more of the most desired or useful plant species. The most interesting case is maize, which only became a staple food some 2,500 or more years after it was first domesticated. Why did it become a staple? Probably both because it was a suitable staple crop (especially when intercropped with beans and squash, as discussed earlier) and because people liked it, so they grew it in large quantities. Over time, and perhaps because of conflict, population pressure, and other forces similar to those that apparently led to domestication in the Near East, people in

Mesoamerica and later North and South America came to rely on maize as their dietary mainstay.

Consequences of the Rise of Food Production

We know that intensive agriculture (permanent rather than shifting cultivation) probably developed in response to population pressure, but we do not know for sure that population pressure was even partly responsible for plant and animal domestication in the first place. Still, population growth certainly accelerated after the rise of food production (see Figure 10–7). There were other consequences too. Paradoxically, perhaps, health seems to have declined. Material possessions, though, became more elaborate.

Accelerated Population Growth

As we have seen, settling down (even before the rise of food production) may have increased the rate of human population growth. But population growth definitely accelerated after the emergence of farming and herding, possibly because the spacing between births was reduced further and therefore fertility (the number of births per mother) increased. Increased fertility may have been advantageous because of the greater value of children in farming and herding economies; there is evidence from recent population studies that fertility rates are higher where children contribute more to the economy.[90]

Not only may parents desire more children to help with chores; the increased workload of mothers may also (but inadvertently) decrease birth spacing. The busier a mother is, the less frequently she may nurse and the more likely her baby will be given supplementary food by other caretakers such as older siblings.[91] Less frequent nursing[92] and greater reliance on food other than mothers' milk may result in an earlier resumption of ovulation after the birth of a baby.

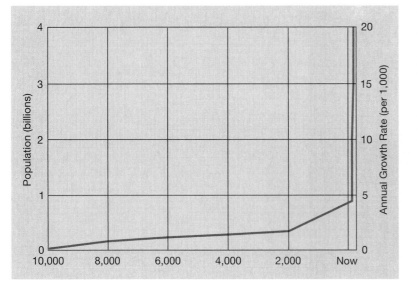

Figure 10–7 Population Growth since 10,000 Years Ago
The rate of population growth accelerated after the emergence of farming and herding 10,000 years ago. The rate of growth accelerated even more dramatically in recent times.

Source: Adapted from Ansley J. Coale, *The History of the Human Population.* Copyright © 1974 by *Scientific American, Inc.*

(Farmers and herders are likely to have animal milk to feed to babies, and also cereals that have been transformed by cooking into soft, mushy porridges.) Therefore the spacing between births may have decreased (and the number of births per mother, in turn, increased) when mothers got busier after the rise of food production.

Declining Health

Although the rise of food production may have led to increased fertility, this does not mean that health generally improved. In fact, it appears that health declined at least sometimes with the transition to food production. The two trends may seem paradoxical, but rapid population growth can occur if each mother gives birth to a large number of babies, even if many of them die early because of disease or poor nutrition.

The evidence that health may have declined sometimes after the rise of food production comes from studies of the bones and teeth of some prehistoric populations, before and after the emergence of food production (see the box titled "You Are What You Eat"). Nutritional and disease problems are indicated by such features as incomplete formation of tooth enamel, nonaccidental bone lesions (incompletely filled-in bone), reduction in stature, and decreased life expectancy. Many of the studied prehistoric populations that relied heavily on agriculture seem to show less adequate nutrition and higher infection rates than populations living in the same areas before agriculture.[93] Some of the agricultural populations are shorter and had lower life expectancies.

The reasons for a decline in health in those populations are not yet clear. Greater malnutrition can result from an overdependence on a few dietary staples that lack some necessary nutrients. Overdependence on a few sources of food may also increase the risk of famine because the fewer the staple crops, the greater the danger to the food supply posed by a weather-caused crop failure. But some or most nutritional problems may be the result of social and political factors, particularly the rise of different socioeconomic classes of people and unequal access, between and within communities, to food and other resources.[94]

Social stratification or considerable socioeconomic inequality seems likely to develop after the rise of food production. The effects of stratification and political dominance from afar on the general level of health may be reflected in the skeletal remains of prehistoric Native Americans who died in what is now Illinois between A.D. 950 and 1300, the period spanning the changeover in that region from hunting and gathering to agriculture. The agricultural people living in the area of Dickson Mounds—burial sites named after the doctor who first excavated them—were apparently in much worse health than their hunter-gatherer ancestors. But curiously, archaeological evidence suggests that they were still also hunting and fishing. A balanced diet was apparently available, but who was getting it? Possibly it was the elites at Cahokia, 110 miles away, where perhaps 15,000–30,000 people lived, who were getting most of the meat and fish. The individuals near Dickson Mounds who collected the meat and fish may have gotten luxury items such as shell necklaces from the Cahokia elites, but many of the people buried at Dickson Mounds were clearly not benefiting nutritionally from the relationship with Cahokia.[95]

The Elaboration of Material Possessions

In the more permanent villages that were established after the rise of food production about 10,000 years ago, houses became more elaborate and comfortable, and construction methods improved. The materials used in construction depended on whether timber or stone was locally available or whether a strong sun could dry mud bricks. Modern architects might find to their surprise that bubble-shaped houses were known long ago in Neolithic Cyprus. Families in the island's town of Khirokitia made their homes in large, domed, circular dwellings shaped like beehives and featuring stone foundations and mud-brick walls. Often, more space was created by dividing the interior horizontally and firmly propping a second floor on limestone pillars.

As this reconstruction shows, transforming grain into flour was a "daily grind," putting a great deal of stress on the lower back and knees. Studies of Neolithic skeletons of women show marks of stress on bone and arthritis, probably reflecting their long hours of work at the grinding stone.

Source: "The Eloquent Bones of Abu Hureyra," Roberto Osti. *Scientific American,* Aug. 1994, p. 73 top.

CURRENT RESEARCH AND ISSUES

You Are What You Eat: Chemical Analyses of Bones and Teeth

Archaeologists study ancient diets in several ways, most of them indirect. They can indirectly infer some of what ancient people ate from recovered food wastes. For example, if you find a lot of corncobs, chances are that the people ate a lot of corn. Plant and animal foods can be identified in the charred remains of cooking fires and (when preserved) in the ancient people's feces, or coprolites. Such inferences are usually biased in favor of hard food sources such as seeds, nuts, and grains (which are likely to be preserved); rarely are the remains of soft plants such as bananas or tubers found. Archaeologists can also indirectly infer diet from the artifacts they find, particularly, of course, ones we can be pretty sure were used in obtaining or processing food. So, for example, if you find a stone with a flat or concave surface that looks like what people use in some places to grind corn, it is very likely that the ancient people also ground grain (or other hard things such as seeds) for food. But plant remains or implements do not tell us how much people relied on particular sources of food.

There is a more direct way to study ancient diets. Anthropologists have discovered that in many ways "you are what you eat." In particular, chemical analyses of bones and teeth, the most common remains found in excavations, can reveal distinctive traces of the foods that metabolically went into the bones and teeth.

One kind of informative chemical analysis involves the ratio of strontium to calcium in bone. This analysis can indicate the relative amounts of plant and animal food in the diet. So, for example, we know from strontium analysis of bones that just before the beginnings of cereal agriculture in the Near East, people were eating a lot of plant food, probably wild cereals that were intensively collected. Then there was a temporary decline in such collecting, suggesting overexploitation of the wild resources or at least their decreasing availability. This problem was presumably solved by the cultivation and domestication (modification) of cereals.

Carbon isotope ratios also can tell us what types of plants people were eating. Trees, shrubs, and temperate-zone grasses (such as rice) have carbon isotope ratios that are different from those of tropical and subtropical grasses (such as millet and corn). People in China were relying heavily on cereals about 7,000–8,000 years ago,

but the cereals were not the same in the north and south. Contrary to what we might expect, the carbon isotope ratios tell us that an originally temperate-zone cereal (rice) was the staple in subtropical southern China; in the more temperate north, an originally tropical or subtropical grass (millet) was most important. The dependence on millet in the north was enormous. It is estimated that 50–80 percent of the diet between 5000 and 500 B.C. came from millet.

In the New World, seed crops such as sunflower, sumpweed, and goosefoot were domesticated in eastern North America long before corn, introduced from Mexico, became the staple. We know this partly from the archaeology; the remains of the early seed crops are older than the remains of corn. Corn, an originally subtropical plant, has a carbon isotope ratio that is different from the ratio for the earlier, temperate-zone seed crops. Thus, the shift in carbon isotope ratios after A.D. 800–900 tells us that corn had become the staple.

Nonchemical analyses of human bones and teeth were traditionally used by physical anthropologists and archaeologists to study similarities and differences between peoples in different geographic regions, between living humans and possible fossil ancestors, and between living humans and other surviving primates. Much of the research involved surface measurements, particularly of the skull (outside and inside). In recent years, physical anthropologists and archaeologists have begun to study the "insides" of bones and teeth. The new kinds of chemical analysis mentioned here are part of that trend. In N. J. van der Merwe's pithy words: "The emphasis in studies of human evolution has . . . shifted from a preoccupation with the brain to an equal interest in the stomach."

Sources: N. J. van der Merwe, "Reconstructing Prehistoric Diet." In Stephen Jones, Robert Martin, and David Pilbeam, eds., *The Cambridge Encyclopedia of Human Evolution* (New York: Cambridge University Press, 1992), pp. 369–72; Clark Spenser Larsen, "Bare Bones Anthropology: The Bioarchaeology of Human Remains." In Peter N. Peregrine, Carol R. Ember, and Melvin Ember, eds., *Archaeology: Original Readings in Method and Practice* (Upper Saddle River, NJ: Prentice Hall, 2002), also in Carol R. Ember, Melvin Ember, and Peter N. Peregrine, eds., *Research Frontiers*, in *New Directions in Anthropology* (Upper Saddle River, NJ: Prentice Hall, CD-ROM, 2004).

Sizable villages of solidly constructed, gabled wooden houses were built in Europe on the banks of the Danube and along the rims of Alpine lakes.[96] Many of the gabled wooden houses in the Danube region were long, rectangular structures that apparently sheltered several family units. In Neolithic times these longhouses had doors, beds, tables, and other furniture that closely resembled those in modern-day societies. We know the people had furniture because miniature clay models have been found at their sites. Several of the chairs and couches seem to be models of padded and upholstered furniture with wooden frames, indicating that Neolithic European artisans were creating fairly sophisticated furnishings.[97] Such furnishings were the result of an advanced tool technology put to use by a people who, because they were staying in one area, could take time to make and use furniture.

For the first time, apparel made of woven textiles appeared. This development was not simply the result of the domestication of flax (for linen), cotton, and wool-growing sheep. These sources of fiber alone could not produce cloth. It was the development by Neolithic society of the spindle and loom for spinning and weaving that made textiles possible. True, textiles can be woven by hand without a loom, but to do so is a slow, laborious process, impractical for producing garments.

The pottery of the early Neolithic was similar to the plain earthenware made by some preagricultural groups and included large urns for grain storage, mugs, cooking pots, and dishes. To improve the retention of liquid, potters in the Near East may have been the first to glaze the earthenware's porous surface. Later, Neolithic ceramics became more artistic. Designers shaped the clay into graceful forms and painted colorful patterns on the vessels.

It is probable that virtually none of these architectural and technological innovations could have occurred until humans became fully sedentary. Nomadic hunting and gathering peoples would have found it difficult to carry many material goods, especially fragile items such as pottery. It was only when humans settled in one place that these goods would have provided advantages, enabling villagers to cook and store food more effectively and to house themselves more comfortably.

There is also evidence of long-distance trade in the Neolithic, as we have noted. Obsidian from southern Turkey was being exported to sites in the Zagros Mountains of Iran and to what are now Israel, Jordan, and Syria in the Levant. Great amounts of obsidian were exported to sites about 190 miles from the source of supply; more than 80 percent of the tools used by residents of those areas were made of this material.[98] Marble was being sent from western to eastern Turkey, and seashells from the coast were traded to distant inland regions. Such trade suggests a considerable amount of contact among various Neolithic communities.

About 3500 B.C., cities first appeared in the Near East. These cities had political assemblies, kings, scribes, and specialized workshops. The specialized production of goods and services was supported by surrounding farming villages, which sent their produce to the urban centers. A dazzling transformation had taken place in a relatively short time. People had not only settled down, but they had also become "civilized," or urbanized. (The word *civilized* literally means to make "citified.") Urban societies seem to have developed first in the Near East and somewhat later around the eastern Mediterranean, in the Indus Valley of northwestern India, in northern China, and in Mexico and Peru. In the next chapter we turn to the rise of these earliest civilizations.

⊚ Summary

1. In the period immediately before plants and animals were domesticated, there seems to have been a shift in many areas of the world to less dependence on big-game hunting and greater dependence on what is called broad-spectrum collecting. The broad spectrum of available resources frequently included aquatic resources such as fish and shellfish and a variety of wild plants, deer and other game. Climatic changes may have been partly responsible for the change to broad-spectrum collecting.

2. In some sites in Europe, the Near East, Africa, and Peru, the switch to broad-spectrum collecting seems to be associated with the development of more permanent communities. In other areas, such as the semiarid highlands of Mesoamerica, permanent settlements may have emerged only after the domestication of plants and animals.

3. The shift to the cultivation and domestication of plants and animals has been referred to as the Neolithic revolution, and it occurred, probably independently, in a number of areas. To date, the earliest evidence of domestication comes from the Near East at about 8000 B.C.

Sophisticated ceramics like this 5000 year old Chinese funeral urn first appeared in the Neolithic era as part of the elaboration of material possessions.

Dating for the earliest domestication in other areas of the Old World is not so clear, but the presence of different domesticated crops in different regions suggests that there were independent centers of domestication in China, Southeast Asia (what is now Malaysia, Thailand, Cambodia, and Vietnam), New Guinea, and Africa some time around or after 6000 B.C. In the New World, there appear to have been several early areas of cultivation and domestication: the highlands of Mesoamerica (about 7000 B.C.), the central Andes around Peru (about the same time, but perhaps even earlier), and the Eastern Woodlands of North America (about 2000 B.C.).

4. Theories about why food production originated remain controversial, but most archaeologists think that certain conditions must have pushed people to switch from collecting to producing food. Some possible causal factors include (1) population growth in regions of bountiful wild resources (which may have pushed people to move to marginal areas where they tried to reproduce their former abundance); (2) global population growth (which filled most of the world's habitable regions and may have forced people to utilize a broader spectrum of wild resources and to domesticate plants and animals); and (3) the emergence of hotter and drier summers and colder winters (which may have favored sedentarism near seasonal stands of wild grain; population growth in such areas may have forced people to plant crops and raise animals to support themselves).

5. Regardless of why food production originated, it seems to have had important consequences for human life. Populations generally increased substantially after plant and animal domestication. Even though not all early cultivators were sedentary, sedentarism did increase with greater reliance on agriculture. Somewhat surprisingly, some prehistoric populations that relied heavily on agriculture seem to have been less healthy than earlier populations that relied on food collection. In the more permanent villages that were established after the rise of food production, houses and furnishings became more elaborate, and people began to make textiles and to paint pottery. These villages have also yielded evidence of increased long-distance trade.

◎ Glossary Terms

agriculture	159	Mesolithic	159
Archaic	159	Neolithic	166
domestication	166	obsidian	168
Epipaleolithic	159	rachis	166
food production	159	sedentarism	159

◎ Critical Questions

1. What factors might cause people to work harder to get food? Explain your answer.

2. How might people have domesticated sheep, goats, and cattle?

3. Do the various theories of the rise of food production explain why domestication occurred in many areas of the world within a few thousand years?

◎ Research Navigator

1. Please go to www.researchnavigator.com and enter your LOGIN NAME and PASSWORD. For instructions on registering for the first time, please view the detailed instructions at the end of Chapter 1.

2. Use Content Select to search the Anthropology database using the keyword "agriculture." Find a recent article on agriculture from an archaeology journal such as *American Antiquity* or *Latin American Antiquity*. Read the article and answer the following questions: What did the researchers learn about prehistoric agriculture? How do their findings help us to understand the way agricultural societies functioned in the past? Do their findings help us to better understand the origins of agriculture?

◎ Discovering Anthropology: Researchers at Work

Read the chapter by Mark Nathan Cohen titled "Were Early Agriculturalists Less Healthy than Food Collectors?" in the accompanying *Discovering Anthropology* reader. Answer the following questions:

1. Describe the basic arguments behind Cohen's question. What benefits did agriculture provide to human groups? What problems may have resulted from agriculture?

2. What does Cohen suggest his comparative data from modern foragers and modern agriculturalists demonstrate about the relative health of the two groups? Do data from ancient skeletons demonstrate a similar or a different pattern?

CHAPTER ELEVEN

Origins of Cities and States

From the time agriculture first developed until about 6000 B.C., people in the Near East lived in fairly small villages. There were few differences in wealth and status from household to household, and apparently there was no governmental authority beyond the village. There is no evidence that these villages had any public buildings or craft specialists or that one community was very different in size from its neighbors. In short, these settlements had none of the characteristics we commonly associate with "civilization."

But sometime around 6000 B.C., in parts of the Near East—and at later times in other places—a great transformation in the quality and scale of human life seems to have begun. For the first time we can see evidence of differences in status among households. For example, some are much bigger than others. Communities begin to differ in size and to specialize in certain crafts. And there are signs that some political officials had acquired authority over several communities, that what anthropologists call "chiefdoms" had emerged.

Somewhat later, by about 3500 B.C., we can see many, if not all, of the conventional characteristics of **civilization:** the first inscriptions, or writing; cities; many kinds of full-time craft specialists; monumental architecture; great differences in wealth and status; and the kind of strong, hierarchical, centralized political system we call the **state** (see Figure 11–1).

This type of transformation has occurred many times and in many places in human history. The most ancient civilizations arose in the Near East around 3500 B.C., in northwestern India and in Peru about 2500 B.C., in northern China around 1750 B.C., in Mexico a few hundred years before the time of Christ, and in tropical Africa somewhat later.[1] At least some of these civilizations evolved independently of the others—for example, those in the New World and those in the Old World. Why did they do so? What conditions favored the emergence of centralized, statelike political systems? What conditions favored the establishment of cities? We ask this last question separately, because archaeologists are not yet certain that all the ancient state societies had cities when they first developed centralized government. In this chapter we discuss some of the things archaeologists have learned or suspect about the growth of ancient civilizations. Our discussion focuses primarily on the Near East and Mexico because archaeologists know the most about the sequences of cultural development in those two areas.

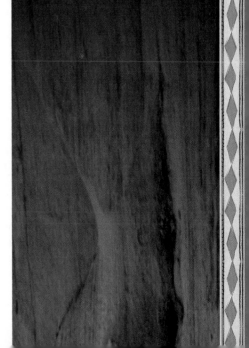

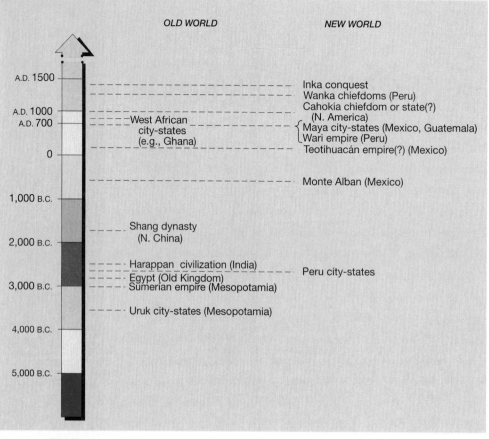

Figure 11–1 The Emergence of Civilization

Archaeological Inferences about Civilization

The most ancient civilizations have been studied by archaeologists rather than historians because those civilizations evolved before the advent of writing. How do archaeologists infer that a particular people in the preliterate past had social classes, cities, or a centralized government?

As we have noted, it appears that the earliest Neolithic societies were *egalitarian;* that is, people did not differ much in wealth, prestige, or power. Some later societies show signs of social inequality, indicated by burial finds. Archaeologists generally assume that inequality in death reflects inequality in life, at least in status and perhaps also in wealth and power. Thus, we can be fairly sure that a society had differences in status if only some people were buried with special objects, such as jewelry or pots filled with food. And we can be fairly sure that high status was assigned at birth rather than achieved in later life if we find noticeable differences in children's tombs. For example, some (but not all) child burials from as early as 5500 to 5000 B.C. at Tell es-Sawwan in Iraq, and from about 800 B.C. at La Venta in Mexico, are filled with statues and ornaments, suggesting that some children had high status from birth.[2] But burials indicating differences in status do not necessarily mean a society had significant dif-

ferences in wealth. It is only when archaeologists find other substantial differences, as in house size and furnishings, that we can be sure the society had different socioeconomic classes of people.

Some archaeologists think that states first evolved around 3500 B.C. in greater Mesopotamia, the area now shared by southern Iraq and southwestern Iran. Archaeologists do not always agree on how a state should be defined, but most think that hierarchical and centralized decision making affecting a substantial population is the key criterion. Other characteristics are usually, but not always, found in these first states. They usually have cities with a substantial part of the population not involved directly in the collection or production of food (which means that people in cities are heavily dependent on people elsewhere); full-time religious and craft specialists; public buildings; and often an official art style. There is a hierarchical social structure topped by an elite class from which the leaders are drawn. The government tries to claim a monopoly on the use of force. (Our own state society says that citizens do not have the right "to take the law into their own hands.") The state uses its force or threat of force to tax its population and to draft people for work or war.[3]

How can archaeologists tell, from the information provided by material remains, whether a society was a state or not? This depends in part on what is used as the criterion for

Reconstruction of the ornaments found with a royal burial from the Sumerian city of Ur. The headdress is made of gold and the necklaces include gold and lapis lazuli. Archaeologists assume that such special treatment indicates elite status.

a state. For example, Henry Wright and Gregory Johnson defined a state as a centralized political hierarchy with at least three levels of administration.[4] But how might archaeologists infer that such a hierarchy existed in some area? Wright and Johnson suggested that the way settlement sites differ in size is one indication of how many levels of administration there were in an area.

During the early Uruk period (just before 3500 B.C.), in what is now southwestern Iran, there were some 50 settlements that seem to fall into three groups in terms of size.[5] There were about 45 small villages, three or four "towns," and one large center, Susa. These three types of settlements seem to have been part of a three-level administration hierarchy, since many small villages could not trade with Susa without passing through a settlement intermediate in size. Because a three-level hierarchy is Wright and Johnson's criterion of a state, they think a state had emerged in the area by early Uruk times.

Evidence from the next period, middle Uruk, suggests more definitely that a state had emerged. This evidence takes the form of clay seals that were apparently used in trading.[6] *Commodity sealings* were used to keep a shipment of goods tightly closed until it reached its destination, and *message sealings* were used to keep track of goods sent and received. The clay seals found in Susa include many message seals and *bullae,* clay containers that served as bills of lading for goods received. The villages, in contrast, had few message seals and

bullae. Again, this finding suggests that Susa administered the regional movement of goods and that Susa was the "capital" of the state.

Let us turn now to the major features of the cultural sequences leading to the first states in southern Iraq.

Cities and States in Southern Iraq

Farming communities older than the first states have not been found in the arid lowland plains of southern Iraq—the area known as Sumer, where some of the earliest cities and states developed (see Figure 11–2). Perhaps silt from the Tigris and Euphrates rivers has covered them. Or, as has been suggested, Sumer may not have been settled by agriculturalists until people learned how to drain and irrigate river-valley soils otherwise too wet or too dry for cultivation. At any rate, small communities depending partly on agriculture had emerged in the hilly areas north and east of Sumer early in the Neolithic. Later, by about 6000 B.C., a mixed herding–farming economy developed in those areas.

The Formative Era

Elman Service called the period from about 5000 to 3500 B.C. the *formative era,* for it saw the coming together of many changes that seem to have played a part in the development of cities and states. Service suggested that with the development of small-scale irrigation, lowland river areas began to attract settlers. The rivers provided not only water for irrigation but also mollusks, fish, and waterbirds for food. And they provided routes by which to import needed raw materials, such as hardwood and stone, that were lacking in Sumer.

Changes during this period suggest an increasingly complex social and political life. Differences in status are reflected in the burial of statues and ornaments with children. Different villages specialized in the production of different goods—pottery in some, copper and stone tools in others.[7] Temples were built in certain places that may have been centers of political as well as religious authority for several communities.[8] Furthermore, some anthropologists think that chiefdoms, each having authority over several villages, had developed by this time.[9]

Sumerian Civilization

By about 3500 B.C., there were quite a few cities in the area of Sumer. Most were enclosed in a fortress wall and surrounded by an agricultural area. About 3000 B.C. all of Sumer was unified under a single government. After that time, Sumer became an empire. It had great urban centers. Imposing temples, commonly set on artificial mounds, dominated the cities. In the city of Warka the temple mound was about 150 feet high. The empire was very complex and included an elaborate system for the administration of justice, codified laws, specialized government officials, a professional standing army, and even sewer systems in the cities. Among

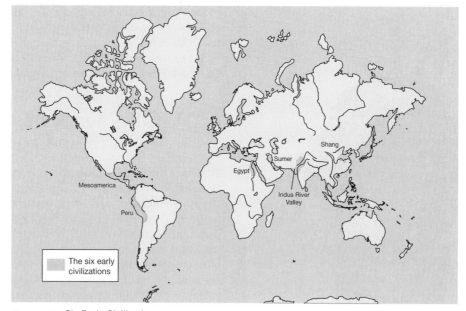

Figure 11–2 Six Early Civilizations

Source: Adapted from *The Origins of the State and Civilization: The Process of Cultural Evolution,* by Elman R. Service. (New York: W. W. Norton, 1975).

the many specialized crafts were brickmaking, pottery, carpentry, jewelry making, leatherworking, metallurgy, basketmaking, stonecutting, and sculpture. Sumerians learned to construct and use wheeled wagons, sailboats, horse-drawn chariots, and spears, swords, and armor of bronze.[10]

As economic specialization developed, social stratification became more elaborate. Sumerian documents describe a system of social classes: nobles, priests, merchants, craftworkers, metallurgists, bureaucrats, soldiers, farmers, free citizens, and slaves. Slaves were common in Sumer; they often were captives, brought back as the spoils of war.

We see the first evidence of writing around 3000 B.C. The earliest Sumerian writings were in the form of ledgers containing inventories of items stored in the temples and records of livestock or other items owned or managed by the temples. Sumerian writing was wedge-shaped, or **cuneiform,** formed by pressing a stylus against a damp clay tablet. For contracts and other important documents, the tablet was fired to create a virtually permanent record. Egyptian writing, or hieroglyphics, appeared about the same time. **Hieroglyphics** were written on rolls woven from papyrus reeds, from which our word *paper* derives.

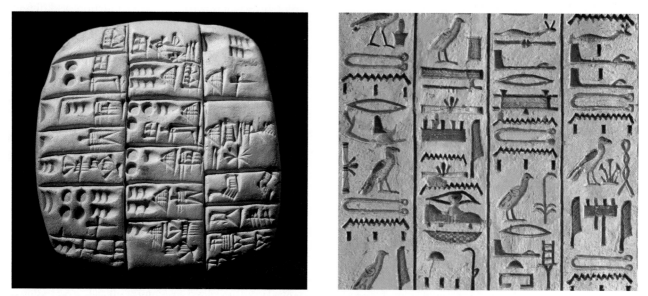

Examples of two of the earliest writing systems on earth. On the left is a cuneiform tablet and on the right is a section of a hieroglyphic panel.

Cities and States in Mesoamerica

Cities and states emerged in Mesoamerica—Mexico and Central America—later than they did in the Near East. The later appearance of civilization in Mesoamerica may be linked to the later emergence of agriculture in the New World, as we saw in the last chapter, and possibly to the near-absence of large animals such as cattle and horses that could be domesticated.[11] We focus primarily on the developments that led to the rise of the city-state of Teotihuacán, which reached its height shortly after the time of Christ. Teotihuacán is located in a valley of the same name, which is the northeastern part of the larger Valley of Mexico.

The Formative Period

The formative period in the area around Teotihuacán (1000–300 B.C.) was characterized initially by small, scattered farming villages on the hilly slopes just south of the Teotihuacán Valley. There were probably a few hundred people in each hamlet, and each of these scattered groups was probably politically autonomous. After about 500 B.C., there seems to have been a population shift to settlements on the valley floor, probably in association with the use of irrigation. Between about 300 and 200 B.C., small "elite" centers emerged in the valley; each had an earthen or stone raised platform. Residences or small temples of poles and thatch originally stood on these platforms. That some individuals, particularly those in the elite centers, were buried in special tombs supplied with ornaments, headdresses, carved bowls, and a good deal of food indicates some social inequality.[12] The various elite centers may indicate the presence of chiefdoms.

The City and State of Teotihuacán

About 150 years before the time of Christ, no more than a few thousand people lived in scattered villages in the Teotihuacán Valley. In A.D. 100, there was a city of 80,000. By A.D. 500, well over 100,000 people, or approximately 90 percent of the entire valley population, seem to have been drawn or coerced into Teotihuacán.[13]

The layout of the city of Teotihuacán, which shows a tremendous amount of planning, suggests that from its beginning the valley was politically unified under a centralized state. Mapping has revealed that the streets and most of the buildings are laid out in a grid pattern following a basic modular unit of 57 square meters. Residential structures are often squares of this size, and many streets are spaced according to multiples of the basic unit. Even the river that ran through the center of the city was channeled to conform to the grid pattern. Perhaps the most outstanding feature of the city is the colossal scale of its architecture. Two pyramids dominate the metropolis, the so-called Pyramid of the Moon and the Pyramid of the Sun. At its base the latter is as big as the great Pyramid of Cheops in Egypt.

The thousands of residential structures built after A.D. 300 follow a standard pattern. Narrow streets separate the one-story buildings, each of which has high, windowless walls. Patios and shafts provide interior light. The layout of rooms suggests that each building consisted of several apartments; more than 100 people may have lived in one of these apartment compounds. There is variation from compound to compound in the size of rooms and the elaborateness of interior decoration, suggesting considerable variation in wealth.[14]

At the height of its power (A.D. 200–500), the metropolis of Teotihuacán encompassed an area larger than imperial Rome.[15] Much of Mesoamerica seems to have been influenced by Teotihuacán. Archaeologically, its influence is suggested by the extensive spread of Teotihuacán-style pottery and architectural elements. Undoubtedly, large numbers of people in Teotihuacán were engaged in production for, and the conduct of, long-distance trade. Perhaps 25 percent of the city's population worked at various specialized crafts, including the manufacture of projectile points and cutting and scraping tools from volcanic obsidian. Teotihuacán was close to major deposits of obsidian, which was apparently in some demand over much of Mesoamerica.

The city of Teotihuacán, which had its peak in 500 A.D., was a planned city built on a grid pattern. At the center was the Pyramid of the Sun, seen in the background on the left here.

NEW PERSPECTIVES ON GENDER

Effects of Imperialism on Women's Status

Archaeologists, and particularly women archaeologists, have begun to pay attention to the gender implications of archaeological materials. Do the findings from excavated houses imply anything about what women and men did where they lived? What do the findings in houses and other places suggest about the division of labor by gender? Can archaeology tell us about women's status in the culture and how it may have changed over time? Recent research suggests that if you look for gender-related results, you can often find some. As the title of a recent book indicated, new kinds of archaeology can be "engendered." For example, archaeologist Cathy Costin has studied the effects of Inka (Inca) imperialism on women's status in a conquered area.

Costin participated in a research project that studied culture change in the Yanamarca Valley of highland Peru. The project focused on the development of chiefdoms among the indigenous Wanka ethnic group between A.D. 1300 and 1470 and on the effects of the Inka conquest at the end of that period. According to the archaeology, most people before the Inka conquest were farmers, but some households specialized part time in the production of pottery, stone tools, and perhaps textiles. Documents written after the arrival of the Spanish suggest that the Wanka had developed chiefdoms about A.D. 1300, possibly as a result of intensified warfare among the various communities. A high level of conflict is inferred from the

locations and configurations of the settlements: Most people lived in fortified (walled) communities located on hills above the valley floor. According to the documentary sources, the Wanka chiefs had achieved their positions because of success as war leaders.

We know from documents that the Wanka were conquered by the Inka during the reign of the emperor Pachakuti (about A.D. 1470). The Wanka region became a province within the Inka empire, and bureaucrats from the capital at Cuzco came to govern the Wanka. The Inka conquerors, including military personnel, formed the highest class in the valley. The Wanka chiefs became vassals of the Inka state and imitators of Inka ways, using Inka-like pottery and building Inka-style additions to their homes. The economy of the valley became more specialized, apparently to meet the needs of the Inka. People in some villages still mostly farmed, but in other villages most households specialized in the production of pottery, stone tools, and other crafts. Skeletal remains indicate that the commoners became healthier and lived longer after the Inka conquest.

How did the Inka conquest affect the status of women? One key to an answer was suggested by the presence in the excavations of several thousand perforated, round ceramic objects. They were spindle whorls, weights used in spinning to keep the thread tight and even. The thread (from llama and alpaca wool) was made

---

Materials found in graves indicate that there was an enormous flow of foreign goods into the city, including precious stones, feathers from colorful birds in the tropical lowlands, and cotton.[16]

The City of Monte Albán

Teotihuacán probably was not the earliest city-state in Mesoamerica. There is evidence of political unification somewhat earlier, about 500 B.C., in the Valley of Oaxaca, in southern Mexico, with the city of Monte Albán at its center. Monte Albán presents an interesting contrast to Teotihuacán. Whereas Teotihuacán seems to have completely dominated its valley, containing almost all its inhabitants and craftspeople, Monte Albán did not. The various villages in the Valley of Oaxaca seem to have specialized in different crafts, and Monte Albán did not monopolize craft production. After the political unification of the valley, cities and towns other than Monte Albán remained important; the popula-

tion of Monte Albán grew only to 30,000 or so. Unlike Teotihuacán, Monte Albán was not an important commercial or market center, it was not laid out in a grid pattern, and its architecture was not much different from that of other settlements in the valley.[17]

Monte Albán did not have the kinds of resources that Teotihuacán had. It was located on top of a mountain in the center of the valley, far from either good soil or permanent water supplies that could have been used for irrigation. Even finding drinking water must have been difficult. No natural resources for trade were nearby, nor is there much evidence that Monte Albán was used as a ceremonial center. Because the city was at the top of a steep mountain, it is unlikely that it could have been a central marketplace for valleywide trade.

Why, then, did Monte Albán rise to become one of the early centers of Mesoamerican civilization? Richard Blanton suggested it may have originally been founded in the late formative period (500–400 B.C.) as a neutral place where representatives of the different political units in the valley

into cloth, which became the major form of tax payment after the Inka took over. Each village had to produce a certain amount of cloth for the state tax collectors. The cloth collected was used to clothe men serving in the army and to "pay" other government personnel. The burden of producing the cloth fell on the traditional spinners and weavers, who we know from the post-Spanish documents were females of all ages.

Just before the Inka conquest, all households excavated had spindle whorls, indicating that the female occupants in all households spun and made cloth. More whorls were found the farther up the mountain the house was located, indicating that women who lived closer to the high grasslands, where the flocks of llamas and alpacas were kept, spun more thread than did women who lived farther down from the pastures. We might expect that elite women would do less work. But, to the contrary, the women in elite households seem to have produced more cloth than the women in commoner households, judging by the number of whorls in the households.

After the Inka conquest, households appear to have produced twice the amount of thread they did before, because there are twice the number of recovered spindle whorls. There is no indication, archaeological or documentary, that the women were freed from other tasks to make more time for spinning, so it would appear that women had to work harder under Inka domination to produce thread and cloth. But the producers do not appear to have benefited from the increased cloth production. Much if not most of the cloth produced was removed from the villages and taken to Inka storage facilities in the capital and redistributed from there.

In addition to working harder for the Inka, women seem to have fared worse than the men when it came to nutrition. Christine Hastorf's chemical analysis of bones from Inka-period graves suggests that women ate less maize (corn) than did men. It seems that the men were "eating out" more than women. Maize was often consumed as chicha beer, a key component of state-sponsored feasts, which were probably attended more by men than women. Men also worked more in state-organized agricultural and production projects, where they probably were rewarded with meat, maize, and chicha for their service to the state.

So, under Inka domination, Wanka women had to produce more and received less. Is this a general effect of imperialism? And, if so, why?

Sources: Elizabeth M. Brumfiel, "Distinguished Lecture in Archeology: Breaking and Entering the Ecosystem—Gender, Class, and Faction Steal the Show," *American Anthropologist,* 94 (1992): 551–67; Joan M. Gero and Margaret W. Conkey, eds., *Engendering Archaeology: An Introduction to Women and Prehistory* (Oxford: Blackwell, 1991); Cathy Lynne Costin, "Cloth Production and Gender Relations in the Inka Empire." In Peter N. Peregrine, Carol R. Ember, and Melvin Ember, eds., *Archaeology: Original Readings in Method and Practice* (Upper Saddle River, NJ: Prentice Hall, 2002), also in Carol R. Ember, Melvin Ember, and Peter N. Peregrine, eds., *Research Frontiers,* in *New Directions in Anthropology* (Upper Saddle River, NJ: Prentice Hall, CD-ROM, 2004); Christine Hastorf, "Gender, Space, and Food in Prehistory," in Gero and Conkey, eds., *Engendering Archaeology.*

could reside to coordinate activities affecting the whole valley. Thus Monte Albán may have been like the cities of Brasília, Washington, D.C., and Athens, all of which were originally founded in "neutral," nonproductive areas. Such a center, lacking obvious resources, would not, at least initially, threaten the various political units around it. Later it might become a metropolis dominating a more politically unified region, as Monte Albán came to do in the Valley of Oaxaca.[18]

Other Centers of Mesoamerican Civilization

In addition to Teotihuacán and Oaxaca, there were other Mesoamerican state societies, which developed somewhat later. For example, there are a number of centers with monumental architecture, presumably built by speakers of Mayan languages, in the highlands and lowlands of modern-day Guatemala and the Yucatán Peninsula of modern-day Mexico.

On the basis of surface appearances, the Mayan centers do not appear to have been as densely populated as Teotihuacán or Monte Albán. But it is now evident that the Mayan centers were more densely populated and more dependent on intensive agriculture than was once thought,[19] and recent translations of Mayan picture writing indicate a much more developed form of writing than previously thought.[20] It is apparent now that Mayan urbanization and cultural complexity were underestimated because of the dense tropical forest that now covers much of the area of Mayan civilization.

The First Cities and States in Other Areas

So far we have discussed the emergence of cities and states in southern Iraq and Mesoamerica whose development is best, if only imperfectly, known archaeologically. But other

Excavation of an ancient culvert at Harappa. Despite large public works like this water control system, there was little display of grandeur at Harappa. Unlike many other ancient civilizations, all Harappan cities were laid out according to the same basic plan.

state societies probably arose more or less independently in many other areas of the world as well (see Figure 14–2). We say "independently" because such states seem to have emerged without colonization or conquest by other states.

Almost at the same time as the Sumerian empire, the great dynastic age was beginning in the Nile Valley in Egypt. The Old Kingdom, or early dynastic period, began about 3100 B.C., with a capital at Memphis. The archaeological evidence from the early centuries is limited, but most of the population appears to have lived in largely self-sufficient villages. Many of the great pyramids and palaces were built around 2500 B.C.[21]

Elsewhere in Africa states also arose. In what is present-day Ethiopia the Axum (or Aksum) state evolved beginning sometime early in the 1st millennium A.D., and ultimately became a center of trade and commerce between Africa and the Arabian Peninsula. Among the unique accomplishments of the Axum state were multistory stone residences built in a singular architectural style. Axum is also notable as being perhaps the first officially Christian state in the world.[22]

In sub-Saharan Africa, by A.D. 800, the savanna and forest zones of western Africa had a succession of city-states. One of them was called Ghana, and it became a major source of gold for the Mediterranean world (as did other states in what came to be known as the "Gold Coast").[23] In the Congo River basin a powerful kingdom had evolved by A.D. 1200, with cities described as having tens of thousands of residences and a king that was recognized as an equal by the Portuguese king in the early 1500s.[24] Farther south, states apparently arose in several areas early in the 2nd millennium A.D. One of these was responsible for the large, circular stone structures known today as the Great Zimbabwe.[25]

In the Indus Valley of northwestern India, a large state society had developed by 2300 B.C. This Harappan civilization did not have much in the way of monumental architecture, such as pyramids and palaces, and it was also unusual in other respects. The state apparently controlled an enormous territory—over a million square kilometers. There was not just one major city but many, each built ac-

cording to a similar pattern and with a municipal water and sewage system.[26]

The Shang dynasty in northern China (1750 B.C.) has long been cited as the earliest state society in the Far East. But recent research suggests that an even earlier one, the Xia dynasty, may have emerged in the same general area by 2200 B.C.[27] In any case, the Shang dynasty had all the earmarks of statehood: a stratified, specialized society; religious, economic, and administrative unification; and a distinctive art style.[28]

In South America, a group of distinct state societies may have emerged as early as 2500 B.C. in the Supe and Pativilca

This bronze ritual vessel shows the unique form and design style of the Shang dynasty. It was used by elites and made by craft specialists.

Artist's reconstruction of what Cahokia may have looked like during its fluorescence.

valleys north of Lima, Peru. The valley contains a group of large cities that seem to have been interdependent—cities on the coast supplied inland cities with fish, while inland cities served as political and economic centers. The cities contain plaza areas and large pyramids, which are thought to be temple structures.[29] After 200 B.C. the major river valleys leading from the Andes to the sea witnessed the development of a complex agricultural system dependent on irrigation. The separate, but similar, states participated in a widespread system of religious symbols and beliefs called Chavín. The various states included the well-known Moche state, creators of some of the most remarkable effigy ceramics ever known, and the Nazca state, the people of which constructed a huge landscape of intaglios (inscribed images and lines) on the hard ground of highland deserts. By A.D. 700, these regional states were integrated into a large, militaristic empire called Wari (or Huari).[30]

And in North America a huge settlement, with over 100 earthen mounds (one of them, Monk's Mound, is the largest pre-Columbian structure north of Mexico), and covering an area of more than 13 square kilometers, developed near present-day St. Louis late in the 1st millennium A.D. The site is called Cahokia, and it was certainly the center of a large and powerful chiefdom. Whether it had achieved a state level of organization is controversial. There is evidence for religious and craft specialists and there is clear social stratification, but whether or not the leaders of Cahokian society were able to govern by force is still unclear.[31]

◎ Theories about the Origin of the State

We have seen that states developed in many parts of the world. Why did they evolve when and where they did? A number of theories have been proposed. We consider those that have been discussed frequently by archaeologists.[32]

Irrigation

Irrigation seems to have been important in many of the areas in which early state societies developed. Irrigation made the land habitable or productive in parts of Mesoamerica, southern Iraq, the Nile Valley, China, and South America. It has been suggested that the labor and management needed for the upkeep of an irrigation system led to the formation of a political elite, the overseers of the system, who eventually became the governors of the society.[33] Proponents of this view believe that both the city and civilization were outgrowths of the administrative requirements of an irrigation system.

Critics note that this theory does not seem to apply to all areas where cities and states may have emerged independently. For example, in southern Iraq, the irrigation systems serving the early cities were generally small and probably did not require extensive labor and management. Large-scale irrigation works were not constructed until after cities had been fully established.[34] Thus, irrigation could not have been the main stimulus for the development of cities and states in Sumer. Even in China, for which the irrigation theory was first formulated, there is no evidence of large-scale irrigation as early as Shang times.[35]

Although large-scale irrigation may not always have preceded the emergence of the first cities and states, even small-scale irrigation systems could have resulted in unequal access to productive land and so may have contributed to the development of a stratified society.[36] In addition, irrigation systems may have given rise to border and other disputes between adjacent groups, thereby prompting people to concentrate in cities for defense and stimulating the development of military and political controls.[37] Finally, as Robert Adams and Elman Service both suggested, the main significance of irrigation, either large or small scale, may have been its intensification of production, a development that in turn may have indirectly stimulated craft specialization, trade, and administrative bureaucracy.[38]

Population Growth, Circumscription, and War

Robert Carneiro has suggested that states may emerge because of population growth in an area that is physically or socially limited. Competition and warfare in such a situation may lead to the subordination of defeated groups, who are obliged to pay tribute and to submit to the control of a more powerful group.[39] Carneiro illustrated his theory by describing how states may have emerged on the northern coast of Peru.

After the people of that area first settled into an agricultural village life, population grew at a slow, steady rate. Initially, new villages were formed as population grew. But in the narrow coastal valleys—blocked by high mountains, fronted by the sea, and surrounded by desert—this splintering-off process could not continue indefinitely. The result, according to Carneiro, was increasing land shortage and warfare between villages as they competed for land. Since the high mountains, the sea, and the desert blocked any escape for losers, the defeated villagers had no choice but to submit to political domination. In this way, chiefdoms may have become kingdoms as the most powerful villages grew to control entire valleys. As chiefs' power expanded over several valleys, states and empires may have been born.

Carneiro noted that physical or environmental circumscription may not be the only kind of barrier that gives rise to a state. Social circumscription may be just as important. People living at the center of a high-density area may find that their migration is blocked by surrounding settlements just as effectively as it could be by mountains, sea, and desert.

Marvin Harris suggested a somewhat different form of circumscription. He argued that the first states with their coercive authority could emerge only in areas that supported intensive grain agriculture (and the possibility of high food production) and were surrounded by areas that could not support intensive grain agriculture. So people in such areas might put up with the coercive authority of a state because they would suffer a sharp drop in living standards if they moved away.[40]

Carneiro suggested that his theory applies to many areas besides the northern coast of Peru, including southern Iraq and the Indus and Nile valleys. Although there were no geographic barriers in areas such as northern China or the Mayan lowlands on the Yucatán Peninsula, the development of states in those areas may have been the result of social circumscription. Carneiro's theory seems to be supported for southern Iraq, where there is archaeological evidence of population growth, circumscription, and warfare.[41] And there is evidence of population growth before the emergence of the state in the Teotihuacán Valley.[42]

But population growth does not necessarily mean population pressure. For example, the populations in the Teotihuacán and Oaxaca valleys apparently did increase prior to state development, but there is no evidence that they had even begun to approach the limits of their resources. More people could have lived in both places.[43] Nor is population growth definitely associated with state formation in all areas where early states arose. For example, according to Wright and Johnson, there was population growth long before states emerged in southwestern Iran, but the population apparently declined just before the states emerged.[44]

In addition, Carneiro's circumscription theory leaves an important logical question unanswered: Why would the victors in war let the defeated populations remain and pay tribute? If the victors wanted the land so much in the first place, why wouldn't they try to exterminate the defeated and occupy the land themselves, which has happened many times in history?

Local and Long-Distance Trade

It has been suggested that trade was a factor in the emergence of the earliest states.[45] Wright and Johnson theorized that the organizational requirements of producing items for export, redistributing the items imported, and defending trading parties would foster state formation.[46] Does the archaeological evidence support such a theory?

In southern Iraq and the Mayan lowlands, long-distance trade routes may indeed have stimulated bureaucratic growth. In the lowlands of southern Iraq, as we have seen, people needed wood and stone for building, and they traded with highland people for those items. In the Mayan lowlands, the development of civilization seems to have been preceded by long-distance trade. Farmers in the lowland regions traded with faraway places in order to obtain salt, obsidian for cutting blades, and hard stone for grinding tools.[47] In southwestern Iran, long-distance trade did not become very important until after Susa became the center of a state society, but short-distance trade may have played the same kind of role in the formation of states.

Kwang-chih Chang put forward a similar theory for the origin of states in China. He suggested that Neolithic societies in the Yellow River valley developed a long-distance trade network, which he called an *interaction sphere*, by about 4000 B.C. Trade spread cultural elements among the societies in the interaction sphere, so that they came to share some common elements (see Figure 11–3). Over time, these societies came to depend on each other both as trade partners and as cultural partners, and around 2000 B.C. they unified into a single political unit under the Shang dynasty.[48] Thus Chang sees political unification in China as an outgrowth of a preexisting system of trade and cultural interaction.

The Various Theories: An Evaluation

Why do states form? As of now, no one theory seems to fit all the known situations. The reason may be that different conditions in different places may have favored the emergence of centralized government. After all, the state, by definition, implies an ability to organize large populations for a collective purpose. In some areas, this purpose may have been the need to organize trade with local or far-off regions. In other cases, the state may have emerged as a way to control defeated populations in circumscribed areas. In still other instances, a combination of factors may have fostered the development of the state type of political system.[49]

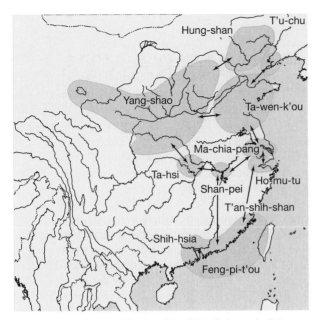

Figure 11–3 Expansion of Regional Neolithic Cultures in China, 4000-3000 B.C.

Source: From *Archaeology of Ancient China*, 4th ed, by K.-C. Chang. (New Haven: Yale, 1986).

The Consequences of State Formation

We have considered several areas where states arose, as well as a number of theories to explain the origin of states. But what were the consequences for the people living in those societies? The consequences seem to have been dramatic.

One of the ways states change the lifestyles of people is by allowing for larger and denser populations.[50] As we have already seen, agriculture itself gives populations the potential to grow, and the development of a state only furthers that potential. Why? Because a state is able to build infrastructure—irrigation systems, roadways, markets—that allows both the production and distribution of agricultural products to become more efficient. States are able to coordinate information as well, and can use that information to manage agricultural production cycles and to anticipate or manage droughts, blights, or other natural disasters. States are also able to control access to land (through laws and a military) and thus can both maintain farmers on the land and prevent others (from either within or outside of the state) from removing the farmers or interfering with their ability to produce food.

With increased efficiency of agricultural production and distribution, states also allow many (if not most) people in the society to be relieved of food production. These people are freed to become craftspeople, merchants, and artists, as well as bureaucrats, soldiers, and political leaders. People may also live apart from agricultural fields, and thus cities with dense populations can arise. Cities can also arise in locations that are not suited to agriculture but that perhaps are suited to trade (such as the cities on rivers in southern Mesopotamia)

or defense (such as on top of a mountain, as in the case of Monte Albán). Art, music, and literature often flourish in such contexts, and these too are often consequences of the rise of states. Organized religion also often develops after states appear. Thus all the hallmarks we associate with civilization can be seen as resulting from the evolution of states.[51]

The development of states can have many negative impacts as well. When states develop, people become governed by force and are no longer able to say "no" to their leaders. Police and military forces can become instruments of oppression and terror.[52] On a less obvious level, the class stratification of states creates differences in access to resources and an underclass of poor, uneducated, and frequently unhealthy people. Health issues are exacerbated by the concentration of people in cities, an environment in which epidemic diseases can flourish.[53] Without direct access to food supplies, people in cities also face the threat of malnutrition or outright starvation if food production and distribution systems fail.[54]

All states appear to be expansionistic, and the emergence of state warfare and conquest seems one of the most striking negative impacts of the evolution of states. In fact, more human suffering can probably be linked to state expansion than to any other single factor. Why do states expand? One basic reason may be that they are able to (see the box "Imperialism, Colonialism, and the State"). States have standing armies ready to fight or be sent to conquer enemies. Another reason for state expansion might be related to the threat of famine and disease, which is more likely with

Shown is a street in the old city of Jaipur, India. The rise of states allows cities with dense populations to develop and, along with them, the many potentials and problems that cities and their populations create.

MIGRANTS AND IMMIGRANTS

Imperialism, Colonialism, and the State

The first city-states seem to have emerged during the Uruk period, roughly the 4th millennium B.C., in the river valleys of southern Mesopotamia, now southern Iraq. From their very beginnings, these first city-states had "foreign trade." This trade may have been indispensable; the riverine environment, though fertile when drained and irrigated, lacked necessary raw materials such as hardwood and stone. The trade with other areas could have been peaceful and balanced, as between equals. After all, it is possible that when one area has something that another wants, and vice versa, the people on both sides could voluntarily arrange to satisfy each other's needs by bargaining and negotiating. But the archaeological evidence from the preliterate Uruk period, as well as the documentary evidence for shortly afterward, suggests that the first city-states in Mesopotamia were engaged in imperialism and colonialism from their very beginnings.

Just like the British and French, who first came to North America to explore and trade and often used force to protect their settlements and access to trade items, the Uruk city-states seem also to have dominated their peripheral, less developed trading "partners." For example, before 3000 B.C. there were fortified towns with Uruk-style pottery and administrative artifacts at river junctions in the north of Mesopotamia. Why did the Uruk people go there? One possibility is that they deliberately built outposts to secure their access to

needed trade goods, including hides and dried meat.

There was no single state involved in this imperialism and colonialism. Southern Mesopotamia (Sumer) was not politically unified until after 3000 B.C. Rather, the various Uruk-period polities of the Tigris and Euphrates river valleys seem to have been intensely competitive. The walls around the cities indicate that they were probably subject to attack by their rivals at any time. The picture is reminiscent of the Greek city-states described by Thucydides. It is also like the picture we get from the hieroglyphic writings of the Maya city-states in and around southern Mexico (A.D. 300–800), which, in a mixture of history and propaganda, extol the triumphs of the various rivalrous rulers. And, of course, we are all familiar with how Britain and Spain and Holland and France were rivalrous before and after the New World was discovered.

We know that the Greek city-states were imperialistic colonizers because we have historical evidence of the fact. Greek-speakers, from Athens and other polities, established colonies all over the Mediterranean—Syracuse in Sicily and Marseilles in France, for example. But what about the Uruk city-states? Why should we think they too were imperialistic colonizers? Archaeologist Guillermo Algaze recently reviewed the evidence. First there was the colonization of the plains of southwestern Iran, which people could get to from southern Mesopotamia in seven to ten days by foot or

---

intensive agriculture.[55] Two of the authors of this text have found that in recent societies resource unpredictability is strongly associated with a higher frequency of warfare, and states fearful of shortfalls in resources may resort to war ahead of time as a means of gaining access to more resources (or of limiting the unpredictability of resources).[56] A third answer to the question of why states tend to expand might be that belligerence is simply part of the nature of states. States often arise through military means, and it may be vital to the continuation of some states that military power be continually demonstrated.[57] Regardless of the causes, war and conquest are the consequences of state formation. Often, too, defeat in war is the fate of states.

The Decline and Collapse of States

When you look over the list of ancient states we have discussed in this chapter—Monte Albán, Teotihuacán, Sumer, pharonic Egypt—you will notice one element common to

them all: Each eventually collapsed; none maintained its power and influence into historic times. Why? It is an important question because, if collapse is the ultimate fate of many if not all states, then we can anticipate that our own state is likely to collapse eventually. Perhaps knowing something about how and why other states have fallen can prevent (or at least hold off) the fall of our own.

One suggested explanation for the decline and collapse of states is environmental degradation. If states originally arose where the environment was conducive to intensive agriculture and harvests big enough to support social stratification, political officials, and a state type of political system, then perhaps environmental degradation—declining soil productivity, persistent drought, and the like—contributed to the collapse of ancient states. Archaeologist Harvey Weiss has suggested that persistent drought helped to bring about the fall of the ancient Akkadian empire, in the Near East. By 2300 B.C., the Akkadians had established an empire stretching 1,300 kilometers from the Persian Gulf in what is now Iraq to the headwaters of the Euphrates River in what is now Turkey. But a century later the empire collapsed. Weiss thinks that a

donkey caravan. Then, and maybe overlapping with the expansion into southwestern Iran, the Uruk polities established outposts or took over already existing settlements to the north and northwest, on the plains of what are now northern Iraq and Syria; these latter settlements were apparently all located at intersections of the important waterways and overland routes.

According to Algaze, the Uruk enclaves and outposts outside southern Mesopotamia fit what comparative historian Philip Curtin calls trade diaspora. Curtin thinks that such movements develop after the emergence of cities, with their vulnerable populations. (An urban population is vulnerable because a city, by definition, is inhabited mostly by people who are dependent for their food on people who live outside the city.) Diaspora have taken various forms, but they all represent ways to organize exchange between areas with different but complementary resources. At one end of the range of possibilities—involving little or no political organization—commercial specialists remove themselves from their own society and settle as aliens somewhere else. At the other end of the range of variation—the most politically organized—the expanding polity is involved from the beginning in the founding of outposts that secure the required trade.

Algaze thinks that the Uruk expansion was motivated by a lack of resources in southern Mesopotamia. But is that a complete explanation? Other areas of the world, at the time and since, have lacked resources, but they did not all become imperialistic colonizers. So what else, in addition to the need for external resources, might explain the Uruk expansion? And how

can we explain why it eventually stopped? Algaze notes that when the Uruk settlers moved into southwestern Iran, they were entering an area that was not so densely settled, so they may have encountered only minimal resistance. Indeed, the various Uruk-period enclaves and outposts outside southern Mesopotamia were apparently larger and more complex than any previous communities in the peripheral areas. Perhaps, then, imperialism and colonialism are possible only in a world of unequals.

Years ago, anthropologist Stanley Diamond argued that "imperialism and colonialism are as old as the State." Does this mean that states are likely to practice imperialism and colonialism if they can get away with it? Or are only some conditions likely to predispose states to imperialism and colonialism? How strongly are imperialism and colonialism linked to state organization anyway? What makes a humane state possible? Perhaps future research, particularly cross-cultural and cross-historical research, will tell us.

Sources: Guillermo Algaze, *The Uruk World System: The Dynamics of Expansion of Early Mesopotamian Civilization* (Chicago: University of Chicago Press, 1993); Melinda A. Zeder, "After the Revolution: Post-Neolithic Subsistence in Northern Mesopotamia," *American Anthropologist,* 96 (1994): 97–126; Philip D. Curtin, *Cross-Cultural Trade in World History* (Cambridge: Cambridge University Press, 1984); Stanley Diamond, *In Search of the Primitive: A Critique of Civilization* (New Brunswick, NJ: Transaction Books, 1974); Joyce Marcus, "Maya Hieroglyphs: History or Propaganda?" In Peter N. Peregrine, Carol R. Ember, and Melvin Ember, eds., *Archaeology: Original Readings in Method and Practice* (Upper Saddle River, NJ: Prentice Hall, 2002), also in Carol R. Ember, Melvin Ember, and Peter N. Peregrine, eds., *Research Frontiers,* in *New Directions in Anthropology* (Upper Saddle River, NJ: Prentice Hall, CD-ROM, 2004).

long-term drought brought the empire down, as well as other civilizations around at that time too. Many archaeologists doubted there was such a widespread drought, but new evidence indicates that the worst dry spell of the past 10,000 years began just as the Akkadians' northern stronghold was being abandoned.[58] The evidence of the drought, windblown dust in sediment retrieved from the bottom of the Persian Gulf, indicates that the dry spell lasted 300 years. Other geophysical evidence suggests that the drought was worldwide.[59]

Environmental degradation may also have contributed to the collapse of Mayan civilization.[60] The Mayans built large temple complexes in the lowland regions of Mexico and the Yucatán Peninsula beginning about A.D. 250, but after about A.D. 750 construction ceased, and by about A.D. 900 the temple complexes appear to have been all but abandoned. Lake sediments show that the region inhabited by the Maya experienced an extended period of drought lasting between roughly A.D. 800 and 1000. The Maya, who depended on rainfall agriculture for subsistence, may not have been able to produce enough food in areas around temple complexes during this long period of drought to feed the resident pop-

ulations. People would have been forced to move into less populated areas to survive, and the temple complexes would have slowly been abandoned.[61]

Environmental degradation may occur for reasons other than natural events. The behavior of humans may sometimes be responsible. Consider the collapse of Cahokia, a city of at least 15,000 people that thrived for a while in the area where the Missouri and Mississippi rivers converge. In the 12th century A.D., Cahokia had large public plazas, a city wall constructed from some 20,000 logs, and massive mounds. But within 300 years only the mounds were left. Silt from flooding covered former croplands and settled areas. Geographer Bill Woods thinks that overuse of woodlands for fuel, construction, and defense led to deforestation, flooding, and persistent crop failure. The result was the abandonment of Cahokia. Timber depletion is also indicated by studies of charcoal from excavations in the area. Apparently the quality of wood used in construction declined over time, suggesting that choice trees got scarcer.[62]

Cahokia is just one example of degradation that may have been caused by human behavior. Another example is the

The history of Ephesus, a former city lying in ruins in what is now western Turkey, illustrates the waxing and waning of states and empires. From about 1000 B.C. to 100 B.C., it was controlled by the Greeks, Lydians, Persians, Macedonians, and Romans, among others.

increasing saltiness of soils caused by evaporation of water from fields that have been irrigated over long periods of time, as in what is now southern Iraq.

Civilizations may sometimes decline because human behavior has increased the incidence of disease. As we noted, many lowland Mayan cities were abandoned between A.D. 800 and 1000, possibly because of drought. But another factor may have been the increasing incidence of yellow fever. The clearing of forests and the consequent increase of breeding sites for mosquitoes may have favored the spread of the disease from areas farther south in Central America. Or the planting of particular trees by the Mayans in their urban areas may have increased the populations of co-resident monkeys who carried the disease (which mosquitoes transmitted to people).[63]

Another reason that some states have collapsed appears to be overextension. This is often one of the reasons given for the decline of the Roman Empire. By the time of its fall, beginning in the 2nd century A.D., the empire had expanded throughout the Mediterranean region and into northwestern Europe. That huge area may simply have been too large to administer. "Barbarian" incursions on the peripheries of the empire went unchecked because it was too difficult, and too costly, to reinforce these far-flung frontiers. Sometimes these incursions became wholesale invasions that were exacerbated by famines, plagues, and poor leadership. By the time the last Roman emperor of the West was deposed in A.D. 476, the empire had withered to virtually nothing.[64]

Finally, internal conflict because of leaders' mismanagement or exploitation has been put forward to explain the collapse of states. For example, Peter Charnais has argued that the Byzantine Empire (the eastern half of the Roman Empire) collapsed because large, powerful landholders had been allowed to take over the land of too many small holders, creating a group of overtaxed, exploited peasants with no interest in maintaining the empire. When the landholders began vying with the emperor for power, civil wars erupted, leading to disunity that left the empire vulnerable to conquest.[65]

Many other ideas have been put forward to explain collapse, ranging from catastrophes to almost mystical factors such as "social decadence," but, as with theories for the origin of states, no single explanation seems to fit all or even most of the situations. While it is still not clear what specific conditions led to the emergence, or collapse, of the state in each of the early centers of civilization, the question of why states form and decline is a lively focus of research today. More satisfactory answers may come out of ongoing and future investigations.

◎ Summary

1. Archaeologists do not always agree on how a state should be defined, but most seem to agree that hierarchical and centralized decision making affecting a substantial population is the key criterion. Most states have cities with public buildings, full-time craft and religious specialists, an official art style, and a hierarchical social structure topped by an elite class from which the leaders are drawn. Most states maintain power with a monopoly

on the use of force. Force or the threat of force is used by the state to tax its population and to draft people for work or war.

2. Early state societies arose within the Near East in what is now southern Iraq and southwestern Iran. Southern Iraq, or Sumer, was unified under a single government just after 3000 B.C. It had writing, large urban centers, imposing temples, codified laws, a standing army, wide trade networks, a complex irrigation system, and a high degree of craft specialization.

3. Probably the earliest city-state in Mesoamerica developed around 500 B.C. in the Valley of Oaxaca, with a capital at Monte Albán. Somewhat later, in the northeastern section of the Valley of Mexico, Teotihuacán developed. At the height of its power, A.D. 200–500, the city-state of Teotihuacán appears to have influenced much of Mesoamerica.

4. City-states arose early in other parts of the New World: in Guatemala, the Yucatán Peninsula of Mexico, Peru, and possibly near St. Louis, Missouri. In the Old World, early states developed in Africa, the Indus Valley of India, and northern China.

5. There are several theories of why states arose. The irrigation theory suggests that the administrative needs of maintaining extensive irrigation systems may have been the impetus for state formation. The circumscription theory suggests that states emerge when competition and warfare in circumscribed areas lead to the subordination of defeated groups, which are obliged to submit to the control of the most powerful group. Theories involving trade suggest that the organizational requirements of producing exportable items, redistributing imported items, and defending trading parties would foster state formation. Which is correct? At this point, no one theory is able to explain the formation of every state. Perhaps different organizational requirements in different areas all favored centralized government.

6. When states arise they have a dramatic impact. Populations grow and become concentrated in cities. Agriculture becomes more efficient, allowing many people to be removed from food production. States provide a context in which what we commonly call civilization—art, music, literature, and organized religion—can develop and flourish. But states also provide a context in which warfare and political terror can flourish. The social differentiation found in states produces an underclass of poor and often unhealthy people. States are prone to epidemic disease and periodic famine.

7. All ancient states collapsed eventually. While we have no good answers to the question of why states collapse, research into this question may have implications for prolonging the lives of our modern state systems.

◎ Glossary Terms

civilization	181	hieroglyphics	184
cuneiform	184	state	181

◎ Critical Questions

1. Cities and states did not appear until after the emergence of food production. Why might food production be necessary, but not sufficient, for cities and states to develop?

2. Like the emergence of food production, the earliest cities and states developed within a few thousand years of each other. What might be the reasons?

3. Can you imagine a future world without states? What conditions might lead to that "state" of the world?

◎ Research Navigator

1. Please go to **www.researchnavigator.com** and enter your LOGIN NAME and PASSWORD. For instructions on registering for the first time, please view the detailed instructions at the end of Chapter 1.

2. Use the link library for Anthropology and explore the links under one of the following topics: Babylon; Egypt, Ancient; India, Ancient; Shang Dynasty. Once you have examined the links, write something that would be suitable for a Web page (or create a "virtual museum" Web page on the ancient state you explored). Have another student read what you wrote (or "visit" your museum) and comment on what they learned.

◎ Discovering Anthropology: Researchers at Work

Read the chapter by Joyce Marcus titled "Maya Hieroglyphs: History or Propaganda?" in the accompanying *Discovering Anthropology* reader. Answer the following questions:

1. Marcus describes a series of "pendulum swings" in the study of Mayan writing. What does she mean by a "pendulum swing"? Give an example.

2. How has the decipherment of Mayan writing led scholars to question the histories it apparently was used to convey?

3. What does Marcus mean by Maya "propaganda"? How might Mayan kings have used "propaganda"?

CHAPTER TWELVE

Human Variation and Adaptation

In any given human population, individuals vary in external features such as skin color or height and in internal features such as blood type or susceptibility to a disease. If you measure the frequencies of such features in different populations, you will typically find differences on average from one population to another. So, for example, some populations are typically darker in skin color than other populations.

Why do these physical differences exist? They may be largely the product of differences in genes. Or they may be largely due to growing up in a particular environment, physical and cultural. Or perhaps they are the result of an interaction between environmental factors and genes.

We turn first to the processes that may singly or jointly produce the varying frequencies of physical traits in different human populations. Then we discuss specific differences in external and internal characteristics and how they might be explained. Finally, we close with a critical examination of racial classification and whether it helps or hinders the study of human variation.

Processes in Human Variation and Adaptation

Mutations—changes in the structure of a gene—are the ultimate source of all genetic variation. Because different genes make for greater or lesser chances of survival and reproduction, natural selection results in more favorable genes becoming more frequent in a population over time. We call this process **adaptation.** Adaptations are genetic changes that give their carriers a better chance to survive and reproduce than individuals without the genetic change who live in the same environment. It is the environment, of course, that favors the reproductive success of some traits rather than others.

How adaptive a gene or trait is depends on the specific environment; what is adaptive in one environment may not be adaptive in another. For example, in the chapter on genetics and evolution, we discussed the advantage that dark moths had over light moths when certain areas of England became industrialized. Predators could not easily see the darker moths against the newly darkened trees, and these moths soon outnumbered the lighter variety. Similarly, human populations live in a great variety of environments, so we would expect natural selection to favor different genes and traits in those different environments. As we shall see, variations in skin color and body build are among the many features that may be at least partly explainable by how natural selection works in different environments.

Adaptation through natural selection does not account for variation in frequencies of neutral traits—that is, traits that do not confer any advantages or disadvantages on their carriers. The sometimes different and sometimes similar frequencies of neutral traits in human populations may result, then, from genetic drift or gene flow. As we discussed in the chapter on genetics and evolution, genetic drift refers to variations in a population that appear because of random processes such as isolation (the "founder effect"), mating patterns, and the random segregation of chromosomes during meiosis. Gene flow involves the exchange of genes between populations. Neither genetic drift nor gene flow are adaptive processes, but they do result in differences between populations. Genetic drift may increase the differences between populations. Gene flow tends to work in the opposite direction—it tends to decrease differences between populations.

Acclimatization

Natural selection may favor certain genes because of certain physical environmental conditions, as in the case of the moths in England. But the physical environment can sometimes produce variation even in the absence of genetic change. As we shall see, climate may influence the way the human body grows and develops, and therefore some kinds of human variation may be explainable largely as a function of environmental variation. We call this process *acclimatization.* **Acclimatization** involves physiological adjustments in individuals to environmental conditions. Acclimatizations may have underlying genetic factors, but they are not themselves genetic. Individuals develop them during their lifetimes, rather than being born with them.

Many acclimatizations are simple physiological changes in the body that appear and disappear as the environment changes. For example, when we are chilled, our bodies attempt to create heat by making our muscles work, a physiological response to the environment that we experience as shivering. Longer exposure to cold weather leads our bodies to increase our metabolic rates so that we generate more internal heat. Both these physiological changes are acclimatizations, one short term (shivering), one longer term (increased metabolic rate).

As we discuss later in this chapter, some long-term acclimatizations are difficult to distinguish from adaptations because they become established as normal operating processes, and they may persist even after the individual moves into an environment that is different from the one that originally fostered the acclimatization. It also appears that some acclimatizations are closely related to genetic adaptations. For example, tanning, an acclimatization among light-skinned people when exposed to high levels of solar radiation, is related to the adaptation of light skin color to environments with low solar radiation.

Influence of the Cultural Environment

Humans are not only influenced by their environments through adaptations and acclimatizations, but, as we shall see in the chapters on food production and on the state,

humans can also dramatically affect their environments. Culture allows humans to modify their environments, and such modifications may lessen the likelihood of genetic adaptations and physiological acclimitizations. For example, the effects of cold may be modified by the culture traits of living in houses, harnessing energy to create heat, and clothing the body to insulate it. In these cultural ways, we alter our "microenvironments." Iron deficiency may be overcome by the culture trait of cooking in iron pots. If a physical environment lacks certain nutrients, people may get them by the culture trait of trading for them; trading for salt has been common in world history. Culture can also influence the direction of natural selection. As we shall see, the culture of dairying seems to have increased the frequency of genes that allow adults to digest milk.[1]

In addition, individual cultures sometimes practice behaviors that lead to physical variations between their members and between members of one culture and another. For example, elites in many highland Andean societies (the Inca, for example) practiced head binding. The heads of elite children were tightly bound with cloth. As the child grew, the binding forced the skull to take on an elongated, almost conical shape. This cultural practice, then, created physical variations among individuals that were intended to identify members of elite groups.[2] Many cultures have practices that are intended to create physical variations that distinguish members of their culture from members of other cultures. The Hebrew Bible, for example, tells the story of how Abraham was instructed by God to circumcise himself and all his male descendants as a sign of the covenant between them.[3] Thus male descendants of Abraham traditionally share a culturally induced physical variation (lack of a foreskin) to identify themselves as a group.

In the next section we discuss some aspects of human (physical) variation for which we have explanations that involve one or more of the processes just described.

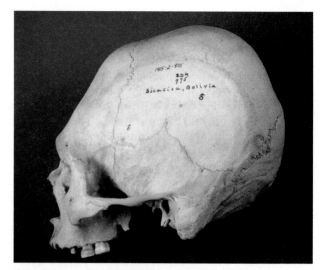

A cranium from Sicasica, Bolivia, showing the effects of head binding. Note how high and flat the forehead is.

Physical Variation in Human Populations

The most noticeable physical variations among populations are those that are external, on the surface—body build, facial features, skin color, and height. No less important are those variations that are internal, such as variation in susceptibility to different diseases and differences in the ability to produce certain enzymes.

We begin our survey with some physical features that appear to be strongly linked to variation in climate, particularly variation in temperature, sunlight, and altitude.

Body Build and Facial Construction

Scientists have suggested that the body build of many birds and mammals may vary according to the temperature of the environment in which they live. Bergmann and Allen, two 19th century naturalists, suggested some general rules for animals, but it was not until the 1950s that researchers began to examine whether these rules applied to human populations.[4] **Bergmann's rule** describes what seems to be a general relationship between body size and temperature: The slenderer populations of a species inhabit the warmer parts of its geographic range, and the more robust populations inhabit the cooler areas.

D. F. Roberts's studies of variation in mean body weight of human populations in regions with widely differing temperatures have provided support for Bergmann's rule.[5] Roberts discovered that the lowest body weights were found among residents of areas with the highest mean annual temperatures, and vice versa. Figure 12–1 shows the relationship between body weight of males and average annual temperature for four different geographic populations. Although the slope of the relationship is slightly different for each group, the trend is the same—with colder temperatures, weight is greater. Looking at the general trend across populations (see the "Total" line), we see that where the mean annual temperatures are about freezing (0°C; 32°F), the average weight for males is about 65 kilograms (143 pounds); where the mean annual temperatures are about 25°C (77°F), men weigh, on the average, about 50 kilograms (110 pounds).

Allen's rule refers to another kind of variation in body build among birds and mammals: Protruding body parts (e.g., limbs) are relatively shorter in the cooler areas of a species' range than in the warmer areas. Research comparing human populations tends to support Allen's rule.[6]

The rationale behind these theories is that the long-limbed, lean body type often found in equatorial regions provides more surface area in relation to body mass and thus facilitates the dissipation of body heat. In contrast, the chunkier, shorter-limbed body type found among residents of cold regions promotes retention of body heat because the amount of surface area relative to body mass is lessened. The build of the Inuit (Eskimo) appears to exemplify Bergmann's

These Samburu people from Kenya illustrate Bergmann's rule. They have the long-limbed, lean body type that is often found in equatorial regions. Such a body type provides more surface area in relation to body mass and thus may facilitate the dissipation of body heat.

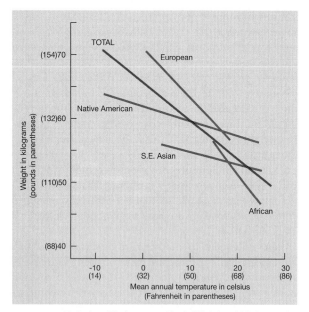

Figure 12–1 Relationship between Body Weight of Males and Average Annual Temperature for Four Major Population Groups.

Source: From D. F. Roberts, "Body Weight, Race, and Climate," *American Journal of Physical Anthropology,* 11 (1953): Fig. 2, reproduced in Stephen Jones, Robert Martin, and David Pilbeam, eds., *The Cambridge Encyclopedia of Human Evolution.*

and Allen's rules. The relatively large bodies and short legs of the Inuit may be adapted to the cold temperatures in which they live.

It is not clear whether differences in body build among populations are due solely to natural selection of different genes under different conditions of cold or heat. Some of the variations may be acclimatizations induced during the life span of individuals.[7] Alphonse Riesenfeld provided experimental evidence that extreme cold can affect body proportions during growth and development. Rats raised under conditions of extreme cold generally showed changes that resemble characteristics of humans in cold environments. These cold-related changes included shortening of the long bones, consistent with Allen's rule.[8]

Like body build, facial structure may also be affected by environment. Riesenfeld found experimentally that the facial width of rats increased in cold temperatures and their nasal openings grew smaller.[9] Because the rats raised in cold environments were genetically similar to those raised in warmer environments, we can confidently conclude that the environment, not genes, brought about these changes in the rats. How much the environment directly affects variation in the human face is not clear. We do know that variation in climate is associated with facial variation. For example, people living in the humid tropics tend to have broad, short, flat noses, whereas people living in climates with low humidity (with cold or hot temperatures) tend to have long, thin noses. A narrow nose may be a more efficient humidifier of drier air than a broad nose.[10]

This Inuit father and son illustrates Allen's rule. Both have relatively large bodies and short limbs, which help them maintain body heat in the cold climate they inhabit.

Skin Color

Human populations obviously differ in average skin color. Many people consider skin color the most important indicator of "race," and they sometimes treat others differently solely on this basis. But anthropologists, in addition to being critical of prejudice, also note that skin color is not a good indicator of ancestry. For example, dark skin is commonly found in sub-Saharan Africa. However, there are natives of southern India whose skin is as dark as or darker than that of many Africans. Yet these people are not closely related to Africans, either genetically or historically.

How can we explain the wide range of skin colors among the peoples of the world? The color of a person's skin depends on both the amount of dark pigment, or melanin, in the skin and the amount of blood in the small blood vessels of the skin.[11] Despite the fact that there is still much to understand about the genetics of skin color, we can explain much of the variation.

The amount of melanin in the skin seems to be related to the climate in which a person lives. **Gloger's rule** states that populations of birds and mammals living in warmer climates have more melanin and, therefore, darker skin, fur, or feathers, than do populations of the same species living in cooler areas. On the whole, this association with climate holds true for people as well as for other mammals and birds.

The populations of darker-skinned humans do live mostly in warm climates, particularly sunny climates (see Figure 12–2). Dark pigmentation seems to have at least one specific advantage in sunny climates. Melanin protects the sensitive inner layers of the skin from the sun's damaging ultraviolet rays; therefore, dark-skinned people living in sunny areas are safer from sunburn and skin cancers than are light-skinned people. Dark skin may also confer other important biological advantages in tropical environments, such as greater resistance to tropical diseases.[12]

What, then, might be the advantages of light-colored skin? Presumably, there must be some benefits in some environments; otherwise, all human populations would tend to have relatively dark skin. Although light-skinned people are more susceptible to sunburn and skin cancers, the ultraviolet radiation that light skin absorbs also facilitates the body's production of vitamin D. Vitamin D helps the body incorporate calcium and thus is necessary for the proper growth and maintenance of bones. Too much vitamin D, however, can cause illness. Thus, the light-colored skin of people in temperate latitudes maximizes ultraviolet penetration, perhaps ensuring production of sufficient amounts of vitamin D for good health, whereas the darker skin of people in tropical latitudes minimizes ultraviolet penetration, perhaps preventing illness from too much vitamin D.[13] Light skin may also confer another advantage in colder environments: It is less likely to be damaged by frostbite.[14]

We now have direct evidence that confirms the connection between solar radiation and skin pigmentation. Anthropologists Nina Jablonski and George Chaplin used data from NASA satellites to determine the average amount of ultraviolet radiation people were exposed to in different parts of the world. They compared these average radiation amounts to data on skin reflectance (the lighter one's skin, the more light it reflects) and found that dark skin is more prevalent where ultraviolet radiation is more intense.

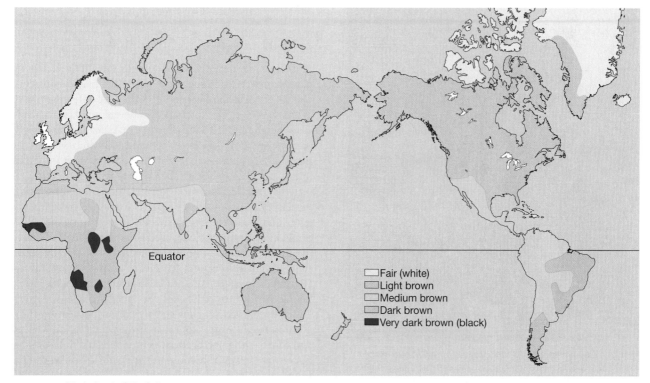

Figure 12–2 Variation in Skin Color

Interestingly, there seems to be one notable exception—Native Americans tend to be lighter-skinned than expected. Jablonski and Chaplin suggest that this is because they are recent migrants to the New World, and their skin colors have not adapted to the varying levels of ultraviolet radiation they encountered in the Americas, just as the skin colors of European colonizers have not.[15]

Adaptation to High Altitude

Oxygen constitutes 21 percent of the air we breathe at sea level. At high altitudes, the percentage of oxygen in the air is the same, but because the barometric pressure is lower, we take in less oxygen with each breath.[16] We breathe more rapidly, our hearts beat faster, and all activity is more difficult. The net effects are discomfort and a condition known as **hypoxia,** or oxygen deficiency.

If high altitude presents such difficulties for many human beings, how is it that populations numbering in the millions can live out their lives, healthy and productive, at altitudes of 6,000, 12,000, or even 17,000 feet? Populations in the Himalayas and the Andes have adapted to their environments and do not display the symptoms suffered by low-altitude dwellers when they are exposed to high altitudes. Moreover, high-altitude dwellers have come to terms physiologically with extreme cold, deficient nutrition, strong winds, rough countryside, and intense solar radiation.[17]

Highland Andean peoples like this Quechua woman and her children, have larger chests and greater lung capacity than people living at low altitude. These differences are thought to be acclimatizations to life at high altitude and the problem of hypoxia, or oxygen deficiency.

Early studies of Andean high-altitude dwellers found that they differed in certain physical ways from low-altitude dwellers. Compared with low-altitude dwellers, high-altitude Andean Indians had larger chests and greater lung capacity, as well as more surface area in the capillaries of the lungs (which was believed to facilitate the transfer of oxygen to the blood).[18] Early researchers thought that genetic changes had allowed the Andeans to maximize their ability to take in oxygen at the lower barometric pressure of their high-altitude environment. Recent research, however, has cast some doubt on this conclusion. It appears now that other populations living at high altitudes do not show the Andean pattern of physical differences. In the Himalayas, for example, low-altitude dwellers and high-altitude dwellers do not differ in chest size or lung size, even though both groups show adequate lung functioning.[19]

Thus, current research does not suggest that high-altitude living requires biological adaptations that are purely genetic. In fact, some evidence suggests that humans who grow up in a high-altitude environment may adapt to hypoxia during their lifetimes, as they mature. For example, Peruvians who were born at sea level but who grew up at high altitudes developed the same amount of lung capacity as people who spent their entire lives at high altitudes.[20] Consistent with a presumed environmental effect, the children of high-altitude Peruvians who grow up in the lowlands do not develop larger chests. What appeared to earlier researchers to be a genetic adaptation among highland Andean populations appears in fact to be an acclimatization that develops early in childhood and persists for the lifetime of an individual. As with other traits that have been studied, it appears that life experiences can have profound effects on how the body grows.

Height

Studies of identical twins and comparisons of the height of parents and children suggest that heredity plays a considerable role in determining height,[21] so genetic differences must at least partly explain differences between populations in average height. But if average height can increase dramatically in a few decades, as in Japan between 1950 and 1980 and in many other countries in recent times,[22] then environmental influences are also likely to be important.

The considerable variation in average height among human populations may be partly explained by temperature differences. The Dutch, in Europe, are among the tallest populations in the world on average, and the Mbuti of Zaire, in central Africa, are among the shortest.[23] We already know that weight is related to mean annual temperature (Bergmann's rule). Weight is also related to height (taller people are likely to be heavier). So, since the taller (heavier) Dutch live in a cooler climate, some of the population variation in height would appear to involve adaptation to heat and cold.[24] Other factors besides heat and cold must also be operating, however, because tall and short peoples can be found in most areas of the world.

Many researchers think that poor nutrition and disease lead to reduced height and weight. In many parts of the world, children in higher social classes are taller on the average than children in lower social classes,[25] and this difference is more marked in economically poorer countries,[26] where the wealth and health differences between the classes are particularly large. During times of war and poor nutrition, children's stature often decreases. For example, in Germany during World War II, the stature of children 7 to 17 years of age declined as compared with previous time periods, despite the fact that stature had generally increased over time.[27]

More persuasive evidence for the effects of poor nutrition and disease comes out of longitudinal studies of the same individuals over time. For example, Reynaldo Martorell found that children in Guatemala who had frequent bouts of diarrhea were on the average over an inch shorter at age 7 than children without frequent diarrhea.[28] Although malnourished or diseased children can catch up in their growth, follow-up research on Guatemalan children suggests that if stunting occurs before 3 years of age, stature at age 18 will still be reduced.[29]

A controversial set of studies links a very different environmental factor to variation in height in human populations. The factor at issue is stress, physical and emotional, in infancy.[30] Contrary to the view that any kind of stress is harmful, it appears that some presumably stressful experiences in infancy are associated with greater height and weight. Experimental studies with rats provided the original stimulus for the studies investigating the possible effect of stress on height. The experiments showed that rats that were

In recent times there has been a dramatic increase in average height, which may be due to one or more environmental factors. Here we see a Chinese American girl who is taller than her mother and almost as tall as her father.

physically handled ("petted") by the experimenters grew to be longer and heavier than rats not petted. Researchers originally thought that this was because the petted rats had received "tender loving care." But someone noticed that the petted rats seemed terrified (they urinated and defecated) when petted by humans, which suggested that the petting might have been stressful. It turned out in subsequent studies that even more obviously stressful experiences such as electric shock, vibration, and temperature extremes also produced rats with longer skeletons as compared with unstressed rats.

Thomas Landauer and John Whiting thought that stress in human infants might similarly produce greater adult height. Many cultures have customs for treating infants that could be physically stressful, including circumcision, branding of the skin with sharp objects, piercing the nose, ears, or lips for the insertion of ornaments, molding and stretching the head and limbs for cosmetic purposes, and vaccination. In addition, Shulamith Gunders and John Whiting suggested that separating the baby from its mother right after birth is another kind of stress. In cross-cultural comparisons by Whiting and his colleagues,[31] it seems that *both* physical stress and mother–infant separation, *if practiced before 2 years of age,* predict greater adult height; males are on the average 2 inches taller in such societies. (It is important to note that the stresses being discussed are short in duration, often a one-time occurrence, and do not constitute prolonged stress or abuse, which can have opposite effects.)

Because the cross-cultural evidence is associational, not experimental, it is possible that the results are due to some factor confounded with infant stress. Perhaps societies with infant stress have better nutrition or have climates that favor tallness. Recently, using new cross-cultural comparisons, J. Patrick Gray and Linda Wolfe attempted to assess different possible predictors of height variation between populations. The predictors compared were nutrition, climate, geography, physical stress, and mother–infant separation. Gray and Wolfe's analysis indicated which of those factors predicted adult height independently of the others. It turned out that geographic region, climatic zone, and customs of infant stress were all significant independent predictors of height.[32] So the results now available clearly show that the effect of infant stress cannot be discounted.

Persuasive evidence for the stress hypothesis also comes from an experimental study conducted in Kenya.[33] Landauer and Whiting arranged for a randomly selected sample of children to be vaccinated before they were 2 years old. Other children were vaccinated soon after they were 2. A few years later the two groups were compared with respect to height. Consistent with the cross-cultural evidence on the possible effect of stress on height, the children vaccinated before the age of 2 were significantly taller than the children vaccinated later. The children vaccinated before the age of 2 were selected randomly for early vaccination, so it is unlikely that nutritional or other differences between the two groups account for their difference in height.

As we noted earlier, in several areas of the world, people have been getting taller. What accounts for this recent trend toward greater height? Several factors may be involved. Some

MIGRANTS AND IMMIGRANTS

Physical Differences between Natives and Immigrants

Physical anthropology in the late 19th century was fascinated with the concept of race. Physical anthropologists focused their careers on identifying and describing, with great detail and accuracy, the particular characteristics that differentiated one "race" of humans from another. There was no debate about the biological reality of human races, as there is today; rather, the idea that races existed seemed obviously true to anyone with eyes. People differed, and those differences could be identified, measured, and compared to show that specific variations were more common among one group of people than another. Some of the greatest scientists of the 19th century—Louis Agassiz, Paul Broca, Francis Galton, Karl Pearson—actively contributed to the identification and description of human "races."

There was a problem, however. The stability of identified so-called "racial" characteristics was untested. It was simply assumed that features used to classify "races," features such as the width of the face and roundness of the head—were stable over long periods of time and under different environmental conditions. If they were not, the characteristics of the supposed "races" might be only short-lived constellations of traits, and not fixed characteristics of human groups created when modern humans spread around the earth.

Franz Boas, the founder of anthropology in the United States, saw an opportunity to test the stability of "racial" characteristics using data on the massive influx of immigrants into the United States at the close of the 19th century. Boas convinced the U.S. Immigration Commission that a large-scale study of immigrants and their children would help the federal government better serve these new citizens. He received funding to conduct a thorough physical study of several thousand immigrant families, and, over the course of several years, collected data on nearly 18,000 individuals.

Boas's results were surprising. He found that immigrants and their children differed in small but statistically significant ways. In particular, he found that cranial shape was not immutable, as had been assumed by physical anthropologists at the time, but rather could change in a single generation. And the direction of change was not always the same. The heads of first-generation offspring born in the United States of relatively long-headed Italians and relatively round-headed Eastern European Jews were more like one another than either was like their parents. What was going on?

Boas provided no clear answer, although he suggested that the similar environment of New York where all these children grew up might have played a role. Boas's study of immigrants proved to be very controversial. At the time it questioned the assumption that "racial" characteristics were stable and unchanging and, in doing so, questioned the entire notion of "race" that had guided physical anthropology for half a century. Interestingly, Boas's study still remains somewhat controversial. In 2003 two groups of scholars published contradictory reanalyses of Boas's original data. One group claimed Boas got it wrong—that Boas overstated his findings and that in reality "racial" features were remarkably stable, the other that Boas basically got it right, despite the comparatively limited statistical analyses available to him. Both agree, however, with Boas that supposedly stable "racial" characteristics can change within a generation.

Sources: C. Loring Brace, "Race" Is a Four Letter Word: The Genesis of the Concept (Oxford; Oxford University Press, 2005); Clarence C. Gravlee, H. R. Bernard, and W. R. Leonard, "Heredity, Environment, and Cranial Form: A Reanalysis of Boas's Immigrant Data." American Anthropologist 105 (2003): 125–38; Corey Sparks and R. L. Jantz, "Changing Times, Changing Faces: Franz Boas's Immigrant Study in Modern Perspective" American Anthropologist 105 (2003): 333–37.

researchers think that it may be the result of improved nutrition and lower incidence of infectious diseases.[34] But it might also be that infant stress has increased as a result of giving birth in hospitals, which usually separate babies from mothers and also subject the newborns to medical tests, including the taking of blood. And various kinds of vaccinations have also become more common in infancy.[35]

In short, differences in human size seem to be the result of both adaptations and acclimatizations, with both of these, in turn, affected by cultural factors such as nutrition and stress.

Susceptibility to Infectious Diseases

Certain populations seem to have developed inherited resistances to particular infectious diseases. That is, populations repeatedly decimated by certain diseases in the past now have a high frequency of genetic characteristics that ameliorate the effects of these diseases. As Arno Motulsky pointed out, if there are genes that protect people from dying when they are infected by one of the diseases prevalent in their area, these genes will tend to become more common in succeeding generations.[36]

A field study of the infectious disease myxomatosis in rabbits supports this theory. When the virus responsible for the disease was first introduced into the Australian rabbit population, more than 95 percent of the infected animals died. But among the offspring of animals exposed to successive epidemics of myxomatosis, the percentage of animals that died from the disease decreased from year to year. The more epidemics the animals' ancestors had lived through, the smaller the percentage of current animals that died of the disease. Thus, the data suggested that the rabbits had developed a genetic resistance to myxomatosis.[37]

Infectious diseases seem to follow a similar pattern among human populations. When tuberculosis first strikes a population that has had no previous contact with it, the disease is usually fatal. But some populations seem to have inherited a resistance to death from tuberculosis. For example, the Ashkenazi Jews in America (those whose ancestors came from central and eastern Europe) are one of several populations whose ancestors survived many years of exposure to tuberculosis in the crowded European ghettos where they had previously lived. Although the rate of tuberculosis infection is identical among American Jews and non-Jews, the rate of tuberculosis mortality is significantly lower among Jews than among non-Jews in the United States.[38] After reviewing other data on this subject, Motulsky thought it likely "that the present relatively high resistance of Western populations to tuberculosis is genetically conditioned through natural selection during long contact with the disease."[39]

We tend to think of measles as a childhood disease that kills virtually no one, and we now have a vaccine against it. But when first introduced into populations, the measles virus can kill large numbers of people. In 1949, the Tupari Indians of Brazil numbered about 200 people. By 1955, two-thirds of the Tupari had died of measles introduced into the tribe by rubber gatherers in the area.[40] Large numbers of people died of measles in epidemics in the Faeroe Islands in 1846, in Hawaii in 1848, in the Fiji Islands in 1874, and among the Canadian Inuit very recently. It is possible that

Permanent settlements and high population densities allow diseases to spread rapidly and produce epidemics. Here shoppers at a supermarket in China wear masks in the hope of preventing the spread of SARS.

where mortality rates from measles are low, populations have acquired a genetic resistance to death from this disease.[41]

But why is a population susceptible to a disease in the first place? Epidemiologist Francis Black suggests that lack of genes for resistance is not the whole answer. A high degree of genetic homogeneity in the population may also increase susceptibility.[42] A virus grown in one host is preadapted to a genetically similar new host and is therefore likely to be more virulent in the new host. For example, the measles virus adapts to a host individual; when it replicates, the viral forms that the host cannot kill are those most likely to survive and continue replicating. When the virus passes to a new host with similar genes, the preadapted virus is likely to kill the new host. If, on the other hand, the next host is very different genetically, the adaptation process starts over again; the virus is not so virulent at first because the host can kill it.

Populations that recently came to an area, and that had a small group of founders (as was probably true for the first Native Americans and the Polynesian seafarers who first settled many islands in the Pacific), tended to have a high degree of genetic homogeneity. Therefore, epidemic diseases introduced by Europeans (such as measles) would be likely to kill many of the natives within the first few years after contact. It is estimated that up to 56 million people died in the New World after contact with Europeans, mostly because of introduced diseases such as smallpox and measles. Similarly caused depopulation occurred widely in the Pacific.[43]

Some researchers suggest that nongenetic factors may also partly explain differential resistance to infectious disease. For example, cultural practices may partly explain the epidemics of measles among the Yanomamö Indians of Venezuela and Brazil. The Yanomamö frequently visit other villages, and that, together with the nonisolation of sick individuals, promoted a very rapid spread of the disease. Because many individuals were sick at the same time, there were not enough healthy people to feed and care for the sick; mothers down with measles could not even nurse their babies. Thus, cultural factors may increase exposure to a disease and worsen its effect on a population.[44]

Epidemics of infectious disease may occur only if many people live near each other. Food collectors, who usually live in small dispersed bands, do not have enough people in and near the community to keep an epidemic going. Without enough people to infect, short-lived microorganisms that cause or carry diseases die out. In contrast, among agriculturalists, there are larger numbers of people in and around the community to whom a disease can spread. Permanent settlements, particularly urban settlements, also are likely to have poor sanitation and contaminated water.[45] Tuberculosis is an example of an infectious disease that, although very old, began to kill large numbers of people only after the emergence of sedentary, larger communities.[46]

Sickle-Cell Anemia

Another biological variation is an abnormality of the red blood cells known as **sickle-cell anemia,** or **sicklemia.** This is a condition in which normal, disk-shaped red blood cells assume a crescent (sickle) shape when deprived of oxygen. The sickle-shaped red blood cells do not move through the body as readily as normal cells, and thus cause more oxygen deficiency and damage to the heart, lungs, brain, and other vital organs. In addition, the red blood cells tend to "die" more rapidly, and the anemia worsens still more.[47]

Sickle-cell anemia is caused by a variant form of the genetic instructions for hemoglobin, the protein that carries oxygen in the red blood cells.[48] Individuals who have sickle-cell anemia have inherited the same allele (Hb^S) from both parents and are therefore homozygous for that gene. Individuals who receive this allele from only one parent are heterozygous; they have one Hb^S allele and one allele for normal hemoglobin (Hb^A). Heterozygotes generally will not show the full-blown symptoms of sickle-cell disease, although in some cases a heterozygous individual may have a mild case of anemia. A heterozygous person has a 50 percent chance of passing on the sickle-cell allele to a child. And if the child later mates with another person who is also a carrier of the sickle-cell allele, the statistical probability is that 25 percent of their children will develop sickle-cell anemia. Without advanced medical care, most individuals with two Hb^S alleles are unlikely to live more than a few years.[49]

Why has the allele for sickle-cell persisted in various populations? If people with sickle-cell anemia do not usually live to reproduce, we would expect a reduction in the frequency of Hb^S to near zero through the process of *normalizing selection.* But the sickle-cell allele occurs fairly often in some parts of the world, particularly in the wet tropical belt of Africa, where frequencies may be between 20 and 30 percent, and in Greece, Sicily, and southern India.[50]

Because the sickle-cell gene occurs in these places much more often than expected, researchers in the 1940s and the 1950s began to suspect that heterozygous individuals (who carry one Hb^S allele) might have a reproductive advantage in a malarial environment.[51] If the heterozygotes were more resistant to attacks of malaria than the homozygotes for normal hemoglobin (who get the Hb^A allele from both parents), the heterozygotes would be more likely to survive and reproduce, and therefore the recessive Hb^S allele would persist at a higher than expected frequency in the population. This kind of outcome is an example of *balancing selection.*[52]

A number of pieces of evidence support the "malaria theory." First, geographic comparisons show that the sickle-cell allele tends to be found where the incidence of malaria is high (see Figure 12–3). Second, as land in the tropics is opened to yam and rice agriculture, the incidence of the sickle-cell allele also increases. Indeed, recent studies suggest malaria may have evolved alongside agriculture in these regions.[53] The reason seems to be that malaria, carried principally by the *Anopheles gambiae* mosquito, becomes more prevalent as tropical forest gives way to more open land where mosquitoes can thrive in warm, sunlit ponds. Indeed, even among peoples of similar cultural backgrounds, the incidence of the sickle-cell allele increases with greater rainfall and surpluses of water. Third, children who are heterozygous for the sickle-cell trait tend to have fewer malarial parasites in their bodies than do homozygous normal individuals, and they are more likely to survive.[54] The sickling trait does not necessarily keep people from contracting malaria, but it greatly decreases the rate of mortality from malaria—and in evolutionary terms, the overall effect is the same.[55] Fourth,

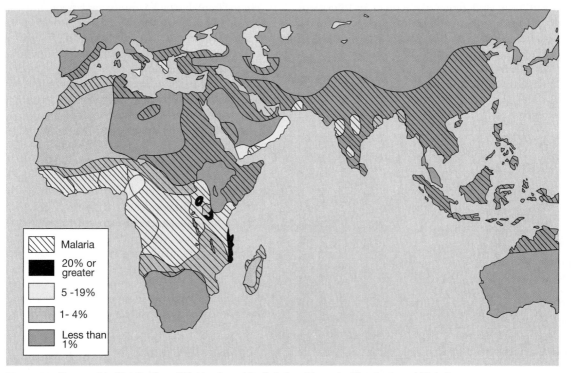

Figure 12–3 Geographic Distribution of Sicklemia and Its Relationship to the Distribution of Malaria

Source: From John Buettner-Janusch, *Physical Anthropology: A Perspective.*

if there is no balancing selection because malaria is no longer present, we should find a rapid decline in the incidence of the sickle-cell allele. Indeed, we find such a decline in populations with African ancestry. Those who live in malaria-free zones of the New World have a much lower incidence of sicklemia than do those who live in malarial regions of the New World.[56]

Hb[S] is not the only abnormal hemoglobin to have a distribution related to malaria. It seems that a number of abnormal hemoglobins may be widespread because of the advantage heterozygotes have against the disease. For example, another abnormal hemoglobin, Hb[E], occurs in populations from India through Southeast Asia and New Guinea where malaria occurs, but Hb[S] is not that common. Why should Hb[E] heterozygotes have resistance to malaria? One possibility is that malarial parasites are less able to survive in an individual's blood with some normal and some abnormal hemoglobin. Abnormal hemoglobin cells are more delicate and live less long, so they may not readily support malarial parasites.[57]

Lactase Deficiency

When American educators discovered that African American schoolchildren very often did not drink milk, they assumed that lack of money or education was the reason. These assumptions provided the impetus for establishing the school milk programs prevalent around the country. However, it now appears that after infancy many people lack an enzyme, lactase I, that is necessary for breaking down the sugar in milk, lactose, into simpler sugars that can be absorbed into the bloodstream.[58] Thus, a person without lactase cannot digest milk properly, and drinking it may cause bloating, cramps, stomach gas, and diarrhea. A study conducted in Baltimore among 312 African American and 221 European American children in grades 1 through 6 in two elementary schools indicated that 85 percent of the African American children and 17 percent of the European American children were milk-intolerant.[59]

More recent studies indicate that lactose intolerance occurs frequently in adults in many parts of the world.[60] The condition is common in Southeast and East Asia, India, the Mediterranean and the Near East, sub-Saharan Africa, and among Native North and South Americans. The widespread incidence of lactose intolerance should not be surprising. After infancy, mammals normally stop producing lactase.[61]

If lactose intolerance in adulthood in mammals is normal, we need to understand why only some human populations have the ability to make lactase I in adulthood and digest lactose. Why would selection favor this genetic ability in some populations but not in others? In the late 1960s, F. J. Simoons and Robert McCracken noted a relationship between lactose absorption and dairying (raising cows for milk). They suggested that with the advent of dairying, individuals with the genetic ability to produce lactase in adulthood would have greater reproductive success, and hence dairying populations would come to have a high proportion of individuals with the ability to break down lactose.[62]

(Top) Milking a cow in Barnstable, Massachusetts. Natural selection may favor production of the enzyme lactase, a genetic way of making milk digestible in dairying populations far from the equator. (Bottom) A Masai woman milking a cow in Kenya. Natural selection may favor the souring of milk, a cultural way of making it digestible in dairying populations close to the equator.

But people in some dairying societies do not produce lactase in adulthood. Rather, they seem to have developed a cultural solution to the problem of lactase deficiency; they transform their milk into cheese, yogurt, sour cream, and other milk products that are low in lactose. To make these low-lactose products, people separate the lactose-rich whey from the curds or treat the milk with a bacterium (*Lactobacillus*) that breaks down the lactose, thus making the milk product digestible by a lactase-deficient person.[63]

So why in some dairying societies did natural selection favor a biological solution (the production in adulthood of the enzyme lactase) rather than the cultural solution? William Durham has collected evidence that natural selection may favor the biological solution in dairying societies farther from the equator. The theory is that lactose behaves biochemically like vitamin D, facilitating the absorption of calcium—but only in people who produce lactase so that they can absorb the lactose. Because people in more temperate latitudes are not exposed to that much sunlight, particularly in the winter, and therefore make less vitamin D in their skin, natural selection may have favored the lactase way of absorbing dietary calcium.[64] In other words, natural selection may favor lactase production in adulthood, as well as lighter skin, at higher latitudes (where there is less sunlight).

This is an example of how culture may influence the way natural selection favors some genes over others. Without dairying, natural selection may not have favored the genetic propensity to produce lactase. This propensity is yet another example of the complex ways in which genes, environment, and culture interact to create human variation.

◎ Race and Racism

Fortunately, internal variations such as lactase deficiency have never been associated with intergroup tensions—perhaps because such differences are not immediately obvious. Unfortunately, the same cannot be said for some of the more obvious external human differences such as skin color.

For as long as any of us can remember, countless aggressive actions—from fistfights to large-scale riots and civil wars—have stemmed from tensions and misunderstandings between various groups commonly referred to by many as "races." *Race* has become such a common term that most of us take the concept for granted, not bothering to consider what it does, and does not, mean. We may talk about the "human race," which means that all humans belong to the same breeding population. Yet we are often asked to check a box to identify our particular "race." We discuss first how biologists sometimes use the term *race;* then we turn to why many biological anthropologists and others now conclude that the concept of race does not usefully apply to humans. We discuss how racial classifications are largely social constructions that have been used to justify discrimination, exploitation, and even the extermination of certain categories of people.

Race as a Construct in Biology

Biological variation is not uniformly distributed in any species. While all members of a species can potentially interbreed with others, most matings take place within smaller groups or breeding populations. Through the processes of natural selection and genetic drift, populations inhabiting different geographic regions will come to exhibit some differences in biological traits. When differences within a species become sufficiently noticeable, biologists may classify different populations into different *varieties,* or *races.* If the term **race** is understood to be just a shorthand or classificatory way that biologists describe slight population variants within a species, the concept of race would probably not be controversial. Unfortunately, as applied to humans, racial classifications have often been confounded with **racism,** the belief that some "races" are innately inferior to others. The misuse and misunderstanding of the term *race* and its association with racist thinking is one reason why many biological anthropologists and others have suggested that the term should not be applied to human biological differences.

A second reason for not applying racial classification to humans is that humans have exhibited so much interbreeding that different populations are not clearly classifiable into discrete groups that can be defined in terms of the presence or absence of particular biological traits.[65] Therefore, many argue that "race" is not scientifically useful for describing human biological variation. The difficulty in employing racial classification is evident by comparing the number of "races" that classifiers come up with. The number of "racial" categories in humans has varied from as few as 3 to more than 37.[66]

How can human groups be clearly divided into "races" if most adaptive biological traits show clines or gradual differences from one region to another?[67] Skin color is a good example of clinal variation. In the area around Egypt, there is a gradient of skin color as one moves from north to south in the Nile Valley. Skin generally becomes darker closer to the equator (south) and lighter closer to the Mediterranean. But other adaptive traits may not have north–south clines, because the environmental predictors may be distributed differently. Nose shape varies with humidity, but clines in humidity do not particularly correspond to variation in latitude. So the gradient for skin color would not be the same as the gradient for nose shape. Because adaptive traits tend to be clinally distributed, there is no line you could draw on a world map that would separate "white" from "black" people or "whites" from "Asians."[68] Only traits that are neutral in terms of natural selection will tend (because of genetic drift) to cluster in regions.[69]

Racial classification is problematic also because there is sometimes more physical, physiological, and genetic diversity *within* a single geographic group that might be called a "race" (e.g., Africans) than there is *between* supposed "racial" groups. Africans vary more among themselves than they do in comparison with people elsewhere.[70] Analyses of all human populations have demonstrated that 93–95% of genetic variation is due to individual differences within populations, while only 3–5% of genetic variation is due to differences among major human population groups.[71] "Race" when applied to humans is a social category, not a scientific one.

Race and Civilization

Many persons hold the racist viewpoint that the biological inferiority of certain groups, which they call "races," is reflected in the supposedly "primitive" quality of their cultures. They will argue that the "developed" nations are "white" and the "underdeveloped" nations are not. (We put terms like "white," which are used as racial categories, in quotes to indicate the problematic nature of the categories.) But to make such an argument ignores much of history. Many of today's so-called underdeveloped nations—primarily in Asia, Africa, and South America—had developed complex and sophisticated civilizations long before European nations expanded and acquired considerable power. The advanced societies of the Shang dynasty in China, the Mayans in Mesoamerica, and the African empire of Ghana were all founded and developed by "nonwhites."

Between 1523 and 1028 B.C., China had a complex form of government, armies, metal tools and weapons, and production and storage facilities for large quantities of grain. The early Chinese civilization also had writing and elaborate religious rituals.[72] From A.D. 300 to 900, the Mayans were a large population with a thriving economy. They built many large and beautiful cities in which were centered great pyramids and luxurious palaces.[73] According to legend, the West African civilization of Ghana was founded during the 2nd century A.D. By A.D. 770, the time of the Sonniki rulers, Ghana had developed two capital cities—one Muslim and the other non-Muslim—each with its own ruler and both supported largely by Ghana's lucrative gold market.[74]

Considering how recently northern Europeans developed cities and central governments, it seems odd that some "whites" should label Africans, Native Americans, and others backward in terms of historical achievement, or biologically inferior in terms of capacity for civilization. But racists, both "white" and "nonwhite," choose to ignore the fact that many populations have achieved remarkable advances in civilization. Most significant, racists refuse to believe that they can acknowledge the achievements of another group without in any way downgrading the achievements of their own.

Race, Conquest, and the Role of Infectious Disease

There are those who would argue that Europeans' superiority accounted for their ability to colonize much of the world during the last few hundred years. But it now appears that Europeans were able to dominate at least partly because many native peoples were susceptible to diseases introduced by the Europeans.[75] Earlier, we discussed how continued exposure to epidemics of infectious diseases, such as tuberculosis and measles, can cause succeeding generations to acquire a genetic resistance to death from such diseases. Smallpox had a long history in Europe and Africa; genetic resistance eventually made it mostly a survivable childhood disease. But in the New World it was quite another story. Cortez and the conquistadores were inadvertently aided by smallpox in their attempt to defeat the Aztecs of Mexico. In 1520, a member of Cortez's army unwittingly transmitted smallpox to the natives. The disease spread rapidly, killing at least 50 percent of the population, and so the Aztecs were at a considerable disadvantage in their battling with the Spanish.[76]

Outbreaks of smallpox repeatedly decimated many Native American populations in North America a century or two later. In the early 19th century, the Massachusett and Narragansett Indians, with populations of 30,000 and 9,000, respectively, were reduced by smallpox to a few hundred members. Extremely high mortality rates were also noted among the Crow, the Blackfoot, and other Native American groups during the 19th century. The germ theory alone may not completely explain these epidemics; Europeans may have deliberately encouraged the spread of one new disease, smallpox, by purposely distributing infected blankets to the natives. Motulsky calls the spread of smallpox "one of the first examples of biological warfare."[77]

Race and Behavior

As an outgrowth of earlier attempts to show that inferior "races" have "primitive" cultures, some scholars have attempted to demonstrate behavioral differences between "races." One of the most active has been psychologist J. Philippe Rushton, whose 1995 book *Race, Evolution, and Behavior* purports to demonstrate behavioral differences between the "Negroid," "Caucasoid," and "Mongoloid" "races" in terms of sexual practices, parenting, social deviance, and family structure, among others.

African metal workers created magnificent works of art like this golden head from Ghana long before Europeans arrived.

Rushton argues that these behaviors have a genetic basis rooted in adaptations to particular environments. He suggests that "Negroids" are adapted to the warm environments of East Africa, where humans first evolved, through a reproductive strategy in which individuals have many offspring but put little energy into their children's upbringing and care. This strategy is known in evolutionary theory as *r-selected,* and is well documented among creatures such as fish, reptiles, and even some mammals (rabbits, for example).[78] Rushton further suggests that as humans left Africa they adapted to the "colder" climates of Asia by adopting a more *K-selected* reproductive strategy, which involves having few offspring but putting lots of energy into their upbringing and care. K-selected strategies are also well documented in the animal world, and it is interesting to note that apes (and humans) are often presented as examples of highly K-selected species.[79]

The data Rushton uses to support his argument come almost entirely from modern nations, many with a history of racial discrimination (such as South Africa, Japan, and the United States). But if genetic differences in behavior do exist among these three "races," differences that have their origins in the exodus of modern humans from Africa more than 100,000 years ago, then those differences should be apparent both between and among all the cultures of the world. That is, "Negroid" cultures should all share behaviors that are clearly different from those of "Caucasoid" cultures, "Caucasoid" cultures should all share behaviors that are different from those of "Mongoloid" cultures, and so on. Do such differences exist?

The authors of this text used information about the 186 cultures composing the Standard Cross-Cultural Sample to test whether Rushton's ideas hold up.[80] We examined 26 separate behaviors that Rushton predicted would differ among the "races." Contrary to Rushton's predictions, most of them showed no differences between the supposed "racial" groups. Only one of them showed the differences that Rushton predicted, and five of them demonstrated a pattern that was the *opposite* of what Rushton predicted. So Rushton's gross division of humans into three "races" does not generally predict variation in human behavior. His ideas appear plainly wrong and do not support the belief that it is scientifically useful to distinguish human "races."[81]

Race and Intelligence

Attempts to document differences in intelligence among the so-called races have a fairly long history. One of the latest attempts was a 1994 book, titled *The Bell Curve,* by Charles Murray and Richard Herrnstein (see the box "Differences in Average IQ Scores").

In the 19th century, European white supremacists tried to find scientific justification for what they felt was the genetically inherited mental inferiority of "blacks." They did this by measuring skulls. It was believed that the larger the skull, the greater the cranial capacity and the bigger (hence, also better) the brain. Although the skull-measuring mania quickly disappeared and is no longer considered seriously as a way to measure intelligence, other "facts" may be used

to demonstrate the presumed intellectual superiority of "white" people—namely, statistics from intelligence tests.

The first large-scale intelligence testing in the United States began with the nation's entry into World War I, in 1917. Thousands of draftees were given the so-called Alpha and Beta IQ tests to determine military assignments. Later, psychologists arranged the test results according to the "racial" categories of "white" and "black" and found what they had expected—"blacks" scored consistently lower than "whites." This result was viewed as scientific proof of the innate intellectual inferiority of "blacks" and was used to justify further discrimination against them, both in and out of the army.[82]

Otto Klineberg's subsequent statistical analyses of IQ-test results demonstrated that "blacks" from northern states scored higher than "blacks" from the South. Although dedicated racists explained that this difference was due to the northward migration of innately intelligent "blacks," most academics attributed the result to the influence of superior education and more stimulating environments in the North. When further studies showed that northern "blacks" scored higher than southern "whites," the better-education-in-the-North theory gained support, but again racists insisted such results were due to northward migration by more intelligent "whites."

As a further test of his conclusions, Klineberg gave IQ tests to "black" schoolgirls born and partly raised in the South who had spent varying lengths of time in New York City. He found that the longer the girls had been in the North, the higher their average IQ. In addition to providing support for the belief that "blacks" are not inherently inferior to "whites," these findings suggested that cultural factors can and do influence IQ scores, and that IQ is not a fixed quantity.

The controversy about race and intelligence was fueled again in 1969 by Arthur Jensen.[83] He suggested that although the IQ scores of American "blacks" overlapped considerably with the IQ scores of "whites," the average score for "blacks" was 15 points lower than the average for "whites." IQ scores presumably have a large genetic component, so the lower average score for "blacks" implied to Jensen that "blacks" were genetically inferior to "whites." But others contend that the evidence presented by Jensen and more recently by Murray and Herrnstein implies no such thing.

The critics of the genetic interpretation point to at least two problems. First, there is widespread recognition now that IQ tests are probably not accurate measures of "intelligence" because they are probably biased in favor of the subculture of those who construct the tests. That is, many of the questions on the test refer to things that "white," middle-class children are familiar with, thus giving such children an advantage.[84] So far, no one has come up with a "culture-fair," or bias-free, test. There is more agreement that, although the IQ test may not measure "intelligence" well, it may predict scholastic success or how well a child will do in the primarily "white"-oriented school system.[85]

A second major problem with a purely genetic interpretation of the IQ difference is that many studies show that IQ scores can be influenced by the social environment.

CURRENT RESEARCH AND ISSUES

Differences in Average IQ Scores—What Do They Mean?

In late 1994, a new book reignited controversy about the relationship between "race" and intelligence. Once again people thought they had evidence of African American "inferiority." But once again there were problems with the evidence. The book was *The Bell Curve,* by Richard Herrnstein and Charles Murray. It purported to show that the intelligence of an individual was largely inherited and unchangeable throughout the life span, that an individual's success was largely based on intelligence, and that African Americans were likely to remain at the bottom of society because they had less intelligence than European Americans. Herrnstein and Murray appealed to a lot of studies to buttress their argument. But their argument was still faulty.

If you look at the average scores on many standard intelligence tests, you might conclude, as racists have, that African Americans are less intelligent than European Americans. The averages are different between the two groups; African Americans typically have lower scores. But what does this average difference mean? Herrnstein and Murray, like many before them, fail to distinguish between a measure, such as a particular IQ test, and what is supposedly being measured, intelligence. If a test only imperfectly measures what it purports to measure, lower average IQ scores merely mean lower scores on that particular IQ test; they do not necessarily reflect lower intelligence. There are many reasons why some smart people might not do well on particular kinds of IQ tests. For example, the way the tests are administered may affect performance, as may lack of familiarity with the format or the experiences and objects referred to. The test might also not measure particular kinds of intelligence such as social "smarts" and creativity.

If African Americans were really less intelligent, more than their average IQ scores would be lower. The whole frequency distribution of their individual scores should also be lower—they should have fewer geniuses and more retarded individuals. That is, the bell-shaped curve showing how their scores are distributed should range lower than the curve for other Americans, and African Americans should also have proportionately fewer scores at the very high end of the scale. But neither expectation is confirmed. According to research by Henry Grubb, the proportion of African Americans at the low end of the scale is not significantly different from the proportion of European Americans. And Grubb and Andrea Barthwell report that, on the basis of IQ tests administered by Mensa (a high-IQ society), the proportion of African Americans at the high end of the scale is not different from the proportion of European Americans. So the available evidence suggests that African Americans have lower average test scores, but not fewer very high scores or more very low scores (proportionately). Why, then, might their average scores be lower?

Grubb and Barthwell point out that the average scores are not lower on all IQ tests. One test that shows no significant difference is an untimed version of an intelligence test using pictures (the pictorial reasoning test). You can administer the pictorial reasoning test in one of two ways—timed or untimed. A person must finish the test by the end of a prescribed, relatively short time period; or the test-taker can respond to the questions without any time limit. African Americans have lower average scores than European Americans on the timed version of the pictorial reasoning test (although not as much lower as on other tests) but not on the untimed version. This finding suggests that a timed test measures or reflects more than just intelligence. What else besides intelligence might affect performance on a timed IQ test?

Familiarity with a particular format or the content could increase performance on a timed test. So could familiarity or comfort with speed. Although they do not have evidence for how African Americans feel about speed, Grubb and Barthwell cite a study that shows that discomfort with speed can affect performance on an IQ test. The study, conducted by A. Lieblich and S. Kugelmass, compared Jewish and Arab children in Israel. The Arab children scored lower than the Jewish children on the parts of a standard Wechsler intelligence test that were timed, but the Arab children scored the same or even higher on the parts that were untimed. Lieblich and Kugelmass concluded that the Arabs' poorer performance on the timed tests may reflect a cultural abhorrence of speed; "Time is of the Devil" is an Arab saying. Speed is not highly valued in some cultures. If unfamiliarity or discomfort with speed can affect performance on an IQ test, then clearly the test is not measuring intelligence only.

Critics have pointed to many other problems with the evidence presented in *The Bell Curve.* But the fundamental problem is the same as with all attempts to use differences in average IQ scores to make judgments about the capability of different groups. IQ tests may not adequately measure what they purport to measure. If they do not—and there are good reasons to think they do not—it is scientifically and morally incorrect to conclude that differences in average scores are caused by genetic differences in intelligence.

Sources: Richard J. Herrnstein and Charles Murray, *The Bell Curve: Intelligence and Class Structure in American Life* (New York: Free Press, 1994); Henry J. Grubb and Andrea G. Barthwell, "Superior Intelligence and Racial Equivalence: A Look at Mensa." Paper presented at the 1996 annual meeting of the Society for Cross-Cultural Research; Henry J. Grubb, "Intelligence at the Low End of the Curve: Where Are the Racial Differences?" *Journal of Black Psychology,* 14 (1987): 25–34; Leon J. Kamin, "Behind the Curve." *Scientific American* (February 1995): 99–103.

Until all people have an equal education and opportunities to achieve, there is no way we can be sure that some people are smarter than others.

Economically deprived children, whether "black" or "white," will generally score lower than affluent "white" or "black" children. And training of children with low IQ scores clearly improves their test scores.[86] More dramatic evidence is provided by Sandra Scarr and her colleagues. "Black" children adopted by well-off "white" families have IQ scores above the average for "whites." And those "blacks" with more European ancestry do not have higher IQ scores.[87] So the average difference between "blacks" and "whites" in IQ cannot be attributed to a presumed genetic difference. For all we know, the 15-point average difference may be due completely to differences in environment or to test bias.

Geneticist Theodosius Dobzhansky reminded us that conclusions about the causes of different levels of achievement on IQ tests cannot be drawn until all people have equal opportunities to develop their potentials. He stressed the need for an open society operating under the democratic ideal, where all persons are given an equal opportunity to develop whatever gifts or aptitudes they possess and choose to develop.[88]

◎ The Future of Human Variation

Laboratory fertilization, subsequent transplantation of the embryo, and successful birth have been accomplished with humans and nonhumans. *Cloning*—the exact reproduction

of an individual from cellular tissue—has been achieved with frogs, sheep, and other animals. And *genetic engineering*—the substitution of some genes for others—is increasingly practiced in nonhuman organisms. Indeed, as we discussed in the chapter on genetics and evolution, genetic engineering is now used in humans to eliminate certain disorders that are produced by defective genes. What are the implications of such practices for the genetic future of humans? Will it really be possible someday to control the genetic makeup of our species? If so, will the effects be positive or negative?

It is interesting to speculate on the development of a "perfect human." Aside from the serious ethical question of who would decide what the perfect human should be like, there is the serious biological question of whether such a development might in the long run be detrimental to the human species, for what is perfectly suited to one physical or social environment may be totally unsuited to another. The collection of physical, emotional, and intellectual attributes that might be "perfect" in the early 21st century might be inappropriate in the 22nd century.[89] Even defects such as the sickle-cell trait may confer advantages under certain conditions, as we have seen.

In the long run, the perpetuation of genetic variability is probably more advantageous than the creation of a "perfect" and invariable human being. In the event of dramatic changes in the world environment, absolute uniformity in the human species might be an evolutionary dead end. Such uniformity might lead to the extinction of the human species if new conditions favored genetic or cultural variations that were no longer present in the species. Perhaps our best hope for maximizing our chances of survival is to tolerate, and even encourage, the persistence of many aspects of human variation, both biological and cultural.[90]

◎ Summary

1. Physical variation—variation in the frequencies of physical traits—from one human population to another is the result of one or more of the following factors: adaptation, acclimatization, and the influence of the social or cultural environment.

2. Some physical variations in human populations involve genetic variation; other variations, including body build, facial construction, and skin color, may be adapted to variation in climate. Still other variations, such as the ability to make lactase, may be adapted partially to variation in cultural environment.

3. Most biological anthropologists today agree that "race" is not a useful way of referring to human biological variation because human populations do not unambiguously fall into discrete groups defined by a particular set of biological traits. Physical traits that are adaptive vary clinally, which makes it meaningless to divide humans into discrete "racial" entities. Rather, it is suggested that "racial" classifications are mostly social categories that are presumed to have a biological basis.

4. Perhaps the most controversial aspect of racial discrimination is the relationship supposed between "racial" categories and intelligence. Attempts have been made to show, by IQ tests and other means, the innate intellectual superiority of one "racial" category over another. But there is doubt that IQ tests measure intelligence fairly. Because evidence indicates that IQ scores are influenced by both genes and environment, conclusions about the causes of differences in IQ scores cannot be drawn until all the people being compared have equal opportunities to develop their potentials.

◎ Glossary Terms

acclimatization	198	hypoxia	202
adaptation	197	race	208
Allen's rule	199	racism	208
Bergmann's rule	199	sickle-cell anemia	
Gloger's rule	201	(sicklemia)	205

◎ Critical Questions

1. Why is skin color used more often than hair or eye color or body proportions in "racial" classifications?
2. If Europeans had been more susceptible to New World and Pacific diseases, would the world be different today?
3. How might studies of natural selection help increase tolerance of other populations?

◎ Research Navigator

1. Please go to **www.researchnavigator.com** and enter your LOGIN NAME and PASSWORD. For instructions on registering for the first time, please view the detailed instructions at the end of Chapter 1.
2. Use Content Select to search the keyword "race" in the Anthropology database. Select three articles from anthropology journals. Try to avoid articles from more general science journals (like *Science News* or *Proceedings of the National Academy of Science*). When you are finished reading these articles, answer the following questions: How is the concept of "race" currently being used in anthropology? Are there differences in how the authors of these articles employ the concept of "race"? If so, what are these differences and how do they affect the author's research?

◎ Discovering Anthropology: Researchers at Work

Read the chapter by C. Loring Brace titled "The Concept of Race in Physical Anthropology" in the accompanying *Discovering Anthropology* reader. Answer the following questions:

1. What does Brace mean when he states that "'race' is whatever people think it should be"?
2. How do geographic populations (or clines) differ from biological races?
3. How might the concept of "race" limit our ability to understand human variation?

CHAPTER THIRTEEN

The Concept of Culture

We all consider ourselves to be unique individuals with our own set of personal opinions, preferences, habits, and quirks. Indeed, all of us are unique; and yet most of us share the feeling that it is wrong to eat dogs, the belief that bacteria or viruses cause illness, the habit of sleeping on a bed. We share many such feelings, beliefs, and habits with most of the people who live in our society. We hardly ever think about the ideas and customs we share, but they constitute what anthropologists refer to as "North American culture."

We tend not to think about our culture because it is so much a part of us that we take it for granted. But when we become aware that other peoples have different feelings from ours, different beliefs, and different habits, we begin to become aware that our culture is different. Most North Americans would never even think of the possibility of eating dog meat if we did not know that people in some other societies commonly do so. We would not realize that our belief in germs was cultural if we were not aware that people in some societies think that illness is caused by witchcraft or evil spirits. We could not become aware that it is our custom to sleep on beds if we were not aware that people in many societies sleep on the floor or on the ground. It is only when we compare ourselves with people in other societies that we become aware of cultural differences and similarities. This is, in fact, the way that anthropology as a profession began. When Europeans began to explore and move to faraway places, they were forced to confront the sometimes striking facts of cultural variation.

Defining Features of Culture

In everyday usage, the word *culture* refers to a desirable quality we can acquire by attending a sufficient number of plays and concerts and visiting art museums and galleries. The anthropologist, however, has a different definition, as Ralph Linton explained:

> *Culture* refers to the total way of life of any society, not simply to those parts of this way which the society regards as higher or more desirable. Thus culture, when applied to our own way of life, has nothing to do with playing the piano or reading Browning. For the social scientist such activities are simply elements within the totality of our culture. This totality also includes such mundane activities as washing dishes or driving an automobile, and for the purposes of cultural

studies these stand quite on a par with "the finer things of life." It follows that for the social scientist there are no uncultured societies or even individuals. Every society has a culture, no matter how simple this culture may be, and every human being is cultured, in the sense of participating in some culture or other.[1]

Culture, then, refers to innumerable aspects of life. Some anthropologists think of culture as the rules or ideas behind behavior.[2] Most anthropologists also include how people customarily behave, including how they interact with others and the habits they share with others. In this view, **culture** is the set of learned behaviors and ideas (including beliefs, attitudes, values, and ideals) that are characteristic of a particular society or other social group. It should be noted that some anthropologists also include *material culture* in culture—things like houses, musical instruments, and tools that are the products of customary behavior.

Different kinds of groups can have cultures. People come to share behaviors and ideas because they communicate with and observe each other. While groups from families to societies share cultural traits, anthropologists have traditionally been concerned with the cultural characteristics of *societies*. Many anthropologists define **society** as a group of people who occupy a particular territory and speak a common language not generally understood by neighboring peoples. By this definition, societies may or may not correspond to countries or nations. There are many countries, particularly the newer ones, that have within their boundaries different peoples speaking mutually unintelligible languages. By our definition of society, such countries are composed of many different societies and therefore many cultures. Also, by our definition of society, some societies may even include more than one country or nation. For example, we would have to say that Canada and the United States form a single society because the two groups generally speak English, live next to each other, and share many common ideas and behaviors. That is why we refer to "North American culture" in this chapter. Not everyone would agree that Canada and the United States form a single society; some would prefer to consider the United States and Canada two different societies because they are separate political entities.

Culture Is Commonly Shared

If only one person thinks or does a certain thing, that thought or action represents a personal habit, not a pattern of culture. For a thought or action to be considered cultural, it must be commonly shared by some population or group of individuals. Even if some behavior is not commonly practiced, it is cultural if most people think it is appropriate. The idea that marriage should involve only two people is cultural in North American society. Most North Americans share this idea and act accordingly when they marry. The role of president or prime minister is not widely shared—after all, there is only one such person at a time—but the role is cultural because most inhabitants of a country with such a position agree that it should exist, and its occupant is generally expected to exhibit certain behaviors. We usually

share many behaviors and ideas with our families and friends (although anthropologists are not particularly concerned with this type of cultural group). We commonly share cultural characteristics with segments of our population whose ethnic or regional origins, religious affiliations, and occupations are the same as or similar to our own. We share certain practices and ideas with most North Americans. And we share some cultural traits with people beyond our society who have similar interests (such as rules for international sporting events) or similar roots (as do the various English-speaking nations).

When we talk about the commonly shared customs of a society, which constitute the central concern of cultural anthropology, we are referring to *a* culture. When we talk about the commonly shared customs of a group within a society, which are a central concern of sociology, we are referring to a **subculture.** And when we study the commonly shared customs of some group that includes different societies, we are talking about a phenomenon for which we do not have a single word—for example, as when we refer to *Western culture* (the cultural characteristics of societies in or derived from Europe) or the *culture of poverty* (the presumed cultural characteristics of poor people the world over).

We must remember that even when anthropologists refer to something as cultural, there is always individual variation, which means that not everyone in a society shares a particular cultural characteristic of that society. For example, it is cultural in North American society for adults to live apart from their parents. But not all adults in our society do so, nor do all adults wish to do so. The custom of living apart from parents is considered cultural because most adults practice that custom. As Edward Sapir noted in the late 1930s, in every society studied by anthropologists—in the simplest as well as the most complex—individuals do not all think and act the same.[3] As we discuss later, individual variation is the source of new culture.[4]

Culture Is Learned

Not all things shared generally by a population are cultural. The typical hair color of a population is not cultural, nor is eating. For something to be considered cultural, it must be learned as well as shared. A typical hair color (unless dyed) is not cultural because it is genetically determined. Humans eat because they must; but what and when and how they eat are learned and vary from culture to culture. Most North Americans do not consider dog meat edible, and indeed the idea of eating dogs horrifies us. But in China, as in some other societies, dog meat is considered delicious. In our society, many people consider a baked ham to be a holiday dish. In several societies of the Middle East, however, including those of Egypt and Israel, eating the meat of a pig is forbidden by sacred writings.

To some extent, all animals exhibit learned behaviors, some of which may be shared by most individuals in a population and may therefore be considered cultural. But different animal species vary in the degree to which their shared behaviors are learned or are instinctive. The sociable ants, for instance, despite all their patterned social behavior, do not

Much of culture is learned by children imitating their parents and other role models.

appear to have much, if any, culture. They divide their labor, construct their nests, form their raiding columns, and carry off their dead—all without having been taught to do so and without imitating the behavior of other ants. In contrast, much of the behavior of humans appears to be culturally patterned.

We are increasingly discovering that our closest biological relatives, the monkeys and the apes, not only learn a wide variety of behaviors on their own, they also learn from each other. Some of their learned responses are as basic as those involved in maternal care; others are as frivolous as the taste for candy. Frans de Waal reviewed seven long-term studies of chimpanzees and identified at least 39 behaviors that were clearly learned from others.[5] When shared and socially learned, these behaviors could be described as cultural. For example, as we discuss in more detail in the chapter on communication and language, vervet monkeys learn to use a certain call in the presence of circling eagles, which prey on the monkeys. The call seems to mean "Watch out—there are eagles around!" Its meaning seems to be shared or understood by the group, because they all respond similarly—they look up—when one individual sounds the call.

The proportion of an animal's life span occupied by childhood seems to reflect the degree to which the animal depends on learned behavior for survival. Monkeys and apes have relatively long childhoods compared to other animals. Humans have by far the longest childhood of any animal, reflecting our great dependence on learned behavior. Although humans may acquire much learned behavior by trial and error and imitation, as do monkeys and apes, most human learned behavior is probably acquired with the aid of spoken, symbolic language.

LANGUAGE   All people known to anthropologists, regardless of their kind of society, have had a complex system of spoken, symbolic communication, what we call *language*. Language is *symbolic* in that a word or phrase can represent what it stands for, *whether or not that thing is present*.

This symbolic quality of language has tremendous implications for the transmission of culture. It means that a human parent can tell a child that a snake, for example, is dangerous and should be avoided. The parent can then describe the snake in great detail—its length, diameter, color, texture, shape, and means of locomotion. The parent can also predict the kinds of places where the child is likely to encounter snakes and explain how the child can avoid them. Should the child encounter a snake, then, he or she will probably recall the symbolic word for the animal, remember as well the related information, and so avoid danger. If symbolic language did not exist, the parent would have to wait until the child actually saw a snake and then, through example, show the child that such a creature is to be avoided. Without language, we probably could not transmit or receive information so efficiently and rapidly, and thus would not be heir to so rich and varied a culture. To sum up, we may say that something is cultural if it is a learned behavior or idea (belief, attitude, value, ideal) that is generally shared by the members of a society or other social group.

◎ Attitudes That Hinder the Study of Cultures

Many of the Europeans who first traveled to faraway places were revolted or shocked by customs they observed. Such reactions are not surprising. People commonly feel that their own behaviors and attitudes are the correct ones and that people who do not share those patterns are immoral or inferior. The person who judges other cultures solely in terms of his or her own culture is **ethnocentric**—that is, he or she holds an attitude called **ethnocentrism.** Most North Americans would think that eating dogs or insects is disgusting, but they clearly do not feel the same way about eating beef. Similarly, they would react negatively to child betrothal, lip plugs, or digging up the bones of the dead.

Our own customs and ideas may appear bizarre or barbaric to an observer from another society. Hindus in India, for example, would consider our custom of eating beef both primitive and disgusting. In their culture, the cow is a sacred animal and may not be slaughtered for food. In many societies a baby is almost constantly carried by someone, in someone's lap, or asleep next to others.[6] People in such societies may think it is cruel of us to leave babies alone for long periods of time, often in devices that resemble cages (cribs and playpens). Even our most ordinary customs—the daily rituals we take for granted—might seem thoroughly absurd when viewed from an outside perspective. An observer of our society might justifiably take notes on certain strange behaviors that seem quite ordinary to us, as the following description shows:

The daily body ritual performed by everyone includes a mouth-rite. Despite the fact that these people are so punctilious about the care of the mouth, this rite involves a practice which strikes the uninitiated stranger as revolting. It was reported to me that the ritual consists of inserting a small bundle of hog hairs into the mouth, along with certain magical powders, and then moving the bundle in a highly formalized series of gestures. In addition to the private mouth-rite, the people seek out a holy-mouth man once or twice a year. These practitioners have an impressive set of paraphernalia, consisting of a variety of augers, awls, probes, and prods. The use of these objects in the exorcism of the evils of the mouth involves almost unbelievable ritual torture of the client. The holy-mouth man opens the client's mouth and, using the above mentioned tools, enlarges any holes which decay may have created in teeth. Magical materials are put into these holes. If there are no naturally occurring holes in the teeth, large sections of one or more teeth are gouged out so that the supernatural substance can be applied. In the client's view, the purpose of these ministrations is to arrest decay and to draw friends. The extremely sacred and traditional character of the rite is evident in the fact that the natives return to the holy-mouth man year after year, despite the fact that their teeth continue to decay.[7]

We are likely to protest that to understand the behaviors of a particular society—in this case, our own—the observer must try to find out what the people in that society say about why they do things. For example, the observer might find out that periodic visits to the "holy-mouth man" are for medical, not magical, purposes. Indeed, the observer,

after some questioning, might discover that the "mouth-rite" has no sacred or religious connotations whatsoever. Actually, Horace Miner, the author of the passage on the "daily rite ritual," was not a foreigner. An American, he described the "ritual" the way he did to show how the behaviors involved might be interpreted by an outside observer.

Ethnocentrism hinders our understanding of the customs of other people and, at the same time, keeps us from understanding our own customs. If we think that everything we do is best, we are not likely to ask why we do what we do or why "they" do what "they" do.

Ethnocentrism is common, but we may not always glorify our own culture. Other ways of life may sometimes seem more appealing. Whenever we are weary of the complexities of civilization, we may long for a way of life that is "closer to nature" or "simpler" than our own. For instance, a young North American whose parent is holding two or three jobs just to provide the family with bare necessities might briefly be attracted to the lifestyle of the !Kung of the Kalahari Desert in the 1950s. The !Kung shared their food and therefore were often free to engage in leisure activities during the greater part of the day. They obtained all their food by men hunting animals and women gathering wild plants. They had no facilities for refrigeration, so sharing a large freshly killed animal was clearly more sensible than hoarding meat that would soon rot. Moreover, the sharing provided a kind of social security system for the !Kung. If a hunter was unable to catch an animal on a certain day, he could obtain

Because we are ethnocentric about many things, it is often difficult to criticize our own customs, some of which might seem shocking to a member of another society. The elderly in America often spend their days alone. In contrast, the elderly in Japan often live in a three-generational family.

MIGRANTS AND IMMIGRANTS

Increasing Cultural Diversity within the Countries of the World

The modern world is culturally diverse in two ways. There are native cultures in every part of the world, and there are migrant or immigrant cultures in most countries. (Migrants are people who have left one place to settle in another, often because they are forced by persecution or genocide to migrate; immigrants are people who have come into a new country, often because they have chosen to.) Parts of populations have moved away from their native places since the dawn of humanity. The first modern-looking humans moved out of Africa only in the last 100,000 years. People have been moving ever since. The people we call Native Americans were actually the first migrants to the New World; most anthropologists think they came from northeast Asia. In the last 200 years the United States and Canada have experienced more extensive immigration. As is commonly said, they have become nations of migrants and immigrants, and Native Americans are now vastly outnumbered by the people and their descendants who came from Europe, Africa, Asia, Latin America, and elsewhere. North America not only has native and regional subcultures, but also ethnic, religious, and occupational subcultures, each with its own distinctive set of culture traits. Thus, North American culture is partly a "melting pot" and partly a mosaic of cultural diversity. Many of us, not just anthropologists, like this diversity. We like to go to ethnic restaurants regularly. We like salsa, sushi, and spaghetti. We compare and enjoy the different geographic varieties of coffee. We like music and artists from other countries. We often choose to wear clothing that may have been manufactured halfway around the world. We like all of these things not only because they may be affordable. We like them mostly, perhaps, because they are different.

Many of the population movements in the world today, as in the past, are responses to persecution and war. The word *diaspora* is often used nowadays to refer to these major dispersions. Most were and are involuntary; people are fleeing danger and death. But not always. Scholars distinguish different types of diaspora, including "victim," "labor," "trade," and "imperial" diasporas. The Africans who were sold into slavery, the Armenians who fled genocide in the early 20th century, the Jews who fled persecution and genocide in various places over the centuries, the Palestinians who fled to the West Bank, Gaza, Jordan, and Lebanon in the mid-20th century, and the Rwandans who fled genocide toward the end of the 20th century may have mostly been victims. The Chinese, Italians, and the Poles may have mostly moved to take advantage of job opportunities, the Lebanese to trade, and the British to extend and service their empire. Often these categories overlap; population movements can and have occurred for more than one reason. Some of the recent diasporas are less one-way than in the past. People are more "transnational," just as economics and politics are more "globalized." The new global communications have facilitated the retention of homeland connections—socially, economically, and politically. Some diasporic communities play an active role in the politics of their homelands, and some nation-states have begun to recognize their far-flung emigrants as important constituencies.

As cultural anthropologists increasingly study migrant and immigrant groups, they focus on how the groups have adapted their cultures to new surroundings, what they have retained, how they relate to the homeland, how they have developed an ethnic consciousness, and how they relate to other minority groups and the majority culture.

Sources: Melvin Ember, Carol R. Ember, and Ian Skoggard, eds., *Encyclopedia of Diasporas: Immigrant and Refugee Cultures Around the World*, 2 volumes (New York: Kluwer Academic/Plenum Publishers, 2004); David Levinson and Melvin Ember, eds., *American Immigrant Cultures: Builders of a Nation*, 2 volumes (New York: Macmillan Reference, 1997).

food for himself and his family from someone else in his band. Then, at some later date the game he caught would provide food for the family of another, unsuccessful hunter. This system of sharing also ensured that persons too young or too old to help with the collecting of food would still be fed.

Could we learn from the !Kung? Perhaps we could in some respects, but we must not glorify their way of life either or think that their way of life might be easily imported into our own society. Other aspects of !Kung life would not appeal to many North Americans. For example, when the nomadic !Kung decided to move their camps, they had to carry all the family possessions, substantial amounts of food and water, and all young children below age 4 or 5. This is a sizable burden to carry for any distance. The !Kung traveled about 1,500 miles in a single year.[8] Thus, for them being nomadic meant that families could not have many possessions. It is unlikely that most North

Americans would find the !Kung way of life enviable in all respects.

Both ethnocentrism and its opposite, the glorification of other cultures, hinder effective anthropological study.

◉ Cultural Relativism

As we discuss in the chapter on theoretical approaches, the early evolutionists tended to think of Western cultures as being at the highest or most progressive stage of evolution, and non-Western cultures were often believed to represent earlier stages of evolution. Not only were these early ideas based on very poor evidence of the details of world ethnography, they were also based on a good deal of ethnocentrism.

Franz Boas and many of his students—like Ruth Benedict, Melville Herskovits, and Margaret Mead—stressed that the early evolutionists did not sufficiently understand the details of the cultures they theorized about, nor did they understand the context in which these customs appeared. They challenged the attitude that Western cultures were obviously superior. The anthropological attitude that a society's customs and ideas should be described objectively and understood in the context of that society's problems and opportunities became known as **cultural relativism.** Does cultural relativism mean that the actions of another society, or of our own, should not be judged? Does our insistence on objectivity mean that anthropologists should not make moral judgments about the cultural phenomena they observe and try to explain? Does it mean that anthropologists should not try to bring about change? Not necessarily. While the concept of cultural relativism remains an important anthropological tenet, anthropologists differ in their interpretation of the principle of cultural relativism.

Many anthropologists are now uncomfortable with the strong form of cultural relativism advocated by Benedict and Herskovits in the 1930s and 1940s, that morality differs in every society and that all patterns of culture are equally valid. What if the people practice slavery, torture, or genocide? If the strong doctrine of relativism is adhered to, then cultural practices such as these are not to be judged, and we should not try to eliminate them. A weaker form of cultural relativism asserts that anthropologists should strive for objectivity in describing a people, and in their attempts to understand the reasons for cultural behavior they should be wary of superficial or quick judgment. Tolerance should be the basic mode unless there is strong reason to behave otherwise.[9] The weak version of cultural relativity does not preclude anthropologists from making judgments or from trying to change behavior they think is harmful. But judgments need not, and should not, preclude accurate description and explanation in spite of any judgments we might have.

But now that we have defined what is cultural, we must ask a further question: How does an anthropologist go about deciding which particular behaviors, values, and beliefs of individuals are cultural?

◉ Describing a Culture

Individual Variation

Describing a particular culture might seem relatively uncomplicated at first. You simply observe what the people in that society do and then record their behavior. But consider the substantial difficulties you might encounter. How would you decide which people to observe? And what would you conclude if each of the first dozen people you observed or talked to behaved quite differently in the same situation? Admittedly, you would be unlikely to encounter such extreme divergence of behaviors. Yet there would tend to be significant individual variation in the actual behaviors observed, even when individuals were responding to the same generalized situation and conforming to cultural expectations.

To understand better how an anthropologist might make sense of diverse behaviors, let us examine the diversity at a professional football game in the United States. When people attend a football game, various members of the crowd behave differently while "The Star-Spangled Banner" is being played. As they stand and listen, some people remove their hats; a child munches popcorn; a veteran of the armed forces stands at attention; a teenager searches the crowd for a friend; and the coaches take a final opportunity to intone secret chants and spells designed to sap the strength of the opposing team. Yet, despite these individual variations, most of the people at the game respond in a basically similar manner: Nearly everyone stands silently, facing the flag. Moreover, if you go to several football games, you will observe that many aspects of the event are notably similar. Although the plays will vary from game to game, the rules of the game are never different, and although the colors of the uniforms of the teams are different, the players never appear on the field dressed in swimsuits.

Although the variations in individual reactions to a given stimulus are theoretically limitless, in fact they tend to fall within easily recognizable limits. The child listening to the anthem may continue to eat popcorn but will probably not do a rain dance. Similarly, it is unlikely that the coaches will react to that same stimulus by running onto the field and embracing the singer. Variations in behavior, then, are confined within socially acceptable limits, and it is part of the anthropologist's goal to find out what those limits are. She or he may note, for example, that some limitations on behavior have a practical purpose: A spectator who disrupts the game by wandering onto the field would be required to leave. Other limitations are purely traditional. In our society it is considered proper for a man to remove his overcoat if he becomes overheated, but others would undoubtedly frown upon his removing his trousers even if the weather were quite warm. Using such observations, the anthropologist discovers the customs and the ranges of acceptable behavior that characterize the society under study.

By focusing on the range of customary behavior, discovered by observing or asking about individual variation, the anthropologist is able to describe cultural characteristics of

CURRENT RESEARCH AND ISSUES

Human Rights and Cultural Relativity

The news increasingly reports what we consider violations of human rights the world over. Examples range from jailing people for expressing political ideas to ethnic massacre. But faced with criticism from the West, people in other parts of the world are saying that the West should not dictate its ideas about human rights to other countries. Indeed, many countries say they have different codes of ethics. Are we in the Western countries being ethnocentric by taking our own cultural ideas and applying them to the rest of the world? Should we instead employ the strong version of the concept of cultural relativism, considering each culture on its own terms? But if we do that, it may not be possible to have a universal standard of human rights.

What we do know is that all cultures have ethical standards, but they do not always emphasize the same things. So, for example, some cultures emphasize individual political rights; others emphasize political order. Some cultures emphasize protection of individual property; others emphasize the sharing or equitable distribution of resources. People in the United States may have freedom to dissent and the right not to have property taken away, but they can be deprived of health insurance or of food if they lack the money to buy them. Cultures also vary markedly in the degree to which they have equal rights for minorities and women. In some societies women are killed when a husband dies or when they disobey a father or brother.

A strong case against the concept of cultural relativism is made by Elizabeth Zechenter. She points out that cultural relativists claim there are no universal principles of morality, but insist on tolerance for all cultures. If tolerance is one universal principle, why shouldn't there be others? She also suggests that the concept of cultural relativism is often used to justify traditions desired by the dominant and powerful. She points to a case in 1996 in Algeria where two teenage girls were raped and murdered because they violated the fundamentalist edict against attending school. Are those girls any less a part of the culture than the fundamentalists? Would it make any difference if most Algerian women supported the murders? Would that make it right? Zechenter does not believe that international treaties such as the Universal Declaration of Human Rights impose uniformity among diverse cultures. Rather, they seek to create a floor below which no society is supposed to fall.

Can the concept of cultural relativism be reconciled with the concept of an international code of human rights? Probably not completely. Paul Rosenblatt recognizes the dilemma but nonetheless thinks that something has to be done to stop torture and "ethnic cleansing," among other practices. He makes the case that "to the extent that it is easier to persuade people whose viewpoints and values one understands, relativism can be a tool for change . . . a relativist's awareness of the values and understanding of the elite makes it easier to know what arguments would be persuasive. (For example, in a society in which the group rather than the individual has great primacy, it might be persuasive to try to show how respect for individual rights benefits the group.)" What do you think?

Sources: Elizabeth M. Zechenter, "In the Name of Culture: Cultural Relativism and the Abuse of the Individual," *Journal of Anthropological Research,* 53 (1997): 319–47; Paul C. Rosenblatt, "Human Rights Violations across Cultures," in *Research Frontiers,* in Carol R. Ember, Melvin Ember, and Peter N. Peregrine, eds., *New Directions in Anthropology* (Upper Saddle River, NJ: Prentice Hall, CD-ROM, 2004).

a group. For example, an anthropologist interested in describing courtship and marriage in our society would initially encounter a variety of behaviors. The anthropologist may note that one couple prefers to go to a movie on a first date, whereas another couple chooses to go bowling; some couples have very long engagements, and others never become engaged at all; some couples emphasize religious rituals in the marriage ceremony, but others are married by civil authorities; and so on. Despite this variability, the anthropologist, after further observation and interviewing, might begin to detect certain regularities in courting practices. Although couples may do many different things on their first and subsequent dates, they nearly always arrange the dates by themselves; they try to avoid their parents when on dates; they often manage to find themselves alone at the end of a date; they put their lips together frequently; and so forth. After a series of more and more closely spaced encounters, a man and woman may decide to declare themselves publicly as a couple, either by announcing that they are engaged or by revealing that they are living together or intend to do so. Finally, if the two of them decide to marry, they must in some way have their union recorded by the civil authorities.

In our society a person who wishes to marry cannot completely disregard the customary patterns of courtship. If a man saw a woman on the street and decided he wanted to marry her, he could conceivably choose a quicker and more direct form of action than the usual dating procedure. He could get on a horse, ride to the woman's home, snatch her up in his arms, and gallop away with her. In Sicily, until the last few decades such a couple would have been considered legally married, even if the woman had never met the man before or had no intention of marrying. But in our society, any man who acted in such a fashion would be arrested and jailed for kidnapping and would probably have his sanity challenged. Such behavior would not be acceptable in our society. Although individual behaviors may vary, most social behavior falls within culturally acceptable limits.

Cultural Constraints

The noted French sociologist Emile Durkheim stressed that culture is something *outside* us exerting a strong coercive power on us. We do not always feel the constraints of our culture because we generally conform to the types of conduct and thought it requires. Standards or rules about what is acceptable behavior are referred to by social scientists as **norms.** The importance of a norm usually can be judged by how members of a society respond when the norm is violated.

Cultural constraints are of two basic types, *direct* and *indirect.* Naturally, the direct constraints are the more obvious. For example, if you choose to wear a casual shorts outfit to a wedding, you will probably be subject to some ridicule and a certain amount of social isolation. But if you choose to wear nothing, you may be exposed to a stronger, more direct cultural constraint—arrest for indecent exposure.

Although indirect forms of cultural constraint are less obvious than direct ones, they are no less effective. Durkheim illustrated this point when he wrote, "I am not obliged to speak French with my fellow-countrymen, nor to use the legal currency, but I cannot possibly do otherwise. If I tried to escape this necessity, my attempt would fail miserably."[10] In other words, if Durkheim had decided he would rather speak Serbo-Croatian than French, nobody would have tried to stop him. But no one would have understood him either. And although he would not have been put into prison for trying to buy groceries with Icelandic money, he would have had difficulty convincing the local merchants to sell him food.

In a series of classic experiments on conformity, Solomon Asch revealed how strong cultural constraints can be. Asch coached the majority of a group of college students to give deliberately incorrect answers to questions involving visual stimuli. A "critical subject," the one student in the room who was not so coached, had no idea that the other participants would purposely misinterpret the evidence presented to them. Asch found that in one-third of the experiments, the critical subjects consistently allowed their own correct perceptions to be distorted by the obviously incorrect statements of the others. And in another 40 percent of the experiments, the critical subject yielded to the opinion of the group some of the time.[11]

The existence of social or cultural constraints, however, is not necessarily incompatible with individuality. Cultural constraints are usually exercised most forcefully around the limits of acceptable behavior. Thus, there is often a broad range of behavior within which individuals can exercise their uniqueness. And individuals do not always give in to the wishes of the majority. In the Asch experiments, many individuals, about one-fourth of the critical subjects, consistently retained their independent opinions in the face of complete disagreement with the majority.

Ideal Versus Actual Cultural Patterns

Every society has ideas (values and norms) about how people in particular situations ought to feel and behave. In everyday terms we speak of these ideas as *ideals;* in anthropology we refer to them as *ideal cultural patterns.* These patterns tend to be reinforced through cultural constraints. But we all know that people do not always behave according to the

In deciding what is cultural behavior, anthropologists look for commonalities, understanding that there is always considerable variation. In North American culture unmarried couples are allowed and even encouraged to spend time with each other, but how they spend their time may vary from settings such as restaurants to informal activities like bike riding.

standards they express. If they did, there would be no need for direct or indirect constraints. Some of our ideal patterns differ from actual behavior because the ideal is outmoded—that is, it is based on the way society used to be. (Consider the ideal of "free enterprise," that industry should be totally free of governmental regulation.) Other ideal patterns may never have been actual patterns and may represent merely what people would like to see as correct behavior.

To illustrate the difference between ideal and actual culture, consider the idealized belief, long cherished in North America, that everybody is "equal before the law," that everybody should be treated in the same way by the police and courts. Of course, we know that this is not always true. The rich, for example, may receive less jail time and be sent to nicer prisons. Nevertheless, the ideal is still part of our culture; most of us continue to believe that the law should be applied equally to all.

How to Discover Cultural Patterns

There are two basic ways in which an anthropologist can discover cultural patterns. When dealing with customs that are overt or highly visible within a society—for example, our custom of sending children to school—the investigator can determine the existence of such practices by direct observation and by interviewing some knowledgeable people. (We discuss methods of gathering evidence more thoroughly in the chapter on explanation and evidence.) When dealing with a particular sphere of behavior that encompasses many individual variations, or when the people studied are unaware of their pattern of behavior, the anthropologist should collect information from a sample of individuals in order to establish what the cultural pattern is.

One example of a cultural pattern that most people in a society are not aware of is how far apart people stand when they are having a conversation. Yet there is considerable reason to believe that unconscious cultural rules govern such behavior. These rules become obvious when we interact with people who have different rules. We may experience considerable discomfort when another person stands too close (indicating too much intimacy) or too far (indicating unfriendliness). Edward Hall reported that Arabs customarily stand quite close to others, close enough, as we have noted, to be able to smell the other person. In interactions between Arabs and North Americans, then, the Arabs will move closer at the same time that the North Americans back away.[12]

If we wanted to arrive at the cultural rule for conversational distance between casual acquaintances, we could study a sample of individuals from a society and determine the *modal response*, or *mode*. The mode is a statistical term that refers to the most frequently encountered response in a given series of responses. So, for the North American pattern of casual conversational distance, we would plot the actual distance for many observed pairs of people. Some pairs may be 2 feet apart, some 2.5, and some 4 feet apart. If we count the number of times every particular distance is observed, these counts provide what we call a *frequency distribution*. The distance with the highest frequency is the *modal pattern*. Very often the frequency distribution takes the form of a *bell-shaped curve*, as shown in Figure 13–1.

There the characteristic being measured is plotted on the horizontal axis (in this case, the distance between conversational pairs), and the number of times each distance is observed (its frequency) is plotted on the vertical axis. If we were to plot how a sample of North American casual conversational pairs is distributed, we would probably get a bell-shaped curve that peaks at around 3 feet.[13] Is it any wonder, then, that we sometimes speak of keeping others "at arm's length"?

Frequency distributions may be calculated on the basis of behaviors exhibited or responses given by all the members of a particular population. But studying everybody is rarely necessary. Instead, most social scientists rely on a subset, or sample, that is believed to be representative of the larger population. The best way to ensure that a sample is representative is to choose a **random sample**—that is, give all individuals an equal chance of being selected for study. If a sample is random, it probably will include examples of all frequent variations of behavior or response exhibited in the society or community in roughly the proportions in which they actually occur.

Because it is relatively easy to make generalizations about public aspects of a culture, such as the existence of executive, legislative, and judicial branches in the U.S. government, or about widely shared norms or behaviors, which almost anyone can identify correctly, random sampling is often not necessary. But in dealing with aspects of culture that are more private, difficult to put into words, or unconscious, the investigator may have to observe or interview a random sample of people in order to generalize correctly about whether or not there are cultural patterns. The reason is that most people may not be aware of others' private behavior and thoughts, such as sexual attitudes and behavior, nor are they aware of unconscious cultural patterns, such as conversational distance. The fact that something is less readily observed publicly or harder to put into words does not imply that it is less likely to be shared. However, it is harder to discover those aspects of culture.

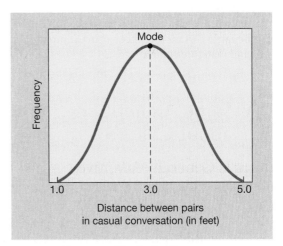

Figure 13–1 Frequency Distribution Curve

Distance between people conversing varies cross-culturally. The faces of the Rajput Indian men on the left are much closer than the faces of the American women on the right.

Although we may be able to discover by interviews and observation that a behavior, thought, or feeling is widely shared within a society, how do we establish that something commonly shared is learned, so that we can call it cultural? Establishing that something is or is not learned may be difficult. Because children are not reared apart from adult caretakers, the behaviors they exhibit as part of their genetic inheritance are not clearly separated from those they learn from others around them. We suspect that particular behaviors and ideas are learned if they vary from society to society. And we suspect purely genetic determinism when particular behaviors or ideas are found in all societies. For example, as we will see in the chapter on language, children the world over seem to acquire language at about the same age, and the structure of their early utterances seems to be similar. These facts suggest that human children are born with an innate grammar. However, although early childhood language seems similar the world over, the particular languages spoken by adults in different societies show considerable variability. This variability suggests that particular languages have to be learned. Similarly, if the courtship patterns of one society differ markedly from those of another, we can be fairly certain that those courtship patterns are learned and therefore cultural.

Some Assumptions about Culture

Culture Is Generally Adaptive

There are some cultural behaviors that, if carried to an extreme, would decrease the chances of survival of a particular society. For example, certain tribes in New Guinea view women as essentially unclean and dangerous individuals

with whom physical contact should be as limited as possible. Suppose the men in one such tribe decided to avoid contact, including sexual contact, with women completely. Clearly, we would not expect such a society to survive for long. Although this example may appear extreme, it indicates that customs that diminish the survival chances of a society are not likely to persist. Either the people clinging to those customs will become extinct, taking the customs with them, or the customs will be replaced, thereby possibly helping the people to survive. By either process, **maladaptive customs**—those that diminish the chances of survival and reproduction—are likely to disappear. The customs of a society that enhance survival and reproductive success are **adaptive** and are likely to persist. Hence, we assume that if a society has survived long enough to be described in the annals of anthropology (the "ethnographic record"), much, if not most, of its cultural repertoire is adaptive, or was at one time.

When we say that a custom is adaptive, however, we mean it is adaptive only with respect to a specific physical and social environment. What may be adaptive in one environment may not be adaptive in another. Therefore, when we ask why a society may have a particular custom, we really are asking if that custom makes sense as an adaptation to that society's particular environmental conditions.

Many cultural behaviors that would otherwise appear incomprehensible to us may be understandable as a society's response to its environment. For example, we might express surprise at certain societies' postpartum sex taboos that prohibit women from engaging in sexual intercourse until their 2-year-olds are ready to be weaned. But in the tropical areas where such taboos exist, they may represent a people's way of adjusting to their physical environment. If there were no such taboo and a mother had another baby soon, she could no longer continue to nurse the older baby. Without its mother's milk, the older child might succumb to *kwashiorkor*, a severe protein-deficiency disease that is common in those tropical areas. The taboo may give infants a better chance to survive.[14] Thus, the long postpartum sex taboo may be an adaptive custom. In nontropical areas where kwashiorkor is not a problem, the same taboo may not be advantageous.

Just as culture represents an adjustment to the physical environment and to biological demands, it may also represent an adjustment to the social environment, that is, to neighboring peoples. For example, we do not know for sure why the Hopi Indians of what is now the state of Arizona began building their settlements on the tops of mesas. They

APPLIED ANTHROPOLOGY

Why the Bedouin Do Not Readily Settle Down

Most countries of the world today want to "develop." They want to increase their crop yields and their exports, build major roads and irrigation projects, and industrialize. Anthropologists interested in development have pointed out that many development schemes have failed in part because they do not adequately consider the culture of the people whose lives they affect. Thus, the international agencies that lend money have increasingly turned for advice to anthropologists to help plan and evaluate development projects.

Governments often view traditional ways of life negatively and fail to recognize that the old ways of life may be adaptive. Because culture is integrated, people cannot be expected to change an aspect of culture that is central to their lives. It is not that people do not want to change, but change is unlikely if it doesn't integrate well with other aspects of their lifestyle.

In many countries of the Middle East, governments want the Bedouin—people who herd animals over vast stretches of semiarid grassland—to settle down. Governments have tried to settle them by force or by enticements, but time after time settlement schemes have failed. In retrospect, such failures are not surprising. The Bedouin continue to try to herd animals near newly constructed settlements, but such grazing often results in human-made deserts near the settlements, so the settlements are abandoned. The traditional Bedouin pattern of herding animals depends on mobility. When the animals eat the tops of the grasses in a particular place, the people need to move on. When water starts drying up in one location, the herds need to be moved. Overgrazing near a settlement and plowing land in a semiarid environment can lead to quick erosion of the soil and the loss of plant cover. After the failure of many settlement schemes, governments may try to encourage a return to more traditional methods of grazing.

It is not that the Bedouin are reluctant to change in all respects. Many Bedouin readily gave up relying on camels for transport in favor of trucks. Trucks are a modern adaptation, yet they still allow mobility. Now the Bedouin are able to get water from wells and transport water to their animals by truck. The adoption of trucks led to other changes in Bedouin life. Small animals can be more readily transported to new pastures by truck, so many Bedouin have given up their dependence on camels and shifted to sheep and goat herding. Money is required to buy trucks and pay for gasoline and repairs, so more time is spent working for wages in temporary jobs.

In the 1980s, Dawn Chatty was asked by the government of the Middle Eastern country of Oman to help design a project to extend basic social services to the Bedouin without coercing them to alter their way of life. It isn't often that governments fund in-depth studies to understand the needs of the people being affected, but Chatty was able to persuade the Oman government that such a study was necessary as a first step. With United Nations funding, she began a study of the Harasiis pastoralists of southern Oman to evaluate their needs. The government wanted some action right away, so the project soon incorporated a mobile health unit that could begin a program of primary care as well as immunization against measles, whooping cough, and polio. After a period of evaluation, the project team also recommended an annual distribution of tents, the establishment of dormitories so children could live at schools, a new system of water delivery, and veterinary and marketing assistance.

Unfortunately, a development project often ends without any guarantee that health and other services will continue to be provided. As Chatty found out, long-term change is not as easy to achieve as short-term change. Along with other applied anthropologists, she continues to push for what Michael Cernea called "putting people first."

Sources: Dawn Chatty, Mobile Pastoralists: Development Planning and Social Change in Oman (New York: Columbia University Press, 1996); Michael M. Cernea, ed., Putting People First: Sociological Variables in Development, 2nd ed. (New York: Oxford University Press, 1991), p. 7.

must have had strong reasons for doing so, because there are many difficulties in building on such sites—the problem of hauling water long distances to the settlements, for instance. It is possible that the Hopi chose to locate their villages on mesa tops for defensive reasons when Athapaskan-speaking groups of Indians (the Navajo and Apache) moved into the Hopi area. In other words, the Hopi may have adjusted their living habits to their social environment.

A given custom represents one society's adaptation to its environment; it does not represent all possible adaptations. Different societies may choose different means of adjusting to the same situation. Thus, among some South American Indian societies where people's diets are low in protein, there is no long postpartum sex taboo, but induced abortion is reported to be a common practice. This practice may serve the same function of spacing out live births and thereby preventing too early weaning of children. The Hopi Indians, when suddenly confronted by the Navajo and Apache, clearly had to take some action to protect themselves. But instead of building their settlements on easily defended mesa tops, they could conceivably have developed a standing army.

Why a society develops a particular response to a problem always requires explanation. The choice may depend largely on whether a particular response is possible, given the existing cultural repertoire. For example, in the Hopi case, a standing army would not have been a likely response to the problem of invaders because the Hopi economy probably could not have supported any large group of full-time specialists such as soldiers. As we shall see in the chapter on food-getting, full-time specialists have to be fed by the regular production of more food than the people involved in food production generally need, and such a level of food production did not exist among the Hopi. The strategy of moving their dwellings to easily defended mesa tops may have been the easiest option.

Although we may assume that societies surviving long enough to be described have had many more adaptive culture traits than maladaptive traits, that does not mean that all culture traits are adaptive. Some, if not many, traits may be neutral in terms of adaptation. That is, they may have no direct relationship to reproductive success. Consider, for example, rules about what to wear at weddings and funerals, how to set the table, and how far to stand from someone. Perhaps someone will uncover survival and reproductive consequences of these shared behaviors, but probably they are neutral in terms of survival. Such neutral traits may once have had adaptive consequences, or they may never have had any.

We must remember that a society is not forced to adapt its culture to changing environmental circumstances. Even in the face of changed circumstances, people may choose not to change their customs. For example, the Tapirapé of central Brazil did not alter their custom of limiting the number of births, even though they suffered severe population losses after contact with Europeans and their diseases. The Tapirapé population fell to fewer than 100 people from over 1,000. Clearly they were on the way to extinction, yet they continued to value small families. Not only did they believe that a woman should have no more than three children, but

they took specific steps to achieve this limitation. They practiced infanticide if twins were born, if the third child was of the same sex as the first two children, and if the possible fathers broke certain taboos during pregnancy or in the child's infancy.[15]

Of course, it is also possible that a people will behave maladaptively even if they try to alter their behavior. After all, although people may alter their behavior according to what they perceive will be helpful to them, what they perceive to be helpful may not prove to be adaptive.

Culture Is Mostly Integrated

When we hear of an unfamiliar cultural pattern, our natural response is to try to imagine how that pattern would work in our own society. We might wonder, for example, what would happen if North American women adopted a long postpartum sex taboo—say, one year of abstinence after the birth of a baby. Such a question is purely whimsical, for the customs of one culture cannot easily be grafted onto another culture. A long postpartum sex taboo presupposes a lack of effective birth-control methods, but our society already has many such methods. Moreover, a long postpartum sex taboo could conceivably affect important aspects of our culture, such as the idea that a happy marriage is a sexy one. The point is that with such a taboo imposed on it, our culture would no longer be the same. Too many aspects of the culture would have to be changed to accommodate the new behavior. This is so because our culture is mostly integrated.

In saying that a culture is mostly *integrated,* we mean that the elements or traits that make up that culture are not just a random assortment of customs but are mostly adjusted to or consistent with one another. One reason anthropologists believe that culture tends to be integrated is that culture is generally adaptive. If certain customs are more adaptive in particular settings, then those "bundles" of traits will generally be found together under similar conditions. For example, the !Kung, as we have mentioned, subsisted by hunting wild animals and gathering wild plants. They were also nomadic, had very small communities, had few material possessions, and shared food within their bands. As we will see, these cultural traits usually occur together when people depend on hunting and gathering for their food.

A culture may also tend to be integrated for psychological reasons. The ideas of a culture—attitudes, values, ideals, and rules for behavior—are stored, after all, in the brains of individuals. Research in social psychology has suggested that people tend to modify beliefs or behaviors that are not cognitively or conceptually consistent with other information.[16] We do not expect cultures to be completely integrated, just as we do not expect individuals to be completely consistent. But if a tendency toward cognitive consistency is found in humans, we might expect that at least some aspects of a culture would tend to be integrated for that reason.

How this pressure for consistency works is not hard to imagine. Children, for example, seem to be very good at remembering *all* the things their parents say. If they ask for something and the parents say no, they may say, "But you said I could yesterday." This pressure for consistency may even make parents change their minds! Of course, not everything one wants to do is consistent with the rest of one's desires, but there surely is pressure from within and without to make it so.

Humans are also capable of rational decision making; they can usually figure out that certain things are not easy to do because of other things they do. For example, if a society has a long postpartum sex taboo, we might expect that most people in the society could figure out that it would be easier to observe the taboo if husband and wife did not sleep in the same bed. Or if people drive on the left side of the road, as in England, it is easier and less dangerous to drive a car with a steering wheel on the right because that placement allows you to judge more accurately how close you are to cars coming at you from the opposite direction.

Consistency or integration of culture traits may also be produced by less conscious psychological processes. As we discuss in the chapters on psychology and culture, religion and magic, and the arts, people may generalize (transfer) their experiences from one area of life to another. For example, where children are taught that it is wrong to express anger toward family and friends, it turns out that folktales parallel the childrearing; anger and aggression in the folktales tend to be directed only toward strangers, not toward family and friends. It seems as if the expression of anger is too frightening, or maladaptive, to be expressed close to home, even in folktales.

The tendency for a culture to be integrated, then, may be cognitively and emotionally, as well as adaptively, induced.

Culture Is Always Changing

When you examine the history of a society, it is obvious that its culture has changed over time. Some of the shared behaviors, beliefs, and values that were common at one time are modified or replaced at another time. In North American society, we only have to consider our attitudes toward sex and marriage to realize that a lot of our culture has changed recently. The impetus for change may come from within the society or from without. From within, the unconscious or conscious pressure for consistency will produce culture change if enough people adjust old behavior and thinking to new. Change can also occur if people try to invent better ways of doing things. Michael Chibnik suggests that people who confront a new problem conduct mental or small "experiments" to decide how to behave. These experiments may give rise to new cultural traits.[17]

A good deal of culture change may be stimulated by changes in the external environment. For example, if people move into an arid area, they will either have to give up farming or develop a system of irrigation. In the modern world, changes in the social environment are probably more frequent stimuli for culture change than changes in the physical environment. Many North Americans, for example, started to think seriously about conserving energy and about using sources of energy other than oil only after oil supplies from the Middle East were curtailed in 1973 and 1974. Different societies have often affected each other, and a significant amount of the radical and rapid culture change that has occurred in the last few hundred years has been due to the imperial expansion of Western societies into other areas of the world. Native Americans, for instance, were forced to alter their lifestyles drastically when they were driven off their lands and confined to reservations. In the chapter on culture change and globalization, we discuss the major patterns of culture change in the modern world, much of it affected by the expansion of the West.

If we assume that cultures are more than random collections of behaviors, beliefs, and values—that they tend to be adaptive, integrated, and changing—then the similarities and differences between them should be understandable. That is, we can expect that similar circumstances within or outside the culture will give rise to, or favor, similar cultural responses. Although we may assume that cultural variation is understandable, the task of discovering which particular

This painting of a beach scene in the early 1900s reminds us of how much cultural ideas about modesty have changed over time.

circumstances favor which particular patterns is a large and difficult one. In the chapters that follow, we hope to convey the main points of what anthropologists think they know about aspects of cultural variation and what they do not know.

We frequently describe particular cultures to illustrate aspects of cultural variation. When we do so, the reader should understand that the description of a particular culture or cultural trait always pertains to a particular time period and sometimes to a specific subgroup. For example, the !Kung of the 1950s were mostly dependent on the collection of wild plants and animals and moved their camp sites frequently, but later they became more sedentary and to engage in wage labor. Whether we focus on some aspect of past behavior or on contemporary behavior depends on what question we want to answer. If we want to maximize our understanding of cultural variation, such as variation in religious belief and practice, it may be important to focus on the earliest descriptions of a group before they were converted to a major world religion. On the other hand, if we want to understand why a people adopted a new religion or how they altered their religion or resisted change in the face of pressure, we need to examine the changes that occurred over time.

⦿ Summary

1. Despite individual differences, the members of a particular society share many behaviors and ideas that constitute their culture.

2. Culture may be defined as the learned behaviors and ideas (beliefs, attitudes, values, and ideals) generally shared by the members of a society or other social group.

3. The size of the group within which cultural traits are shared can vary from a particular society or a segment of that society to a group that transcends national boundaries. When anthropologists refer to *a* culture, they usually are referring to the cultural patterns of a particular society—that is, a particular territorial population speaking a language not generally understood by neighboring territorial populations.

4. A defining feature of culture is that it is learned. Although other animals exhibit some cultural behavior, humans are unusual in the number and complexity of the learned patterns that they transmit to their young. And they have a unique way of transmitting their culture: through spoken, symbolic language.

5. Ethnocentrism, judging other cultures in terms of your own, and its opposite—the glorification of other cultures—impede anthropological inquiry. An important tenet in anthropology is the principle of cultural relativism: the attitude that a society's customs and ideas should be studied objectively and understood in the context of that society's culture. But when it comes to some cultural practices such as torture, slavery, or genocide, most anthropologists can no longer adhere to the strong form of cultural relativism that asserts that all cultural practices are equally valid.

6. Anthropologists seek to discover the customs and ranges of acceptable behavior that constitute the culture of a society under study. In doing so, they focus on general or shared patterns of behavior rather than on individual variations. When dealing with practices that are highly visible, or with beliefs that are almost unanimous, the investigator can rely on observation or on a few knowledgeable persons. With less obvious behaviors or attitudes, the anthropologist must collect information from a sample of individuals. The mode of a frequency distribution can then be used to express the cultural pattern.

7. Every society develops a series of ideal cultural patterns that represent what most members of the society believe to be the correct behavior in particular situations. A society's ideal cultural patterns, however, do not always agree with its actual cultural patterns.

8. One important factor that limits the range of individual variation is the culture itself, which acts directly or indirectly as a constraint on behavior. The existence of cultural constraints, however, is not necessarily incompatible with individuality.

9. Several assumptions are frequently made about culture. First, culture is generally adapted to the particular conditions of its physical and social environment. What may be adaptive in one environment may not be adaptive in another. Some cultural traits may be neutral in terms of adaptation, some may merely have been adaptive in the past, and still others may be maladaptive. Second, culture is mostly integrated, in that the elements or traits that make up the culture are mostly adjusted to or consistent with one another. Third, culture is always changing.

⦿ Glossary Terms

adaptive customs	224	maladaptive customs	224
cultural relativism	220	norms	222
culture	216	random sample	223
ethnocentric	217	society	216
ethnocentrism	217	subculture	216

⦿ Critical Questions

1. Would it be adaptive for a society to have everyone adhere to the cultural norms? Why do you think so?

2. Why does culture change more rapidly in some societies than in others? What external and internal factors might affect the rapidity of culture change?

3. Does the concept of cultural relativism promote international understanding, or does it hinder attempts to have international agreement on acceptable behavior, such as human rights?

⊚ Research Navigator

1. Please go to **www.researchnavigator.com** and enter your LOGIN NAME and PASSWORD. For instructions on registering for the first time, please view the detailed instructions at the end of Chapter 1.

2. Using ContentSelect select "Anthropology" and look for an article on how some aspect of cultural or social life has changed for immigrants or migrants (try using search words such as immigrants, migrants, or diaspora). Describe the traditional pattern and how a custom has changed.

⊚ Discovering Anthropology: Researchers at Work

Read the chapter by Regina Smith Oboler, "Nandi: From Cattle-Keepers to Cash-Crop Farmers," in the accompanying *Discovering Anthropology* reader, and answer the following questions:

1. Who are the Nandi? Give a brief description of them, and include the time period and community being described by Oboler.

2. As you read about the Nandi, you may be surprised by some of their customs. Indicate which specific customs surprise you. Describe whether you think you are reacting simply because their customs are different from your customs, whether you are being ethnocentric, or if you prefer their customs.

3. Anthropologists have to learn *not* to judge behavior in another culture in terms of their own culture. Give an example from Regina Smith Oboler's fieldwork among the Nandi.

History of Theoretical Orientations

In anthropology, as in any discipline, there is a continual ebb and flow of ideas. One theoretical orientation will arise and may grow in popularity until another is proposed in opposition to it. Often, one orientation will capitalize on those aspects of a problem that a previous orientation ignored or played down. In our survey of the orientations that have developed since the emergence of cultural anthropology as a professional discipline, we follow an approximate historical sequence. As we discuss each school of thought, we will indicate what kinds of information or phenomena it emphasizes (if it does) as explanatory factors. Some of these orientations have passed into history by now; others continue to attract adherents.

Early Evolutionism

In the early years of anthropology, the prevailing view was that culture generally develops (or evolves) in a uniform and progressive manner. It was thought that most societies pass through the same series of stages, to arrive ultimately at a common end. The sources of culture change were generally assumed to be embedded within the culture from the beginning, and therefore the ultimate course of development was thought to be internally determined. Two 19th-century anthropologists whose writings exemplified the theory that culture generally evolves uniformly and progressively were Edward B. Tylor (1832–1917) and Lewis Henry Morgan (1818–1889).

Tylor maintained that culture evolved from the simple to the complex and that all societies passed through three basic stages of development: from savagery through barbarism to civilization.[1] "Progress" was therefore possible for all. To account for cultural variation, Tylor and other early evolutionists postulated that different contemporary societies were at different stages of evolution. According to this view, the "simpler" peoples of the day had not yet reached "higher" stages. Thus, simpler contemporary societies were thought to resemble ancient societies. The more advanced societies, on the other hand, testified to cultural evolution by exhibiting what Tylor called *survivals*—traces of earlier customs that survive in present-day cultures. The making of pottery is an example of a survival in the sense used by Tylor. Earlier peoples made their cooking pots out of clay; today we generally make them out of metal because it is more durable. But we still prefer dishes made out of clay.

Tylor believed there was a kind of psychic unity among all peoples that explained parallel evolutionary sequences in different cultural traditions. In other words, because of the basic similarities common to all peoples, different societies often find the same solutions to the same problems independently. But Tylor also noted that cultural traits may spread from one society to another by simple **diffusion**—the borrowing by one culture of a trait belonging to another as the result of contact between the two.

Another 19th-century proponent of uniform and progressive cultural evolution was Lewis Henry Morgan. A lawyer in upstate New York, Morgan became interested in the local Iroquois Indians and defended their reservation in a land-grant case. In gratitude, the Iroquois "adopted" Morgan.

In his best-known work, *Ancient Society,* Morgan postulated several sequences in the evolution of human culture. For example, he speculated that the family evolved through six stages. Human society began as a "horde living in promiscuity," with no sexual prohibitions and no real

Simplicity of technology should not be taken to imply backwardness. The Eskimo developed very ingenious ways of dealing with their difficult environment. Constructing an igloo out of specially-shaped blocks of ice is not easy.

family structure. Next was a stage in which a group of brothers was married to a group of sisters and brother–sister matings were permitted. In the third stage, group marriage was practiced, but brothers and sisters were not allowed to mate. The fourth stage was characterized by a loosely paired male and female who still lived with other people. Then came the husband-dominant family, in which the husband could have more than one wife simultaneously. Finally, the stage of civilization was distinguished by the monogamous family, with just one wife and one husband who were relatively equal in status.[2]

Morgan believed that family units became progressively smaller and more self-contained as human society developed. But his postulated sequence for the evolution of the family is not supported by the enormous amount of ethnographic data that has been collected since his time. For example, no recent society generally practices group marriage or allows brother–sister mating. (In the chapter on marriage and the family, we discuss how recent cultures have varied in regard to marriage customs.)

Karl Marx was struck by the parallels between Morgan's evolutionism and his own theory of history. Marx and his co-worker, Friedrich Engels, devised a theory in which the institutions of monogamy, private property, and the state were assumed to be chiefly responsible for the exploitation of the working classes in modern industrialized societies. Marx and Engels extended Morgan's evolutionary scheme to include a future stage of cultural evolution in which monogamy, private property, and the state would cease to exist and the "communism" of primitive society would once more come into being.[3]

The evolutionism of Tylor, Morgan, and others of the 19th century is largely rejected today. For one thing, their theories cannot satisfactorily account for cultural variation. The "psychic unity of mankind" or "germs of thought" that were postulated to account for parallel evolution cannot also account for cultural differences. Another weakness in the early evolutionist theories is that they cannot explain why some societies have regressed or even become extinct. And finally, although other societies may have progressed to "civilization," some of them have not passed through all the stages. Thus, early evolutionist theory cannot explain the details of cultural evolution and variation as anthropology now knows them.

Diffusionism

In the late 19th and early 20th centuries, while the cultural evolutionism of Tylor and Morgan was still popular, diffusionism began to take hold among anthropologists in several parts of the world. The two main schools with a diffusionist viewpoint were the British and the German-Austrian.

The main spokesmen for the British school of diffusionism were G. Elliott Smith, William J. Perry, and W.H.R. Rivers. Smith and Perry stated that most aspects of higher civilization were developed in Egypt (which was relatively advanced because of its early development of agriculture)

This advertisement aludes to the fact that people in the New World were the first to grow and smoke tobacco. Smoking is now widely diffused. Why is not completely understood.

and were then diffused throughout the world as other peoples came into contact with the Egyptians.[4] The British diffusionists thought that the independent parallel evolution of a particular cultural trait in two widely removed areas of the world was extremely rare. People, they believed, are inherently uninventive and invariably prefer to borrow the inventions of another culture rather than develop ideas for themselves. This viewpoint was never widely accepted, and it has now been abandoned completely.

Inspired by Fredrick Ratzel, Fritz Graebner and Father Wilhelm Schmidt led the early 20th-century German-Austrian diffusionist school. This school also held that people borrow from other cultures because they are basically uninventive themselves. Graebner and Schmidt suggested that cultural traits can diffuse as a group, as well as singly, over great distances.[5] In contrast to Smith and Perry of the British school, who assumed that all cultural traits originated in one place (Egypt) and filtered out to cultures throughout the world, the German-Austrian school suggested the existence and diffusion of several different cultural complexes (plural in German, *Kulturkreise*).[6] Like the British diffusionists, however, the *Kulturkreis* (singular) school provided little documentation for the historical relationships it assumed.

A separate American diffusionist school of thought, led by Clark Wissler and Alfred Kroeber, also arose in the first few decades of the 20th century. It was similar in method to the German-Austrian school but more modest in its claims. The American diffusionists attributed the characteristic features of a culture area to a geographical *culture center,* where the traits were first developed and from which they then diffused outward. This theory led Wissler to formulate his age-area principle: If a given trait diffuses outward from a single culture center, it follows that the most widely distributed traits found to exist around such a center must be the oldest traits.[7]

Although most anthropologists today acknowledge the spread of traits by diffusion, few try to account for most aspects of cultural development and variation in terms of diffusion. For one thing, the diffusionists dealt only in a very superficial way with the question of how cultural traits are transferred from one society to another. The failing was a serious one, because one of the things we want to explain is why a culture accepts, rejects, or modifies a trait that one of its neighbors has. Also, even if it could be demonstrated how and why a trait diffused outward from a cultural center, we would still be no closer to an explanation of how or why the trait developed within that center in the first place.

The beginning of the 20th century brought the end of evolutionism's reign in cultural anthropology. Its leading opponent was Franz Boas (1858–1942), whose main disagreement with the evolutionists involved their assumption that universal laws governed all human culture. Boas pointed out that these 19th-century individuals lacked sufficient data (as did Boas himself) to formulate many useful generalizations. Boas almost single-handedly trained the first generation of American anthropologists, including (among others) Alfred Kroeber, Robert Lowie, Edward Sapir, Melville Herskovits, and Margaret Mead.[8]

Historical Particularism

Boas stressed the apparently enormous complexity of cultural variation, and perhaps because of this complexity he believed it was premature to formulate universal laws. He felt that single cultural traits had to be studied in the context of the society in which they appeared. In 1896, Boas published an article entitled "The Limitation of the Comparative Method of Anthropology,"[9] which dealt with his objections to the evolutionist approach. In it, he stated that anthropologists should spend less time developing theories based on insufficient data. Rather, they should devote their energies to collecting as much data as possible, as quickly as possible, before cultures disappeared (as so many already had, after contact with foreign societies). He asserted that only after this body of data was gathered could valid interpretations be made and theories proposed.

Boas expected that if a tremendous quantity of data was collected, the laws governing cultural variation would emerge from the mass of information by themselves. According to the method he advocated, the essence of science is to mistrust all expectations and to rely only on facts. But, the "facts" that are recorded, even by the most diligent observer, will necessarily reflect what that individual considers important. Collecting done without some preliminary

The presence or absence of fathers has important consequences for psychological development and some societies have much more father presence than others. This Tongan father in the South Pacific is shown with his family.

theorizing, without ideas about what to expect, is meaningless, for the facts that are most important may be ignored while irrelevant ones may be recorded. Although it was appropriate for Boas to criticize previous "armchair theorizing," his concern with innumerable local details did not encourage a belief that it might be possible to explain the major variations in culture that anthropologists observe.

Psychological Approaches

In the 1920s, some American anthropologists began to study the relationship between culture and personality. While there are varying opinions about how the culture-and-personality school got started, the writings of Sigmund Freud and other psychoanalysts were undoubtedly influential. Edward Sapir, one of Boas's earliest students, reviewed psychoanalytical books and seems to have influenced two other students of Boas—Ruth Benedict and Margaret Mead—who became early proponents of a psychological orientation.[10]

In *Patterns of Culture,* Benedict argued not only that cultures are patterned but also that different cultures could be characterized in terms of different personality types. In contrast to Benedict, Mead did not attempt to describe cultures in terms of personality types. But for Mead as well as Benedict, culture and personality were strongly linked. After studying three societies in New Guinea, Mead suggested that each of those societies had a different pattern of sex differences in personality. In other words, men and women were different psychologically in the three societies, and the differences were not the same across the three societies. If the women in one could act like the men in another, Mead concluded that culture, not biology, was mainly responsible for personality differences between the sexes. Although many of Benedict's and Mead's assertions were later challenged, the research of these two women aroused a great deal of interest in personality and culture and in anthropology in general.

In seminars at Columbia University in the 1930s and 1940s, Ralph Linton, an anthropologist, and Abram Kardiner, a psychoanalyst, developed important ideas for culture-and-personality studies. Kardiner suggested that in every culture there is a *basic personality* that is produced by certain shared cultural experiences. In other words, just as a child's later personality may be shaped by his or her earlier experiences, so the personality of adults in a society should be shaped by common cultural experiences. These shared experiences derive from the society's **primary institutions,** which have to do with the customary ways of making a living, the customary composition of the family, and the customs of childrearing. The basic personality structure, in turn, gives rise to the aspects of culture, called **secondary institutions,** that are created to satisfy and reconcile the needs and conflicts that constitute the basic personality structure. These institutions—which include ritual, religion, and folklore—are considered secondary because they presumably stem from the basic personality structure.[11]

Not all psychological anthropologists use Kardiner's entire scheme. But most assume that there is a set of typical personality characteristics in a society, whether they call it "basic personality," "national character," or "modal personality." And most accept Kardiner's assumption that the typical personality is produced by certain aspects of cultural experience, particularly the customs of childrearing.

During World War II and shortly thereafter, the culture-and-personality orientation was applied to complex societies. Most of these studies of national character attributed the apparent personality traits of different nations to aspects of childrearing. For example, three studies suggested that adult Japanese were compulsive because of the strict toilet training they received as children.[12] Similarly, the manic-depressive swings in emotion believed to be common among Russians were attributed by Geoffrey Gorer and John Rickman to the practice in Soviet nurseries of swaddling infants from birth.[13] (Swaddling involves wrapping cloth strips around an infant's body to keep arms and legs immobile.) This practice was thought to cause anger and frustration in the infant that were later expressed in the adult as manic-depressive behavior.

Unfortunately, because it was wartime, the investigators working on Japanese compulsiveness were unable to do any fieldwork. The anthropologists studying Russian character were also forced to use indirect research methods. Later, when researchers were able to obtain firsthand data from more representative samples of subjects, they discovered that the conclusions of the earlier studies were not always reliable.

For example, it was found that the toilet-training practices of the Japanese were not particularly strict. In other words, the early studies of national character had been crude attempts of analysis from a distance and were not always accurate about personality differences between complex societies.

As time went on, the focus of the psychological approach changed. While retaining their interest in Freudian theories and the relation between child training and adult personality, some anthropologists began to investigate the possible determinants of variation in child-training practices. For example, in a comparative study, Herbert Barry, Irvin Child, and Margaret Bacon suggested that the future food supply in herding and agricultural societies is best ensured by adherence to an established routine, because mistakes may jeopardize a year's food supply. In most hunting and fishing societies, however, mistakes will affect only the daily food supply. Therefore, adherence to routine is not so essential, and individual initiative may be encouraged. As the investigators predicted, the cross-cultural evidence indicates that agricultural societies are apt to stress obedience and responsibility in their child training, whereas hunting and fishing societies tend to emphasize independence and self-reliance.[14]

In addition to exploring the determinants of different patterns of child training, some studies have elaborated on Kardiner's suggestion that personality traits and processes may account for cross-cultural associations between one cultural pattern and another. The argument in these studies is that certain culture traits produce certain psychological characteristics, which in turn give rise to other culture traits. Such a mediating influence of personality is suggested, for example, by the work of John Whiting and Irvin Child on cultural explanations of illness.[15] They suggest that severe punishment for aggression in childhood (a cultural characteristic) may lead to an exaggerated preoccupation with aggression in adulthood (a psychological characteristic), which may in turn predispose adults to believe that aggressive behavior causes illness (a cultural characteristic).

To generalize about the psychological approach to cultural anthropology, then, we may say that it tries to understand how psychological factors and processes may help to explain cultural practices.

Functionalism

In Europe the reaction against evolution was not as dramatic as in the United States, but a clear division between the diffusionists and those who came to be known as functionalists emerged by the 1930s. **Functionalism** in social science looks for the part (function) some aspect of culture or social life plays in maintaining a cultural system. Two quite different schools of functionalism arose in conjunction with two British anthropologists—Bronislaw Malinowski (1884–1942) and Arthur Reginald Radcliffe-Brown (1881–1955).

Malinowski's version of functionalism assumes that all cultural traits serve the needs of *individuals* in a society.

That is, the function of a culture trait is its ability to satisfy some *basic* or *derived need* of the members of the group. The basic needs include nutrition, reproduction, bodily comfort, safety, relaxation, movement, and growth. Some aspects of the culture satisfy these basic needs. In doing so, they give rise to derived needs that must also be satisfied. For example, culture traits that satisfy the basic need for food give rise to the secondary, or derived, need for cooperation in food collection or production. Societies will in turn develop forms of political organization and social control that guarantee the required cooperation. How did Malinowski explain such things as religion and magic? He suggested that since humans always live with a certain amount of uncertainty and anxiety, they need stability and continuity. Religion and magic are functional in that they serve those needs.[16]

Unlike Malinowski, Radcliffe-Brown felt that the various aspects of social behavior *maintain* a *society's social structure* rather than satisfying individual needs. By social structure, he meant the total network of existing social relationships in a society.[17] Since Radcliffe-Brown's version of functionalism emphasized the social structure as the system to be maintained, the phrase *structural-functionalism* is often used to describe his approach.

An example of Radcliffe-Brown's structural-functionalist approach is his analysis of the ways in which different societies deal with the tensions that are likely to develop among people related through marriage. To reduce potential tension between in-laws, he suggested, societies do one of two things. They may develop strict rules forbidding the persons involved ever to interact face to face (as do the Navajos, for example, in requiring a man to avoid his mother-in-law). Or they may allow mutual disrespect and teasing between the in-laws. Radcliffe-Brown suggested that avoidance is likely to occur between in-laws of different generations, whereas disrespectful teasing is likely between in-laws of the same generation.[18] Both avoidance and teasing, he suggested, are ways to avoid real conflict and help maintain the social structure. (American mother-in-law jokes may also help relieve tension.)

The major objection to Malinowski's functionalism is that it cannot readily account for cultural variation. Most of the needs he identified, such as the need for food, are universal: All societies must deal with them if they are to survive. Thus, while the functionalist approach may tell us why all societies engage in food-getting, it cannot tell why different societies have different food-getting practices. In other words, functionalism does not explain why certain specific cultural patterns arise to fulfill a need that might be fulfilled just as easily by any of a number of alternative possibilities.

A major problem of the structural-functionalist approach is that it is difficult to determine whether a particular custom is in fact functional in the sense of contributing to the maintenance of the social system. In biology, the contribution an organ makes to the health or life of an animal can be assessed by removing it. But we cannot subtract a cultural trait from a society to see if the trait really does contribute to the maintenance of that group. It is conceivable that certain customs within the society may be neutral or even detrimental to its maintenance.

We cannot assume that all of a society's customs are functional merely because the society is functioning at the moment. And even if we are able to assess whether a particular custom is functional, this theoretical orientation fails to deal with the question of why a particular society chooses to meet its structural needs in a particular way. A given problem does not necessarily have only one solution. We still must explain why one of several possible solutions is chosen.

Neoevolution

The evolutionary approach to cultural variation did not die with the 19th century. Beginning in the 1940s, Leslie A. White (1900–1975) attacked the Boasian emphasis on historical particularism and championed the evolutionist orientation.

Though quickly labeled a neoevolutionist, White rejected the term, insisting that his approach did not depart significantly from the theories adopted in the 19th century. What White did add to the classical evolutionist approach was a conception of culture as an energy-capturing system. According to his "basic law" of cultural evolution, "other factors remaining constant, *culture evolves as the amount of energy harnessed per capita per year is increased or as the efficiency of the instrumental means of putting the energy to work is increased*."[19] In other words, a more advanced technology gives humans control over more energy (human, animal, solar, and so on), and cultures expand and change as a result.

White's orientation has been criticized for the same reasons that the ideas of Tylor and Morgan were. In describing what has happened in the evolution of human culture, he assumed that cultural evolution is determined strictly by conditions (preeminently technological ones) inside the culture. That is, he explicitly denied the possibility of environmental, historical, or psychological influences on cultural evolution. The main problem with such an orientation is that it cannot explain why some cultures evolve while others either do not evolve or become extinct. Thus, White's theory of energy capture as the mechanism of cultural evolution sidesteps the question of why only some cultures are able to increase their energy capture.

Julian H. Steward (1902–1972), another later evolutionist, divided evolutionary thought into three schools: unilinear, universal, and multilinear.[20] Steward believed that Morgan and Tylor's theories exemplified the unilinear approach to cultural evolution, the classical 19th-century orientation that attempted to place particular cultures on the rungs of a sort of evolutionary ladder. Universal evolutionists such as Leslie White, on the other hand, were concerned with culture in the broad sense, rather than with individual cultures. Steward classified himself as a multilinear evolutionist: one who deals with the evolution of particular cultures and only with demonstrated sequences of parallel culture change in different areas.

Steward was concerned with explaining specific cultural differences and similarities. Consequently, he was critical of

White's vague generalities and his disregard of environmental influences. White, on the other hand, asserted that Steward fell into the historical-particularist trap of paying too much attention to particular cases.

Marshall Sahlins (born 1930) and Elman Service (1915–1996), who were students and colleagues of both White and Steward, combined the views of those two individuals by recognizing two kinds of evolution—specific and general.[21] **Specific evolution** refers to the particular sequence of change and adaptation of a particular society in a given environment. **General evolution** refers to a general progress of human society, in which higher forms (having higher energy capture) arise from and surpass lower forms. Thus, specific evolution is similar to Steward's multilinear evolution, and general evolution resembles White's universal evolution. Although this synthesis does serve to integrate the two points of view, it does not give us a way of explaining why general evolutionary progress has occurred. But, unlike the early evolutionists, some of the later evolutionists did suggest a mechanism to account for the evolution of particular cultures—namely, adaptation to particular environments.

Structuralism

Claude Lévi-Strauss (born 1908) has been the leading proponent of an approach to cultural analysis called **structuralism.** Lévi-Strauss's structuralism differs from that of Radcliffe-Brown. Whereas Radcliffe-Brown concentrated on how the elements of a society function as a system, Lévi-Strauss concentrates more on the origins of the systems themselves. He sees culture, as expressed in art, ritual, and the patterns of daily life, as a surface representation of the underlying structure of the human mind. Consider, for example, how he tries to account for what anthropologists call a *moiety system.* Such a system is said to exist if a society is divided into two large intermarrying kin groups (each called a *moiety,* probably derived from the French word *moitié,* meaning "half"). Lévi-Strauss says that moiety systems reflect the human mind's predisposition to think and behave in terms of *binary oppositions* (contrasts between one thing and another).[22] Clearly, a moiety system involves a binary opposition: You are born into one of two groups and you marry someone in the other. The problem with Lévi-Strauss's explanation of moieties is that he is postulating a constant—the human mind's supposed dualism—to account for a cultural feature that is not universal. Moiety systems are found in only a relatively small number of societies, so how could something that is universal explain something else that is not?

Lévi-Strauss's interpretations of cultural phenomena (which tend to be far more involved and difficult to follow than the example just described) have concentrated on the presumed cognitive processes of people, the ways in which people supposedly perceive and classify things in the world around them. In studies such as *The Savage Mind* and *The Raw and the Cooked,* he suggested that even technologically simple groups often construct elaborate systems of classification of plants and animals, not only for practical purposes but also out of a need for such intellectual activity.[23]

Structuralism has influenced thinking not only in France; Britain too has been receptive. But the British structuralists, such as Edmund Leach, Rodney Needham, and Mary Douglas, do not follow Lévi-Strauss in looking for panhuman or universal principles in the human mind. Rather, they concentrate on applying structural analysis to particular societies and particular social institutions.[24] For example, Mary Douglas discusses an argument that took place in her home over whether soup is an "appropriate" supper. She suggests that meals (in her household and in culturally similar households) have certain structural principles. They have contrasts—hot and cold, bland and spiced, liquid and semi-liquid—and various textures. They must incorporate cereals, vegetables, and animal protein. Douglas concludes that if the food served does not follow these principles, it cannot be considered a meal![25]

Some structuralist writings have been criticized for their concentration on abstruse, theoretical analysis at the expense of observation and evidence. For example, it is not always clear how Lévi-Strauss derived a particular structuralist interpretation, and in the absence of any systematically collected supporting evidence, the reader must decide whether the interpretation seems plausible. Thus, Lévi-Strauss's studies have come to be regarded by many as vague and untestable, as self-contained intellectual constructs with little explanatory value. Moreover, even if there are some universal patterns that underlie cultural phenomena, universals or constants cannot explain cultural differences.

Ethnoscience

Lévi-Strauss's structuralist approach involves intuitively grasping the rules of thought that may underlie a given culture. An ethnographic approach known as **ethnoscience** attempts to derive these rules from a logical analysis of ethnographic data that are kept as free as possible from contamination by the observer's own cultural biases.

The approach of ethnoscience is similar to that of Lévi-Strauss insofar as both are influenced by the methodology of descriptive linguistics, but there the similarity ends. Rather than collecting data according to a predetermined set of anthropological categories, the ethnoscientist seeks to understand a people's world from their point of view. Studying their language, and particularly the words they use to describe what they do, ethnoscientists try to formulate the rules that generate acceptable behavior in the culture. The rules in question are believed to be comparable to the grammatical rules that generate the correct use of the language. Ethnoscience was an early kind of *cognitive anthropology.*[26]

Many ethnoscientists think that if we can discover the rules that generate correct cultural behavior, we can explain much of what people do and why they do it. Probably individuals do generally act according to the conscious and unconscious rules they have internalized. But we still need to understand why a particular society has developed the particular cultural rules it has. Just as a grammar does not explain how a language came to be what it is, so the ethnoscientific discovery of a culture's rules does not explain why those rules developed.

Cultural Ecology

Some anthropologists are concerned mostly with the influence of environment on culture. Julian Steward was one of the first to advocate the study of **cultural ecology**—the analysis of the relationship between a culture and its environment. Steward felt that the explanation for some aspects of cultural variation could be found in the adaptation of societies to their particular environments. But rather than merely hypothesize that the environment did or did not determine cultural variation, Steward wished to resolve the question *empirically*—that is, he wanted to carry out investigations to evaluate his viewpoint.[27]

Steward felt, however, that cultural ecology must be separated from *biological ecology,* the study of the relationships between organisms and their environment. Later cultural ecologists, such as Andrew Vayda and Roy Rappaport, wished to incorporate principles of biological ecology into the study of cultural ecology in order to make a single science of ecology.[28] In their view, cultural traits, just like biological traits, can be considered adaptive or maladaptive. Cultural ecologists assume that cultural adaptation involves the mechanism of *natural selection*—the more frequent survival and reproduction of the better adapted. Environment, including the physical and social environments, affects the development of culture traits in that "individuals or populations behaving in certain different ways have different degrees of success in survival and reproduction and, consequently, in the transmission of their ways of behaving from generation to generation."[29]

Consider how culture and environment may interact among the Tsembaga, who live in the interior of New Guinea.[30] The Tsembaga are horticulturalists, living mainly on the root crops and greens they grow in home gardens. They also raise pigs. The pigs are seldom eaten; instead, they serve other useful functions. They keep residential areas clean by consuming garbage, and they help prepare the soil for planting by rooting in it. Small numbers of pigs are easy to keep; they run free all day, returning at night to eat whatever substandard tubers are found in the course of their owners' harvesting of their daily rations. Thus pigs, which require a minimum of maintenance, serve the Tsembaga both as janitors and as cultivating machines.

But problems arise when the pig herd grows large. Often there are not enough substandard tubers, and then the pigs must be fed human rations. Also, although a small number of pigs will clean up yards and soften the soil in the gardens, a large herd is likely to intrude upon garden crops. Pigs can even break up communities. If one person's pig invades a neighbor's garden, the garden owner often retaliates by killing the offending pig. In turn, the dead animal's owner may kill the garden owner, the garden owner's wife, or one of his pigs. As the number of such feuds increases, people

Sometimes you can have too many pigs. A pig feast solves this problem and maintains or creates close ties between groups. Here we see preparations for a pig feast on the island of Tanna in the New Hebrides.

begin to put as much distance as possible between their pigs and other people's gardens.

Rappaport suggests that to cope with the problem of pig overpopulation, the Tsembaga developed an elaborate cycle of rituals involving the slaughter of large numbers of surplus pigs. The cultural practice of ritual pig feasts can be viewed as a possible adaptation to environmental factors that produce a surplus pig population. But it is hard to know if the ritual pig feasts are more adaptive than other possible solutions to the problem of pig overpopulation. For example, it might be more adaptive to slaughter and eat pigs regularly so that pig herds never get too large. Without being able to contrast the effects of alternative solutions, a cultural ecologist studying a single society may find it difficult to obtain evidence that a custom already in place is more adaptive than other possible solutions to the problem.

More recent ecological anthropologists have criticized the earlier ecologists for having an overly narrow view of a bounded culture in an isolated environment and have considered the environment in a broader context—moving well beyond the local ecosystem to national and even international levels.[31] As we will discuss shortly, there are hardly any people on earth who are not affected in important ways by larger political, social, and environmental forces.

Political Economy

Like cultural ecology, the school of thought known as **political economy** assumes that external forces explain the way a society changes and adapts. But it is not the natural environment, or the social environment in general, that is central to the approach of political economy. What is central is the social and political impact of those powerful state societies (principally Spain, Portugal, Britain, and France) that transformed the world by colonialism and imperialism after the mid-1400s and fostered the development of a worldwide economy or world system.[32] Scholars now realize that imperialism is at least 5,000 years old; most if not all of the first civilizations were imperialistic. Imperialistic expansion of the first state societies was

Workers in China make sneakers for an American corporation.

linked to expanding commercialization, the growth of buying and selling.[33] Today, of course, the entire world is linked commercially.

Some of the earliest figures associated with the political economy approach in anthropology were trained at Columbia University when Julian Steward was a professor there. For those students, Steward's cultural ecology was insufficiently attentive to recent world history. For example, Eric Wolf and Sidney Mintz argued that the communities they studied in Puerto Rico developed as they did because of colonialism and the establishment of plantations to supply sugar and coffee to Europe and North America.[34] And Eleanor Leacock, who studied the Montagnais-Naskapi Indians of Labrador, suggested that their system of family hunting territories was not an old characteristic, present before European contact, but developed instead out of the Indians' early involvement in the European-introduced fur trade.[35]

Central to the later and continuing intellectual development of political economy in anthropology are the writings, published in the 1960s and 1970s, of two political sociologists, André Gunder Frank and Immanuel Wallerstein. Frank suggested that the development of a region (Europe, for example) depended on the suppression of development or underdevelopment of other regions (the New World, Africa). He argued that if we want to understand why a country remains underdeveloped, we must understand how it is exploited by developed nations.[36] Frank is concerned with what happened in the underdeveloped world. Wallerstein is more concerned with how capitalism developed in the privileged countries and how the expansionist requirements of the capitalist countries led to the emergence of the world system.[37]

The political economy or world-system view has inspired many anthropologists to study history more explicitly and to explore the impact of external political and economic processes on local events and cultures in the underdeveloped world. In the past, when anthropologists first started doing fieldwork in the far corners of the world, they could imagine that the cultures they were studying or reconstructing could be investigated as if those cultures were more or less isolated from external influences and forces. In the modern world, such isolation hardly exists. The political economy approach has reminded us that the world, every part of it, is interconnected, for better or worse.

Sociobiology, Behavioral Ecology, and Evolutionary Biology/Psychology

Also related to cultural ecology is the idea that natural selection can operate on the behavioral or social characteristics of populations (and not just on their physical traits). **Behavioral ecology** (earlier, **sociobiology;** now often referred to as **evolutionary biology** or **evolutionary psychology**) was developed mainly by biologists. It involves the application of biological evolutionary principles to the social behavior of animals, including humans. Some cultural anthropologists have employed theory in behavioral ecology to explain some aspects of cultural variation.[38]

How is behavioral ecology different from cultural ecology? Although both orientations assume the importance of natural selection in cultural evolution, they differ in important ways. Cultural ecology focuses mostly on what biologists would call **group selection:** Cultural ecologists talk mostly about how a certain behavioral or social characteristic may be adaptive for a group or society in a given environment. (A newly emergent behavioral or social trait that is adaptive is likely to be passed on to future generations by cultural transmission.) In contrast, behavioral ecology focuses mostly on what biologists call **individual selection:** Behavioral ecologists talk mostly about how a certain characteristic may be adaptive for an individual in a given environment.[39] By *adaptive* is meant the ability of individuals to get their genes into future generations. This viewpoint implies that behavior is transmitted in some way (by genes or learning) to persons who share your genes (usually offspring).[40] If a certain behavior is adaptive for individuals in a particular environment, it should become more widespread in future generations as the individuals with those traits increase in number.

Whereas a cultural ecologist such as Rappaport might consider how ritual pig feasts were adaptive for the Tsembaga as a whole, behavioral ecologists would insist that to speak of adaptation it must be shown how the pig feasts benefited individuals and their closest kin. Behavioral ecologists might raise the following possibilities regarding pig feasts. Do the people who organize pig feasts have more children? If so, then pig feasts may benefit an individual reproductively. Are people who have excess pigs more likely to be killed because their pigs destroy others' gardens? If so, then finding a way to cut down on pigs benefits the survival chances and hence the reproductive chances of individuals. We do not know of a direct comparison of the predictions of cultural ecology and behavioral ecology, but these questions may convey how the behavioral ecology approach is different.

In general, behavioral ecological theory does not expect that "social good" will prevail unless "individual good" underlies it. Take the idea of conserving the earth's resources for the long-term benefit of others. If individuals and families are seeking to maximize their own benefits, behavioral ecology would not expect conservation practices unless an individual or family saw short-term negative effects of their not conserving. Indeed, Bobbi Low finds cross-culturally that conservation ideas (reasons to leave resources untouched) are very rare, occurring in only 5 percent of the societies surveyed.[41]

This is not to say that behavioral ecology cannot explain some kinds of altruism—when a person does something apparently for the good of another person. Adopting or caring for a child of a relative may help perpetuate your own genes. Sharing food with others today may increase your own food intake in the future. But behavioral ecology has difficulty explaining human behaviors that appear to be completely altruistic with no apparent gain for the altruist. How can we explain why so many people in the United States and other countries believe in the value of conservation? And why did some people in Nazi Germany, at risk to their own safety, hide people from the Nazis?

Feminist Approaches

Women have played an important role in the history of anthropology. Margaret Mead, Ruth Benedict, and Mary Douglas are just a few of the women who have made lasting contributions to the discipline. Yet the study of women and women's roles in other cultures was relatively rare, and by the 1960s women anthropologists began asking why women were not a more important focus of research. One group of scholars argued that women were in subservient positions in all cultures, and hence were largely "invisible" to the anthropologists studying those cultures. Another group argued that while women historically held positions of power and authority in many cultures, the impact of colonization and capitalism had moved them into subservient positions. In either case, it became clear to these scholars that a focused effort on studying the roles of women was necessary, and feminist anthropology was born.

Feminist anthropology is a highly diverse area of research. Feminist anthropologists share an interest in the role of women in culture, but vary widely in how they approach this common interest. Some feminist anthropologists take an overtly political stance, seeing their task as identifying ways in which women are exploited and working to overcome them. Others simply try to understand women's lives and how they differ from those of men. In some cases, entirely new understandings of other cultures have come from feminist scholarship. For example, Annette Wiener studied the same culture that Malinowski had, in the Trobriand Islands, and found that Malinowski had overlooked an entire women-run economic system.[42] Similarly, Sally Slocum pointed out that while hunting was a focus for paleoanthropologists interested in human origins, the gathering of wild foods, typically a female activity, was hardly discussed at all, even though gathered foods are more important than hunted foods in the diets of some recent foragers. Slocum's work forced paleoanthropologists to consider the role of

Women have recently become a more important focus of research in anthropology. A Trobriand Island woman in Papua New Guinea stacks yams during the yam harvest festival.

gathered foods and, consequently, of women, in human evolution.[43]

One of the most important effects feminist research has had on anthropology is the recognition that perceptions of other cultures are shaped by the observer's culture and how the observer behaves in the field. Male researchers may not be able to ask about or observe some women's roles, just as women may not be able to ask about or observe some men's roles. More broadly, feminist scholarship suggested that the scientific approach was only one way of studying other cultures, and that different ways of studying other cultures might lead to different understandings. From this insight grew two powerful theoretical agendas that continue to affect anthropology today.

One agenda stemming from feminist scholarship is that science is inherently male in its orientation and that its impact on the world has been to further the subjugation of women. But female scientists would strongly dis-

agree: Science is neither male nor female. A second agenda, less radical than the first, is to experiment with alternative ways of studying and describing other cultures, ways that give more voice to the people being studied and that allow for the feelings, opinions, and insights of the observer to be openly expressed in anthropological writing. Many of these feminist anthropologists have used personal narratives, storytelling, and even poetry as ways to express their understanding of the cultures they have studied.[44]

Interpretive Approaches

The "literary turn" in anthropology, in which anthropologists began to experiment with fiction, personal insights, and even poetry as forms of ethnography, did not come solely out of feminist anthropology. Since the 1960s, writers in the field of literary criticism have influenced the development of a variety of "interpretive" approaches in

CURRENT RESEARCH AND ISSUES

Evaluating Alternative Theories

In working among the Abelam of New Guinea, Richard Scaglion was puzzled why they invest so much energy in growing giant ceremonial yams, sometimes more than 10 feet long. And why do they abstain from sex for six months while they grow them? Of course, to try to understand, we need to know much more about the Abelam way of life. Scaglion had read about them, lived among them, and talked to them, but, as many ethnographers have discovered, answers to *why* questions don't just leap out at you. Answers, at least tentative ones, often come from theoretical orientations that suggest how or where to look for answers. Scaglion considers several possibilities. As Donald Tuzin had suggested for a nearby group, the Plains Arapesh, yams may be symbols of, or stand for, shared cultural understandings. (Looking for the meanings of symbols is a kind of interpretative approach to ethnographic data.) The Abelam think of yams as having souls that appreciate tranquillity. Yams also have family lines; at marriage, the joining of family lines is symbolized by planting different yam lines in the same garden. During the yam-growing cycle (remember that yams appreciate tranquillity), lethal warfare and conflict become channeled mostly into competitive but nonlethal yam-growing contests. So yam growing may be functional in the sense that it helps to foster harmony.

Then again, ceremonial yam growing may have adaptive ecological consequences. Just as the Tsembaga pig feasts seemed to keep human population in line with resources, Scaglion thinks that ceremonial yam growing did too. Growing pig populations damage gardens and create conflicts, but during competitive yam ceremonies pigs are also given away, so the pig population declines. Wild animals that are hunted also have a chance to replenish themselves because hunting is frowned upon during the yam-growing cycle.

As Scaglion's discussion illustrates, theoretical orientations help researchers derive explanations. They do not have to be "rival" explanations, in the sense that one has to be right and others wrong; more than one theory may help explain some phenomenon. But we can't assume that just because a theory sounds good, it is correct and helps us to understand. The important point is that we need something more to evaluate theory. As we discuss in the next chapter, we have to find ways to test a theory against evidence. Until we do that, we really don't know how many, or if indeed any, of the theories available are helpful.

Source: Richard Scaglion, "Abelam: Giant Yams and Cycles of Sex, Warfare and Ritual," in *Portraits of Culture,* in Carol R. Ember, Melvin Ember, and Peter N. Peregrine, eds., *New Directions in Anthropology* (Upper Saddle River, NJ: Prentice Hall, CD-ROM, 2004).

cultural anthropology, particularly with respect to ethnography.[45] Clifford Geertz (born 1926) popularized the idea that a culture is like a literary text that can be analyzed for meaning, as the ethnographer interprets it. According to Geertz, ethnographers choose to interpret the meaning of things in their field cultures that are of interest to themselves. Then they try to convey their interpretations of cultural meaning to people of their own culture. Thus, according to Geertz, the ethnographer is a kind of selective intercultural translator.[46]

For many interpretive anthropologists, the goal of anthropology is to understand what it means to be a person living in a particular culture, rather than to explain why cultures vary. The task of understanding meaning, these scholars claim, cannot be achieved scientifically, but can only be approached through forms of literary analysis. Among the most important of these is **hermeneutics**—the study of meaning. Using hermeneutics an anthropologist might examine a particular behavior, closely examining the interactions of people, the language they use, and the symbols they employ (both physical and linguistic) to derive what that behavior means to the people engaged in it. One of the most famous examples is Geertz's analysis of cockfighting on the Indonesian island of Bali, which he suggests reflects, and thus allows us to comprehend, the Balinese worldview.[47]

A key facet of interpretive analyses is that they are openly subjective and personal. Geertz's interpretation of the Balinese cockfight is neither right nor wrong—it is simply his. Another anthropologist viewing the same phenomenon might come to a completely different interpretation. Interpretive anthropologists accept this as part of the nature of being human. They suggest that no human sees the world in quite the same way, so that no interpretation of human behavior can or should be the same. Anthropology, then, becomes a reflection of the anthropologist as much as it is a description of other peoples. For many anthropologists this self-centered approach makes interpretive anthropology very unappealing; for others, it is the only truthful way to work.

Some anthropologists think that interpretation is the only achievable goal in cultural anthropology because they do not believe it is possible to describe or measure cultural phenomena (and other things involving humans) in objective or unbiased ways. Scientific anthropologists do not agree. To be sure, interpretive ethnographies might provide insights. But we do not have to believe what an interpretation suggests, no matter how eloquently it is stated. (We are rarely given objective evidence to support the interpretation.) Scientific researchers have developed many techniques for minimizing bias and increasing the objectivity of measurement. Thus, interpretative anthropologists who deny the possibility of scientific understanding of human behavior and thinking may not know how much has been achieved so far by scientific studies of cultural phenomena, which we try to convey in the chapters that follow.

As Dan Sperber has suggested, the task of interpretation in cultural anthropology is clearly different from the task of explanation.[48] The goal of interpretation is to convey intuitive understanding of human experiences in a *particular* culture (intuitive in the sense of not requiring conscious reasoning or systematic methods of inquiry). Thus the interpretative ethnographer is like a novelist (or literary critic). In contrast, the goal of explanation is to provide causal and general understanding of cultural phenomena (causal in the sense of mechanisms that account for why something comes to be shared in a population, and general in the sense of applying to a number of similar cases).

Does the goal (interpretation vs. explanation) preclude or invalidate the other? We don't think so. We share Sperber's view that interpretation and explanation are not opposed goals: they just are different kinds of understanding. Indeed, an intuitive interpretation described in causal and general terms might turn out, when scientifically tested, to be a powerful explanation!

Postmodernist Approaches

Feminist and interpretive approaches often assume that all knowledge is subjective. Postmodern scholars take this idea a step further. Not only is all knowledge subjective, it is also actively shaped by the political powers-that-be. One of the most influential postmodern theorists is the French philosopher Michel Foucault (1926–1984). Foucault argued that those in political power were able to shape the way accepted truths were defined. In the modern age, truth is defined through science, and science, in turn, is controlled by Western political and intellectual elites.[49] Science, then, is not only a way of understanding the world, it is a way of controlling and dominating it.

For anthropologists who accept the postmodern view of science, anthropology is just another tool used by dominant powers to control others. By studying others "objectively" we dehumanize the people being studied. Turning people into objects for study allows them to become objects that can be molded and used by the political powers-that-be.

How can anthropology continue to exist if its efforts contribute to the domination and control of others? This seems counter to anthropology's commitment to cultural relativism. Postmodern scholars answer that anthropology must transform itself into a purely activist discipline that seeks to express the voices of the dominated rather than to study or interpret them. Anthropology should be a conduit for the disenfranchised and subjugated to be heard. But even so, does that preclude anthropology from being scientific?

While postmodern, interpretive, and some feminist approaches have challenged the very foundations of anthropology, anthropology as a discipline continues to thrive. In part, this is because anthropology has learned important lessons from the work of feminist, interpretive, and postmodern scholars. No anthropologist working today could ignore women's roles, for example. It is no longer possible to ignore half of humanity. Understanding meaning is now a parallel goal of anthropology along with explaining variation. Anthropologists realize that their knowledge of others is possibly subjective and imperfect, but that doesn't mean it is impossible to study humans and their cultures scientifically.

The Hypothesis-Testing Orientation

The intellectuals who developed science in the mid-17th century understood very well that human knowledge of the world could be biased and incomplete. Rather than rejecting the possibility of objective understanding, as postmodern and interpretive anthropologists have argued, the founders of science created a way of generating understanding based on the rigorous testing of ideas. As anthropologist Philip Salzman explains:

> The scientific method, the heart of science, was invented because it was understood that human error, wish-fulfillment, duplicity, dishonesty, and weakness would commonly distort research findings. The scientific requirements that the procedures of all studies must be specified in detail so that others could repeat them, and the actual replication of findings by other scientists in other venues, were established to minimize the distorting effects of human subjectivity and moral weakness in the quest for knowledge.[50]

Many anthropologists continue to believe that objective knowledge is possible through science. Still, if the goal of anthropology is to understand what it means to be a human in a different cultural context, as interpretive anthropologists believe, then science may not be an appropriate method for all of anthropology. The task of explanation is just different from the task of interpretation.

One can pursue explanations with or without a particular theoretical orientation. Indeed, an increasing number of contemporary cultural anthropologists would explicitly deny that they prefer any particular theoretical orientation, subject interest, or method of research. Rather, they think of themselves as having a *hypothesis-testing* orientation. Any type of theory might be considered and a variety of research methods might be employed by such anthropologists. It all depends on the questions they are asking. The overarching goal is to test possible explanations because they believe that any explanation should be exposed to the possibility of being falsified by some set of systematically collected data. In the absence of such a test, these anthropologists would say that we are entitled or even obliged to be skeptical about the validity of any suggested explanation.

Summary

1. Which aspects of life anthropologists concentrate on usually reflects their theoretical orientation, subject interest, or preferred method of research.

2. A theoretical orientation is usually a general attitude about how cultural phenomena are to be explained.

3. The prevailing theoretical orientation in anthropology during the 19th century was based on a belief that culture generally evolves in a uniform and progressive manner: That is, most societies were believed to pass through the same series of stages, to arrive ultimately at a common end. Two proponents of this early theory of cultural evolution were Edward B. Tylor and Lewis Henry Morgan.

4. The diffusionist approach, popular in the late 19th and early 20th centuries, was developed by two main schools—the British and the German-Austrian. In general diffusionists believed that most aspects of high civilization had emerged in culture centers from which they then diffused outward.

5. During the early 20th century the leading opponent of evolutionism was Franz Boas, whose historical particularism rejected the way in which early evolutionists had assumed that universal laws governed all human culture. Boas stressed the importance of collecting as much anthropological data as possible, from which the laws governing cultural variation would supposedly emerge by themselves.

6. The psychological orientation in anthropology, which began in the 1920s, seeks to understand how psychological factors and processes may help us explain cultural practices.

7. Functionalism in social science looks for the part (function) some aspect of culture or social life plays in maintaining a cultural system. There are two quite different schools of functionalism. Malinowski's version of functionalism assumes that all cultural traits serve the needs of *individuals* in a society. Radcliffe-Brown's felt that the various aspects of social behavior maintain a *society's social structure* rather than satisfying individual needs.

8. In the 1930s, the evolutionary approach to cultural development was revived by Leslie A. White. White believed that technological development, or the amount of energy harnessed per capita, was the main driving force creating cultural evolution. Anthropologists such as Julian H. Steward, Marshall Sahlins, and Elman Service have also presented evolutionary viewpoints.

9. Claude Lévi-Strauss has been the leading proponent of structuralism. Lévi-Strauss sees culture, as it is expressed

in art, ritual, and the patterns of daily life, as a surface representation of the underlying patterns of the human mind.

10. Whereas Lévi-Strauss's structuralist approach involves intuitively grasping the rules of thought that may underlie a given culture, an ethnographic approach known as ethnoscience attempts to derive these rules from a logical analysis of data—particularly the words people use to describe their activities. In this way, the ethnoscientist tries to formulate the rules that generate acceptable behavior in a given culture. Cognitive anthropology has its roots in ethnoscience.

11. Cultural ecology seeks to understand the relationships between cultures and their physical and social environments. Cultural ecologists ask how a particular culture trait may be adaptive in its environment.

12. The theoretical orientation called political economy focuses on the impact of external political and economic processes, particularly as connected to colonialism and imperialism, on local events and cultures in the underdeveloped world. The political economy approach has reminded us that all parts of the world are interconnected for better or worse.

13. Behavioral ecology (earlier, sociobiology; now often referred to as evolutionary biology or evolutionary psychology) involves the application of biological evolutionary principles to the social behavior of animals, including humans.

14. Feminist approaches were born from the realization that the study of women and women's roles in other cultures was relatively rare. Some feminist anthropologists take an overtly political stance, seeing their task as identifying ways in which women are exploited and working to overcome them. Others simply try to understand women's lives and how they differ from those of men.

15. For many interpretive anthropologists, the goal of anthropology is to understand what it means to be a person living in a particular culture, rather than to explain why cultures vary. The task of understanding meaning, these scholars claim, cannot be achieved scientifically, but can only be approached through forms of literary analysis.

16. Postmodernists take the interpretative idea that all knowledge is subjective further, arguing that knowledge is actively shaped by the political powers-that-be.

17. There are cultural anthropologists who do not follow any particular theoretical orientation or prefer any particular subject matter or method of research. These anthropologists think of themselves as having a hypothesis-testing orientation.

◎ Glossary Terms

behavioral ecology	239	individual selection	240
cultural ecology	238	political economy	239
diffusion	232	primary institutions	235
ethnoscience	237	secondary institutions	235
evolutionary biology	239	sociobiology	239
evolutionary psychology	239	specific evolution	237
functionalism	235	structuralism	237
general evolution	237	theoretical orientation	231
group selection	240		
hermenutics	242		

◎ Critical Questions

1. Does a theoretical orientation enhance one's way of looking at the world, or does it blind one to other possibilities? Explain your answer.

2. In anthropology as in many other fields, one theoretical orientation will arise and may grow in popularity until another is proposed in opposition to it. Is this kind of rejection healthy for a discipline? If so, why? If not, why not?

3. Although anthropology is holistic in including the study of humans as both biological organisms and as cultural or social organisms, cultural and biological theories are rarely considered together. Why do you think? Explain why you think that this helps or hinders cultural anthropology.

◎ Research Navigator

1. Please go to **www.researchnavigator.com** and enter your LOGIN NAME and PASSWORD. For instructions on registering for the first time, please view the detailed instructions at the end of Chapter 1.

2. Using ContentSelect select "Anthropology." Search for an article that includes a discussion of one of the theorists mentioned in this chapter. Summarize the article and give an example of one of the following: 1) how the theoretical approach of that person was used by the author; 2) how and why the theorist was mentioned; or 3) how research was derived from the theoretical approach.

◎ Discovering Anthropology: Researchers at Work

Read Richard Scaglion, "Abelam: Giant Yams and Cycles of Sex, Warfare and Ritual" in the *Discovering Anthropology* reader accompanying your textbook and answer the following questions:

1. Describe what Scaglion means by the "ethnographic present." Does using that concept allow for studying cultural change?

2. Pick two of the theoretical orientations you have read about in this chapter, then indicate how they might point toward an explanation of some aspects of the yam-growing cycle.

CHAPTER FIFTEEN

Explanation and Evidence

Anthropologists in the field try to arrive at accurate answers to descriptive questions. How do the people make a living? How do they marry? What gods do they believe in? But as important as accurate description is, it is not the ultimate goal of anthropology. Anthropologists want to *understand*—to know *why* people have certain customs or beliefs, not just to see that they *do* have them. As difficult as the *how* and *what* questions are to answer, the *why* questions are even harder. *Why* questions deal with explanations, which are harder to generate and harder to evaluate. In science, to understand is to explain, and so the major goal of science is to arrive at trustworthy explanations.[1]

For many anthropologists, the plausibility or persuasiveness of an explanation cannot be considered a sufficient reason to accept it. The explanation must also be tested and supported by objective evidence that could conceivably have falsified it. And even when it is supported, there still may be grounds for skepticism. According to the scientific orientation, all knowledge is uncertain and therefore subject to increasing or decreasing confirmation as new tests are made. If this is true—and it may be uncomfortable to acknowledge—it means that we will never arrive at absolute truth. On the other hand, and this is encouraging, we should be able to achieve a more reliable understanding if we keep testing our theories.

This chapter is concerned largely with scientific understanding—what it means to explain, and what kinds of evidence are needed to evaluate an explanation. We also discuss the various types of research that are conducted in cultural anthropology, from ethnography and ethnohistory to cross-cultural and other types of comparisons.

Explanations

An **explanation** is an answer to a *why* question. There are many types of explanations, some more satisfying than others. For example, suppose we ask why a society has a long postpartum sex taboo. We could guess that the people in that society want to abstain from sex for a year or so after the birth of a baby. Is this an explanation? Yes, because it does suggest that people have a purpose in practicing the custom; it therefore partly answers the *why* question. But such an explanation would not be very satisfying because it does not specify what the purpose of the custom might be. How about the idea that people have a long postpartum sex taboo because it is their tradition? Yes, that too is an explanation, but it is not satisfactory for a different reason. It is a *tautology;* that is, the thing to be explained (the taboo) is being explained by itself, by its prior existence. To explain something in terms of tradition is to say that people do it because they already do it, which is not informative. What kinds of explanations are more satisfactory, then? In science, there are two kinds of explanations that investigators try to achieve: associations and theories.

Associations or Relationships

One way of explaining something (an observation, an action, a custom) is to say how it conforms to a general principle or relationship. So to explain why the water left outside in the basin froze, we say that it was cold last night and that water freezes at 32°F. The statement that water solidifies (becomes ice) at 32° is a statement of a relationship or association between two **variables**—things or quantities that vary. In this case, variation in the state of water (liquid vs. solid) is related to variation in the temperature of the air (above vs. below 32°F). The truth of the relationship is suggested by repeated observations. In the physical sciences, such relationships are called **laws** when they are accepted by almost all scientists. We find such explanations satisfactory because they allow us to predict what will happen in the future or to understand something that has happened regularly in the past.

In the social sciences, associations are usually stated *probabilistically*; that is, we say that two or more variables tend to be related in a predictable way, which means that there are usually some exceptions. For example, to explain why a society has a long postpartum sex taboo, we can point to the association (or correlation) that John Whiting found in a worldwide sample of societies: Societies with apparently low-protein diets tend to have long postpartum sex taboos.[2] We call the relationship between low-protein diets and the sex taboo a **statistical association,** which means that the observed relationship is unlikely to be due to chance.

Theories

Even though laws and statistical associations explain by relating what is to be explained to other things, we want to know more: why those laws or associations exist. Why does water freeze at 32°F? Why do societies with low-protein diets tend to have long postpartum sex taboos? Therefore, scientists try to formulate theories that will explain the observed relationships (laws and statistical associations).[3]

Theories—explanations of laws and statistical associations—are more complicated than the observed relationships they are intended to explain. It is difficult to be precise about what a theory is. By way of example, let us return to the question of why some societies have long postpartum sex taboos. We have already seen that a known statistical association can be used to help explain it. In general (but not always), if a society has a low-protein diet, it will have a long postpartum sex taboo. But most people would ask additional questions: Why does a low-protein diet explain the taboo?

What is the mechanism by which a society with such a diet develops the custom of a long postpartum sex taboo? A theory is intended to answer such questions.

In the chapter on the concept of culture, we briefly discussed John Whiting's theory that a long postpartum sex taboo may be an adaptation to certain conditions. Particularly in tropical areas, where the major food staples are low in protein, babies are vulnerable to the protein-deficiency disease called kwashiorkor. But if a baby could continue to nurse for a long time, it might have more of a chance to survive. The postpartum sex taboo might be adaptive, Whiting's theory suggests, because it increases the likelihood of a baby's survival. That is, if a mother puts off having another baby for a while, the first baby might have a better chance to survive because it can be fed mother's milk for a longer time. Whiting suggests that parents may be aware, whether unconsciously or consciously, that having another baby too soon might jeopardize the survival of the first baby, and so they might decide that it would be a good idea to abstain from intercourse for more than a year after the birth of the first baby.

As this example of a theory illustrates, there are differences between a theory and an association. A theory is more complicated, containing a series of statements. An association usually states quite simply that there is a relationship between two or more measured variables. Another difference is that, although a theory may mention some things that are observable, such as the presence of a long postpartum sex taboo, parts of it are difficult or impossible to observe directly. For example, with regard to Whiting's theory, it would be difficult to find out if people had deliberately or unconsciously decided to practice a long postpartum sex taboo because they recognized that babies would thereby have a better chance to survive. Then, too, the concept of adaptation—that some characteristic promotes greater reproductive success—is difficult to verify because it is difficult to find out whether different individuals or groups have different rates of reproduction because they do or do not practice the supposedly adaptive custom. Thus, some concepts or implications in a theory are unobservable (at least at the present time), and only some aspects may be observable. In contrast, statistical associations or laws are based entirely on observations.[4]

Why Theories Cannot Be Proved

Many people think that the theories they learned in physics or chemistry courses have been proved. Unfortunately, many students get that impression because their teachers present "lessons" in an authoritative manner. It is now generally agreed by scientists and philosophers of science that although some theories may have considerable evidence supporting them, no theory can be said to be proved or unquestionably true. This is because many of the concepts and ideas in theories are not directly observable and therefore not directly verifiable. For example, scientists may try to

CURRENT RESEARCH AND ISSUES

Science and Humanism

This chapter deals largely with the scientific view of understanding, but there are anthropologists who question whether the scientific approach is desirable or possible. They often describe themselves as humanists who use the human capacity to intuit, empathize, evoke, interpret, and illuminate as ways to understand. This orientation offers a very different kind of understanding because, compared with that offered by science, it does not insist on objectivity, nor does it insist on putting insights to empirical tests as science does. This is not to say that scientists do not intuit or interpret. They often do in the process of deriving theories, which involves creative leaps of imagination. And scientists, like anyone else, may empathize with the plight of the people they study. But the crucial difference between the humanistic and scientific orientations lies in the end result. For humanists, interpretation or evocation is the goal; for scientists, the goal is testing interpretations to see if they may be wrong.

Is objectivity possible? Or, because we are humans observing other humans, can we only be subjective? Objectivity requires trying to get at the truth despite the observer's subjective desires or needs. Is that possible? Can any human be unbiased? In an absolute sense, no one can be completely free of bias. But science has ways to strive for objectivity; it does not need to assume that every human is completely unbiased. Remember that even when humans engage in physical science, they are often the observers or the creators of the instruments that do the observation. When an instrument points to a number, two persons may get slightly different readings because they look at the instrument from different angles. But neither person will be far off the mark, and the average of readings by two or more individuals will be very close to the "true" score.

But do we see other people objectively? Undoubtedly, some things about them are harder to "see" than others. It is easier to know objectively that wives and husbands usually sit down to dinner together, harder to "see" how they feel about one another. Suppose you are in a society where you never observe any obvious expression of affection between husbands and wives. At first, your own cultural bias might lead you to think that such couples don't care for each other much. Such an observation might indeed be biased (and not objective) if it turned out that couples privately express affection to each other but avoid public expressions. Or it might be that couples communicate their affection for each other in ways you didn't notice. But that doesn't mean that you wouldn't be able to figure this out eventually. In trying to understand the meaning of female–male relationships, you might very well try to establish close, personal relationships with some families. You might then ask people to tell you stories to try to see how they portrayed relations between husband and wife. In short, a humanistic approach might help you understand how couples really feel about each other. But a scientist might go through the same procedure too in order to come to a tentative understanding.

As this example illustrates, humanistic understanding and science are really not incompatible. Both the scientist and the humanist would agree on the need to convey what a culture is like (e.g., with regard to how couples feel about each other). But scientists would insist on more. First, they would try to verify, perhaps by systematic interviewing, how commonly a feeling is shared in the culture; second, they would want to explain why this feeling is common in some cultures but not in others. Therefore, they would have to create a theory to explain the variation and then collect evidence to test the theory to see if it might be wrong.

If humans are always biased observers, how can humanists convey the meaning behind other cultures? Aren't humanists trying to get close to the "truth" too? The poet Marianne Moore wrote that poetry gives us "imaginary gardens with real toads in them." Can imagination, humanistic or scientific, be meaningful without at least some real toads?

Sources: James Lett, "Scientific Anthropology," in David Levinson and Melvin Ember, eds., *Encyclopedia of Cultural Anthropology*, 4 vols. (New York: Henry Holt, 1996). The quote from Marianne Moore is from John Timpane, "Essay: The Poetry of Science," *Scientific American* (July 1991): 128.

explain how light behaves by postulating that it consists of particles called photons, but photons cannot be observed, even with the most powerful microscope. So exactly what a photon looks like and exactly how it works remain in the realm of the unprovable. The photon is a **theoretical construct,** something that cannot be observed or verified directly. Because all theories contain such constructs, theories cannot be proved entirely or with absolute certainty.[5]

Why should we bother with theories, then, if we cannot prove that they are true? Perhaps the main advantage of a theory as a kind of explanation is that it may lead to new understanding or knowledge. A theory can suggest new relationships or imply new predictions that might be supported or confirmed by new research. For example, Whiting's theory about long postpartum sex taboos has implications that could be investigated by researchers. Because the theory discusses how a long postpartum sex taboo might be adaptive, we would expect that certain changes would result in the taboo's disappearance. For example, suppose people adopted either mechanical birth-control devices or began to give supplementary high-protein foods to babies. With birth control, a family could space births without abstaining from sex, so we would expect the custom of postpartum abstinence to disappear. So, too, we would expect it to disappear with protein supplements for babies, because kwashiorkor would then be less likely to afflict the babies. Whiting's ideas might also prompt investigators to try to find out whether parents are consciously or unconsciously aware of the problem of close birth spacing in areas with low supplies of protein.

Although theories cannot be proved, they are rejectable. The method of **falsification,** which shows that a theory seems to be wrong, is the main way that theories are judged.[6] Scientists derive implications or predictions that should be true if the theory is correct. So, for example, Whiting predicted that societies with long postpartum sex taboos would be found more often in the tropics than in temperate regions and that they would be likely to have low-protein food supplies. Such predictions of what might be found are called **hypotheses.** If the predictions turn out not to be correct, the researcher is obliged to conclude that there may be something wrong with the theory or something wrong with the test of the theory. Theories that are not falsified are accepted for the time being because the available evidence seems to be consistent with them. But remember that no matter how much the available evidence seems to support a theory, we can never be certain it is true. There is always the possibility that some implication of it, some hypothesis derivable from it, will not be confirmed in the future.

◉ Generating Theories

In the previous chapter we discussed theoretical orientations that are popular in cultural anthropology. Most orientations merely suggest where to look for answers to questions; they do not by themselves suggest particular explanations for particular phenomena. You cannot directly deduce a theory from a theoretical orientation. For example, an anthropologist with an ecological theoretical orientation is likely to say that some particular custom exists because it is or used to be adaptive. But exactly how a particular custom may be adaptive must still be specified; the mechanism of its adaptiveness is not automatically suggested by the theoretical orientation. Whiting's theory suggests specific conditions under which the long postpartum sex taboo might be adaptive. The theory does not just say that the taboo is adaptive. How, then, does an anthropologist develop an explanation or theory for some particular phenomenon?

It is difficult to specify any one procedure that is guaranteed to produce a theory, because developing a theory requires creative imagination, and no discovery procedure by itself necessarily generates creativity. Too much dependence on a particular theoretical orientation may, in fact, be detrimental, because it may blind the investigator to other possibilities. A more important factor in generating a theory may be the investigator's belief that it is possible to do so. A person who believes that something is explainable will be more apt to notice possibly connected facts, as well as to recall possibly relevant considerations, and put them all together in some explanatory way.

We can point to two types of procedures that have helped anthropologists produce explanations of cultural phenomena: *single-case analysis* and a *comparative study.* In analyzing a single case, the anthropologist may be interested in explaining a particular custom. While in the field, ethnographers may ask informants why they practice (or think they practice) the custom. Sometimes such inquiries will elicit a plausible explanation. But more often than not, the informants merely answer, "We have always done it that way." The investigator may then make a kind of mental search through other features of the society or its environment that may be connected with the custom. If possible, the anthropologist may try to view the situation historically, to see if the custom appeared rather recently. If it did, what possible explanatory conditions appeared just before the custom?

An anthropologist may also generate an explanation by comparing different societies that share this characteristic in order to determine what other characteristics regularly occur along with it. Societies in which the characteristic is lacking would also be considered, because a possible cause of that characteristic should be absent in those societies. If a characteristic occurs regularly in different cultures along with certain other features, we can be reasonably certain that the possible causes of that characteristic have been narrowed down. It must be remembered, however, that the investigator is not a computer. It is not necessary to search through all the characteristics that might be shared by different cultures. The investigator usually looks only at those traits that can plausibly be connected. Here is where an individual's theoretical orientation generally comes into play, since that orientation usually points to the possible importance of one particular set of factors over others.

◉ Evidence: Testing Explanations

In any field of investigation, theories are generally the most plentiful commodity, apparently because of the human predisposition to try to make sense of the world. It is necessary, then, for us to have procedures that enable us to select from among the many available theories those that are more likely to be correct. "Just as mutations arise naturally but are not all beneficial, so hypotheses [theories] emerge naturally but are not all correct. If progress is to occur, therefore, we require a superfluity of hypotheses and also a mechanism of selection."[7] In other words, generating a theory or interpretation is not enough. We need some reliable method of testing whether or not that interpretation is likely to be correct.

If an interpretation is not correct, it may detract from our efforts to achieve understanding by misleading us into thinking the problem is already solved.

The strategy in all kinds of testing in science is to predict what one would expect to find if a particular interpretation were correct, and then to conduct an investigation to see if the prediction is generally consistent with the data. If the prediction is not supported, the investigator is obliged to accept the possibility that the interpretation is wrong. If, however, the prediction holds true, then the investigator is entitled to say that there is evidence to support the theory. Thus, conducting research designed to test expectations derived from theory allows researchers to eliminate some interpretations and to accept others, at least tentatively.

Operationalization and Measurement

We test predictions derived from a theory to see if the theory may be correct, to see if it is consistent with observable events or conditions in the real world. A theory and the predictions derived from it are not useful if there is no way to measure the events or conditions mentioned in the predictions. If there is no way of relating the theory to observable events, it does not matter how good the theory sounds; it is still not a useful scientific theory.[8] To transform theoretical predictions into statements that might be verified, a researcher provides an **operational definition** of each of the concepts or variables mentioned in the prediction. An operational definition is a description of the procedure that is followed to measure the variable.[9]

Whiting predicted that societies with a low-protein diet would have a long postpartum sex taboo. Amount of protein in the diet is a variable; some societies have more, others have less. Length of the postpartum sex taboo is a variable; a society may have a short taboo or a long taboo. Whiting op-

erationally defined the first variable, *amount of protein,* in terms of staple foods.[10] For example, if a society depended mostly on root and tree crops (cassava, bananas), Whiting rated the society as having low protein. If the society depended mostly on cereal crops (wheat, barley, corn, oats), he rated it as having moderate protein, because cereal crops have more protein by weight than root and tree crops. If the society depended mostly on hunting, fishing, or herding for food, he rated it as having high protein. The other variable in Whiting's prediction, *length of postpartum sex taboo,* was operationalized as follows: A society was rated as having a long taboo if couples customarily abstained from sex for more than a year after the birth of a baby; abstention for a year or less was considered a short taboo.

Specifying an operational definition for each variable is extremely important because it allows other investigators to check a researcher's results.[11] Science depends on *replication,* the repetition of results. Only when many researchers observe a particular association can we call that association or relationship a law. Providing operational definitions is also extremely important because it allows others to evaluate whether a measure is appropriate. Only when we are told exactly how something was measured can we judge whether the measure reflects what it is supposed to reflect. Specifying measures publicly is so important in science that we are obliged to be skeptical of any conclusions offered by a researcher who fails to say how variables were measured.

To **measure** something is to say how it compares with other things on some scale of variation.[12] People often assume that a measuring device is always a physical instrument, such as a scale or a ruler, but physical devices are not the only way to measure something. *Classification* is also a form of measurement. When we classify persons as male or female or employed versus unemployed, we are dividing them into *sets.* Deciding which set they belong to is a kind

The Yanomamö Indians of Brazil depend on root crops. The Masai pastoralists of Kenya depend largely on milk and other products of their cattle.

Anthropologist Margaret Kieffer interviews Mayan woman in Guatemala.

of measurement because doing so allows us to compare them. We can also measure things by deciding which cases or examples have more or less of something (e.g., more or less protein in the diet). The measures employed in physical science are usually based on scales that allow us to assign numbers to each case; we measure height in meters and weight in grams, for example. However we measure our variables, the fact that we can measure them means that we can test our hypotheses to see if the predicted relationships actually exist, at least most of the time.

Sampling

After deciding how to measure the variables in some predicted relationship, the investigator must decide how to select which cases to study to see if the predicted relationship holds. If the prediction is about the behavior of people, the sampling decision involves which people to observe. If the prediction is about an association between societal customs, the sampling decision involves which societies to study. Investigators must decide not only which cases to choose but also how many to choose. No researcher can investigate all the possible cases, so choices must be made. Some choices are better than others. In the chapter on the concept of culture, we talked about the advantages of random sampling. A random sample is one in which all cases selected had an equal chance of being included in the sample. Almost all statistical tests used to evaluate the results of research require random sampling, because only results based on a random sample can be assumed to be probably true for some larger set or universe of cases.

Before researchers can sample randomly, they must specify the **sampling universe,** that is, the list of cases to be sampled from. Suppose an anthropologist is doing fieldwork in a society. Unless the society is very small, it is usually not practical to use the whole society as the sampling universe. Because most fieldworkers want to remain in a community for a considerable length of time, the community usually

becomes the sampling universe. If a cross-cultural researcher wants to test an explanation, it is necessary to sample the world's societies. But we do not have descriptions of all the societies, past and present, that have existed in the world. So samples are usually drawn from published lists of described societies that have been classified or coded according to standard cultural variables,[13] or they are drawn from the *Human Relations Area Files (HRAF) Collection of Ethnography,* an indexed, annually growing collection of original ethnographic books and articles on more than 385 societies past and present around the world.[14]

Random sampling is not often employed in anthropology, but a nonrandom sample might still be fairly representative if the investigator has not personally chosen the cases for study. We should be particularly suspicious of any sample that may reflect the investigator's own biases or interests. For example, if an investigator picks only the people with whom he or she is friendly, the sample is suspicious. If cross-cultural researchers select sample societies because ethnographies on them happen to be on their own bookshelves, such samples are also suspicious. A sampling procedure should be designed to get a fair representation of the sampling universe, not a biased selection. If we want to increase our chances of getting a representative sample, we have to use a random-sampling procedure. To do so, we conventionally number the cases in the statistical universe and then use a table of random numbers to draw our sample cases.

Statistical Evaluation

When researchers have measured the variables of interest for all the sample cases, they are ready to see if the predicted relationship actually exists in the data. Remember, the results may not turn out to be what the theory predicts. Sometimes researchers construct a *contingency table,* like that shown in Table 15–1, to see if the variables are associated as predicted. In Whiting's sample of 172 societies, each case is assigned

A thermometer provides a way of comparing or measuring the "heat" of different locations or over different time periods. While the physical sciences often use physical instruments and the social sciences often use humans to observe, all measurements compare things on some scale of variation.

to a box, or cell, in the table, depending on how the society is measured on the two variables of interest. For example, a society that has a long postpartum sex taboo and a low-protein diet is placed in the third row of the Long Duration column. (In Whiting's sample [see Table 15–1] there are 27 such societies.) A society that has a short postpartum sex taboo and a low-protein diet is placed in the third row in

Table 15–1 Association between Availability of Protein and Duration of Postpartum Sex Taboo

AVAILABILITY OF PROTEIN	DURATION OF POSTPARTUM SEX TABOO		
	Short (0–1 Year)	Long (More Than 1 Year)	Total
High	47	15	62
Medium	38	25	63
Low	20	27	47
Total	105	67	172

Source: Adapted from John W. M. Whiting, "Effects of Climate on Certain Cultral Practices," in Ward H. Goodenough, ed., *Explorations in Cultural Anthropology* (New York: McGraw-Hill, 1964), p. 520.

the Short Duration column. (There are 20 such societies in the sample.) The statistical question is: Does the way the cases are distributed in the six cells of the table generally support Whiting's prediction? If we looked just at the table, we might not know what to answer. Many cases appear to be in the expected places. For example, most of the high-protein cases (47 of 62) have short taboos, and most of the low-protein cases (27 of 47) have long taboos. But there are also many exceptions (e.g., 20 cases have low protein and a short taboo). So, although many cases appear to be in the expected places, there are also many exceptions. Do the exceptions invalidate the prediction? How many exceptions would compel us to reject the hypothesis? Here is where we resort to *statistical tests of significance.*

Statisticians have devised various tests that tell us how "perfect" a result has to be for us to believe that there is probably an association between the variables of interest, that one variable generally predicts the other. Essentially, every statistical result is evaluated in the same objective way. We ask: What is the chance that this result is purely accidental, that there is no association at all between the two variables? Although some of the mathematical ways of answering this question are complicated, the answer always involves a **probability value** (or **p-value**)—the likelihood that the observed result or a stronger one could have occurred by chance. The statistical test used by Whiting gives a *p*-value of less than .01 ($p < .01$) for the observed result. In other words, there is less than 1 chance out of 100 that the relationship observed is purely accidental. A *p*-value of less than .01 is a fairly low probability; most social scientists conventionally agree to call any result with a *p*-value of .05 or less (5 or fewer chances out of 100) a **statistically significant,** or probably true, result. When we describe relationships or associations in the rest of this book, we are almost always referring to results that have been found to be statistically significant.

But why should a probably true relationship have any exceptions? If a theory is really correct, shouldn't *all* the cases fit? There are many reasons why we can never expect a perfect result. First, even if a theory is correct (e.g., if a low-protein diet really does favor the adoption of a long postpartum sex taboo), there may still be other causes that we have not investigated. Some of the societies could have a long taboo even though they have high protein. For example, societies that depend mostly on hunting for their food, and would therefore be classified as having a high-protein diet, may have a problem carrying infants from one campsite to another and may practice a long postpartum sex taboo so that two infants will not have to be carried at the same time.

Exceptions to the predicted relationship might also occur because of *cultural lag.*[15] Culture lag occurs when change in one aspect of culture takes time to produce change in another aspect. Suppose that a society recently changed crops and is now no longer a low-protein society but still practices the taboo. This society would be an exception to the predicted relationship, but it might fit the theory if it stopped practicing the taboo in a few years. Measurement inaccuracy is another source of exceptions. Whiting's measure of protein, which is based on the major sources of food, is not a very precise measure of protein in the diet. It does not take into account the possibility that a "tree-crop" society might get a lot of protein from fishing or raising pigs. So it might turn out that some supposedly low-protein societies have been misclassified, which may be one reason why there are 20 cases in the lowest cell in the left-hand column of Table 15–1. Measurement error usually produces exceptions.

Significant statistical associations that are predictable from a theory offer tentative support for the theory. But much more is needed before we can be fairly confident about the theory. Replication is needed to confirm whether the predictions can be reproduced by other researchers using other samples. Other predictions should be derived from the theory to see if they too are supported. The theory should be pitted against alternative explanations to see which theory works better. We may have to combine theories if the alternative explanations also predict the relationship in question. The research process in science thus requires time and patience. Perhaps most important, it requires that researchers be humble. No matter how wonderful one's own theory seems, it is important to acknowledge that it may be wrong. If we don't acknowledge that possibility, we can't be motivated to test our theories. If we don't test our theories, we can never tell the difference between a better or worse theory, and we will be saddled forever with our present ignorance. In science, knowledge or understanding is explained variation. Thus, if we want to understand more, we have to keep testing our beliefs against sets of objective evidence that could contradict our beliefs.

Types of Research in Cultural Anthropology

Cultural anthropologists use several methods to conduct research. Each has certain advantages and disadvantages in generating and testing explanations. The types of research in cultural anthropology can be classified according to two criteria. One is the spatial scope of the study—analysis of a single society, analysis of societies in a region, or analysis of a worldwide sample of societies. The other criterion is the temporal scope of the study—historical versus nonhistorical. Combinations of these criteria are shown in Table 15–2.

Ethnography

Around the beginning of the 20th century, anthropologists realized that if they were to produce anything of scientific value, they would have to study their subject in depth. To describe cultures more accurately, they started to live among the people they were studying. They observed, and even took part in, the important events of those societies and carefully questioned the people about their native customs. This method is known as **participant-observation.** Participant-observation always involves **fieldwork,** which is firsthand experience with the people being studied, but fieldwork may also involve other methods, such as conducting a census or a survey.[16]

Fieldwork, the cornerstone of modern anthropology, is the means by which most anthropological information is obtained. Regardless of other methods that anthropologists may use, participant-observation, usually for a year or more, is regarded as fundamental. In contrast to the casual descriptions of travelers and adventurers, anthropologists' descriptions record, describe, analyze, and eventually formulate a picture of the culture, or at least part of it.[17] After doing fieldwork, an anthropologist may prepare an *ethnography,* a description and analysis of a single society.

How an anthropologist goes about doing long-term participant-observation in another culture—and, more important, doing it well—is not so straightforward. Much of it depends on the person, the culture, and the interaction between the two. Without a doubt, the experience is physically and psychologically demanding, comparable often to a rite of passage. Although it helps enormously to learn the local language before one goes, often it is not possible to do so, and so most anthropologists find themselves struggling to communicate in addition to trying to figure out how to behave properly. Participant-observation carries its own dilemma. Participation implies living like the people you have come to study, trying to understand subjectively what they think and feel by doing what they do, whereas observation implies a certain amount of objectivity and detachment.[18] Because participant-observation is such a personal experience, it is not surprising that anthropologists have begun to realize that *reflecting* on their experiences and their personal interaction with the people they live with is an important part of understanding the enterprise.

Table 15–2   Types of Research in Cultural Anthropology

Scope	Nonhistorical	Historical
Single society	Ethnography Within-culture comparison	Ethnohistory Within-culture comparison
Region	Controlled comparison	Controlled comparison
Worldwide sample	Cross-cultural research	Cross-historical research

Ethnohistorians need to analyze pieces of information from a variety of sources such as the accounts of explorers in the Pacific. Pictured here is a painting of the arrival of a French explorer in Maui, Hawaii in the late 1700s.

An essential part of the participant-observation process is finding some knowledgeable people who are willing to work with you (anthropologists call them *informants*), to help you interpret what you observe and tell you about aspects of the culture that you may not have a chance to see, or may not be entitled to see. For example, it is not likely that you will see many weddings in a village of 200 people in a year or two of fieldwork. So how can you know who will be a good informant? It is obviously important to find people who are easy to talk to and who understand what information you need. But how do you know who is knowledgeable? You can't just assume that the people you get along with have the most knowledge. (Besides, knowledge is often specialized; one person may know a whole lot more about some subjects than others.) At a minimum, you have to try out a few different people to compare what they tell you about a subject. What if they disagree? How do you know who is more trustworthy or accurate? Fortunately, formal methods have been developed to help select the most knowledgeable informants. One method called the "cultural consensus model" relies on the principle that those things that most informants agree on are probably cultural. After you establish which things appear to be cultural by asking a sample of informants the same questions about a particular cultural domain, it will be easy to discover which informants are very likely to give answers that closely match the cultural consensus. These individuals are your best bets to be the most knowledgeable in that domain.[19] It may seem paradoxical, but the most knowledgeable and helpful individuals are not necessarily "typical" individuals. Many anthropologists have pointed out that key informants are likely to feel somewhat marginal in their culture. After all, why would they want to spend so much time with the visiting anthropologist?[20]

Participant-observation is valuable for understanding some aspects of culture, particularly the things that are the most public, readily talked about, and most widely agreed upon. But more systematic methods are important too: mapping, house-to-house censuses, behavior observations (e.g., to determine how people spend their time), as well as focused interviews with a sample of informants.

Ethnographies and ethnographic articles on particular topics provide much of the essential data for all kinds of studies in cultural anthropology. To make a comparison of societies in a given region or worldwide, an anthropologist would require ethnographic data on many societies. With regard to the goal of generating theory, ethnography, with its in-depth, firsthand, long-term observation, provides an investigator with a wealth of descriptive material covering a wide range of phenomena. Thus, it may stimulate interpretations about the way different aspects of the culture are related to each other and to features of the environment. The ethnographer in the field has the opportunity to get to know the context of a society's customs by directly asking the people about those customs and by observing the phenomena that appear to be associated with those practices. In addition, the ethnographer who develops a possible explanation for some custom can test that hunch by collecting new information related to it. In this sense, the ethnographer is similar to a physician who is trying to understand why a patient has certain symptoms of illness.

Although ethnography is extremely useful for generating explanations, a field study of a single site does not generally provide sufficient data to test a hypothesis. For example, an ethnographer may think that a particular society practices *polygyny* (one man married to two or more women simultaneously) because it has more women than men. But the ethnographer could not be reasonably sure that this explanation was correct unless the results of a comparative study of a sample of societies showed that most polygynous societies have more women than men. After all, the fact that one society has both these conditions could be a historical accident rather than a result of some necessary connection between the two conditions.

CURRENT RESEARCH AND ISSUES

Fieldwork: How Can We Know What Is True?

Hardly any cultural anthropologist disputes the value of fieldwork in another culture, both for what it contributes to understanding others and for what it contributes to understanding yourself and your own culture. Probably it is the immersion that does it. Living with other people (participant-observation) allows you to see things you would not otherwise notice. At the same time, you cannot help but realize how the smallest habitual things you do, which you may have thought were just natural, are just wrong in your field site. At the beginning, there is culture shock because there is so much you don't comprehend. And at the end, there is culture shock when you return home. All of a sudden, many things in your own society now seem strange. Indeed, the experience is so profound that most cultural anthropologists feel that fieldwork provides them with the "deepest" kind of knowledge. Not just deep, but real.

Although few people doubt the value of fieldwork, there have been challenges about its veracity. Consider the controversy over the fieldwork of Margaret Mead, who lived on a small island in American Samoa in the 1920s and wrote about the sexual freedom of adolescents in *Coming of Age in Samoa*. Derek Freeman, who worked in Western Samoa largely in the 1960s, wrote a scathing critique of Mead's fieldwork in his *Margaret Mead and Samoa: The Making and Unmaking of an Anthropological Myth*. Essentially, Freeman said that Mead got most things wrong. For example, he stated that the Samoans are puritanical in their sexuality. If both did fieldwork, and fieldwork gives us real, deep knowledge, shouldn't they both be right? But how can they be? Was one a good fieldworker and the other not? How can we know what is true?

Paul Shankman suggests that both might be partly right if we recognize several things. First, he points out that we can speak of sexual permissiveness and sexual restrictiveness only in comparative terms. We need to understand that Mead did her fieldwork at a time when premarital sex was uncommon in the United States, but sex patterns changed subsequently. So, in contrast with

American girls during Mead's time, Samoan girls may have seemed more sexually free. Second, Samoa changed a great deal over time with missionization, colonialization, World War II, and commercialization. Third, Samoa was variable—American Samoa versus Western Samoa, rural versus urban. So what the two fieldworkers experienced may have been quite different, and therefore they could both be right. But, in fact, Shankman suggests that if we ignore Mead's and Freeman's conclusions about permissive or restrictive sexuality, if we separate ideal from actual behavior, and if we look at actual data on individual sexual behavior as collected by both Mead and Freeman, the two fieldworkers are not all that different: Samoans are in the middle of the worldwide range of cultures in regard to the occurrence of premarital sex.

What do we conclude from this controversy? As many anthropologists are now pointing out, it is important to reflect on the possible influences of the context of the fieldwork, the qualities of the person doing it, how that person interacts with the people she or he lives with, and the kinds of methods used to try to verify conclusions. Others point out that reflection, although important, is not enough. If we want to be more sure that we are understanding correctly, it is not sufficient to assume that the traditional style of fieldwork (participant-observation and interviewing of a few selected informants) can always discover the truth in a field situation. Particularly for those behaviors that are private, or more variable, or not easily verbalized, anthropological fieldworkers should consider interviewing a representative sample of people and using tests of informant accuracy.

Sources: Paul Shankman, "Sex, Lies, and Anthropologists: Margaret Mead, Derek Freeman, and Samoa," in *Research Frontiers,* in Carol R. Ember, Melvin Ember, and Peter N. Peregrine eds., *New Directions in Anthropology* (Upper Saddle River, NJ: Prentice Hall, CD-ROM, 2004); Melvin Ember, "Evidence and Science in Ethnography: Reflections on the Freeman–Mead Controversy," *American Anthropologist,* 87 (1985): 906–909.

ETHICS IN FIELDWORK   Anthropologists have many ethical obligations—to the people they study, their anthropological colleagues, to the public and world community, and even to their employers and their own and host countries. But anthropologists agree that should a conflict arise in ethical obligations, the most important obligation is to protect the interests of the people they study. According to the pro-

fession's code of ethics, anthropologists should tell people in the field site about the research and they should respect the right of people to remain anonymous if they so choose.[21] It is for this reason that informants are often given "pseudonyms" or fake names; many anthropologists have extended this principle to using a fake name for the community as well. But the decision to create a fake name for a community is questionable in many circumstances.[22] First, anthropologists "stick out" and it is not hard for anyone interested to figure out where they lived and worked. Governments may have to be asked for research clearance, which means that they know where the anthropologist is going to do the fieldwork. Second, people who are studied are often proud of their place and their customs and they may be insulted if their community is called something else. Third, important geographic information is often vital to understanding the community. You have to reveal if it is located at the confluence of two major rivers, or if it is the trading center of the region. And lastly, it may be difficult for a future anthropologist to conduct a follow-up study if the community is disguised. Of course, if a community were truly in danger there would be no question that an anthropologist has an obligation to try to protect it.

Honest, objective reporting is also an obligation to the anthropological profession, to the public at large, and to the observed community. But suppose a custom or trait that appears perfectly reasonable to the observed community is considered objectionable by outsiders? Such customs could range from acts that outsiders consider criminal, such as infanticide, to those that are considered repugnant, such as eating dogs. An anthropologist may believe that publication of the information could bring harm to the population. Kim Hill and Magdalena Hurtado faced this situation when they realized that infanticide rates were high in the group they studied in South America. They did not want to play up their findings, nor did they want to dissimulate. After they met with community leaders to discuss the situation, they agreed not to publish their findings in Spanish to minimize the possibility that the local media or neighboring groups might learn of their findings.[23]

Everyday decisions like how to compensate people for their time are not easy either. Nowadays, many if not most informants expect to be paid or receive gifts. But in the early days of anthropology, in places where money was not an important part of the native economy, the decision to pay people was not a clear ethical choice. If money is rare, paying people increases the importance of money in that economy. Even nonmonetary gifts can increase inequalities or create jealousies. On the other hand, doing nothing by way of compensation doesn't seem right either. As an alternative some anthropologists try to find some community project that they can help with—that way, everyone benefits. This is not to say that the anthropologist is necessarily a burden on the community. People often like to talk about their customs, and they may want others to appreciate their way of life. And anthropologists are often amusing. They may ask "funny" questions, and when they try to say or do customary things they often do them all wrong. Probably every anthropologist has been laughed at sometimes in the field.

Within-Culture Comparisons

Ethnographers could test a theory within one society if they decide to compare individuals, families, households, communities, or districts. The natural variability that exists can be used to create a comparison. Suppose we want to verify Whiting's assumption that in a society with a low-protein diet, longer postpartum taboos enhance the survival of babies. Although almost all couples might practice a long postpartum sex taboo because it is customary, some couples might not adhere to the taboo consistently and some couples might not conceive quickly after the taboo is lifted. So we would expect some variation in spacing between births. If we collected information on the births of each mother and the survival outcome of each birth, we would be able to compare the survival rates of children born a short time after the mother's last pregnancy with those of children born after longer intervals. A significantly higher survival rate for the births after longer intervals would support Whiting's theory. What if some communities within the society had access to more protein than others? If Whiting's theory is correct, those communities with more protein should also have a higher survival rate for babies. If there were variation in the length of the postpartum sex taboo, the communities with more protein should have shorter taboos.

Whether or not we can design intracultural tests of hypotheses depends on whether we have sufficient variability in the variables in our hypotheses. More often than not we do, and we can make use of that variation to test hypotheses within a culture.

Regional Controlled Comparisons

In a regional controlled comparison, the anthropologist compares ethnographic information obtained from societies found in a particular region—societies that presumably have similar histories and occupy similar environments. The anthropologist who conducts a regional comparison is apt to be familiar with the complex of cultural features associated with that region. These features may provide a good understanding of the context of the phenomenon that is to be explained. An anthropologist's knowledge of the region under study, however, is probably not as great as the ethnographer's knowledge of a single society. Still, the anthropologist's understanding of local details is greater in a regional comparison than in a worldwide comparison. The worldwide comparison is necessarily so broad that the investigator is unlikely to know a great deal about any of the societies being compared.

The regional controlled comparison is useful not only for generating explanations but also for testing them. Because some of the societies being compared will have the characteristic that is to be explained and some will not, the anthropologist can determine whether the conditions hypothesized to be related are in fact related, at least in that region. We must remember, however, that two or more conditions may be related in one region for reasons peculiar to that region. Therefore, an explanation supported in one region may not fit others.

Cross-Cultural Research

Anthropologists can generate interpretations on the basis of worldwide comparisons by looking for differences between those societies having and those lacking a particular characteristic. But the most common use of worldwide comparisons has been to test explanations. An example is Whiting's test of his theory about the adaptive functions of a long postpartum sex taboo. Recall that Whiting hypothesized that if his theory were correct, variation in protein supplies in the adult diet should predict variation in the duration of the postpartum sex taboo. Cross-cultural researchers first identify conditions that should generally be associated if a particular theory is correct. Then they look at a worldwide sample of societies to see if the expected association generally holds true. While it is possible for a cross-cultural researcher to choose any set of societies upon which to test theories and hypotheses, it is preferable to avoid personal bias in the selection of the sample societies. One of the worst possible samples would be to choose the ethnographies from your own bookshelf. (You are unlikely to have collected them in a random way.) As we indicated in the sampling section, most cross-culturalists choose a published sample of societies that was not constructed for any specific hypothesis test. Two of the most widely used samples are the Standard Cross-Cultural (SCCS) sample of 186 societies and the annually-growing HRAF Collection of Ethnography. Since HRAF actually contains full-text ethnographies that are subject-indexed by paragraph, a researcher can fairly quickly find information to code a new variable across a large number of societies. In contrast, the SCCS sample contains pointers to ethnography, not ethnographies themselves. However, thousands of variables have now been coded by other researchers for this sample, so researchers who want to use data coded by others tend to use this sample.[24]

The advantage of cross-cultural research is that the conclusion drawn from it is probably applicable to most societies, if the sample used for testing has been more or less randomly selected and therefore is representative of the world. In other words, in contrast with the results of a regional comparison, which may or may not be applicable to other regions, the results of a cross-cultural study are probably applicable to most societies and most regions.

As we have noted, the greater the number of societies examined in a study, the less likely it is that the investigator will have detailed knowledge of the societies involved. So if a cross-cultural test does not support a particular explanation, the investigator may not know enough about the sample societies to know how to modify the interpretation or come up with a new one. In this situation, the anthropologist may reexamine the details of one or more particular societies in order to stimulate fresh thinking on the subject. Another limitation of cross-cultural research, as a means of both generating and testing explanations, is that only those explanations for which the required information is generally available in ethnographies can be tested. An investigator interested in explaining something that has not been generally described must resort to some other research strategy to collect data.

Historical Research

Ethnohistory consists of studies based on descriptive materials about a single society at more than one point in time. It provides the essential data for historical studies of all types,

just as ethnography provides the essential data for all nonhistorical types of research. Ethnohistorical data may consist of sources other than the ethnographic reports prepared by anthropologists—accounts by explorers, missionaries, traders, and government officials. Ethnohistorians, like historians, cannot simply assume that all the documents they find are simply descriptions of fact; they were written by very different kinds of people with very different goals and purposes. So they need to separate carefully what may be fact from what may be speculative interpretation. To reconstruct how a culture changed over hundreds of years, where the natives left few or no written accounts, anthropologists have to seek out travelers' accounts and other historical documents that were written by non-natives. Mary Helms had to do this when she decided to do fieldwork among the Miskito of Nicaragua, to reconstruct how their life had changed under the conditions of European colonialism. She was particularly interested in discovering why the Miskito were able to preserve a lot of political independence.[25]

In terms of generating and testing hypotheses, studies of single societies over time tend to be subject to the same limitations as studies of single societies confined to a single period. Like their nonhistorical counterparts, studies that concentrate on a single society observed through time are likely to generate more than one hypothesis, but they do not generally provide the opportunity to establish with reasonable certainty which of those hypotheses is correct. Cross-cultural historical studies (of which we have only a few examples thus far) suffer from the opposite limitation. They provide ample means of testing hypotheses through comparison, but they are severely constrained, because of the necessity of working with secondhand data, in their ability to generate hypotheses derived from the available data.

There is, however, one advantage to historical studies of any type. The goal of theory in cultural anthropology is to explain variation in cultural patterns, that is, to specify what conditions will favor one cultural pattern rather than another. Such specification requires us to assume that the supposed causal, or favoring, conditions antedated the pattern to be explained. Theories or explanations, then, imply a sequence of changes over time, which are the stuff of history. Therefore, if we want to come closer to an understanding of the reasons for the cultural variations we are investigating, we should examine historical sequences. They will help us determine whether the conditions we think caused various phenomena truly antedated those phenomena and thus might more reliably be said to have caused them. If we can examine historical sequences, we may be able to make sure that we do not put the cart before the horse.

The major impediment to historical research is that collecting and analyzing historical data—particularly when they come from the scattered accounts of explorers, missionaries, and traders—tends to be very time-consuming. It may be more efficient to test explanations nonhistorically first, in order to eliminate some interpretations. Only when an interpretation survives a nonhistorical test should we look to historical data to test the presumed sequence.

In the chapters that follow, we discuss not only what we strongly suspect about the determinants of cultural variation but also what we do not know or only dimly suspect. We devote a lot of our discussion to what we do not know—what has not yet been the subject of research that tests hypotheses and theories—because we want to convey a sense of what cultural anthropology might discover in the future.

◎ Summary

1. Scientists try to achieve two kinds of explanations—associations (observed relationships between two or more variables) and theories (explanations of associations).

2. A theory is more complicated than an association. Some concepts or implications in a theory are unobservable; an association is based entirely on observations.

3. Theories can never be proved with absolute certainty. There is always the possibility that some implication, some derivable hypothesis, will not be confirmed by future research.

4. A theory may be rejectable through the method of falsification. Scientists derive predictions that should be true if the theory is correct. If the predictions turn out to be incorrect, scientists are obliged to conclude that there may be something wrong with the theory.

5. To make a satisfactory test, we have to specify operationally how we measure the variables involved in the relationships we expect to exist, so that other researchers can try to replicate, or repeat, our results.

6. Tests of predictions should employ samples that are representative. The most objective way to obtain a representative sample is to select the sample cases randomly.

7. The results of tests are evaluated by statistical methods that assign probability values to the results. These values allow us to distinguish between probably true and probably accidental results.

8. Cultural anthropologists use several different methods to conduct research. Each has certain advantages and disadvantages in generating and testing explanations. The types of research in cultural anthropology can be classified according to two criteria: the spatial scope of the study (analysis of a single society, analysis of several or more societies in a region, or analysis of a worldwide sample of societies) and the temporal scope of the study (historical vs. nonhistorical). The basic research methods, then, are ethnography and ethnohistory, historical and nonhistorical regional controlled comparisons, and historical and nonhistorical cross-cultural research.

◎ Glossary Terms

◎ Critical Questions

1. Are theories important? Explain why or why not.
2. Can a unique event be explained? Explain your answer.
3. How does measurement go beyond observation?
4. Why is scientific understanding always uncertain?
5. If two ethnographers describing the same culture disagree, how do we decide who's right?

◎ Research Navigator

1. Please go to www.researchnavigator.com and enter your LOGIN NAME and PASSWORD. For instructions on registering for the first time, please view the detailed instructions at the end of Chapter 1.
2. Using Link Library go to the Cultural Anthropology section of Anthropology. Using the Anthro-Tech site find a Web site devoted to ethnography and find one related to cross-cultural research (Hint: Go to the Human Relations Area Files site). How are they different and similar?

◎ Discovering Anthropology: Researchers at Work

Read the chapter by Carol R. Ember and Melvin Ember, "On Cross-Cultural Research," in *Discovering Anthropology* and answer the following questions:

1. Give a few examples of questions that can be answered by cross-cultural research.
2. What are the basic assumptions and steps in a cross-cultural study?

lish have agreed to call the color of grass *green,* even though we have no way of comparing precisely how two persons actually experience this color. What we share is the agreement to call similar sensations *green.* Any system of language consists of publicly accepted symbols by which individuals try to share private experiences. Spoken or vocal language is probably the major transmitter of culture, allowing us to share and pass on our complex configuration of attitudes, beliefs, and patterns of behavior.

Nonverbal Human Communication

As we all know from experience, the spoken word does not communicate all that we know about a social situation. We can usually tell when someone says, "It was good to meet you," whether he or she really means it. We can tell if people are sad from their demeanor, even if they just say, "I'm fine," in response to the question "How are you?"

Obviously, our communication is not limited to spoken language. We communicate directly through facial expression, body stance, gesture, and tone of voice and indirectly through systems of signs and symbols, such as writing, algebraic equations, musical scores, dancing, painting, code flags, and road signs. As Anthony Wilden put it, "every act, every pause, every movement in living and social systems is also a message; silence is communication; short of death it is impossible for an organism or person not to communicate."[2] How can silence be a communication? Silence may reflect companionship, as when two people work side by side on a project, but silence can also communicate unfriendliness. An anthropologist can learn a great deal from what people in a society do not talk about. For example, in India, sex is not supposed to be talked about. HIV infection is spreading very fast in India, so the unwillingness of people to talk about sex makes it extraordinarily difficult for medical anthropologists and health professionals to do much to reduce the rate of spread.[3]

Some nonverbal communication appears to be universal in humans. For example, humans the world over appear to understand facial expression in the same way; that is, they are able to recognize a happy, sad, surprised, angry, disgusted, or afraid face. How the face is represented in art appears to evoke similar feelings in many different cultures. As we explore later in the arts chapter, masks intended to be frightening have sharp, angular features and inward- and downward-facing eyes and eyebrows. But nonverbal communication is also culturally variable. In the chapter on the concept of culture, we discussed how the distance between people standing together is culturally variable. In the realm of facial expression, different cultures have different rules about the emotions that are acceptable to express. One study compared how Japanese and Americans express emotion. Individuals from both groups were videotaped while they were shown films intended to evoke feelings of fear and disgust. When the subjects saw the films by themselves, without other people present, they showed the same kinds of facial expressions of fear and disgust. But there was a cultural effect too. When an authority figure was present during the videotaping, the Japanese subjects tried to mask their negative feelings with a half-smile more often than did the Americans.[4] Many gestures are culturally variable. In some cultures an up and down nod of the head means "yes," in others it means "no."

Kinesics is the study of communication by nonverbal or nonvocal means, including posture, mannerisms, body movement, facial expressions, and signs and gestures. Informally we may refer to nonverbal communication as "body language." As noted above, some aspects of body language, such as facial expressions of emotion, may be human universals. Specific signs and gestures are often culturally variable and the cause of cultural misunderstandings. Nonverbal communication can even involve the voice. Consider how we might know that a person is not fine even though she just said "I'm fine." We can tell a lot by tone of voice. A depressed person might speak very quietly and use a flat tone of voice. If a person thought about explaining what was really wrong but thought better of it, a significant pause or silence might come before the words "I'm fine." Even a person's **accent** (differences in pronunciation) can tell a lot about the person's background, such as place of origin and education. There are also nonverbal (nonword) sounds that people make—grunts, laughs, giggles, moans, and sighs. **Paralanguage** refers to all the optional vocal features or silences that communicate meaning apart from the language itself. While body language and some forms of paralanguage enable humans to communicate without spoken language, language spoken by humans probably never occurs without kinetic communication and paralanguage.[5]

Nonhuman Communication

Systems of communication are not unique to human beings, nor is communication by sound. Other animal species communicate in a variety of ways. One way is by sound. A bird may communicate by a call that "this is my territory"; a squirrel may utter a cry that leads other squirrels to flee from danger. Another means of animal communication is odor. An ant releases a chemical when it dies, and its fellows then carry it away to the compost heap. Apparently the communication is highly effective; a healthy ant painted with the death chemical will be dragged to the funeral heap again and again. Another means of communication, body movement, is used by bees to convey the location of food sources. Karl von Frisch discovered that the black Austrian honeybee—by choosing a round dance, a wagging dance, or a short, straight run—can communicate not only the precise direction of the source of food but also its distance from the hive.[6]

One of the biggest scholarly debates is the degree to which nonhuman animals, particularly nonhuman primates, differ from humans in their capacity for language. Some scholars see so much discontinuity that they postulate that humans must have acquired (presumably through mutation) a specific genetic capability for language. Others see much more continuity between humans and nonhuman primates and point to research that shows much more cognitive capacity in nonhuman primates than previously thought possible. They point out that the discontinuity the-

Apes lack the human capacity for speech, so researchers have explored the capacity of chimpanzees and other apes to communicate with hand gestures. A variety of signs from American Sign Language, used by the hearing impaired, are shown on the left. Researcher Joyce Butler teaches Nim, a chimpanzee, a sign for "drink."

orists are constantly raising the standards for the capacities thought necessary for language.[7] For example, in the past, only human communication was thought to be symbolic. But recent research suggests that some monkey and ape calls in the wild are also symbolic.

When we say that a call, word, or sentence is **symbolic communication,** we mean at least two things. First, the communication has meaning even when its *referent* (whatever is referred to) is not present. Second, the meaning is arbitrary; the receiver of the message could not guess its meaning just from the sound(s) and does not know the meaning instinctively. In other words, symbols have to be learned. There is no compelling or "natural" reason that the word *dog* in English should refer to a smallish four-legged omnivore that is sometimes the bane of letter carriers.

Vervet monkeys in Africa are not as closely related to humans as are African apes. Nevertheless, scientists who have observed vervet monkeys in their natural environment consider at least three of their alarm calls to be symbolic because each of them *means* (refers to) a different kind of predator—eagles, pythons, or leopards—and monkeys react differently to each call. For example, they look up when they hear the "eagle" call. Experimentally, in the absence of the referent, investigators have been able to evoke the normal reaction to a call by playing it back electronically. Another indication that the vervet alarm calls are symbolic is that infant vervets appear to need some time to learn the referent for each. When they are very young, infants apply a particular call to more animals than adult vervets apply the call to. So, for example, infant vervets will often make the eagle warning call when they see any flying bird. The infants learn the appropriate referent apparently through adult vervets' repetition of infants' "correct" calls; in any case, the infants gradually learn to restrict the call to eagles. This process is probably not too different from the way a North American infant in an English-speaking family first applies the "word" *dada* to all adult males and gradually learns to restrict it to one person.[8]

All of the nonhuman vocalizations we have described so far enable individual animals to convey messages. The sender gives a signal that is received and "decoded" by the receiver, who usually responds with a specific action or reply. How is human vocalization different? Since monkeys and apes appear to use symbols at least some of the time, it is not appropriate to emphasize symbolism as the distinctive feature of human language. However, there is a significant quantitative difference between human language and other primates' systems of vocal communication. All human languages employ a much larger set of symbols.

Another often-cited difference between human and nonhuman vocalizations is that the other primates' vocal systems are *closed*—that is, different calls are not combined to produce new, meaningful utterances. In contrast, human languages are *open* systems, governed by complex rules about how sounds and sequences of sounds can be combined to produce an infinite variety of meanings.[9] For example, an English speaker can combine *care* and *full* (*careful*) to mean one thing, then use each of the two elements in other combinations to mean different things. *Care* can be used to make *carefree, careless,* or *caretaker; full* can be used to make *powerful* or *wonderful.* And because language is a system of shared symbols, it can be re-formed into an infinite variety of expressions and be understood by all who share these symbols. In this way, for example, T. S. Eliot could form a sentence never before formed—"In the room the women come and go/talking of Michelangelo"[10]—and the sense of his sentence, though not necessarily his private meaning, could be understood by all speakers of English.

While no primatologist disputes the complexity and infinite variety with which human languages can combine sounds, the closed versus open distinction has been called into question by research on cotton-top tamarins, pygmy marmosets, capuchin monkeys, and rhesus macaques. These nonhuman primates also combine calls in orderly sequences,[11] but not nearly as much as humans do.

Another trait thought to be unique to humans is the ability to communicate about past or future events. But Sue Savage-Rumbaugh has observed wild bonobos leaving what appear to be messages to other bonobos to follow a trail. They break off vegetation where trails fork and point the broken plants in the direction to follow.

Perhaps most persuasive are the successful attempts to teach apes to communicate with humans and with each other using human-created signs. These successes have led many scholars to question the traditional assumption that the gap between human and other animal communication is enormous. Even a parrot, which has a small brain, has been taught to communicate with a human trainer in ways once thought impossible. Alex (the parrot) can correctly an-

swer questions in English about what objects are made of, how many objects of a particular type there are, and even what makes two objects the same or different.[12] When he is not willing to continue a training session, Alex says: "I'm sorry . . . Wanna go back."[13] Chimpanzees Washoe and Nim and the gorilla Koko were taught hand signs based on American Sign Language (ASL; used by the hearing impaired in the United States). The chimpanzee Sarah was trained with plastic symbols. Subsequently, many chimpanzees were trained on symbol keyboards connected to computers. For example, Sherman and Austin began to communicate with each other about actions they were intending to do, such as the types of tools they needed to solve a problem. And they were able to classify items into categories, such as "food" and "tools." Some of the best examples of linguistic ability come from a chimpanzee named Kanzi. In contrast to other apes, Kanzi initially learned symbols just by watching his mother being taught, and he spontaneously began using the computer symbols to communicate with humans, even indicating his intended actions. Kanzi did not need rewards or to have his hands put in the right position. And he understood a great deal of what was spoken to him in English. For example, when he was 5 years old, Kanzi heard someone talk about throwing a ball in the river, and he turned around and did so. Kanzi has come close to having a primitive English grammar when he strings symbols together.[14] If chimpanzees and other primates have the capacity to use nonspoken language and even to understand spoken language, then the difference between humans and nonhumans may not be as great as people used to think.

Are these apes really using language in some minimal way? Many investigators do agree about one thing—nonhuman primates have the ability to "symbol," to refer to something (or a class of things) with an arbitrary "label" (gesture or sequence of sounds).[15] For example, the gorilla Koko (with a repertoire of about 375 signs) extended the sign for *drinking straw* to plastic tubing, hoses, cigarettes, and radio antennae. Washoe originally learned the sign *dirty* to refer to feces and other soil and then began to use it insultingly, as in "dirty Roger," when her trainer Roger Fouts refused to give her things she wanted. Even the mistakes made by the apes suggest that they are using signs symbolically, just as words are used in spoken language. For example, the sign *cat* may be used for dog if the animal learned *cat* first (just as our daughter Kathy said "dog" to all pictures of four-footed animals, including elephants, when she was 18 months old).

When we discuss the structure of sounds (phonology) later in this chapter, we will see that every human language has certain ways of combining sounds and ways of not combining those sounds. Apes do not have anything comparable to linguistic rules for allowed and not allowed combinations of sounds. In addition, humans have many kinds of discourse. We make lists and speeches, tell stories, argue, and recite poetry. Apes do none of these things.[16] But apes do have at least some of the capacities for language. Therefore, understanding their capacities may help us better understand the evolution of human language.

The Origins of Language

How long humans have had spoken language is not known. Some think that the earliest *Homo sapiens,* perhaps 100,000 years ago, may have had the beginnings of language. Others believe that language developed only in the last 40,000 years or so, with the emergence of modern humans. Because the only unambiguous remains of language are found on written tablets, and the earliest stone tablets date back only about 5,000 years,[17] pinpointing the emergence of earliest languages remains speculative. Theories about when language developed are based on nonlinguistic information such as when cranial capacity expanded dramatically, when complex technology and symbolic artifacts (such as art) started to be made, and when the anatomy of the throat, as inferred from fossil remains, began to resemble what we see in modern humans.

Perhaps the majority of scholars believe that spoken language was a radical departure from communication that preceded it. However, as we have noted, based on observations of nonhuman primates in the wild and in the laboratory, many primatologists have questioned whether there is an enormous gap between nonhuman primate and human communicational capacities. In fact, some think that all the brain prerequisites for language were in place before the evolutionary split between apes and humans, and they view the emergence of spoken language as a quantitative rather than a qualitative difference.[18] These two points of view have led to lively debate.

Noam Chomsky and other theoreticians of grammar suggest that there is an innate *language-acquisition device* in the human brain, as innate to humans as call systems are to other animals.[19] If humans are unique in having an innate capacity for language, then some mutation or series of mutations had to be favored in human evolution, not before the human line separated from apes. Whether such a mechanism in fact exists is not clear. But we do know that the actual development of individual language is not completely biologically determined; if it were, all human beings would speak the same brain-generated language. Instead, about 4,000 to 5,000 mutually unintelligible languages have been identified. More than 2,000 of them were still spoken as of recently, most by peoples who did not traditionally have a system of writing.

Can we learn anything about the origins of language by studying the languages of nonliterate (no writing) and technologically simpler societies? The answer is no, because such languages are not simpler or less developed than ours. The sound systems, vocabularies, and grammars of technologically simpler peoples are in no way inferior to those of peoples with more complex technology.[20] Of course, people in other societies, and even some people in our own society, will not be able to name the sophisticated machines used in our society. All languages, however, have the potential for doing so. As we will see later in this chapter, all languages possess the amount of vocabulary their speakers need, and all languages expand in response to cultural changes. A language that lacks terminology for some of our conveniences may have a rich vocabulary for events or natural phenomena that are of particular importance to the people in that society.

If there are no primitive languages, and if the earliest languages have left no traces that would allow us to reconstruct them, does that mean we cannot investigate the origins of language? Some linguists think that understanding the way children acquire language, which we discuss shortly, can help us understand the origins of language. Other linguists have suggested that an understanding of how creole languages develop will also tell us something about the origins of language.

Creole Languages

Some languages developed in various areas where European colonial powers established commercial enterprises that relied on imported labor, generally slaves. The laborers in one place often came from several different societies and in the beginning would speak with their masters and with each other in some kind of *pidgin* (simplified) version of the masters' language. Pidgin languages lack many of the building blocks found in the languages of whole societies, building blocks such as prepositions (*to, on,* and so forth) and auxiliary verbs (designating future and other tenses). Many pidgin languages developed into and were replaced by so-called *creole languages,* which incorporate much of the vocabulary of the masters' language but also have a grammar that differs from it and from the grammars of the laborers' native languages.[21]

Derek Bickerton argues that there are striking grammatical similarities in creole languages throughout the world. This similarity, he thinks, is consistent with the idea that some grammar is inherited by all humans. Creole languages, therefore, may resemble early human languages. All creoles use intonation instead of a change in word order to ask a question. The creole equivalent of the question "Can you fix this?" would be "You can fix this?" The creole version puts a rising inflection at the end; in contrast, the English version reverses the subject and verb without much inflection at the end. All creoles express the future and the past in the same grammatical way, by the use of particles (such as the English *shall*) between subject and verb, and they all employ double negatives, as in the Guyana English creole "Nobody no like me."[22]

It is possible that many other things about language are universal, that all languages are similar in many respects, because of the way humans are "wired" or because people in all societies have similar experiences. For example, names for frogs may usually contain *r* sounds because frogs make them.[23]

Children's Acquisition of Language

Apparently a child is equipped from birth with the capacity to reproduce all the sounds used by the world's languages and to learn any system of grammar. Research on 6-months-old infants finds that they can distinguish sounds of approximately 600 consonants and 200 vowels—all the sounds of all the languages of the world. But by about the time of their first birthdays, babies become better at recognizing the salient sounds and sound clusters of their parents or caretakers and become less adept at distinguishing those of other languages.[24]

Children's acquisition of the structure and meaning of language has been called the most difficult intellectual achievement in life. If that is so, it is pleasing to note that they accomplish it with relative ease and vast enjoyment. Many believe that this "difficult intellectual achievement" may in reality be a natural response to the capacity for language that is one of humans' genetic characteristics. All over the world children begin to learn language at about the same age, and in no culture do children wait until they are 7 or 10 years old. By 12 or 13 months of age, children are able to name a few objects and actions, and by 18 to 20 months they can make one key word stand for a whole sentence: "Out!" for "Take me out for a walk right now"; "Juice!" for "I want some juice now." Evidence suggests that children acquire the concept of a word as a whole, learning sequences of sounds that are stressed or at the ends of words (e.g., "raffe" for giraffe). Even hearing-impaired children learning signs in ASL tend to acquire and use signs in a similar fashion.[25]

Children the world over tend to progress to two-word sentences at about 18 to 24 months of age. In their sentences they express themselves in "telegraph" form—using nounlike words and verblike words but leaving out the seemingly less important words. So a two-word sentence such as "Shoes off" may stand for "Take my shoes off," or "More milk" may stand for "Give me more milk, please."[26] They do not utter their two words in random order, sometimes saying "off" first, other times saying "shoes" first. If a child says "Shoes off," then he or she will also say "Clothes off" and "Hat off." They seem to select an order that fits the conventions of adult language, so they are likely to say "Daddy eat," not "Eat Daddy." In other words, they tend to put the subject first, as adults do. And they tend to say "Mommy coat" rather than "Coat Mommy" to indicate "Mommy's coat."[27] Adults do not

utter sentences such as "Daddy eat," so children seem to know a lot about how to put words together with little or no direct teaching from their caretakers. Consider the 5-year-old who, confronted with the unfamiliar "Gloria in Excelsis," sings quite happily, "Gloria eats eggshells." To make the words fit the structure of English grammar is more important than to make the words fit the meaning of the Christmas pageant.

If there is a basic grammar imprinted in the human mind, we should not be surprised that children's early and later speech patterns seem to be similar in different languages. We might also expect children's later speech to be similar to the structure of creole languages. And it is, according to Derek Bickerton.[28] The "errors" children make in speaking are consistent with the grammar of creoles. For example, English-speaking children 3 to 4 years old tend to ask questions by intonation alone, and they tend to use double negatives, such as "I don't see no dog," even though the adults around them do not speak that way and consider the children's speech "wrong."

But some linguists argue that the evidence for an innate grammar is weak because children the world over do not develop the same grammatical features at similar ages. For example, word order is a more important determinant of meaning in English than in Turkish; the endings of words are more important in Turkish. The word at the beginning of the sentence in English is likely to be the subject. The word with a certain ending in Turkish is the likely subject. Consistent with this difference, English-speaking children learn word order earlier than Turkish children do.[29]

Future research on children's acquisition of language and on the structure of creole languages may bring us closer to an understanding of the origins of human language. But even if much of grammar is universal, we still need to understand how and why the thousands of languages in the world vary, which brings us to the conceptual tools linguists have had to invent in order to study languages.

◎ Descriptive Linguistics

In every society children do not need to be taught "grammar" to learn how to speak. They begin to grasp the essential structure of their language at a very early age, without direct instruction. If you show English-speaking children a picture of one "gork" and then a picture of two of these creatures, they will say there are two "gorks." Somehow they know that adding an *s* to a noun means more than one. But they do not know this consciously, and adults may not either. One of the most surprising features of human language is that meaningful sounds and sound sequences are combined according to rules that often are not consciously known by the speakers.

These rules should not be equated with the "rules of grammar" you were taught in school so that you would speak "correctly." Rather, when linguists talk about rules, they are referring to the patterns of speaking that are discoverable in actual speech. Needless to say, there is some overlap between the actual rules of speaking and the rules taught in school. But there are rules that children never hear about in school,

A lot of language instruction is by pointing to something and saying what it is called.

because their teachers are not linguists and are not aware of them. When linguists use the term *grammar,* they are *not* referring to the prescriptive rules that people are supposed to follow in speaking. Rather, *grammar* to the linguist consists of the actual, often unconscious principles that predict how most people talk. As we have noted, young children may speak two-word sentences that conform to a linguistic rule, but their speech is hardly considered "correct."

Discovering the mostly unconscious rules operating in a language is a very difficult task. Linguists have had to invent special concepts and methods of transcription (writing) to permit them to describe: (1) the rules or principles that predict how sounds are made and how they are used (slightly varying sounds are often used interchangeably in words without creating a difference in meaning—this aspect of language is called **phonology**); (2) how sound sequences (and sometimes even individual sounds) convey meaning and how meaningful sound sequences are strung together to form words (this aspect is called **morphology**); and (3) how words are strung together to form phrases and sentences (this aspect is called **syntax**).

Understanding the language of another people is an essential part of understanding the culture of that people. Although sometimes what people say is contradicted by their observed behavior, there is little doubt that it is hard to understand the beliefs, attitudes, values, and worldview of a people without understanding their language and the nuances of how that language is used. Even behavior, which theoretically one can observe without understanding language, usually cannot be readily understood without interpretation. Imagine that you see people go by a certain rock and seemingly walk out of their way to avoid it. Suppose they believe that an evil spirit resides there. How could you possibly know that without being able to ask and to understand their answer?

Phonology

Most of us have had the experience of trying to learn another language and finding that some sounds are exceedingly difficult to make. Although the human vocal tract theoretically can make a very large number of different sounds—**phones,** to linguists—each language uses only some of them. It is not that we cannot make the sounds that are strange to us; we just have not acquired the habit of making those sounds. And until the sounds become habitual for us, they continue to be difficult to form.

Finding it difficult to make certain sounds is only one of the reasons we have trouble learning a "foreign" language. Another problem is that we may not be used to combining certain sounds or making a certain sound in a particular position in a word. Thus, English speakers find it difficult to combine *z* and *d,* as Russian speakers often do (because we never do so in English), or to pronounce words in Samoan, a South Pacific language, that begin with the sound English speakers write as *ng,* even though we have no trouble putting that sound at the end of words, as in the English *sing* and *hitting.*

In order to study the patterning of sounds, linguists who are interested in *phonology* have to write down speech utterances

as sequences of sound. This task would be almost impossible if linguists were restricted to using their own alphabet (say, the one we use to write English), because other languages use sounds that are difficult to represent with the English alphabet or because the alphabet we use in English can represent a particular sound in different ways. (English writing represents the sound *f* by *f* as in *food,* but also as *gh* in *tough* and *ph* in *phone.*) In addition, in English different sounds may be represented by the same letter. English has 26 letters but more than 40 significant sounds (sounds that can change the meaning of a word).[30] To overcome these difficulties in writing sounds with the letters of existing writing systems, linguists have developed systems of transcription with special alphabets in which each symbol represents only one particular sound.

Once linguists have identified the sounds or phones used in a language, they try to identify which sounds affect meaning and which sounds do not. One way is to start with a simple word like *lake* and change the first sound to *r* to make the word *rake.* The linguist will ask if this new combination of sounds means the same thing. An English speaker would say *lake* means something completely different from *rake.* These minimal contrasts enable linguists to identify a **phoneme** in a language—a sound or set of sounds that makes a difference in meaning in that language.[31] So the sound *l* in *lake* is different phonemically from the sound *r* in *rake.* The ways in which sounds are grouped together into phonemes vary from language to language. We are so used to phonemes in our own language that it may be hard to believe that the contrast between *r* and *l* may not make a difference in meaning in some languages. For example, in Samoan, *l* and *r* can be used interchangeably in a word without changing the meaning (therefore, these two sounds belong to the same phoneme in Samoan). So Samoan speakers may say "Leupena" sometimes and "Reupena" at other times when they are referring to someone who in English would be called "Reuben."

English speakers may joke about languages that "confuse" *l* and *r,* but they are not usually aware that we do the same thing with other sets of sounds. For example, in English, the word we spell *and* may be pronounced quite differently by two different English speakers without changing the meaning, and no one would think that a different word was spoken. We can pronounce the *a* in *and* as in the beginning of the word *air,* or we can pronounce it as the *a* in *bat.* If you say those varying *a* sounds and try to think about how you are forming them in your mouth, you will realize that they are two different sounds. English speakers might recognize a slight difference in pronunciation but pay little or no attention to it because the two ways to pronounce the *a* in *and* do not change the meaning. Now think about *l* and *r.* If you form them in your mouth, you will notice that they are only slightly different with respect to how far the tongue is from the ridge behind the upper front teeth. Languages do tend to consider sounds that are close as belonging to the same phoneme, but why they choose some sounds and not others to group together is not yet fully understood.

Some recent research suggests that infants may learn early to ignore meaningless variations of sound (those that are part of the same phoneme) in the language they hear at home. It turns out that as early as 6 months of age, infants "ignore" sound shifts within the same phoneme of their own language, but they "hear" a sound shift within the phoneme of another language. Researchers are not sure how babies learn to make the distinction, but they seem to acquire much of the phonology of their language very early indeed.[32]

After discovering which sounds are grouped into phonemes, linguists can begin to discover the sound sequences that are allowed in a language and the usually unconscious rules that predict those sequences. For example, words in English rarely start with three nonvowel sounds. But when they do, the first sound or phone is always an *s,* as in *strike* and *scratch.*[33] (Some other words in English may start with three consonants but only two sounds are involved, as in *chrome,* where the *ch* stands for the sound in *k.*) Linguists' descriptions of the patterning of sounds (phonology) in different languages may allow them to investigate why languages vary in their sound rules.

Why, for example, are two or more consonants strung together in some languages, whereas in other languages vowels are *almost* always put between consonants? The Samoan language now has a word for "Christmas" borrowed from English, but the borrowed word has been changed to fit the rules of Samoan. In the English word, two consonants come first, *k* and *r,* which we spell as *ch* and *r.* The Samoan word is *Kerisimasi* (pronounced as if it were spelled Keh-ree-see-mah-see). It has a vowel after each consonant, or five consonant–vowel syllables.

Why do some languages like Samoan alternate consonants and vowels more or less regularly? Recent cross-cultural research suggests three predictors of this variation. One predictor is a warmer climate. Where people live in warmer climates, the typical syllable is more likely to be a consonant–vowel syllable. Linguists have found that consonant–vowel syllables provide the most contrast in speech. Perhaps when people converse outdoors at a dis-

APPLIED ANTHROPOLOGY

Can Languages Be Kept from Extinction?

Not only animal and plant species are endangered; many peoples and their languages are too. In the last few hundred years, and continuing in some places today, Western expansion and colonization have led to the depopulation and extinction of many native societies, mainly as a result of introduced disease and campaigns of extermination. Thus, many languages disappeared with the peoples that spoke them. More than 50 aboriginal languages in Australia of approximately 200 disappeared relatively quickly as a result of massacre and disease.

Today native languages are endangered more by the fact that they are not being passed on to children. Political and economic dominance by speakers of Western languages undoubtedly plays an enormous role in this process. First, schooling is usually conducted in the dominant language. Second, when another culture is dominant, the children themselves may prefer to speak in the language perceived to have higher prestige; indeed, parents sometimes encourage this tendency. Almost all the languages of aboriginal Australia are now gone. This is a worldwide trend. Michael Krauss, a linguist who tracks disappearing languages, estimates that 90 percent of the world's languages are endangered. Here is another example: Only 2 of the 20 native Alaskan languages are currently being taught to children, who therefore speak English only.

What can be done? Krauss, who is particularly interested in native Alaskan languages, is trying to do some-

thing. With help from the state government of Alaska, Krauss is developing materials on native languages to help teachers promote bilingual education as a way of preserving native languages. A very different approach has been taken by H. Russell Bernard, who believes that "to keep a language truly alive we must produce authors." With the help of computer technology, which allows reconfiguring a keyboard to produce special characters for sounds, Bernard has taught native speakers to write their native languages directly on computers. These texts then become the basis for dictionaries. So far, more than 80 people, speaking 12 endangered languages, have become authors in Mexico and South America. Although these authors may not be using the standardized characters used by linguists to represent sounds, they are producing "written" materials that might otherwise be lost forever. These texts provide more than just information about language. In their works the authors convey ideas about curing illness, acquiring food, raising children, and settling disputes.

We are not sure when humans first developed spoken language. But the enormous linguistic diversity on this planet took a long time to develop. Unfortunately, it may take only a short time for that diversity to become a thing of the past.

Sources: Seth Shulman, "Nurturing Native Tongues," *Technology Review* (May/June 1993): 16; Janet Holmes, *An Introduction to Sociolinguistics* (London: Longman, 1992), pp. 61–62.

tance, which they are likely to do in a warmer climate, they need more contrast between sounds to be understood. A second predictor of consonant–vowel alternation is literacy. Languages that are written have fewer consonant–vowel syllables. If communication is often in written form, meaning does not have to depend so much on contrast between adjacent sounds. A third (indeed the strongest) predictor of consonant–vowel alternation is the degree to which babies are held by others. Societies with a great deal of baby-holding have a lot of consonant–vowel syllables. Later, in the chapter on the arts, you will read about research that relates baby-holding to a societal preference for regular rhythm in music. The theory is that when babies are held on a person much of the day, they begin to associate regular rhythm with pleasurable experiences. The baby senses the regular rhythm of the caretaker's heartbeats or the caretaker's rhythmic work, and the reward value of that experience generalizes to a preference for all regular rhythms in adult life, including apparently a regular consonant–vowel alternation in adult speech. Compare the rhythm of the Samoan word *Kerisimasi* with the English word *Christmas*.[34]

Morphology

A phoneme in a language usually does not mean something by itself. Usually phonemes are combined with other phonemes to form a meaningful sequence of sounds. *Morphology* is the study of sequences of sounds that have meaning. Often these meaningful sequences of sounds make up what we call *words*, but a word may be composed of a number of smaller meaningful units. We take our words so much for granted that we do not realize how complicated it is to say what words are. People do not usually pause very much between words when they speak; if we did not know our language, a sentence would seem like a continuous stream of sounds. This is how we first hear a foreign language. It is only when we understand the language and write down what we say that we separate (by spaces) what we call words. But a word is really only an arbitrary sequence of sounds that has a meaning; we would not "hear" words as separate units if we did not understand the language spoken.

Because anthropological linguists traditionally investigated unwritten languages, sometimes without the aid of interpreters, they had to figure out which sequences of sounds conveyed meaning. And because words in many languages can often be broken down into smaller meaningful units, linguists had to invent special words to refer to those units. Linguists call the smallest unit of language that has a meaning a **morph**. Just as a phoneme may have one or more phones, one or more morphs with the same meaning may make up a **morpheme**. For example, the prefix *in-*, as in *indefinite*, and the prefix *un-*, as in *unclear*, are morphs that belong to the morpheme meaning *not*. Although some words are single morphs or morphemes (e.g., *for* and *giraffe* in English), many words are a combination of morphs, generally prefixes, roots, and suffixes. Thus *cow* is one word, but the word *cows* contains two meaningful units—a root (*cow*) and a suffix (pronounced like *z*) meaning more than one.

The **lexicon** of a language, which a dictionary approximates, consists of words and morphs and their meanings.

It seems likely that the intuitive grasp children have of the structure of their language includes a recognition of morphology. Once they learn that the morph */-z/* added to a noun-type word indicates more than one, they plow ahead with *mans, childs;* once they grasp that the morpheme class pronounced */-t/* or */-d/* or */-ed/* added to the end of a verb indicates that the action took place in the past, they apply that concept generally and invent *runned, drinked, costed.* They see a ball roll near*er* and near*er,* and they transfer that concept to a kite, which goes upp*er* and upp*er.* From their mistakes as well as their successes, we can see that children understand the regular uses of morphemes. By the age of 7, they have mastered many of the irregular forms as well—that is, they learn which morphs of a morpheme are used when.

The child's intuitive grasp of the dependence of some morphemes on others corresponds to the linguist's recognition of free morphemes and bound morphemes. A *free* morpheme has meaning standing alone—that is, it can be a separate word. A *bound* morpheme displays its meaning only when attached to another morpheme. The morph pronounced */-t/* of the bound morpheme meaning *past tense* is attached to the root *walk* to produce *walked;* but the */-t/* cannot stand alone or have meaning by itself.

In English, the meaning of an utterance (containing a subject, verb, object, and so forth) usually depends on the order of the words. "The dog bit the child" is different in meaning from "The child bit the dog." But in many other languages, the grammatical meaning of an utterance does not depend much, if at all, on the order of the words. Rather, meaning may be determined by how the morphs in a word are ordered. For example, in Luo, a language of East Africa, the same bound morpheme may mean the subject or object of an action. If the morpheme is the prefix to a verb, it means the subject; if it is the suffix to a verb, it means the object. Another way that grammatical meaning may be conveyed is by altering or adding a bound morpheme to a word to indicate what part of speech it is. For example, in Russian, the word for "mail" when it is the subject of a sentence is pronounced something like "pawchtah." When "mail" is used as the object of a verb, as in "I gave her the mail," the ending of the word changes to "pawchtoo." And if I say, "What was in the mail?" the word becomes "pawchtyeh."

Some languages have so many bound morphemes that they might express as a complex but single word what is considered a sentence in English. For example, the English sentence "He will give it to you" can be expressed in Wishram, a Chinookan dialect that was spoken along the Columbia River in the Pacific Northwest, as *acimluda* (a-c-i-m-l-ud-a, literally "will-he-him-thee-to-give-will"). Note that the pronoun *it* in English is gender-neutral; Wishram requires that *it* be given a gender, in this case, "him."[35]

Syntax

Because language is an open system, we can make up meaningful utterances that we have never heard before. We are constantly creating new phrases and sentences. Just as they do for morphology, speakers of a language seem to have an intuitive grasp of *syntax*—the rules that predict how phrases and sentences are generally formed. These "rules" may be partly learned in school, but children know many of them even before they get to school. In adulthood, our understanding of morphology and syntax is so intuitive that we can even understand a nonsense sentence, such as this famous one from Lewis Carroll's *Through the Looking Glass:*

> 'Twas brillig, and the slithy toves
>
> Did gyre and gimble in the wabe

Simply from the ordering of the words in the sentence, we can surmise which part of speech a word is, as well as its function in the sentence. *Brillig* is an adjective; *slithy* an adjective; *toves* a noun and the subject of the sentence; *gyre* and *gimble* verbs; and *wabe* a noun and the object of a prepositional phrase. Of course, an understanding of morphology helps too. The *-y* ending in *slithy* is an indication that the latter is an adjective, and the *-s* ending in *toves* tells us that we most probably have more than one of these creatures. In addition to producing and understanding an infinite variety of sentences, speakers of a language can tell when a sentence is not "correct" without consulting grammar books. For example, an English speaker can tell that "Child the dog the hit" is not an acceptable sentence but "The child hit the dog" is fine. There must, then, be a set of rules underlying how phrases and sentences are constructed in a language.[36] Speakers of a language know these implicit rules of syntax but are not usually consciously aware of them. The linguist's description of the syntax of a language tries to make these rules explicit.

⊚ Historical Linguistics

The field of **historical linguistics** focuses on how languages change over time. Written works provide the best data for establishing such changes. For example, the following passage from Chaucer's *Canterbury Tales,* written in the English of the 14th century, has recognizable elements but is different enough from modern English to require a translation.

> A Frere ther was, a wantowne and a merye,
>
> A lymytour, a ful solempne man.
>
> In alle the ordres foure is noon that kan
>
> So muche of daliaunce and fair language.
>
> He hadde maad ful many a mariage
>
> Of yonge wommen at his owene cost.
>
> Unto his ordre he was a noble post.
>
> Ful wel biloued and famulier was he
>
> With frankeleyns ouer al in his contree,

> And with worthy wommen of the toun;
>
> For he hadde power of confessioun,
>
> As seyde hymself, moore than a curat,
>
> For of his ordre he was licenciat.

> A Friar there was, wanton and merry,
>
> A limiter [a friar limited to certain districts], a full solemn [very important] man.
>
> In all the orders four there is none that knows
>
> So much of dalliance [flirting] and fair [engaging] language.
>
> He had made [arranged] many a marriage
>
> Of young women at his own cost.
>
> Unto his order he was a noble post [pillar].
>
> Full well beloved and familiar was he
>
> With franklins [wealthy landowners] all over his country
>
> And also with worthy women of the town;
>
> For he had power of confession,
>
> As he said himself, more than a curate,
>
> For of his order, he was a licentiate [licensed by the Pope].[37]

In this passage we can recognize several changes. Many words are spelled differently today, and in some cases, meaning has changed: *Full,* for example, would be translated today as *very.* What is less evident is that changes in pronunciation have occurred. For example, the *g* in *mariage* (marriage) was pronounced *zh,* as in the French from which it was borrowed, whereas now it is usually pronounced like either *g* in *George.* Because languages spoken in the past leave no traces unless they were written, and most of the languages known to anthropology were not written by their speakers, you might think that historical linguists can study linguistic change only by studying written languages such as English. But that is not the case. Linguists can reconstruct changes that have occurred by comparing contemporary languages that are similar. Such languages show phonological, morphological, and syntactical similarities because they usually derive from a common ancestral language. For example, Romanian, Italian, French, Spanish, and Portuguese have many similarities. On the basis of these similarities, linguists can reconstruct what the ancestral language was like and how it changed into what we call the Romance languages. Of course, these

This reproduced page dates from a 1433 book authored by John Lydgate. The language is described by linguists as Middle English, spanning approximately 1100–1500.

Language Families and Culture History

Latin is the ancestral language of the Romance languages. We know this from documentary (written) records. But if the ancestral language of a set of similar languages is not known from written records, linguists still can reconstruct many features of that language by comparing the derived languages. (Such a reconstructed language is called a **proto-language.**) That is, by comparing presumably related languages, linguists can become aware of the features that many of them have in common, features that were probably found in the common ancestral language. The languages that derive from the same protolanguage are called a *language family.* Most languages spoken today can be grouped into fewer than 30 families. The language family that English belongs to is called *Indo-European,* because it includes most of the languages of Europe and some of the languages of India. About 50 percent of the world's more than 6 billion people speak Indo-European languages.[38] Another very large language family, now spoken by more than a billion people, is Sino-Tibetan, which includes the languages of northern and southern China as well as those of Tibet and Burma.

The field of historical linguistics got its start in 1786, when a British scholar living in India, Sir William Jones, noticed similarities between Sanskrit, a language spoken and written in ancient India, and classical Greek, Latin, and more recent European languages.[39] In 1822, Jakob Grimm, one of the brothers Grimm of fairytale fame, formulated rules to describe the sound shifts that had occurred when the various Indo-European languages diverged from each other. So, for example, in English and the other languages in the Germanic branch of the Indo-European family, *d* regularly shifted to *t* (compare the English *two* and *ten* with the Latin *duo* and *decem*) and *p* regularly shifted to *f* (English *father* and *foot*, Latin *pater* and *pes*). Scholars generally agree that the Indo-European languages derive from a language spoken 5,000 to 6,000 years ago.[40] The ancestral Indo-European language, many of whose features have now been reconstructed, is called *proto-Indo-European,* or *PIE* for short. Figure 16–1 shows the branches and some existing languages of the family.

Where did PIE originate? Some linguists believe that the approximate location of a protolanguage is suggested by the words for plants and animals in the derived languages. More specifically, among these different languages, the words that are **cognates**—that is, words that are similar in sound and meaning—presumably refer to plants and animals that were present in the original homeland. So if we know where those animals and plants were located 5,000 to 6,000 years ago, we can guess where PIE people lived. Among all the cognates for trees in the Indo-European languages, Paul Friedrich has identified 18 that he believes were present in the eastern Ukraine in 3000 B.C. On this basis he suggests that the eastern Ukraine was the PIE homeland.[41] Also consistent with this hypothesis is the fact that the Balto-Slavic subfamily of Indo-European, which includes most of the languages in and around the former Soviet Union, has the most tree names (compared with other subfamilies) that are similar to the reconstructed form in proto-Indo-European.[42]

reconstructions can easily be tested and confirmed because we know from many surviving writings what the ancestral language, Latin, was like; and we know from documents how Latin diversified as the Roman Empire expanded. Thus, common ancestry is frequently the reason why neighboring, and sometimes even separated, languages show patterns of similarity.

But languages can be similar for other reasons too. Contact between speech communities, often with one group dominant over another, may lead one language to borrow from the other. For example, English borrowed a lot of vocabulary from French after England was conquered by the French-speaking Normans in A.D. 1066. Languages may also show similarities even though they do not derive from a common ancestral language and even though there has been no contact or borrowing between them. Such similarities may reflect common or universal features of human cultures or human brains or both. (As we noted earlier in the chapter, the grammatical similarities exhibited by creole languages may reflect how the human brain is "wired.") Finally, even unrelated and separated languages may show some similarities because of the phenomenon of convergence; similarities can develop because some processes of linguistic change may have only a few possible outcomes.

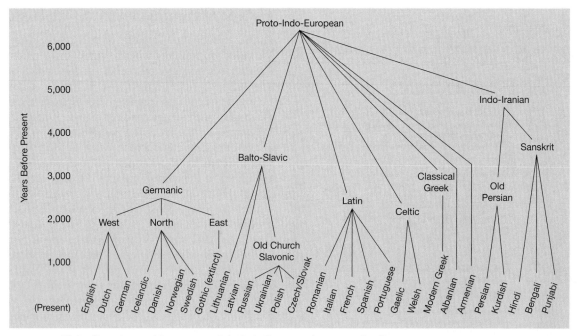

Figure 16–1 Major Branches and Languages of the Indo-European Language Family

Marija Gimbutas thinks we can even identify the proto-Indo-Europeans archaeologically. She believes that the PIE people were probably the people associated with what is known as the Kurgan culture (5000 to 2000 B.C.), which spread out from the Ukraine around 3000 B.C. The Kurgan people were herders, raising horses, cattle, sheep, and pigs. They also relied on hunting and grain cultivation. Burials suggest differences in wealth and special status for men.[43] Why the Kurgan and linguistically similar people were able to expand to many places in Europe and the Near East is not yet clear. Some have suggested that horses and horsedrawn wagons and perhaps horseback riding provided important military advantages.[44] In any case, it is clear that many Kurgan cultural elements were distributed after 3000 B.C. over a wide area of the Old World.

Colin Renfrew disagrees with the notion that the Ukraine was the homeland of PIE. He thinks that PIE is 2,000 to 3,000 years older than Kurgan culture and that the PIE people lived in a different place. Renfrew locates the PIE homeland in eastern Anatolia (Turkey) in 7000 to 6000 B.C., and he suggests, on the basis of archaeological evidence, that the spread of Indo-European to Europe and what is now Iran, Afghanistan, and India accompanied the spread of farming to those areas.[45]

Just as some historical linguists and archaeologists have suggested when and where the PIE people may have lived originally and how they may have spread, other linguists and archaeologists have suggested culture histories for other language families. For example, the Bantu languages in Africa (spoken by perhaps 100 million people) form a subfamily of the larger Niger-Congo family of languages. Bantu speakers currently live in a wide band across the center of Africa and down the eastern and western sides of southern Africa. All of the Bantu languages presumably derive from people who spoke proto-Bantu. But where was their homeland?

As in the case of proto-Indo-European, different theories have been proposed. But most historical linguists now agree with Joseph Greenberg's suggestion that the origin of Bantu was in what is now the Middle Benue area of eastern Nigeria.[46] The point of origin is presumably where there is the greatest diversity of related languages and *dialects* (varying forms of a language); it is assumed that the place of origin has had the most time for linguistic diversity to develop, compared with an area only recently occupied by a related language. For example, England has more dialect diversity than New Zealand or Australia.

Why were the Bantu able to spread so widely over the last few thousand years? Anthropologists have only begun to guess.[47] Initially, the Bantu probably kept goats and practiced some form of agriculture and thereby were able to spread, displacing hunter-gatherers in the area. As the Bantu speakers expanded, they began to cultivate certain cereal crops and herd sheep and cattle. Around this time, after 1000 B.C., they also began to use and make iron tools, which may have given them significant advantages. In any case, by 1,500 to 2,000 years ago, Bantu speakers had spread throughout central Africa and into the northern reaches of southern Africa. But speakers of non-Bantu languages still live in eastern, southern, and southwestern Africa.

◎ The Processes of Linguistic Divergence

The historical or comparative linguist hopes to do more than record and date linguistic divergence. Just as the physical anthropologist may attempt to develop explanations for human variation, so the linguist investigates the possible causes of linguistic variation. Some of the divergence undoubtedly comes about gradually. When groups of people speaking the same language lose communication with one another because they become separated, either physically or socially, they begin to accumulate small changes in phonology, morphology, and syntax (which occur continuously in any language). These variant forms of language are considered **dialects** when the differences in phonology, morphology, and syntax are not great enough to produce unintelligibility. (Dialects should not be confused with accents, which are merely differences in pronunciation.) Eventually, if the separation continues, the former dialects of the same language will become separate languages; that is, they will become mutually unintelligible, as German and English now are.

Geographic barriers, such as large bodies of water, deserts, and mountains, may separate speakers of what was once the same language, but distance by itself can also produce divergence. For example, if we compare dialects of English in the British Isles, it is clear that the regions farthest away from each other are the most different linguistically (compare the northeast of Scotland and London).[48] In northern India, hundreds of semi-isolated villages and regions developed hundreds of local dialects. Today, the inhabitants of each village understand the dialects of the surrounding villages and, with a little more difficulty, the dialects of the next circle of villages. But slight dialect shifts accumulate village by village, and it seems as if different languages are being spoken at the opposite ends of the region, which are separated by more than a thousand miles.[49]

Even where there is little geographic separation there may still be a great deal of dialect differentiation because of social distance. So, for example, the spread of a linguistic feature may be halted by religious, class, or other social differences that inhibit communication.[50] In the village of Khalapur in northern India, John Gumperz found substantial differences in speech between the Untouchables and other groups. Members of the Untouchables have work contacts with members of other groups but no friendships.[51] Without friendships and the easy communication between friends, dialect differentiation can readily develop.

Whereas isolation brings gradual divergence between speech communities, contact results in greater resemblance. This effect is particularly evident when contact between mutually unintelligible languages introduces borrowed words, which usually name some new item borrowed from the other culture—*tomato, canoe, sushi,* and so on. Bilingual groups within a culture may also introduce foreign words, especially when the mainstream language has no real equivalent. Thus, *salsa* has come into English, and *le weekend* into French.

Conquest and colonization often result in extensive and rapid borrowing, if not linguistic replacement. The Norman conquest of England introduced French as the language of the new aristocracy. It was 300 years before the educated classes began to write in English. During this time the English borrowed words from French and Latin, and the two languages—English and French—became more alike than they would otherwise have been. About 50 percent of the English general vocabulary originated in French. As this example suggests, different social classes may react to language contact differentially. For example, English aristocrats eventually called their meat "pork" and "beef" (derived from the French words), but the people who raised the animals and prepared them for eating continued (at least for a while) to refer to the meat as "pig" and "bull," the original Anglo-Saxon words.

In those 300 years of extensive contact, the grammar of English remained relatively stable. English lost most of its inflections or case endings, but it adopted little of the French grammar. In general, the borrowing of words, particularly free morphemes,[52] is much more common than the borrowing of grammar.[53] As we might expect, borrowing by one language from another can make the borrowing language more different from its *sibling languages* (those derived from a common ancestral language) than it would otherwise be. Partly as a result of the French influence, the English vocabulary looks quite different from the languages to which it is actually most similar in terms of phonology and grammar—German, Dutch, and the Scandinavian languages.

Relationships between Language and Culture

Some attempts to explain the diversity of languages have focused on the possible interactions between language and other aspects of culture. On the one hand, if it can be shown that a culture can affect the structure and content of its language, then it would follow that linguistic diversity derives at least in part from cultural diversity. On the other hand, the direction of influence between culture and language might work in reverse: Linguistic features and structures might affect other aspects of the culture.

Cultural Influences on Language

One way a society's language may reflect its corresponding culture is in **lexical content,** or vocabulary. Which experiences, events, or objects are singled out and given words may be a result of cultural characteristics.

BASIC WORDS FOR COLORS, PLANTS, AND ANIMALS
Early in the 20th century many linguists pointed to the lexical domain (vocabulary) of color words to illustrate the supposed truth that languages vary arbitrarily or without apparent reason. Different languages not only had different numbers of basic color words (from 2 to 12 or so; for example, the words *red, green,* and *blue* in English), but they also, it was thought, had no consistency in the way they classified or divided the colors of the spectrum. But findings from a comparative (cross-linguistic) study contradicted these traditional presumptions about variation in the number and meaning of basic color words. On the basis of their study of at first 20 and later over 100 languages, Brent Berlin and Paul Kay found that languages did not encode color in completely arbitrary ways.[54]

Although different languages do have different numbers of basic color words, most speakers of any language are very likely to point to the same color chips as the best representatives of particular colors. For example, people the world over mean more or less the same color when they are asked to select the best "red." Moreover, there appears to be a nearly universal sequence by which basic color words are added to a language.[55] If a language has just two basic color words, its speakers will always refer to "black" (or dark) hues and "white" (or light) hues. If a language

The word *sushi* has been borrowed in North America to identify a Japanese style of food.

has three basic color words, the third word will nearly always be "red." The next category to appear is either "yellow" or "grue" (green/blue); then different words for green and blue; and so on. To be sure, we usually do not see the process by which basic color words are added to a language. But we can infer the usual sequence because, for example, if a language has a word for "yellow," it will almost always have a word for "red," whereas having a word for "red" does not mean that the language will have a word for "yellow."

What exactly is a *basic* color word? All languages, even the ones with only two basic color terms, have many different ways of expressing how color varies. For example, in English we have words such as turquoise, blue-green, scarlet, crimson, and sky blue. Linguists do not consider these to be basic color words. In English the basic color words are *white, black, red, green, yellow, blue, brown, pink, purple, orange,* and *gray.* One feature of a basic color word is that it consists of a single morph; it cannot include two or more units of meaning. This feature eliminates combinations such as *blue-green* and *sky blue.* A second feature of a basic color word is that the color it represents is not generally included in a higher-order color term. For example, scarlet and crimson are usually considered variants of red, turquoise a variant of blue. A third feature is that basic terms tend to be the first-named words when people are asked for color words. Finally, for a word to be considered a basic color word, many individual speakers of the language have to agree on the central meaning (in the color spectrum) of the word.[56]

Why do different societies (languages) vary in number of basic color terms? Berlin and Kay suggest that the number of basic color terms in a language increases with technological specialization as color is used to decorate and distinguish objects.[57] Cross-linguistic variation in the number of basic color terms does not mean that some languages

make more color distinctions than others. Every language could make a particular distinction by combining words (e.g., "fresh leaf" for green); a language need not have a separate basic term for that color.

There may also be many basic color terms because of a biological factor.[58] Peoples with darker (more pigmented) eyes seem to have more trouble distinguishing colors at the dark (blue-green) end of the spectrum than do peoples with lighter eyes. It might be expected, then, that peoples who live nearer the equator (who tend to have darker eyes, presumably for protection against damaging ultraviolet radiation) would tend to have fewer basic color terms. And they do.[59] Moreover, it seems that both cultural and biological factors are required to account for cross-linguistic variation in the number of basic color terms. Societies tend to have six or more such terms (with separate terms for blue and green) only when they are relatively far from the equator and only when their cultures are more technologically specialized.[60] As we will see in later chapters, technological specialization tends to go with larger communities, more centralized governments, occupational specialization, and more social inequality. Societies with such traits are often referred to in a shorthand way as more "complex," which should not be taken to mean "better."

Echoing Berlin and Kay's finding that basic color terms seem to be added in a more or less universal sequence, Cecil Brown has found what seem to be developmental sequences in other lexical domains. Two such domains are general, or *life-form,* terms for plants and for animals. Life-form terms are higher-order classifications. All languages have lower-order terms for specific plants and animals. For example, English has words such as *oak* and *pine, sparrow,* and *salmon.* English speakers make finer distinctions too— *pin oak* and *white pine, white-throated sparrow,* and *red salmon.* But why in some languages do people have a larger number of general terms such as *tree, bird,* and *fish?* It seems that these general terms show a universal developmental sequence too. That is, general terms seem to be added in a somewhat consistent order. After "plant" comes a term for "tree"; then one for "grerb" (small, green, leafy, nonwoody plant); then "bush" (for plants between tree and grerb in size); then "grass"; then "vine."[61] The life-form terms for animals also seem to be added in sequence; after "animal" comes a term for "fish," then "bird," then "snake," then "wug" (for small creatures other than fish, birds, and snakes—for example, worms and bugs), then "mammal."[62]

More complex societies tend to have a larger number of general, or life-form, terms for plants and animals than do simpler societies, just as they tend to have a larger number of basic color terms. Why? And do all realms or domains of vocabulary increase in size as social complexity increases? If we look at the total vocabulary of a language (as can be counted in a dictionary), more complex societies do have larger vocabularies.[63] But we have to remember that complex societies have many kinds of specialists, and dictionaries will include the terms used by such specialists. If we look instead at the nonspecialist **core vocabulary** of languages, it seems that all languages have a core vocabulary of about the same size.[64] Indeed, although some domains increase in size with social complexity, some remain the same and still others decrease. An example of a smaller vocabulary domain in complex societies is that of specific names for plants. Urban North Americans may know general terms for plants, but they know relatively few names for specific plants. The typical individual in a small-scale society can commonly name 400 to 800 plant species; a typical person in our own and similar societies may be able to name only 40 to 80.[65] The number of life-form terms is larger in societies in which ordinary people know less about particular plants and animals.[66]

The evidence now available strongly supports the idea that the vocabulary of a language reflects the everyday distinctions that are important in the society. Those aspects of environment or culture that are of special importance will receive greater attention in the language.

GRAMMAR Most of the examples we could accumulate would show that a culture influences the names of things visible in its environment. Evidence for cultural influence on the grammatical structure of a language is less extensive. Harry Hoijer draws attention to the verb categories in the language of the Navajo, a traditionally nomadic people. These categories center mainly in the reporting of events, or "eventings," as he calls them. Hoijer notes that in "the reporting of actions and events, and the framing of substantive concepts, Navajo emphasizes movement and specifies the nature, direction, and status of such movement in considerable detail."[67] For example, Navajo has one category for eventings that are in motion and another for eventings that have ceased moving. Hoijer concludes that the emphasis on events in the process of occurring reflects the Navajo's nomadic experience over the centuries, an experience also reflected in their myths and folklore.

A linguistic emphasis on events may or may not be generally characteristic of nomadic peoples; as yet, no one has investigated the matter cross-culturally or comparatively. But there are indications that systematic comparative research would turn up other grammatical features that are related to cultural characteristics. For example, many languages lack the possessive transitive verb we write as "have," as in "I have." Instead, the language may say something such as "it is to me." A cross-cultural study has suggested that a language may develop the verb "have" after the speakers of that language have developed a system of private property or personal ownership of resources.[68] As we shall see later, in the chapter on economic systems, the concept of private property is far from universal and tends to occur only in complex societies with social inequality. In contrast, many societies have some kind of communal ownership, by kin groups or communities. How people talk about owning seems to reflect how they own; societies that lack a concept of private property also lack the verb "have."

Linguistic Influences on Culture: The Sapir–Whorf Hypothesis

There is general agreement that culture influences language. But there is less agreement about the opposite possibility—that language influences other aspects of culture. Edward Sapir and Benjamin Lee Whorf suggested that language is a force in its own right, that it affects how individuals in a society perceive and conceive reality. This suggestion is known as the *Sapir–Whorf hypothesis.*[69] In comparing the English language with Hopi, Whorf pointed out that English-language categories convey discreteness with regard to time and space, but Hopi does not. English has a discrete past, present, and future, and things occur at a definite time. Hopi expresses things with more of an idea of ongoing processes without time being apportioned into fixed segments. According to Ronald Wardhaugh, Whorf believed that these language differences lead Hopi and English speakers to see the world differently.[70]

As intriguing as that idea is, the relevant evidence is mixed. Linguists today do not generally accept the view that language coerces thought, but some suspect that particular features of language may facilitate certain patterns of thought.[71] The influences may be clearest in poetry and metaphors, where words and phrases are applied to other than their ordinary subjects, as in "all the world's a stage."[72] One of the serious problems in testing the Sapir–Whorf hypothesis is that researchers need to figure out how to separate the effects of other aspects of culture from the effects of language.

One approach that may reveal the direction of influence between language and culture is to study how children in different cultures (speaking different languages) develop concepts as they grow up. If language influences the formation of a particular concept, we might expect that children will acquire that concept earlier in societies where the languages emphasize that concept. For example, some languages make more of gender differences than others. Do children develop gender identity earlier when their language emphasizes gender? (Very young girls and boys seem to believe they can switch genders by dressing in opposite-sex clothes, suggesting that they have not yet developed a stable sense that they are unchangeably girls or boys.) Alexander Guiora and his colleagues have studied children growing up in Hebrew-speaking homes (Israel), English-speaking homes (the United States), and Finnish-speaking homes (Finland). Hebrew has the most gender emphasis of the three languages; all nouns are either masculine or feminine, and even second-person and plural pronouns are differentiated by gender. English emphasizes gender less, differentiating by gender only in the third-person singular (*she* or *her* or *hers, he* or *him* or *his*). Finnish emphasizes gender the least; although some words, such as *man* and *woman*, convey gender, differentiation by gender is otherwise lacking in the language. Consistent with the idea that language may influence thought, Hebrew-speaking children acquire the concept of stable gender identity the earliest on the average, Finnish-speaking children the latest.[73]

Another approach is to predict from language differences how people may be expected to perform in experiments. Comparing the Yucatec Mayan language and English, John Lucy predicted that English speakers might recall the *number* of things presented more than Yucatec Mayan speakers. For most classes of nouns, English requires a linguistic way of indicating whether something is singular or plural. You cannot say "I have dog" (no indication of number), but must say "I have a dog," "I have dogs," or "I have one (two, three, several, many) dogs." Yucatec Maya, like English, can indicate a plural, but allows the noun to be neutral with regard to number. For example, the translated phrase there-is-dog-over-there (*yàan pèek té'elo'*) can be left ambiguous about whether there is one or more than one dog. In English, the same ambiguity would occur in the sentence "I saw deer over there," but English does not often allow ambiguity for animate or inanimate nouns.[74] In a number of experiments, Yucatec Mayan and American English speakers were equally likely to recall the objects in a picture, but they differed in how often they described the number of a particular object in the picture. Yucatec Mayan speakers did so less often, consistent with their language's lack of insistence on indicating number.[75] So the salience of number in the experiments was probably a consequence of how the languages differ. Of course, it is possible that salience of number is created by some other cultural feature, such as dependence on money in the economy.

The Ethnography of Speaking

Traditionally, linguists concentrated on trying to understand the structure of a language, the usually unconscious rules that predict how the people of a given society typically speak. In recent years, many linguists have begun to study how people in a society vary in how they speak. This type of linguistic study, *sociolinguistics,* is concerned with the *ethnography of speaking*—that is, with cultural and subcultural patterns of speech variation in different social contexts.[76] The sociolinguist might ask, for example, what kinds of things one talks about in casual conversation with a stranger. A foreigner may know English vocabulary and grammar well but may not know that one typically chats with a stranger about the weather or where one comes from, and not about what one ate that day or how much money one earns. A foreigner may be familiar with much of the culture of a North American city, but if that person divulges the real state of his or her health and feelings to the first person who says, "How are you?" he or she has much to learn about "small talk" in North American English.

Similarly, North Americans tend to get confused in societies where greetings are quite different from ours. People in some other societies may ask as a greeting, "Where are you going?" or "What are you cooking?" Some Americans may think such questions are rude; others may try to answer in excruciating detail, not realizing that only vague answers are expected, just as we don't really expect a detailed answer when we ask people how they are.

Social Status and Speech

That a foreign speaker of a language may know little about the small talk of that language is but one example of the sociolinguistic principle that what we say and how we say it are not wholly predictable by the rules of our language. Who we are socially and whom we are talking to may greatly affect what we say and how we say it.

In a study interviewing children in a New England town, John Fischer noted that in formal interviews, children were likely to pronounce the ending in words such as *singing* and *fishing,* but in informal conversations they said "*singin'*" and "*fishin'*." Moreover, he noted that the phenomenon also appeared to be related to social class; children from higher-status families were less likely to drop the ending than were children from lower-status families. Subsequent studies in English-speaking areas tend to support Fischer's observations with regard to this speech pattern. Other patterns are observed as well. For example, in Norwich, England, lower classes tend to drop the *h* in words such as *hammer,* but in all classes the pattern of dropping the *h* increases in casual situations.[77]

Research has shown that English people from higher-class backgrounds tend to have more *homogeneous* speech, conforming more to what is considered standard English (the type of speech heard on television or radio), whereas people from lower-class backgrounds have very *heterogeneous* speech, varying in their speaking according to the local or dialect area they come from.[78] In some societies, social status differences may be associated with more marked differentiation of words. Clifford Geertz, in his study of Javanese, showed that the vocabularies of the three rather sharply divided groups in Javanese society—peasants, townspeople, and aristocrats—reflect their separate positions. For example, the concept *now* is expressed differently in these three groups. A peasant will use *saiki* (considered the lowest

Strangers shake hands when they meet; friends touch each other more warmly. How we speak to others also differs according to the degree of friendship.

and roughest form of the word); a townsman will use *saniki* (considered somewhat more elegant); and an aristocrat will use *samenika* (the most elegant form).[79]

Status relationships between people can also influence the way they speak to each other. Terms of address are a good example. In English, forms of address are relatively simple. One is called either by a first name or by a title (such as *Doctor, Professor, Ms.,* or *Mister*) followed by a last name. A study by Roger Brown and Marguerite Ford indicates that terms of address in English vary with the nature of the relationship between the speakers.[80] The reciprocal use of first names generally signifies an informal or intimate relationship between two persons. A title and last name used reciprocally usually indicates a more formal or businesslike relationship between individuals who are roughly equal in status. Nonreciprocal use of first names and titles in English is reserved for speakers who recognize a marked difference in status between them. This status difference can be a function of age, as when a child refers to her mother's friend as Mrs. Miller and is in turn addressed as Sally, or can be due to occupational hierarchy, as when a person refers to his boss as Ms. Ramirez and is in turn addressed as Joe. In some cases, generally between boys and between men, the use of the last name alone represents a middle ground between the intimate and the formal usages.

Gender Differences in Speech

In many societies the speech of men differs from the speech of women. The variation can be slight, as in our own society, or more extreme, as with the Carib Indians in the Lesser Antilles of the West Indies, among whom women and men use different words for the same concepts.[81] In Japan, males and females use entirely different words for numerous concepts (e.g., the male word for water is *mizu*, the female version is *ohiya*), and females often add the polite prefix *o-* (females will tend to say *ohasi* for chopsticks; males will tend to say *hasi*).[82] In the United States and other Western societies, there are differences in the speech of females and males, but they are not as dramatic as in the Carib and Japanese cases. For example, earlier we noted the tendency for the *g* to be dropped in words such as *singing* when the situation is informal and when the social class background is lower. But there is also a gender difference. Women are more likely than men to keep the *g* sound and less likely than men to drop the *h* in words such as *happy*. In Montreal, women are less likely than men to drop the *l* in phrases such as *il fait* ("he does") or in the idiom *il y a* ("there is/are").[83]

Gender differences occur in intonation and in phrasing of sentences as well. Robin Lakoff found that in English women tend to answer questions with sentences that have rising inflections at the end instead of a falling intonation associated with a firm answer. Women also tend to add questions to statements, such as "They caught the robber last week, didn't they?"[84]

One explanation for the gender differences, particularly with regard to pronunciation, is that women in many societies may be more concerned than men with being "correct."[85] (Not in the linguist's sense; it is important to remember that linguists do not consider one form of speech more correct than another, just as they do not consider one dialect superior to another. All are equally capable of expressing a complex variety of thoughts and ideas.) In societies with social classes, what is considered more correct by the average person may be what is associated with the upper class. In other societies, what is older may be considered more correct. For example, in the Native American language of Koasati, which used to be spoken in Louisiana, males and females used different endings in certain verbs. The differences seemed to be disappearing in the 1930s, when the research on Koasati was done. Young girls had begun to use the male forms and only older women still used the female forms. Koasati men said that the women's speech was a "better" form of speech.[86] Gender differences in speech may parallel some of the gender differences noted in other social behavior (as we will see in the chapter on sex, gender, and culture): Girls are more likely than boys to behave in ways that are acceptable to adults.

There are not enough studies to know just how common it is for women to exhibit more linguistic "correctness." We do know of some instances where it is not the case. For example, in a community in Madagascar where people speak Merina, a dialect of Malagasy, it is considered socially correct to avoid explicit directives. So instead of directly ordering an action, a Merina speaker will try to say it indirectly. Also, it is polite to avoid negative remarks, such as expressing anger toward someone. In this community, however, it is women, not men, who often break the rules; women speak more directly and express anger more often.[87] This difference may be related to the fact that women are more involved in buying and selling in the marketplace.

Some researchers have questioned whether it is correctness that is at issue. Rather, we may be dealing in these examples with unequal prestige and power. Women may try to raise their status by conforming more to standard speech. When they answer a question with a rising inflection, they may be expressing uncertainty and a lack of power. Alternatively, perhaps women want to be more cooperative conversationalists. Speaking in a more "standard" fashion is consistent with being more likely to be understood by others. Answering a question with another question leads to continued conversation.[88]

Men and women typically differ in what they talk about, or do not talk about. Deborah Tannen offers some examples. When women hear about someone else's troubles they are likely to express understanding of the other's feelings; in contrast, men are likely to offer solutions. Men tend not to ask for directions; women do. Women tend to talk a lot in private settings; men talk more in public settings. These and other differences can cause friction and misunderstanding between the genders. When women express their troubles and men offer solutions, women feel that their feelings are not understood; men are frustrated that the women do not take their solutions seriously. Men may prefer to sit at home quietly and feel put upon to have to engage in conversation; women feel slighted when men avoid extended conversations with them. Why these differences? Tannen suggests that misunderstanding between men and women arises because boys

NEW PERSPECTIVES ON GENDER

Does the English Language Promote Sexist Thinking?

Does English promote sexist thinking, or does the language merely reflect gender inequalities that already exist? For those who wish to promote gender equality, the answers to these questions are important because if language influences thought (along the lines put forward by Edward Sapir and Benjamin Whorf), then linguistic change will be necessary in order to bring about change in the culture of gender. If it is the other way around, that is, if language reflects inequality, then social, economic, and political changes have to come before we can expect substantial linguistic change to occur.

Leaving aside for the moment which changes first, how does English represent gender inequity? Consider the following written by Benjamin Lee Whorf: "Speech is the best show man puts on. . . . Language helps man in his thinking." While *man* in English technically refers to all humans and *his* technically refers to the thinking of a single person of either gender, the frequent use of such words could convey the idea that males are more important. Similarly, do the words *chairman, policeman, businessman,* and *salesman* convey that males are supposed to have those jobs? What is conveyed when there are two words for the two genders, as in *actor* and *actress* and *hero* and *heroine*? Usually the base word is male and the suffix is added for the female form. Does the suffix convey that the female form is an afterthought or less important?

It is not just the structure of the language that may convey gender inequality. How come in the pairs *sir/madam, master/mistress, wizard/witch,* the female version has acquired negative connotations? Men might be called animal names, such as wolves, rats, or pigs. But more animal images seem to be applied to women. They can be *chicks, henpeckers, cows, dogs, bitches, kittens,* or *birds.* Coming back to the original questions, how would we know whether language promotes sexism or sexism influences language? One way to find out is to do experimental studies, such as the one conducted by Fatemeh Khosroshashi. Some individuals were asked to read texts written with *man* and *he* and *his* referring to people; others were asked to read texts with more gender-neutral phrasing. Individuals were subsequently asked to draw pictures to go with the texts. The ones who read the texts with more male terminology drew more accompanying pictures of men, strongly suggesting that the use of the terms *man, he,* and *his* conveyed

the thought that the people in the text were men, not women, *because* of the vocabulary used. We need more such studies to help address the intellectual question of which comes first, linguistic or nonlinguistic culture.

It would be important to know whether societies with more "male-oriented" language are more male-dominated than are societies without such distinctions. We don't have that kind of comparative research yet. But one study by Robert and Ruth Munroe looked at the *proportion* of female and male nouns in ten languages (six Indo-European, four other than Indo-European) in which nouns have gender. Although none of those societies could be described as having a female bias, the Munroes were able to ask whether those societies with less male bias in social customs (e.g., all children are equally likely to inherit property) have a higher proportion of female nouns than male nouns (more female than male nouns). The answer appears to be yes. Although this study does not reveal what came first, studies like it are important if we want to discover how language differences may be related to other aspects of culture. If male-oriented languages are not related to male dominance, then it is not likely that sexist thinking is a consequence of language.

On the assumption that language may influence thought, many are pushing for changes in the way English is used, if not structured. It is hard to get English speakers to adopt a gender-neutral singular pronoun to replace *he.* Attempts to do so go back to the 18th century and include suggestions of *tey, thon, per,* and *s/he.* Although these efforts have not succeeded, the way English is written and spoken has begun to change. Words or phrases such as *chair* (or *chairperson*), *police officer,* and *sales assistant* (*salesperson*) have begun to replace their former *man* versions. If Whorf were writing his sentence now, it probably would be written: "Speech is the best show humans put on. . . . Language helps people think."

Sources: Janet Holmes, *An Introduction to Sociolinguistics,* 2nd ed. (London: Longman, 2001), pp. 305–16; Suzanne Romaine, *Language in Society: An Introduction to Sociolinguistics* (Oxford: Oxford University Press, 1994), pp. 105–16; Richard Wardhaugh, *An Introduction to Sociolinguistics,* 4th ed. (Oxford: Blackwell, 2002), p. 317; Robin Lakoff, "Language and Woman's Place," *Language in Society,* 2 (1973): 45–80; Fatemeh Khosroshashi, "Penguins Don't Care, but Women Do: A Social Identity Analysis of a Whorfian Problem," *Language in Society,* 18 (1989): 505–25; Robert L. Munroe and Ruth H. Munroe, "A Cross-Cultural Study of Sex, Gender and Social Structure," *Ethnology,* 8 (1969): 206–11.

and girls grow up in somewhat different cultures. Girls typically play in small groups, talk frequently, and are intimate with others. Boys more often play in large groups in which jockeying for status and attention are more of a concern. Higher-status individuals give directions and solutions; they

do not seek directions or solutions. So asking for directions is like acknowledging lower status. But large play groups resemble public settings, and so later in life men feel more comfortable speaking in public. Women, in contrast, are more comfortable speaking in small, intimate groups.[89]

Multilingualism and Codeswitching

For many people the ability to speak more than one language is a normal part of life. One language may be spoken at home and another in school, the marketplace, or government. Or more than one language may be spoken at home if family members come from different cultures and still other languages are spoken outside. Some countries explicitly promote multilingualism. For example, Singapore has four official languages—English, Mandarin (one of the Chinese languages), Tamil, and Malay. English is stressed for trade, Mandarin as the language of communication with most of China, Malay as the language of the general region, and Tamil as the language of an important ethnic group. Moreover, most of the population speaks Hokkien, another Chinese language. Education is likely to be in English and Mandarin.[90]

What happens when people who know two or more languages communicate with each other? Very often you find

MIGRANTS AND IMMIGRANTS

Why Are "Mother Tongues" Retained, and For How Long?

The longer an immigrant group lives in another country, the more they incorporate the culture of their new home. At some point the original language is no longer even partially understood. Consider people who originally came from Wales, the region west of England in Great Britain. In that region, until about 100 years ago, most people spoke the Welsh language, which belongs to the Celtic subfamily of Indo-European along with Irish and Scottish Gaelic and Breton. (Celtic is a different subfamily from the one English belongs to, which is Germanic.) In 1729, the Welsh in Philadelphia established the Welsh Society, the oldest ethnic organization in the United States. Many of the members, if not all, spoke Welsh in addition to English at that time. But by the 20th century, hardly any of their descendants did.

If immigrant groups eventually lose their "mother tongues" in many if not most countries, this doesn't mean that the process occurs at the same speed in every group. Why is that? Why do some immigrant groups lose their language faster than others? Is it because they do not live in tightly knit ethnic enclaves? Or because they marry outside their ethnic group? Or because they do not have traditional festivals or celebrations marking their separate identity? A comparative study by Robert Schrauf discovered the most likely reasons. First, Schrauf assessed the degree to which immigrant groups coming to North America retained their native language over time. The greatest retention was defined as when the third generation (the grandchildren of immigrants) continued to use the native language. Examples were Chicanos, Puerto Ricans, Cubans, and Haitians. On the other hand, in some groups the third generation had no comprehension of the native language except for isolated words. Even the second generation (the children of immigrants) mostly spoke and understood only English. Examples were Italians, Armenians, and Basques. Chinese and Koreans were in the middle, with some evidence that the third generation understands a little of the native language. Schrauf then measured seven social factors that might explain longer versus shorter retention of the mother tongue. He looked at whether the

group lived in tightly knit communities, retained religious rituals from the old country, had separate schools and special festivals, visited their homeland, did not intermarry, or worked with others of their ethnic group.

Schrauf used data on 11 North American ethnic groups drawn from the HRAF Collection of Ethnography. The major advantage of the HRAF materials is that ethnographies written for more general purposes, or for purposes other than linguistic ones, contain a wealth of information concerning sociocultural features of ethnic groups that may be tested for their possible effects on language retention and loss.

We might suspect that all of the factors measured by Schrauf would lead people to retain their native language (and presumably other native cultural patterns). But not all do, apparently. Only living in tightly knit communities and retaining religious rituals strongly predict retention of the mother tongue in the home into the third generation. Why? Possibly because living in an ethnic community and religious ritual are experienced early in life: conditions associated with early socialization might have more lasting effects than conditions experienced later in life, such as schooling, visits to the homeland, marriage, and work. Participation in celebrations and festivals is probably important too, but it does not have quite as strong an effect, perhaps because celebrations and festivals are not everyday experiences.

As always, in the case of research, this study raises questions for future research. Would the same effects be found outside of North America? Would the results be the same if we looked also at other immigrant groups in North America? Do some immigrant groups live in close-knit communities because of discrimination or choice? If choice, are some groups more interested in assimilating than others? And if so, why?

Sources: D. Douglas Caulkins, "Welsh," in David Levinson and Melvin Ember, eds., *American Immigrant Cultures: Builders of a Nation,* 2 vols. (New York: Macmillan Reference USA, 1997), vol. 2, pp. 935–41; Robert W. Schrauf, "Mother Tongue Maintenance Among North American Ethnic Groups," *Cross-Cultural Research,* 33 (1999): 175–92.

them **codeswitching,** using more than one language in the course of conversing.[91] Switching can occur in the middle of a Spanish-English bilingual sentence, as in "No van a bring it up in the meeting" ("They are not going to bring it up in the meeting").[92] Or switching can occur when the topic or situation changes, such as from social talk to school-work. Why do speakers of more than one language sometimes switch? Although speakers switch for a lot of different reasons, what is clear is that the switching is not a haphazard mix that comes from laziness or ignorance. Codeswitching involves a great deal of knowledge of two or more languages and an awareness of what is considered appropriate or inappropriate in the community. For example, in the Puerto Rican community in New York City, codeswitching within the same sentence seems to be common in speech among friends, but if a stranger who looks like a Spanish speaker approaches, the language will shift entirely to Spanish.[93] (We discuss interethnic communication more in the chapter on applied and practicing anthropology.)

Although each community may have its own rules for codeswitching, variations in practice may need to be understood in terms of the broader political and historical context. For example, German speakers in Transylvania, where Romanian is the national language, hardly ever codeswitch to Romanian. Perhaps the reason is that, before the end of World War II, German speakers were a privileged economic group who looked down upon landless Romanians and their language. Under socialism, the German speakers lost their economic privilege, but they continued to speak German among themselves. In the rare cases that Romanian is used among German speakers, it tends to be associated with low-status speech, such as singing bawdy songs. The opposite situation occurred in a Hungarian region of German-speaking Austria. The people of this agricultural region, annexed to Austria in 1921, were fairly poor peasant farmers. After World War II, business expansion began to attract labor from rural areas, so many Hungarians eagerly moved into jobs in industry. German was seen by the younger generations as a symbol of higher status and upward mobility; not surprisingly, codeswitching between Hungarian and German became part of their conversations. Indeed, in the third generation, German has become the language of choice, except when speaking to the oldest Hungarians. The Hungarian–Austrian situation is fairly common in many parts of the world, where the language of the politically dominant group ends up being "linguistically dominant."[94]

Writing and Literacy

Most of us have come to depend on writing for so many things that it is hard to imagine a world without it. Yet humans spent most of their history on earth without written language and many, if not most, important human achievements predate written language. Parents and other teachers passed on their knowledge by oral instruction and demonstration. Stories, legends, and myths abounded—the stuff we call oral literature—even in the absence of writing. This is not to say that writing is not important. Far more information and far more literature can be preserved for a longer period of time with a

Children do not need help learning the language spoken in their homes. However, reading and writing cannot usually be learned without instruction. Nowadays children in most cultures are expected to learn to read and write in school. These Trobriand children from Papua New Guinea are allowed to wear their traditional clothes to school once a week.

writing system. The earliest writing systems are only about 6,000 years old and are associated with early cities and states. Early writing is associated with systematic record-keeping—keeping of ledgers for inventorying goods and transactions. In early times probably only the elite could read and write—indeed it is only recently that universal literacy (the ability to read and write) has become the goal of most countries. But in most countries the goal of universal literacy is far from achieved. Even in countries with universal education the quality of education and the length of education varies considerably between subcultures and genders. Just as some ways of speaking are considered superior to others, a high degree of literacy is usually considered superior to illiteracy.[95] But literacy in what language or languages? As we discussed in the box on endangered languages, recent efforts to preserve languages have encouraged writing of texts in languages that were only spoken previously. Obviously, there will be few texts in those languages; other languages have vast numbers of written texts. As more and more accumulated knowledge is written and stored in books, journals, and databases, attainment of literacy in those written languages will be increasingly critical to success. And texts do not only convey practical knowledge—they may also convey attitudes, beliefs, and values that are characteristic of the culture associated with the language in which the texts are written.

Summary

1. The essential function language plays in all societies is that of communication. Although human communication is not limited to spoken language, such language is

of overriding importance because it is the primary vehicle through which culture is shared and transmitted.

2. Systems of communication are not unique to humans. Other animal species communicate in a variety of ways—by sound, odor, body movement, and so forth. The ability of chimpanzees and gorillas to learn and use sign language suggests that symbolic communication is not unique to humans. Still, human language is distinctive as a communication system in that its spoken and symbolic nature permits an infinite number of combinations and recombinations of meaning.

3. Nonverbal human communication includes posture, mannerisms, body movement, facial expressions, and signs and gestures. Nonverbal human communication also includes tone of voice, accent, nonword sounds, and all the optional vocal features that communicate meaning apart from the language itself.

4. Descriptive (or structural) linguists try to discover the rules of phonology (the patterning of sounds), morphology (the patterning of sound sequences and words), and syntax (the patterning of phrases and sentences) that predict how most speakers of a language talk.

5. By comparative analysis of cognates and grammar, historical linguists test the notion that certain languages derive from a common ancestral language, or protolanguage. The goals are to reconstruct the features of the protolanguage, to hypothesize how the offspring languages separated from the protolanguage or from each other, and to establish the approximate dates of such separations.

6. When two groups of people speaking the same language lose communication with each other because they become separated either physically or socially, they begin to accumulate small changes in phonology, morphology, and syntax. If the separation continues, the two former dialects of the same language will eventually become separate languages—that is, they will become mutually unintelligible.

7. Whereas isolation brings about divergence between speech communities, contact results in greater resemblance. This effect is particularly evident when contact between mutually unintelligible languages introduces borrowed words, most of which name some new item borrowed from the other culture.

8. Some attempts to explain the diversity of languages have focused on the possible interaction between language and other aspects of culture. On the one hand, if it can be shown that a culture can affect the structure and content of its language, then it would follow that linguistic diversity derives at least in part from cultural diversity. On the other hand, the direction of influence between culture and language might work in reverse; the linguistic structures might affect other aspects of the culture.

9. In recent years, some linguists have begun to study variations in how people actually use language when speaking. This type of linguistic study, called sociolinguistics, is concerned with the ethnography of speaking—that is, with cultural and subcultural patterns of speaking in different social contexts.

10. In bilingual or multilingual populations, codeswitching (using more than one language in the course of conversing) has become increasingly common.

11. Written language dates back only about 6,000 years, but writing and written records have become increasingly important; literacy is now a major goal of most countries.

⊚ Glossary Terms

accent	262	morpheme	269
codeswitching	280	morphology	267
cognates	271	paralanguage	262
core vocabulary	274	phones	267
dialects	273	phoneme	267
historical linguistics	270	phonology	267
kinesics	262	protolanguage	271
lexical content	273	syntax	267
lexicon	269	symbolic communication	263
morph	269		

⊚ Critical Questions

1. Why might natural selection have favored the development of true language in humans but not in apes?

2. Would the world be better off with many different languages spoken or with just one universal language? Why do you think so?

3. Discuss some new behavior or way of thinking that led people to adopt or invent new vocabulary or some new pattern of speech.

⊚ Research Navigator

1. Using ContentSelect (Anthropology) find an article on gender differences in children's speech in Japan. Summarize some of the differences in children's behavior as well as in speech.

2. Using Link Library for Anthropology look for Linguistics sites. Explore a site on teaching and preserving indigenous languages.

⊚ Discovering Anthropology: Researchers at Work

Read the chapter by Jane H. Hill, "Do Apes Have Language?" in *Discovering Anthropology* and answer the following questions.

1. Jane Hill raises the question of whether apes have language. Briefly, what is her answer to the question?

2. Chimpanzees have learned signs from American Sign Language but they have not been able to learn to speak words. Why not?

domestication in the Near East. Lewis Binford and Kent Flannery suggested that some change, not necessarily environmental, in external circumstances must have induced or favored the changeover to food production.[44] As Flannery pointed out, there is no evidence of a great economic incentive for hunter-gatherers to become food producers. In fact, as we have seen, some contemporary hunter-gatherers may actually obtain adequate nutrition with far less work than many agriculturalists.

Binford and Flannery thought that the incentive to domesticate animals and plants may have been a desire to reproduce what was wildly abundant in the most bountiful or optimum hunting-gathering areas. Because of population growth in the optimum areas, people might have moved to surrounding areas containing fewer wild resources. It would have been in those marginal areas that people turned to food production in order to reproduce what they used to have.

The Binford-Flannery model seems to fit the archaeological record in the Levant, the southwestern part of the Fertile Crescent, where population increase did precede the first signs of domestication.[45] But as Flannery admitted, in some regions, such as southwestern Iran, the optimum hunting-gathering areas do not show population increase before the emergence of domestication.[46]

The Binford-Flannery model focuses on population pressure in a small area as the incentive to turn to food production. Mark Cohen theorized that it was population pressure on a global scale that explains why so many of the world's peoples adopted agriculture within the span of a few thousand years.[47] He argued that hunter-gatherers all over the world gradually increased in population, so that by about 10,000 years ago the world was more or less filled with food collectors. Thus, people could no longer relieve population pressure by moving to uninhabited areas. To support their

MIGRANTS AND IMMIGRANTS

Food on the Move

People in North America get most of their food from stores. Where the food comes from originally—where it was first grown or raised—is unknown to most people. Partly this is because relatively few are directly involved in food-getting (less than 2 percent of the workers in the United States). Even when you count all the activities related to food-getting, such as marketing and transportation, only 14 percent of U.S. workers have anything to do with the production and distribution of food. But nowadays many of the foods we buy in markets—tacos, salsa, bagels, pasta, pizza, sausage, soy sauce, and teriyaki—have become mainstream "North American" food. Where did these foods come from? Originally they were eaten only by ethnic and immigrant minorities who came to the United States and Canada. Some, but not all, of their foods caught on and became widely consumed. They became, in short, as "American" as apple pie.

The ingredients in many of these food items resulted from previous movements of people even further back in time. Consider the ingredients in pizza, a favorite food now for many of us. The dough is made from wheat flour, which was first grown in the Middle East, perhaps as much as 10,000 years ago. How do anthropologists know that? Archaeologists have discovered wheat kernels that old in Middle Eastern sites, and they have found flat stones and stone rolling pins from that time that we know were used to grind kernels into flour (we can tell from microscopic analysis of the residue on the stone). What about other ingredients that may be found in pizza? Cheese was first made in the Middle East too, at least 5,000 years ago (we have writings from that time that mention cheese). Tomatoes were first grown in South America, probably several thousand years ago. They got to Italy, the birthplace of the tomato pie (which became transformed into pizza), less than 200 years ago. Just 100 years ago, tomatoes (the key ingredient in pizza for some) were so new in eastern Europe that people were afraid to eat them because their leaves are poisonous to humans and some other animals. Another food we associate with Italian cuisine, spaghetti-type noodles, came to Italy (from China) less than 500 years ago. So the major ingredients of pizza, just like round-noodle *pasta*, are all not native to Italy.

The amazing thing about foods is that they so often travel far and wide, generally carried by the people who like to eat them. And some of our foods, when alive, also travel widely. For example, the bluefin tuna (which can weigh more than a thousand pounds) swims thousands of miles from feeding to breeding grounds in the North Atlantic, Mediterranean, and Caribbean. This largest of all existing fishes is being hunted into extinction because its meat is so prized for what the Japanese call *sushi*, a kind of food that has spread from Japan throughout the world.

Sources: Michelle Diament, "Diversifying Their Crops: Agriculture schools, focusing on job prospects, reach out to potential students from cities and suburbs," *The Chronicle of Higher Education,* May 6, 2005, pp. A32–34; Andrew C. Revkin, "Tracking the Imperiled Bluefin From Ocean to Sushi Platter," *The New York Times,* May 3, 2005, pp. F1, F4.

increasing populations, they would have had to exploit a broader range of less desirable wild foods; that is, they would have had to switch to broad-spectrum collecting, or they would have had to increase the yields of the most desirable wild plants by weeding, protecting them from animal pests, and perhaps deliberately planting the most productive among them. Cohen suggested that people might have tried a variety of these strategies to support themselves but would generally have ended up depending on cultivation because that would have been the most efficient way to allow more people to live in one place.

Recently, some archaeologists have returned to the idea that climatic change played a role in the emergence of agriculture. It seems clear from the evidence now available that the climate of the Near East about 13,000 to 12,000 years ago became more seasonal; the summers got hotter and drier and the winters became colder. These climatic changes may have favored the emergence of annual species of grain that archaeologically we see proliferating in many areas of the Near East.[48] Some food collectors intensively exploited the seasonal grains, developing an elaborate technology for storing and processing the grains and giving up their previous nomadic existence to do so. The transition to agriculture may have occurred when sedentary food collection no longer provided sufficient resources for the population. This change could have happened for a number of reasons. First, sedentarization itself may have led to shortages of resources, either because population increased with sedentarization[49] or because people in permanent villages depleted the local wild resources nearby.[50] Second, climate change may have reduced the available stands of wild grain. In at least one area of the Near East, the onset of drier and cooler weather may have led food collectors to try to cultivate their food supplies.[51] Change to a more seasonal climate might also have led to a shortage of certain nutrients for food collectors. In the dry seasons certain nutrients would have been less available. For example, grazing animals become lean when grasses are not plentiful, and so meat from hunting would have been in short supply in the dry seasons. Although it may seem surprising, some recent hunter-gatherers have starved when they had to rely on lean meat. If they could have somehow increased their carbohydrate or fat intake, they might have been more likely to get through the periods of lean game.[52] So it is possible that some wild-food collectors in the past thought of planting crops to get them through the dry seasons when hunting, fishing, and gathering did not provide enough carbohydrates and fat for them to avoid starvation.

⊚ The Spread and Intensification of Food Production

Whatever the reasons for the switch to food production, we still need to explain why food production has supplanted food collection as the primary mode of subsistence. We cannot assume that collectors would automatically adopt production as a superior way of life once they understood the process of domestication. After all, as we have noted, domestication may entail more work and provide less security than the food-collecting way of life.

The spread of agriculture may be linked to the need for territorial expansion. As a sedentary, food-producing population grew, it may have been forced to expand into new territory. Some of this territory may have been vacant, but much of it was probably already occupied by food collectors. Although food production is not necessarily easier than collection, it is generally more productive per unit of land. Greater productivity enables more people to be supported in a given territory. In the competition for land between the faster-expanding food producers and the food collectors, the food producers may have had a significant advantage: They had more people in a given area. Thus, the foraging groups may have been more likely to lose out in the competition for land. Some groups may have adopted cultivation, abandoning the foraging way of life in order to survive. Other groups, continuing as food collectors, may have been forced to retreat into areas not desired by the cultivators. Today, as we have seen, the small number of remaining food collectors inhabit areas not particularly suitable for cultivation—dry lands, dense tropical forests, and polar regions.

Just as prior population growth might account for the origins of domestication, so at later periods further population growth and ensuing pressure on resources might at least partly explain the transformation of horticultural systems into intensive agricultural systems. Ester Boserup suggested that intensification of agriculture, with a consequent increase in yield per acre, is not likely to develop naturally out of horticulture because intensification requires much more work.[53] She argued that people will be willing to intensify their labor only if they have to. Where emigration is not feasible, the prime mover behind intensification may be prior population growth. The need to pay taxes or tribute to a political authority may also stimulate intensification.

Boserup's argument about intensification is widely accepted. However, her assumption that more work is required with intensive agriculture has recently been questioned. Comparing horticultural (swidden or shifting) rice production with rice produced on permanent fields using irrigation, Robert Hunt found that *less,* not more, labor is required with irrigation.[54] Still, population increase may generally provide the impetus to intensify production in order to increase yields to support the additional people.

Intensive agriculture has not yet spread to every part of the world. Horticulture continues to be practiced in certain tropical regions, and there still are some pastoralists and food collectors. Some environments may make it somewhat more difficult to adopt certain subsistence practices. For example, intensive agriculture cannot supplant horticulture in some tropical environments without tremendous investments in chemical fertilizers and pesticides, not to mention the additional labor required.[55] And enormous amounts of water may be required to make agriculturalists out of foragers and pastoralists who now exploit semiarid environments. However, difficulty is not impossibility. Anna Roosevelt points out that although horticulture was a common food-getting strategy in Amazonia in recent times, archaeological evidence indicates that there were complex societies practicing intensive agriculture on raised, drained fields in the past.[56] The physical environment does not completely control what can be done with it.

◎ Summary

1. Food collection or foraging—hunting, gathering, and fishing—depends on wild plants and animals and is the oldest human food-getting technology. There is a lot of variation with regard to which food-getting activity is most important to the society. Recent foragers depended most on fishing, followed by gathering and hunting. Today, only a small number of societies depend largely on food collection and they tend to inhabit marginal environments.

2. Food collectors can be found in various physical habitats. Most food collectors are nomadic, and population density is low. Usually, the small bands consist of related families, with the division of labor along age and gender lines only. Personal possessions are limited, individuals' land rights are seldom recognized, and people are not differentiated by class.

3. Beginning about 10,000 years ago, certain peoples in widely separated geographic locations began to make the revolutionary changeover to food production—the cultivation and raising of plants and animals. Over the centuries, food production began to supplant food collection as the predominant mode of subsistence.

4. Horticulturalists farm with relatively simple tools and methods and do not cultivate fields permanently. Their food supply is sufficient to support larger, more densely populated communities than can be fed by food collection. Their way of life is sedentary, although communities may move after some years to farm a new series of plots.

5. Intensive agriculture is characterized by techniques such as fertilization and irrigation that allow fields to be cultivated permanently. In contrast with horticultural societies, intensive agriculturalists are more likely to have towns and cities, a high degree of craft specialization, large differences in wealth and power, and more complex political organization. They are also more likely to face food shortages. In the modern world, intensive agriculture is increasingly mechanized and geared to production for a market.

6. Pastoralism is a subsistence technology involving principally the raising of large herds of animals. It is generally found in low-rainfall areas. Pastoralists tend to be nomadic, to have small communities consisting of related families, and to depend significantly on trade because they do not produce items (including certain types of food) they need.

7. Anthropologists generally agree that the physical environment normally exercises a restraining rather than a determining influence on how people in an area get their food; technology and social and political factors may be more important.

8. We see the first evidence of a changeover to food production in the Near East about 8000 B.C. Theories about why food production originated remain controversial, but most archaeologists think that certain conditions must have pushed people to switch from collecting to producing food. Some possible causal factors include (1) population growth in regions of bountiful wild resources, which may have pushed people to move to marginal areas where they tried to reproduce their former abundance; (2) global population growth, which filled most of the world's habitable regions and may have forced people to utilize a broader spectrum of wild resources and to domesticate plants and animals; and (3) the emergence of hotter and drier summers and colder winters, which may have favored sedentarization near seasonal stands of wild grain; population growth in such areas may have forced people to plant crops and raise animals to support themselves.

9. Because food producers can support more people in a given territory than food collectors can, they may have had a competitive advantage in confrontations with food collectors.

◎ Glossary Terms

cash crops	289	intensive agriculture	289
commercialization	291	pastoralism	291
extensive or shifting cultivation	286	prairie	294
food collection	284	savanna	294
food production	286	slash-and-burn	287
foragers	284	steppe	294
horticulture	286	subsistence economy	283
hunter-gatherers	284		

◎ Critical Questions

1. Why might meat be valued more than plant foods in many societies?

2. Why might foragers be less likely than intensive agriculturalists to suffer from food shortages?

3. Why do certain foods in a society come to be preferred?

⊚ Research Navigator

1. Please go to **www.researchnavigator.com** and enter your LOGIN NAME and PASSWORD. For instructions on registering for the first time, please view the detailed instructions at the end of Chapter 1.

2. Using ContentSelect select "Anthropology." Find an article on a food-collecting society (hunter-gatherers or foragers) and a food-producing society (horticultural or intensive agricultural). Summarize what each article is about.

3. Using Link Library for Anthropology find a Web site about hunter-gatherers or foragers and describe its major contents.

⊚ Discovering Anthropology: Researchers at Work

Read the chapter by Burton Pasternak, "Han: Pastoralists and Farmers on a Chinese Frontier," in *Discovering Anthropology* and answer the following questions.

1. The Han Chinese traditionally depended on intensive agriculture. The Mongols traditionally depended on pastoralism. What happened to the Han when they moved beyond the Great Wall to a grassland environment?

2. How has the change to more pastoralism affected marriage and family among the Han?

3. How have the Mongols changed?

The following pages contain maps that have been adapted from the *DK Atlas of World History: Mapping the Human Journey* and *Atlas of Anthropology*, produced by Dorling Kindersley. Each map focuses on a topic that is discussed in more detail within the text itself and is intended to bring the richness of anthropology to life.

Maps

The Living Primates
The Spread of Modern Humans
The Spread of Agriculture
The First Civilizations
The Spread of Writing
European Expansion in the 16th Century
Biological Exchanges
Trading in Human Lives
Migration in the 19th Century
Trade in the 19th Century

 Prentice Hall would sincerely like to thank Dorling Kindersley for helping to put this feature together.

The Living Primates

The great apes are the chimpanzees, gorillas, and Asian orangutans, while the lesser, smaller apes are the gibbons and siamangs of South and Southeast Asia.Primates are the mammalian order that includes apes, monkeys, and humans. Prosimians, the most primitive of primates, are mainly small, solitary nocturnal creatures. Anthropoids, including apes, monkeys and ourselves, have larger bodies, and are organized on social groups. All primates have well developed visual sense, forward-directed eyes, and larger brains for their body sizes than other mammals. Most live in the tropics, and move around in a variety of different ways.

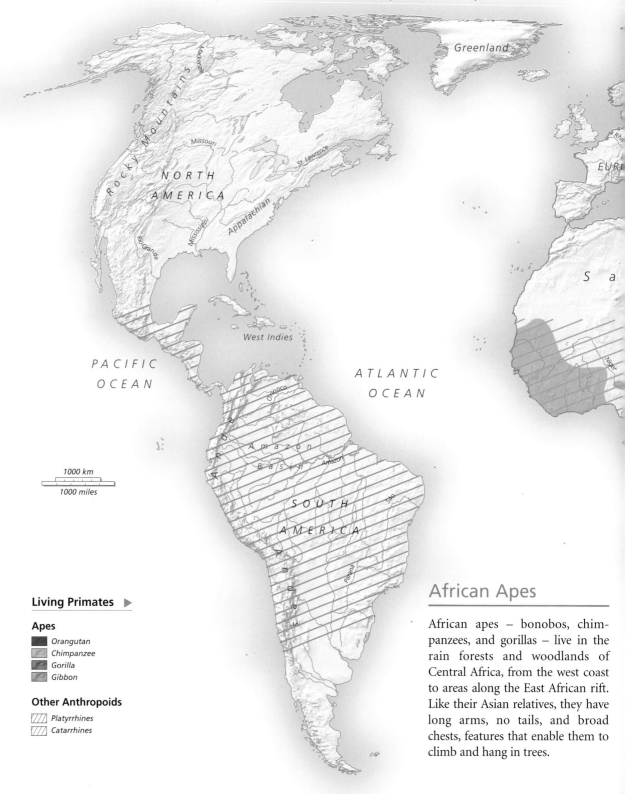

Living Primates ▶

Apes
- ■ Orangutan
- ▨ Chimpanzee
- ▨ Gorilla
- ▨ Gibbon

Other Anthropoids
- ▨ Platyrrhines
- ▨ Catarrhines

African Apes

African apes – bonobos, chimpanzees, and gorillas – live in the rain forests and woodlands of Central Africa, from the west coast to areas along the East African rift. Like their Asian relatives, they have long arms, no tails, and broad chests, features that enable them to climb and hang in trees.

Asian Apes

Gibbons and their relatives, the siamangs and orangutans, are confined to South and Southeast Asia. Gibbons are the smallest and most anatomically primitive of all apes, retaining many monkeylike traits. Orangutans are the largest arboreal mammals. Once widespread, they are now confined to forested regions of Borneo and Sumatra.

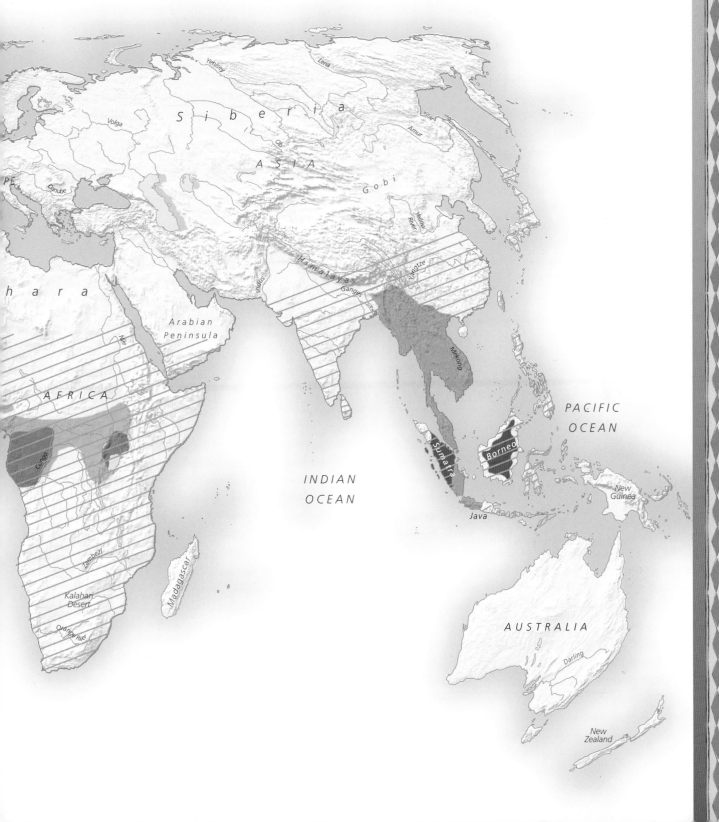

The Spread of Modern Humans

Fully modern humans evolved in Africa, probably between 200,000 and 100,000 years ago. By 30,000 years ago, they had colonized much of the globe. Rising temperatures at the end of the last Ice Age allowed plants and animals to become more abundant, and new areas were settled. By 8000 BC, larger populations and

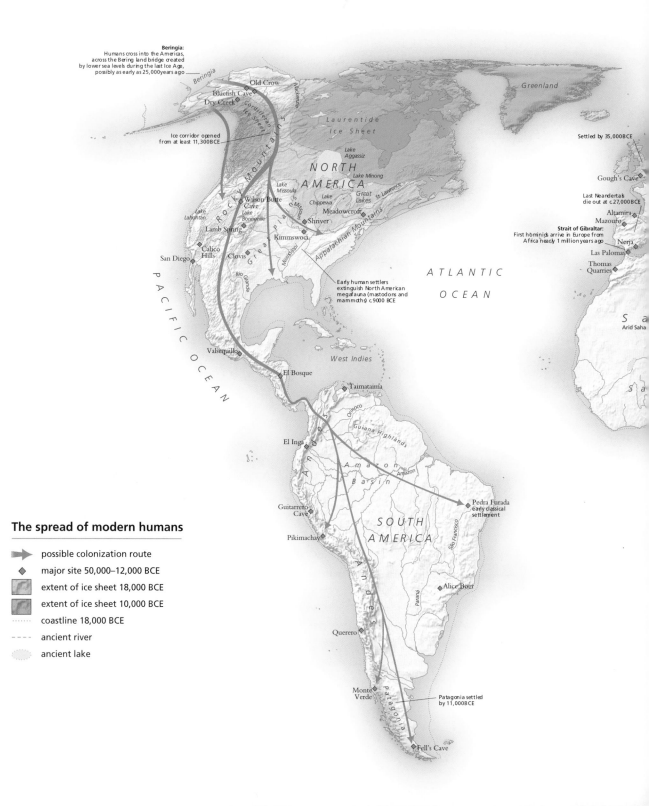

The spread of modern humans

- possible colonization route
- major site 50,000–12,000 BCE
- extent of ice sheet 18,000 BCE
- extent of ice sheet 10,000 BCE
- coastline 18,000 BCE
- ancient river
- ancient lake

intense hunting had contributed to the near extinction of large mammals, such as mastodons and mammoths. In the Near East, groups of hunter gatherers were living in permanent settlements, harvesting wild cereals, and experimenting with the domestication of local animals. The transition to agriculture was under way.

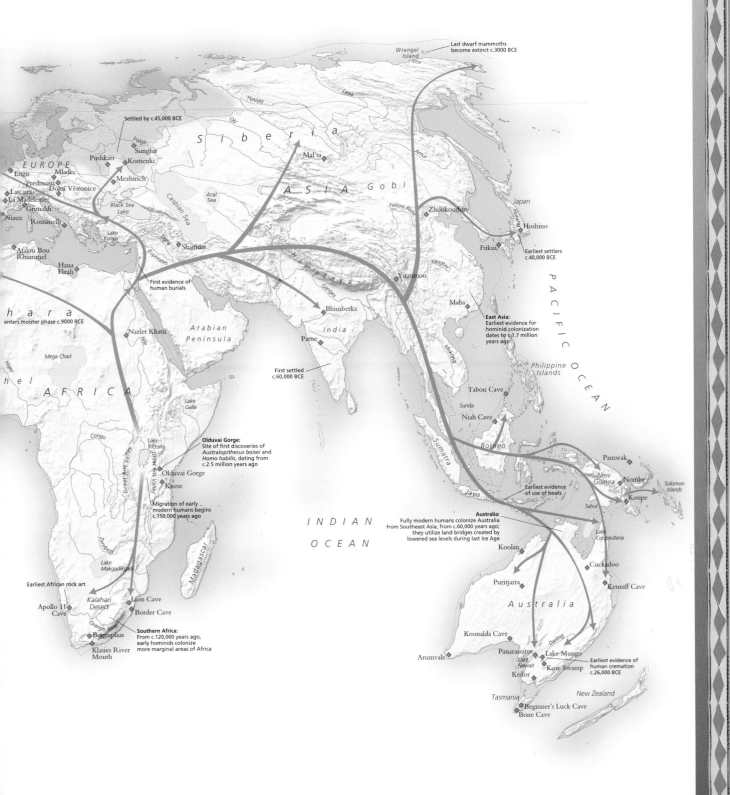

Last dwarf mammoths become extinct c.3000 BCE

Wrangel Island

Yenisei

Lena

Settled by c.45,000 BCE

Ob

S i b e r i a

Volga
Sunghir
Pushkari • Kostienki
Mezhirich

EUROPE
Engis • Mladec
Predmosti
Dolní Věstonice
Lascaux
La Madeleine
Grimaldi
Niaux • Romanelli

Black Sea Lake

Caspian Sea

Aral Sea

Mal'ta

A S I A   *Gobi*

Amur

Japan

Zhoukoudian

Yellow River

Hoshino

Earliest settlers c.40,000 BCE

Fukui

Afalou Bou Rhummel
Haua Fleah

Lake Konya
Tigris
Euphrates
Shanidar

First evidence of human burials

Yangtze

Yuanmou

Maba

East Asia:
Earliest evidence for hominid colonization dates to c.1.7 million years ago

PACIFIC OCEAN

h a r a
enters moister phase c.9000 BCE

Nazlet Khatir

Nile

Arabian Peninsula

Indus
Ganges

Himalayas

Bhimbetka

I n d i a

Mekong

Philippine Islands

Mega Chad

Niger

h e l   AFRICA

Lake Galla

Patne

First settled c.60,000 BCE

Tabon Cave

Sunda

Niah Cave

Borneo

Pamwak

Congo

Lake Victoria

Olduvai Gorge:
Site of first discoveries of *Australopithecus boisei* and *Homo habilis*, dating from c.2.5 million years ago

Olduvai Gorge
Kisese

Great Rift Valley

Migration of early modern humans begins c.150,000 years ago

Sumatra
Java

Earliest evidence of use of boats

New Guinea • Nombe

Sahul

Kosipe

Solomon Islands

INDIAN OCEAN

Australia:
Fully modern humans colonize Australia from Southeast Asia, from c.60,000 years ago; they utilize land bridges created by lowered sea levels during last Ice Age

Lake Carpentaria

Zambezi

Lake Makgadikgadi

Madagascar

Koolan

Cuckadoo

Earliest African rock art

Kalahari Desert
Lion Cave

Apollo 11 Cave
Border Cave

Orange River

Boomplaas

Klasies River Mouth

Southern Africa:
From c.120,000 years ago, early hominids colonize more marginal areas of Africa

Puritjarra

A u s t r a l i a

Kenniff Cave

Koonalda Cave

Darling

Arumvale

Panaramitee
Lake Nawai

Lake Mungo

Earliest evidence of human cremation c.26,000 BCE

Keilor

Kow Swamp

Tasmania

New Zealand

Beginner's Luck Cave
Bone Cave

The Spread of Agriculture

The appearance of farming transformed the face of the Earth. It was not merely a change in subsistence, it also transformed the way in which our ancestors lived. Agriculture, and the vastly greater crop yields it produced, enabled larger groups of people to live together, often in permanent villages. After agriculture emerged, craft, religious, and political specialization became more likely, and the first signs of social

The spread of agriculture ▶

▨	areas of early agriculture, with dates of first domestication of plants and animals
➤	diffusion of agricultural skills

Staple crops under cultivation by c.4000 BCE

🌾	wheat
🌾	barley
🌾	millet
🌽	maize
🌾	rice

Wild ancestors of domesticated animals

🐗	aurochs (wild cattle)
🐗	pig

🐑	sheep
🐫	ass
🐪	dromedary camel
🐎	horse
🐫	bactrian camel
🐂	gaur (wild ox)
🐃	buffalo
🐓	chicken
🐐	goat
🐑	yak
🦃	turkey
🦙	guanaco (llama)
🐹	guinea pig
🦙	alpaca
🐂	banteng

Mediterranean:
olive
grape
turnip
leek
plum
pear
cabbage
lettuce
rapeseed

Eastern North America:
sunflower
sumpweed
tepary bean

Central America:
maize
sweet potato
manioc
squash
bottle gourd
tomato
avocado
cotton

South America:
manioc
potato
cotton
peanut
squash
bottle gourd
chilli pepper
lima bean

inequality appeared. In 5000 B.C., only a limited number of regions were fully dependent on agriculture. In many parts of the globe, small-scale farming began to supplement hunting and gathering, the first steps in the gradual transition to the sedentary agricultural way of life.

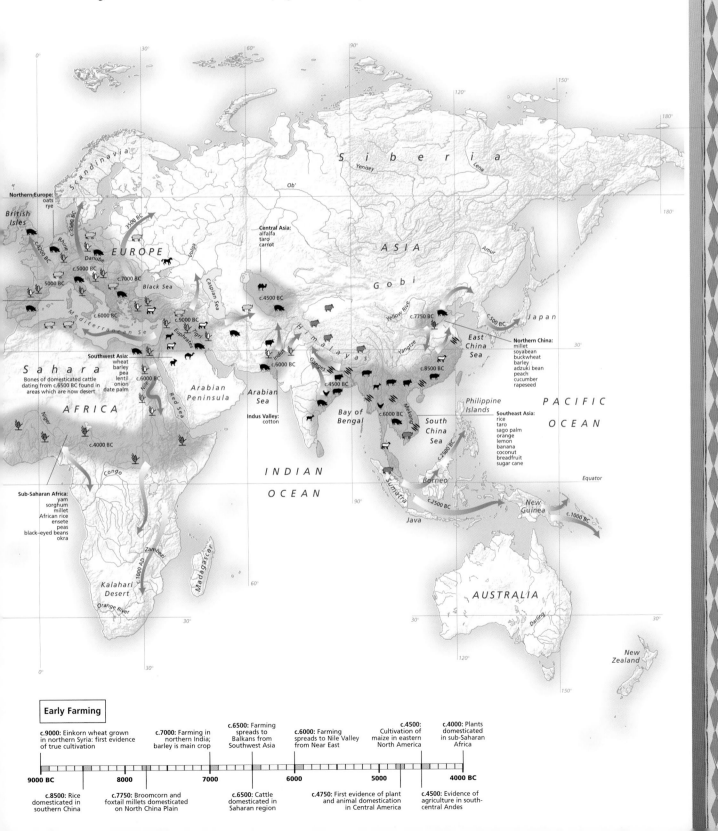

Early Farming

c.9000: Einkorn wheat grown in northern Syria: first evidence of true cultivation

c.7000: Farming in northern India; barley is main crop

c.6500: Farming spreads to Balkans from Southwest Asia

c.6000: Farming spreads to Nile Valley from Near East

c.4500: Cultivation of maize in eastern North America

c.4000: Plants domesticated in sub-Saharan Africa

9000 BC	8000	7000	6000	5000	4000 BC

c.8500: Rice domesticated in southern China

c.7750: Broomcorn and foxtail millets domesticated on North China Plain

c.6500: Cattle domesticated in Saharan region

c.4750: First evidence of plant and animal domestication in Central America

c.4500: Evidence of agriculture in south-central Andes

The First Civilizations

The period between 5000 and 2500 B.C. saw the development of complex urban civilizations in the fertile river valleys of the Nile, Tigris, Euphrates, and Indus. Mesopotamian city states formed small kingdoms, which competed with one another. A literate elite ruled over each civilization, and their artisans experimented with new technologies such as bronze and copper metallurgy. Many village societies developed important ritual centers or buried their dead in communal sepulchers.

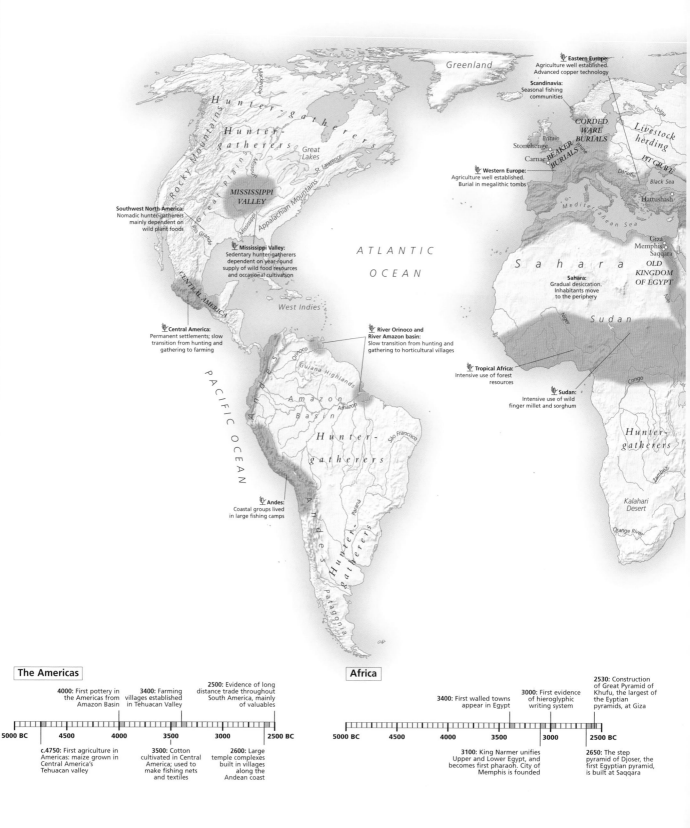

Eastern Europe: Agriculture well established. Advanced copper technology

Scandinavia: Seasonal fishing communities

CORDED WARE BURIALS

Stonehenge

Carnac *BEAKER BURIALS*

Livestock herding

PIT GRAVE

Western Europe: Agriculture well established. Burial in megalithic tombs

Hattushash

Giza
Memphis
Saqqara

OLD KINGDOM OF EGYPT

S a h a r a

Sahara: Gradual desiccation. Inhabitants move to the periphery

S u d a n

Southwest North America: Nomadic hunter-gatherers mainly dependent on wild plant foods

MISSISSIPPI VALLEY

Hunter-gatherers

Hunter-gatherers

Greenland

Great Lakes

Mississippi Valley: Sedentary hunter-gatherers dependent on year-round supply of wild food resources and occasional cultivation

ATLANTIC OCEAN

Central America: Permanent settlements; slow transition from hunting and gathering to farming

West Indies

River Orinoco and River Amazon basin: Slow transition from hunting and gathering to horticultural villages

Tropical Africa: Intensive use of forest resources

Sudan: Intensive use of wild finger millet and sorghum

Guiana Highlands

A m a z o n   B a s i n

Hunter-gatherers

Hunter-gatherers

Andes: Coastal groups lived in large fishing camps

PACIFIC OCEAN

A n d e s

Patagonia

Hunter-gatherers

Kalahari Desert

Orange River

The Americas

4000: First pottery in the Americas from Amazon Basin

3400: Farming villages established in Tehuacan Valley

2500: Evidence of long distance trade throughout South America, mainly of valuables

5000 BC — 4500 — 4000 — 3500 — 3000 — 2500 BC

c.4750: First agriculture in Americas: maize grown in Central America's Tehuacan valley

3500: Cotton cultivated in Central America; used to make fishing nets and textiles

2600: Large temple complexes built in villages along the Andean coast

Africa

3400: First walled towns appear in Egypt

3000: First evidence of hieroglyphic writing system

2530: Construction of Great Pyramid of Khufu, the largest of the Eyptian pyramids, at Giza

5000 BC — 4500 — 4000 — 3500 — 3000 — 2500 BC

3100: King Narmer unifies Upper and Lower Egypt, and becomes first pharaoh. City of Memphis is founded

2650: The step pyramid of Djoser, the first Egyptian pyramid, is built at Saqqara

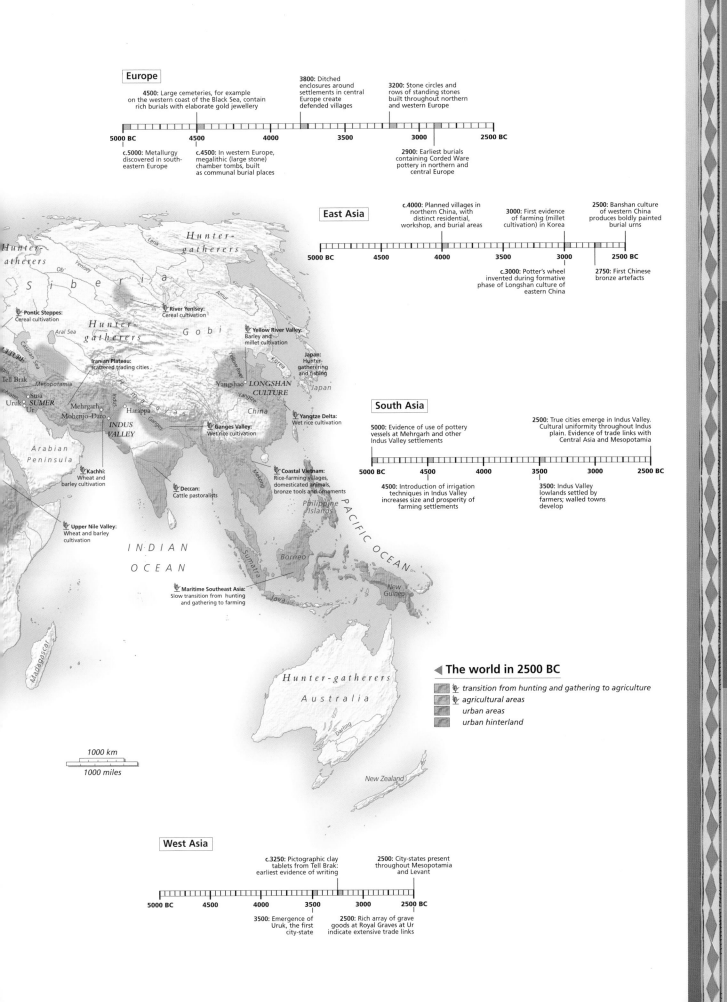

Europe

4500: Large cemeteries, for example on the western coast of the Black Sea, contain rich burials with elaborate gold jewellery

3800: Ditched enclosures around settlements in central Europe create defended villages

3200: Stone circles and rows of standing stones built throughout northern and western Europe

5000 BC — 4500 — 4000 — 3500 — 3000 — 2500 BC

c.5000: Metallurgy discovered in south-eastern Europe

c.4500: In western Europe, megalithic (large stone) chamber tombs, built as communal burial places

2900: Earliest burials containing Corded Ware pottery in northern and central Europe

East Asia

c.4000: Planned villages in northern China, with distinct residential, workshop, and burial areas

3000: First evidence of farming (millet cultivation) in Korea

2500: Banshan culture of western China produces boldly painted burial urns

5000 BC — 4500 — 4000 — 3500 — 3000 — 2500 BC

c.3000: Potter's wheel invented during formative phase of Longshan culture of eastern China

2750: First Chinese bronze artefacts

South Asia

5000: Evidence of use of pottery vessels at Mehrgarh and other Indus Valley settlements

2500: True cities emerge in Indus Valley. Cultural uniformity throughout Indus plain. Evidence of trade links with Central Asia and Mesopotamia

5000 BC — 4500 — 4000 — 3500 — 3000 — 2500 BC

4500: Introduction of irrigation techniques in Indus Valley increases size and prosperity of farming settlements

3500: Indus Valley lowlands settled by farmers; walled towns develop

West Asia

c.3250: Pictographic clay tablets from Tell Brak: earliest evidence of writing

2500: City-states present throughout Mesopotamia and Levant

5000 BC — 4500 — 4000 — 3500 — 3000 — 2500 BC

3500: Emergence of Uruk, the first city-state

2500: Rich array of grave goods at Royal Graves at Ur indicate extensive trade links

◀ **The world in 2500 BC**

- transition from hunting and gathering to agriculture
- agricultural areas
- urban areas
- urban hinterland

Map labels:

Hunter-gatherers (Siberia)

Hunter-gatherers

Lena

Ob'

Yenisey

Amur

Gobi

Pontic Steppes: Cereal cultivation

Aral Sea

Caspian Sea

River Yenisey: Cereal cultivation

Yellow River Valley: Barley and millet cultivation

Yellow River

Korea

Japan: Hunter-gathering and fishing

Japan

Iranian Plateau: scattered trading cities

Tell Brak

Mesopotamia

Susa

Uruk *SUMER*

Ur

Yangshao *LONGSHAN CULTURE*

Yangtze

China

Yangtze Delta: Wet rice cultivation

Mehrgarh

Indus

Harappa

Mohenjo-Daro

INDUS VALLEY

Ganges

Ganges Valley: Wet rice cultivation

Kachhi: Wheat and barley cultivation

Arabian Peninsula

Deccan: Cattle pastoralists

Coastal Vietnam: Rice-farming villages, domesticated animals, bronze tools and ornaments

Mekong

Philippine Islands

Upper Nile Valley: Wheat and barley cultivation

INDIAN OCEAN

Sumatra

Borneo

New Guinea

PACIFIC OCEAN

Maritime Southeast Asia: Slow transition from hunting and gathering to farming

Java

Madagascar

Hunter-gatherers

Australia

Darling

New Zealand

1000 km

1000 miles

The Spread of Writing

The precursors of the first known writing and numerical systems were clay counting tokens, used in south-west Asia before c.3400 BC to record quantities of stored goods. They were eventually sealed in clay envelopes, and marked on the outside with signs indicating their contents – the first written symbols. Within a thousand years, writing and numerical systems had spread throughout western Asia. Writing became a powerful tool of government, and a means of communicating, codifying laws, and recording history.

Central America: Earliest known script, Zapotec pictographic, c.600 BC Maya script (pictographic/syllabic) evolves c.300 AD

The evolution and spread of major scripts ▶

- Sumerian cuneiform
- spread of cuneiform
- Egyptian hieroglyphic
- spread of hieroglyphic
- Phoenician alphabet
- spread of alphabet
- Chinese script
- spread of Chinese script
- Mesoamerican script
- Runic script
- Indus sctipt

Major developments in writing, counting, and calendrical systems

c.3400: Sumerians use clay counting tokens and first written symbols

c.3000: Development of Egyptian hieroglyphic writing system

c.2500: Egyptian calendar pioneers division of day into 24 units

c.1400: First written inscriptions in China, on Shang oracle bones

c.1100: Introduction of Phoenician alphabet

46: Julian calendrical reforms; 'Year of Confusion' is 445 days long

3500 BC · 3000 BC · 2500 BC · 2000 BC · 1500 BC · 1000 BC · 500 BC · 1 CE

c.3250: Earliest writing in the world; clay pictographic tablets from Tell Brak, Syria

c.2000: Appearance of Cretan hieroglyphic writing

c.600: First Greek coins
c.600: First Central American script (Zapotec)

c.500: Hebrews evolve use of 7-day weeks
c.500: First coins used in China

Runic script: Script of Germanic peoples. First appears 3rd century CE. Runic symbols arranged in alphabetic order (*futhark*), perhaps based on Latin alphabet

Europe 100 BC

Italy 600 BC

Rome

Greece 750 BC

Athens

Memphis

Hittites 1500 BC

Urartians 1500 BC

Hurrians 1200 BC

Elamites 3000 BC

Persepolis

Persia 500 BC

Tell Brak

Cuneiform: Earliest writing system Sumerian, c.3500 BC Pictographic/syllabic

Possible influence on script of India 250 BC

Korea 3rd century AD

Japan 8th century AD

Anyang

Pataliputra

Cretan scripts: Undeciphered Cretan hieroglyphic (c.2000 BC), may have been influenced by Egyptian scripts. Linear A (c.1750 BC) pictographic Linear B (c.1600 BC) syllabic

Phoenicia (Levantine coast), c.1100 BC

Proto-Canaanite 1500 BC

South Arabia c.1300 BC

North Arabia 550 BC

Ethiopia 550 BC

Egypt (Coptic) 100 BC

Hieroglyphic: Egypt, c.3000 BC Pictographic/syllabic (Phonetic element of Egyptian writing system adopted in Sinai (Proto-Sinaitic) and Syria/Palestine (Proto-Canaanite), c.1500 BC

Indus Valley script: Poorly understood pictographic script from Harappan civilization, c.2500–1700 BC

Chinese script: China, c.1400 BC Pictographic origins; evolves into a combination of phonetic, syllabic and ideographic

Modern form (3rd century to present day)

Greater Seal (W. Zhou)

Oracle–bone form (Shang dynasty)

EUROPE · ASIA · AFRICA · Siberia · Gobi · India · Sahara

Mediterranean Sea · Black Sea · Aral Sea · Caspian

Yenisey · Lena · Ob · Yellow River · Yangtze · Ganges · Mekong · Nile · Niger · Zambezi · Orange River · Darling

INDIAN OCEAN · PACIFIC OCEAN

Kalahari Desert · Madagascar · New Guinea · AUSTRALIA · New Zealand

1000 km
1000 miles

European Expansion in the 16th Century

The 16th century saw the expansion of several of the great European nations far beyond their continental limits. Explorers searching for new sources of luxury goods and precious metals began to open up new territories which monarchs such as Philip II of Spain quickly built up into great empires in the "New World." The Spanish and Portuguese, inspired by the voyages of Columbus and da Gama, led the way, closely followed by the Dutch and the English. The explorers were aided by technological advances in shipbuilding, navigational equipment, and cartography. At the start of the 16th century, the Americas were virtually unknown to Europeans; by 1700, outposts of a greater European empire had been established almost everywhere the explorers landed.

Spain and Portugal were the leaders of world exploration in the 16th century. In search of maritime trade routes to Asia, the Portuguese found sea lanes through the Atlantic and Indian oceans to India. By 1512, fortified trading posts were in place at Goa and Malacca, and they had reached the "Spice Islands" of the Moluccas in eastern Indonesia. The Spanish, taking a westward route, found the Caribbean islands and the Americas instead. Magellan's three-year global circumnavigation revealed a western route through the Strait of Magellan and across the Pacific Ocean. English and French mariners sought northern passages to Asian markets and their voyages paved the way for the establishment of European settlements in North America.

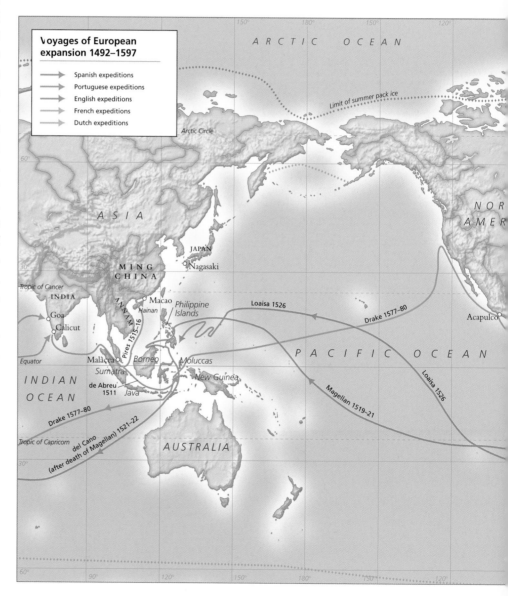

Voyages of European expansion 1492–1597

- → Spanish expeditions
- → Portuguese expeditions
- → English expeditions
- → French expeditions
- → Dutch expeditions

Voyages of expansion 1492–1590

1492: Columbus, in search of Asia, reaches Cuba and the Bahamas

1509–16: Portuguese voyages to Moluccas, Malacca, and Macao

1532: Cartier explores Strait of Belle Isle and St Lawrence

1576: Frobisher reaches Baffin Island

1490   1510   1530   1550   1570   1590

1498: Vasco da Gama rounds Cape of Good Hope and reaches India

1500: Cabral sights Brazilian coast on voyage to India

1519–22: Magellan and del Cano complete first global circumnavigation reaching Moluccas via the Philippine Islands

1553: Willoughby reaches Archangel on Northeast Passage

1577–80: Drake circumnavigates globe

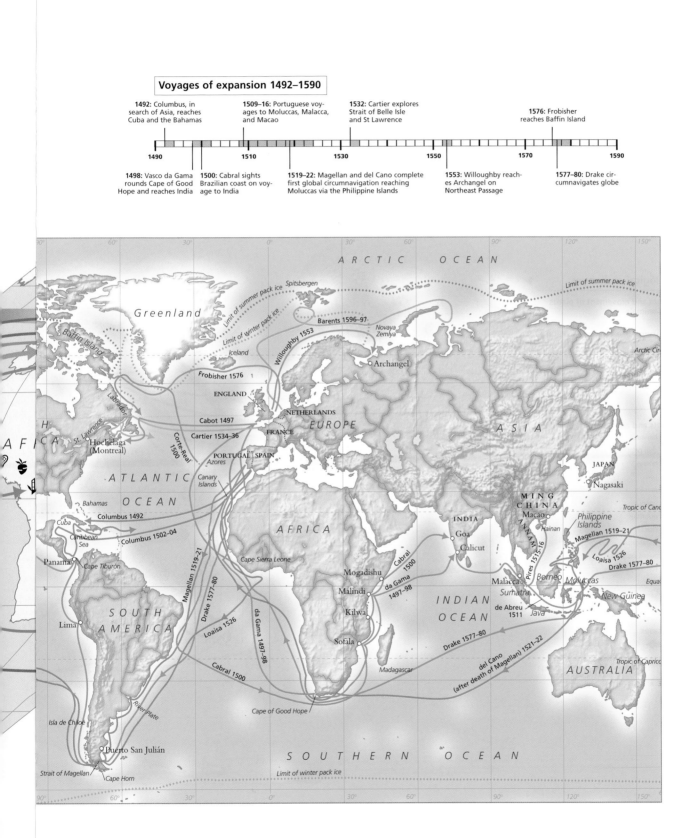

Trading in Human Lives

The use of slaves seems to have been endemic in many human societies. Normally taken as prisoners of war, slaves were also acquired as a form of tribute. The establishment of European colonies and overseas empires between the 16th and 19th centuries saw the creation of a slave trade on an industrial scale, a commerce which laid the foundations for pan-global trading networks. Trading concerns such as the English and Dutch East India companies developed trade on a larger scale than ever before; but it was the need to supply labor for the plantations of the Americas which led to the greatest movement of peoples across the face of the earth.

Slaves in the New World

The great plantation systems and mining concerns that arose in the New World from the 16th century onward demanded large reservoirs of labor. Though the Spanish and Portuguese initially used enslaved indigenous people, they soon required a more reliable source of labor. The Portuguese began bringing African slaves to the Caribbean and Brazil in the early 16th century. The cotton plantations of the southern US, which boomed in the early 19th century, were a key factor in sustaining the Atlantic trade.

The Atlantic slave trade

From the late 15th to the early 19th century, European merchants – especially the British and Portuguese – carried on a massive trade in African slaves across the Atlantic. As well as utilizing the established sources of slaves from the Central and West African kingdoms, they also raided coastal areas of West Africa for additional supplies of slaves. European manufactured goods, especially guns, were exchanged for slaves destined to work as agricultural laborers on plantations in the Caribbean and the tropical Americas. Slaves transported to the western hemisphere may have numbered 12 million or more.

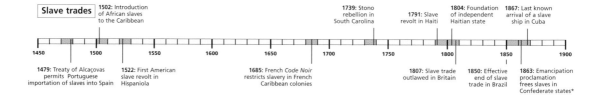

Slave trades

1502: Introduction of African slaves to the Caribbean

1739: Stono rebellion in South Carolina

1791: Slave revolt in Haiti

1804: Foundation of independent Haitian state

1867: Last known arrival of a slave ship in Cuba

1450   1500   1550   1600   1650   1700   1750   1800   1850   1900

1479: Treaty of Alcaçovas permits Portuguese importation of slaves into Spain

1522: First American slave revolt in Hispaniola

1685: French *Code Noir* restricts slavery in French Caribbean colonies

1807: Slave trade outlawed in Britain

1850: Effective end of slave trade in Brazil

1863: Emancipation proclamation frees slaves in Confederate states*

Voyages of expansion 1492–1590

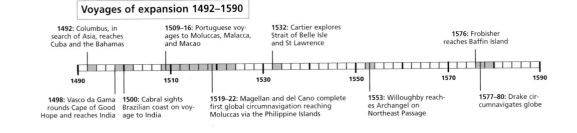

1492: Columbus, in search of Asia, reaches Cuba and the Bahamas

1509–16: Portuguese voyages to Moluccas, Malacca, and Macao

1532: Cartier explores Strait of Belle Isle and St Lawrence

1576: Frobisher reaches Baffin Island

1490   1510   1530   1550   1570   1590

1498: Vasco da Gama rounds Cape of Good Hope and reaches India

1500: Cabral sights Brazilian coast on voyage to India

1519–22: Magellan and del Cano complete first global circumnavigation reaching Moluccas via the Philippine Islands

1553: Willoughby reaches Archangel on Northeast Passage

1577–80: Drake circumnavigates globe

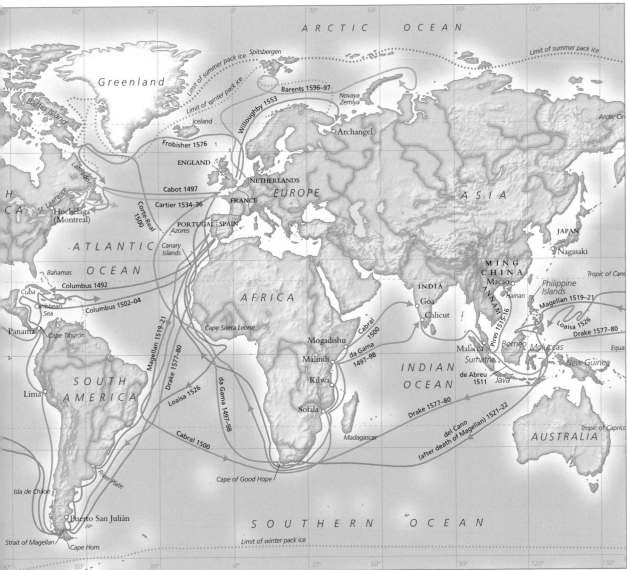

Biological Exchanges

European expansion had a profound biological impact. Travelers transported numerous species of fruits, vegetables, and animals from the Americas to Europe. At the same time, settlers introduced European species to the Americas and Oceania. Horses, pigs, and cattle were transported to the western hemisphere where, without natural predators, their numbers increased spectacularly. The settlers consciously introduced food crops, such as wheat, grapes, apples, peaches, and citrus fruits. Some plants, such as nettles, dandelions, and

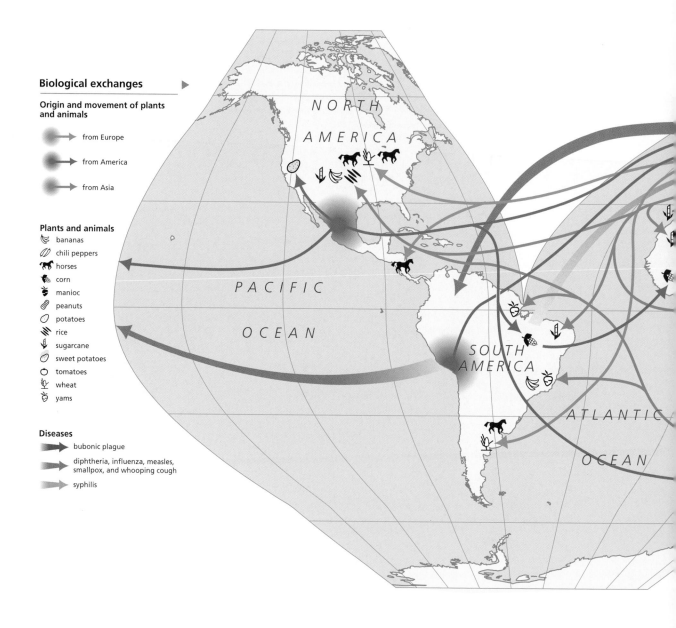

Biological exchanges ▶

Origin and movement of plants and animals

→ from Europe

→ from America

→ from Asia

Plants and animals
- 🍌 bananas
- 🌶 chili peppers
- 🐎 horses
- 🌽 corn
- 🌱 manioc
- 🥜 peanuts
- 🥔 potatoes
- 🌾 rice
- 🌿 sugarcane
- 🍠 sweet potatoes
- 🍅 tomatoes
- 🌾 wheat
- 🌰 yams

Diseases
- ➤ bubonic plague
- ➤ diphtheria, influenza, measles, smallpox, and whooping cough
- ➤ syphilis

other weeds were inadvertently dispersed by the winds or on the coats of animals. European expansion also led to a spread of European diseases. Vast numbers of indigenous American peoples died from measles and smallpox, which broke out in massive epidemics among populations with no natural or acquired immunity. During the 16th century, syphilis – thought now to be the result of the fusion of two similar diseases from Europe and the New World – killed a million Europeans.

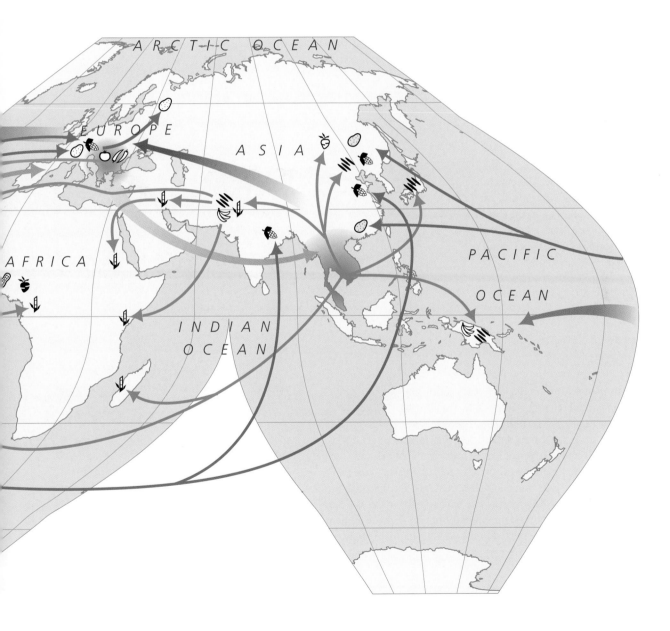

Trading in Human Lives

The use of slaves seems to have been endemic in many human societies. Normally taken as prisoners of war, slaves were also acquired as a form of tribute. The establishment of European colonies and overseas empires between the 16th and 19th centuries saw the creation of a slave trade on an industrial scale, a commerce which laid the foundations for pan-global trading networks. Trading concerns such as the English and Dutch East India companies developed trade on a larger scale than ever before; but it was the need to supply labor for the plantations of the Americas which led to the greatest movement of peoples across the face of the earth.

Slaves in the New World

The great plantation systems and mining concerns that arose in the New World from the 16th century onward demanded large reservoirs of labor. Though the Spanish and Portuguese initially used enslaved indigenous people, they soon required a more reliable source of labor. The Portuguese began bringing African slaves to the Caribbean and Brazil in the early 16th century. The cotton plantations of the southern US, which boomed in the early 19th century, were a key factor in sustaining the Atlantic trade.

The Atlantic slave trade

From the late 15th to the early 19th century, European merchants – especially the British and Portuguese – carried on a massive trade in African slaves across the Atlantic. As well as utilizing the established sources of slaves from the Central and West African kingdoms, they also raided coastal areas of West Africa for additional supplies of slaves. European manufactured goods, especially guns, were exchanged for slaves destined to work as agricultural laborers on plantations in the Caribbean and the tropical Americas. Slaves transported to the western hemisphere may have numbered 12 million or more.

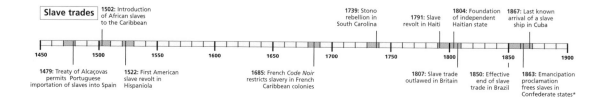

Slave trades

1502: Introduction of African slaves to the Caribbean

1739: Stono rebellion in South Carolina

1791: Slave revolt in Haiti

1804: Foundation of independent Haitian state

1867: Last known arrival of a slave ship in Cuba

| 1450 | 1500 | 1550 | 1600 | 1650 | 1700 | 1750 | 1800 | 1850 | 1900 |

1479: Treaty of Alcaçovas permits Portuguese importation of slaves into Spain

1522: First American slave revolt in Hispaniola

1685: French *Code Noir* restricts slavery in French Caribbean colonies

1807: Slave trade outlawed in Britain

1850: Effective end of slave trade in Brazil

1863: Emancipation proclamation frees slaves in Confederate states*

Other slave trades

By the 9th and 10th centuries, a number of complex slave-trading routes were in existence in Europe and the Near East. Viking and Russian merchants traded in slaves from the Balkans who were often sold to harems in southern Spain and North Africa. The Baghdad Caliphate drew slaves from western Europe via the ports of Venice, Prague, and Marseille, and Slavic and Turkic slaves from eastern Europe and Central Asia. In the 13th century, the Mongols sold slaves at Karakorum and in the Volga region. There was long-standing commerce in African slaves – primarily from East Africa before European mariners entered the slave trade. Between the 9th and 19th centuries Muslim merchants may have transported as many as 14 million across the Sahara by camel caravan and through East African ports, principally to destinations in the Indian Ocean basin.

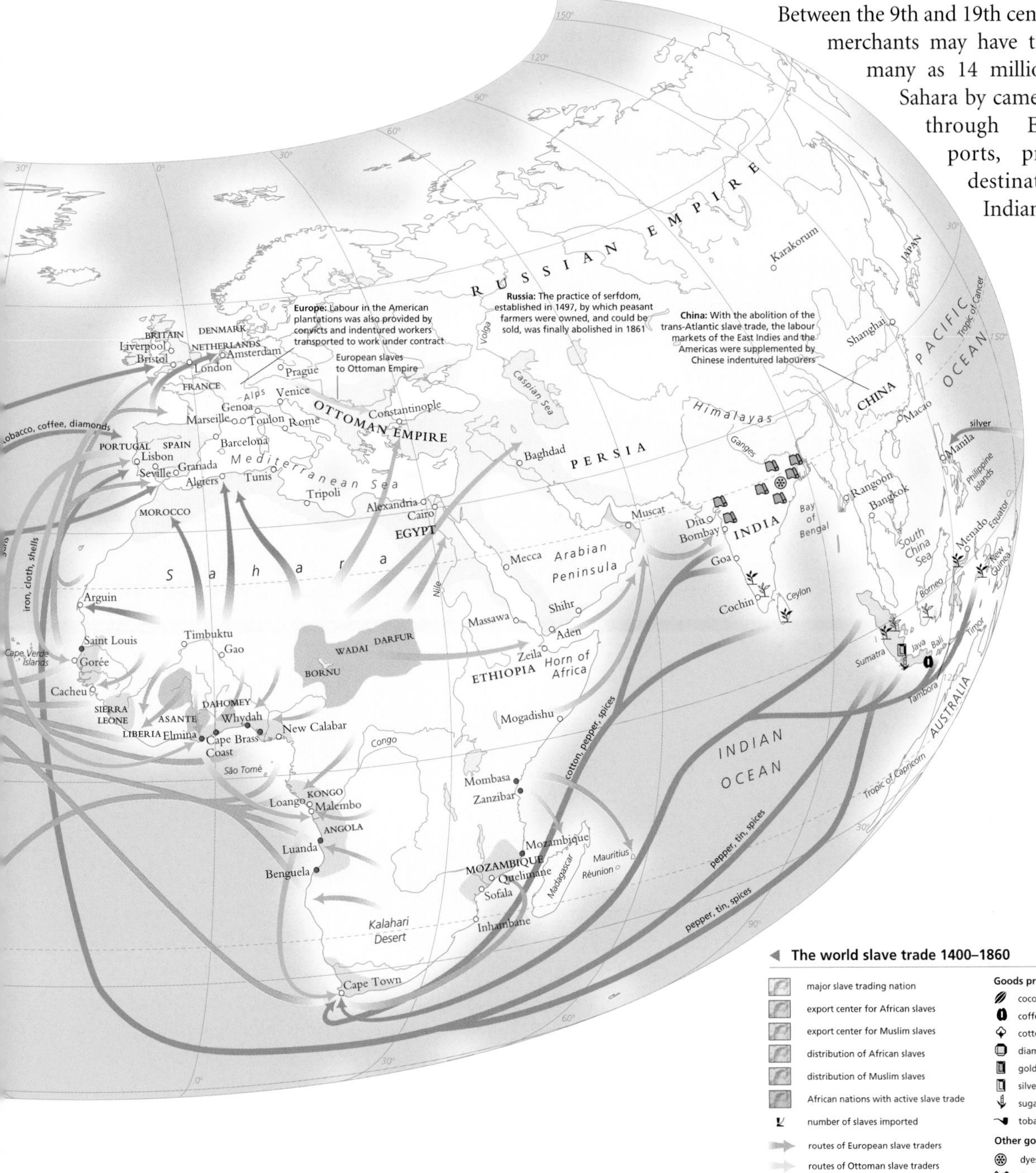

Russia: The practice of serfdom, established in 1497, by which peasant farmers were owned, and could be sold, was finally abolished in 1861

Europe: Labour in the American plantations was also provided by convicts and indentured workers transported to work under contract

European slaves to Ottoman Empire

China: With the abolition of the trans-Atlantic slave trade, the labour markets of the East Indies and the Americas were supplemented by Chinese indentured labourers

◄ The world slave trade 1400–1860

major slave trading nation	
export center for African slaves	
export center for Muslim slaves	
distribution of African slaves	
distribution of Muslim slaves	
African nations with active slave trade	

🌾 number of slaves imported

→ routes of European slave traders

→ routes of Ottoman slave traders

→ routes of Saharan slave traders

→ routes of Arab slave traders

→ exports of Muslim slaves from Southeast Asia

→ goods exported in exchange for slaves

→ goods exported for slaves

→ European exports to Africa

• slave factory

Goods produced using slaves

- 🖊 cocoa beans
- ◉ coffee
- ♦ cotton
- 💠 diamonds
- 🟫 gold
- 🟦 silver
- ↓ sugar
- 🌿 tobacco

Other goods traded

- ⊛ dyestuffs
- 🪶 furs and hides
- 🌿 pepper
- 🧵 silk and textiles
- 🌾 spices
- 🟫 tin

Goods imported for slaves

- 🐟 salt cod

Migration in the 19th Century

The technical innovations of the Industrial Revolution made the 19th-century world a much smaller place. Railroads could quickly transport large human cargoes across continents, the Suez and Panama canals reduced travel times – sometimes by as much as 50%, and ships became larger, faster, and more seaworthy. The mechanization and centralization of industry required the concentration of labor on a scale never seen before. At the same time, the European imperial powers were exploiting their tropical possessions for economic benefit. Cash crops, grown on large plantations, needed a plentiful supply of labor as well. Political upheaval, wars, and economic hardship provided the most dramatic impetus to emigration – especially in the Russian Empire and Central Europe, and in southeastern China.

Migration in the 19th century

More than 80 million people emigrated from their country of origin during the 19th and early 20th centuries. Over half of them moved across the Atlantic to North and South America. The end of the American Civil War in 1865, and the opening up of Native American land to settlers saw the greatest period of immigration to the US and Canada. In the Russian Empire, movement was eastward from European Russia into Siberia and the Caspian region. Europeans moved south and east to take up employment in the colonies, while indentured laborers traveled to the Americas, Africa, and Southeast Asia.

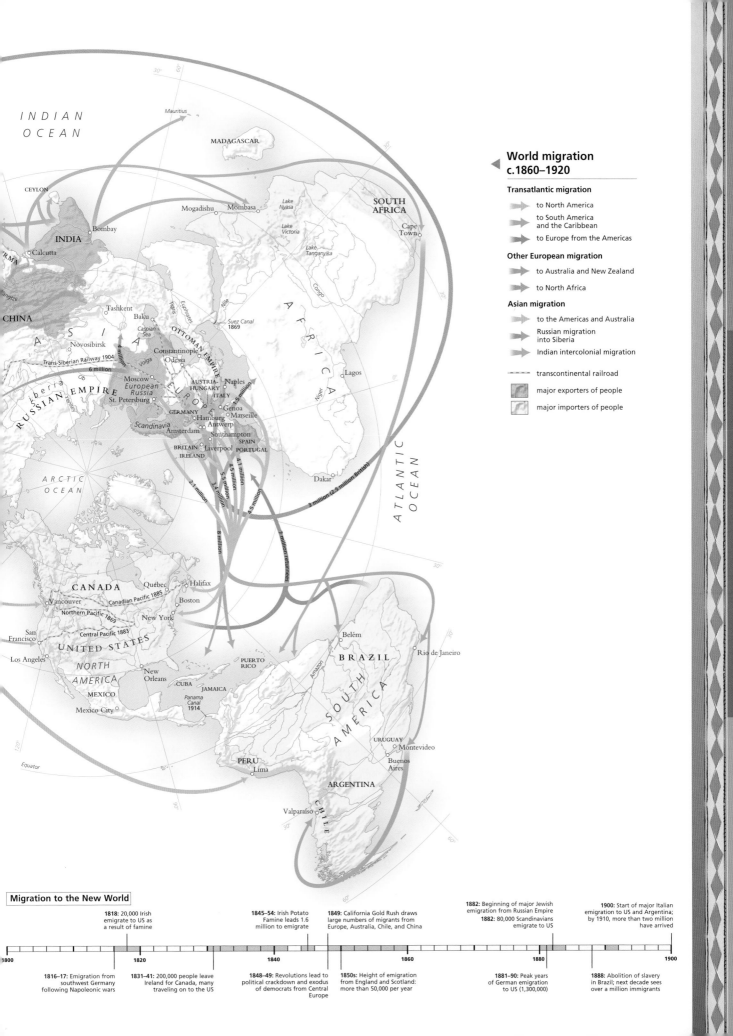

Trade in the 19th Century

In the first half of the 19th century, world trade and industry was dominated by Britain; by the 1870s, the industrial balance was shifting in favor of other nations, especially Germany, France, Russia, and the US, with rapid industrialization occurring throughout most of Europe by the end of the century. A stable currency, a standard (for example, the price of gold) against which the currency's value could be measured, and an effective private banking system were seen as essential to the growth and success of every industrializing nation. The major industrial nations also began to invest heavily overseas. Their aims were the discovery and exploitation of cheaper raw materials, balanced by the development of overseas markets for their products.

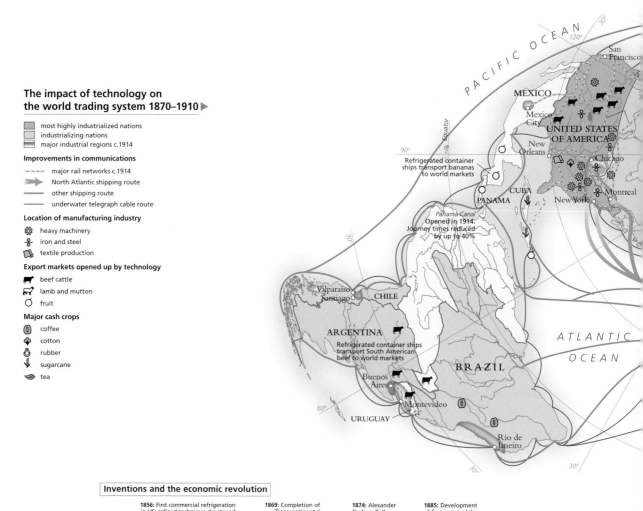

The impact of technology on the world trading system 1870–1910 ▶

- most highly industrialized nations
- industrializing nations
- major industrial regions c.1914

Improvements in communications

- major rail networks c.1914
- North Atlantic shipping route
- other shipping route
- underwater telegraph cable route

Location of manufacturing industry

- heavy machinery
- iron and steel
- textile production

Export markets opened up by technology

- beef cattle
- lamb and mutton
- fruit

Major cash crops

- coffee
- cotton
- rubber
- sugarcane
- tea

Inventions and the economic revolution

1856: First commercial refrigeration in US; refined technique developed in Australia by 1859	**1869:** Completion of Transcontinental Railroad in US	**1874:** Alexander Graham Bell patents telephone	**1885:** Development of first automobile by Daimler and Benz	

1835   1845   1855   1865   1875   1885   1895

1838: Invention of first electric telegraph in Britain

1856: Bessemer invents process for mass production of steel

1863: Construction of London Underground begins

1880s: Refrigerated ships transport cheese, butter, and meat from New Zealand

1895: Invention of wireless telegraphy (radio) by Marconi

The Impact of the Industrial Revolution

World industrial output from 1870–1914 increased at an extraordinary rate: coal production by as much as 650%; steel by 2500%; steam engine capacity by over 350%. Technology revolutionized the world economy: the invention of refrigerated ships meant that meat, fruit, and other perishables could be shipped to Europe from as far away as New Zealand; sewing machines and power looms allowed the mass production of textiles and clothing; telephones, telegraphs, and railroads made communications faster.

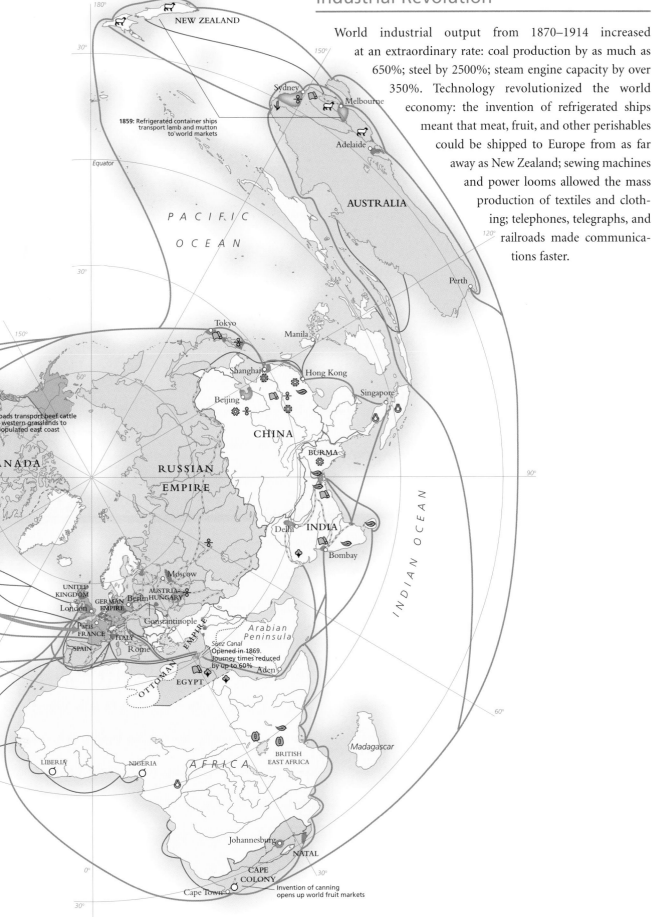

NEW ZEALAND

Sydney

Melbourne

1859: Refrigerated container ships transport lamb and mutton to world markets

Adelaide

Equator

PACIFIC OCEAN

AUSTRALIA

Perth

Tokyo

Manila

Shanghai

Hong Kong

Beijing

Singapore

CHINA

BURMA

railroads transport beef cattle from western grasslands to the populated east coast

CANADA

RUSSIAN EMPIRE

Delhi

INDIA

Bombay

INDIAN OCEAN

Moscow

UNITED KINGDOM

AUSTRIA–HUNGARY

London

Berlin

GERMAN EMPIRE

Paris

Constantinople

Arabian Peninsula

FRANCE

ITALY

Rome

SPAIN

OTTOMAN EMPIRE

Suez Canal
Opened in 1869.
Journey times reduced by up to 60%

Aden

EGYPT

LIBERIA

NIGERIA

AFRICA

BRITISH EAST AFRICA

Madagascar

Johannesburg

NATAL

CAPE COLONY

Cape Town

Invention of canning opens up world fruit markets

Economic Systems

When we think of economics, we think of things and activities involving money. We think of the costs of goods and services, such as food, rent, haircuts, and movie tickets. We may also think of factories, farms, and other enterprises that produce the goods and services we need, or think we need. In industrial societies, workers may stand before a moving belt for eight hours, tightening identical bolts that glide by. For this task they are given bits of paper that may be exchanged for food, shelter, and other goods or services. But many societies—indeed, most that are known to anthropology—did not have money or the equivalent of the factory worker. Still, all societies have economic systems, whether or not they involve money. All societies have customs specifying how people gain access to natural resources; customary ways of transforming or converting those resources, through labor, into necessities and other desired goods and services; and customs for distributing and perhaps exchanging goods and services.

As we shall see in this chapter, a great deal of the cross-cultural variation in economic systems is related to how a society gets its food. However, other aspects of the culture also affect the economic system. These other influences, which we cover in subsequent chapters, include the presence or absence of social (class and gender) inequality, family and kinship groups, and the political system.

✦

The Allocation of Resources

Natural Resources: Land

Every society has access to natural resources—land, water, plants, animals, minerals—and every society has cultural rules for determining who has access to particular resources and what can be done with them. In societies like the United States, where land and many other things may be bought and sold, land is divided into precisely measurable units, the borders of which may be visible or invisible. Relatively small plots of land and the resources on them are usually owned by individuals. Large plots of land are generally owned collectively. The owner may be a government agency, such as the National Park Service, which owns land on behalf of the entire population of the United States. Or the owner may be a corporation—a private collective of shareholders. In the United States, property ownership entails a more or less exclusive right to use land or other resources (called *usufruct*) in whatever ways the owner wishes, including the right to withhold or prevent use by others. In the United States and many other societies, property ownership also includes the right to "alienate" property—that is, to sell, give away, bequeath, or destroy the resources owned. This type of property ownership is often referred to as a *private property* system.

Private property in regard to land is uncommon among most food collectors and most horticulturalists. There is no individual ownership of land or ownership by a group of unrelated people. If there is collective ownership, it is always by groups of related people (kinship groups) or by territorial groups (bands or villages). Land is not bought and sold.

Society specifies what is considered property and the rights and duties associated with that property.[1] These specifications are social in nature, for they may be changed over time. For example, France declared all its beaches to be public, thereby stating, in effect, that the ocean shore is not a resource that can be owned by an individual. As a result, all the hotels and individuals that had fenced off portions of the best beaches for their exclusive use had to remove the barriers. Even in countries with private property, such as the United States, people cannot do anything that they want with their property. Federal, state, and local governments have adopted legislation to prevent the pollution of the air and the water supply. Such regulation may be new, but the rights of ownership in the United States have been limited for some time. For example, land may be taken by the government for use in the construction of a highway; compensation is paid, but the individual cannot prevent confiscation. Similarly, people are not allowed to burn their houses or to use them as brothels or munitions arsenals. In short, even with an individualistic system of ownership, property is not entirely private.

How societies differ in their rules for access to land and other natural resources seems to be related in part to how they differ in food-getting. Let us now examine how food collectors, horticulturalists, pastoralists, and intensive agriculturalists structure rights to land in different ways. We look at traditional patterns first. As we shall see later, traditional rights to land have been considerably affected by state societies that have spread to and colonized native societies in the New World, Africa, and Asia.

FOOD COLLECTORS   As we have noted, members of food-collecting societies generally do not have private ownership of land. The reason is probably that land itself has no intrinsic value for food collectors; what is of value is the presence of game and wild plant life on the land. If game moves away or food resources become less plentiful, the land is less valuable. Therefore, the greater the possibility that the wild food supply in a particular locale will fluctuate, the less desirable it is to parcel out small areas of land to individuals and the more advantageous it is to make land ownership communal. The Hadza of Tanzania, for example, do not believe that they have exclusive rights over the land on which they hunt. Any member of the group can hunt, gather, or draw water wherever he or she likes.[2] This is not to say that private ownership of land does not exist among foragers. Among foragers heavily dependent on fishing in rivers, individual or family ownership is more common,[3] perhaps because the fishing in rivers is more predictable than other

kinds of foraging. Although food collectors rarely practice anything resembling individual ownership of land or other resources, there is considerable variation in the extent of communal ownership. In some societies, such as the Hadza, groups do not claim or defend particular territories. In fact, the Hadza do not even restrict use of their land to members of their own language group. But the Hadza are somewhat unusual. It is more common in food-collecting societies for a group of individuals, usually kin, to "own" land. To be sure, such ownership is not usually exclusive; typically some degree of access is provided to members of neighboring bands.[4]

At the other extreme, local groups in some foraging societies try to maintain exclusive rights to particular territories. The Owens Valley Paiute in the California part of the Great Basin lived all year in permanent villages along streams. A group of villagers claimed and defended a particular territory against intruders, who may or may not have been other Owens Valley Paiute.

Why have some food collectors been more territorial than others? One suggestion is that when the plants and animals collected are predictably located and abundant, groups are more likely to be sedentary and to try to maintain exclusive control over territories. In contrast, when plant and animal resources are unpredictable in location or amount, territoriality will tend to be minimal.[5] Territorial food collectors appear to have predictably located resources *and* more permanent villages, so it is hard to know which factor is more important in determining whether territory will be defended.

HORTICULTURALISTS   Like food collectors, most horticulturalists do not have individual or family ownership of land. This may be because rapid depletion of the soil necessitates letting some of the land lie fallow for a period of years or abandoning an area after a few years and moving to a new location. There is no reason for individuals or families to claim permanent access to land that, given available technology, is not usable permanently. But, in contrast to food collectors, horticulturalists are more likely to allocate particular plots of land to individuals or families for their use, although these individuals or families do not commonly own the land in our sense of potentially permanent ownership.

Among the Mundurucu of Brazil, the village controls the rights to use land. People in the community can hunt and fish where they like, and they have the right to clear a garden plot wherever land belonging to the community is not being used. Gardens can be cultivated for only two years before the soil is exhausted; then the land reverts to the community. The Mundurucu distinguish between the land and the produce on the land, so that a person who cultivates the land owns the produce. Similarly, the person who kills an animal or catches a fish owns it, no matter where it was obtained. But because all food is shared with others, it does not really matter who owns it. Rights to land became more individualized when Mundurucu men began to tap rubber trees for sale. Rights to a particular path in the forest where trees were tapped could not be bought and sold, but the rights could be inherited by a son or son-in-law.[6]

CURRENT RESEARCH AND ISSUES

Does Communal Ownership Lead to Economic Disaster?

A common idea in Western thought is that when land or other resources are held in common, serious damage results because individuals do not see it in their own interest to protect those resources. In a paper called "The Tragedy of the Commons," Garrett Hardin suggested that if animals are grazed on common land, it is economically rational for individual animal owners to graze as many animals as possible, since they do not incur the pasture costs. According to Hardin, tragedy results because pasture is degraded by overgrazing, and productivity falls. Similarly, why shouldn't a fisher take as much fish as possible from the ocean, a kind of commons, and not worry about the consequences? On the other hand, if the resource is privately owned, individuals might try to conserve their resources because degrading those resources will cost them in the long run by decreasing their yields. The theory, then, is that in order to minimize costs and maximize yields, private owners will find it rational to conserve their resources.

Is it really true that communal ownership tends to result in overexploitation of resources and lower yields, and private ownership tends to result in conservation of resources and higher yields? We do not have enough studies yet to generalize, but we do know about instances where communal grazing lands have been more productive than private grazing lands in comparable climates. For example, the Borana of Ethiopia, who have communal grazing, produce more animal protein per acre at lower cost than Australian cattle ranches, although the climates are similar. And there are instances, such as the overgrazing in the Great American Desert (described in the box "The Effect of Food-Getting on the Environment" in the preceding chapter), where private ownership did lead to degradation of the environment.

We have to remember that communal ownership does not mean that anyone can graze animals or fish at any time. Communities and kin groups often govern rights to pasturage or fishing, and only members of the group have rights of access and use. As we saw in the last chapter, pastoralists such as the Basseri have well-defined, socially arranged travel routes, moving their herds when conditions demand. For traditional pastoralists, mobility is often the key to prevent overgrazing. Similarly, many groups that fish have strict rules regulating access to fishing grounds, and some have conservation rules as well. For example, the Palauans of Micronesia usually allow only members of a cluster of villages to fish in the adjacent lagoon waters inside the fringing reef. Traditionally, people took only what they could eat, and there were "laws" governing the times that people could fish for certain species.

Restricted access to communal property may be the main way that pastoralists and fishers prevent degradation of their environment. Some groups, such as the Palauans, clearly have conservation rules. But we do not know how many pastoralists and fishers have such rules. For example, the Ponam of New Guinea do not appear to conserve fish resources, even though they restrict access to their communal fishing territories. They do value the prestige associated with generosity, and consequently they try to collect more fish than they need in order to give some away.

Development and commercialization may be more important than private versus communal ownership in leading to overgrazing or overfishing, at least initially. In Palau, which had traditional conservation practices, serious overfishing became a problem apparently only when people started to sell fish to Japanese colonists for imported trade goods. Some of those goods (nets and motors) helped to make fishing easier. Eventually, overfishing resulted in reduced catches and increased costs of fishing, and the Palauans had to buy much of their fish in imported cans. In arid areas of the Sahel in Africa, development may have led to pastoral overgrazing. Boreholes were built by development agencies to increase the water supply, but this practice often made people reluctant to move to new grazing land, so local land was overgrazed. In addition, the development of irrigation agriculture nearby decreased the amount of land available for pasturage.

So which is more likely in general to lead to conservation, communal ownership or private ownership? We cannot say yet. We need more systematic comparisons of many cases of the two types of systems to tell us.

Sources: Garrett Hardin, "The Tragedy of the Commons," *Science,* 162 (1968): 1243–48; Bonnie M. McCay and James M. Acheson, "Introduction," and James G. Carrier, "Marine Tenure and Conservation in Papua New Guinea," in Bonnie M. McCay and James M. Acheson, eds., *The Question of Commons: The Culture and Ecology of Communal Resources* (Tucson: University of Arizona Press, 1987); Michael M. Horowitz, "Donors and Deserts: The Political Ecology of Destructive Development in the Sahel," in Rebecca Huss-Ashmore and Solomon H. Katz, eds., *African Food Systems in Crisis. Part Two: Contending with Change* (New York: Gordon and Breach, 1990); R. E. Johannes, *Words of the Lagoon: Fishing and Marine Lore in the Palau District of Micronesia* (Berkeley: University of California Press, 1981); Robert Dirks, "Hunger and Famine," in *Research Frontiers* in Carol R. Ember, Melvin Ember, and Peter N. Peregrine eds., *New Directions in Anthropology* (Upper Saddle River, NJ: Prentice Hall, CD-ROM, 2004); John J. Poggie, personal communication, 1994.

PASTORALISTS The territory of pastoral nomads usually far exceeds that of most horticultural societies. Since their wealth ultimately depends on mobile herds, uncultivated pasture for grazing, and water for drinking, pastoralists often combine the adaptive potential of both food collectors and horticulturalists. Like food collectors, they generally need to know the potential of a large area of land. The Basseri, described in the last chapter, moved over an area of 15,000 square miles to obtain supplies of grass and water. And, like horticulturalists, pastoralists must move on when a resource is exhausted (in this case, until grass renews itself). Also like horticulturalists, they depend for subsistence on human manipulation of a natural resource—animals—as opposed to the horticulturalists' land.

Because land is only good if there is sufficient pasture and water, there would be considerable risk to individuals or families to own land that did not predictably have grass and water. So, like most foragers and horticulturalists, community members generally have free access to pasture land.[7] Although grazing land tends to be communally held, it is customary among pastoralists for animals to be owned by individuals.[8] Fredrik Barth argued that if animals were not so owned, the whole group might be in trouble because the members might be tempted to eat up their productive capital—their animals—in bad times. When animals are owned individually, a family whose herd drops below the minimum number of animals necessary for survival can drop out of nomadic life, at least temporarily, and work for wages in sedentary agricultural communities. But in so doing, such a family does not jeopardize other pastoral families. On the other hand, if the fortunate were to share their herds with the

unfortunate, all might approach bankruptcy. Thus, Barth argued, individual ownership is adaptive for a pastoral way of life.[9]

John Dowling questioned that interpretation. As he pointed out, pastoral nomads are not the only ones who have to save some of their "crop" for future production. Horticulturalists also must save some of their crop, in the form of seeds or tubers, for future planting. But horticulturalists generally lack private ownership of productive resources, so the necessity to save for future production cannot explain private ownership of animals in pastoral societies. Dowling suggested that private ownership will develop only in pastoral societies that depend on selling their products to non-pastoralists.[10] Thus, it may be the opportunity to sell their products as well as their labor that explains both the possibility of dropping out of nomadic life and the private ownership of animals among most pastoralists.

As among hunter-gatherers, pastoralists vary in how much a group actually has ownership rights to the territories through which they move their animals. The Basseri have rights to pass through certain areas, including agricultural areas and even cities, but they do not own the entire territory. The Baluch, another pastoralist group in the border region between Iran, Pakistan, and Afghanistan, claim a "tribal" territory, which they defend by force, if necessary.[11]

INTENSIVE AGRICULTURALISTS Individual ownership of land resources—including the right to use the resources and the right to sell or otherwise dispose of them—is common among intensive agriculturalists. The development of such ownership is partly a result of the possibility of using

A Surui village in the Amazon with cleared land for horticulture in the foreground and the surrounding rainforest in the background.

land season after season, which gives the land more or less permanent value. But the concept of individual ownership is also partly a political and social matter. So, for example, the occupation and cultivation of frontier land in the United States was transformed by law into individual ownership. Under the Homestead Act of 1862, if a person cleared a 160-acre piece of land and farmed it for five years, the federal government would consider that person the owner of the land. This practice is similar to the custom in some societies by which a kin group, a chief, or a community is obligated to assign a parcel of land to anyone who wishes to farm it. The difference is that once the American homesteader had become the owner of the land, the laws of the country gave the homesteader the right to dispose of it at will by selling or giving it away. Once individual ownership of land has become established, property owners may use their economic, and hence political, power to pass laws that favor themselves. In the early years of the United States, only property owners could vote.

Private individual ownership is usually associated with intensive agriculture, but not always. As we mentioned in the preceding chapter, intensive agriculture is usually associated with more complex political systems and with differences in wealth and power, so we need to understand the larger political and social context in order to understand particular systems of land allocation. For example, under the feudal and manor systems in much of medieval Europe, land and protection were granted by a higher aristocrat to a lower aristocrat (vassal) in exchange for military service and other obligations. If the vassal had no heirs, the land reverted to the higher aristocrat. Most of the farming was done by commoners—tenants and serfs. Tenants were granted land by the lord of a manor in return for labor, a portion of the crops, and military service when needed. Tenancy could be passed on to the children, and tenants technically were free to leave, but it was not easy to leave. Serfs, who had similar obligations to the lord of the manor, were bound to the land and could not leave, but neither could they be ejected.

In recent times, some communist and socialist nations with intensive agriculture formed agricultural collectives. For example, after World War II, the small farm holdings in a village in Bulgaria named Zamfirovo were incorporated into a village cooperative. Most of the villagers worked as laborers on the new cooperative, but every household was allocated a small plot by the cooperative on which to grow its own grain, vegetables, and grapes. These plots were fairly productive, and Westerners often attributed their productivity to private enterprise. But the cooperative provided much of the labor needed to plant and plow these plots, so they could hardly be considered private property. In 1989, after the overthrow of the communist regime, the cooperative was dissolved, and the land was divided and sold to private owners.[12]

COLONIALISM, THE STATE, AND LAND RIGHTS

Almost universally around the world, colonial conquerors and settlers have taken land away from the natives or aborigines. Even if the natives were given other land in exchange, as in Brazil and the United States, these reservations were often, if not always, poorer in potential than the original land. (If the reservation land hadn't been poorer in quality, the settlers would have taken it for themselves.) In addition, the new centralized governments often tried to change how land was owned by the natives, almost always in the direction of individual or private ownership. If kin groups or larger social entities owned the land, it would be more difficult for the settlers to get the natives to give it up, either by sale or threat. Individual owners could be dispossessed more easily.[13]

The newcomers who benefited from these forced changes were not always people of European background, but they were always people from expanding state societies. Beginning in the late 15th century, the expanding groups came mostly from Western Europe. But in recent times, as well as in the millennia before and after the time of Christ, conquerors and settlers have come from India, China, Japan, Arabia, Scandinavia, Russia, and other countries. This is not to say that native peoples in Africa, Asia, and the New World were never guilty of conquering and exploiting others on their continents or elsewhere. They were. The Aztecs in Mexico and Central America, the native kingdoms in West Africa after about 800 years ago, and the Arabs after the rise of Islam were just some of the expanding state societies of the past, before the rise of the West. Wherever there have been "civilized" (urban) societies, there have been imperialism and colonialism.

In North America, the British recognized the principle that lands not ceded to the crown would be Indian hunting grounds, but such recognition of rights by the British and then by the United States remained in force only as long as the various Indian groups remained numerous enough to constitute a threat to the settlers. President Andrew Jackson, for example, called for removal of all eastern Native American groups to "permanent" settlements west of the

Colonial governments have often taken land away from native peoples to establish enterprises such as plantations. Even after independence such lands remain as private enterprises. A Nepali girl harvests tea on a tea plantation.

Mississippi. Some 90,000 people were removed. But as settlers moved west, the reservations were often reduced in size. Government agents usually assumed that communal forms of ownership were detrimental to progress and enacted laws to assign land to individuals.[14] In much of colonial Africa, governments ceded land to European-owned companies for development. Reserves were established for large native populations, who then were invariably forced to work as laborers on European-owned plantations and in European-owned mines. In Kenya, for example, Europeans, who constituted less than 1 percent of the population, acquired access to or control of 20 percent of the land, mostly in the highlands, where there was the greatest potential for commercial production of tea and coffee.[15]

The taking of land by state authorities does not just happen with colonialism and imperialism. Indigenous revolutionary movements have collectivized land, as in Russia, or broken up large private landholdings, as in Mexico. Typically, state authorities do not like communal land-use systems. Mobile pastoralists are particularly viewed unfavorably by state authorities, because their mobility makes them difficult to control. Governments usually try to settle pastoralists or break up communally held pasture into small units.[16]

Technology

In order to convert resources to food and other goods, every society makes use of a technology, which includes tools, constructions (such as fish traps), and required skills (such as how and where to set up a fish trap). Societies vary considerably in their technologies and in the way access to technology is allocated. For example, food collectors and pastoralists typically have fairly small tool kits. They must limit their tools, and their material possessions in general, to what they can comfortably carry with them. As for access to technology, food collectors and horticulturalists generally allow equal opportunity. In the absence of specialization, most individuals have the skills to make what they need. But in an industrial society like our own, the opportunity to acquire or use a particular technology (which may be enormously expensive as well as complex) is hardly available to all. Most of us may be able to buy a drill or a hammer, but few of us can buy the factory that makes it.

The tools most needed by food collectors are weapons for the hunt, digging sticks, and receptacles for gathering and carrying. Andaman Islanders used bows and arrows for hunting game and large fish. Australian aborigines developed two types of boomerangs: a heavy one for a straight throw in killing game and a light, returning one for playing games or for scaring birds into nets strung between trees. The Semang of Malaya used poisoned darts and blowguns. The Mbuti of the Congo trap elephants and buffalo in deadfalls and nets. Of all food collectors, the Inuit probably had the most sophisticated weapons, including harpoons, compound bows, and ivory fishhooks. Yet the Inuit also had relatively fixed settlements with available storage space and dog teams and sleds for transportation.[17]

Among food collectors, tools are considered to belong to the person who made them. There is no way of gaining superiority over others through possession of tools, because whatever resources for toolmaking are available to one are available to all. In addition, the custom of sharing applies to tools as well as to food. For example, Elizabeth Thomas, speaking of the !Kung, said, "The few possessions that Bushmen have are constantly circulating among the members of their groups."[18]

Pastoralists, like food collectors, are somewhat limited in their possessions, for they too are nomadic. But pastoralists can use their animals to carry some possessions. Each family owns its own tools, clothes, and perhaps a tent, as well as its own livestock. The livestock are the source of other needed articles, for the pastoralists often trade their herd products for the products of the townspeople. Horticulturalists, on the other hand, are more self-sufficient than pastoralists. The knife for slashing and the hoe or stick for digging are their principal farming tools. What a person makes is considered his or her own, yet everyone is often obligated to lend tools to others. In Chuuk society, the owner of a canoe has first use of it; the same is true for farming implements. Yet if a close relative needs the canoe and finds it unused, the canoe may be taken without permission. A distant relative or neighbor must ask permission to borrow any tools, but the owner may not refuse. If owners were to refuse, they would risk being scorned and refused if they were to need tools later.

Societies with intensive agriculture and industrialized societies are likely to have tools made by specialists, which means that tools must be acquired by trade or purchase. Probably because complex tools cost a considerable amount of money, they are less likely than simple tools to be shared except by those who contributed to the purchase price. For example, a diesel-powered combine requires a large amount of capital for its purchase and upkeep. The person who has supplied the capital is likely to regard the machine as individual private property and to regulate its use and disposal. The owner must then use the machine to produce enough surplus to pay for its cost and upkeep as well as for its replacement. The owner may rent the machine to neighboring farmers during slack periods to obtain a maximum return on the investment.

Expensive equipment, however, is not always individually owned in societies with intensive agriculture or industrialized economies. Even in capitalist countries, there may be collective ownership of machines by cooperatives or co-ownership with neighbors.[19] Governments often own very expensive equipment or facilities that benefit some productive group as well as the public: Airports benefit airlines and travelers; highways benefit truckers, commuters, and travelers; dams benefit power and water companies as well as the consumers of water. Such resources are owned collectively by the whole society. Rights of use depend on the facility. Anyone can use a highway, but only contributing municipalities can draw upon the water in a dam. Other productive resources in industrial societies, such as factories or service companies, may be owned jointly by shareholders, who purchase a portion of a corporation's assets in return for a proportionate share of its earnings. The proportion of technology and facilities owned by various levels of government also reflects the type of political-economic system—socialist and communist countries have more public ownership than do capitalist countries.

The Conversion of Resources

In all societies, resources have to be transformed or converted through labor into food, tools, and other goods. These activities constitute what economists call *production*. In this section, after briefly reviewing different types of production, we examine what motivates people to work, how societies divide up the work to be done, and how they organize work. As we shall see, some aspects of the conversion of natural resources are culturally universal, but there is also an enormous amount of cultural variation.

Types of Economic Production

At the times they were first described, most of the societies known to anthropology had a *domestic*—family or kinship—mode of production. People labored to get food and to produce shelter and implements for themselves and their kin. Usually families had the right to exploit productive resources and control the products of their labor. Even part-time specialists, such as potters, could still support themselves without that craft if they needed to. At the other extreme are *industrial* societies, where much of the work is based on mechanized production, as in factories but also in mechanized agriculture. Because machines and materials are costly, only some individuals (capitalists), corporations, or governments can afford the expenses of production. Therefore, most people in industrial societies labor for others as wage earners. Although wages can buy food, people out of work lose their ability to support themselves, unless they are protected by welfare payments or unemployment insurance. Then there is the *tributary* type of production system, found in nonindustrial societies in which most people still produce their own food but an elite or aristocracy controls a portion of production (including the products of specialized crafts). The feudal societies of medieval western Europe were examples of tributary production, as was czarist Russia under serfdom.[20]

Many people have suggested that our own and other developed economies are now moving from *industrialism* to *postindustrialism*. In many areas of commerce, computers have radically transformed the workplace. Computers "drive" machines and robots, and much of the manual work required in industry is disappearing. Businesses are now more knowledge- and service-oriented. Information is more accessible with telecommunication, so much so that *telecommuting* has entered our vocabulary to describe how people can now work (for wages) at home. This economic transformation has important implications for both home life and the workplace. With inexpensive home computers and speedy data transmission by telephone and other means,

more and more people are able to work at home. In addition, when information and knowledge become more important than capital equipment, more and more people can own and have access to the productive resources of society.[21] If "who owns what" partly determines who has political and other influence, the wider ownership of resources that is possible in postindustrial society may eventually translate into new, more democratic political forms and processes.

Incentives for Labor

Why do people work? Probably all of us have asked ourselves this question. Our concern may not be why other people are working, but why we have to work. Clearly, part of the answer is that work is necessary for survival. Although there are always some able-bodied adults who do not work as much as they should and rely on the labor of others, no society would survive if most able-bodied adults were like that. In fact, most societies probably succeed in motivating most people to want to do (and even enjoy) what they have to do. But are the incentives for labor the same in all societies? Anthropologists think the answer is both yes and no. One reason people may work is because they must. But why do people in some societies apparently work *more* than they must?

We can be fairly certain that a particular and often-cited motive—the profit motive, or the desire to exchange something for more than it costs—is not universal or always the dominant motive. There can be no profit motive among people who produce food and other goods primarily for their own consumption, as do most food collectors, most horticulturalists, and even some intensive agriculturalists. Such societies have what we call a *subsistence economy,* not a money or commercial economy. Anthropologists have noticed that people in subsistence economies (with a domestic mode of production) often work less than people in commercial economies (with tributary or industrial modes of production). Indeed, food collectors appear to have a

In postindustrial economies, computers and robots rather than people do much of the work in factories. There are few people in this Bavarian brewery.

considerable amount of leisure time, as do many horticulturalists. It has been estimated, for example, that the men of the horticultural Kuikuru tribe in central Brazil spent about three and a half hours a day on subsistence. It appears that the Kuikuru could have produced a substantial surplus of manioc, their staple food, by working 30 minutes more a day.[22] Yet they and many other peoples do not produce more than they need. Why should they? They cannot store a surplus for long because it would rot; they cannot sell it because there is no market nearby; and they do not have a political authority that might collect it for some purpose. Although we often think "more is better," a food-getting strategy with such a goal might even be disastrous, especially for food collectors. The killing of more animals than a group could eat might seriously jeopardize the food supply in the future, because overhunting could reduce reproduction among the hunted animals.[23] Horticulturalists might do well to plant a little extra, just in case part of the crop failed, but a great deal extra would be a tremendous waste of time and effort.

It has been suggested that when resources are converted primarily for household consumption, people will work harder if they have more consumers in the household. That is, when there are few able-bodied workers and a proportionately large number of consumers (perhaps because there are many young children and elderly people), the workers have to work harder. But when there are proportionately more workers, they can work less. This idea is called *Chayanov's rule.*[24] Alexander Chayanov found this relationship in data on rural Russians before the Russian Revolution.[25] But it appears to work in other places too. Paul Durrenberger and Nicola Tannenbaum collected data in Thailand in several villages and found general support for Chayanov's rule.[26] And Michael Chibnik found support for Chayanov's rule when he compared data from 12 communities in five areas of the world. The communities ranged in complexity from New Guinea horticulturalists to commercial Swiss farmers. Although Chayanov restricted his theory to farmers who mostly produced food for their own consumption and did not hire labor, Chibnik's analysis suggests that Chayanov's rule applies even for hired labor.[27] However, Durrenberger and Tannenbaum found that political and social factors explained some of the variability in household production. For example, in the villages that lacked social classes, families with a high ratio of workers to consumers produced less, apparently to avoid doing much better than other families. In contrast, in the villages that had social classes, households with a high ratio of workers to consumers produced more, and gained prestige from their efforts.[28]

But there appear to be many societies, even with subsistence economies, in which some people work harder than they need to just for their own families' subsistence. What motivates them to work harder? It turns out that many subsistence economies are not oriented just to household consumption. Rather, sharing and other transfers of food and goods often go well beyond the household, sometimes including the whole community or even groups of communities, as we will see later in this chapter. In such societies, social rewards come to those who are generous, who give

things away. Thus, people who work harder than they have to for subsistence may be motivated to do so because they thereby gain respect or esteem.[29] In many societies too, as we shall see in subsequent chapters, extra food and goods may be needed at times for special purposes and occasions; goods and services may be needed to arrange and celebrate marriages, to form alliances, and to perform rituals and ceremonies (including what we would call sporting events). Thus, how the culture defines what one works for and what is needed may go beyond what is necessary.

In commercial economies such as our own—where foods, other goods, and services are sold and bought—people seem to be motivated to keep any extra income for themselves and their families. Extra income is converted into bigger dwellings, more expensive furnishings and food, and other elements of a "higher" standard of living. But the desire to improve one's standard of living is probably not the only motive operating. Some people may work partly to satisfy a need for achievement,[30] or because they find their work enjoyable. In addition, just as in precommercial societies, some people may work partly to gain respect or influence by giving some of their income away. Not only do we respect philanthropists and movie stars for giving to charities; our society encourages such giving by making it an allowable tax deduction. Still, the emphasis on giving in commercial societies is clearly less developed than in subsistence economies. We consider charity by the religious or rich appropriate and even admirable, but we would think it foolish or crazy for people to give so much away that they become poverty-stricken.

Forced and Required Labor

Thus far we have mostly discussed *voluntary labor*—voluntary in the sense that no formal organization within the society compels people to work and punishes them for not working. Social training and social pressure are powerful enough to persuade an individual to perform some useful

The Great Wall of China, like many monumental works in ancient societies, was built with forced labor.

Division of Labor

All societies have some division of labor, some customary assignment of different kinds of work to different kinds of people. Universally, males and females and adults and children do not do the same kinds of work. In a sense, then, division of labor by gender and age is a kind of universal specialization of labor. Many societies known to anthropology divide labor only by gender and age; other societies have more complex specialization.

BY GENDER AND AGE All societies make use of gender differences to some extent in their customary assignment of labor. In the chapter on sex, gender, and culture, we discuss the division of labor by gender in detail.

Age is also a universal basis for division of labor. Clearly, children cannot do work that requires a great deal of strength. But in many societies girls and boys contribute much more in labor than do children in our own society. For example, they help in animal tending, weeding, and harvesting and do a variety of domestic chores such as child care, fetching water and firewood, and cooking and cleaning. In agricultural communities in the Ivory Coast, children's tasks mirror the tasks of same-sex adults (see Figure 18–1).

A boat-builder specialist working in Barbados.

task. In both food-collecting and horticultural societies, individuals who can stand being the butt of jokes about laziness will still be fed. At most, they will be ignored by the other members of the group. There is no reason to punish them and no way to coerce them to do the work expected of them.

More complex societies have ways of forcing people to work for the authorities, whether those authorities are kings or presidents. An indirect form of forced labor is taxation. The average tax in the United States (local, state, and federal) is about 33 percent of income, which means that the average person works four months out of the year for the various levels of government. If a person decides not to pay the tax, the money will be taken forcibly or the person may be put in prison.

Money is the customary form of tax payment in a commercial society. In a politically complex but nonmonetary society, persons may pay their taxes in other ways—by performing a certain number of hours of labor or by giving up a certain percentage of what they produce. The **corvée,** a system of required labor, existed in the Inca Empire in the central Andes before the Spanish conquest. Each male commoner was assigned three plots of land to work: a temple plot, a state plot, and his own plot. The enormous stores of food that went into state warehouses were used to supply the nobles, the army, the artisans, and all other state employees. If labor became overabundant, the people were still kept occupied; it is said that one ruler had a hill moved to keep some laborers busy. In addition to subsistence work for the state, Inca commoners were subject to military service, to duty as personal servants for the nobility, and to other "public" service.[31]

The draft, or compulsory military service, is also a form of corvée, in that a certain period of service is required, and failure to serve can be punished by a prison term or involuntary exile. Emperors of China had soldiers drafted to defend their territory and to build the Great Wall along the northern borders of the empire. The wall extends over 1,500 miles, and thousands were drafted to work on it. Slavery is the most extreme form of forced work, in that slaves have little control over their labor. Because slaves constitute a category or class of persons in many societies, we discuss slavery more fully in the chapter on social stratification.

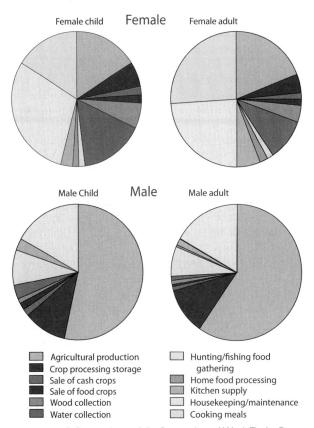

Figure 18–1 A Comparison of the Proportion of Work Tasks Done by Adults and Children.

Source: From James A. Levine, Robert Weisell, Simon Chevassus, Claudio D. Martinez, and Barbara Burlingame. "The Distribution of Work Tasks for Male and Female Children and Adults Separated by Gender" in "Looking at Child Labor," *Science 296* (10 May 2002): 1025.

In some societies, a child that is 6 years old is considered old enough to be responsible for a younger sibling for a good part of the day.[32] Animal tending is often important work for children. Children in some societies spend more time at this task than adults.[33]

Why do children do so much work in some societies? If adults, particularly mothers, have heavy workloads, and children are physically and mentally able to do the work, a good part of the work is likely to be assigned to children.[34] As we have seen, food producers probably have more work than food collectors, so we would expect that children would be likely to work more where there is herding and farming. Consistent with this expectation, Patricia Draper and Elizabeth Cashdan found differences in children's work between nomadic and settled !Kung. Even though recently settled !Kung have not switched completely from food collection to food production, children's as well as adults' activities have changed considerably. The children living in nomadic camps had virtually no work at all; adults did all the gathering and hunting. But the settled children were given lots of chores, ranging from helping with animals to helping with the harvest and food processing.[35]

What we have said about the !Kung should not imply that children in foraging societies always do little work. For example, among the Hadza of Tanzania, children between the ages of 5 and 10 are able to get one-third to one-half of their calories as they forage with their mothers. The Hadza also have more children than the !Kung.[36] Is there a relationship between children's work and fertility? When children in a society do a great deal of work, parents may value them more and may consciously want to have more children.[37] This may be one of the reasons why birth rates are especially high in intensive agricultural societies where workloads are very high.[38]

In some societies, work groups are formally organized on the basis of age. Among the Nyakyusa of southeastern Africa, for example, cattle are the principal form of wealth, and boys that are 6 to 11 years old herd the cattle for their parents' village. The boys join together in herding groups to tend the cattle of their fathers and of any neighboring families that do not have a son of herding age.[39]

BEYOND GENDER AND AGE   In societies with relatively simple technologies, there is little specialization of labor beyond that of gender and age. But as a society's technology becomes more complex and it is able to produce large quantities of food, more of its people are freed from subsistence work to become specialists in some other tasks—canoe builders, weavers, priests, potters, artists, and the like.

In contrast with food collectors, horticultural societies may have some part-time specialists. Some people may devote special effort to perfecting a particular skill or craft—pottery making, weaving, house building, doctoring—and in return for their products or services be given food or other gifts. Among some horticultural groups, the entire village may specialize part time in making a particular product, which can then be traded to neighboring people.

With the development of intensive agriculture, full-time specialists—potters, weavers, blacksmiths—begin to appear.

The trend toward greater specialization reaches its peak in industrialized societies, where workers develop skills in one small area of the economic system. The meaninglessness and dehumanizing effect of much of industrialized work was depicted by Charlie Chaplin in the film *Modern Times*. When his character left the factory after repeatedly tightening the same kind of bolt all day long, he could not stop his arms from moving, as if they were still tightening bolts. Full-time specialization means more than producing a product or providing a service full time. Such specialization makes people dependent on the necessity to sell their labor or products in order to make a living. In societies with full-time occupational specialization, different jobs are usually associated with differences in prestige, wealth, and power, as we shall see in the chapter on social stratification.

The Organization of Labor

The degree to which labor has to be organized reaches its peak in industrial societies, which have great occupational specialization and complex political organization. The coordination required to produce an automobile on an assembly line is obvious; so is the coordination required to collect taxes from every wage earner.

In many food-collecting and horticultural societies there is little formal organization of work. Work groups tend to be organized only when productive work requires it and to dissolve when they are no longer needed. Furthermore, the groups so organized often have changing composition and leadership; participation tends to be individualistic and voluntary.[40] Perhaps this flexibility is possible because when virtually everyone has the same work to do, little instruction is needed, and almost anyone can assume leadership. Still, some types of work require more organization than others. Hunting big game usually requires coordinated efforts by a large number of hunters; so might catching fish in large nets. For example, on Moala, a Fijian island in the Pacific, net fishing is a group affair. Saturday is the most popular day for communal netting. A party of 20 to 30 women wade out on the reef and make a semicircle of nets. At a signal from an experienced woman, usually the chief's wife, the women move together at the ends, forming a circle. After the fish are caught in the nets, the women bite them on the backs of their heads to kill them and put them in baskets that they carry ashore. A larger fish drive is undertaken by the village, or several villages, around Christmas. The day before, more than 100 people make a "sweep," some 1,600 yards long, from coconut fronds. The next day, the men, women, and children all participate in the surround, catching thousands of fish.[41]

Kinship ties are an important basis for work organization, particularly in nonindustrial societies. For example, among the horticultural Kapauku of western New Guinea, the male members of a village are a kin group, and all work together to build drainage ditches, large fences, and bridges.[42] With increasing technological complexity, the basis of work organization begins to shift to more formally organized groups.[43] In modern industrial societies, the predominant basis of organization is the *contract*—the agreement between

Sharing can occur even in a socially stratified society. Here we see men in a village in Yunnan, China, cutting the meat from a steer into 72 portions for the families of the village.

employers and employees whereby the latter perform a specified amount of work for a specified amount of wages. Although the arrangement may be entered into voluntarily, laws and the power of the state enforce the obligation of the parties to abide by the contract.

Making Decisions About Work

Food collectors ignore many of the plant and animal species in their environment, choosing to go after only some. Why? The people may say that some animals are taboo whereas others are delicious. But where do such customary beliefs come from? Are they adaptive? And if there are no customary preferences for certain plants and animals, how can we explain why a food collector will go after certain foods and ignore others on a particular day? Food producers also make choices constantly. For example, a farmer has to decide when to plant, what to plant, how much to plant, when to harvest, how much to store, and how much to give away or sell. Researchers have tried to explain why certain economic decisions become customary and why individuals make certain economic choices in their everyday lives.

A frequent source of ideas about choices is **optimal foraging theory,** which was developed originally by students of animal behavior and which has been applied to decision making by food collectors. Optimal foraging theory assumes that individuals seek to maximize the returns, in calories and nutrients, on their labor in deciding which animals and plants to hunt or collect. Natural selection should favor optimal foraging because "good" decisions would increase the chances of survival and reproduction. Research in different food-collecting societies supports the optimal foraging model.[44] For example, the Aché of eastern Paraguay consistently prefer to hunt peccaries (wild piglike mammals) rather than armadillos. Although peccaries take much longer to find and are harder to kill than armadillos, a day spent hunting peccaries yields more than 4,600 calories per hour of work, whereas hunting armadillos yields only about 1,800 calories an hour.[45] Other factors in addition to calorie yield, such as predictability of resources, may also influence which

foods are collected. For example, the !Kung of the Kalahari Desert depend largely on mongongo nuts, even though these nuts yield fewer calories per hour of work than does meat. But mongongo nuts in season are more dependable than game is. Once a group of !Kung hikes to a grove of ripe mongongo nuts, they know they can obtain food there until the supply is exhausted; they are not as certain of getting game when they seek it.[46] Similarly on Ifaluk, an atoll in the Federated States of Micronesia where fishing is the main source of animal protein, men most often choose to fish in the place where there is the highest return on average. But they do not always fish there; if the return on a previous day was lower than average, they tend to choose other spots.[47]

How does a farmer decide whether to plant a particular crop and how much land and labor to devote to it? Christina Gladwin and others suggested that farmers make decisions in steps, with each choice point involving a yes or no answer. For example, in the high-altitude region of Guatemala, farmers could choose to plant about eight crops, or combinations of them, such as corn and beans, which grow together well. A farmer will quickly exclude some choices because of the answers to certain questions: Can I afford the seed and fertilizer? Can this crop be watered adequately? Is the altitude appropriate? And so on. If any of the answers is no, the crop is not planted. By a further series of yes or no decisions, farmers presumably decide which of the remaining possibilities will be planted.[48]

Individuals may not always be able to state clearly their rules for making decisions, nor do they always have complete knowledge about the various possibilities, particularly when some of the possibilities are new. That does not mean, however, that economic choices cannot be predicted or explained by researchers. For example, Michael Chibnik found that men in two villages in Belize, in Central America, were not able to say why they devoted more or less time to working for wages versus growing crops. But their behavior was still predictable. Older men grew crops because wage labor was more physically demanding; and in the village with a higher cost of living, men were more likely to work for wages.[49]

The Distribution of Goods and Services

Goods and services are distributed in all societies by systems that, however varied, can be classified under three general types: reciprocity, redistribution, and market or commercial exchange.[50] The three systems often coexist in a society, but one system usually predominates. The predominant system seems to be associated with the society's food-getting technology and, more specifically, its level of economic development.

Reciprocity

Reciprocity consists of giving and taking without the use of money; it mainly takes the form of gift giving or generalized reciprocity. There may also be exchanges of equal value (trade) or balanced reciprocity, without the use of money.[51]

GENERALIZED RECIPROCITY   When goods or services are given to another, without any apparent expectation of a return gift, we call it **generalized reciprocity.** Generalized reciprocity sustains the family in all societies. Parents give food, clothing, and labor to children because they want to or perhaps feel obliged to, but they do not usually calculate exactly how their children will reciprocate years later. These gifts are one-way transfers. In this sense, all societies have some kind of generalized reciprocity. But some societies depend on it almost entirely to distribute goods and services.

Lorna Marshall recounted how the !Kung divided an eland brought to a site where five bands and several visitors were camping—more than 100 people in all. The owner of the arrow that had first penetrated the eland was, by custom, the owner of the meat. He first distributed the forequarters to the two hunters who had aided him in the kill. After that, the distribution depended on kinship: Each hunter shared with his wives' parents, wives, children, parents, and siblings, and they in turn shared with their kin. Sixty-three gifts of raw meat were recorded, after which further sharing of raw and cooked meat was begun. The !Kung distribution of large game—clearly, generalized reciprocity—is common among foragers. But giving away is not limited to game. For example, when Marshall left the band that had sponsored her in 1951, she gave each woman in the band a present of enough cowrie shells to make a necklace—one large shell and 20 small ones. When she returned in 1952, there were no cowrie-shell necklaces and hardly a single shell among the people in the band. Instead, the shells appeared by ones and twos in the ornaments of the people of neighboring bands.[52]

Although generalized reciprocity may seem altruistic or unselfish, researchers have suggested that giving may in fact benefit the givers in various ways. For example, parents who help their children may not only perpetuate their genes (the ultimate biological benefit) but may also be likely to receive care and affection from their grown-up children when the parents are old. And giving parents may be happier and enjoy life more than nongiving parents. So, in the shorter as well as the longer run, givers may derive economic and psychological benefits, in addition to reproductive benefits.

Parent–child giving may seem easy to understand, but giving beyond the family is more of a problem. Why do some societies rely more on generalized reciprocity than others, particularly beyond the family? Sharing may be most likely when people are not sure they can get the food and water they need. In other words, sharing may be most likely if resources are unpredictable. So a !Kung band may share its water with other bands because they may have water now but not in the future. A related group in the Kalahari, the G//ana,[53] has been observed to share less than other groups. It turns out that the resources available to the G//ana are more predictable, because the G//ana supplement their hunting and gathering with plant cultivation and goat herding. Cultivated melons (which store water) appear to buffer the G//ana against water shortages, and goats to buffer them against shortages of game. Thus, whereas the !Kung distribute the meat right after a kill, the G//ana dry it and then store it in their houses.[54]

The idea that unpredictability favors sharing may also explain why some foods are more often shared than others. Wild game, for example, is usually unpredictable; when hunters go out to hunt, they cannot be sure that they will come back with meat. Wild plants, on the other hand, are more predictable; gatherers can be sure when they go out that they will come back with at least some plant foods. In any case, it does appear that game tends to be shared by food collectors much more than wild plant foods.[55] Even among people who depend largely on horticulture, such as the Yanomamö of Venezuela and Brazil, food items that are less predictably obtained (hunted game and fish) are shared more often than the more predictably obtained garden produce.[56] But while meat is shared more than plant food, foraged or cultivated plants are often shared by horticulturalists. Why? Sharing plant food may be advantageous to horticulturalists who are some distance from their gardens because they may not have to go as often. And sharing may solidify a social relationship so that other families will help in times of need, such as sickness or accident, that makes it hard to work.[57] Does food sharing increase the food supply for an individual? Calculations for the Aché of eastern Paraguay, who get most of their food from hunting when they go on food-collecting trips, suggest that the average individual gets more food when food is shared. Even the males who actually do the hunting get more, although the benefits are greater for the females and children on the trip.[58] Mathematically, the risk that an individual food collector will not find enough food on a particular day will be appreciably reduced if at least six to eight adult collectors share the food they collect. Food-collecting bands may often contain only 25 to 30 people, which is about the size that is needed to ensure that there are six to eight adult collectors.[59]

Although giving things to others may be expected in some societies, this does not necessarily mean that everyone does so willingly or without some social pressure. For example, the !Kung call "far-hearted" anyone who does not give gifts, and they express their disapproval openly. The necessity to reduce tensions, to avoid envy and anger, and to keep all social relations peaceful, not only within their own band but among all !Kung bands, creates continuing cross-currents of obligation and friendship. These are maintained, renewed,

MIGRANTS AND IMMIGRANTS

Working Abroad to Send Money Home

Throughout recorded history, people have been going to other places to make a living. They do it not just because they need jobs to support themselves, but also to support their families back home. Indeed, the people left behind might suffer terribly, or even starve, without the money sent back to them (which economists call "remittances"). Going to another country to work temporarily generated more than $100 billion in remittances in 2003. In the 19th century, men from China were recruited to come to North America to build the transcontinental railroads, and Italians were recruited to work on building the railroads in New York State, New Jersey, Connecticut, and Massachusetts. In the years after World War II, when West German businesses were short of labor because so many people had been killed in the war, men from Turkey were recruited to come to Germany to fill the available jobs. Now, 30–40 years later, they make up a sizeable proportion of the population. Most if not all of the labor-short countries in western Europe (including England and France, the Netherlands, Sweden, Norway, Italy, and Spain) have attracted considerable numbers of immigrants in recent years. Indeed, much like the U.S. before them, the countries of western Europe are now becoming quite diverse culturally.

We may think that many if not most immigrants want to stay in the countries they have moved to. But this was not always true in the past, and it is not always true today. Many in the past just wanted to stay a few years. They wanted to earn money to help relatives back home, and maybe (if they were lucky) they could earn enough money to return home themselves and buy a farm or other small business. They often didn't become citizens in the new country because they didn't intend to stay. But until recently most immigrants never went home again, and by the second or third generation they had lost their native languages. In the last few decades people who move to other countries to work often go home again—and again and again. They have become "transnationals," fluent in at least two languages, and comfortable living in different countries alternately. They may even retain two (or more) citizenships. Consider how different this is from many past immigrants who were highly motivated to "pass." It is not clear yet what explains why some people are more comfortable now with not passing. Could it be that some places are less ethnocentric than in the past? If so, why is that?

Not all moves to another country turn out well for the migrants. Consider the poor young women from Sri Lanka who are recruited to work as housemaids in other countries. They may be burned or beaten if their work is deemed unacceptable, and they may return home with no money saved from their work time abroad. One in every 19 citizens of Sri Lanka now works abroad, most of them as housemaids. For a country like Sri Lanka, migration has become a safety valve for the economy. The Sri Lankan economy may be advantaged by the remittances received, but not without suffering for some of the migrants.

Sources: Melvin Ember, Carol R. Ember, and Ian Skoggard, eds., *Encyclopedia of Diasporas: Immigrant and Refugee Cultures Around the World*, 2 vols. (New York: Kluwer Academic/Plenum, 2004); Amy Waldman, "Sri Lankan Maids' High Price for Foreign Jobs," *The New York Times*, May 8, 2005, pp. 1, 20.

---

or established through the generalized reciprocity of gift giving. In a sense, one can say that in exchange for a gift, one gains prestige or perhaps "social credit" for a potential return at some indefinite time in the future. But this gain clearly is not based on explicit return considerations. Among the !Kung as well as other foraging groups, a person who does not hunt will still get a share of meat.

Day-to-day unpredictability is one thing; more prolonged scarcity is another. What happens to a system of generalized reciprocity when resources are scarce because of a drought or other disaster? Does the ethic of giving break down? Evidence from a few societies suggests that the degree of sharing may actually *increase* during the period of food shortage.[60] For example, in describing the Netsilik Inuit, Asen Balikci said, "Whenever game was abundant, sharing among non-relatives was avoided, since every family was supposedly capable of obtaining the necessary catch. In situations of scarcity, however, caribou meat was more evenly distributed throughout camp."[61] Sharing may increase during mild scarcity because people can minimize their deprivation, but generalized reciprocity may be strained by extreme scarcity. Ethnographic evidence from a few societies suggests that during famine, when individuals are actually dying from hunger, sharing may be limited to the household.[62]

Researchers generally have difficulty explaining sharing because they assume that, other things being equal, individuals would tend to be selfish. Most of the ideas about sharing have postulated that sharing is, in fact, advantageous to individuals in certain circumstances. And it is in those circumstances that societies have found ways to make sharing a moral issue or to otherwise make nonsharers extremely uncomfortable. But experimental evidence suggests that sharing is likely even with people who do not know each other or who have no expectation of any return in the future from that person. Experimenters set up "games" in which they can control for or eliminate certain responses. For example, in one game a particular player is given a certain amount of money and he or she decides how much of the money to offer to the second player in the game. The second player can accept or reject the offer. If the division is rejected, no one gets any money. If the division is accepted, both players receive the proposed division. If selfishness were normal, one would expect that the proposer of the division would try to give away as little as possible and the second player should always accept whatever is offered because otherwise nothing is gained. Surprisingly, equal divisions are commonly proposed and low offers are commonly rejected because they are viewed as unfair. If a person views the offer as unfair and forfeits any money, he or she seems willing to "punish" the greedy individual. While such experiments were mostly done at first in Western societies, we now have results from over 15 other societies that largely confirm the earlier results.[63] And there is now evidence suggesting that cooperation may even evoke pleasure. Researchers studying brain activity in women, who are playing a game allowing either cooperative or greedy strategies, found to their surprise that cooperation made certain areas of the brain light up. These areas are normally associated with pleasure, such as when eating desserts. So cooperation may be more "natural" than some people think.[64]

BALANCED RECIPROCITY   **Balanced reciprocity** is explicit and short term in its expectations of return. In contrast to generalized reciprocity or a one-way transfer, which has no expectation of a return, balanced reciprocity involves either an immediate exchange of goods or services or an agreed-upon exchange over a limited period of time. The !Kung, for instance, trade with the Tswana Bantu: a gemsbok hide for a pile of tobacco, five strings of beads made from ostrich eggshells for a spear, three small skins for a good-sized knife.[65] In the 1600s, the Iroquois of the North American Northeast traded deerskin to Europeans for brass kettles, iron hinges, steel axes, woven textiles, and guns.[66] The !Kung and Iroquois acquired trade goods by balanced reciprocity, but such exchanges were not crucial to their economies.

In contrast, some societies depend much more heavily on balanced reciprocity. For example, the Efe, who hunt and gather in the Ituri forest of central Africa, get most of their calories from manioc, peanuts, rice, and plaintains grown by another group—the agricultural Lese. Efe men and women provide labor to the Lese, and in exchange receive a portion of the harvest as well as goods such as metal pots and spears.[67] Pastoralists, too, are rarely self-sufficient, as we mentioned in the preceding chapter. They have to trade their pastoral products to agriculturalists to get the grain and other things they need.

Balanced reciprocity may mostly involve labor. Cooperative work parties usually exchange or balance gifts of labor. A cooperative work party, or *kuu*, among the Kpelle of Liberia may number from 6 to 40 persons, all of whom are generally relatives or friends. In addition to promising return work on a particular date, each farmer rewards the work party's hard day's labor by providing a feast and sometimes rhythmic music to work by.[68] When we say that an exchange is balanced, we do not mean to imply that the things exchanged are exactly equivalent in value or that the exchange is purely economic. In the absence of a money economy, where there is no explicit standard by which value can be judged, there is no way to assess value objectively. The point is that the parties in balanced reciprocity are freely giving each other the respective goods and services they each want; they are not coerced into doing so, so presumably they are not conceiving of the exchange as unbalanced.[69] And when something is valued, it may be valued for other than economic reasons. The exchange itself may also be fun, adventuresome, or aesthetically pleasing, or it may enhance social relationships.

Because exchanges can have different motivations, they can have different meanings. Consequently, some economic anthropologists now want to distinguish between gift and commodity exchanges. *Gift exchanges* are personal and involve the creation or perpetuation of some kind of enduring relationship between people and groups. In our society, the exchange of dinner invitations or Christmas gifts is motivated by social considerations; we are not interested only in the actual food or objects received. As we shall see shortly, some of the exchanges involved in the famous *kula* ring seem mostly to be motivated by the desire to establish or cement trade partnerships. In contrast, *commodity exchanges,* which can occur even in the absence of money, focus on the objects or services received—the transaction itself is the motive. When the transaction is completed, the relationship between the parties involved usually ends.[70]

The* Kula *Ring   The horticultural Trobriand Islanders, who live off the eastern coast of New Guinea, worked out an elaborate scheme for trading ornaments, food, and other necessities with the people of neighboring islands. The trade is essential, for some of the islands are small and rocky and cannot produce enough food to sustain their inhabitants, who specialize instead in canoe building, pottery making, and other crafts. Other islands produce far more yams, taro, and pigs than they need. According to Uberoi, the trade in necessary items is carefully hidden beneath the panoply of the ***kula* ring,** the ceremonial exchange of valued shell ornaments classically described by Bronislaw Malinowski.[71]

Two kinds of ornaments are involved in the ceremonial exchanges—white shell armbands (*mwali*), which travel around the circle of islands in a counterclockwise direction, and red shell necklaces (*soulava*), which travel in a clockwise direction (see Figure 18–2). The possession of one or more of these ornaments allows a man to organize an expedition to the home of one of his trading partners on another island. The high point of an expedition is the ceremonial giving of the valued *kula* ornaments. Each member of the expedition receives a shell ornament from his trading partner and then remains on the island for two or three days as the guest of that person. During the visit the trading of necessities goes on. Some of the exchange takes the form of gift giving between trading partners. There is also exchange or barter between expedition members and others on the island. By the time the visitors leave, they have accomplished a year's trading, without seeming to do so.

But the practical advantages of the *kula* ring are not the only gains. There may be purely social ones, for goods are traded with ease and enjoyment. A trading expedition takes on the flavor of adventure rather than business. Many of the traditions of the islands are kept alive: Myth, romance, ritual, and history are linked to the circulating ornaments, especially the larger, finer pieces, which are well known and recognized as heirlooms. The *kula* ring also permits wide ownership of valuables. Instead of possessing one valued object permanently, a man is able to possess many valued things within his lifetime, each for a year or so. Each object, when it is received, arouses enthusiasm in a way that one lifelong possession could not.[72]

Whatever the reasons for the origin of the *kula* ring, which may date back nearly 2,000 years, it continued to be an important institution after Papua New Guinea became an independent country. For example, active participation in the *kula* ring helped candidates in the 1960s and the 1970s to be elected to the national parliament.[73]

The *kula* is not the only form of exchange in Trobriand life. For example, on the two days following a burial, the kin of the deceased give yams, taro, and valuables to those who helped care for the deceased before death, to those who participated in the burial ceremonies, and to those who came to mourn the deceased. After these initial exchanges, the hamlet settles into mourning. Women from other hamlets bring food to the people in mourning, and the mourning women prepare bundles of banana leaves and weave skirts of banana fiber for later distribution. Husbands help their wives accumulate valuables to "buy" extra bundles of banana leaves. Then the women's mortuary ceremony is held. It is very competitive—each of the mourning women tries to distribute the most bundles and skirts. As many as 5,000 bundles and 30 skirts might be distributed by one mourning woman in a single day. Each of these giveaways completes a balanced reciprocity: The giver is reciprocating for gifts of goods and services received in the past. A woman's brothers gave her yams and taro during the year. She gives her brothers' wives bundles or skirts, which are also given to those who helped make the special mourning skirts and to those who brought or cooked food during the mourning period.[74]

Sometimes the line between generalized and balanced reciprocity is not so clear. Consider our gift giving at Christmas. Although such gift giving may appear to be generalized reciprocity, there may be strong expectations of balance. Two friends or relatives may try to exchange presents of fairly equal value, based on calculations of what last year's gift cost. If a person receives a $5 present when he or she gave a $25 present, that person will be hurt and perhaps angry. On the other hand, a person who receives a $500 present when he or she gave a $25 present may well be dismayed.

KINSHIP DISTANCE AND TYPE OF RECIPROCITY

Most food-collecting and horticultural societies depend on some form of reciprocity for the distribution of goods and labor. Marshall Sahlins suggested that the form of the reciprocity depends largely on the kinship distance between persons. Generalized reciprocity may be the rule for family members and close kinsmen. Balanced reciprocity may be practiced among equals who are not closely related. Persons who would consider it inappropriate to trade with their own families will trade with neighboring groups.[75] In general, the importance of reciprocity declines with economic development.[76] In societies with intensive agriculture, and even more so in industrialized societies, reciprocity distributes only a small proportion of goods and services.

RECIPROCITY AS A LEVELING DEVICE

Reciprocal gift giving may do more than equalize the distribution of goods within a community, as in the !Kung's sharing. It may also tend to equalize the distribution of goods between communities.

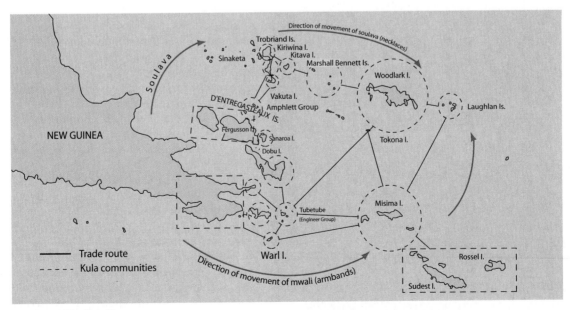

Figure 18–2 The *Kula* Ring

In the kula *ring, red shell necklaces (*soulava*) travel in a clockwise direction; white shell armbands (*mwali*) travel counterclockwise. The solid lines show the overseas trade routes. The dashed circles identify the* kula *communities, and the dashed rectangles show the areas indirectly affected by the* kula.

Many Melanesian societies in and near New Guinea have the custom of holding pig feasts in which 50, 100, or even 2,000 pigs are slaughtered. Andrew Vayda, Anthony Leeds, and David Smith suggested that these enormous feasts, though apparently wasteful, are just one of the outcomes of a complex of cultural practices that are highly advantageous. The people of these societies cannot accurately predict how much food they will produce during the year. Some years there will be bumper crops and other years very poor crops, because of fluctuations in the weather. So it might be wise to overplant just in case the yield is poor. Yet overplanting results in overproduction during average and exceptionally good years. What can be done with this extra food? Root crops such as yams and taro do not keep well over long periods, so any surplus is fed to pigs, which become, in effect, food-storing repositories. Pigs are then available for needed food during lean times. But if there are several years of surpluses, pigs can become too much of a good thing. Pigs wanting food can destroy yam and taro patches. When the pig population grows to menacing proportions, a village may invite other villages to a gigantic feast that results in a sharp reduction of the pig population and keeps the fields from being overrun. Over the years the pig feasts serve to equalize the food consumption, and especially the protein consumption, of all the villages that participate in the feasts.[77] Thus, the custom of pig feasts may be a way for villages to "bank" surplus food by storing up "social credit" with other villages, which will return that credit in subsequent feasts.

A man on the Northwest Pacific coast (southeastern Alaska) wears a "potlatch hat" showing how many potlatches he has had.

In some Melanesian societies, the pig feasts foster an element of competition among the men who give them. "Big men" may try to bolster their status and prestige by the size of their feasts. A reputation is enhanced not by keeping wealth but by giving it away. A similar situation existed among many Native American groups of the Pacific Northwest, where a chief might attempt to enhance his status by holding a **potlatch.** At a potlatch, a chief and his group would give away blankets, pieces of copper, canoes, large quantities of food, and other items to their guests. The host chief and his group would later be invited to other potlatches.

The competitive element in the potlatch appears to have intensified after contact with Europeans. Because of the fur trade, the number of trade goods increased, and so more items could be given away. Possibly more important was the population decline among the Indians, caused by diseases such as smallpox that were introduced by European traders. Distant relatives of chiefs who had no direct heirs might compete for the right to the title, each attempting to give away more than the others.[78] Chiefs may also have attempted to attract men to their half-empty villages by spectacular giveaways.[79] Decimated groups might have coalesced in order to maintain the potlatching. For example, when the Tlingit population declined to a low in the 1910s, kin groups coalesced in order to assemble enough resources for a potlatch.[80] Although the potlatch system seems wasteful in that goods were often destroyed in the competition, the system probably also served to equalize the distribution of goods among competing groups.

The Pomo Indians of central California had another way to bank credit for previous generosity. A village with an overabundance of fish or acorns might invite another village to a feast. In return for surplus fish or acorns, the guests would give the host village a certain number of beads. Before beginning the journey to the feast, the chief of the guest village would obtain from each family as many strings of beads as possible. After a few days of feasting at the host village, the chief would trade the beads for the supply of surplus fish or acorns. Each member of the visiting village would be given an equal share of the food, regardless of how many beads had been contributed. But the members of a village would not be invited to a feast unless they brought beads to trade, and they could not obtain beads unless they had given food away themselves sometime in the past. Thus, giving away food and receiving beads in return served as a means of storing social credit for times of scarcity. Later, if food was scarce in the former host village, the villagers could use the beads they had acquired by giving in the past to obtain food from another village with a surplus. The trade feasts, then, had the effect of equalizing the consumption of food not only within a village but over a fairly widespread area.[81]

On one level of analysis, the Melanesian pig feasts, the Pacific Northwest potlatches, and the Pomo trade feasts were all reciprocal exchanges between communities or villages. But these exchanges were not just intercommunity versions of reciprocal gift giving between individuals. Because these feasts were organized by people who collected goods, they also involved another mode of distribution, which anthropologists call *redistribution.*

Redistribution

Redistribution is the accumulation of goods or labor by a particular person, or in a particular place, for the purpose of subsequent distribution. Although redistribution is found in all societies, it becomes an important mechanism only in societies that have political hierarchies—that is, chiefs or other specialized officials and agencies. In all societies, there is some redistribution, at least within the family. Members of the family pool their labor, products, or income for the common good. But in many societies, there is little or no redistribution beyond the family. It seems that redistribution on a territorial basis emerges when there is a political apparatus to coordinate centralized collection and distribution of goods or to mobilize labor for some public purpose.

In the African state of Bunyoro, in western Uganda, for example, the king (called the *mukama*) retained much of the wealth for himself and his close kin. The *mukama* had the authority to grant the use of land and all other natural resources to his subordinate chiefs, and they in turn granted it to the common people. In return, everyone was required to give the *mukama* large quantities of food, crafts, and even labor services. The *mukama* then redistributed these goods and services, in theory at least, to all the people. The *mukama* was praised with names that emphasized his generosity: *Agutamba* ("he who relieves distress") and *Mwebingwa* ("he to whom the people run for help"). But it is clear that much of what the king redistributed did not find its way back to the common people, who produced the bulk of the goods. Instead, the wealth was distributed largely according to rank within the state.[82]

Other redistribution systems are more equal. For example, among the Buin of Melanesia, "the chief is housed, dressed, and fed exactly like his bondsman."[83] Even though the chief owns most of the pigs, everyone shares equally in the consumption of the wealth. In general, where redistribution is important, as in societies with higher levels of productivity, the wealthy are more likely than the poor to benefit from the redistributions.[84]

Why do redistribution systems develop? Elman Service suggested that they develop in agricultural societies that contain subregions suited to different kinds of crops or natural resources. Food collectors can take advantage of environmental variation by moving to different areas. With agriculture, the task is more difficult; it might be easier to move different products across different regions.[85] If the demand for different resources or products becomes too great, reciprocity between individuals might become awkward. So it might be more efficient to have someone—a chief, perhaps—coordinate the exchanges. We saw in the Pomo trade feasts that, although whole communities appeared to be engaged in reciprocal exchanges, the collection of surplus food and beads was handled by village chiefs.

Marvin Harris agreed that redistribution becomes more likely with agriculture, but for a somewhat different reason. He argued that competitive feasting, as in New Guinea, is adaptive because it encourages people to work harder to produce somewhat more than they need. Why would this feature be adaptive? Harris argued that with agriculture, people really have to produce more than they need so that they can protect themselves against crises such as crop failure. The groups that make feasts may be indirectly ensuring themselves against crises by storing up social credit with other villages, who will reciprocate by making feasts for them in the future. On the other hand, inducements to collect more than they need may not be advantageous to food-collecting groups, who might lose in the long run by overcollecting.[86]

Market or Commercial Exchange

When we think of markets we usually think of bustling, colorful places where goods are bought and sold. The exchanges usually involve money. In our own society we have supermarkets and the stock market and other places for buying and selling that we call shops, stores, and malls. In referring to **market** or **commercial exchange,** economists and economic anthropologists are referring to exchanges or transactions in which the "prices" are subject to supply and demand, whether or not the transactions actually occur in a marketplace.[87] Market exchange involves not only the exchange (buying and selling) of goods but also transactions of labor, land, rentals, and credit.

On the surface, many market exchanges resemble balanced reciprocity. One person gives something and receives something in return. How, then, does market exchange differ from balanced reciprocity? It is easy to distinguish market exchange from balanced reciprocity when money is directly involved, since reciprocity is defined as not involving money. But market exchange need not always involve money directly.[88] For example, a landowner grants a tenant farmer the right to use the land in exchange for a portion of the crop. So, to call a transaction market exchange, we have to ask whether supply and demand determine the price. If a tenant farmer gave only a token gift to the landowner, we would not call it market exchange, just as a Christmas gift to a teacher is not payment for teaching. If tenants, however, are charged a large portion of their crops when the supply of land is short, or if landowners lower their demands when few people want to tenant-farm, then we would call the transactions market or commercial exchange. The forces of supply and demand create considerable risk for those dependent on monetary exchange for life's necessities. A wage earner who loses a job may not be able to afford food or shelter; a farmer relying on a cash crop may not get a price sufficient to support the family. Societies with monetary exchange usually have considerable inequities in wealth and power.

KINDS OF MONEY   Although market exchange need not involve money, most commercial transactions, particularly nowadays, do involve what we call money. Some anthropologists define money according to the functions and characteristics of the **general-purpose money** used in our own and other complex societies, for which nearly all goods, resources, and services can be exchanged. According to this definition, money performs the basic functions of serving as an accepted medium of exchange, a standard of value, and a store of wealth. As a medium of exchange, it allows all goods and services to be valued in the same objective way; we say that an object or service is worth so much money.

Also, money is nonperishable, and therefore savable or storable, and almost always transportable and divisible, so transactions can involve the buying and selling of goods and services that differ in value.

Although money can technically be anything, the first money systems used rare metals such as gold and silver. These metals are relatively soft and therefore can be melted and shaped into standard sizes and weights. The earliest standardized coins we know of are said to have been made by the Lydians in Asia Minor and the Chinese, in the 7th century A.D. It is important to realize that money has little or no intrinsic value; rather, it is society that determines its value. In the United States today, paper bills, bank checks, and credit and debit cards are fully accepted as money, and money is increasingly transferred electronically.

General-purpose money is used both for commercial transactions (buying and selling) and for noncommercial transactions (payment of taxes or fines, personal gifts, contributions to religious and other charities). General-purpose money provides a way of condensing wealth: Gold dust or nuggets are easier to carry around than bushels of wheat; paper bills, a checkbook, and plastic cards are handier than a herd of sheep or goats.

In many societies, money is not an all-purpose medium of exchange. Many peoples whose food production per capita is not sufficient to support a large population of nonproducers of food have **special-purpose money.** This consists of objects of value for which only some goods and services can be exchanged on the spot or through balanced reciprocity. In some parts of Melanesia, pigs are assigned value in terms of shell money—lengths of shells strung together in units each roughly as long as the distance covered by a man's outstretched arms. According to its size, a pig will be assigned a value in tens of such units up to 100.[89] But shell money cannot be exchanged for all the goods or services a person might need. Similarly, a Pacific Northwest native could exchange food, but not most other goods and services, for a "gift of wealth," such as blankets. The gift was a "receipt" that entitled the person to receive an equal amount of food, but little else, later.

DEGREES OF COMMERCIALIZATION   Most societies were not commercialized at all, or only barely so, when first described in the ethnographic record by explorers, missionaries, and anthropologists. That is, most societies as first described did not rely on market or commercial exchange to distribute goods and services. But commercial exchange has become the dominant form of distribution in the modern world. Most societies of the ethnographic past are now incorporated into larger nation-states; for example, the Trobriand Islanders and other societies in Melanesia are now districts in the nation of Papua New Guinea. Selling today goes far beyond the nation-state. The world is now a multinational market.[90]

But there is considerable variation in the degree to which societies today depend on market or commercial exchange. Many societies still allocate land without purchase and distribute food and other goods primarily by reciprocity and redistribution, participating only peripherally in market ex-

change. These are societies in transition; their traditional subsistence economies are becoming commercialized. Among the Luo of western Kenya, for example, most rural families still have land that was allocated to them by their kin groups. The food they eat they mostly produce themselves. But many men also work for wages—some nearby, others far away in towns and cities, where they spend a year or two. These wages are used to pay government taxes, to pay for children's schooling, and to buy commercially produced items, such as clothes, kerosene lamps, radios, fish from Lake Nyanza, tea, sugar, and coffee. Occasionally, families sell agricultural surpluses or craft items such as reed mats. Economies such as that of the rural Luo are not fully commercialized, but they may become so in the future. In the chapter on culture change and globalization, we discuss some of the implications and effects of this transition to a more commercialized economy—a transition that is a worldwide phenomenon.

What anthropologists call *peasant economies* are somewhat more commercialized than transitional subsistence economies such as that of the Luo. Although **peasants** also produce food largely for their own consumption, they regularly sell part of their surplus (food, other goods, or labor) to others, and land is one of the commodities they buy, rent, and sell. But, although their production is somewhat commercialized, peasants still are not like the fully commercialized farmers in industrialized societies, who rely on the market to exchange all or almost all of their crops for all or almost all of the goods and services they need.

In fully commercialized societies such as our own, market or commercial exchange dominates the economy; prices and wages are regulated, or at least significantly affected, by the forces of supply and demand. A modern industrial or postindustrial economy may involve international as well as national markets in which everything has a price, stated in the same money terms—natural resources, labor, goods, services, prestige items, religious and ceremonial items. Reciprocity is reserved for family members and friends or remains behind the scenes in business transactions. Redistribution, however, is an important mechanism. It is practiced in the form of taxation and the use of public revenue for transfer payments and other benefits to low-income families—welfare, Social Security, health care, and so on. But commercial exchange is the major way goods and services are distributed.

WHY DO MONEY AND MARKET EXCHANGE DEVELOP?   Most economists think that money is invented in a society, or copied from another society, when trade increases and barter becomes increasingly inefficient. The more important or frequent trade is, the more difficult it is to find a person who can give something you want and wants something you have to give. Money makes it easy to trade. It is a valuable that may be exchanged for *anything,* and so it is an efficient medium of exchange when trade becomes important. In contrast, many anthropologists do not link the origins of money or market exchange to the necessities of trade. Instead, they link the origins of money to various noncommercial "payments," such as the *kula* valuables, the Pomo beads, and the taxes that have to be paid to a political authority. All of the available explanations of money suggest

APPLIED ANTHROPOLOGY

Impact of the World System—Deforestation of the Amazon

When we speak of the economic system of a people, we must keep in mind that probably no group has ever been completely isolated from outside economic, political, social, or environmental events. In the modern world, with the expanding demand and opportunity of a growing world market economy, even the most self-sufficient groups cannot avoid the effects of their connections to the outside world.

Consider the great rain forest drained by the Amazon River and its tributaries. Covering more than a billion acres, it is not only the home to many largely self-sufficient indigenous cultures; it also supports about 50 percent of all the earth's plants and animals. Yet the Amazon forest and other tropical forests are disappearing at an alarming rate because of their increased use. Some have suggested that the world demand for wood, hamburger, and gold is largely responsible for the diminution of the Amazon forest.

Like many tropical forests, the Amazon has large numbers of desirable hardwood trees. Forests in Africa and Asia are already largely depleted, so the demand for wood from the Amazon has grown considerably. In addition, the Amazon Development Agency in Brazil has offered incentives to clear forest for cattle ranching, which can provide hamburger to fast-food restaurants. There is little concern that a few seasons of overgrazing can make it impossible even for grasses to grow in the soils of the former forest.

The indigenous people often find themselves in a land squeeze, with loggers, cattle ranchers, and miners trying to encroach on their territory. With less land, food-getting and traditional economic practices are in jeopardy. But it is naive to assume that the indigenous people are interested only in maintaining their traditional economies. They often accept the dilemma of economic development: They might lose some land, but selling

rights to loggers and miners brings in money, which they can use to buy things they need and want. Development experts and applied anthropologists are searching for ways to achieve development without destroying or degrading the environment. For example, indigenous groups are encouraged to gather Brazil nuts, a wild but renewable resource, for sale. Others are encouraged to harvest latex (natural rubber) and hearts of palm. Medicinal plants have economic value to multinational pharmaceutical and biotechnical companies, which have discovered that the conservation of biodiversity may be economically advantageous to themselves as well as to the local people and to scientists who want to study the diversity.

Can development be sustainable? That is, are resources (such as hardwoods) renewable, so that both economic productivity and the environment can be protected? Even if some kind of sustainable development is possible, organizing it may require concerted effort by all involved, which requires participation by all in decision making. Whether we like it or not, economic development and the desire for it are not going to go away. But we need to do more than applaud or bemoan economic development. In particular, we need research that reveals what impact particular changes will have on people, other animals, plants, and the environment. Most of all, for the sake of human rights, we need to listen to the people whose lives will be most affected, to understand their needs as well as those of the developers.

Sources: Marguerite Holloway, "Sustaining the Amazon," *Scientific American* (July 1993): 91–9; Emilio F. Moran, *Through Amazon Eyes: The Human Ecology of Amazonian Populations* (Iowa City: University of Iowa Press, 1993); Robert Winterbottom, "The Tropical Forestry Plan: Is It Working?" in Pamela J. Puntenney, ed., *Global Ecosystems: Creating Options through Anthropological Perspectives,* NAPA Bulletin 15 (1995): 60–70.

that money will be found mostly in societies at higher levels of economic development; and indeed it is. When simpler societies have money, dominant and more complex societies have usually introduced it.[91]

Most theories about the development of money and market exchange assume that producers have regular surpluses they want to exchange. But why do people produce surpluses in the first place? Perhaps they are motivated to produce extra only when they want to obtain goods from a distance and the suppliers of such goods are not well known to them, making reciprocity less likely as a way to obtain those goods. So some theorists suggest that market exchange begins with

external, or intersocietal, trade; kin would not likely be involved, so transactions would involve bargaining, and therefore market exchange, by definition. Finally, some argue that as societies become more complex and more densely populated, social bonds between individuals become less kinlike and friendly, and therefore reciprocity becomes less likely.[92] Perhaps this is why traders in developing areas are often foreigners or recent immigrants.[93]

In any case, Frederic Pryor's cross-cultural research supports the notion that all types of market exchange—goods, labor, land, and credit—are more likely with higher levels of economic productivity. Pryor also found that market

Fiesta sponsors spend a great deal of money for food and drink as well as for musicians and dancers. Here we see a fiesta in Oaxaca, Mexico.

exchange of goods appears at lower levels of economic development than market exchange of labor and credit; market exchange of land, probably because it is associated with private property (individual ownership), appears mostly at the highest levels of productivity. Perhaps surprisingly, smaller societies tend to have more market exchange or trade with other societies. Larger societies can presumably get more of what they need from inside the society; for example, until recently China had relatively little foreign trade throughout much of its history.[94]

POSSIBLE LEVELING DEVICES IN COMMERCIAL ECONOMIES   As we will see in the next chapter, societies that depend substantially on market or commercial exchange tend to have marked differences in wealth among the people. Nonetheless, there may be mechanisms that lessen the inequality, that act at least partially as leveling devices. Some anthropologists have suggested that the fiesta complex in highland Indian communities of Latin America may be a mechanism that tends to equalize income.[95] In these peasant villages, fiestas are held each year to celebrate important village saints. The outstanding feature of this system is the extraordinary amount of money and labor a sponsoring family must contribute. Sponsors must hire ritual specialists, pay for church services, musicians, and costumes for dancers, and cover the complete cost of food and drink for the entire community. The costs incurred can very easily amount to a year's wages.[96]

Some anthropologists have suggested that, although the richer Indians who sponsor fiestas are clearly distributing a good deal of wealth to the poorer members of their own and other communities, the fiestas do not really level wealth at all. First, true economic leveling would entail the redistribution of important productive resources such as land or

animals; the fiesta only temporarily increases the general level of consumption. Second, the resources expended by the sponsors are usually extra resources that have been accumulated specifically for the fiesta, which is why the sponsors are always appointed in advance. Third, and perhaps most important, the fiestas do not seem to have reduced long-term wealth distinctions within the villages.[97]

In nations such as ours, can the income tax and the social-assistance programs it pays for, such as welfare and disaster relief, be thought of as leveling devices? Theoretically, our tax system is supposed to work that way, by taxing higher incomes at higher rates. But we know that in fact it doesn't. Those in higher income brackets can often deduct an appreciable amount from their taxable incomes and therefore pay taxes at a relatively low rate. Our tax system may help some to escape extreme poverty, but, like the fiesta system, it has not eliminated marked distinctions in wealth.

⊚ Summary

1. All societies have economic systems, whether or not these involve the use of money. All societies have customs specifying access to natural resources; customary ways of transforming or converting those resources, through labor, into necessities and other desired goods and services; and customs for distributing and perhaps exchanging goods and services.

2. Regulation of access to natural resources is a basic factor in all economic systems. The concept of individual or private ownership of land—including the right to use its resources and the right to sell or otherwise dispose of them—is common among intensive agriculturalists. In contrast, food collectors, horticulturalists, and pas-

toralists generally lack individual ownership of land. Among pastoral nomads, however, animals are considered family property and are not usually shared.

3. Every society makes use of a technology, which includes tools, constructions, and required skills. Even though food collectors and horticulturalists tend to think of tools as "owned" by the individuals who made them, the sharing of tools is so extensive that individual ownership does not have much meaning. Among intensive agriculturalists, toolmaking tends to be a specialized activity. Tools tend not to be shared, except mainly by those who have purchased them together.

4. Incentives for labor vary cross-culturally. Many societies produce just for household consumption; if there are more consumers, producers work harder. In some subsistence economies, people may work harder to obtain the social rewards that come from giving to others. Forced labor generally occurs only in complex societies.

5. Division of labor by gender is universal. In many nonindustrial societies, large tasks are often accomplished through the cooperative efforts of a kinship group. Such cooperation is not as prevalent in industrialized societies. In general, the more technically advanced a society is, the more surplus food it produces and the more some of its members engage in specialized work.

6. The organization of labor reaches its peak in complex societies; work groups tend to be formally organized, and sometimes there is an enforced obligation to participate. In food-collecting and horticultural societies, in contrast, there is little formal organization of work.

7. Goods and services are distributed in all societies by systems that can be classified under three types: reciprocity, redistribution, and market or commercial exchange. Reciprocity is giving and taking without the use of money and generally assumes two forms: generalized reciprocity and balanced reciprocity. Generalized reciprocity is gift giving without any immediate or planned return. In balanced reciprocity, individuals exchange goods and services immediately or in the short term.

8. Redistribution is the accumulation of goods or labor by a particular person, or in a particular place, for the purpose of subsequent distribution. It becomes an important mechanism of distribution only in societies with political hierarchies.

9. Market or commercial exchange, where "prices" depend on supply and demand, tends to occur with increasing levels of economic productivity. Especially nowadays, market exchange usually involves an all-purpose medium of exchange—money. Most societies today are at least partly commercialized; the world is becoming a single market system.

◎ Glossary Terms

◎ Critical Questions

1. What conditions might enable us to achieve a world of sustainable resources?
2. What are the possible effects of a postindustrial economy in which a large proportion of the population has inexpensive access to computers and information?
3. Do you expect any appreciable change in the amount of resources privately owned in the future? State your reasons.

◎ Research Navigator

1. Please go to www.researchnavigator.com and enter your LOGIN NAME and PASSWORD. For instructions on registering for the first time, please view the detailed instructions at the end of Chapter 1.
2. Using the *New York Times* section find an article on the impact of AIDs on economies in Africa.
3. Using Link Library choose Anthropology and then Cultural Anthropology. Under Cultural Anthropology you will find "Tutorials." Choose "Economic Anthropology" and read about Non-Market Economies. Cite something new that you have learned.

◎ Discovering Anthropology: Researchers at Work

Read "Yanomamö: Varying Adaptations of Foraging Agriculturalists" by Raymond B. Hames in *Discovering Anthropology* and answer these case study questions:

1. Why does Hames refer to the Yanomamö as "foraging horticulturalists"?
2. Customary behavior in all societies varies somewhat over time as well as over space. What kinds of differences did Hames find in food-getting and economy between lowland and highland groups?
3. Hames measured how people spend their time during the day. What differences did he find between women and men's work? Which gender generally worked more? Does the conclusion change depending on how work is defined?

CHAPTER NINETEEN

Social Stratification: Class, Ethnicity, and Racism

A long-enduring value in the United States is the belief that "all men are created equal." These famous words from the American Declaration of Independence do not mean that all people are equal in wealth or status but rather that all (including women nowadays) are supposed to be equal before the law. Equality before the law is the ideal. But the ideal is not always the actuality. Some people have advantages in legal treatment, and they generally also tend to have advantages of other kinds, including economic advantages. Without exception, recent and modern industrial and postindustrial societies such as our own are *socially stratified*—that is, they contain social groups such as families, classes, or ethnic groups that have unequal access to important advantages such as economic resources, power, and prestige.

Hasn't such inequality always existed? Anthropologists, based on firsthand observations of recent societies, would say not. To be sure, even the simplest societies (in the technological sense) have some differences in advantages based on age, ability, or gender—adults have higher status than children, the skilled more than the unskilled, men more than women (we discuss gender stratification in the next chapter). But anthropologists would argue that *egalitarian* societies exist where *social groups* (e.g., families) have more or less the same access to rights or advantages. As we noted in the last chapter, the economic systems of many food collectors and horticulturalists promote equal access to economic resources for all families in the community. Moreover, such societies also tend to emphasize the sharing of food and other goods, which tends to equalize any small inequalities in resources between families. Until about 10,000 years ago, all human societies depended on food they hunted, gathered, and/or fished. And so we might expect that egalitarianism characterized most of human history. That is indeed what archaeology suggests. Substantial inequality generally appears only with permanent communities, centralized political systems, and intensive agriculture, which are cultural features that began to appear in the world only in the last 10,000 years. Before that time, then, most societies were probably egalitarian. In the world today, egalitarian societies have all but disappeared because of two processes—the global spread of commercial or market exchange and the voluntary or involuntary incorporation of many diverse people into large, centralized political systems. In modern societies, some groups have more advantages than others. These groups may include *ethnic* groups. That is, ethnic diversity is almost always associated with differential access to advantages. When ethnic diversity is also associated with differences in physical features such as skin color, the social stratification may involve *racism,* the belief that some "racial" groups are inferior.

Systems of social stratification are strongly linked to the customary ways in which economic resources are allocated, distributed, and converted through labor into goods and services. So we would not expect much inequality if all people had relatively equal access to economic resources. But stratification cannot be understood solely in terms of economic resources; there are other benefits such as prestige and power that may be unequally distributed. We first examine how societies vary in their systems of stratification. Then we turn to possible explanations of why they vary.

※

Variation in Degree of Social Inequality

Societies vary in the extent to which social groups, as well as individuals, have unequal access to advantages. In this chapter we are concerned with differential or unequal access to three types of advantages: (1) wealth or economic resources, (2) power, and (3) prestige. **Economic resources** are things that have value in a culture; they include land, tools and other technology, goods, and money. **Power,** a second but related advantage, is the ability to make others do what they do not want to do; power is influence based on the threat of force. When groups in a society have rules or customs that give them unequal access to wealth or resources, they generally also have unequal access to power. So, for example, when we speak of a "company town" in the United States, we are referring to the fact that the company that employs most of the residents of the town usually has considerable control over them. Finally, there is the advantage of **prestige.**

When we speak of prestige, we mean that someone or some group is accorded particular respect or honor. Even if it is true that there is always unequal access by individuals to prestige (because of differences in age, gender, or ability), there are some societies in the ethnographic record that have no social groups with unequal access to prestige.

Thus, anthropologists conventionally distinguish three types of society in terms of the degree to which different social groups have unequal access to advantages: *egalitarian, rank,* and *class societies* (see Table 19–1). Some societies in the ethnographic record do not fit easily into any of these three types; as with any classification scheme, some cases seem to straddle the line between types.[1] **Egalitarian societies** contain no social groups with greater or lesser access to economic resources, power, or prestige. **Rank societies** do not have very unequal access to economic resources or to power, but they do contain social groups with unequal access to prestige. Rank societies, then, are partly stratified. **Class societies** have unequal access to all three advantages—economic resources, power, and prestige.

Table 19–1 Stratification in Three Types of Societies				
	SOME SOCIAL GROUPS HAVE GREATER ACCESS TO:			
Type of Society	Economic Resources	Power	Prestige	Examples
Egalitarian	No	No	No	!Kung, Mbuti, Australian aborigines, Inuit, Aché, Yanomamö
Rank	No	No	Yes	Samoans, Tahiti, Trobriand Islands, Ifaluk
Class/caste	Yes	Yes	Yes	United States, Canada, Greece, India, Inca

Egalitarian Societies

Egalitarian societies can be found not only among foragers such as the !Kung, Mbuti, Australian aborigines, Inuit, and Aché, but also among horticulturalists such as the Yanomamö and pastoralists such as the Lapps. An important point to keep in mind is that egalitarian does not mean that all people within such societies are the same. There will always be differences among individuals in age and gender and in such abilities or traits as hunting skill, perception, health, creativity, physical prowess, attractiveness, and intelligence. According to Morton Fried, egalitarian means that within a given society "there are as many positions of prestige in any given age/sex grade as there are persons capable of filling them."[2] For instance, if a person can achieve high status by fashioning fine spears, and if many persons in the society fashion such spears, then many acquire high status as spear makers. If high status is also acquired by carving bones into artifacts, and if only three people are considered expert carvers of bones, then only those three achieve high status as carvers. But the next generation might produce eight spear makers and 20 carvers. In an egalitarian society, the number of prestigious positions is adjusted to fit the number of qualified candidates. We would say, therefore, that such a society is not socially stratified.

There are, of course, differences in position and prestige arising out of differences in ability. Even in an egalitarian society, differential prestige exists. But, although some persons may be better hunters or more skilled artists than others, there is still *equal access* to status positions for people of the same ability. Any prestige gained by achieving high status as a great hunter, for instance, is neither transferable nor inheritable. Because a man is a great hunter, it is not assumed that his sons are also great hunters. There also may be individuals with more influence, but it cannot be inherited, and there are no groups with appreciably more influence over time. An egalitarian society keeps inequality at a minimal level.

Any differences in prestige that do exist are not related to economic differences. Egalitarian groups depend heavily on *sharing,* which ensures equal access to economic resources despite differences in acquired prestige. For instance, in some egalitarian communities, some members achieve higher status through hunting. But even before the hunt begins, how the animal will be divided and distributed among the members of the band has already been decided according to custom. The culture works to separate the status achieved by members—recognition as great hunters—from actual possession of the wealth, which in this case would be the slain animal.

Just as egalitarian societies do not have social groups with unequal access to economic resources, they also do not have social groups with unequal access to power. As we will see later in the chapter on political organization, unequal access to power by social groups seems to occur only in state societies, which have full-time political officials and marked differences in wealth. Egalitarian societies use a number of customs to keep leaders from dominating others. Criticism and ridicule can be very effective. The Mbuti of central Africa shout down an overassertive leader. When a Hadza man (in Tanzania) tried to get people to work for him, other Hadza made fun of him. Disobedience is another strategy. If a leader tries to command, people just ignore the command. In extreme cases, a particularly domineering leader may be killed by community agreement; this behavior was reported among the !Kung and the Hadza. Finally, particularly among more nomadic groups, people may just move away from a leader they don't like. The active attempts to put down upstarts in

In egalitarian societies, such as among the Mbuti hunter-gatherers, houses tend to look the same.

many egalitarian societies prompts Christopher Boehm to suggest that dominance comes naturally to humans. Egalitarian societies work hard to reverse that tendency.[3] The Mbuti provide an example of a society almost totally equal: "Neither in ritual, hunting, kinship nor band relations do they exhibit any discernible inequalities of rank or advantage."[4] Their hunting bands have no leaders, and recognition of the achievement of one person is not accompanied by privilege of any sort. Economic resources such as food are communally shared, and even tools and weapons are frequently passed from person to person. Only within the family are rights and privileges differentiated.

Foraging societies with extensive sharing of resources are more readily labeled egalitarian as compared with some pastoral societies where households may vary considerably in the number of animals they own. Should we consider a pastoral society with unequal distribution of animals egalitarian? Here there is controversy. One important issue is whether unequal ownership persists through time—that is, inherited. If vagaries of weather, theft, and gifts of livestock to relatives make livestock ownership fluctuate over time, wealth differences may mostly be temporary. A second important issue is whether the inequalities in livestock ownership make any difference in the ease of acquiring other "goods," such as prestige and political power. If wealth in livestock is ephemeral and is not associated with differential access to prestige and power, then some anthropologists would characterize such pastoral societies as egalitarian.[5] It is easy to imagine how an egalitarian society with some wealth differences, as opposed to one with no wealth differences, could become a rank or a class society. All you would need is a mechanism for retaining more wealth in some families over time.

Rank Societies

Most societies with social *ranking* practice agriculture or herding, but not all agricultural or pastoral societies are ranked. Ranking is characterized by social groups with unequal access to prestige or status but *not* significantly unequal access to economic resources or power. Unequal access to prestige is often reflected in the position of chief, a rank to which only some members of a specified group in the society can succeed.

Unusual among rank societies were the 19-century Native Americans who lived along the northwestern coast of the United States and the southwestern coast of Canada. An example were the Nimpkish, a Kwakiutl group.[6] These societies were unusual because their economy was based on food collecting. But huge catches of salmon—which were preserved for year-round consumption—enabled them to support fairly large and permanent villages. These societies were similar to food-producing societies in many ways, not just in their development of social ranking. Still, the principal means of proving one's high status was to give wealth away. The tribal chiefs celebrated solemn rites by grand feasts called *potlatches* at which they gave gifts to every guest.[7]

In rank societies, the position of chief is at least partly hereditary. The criterion of superior rank in some Polynesian societies, for example, was genealogical. Usually the eldest son succeeded to the position of chief, and different kinship groups were differentially ranked according to their genealogical distance from the chiefly line. In rank societies, chiefs are often treated with deference by people of lower rank. For example, among the Trobriand Islanders of Melanesia, people of lower rank must keep their heads lower than a person of higher rank. So, when a chief is standing, commoners must bend low. When commoners have to walk past a chief who happens to be sitting, he may rise and they will bend. If the chief chooses to remain seated, they must crawl.[8]

While there is no question that chiefs in a rank society enjoy special prestige, there is some controversy over whether they really do not also have material advantages. Chiefs may sometimes look as if they are substantially richer than commoners, for they may receive many gifts and have larger storehouses. In some instances, the chief may even be called the "owner" of the land. However, Marshall Sahlins maintains that the chief's storehouses only house temporary accumulations for feasts or other redistributions. And although the chief may be designated the "owner" of the land, others have the right to use the land. Furthermore, Sahlins suggests that the chief in a rank society lacks power because he usually cannot make people give him gifts or force them to work on communal projects. Often the chief can encourage production only by working furiously on his own cultivation.[9]

This picture of economic equality in rank societies is beginning to be questioned. Laura Betzig studied patterns of food sharing and labor on Ifaluk, a small atoll in the Western Carolines.[10] Chiefly status is inherited geneaologically in the female line, although most chiefs are male. (In the sex, gender, and culture chapter, we discuss why political leaders are usually male, even in societies structured around women.) As in other chiefly societies, Ifaluk chiefs are accorded deference. For example, during collective meals prepared by all the island women, chiefs were served first and were bowed to. The Ifaluk chiefs are said to control the fishing areas. Were the catches equitably distributed? Betzig measured the amount of fish each household got. All the commoners received an equal share, but the chiefs got extra fish; their households got twice as much per person as other households. Did the chiefs give away more later?

Theoretically, it is generosity that is supposed to even things out, but Betzig found that the gifts from chiefs to other households did not equal the amount the chiefs received from others. Furthermore, while everyone gave to the chiefs, the chiefs gave mostly to their close relatives. On Ifaluk, the chiefs did not work harder than others; in fact, they worked less. Is this true in other societies conventionally considered to be rank societies? We do not know. However, we need to keep in mind that the chiefs in Ifaluk were not noticeably better off either. If they lived in palaces with servants, had elaborate meals, or were dressed in fine clothes and jewelry, we would not need measures of food received or a special study to see if the chiefs had greater access to economic resources, because their wealth would be obvious.

In societies with rank and class, deference is usually shown to political leaders, as in the case of this Fon chief in the lowlands of Cameroon, Africa.

But rank societies may not have had as much economic equality as we used to think.

 Class Societies

In class societies, as in rank societies, there is unequal access to prestige. But, unlike rank societies, class societies are characterized by groups of people that have substantially greater or lesser access to economic resources and power. That is, not every social group has the same opportunity to obtain land, animals, money, or other economic benefits or the same opportunity to exercise power that other groups have. Fully stratified or class societies range from somewhat open to virtually closed class, or *caste*, systems.

Open Class Systems

A **class** is a category of persons who all have about the same opportunity to obtain economic resources, power, and prestige. Different classes have differing opportunities. We call class systems *open* if there is some possibility of moving from one class to another. Since the 1920s, there have been many studies of classes in towns and cities in the United States. Researchers have produced profiles of these different communities—known variously as Yankee City, Middle-

town, Jonesville, and Old City—all of which support the premise that the United States has distinguishable, though somewhat open, social classes. Both W. Lloyd Warner and Paul Lunt's Yankee City study[11] and Robert and Helen Lynd's Middletown study[12] concluded that the social status or prestige of a family is generally correlated with the occupation and wealth of the head of the family. Class systems are by no means confined to the United States. They are found in all nations of the modern world.

Although class status is not fully determined at birth in open class societies, there is a high probability that most people will stay close to the class into which they were born and will marry within that class. Classes tend to perpetuate themselves through the inheritance of wealth. John Brittain suggested that, in the United States, the transfer of money through bequests accounts for much of the wealth of the next generation. As we might expect, the importance of inheritance seems to increase at higher levels of wealth. That is, the wealth of richer people comes more from inheritance than does the wealth of not-so-rich people.[13]

Other mechanisms of class perpetuation may be more subtle, but they are still powerful. In the United States there are many institutions that make it possible for an upper-class person to have little contact with other classes. Private day and boarding schools put upper-class children in close contact mostly with others of their class. Attending these

People of the same social class tend to socialize together, where they live or where they vacation. Pictured here is an upscale hotel in Victoria, British Columbia.

schools makes it more likely they will get into universities with higher prestige. Debutante balls and exclusive private parties ensure that young people meet the "right people." Country clubs, exclusive city clubs, and service in particular charities continue the process of limited association. People of the same class also tend to live in the same neighborhoods. Before 1948, explicit restrictions kept certain groups out of particular neighborhoods, but after the U.S. Supreme Court ruled such discrimination unconstitutional, more subtle methods were developed. For instance, zoning restrictions may prohibit multiple-family dwellings in a town or neighborhood and lots below a certain acreage.[14]

Identification with a social class begins early in life. In addition to differences in occupation, wealth, and prestige, social classes vary in many other ways, including religious affiliation, closeness to kin, ideas about childrearing, job satisfaction, leisure-time activities, style of clothes and furniture, and (as noted in the chapter on communication and language) even in styles of speech.[15] People from each class tend to be more comfortable with those from the same class; they talk similarly and are more likely to have similar interests and tastes.

Class boundaries, though vague, have been established by custom and tradition; sometimes they have been reinforced by the enactment of laws. Many of our laws serve to protect property and thus tend to favor the upper and upper-middle classes. The poor, in contrast, seem to be disadvantaged in our legal system. The crimes the poor are most likely to commit are dealt with harshly by the courts, and poor people rarely have the money to secure effective legal counsel.

In open class systems it is not always clear how many classes there are. In Stanley Barrett's study of "Paradise," Ontario, some people thought that in the past there were only two classes. One person said, "There was the hierarchy, and

the rest of us." Another said that there were three classes: "The people with money, the in-between, and the ones who didn't have anything." Many said there were four: "The wealthy businessmen, the middle class, blue collar workers, and the guys that were just existing."[16] A few insisted that there were five classes. With the breakdown of the old rigid class structure, there are more people in the middle.[17]

DEGREE OF OPENNESS   Some class systems are more open than others; that is, it is easier in some societies to move from one class position to another. Social scientists typically compare the class of a person with the class of his or her parent or parents to measure the degree of mobility. Although most people aspire to move up, mobility also includes moving down. Obtaining more education, particularly a university education, is one of the most effective ways to move upward in contemporary societies. For example, in the United States, college-educated individuals have on average 60 percent more income than those without a college education.[18] In fact, in many countries educational attainment predicts one's social class better than parents' occupation does.[19]

How do the United States and Canada compare with other countries in degree of class mobility? Canada and Sweden have more mobility than the United States, France, and Britain. Japan and Italy have less mobility. If we focus on the ease of moving into the highest class, Italy, France, Spain, Germany, and Japan are more difficult than Britain and the United States.[20]

Class openness also varies over time. In "Paradise," Ontario, Barrett found that the rigid stratification system of the 1950s opened up considerably as new people moved into the community. No one disputed who belonged to the elite in the past. They were of British background, lived in the largest houses, had new cars, and vacationed in Florida.

Moreover, they controlled all the leadership positions in the town. By the 1980s, though, the leaders came mostly from the middle and working classes.[21]

DEGREE OF INEQUALITY   Degree of class mobility, however, is not the same as degree of economic inequality. For example, Japan, Italy, and Germany have less mobility than the United States, but less inequality (see below). Degree of inequality can vary considerably over time. In the United States, inequality has fluctuated considerably from the 1900s to the present. The greatest inequality was just before the 1929 stock market crash, when the top 1 percent had 42.6 percent of all the wealth. The least inequality was in the mid-1970s after the stock market declined by 42 percent. Then the top 1 percent controlled 17.6 percent of the wealth.

Change over time in the degree of inequality sometimes appears to have economic causes; for example, the 1929 crash made the wealthy less wealthy. But some of the change over time is due to shifts in public policy. During the New Deal of the 1930s, tax changes and work programs shifted more income to ordinary people; in the 1980s, tax cuts for the wealthy helped the rich get richer. In the 1990s, the rich continued to get richer and the poor got poorer.[22] One way of calculating the disparity between rich and poor is to use the ratio of income held by the top fifth of the households divided by the income held by the bottom fifth. Comparatively speaking, the United States presently has more inequality than any of the countries in western Europe, with a ratio of 9 to 1 (see Figure 19–1). That is, the top 20 percent of U.S. households controls nine times the wealth controlled by the bottom 20 percent. Norway, on the other hand, has a ratio of about 3.5 to 1. And Germany has a ratio of about 4.5 to 1. The degree of inequality in the United States exceeds that of India, with a ratio of about 5.5 to 1. South Africa and Brazil are among the most unequal countries, with ratios of 22 to 1 and 24 to 1, respectively.

Recognition of Class

Societies that have open class systems vary in the degree to which members of the society recognize that there are classes, albeit somewhat open classes. The United States is unusual in that despite objective evidence of multiple social classes, many people deny their existence. The ideology that hard work and strong character can transform anyone into a success appears to be so powerful that it masks the realities of social inequality.[23] A recent poll found that more people in the United States now believe that the chance of moving up has improved in the last few decades when in reality mobility has declined.[24] When we were growing up we were told that "Anyone can be President of the United States." As "proof" people pointed to a few individuals who rose from humble beginnings. But consider the odds. How many presidents have come from poor families? How many were not European in background? How many were not Protestant? (And, as we discuss in the next chapter, how many were not male?) So far, all of the presidents of the United States have been European in ancestry, all but one have been Protestant, and all have been male. And only a handful came from humble beginnings. In the Canadian town of "Paradise" the ideology of "classlessness" became more prevalent over time, paralleling the trend in the United States where most people see themselves as "middle class."[25] The paradox of an open class system is that to move up in the social ladder people seem to have to believe that it is possible to do so. However, it is one thing to believe in mobility; it is another thing to deny the existence of classes. Why might people need to deny that classes exist?

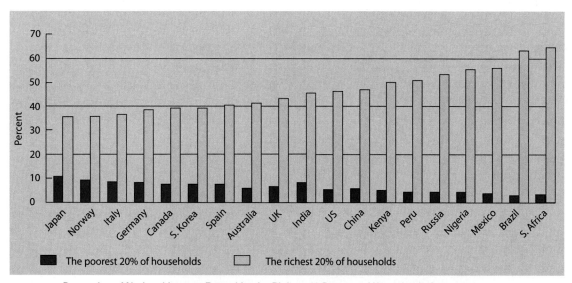

■ The poorest 20% of households   □ The richest 20% of households

Figure 19–1 Proportion of National Income Earned by the Richest 20 Percent of Households Compared with the Poorest 20 Percent: Selected Country Comparisons

Source: These data are abstracted from *2001 World Development Indicators.* Washington, D.C.: The World Bank, 2001, pp. 70–73.

Caste Systems

Some societies have classes that are virtually closed called castes. A **caste** is a ranked group in which membership is determined at birth, and marriage is restricted to members of one's own caste. The only way you can belong is by being born into the group; and since you cannot marry outside the group, your children cannot acquire another caste status either. In India, for example, there are several thousand hereditary castes. Although the precise ranking of these thousands of groups is not clear, there appear to be four main levels of hierarchy. The castes in India are often thought to be associated with different occupations, but that is not quite true. Most Indians live in rural areas and have agricultural occupations, but their castes vary widely.[26]

Castes may exist in conjunction with a more open class system. Indeed, in India today, members of a low caste who can get wage-paying jobs, chiefly those in urban areas, may improve their social standing in the same ways available to people in other class societies. In general, however, they still cannot marry someone in a higher caste, so the caste system is perpetuated.

Questions basic to all stratified societies, and particularly to a caste society, were posed by John Ruskin, a 19th-century British essayist: "Which of us . . . is to do the hard and dirty work for the rest—and for what pay? Who is to do the pleasant and clean work, and for what pay?"[27] In India those questions have been answered by the caste system, which mainly dictates how goods and services are exchanged, particularly in rural areas.[28] Who is to do the hard and dirty work for the rest of society is clearly established: A large group of Untouchables forms the bottom of the hierarchy. Among the Untouchables are subcastes such as the Camars, or leatherworkers, and the Bhangis, who traditionally are sweepers. At the top of the hierarchy, performing the pleasant and clean work of priests, are the Brahmans. Between the two extremes are thousands of castes and subcastes. In a typical village, the potter makes clay drinking cups and large water vessels for the entire village population. In return, the principal landowner gives him a house site and supplies him twice yearly with grain. Some other castes owe the potter their services: The barber cuts his hair; the sweeper carries away his rubbish; the washer washes his clothes; the Brahman performs his children's weddings. The barber serves every caste in the village except the Untouchables; he, in turn, is served by half of the others. He has inherited the families he works for, along with his father's occupation. All castes help at harvest and at weddings for additional payment, which sometimes includes a money payment.

This description is, in fact, an idealized picture of the caste system of India. In reality, the system operates to the advantage of the principal landowning caste—sometimes the Brahmans and sometimes other castes. Also, it is not carried on without some resentment; signs of hostility are shown toward the ruling caste by the Untouchables and other lower castes. The resentment does not appear to be against the caste system as such. Instead, the lower castes exhibit bitterness at their own low status and strive for greater equality. For instance, one of the Camars' traditional services is to remove dead cattle; in return, they can have the meat to eat and the hide to tan for their leatherworking. Because handling dead animals and eating beef are regarded as unclean acts, the Camars of one village refused to continue this service. Thus, they lost a source of free hides and food in a vain attempt to escape unclean status.

Since World War II, the economic basis of the caste system in India has been undermined somewhat by the growing practice of giving cash payment for services. For instance, the son of a barber may be a teacher during the week, earning a cash salary, and confine his haircutting to weekends. But he still remains in the barber caste (Nai) and must marry within that caste.

Perpetuation of the caste system is ensured by the power of those in the upper castes, who derive three main advan-

India has witnessed a marked increase in service and high technology jobs as companies around the world outsource many of their service activities to India. Caste is less important now for jobs.

tages from their position: economic, prestige, and sexual gains. The economic gain is the most immediately apparent. An ample supply of cheap labor and free services is maintained by the threat of sanctions. Lower-caste members may have their use of a house site withdrawn; they may be refused access to the village well or to common grazing land for animals; or they may be expelled from the village. Prestige is also maintained by the threat of sanctions; the higher castes expect deference and servility from the lower castes. The sexual gain is less apparent but equally real. The high-caste male has access to two groups of females, those of his own caste and those of lower castes. High-caste females are kept free of the "contaminating" touch of low-caste males because low-caste males are allowed access only to low-caste women. Moreover, the constant reminders of ritual uncleanness serve to keep the lower castes "in their place." Higher castes do not accept water from Untouchables, sit next to them, or eat at the same table with them.

Japan also had a caste group within a class society. Now called *burakumin* (instead of the pejorative *Eta*), this group traditionally had occupations that were considered unclean.[29] Comparable to India's Untouchables, they were a hereditary, endogamous (in-marrying) group. Their occupations were traditionally those of farm laborer, leatherworker, and basket weaver; their standard of living was very low. The burakumin are physically indistinguishable from other Japanese.[30] Discrimination against the burakumin was officially abolished by the Japanese government in 1871, but it was not until the 20th century that the burakumin began organizing to bring about change. These movements appear to be paying off as more active steps have been taken recently by the Japanese government to alleviate discrimination and poverty. As of 1995, 73 percent of burakumin marriages were with non-burakumin. In public opinion polls, two-thirds of burakumin now said that they had not encountered discrimination. However, most burakumin still live in segregated neighborhoods where unemployment, crime, and alcoholism rates are high.[31]

We turn now to some situations where the caste system appears to be associated with differences in physical appearance. In Rwanda, a country in east-central Africa, a long-time caste system was overthrown, first by an election and then by a revolution in 1959 to 1960. Three castes had existed, each distinguished from the others by physical appearance and occupation.[32] It is believed that the three castes derived from three different language groups that came together through migration and conquest. Later, however, they began to use a common language, although remaining endogamous and segregated by hereditary occupations. The taller and leaner ruling caste, the Tutsi, constituted about 15 percent of the population. They were the landlords and practiced the prestigious occupation of herding. The shorter and stockier agricultural caste, the Hutu, made up about 85 percent of the population. As tenants of the Tutsi, they produced most of the country's food. The much shorter Twa, accounting for less than 1 percent of the population, were foragers who formed the lowest caste.

Colonial rule, first by the Germans and then by the Belgians after World War I, strengthened Tutsi power. When the Hutu united to demand more of the rewards of their labor in 1959, the king and many of the Tutsi ruling caste were driven out of the country. The Hutu then established a republican form of government and declared independence from Belgium in 1962. In this new government, however, the forest-dwelling Twa were generally excluded from full citizenship. In 1990, Tutsi rebels invaded from Uganda, and attempts were made to negotiate a multiparty government. However, civil war continued, and in 1994 alone over a million people, mostly Tutsi, were killed. Almost 2 million refugees, mostly Hutu, fled to Zaire as the Tutsi-led rebels established a new government.[33]

In the United States, African Americans used to have more of a castelike status determined partly by the inherited characteristic of skin color. Until recently, some states had laws prohibiting an African American from marrying a European American. When interethnic marriage did occur, children of the union were often regarded as having lower status than European American children, even though they may have had blond hair and light skin. In the South, where treatment of African Americans as a caste was most apparent, European Americans refused to eat with African Americans or sit next to them at lunch counters, on buses, and in schools. Separate drinking fountains and toilets reinforced the idea of ritual uncleanness. The economic advantages and gains in prestige enjoyed by European Americans are well documented.[34] In the following sections, on slavery, racism, and inequality, we discuss the social status of African Americans in more detail.

Slavery

Slaves are persons who do not own their own labor, and as such they represent a class. We may associate slavery with a few well-known examples, such as ancient Egypt, Greece, and Rome or the southern United States, but slavery has existed in some form in almost every part of the world at one time or another, in simpler as well as in more complex societies. Slaves are often obtained from other cultures directly: kidnapped, captured in war, or given as tribute. Or they may be obtained indirectly as payment in barter or trade. Slaves sometimes come from the same culture; one became a slave as payment of a debt, as a punishment for a crime, or even as a chosen alternative to poverty. Slave societies vary in the degree to which it is possible to become freed from slavery.[35] Sometimes the slavery system has been a closed class, or caste, system, sometimes a relatively open class system. In different slave-owning societies, slaves have had different, but always some, legal rights.[36]

In ancient Greece, slaves often were conquered enemies. Because city-states were constantly conquering one another or rebelling against former conquerors, slavery was a threat to everyone. After the Trojan War, the transition of Hecuba from queen to slave was marked by her cry, "Count no one happy, however fortunate, before he dies."[37] Nevertheless, Greek slaves were considered human beings, and they could even acquire some higher-class status along with freedom. Andromache, Hecuba's daughter-in-law, was taken as a slave and concubine by one of the Greek heroes. When his legal wife produced no

CURRENT RESEARCH AND ISSUES

Is Global Inequality Increasing?

When people support themselves by what they collect and produce themselves, as most people did until a few thousand years ago, it is difficult to compare the standards of living of different societies because we cannot translate what people have into market or monetary value. It is only where people are at least partly involved in the world market economy that we can measure the standard of living in monetary terms. Today this comparison is possible for most of the world. Many people in most societies depend on buying and selling for a living; and the more people who depend on international exchange, the more possible it is to compare them in terms of standard economic indicators. We do not have such indicators for all the different societies, but we do have them for many countries. Those indicators suggest that the degree of economic inequality in the world is not only very substantial but has generally increased over time.

To convey just how economically unequal the world is, consider this. Surveying households in 91 countries, Branko Milanovic calculated that the richest 1 percent of people in the world have as much total income as 57 percent of the people at the bottom. Over one billion people on earth live on less than one U.S. dollar a day. This level of inequality exceeds the degree of inequality within any individual country. The disparities are not just in terms of income; there are vast inequalities in literacy, access to clean water, and mortality from a wide range of diseases.

Global inequality has increased substantially in the last three decades. To measure the changes, we can compare the ratio between the richest and poorest fifths over time. In 1997, the ratio was 70.4 to 1, which is calculated by dividing the income for the top fifth by the income for the bottom fifth. That ratio has increased since the 1970s, when the ratio was 33.7 to 1. Higher inequality over time does not necessarily mean that the poor are worse off than before; it is possible that the rich can get much richer and the poor remain the same. However, it does seem that the poor have gotten poorer and the rich have gotten richer. Between 1988 and 1993 Milanovic calculated that the real incomes of the bottom 5 percent dropped by 25 percent, while the incomes of the richest 20 percent grew by about 12 percent.

If the world as a whole is seeing improvements in technology and economic development, why is inequality in the world increasing? As we shall see later, in the chapter on culture change and globalization, it is often the rich within a society who benefit most from new technology, at least initially. They are not only the most likely to be able to afford it, they also are the only ones who can afford to take the risks that it involves. The same may be true for nations. Those that already have capital are more likely than the poorer nations to take advantage of improvements in technology. In addition, the poorer countries generally have the highest rates of population growth, so income per capita can fall if population increases faster than the rate of economic development. Economists tell us that a developing country may, at least initially, experience an increase in inequality, but the inequality often decreases over time. Will the inequalities among countries also decrease as the world economy develops further?

The picture is not entirely bleak. It is true that the disparity between rich and poor countries has increased in recent years, but it is also true that the world economy has improved in some respects. The United Nations has computed a "human development index" for 114 countries, combining measures of life expectancy, literacy, and a measure of per capita purchasing power. According to this index, all countries but Zambia have improved over a period of 30 years, many of them substantially. For example, a child in the world today can expect to live 8 more years than 30 years ago. Literacy has increased from 47 percent in 1970 to 73 percent in 1999. The most progress has occurred in East Asia and the Pacific, the least in sub-Saharan Africa. World leaders at the United Nations Millenium Declaration have committed themselves to a number of goals by the year 2015, including halving the proportion of people living in extreme poverty and halving the proportion of people suffering from hunger. Even if those goals are achieved, much more will remain to be done if we are to achieve a more equal world.

Sources: Human Development Report 2001, published for the United Nations Development Programme (New York: Oxford University Press, 2001), pp. 9–25; Branko Milanovic, *The Economic Journal,* 112 (2002): 51–92; *State of the World 1994: A Worldwatch Institute Report on Progress toward a Sustainable Society* (New York: Norton, 1994), pp. 1–8; Peter Donaldson, *Worlds Apart: The Economic Gulf between Nations* (London: British Broadcasting Corporation, 1971); Philips Foster, *The World Food Problem: Tackling the Causes of Undernutrition in the Third World* (Boulder, CO: Lynne Rienner, 1992), pp. 149–51.

children, Andromache's slave son became heir to his father's throne. Although slaves had no rights under law, once they were freed, either by the will of their master or by purchase, they and their descendants could become assimilated into the dominant group. In other words, slavery in Greece was not seen as the justified position of inferior people. It was regarded, rather, as an act of fate—"the luck of the draw"—that relegated one to the lowest class in society.

Among the Nupe, a society in central Nigeria, slavery was of quite another type.[38] The methods of obtaining slaves—as part of the booty of warfare and, later, by purchase—were similar to those of Europeans, but the position of the slaves was very different. Mistreatment was rare. Male slaves were given the same opportunities to earn money as other dependent males in the household—younger brothers, sons, or other relatives. A slave might be given a garden plot of his own to cultivate, or he might be given a commission if his master was a craftsman or a tradesman. Slaves could acquire property, wealth, and even slaves of their own. But all of a slave's belongings went to the master at the slave's death.

Manumission—the granting of freedom to slaves—was built into the Nupe system. If a male slave could afford the marriage payment for a free woman, the children of the resulting marriage were free; the man himself, however, remained a slave. Marriage and concubinage were the easiest ways out of bondage for a slave woman. Once she had produced a child by her master, both she and the child had free status. The woman, however, was only figuratively free; if a concubine, she had to remain in that role. As might be expected, the family trees of the nobility and the wealthy were liberally grafted with branches descended from slave concubines.

The most fortunate slaves among the Nupe were the house slaves. They could rise to positions of power in the household as overseers and bailiffs, charged with law enforcement and judicial duties. (Recall the Old Testament story of Joseph, who was sold into slavery by his brothers. Joseph became a household slave of the pharaoh and rose to the position of second in the kingdom because he devised an ingenious system of taxation.) There was even a titled group of Nupe slaves, the Order of Court Slaves, who were trusted officers of the king and members of an elite. Slave status in general, though, placed one at the bottom of the social ladder. In the Nupe system, few slaves, mainly princes from their own societies, ever achieved membership in the titled group. Nupe slavery was abolished at the beginning of the 20th century.

In the United States, slavery originated as a means of obtaining cheap labor, but the slaves soon came to be regarded as deserving of their low status because of their alleged inherent inferiority. Because the slaves were from Africa and dark-skinned, some European Americans justified slavery and the belief in "black" people's inferiority by quoting Scripture out of context ("They shall be hewers of wood and drawers of water"). Slaves could not marry or make any other contracts, nor could they own property. In addition, their children were also slaves, and the master had sexual rights over the female slaves. Because the status of slavery was determined by birth in the United States, slaves constituted a caste. During the days of slavery, therefore, the United States had both a caste and a class system. And even after the abolition of slavery, as we have noted, some castelike elements remained. It is important to note that these castelike elements were not limited to the American South where slavery had been practiced. For example, although Indiana was established as a "free" state in 1816, in its first constitution "Negros" did not have the right to vote nor could they intermarry with "Whites." In the constitution of 1851 Indiana did not allow "Negros" to come into the state, nor did it allow the existing African American residents to attend public schools even though they had to pay school taxes.[39] In Muncie, Indiana, in the first half the 20th century, there was customary segregation in shows, restaurants, and parks. It was not until the 1950s that the public swimming pool was desegregated.[40]

As for why slavery may have developed in the first place, cross-cultural research is as yet inconclusive. We do know, however, that slavery is not an inevitable stage in economic development, contrary to what some have assumed. In other words, slavery is not found mainly in certain economies, such as those dependent on intensive agriculture. Unlike the United States until the Civil War, many societies with intensive agriculture did not develop any variety of slavery. Also, the hypothesis that slavery develops where available resources are plentiful but labor is scarce is not supported by the cross-cultural evidence. All we can say definitely is that slavery does not occur in developed or industrial economies; either it disappears or it was never present in them.[41]

Racism and Inequality

Racism is the belief that some "races" are inferior to others. In a society composed of people with noticeably different physical features, such as differences in skin color, racism is almost invariably associated with social stratification. Those "races" considered inferior make up a larger proportion of the lower social classes or castes. Even in more open class systems, where individuals from all backgrounds can achieve higher status positions, individuals from "racial" groups deemed inferior may be subject to discrimination in housing or may be more likely to be searched or stopped by the police.

In some societies, such as the United States, the idea that humans are divided into "races" is taken so much for granted that people are asked for their "race" on the census. Most Americans probably assume that "races" are real, meaningful categories, reflecting important biological variation. But that is not necessarily the case. You may have noticed that we put "races" in quotes. We have done so deliberately because most anthropologists are persuaded that "race" is a meaningless concept as applied to humans. To understand why we say that, we first need to consider what the concept of *race* means in biology.

Race as a Construct in Biology

While all members of a species can potentially interbreed with others, most reproduction takes place within smaller groups or breeding populations. Through time, populations inhabiting different geographic regions may develop some differences in biological traits. Biologists may then classify different geographic populations into different *varieties,* or

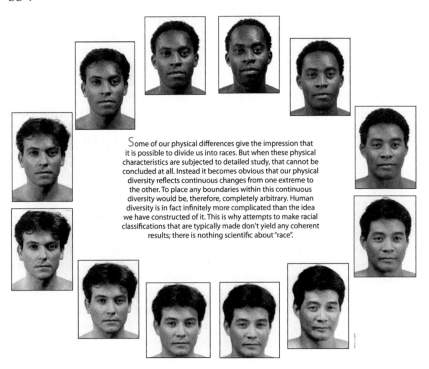

Some of our physical differences give the impression that it is possible to divide us into races. But when these physical characteristics are subjected to detailed study, that cannot be concluded at all. Instead it becomes obvious that our physical diversity reflects continuous changes from one extreme to the other. To place any boundaries within this continuous diversity would be, therefore, completely arbitrary. Human diversity is in fact infinitely more complicated than the idea we have constructed of it. This is why attempts to make racial classifications that are typically made don't yield any coherent results; there is nothing scientific about "race".

It is an illusion that there are races. The diversity of human beings is so great and so complicated that it is impossible to classify the 5.8 billions of individuals into discrete "races".

races. If the term *race* is understood to be just a shorthand or classificatory way in which biologists describe variation within a species from one population to the next, the concept of race would probably not be controversial. But, as applied to humans, racial classifications have often been thought to imply that some "races" are innately inferior to others.

The misuse and misunderstanding of the term *race,* and its association with racist thinking, are two of the reasons that many anthropologists and others have suggested that the concept of race may hinder the search to explain the development of biological differences in humans. In any case, racial classifications are not scientifically useful in that search because different populations are not clearly classifiable into discrete groups that can be defined in terms of the presence or absence of particular sets of biological traits.[42] Population A may have a higher frequency of trait X than population B, but in regard to the frequency of trait Y the two populations may not be distinguishable. So biological characteristics in humans often vary from one population to another in uncorrelated ways. This situation makes racial classification a very arbitrary undertaking when it comes to humans. Compare the number of "races" that different classifiers have come up with. The number of supposed racial categories has varied from as few as three to more than 37.[43]

How can groups be clearly divided into "races" if most adaptive biological traits show gradual, but not always correlated, differences from one region to a neighboring region?[44] Skin color is a good example. Darker skin appears to protect the body from damaging ultraviolet radiation, and natural selection seems to have favored individuals with darker skin in environments with more sunlight. In the area around Egypt, there is a gradient of skin color as you move from north to south in the Nile Valley. Skin generally becomes darker closer to the equator (which is south) and lighter closer to the Mediterranean. Other adaptive traits

may not have north–south gradients, because the environmental predictors may be distributed differently. Nose shape varies with humidity, but **clines,** or gradients of varying frequencies, in humidity do not particularly correspond to variation in latitude. So the gradient for nose shape would not be the same as the gradient for skin color.

Because adaptive traits tend to be distributed in clines, there is no line you could draw on a world map that would separate "white" from "black" people, or "whites" from "Asians."[45] Only traits that are neutral in terms of adaptation or natural selection will tend to cluster in regions.[46] It should also be noted that the traits we have mentioned are superficial surface features. Human populations do vary biologically in some ways, but it is important to realize that few of these ways are correlated with each other. And all humans are nearly alike genetically under the skin.

Race as a Social Category

If race, in the opinion of many biological anthropologists, is not a particularly useful device for classifying humans, how come it is so widely used as a category in various societies? Anthropologists suggest the reasons are social. That is, racial classifications are social categories to which individuals are assigned, by themselves and others, to separate "our" group from others. We have seen that people tend to be *ethnocentric,* to view their culture as better than other cultures. Racial classifications may reflect the same tendency to divide "us" from "them," except that the divisions are supposedly based on biological differences.[47] The "them" are almost always viewed as inferior to "us."

We know that racial classifications have often been, and still are, used by certain groups to justify discrimination, exploitation, or genocide. The "Aryan race" was supposed to be the group of blond-haired, blue-eyed, white-skinned

Members of minority ethnic groups are more often at the bottom of the socioeconomic "ladder," but not always, as these pictures from the United States illustrate.

people whom Adolf Hitler wanted to dominate the world, to which end he and others attempted to destroy as many members of the Jewish "race" as they could. (It is estimated that 6 million Jews and others were murdered in what is now called the Holocaust.[48]) But who were the Aryans? Technically, Aryans are any people, including the German-speaking Jews in Hitler's Germany, who speak one of the Indo-European languages. The Indo-European languages include such disparate modern tongues as Greek, Spanish, Hindi, Polish, French, Icelandic, German, Gaelic, and English. And many Aryans speaking these languages have neither blond hair nor blue eyes. Similarly, all kinds of people may be Jews, whether or not they descend from the ancient Near Eastern population that spoke the Hebrew language. There are light-skinned Danish Jews and darker Jewish Arabs. One of the most orthodox Jewish groups in the United States is based in New York City and is composed entirely of African Americans.

The arbitrary and social basis of most racial classifications becomes apparent when you compare how they differ from one place to another. Consider, for example, what used to be thought about the "races" in South Africa. Under apartheid, which was a system of racial segregation and discrimination, someone with mixed "white" and "black" ancestry was considered "colored." However, when important people of African ancestry (from other countries) would visit South Africa, they were often considered "white." Chinese were considered "Asian"; but the Japanese, who were important economically to South Africa, were considered "white."[49] In some parts of the United States, laws against interracial marriage continued in force through the 1960s. You would be considered a "negro" if you had an eighth or more "negro" ancestry (if one or more of your eight grandparents were "negro"). So only a small amount of "negro" ancestry made a person "negro." But a small amount of "white"

ancestry did not make a person "white." Biologically speaking, this makes no sense, but socially it was another story.[50]

If people of different "races" are viewed as inferior, they are almost inevitably going to end up on the bottom of the social ladder in a socially stratified society. Discrimination will keep them out of the better-paying or higher-status jobs and in neighborhoods that are poorer. As the box "Unequal in Death" shows, people of different "races" also suffer from differential access to health care and have more health problems.

Ethnicity and Inequality

If "race" is not a scientifically useful category because people cannot be clearly divided into different "racial" categories based on sets of physical traits, then racial classifications such as "black" and "white" in the United States might better be described as *ethnic* classifications. How else can we account for the following facts? Groups that now in the United States are thought of as "white" were earlier thought of as belonging to inferior "races." For example, in the latter half of the 19th century, newspapers would often talk about the new immigrants from Ireland as belonging to the Irish "race." Similarly, before World War II, Jews were thought of as a separate "racial" group, and only became "white" afterward.[51] It is hard to escape the idea that changes in "racial" classification occurred as the Irish, Jews, and other immigrant groups became more accepted by the majority in the United States.[52]

It is apparent that *ethnic groups* and *ethnic identities* emerge as part of a social and political process. The process of defining **ethnicity** usually involves a group of people emphasizing common origins and language, shared history, and selected cultural difference such as a difference in religion.

APPLIED ANTHROPOLOGY

Unequal in Death: African Americans Compared with European Americans

Everyone dies of something. Yet, if you consider cardiovascular disease, the leading cause of death in the United States, it turns out that after controlling for the effects of age and gender, African Americans die more often from that disease than European Americans. The same kind of disparity occurs also with almost every other major cause of death—cancer, cirrhosis of the liver, diabetes, injuries, infant mortality, and homicide. Medical anthropologists and health policy researchers want to know why. Without such understanding, it is hard to know how to reduce the disparity.

One reason may be subtle discrimination by the medical profession itself. For example, a European American with chest pain in the United States is more likely than an African American to be given an angiogram, a medical procedure that injects radioactive dye into the heart to look for deficits in blood flow through the coronary arteries that supply blood to the heart. And even if coronary heart disease is detected by an angiogram, an African American is less likely to receive bypass surgery. Thus, the death rate from cardiovascular disease may be higher for African Americans than for European Americans because of unequal medical care.

Yet, while some difference in mortality may be due to disparity in medical treatment, this could only be part of the picture. African Americans may be more prone to cardiovascular disease because they are about twice as likely as European Americans to have high rates of hypertension (high blood pressure). But why the disparity in hypertension? Three possible explanations, not mutually exclusive, are discussed in the research literature. The first is a possible difference in genetics. The second is a difference in lifestyle. The third is class difference.

Most of the Africans that came to the Americas were forcibly taken as slaves between the 16th and 19th centuries, largely from West Africa. In one comparative study of hypertension, African Americans had much higher blood pressure than Africans in Nigeria and Cameroon, even in urban areas. People with African ancestry in the Caribbean were in the middle of the range. Lifestyle differences were also vast—the West Africans had plenty of exercise, were lean, and had low-fat and low-salt diets. Any possible difference in genes would seem to be insignificant. Jared Diamond has suggested that individuals who could retain salt would have been most likely to survive the terrible conditions of the sailing ships that brought slaves to the New World. Many died from diarrhea and dehydration (salt-depleting conditions) on those voyages. Retention of salt would have been a genetic advantage then, but disadvantageous in places such as the United States with high-salt, high-fat diets. Critics of this theory suggest that salt-depleting diseases were not the leading causes of death in the slave voyages; tuberculosis and violence were more frequent causes of death. Furthermore, critics say that the slave-ship theory would predict little genetic diversity in African American populations with respect to hypertension, but in fact there is great diversity.

Hypertension could be related also to differences in lifestyle and wealth. As we noted in the section on racism and inequality, African Americans in the United States are disproportionately poorer. Study after study has noted that healthier lifestyle habits are generally correlated with higher positions on the socioeconomic ladder. Moreover, individuals from higher social positions are more likely to have health insurance and access to care in superior hospitals. But even after correcting for factors such as obesity, physical activity, and social class, the health differential persists—African Americans still have a much higher incidence of hypertension than European Americans.

William Dressler suggests that stress is another possible cause of higher rates of hypertension. Despite increased economic mobility in recent years, African Americans are still subject to prejudice and may consequently have more stress even if they have higher income. Stress is related to higher blood pressure. In a color-conscious society, a very dark-skinned individual walking in a wealthy neighborhood at night may be thought not to live there and may be stopped by the police. If Dressler is correct, darker-skinned African Americans who have objective indicators of higher status should have much higher blood pressure than would be expected from their relative education, age, body mass, or social class alone. And that seems to be true. Racism may affect health.

Sources: William W. Dressler, "Health in the African American Community: Accounting for Health Inequalities," *Medical Anthropological Quarterly* 7 (1993): 325–45; Richard S. Cooper, Charles N. Rotimi, and Ryk Ward, "The Puzzle of Hypertension in African-Americans," *Scientific American* (February 1999): 56–63; Jared Diamond, "The Saltshaker's Curse—Physiological Adaptations That Helped American Blacks Survive Slavery May Now Be Predisposing Their Descendants to Hypertension," *Natural History* (10), October 1991.

Those doing the defining can be outside or inside the ethnic group. Outsiders and insiders often perceive ethnic groups differently. In a country with one large core majority group, often the majority group doesn't think of itself as an ethnic group. Rather, they consider only the minority groups to have ethnic identities. For example, in the United States it is not common for the majority to call themselves European Americans, but other groups may be called African Americans, Asian Americans, or Native Americans. The minority groups, on the other hand, may have different named identities.[53] Asian Americans may identify themselves more specifically as Japanese Americans, Korean Americans, Chinese Americans, or Hmong. The majority population often uses derogatory names to identify people who are different. The majority may also tend to lump people of diverse ethnicities together. Naming a group establishes a boundary between it and other ethnic groups.[54]

Ethnic identity may be manipulated, by insiders and by outsiders, in different situations. A particularly repressive regime that emphasizes nationalism and loyalty to the state may not only suppress the assertiveness of ethnic claims; it may also act to minimize communication among people who might otherwise embrace the same ethnic identity.[55] More democratic regimes may allow more expression of difference and celebrate ethnic difference. However, manipulation of ethnicity does not come just from the top. It may be to the advantage of minority groups to lobby for more equal treatment as a larger entity, such as Asian American, rather than as Japanese, Chinese, Hmong, Filipino, or Korean American. Similarly, even though there are hundreds of American Indian groups, originally speaking different languages, there may be political advantages for all if they are treated as Native Americans.

In many multiethnic societies, ethnicity and diversity are things to be proud of and celebrated. Shared ethnic identity often makes people feel comfortable with similar people and gives them a strong sense of belonging. Still, ethnic differences in multiethnic societies are usually associated with inequities in wealth, power, and prestige. In other words, ethnicity is part of the system of *stratification*.

Although there are some people who believe that inequities are deserved, the origins of ethnic stereotypes, prejudice, and discrimination usually follow from historical and political events that give some groups dominance over others. For example, even though there were many early stories of help given by native peoples to the English settlers in the 17th century in the land now known as North America, the English were the invaders, and negative stereotypes about native peoples developed to justify taking their land and their lives. Referring to the negative stereotypes of Native Americans that developed, J. Milton Yinger said: "One would almost think that it had been the Indian who had invaded Europe, driven back the inhabitants, cut their population to one-third of its original size, unilaterally changed treaties, and brought the dubious glories of firewater and firearms."[56]

Similarly, as we noted in the section on slavery, African slaves were initially acquired as cheap labor, but inhumane treatment of slaves was justified by beliefs about their inferiority. Unfortunately, stereotypes can become self-fulfilling

prophesies, especially if those discriminated against come to believe the stereotypes. It is easy to see how this can happen. If there is a widespread belief that a group is inferior, and that group is given inferior schools and little chance for improvement or little chance for a good job, the members of that group may acquire few skills and not try hard. The result is often a vicious cycle.[57]

And yet, the picture is not all bleak. Change has occurred. The ethnic identity forged by a minority group can help promote political activism, such as the nonviolent civil rights movement in the United States in the 1960s. That activism, helped by some people in the more advantaged groups, helped break down many of the legal barriers and segregationist practices that reinforced inequality.

The traditional barriers in the United States have mostly been lifted in recent years, but the "color line" has not disappeared. African Americans are found in all social classes, but they remain underrepresented in the wealthiest group and overrepresented at the bottom. Discrimination may be lessened, but it is still not gone. In research done with matched pairs of "whites" and "blacks" applying for jobs or for housing, discrimination is still evident.[58] Thus, African Americans may have to be better than others to get promoted, or it may be assumed that they got ahead just because they were African American and were hired because of affirmative action programs. European Americans often expect African Americans to be "ambassadors," to be called on mainly for knowledge about how to handle situations involving other African Americans. African Americans may work with others, but they usually go home to African American neighborhoods. Or they may live in mixed neighborhoods and experience considerable isolation. Few African Americans can completely avoid the anguish of racism.[59]

◉ The Emergence of Stratification

Anthropologists are not certain why social stratification developed. Nevertheless, they are reasonably sure that higher levels of stratification emerged relatively recently in human history. Archaeological sites dating before about 8,000 years ago do not show extensive evidence of inequality. Houses do not appear to vary much in size or content, and different communities of the same culture are similar in size and otherwise. Signs of inequality appear first in the Near East, about 2,000 years after agriculture emerged in that region. Inequality in burial suggests inequality in life. Particularly telling are unequal child burials. It is unlikely that children could achieve high status by their own achievements. So when archaeologists find statues and ornaments only in some children's tombs, as at the 7,500-year-old site of Tell es-Sawwan in Iraq,[60] the grave goods suggest that those children belonged to a higher-ranking family or a higher class.

Another indication that stratification is a relatively recent development in human history is the fact that certain cultural features associated with stratification also developed relatively recently. For example, most societies that depend primarily on agriculture or herding have social classes.[61] Agriculture and herding developed within the past 10,000 years, so we may assume that most food collectors in the distant past lacked social classes. Other recently developed cultural features associated with class stratification include fixed settlements, political integration beyond the community level, the use of money as a medium of exchange, and the presence of at least some full-time specialization.[62]

In 1966, the comparative sociologist Gerhard Lenski suggested that the trend since 8,000 years ago toward increasing inequality was reversing. He argued that inequalities of power and privilege in industrial societies—measured in terms of the concentration of political power and the distribution of income—are less pronounced than inequalities in complex preindustrial societies. Technology in industrialized societies is so complex, he suggested, that those in power are compelled to delegate some authority to subordinates if the system is to work. In addition, a decline in the birth rate in industrialized societies, coupled with the need for skilled labor, has pushed the average wage of workers far above the subsistence level, resulting in greater equality in the distribution of income. Finally, Lenski also suggested that the spread of the democratic ideology, and particularly its acceptance by elites, has significantly broadened the political power of the lower classes.[63] A few studies have tested and supported Lenski's hypothesis that inequality has decreased with industrialization. In general, nations that are highly industrialized exhibit a lower level of inequality than nations that are only somewhat industrialized.[64] But, as we have seen, even the most industrialized societies may still have an enormous degree of inequality.

Why did social stratification develop in the first place? On the basis of his study of Polynesian societies, Marshall Sahlins suggested that an increase in agricultural productivity results in social stratification.[65] According to Sahlins, the degree of stratification is directly related to the production of a surplus, which is made possible by greater technological efficiency. The higher the level of productivity and the larger the agricultural surplus, the greater the scope and complexity of the distribution system. The status of the chief, who serves as redistributing agent, is enhanced. Sahlins argued that the differentiation between distributor and producer inevitably gives rise to differentiation in other aspects of life:

> First, there would be a tendency for the regulator of distribution to exert some authority over production itself—especially over productive activities which necessitate subsidization, such as communal labor or specialist labor. A degree of control of production implies a degree of control over the utilization of resources, or, in other words, some preeminent property rights. In turn, regulation of these economic processes necessitates the exercise of authority in interpersonal affairs; differences in social power emerge.[66]

Sahlins later rejected the idea that a surplus leads to chiefships, postulating instead that the relationship may be the other way around—that is, leaders encourage the develop-

ment of a surplus so as to enhance their prestige through feasts, potlatches, and other redistributive events.[67] Of course, both trajectories are possible—surpluses may generate stratification, and stratification may generate surpluses; they are not mutually exclusive.

Lenski's theory of the causes of stratification is similar to Sahlins's original idea. Lenski, too, argued that production of a surplus is the stimulus in the development of stratification, but he focused primarily on the conflict that arises over control of that surplus. Lenski concluded that the distribution of the surplus will be determined on the basis of power. Thus, inequalities in power promote unequal access to economic resources and simultaneously give rise to inequalities in privilege and prestige.[68]

The "surplus" theories of Sahlins and Lenski do not really address the question of why the redistributors or leaders will want, or be able, to acquire greater control over resources. After all, the redistributors or leaders in many rank societies do not have greater wealth than others, and custom seems to keep things that way. One suggestion is that as long as followers have mobility, they can vote with their feet by moving away from leaders they do not like. But when people start to make more permanent "investments" in land or technology (e.g., irrigation systems or weirs for fishing), they are more likely to put up with a leader's aggrandizement in exchange for protection.[69] Another suggestion is that access to economic resources becomes unequal only when there is population pressure on resources in rank or chiefdom societies.[70] Such pressure may be what induces redistributors to try to keep more land and other resources for themselves and their families.

C. K. Meek offered an example of how population pressure in northern Nigeria may have led to economic stratification. At one time, a tribal member could obtain the right to use land by asking permission of the chief and presenting him with a token gift in recognition of his higher status. But by 1921, the reduction in the amount of available land had led to a system under which applicants offered the chief large payments for scarce land. As a result of these payments, farms came to be regarded as private property, and differential access to such property became institutionalized.[71]

Future research by archaeologists, sociologists, historians, and anthropologists should provide more understanding of the emergence of social stratification in human societies and how and why it may vary in degree.

⊚ Summary

1. Without exception, recent and modern industrial and postindustrial societies such as our own are socially stratified—that is, they contain social groups such as families, classes, or ethnic groups that have unequal access to important advantages, such as economic resources, power, and prestige. Anthropologists, based on firsthand observations, would say that such inequality has not always existed among the societies they have studied. While even the simplest societies (in the tech-

nological sense) have some differences in advantages based on age, ability, or gender—adults have higher status than children, the skilled more than the unskilled, men more than women (we discuss gender stratification in the next chapter)—anthropologists would argue that egalitarian societies exist where social groups (e.g., families) have more or less the same access to rights or advantages.

2. The presence or absence of customs or rules that give certain groups unequal access to economic resources, power, and prestige can be used to distinguish three types of societies. In egalitarian societies, social groups do not have unequal access to economic resources, power, or prestige; they are unstratified. In rank societies, social groups do not have very unequal access to economic resources or power, but they do have unequal access to prestige. Rank societies, then, are partially stratified. In class societies, social groups have unequal access to economic resources, power, and prestige. They are more completely stratified than are rank societies.

3. Stratified societies range from somewhat open class systems to caste systems, which are extremely rigid, since caste membership is fixed permanently at birth.

4. Slaves are persons who do not own their own labor; as such, they represent a class and sometimes even a caste. Slavery has existed in various forms in many times and places, regardless of "race" and culture. Sometimes slavery is a rigid and closed, or caste, system; sometimes it is a relatively open class system.

5. Within a society composed of people from widely divergent backgrounds and different physical features, such as skin color, racism is almost invariably associated with social stratification. Those "races" considered inferior make up a larger proportion of the lower social classes or castes. In the opinion of many biological anthropologists, "race" is not a scientifically useful device for classifying humans. "Racial" classifications should be recognized for what they mostly are—social categories to which individuals are assigned, by themselves and others, on the basis of supposedly shared biological traits.

6. In multiethnic societies, ethnic differences are usually associated with inequities in wealth, power, and prestige. In other words, ethnicity is part of the system of stratification.

7. Social stratification appears to have emerged relatively recently in human history, about 8,000 years ago. This conclusion is based on archaeological evidence and on the fact that certain cultural features associated with stratification developed relatively recently.

8. One theory suggests that social stratification developed as productivity increased and surpluses were produced. Another suggestion is that stratification can develop only when people have "investments" in land or technology and therefore cannot move away from leaders they do not like. A third theory suggests that stratification emerges only when there is population pressure on resources in rank societies.

◎ Glossary Terms

caste	330	manumission	333
class	327	power	324
class societies	324	prestige	324
clines	334	races	334
economic resources	324	racism	333
egalitarian societies	324	rank societies	324
ethnicity	335	slaves	331

◎ Critical Questions

1. What might be some of the social consequences of large differences in wealth? Explain your reasoning.

2. Is an industrial or a developed economy incompatible with a more egalitarian distribution of resources? Why or why not?

3. In a multiethnic society, does ethnic identity help or hinder social equality? Explain your answer.

4. Why do you suppose the degree of inequality has decreased in some countries in recent years?

◎ Research Navigator

1. Please go to www.researchnavigator.com and enter your LOGIN NAME and PASSWORD. For instructions on registering for the first time, please view the detailed instructions at the end of Chapter 1.

2. Using ContentSelect and Anthropology look for two articles on race or racism. Compare what you have read in these articles to what you have learned in this chapter.

3. Using Link Library look for a Web site on "social class" or "social stratification" and try to find information on social class differences or ways that class is perpetuated. Describe your findings noting the country or culture that you found described.

◎ Discovering Anthropology: Researchers at Work

Read "Haitians: From Political Repression to Chaos" by Robert Lawless in *Discovering Anthropology*. Answer the questions below.

1. In what ways does Lawless suggest that the elite in Haiti maintain their power?

2. Why does Lawless say that "Voodoo" is an egalitarian religion?

3. Explain what role slavery played in Haitian history.

sex.[99] But societies that are generally restrictive about heterosexuality are not necessarily restrictive about homosexuality. Societies restrictive about premarital sex are neither more nor less likely to restrict homosexuality. In the case of extramarital sex, the situation is somewhat different. Societies that have a considerable amount of male homosexuality tend to disapprove of males having extramarital heterosexual relationships.[100] If we are going to explain restrictiveness, then, it appears we have to consider heterosexual and homosexual restrictiveness separately.

Let us consider homosexual restrictiveness first. Why do homosexual relationships occur more frequently in some societies, and why are some societies intolerant of such relationships? There are many psychological interpretations of why some people become interested in homosexual relationships, and many of these interpretations relate the phenomenon to early parent–child relationships. So far, the research has not yielded any clear-cut predictions, although several cross-cultural predictors about male homosexuality are intriguing.

One such finding is that societies that forbid abortion and infanticide for married women (most societies permit these practices for illegitimate births) are likely to be intolerant of male homosexuality.[101] This and other findings are consistent with the point of view that homosexuality is less tolerated in societies that would like to increase population. Such societies may be intolerant of all kinds of behaviors that minimize population growth. Homosexuality would have this effect, if we assume that a higher frequency of homosexual relations is associated with a lower frequency of heterosexual relations. The less frequently heterosexual relations occur, the lower the number of conceptions there might be. Another indication that intolerance may be related to a desire for population growth is that societies with famines and severe food shortages are more likely to allow homosexuality. Famines and food shortages suggest population pressure on resources; under these conditions, homosexuality and other practices that minimize population growth may be tolerated or even encouraged.[102]

The history of the Soviet Union may provide some other relevant evidence. In 1917, in the turmoil of revolution, laws prohibiting abortion and homosexuality were revoked and reproduction was discouraged. But in the period 1934 to 1936 the policy was reversed. Abortion and homosexuality were again declared illegal, and homosexuals were arrested. At the same time, awards were given to mothers who had more children.[103] Population pressure may also explain why our own society has become somewhat more tolerant of homosexuality recently. Of course, population pressure does not explain why certain individuals become homosexual or why most individuals in some societies engage in such behavior, but it might explain why some societies view such behavior more or less permissively.

Let us now turn to heterosexual behavior. What kinds of societies are more permissive than others? Although we do not yet understand the reasons, we do know that greater restrictiveness toward premarital sex tends to occur in more complex societies—societies that have hierarchies of political officials, part-time or full-time craft specialists, cities and towns, and class stratification.[104] It may be that as social inequality increases and various groups come to have differential wealth, parents become more concerned with preventing their children from marrying "beneath them." Permissiveness toward premarital sexual relationships might lead a person to become attached to someone not considered a desirable marriage partner. Even worse, from the family's point of view, such "unsuitable" sexual liaisons might result in a pregnancy that could make it impossible for a girl to marry "well." Controlling mating, then, may be a way of trying to control property. Consistent with this view is the finding that virginity is emphasized in rank and stratified societies, in which families are likely to exchange goods and money in the course of arranging marriages.[105]

The biological fact that humans depend on sexual reproduction does not by itself help explain why females and males differ in so many ways across cultures, or why societies vary in the way they handle male and female roles. We are only beginning to investigate these questions. When we eventually understand more about how and why females and males are different or the same in roles, personality, and sexuality, we may be better able to decide how much we want the biology of sex to shape our lives.

◎ Summary

1. That humans reproduce sexually does not explain why males and females tend to differ in appearance and behavior, and to be treated differently, in all societies.

2. All or nearly all societies assign certain activities to females and other activities to males. These worldwide gender patterns of division of labor may be explained by male–female differences in strength, by differences in compatibility of tasks with child care, or by economy-of-effort considerations and/or the expendability of men.

3. Perhaps because women almost always have infant- and child-care responsibilities, men in most societies contribute more to primary subsistence activities, in terms of calories. But women contribute substantially to primary subsistence activities in societies that depend heavily on gathering and horticulture and in which warfare occurs while primary subsistence work has to be done. When primary and secondary subsistence work are counted, women typically work more hours than men. In most societies men are the leaders in the political arena, and warfare is almost exclusively a male activity.

4. The relative status of women compared with that of men seems to vary from one area of life to another. Whether women have relatively high status in one area does not necessarily indicate that they will have high status in another. Less complex societies, however, seem to approach more equal status for males and females in a variety of areas of life.

5. Recent field studies have suggested some consistent female–male differences in personality: Boys tend to be

more aggressive than girls, and girls seem to be more re-sponsible and helpful than boys.

6. Although all societies regulate sexual activity to some extent, societies vary considerably in the degree to which various kinds of sexuality are permitted. Some societies allow both masturbation and sex play among children, whereas others forbid such acts. Some societies allow premarital sex; others do not. Some allow extramarital sex in certain situations; others forbid it generally.

7. Societies that are restrictive toward one aspect of het-erosexual sex tend to be restrictive with regard to other aspects. And more complex societies tend to be more restrictive toward premarital heterosexual sex than less complex societies.

8. Societal attitudes toward homosexuality are not com-pletely consistent with attitudes toward sexual relation-ships between the sexes. Societal tolerance of homosexuality is associated with tolerance of abortion and infanticide and with famines and food shortages.

◎ Glossary Terms

compatibility-with child-care theory	344	primary subsistence activities	345
economy-of-effort theory	344	secondary subsistence activities	345
expendability theory	344	sex differences	341
gender differences	341	sexually dimorphic	342
gender roles	343	strength theory	343
gender stratification	349		

◎ Critical Questions

1. Would you expect female–male differences in person-ality to disappear in a society with complete gender equality in the workplace?

2. Under what circumstances would you expect male–female differences in athletic performance to disappear?

3. What conditions make the election of a female head of state most likely?

◎ Research Navigator

1. Please go to www.researchnavigator.com and enter your LOGIN NAME and PASSWORD. For instructions on registering for the first time, please view the detailed instructions at the end of Chapter 1.

2. In the early days of anthropology the focus of ethnog-raphy tended to be on men. With the emergence of the feminist movement an increasing number of studies of gender focused on women. Using Link Library/Anthro-pology look for sites related to "gender" and see how many of those sites focus on women's versus men's is-sues. What kinds of men's issues are discussed?

3. Using ContentSelect/Anthropology look for two arti-cles on aspects of sexuality that have not been discussed much in this chapter. Possibilities include female ho-mosexuality, transgenders, bisexuality, transvestites, or contraception.

◎ Discovering Anthropology: Researchers at Work

Read "Andean Mestizos: Growing Up Female and Male" by Lauris McKee in *Discovering Anthropology* and answer the following questions:

1. Which of the Andean Mestizos' ideas about conception, pregnancy, and birth are different from those of your own culture? (Identify your own culture in your answer.)

2. According to McKee, what do the Mestizos say is the rea-son for the shorter breast-feeding of girls?

3. What are the consequences of the gender difference in breast-feeding? Are the parents aware of these conse-quences?

Marriage and the Family

Whatever a society's attitudes toward male–female relationships, one such relationship is found in virtually all societies—marriage. Why marriage is customary in nearly every society we know of is a classic and perplexing question, and one we attempt to deal with in this chapter.

The universality of marriage does not mean that everyone in every society gets married. It means only that most, usually nearly all, people in every society get married at least once in their lifetime. In addition, when we say that marriage is universal, we do not mean that marriage and family customs are the same in all societies. On the contrary, there is much variation from society to society in how one marries, whom one marries, and even how many persons a person can be married to simultaneously.

Families also are universal. All societies have parent–child social groups, although the form and size of families may vary from one society to another. Some societies have large extended families with two or more related parent–child groups; others have smaller independent families. Today, marriage is not always the basis for family life. One-parent families are becoming increasingly common in our own and other societies. Marriage has not disappeared in these places—it is still customary to marry—but more individuals are choosing now to have children without being married.

 Marriage

When anthropologists speak of marriage, they do not mean to imply that couples everywhere must get marriage certificates or have wedding ceremonies, as in our own society. **Marriage** merely means a socially approved sexual and economic union, usually between a woman and a man. It is presumed, by both the couple and others, to be more or less permanent, and it subsumes reciprocal rights and obligations between the two spouses and between spouses and their future children.[1]

It is a socially approved sexual union in that a married couple does not have to hide the sexual nature of their relationship. A woman might say, "I want you to meet my husband," but she could not say, "I want you to meet my lover" without causing some embarrassment in most societies. Although the union may ultimately be dissolved by divorce, couples in all societies begin marriage with some idea of permanence in mind. Implicit too in marriage are reciprocal rights and obligations. These may be more or less specific and formalized regarding matters of property, finances, and childrearing.

Marriage entails both a sexual and an economic relationship, as George Peter Murdock noted: "Sexual relations can occur without economic cooperation, and there

Weddings in some societies are very elaborate. A Minangkabau bride dressed in elaborate clothes sits in the windowsill of a home in Padang, West Sumatra, Indonesia.

can be a division of labor between men and women without sex. But marriage unites the economic and the sexual."[2]

As we will see, the event that marks the commencement of marriage varies in different societies. A Winnebago bride, for example, knew no formal ritual such as a wedding ceremony. She went with her groom to his parents' house, took off her "wedding" clothes and finery, gave them to her mother-in-law, received plain clothes in exchange, and that was that.[3]

Rare Types of Marriage

In addition to the usual male–female marriages, some societies recognize marriages between persons of the same biological sex. But such marriages are not typical in any known society and they often do not fit the definition of marriage that we have given above. Aside from the fact that these unions are not between a male and a female, they are not necessarily sexual unions, as we will see. But these "marriages" are socially approved unions, usually modeled after regular marriages, and they often entail a considerable number of reciprocal rights and obligations. Sometimes the marriages involve an individual who is considered a "woman" or "man," even though "she" or "he" is not that sex biologically. As we noted in the previous chapter, the Cheyenne Indians allowed a married man to take as a second wife a biological man belonging to the third (two-spirits) gender formerly known as a *berdache*.[4]

Although it is not clear that the Cheyenne male–male marriages involved homosexual relationships, it is clear that temporary homosexual marriages did occur among the Azande of Africa. Before the British took control over what is now Sudan, Azande warriors who could not afford wives often married "boy-wives" to satisfy their sexual needs. As in normal marriages, gifts (although not as substantial) were given by the "husband" to the parents of his boy-wife. The husband performed services for the boy's parents and could sue any other lover of the boy in court for adultery. The boy-

wives not only had sexual relations with their husbands but also performed many of the chores female wives traditionally performed for their husbands.[5]

Female–female marriages are reported to have occurred in many African societies, but there is no evidence of any sexual relationship between the partners. It seems, rather, that female–female marriages were a socially approved way for a woman to take on the legal and social roles of a father and husband.[6] For example, among the Nandi, a pastoral and agricultural society of Kenya, about 3 percent of the marriages are female–female marriages. Such marriages appear to be a Nandi solution to the problem of a regular marriage's failure to produce a male heir to property. The Nandi solution is to have the woman, even if her husband is still alive, become a "husband" to a younger female and "father" the younger woman's children. The female husband provides the marriage payments required for obtaining a wife, renounces female work, and takes on the obligations of the husband to that woman. Although no sexual relations are permitted between the female husband and the new wife (or between the female husband and her own husband), the female husband arranges a male consort so that the new wife can have children. Those children, however, consider the female husband to be their father because she (or more aptly the gender role "he") is the socially designated father. If asked who their father is, a child of such a marriage will name the female who is the husband.[7]

Why Is Marriage Universal?

Because virtually all societies practice female–male marriage as we have defined it, we can assume that the custom is adaptive. But saying that does not specify exactly how it may be adaptive. Several interpretations have traditionally been offered to explain why all human societies have the custom of marriage. Each suggests that marriage solves problems found in all societies—how to share the products of a gender division of labor; how to care for infants, who are dependent for a long time; and how to minimize sexual competition. To evaluate the plausibility of these interpretations, we must ask whether marriage provides the best or the only reasonable solution to each problem. After all, we are trying to explain a custom that is presumably a universal solution. The comparative study of other animals, some of which have something like marriage, may help us to evaluate these explanations.

Gender Division of Labor

We noted in the preceding chapter that every society known to anthropology has had a gender division of labor. Males and females in every society perform different economic activities. This gender division of labor has often been cited as a reason for marriage.[8] As long as there is a division of labor by gender, society has to have some mechanism by which women and men share the products of their labor. Marriage would be one way to solve that problem. But it seems unlikely that marriage is the only possible solution. The hunter-gatherer rule of sharing could be extended to include all the products brought in by both women and men. Or a small group of men and women, such as brothers and sisters, might be pledged to cooperate economically. Thus, although marriage may solve the problem of sharing the fruits of a division of labor, it clearly is not the only possible solution.

Prolonged Infant Dependency

Humans exhibit the longest period of infant dependency of any primate. The child's prolonged dependence places the greatest burden on the mother, who is the main child caregiver in most societies. The burden of prolonged child care by human females may limit the kinds of work they can do. They may need the help of a man to do certain types of work, such as hunting, that are incompatible with child care. Because of this prolonged dependency, it has been suggested, marriage is necessary.[9] But here the argument becomes essentially the same as the division-of-labor argument, and it has the same logical weakness. It is not clear why a group of women and men, such as a hunter-gatherer band, could not cooperate in providing for dependent children without marriage.

Sexual Competition

Unlike most other female primates, the human female may engage in intercourse at any time throughout the year. Some scholars have suggested that more or less continuous female sexuality may have created a serious problem—considerable sexual competition between males for females. It is argued that society had to prevent such competition in order to survive, that it had to develop some way of minimizing the rivalry among males for females in order to reduce the chance of lethal and destructive conflict.[10]

There are several problems with this argument. First, why should continuous female sexuality make for more sexual competition in the first place? One might argue the other way around. There might be more competition over the scarcer resources that would be available if females were less frequently interested in sex. Second, males of many animal species, even some that have relatively frequent female sexuality (as do many of our close primate relatives), do not show much aggression over females. Third, why couldn't sexual competition, even if it existed, be regulated by cultural rules other than marriage? For instance, society might have adopted a rule whereby men and women circulated among all the opposite-sex members of the group, each person staying a specified length of time with each partner. Such a system presumably would solve the problem of sexual competition. On the other hand, such a system might not work particularly well if individuals came to prefer certain other individuals. Jealousies attending those attachments might give rise to even more competition.

Other Mammals and Birds: Postpartum Requirements

None of the theories we have discussed explains convincingly why marriage is the only or the best solution to a particular problem. Also, we now have some comparative evidence on mammals and birds that casts doubt on those theories.[11] How can evidence from other animals help us evaluate theories about human marriage? If we look at the animals that, like humans, have some sort of stable female–male mating, as compared with those that are completely promiscuous, we can perhaps see what sorts of factors may predict male–female bonding in the warm-blooded animal species. Most species of birds, and some mammals such as wolves and beavers, have "marriage." Among 40 mammal and bird species, none of the three factors discussed above—division of labor, prolonged infant dependency, and greater female sexuality—predicts or is correlated strongly with male–female bonding. With respect to division of labor by sex, most other animals have nothing comparable to a humanlike division of labor, but many have stable female–male matings anyway. The two other supposed factors—prolonged infant dependency and female sexuality—predict just the opposite of what we might expect. Mammal and bird species that have longer dependency periods or more female sexuality are less likely to have stable matings.

Does anything predict male–female bonding? One factor does among mammals and birds, and it may also help explain human marriage. Animal species in which females can simultaneously feed themselves and their babies after birth (*postpartum*) tend not to have stable matings; species in which postpartum mothers cannot feed themselves and their babies at the same time tend to have stable matings. Among the typical bird species, a mother would have difficulty feeding herself and her babies simultaneously. Because the young cannot fly for a while and must be protected in a nest, the mother risks losing them to other animals if she goes off to obtain food. But if she has a male bonded to her (as most bird species do), he can bring back food or take a turn watching the nest. Among animal species that have no postpartum feeding problem, babies almost immediately after birth are able to travel with the mother as she moves about to eat (as do grazers such as horses), or the mother can transport the babies as she moves about to eat (as do baboons and kangaroos). We think the human female has a postpartum feeding problem. When humans lost most of their body hair, babies could not readily travel with the mother by clinging to her fur. And when humans began to depend on certain kinds of food-getting that could be dangerous (such as hunting), mothers could not engage in such work with their infants along.[12]

Recent research on the Hadza foragers of Tanzania appears to support this view. Frank Marlowe found that the caloric contribution of mothers and fathers depends on whether or not they have a nursing infant. Women may generally contribute more calories than men to the diet, but married women who are nursing contribute substantially less than other married women. The lower contribution of nursing mothers appears to be made up by the father. Fathers with nursing children contribute significantly more food to the household than fathers with older children.[13]

Even if we assume that human mothers have a postpartum feeding problem, we still have to ask if marriage is the most likely solution to the problem. We think so, because other conceivable solutions probably would not work as well. For example, if a mother took turns babysitting with another mother, neither might be able to collect enough food for both mothers and the two sets of children dependent on them. But a mother and father share the same set of children, and therefore it would be easier for them to feed themselves and their children adequately. Another possible solution is no pair bonding at all, just a promiscuous group of males and females. But in that kind of arrangement, we think, a particular mother probably would not always be able to count on some male to watch her baby when she had to go out for food or to bring her food when she had to watch her baby. Thus, it seems to us that the problem of postpartum feeding by itself helps to explain why some animals, including humans, have relatively stable male–female bonds.[14] Of course, there is still the question of whether research on other animals can be applied to human beings. We think it can, but not everybody will agree.

◎ How Does One Marry?

When we say that marriage is a socially approved sexual and economic union, we mean that all societies have some way of marking the onset of a marriage, but the ways of doing so vary considerably. For reasons that we don't fully understand, some cultures mark marriages by elaborate rites and celebrations; others mark marriages in much more informal ways. And most societies have economic transactions before, during, or even after the onset of the marriages.

Marking the Onset of Marriage

Many societies have ceremonies marking the beginning of marriage. But others, such as the Taramiut Inuit, the Trobriand Islanders of the South Pacific, and the Kwoma of New

"I do love you. But, to be perfectly honest, I would have loved any other lovebird who happened to turn up."

(Rothco Cartoons)

Guinea, use different social signals to indicate that a marriage has taken place. Among the Taramiut Inuit, the betrothal is considered extremely important and is arranged between the parents at or before the time their children reach puberty. Later, when the youth is ready, he moves in with his betrothed's family for a trial period. If all goes well—that is, if the girl gives birth to a baby within a year or so—the couple are considered married. At this time, the wife goes with her husband to his camp.[15]

In keeping with the general openness of their society's attitudes toward sexual matters, a Trobriand couple advertise their desire to marry "by sleeping together regularly, by showing themselves together in public, and by remaining with each other for long periods at a time."[16] When a girl accepts a small gift from a boy, she demonstrates that her parents favor the match. Before long, she moves to the boy's house, takes her meals there, and accompanies her husband all day. Then the word goes around that the two are married.[17]

The Kwoma of New Guinea practice a trial marriage followed by a ceremony that makes the couple husband and wife. The girl lives for a while in the boy's home. When the boy's mother is satisfied with the match and knows that her son is too, she waits for a day when he is away from the house. Until that time, the girl has been cooking only for herself, and the boy's food has been prepared by his womenfolk. Now the mother has the girl prepare his meal. The young man returns and begins to eat his soup. When the first bowl is nearly finished, his mother tells him that his betrothed cooked the meal, and his eating it means that he is now married. At this news, the boy customarily rushes out of the house, spits out the soup, and shouts, "Faugh! It tastes bad! It is cooked terribly!" A ceremony then makes the marriage official.[18]

Just in the last three decades "living together" has become more of an option in the United States and other Western countries. For most, living together is a prelude to marriage or kind of a trial marriage. For some, living together has become an alternative to marriage. Statistics in the United States suggest that a third of married women under age 45 have lived together with a man for at least some time period.[19]

Among those societies that have ceremonies marking the onset of marriage, feasting is a common element. It expresses publicly the unification of the two families by marriage. The Reindeer Tungus of Siberia set a wedding date after protracted negotiations between the two families and their larger kin groups. Go-betweens assume most of the responsibility for the negotiating. The wedding day opens with the two kin groups, probably numbering as many as 150 people, pitching their lodges in separate areas and offering a great feast. After the groom's gifts have been presented, the bride's dowry is loaded onto reindeer and carried to the groom's lodge. There the climax of the ceremony takes place. The bride takes the wife's place—that is, at the right side of the entrance of the lodge—and members of both families sit in a circle. The groom enters and follows the bride around the circle, greeting each guest, while the guests, in their turn, kiss the bride on the mouth and hands. Finally, the go-betweens spit three times on the bride's hands, and the couple are formally husband and wife. More feasting and revelry bring the day to a close.[20]

In many cultures, marriage includes ceremonial expressions of hostility. Mock fights are staged in many societies. On occasion, hostility can have genuinely aggressive overtones, as among the Gusii of Kenya:

> Five young clansmen of the groom come to take the bride and two immediately find the girl and post themselves at her side to prevent her escape, while the others receive the final permission of her parents. When it has been granted the bride holds onto the house posts and must be dragged outside by the young men. Finally she goes along with them, crying and with her hands on her head.[21]

But the battle is not yet over. Mutual antagonism continues right onto the marriage bed, even up to and beyond coitus. The groom is determined to display his virility; the bride is equally determined to test it. "Brides," Robert and Barbara LeVine remarked, "are said to take pride in the length of time they can hold off their mates." Men can also win acclaim. If the bride is unable to walk the following day, the groom is considered a "real man."[22] Such expressions of hostility usually occur in societies in which the two sets of kin are actual or potential rivals or enemies. In many societies, it is common to marry women from "enemy" villages.

As this example suggests, marriage ceremonies often symbolize important elements of the culture. Whereas the Gusii ceremony may symbolize hostility between the two families, in other societies the ceremony may promote harmony between the families. For example, on the Polynesian island of Rotuma, a female clown is an important part of the ceremony. She is responsible for creating an enjoyable, joking atmosphere that facilitates interaction between the two sides.[23]

Economic Aspects of Marriage

"It's not man that marries maid, but field marries field, vineyard marries vineyard, cattle marry cattle." In its down-to-earth way, this German peasant saying indicates that in many societies marriage involves economic considerations. In our culture, economic considerations may or may not be explicit. However, in about 75 percent of the societies known to anthropology,[24] one or more explicit economic transactions take place before or after the marriage. The economic transaction may take several forms: bride price, bride service, exchange of females, gift exchange, dowry, or indirect dowry. The distribution of those forms among societies that have economic marriage transactions is shown in Figure 21–1.

BRIDE PRICE   Bride price or **bride wealth** is a gift of money or goods from the groom or his kin to the bride's kin. The gift usually grants the groom the right to marry the bride and the right to her children. Of all the forms of economic transaction involved in marriage, bride price is the most common. In one cross-cultural sample, 44 percent of the societies with economic transactions at marriage practiced bride price; in almost all of those societies the bride price was substantial.[25] Bride price occurs all over the world but is especially common in Africa and Oceania. Payment can be made in different currencies; livestock and food are two of the more common. With the increased importance of commercial exchange, money has increasingly become part of the bride price payments. Among the Nandi, the bride price consists of about five to seven cattle, one or two sheep

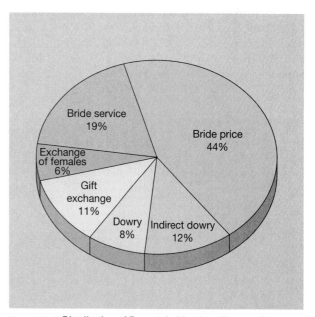

Figure 21–1 Distribution of Economic Marriage Transactions Among Societies That Have Them
Note that there are societies in the ethnographic record (25 percent) that lack any substantial economic transactions at marriage.

Source: Based on data from Alice Schlegel and Rohn Eloul, "Marriage Transactions: Labor, Property, and Status," *American Anthropologist* 90 (1988): 291–309.

and goats, cowrie shells, and money equivalent to the value of one cow. Even in unusual female–female marriages, the female "husband" must pay a bride price to arrange the marriage and be considered the "father."[26]

The Subanun of the Philippines have an expensive bride price—several times the annual income of the groom plus three to five years of bride service (described in the next section).[27] Among the Manus of the Admiralty Islands off New Guinea, a groom requires an economic backer, usually an older brother or an uncle, if he is to marry, but it will be years before he can pay off his debts. Depending on the final bride price, payments may be concluded at the time of the marriage, or they may continue for years afterward.[28]

Despite the connotations that bride price may have for us, the practice does not reduce a woman to the position of slave—although it is associated, as we shall see, with relatively low status for women. The bride price may be important to the woman and her family. Indeed, the fee they receive can serve as a security. If the marriage fails through no fault of hers and the wife returns to her kin, the family might not return the bride price to the groom. On the other hand, the wife's kin may pressure her to remain with her husband, even though she does not wish to, because they do not want to return the bride price or are unable to do so. A larger bride price is associated with more difficulty in obtaining a divorce.[29]

What kinds of societies are likely to have the custom of bride price? Cross-culturally, societies with bride price are likely to practice horticulture and lack social stratification. Bride price is also likely where women contribute a great deal to primary subsistence activities[30] and where they contribute more than men to all kinds of economic activities.[31] Although these findings might suggest that women are highly valued in such societies, recall that the status of women relative to men is not higher in societies in which women contribute a lot to primary subsistence activities. Indeed, bride price is likely to occur in societies in which men make most of the decisions in the household,[32] and decision making by men is one indicator of lower status for women.

BRIDE SERVICE   Bride service, which is the next most common type of economic transaction at marriage—occurring in about 19 percent of the societies with economic transactions—requires the groom to work for the bride's family, sometimes before the marriage begins, sometimes after. Bride service varies in duration. In some societies it lasts for only a few months; in others, as long as several years. Among the North Alaskan Eskimo, for example, the boy works for his in-laws after the marriage is arranged. To fulfill his obligation, he may simply catch a seal for them. The marriage may be consummated at any time while he is in service.[33] In some societies, bride service sometimes substitutes for bride price. An individual might give bride service in order to reduce the amount of bride price required. Native North and South American societies were likely to practice bride service, particularly if they were egalitarian food collectors.[34]

EXCHANGE OF FEMALES   Of the societies that have economic transactions at marriage, 6 percent have the custom whereby a sister or female relative of the groom is exchanged for the bride. Among these societies are the Tiv of West Africa and the Yanomamö of Venezuela-Brazil. These societies tend to be horticultural, egalitarian, and to have a relatively high contribution of women to primary subsistence.[35]

GIFT EXCHANGE   Gift exchange, which involves the exchange of gifts of about equal value by the two kin groups about to be linked by marriage, occurs somewhat more often than the exchange of females (about 11 percent of those with economic transactions).[36] For example, among the Andaman Islanders, as soon as a boy and girl indicate their intention to marry, their respective sets of parents cease all communication and begin sending gifts of food and other objects to each other through a third party. This arrangement

Quilts that are part of a dowry in the Kyrgyz Republic.

continues until the marriage is completed and the two kin groups are united.[37]

DOWRY A **dowry** is usually a substantial transfer of goods or money from the bride's family to the bride, the groom, or the couple.[38] Unlike the types of transactions we have discussed so far, the dowry, which occurs in about 8 percent of the societies with economic transactions, is usually not a transaction between the kin of the bride and the kin of the groom. A family has to have wealth to give a dowry, but because the goods go to the new household, no wealth comes back to the family that gave the dowry. Payment of dowries was common in medieval and Renaissance Europe, where the size of the dowry often determined the desirability of the daughter. The custom is still practiced in parts of eastern Europe and in sections of southern Italy and France, where land is often the major item provided by the bride's family. Parts of India also practice the dowry.

In contrast to societies with bride price, societies with dowry tend to be those in which women contribute relatively little to primary subsistence activities, there is a high degree of social stratification, and a man is not allowed to be married to more than one woman simultaneously.[39] Why does dowry tend to occur in these types of societies? One theory suggests that the dowry is intended to guarantee future support for a woman and her children, even though she will not do much primary subsistence work. Another theory is that the dowry is intended to attract the best bridegroom for a daughter in monogamous societies with a high degree of social inequality. The dowry strategy is presumed to increase the likelihood that the daughter and her children will do well reproductively. Both theories are supported by recent cross-cultural research, with the second predicting dowry better.[40] But many stratified societies (including our own) in which women and men have only one spouse at a time do not practice dowry. Why this is so still needs to be explained.

INDIRECT DOWRY The dowry is provided by the bride's family to the bride, the groom, or the couple. But sometimes the payments to the bride originate from the groom's family. Because the goods are sometimes first given to the bride's father, who passes most if not all of them to her, this kind of transaction is called **indirect dowry.**[41] Indirect dowry occurs in about 12 percent of the societies in which marriage involves an economic transaction. For example, among the Basseri of southern Iran, the groom's father assumes the expense of setting up the couple's new household. He gives cash to the bride's father, who uses at least some of the money to buy his daughter household utensils, blankets, and rugs.[42]

Restrictions on Marriage: The Universal Incest Taboo

Hollywood and its press agents notwithstanding, marriage is not always based solely on mutual love, independently discovered and expressed by the two life-partners-to-be. Nor is it based on sex or wealth alone. Even when love, sex, and economics are contributing factors, regulations specify whom one may or may not marry. Perhaps the most rigid regulation, found in *all* cultures, is the **incest taboo,** which prohibits sexual intercourse or marriage between some categories of kin.

The most universal aspect of the incest taboo is the prohibition of sexual intercourse or marriage between mother and son, father and daughter, and brother and sister. No society in recent times has permitted either sexual intercourse or marriage between those pairs. A few societies in the past, however, did permit incest, mostly within the royal and aristocratic families, though generally it was forbidden to the rest of the population. For example, the Incan and Hawaiian royal families allowed marriage within the family. Probably the best-known example of allowed incest involved Cleopatra of Egypt.

It seems clear that the Egyptian aristocracy and royalty indulged in father–daughter and brother–sister marriages. Cleopatra was married to two of her younger brothers at different times.[43] The reasons seem to have been partly religious—a member of the family of the pharaoh, who was considered a god, could not marry any "ordinary" human—and partly economic, for marriage within the family kept the royal property undivided. In Egypt, between 30 B.C. and A.D. 324, incest was allowed not just in the royal family; an estimated 8 percent of commoner marriages were brother–sister marriages.[44]

But, despite these exceptions, the fact remains that no culture we know of today permits or accepts incest within the nuclear family. Why is the familial incest taboo universal? Several explanations have been suggested.

Childhood-Familiarity Theory

The childhood-familiarity theory, suggested by Edward Westermarck, was given a wide hearing in the early 1920s. Westermarck argued that persons who have been closely associated with each other since earliest childhood, such as siblings, are not sexually attracted to each other and therefore would avoid marriage with each other.[45] This theory was subsequently rejected because of evidence that some children were sexually interested in their parents and siblings. Studies have suggested, however, that there might be something to Westermarck's theory.

Yonina Talmon investigated marriage patterns among the second generation of three well-established collective communities (*kibbutzim*) in Israel. In these collectives, children live with many members of their peer group in quarters separate from their families. They are in constant interaction with their peers, from birth to maturity. The study revealed that among 125 couples, there was "not one instance in which both mates were reared from birth in the same peer group,"[46] despite parental encouragement of marriage within the peer group. Children reared in common not only avoided marriage, they also avoided any sexual relations among themselves.

Talmon stated that the people reared together firmly believed that overfamiliarity breeds sexual disinterest. As one

Children on an Israeli Kibbutz live together
as well as go to school together.

of them told her, "We are like an open book to each other. We have read the story in the book over and over again and know all about it."[47] Talmon's evidence reveals not only the onset of disinterest and even sexual antipathy among children reared together, but a correspondingly heightened fascination with newcomers or outsiders, particularly for their "mystery."

Arthur Wolf's study of the Chinese in northern Taiwan also supports the idea that something about being reared together produces sexual disinterest. Wolf focused on a community still practicing the Chinese custom of *t'ung-yang-hsi,* or "daughter-in-law raised from childhood":

> When a girl is born in a poor family . . . she is often given away or sold when but a few weeks or months old, or one or two years old, to be the future wife of a son in the family of a friend or relative which has a little son not betrothed in marriage. . . . The girl is called a "little bride" and taken home and brought up in the family together with her future husband.[48]

Wolf's evidence indicates that this arrangement is associated with sexual difficulties when the childhood "couple" later marry. Informants implied that familiarity results in disinterest and lack of stimulation. As an indication of their disinterest, these couples produce fewer offspring than spouses not raised together, they are more likely to seek extramarital sexual relationships, and they are more likely to get divorced.[49]

The Talmon and Wolf studies suggest, then, that children raised together are not likely to be sexually interested in each other when they grow up. Such disinterest is consistent with Westermarck's notion that the incest taboo may be more an avoidance of certain matings than a prohibition of them. There is one other piece of evidence consistent with this explanation of the incest taboo. Hilda and Seymour Parker

compared two samples of fathers: those who had sexually abused their daughters and those who supposedly had not.[50] To maximize their similarities otherwise, the Parkers selected the two samples of fathers from the same prisons and psychiatric facilities. The Parkers found that the fathers who had committed incest with their daughters were much more likely than the other sample of fathers to have had little to do with bringing up their daughters, because they were not at home or hardly at home during the daughters' first three years of life. In other words, the fathers who avoided incest had been more closely associated with their daughters in childhood. That finding is consistent with Westermarck's suggestion that the incest taboo is a result of familiarity in childhood.

Although Westermarck was talking about the development of sexual aversion during early childhood, some researchers have asked how the childhood-familiarity theory could explain the extension of incest taboos to first cousins. The familiarity argument implies that first-cousin marriage should be prohibited in societies in which first cousins grow up together in the same community. But that is not the case. Such societies are not more likely to prohibit first-cousin marriage.[51]

Even if there is something about familiarity in childhood that normally leads to sexual disinterest,[52] we still are left with the question of why societies have to prohibit marriages that would voluntarily be avoided because of disinterest. And why do many couples remain actively interested in each other sexually after years of marriage?

Freud's Psychoanalytic Theory

Sigmund Freud proposed that the incest taboo is a reaction against unconscious, unacceptable desires.[53] He suggested that the son is attracted to his mother (as the daughter is to her father) and as a result feels jealousy and hostility toward his father. But the son knows that these feelings cannot continue, for they might lead the father to retaliate against him; therefore, they must be renounced or repressed. Usually the feelings are repressed and retreat into the unconscious. But the desire to possess the mother continues to exist in the unconscious, and, according to Freud, the horror of incest is a reaction to, or a defense against, the forbidden unconscious impulse.

Although Freud's theory may account for the aversion felt toward incest, or at least the aversion toward parent–child incest, it does not explain why society needs an explicit taboo, particularly on brother–sister incest. Nor does it account for the findings of sexual disinterest we discussed in connection with the Westermarck hypothesis.

Family-Disruption Theory

The family-disruption theory, often associated with Bronislaw Malinowski,[54] can best be summed up as follows: Sexual competition among family members would create so much rivalry and tension that the family could not function as an effective unit. Because the family must function effectively for society to survive, society has to curtail competition within the family. The familial incest taboo is thus imposed to keep the family intact.

But there are inconsistencies in this approach. Society could have shaped other rules about the sexual access of one member of the family to another that would also eliminate potentially disruptive competition. Also, why would brother–sister incest be so disruptive? As we noted, such marriages did exist in ancient Egypt. Brother–sister incest would not disrupt the authority of the parents if the children were allowed to marry when mature. The family-disruption theory, then, does not explain the origin of the incest taboo.

Cooperation Theory

The cooperation theory was proposed by the early anthropologist Edward B. Tylor and was elaborated by Leslie A. White and Claude Lévi-Strauss. It emphasizes the value of the incest taboo in promoting cooperation among family groups and thus helping communities to survive. As Tylor saw it, certain operations necessary for the welfare of the community can be accomplished only by large numbers of people working together. In order to break down suspicion and hostility between family groups and make such cooperation possible, early humans developed the incest taboo to ensure that individuals would marry members of other families. The ties created by intermarriage would serve to hold the community together. Thus, Tylor explained the incest taboo as an answer to the choice "between marrying out and being killed out."[55]

The idea that marriage with other groups promotes cooperation sounds plausible, but is there evidence to support it? After all, there are societies such as the Gusii in which marriage is often between hostile groups. But is that society an exception? Does marriage promote cooperation? Because people in all recent societies marry outside the family, we cannot test the idea that such marriages promote cooperation more than marriages within the family. We can, however, ask whether other kinds of out-marriage, such as marriage with other communities, promote cooperation with those communities. The evidence on that question does not support the cooperation theory. There is no greater peacefulness between communities when marriages are forbidden within the community and always arranged with other communities than when they are not.[56]

But even if marriage outside the family promoted cooperation with other groups, why would it be necessary to prohibit all marriages within the family? Couldn't families have required some of their members to marry outside the family if they thought it necessary for survival but permitted incestuous marriages when such alliances were not needed? Although the incest taboo might enhance cooperation between families, the need for cooperation does not adequately explain the existence of the incest taboo in all societies; other customs might also promote alliances. Furthermore, the cooperation theory does not explain the sexual aspect of the incest taboo. Societies could conceivably allow incestuous sex and still insist that children marry outside the family.

Inbreeding Theory

One of the oldest explanations for the incest taboo is the inbreeding theory. It focuses on the potentially damaging consequences of inbreeding or marrying within the family. People within the same family are likely to carry the same harmful recessive genes. Inbreeding, then, will tend to produce offspring who are more likely to die early of genetic disorders than are the offspring of unrelated spouses. For many years this theory was rejected because, on the basis of dog-breeding practices, it was thought that inbreeding need not be harmful. The inbreeding practiced to produce prize-winning dogs, however, is not a good guide to whether inbreeding is harmful; dog breeders don't count the runts they cull when they try to breed for success in dog shows. We now have a good deal of evidence, from humans as well as other animals, that the closer the degree of inbreeding, the more harmful the genetic effects.[57]

Genetic mutations occur frequently. Although many pose no harm to the individuals who carry a single recessive gene, matings between two persons who carry the same gene often produce offspring with a harmful or lethal condition. Close blood relatives are much more likely than unrelated individuals to carry the same harmful recessive gene. So if close relatives mate, their offspring have a higher probability than the offspring of nonrelatives of inheriting the harmful trait.

One study compared children produced by familial incest with children of the same mothers produced by nonincestuous unions. About 40 percent of the incestuously produced children had serious abnormalities, compared with about 5 percent of the other children.[58] Matings between other kinds of relatives not as closely related also show harmful, but not as harmful, effects of inbreeding. These results are consistent with inbreeding theory. The likelihood that a child will inherit a double dose of a harmful recessive gene is lower the more distantly the child's parents are related.

Also consistent with inbreeding theory is the fact that rates of abnormality are consistently higher in the offspring of uncle–niece marriages (which are allowed in some societies) than in the offspring of cousin marriages; for the offspring of uncle–niece marriages, the likelihood of inheriting a double dose of a harmful recessive is twice that for the offspring of first cousins.[59]

Although most scholars acknowledge the harmful effects of inbreeding, some question whether people in former days would have deliberately invented or borrowed the incest taboo because they knew that inbreeding was biologically harmful. William Durham's cross-cultural survey suggests that they did. Ethnographers do not always report the perceived consequences of incest, but in 50 percent of the reports Durham found, biological harm to the offspring was mentioned.[60] For example, Raymond Firth reported on the Tikopia, who live on an island in the South Pacific:

> The idea is firmly held that unions of close kin bear with them their own doom, their *mara*. . . . The idea [*mara*] essentially concerns barrenness. . . . The peculiar barrenness of an incestuous union consists not in the absence of children, but in their illness or death, or some other mishap. . . . The idea that the offspring of a marriage between near kin are weakly and likely to die young is stoutly held by these natives and examples are adduced to prove it.[61]

So, if the harm of inbreeding was widely recognized, people may have deliberately invented or borrowed the incest taboo.[62] But whether or not people actually recognized the harmfulness of inbreeding, the demographic consequences of the incest taboo would account for its universality, since reproductive and hence competitive advantages probably accrued to groups practicing the taboo. Thus, although cultural solutions other than the incest taboo might provide the desired effects assumed by the family-disruption theory and the cooperation theory, the incest taboo is the only possible solution to the problem of inbreeding.

As is discussed toward the end of the next section, a society may or may not extend the incest taboo to first cousins. That variation is also predictable from inbreeding theory, which provides additional support for the idea that the incest taboo was invented or borrowed to avoid the harmful consequences of inbreeding.

 ## Whom Should One Marry?

Probably every child in our society knows the story of Cinderella—the poor, downtrodden, but lovely girl who accidentally meets, falls in love with, and eventually marries a prince. It is a charming tale, but as a guide to mate choice in our society it is misleading. The majority of marriages simply do not occur in so free and coincidental a way in any society. In addition to the incest taboo, societies often have

A priest in India prays for young women to get good husbands and to have many sons. Marriages are often still arranged.

rules restricting marriage with other persons, as well as preferences about which other persons are the most desirable mates.

Even in a modern, urbanized society such as ours, where theoretically mate choice is free, people tend to marry within their own class and geographic area. For example, studies in the United States consistently indicate that a person is likely to marry someone who lives close by.[63] Neighborhoods are frequently made up of people from similar class backgrounds, so it is unlikely that many of these alliances are Cinderella stories.

Arranged Marriages

In an appreciable number of societies, marriages are arranged; negotiations are handled by the immediate families or by go-betweens. Sometimes betrothals are completed while the future partners are still children. This was formerly the custom in much of Hindu India, China, Japan, and eastern and southern Europe. Implicit in the arranged marriage is the conviction that the joining together of two kin groups to form new social and economic ties is too important to be left to free choice and romantic love.

An example of a marriage arranged for reasons of prestige comes from Clellan Ford's study of the Kwakiutl of British Columbia. Ford's informant described his marriage as follows:

> When I was old enough to get a wife—I was about 25—my brothers looked for a girl in the same position

MIGRANTS AND IMMIGRANTS

Arranging Marriages in the Diaspora

What happens when people move from a place with arranged marriage to a place where marriage is based on free choice and romantic love? Many people around the world or their parents are from places that reject love marriage because it could fizzle out. Love was not considered a sufficient basis for marriage. So parents and other kin, or hired go-betweens, would select your marriage partner, preferably someone from the same socioeconomic background. For example, in many parts of South Asia until recently, one was supposed to marry someone from the same caste and class. Many immigrant parents still insist that their children's marriages be arranged. But this is changing. Consider how some young South Asians in England are "arranging" their own marriages.

Go-betweens are replaced by Web sites, chat rooms, and personal advertisements on the internet. A couple who "meet" first electronically might then arrange to meet face-to-face, in what's called "South Asian speed dating"; they agree to meet and talk—for just three minutes—at a restaurant or bar, and then they move on. The participants, who are in their 20s and middle class, consider themselves hip. They are quite comfortable blending behaviors from West and East. But many marriages are still arranged by relatives or go-betweens. Is it because there is discrimination against South Asians and therefore it is difficult to meet and marry other kinds of people? Is the same true for South Asians in the United States?

The U.S. has had a long history of discrimination against people of color, and South Asians generally have darker skins. So they may also encounter social barriers. Most immigrant groups in the past and present have had restricted opportunities to meet and marry people from different ethnic and class backgrounds. Poor people didn't belong to country clubs.

Certain ethnic groups were not admitted, or only admitted sparingly, to Ivy League colleges. To be sure, some people were able to "move up" economically, and this provided more opportunities to meet people from other backgrounds. But marriages were generally restricted to your own class, religion, and locality. And this is still true for the most part. We might expect then that immigrants who come from South Asia would continue to practice arranged marriage. And many do. Young people may say that they would prefer to have a love marriage. But they wouldn't dream of marrying someone who was not like them. And so their parents hire a matchmaker to find them a spouse.

Rakhi is a lawyer in New York City. She is the daughter of Sikh immigrants from Punjab, India. (The Sikhs are a religious group.) As a young girl, Rakhi had built a shrine to an American movie star in her bedroom. But at the age of 27 she decided to marry someone like herself. But she was focused on her career and didn't have time to date. So her mother enlisted the help of a Sikh matchmaker who had been instructed by the mother of a man named Ranjeet to find a wife for him. Ranjeet also had thought he would marry for love. "But seeing how different cultures treated their families, I realized the importance of making the right match." When the matchmaker organized a party to which she invited Rakhi and Ranjeet (and their mothers), Rakhi's mother whispered: "I think he's the one." After the two young people dated secretly for two months, the matchmaker was once again summoned, this time to negotiate the marital arrangements. Some time later Rakhi and Ranjeet were married in a Sikh temple in a New York suburb.

Sources: Lizette Alvarez, "Arranged Marriages Get a Little Rearranging," *The New York Times,* June 22, 2003, p. 1.3; Stephen Henderson, "Weddings: Vows; Rakhi Dhanoa and Ranjeet Purewal," *The New York Times,* August 18, 2002, p. 9.2.

---

that I and my brothers had. Without my consent, they picked a wife for me—Lagius' daughter. The one I wanted was prettier than the one they chose for me, but she was in a lower position than me, so they wouldn't let me marry her.[64]

In many places arranged marriages are beginning to disappear, and couples are beginning to have more say about their marriage partners. As recently as 1960, marriages were still arranged on the Pacific island of Rotuma, and sometimes the bride and groom did not meet until the wedding day. Today weddings are much the same, but couples are allowed to "go out" and have a say about whom

they wish to marry.[65] In a small Moroccan town, arranged marriages are still the norm, although a young man may ask his mother to make a marriage offer to a particular girl's parents, who may ask her whether she wants to accept the marriage offer. But dating is still not acceptable, so getting acquainted is hard to arrange.[66]

Exogamy and Endogamy

Marriage partners often must be chosen from outside one's own kin group or community; this is known as a rule of **exogamy.** Exogamy can take many forms. It may mean marrying outside a particular group of kin or outside a particular village or group of villages. Often, then, spouses come from a distance. For example, in Rani Khera, a village in India, 266 married women had come from about 200 different villages averaging between 12 and 24 miles away; 220 local women had gone to 200 other villages to marry. As a result of these exogamous marriages, Rani Khera, a village of 150 households, was linked to 400 other nearby villages.[67] When there are rules of exogamy, violations are often believed to cause harm. On the islands of Yap in Micronesia, people who are related through women are referred to as "people of one belly." The elders say that if two people from the same kinship group married, they would not have any female children and the group would die out.[68]

People in societies with very low population densities often have to travel considerable distances to meet mates. A study of foragers and horticulturalists found a clear relationship between population density and the distance between the communities of the husband and wife—the lower the density, the greater the marriage distance. Because foragers generally have lower densities than horticulturalists, they generally have further to go to find mates. Among the !Kung, for instance, the average husband and wife had lived 65 kilometers (40 miles) from each other before they were married.[69]

A rule of **endogamy** obliges a person to marry within some group. The caste groups of India traditionally have been endogamous. The higher castes believed that marriage with lower castes would "pollute" them, and such unions were forbidden. Caste endogamy is also found in some parts of Africa. In East Africa, a Masai warrior would never stoop to marry the daughter of an ironworker, nor would a former ruling caste Tutsi in Rwanda, in central Africa, think of marrying a person from the hunting caste Twa.

Cousin Marriages

Kinship terminology for most people in the United States does not differentiate between types of cousins. In some other societies such distinctions may be important, particularly with regard to first cousins; the terms for the different kinds of first cousins may indicate which cousins are suitable marriage partners (sometimes even preferred mates) and which are not. Although most societies prohibit marriage with all types of first cousins,[70] some societies allow and even prefer particular kinds of cousin marriage.

Cross-cousins are children of siblings of the opposite sex; that is, a person's cross-cousins are father's sisters' children and mother's brothers' children. **Parallel cousins** are children of siblings of the same sex; a person's parallel cousins, then, are father's brothers' children and mother's sisters' children (see Figure 21–2). The Chippewa Indians used to practice cross-cousin marriage, as well as cross-cousin joking. With his female cross-cousins, a Chippewa man was expected to exchange broad, risqué jokes, but he would not do so with his parallel cousins, with whom severe propriety was the rule. In general, in any society in which cross-cousin marriage is allowed but parallel-cousin is not, there is a joking relationship between a man and his

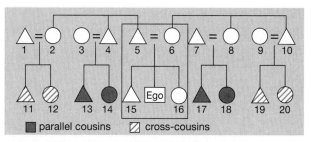

Figure 21–2 Cross-Cousin and Parallel Cousins
Anthropologists use symbols to represent kinship relationships. A triangle represents a male; a circle a female; an "=" sign a marriage; a vertical line "the children of"; and a horizontal connector for siblings. Often there is a focus of the diagram (an "ego") designated by a square. The rectangle in the figure surrounds a nuclear family unit consisting of ego, ego's two siblings—a brother (15) and sister (16), and the parents (5 and 6—5 is the father of ego and 6 is the mother). Ego's cousins (as well as the cousins of ego's siblings are 11–14 on the father's side of the family and 17–20 on the mother's side of the family. Also shown are the father's and mother's brothers and sisters and their spouses.

To consider which cousins are parallel cousins and which are cross-cousins let us look at the links between ego and the cousins. If the link is the same sex (i.e., through mother's sister or father's brother) we call the cousins "parallel cousins." In the diagram ego's parallel cousins are 13, 14, 17, and 18. Cross-cousins are linked through the opposite sex. So ego's cross-cousins would be father's sister's children (11, 12) or mother's brother's children (19, 20). To specify which parallel or cross-cousins we are referring to, we can use the terms "matrilateral (mother's side)" or "patrilateral (father's side)."

female cross-cousins. This attitude contrasts with the formal and very respectful relationship the man maintains with female parallel cousins. Apparently, the joking relationship signifies the possibility of marriage, whereas the respectful relationship signifies the extension of the incest taboo to parallel cousins.

When first-cousin marriage is allowed or preferred, it is usually with some kind of cross-cousin. Parallel-cousin marriage is fairly rare, but Muslim societies usually prefer such marriages, allowing other cousin marriages as well. The Kurds, who are mostly Sunni Muslims, prefer a young man to marry his father's brother's daughter (for the young woman this would be her father's brother's son). The father and his brother usually live near each other, so the woman will stay close to home in such a marriage. The bride and groom are also in the same kin group, so marriage in this case also entails kin group endogamy.[71]

What kinds of societies allow or prefer first-cousin marriage? There is evidence from cross-cultural research that cousin marriages are most apt to be permitted in relatively large and densely populated societies. Perhaps this is because the likelihood of such marriages, and therefore the risks of inbreeding, are minimal in those societies. Many small, sparsely populated societies, however, permit or even sometimes prefer cousin marriage. How can these cases be explained? They seem to cast doubt on the interpretation that cousin marriage should be prohibited in sparsely populated societies, in which marriages between close relatives are more likely just by chance and the risks of inbreeding should be greatest. It turns out that most of the small societies that permit cousin marriage have lost a lot of people to epidemics. Many peoples around the world, particularly in the Pacific and in North and South America, suffered severe depopulation in the first generation or two after contact with Europeans, who introduced diseases (such as measles, pneumonia, and smallpox) to which the native populations had little or no resistance. Such societies may have had to permit cousin marriage in order to provide enough mating possibilities among the reduced population of eligible mates.[72]

Levirate and Sororate

In many societies, cultural rules oblige individuals to marry the spouse of deceased relatives. **Levirate** is a custom whereby a man is obliged to marry his brother's widow. **Sororate** obliges a woman to marry her deceased sister's husband. Both customs are exceedingly common, being the obligatory form of second marriage in a majority of societies known to anthropology.[73]

Among the Chukchee of Siberia, levirate obliges the next oldest brother to become the successor husband. He cares for the widow and children, assumes the sexual privileges of the husband, and unites the deceased's reindeer herd with his own, keeping it in the name of his brother's children. If there are no brothers, the widow is married to a cousin of her first husband. The Chukchee regard the custom more as a duty than as a right. The nearest relative is obliged to care for a woman left with children and a herd.[74]

How Many Does One Marry?

We are accustomed to thinking of marriage as involving just one man and one woman at a time—**monogamy**—but most societies known to anthropology have allowed a man to be married to more than one woman at the same time—**polygyny.** At any given time, however, the majority of men in societies permitting polygyny are married monogamously; few or no societies have enough women to permit most men to have at least two wives. Polygyny's mirror image—one woman being married to more than one man at the same time, called **polyandry**—is practiced in very few societies. Polygyny and polyandry are the two types of **polygamy,** or plural spouse marriage. **Group marriage,** in which more than one man is married to more than one woman at the same time, sometimes occurs but is not customary in any known society. The four possible forms of marriage are illustrated in Table 21–1.

Polygyny

The Old Testament has many references to men with more than one wife simultaneously: King David and King Solomon are just two examples of men polygynously married. Just as in the society described in the Old Testament, polygyny in many societies is a mark of a man's great wealth

Table 21–1   Four Possible Forms of Marriage

Form of Marriage	Males	Females
Monogamy	Δ	= O
Polygamy		
Polygyny	Δ	= O + O +
Polyandry	Δ + Δ +	= O
Group marriage	Δ + Δ +	= O + O +

Δ represents male; O, female; and =, marriage.

or high status. In such societies only the very wealthy can, and are expected to, support more than one wife. Some Muslim societies, especially Arabic-speaking ones, still view polygyny in this light. But a man does not always have to be wealthy to be polygynous; indeed, in some societies in which women are important contributors to the economy, it seems that men try to have more than one wife in order to become wealthier.

Among the Siwai, a society in the South Pacific, status is achieved through feast giving. Pork is the main dish at these feasts, so the Siwai associate pig raising with prestige. This great interest in pigs sparks an interest in wives, because in Siwai society women raise the food needed to raise pigs. Thus, although having many wives does not in itself confer status among the Siwai, the increase in pig herds that may result from polygyny is a source of prestige for the owner.[75]

Polygynously married Siwai men do seem to have greater prestige, but they complain that a household with multiple wives is difficult. Sinu, a Siwai, described his plight:

> There is never peace for a long time in a polygynous family. If the husband sleeps in the house of one wife, the other one sulks all the next day. If the man is so stupid as to sleep two consecutive nights in the house of one wife, the other one will refuse to cook for him, saying, "So-and-so is your wife; go to her for food. Since I am not good enough for you to sleep

Polygyny is practiced by some in this country, even though it is prohibited by law.

CURRENT RESEARCH AND ISSUES

The Husband–Wife Relationship: Variation in Love, Intimacy, and Sexual Jealousy

Americans believe that love should be a basis of marriage. Does this ideal characterize most societies? We know the answer to that question: No. In fact, in many places romantic love is believed to be a poor basis for marriage and is strongly discouraged. However, even though romantic love may not be a basis for marriage everywhere, it does occur almost everywhere. A recent cross-cultural survey suggests that about 88 percent of the world's societies show signs of romantic love—accounts of personal longing, love songs or love depicted in folklore, elopement because of affection, and passionate love described by informants quoted in ethnographies. So if love is nearly universal, why is it often discouraged as a basis for marriage?

Three conditions appear to predict such discouragement. One is that the husband and wife live in an extended family. In this situation, the family seems more concerned with how the in-marrying person gets along with others, and less concerned with whether the husband and wife love each other. A second condition predicting the discouragement of romantic love as a basis for marriage is that one of the spouses does most of the primary subsistence work or earns most of the couple's income. Third, romantic love is unlikely when men have more sexual freedom than women. In general, then, romantic love is discouraged as a basis for marriage under conditions of inequality—if one of the spouses is highly dependent on the other or the other's kin or the woman has fewer sexual rights than the man.

Intimacy is different from romantic love. It refers to how close the married couple are to each other—eating together, sleeping in the same bed, spending their leisure time together, as well as having frequent sex. In some societies couples are together a lot; in others they spend very little time together. Foraging societies seem on average to have more marital intimacy than more complex herding and agricultural societies, but the reasons are not entirely clear. Also, a high involvement in war seems to detract from intimacy.

When it comes to sexual jealousy, men are far more likely to be violent than women. Incidentally, infidelity is the most frequently reported reason for a husband to divorce a wife. Anthropologists with a biological orientation point out that fathers always have some uncertainty about whether their children are theirs, so males are much more likely for that reason alone to try to guard against rival males. But how can we account for the considerable variation in jealousy from one society to another? It does seem that the more a society emphasizes the importance of getting married, the more it limits sex to the marriage relationship, the more it emphasizes property, and the more its males appear to exhibit sexual jealousy.

How are these various aspects of marriage related to each other? Does romantic love as a basis for marriage increase or decrease sexual jealousy? Does romantic love predict intimacy, or is romantic love more likely with less frequent contact between the spouses? We are still far from understanding how these different aspects are related. All we know is that an emphasis on love and intimacy does not preclude marital violence or marital dissolution.

Sources: Lewellyn Hendrix, "Varieties of Marital Relationships," in *Cross-Cultural Research for Social Science,* in Carol R. Ember, Melvin Ember, and Peter N. Peregrine, eds., *New Directions in Anthropology* (Upper Saddle River, NJ: Prentice Hall, CD-ROM, 2004); Laura Betzig, "Causes of Conjugal Dissolution: A Cross-Cultural Study," *Current Anthropology* 30 (1989): 654–76. William R. Jankowiak and Edward F. Fischer, "A Cross-Cultural Perspective on Romantic Love," *Ethnology,* 31 (1992): 149–55; Victor C. de Munck and Andrey Korotayev, "Sexual Equality and Romantic Love: A Reanalysis of Rosenblatt's Study on the Function of Romantic Love," *Cross-Cultural Research,* 33 (1999): 265–73.

I ask this boon, will you be MY VALENTINE?

The Valentine, as in this 19th century British card, symbolizes romantic love.

with, then my food is not good enough for you to eat." Frequently the co-wives will quarrel and fight. My uncle formerly had five wives at one time and the youngest one was always raging and fighting the others. Once she knocked an older wife senseless and then ran away and had to be forcibly returned.[76]

Jealousy between co-wives is reported in many polygynous societies, but it seems not to be present in some. For example, Margaret Mead reported that married life among the Arapesh of New Guinea, even in the polygynous marriages, was "so even and contented that there is nothing to relate of it at all."[77] Why might there be little or no jealousy between co-wives in a society? One possible reason is that a man is married to two or more sisters—**sororal polygyny;** it seems that sisters, having grown up together, are more likely to get along and cooperate as co-wives than are co-wives who are not also sisters—**nonsororal polygyny.** Other customs may also lessen jealousy between co-wives:

1. Co-wives who are not sisters tend to have separate living quarters; sororal co-wives almost always live together. Among the Plateau Tonga in Africa, who practice nonsororal polygyny, the husband shares his personal goods and his favors among his wives, who live in separate dwellings, according to principles of strict equality. The Crow Indians practiced sororal polygyny, and co-wives usually shared a tepee.

2. Co-wives have clearly defined equal rights in matters of sex, economics, and personal possessions. For example, the Tanala of Madagascar require the husband to spend a day with each co-wife in succession. Failure to do so constitutes adultery and entitles the slighted wife to sue for divorce and alimony of up to one-third of the husband's property. Furthermore, the land is shared equally among all the women, who expect the husband to help with its cultivation when he visits them.

3. Senior wives often have special prestige. The Tonga of Polynesia, for example, grant to the first wife the status of "chief wife." Her house is to the right of her husband's and is called the "house of the father." The other wives are called "small wives," and their houses are to the left of the husband's. The chief wife has the right to be consulted before the small wives, and her husband is expected to sleep under her roof before and after a journey. Although this rule might seem to enhance the jealousy of the secondary wives, later wives are usually favored somewhat because they tend to be younger and more attractive. By this custom, then, the first wife may be compensated for her loss of physical attractiveness by increased prestige.[78]

We must remember that, although jealousy is commonly mentioned in polygynous marriages, people who practice polygyny think it has considerable advantages. In a study conducted by Philip and Janet Kilbride in Kenya, female as well as male married people agreed that polygyny had economic and political advantages. Because they tend to be large, polygynous families provide plenty of farm labor and extra food that can be marketed. They also tend to be influential in their communities and are likely to produce individuals who become government officials.[79] And in South Africa, Connie Anderson found that women choose to be married to a man with other wives because the other wives could help with child care and household work, provide companionship, and allow more freedom to come and go. Some women said they chose polygynous marriages because there was a shortage of marriageable males.[80]

How can we account for the fact that polygyny is allowed and often preferred in most of the societies known to anthropology? Ralph Linton suggested that polygyny derives from a general male primate urge to collect females.[81] But if that were so, then why wouldn't all societies allow polygyny? Other explanations of polygyny have been suggested. We restrict our discussion here to those that statistically and strongly predict polygyny in worldwide samples of societies.

One theory is that polygyny will be permitted in societies that have a long **postpartum sex taboo.**[82] In these societies, a couple must abstain from intercourse until their child is at least a year old. John Whiting suggested that couples abstain from sexual intercourse for a long time after their child is born for health reasons. A Hausa woman reported:

> A mother should not go to her husband while she has a child she is suckling. If she does, the child gets thin; he dries up, he won't be strong, he won't be healthy. If she goes after two years it is nothing, he is already strong before that, it does not matter if she conceives again after two years.[83]

The symptoms the woman described seem to be those of *kwashiorkor*. Common in tropical areas, kwashiorkor is a protein-deficiency disease that occurs particularly in children suffering from intestinal parasites or diarrhea. By observing a long postpartum sex taboo, and thereby ensuring that her children are widely spaced, a woman can nurse each child longer. If a child gets protein from mother's milk during its first few years, the likelihood of contracting kwashiorkor may be greatly reduced. Consistent with Whiting's interpretation is the fact that societies with low-protein staples (those whose principal foods are root and tree crops such as taro, sweet potatoes, bananas, and breadfruit) tend to have a long postpartum sex taboo. Societies with long postpartum sex taboos also tend to be polygynous. Perhaps, then, a man's having more than one wife is a cultural adjustment to the taboo. As a Yoruba woman said,

> When we abstain from having sexual intercourse with our husband for the two years we nurse our babies, we know he will seek some other woman. We would rather have her under our control as a co-wife so he is not spending money outside the family.[84]

Even if we agree that men will seek other sexual relationships during the period of a long postpartum sex taboo, it is not clear why polygyny is the only possible solution to the problem. After all, it is conceivable that all of a man's wives might be subject to the postpartum sex taboo at the same time. Furthermore, there may be sexual outlets outside marriage.

Another explanation of polygyny is that it is a response to an excess of women over men. Such an imbalanced sex ratio may occur because of the prevalence of warfare in a society. Because men and not women are generally the warriors, warfare almost always takes a greater toll of men's lives. Given that almost all adults in noncommercial societies are married, polygyny may be a way of providing spouses for surplus women. Indeed, there is evidence that societies with imbalanced sex ratios in favor of women tend to have both polygyny and high male mortality in warfare. Conversely, societies with balanced sex ratios tend to have both monogamy and low male mortality in warfare.[85]

A third explanation is that a society will allow polygyny when men marry at an older age than women. The argument is similar to the sex ratio interpretation. Delaying the age of marriage for men would produce an artificial, though not an actual, excess of marriageable women. Why marriage for men is delayed is not clear, but the delay does predict polygyny.[86]

Is one of these explanations better than the others, or are all three factors—long postpartum sex taboo, an imbalanced sex ratio in favor of women, and delayed age of marriage for men—important in explaining polygyny? One way of trying to decide among alternative explanations is to do what is called a *statistical-control analysis,* which allows us to see if a particular factor still predicts when the effects of other possible factors are removed. In this case, when the possible effect of sex ratio is removed, a long postpartum sex taboo no longer predicts polygyny and hence is probably not a cause of polygyny.[87] But both an actual excess of women and a late age of marriage for men seem to be strong predictors of polygyny. Added together, these two factors predict even more strongly.[88]

Behavioral ecologists have also suggested ecological reasons why both men and women might prefer polygynous marriages. If there are enough resources, men might prefer polygyny because they can have more children if they have more than one wife. If resources are highly variable and men control resources, women might find it advantageous to marry a man with many resources even if she is a second wife. A recent study of foragers suggests that foraging societies in which men control hunting or fishing territories are more likely to be polygynous. This finding is consistent with the theory, but the authors were surprised that control of gathering sites by men did not predict polygyny.[89] The main problem with the theory of variable resources and their marital consequences is that many societies, particularly in the "modern" world, have great variability in wealth, but little polygyny. So behavioral ecologists have had to argue that polygyny is lacking because of socially imposed constraints. But why are those constraints imposed? The sex-ratio interpretation can explain the absence of polygyny in most commercialized modern societies. First, very complex societies have standing armies and male mortality in warfare is rarely as high *proportionately* as in simpler societies. Second with commercialization there are more possibilities for individuals to support themselves without being married. Degree of disease in the environment may also be a factor.

Bobbi Low has suggested that a high incidence of disease may reduce the prevalence of "healthy" men. In such cases it may be to a woman's advantage to marry a "healthy" man even if he is already married, and it may be to a man's advantage to marry several unrelated women to maximize genetic variation (and disease resistance) among his children. Indeed, societies with many pathogens are more likely to have polygyny.[90] Further research is needed to compare the degree of disease explanation of polygyny with the imbalanced sex-ratio explanation.

Polyandry

George Peter Murdock's "World Ethnographic Sample" included only four societies (less than 1 percent of the total) in which polyandry, or the marriage of several men to one woman, was practiced.[91] When the husbands are brothers we call it **fraternal polyandry;** if they are not brothers, it is **nonfraternal polyandry.** Some Tibetans, the Toda of India, and the Sinhalese of Sri Lanka have practiced fraternal polyandry. Among the Tibetans who practice fraternal polyandry, biological paternity seems to be of no particular concern; there is no attempt to link children biologically to a particular brother, and all children are treated the same.[92]

One possible explanation for the practice of polyandry is a shortage of women. The Toda practiced female infanticide;[93] the Sinhalese had a shortage of women but denied the practice of female infanticide.[94] A correlation between shortage of women and polyandry would account for why polyandry is so rare in the ethnographic record; an excess of men is rare cross-culturally.

Another possible explanation is that polyandry is an adaptive response to severely limited resources. Melvyn Goldstein studied Tibetans who live in the northwestern corner of Nepal, above 12,000 feet in elevation. Cultivable land is extremely scarce there, with most families having less than an acre. The people say they practice fraternal polyandry in order to prevent the division of a family's farm and animals. Instead of dividing up their land among them and each taking a wife, brothers preserve the family farm by sharing a wife. Although not recognized by the Tibetans, their practice of polyandry minimizes population growth. There are as many women as men of marriageable age. But about 30 percent of the women do not marry, and, although these women do have some children, they have far fewer than married women. Thus, the practice of polyandry minimizes the number of mouths to feed and therefore maximizes the standard of living of the polyandrous family. In contrast, if the Tibetans practiced monogamy and almost all women married, the birth rate would be much higher and there would be more mouths to feed with the severely limited resources.[95]

 The Family

Although family form varies from one society to another and even within societies, all societies have families. A **family** is a social and economic unit consisting minimally of one or more parents and their children. Members of a family always have certain reciprocal rights and obligations, particularly economic ones. Family members usually live in one household, but common residence is not a defining feature of families. In our society, children may live away while they go to college. Some members of a family may deliberately set up separate households in order to manage multiple business enterprises while maintaining economic unity.[96] In simpler societies, the family and the household tend to be indistinguishable; it is only in more complex societies, and in societies becoming dependent on commercial exchange, that some members of a family may live elsewhere.[97]

The family provides a learning environment for children. Although some animals, such as fish, do take care of themselves after birth or hatching, no mammal is able to care for itself at birth, and a human is exceptional in that he or she is unable to do so until many years later. Since humans mature late biologically, they have few if any inborn or instinctive responses that will simplify adjustment to their surroundings. Consequently, they have to learn a repertoire of beliefs and habits (most of which are cultural) in order to become functioning adults in society. A family cares for and protects children while they acquire the cultural behavior, beliefs, and values necessary for their own, and their society's, survival.

Variation in Family Form

Most societies have families that are larger than the single-parent family (the parent in such families is usually the mother, in which case the unit is called the **matrifocal family**), the monogamous (single-couple) family (called the **nuclear family**), or the polygamous (usually polygynous) family. The **extended family** is the prevailing form of family in more than half the societies known to anthropology.[98] It may consist of two or more single-parent, monogamous, polygynous, or polyandrous families linked by a blood tie. Most commonly, the extended family consists of a married couple and one or more of the married children, all living in the same house or household. The constituent nuclear families are normally linked through the parent–child tie. An extended family, however, is sometimes composed of families linked through a sibling tie. Such a family might consist of two married brothers, their wives, and their children. Extended families may be very large, containing many relatives and including three or four generations.

Extended-Family Households

In a society composed of extended-family households, marriage does not bring as pronounced a change in lifestyle as it does in our culture, where the couple typically moves to a new residence and forms a new, and basically independent, family unit. In extended families, the newlyweds are assimilated into an existing family unit. Margaret Mead described such a situation in Samoa:

> In most marriages there is no sense of setting up a new and separate establishment. The change is felt in the change of residence for either husband or wife and in the reciprocal relations which spring up between the two families. But the young couple live in the main household, simply receiving a bamboo pillow, a mosquito net and a pile of mats for their bed. . . . The wife works with all the women of the household and waits on all the men. The husband shares the enterprises of the other men and boys. Neither in personal service given or received are the two marked off as a unit.[99]

A young couple in Samoa, as in other societies with extended families, generally has little decision-making power over the governing of the household. Often the responsibility of running the household rests with the senior male. Nor can the new family accumulate its own property and become independent; it is a part of the larger corporate structure:

The Kazak extended family collectively herds their livestock. The youngest son inherits the house. The older son will build his house nearby when he marries.

CURRENT RESEARCH AND ISSUES

One-Parent Families: Why the Recent Increase?

Not only is the custom of marriage almost universal, but in most societies known to anthropology most people marry. And they usually remarry if they divorce. This means that, except for the death of a spouse or temporarily during times of divorce or separation, one-parent families are relatively uncommon in most societies.

In many Western countries, however, there has been a dramatic increase recently in the percentage of one-parent families, most of which (about 90 percent) are female-headed families. For example, in the 1960s about 9 percent of families in the United States were one-parent families, but in the mid-1980s the figure jumped to about 24 percent. Whereas Sweden once led the Western countries in percentage of one-parent families—about 13 percent in the 1970s—the United States now has the highest percentage.

Before we examine the reasons for the increase, we need to consider that there are a variety of ways to become a one-parent family. First, many one-parent families result from the divorce or separation of two-parent families. Second, many one-parent families result from births out of wedlock. In addition, some result from the death of a spouse and others from the decision by a single person to have a child.

Many researchers suggest that the ease of divorce is largely responsible for the increase in one-parent families. On the face of it, this explanation seems plausible. But it is flawed. In many countries during the late 1960s and early 1970s, changes in the law made getting a divorce much easier, and the percentage of one-parent families did rise after that. But why did so many countries ease divorce restrictions at the same time? Did attitudes about marriage change first? A high divorce rate by itself will make for a higher percentage of one-parent households only if individuals do not remarry quickly. In the United States, for example, remarriage rates did decline sharply in the mid-1960s, particularly among younger, better educated women, and so the percentage of one-parent households may have risen for that reason. In many other countries, divorce rates stabilized in the 1980s, but the percentage of one-parent families still increased. Thus, easier divorce does not fully explain the increase in number of one-parent families.

Although some parents are clearly choosing to stay single, many might prefer to marry if they could find an appropriate spouse. In some countries, and among some ethnic groups within some countries, there are many fewer males than females, and sometimes a high proportion of the males have poor economic prospects. In the former Soviet Union, there are many more women than men because males are more likely to have died from war, alcoholism, and accidents. The United States does not have such a skewed sex ratio, but in some neighborhoods, particularly poor neighborhoods, there are very high mortality rates for young males. And many males in such neighborhoods do not have work. One study by Daniel Lichter and his col-

So the young people bide their time. Eventually, when the old man dies or retires, they will own the homestead, they will run things. When their son grows up and marries, he will create a new subsidiary family, to live with them, work for the greater glory of *their* extended family homestead, and wait for them to die.[100]

The extended family is more likely than the independent nuclear family to perpetuate itself as a social unit. In contrast with the independent nuclear family, which by definition disintegrates with the death of the senior members (the parents), the extended family is always adding junior families (monogamous, polygamous, or both), whose members eventually become the senior members when their elders die.

Possible Reasons for Extended-Family Households

Why do most societies known to anthropology commonly have extended-family households? Extended-family households are found most frequently in societies with sedentary agricultural economies, so economic factors may play a role in determining household type. M. F. Nimkoff and Russell Middleton suggested how agricultural life, as opposed to hunting-gathering life, may favor extended families among agriculturalists. The extended family may be a social mechanism that prevents the economically ruinous division of family property in societies in which property such as cultivated land is important. Conversely, the need for mobility in hunter-gatherer societies may make it difficult to maintain extended-family households. During certain seasons,

leagues estimated that for every 100 African American women between the ages of 21 and 28, there were fewer than 80 available African American men. If we count only men who are employed full or part time, the number of available men per 100 women drops below 50. And a recent comparison of 85 countries finds that single parenthood is much more likely when there is higher male unemployment as well as when there are fewer men than women of a comparable age. So there may be considerable merit to the argument that one-parent families (usually headed by women) will be likely when a spouse (particularly an employed one) is hard to find.

Another popular explanation for the rise in number of one-parent families is that, in contrast to the past, women can manage without husbands because of support from the state. This scenario seems to fit Sweden, where unmarried and divorced mothers receive many social supports and allowances for maternity and educational leave. But Iceland has few social supports from the government and yet has the highest rate of out-of-wedlock births of all the Scandinavian countries. In the United States, the welfare argument fails to predict changes over time. The program called Aid to Families with Dependent Children provided aid largely to single mothers. If the theory about government help was correct, increases in such aid would generally predict increases in the percentage of mother-headed households. But, in fact, during the 1970s the percentage of families receiving aid and the value of aid decreased, while the percentage of mother-headed households increased. In the 1980s it was more difficult to go "on welfare," but the percentage of mother-headed households increased anyway.

Women might be more able to manage alone if they have high-paying employment, and therefore we might expect more one-parent families by choice, as more women enter the job market. But, although this may explain the choices of some women, recent research finds that employed women generally are *more* rather than less likely to marry.

In any case, there seems to be a general association between commercial economies and the possibility of one-parent families. Is there something about subsistence economies that promotes marriage and something about commercial economies that detracts from it? Although marriage is not universally based on love or companionship, it entails a great deal of economic and other kinds of interdependence, particularly in not-so-commercial economies. Market economies allow other possibilities; goods and services can be bought and sold, and governments may take over functions normally handled by kin and family. So the one-parent family is likely to remain an option—either a choice or a necessity—for some people.

Sources: Alisa Burns and Cath Scott, *Mother-Headed Families and Why They Have Increased* (Hillsdale, NJ: Lawrence Erlbaum Associates, 1994); David Popenoe, *Disturbing the Nest: Family Change and Decline in Modern Societies* (New York: Aldine, 1988); Daniel T. Lichter, Diane K. McLaughlin, George Kephart, and David J. Landry, "Race and the Retreat from Marriage: A Shortage of Marriageable Men?" *American Sociological Review,* 57 (1992): 781–99; Nigel Barber, "Paternal Investment Prospects and Cross-National Differences in Single Parenthood," *Cross-Cultural Research,* 37 (2003): 163–77.

the hunter-gatherers may be obliged to divide into nuclear families that scatter into other areas.[101]

But agriculture is only a weak predictor of extended-family households. Many agriculturalists lack them, and many nonagricultural societies have them. A different theory is that extended-family households come to prevail in societies that have incompatible activity requirements—that is, requirements that cannot be met by a mother or a father in a one-family household. In other words, extended-family households are generally favored when the work a mother has to do outside the home (cultivating fields or gathering foods far away) makes it difficult for her to also care for her children and do other household tasks. Similarly, extended families may be favored when the required outside activities of a father (warfare, trading trips, or wage labor far away) make it difficult for him to do the subsistence work required

of males. There is cross-cultural evidence that societies with such incompatible activity requirements are more likely to have extended-family households than societies with compatible activity requirements, regardless of whether or not the society is agricultural. Even though they have incompatible activity requirements, however, societies with commercial or monetary exchange may not have extended-family households. In commercial societies, a family may be able to obtain the necessary help by "buying" the required services.[102]

Of course, even in societies with money economies, not everyone can buy required services. Those who are poor may need to live in extended families, and extended-family living may become more common even in the middle class when the economy is depressed. As a popular magazine noted,

Whatever happened to the all-American nuclear family—Mom, Pop, two kids and a cuddly dog, nestled under one cozy, mortgaged roof? What happened was an economic squeeze: layoffs, fewer jobs for young people, more working mothers, a shortage of affordable housing and a high cost of living. Those factors, along with a rising divorce rate, a trend toward later marriages and an increase in the over sixty-five population, all hitting at once, are forcing thousands of Americans into living in multigenerational families.[103]

In many societies there are kin groups even larger than extended families. The next chapter discusses the varieties of such groupings.

◎ Summary

1. All societies known today have the custom of marriage. Marriage is a socially approved sexual and economic union usually between a man and a woman that is presumed to be more or less permanent and that subsumes reciprocal rights and obligations between the two spouses and between the spouses and their children.

2. The way marriage is socially recognized varies greatly; it may involve an elaborate ceremony or none at all. Variations include childhood betrothals, trial-marriage periods, feasting, and the birth of a baby.

3. Marriage arrangements often include an economic element. The most common form is the bride price, in which the groom or his family gives an agreed-upon amount of money or goods to the bride's family. Bride service exists when the groom works for the bride's family for a specified period. In some societies, a female from the groom's family is exchanged for the bride; in others, gifts are exchanged between the two families. A dowry is a payment of goods or money by the bride's family, usually to the bride. Indirect dowry is provided by the groom's family to the bride, sometimes through the bride's father.

4. No society in recent times has allowed sex or marriage between brothers and sisters, mothers and sons, or fathers and daughters.

5. Every society tells people whom they cannot marry, whom they can marry, and sometimes even whom they should marry. In quite a few societies, marriages are arranged by the couple's kin groups. Implicit in arranged marriages is the conviction that the joining of two kin groups to form new social and economic ties is too important to be left to free choice and romantic love. Some societies have rules of exogamy, which require marriage outside one's own kin group or community; others have rules of endogamy, requiring marriage within one's group. Although most societies prohibit all first-cousin marriages, some permit or prefer marriage with cross-cousins (children of siblings of the opposite sex) and parallel cousins (children of siblings of the same sex). Many societies have customs providing for the remarriage of widowed persons. Levirate is a custom whereby a man marries his brother's widow. Sororate is the practice whereby a woman marries her deceased sister's husband.

6. We think of marriage as involving just one man and one woman at a time (monogamy), but most societies allow a man to be married to more than one woman at a time (polygyny). Polyandry, the marriage of one woman to several husbands, is rare.

7. The prevailing form of family in most societies is the extended family. It consists of two or more single-parent, monogamous (nuclear), polygynous, or polyandrous families linked by blood ties.

◎ Glossary Terms

bride price (or bride wealth)	363	matrifocal family	375
bride service	364	monogamy	371
cross-cousins	370	nonfraternal polyandry	374
dowry	365	nonsororal polygyny	373
endogamy	370	nuclear family	375
exogamy	369	parallel cousins	370
extended family	375	polyandry	371
family	374	polygamy	371
fraternal polyandry	374	polygyny	371
group marriage	371	postpartum sex taboo	373
incest taboo	365	sororal polygyny	373
indirect dowry	365	sororate	371
levirate	371		
marriage	359		

◎ Critical Questions

1. Will it remain customary in our society to marry? Why do you think it will or will not?

2. Do you think extended-family households will become more common in our society? Why?

3. Why is polyandry so much less common than polygyny?

◎ Research Navigator

1. Please go to www.researchnavigator.com and enter your LOGIN NAME and PASSWORD. For instructions on registering for the first time, please view the detailed instructions at the end of Chapter 1.

2. Using ContentSelect to find two articles on marriage and family that interest you. Find one relevant to your own society and another from a different continent. Briefly summarize the articles.

3. Using Link Library (Anthropology/Marriage) find the Web site called "Marriage and Family Life." Pick a topic that is not covered in this chapter and briefly describe the issues raised.

◎ Discovering Anthropology: Researchers at Work

Read Alan Howard and Jan Rensel's "Rotuma: Interpreting a Wedding" in *Discovering Anthropology* and answer the following questions:

1. Howard and Rensel suggest that weddings among the Rotuma express their core values. What core values are expressed in their weddings?

2. How has courtship and marriage changed?

3. Compare the essential features of weddings in your culture (make sure to mention the name of your culture) with those described for the Rotuma.

Marital Residence and Kinship

In the United States and Canada, as well as in many other industrial societies, a young man and woman usually establish a place of residence apart from their parents or other relatives when they marry, if they have not already moved away before that. Our society is so oriented toward this pattern of marital residence—*neolocal (new-place) residence*—that it seems to be the obvious and natural one to follow. Some upper-income families begin earlier than others to train their children to live away from home by sending them to boarding schools at age 13 or 14 or to sleep-away summer camps. Young adults of all income levels learn to live away from home most of the year if they join the army or attend an out-of-town college. In any case, when a young person marries, he or she generally lives apart from family.

So familiar is neolocal residence to us that we tend to assume that all societies must practice the same pattern. On the contrary, of the 565 societies in George Peter Murdock's "World Ethnographic Sample," only about 5 percent followed this practice.[1] About 95 percent of the world's societies have had some other pattern of residence whereby a new couple settles within, or very close to, the household of the parents or some other close relative of either the groom or the bride. When married couples live near kin, it stands to reason that kinship relationships will figure prominently in the social life of the society. Marital residence largely predicts the types of kin groups found in a society, as well as how people refer to and classify their various relatives.

As we will see, kin groups that include several or many families and hundreds or even thousands of people are found in many societies and structure many areas of social life. Kin groups may have important economic, social, political, and religious functions.

❊

◎ Patterns of Marital Residence

In societies in which newly married couples customarily live with or close to their kin, the pattern of residence varies. Children in all societies are required to marry outside the nuclear family, because of the incest taboo, and, with few exceptions, couples in almost all societies live together after they are married. Therefore some children have to leave home when they marry. But which married children remain at home and which reside elsewhere? Societies vary in the way they deal with this question, but there are not many different patterns. The prevailing one could be one of the following (the percentages of each in the ethnographic record do not sum to 100 because of rounding):

1. **Patrilocal residence.** The son stays and the daughter leaves, so that the married couple lives with or near the husband's parents (67 percent of all societies).
2. **Matrilocal residence.** The daughter stays and the son leaves, so that the married couple lives with or near the wife's parents (15 percent of all societies).
3. **Bilocal residence.** Either the son or the daughter leaves, so that the married couple lives with or near either the wife's or the husband's parents (7 percent of all societies).
4. **Avunculocal residence.** Both son and daughter normally leave, but the son and his wife settle with or near his mother's brother (4 percent of all societies).[2]

In these definitions, we use the phrase "the married couple lives *with or near*" a particular set of in-laws. When couples live with or near the kin of a spouse, the couple may live in the same household with those kin, creating an *extended-family* household, or they may live separately in an *independent-family* household, but nearby. (Because matrilocal, patrilocal, and avunculocal residence specify just one pattern, they are often called nonoptional or **unilocal residence** patterns.)

A fifth pattern of residence is neolocal, in which the newly married couple does not live with or near kin.

5. **Neolocal residence.** Both son and daughter leave; married couples live apart from the relatives of both spouses (5 percent of all societies).

Figure 22–1 graphically shows the percentage of societies in the ethnographic record that practice each of the five marital residence patterns.

How does place of residence affect the social life of the couple? Because the pattern of residence governs with whom or near whom individuals live, it largely determines which people those individuals interact with and have to depend on. If a married couple is surrounded by the kin of the husband, for example, the chances are that those relatives will figure importantly in the couple's future. Whether the couple lives with or near the husband's or the wife's kin can also be expected to have important consequences for the status of the husband or wife. If married couples live patrilocally, as occurs in most societies, the wife may be far from her own kin. In any case, she will be an outsider among a group of male relatives who have grown up together. The feeling of being an outsider is particularly strong when the wife has moved into a patrilocal extended-family household.

Among the Tiv of central Nigeria,[3] the patrilocal extended family consists of the "great father," who is the head of the household, and his younger brothers, his sons, and his younger brothers' sons. Also included are the in-marrying

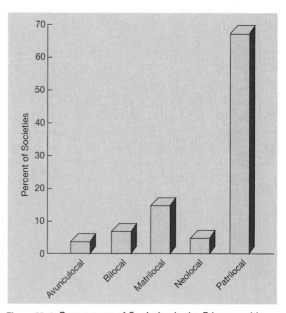

Figure 22–1 Percentage of Societies in the Ethnographic Record with Various Marital Residence Patterns

Source: Calculated from Allan D. Coult and Robert W. Habenstein, *Cross Tabulations of Murdock's World Ethnographic Sample* (Columbia: University of Missouri Press, 1965).

wives and all unmarried children. (The sisters and daughters of the household head who have married would have gone to live where their husbands lived.) Authority is strongly vested in the male line, particularly the oldest of the household, who has authority over bride price, disputes, punishment, and plans for new buildings.

In many societies known to anthropology, the bride goes to live with or near the husband's family. In the town of Itako, Japan, a bride is transported to the bridegroom's place.

A somewhat different situation exists if the husband comes to live with or near his wife's parents. In this case, the wife and her kin take on somewhat greater importance, and the husband is the outsider. As we shall see, however, the matrilocal situation is not quite the mirror image of the patrilocal, because in matrilocal societies the husband's kin often are not far away. Moreover, even though residence is matrilocal, women often do not have as much to say in decision making as their brothers do.

If the married couple does not live with or near the parents or close kin of either spouse, the situation is again quite different. It should not be surprising that relatives and kinship connections do not figure very largely in everyday life in neolocal residence situations.

Marital residence determines which kin will live, or not live, in the immediate vicinity of the married couple. Toward the end of this chapter we consider the factors that may explain residential variation; these same factors may also help explain the types of kinship groups that develop.

◎ The Structure of Kinship

In noncommercial societies, kinship connections structure many areas of social life—from the kind of access an individual has to productive resources to the kind of political alliances formed between communities and larger territorial groups. In some societies, in fact, kinship connections have an important bearing on matters of life and death.

Recall the social system described in Shakespeare's *Romeo and Juliet*. The Capulets and the Montagues were groups of kin engaged in lethal competition with each other, and the fatal outcome of Romeo and Juliet's romance was related to that competition. Although Romeo and Juliet's society had a commercial economy (but not, of course, an industrialized one), the political system of the city they lived in was a reflection of the way kinship was structured. Sets of kin of common descent lived together, and the various kin groups competed, and sometimes fought, for a prominent, or at least secure, place in the political hierarchy of the city-state.

If a preindustrial commercial society could be so structured by kinship, we can imagine how much more important kinship connections and kin groups are in many noncommercial societies that lack political mechanisms such as princes and councils of lords who try to keep the peace and initiate other activities on behalf of the community. It is no wonder that anthropologists often speak of the web of kinship as providing the main structure of social action in noncommercial societies.

If kinship is important, there is still the question of which set of kin a person affiliates with and depends on. After all, if every single relative were counted as equally important, there would be an unmanageably large number of people in each person's kinship network. Consequently, in most societies in which kinship connections are important, rules allocate each person to a particular and definable set of kin.

Types of Affiliation with Kin

We distinguish three main types of affiliation with kin: *unilineal descent, ambilineal descent,* and *bilateral kinship.* The first two types (unilineal descent and ambilineal descent) are based on **rules of descent,** which are rules that connect individuals with particular sets of kin because of known or presumed common ancestry. By the particular rule of descent operating in their society, individuals can know more or less immediately which set of kin to turn to for support and help. As we shall see, bilateral kinship is not based on rules of descent or ancestry and does not create clear and unambiguous groups.

Unilineal descent refers to the fact that a person is affiliated with a group of kin through descent links of one sex only—either males only or females only. Thus unilineal descent can be either patrilineal or matrilineal.

1. **Patrilineal descent** affiliates an individual with kin of both sexes related to him or her *through men only.* As Figure 22–2 indicates, in patrilineal systems the children in each generation belong to the kin group of their father; their father, in turn, belongs to the group of his father; and so on. Although a man's sons and daughters are

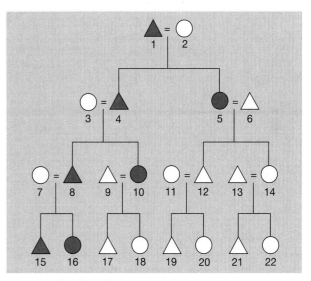

Figure 22–2 Patrilineal Descent

Individuals 4 and 5, who are the children of 1 and 2, affiliate with their father's patrilineal kin group, represented by the color red. In the next generation, the children of 3 and 4 also belong to the red kin group, since they take their descent from their father, who is a member of that group. However, the children of 5 and 6 do not belong to this patrilineal group, since they take their descent from their father, who is a member of a different group. That is, although the mother of 12 and 14 belongs to the red partrilineal group, she cannot pass on her descent affiliation to her children, and since her husband (6) does not belong to her patrilineage, her children (12 and 14) belong to their father's group. In the fourth generation, only 15 and 16 belong to the red patrilineal group, since their father is the only male member of the preceding generation who belongs to the red patrilineal group. In this diagram, then, 1, 4, 5, 8, 10, 15, and 16 are affiliated by the patrilineal descent; all the other individuals belong to other patrilineal groups.

CURRENT RESEARCH AND ISSUES

Neolocality and Adolescent Rebellion: Are They Related?

In our society it is taken for granted that adolescence means turmoil and parent–child conflict. Teenagers, parents, and educators worry about how to reduce the conflict. But few in our society ask why the conflict occurs in the first place. Is it "natural" for adolescents to be rebellious? Are they rebellious in all cultures? If not, why do we have conflict in our society?

This issue was first raised by Margaret Mead. In her best-selling *Coming of Age in Samoa* (originally published in 1928), she said that conflict during adolescence was minimal in Samoa. Some researchers have recently criticized her analysis (see the discussion in the chapter on psychology and culture), but many field and comparative studies by anthropologists have since found that adolescence is not experienced in the same way in all societies. For example, in their systematic cross-cultural study of adolescence, Alice Schlegel and Herbert Barry concluded that relations between adolescents and their families were generally harmonious around the world. They suggested that when family members need each other throughout their lives, independence, as expressed in adolescent rebelliousness, would be foolhardy. Indeed, Schlegel and Barry found that adolescents are likely to be rebellious only in societies, like our own, that have neolocal residence and considerable job and geographic mobility.

Why should this be? We might speculate that adolescent rebellion is an elaborate psychodrama played out by both parents and children to prepare themselves for separation. Children spend a considerable part of their lives being dependent on their parents. But they know they must move away, and that prospect may arouse anxiety. Children want to be independent, but independence is scary. Dependence is nice in some ways—at least it can make life easier (someone else cooks for you and so on)—but it is also less grown-up than independence. So what pushes a child to leave? Perhaps the conflict itself propels the departure. Teenagers ask for things they want, but they may know, at least unconsciously, that their parents will say no. And parents often do say no, so the teenagers get angry and can't wait to be on their own. Parents are also ambivalent. They want their children to grow up, but they miss them when they leave. After a period of conflict, it may be a relief for all concerned when parents and children go their separate ways.

What if our social structure was different? What if parents and children knew that some of the children were going to spend the rest of their lives with or near the parents? And even those children who moved away, as some would have to in societies practicing matrilocal, patrilocal, avunculocal, or bilocal residence, would know they were going to spend the rest of their lives with or near their in-laws. Could teenagers in non-neolocal societies afford to have serious conflict with their parents? Could the parents afford to have serious conflict with the teenagers who will be staying put after their marriages? We think not. We suggest that adolescent conflict would

---

all members of the same descent group, affiliation with that group is transmitted only by the sons to their children. Just as patrilocal residence is much more common than matrilocal residence, patrilineal descent is more common than matrilineal descent.

2. **Matrilineal descent** affiliates an individual with kin of both sexes related to him or her *through women only*. In each generation, then, children belong to the kin group of their mother (see Figure 22–3). Although a woman's sons and daughters are all members of the same descent group, only her daughters can pass on their descent affiliation to their children.

Some have questioned the existence of unilineal descent and descent groups, suggesting that theorists have only imagined them. Reality could not possibly have been like that. But recent ethnohistorical analyses confirm that Native North American societies, like the Omaha, really did have patrilineal descent groups in the 19th century[4] and the Chuuk (in the Pacific) still have functioning matrilineal groups, despite many years of Western contact.[5]

Unilineal rules of descent affiliate an individual with a line of kin extending back in time and into the future. By virtue of this line of descent, whether it extends through males or females, some very close relatives are excluded. For example, in a patrilineal system, your mother and your mother's parents do not belong to your patrilineal group, but your father and his father (and their sisters) do. In your own generation in a matrilineal or patrilineal system, some cousins are excluded, and in your children's generation, some of your nieces and nephews are excluded.

However, although unilineal rules of descent exclude certain relatives from membership in one's kin group, just as practical considerations restrict the effective size of kinship

be very disadvantageous in a non-neolocal society, and therefore we would expect its minimization or suppression when the residence pattern is other than neolocal.

There is another reason why rebelliousness might be associated with neolocality; it has to do with the fact that neolocality is predicted by commercial exchange. In the modern world, commercial societies are likely to have a great deal of occupational specialization and people with many different values. Thus children are presented with a great many choices in a rapidly changing culture. Let us consider the effect of a rapidly changing technology. If children have to know and do things that the parents do not know about, how can we expect the children to want to follow in their parents' footsteps?

But a rapidly changing culture is not necessarily accompanied by parent–child conflict. Other conditions are probably also necessary to generate the conflict, if the situation in a Moroccan town is any guide. As part of a comparative research project on adolescence, Susan and Douglas Davis interviewed young people in a small town in Morocco. The culture had changed a lot recently. Parents mostly worked at jobs in and related to agriculture; children aspired to white-collar jobs. Grandparents rarely saw a car; teenagers took trains to the capital. Only a few parents had gone to school; most teenagers did. Yet the Davises reported little serious parent–child conflict, despite the cultural changes. For example, 40 percent of the teenagers said that they had never disagreed with their mothers. Perhaps we need to consider other facets of the culture. For one thing, Morocco has an authoritarian political structure with a monarchy and a clear pyramid of offices; perhaps parent–child conflict is unlikely in such a political system because it emphasizes

and requires obedience. A second possible consideration is that group life is more important than the individual. The family is the most important social group, and as such cannot tolerate adolescent rebelliousness. A third possible consideration is that adults are supposed to avoid open conflict. The study by the Davises implies that adolescent rebelliousness is likely only in societies like the United States that emphasize individuality, personal autonomy, and individual achievement.

What we need is research that tries to untangle the various causal possibilities. To discover the possible effect of neolocality, rapid change, cultural emphasis on individual autonomy, or an authoritarian political system, we need to study samples of cultures that have different combinations of those traits. It is possible that they all are influential, or that some are more important than others, or that some cause the others. Whatever we discover in the future about the causality, we know now that adolescent rebelliousness is not inevitable or natural, that it is probably linked to some other aspects of cultural variation—as Margaret Mead suggested many years ago.

Sources: Margaret Mead, Coming of Age in Samoa (New York: Morrow, 1928); Alice Schlegel and Herbert Barry III, Adolescence: An Anthropological Inquiry (New York: Free Press, 1991); Melvin Ember, "The Emergence of Neolocal Residence," Transactions of the New York Academy of Sciences 30 (1967): 291–302; Susan Schaefer Davis, "Rebellious Teens? A Moroccan Instance," paper presented at the annual meeting of the Middle East Studies Association, November 1993; Susan Schaefer Davis, "Morocco: Adolescents in a Small Town," in Portraits of Culture, in Carol R. Ember, Melvin Ember, and Peter N. Peregrine, eds., New Directions in Anthropology (Upper Saddle River, NJ: Prentice Hall, CD-ROM, 2004).

networks in our own society, the excluded relatives are not necessarily ignored or forgotten. Indeed, in many unilineal societies they may be entrusted with important responsibilities. For example, when a person dies in a patrilineal society, some members of his or her mother's patrilineal descent group may customarily be accorded the right to perform certain rituals at the funeral.

Unilineal rules of descent can form clear-cut, and hence unambiguous, groups of kin, which can act as separate units even after the death of individual members. Referring again to Figures 22–2 and 22–3, we can see that the individuals in the highlight color belong to the same patrilineal or matrilineal descent group without ambiguity; individuals in the fourth generation belong to the group just as much as those in the first generation. Say the patrilineal group has a name, the Hawks. Individuals know whether or not they are Hawks. If not, they belong to some other group, for each person

belongs to only one line of descent. This fact is important if kin groups are to act as separate, nonoverlapping units. It is difficult for people to act together unless they know exactly who should get together. And it is easier for individuals to act together as a group if each one belongs to only one such group or line.

In contrast to unilineal descent, **ambilineal descent** affiliates an individual with kin related to him or her through men *or* women. In other words, some people in the society affiliate with a group of kin through their fathers; others, through their mothers. Consequently, the descent groups show both female and male genealogical links, as illustrated in Figure 22–4.

These three rules of descent (patrilineal, matrilineal, and ambilineal) are usually, but not always, mutually exclusive. Most societies can be characterized as having only one rule of descent, but sometimes two principles are used to affiliate

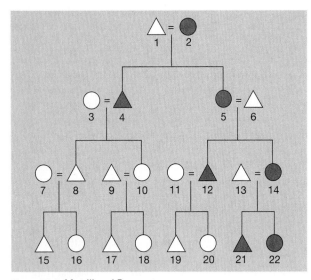

Figure 22–3 Matrilineal Descent

Individuals 4 and 5, who are the children of 1 and 2, affiliate with their mother's kin group, represented by the color green. In the next generation, the children of 5 and 6 also belong to the green kin group, since they take their descent from their mother, who is a member of that group. However, the children of 3 and 4 do not belong to this matrilineal group, since they take their descent from their mother, who is a member of a different group; their father, although a member of the green matrilineal group, cannot pass his affiliation on to them under the rule of matrilineal descent. In the fourth generation, only 21 and 22 belong to the green matrilineal group, since their mother is the only female member of the preceding generation who belongs. Thus, individuals 2, 4, 5, 12, 14, 21, and 22 belong to the same matrilineal group.

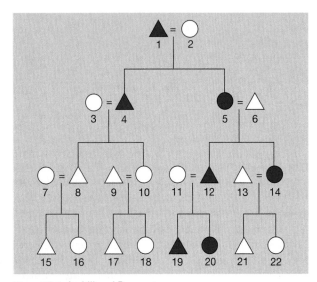

Figure 22–4 Ambilineal Descent

A hypothetical ambilineal group of kin is indicated by the color blue. Members 4 and 5 belong to this group because of a male link, their father (1); members 12 and 14 belong because of a female link, their mother (5); and members 19 and 20 belong because of a male link, their father (12). This is a hypothetical example because any combination of lineal links is possible in an ambilineal descent group.

individuals with different sets of kin for different purposes. Some societies have, then, what is called **double descent or double unilineal descent,** whereby an individual affiliates for some purposes with a group of matrilineal kin and for other purposes with a group of patrilineal kin. Thus, two rules of descent, each traced through links of one sex only, are operative at the same time. For example, if there is a patrilineal system and a matrilineal one, individuals would belong to two groups at birth: the matrilineal group of the mother and the patrilineal group of the father. Imagine combining Figures 22–2 and 22–3. Individuals 4 and 5 would belong to both the patrilineal group (red in Figure 22–2) to which their father belongs and the matrilineal group (green in Figure 22–3) to which their mother belongs.

The way a society assigns names does not necessarily convey any information about a rule of descent. It is customary in North American society for children to have a last, or "family," name—usually their father's last name. All the people with the same last name do not conceive of themselves as descended from the same common ancestor; all Smiths do not consider themselves related. Nor do such people act together for any particular purpose. And many societies, even with rules of descent, do not give individuals the name of their kin group or of their father or mother. For example, among the patrilineal Luo of Kenya, babies were traditionally given names that described the circumstances of their birth (such as "born-in-the-morning"); their names did not include their father's or kin group's name. Only after the British established a colony in Kenya, and continuing after independence, did children get their father's personal name as a family name.

Many societies, including our own, do not have lineal (matrilineal, patrilineal, or ambilineal) descent groups—sets of kin who believe they descend from a common ancestor. These are societies with **bilateral kinship.** *Bilateral* means "two-sided," and in this case it refers to the fact that one's relatives on both the mother's and father's sides are equal in importance or, more usually, in unimportance. Kinship reckoning in bilateral societies does not refer to common descent but rather is horizontal, moving outward from close to more distant relatives rather than upward to common ancestors (see Figure 22–5).

The term **kindred** describes a person's bilateral set of relatives who may be called upon for some purpose. Most bilateral societies have kindreds that overlap in membership. In North America, we think of the kindred as including the people we might invite to weddings, funerals, or some other ceremonial occasion; a kindred, however, is not usually a definite group. As anyone who has been involved in creating a wedding invitation list knows, a great deal of time may be spent deciding which relatives ought to be invited and which ones can legitimately be excluded. Societies with bilateral kinship differ in precisely how distant relatives have to be before they are lost track of or before they are not included in ceremonial activities. In societies such as our own, in which kinship is relatively unimportant, fewer relatives are included in the kindred. In other bilateral societies,

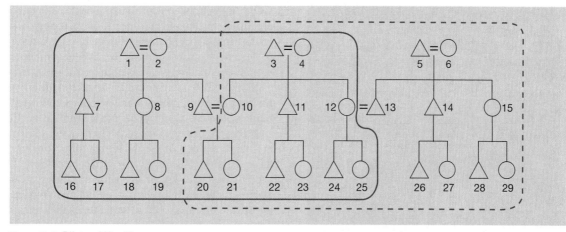

Figure 22–5 Bilateral Kinship

In a bilateral system the kindred is ego-centered; hence, it varies with different points of reference (except for brothers and sisters). In any bilateral society, the kindred minimally includes parents, grandparents, aunts, uncles, and first cousins. So, if we look at the close kindred of the brother and sister 20 and 21 (enclosed by the solid line), it would include their parents (9 and 10), their aunts and uncles (7, 8, 11, 12), their grandparents (1, 2, 3, 4), and their first cousins (16–19, 22–25). But the kindred of the brother and sister 24 and 25 (shown by the dashed line) includes only some of the same people (3, 4, 10–12, 20–23); in addition, the kindred of 24 and 25 includes people not in the kindred of 20 and 21 (5, 6, 13–15, 26–29).

however, where kinship connections are somewhat more important, more would be included.

The distinctive feature of bilateral kinship is that, aside from brothers and sisters, no two persons belong to exactly the same kin group. Your kindred contains close relatives spreading out on both your mother's and father's sides, but the members of your kindred are affiliated only by way of their connection to you (**ego,** or the focus). Thus, the kindred is an *ego-centered* group of kin. Because different people (except for brothers and sisters) have different mothers and fathers, your first cousins will have different kindreds, and even your own children will have a different kindred from yours. It is the ego-centered nature of the kindred that makes it difficult for it to serve as a permanent or persistent group. The only thing the people in a kindred have in common is the ego who brings them together. A kindred usually has no name, no common purpose, and only temporary meetings centered around the ego.[6] Furthermore, because everyone belongs to many different and overlapping kindreds, the society is not divided into clear-cut groups.

While kindreds may not form clear-cut groups as in a unilineal society, this does not mean that the kindred cannot be turned to for help. In a bilateral society, the kindred may provide social insurance against adversity. Among the Chipewyan of subarctic Canada, for example, people would borrow a fishing net from a kindred member, or ask a kindred member to provide child care for a young person whose parent was ill. But recently, with the national and provincial governments providing resources such as housing and medical assistance, and with the increase in opportunities for wage labor, the kindred has ceased to be the main source of help for people in need. Aid from the state is making kinship less useful.[7]

Variation in Unilineal Descent Systems

In a society with unilineal descent, people usually refer to themselves as belonging to a particular unilineal group or set of groups because they believe they share common descent in either the male (patrilineal) or female (matrilineal) line. Several types of unilineal descent groups are distinguished by anthropologists: lineages, clans, phratries, and moieties.

LINEAGES   A **lineage** is a set of kin whose members trace descent from a common ancestor through known links. There may be **patrilineages** or **matrilineages,** depending on whether the links are traced through males only or through females only. Lineages are often designated by the name of the common male or female ancestor. In some societies, people belong to a hierarchy of lineages. That is, they first trace their descent back to the ancestor of a minor lineage, then to the ancestor of a larger and more inclusive major lineage, and so on.

CLANS   A **clan** (also sometimes called a **sib**) is a set of kin whose members believe themselves to be descended from a common ancestor, but the links back to that ancestor are not specified. In fact, the common ancestor may not even be known. Clans with patrilineal descent are called **patriclans;** clans with matrilineal descent are called **matriclans.** Clans often are designated by an animal name (Bear, Wolf), called a **totem,** which may have some special significance for the group and, at the very least, is a means of group identification. The word *totem* comes from the Ojibwa Indian word *ototeman,* "a relative of mine." In some societies, people

Totem poles often symbolize the history of a descent group. A totem pole in Ketchikan, Alaska.

have to observe taboos relating to their clan totem animal. For example, clan members may be forbidden to kill or eat their totem.

Although it may seem strange that an animal or plant should be a symbol of a kin group, animals as symbols of groups are familiar in our own culture. Football and baseball teams, for example, are often named for animals (Detroit Tigers, Baltimore Ravens, Philadelphia Eagles, Chicago Bears). Voluntary associations, such as men's clubs, are sometimes called by the name of an animal (Elks, Moose, Lions). Entire nations may be represented by an animal; we speak, for instance, of the American Eagle and the British Lion.[8] Why humans so often choose animal names to represent groups is an intriguing question for which we have no tested answer as yet.

PHRATRIES A **phratry** is a unilineal descent group composed of supposedly related clans or sibs. As with clans, the descent links in phratries are unspecified.

MOIETIES When a whole society is divided into two unilineal descent groups, we call each group a **moiety.** (The word *moiety* comes from a French word meaning "half.") The people in each moiety believe themselves to be descended from a common ancestor, although they cannot specify how. Societies with moiety systems usually have relatively small populations (fewer than 9,000 people). Societies with phratries and clans tend to be larger.[9]

COMBINATIONS Although we have distinguished several different types of unilineal descent groups, we do not wish to imply that all unilineal societies have only one type of descent group. Many societies have two or more types in various combinations. For example, some societies have lineages and clans; others may have clans and phratries but no lineages; and still others may have clans and moieties but neither phratries nor lineages. Aside from the fact that a society that has phratries must also have clans (since phratries are combinations of clans), all combinations of descent groups are possible. Even if societies have more than one type of unilineal kin group—for example, lineages and clans—there is no ambiguity about membership. Small groups are simply subsets of larger units; the larger units include people who say they are unilineally related further back in time.

Patrilineal Organization

Patrilineal organization is the most frequent type of descent system. The Kapauku Papuans, a people living in the central highlands of western New Guinea, are an example of a patrilineal society with various types of descent groups.[10] The hierarchy of groups to which the Kapauku are affiliated by virtue of the patrilineal descent system plays an extremely important part in their lives. Every Kapauku belongs to a patrilineage, to a patriclan that includes his or her lineage, and to a patriphratry that includes his or her clan.

The male members of a patrilineage—all the living males who can trace their actual relationship through males to a common ancestor—constitute the male population of a single village or, more likely, a series of adjoining villages. In other words, the lineage is a *territorial unit.* The male members of the lineage live together by virtue of a patrilocal rule of residence and a fairly stable settlement pattern. A son stays near his parents and brings his wife to live in or near his father's house; the daughters leave home and go to live with their husbands. If the group lives in one place over a long period, the male descendants of one man will live in the same territory. If the lineage is large, it may be divided into sublineages composed of people who trace their descent from one of the sons of the lineage ancestor. The male members of a sublineage live in a contiguous block within the larger lineage territory.

The members of the same patrilineage address each other affectionately, and within this group law and order are maintained by a headman. Killing within the lineage is considered a serious offense, and any fighting that takes place is done with sticks rather than lethal weapons such as spears. The sublineage headman tries to settle grievances within the sublineage as quickly and as peacefully as possible. If a sublineage mate commits a crime against outsiders, all members of the sublineage may be considered responsible and their property seized, or a member of the sublineage may be killed in revenge by the victim's kin.

The Kapauku also belong to larger and more inclusive patrilineal descent groups—clans and phratries. All the people of the same clan believe they are related to each other in the father's line, but they are unable to say how they are related. If a member of the patriclan eats the clan's plant or animal totem, it is believed that the person will become deaf. A Kapauku is also forbidden to marry anyone from his or her clan. In other words, the clan is exogamous.

Unlike the members of the patrilineage, the male members of the patriclan do not all live together. Thus, the lineage is the largest group of patrilineal kinsmen that is localized. The lineage is also the largest group of kinsmen that acts together politically. Among clan members there is no mechanism for resolving disputes, and members of the same patriclan (who belong to different lineages) may even go to war with one another.

The most inclusive patrilineal descent group among the Kapauku is the phratry, each of which is composed of two or more clans. The Kapauku believe that the phratry was originally one clan, but that in a conflict between brothers of the founding family the younger brother was expelled and he formed a new clan. The two resulting clans are viewed as patrilineally related, since their founders are said to have been brothers. The members of a phratry observe all the totemic taboos of the clans that belong to that phratry. Intermarriage of members of the same clan is forbidden, but members of the same phratry, if they belong to different clans, may marry.

The Kapauku, then, have lineages with demonstrated kinship links and two kinds of descent groups with unknown descent links (clans and phratries).

Matrilineal Organization

Although societies with matrilineal descent seem in many respects like mirror images of their patrilineal counterparts, they differ in one important way. That difference has to do with who exercises authority. In patrilineal systems, descent affiliation is transmitted through males, and it is also the males who exercise authority. Consequently, in the patrilineal system, lines of descent and of authority converge. In a matrilineal system, however, although the line of descent passes through females, females rarely exercise authority in their kin groups. Usually males do. Thus, the lines of authority and descent do not converge.[11] Anthropologists do not completely understand why this is so, but it is an ethnographic fact. In any case, since males exercise authority in the kin group, an individual's mother's brother becomes an important authority figure, because he is the individual's closest male matrilineal relative in the parental generation. The individual's father does not belong to the individual's own matrilineal kin group and thus has no say in kin group matters.

The divergence of authority and descent in a matrilineal system has some effect on community organization and marriage. Most matrilineal societies practice matrilocal residence. Daughters stay at home after marriage and bring their husbands to live with them; sons leave home to join their wives. But the sons who are required to leave will be the ones who eventually exercise authority in their kin groups. This situation presents a problem. The solution that seems to have been arrived at in most matrilineal societies is that, although the males move away to live with

their wives, they usually do not move too far away; indeed, they often marry women who live in the same village. Thus, matrilineal societies tend not to be locally exogamous—that is, members often marry people from inside the village—whereas patrilineal societies are often locally exogamous.[12]

The matrilineal organization on Chuuk, a group of small islands in the Pacific, illustrates the general pattern of authority in matrilineal systems.[13] The Chuukese have both matrilineages and matriclans. The matrilineage is a property-owning group whose members trace descent from a known common ancestor in the female line. The female lineage members and their husbands occupy a cluster of houses on the matrilineage's land. The property of the lineage group is administered by the oldest brother of the group, who allocates the productive property of his matrilineage and directs the work of the members. He also represents the group in dealings with the district chief and all outsiders, and he must be consulted on any matter that affects the group. There is also a senior woman of the lineage who exercises some authority, but only insofar as the activities of the women are concerned. She may supervise the women's cooperative work (they usually work separately from the men) and manage the household.

Within the nuclear family, the father and mother have the primary responsibility for raising and disciplining their children. When a child reaches puberty, however, the father's right to discipline or exercise authority over the child ceases. The mother continues to exercise her right of discipline, but her brother may interfere. A woman's brother rarely interferes with his sister's child before puberty, but after puberty he may exercise some authority, especially since he is an elder in the child's own matrilineage. On Chuuk, men rarely move far from their birthplace. As Ward Goodenough pointed out, "Since matrilocal residence takes the men away from their home lineages, most of them marry women whose lineage houses are within a few minutes' walk of their own."[14]

Although there are some differences between patrilineal and matrilineal systems, there are many similarities. In both types of systems there may be lineages, clans, phratries, and moieties, alone or in any combination. These kin groups, in either matrilineal or patrilineal societies, may perform any number of functions. They may regulate marriage, they may come to each other's aid economically or politically, and they may perform rituals together.

◎ Functions of Unilineal Descent Groups

Unilineal descent groups exist in societies at all levels of cultural complexity.[15] Apparently, however, they are most common in noncommercial food-producing, as opposed to food-collecting, societies.[16] Unilineal descent groups often have important functions in the social, economic, political, and religious realms of life.

NEW PERSPECTIVES ON GENDER

Variation in Residence and Kinship: What Difference Does It Make to Women?

When we say that residence and kinship have profound effects on people's lives, what exactly do we mean? We may imagine that it is hard for a woman in a patrilocal society to move at marriage into another village where her husband has plenty of relatives and she has few. But do we have evidence of that? Most ethnographies usually do not give details about people's feelings, but some do. For example, Leigh Minturn gives us the text of a letter that one new Rajput bride (who grew up in the village of Khalapur, India) sent to her mother shortly after she married into her husband's village. The letter was written when the bride had been gone six weeks, but she repeatedly asked if her mother, her father, and her aunts had forgotten her. She begged to be called home and said her bags were packed. She described herself as "a parrot in a cage" and complained about her in-laws. The bride's mother was not alarmed; she knew that such complaints were normal, reflections of her daughter's separation anxiety. Seven years later, when Minturn returned to India, the mother reported the daughter to be happy. Still, a few other brides did have more serious symptoms: ghost possession, 24- to 36-hour comas, serious depression, or suicide. What research has not told us is whether these serious symptoms are present more often in patrilocal, patrilineal societies than in other societies, particularly matrilocal,

matrilineal societies. Conversely, do men have some symptoms in matrilocal, matrilineal societies that they do not have in patrilocal societies? We do not know.

What about the status of women? Some research suggests that matrilocality and matrilineality enhance some aspects of women's status, but perhaps not as much as we might think. Even in matrilineal societies, men are usually the political leaders. The main effect of matrilocality and matrilineality appears to be that women control property, but they also tend to have more domestic authority in the home, more equal sexual restrictions, and more value placed on their lives. Alice Schlegel pointed out that women's status is not always relatively high in matrilineal societies, because they can be dominated by the husband or by brothers (because brothers play important roles in their kin groups). It is only when neither the husband nor the brother dominates that women may have considerable control over their own lives. Certainly the combination of matrilocality and matrilineality is better for women's status than patrilocality and patrilineality. Matrilocality and matrilineality might not enhance women's status because of the dominance of male matrilineal kin, but patrilocality and patrilineality are very likely to detract from women's status. Norma Diamond stated that even after the Chinese Communist revolution, which abolished the landholding estates of

Regulating Marriage

In unilineal societies, individuals are not usually permitted to marry within their own unilineal descent groups. In some, however, marriage may be permitted within more inclusive kin groups but prohibited within smaller kin groups. In a few societies, marriage within the kin group is actually preferred.

But, in general, the incest taboo in unilineal societies is extended to all presumed unilineal relatives. For example, on Chuuk, which has matriclans and matrilineages, a person is forbidden by the rule of descent group exogamy to marry anyone from her or his matriclan. The matrilineage is included within the matriclan, so the rule of descent group exogamy also applies to the matrilineage. Among the Kapauku, who have patriphratries, patriclans, and patrilineages, the largest descent group that is exogamous is the patriclan. The

phratry may once have been exogamous, but the exogamy rule no longer applies to it. Some anthropologists have suggested that rules of exogamy for descent groups may have developed because the alliances between descent groups generated by such rules may be selectively favored under the conditions of life faced by most unilineal societies.

Economic Functions

Members of a person's lineage or clan are often required to side with that person in any quarrel or lawsuit, to help him or her get established economically, to contribute to a bride price or fine, and to support the person in life crises. Mutual aid often extends to economic cooperation on a regular basis. The unilineal descent group may act as a corporate unit in landownership. For example, house sites and farmland are owned by a lineage among the Chuukese and the Kapauku.

patrilineages and gave women access to education as well as jobs outside the home, male dominance continued. The mode of production and labor changed, but patrilocality did not. Women were still usually the in-marrying strangers, and members of the patrilineage became a work team on the collective farm. Diamond pointed out that those few women who became local leaders were likely to have atypical marriages that allowed them to live in the villages of their birth.

Residence and descent also predict societal attempts to control reproduction. According to Suzanne Frayser, patrilineal societies have several sexual and reproductive dilemmas. One dilemma is the contradiction between the importance of males in kinship and the women's role in reproduction. If patrilineal societies denigrate women too much, women may try to decrease their reproduction. If patrilineal societies exalt women too much, that exaltation may detract from the value of men. A second dilemma has to do with paternity, which is essential for patrilineal descent but harder than maternity to be certain of. Frayser argued that because kin group links are traced through males in patrilineal societies, they will do more to ensure that the man a woman marries is the father. Frayser suggested that patrilineal societies therefore will be more restrictive about a woman's sexuality. Indeed, the results of her cross-cultural study indicate that patrilineal societies are more likely than other societies to prohibit premarital and extramarital sex for women, and they are more likely to make it very difficult for a woman to divorce her husband.

Of course we have to remember that there is considerable variation within patrilocal/patrilineal societies and matrilocal/matrilineal societies. In the patrilineal society that Audrey Smedley studied—the Birom of the Jos Plateau in Nigeria—women were formally barred from owning property, from holding political offices, and from major decision making. Yet, her fieldwork revealed that in everyday life they had considerable autonomy in their personal lives, including the legal right to take on lovers. Indeed, they had considerable indirect influence on decision making and were strong supporters of the patrilineal system. Smedley speculates that in some environmental circumstances women support patrilineality because it serves their interests and those of their children too. For example, male crops are highly valued, but such crops are grown on the more dangerous plains where men risked death at the hands of raiders from other groups. Food was scarce, so it may have been adaptive for everyone, including women, to give special status to men for growing crops in dangerous places.

Sources: Leigh Minturn, *Sita's Daughters: Coming Out of Purdah: The Rajput Women of Khalapur Revisited* (New York: Oxford University Press, 1993), pp. 54–71; Martin King Whyte, *The Status of Women in Preindustrial Societies* (Princeton, NJ: Princeton University Press, 1978), pp. 132–34; Alice Schlegel, "The Status of Women," in *Cross-Cultural Research for Social Science,* in Carol R. Ember, Melvin Ember, and Peter N. Peregrine, eds., *New Directions in Anthropology* (Upper Saddle River, NJ: Prentice Hall, CD-ROM, 2004); Norma Diamond, "Collectivization, Kinship, and the Status of Women in Rural China," in Rayna R. Reiter, *Toward an Anthropology of Women* (New York: Monthly Review Press, 1975); Audrey Smedley, *Women Creating Patriliny* (Walnut Creek, CA: AltaMira Press, 2004); Suzanne G. Frayser, *Varieties of Sexual Experience* (New Haven, CT: HRAF Press, 1985), pp. 338–47.

Descent group members may also support one another in such enterprises as clearing virgin bush or forest for farmland and providing food and other items for feasts, potlatches, curing rites, and ceremonial occasions, such as births, initiations, marriages, and funerals.

Money earned—either by harvesting a cash crop or by leaving the community for a time to work for cash wages—is sometimes viewed by the descent group as belonging to all. In recent times, however, young people in some places have shown an unwillingness to part with their money, viewing it as different from other kinds of economic assistance.

Political Functions

The word *political,* as used by members of an industrialized society, generally does not apply to the vague powers that may be entrusted to a headman or the elders of a lineage or clan. But these persons may have the right to assign land for use by a lineage member or a clan member. Headmen or elders may also have the right to settle disputes between two members within a lineage, although they generally lack power to force a settlement. And they may act as intermediaries in disputes between a member of their own clan and a member of an opposing kin group.

Certainly one of the most important political functions of unilineal descent groups is their role in warfare—the attempt to resolve disputes within and without the society by violent action. In societies without towns or cities, the organization of such fighting is often in the hands of descent groups. The Tiv of central Nigeria, for instance, know very well at any given moment which lineages they will fight against, which lineages they will join as allies in case of a fight, which they will fight against using only sticks, and which must be attacked using bows and arrows.

MIGRANTS AND IMMIGRANTS

Blood Is Thicker than Water

With the spread of money economies, many societies no longer have kin groups like lineages, clans, phratries, and moieties—kin groups larger than families, sometimes much larger (possibly with hundreds and sometimes thousands of members). But if large kin groups are disappearing in the modern world, that doesn't mean they are completely gone. Lineages continue to be important for many Chinese, and for people in various parts of Africa and on islands in the Pacific. Lineages and clans in some places still "own" the cultivable land and other valuable property. Kinship may be particularly useful when it comes time to migrate to other countries. When that time comes, and it comes for millions of people every year, "blood is thicker than water," as the old saying goes. Migrants generally look to settle, at least at first, near or with relatives. The relatives may be genealogically close (siblings, uncles, aunts). Or they may be more distantly related, members of one's lineage or clan. Probably the most common reason migrants use kinship connections is that they need help, at least for a while, to make a living in the new country.

When looking for help from lineage mates or clansmen, you may not know exactly how you are related to them. All you might be able to say is that they belong to your lineage or clan. You know because they say they are "Li," "Park," or "Bear" like you. (Clans in some societies are believed to have animal ancestors.) It's like having an automatic friend in the new place, which can be very useful, particularly if you don't have close relatives there. Indeed, if you come from a region that has lineages, the first person you might look up (even before you leave home) might be a lineage mate.

This is often what happens when Chinese from the Hong Kong area go abroad to seek their fortune. Consider the lineage known as the "Man," one of the five major lineages that dominated political life until the 1960s in the Hong Kong New Territories. Anthropologist James L. Watson has studied this group for more than 35 years, in the area around Hong Kong and in other parts of the world to which they have migrated. He has particularly tracked people from the village of San Tin, located on what used to be one of the front lines of the Cold War, 400 yards south of the border between British-controlled Hong Kong and Communist-controlled China.

People involved in the San Tin diaspora began to move away in the late 1950s. They had little money or assets. By the mid-1970s, they had managed to establish a chain of Chinese restaurants in England and other parts of Europe. Today, most of the grandchildren of the original migrants are wealthy professionals and some are multimillionaires. Many in the current generation cannot speak or read Cantonese, the Chinese language of their ancestors. They now speak English, Dutch, or German.

The people who consider themselves members of the Man lineage trace their descent from Man Sai-go, the ancestor who settled near San Tin in the 14th century. Today, there are about 4,000 people who claim descent from Man Sai-go, living in more than 20 countries. The exact number is known only to the lineage master (*zushang*) and elders who manage the ancestral estates (properties in land and other assets). For nearly 600 years, the Man survived on a kind of rice grown in the salty paddies along the Shenzhen River, which became the border between British Hong Kong and China in 1898. San Tin's farmers faced a crisis in the early 1950s. The markets for their rice were located on the Chinese side of the river, which was no longer regularly accessible. Unlike other lineages in the area, the Man could not convert to growing vegetables or white rice (which could not be grown in their salty paddies). They had two choices: go to Hong Kong to work in its booming factories or migrate to England to work in Chinese restaurants. Just before migration to England was banned by the British authorities in 1962, 85–90 percent of San Tin's able-bodied men left for Britain, lineage mates following lineage mates, to work in factories and hotels, as well as restaurants.

The village of San Tin became a remittance economy, wives and children and elders left behind, supported by the money sent home by the migrants who returned to San Tin for a visit every few years and then went back to Europe to work. Many of the migrants, when they retired, decided to join their children's families in the diaspora, and never again returned to San Tin.

The history of San Tin and its people illustrates how a supposedly premodern form of kinship, the Chinese lineage, is still very much alive in the modern world.

Sources: Caroline B. Brettell, "Migration," in David Levinson and Melvin Ember, eds., *Encyclopedia of Cultural Anthropology*, 4 vols. (New York: Henry Holt, 1996), vol. 3, pp. 793–797; Adam McKeown, "Chinese Diaspora," in Melvin Ember, Carol R. Ember, and Ian Skoggard, eds., *Encyclopedia of Diasporas: Immigrant and Refugee Cultures Around the World*, 2 vols. (New York: Kluwer Academic/Plenum, 2005), vol. 1, pp. 65–76; James L. Watson, "Presidential Address: Virtual Kinship, Real Estate, and Diaspora Formation—the Man Lineage Revisited," *Journal of Asian Studies* 63 (2004): 893–910.

Trobriand Islanders have avunculocal residence and matrilineal descent groups.

Religious Functions

A clan or lineage may have its own religious beliefs and practices, worshiping its own gods or goddesses and ancestral spirits. The Tallensi of West Africa revere and try to pacify their ancestors. They view life as we know it as only a part of human existence; for them, life existed before birth and will continue after death. The Tallensi believe that the ancestors of their descent groups have changed their form but have retained their interest in what goes on within their society. They can show their displeasure by bringing sudden disaster or minor mishap and their pleasure by bringing unexpected good fortune. But people can never tell what will please them; ancestral spirits are, above all, unpredictable. Thus, the Tallensi try to account for unexplainable happenings by attributing them to the ever-watchful ancestors. Belief in the presence of ancestors also provides security; if their ancestors have survived death, so will they. The Tallensi religion is thus a descent-group religion. The Tallensi are not concerned with other people's ancestors; they believe it is only one's own ancestors who plague or protect one.[17]

 Ambilineal Systems

Societies with ambilineal descent groups are far less numerous than unilineal or even bilateral societies. Ambilineal societies, however, resemble unilineal ones in many ways.

For instance, the members of an ambilineal descent group believe that they are descended from a common ancestor, although frequently they cannot specify all the genealogical links. The descent group is commonly named and may have an identifying emblem or even a totem; land and other productive resources may be owned by the descent group; and myths and religious practices are often associated with the group. Marriage is often regulated by group membership, just as in unilineal systems, although kin group exogamy is not nearly as common as in unilineal systems. Moreover, ambilineal societies resemble unilineal ones in having various levels or types of descent groups. They may have lineages and higher orders of descent groups, distinguished (as in unilineal systems) by whether or not all the genealogical links to the supposed common ancestors are specified.[18]

The Samoans of the South Pacific are an example of an ambilineal society.[19] Samoa has two types of ambilineal descent groups, corresponding to what would be called clans and subclans in a unilineal society. Both groups are exogamous. Associated with each ambilineal clan are one or more chiefs. A group takes its name from the senior chief; subclans, of which there are always at least two, may take their names from junior chiefs.

The distinctiveness of the Samoan ambilineal system, compared with unilineal systems, is that because people may be affiliated with an ambilineal group through their father or mother (and the parents, in turn, could be affiliated with any of their parents' groups), there are a number of ambilineal groups to which individuals could belong. Affiliation with a Samoan descent group is optional, and people may theoretically affiliate with any or all of the ambilineal groups to which they are related. In practice, however, people are primarily associated with one group—the ambilineal group whose land they actually live on and cultivate—although they may participate in the activities (e.g., house building) of several groups. Because a person may belong to more than one ambilineal group, the society is not divided into separate kin groups, in contrast with unilineal societies. Consequently, the core members of each ambilineal group cannot all live together, as they could in unilineal societies, because each person belongs to more than one group and cannot live in several places at once.

Not all ambilineal societies have the multiple descent group membership that occurs in Samoa. In some ambilineal societies, a person may belong at any one time to only one group. In such cases, the society can be divided into separate, nonoverlapping groups of kin.

Explaining Variation in Residence

Questions can be raised as to why different societies have different patterns of residence. If in most societies married couples live with or near kin, as in patrilocal, matrilocal, bilocal, and avunculocal patterns of residence, then why in some societies, such as our own, do couples typically live apart from kin? And, among the societies in which couples

In some cultures people worship or give gifts to ancestral spirits, as is common in China.

live with or near kin, why do most choose the husband's side (patrilocal residence), but some the wife's side (matrilocal residence)? Why do some non-neolocal societies allow a married couple to go to either the wife's or the husband's kin (bilocal residence), whereas most others do not allow a choice?

Neolocal Residence

Many anthropologists have suggested that neolocal residence is related to the presence of a money or commercial economy. They argue that when people can sell their labor or their products for money, they can buy what they need to live, without having to depend on kin. Because money is not perishable, unlike crops and other foods in a world largely lacking refrigeration, it can be stored for exchange at a later time. Thus, a money-earning family can resort to its own savings during periods of unemployment or disability, or it might be able to rely on monetary aid from the government, as in our own society. This strategy is impossible in nonmoney economies, where people must depend on relatives for food and other necessities if for some reason they cannot provide their own.

There is cross-cultural evidence to support this interpretation. Neolocal residence tends to occur in societies with monetary or commercial exchange, whereas societies without money tend to have patterns of residence that locate a couple near or with kin.[20] The presence of money, then, partially accounts for neolocal residence: Money seems to allow couples to live on their own. Still, this fact does not quite explain why they choose to do so.

One reason may be that in commercial societies, couples do better on their own because the jobs available require physical or social mobility. Or perhaps couples prefer to live apart from kin because they want to avoid some of the interpersonal tensions and demands that may be generated by living with or near kin. But why couples, when given money, should *prefer* to live on their own is not completely understood.

Matrilocal versus Patrilocal Residence

It is traditionally assumed that in societies in which married children live near or with kin, the pattern of residence will tend to be patrilocal if males contribute more to the economy and matrilocal if women contribute more. However plausible that assumption may seem, the cross-cultural evidence does not support it. Where men do most of the primary subsistence work, residence is patrilocal no more often than would be expected by chance. Conversely, where women do an equal amount or more of the subsistence work, residence is no more likely to be matrilocal than patrilocal.[21] And if we counted all work inside and outside the home, most societies should be matrilocal because women usually do more. But that is not true either; most societies are not matrilocal.

We can predict whether residence will be matrilocal or patrilocal, however, from the type of warfare practiced in the society. In most societies known to anthropology, neighboring communities or districts are enemies. The type of warfare that breaks out periodically between such groups is called *internal*, because the fighting occurs between groups that speak the same language. In other societies, the warfare is never within the same society but only with other language groups. This pattern of warfare is referred to as purely *external*. Cross-cultural evidence suggests that in societies where warfare is at least sometimes internal, residence is almost always patrilocal rather than matrilocal. In contrast, residence is usually matrilocal when warfare is purely external.[22]

How can we explain this relationship between type of warfare and matrilocal versus patrilocal residence? One theory is that patrilocal residence tends to occur with internal warfare because there may be concern over keeping sons close to home to help with defense. Because women do not usually constitute the fighting force in any society, having sons reside at home after marriage might be favored as a means of maintaining a loyal and quickly mobilized fighting force in case of surprise attack from nearby. If warfare is purely external, however, people may not be so concerned about keeping their sons at home because families need not fear attack from neighboring communities or districts.

With purely external warfare, then, the pattern of residence may be determined by other considerations, especially economic ones. If in societies with purely external warfare the women do most of the primary subsistence work, families might want their daughters to remain at home after marriage, so the pattern of residence might become matrilocal. If warfare is purely external but men still do more of the primary subsistence work, residence should still be patrilocal. Thus, the need to keep sons at home after marriage when there is internal warfare may take precedence over any considerations based on division of labor. It is perhaps only when internal warfare is nonexistent that a female-dominant division of labor may give rise to matrilocal residence.[23]

The frequent absence of men because of long-distance trade or wage labor in distant places may also provide an impetus for matrilocal residence even after warfare ceases. For example, among the Miskito of eastern Central America, matrilocality allowed domestic and village life to continue without interruption when men were away from home for long periods of time, working as lumberers, miners, and river transporters. These jobs were not always available, but when they were the men went away to work at them in order to earn money. Even though some men would always be away from home, the Miskito continued to get food in their traditional ways, from farming (done mostly by the women) and from hunting and fishing (which was mostly men's work).[24]

Bilocal Residence

In societies that practice bilocal residence, a married couple goes to live with or near either the husband's or the wife's parents. Although this pattern seems to involve a choice for the married couple, theory and research suggest that bilocal residence may occur out of necessity instead. Elman Service suggested that bilocal residence is likely to occur in societies that have recently suffered a severe and drastic loss of population because of the introduction of new infectious diseases.[25] Over the last 400 years, contact with Europeans in many parts of the world has resulted in severe population losses among non-European societies that lacked resistance to the Europeans' diseases. If couples need to live with some set of kin in order to make a living in noncommercial societies, it seems likely that couples in depopulated, noncommercial societies might have to live with whichever spouse's parents and other relatives are still alive. This interpretation is supported by the cross-cultural evidence. Recently depopulated societies tend to have bilocal residence or frequent departures from unilocality, whereas societies that are not recently depopulated tend to have one pattern or another of unilocal residence.[26]

In hunter-gatherer societies, a few other circumstances may also favor bilocal residence. Bilocality tends to be found among those hunter-gatherers who have very small bands or unpredictable and low rainfall. Residential "choice" in these cases may be a question of adjusting marital residence to where the couple will have the best chance to survive or to find close relatives with whom to live and work.[27] Figure 22–6 illustrates the main predictors of the various marital residence patterns.

Avunculocal Residence

Now that we have learned about matrilineal systems, the avunculocal pattern of residence, whereby married couples live with or near the husband's mother's brother, may become clearer. Although avunculocal residence is relatively rare, just about all avunculocal societies are matrilineal. As we have seen, the mother's brother plays an important role in decision making in most matrilineal societies. Aside from his brothers, who is a boy's closest male matrilineal relative? His mother's brother. Going to live with the mother's brother, then, provides a way of localizing male *matrilineal* relatives. But why should some matrilineal societies practice that form of residence? The answer may involve the prevailing type of warfare.

Avunculocal societies, in contrast with matrilocal societies, fight internally. Just as patrilocality may be a response to keep patrilineally related men home after marriage, so avunculocality may be a way of keeping related—in this case, matrilineally related—men together after marriage to provide for quick mobilization in case of surprise attack from

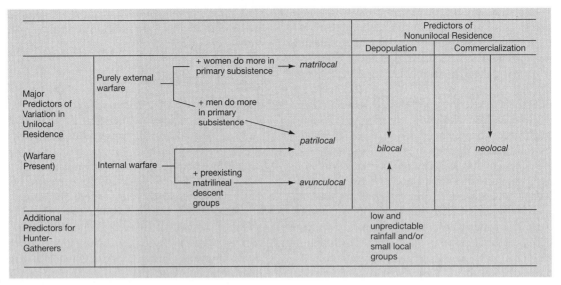

Figure 22–6 The Main Predictors of Marital Residence Patterns
An arrow indicates the suggested causal direction.

Source: Adapted from Melvin Ember and Carol R. Ember, *Marriage, Family, and Kinship: Comparative Studies of Social Organization* (New Haven, CT: HRAF Press, 1983).

nearby. Societies that already have strong, functioning matrilineal descent groups may choose initially, when faced with the emergence of fighting close to home, to switch to avunculocality rather than patrilocality. This is assuming that the close warfare results in high male mortality, which might make it more difficult to trace descent patrilineally than matrilineally. So such a society might begin to practice avunculocality rather than switch to patrilocality. Avunculocal residence would keep a higher number of related men together after marriage, compared with patrilocality, because there would be more possible links through women than through men if many men were dying relatively young in the warfare.[28]

The Emergence of Unilineal Systems

Unilineal kin groups play very important roles in the organization of many societies. But not all societies have such groups. In societies that have complex systems of political organization, officials and agencies take over many of the functions that might be performed by kin groups, such as the organization of work and warfare and the allocation of land. But not all societies that lack complex political organization have unilineal descent systems. Why, then, do some societies have unilineal descent systems, but others do not?

It is generally assumed that unilocal residence, patrilocal or matrilocal, is necessary for the development of unilineal descent. Patrilocal residence, if practiced for some time in a society, will generate a set of patrilineally related males who live in the same territory. Matrilocal residence over time will similarly generate a localized set of matrilineally related females. It is no wonder, then, that matrilocal and patrilocal

residence are cross-culturally associated with matrilineal and patrilineal descent, respectively.[29]

But, although unilocal residence might be necessary for the formation of unilineal descent groups, it is apparently not the only condition required. For one thing, many societies with unilocal residence lack unilineal descent groups. For another, merely because related males or related females live together by virtue of a patrilocal or matrilocal rule of residence, it does not necessarily follow that the related people will actually view themselves as a descent group and function as such. Thus, it appears that other conditions are needed to supply the impetus for the formation of unilineal descent groups.

There is evidence that unilocal societies that engage in warfare are more apt to have unilineal descent groups than unilocal societies without warfare.[30] It may be, then, that the presence of fighting in societies lacking complex systems of political organization provides an impetus to the formation of unilineal descent groups. Unilineal descent groups provide individuals with unambiguous groups of persons who can fight or form alliances as discrete units.[31] There is no ambiguity about an individual's membership. It is perfectly clear whether someone belongs to a particular clan, phratry, or moiety. It is this feature of unilineal descent groups that enables them to act as separate and distinct units—mostly, perhaps, in warfare.

Explaining Ambilineal and Bilateral Systems

Why do some societies have ambilineal descent groups? Although the evidence is not clear cut, it may be that societies with unilineal descent groups are transformed into ambilineal ones under special conditions, particularly in the presence of depopulation. We have already noted that depopulation may transform a previously unilocal society into a bilocal society. If that previously unilocal society also had unilineal descent groups, the descent groups may become transformed into ambilineal groups. If a society used to be patrilocal and patrilineal, for example, but some couples began to live matrilocally, then their children would be associated through their mother with a previously patrilineal descent group on whose land they may be living. Once this situation happens regularly, the unilineal principle may become transformed into an ambilineal principle.[32] Thus, ambilineal descent systems may have developed recently as a result of depopulation caused by the introduction of European diseases.

The conditions that favor bilateral systems are in large part opposite to those favoring unilineal descent. As we discussed, unlineal descent seems to develop in a nonstate society with unilocal residence that has warfare. If one needs an unambigious set of allies, bilateral systems are unlikely to provide them. Recall that bilateral systems are ego-centered; and every person, other than siblings, has a slightly different set of kin to rely on. Consequently, in bilateral societies it is often not clear to whom one can turn and which person has responsibility for aiding another. Such ambiguity, however, might not be a liability in societies without warfare. In complex political systems that organize fighting on behalf of large populations, a standing army usually provides the fighting force and mobilization of kin is not so important. Perhaps because warfare is somewhat less likely in foraging societies,[33] bilateral systems may often develop in foraging societies, just like bilaterality is likely in more complex societies because they don't need to rely on descent groups for war. Neolocal residence, which becomes more common with commercialization and market exchange, also works against unilineal descent, and therefore also makes a bilateral system more likely.

Kinship Terminology

Our society, like all others, refers to a number of different kin by the same **classificatory term.** Most of us probably never stop to think about why we name relatives the way we do. For example, we call our mother's brother and father's brother (and often mother's sister's husband and father's sister's husband) by the same term—*uncle.* It is not that we are unable to distinguish between our mother's or father's brother or that we do not know the difference between **consanguineal kin** (blood kin) and **affinal kin** (kin by marriage, or what we call *in-laws*). Instead, it seems that in our society we do not usually find it necessary to distinguish between various types of uncles.

However natural our system of classification may seem to us, countless field studies by anthropologists have revealed that societies differ markedly in how they group or distinguish relatives. The kinship terminology used in a society may reflect its prevailing kind of family, its rule of residence, its rule of descent, and other aspects of its social organization. Kin terms may also give clues to prior features of the

society's social system, if, as many anthropologists believe,[34] the kin terms of a society are very resistant to change. The major systems of kinship terminology are the Omaha system, the Crow system, the Iroquois system, the Sudanese system, the Hawaiian system, and the Inuit (Eskimo) system.

Because it is the most familiar to us, let us first consider the kinship terminology system employed in our own and many other commercial societies. But it is by no means confined to commercial societies. In fact, this system is found in many Inuit societies.

Inuit, or Eskimo, System

The distinguishing features of the Inuit, or Eskimo, system (see Figure 22–7) are that all cousins are lumped together under the same term but are distinguished from brothers and sisters, all aunts are lumped under the same term and distinguished from mother, and all uncles are lumped under the same term and distinguished from father. In Figure 22–7 and in subsequent figures, the kin types that are referred to by the same term are colored and marked in the same way; for example, in the Inuit system, kin types 2 (father's brother) and 6 (mother's brother) are referred to by the same term (*uncle* in English). Note that in this system, in contrast to the others we will examine, no other relatives are generally referred to by the same terms used for members of the nuclear family—mother, father, brother, and sister.

The Inuit type of kinship terminology is not generally found where there are unilineal or ambilineal descent groups; the only kin group that appears to be present is the bilateral kindred.[35] Remember that the kindred in a bilateral kinship system is an ego-centered group. Although relatives on both my mother's and my father's sides are equally important, my most important relatives are generally those closest to me. This is particularly true in our society, where the nuclear family generally lives alone, separated from and not particularly involved with other relatives except on ceremonial occasions. Because the nuclear family is most important, we would expect to find that the terminology for kin types in the nuclear family is different from the terminology for all other relatives. And the mother's and father's sides are equally important (or unimportant), so it makes sense that we use the same terms (*aunt, uncle,* and *cousin*) for both sides of the family.

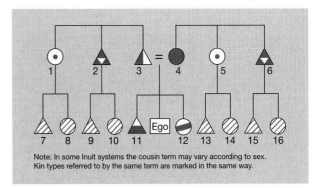

Note: In some Inuit systems the cousin term may vary according to sex. Kin types referred to by the same term are marked in the same way.

Figure 22–7 Inuit (Eskimo) Terminology System

Omaha System

The Omaha system of kin terminology is named after the Omaha of North America, but the system is found in many societies around the world, usually those with patrilineal descent.[36] Referring to Figure 22–8, we can see immediately which types of kin are lumped together in an Omaha system. First, father and father's brother (numbers 2 and 3) are both referred to by the same term. This way of classifying relatives contrasts markedly with ours, in which no term that applies to a member of the nuclear family (father, mother, brother, sister) is applied to any other relative. What could account for the Omaha system of lumping? One interpretation is that father and father's brother are lumped in this system because most societies in which this system is found have patrilineal kin groups. Both father and father's brother are in the parental generation of my patrilineal kin group and may behave toward me similarly. My father's brother also probably lived near me as a child, since patrilineal societies usually have patrilocal residence. The term for father and father's brother, then, might be translated "male member of my patrilineal kin group in my father's generation."

A second lumping, which at first glance appears similar to the lumping of father and father's brother, is that of mother and mother's sister (4 and 5), both of whom are called by the same term. But more surprisingly, mother's brother's daughter (16) is also referred to by this term. Why? If we think of the term as meaning "female member of my mother's patrilineage of *any* generation," then the term makes sense. Consistent with this view, all the male members of my mother's patrilineage of any generation (mother's brother, 6; mother's brother's son, 15) are also referred to by one term.

It is apparent, then, that relatives on the father's and the mother's sides are grouped differently in this system. For members of my mother's patrilineal kin group, I lump all male members together and all female members together regardless of their generation. Yet, for members of my father's patrilineal kin group, I have different terms for the male and female members of different generations. George Peter Murdock suggested that a society lumps kin types when there are more similarities than differences among them.[37]

Using this principle, and recognizing that societies with an Omaha system usually are patrilineal, I realize that my father's patrilineal kin group is the one to which I belong and in which I have a great many rights and obligations. Consequently, persons of my father's generation are likely to behave quite differently toward me than are persons of my own generation. Members of my patrilineal group in my father's generation are likely to exercise authority over me, and I am required to show them respect. Members of my patrilineal group in my own generation are those I am likely to play with as a child and to be friends with. Thus, in a patrilineal system, persons on my father's side belonging to different generations are likely to be distinguished. On the other hand, my mother's patrilineage is relatively unimportant to me (since I take my descent from my father). And because my residence is probably patrilocal, my mother's relatives will probably not even live near me. Thus, inasmuch as my mother's patrilineal relatives are comparatively unimportant in such a system, they become similar enough to be lumped together.

Finally, in the Omaha system, I refer to my male parallel cousins (my father's brother's son, 9; and my mother's sister's son, 13) in the same way I refer to my brother (11). I refer to my female parallel cousins (my father's brother's daughter, 10; and my mother's sister's daughter, 14) in the same way I refer to my sister (12). Considering that my father's brother and mother's sister are referred to by the same terms I use for my father and mother, this lumping of parallel cousins with **siblings** (brothers and sisters) is not surprising. If I call my own mother's and father's children (other than myself) "Brother" and "Sister," then the children of anyone whom I also call "Mother" and "Father" ought to be called "Brother" and "Sister" as well.

Crow System

The Crow system, named after another North American culture, has been called the mirror image of the Omaha system. The same principles of lumping kin types are employed, except that the Crow system is associated with matrilineal descent,[38] so the individuals in my mother's matrilineal group (which is my own) are not lumped across generations, whereas the individuals in my father's matrilineal group are. Comparing Figure 22–9 with Figure 22–8, we find that the lumping and separating of kin types are much the same in both, except that the lumping across generations in the Crow system appears on the father's side rather than on the mother's side. In other words, I call both my mother and my mother's sister by the same term (since both are female

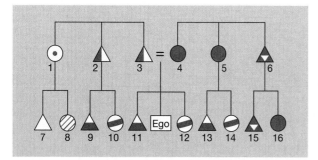

Figure 22–8 Omaha Kinship Terminology System

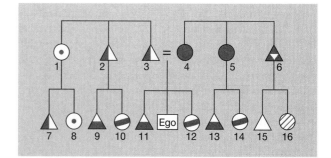

Figure 22–9 Crow Kinship Terminology System

members of my matrilineal descent group in my mother's generation). I call my father, my father's brother, and my father's sister's son by the same term (all male members of my father's matrilineal group in any generation). I call my father's sister and my father's sister's daughter by the same term (both female members of my father's matrilineal group). And I refer to my parallel cousins in the same way I refer to my brother and sister.

Iroquois System

The Iroquois system, named after the Iroquois of North America, is similar to both the Omaha and Crow systems in the way in which I refer to relatives in my parents' generation (see Figure 22–10). That is, my father and my father's brother (2 and 3) are referred to by the same term, and my mother and my mother's sister (4 and 5) are referred to by the same term. However, the Iroquois system differs from the Omaha and Crow systems regarding my own generation. In the Omaha and Crow systems, one set of cross-cousins was lumped in the kinship terminology with the generation above. In the Iroquois system both sets of cross-cousins (mother's brother's children, 15 and 16; and father's sister's children, 7 and 8) are referred to by the same terms, distinguished by sex. That is, mother's brother's daughter and father's sister's daughter are both referred to by the same term. Also, mother's brother's son and father's sister's son are referred to by the same term. Parallel cousins always have terms different from those for cross-cousins and are sometimes, but not always, referred to by the same terms as one's brother and sister.

Like the Omaha and Crow systems, the Iroquois system has different terms for relatives on the father's and mother's sides. Such differentiation tends to be associated with unilineal descent, which is not surprising since unilineal descent involves affiliation with either mother's or father's kin. Why Iroquois, rather than Omaha or Crow, terminology occurs in a unilineal society requires explanation. One possible explanation is that Omaha or Crow is likely to occur in a developed, as opposed to a developing or decaying, unilineal system.[39] Another possibility is that Iroquois terminology emerges in societies that prefer marriage with both cross-cousins,[40] who are differentiated from other relatives in an Iroquois system.

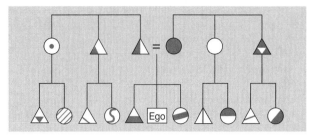

Figure 22–11 Sudanese Kinship Terminology System

Sudanese System

Unlike the Omaha, Crow, and Iroquois systems, the Sudanese system usually does not lump any relatives in the parents' and ego's generations. That is, the Sudanese system is usually a *descriptive system,* in which a different descriptive term is used for *each* of the relatives, as shown in Figure 22–11. What kinds of societies are likely to have such a system? Although societies with Sudanese terminology are likely to be patrilineal, they probably are different from most patrilineal societies that have Omaha or Iroquois terms. Sudanese terminology is associated with relatively great political complexity, class stratification, and occupational specialization. It has been suggested that under such conditions, a kinship system may reflect the need to make fine distinctions among members of descent groups who have different opportunities and privileges in the occupational or class system.[41]

The Omaha, Crow, Iroquois, and Sudanese systems, although different from one another and associated with somewhat different predictors, share one important feature: The terms used for the mother's and father's side of the family are not the same. If you imagine folding the kinship terminology diagrams in half, the two sides would not be the same. As we have seen in the Inuit system, however, the terms on the mother's and father's side of the family are *exactly* the same. This feature suggests that the two sides of the family are equally important or equally unimportant. The Hawaiian system discussed next also has the same terms on both sides, but kinship outside the nuclear family is more important.

Hawaiian System

The Hawaiian system of kinship terminology is the least complex in that it uses the smallest number of terms. In this system, all relatives of the same sex in the same generation are referred to by the same term (see Figure 22–12). Thus,

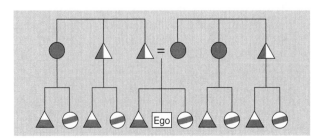

Figure 22–12 Hawaiian Kinship Terminology System

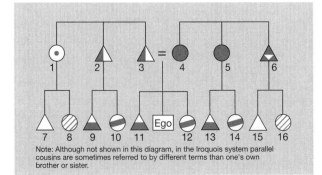

Note: Although not shown in this diagram, in the Iroquois system parallel cousins are sometimes referred to by different terms than one's own brother or sister.

Figure 22–10 Iroquois Terminology System

all my female cousins are referred to by the same term as my sister; all male cousins are referred to by the same term as my brother. Everyone known to be related to me in my parents' generation is referred to by one term if female (including my mother) and by another term if male (including my father).

The fact that societies with Hawaiian kin terminology tend not to have unilineal descent groups[42] helps explain why kinship terms are the same on both sides of the family. Why are the terms for mother, father, sister, and brother used for other relatives? Perhaps because societies with Hawaiian terminology are likely to have large extended families[43] to which every type of relative in Figure 22–12 may belong because of alternative (bilocal) residence patterns.[44] So, in contrast to our own society, many kin are very important, a fact that seems to be reflected in the practice of referring to other relatives with the same terms that are used for nuclear family members.

◉ Summary

1. In our society, and in many other industrial societies, a newly married couple usually establishes a place of residence apart from parents or relatives (neolocal residence). But about 95 percent of the world's societies have some pattern of residence whereby the new couple settles within or very close to the household of the parents or some other close relative of the groom or bride.

2. The four major patterns in which married couples live with or near kinsmen are these:
   a. Patrilocal residence: The couple lives with or near the husband's parents (67 percent of all societies).
   b. Matrilocal residence: The couple lives with or near the wife's parents (15 percent of all societies).
   c. Bilocal residence: The couple lives with or near either the husband's parents or the wife's parents (7 percent of all societies).
   d. Avunculocal residence: The son and his wife settle with or near his mother's brother (4 percent of all societies).

3. In most societies where kinship is important, rules of affiliation allocate each person to a particular and definable set of kin. The three main types of affiliation with kin are: unilineal descent, ambilineal descent, and bilateral kinship.

4. Unilineal descent and ambilineal descent are based on rules of descent, which are rules that connect individuals with particular sets of kin because of known or presumed common ancestry. Unilineal descent refers to the fact that a person is affiliated with a group of kin through descent links of one sex only—either males only or females only. Thus unilineal descent can be either patrilineal or matrilineal.
   a. Patrilineal descent affiliates individuals with kin of both sexes related to them through men only. In each generation, then, children belong to the kin group of their father.

   b. Matrilineal descent affiliates individuals with kin related to them through women only. In each generation, then, children belong to the kin group of their mother.

5. Ambilineal descent affiliates individuals with kin related to them through either men or women. Consequently, the descent groups show both female and male genealogical links.

6. Societies without lineal descent rules are bilateral societies. Relatives on both the mother's and father's sides of the family are of equal importance or, more usually, unimportance. Kindreds are ego-centered sets of kin who may be called together temporarily for some purpose.

7. With unilineal descent people usually refer to themselves as belonging to a particular unilineal group or set of groups because they believe they share common descent in either the male or the female line. These people form what is called a unilineal descent group. There are several types, and a society may have more than one type.
   a. Lineages are sets of kin whose members trace descent from a common ancestor through known links.
   b. Clans are sets of kin who believe they are descended from a common ancestor but cannot specify the genealogical links.
   c. Phratries are groups of supposedly related clans.
   d. Moieties are said to exist when the whole society is divided into two unilineal descent groups without specified links to the supposed common ancestor of each.

8. Unilineal descent groups are most common in societies in the middle range of cultural complexity—that is, in noncommercial food-producing, as opposed to food-collecting, societies. In such societies, unilineal descent groups often have important functions in the social, economic, political, and religious realms of life.

9. Societies differ markedly in how they group or distinguish relatives under the same or different kinship terms. The major systems of terminology are the Inuit (Eskimo), Omaha, Crow, Iroquois, Sudanese, and Hawaiian systems.

◉ Glossary Terms

affinal kin	397	double descent or double unilineal descent	386
ambilineal descent	385		
avunculocal residence	382	ego	387
bilateral kinship	386	kindred	386
bilocal residence	382	lineage	387
clan or sib	387	matriclans	387
classificatory term	397	matrilineage	387
consanguineal kin	397	matrilineal descent	384
		matrilocal residence	382

Critical Questions

1. What other things about our society would change if we practiced other than neolocal residence?
2. Why does kinship provide the main structure of social action in noncommercial societies?
3. Why might it be important for unilineal descent groups to be nonoverlapping in membership?

Research Navigator

1. Please go to www.researchnavigator.com and enter your LOGIN NAME and PASSWORD. For instructions on registering for the first time, please view the detailed instructions at the end of Chapter 1.

2. Using Link Library (Anthropology) click on kinship and find the tutorial site. Describe kinship groups and how they function in two different societies (pick two different kinds of kinship systems). Use the instructional information to help with concepts you are having trouble with.

Discovering Anthropology: Researchers at Work

Read William L. Anderson's "Cherokee: The European Impact on the Cherokee Culture" in the accompanying *Discovering Anthropology* reader. Answer the following questions.

1. Describe the patterns of marital residence and descent practiced by the Cherokee.
2. What functions did the kin groups have?
3. How did European contact affect patterns of residence and descent?

CHAPTER TWENTY-THREE

Associations and Interest Groups

Samuel Johnson, the 18th-century English author, was once asked to describe James Boswell, his companion and biographer. "Boswell," he boomed, "is a very clubable man." Johnson did not mean that Boswell deserved to be attacked with bludgeons. He was referring to Boswell's fondness for all sorts of clubs and associations, a fondness he shared with many of his contemporaries. The tendency to form associations was not unique to 18th-century England.

The notion of clubs may make us think of something extracurricular and not very important, but associations play very important roles in the economy and political life of many societies. In this chapter we examine the various kinds of associations formed in different societies, how these groups function, and what general purposes they serve. When we speak of **associations,** we mean different kinds of groups that are not based on kinship, as discussed in the preceding chapter, or on territory, which we take up in the next chapter. Associations, then, are nonkin and nonterritorial groups; and, although they vary, they also have several common characteristics: (1) some kind of formal, institutionalized structure; (2) the exclusion of some people; (3) members with common interests or purposes; and (4) members with a discernible sense of pride and feeling of belonging. Contemporary American society has an abundance of *interest groups*—to use the terminology of the political scientist—that display these general characteristics of associations. Such groups vary considerably in size and social significance, ranging from national organizations such as the Democratic and Republican parties to more local organizations such as college sororities and fraternities.

But societies differ considerably in the degree to which they have such associations and, if they do have them, in what kind they have. To make our discussion somewhat easier, we focus on two dimensions of how associations vary from one society to another. One is whether or not recruitment into the association is voluntary. In U.S. society, with the exception of the government's right to draft men into the military, just about all associations are voluntary—that is, people can choose to join or not join. But in many societies, particularly the more egalitarian ones, membership is nonvoluntary: All people of a particular category must belong.

A second dimension of variation in associations is what qualifies a person for membership. There are two possible kinds of qualifications: those that are achieved and those that are ascribed. **Achieved qualities** are those a person acquires during his or her lifetime, such as superior skills in a sport or the skills required to be an electrician. **Ascribed qualities** are those determined for a person at birth, either because of genetic makeup (e.g., sex) or because of family background (ethnicity, place of birth, religion, social class). We speak of two kinds of ascribed qualities or characteristics: **universally ascribed qualities,** those that are found in all societies, such as age and sex; and **variably ascribed qualities,** those that are found only in some societies, such as ethnic, religious, or social class differences.

Table 23–1 gives these two dimensions of variation in associations—voluntary versus nonvoluntary recruitment and criteria for membership—and some kinds of associations that fit neatly into our classification. Some associations do not fit so neatly—for example, the criteria that qualify someone for Girl Scout membership include an interest in joining, an achieved quality, as well as biological sex, an ascribed characteristic.

 Nonvoluntary Associations

Although complex societies may have nonvoluntary associations, such associations are more characteristic of relatively unstratified or egalitarian societies. In relatively unstratified societies, associations tend to be based on the universally ascribed characteristics of age and sex. Such associations take two forms: age-sets and male or female (unisex) associations.

Age-Sets

All societies use a vocabulary of age terms, just as they use a vocabulary of kinship terms. For instance, as we distinguish among *brother, uncle,* and *cousin,* so we differentiate *infant,* *adolescent,* and *adult. Age terms* refer to categories based on age, or age-grades. An **age-grade** is simply a category of persons who happen to fall within a particular culturally distinguished age range. **Age-set,** on the other hand, is the term for a group of persons of similar age and the same sex who move through some or all of life's stages together. For example, all the boys of a certain age range in a particular district might simultaneously become ceremonially initiated into "manhood." Later in life, the group as a whole might become "elders," and still later "retired elders." Entry into an age-set system is generally nonvoluntary and is based on the universally ascribed characteristics of sex and age.

Kinship forms the basis of the organization and administration of most noncommercial societies. In some noncommercial societies, however, age-sets crosscut kinship ties

Table 23–1	Some Examples of Associations	
Membership	**Criteria**	**Recruitment**
	Voluntary	**Nonvoluntary**
UNIVERSALLY ASCRIBED		Age-set Most unisex associations
VARIABLY ASCRIBED	Ethnic associations Regional associations	Conscripted army
ACHIEVED	Occupational associations Political parties Special interest groups	

Some circumstances have changed, but the age-sets of the Nandi of Kenya still have importance. This young Nandi man (in a suit) is told by a traditional spiritual leader (in a skin cloak): "In the past, when our young warriors went out for the first time, we gave them spears and shields and told them to bring back wealth to the community. Today we give you a pen and paper and ask the same."

and form strong supplementary bonds. Two such societies are the Karimojong of East Africa and the Shavante of Brazil.

KARIMOJONG AGE-SETS The Karimojong number some 60,000 people. Predominantly cattle herders, they occupy about 4,000 acres of semiarid country in northeastern Uganda. Their society is especially interesting because of its organization into combinations of age-sets and generation-sets. These groupings provide "both the source of political authority and the main field within which it is exercised."[1]

A Karimojong age-set comprises all the men who have been initiated into manhood within a span of about five to six years. A generation-set consists of a combination of five such age-sets, covering 25 to 30 years. Each generation-set is seen as "begetting" the one that immediately follows it, and at any one time two generation-sets are in existence. The senior unit—whose members perform the administrative, judicial, and priestly functions—is closed; the junior unit, whose members serve as warriors and police, continues to recruit. When all five age-sets in the junior generation-set are established, that generation-set will be ready—actually impatient—to assume the status of its senior predecessor. Eventually, grumbling but realistic, the elders agree to a succession ceremony, moving those who were once in a position of obedience to a position of authority.

Once initiated, a boy has become a man, one with a clearly defined status and the ultimate certainty of exercising full authority together with his set partners. Indeed, a Karimojong is not expected to marry—and is certainly barred from starting a family—until he has been initiated. The initiation ceremony itself illustrates the essential political and social characteristics of the age-set system. Without the authority of the elders, the ceremony cannot be held; throughout the proceedings their authority is explicit. The father–son relationship of adjacent generation-sets is emphasized, for fathers are initiating their sons.

The Karimojong age system, then, comprises a cyclical succession of four generation-sets in a predetermined continuing relationship. The *retired generation-set* consists of elders who have passed on the mantle of authority, since most of the five age-sets within the retired generation-set are depleted, if not defunct. The *senior generation-set* contains the five age-sets that actively exercise authority. The *junior generation-set* is still recruiting members and, although obedient to elders, has some administrative powers. The noninitiates are starting a generation-set. Figure 23–1 illustrates the Karimojong age system.

SHAVANTE AGE-SETS The Shavante inhabit the Mato Grasso region of Brazil. Right into the middle of the 20th century they were hostile to Brazilians of European ancestry who tried to move into their territory. It was not until the 1950s that peaceful contact with the 2,000 or so Shavante was achieved. Although the Shavante practice some agriculture, they rely primarily on food collection. Wild roots, nuts, and fruits are their staple foods, and hunting is

In the beginning of the 19th century the Cheyenne had five military associations: the Fox, Dog, Shield, Elk (or Hoof Rattle), and Bowstring (or Contrary). The last-named association was annihilated by the Pawnee in the middle of the 19th century. Later, two new associations were established, the Wolf and Northern Crazy Dogs. Although the various associations may have had different costumes, songs, and dances, they were alike in their internal organization, each being headed by four leaders who were among the most important war chiefs.

When various Plains groups were confined to reservations, the military associations lost many of their old functions, but they did not entirely disappear. For example, among the Lakota, warrior societies continue to be an important part of social life because many men and women have engaged in military activity on behalf of the United States in World Wars I and II, in Korea and Vietnam, and in the wars in the Persian Gulf. Returning soldiers continue to be welcomed with traditional songs of honor and victory dances.[15]

Regional Associations

Regional associations bring together migrants from a common geographic background. Thus, they are often found in urban centers, which traditionally have attracted settlers from rural areas. In the United States, for example, migrants from rural Appalachia have formed associations in Chicago and Detroit. Many of these organizations have become vocal political forces in municipal government. Regional associations often form even when migrants have come from a considerable distance. For example, in the Chinatowns of the United States and Canada, there are many associations based on district of origin in China as well as on surname. The regional and family organizations are in turn incorporated into more inclusive ethnic associations, as we shall see later in this chapter.[16]

William Mangin described the role of regional associations in helping rural migrants adapt to urban life in Lima, Peru.[17] During the 1950s, Mangin studied a group of migrants from the rural mountains, the *serranos* from Ancash. Typically these *serranos*, about 120,000 in number, lived in a slumlike urban settlement called a *barriada*. The *barriada* was not officially recognized by either the national government or the city authorities. Accordingly, it lacked all usual city services, such as water supply, garbage removal, and police protection. Its inhabitants had left their rural birthplaces for reasons typical of such population movements, wherever they occur. These reasons were social and economic; most were related to population and land pressure, but the higher expectations associated with the big city—better education, social mobility, wage labor—were also compelling considerations.

Typically, also, the *serranos* from Ancash formed a regional association. Club membership was open to both sexes. Men generally controlled the executive positions, and club leaders were often men who had achieved political power in their hometowns. Women, who had relatively less economic and social freedom, nevertheless played an important part in club activities.

The *serrano* regional association performed three main services for its members. First, it lobbied the central government on matters of community importance—for example, the supplying of sewers, clinics, and similar public services. A club member had to follow a piece of legislation through the channels of government to make certain it was not forgotten or abandoned. Second, the *serrano* association assisted in acculturating newly arrived *serranos* to the urban life in Lima. The most noticeable rural traits—coca chewing and hairstyle and clothing peculiarities—were the first to disappear, with the men generally able to adapt faster than the women. The association also provided opportunities for fuller contact with the national culture. And finally, the group organized social activities such as fiestas, acted as the clearinghouse for information transmitted to and from the home area, and supplied a range of other services to help migrants adapt to their new environment while retaining ties to their birthplace.

The functions of regional associations may change over time as social conditions change. For example, during the plantation period in Hawaii, many Filipino migrants joined hometown associations that served as mutual aid societies. As more and more Filipinos went to Hawaii, however, more people had kin to whom they could turn. The hometown associations continue to have some economic functions, such as assistance in times of emergency, serious illness, or death, and some scholarship aid, but meetings are infrequent and most members do not attend. Those members who are active seem to want the recognition and prestige that can be attained through leadership positions in the hometown association, which is much more than they can achieve in the wider Hawaiian arena.[18]

Although regional clubs may help to integrate their members into a more complex urban or changing environment, the presence of many such groups may increase divisiveness and rivalry among groups. In some areas the smaller groups have banded together and become quite powerful. For example, within each Chinatown of a major U.S. or Canadian city, the various regional and family associations formed a Chinese Benevolent Association. This larger association, usually controlled by the wealthiest Chinese merchants, acts to oversee business, settle disputes, and organize against discrimination from the outside.[19] Thus, by banding together, the regional and family associations formed ethnic associations.

Ethnic Associations

Various types of ethnic associations or interest groups are found in cities all over the world. Membership in these associations is based largely on ethnicity. Ethnic associations are particularly widespread in urban centers of West Africa. There, accelerated cultural change, reflected in altered economic arrangements, in technological advances, and in new urban living conditions, has weakened kinship relations and

MIGRANTS AND IMMIGRANTS

Ethnic Associations in "Chinatowns"

When immigrants come to a new country, they often first live in urban neighborhoods that mostly contain people like themselves, people from the same regions and even from the same towns and villages. These neighborhoods are called "Chinatowns," "Korea Towns," and the like. These ethnic neighborhoods often have associations, nonkin and nonterritorial groups that protect their members in a variety of ways, which is probably why people wanted to live in the neighborhood in the first place. According to the constitution of the Chinese Benevolent Association in Victoria, British Columbia (a ferry ride from Vancouver), that association was established in order "to undertake social welfare, to settle disputes, to aid the poor and the sick, to eliminate evils within the community, and to defend the community against external threat" (Thompson 2004).

Many Chinatowns grew up in the United States and Canada since the middle of the 19th century. After perhaps working first on the railroads, which recruited them to come to North America, the Chinese immigrants would settle in San Francisco or Vancouver. Often they joined an association of people with the same surname. This set of people considered themselves vaguely related (after all, they did have the same surname) but they usually couldn't trace how or even *if* they were related. Or the neighborhood contained people from the same district in China, with the same dialect. Some people migrated eastward, to the urban centers of New York, Boston, Philadelphia, Montreal, and Toronto. Most if not all of the "Chinatowns" continue to exist, even if subsequent generations have moved away from them. Suburban Chinese-Americans often come to Chinatown on the weekend to visit with relatives and to shop for traditional foods. They are not different from other immigrants in this respect; most immigrants retain their food preferences for generations.

The earliest Chinese immigrants established themselves in various kinds of small business—hand laundries, restaurants, groceries. Such businesses were cheap to start up, and workers who were family members did not have to be paid much to keep them. Hand laundries were the first to disappear as the immigrants and their descendants prospered, and as many people in the general population started to do their laundry in machines at home or in a nearby "laundromat." Now, instead of working in the old family businesses, the descendants of people who used to live in Chinatown often go to college and become doctors and other professionals. Their jobs could be anyplace. Upward mobility often means geographic mobility: people often have to chase the job rather than stay close to home, if they want to maximize their income. This is true for many immigrant groups, not just the people from "Chinatown." When people move away from the old neighborhood, the ethnic association loses its attraction and value. In a generation or two, it may be gone. Just as you may have less opportunity to see cousins and other relatives when you move away, you are also unlikely to participate in your ancestral ethnic association when your job requires you to live in a new place. Mobility has costs as well as benefits.

Sources: Richard H. Thompson, "Chinatowns: Immigrant Communities in Transition," in Carol R. Ember, Melvin Ember, and Peter N. Peregrine eds., *New Directions in Anthropology* (Upper Saddle River, NJ: Prentice Hall, CD-ROM, 2004)—also in Carol R. Ember, Melvin Ember, and Peter N. Peregrine, eds., *Discovering Anthropology: Researchers at Work* (Upper Saddle River, NJ: Prentice Hall, 2006, shrink-wrapped with this volume); Caroline B. Brettell and Robert V. Kemper, "Migration and Cities," in Melvin Ember and Carol R. Ember, eds., *Encyclopedia of Urban Cultures: Cities and Cultures Around the World*, 4 vols. (Danbury, CT: Grolier/Scholastic, 2002, vol. 1, pp. 30–38); Richard H. Thompson, "Assimilation," in David Levinson and Melvin Ember, eds., *Encyclopedia of Cultural Anthropology*, 4 vols. (New York: Henry Holt, vol. 1, pp. 112–116).

other traditional sources of support and solidarity.[20] Sometimes it is difficult to say whether a particular association is ethnic or regional in origin; it may be both.

Tribal unions are frequently found in Nigeria and Ghana. These are typical of most such associations in that they are extraterritorial—that is, they recruit members who have left their tribal locations; also, they have a formal constitution, and they have been formed to meet certain needs arising out of conditions of urban life. One such need is to keep members

in touch with their traditional culture. The Ibo State Union, for example, in addition to providing mutual aid and financial support in case of unemployment, sickness, or death, performs the service of "fostering and keeping alive an interest in tribal song, history, language and moral beliefs and thus maintaining a person's attachment to his native town or village."[21] Some tribal unions collect money to improve conditions in their ancestral homes. Education, for example, is an area of particular concern. Others publish newsletters that report members' activities. Most unions have a young membership that exercises a powerful democratizing influence in tribal councils, and the organizations provide a springboard for those with national political aspirations.

West African occupational clubs also fall into the ethnic category. African versions of trade unions are organized along tribal as well as craft lines, and their principal concern is the status and remuneration of their members as workers. The Motor Drivers' Union of Keta, in Ghana, was formed to fund insurance and legal costs, to contribute to medical care in case of accident or illness, and to help pay for funeral expenses.

Friendly societies differ from tribal unions in that their objectives are confined for the most part to mutual aid. Such a club was formed by the wives of Kru migrants in Freetown, Sierra Leone. Kru men normally go to sea, still a hazardous occupation. The club is classified into three grades. An admission fee permits entry into the lowest grade. Elevation to higher grades depends on further donations. At the death of a member or her husband, the family receives a lump sum commensurate with her status in the club.[22]

Rotating Credit Associations

A common type of mutual aid society is the *rotating credit association.* The basic principle is that each member of the group agrees to make a regular contribution, in money or in kind, to a fund, which is then handed over to each member in rotation.[23] The regular contributions promote savings by each member, but the lump sum distribution enables the recipient to do something significant with the money. These associations are found in many areas of East, South, and Southeast Asia, Africa (particularly West Africa), and the West Indies.[24] They usually include a small number of people, perhaps between 10 or 30, so that rotations do not take that long. The associations are usually informal and may last only as long as one rotation.

How do these systems work? What prevents someone from quitting after getting a lump sum? Ethnographic evidence indicates that defaulting on regular contributions is so rare that participants consider it unthinkable. Once a person joins a rotating credit association, there is strong social pressure to continue paying regularly. A person who joins does not have to fill out paperwork, as in a bank. All that is needed is a reputation for trustworthiness. There is often a social component to the association. Some have regular meetings with socializing and entertainment.[25] A rotating credit association may have one of three types of distribution. In some, a leader may decide the order of rotation, usually making the judgment on perceived need. In others, distribution is based on a random drawing or the roll of dice. The third method is based on who is willing to pay the highest interest.[26]

The principle of a rotating credit association often has roots in traditional sharing systems. For example, among the Kikuyu, related women would work together to weed or harvest each other's fields in turn. When a person had special expenses, such as a funeral, there would be a contribution party and everyone who came would make a contribution. Nici Nelson describes a very successful rotating credit association that developed in a squatter area of Nairobi. The founding woman organized a group of women of similar economic status who came from the Kiambu district of Kenya. Early in 1971 the group had about 20 members, but expanded to about 30. In a few years the founder also started a land-buying cooperative. While the rotating credit association remained embedded in the cooperative, eventually it lost its usefulness as members became wealthy enough to have bank accounts of their own. It disbanded in the 1990s. At one point, men tried to join,

Entrance to the Cuban-Chinese Lung Kong Association in Havana, Cuba.

but the women refused to allow it. One woman said: "They will take over and not let us speak in our own cooperative."[27]

In Ghana, despite 30 years of national banking institutions, most saving methods are still informal. In 1991 it was estimated that 55 percent of the money in the country was saved informally. Rotating credit associations flourish. Women are more likely to join rotating credit associations than men, and the associations or clubs tend to be sex-segregated. The club names often reflect their emphasis on mutual aid. One club in the Accra Makola Market has a name that translates as "Our Well-Being Depends on Others."[28] Most of the savings are used to provide capital for trading activities.

In societies that depend on sharing, saving money is difficult. Others may ask you for money, and there may be an obligation to give it to them. However, if there is a rotating credit association, you can say that you are obliged to save for your contribution and people will understand. Rotating credit associations also appear to work well when people find it hard to delay gratification. The social pressure of the group appears sufficient to push people to save enough for their regular contribution and the windfall you get when your turn comes is gratifying.[29]

When people move far outside their homelands, they may make even more use of such associations. For example, rotating credit associations in Korea go back to 1633. In the Los Angeles area, Koreans are even more likely to use rotating credit associations, mostly to accumulate sums for business.[30]

Multiethnic Associations

Although many voluntary associations draw on people from the same regional or ethnic background, increasingly in the modern world voluntary groups draw members from many different backgrounds. For example, the Kafaina, or Wok Meri ("women's work"), associations in Papua New Guinea are savings and loan associations that link thousands of women from different tribal areas.[31] Originally, there were smaller groups that started as savings associations in particular localities, but links between groups developed as women who married out of a village encouraged a relative back home or in another village to start a "daughter" group. "Mother–daughter" visits between groups can last for three days, as one group hosts another and the groups exchange money. All money received from another group is placed in a netbag that is hidden and cannot be touched, so the savings grow over time. When a group accumulates a certain amount, a building the size of a men's house is built for the association and a very large ceremony is held.

Does the development of these women's associations translate into new power for women in their traditionally male-dominated societies? That has yet to happen (see the box "Do Separate Women's Associations Increase Women's Status and Power?"). Apparently frustrated by their exclusion from local politics, the women are increasingly participating in the Kafaina movement. They may have intergroup exchanges and they may now engage in public speaking, but so far their arena is still separate from the men's arena.

Just as the Kafaina women's associations seem to be a response to perceived deprivation, the formation of associations with multiethnic or regional membership is not unusual where colonialism or other political domination is recognized as a common problem. For example, in Alaska in the 1960s, Native Americans felt threatened by proposals for economic development that they thought would threaten their subsistence resources. Many regional and ethnic associations formed during this crisis, but perhaps more significant from the point of view of achieving substantial compensation and titles to land was the formation of a pan-Alaska association called the Alaska Federation of Natives. What made the amalgamation possible? Like the leaders of multiethnic movements in many places, the leaders at the highest levels seem to have had a lot of things in common. They were educated, urban dwellers who worked at professional occupations. Perhaps most important, many of them had attended the same schools.[32]

Multiethnic and multiregional associations have often been involved in independence movements all over the world. Often, revolutionary political parties develop out of such associations and lead the efforts to gain independence.

The Kafaina women's savings and loan associations in New Guinea often encourage relatives to start "daughter" organizations. At a ceremony for the new organization, a "daughter" doll is displayed.

Why independence movements develop in some places but not in others is not yet understood.

Other Interest Groups

Societies such as the United States consist of people from many different ethnic backgrounds. Often there are voluntary ethnic and regional associations. But the majority of the voluntary associations in our own and other complex societies have members who belong because of common, achieved interests. These common interests include occupation (so we have trade unions and professional associations), political affiliation (as in national political parties and political action groups), recreation (sports and game clubs, fan clubs, music and theater groups), charities, and social clubs. The larger and more diversified the society, the more different kinds of associations there are. They bring together people with common interests, aspirations, or qualifications, and they provide opportunities to work for social causes, for self-improvement, or to satisfy a need for new and stimulating experiences. We join clubs and other interest groups because we want to achieve particular goals. Not the least of such goals is identification with a "corporate" group and through it the acquisition of status and influence.

Joining clubs is much more important in some societies than in others. Norway is an example of a society with a rich organizational life. Even in areas with small communities there are many different clubs. For example, Douglas Caulkins found that in the municipality of Volda, a town of about 7,000, there were 197 organizations. People were expected to be active in at least a couple of organizations, and these groups met regularly. In fact, there were so many meetings that organizations were expected to coordinate their calendars so that the meetings would not interfere with one another.[33] Why some societies, like Norway, have so much involvement with voluntary associations is not well understood. Nor do we understand what the consequences of such involvement may be. Norway happens to have a particularly low crime rate and it scores high on other indicators of social and economic health.[34] Does the complexity of its organizational life and its many overlapping involvements play a role in its social health? We don't know, because cross-cultural studies to test that possibility have not been done.

Explaining Variation in Associations

Anthropologists are not content to provide descriptions of the structure and operation of human associations. They also seek to understand why different types of associations develop. For example, what may account for the development of age-set systems? S. N. Eisenstadt's comparative study of African age-sets led him to the hypothesis that when kinship groups fail to carry out functions important to the integration of society—such as political, educational, and economic functions—age-set systems arise to fill the void. Age-set systems may provide a workable solution to a society's need for functional divisions among its members, because age is a criterion that can be applied to all members of society in the allocation of roles.[35] But it is not at all clear why age-set systems arise to fill the void left by lack of kinship organization. Many societies have kin structures that are limited in scope, yet the majority of them have not adopted an age-set system.

B. Bernardi, in his critical evaluation of Nilo-Hamitic age-set systems, also suggested that age-set systems arise to make up for a deficiency in social organization.[36] But, in contrast with Eisenstadt, Bernardi specifically suggested why more social organization is necessary and what particular deficiencies in the previous form of organization should favor development of age-sets. He hypothesized that age-set systems arise in societies that have a history of territorial rivalry, lack central authority, and have only dispersed kin groups. When all three factors are present, he argued, the need for a mechanism of territorial integration is supplied by an age-set system.

One cross-cultural study suggests that territorial rivalry, as indicated by warfare, may favor the development of age-set systems, but this study found no evidence to support Bernardi's hypothesis that age-sets develop in societies that lack central authority and have only dispersed kin groups.[37] So it does not seem that age-set societies are deficient in political or kinship organization. An alternative explanation, which is consistent with the cross-cultural evidence, is that age-set systems arise in societies that have both frequent warfare and local groups that change in size and composition throughout the year. In such situations, men may not always be able to rely on their kinsmen for cooperation in warfare because the kinsmen are not always nearby. Age-sets, however, can provide allies *wherever* one happens to be.[38] This interpretation suggests that age-set systems arise *in addition to,* rather than as alternatives to, kin-based and politically based forms of integration.[39]

As for voluntary associations whose membership is variably ascribed—that is, determined at birth but not found in all persons of a given age-sex category—it is difficult to say exactly what causes them to arise. As already noted, there are suggestions that voluntary associations of all types become more numerous, and more important, as the society harboring them advances in technology, complexity, and scale. No definitive evidence is yet available to support this explanation, but the following trends seem to be sufficiently established to merit consideration.

First, there is urbanization. Developing societies are becoming urban, and as their cities grow, so does the number of people separated from their traditional kinship ties and local customs. It is not surprising, then, that the early voluntary associations should be mutual aid societies, established first to take over kin obligations in case of death and later broadening their benefits in other directions. In this respect, the recent associations of the developing African societies closely resemble the early English laboring-class associations. Those clubs also served to maintain the city migrants' contacts with former traditions and culture. The regional associations in Latin America resemble the regional associations of European immigrants in the United States. Such associations also seem to arise in response to the migrants' or immigrants' needs in the new home.

Second, there is an economic factor. Migrants and immigrants try to adapt to new economic conditions, and group interests in the new situations have to be organized, promoted, and protected.

Why, then, do variably ascribed associations tend to be replaced by clubs of the achieved category in highly industrialized societies? Perhaps the strong focus on specialization in industrialized societies is reflected in the formation of specialized groups. Possibly the emphasis on achievement in industrialized societies is another contributing factor. Perhaps, too, the trend toward uniformity, encouraged by mass marketing and the mass media, is progressively weakening the importance of regional and ethnic distinctions. The result seems to be that the more broadly based organizations are being replaced by more narrowly based associations that are more responsive to particular needs not being met by the institutions of mass society.

⊚ Summary

1. Associations or interest groups have the following characteristics in common: (a) some kind of formal, institutional structure exists; (b) some people are excluded from membership; (c) membership is based on commonly shared interests or purposes; and (d) there is a clearly discernible sense of mutual pride and belonging. Membership varies according to whether or not it is voluntary and whether the qualities of members are universally ascribed, variably ascribed, or achieved.

2. Age-sets are nonvoluntary associations whose members belong because of universally ascribed characteristics—that is, groups of persons of similar age and sex who move through life's stages together. Entry into the system is usually by an initiation ceremony. Transitions to new stages are usually marked by succession rituals. Unisex associations restrict membership to one sex. In noncommercial societies membership in such associations (usually male) is generally nonvoluntary.

3. Regional and ethnic organizations are voluntary associations whose members belong because of variably ascribed characteristics. Both usually occur in societies where technological advance is accelerating, bringing with it economic and social complexity. Despite a variety of types, regional and ethnic associations have in common an emphasis on (a) helping members adapt to new conditions; (b) keeping members in touch with home-area traditions; and (c) promoting improved living conditions for members who have recently migrated to urban areas.

4. Associations whose members belong because of variably ascribed characteristics tend to be replaced in highly industrialized societies by associations whose membership is based on achieved qualities.

⊚ Glossary Terms

achieved qualities	404	unisex association	406
age-grade	404	universally ascribed qualities	404
age-set	404		
ascribed qualities	404	variably ascribed qualities	404
associations	403		

⊚ Critical Questions

1. How could young people who might join gangs be encouraged not to?

2. What associations do you belong to, and why?

3. Many formerly unisex associations have opened their membership to the opposite sex. What might be the results of this change?

⊚ Research Navigator

1. Please go to www.researchnavigator.com and enter your LOGIN NAME and PASSWORD. For instructions on registering for the first time, please view the detailed instructions at the end of Chapter 1.

2. Using Link Library (Anthropology/Cultural Anthropology) find the Web site "Proseminar in Sociocultural Anthropology." You will find a discussion of anthropology organizations. Name and briefly describe two of them. In the context of what we discussed in the chapter, indicate what the purposes of the association are and what type of association it is (e.g., a nonvoluntary association based on ascribed characteristics, a voluntary association based on achieved characteristics, etc.).

⊚ Discovering Anthropology: Researchers at Work

Read Richard H. Thompson's "Chinatowns: Immigrant Communities in Transition" in *Discovering Anthropology*. Answer the following questions.

1. Describe the role that associations played in the earliest Chinatowns.

2. According to Thompson, the traditional associations were more important to certain classes of Chinese Americans. Explain.

3. Describe some of the tensions between the generations.

CHAPTER TWENTY-FOUR

Political Life: Social Order and Disorder

For people in the United States, the phrase *political life* has many connotations. It may call to mind the various branches of government: the executive branch, from the president on the national level to governors on the state level to mayors on the local level; legislative institutions, from Congress to state legislatures to city councils; and administrative bureaus, from federal government departments to local agencies.

Political life may also evoke thoughts of political parties, interest groups, lobbying, campaigning, and voting. In other words, when people living in the United States think of political life, they may think first of "politics," the activities (not always apparent) that influence who is elected or appointed to political office, what public policies are established, how they get established, and who benefits from those policies.

But in the United States and in many other countries, *political life* involves even more than government and politics. Political life also involves ways of preventing or resolving troubles and disputes both within and outside the society. Internally, a complex society such as ours may employ mediation or arbitration to resolve industrial disputes, a police force to prevent crimes or track down criminals, and courts and a penal system to deal with lawbreakers as well as with social conflict in general. Externally, such a society may establish embassies in other nations and develop and utilize its armed forces both to maintain security and to support domestic and foreign interests.

By means of all these informal and formal political mechanisms, complex societies establish social order and minimize, or at least deal with, social disorder.

Formal governments have become more and more widespread around the world over the last 100 years, as powerful colonizing countries have imposed political systems upon others or as people less formally organized realized that they needed governmental mechanisms to deal with the larger world. But many societies known to anthropology did not have political officials or political parties or courts or armies. Indeed, the band or village was the largest autonomous political unit in 50 percent of the societies in the ethnographic record, as of the times they were first described. And those units were only informally organized; that is, they did not have individuals or agencies formally authorized to make and implement policy or resolve disputes. Does this mean they did not have political life? If we mean political life as we know it in our own society, then the answer has to be that they did not. But if we look beyond our formal institutions and mechanisms—if we ask what functions these institutions and mechanisms perform—we find that all societies have had political activities and beliefs to create and maintain social order and cope with social disorder.

Many of the kinds of groups we discussed in the three previous chapters, on families, descent groups, and associations, have political functions. But when anthropologists talk about *political organization* or *political life,* they are particularly focusing on activities and beliefs pertaining to *territorial groups.* Territorial groups, in whose behalf political activities may be organized, range from small communities, such as bands and villages, to large communities, such as towns and cities, to multilocal groups, such as districts or regions, entire nations, or even groups of nations.

As we shall see, the different types of political organization, as well as how people participate in politics and how they cope with conflict, are often strongly linked to variation in food-getting, economy, and social stratification.

◉ Variation in Types of Political Organization

Societies in the ethnographic record vary in *level of political integration*—that is, the largest territorial group on whose behalf political activities are organized—and in the degree to which political authority is centralized or concentrated in the integrated group. When we describe the political integration of particular societies, we focus on their traditional political systems. In many societies known to anthropology, the small community (band or village) was traditionally the largest territorial group on whose behalf political activities were organized. The authority structure in such societies did not involve any centralization; there was no political authority whose jurisdiction included more than one community. In other societies political activities were traditionally organized sometimes on behalf of a multilocal group, but there was no permanent authority at the top. And in still other societies political activities were often traditionally organized on behalf of multilocal territorial groups, and there was a centralized or supreme political authority at the top. In the modern world, however, every society has been incorporated into some larger, centralized political system.

Elman Service suggested that most societies can be classified into four principal types of political organization: bands, tribes, chiefdoms, and states.[1] Although Service's classification does not fit all societies, it is a useful way to show how societies vary in trying to create and maintain social order. We often use the present tense in our discussion, because that is the convention in ethnographic writing, but the reader should remember that most societies that used to be organized at the band, tribe, or chiefdom level are now incorporated into larger political entities. With a handful of exceptions, there are no politically autonomous bands or tribes or chiefdoms in the world anymore.

Band Organization

Some societies were composed of fairly small and usually nomadic groups of people. Each of these groups is conventionally called a **band** and is politically autonomous. That is, in **band organization** the local group or community is the largest group that acts as a political unit. Because most recent food collectors had band organization, some anthropologists contend that this type of political organization characterized nearly all societies before the development of agriculture, or until about 10,000 years ago. But we have to remember that almost all of the described food-collecting societies are or were located in marginal environments; and almost all were affected by more dominant societies nearby.[2] So it is possible that what we call "band organization" may not have been typical of food collectors in the distant or prehistoric past.

Bands are typically small, with less than 100 people usually, often considerably less. Each small band occupies a large territory, so population density is low. Band size often varies by season, with the band breaking up or recombining according to the food resources available at a given time and place. Inuit bands, for example, are smaller in the winter, when food is hard to find, and larger in the summer, when there is sufficient food to feed a larger group.

Political decision making within the band is generally informal. The "modest informal authority"[3] that does exist can be seen in the way decisions affecting the group are made. Because the formal, permanent office of leader typically does not exist, decisions such as when camp has to be moved or how a hunt is to be arranged are either agreed upon by the community as a whole or made by the best-qualified member. Leadership, when it is exercised by an individual, is not the consequence of bossing or throwing one's weight about. Each band may have its informal **headman,** or its most proficient hunter, or a person most accomplished in rituals. There may be one person with all these qualities, or several persons, but such a person or persons will have gained status through the community's recognition of skill, good sense, and humility. Leadership, in other words, stems not from power but from influence, not from office but from admired personal qualities.

In Inuit bands, each settlement may have its headman, who acquires his influence because the other members of the community recognize his good judgment and superior skills. The headman's advice concerning the movement of the band and other community matters is generally heeded, but he possesses no permanent authority and has no power to impose sanctions of any kind. Inuit leaders are male, but men often consult their wives in private, and women who hunt seem to have more influence than those who do not.[4] In any case, leadership exists only in a very restricted sense, as among the Iglulik Inuit, for example:

> Within each settlement . . . there is as a rule an older man who enjoys the respect of the others and who decides when a move is to be made to another hunting center, when a hunt is to be started, how the spoils are to be divided, when the dogs are to be fed. . . . He is called *isumaitoq,* "he who thinks." It is not always the oldest man, but as a rule an elderly man who is a clever hunter or, as head of a large family, exercises great authority. He cannot be called a chief; there is no obligation to follow his counsel; but they do so in most cases, partly because they rely on his experience, partly because it pays to be on good terms with this man.[5]

A summary of the general features of band organization can be found in Table 24–1. Note, however, that there are exceptions to these generalizations. For example, not all known food collectors are organized at the band level or have all the features of a band type of society. Classic exceptions are the Native American societies of the Northwest Pacific coast, who had enormous resources of salmon and other fish, relatively large and permanent villages, and political organization beyond the level of the typical band societies in the ethnographic record.

Tribal Organization

When local communities mostly act autonomously but there are kinship groups (such as clans or lineages) or associations (such as age-sets) that can potentially integrate several local groups into a larger unit (**tribe**), we say that the society has **tribal organization.** Unfortunately, the term *tribe* is sometimes used to refer to an entire society; that is, an entire language group may be called a tribe. But a tribal type of political system does not usually permit the entire society to act as a unit; all the communities in a tribal society may be linked only occasionally for some political (usually

Table 24–1   Suggested Trends in Political Organization and Other Social Characteristics

Type of Organization	Highest Level of Political Integration	Specialization of Political Officials	Predominant Mode of Subsistence	Community Size and Population Density	Social Differentiation	Major Form of Distribution
Band	Local group or band	Little or none: informal leadership	Food collecting	Very small communities, very low density	Egalitarian	Mostly reciprocity
Tribe	Sometimes multilocal group	Little or none: informal leadership	Extensive (shifting) agriculture and/or herding	Small communities, low density	Egalitarian	Mostly reciprocity
Chiefdom	Multilocal group	Some	Extensive or intensive agriculture and/or herding	Large communities, medium density	Rank	Reciprocity and redistribution
State	Multilocal group, often entire language group	Much	Intensive agriculture and herding	Cities and towns, high density	Class and caste	Mostly market exchange

In many egalitarian societies, leadership shifts informally from one person to another. In much of New Guinea there is more competition for achieving "big" status. On Vanatinai the women compete as well as the men, so there are "big women" as well as "big men." Here a "big woman" paints the face of her cousin's widow for a feast honoring the dead man.

military) purpose. Thus, what distinguishes tribal from band political organization is the presence in the former of some multilocal, but not usually societywide, integration. The multilocal integration, however, is *not permanent,* and it is *informal* in the sense that it is not headed by political officials. Frequently, the integration is called into play only when an outside threat arises; when the threat disappears, the local groups revert to self-sufficiency.[6] Tribal organization may seem fragile—and, of course, it usually is—but the fact that there are social ways to integrate local groups into larger political entities means that societies with tribal organization are militarily a good deal more formidable than societies with band organization.

Societies with tribal political organization are similar to band societies in their tendency to be egalitarian (see Table 24–1). At the local level, informal leadership is also characteristic. In those tribal societies where kinship provides the basic framework of social organization, the elders of the local kin groups tend to have considerable influence; where age-sets are important, a particular age-set is looked to for leadership. But, in contrast to band societies, societies with tribal organization generally are food producers. And because cultivation and animal husbandry are generally more productive than hunting and gathering, the population density of tribal societies is generally higher, local groups are larger, and the way of life is more sedentary than in hunter-gatherer bands.

KINSHIP BONDS   Frequently communities are linked to each other by virtue of belonging to the same kin group, usually a unilineal group such as a lineage or clan. A **segmentary lineage system** is one type of tribal integration based on kinship. A society with such a system is composed of segments, or parts, each similar to the others in structure and function. Every local segment belongs to a hierarchy of lineages stretching farther and farther back genealogically. The hierarchy of lineages, then, unites the segments into larger and larger genealogical groups. The closer two groups are genealogically, the greater their general closeness. In the event of a dispute between members of different segments, people related more closely to one contestant than to another take the side of their nearest kinsman.

The Tiv of northern Nigeria offer a classic example of a segmentary lineage system, one that happens to link all the Tiv into a single genealogical structure or tribe. The Tiv are a large society, numbering more than 800,000. Figure 24–1 is a representation of the Tiv lineage structure as described by Paul Bohannan. In the figure, there are four levels of lineages. Each of the smallest lineages, symbolized by a through *h,* is in turn embedded in more inclusive lineages. So minimal lineages *a* and *b* are together in lineage *1.* Lineages *1* and *2* are embedded in lineage *A.* Territorial organization follows lineage hierarchy. As shown in the bottom of the figure, the most closely related lineages have territories near each other. Minimal lineages *a* and *b* live next to each other; their

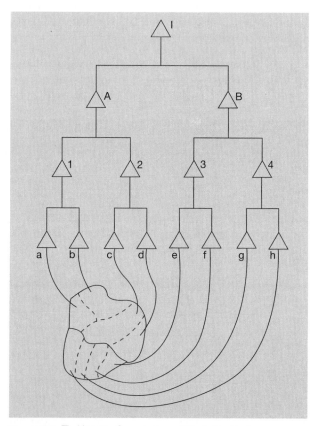

Figure 24–1 Tiv Lineage Segments and Their Territories

Source: Adapted from Paul Bohannan, "The Migration and Expansion of the Tiv," *Africa,* 24 (1954): 3.

combined territory is the territory of their higher-order lineage, *I*. Lineage *A* in turn has a territory that is differentiated from lineage *B*. All of Tivland is said to descend from one ancestor, represented by *I*.[7]

Tiv lineage organization is the foundation of Tiv political organization. A look at Figure 24–1 helps to explain how. A dispute between lineages (and territories) *a* and *b* remains minor, since no more than "brother" segments are involved. But a dispute between *a* and *c* involves lineages *1* and *2* as well, with the requirement that *b* assist *a* and *d* support *c*. This process of mutual support, called **complementary opposition,** means that segments will unite only in a confrontation with some other group. Groups that will fight with each other in a minor dispute might coalesce at some later time against a larger group.

The segmentary lineage system was presumably very effective in allowing the Tiv to intrude into new territory and take land from other tribal societies with smaller descent groups. Individual Tiv lineage segments could call on support from related lineages when faced with border troubles. Conflicts within the society—that is, between segments—especially in border areas, were often turned outward, "releasing internal pressure in an explosive blast against other peoples."[8]

Segmentary lineage systems may have military advantages even when they do not unite the entire society. A classic example is the Nuer of the Upper Nile region, who had tribal, but not societywide, organization because of their segmentary lineages. In the early 1800s, the Nuer had a territory of about 8,700 square miles and the neighboring Dinka had ten times that much. But by 1890, the Nuer had cut a 100-mile swath through Dinka territory, increasing Nuer territory to 35,000 square miles. Even though the Nuer and Dinka were culturally very similar, the segmentary lineage organization of the Nuer seems to have given them a significant military advantage in their incursions into Dinka territory.[9]

A segmentary lineage system may generate a formidable military force, but the combinations of manpower it produces are temporary, forming and dissolving as the occasion demands.[10] Tribal political organization does not make for a political system that more or less permanently integrates a number of communities.

AGE-SET SYSTEMS In the previous chapter we described age-set systems in general. Here we discuss how age-sets can function as the basis of a tribal type of political organization, as among the Karimojong of northeastern Uganda.[11]

The Karimojong age-set system has an important bearing on day-to-day tribal life. As herders, Karimojong adults are often separated from their usual settlements. Herders will meet, mingle for a while, then go their separate ways, but each may call upon other members of his age-set wherever he goes. The age-set system is important among the Karimojong because it immediately allocates to each individual a place in the system and thereby establishes for him an appropriate pattern of response. A quarrel in camp will be settled by the representatives of the senior age-set who are present, regardless of which section of the tribe they may belong to.

Among the Karimojong, political leaders are not elected from among the elders of a particular age-set, nor are they appointed; they acquire their positions informally. Usually a man's background, and the ability he has demonstrated in public debates over a period of time, will result in his being considered by the men of his neighborhood to be their spokesman. His function is to announce what course of action seems required in a particular situation, to initiate that action, and then to coordinate it after it has begun.

Most political leaders exercise their authority within the local sphere because the pastoral nature of the Karimojong economy, with its dispersed groups and movement from one feeding ground to another, offers no alternative. From time to time an elder may acquire the status of a prophet and be awarded respect and obedience on a tribal scale. He will be called upon to lead sacrifices (to avert misfortune), to undertake rainmaking (to bring prosperity), and so on. Yet even a prophet's prestige and authority do not warrant him a position of overlord or chief.[12]

Chiefdom Organization

Whereas a tribe has some informal mechanism that can integrate more than one community, a **chiefdom** has some *formal* structure that integrates more than one community into a political unit. The formal structure could consist of a council with or without a chief, but most commonly there is a person—the **chief**—who has higher rank or authority than others. Most societies at the chiefdom level of organization contain more than one multicommunity political unit or chiefdom, each headed by a district chief or a council. There may also be more than one level of chief beyond the community, such as district chiefs and higher-level chiefs. Compared with tribal societies, societies with chiefdoms are more densely populated and their communities more permanent, partly as a consequence of their generally greater economic productivity (see Table 24–1).

The position of chief, which is sometimes hereditary and generally permanent, bestows high status on its holder. Most chiefdoms have social ranking and accord the chief and his family greater access to prestige. The chief may redistribute goods, plan and direct the use of public labor, supervise religious ceremonies, and direct military activities on behalf of the chiefdom. In South Pacific chiefdoms, the chiefs carried out most of these duties. In Fijian chiefdoms, for example, the chief was responsible for the redistribution of goods and the coordination of labor:

> [The chief] could summon the community's labor on his own behalf, or on behalf of someone else who requested it, or for general purposes. . . . Besides his right to summon labor he accumulated the greater proportion of the first fruits of the yam crop . . . and he benefited from other forms of food presentation, or by the acquisition of special shares in ordinary village distribution. . . . Thus, the paramount [chief] would collect a significant part of the surplus production of

the community and redistribute it in the general welfare.[13]

In contrast to leaders in tribal societies, who generally have to earn their privileges by their personal qualities, hereditary chiefs are said to have those qualities in their "blood." A high-ranking chief in Polynesia, a huge triangular area of islands in the South Pacific, inherited special religious power called *mana. Mana* sanctified his rule and protected him.[14] Chiefs in Polynesia had so much religious power that missionaries could convert people to Christianity only after their chiefs had been converted.[15]

In most chiefdoms, the chiefs did not have the power to compel people to obey them; people would act in accordance with the chief's wishes because the chief was respected and often had religious authority. But in the most complex paramount chiefdoms, such as those of Hawaii and Tahiti, the chiefs seemed to have more compelling sanctions than the "power" of respect or *mana.* Substantial amounts of goods and services collected by the chiefs were used to support subordinates, including specialists such as high priests, political envoys, and warriors who could be sent to quell rebellious factions.[16] When redistributions do not go to everybody—when chiefs are allowed to keep items for their own purposes—and when a chief begins to use armed force, the political system is on the way to becoming what we call a state.

State Organization

A **state,** according to one more or less standard definition, is "an autonomous political unit, encompassing many communities within its territory and having a centralized government with the power to collect taxes, draft men for work or war, and decree and enforce laws."[17] States, then, have a complex, centralized political structure that includes a wide range of permanent institutions with legislative, executive, and judicial functions and a large bureaucracy. Central to this definition is the concept of legitimate force used to implement policies both internally and externally. In states, the government tries to maintain a monopoly on the use of physical force.[18] This monopoly can be seen in the development of formal and specialized instruments of social control: a police force, a militia, or a standing army.

Just as a particular society may contain more than one band, tribe, or chiefdom, so may it contain more than one state. The contiguously distributed population speaking a single language may or may not be politically unified in a single state. Ancient Greece was composed of many city-states; so, too, was Italy until the 1870s. German speakers are also not politically unified; Austria and Germany are separate states, and Germany itself was not politically unified until the 1870s. We say that a society has **state organization** when it is composed of one or more political units that are states.

A state may include more than one society. Multisociety states often are the result of conquest or colonial control when the dominant political authority, itself a state, imposes a centralized government over a territory with many different societies and cultures, as the British did in Nigeria and Kenya.

Colonialism is a common feature of state societies. But not all colonialisms are alike. Archaeology and history tell us about various kinds of colonialism. The expanding state society may send people to build a new imperial settlement in some other place to trade or protect trade routes, like the

Presenting *kava,* a special drink, to a chief in Fiji. The chief wears a tie.

MIGRANTS AND IMMIGRANTS

The Growth of Cities

Humans are a social bunch. They generally live in groups or communities. These groups range in size from bands to villages to town and cities. Each may function as a political entity; activities are organized in their behalf by headmen, mayors, councils, and other political "officials" and groups. Nearly half of the world's human population now lives in cities, which are usually defined as communities where few are directly involved in food getting. An even larger proportion of humanity will be urban dwellers 30 years from now.

The explosive growth of cities over the past century or so is not due to more births than deaths in the cities. Rather cities have grown mostly because of migration from rural areas of the country, and from rural areas in other countries. Recall the exodus of the Irish to Britain and the U.S. because of the "potato famine," the massive migrations from the villages of Germany, Italy, and Greece in the 19th and 20th centuries, and the huge migrations particularly in the last 50 years from rural Mexico and China. It is probably safe to say that many millions of people in many parts of the world would move to the U.S., Canada, and Western Europe tomorrow, if they could. Poverty is one "push" factor. Flight from persecution is another. Many parts of the world are not safe, particularly for poor people. Or other places look more promising. Think of the state of California in the U.S. The vast majority of its inhabitants were born elsewhere. True, in the modern world it is possible for some people to go "home" for a visit, even halfway around the world. But for many migrants, now and in the recent past, the move was one way. Because you may have run away from poverty, persecution, and war, you couldn't (or wouldn't) go home again.

An increasing number of anthropologists call themselves "urban anthropologists." They study why people move, and how they adjust to new places. They do so because so many people are moving now. There are villages in rural Spain and France that are mostly empty during the week. The owners live and work in Barcelona or Paris, and they hardly ever go "home." Indeed, their village houses may not even be available to them much, because they are usually rented to tourists! From across the Atlantic, no less.

Cities everywhere have problems, even in the most developed countries. It is difficult and expensive to provide water, power, sanitation, and other services to perhaps millions of city-dwellers. Yet in every country people are leaving rural areas and going to cities for a variety of reasons. Some are political refugees, like the Hmong from Laos who live now in St. Paul, Minnesota. Then there are the people from Congo and Sudan, from Kosovo and Northern Ireland, who have fled civil wars. There are other reasons to leave too. Technological improvements may have reduced the need for rural labor, which happened in the U.S. South after the 1930s. Or the rural opportunities cannot support the increased number of mouths to be fed. Where do they go? Usually not to other rural areas but rather to cities, often in other countries, where there are jobs available. In the more urbanized countries the cities have acquired "suburbs," where many of the people in a metropolitan area may actually live. But hardly anyone is left on the farm—only just a few percent of the population in the more developed countries.

In the last half of the 20th century, with the building of suburbs, there seems to have been a turning away from cities in many countries. Cities lost population as people moved to the suburbs to have more living space, or a garden, or "better" schools for their children, or to escape from the threat of violence. But recently the flow has started to reverse, in North America and elsewhere. The suburbanites are coming back to the cities, perhaps because people are getting tired of commuting longer and longer distances to jobs and recreation. This is particularly so with wealthier people whose children have grown up and moved away, and with more people living until older ages, many want to move closer to the places where they mostly spend their time. Despite the social inequality and violence, cities have always been the places to go for jobs and other activities. Concerts, theaters, restaurants, museums, amusement parks, hospitals, and professional sports stadiums have always been located in cities or nearby.

The "push" out of the rural areas, the "pull" of the cities, is hard to resist, despite the enormous political problems of urban living. As the old song laments, "Howya goin' keep 'em down on the farm after they've seen Paree?"

Source: Melvin Ember and Carol R. Ember, eds., *Encyclopedia of Urban Cultures: Cities and Cultures Around the World,* 4 vols. (Danbury, CT: Grolier/Scholastic, 2002).

British, Spanish, and others did. Or the colonial power may displace and move parts of the original population, as the Inka empire did.[19] Most of the expanding state societies we know about are usually called *empires.* They incorporated other societies and states. The extension of U.S. power in modern times, for example, by persuading other countries to let the U.S. build military bases, has led some commentators to refer to an American empire, even though the U.S. did not always establish colonies where they had economic and political control.[20]

Nearly all of the multisociety states that emerged after World War II were the results of successful independence movements against colonial powers.[21] Most have retained their political unity despite the fact that they still contain many different societies. For example, Nigeria remains unified despite a civil war; the eastern section called Biafra (mostly populated by people of Ibo culture) tried unsuccessfully 30 years ago to secede, and subsequently there has been serious conflict among some of the constituent societies.

Multisociety or multiethnic states may also form voluntarily, in reaction to external threat. Switzerland comprises cantons, each of which speaks mainly French, German, Italian, or Romansch; the various cantons confederated originally to shake off control by the Holy Roman Empire. But some states have lost their unity recently, including the former Union of Soviet Socialist Republics (USSR) and much of Yugoslavia.

In addition to their strictly political features, state-organized societies are generally supported by intensive agriculture. The high productivity of the agriculture allows for the emergence of cities, a high degree of economic and other kinds of specialization, and market or commercial exchange. In addition, state societies usually have class stratification (see Table 24–1). Cities have grown tremendously in the last 100 years, largely as a result of migration and immigration.

When states come into existence, people's access to scarce resources is radically altered. So, too, is their ability not to listen to leaders: You cannot refuse to pay taxes and go unpunished. Of course, the rulers of a state do not maintain the social order by force alone. The people must believe, at least to some extent, that those in power have a legitimate right to govern. If the people think otherwise, history suggests that those in power may eventually lose their ability to control. Witness the recent downfall of Communist parties throughout most of eastern Europe and the former Soviet Union.

So force and the threat of force are not enough to explain the legitimacy of power, and the inequities that occur commonly, in state societies. But then what does? There are various theories. The rulers of early states often claimed divine descent to buttress their legitimacy, but this claim is rare nowadays. Another theory is that if parents teach their children to accept all authority, such lessons may generalize to the acceptance of political authority. Some analysts think that people accept state authority for no good reason; the rulers are just able to fool them. Finally, some theorists think that states must provide people with real or rational advantages; otherwise people would not think that the rulers de-

serve to exercise authority. Legitimacy is not an all-or-none phenomenon; it varies in degree. Why it has varied, in different times and places, remains a classic question in the social sciences, including anthropology, as well as in philosophy and other humanistic disciplines.[22]

A state society can retain its legitimacy, or at least its power, for a long time. For example, the Roman Empire was a complex state society that dominated the Mediterranean and Near East for hundreds of years. It began as a city-state that waged war to acquire additional territory. At its height, the Roman Empire embraced more than 55 million people[23]; the capital city of Rome had a population of well over a million.[24] The empire included parts of what are now Great Britain, France, Spain, Portugal, Germany, Rumania, Turkey, Greece, Armenia, Egypt, Israel, and Syria.

Another example of a state society was the kingdom of Nupe in West Africa, now part of the nation-state of Nigeria. As is characteristic of state societies, Nupe society was rigidly stratified. At the top of the social system was the king, or *etsu.* Beneath the king, members of the royal family formed the highest aristocratic class. Next in order were two other classes of nobility, the local chiefs and the military leaders. At the bottom were the commoners, who had neither prestige nor power and no share in political authority.

The Nupe king possessed ultimate authority in many judicial matters. Minor disputes and civil cases were handled by local village councils, but serious criminal cases were the prerogative of the king. Such cases, referred to as "crimes for the king," were brought before the royal court by the king's local representatives. The king and his counselors judged the cases and determined suitable punishments.

The most powerful influence of the state over the Nupe people was in the area of taxation. The king was given the power to impose taxes and collect them from every household. Payment was made either in money (cowrie shells originally and, later, British currency) or certain gifts, such as cloth, mats, and slaves. Much of the revenue collected was kept by the king, and the remainder was shared with his local representatives and lords. In return for the taxes they paid, the people received security—protection against invasion and domestic disorder.[25]

Factors Associated with Variation in Political Organization

The kinds of political organization we call band, tribal, chiefdom, and state are points on a continuum of levels of political integration or unification, from small-scale local autonomy to large-scale regional unification. There also is variation in political authority, from a few temporary and informal political leaders to large numbers of permanent, specialized political officials, from the absence of coercive political power to the monopoly of public force by a central authority. These aspects of variation in political organization are generally associated with shifts from food collection to more intensive food production, from small to large communities, from low to high population densities, from an emphasis on reciprocity to redistribution to market

Popular will can change governments. Massive protest in Ukraine led a newly elected president to resign.

exchange, and from egalitarian to rank to fully stratified class societies.

The associations just outlined, which seem to be confirmed by the available cross-cultural evidence, are summarized in Table 24–1. With regard to the relation between level of subsistence technology and political complexity, one cross-cultural study employing a small random sample of societies found that the greater the importance of agriculture in a society, the larger the population that is politically unified and the greater the number and types of political officials.[26] A massive cross-cultural survey reported a similar trend: The more intensive the agriculture, the greater the likelihood of state organization; conversely, societies with no more than local political institutions are likely to depend on hunting, gathering, and fishing.[27]

With regard to community size, the first of these studies also suggested that the larger the leading community, the wider the range of political officials in the society.[28] Robert Textor presented a similar finding: Societies with state organization tend to have cities and towns, whereas those with only local political organization are more likely to have communities with an average population of fewer than 200 persons.[29] Cross-cultural research also tends to confirm that societies with higher levels of political integration are more likely to exhibit social differentiation, especially in the form of class distinctions.[30]

Does this evidence provide us with an explanation for why political organization varies? Clearly, the data indicate that several factors are associated with political development, but exactly why changes in organization occur is not yet understood. Although economic development may be a necessary condition for political development,[31] that relation does not fully explain why political organization should become more complex just because the economy can support it. Some theorists have suggested that competition between

groups may be a more important reason for political consolidation. For example, Elman Service suggested competition as a reason why a society might change from a band level of political organization to a tribal level. Band societies are generally hunter-gatherers. With a changeover to agriculture, population density and competition between groups may increase. Service believed that such competition would foster the development of some informal organization beyond the community—namely, tribal organization—for offense and defense.[32] Indeed, as we saw in the chapters on marital residence and kinship, and associations, both unilineal kinship groups and age-set systems seem to be associated with warfare.

Among agriculturalists, defensive needs might also be the main reason for switching from informal multivillage political organization to more formal chiefdom organization. Formally organized districts are probably more likely to defeat autonomous villages or even segmentary lineage systems.[33] In addition, there may be economic reasons for political development. With regard to chiefdoms, Service suggested that chiefdoms will emerge when redistribution between communities becomes important or when large-scale coordinated work groups are required. The more important these activities are, the more important—and hence more "chiefly"—the organizer and his family presumably become.[34] But redistribution is far from a universal activity of chiefs.[35]

Theory and research on the anthropology of political development have focused mostly on the high end of the scale of political complexity, and particularly on the origins of the first state societies. Those earliest states apparently rose independently of one another, after about 3500 B.C., in what are now southern Iraq, Egypt, northwestern India, northern China, and central Mexico. Several theories have been proposed to explain the rise of the earliest states, but no one theory seems to fit all the known archaeological sequences culminating in early state formation. The reason may be that different conditions in different places favored the emergence of centralized government. The state, by definition, implies the power to organize large populations for collective purposes. In some areas, the impetus may have been the need to organize necessary local or long-distance trade or both. In other areas, the state may have emerged as a way to control defeated populations that could not flee. In still other instances, other factors or a combination of factors may have fostered the development of states. It is still not clear what the specific conditions were that led to the emergence of the state in each of the early centers.[36]

The Spread of State Societies

The state level of political development has come to dominate the world. Societies with states have larger communities and higher population densities than do band, tribal, and chiefdom societies. They also have armies that are ready to fight at almost any time. State systems that have waged war against chiefdoms and tribes have almost always won, and the result has usually been the political incorporation of the losers. For example, the British and, later, the U.S. colonization of much of North America led to the defeat and incorporation of many Native American societies.

The defeat and incorporation of the Native Americans was at least partly due to the catastrophic depopulations they suffered because of epidemic diseases, such as smallpox and measles, that European colonists introduced. Catastrophic depopulation was commonly the outcome of the first contacts between European Americans and the natives of North and South America, as well as the natives of the far islands in the Pacific. People in the New World and the Pacific had not been exposed, and therefore were not resistant, to the

diseases the European Americans carried with them when they began to colonize the world. Before the expansion of Europeans, the people of the New World and the Pacific had been separated for a long time from the people and diseases on the geographically continuous landmass we separate into Europe, Africa, and Asia. Smallpox, measles, and the other former scourges of Europe had largely become childhood diseases that most individuals of European ancestry survived.[37]

Whether by depopulation, conquest, or intimidation, the number of independent political units in the world has decreased strikingly in the last 3,000 years, and especially in the last 200 years. Robert Carneiro estimated that in 1000 B.C., there may have been between 100,000 and 1 million separate political units in the world; today there are fewer than 200.[38] In the ethnographic record, about 50 percent of the 2,000 or so societies described within the last 150 years had only local political integration. That is, the highest level of political integration in one out of two recent societies was the local community.[39] Thus, most of the decrease in the number of independent political units has occurred fairly recently.

But the recent secessions from the former Soviet Union and Yugoslavia and other separatist movements around the world suggest that ethnic rivalries may make for departures from the trend toward larger and larger political units. Ethnic groups that have been dominated by others in multinational states may opt for political autonomy, at least for a while. On the other hand, the separate nations of Western Europe are becoming more unified every day, both politically and economically. So the trend toward larger and larger political units may be continuing, even if there are departures from it now and then.

Extrapolating from past history, a number of investigators have suggested that the entire world will eventually come to be politically integrated, perhaps as soon as the 23rd century and no later than A.D. 4850.[40] Only the future will tell if this prediction will come true. And only the future will

In the governance structure of the European Union (EU), the executive branch (the European Commission) consists of one representative from each EU country.

tell if further political integration in the world will occur peacefully—with all parties agreeing—or by force or the threat of force, as has happened so often in the past.

Variation in Political Process

Anthropologists are increasingly interested in the politics, or political processes, of the societies they study: who acquires influence or power, how they acquire it, and how political decisions are made. But even though we have descriptive accounts of politics in many societies, there is still little comparative or cross-cultural research on what may explain variation in politics.[41]

Getting to Be a Leader

In those societies that have hereditary leadership, which is common in rank societies and in state societies with monarchies, rules of succession usually establish how leadership is inherited. Such leaders are often identifiable in some obviously visible way; they may be permanently marked or tattooed, as in chiefdoms in Polynesia, or they may wear elaborate dress and insignia, as in class-stratified societies (see the discussion of body adornment in the chapter on the arts). But for societies whose leaders are *chosen,* either as informal leaders or as political officials, we need a lot more research to understand why some kinds of people are chosen over others.

A few studies have investigated the personal qualities of leaders in tribal societies. One study, conducted among the Mekranoti-Kayapo of central Brazil, found that leaders, in contrast to followers, tend to be rated by their peers as higher in intelligence, generosity, knowledgeability, ambitiousness, and aggressiveness. Leaders also tend to be older and taller. And despite the egalitarian nature of Mekranoti society (at least with respect to sharing resources), sons of leaders are more likely than others to become leaders.[42]

Research in another Brazilian society, the Kagwahiv of the Amazon region, suggests another personal quality of leaders: They seem to have positive feelings about their fathers and mothers.[43] In many respects, studies of leaders in the United States show them to be not that different from their counterparts in Brazil. But there is one major difference: Mekranoti and Kagwahiv leaders are not wealthier than others; in fact, they give their wealth away. U.S. leaders are generally wealthier than others.[44]

"BIG MEN" In some egalitarian tribal societies, the quest for leadership seems quite competitive. In parts of New Guinea and South America, "big men" compete with other ambitious men to attract followers. Men who want to compete must show that they have magical powers, success in gardening, and bravery in war. But, most important, they have to collect enough goods to throw big parties at which the goods are given away. Big men have to work very hard to attract and keep their followings, for dissatisfied followers can always join other aspiring men.[45] The wives of big men are often leaders too. Among the Kagwahiv, for example, a headman's wife is usually the leader of the women in the community; she is responsible for much of the planning for feasts and often distributes the meat at them.[46]

Although the phenomenon of big men leaders is common throughout New Guinea, researchers are beginning to see variation in the type and extent of "bigmanship" in different areas of New Guinea. For example, in the southern Highlands, groups of men (not just big men) may engage in large-scale giveaways, so big men are not so different from ordinary men. In the northwestern Highlands, on the other hand, big men stand out from other men in striking ways. They make policy for groups of people and organize collective events, they have substantial access to pigs or to valuables acquired in exchanges, and they have control over a substantial amount of labor (more than one wife and fellow kin).[47]

We know that some big men are "bigger" than others, but how does a man get to be a big man? Among the Kumdi-Engamoi, a central Highlands group, a man who wants to be considered a *wua nium* (literally, a "great-important-wealthy man") needs to have many wives and daughters, because the amount of land controlled by a man and how much can be produced on that land depend on the number of women in his family. The more wives he has, the more land he is given to cultivate. He must also be a good speaker. Everyone has the right to speak and give speeches, but to get to be known as a big man requires speaking well and forcefully and knowing when to sum up a consensus. It usually takes a man until his thirties or forties to acquire more than one wife and to make his name through exchanges. When a man wants to inaugurate an exchange, he needs to get shells and pigs from his family and relatives. Once he has achieved a reputation as a *wua nium*, he can keep it only if he continues to perform well—that is, if he continues to distribute fairly, make wise decisions, speak well, and conduct exchanges.[48]

"BIG WOMEN" In contrast to most of mainland New Guinea, the islands off the southeastern coast are characterized by matrilineal descent. But, like the rest of New Guinea, the islands also have a shifting system of leadership in which people compete for "big" status. Here, though, the people competing are women as well as men, and so there are "big women" as well as "big men." On the island of Vanatinai, for example, women and men compete with each other to exchange valuables. Women lead canoe expeditions to distant islands to visit male as well as female exchange partners, women mobilize relatives and exchange partners to mount large feasts, and the women get to keep the ceremonial valuables exchanged, at least for a while.[49]

The prominence of women on Vanatinai may be linked to the disappearance of warfare—the colonial powers imposed peace; we call this "pacification." Interisland exchanges became frequent when war became rarer in the early 20th century, giving women and men more freedom to travel. For men, but not women, war provided a path to leadership; champion warriors would acquire great renown and influence. It is not that women did not participate in war; they did, which is unusual cross-culturally, but a woman could not become a war leader. Now, in the absence of war, women have an opportunity through exchanges to become leaders, or "big women."

In one respect, however, women have less of an opportunity to acquire influence now. There are local government councils now, but all the councillors are male. Why? Some women were nominated for the posts, but they withdrew in embarrassment because they could not speak English. Big men or big women do not automatically have a path to these new positions; it is mostly young males who know English who become the councillors. But this situation may change. With the opening of a government primary school in 1984, both girls and boys are learning English, so women in the future may be more likely to achieve leadership by becoming councillors.

Political Participation

Political scientist Marc Ross conducted cross-cultural research on variation in degree of political participation. Ross phrased the research question: "Why is it that in some polities there are relatively large numbers of persons involved in political life, while in others political action is the province of very few?"[50]

Political participation in preindustrial societies ranges from widespread to low or nonexistent. In 16 percent of the societies examined, there is widespread participation; decision-making forums are open to all adults. The forums may be formal (councils and other governing bodies) or informal. Next in degree of political participation are societies (37 percent) that have widespread participation by some but not all adults (men but not women, certain classes but not others). Next are societies (29 percent) that have some but not much input by the community. Finally, 18 percent of the societies have low or nonexistent participation, which means that leaders make most decisions, and involvement of the average person is very limited.

Degree of political participation seems to be high in small-scale societies, as well as in modern democratic nation-states, but not in between (feudal states and preindustrial empires). Why? In small-scale societies leaders do not have the power to force people to act; thus a high degree of political participation may be the only way to get people to go along with decisions. In modern democracies, which have many powerful groups outside the government—corporations, unions, and other associations are examples—the central authorities may only theoretically have the power to force people to go along; in reality, they rely mostly on voluntary compliance. For example, the U.S. government failed when it tried with force (Prohibition, 1920–1933) to stop the manufacture, transport, and sale of alcoholic beverages.

Another factor may be early family experiences. Recently some scholars have suggested that the type of family people are raised in predicts the degree of political participation in a society. A large extended family with multiple generations tends to be hierarchical, with the older generations having more authority. Children may learn that they have to obey

and subordinate their wishes to their elders. Societies with polygyny also seem to have less political participation. The ways of interacting in the family may carry over to the political sphere.[51]

A high degree of political participation seems to have an important consequence. In the modern world, democratically governed states rarely go to war with each other.[52] So, for example, the United States invaded three countries—Grenada, Panama, and Iraq—between 1980 and 1993 but no democracies. Similarly, it appears that more participatory, that is, more "democratic," political units in the ethnographic record fight with each other significantly less often than do less participatory political units, just as seems to be the case among modern nation-states.[53] Does this mean that democracies are more peaceful in general? Here there is more controversy. Judging by the frequency of war, modern democratic states do not look very different from autocratic states in their tendency to go to war. However, if you look at the severity of war as measured by casualty rates, democratic societies do look less warlike.[54] Exactly why more participation or more democracy is likely to lead to peace remains to be established. But there are policy implications of the relationship, which we explore in the chapter on global social problems.

⊙ Resolution of Conflict

As we noted in the beginning of this chapter, political life involves more than the making of policy, its administration, and its enforcement. Political life also involves the resolution of conflict, which may be accomplished peacefully by avoidance, community action, mediation or the negotiation of compromises, apology, appeal to supernatural forces, or adjudication by a third party. As we shall see, the procedures used usually vary with degree of social complexity; decisions by third parties are more likely in hierarchical societies.[55] But peaceful solutions are not always possible, and disputes may erupt into violent conflict. When violence occurs within a political unit in which disputes are usually settled peacefully, we call such violence crime, particularly when committed by an individual. When the violence occurs between groups of people from separate political units—groups between which there is no procedure for settling disputes—we usually call such violence *warfare*. When violence occurs between subunits of a population that had been politically unified, we call it *civil war*.

Peaceful Resolution of Conflict

Most modern industrialized states have formal institutions and offices, such as police, district attorneys, courts, and penal systems, to deal with minor disputes and more serious conflicts that may arise in society. All these institutions generally operate according to **codified laws**—that is, a set of explicit, usually written rules stipulating what is permissible and what is not. Transgression of the law by individuals gives the state the right to take action against them. The state has a monopoly on the legitimate use of force in the society, for

CURRENT RESEARCH AND ISSUES

Democracy and Economic Development: How and Why Are They Related?

The subsistence economies traditionally studied by anthropologists are becoming more and more commercialized as people increasingly produce goods and services for a market. And the pace of economic development is quickening, particularly in places that until recently lacked industrial wage labor, as their economies are increasingly integrated into the same world system. What effect, if any, does economic development have on political participation? Can we speculate about the future on the basis of comparative research?

Most of the comparative research on the relationship between economic development and political participation has been cross-national, comparing data on different countries. Some countries are more democratic than others, on the basis of such characteristics as contested elections, an elected head of state, an elected powerful legislature, and the protection of civil liberties. In capitalist countries, more democracy is generally associated with higher levels of economic development, as measured by indicators such as per capita output; in countries that are not very industrialized, there is little democracy at the national level. Why should more democracy be associated with more economic development? The prevailing opinion is that economic development increases the degree of social equality in the country, and the more equality among interest groups, the more they demand participation in the political process, and hence the more democracy. Or, to put this theory another way, as the economy develops, the more what we might call the middle and working classes can demand rewards and power, and therefore the less power the elite can retain.

What about the societies usually studied by anthropologists, what we call the cross-cultural or ethnographic record? We know that some of the highest levels of political participation occur in the least complex societies, such as foraging societies. Many adults in such societies have a say in decisions, and leadership is informal; leaders can retain their roles only if people voluntarily go along with them. Concentrated power and less political participation are more likely in chiefdoms and states than in band and tribal societies. The more hierarchical chiefdoms and states usually depend on agriculture, particularly intensive agriculture, which can produce more goods and services per capita than foraging economies

can. So the relationship between economic development and political participation in the ethnographic record is *opposite* to what we find cross-nationally. That is, the more economic development, the less political participation in the societies studied by anthropologists. Why should this be so? It seems that social equality *decreases* with economic development in the ethnographic record (which does not include many industrialized societies). In that record, an economically developed society is likely to have features such as plowing, fertilizers, and irrigation, which make permanent cultivation of the fields and permanent communities possible. Such intensive agricultural activity is more conducive to concentrated wealth than is hunter-gatherer subsistence or shifting cultivation (horticulture). Thus, in the ethnographic record, the more economically developed societies have more social inequality and therefore less democracy.

The two sets of findings, the cross-national and the cross-cultural, are not that hard to reconcile. Social and economic inequality appears to work against democracy and extensive political participation. Social inequality increases with the switch from foraging to agriculture. But social inequality decreases with the switch from preindustrial agriculture to high (industrial) levels of economic development. Political participation decreases with the first switch and increases with the second, because social inequality first increases and then decreases.

So what does comparative research suggest about the future? If the middle and working classes feel they are not getting a fair return on their labor, their demands should increase. The elite may be willing to satisfy those increased demands; if they do, their power will be reduced. In either case, unless the elite try to retain their power at any cost, there should be more political participation and more democracy, at least in the long run.

Sources: Kenneth A. Bollen, "Liberal Democracy: Validity and Method Factors in Cross-National Measures," *American Journal of Political Science,* 37 (1993): 1207–30; Edward N. Muller, "Economic Determinants of Democracy," and Melvin Ember, Carol R. Ember, and Bruce Russett, "Inequality and Democracy in the Anthropological Record," in Manus I. Midlarsky, ed., *Inequality, Democracy, and Economic Development* (Cambridge, UK: Cambridge University Press, 1997), pp. 133–55 and 110–30, respectively. Marc Howard Ross, "Political Participation," in *Cross-Cultural Research for Social Science,* in Carol R. Ember, Melvin Ember, and Peter N. Peregrine, eds., *New Directions in Anthropology* (Upper Saddle River, NJ: Prentice Hall, CD-ROM, 2004).

it alone has the right to coerce subjects into agreement with regulations, customs, political edicts, and procedures.

Many societies lack such specialized offices and institutions for dealing with conflict. Yet, because all societies have peaceful, regularized ways of handling at least certain disputes, some anthropologists speak of the *universality of law*. E. Adamson Hoebel, for example, stated the principle as follows:

> Each people has its system of social control. And all but a few of the poorest of them have as a part of the control system a complex of behavior patterns and institutional mechanisms that we may properly treat as law. For, "anthropologically considered, law is merely one aspect of our culture—the aspect which employs the force of organized society to regulate individual and group conduct and to prevent redress or punish deviations from prescribed social norms."[56]

Law, then, whether informal as in simpler societies, or formal as in more complex societies, provides a means of dealing peacefully with whatever conflicts develop. That does not mean that conflicts are always resolved peacefully. But that also does not mean that people cannot learn to resolve their conflicts peacefully. The fact that there are societies with little or no violent conflict means that it may be possible to learn from them; it may be possible to discover how to avoid violent outcomes of conflicts. How come South Africa could move relatively peacefully from a society dominated by people from Europe to one with government and civil rights shared by all groups? On the other hand, Bosnia had very violent conflict between ethnic groups and needed intervention by outside parties to keep the warring sides apart.[57]

AVOIDANCE   Violence can often be avoided if the parties to a dispute voluntarily avoid each other or are separated until emotions cool down. Anthropologists have frequently remarked that foragers are particularly likely to make use of this technique. People may move to other bands or move their dwellings to opposite ends of camp. Shifting horticulturalists may also split up when conflicts get too intense. Avoidance is obviously easier in societies, such as band societies, that are nomadic or seminomadic and in which people have temporary dwellings. And avoidance is more feasible when people live independently and self-sufficiently (e.g., in cities and suburbs).[58] But even if conditions in such societies may make avoidance easier, we still need to know why some societies use avoidance more than confrontation as a way of resolving conflict.

COMMUNITY ACTION   Societies have found various ways of resolving disputes peacefully. One such way involves action by a group or the community as a whole; collective action is common in simpler societies that lack powerful authoritarian leaders.[59] Many Inuit societies, for example, frequently resolve disputes through community action. Within local groups, kinship ties are not particularly emphasized, and the family is regarded as autonomous in most matters. They believe that spirits, particularly if displeased,

can determine much of a person's fate. Consequently, people carry out their daily tasks within a complex system of taboos. This system is so extensive that the Inuit, at least in the past, may have had no need for a formal set of laws.

Nevertheless, conflicts do arise and have to be resolved. Accordingly, *principles* act as guides to the community in settling trouble cases. An individual's failure to heed a taboo or to follow the suggestions of a shaman leads to expulsion from the group, because the community cannot accept a risk to its livelihood. A person who fails to share goods voluntarily will find them confiscated and distributed to the community, and he or she may be executed in the process. A single case of murder, as an act of vengeance (usually because of the abduction of a wife or as part of a blood feud), does not concern the community, but repeated murders do. Franz Boas gave a typical example:

> There was a native of Padli by the name Padlu. He had induced the wife of a native of Cumberland Sound to desert her husband and follow him. The deserted husband, meditating revenge . . . visited his friends in Padli, but before he could accomplish his intention of killing Padlu, the latter shot him. . . . A brother of the murdered man went to Padli to avenge the death . . . but he also was killed by Padlu. A third native of Cumberland Sound, who wished to avenge the death of his relatives, was also murdered by him.

> On account of these outrages the natives wanted to get rid of Padlu, but yet they did not dare to attack him. When the *pimain* (headman) of the Akudmurmuit learned of these events he started southward and *asked every man in Padli whether Padlu should be killed. All agreed;* so he went with the latter deer hunting . . . and . . . shot Padlu in the back.[60]

The killing of an individual is the most extreme action a community can take—we call it *capital punishment.* The community as a whole or a political official or a court may decide to administer such punishment, but capital punishment seems to exist in nearly all societies, from the simplest to the most complex.[61] It is often assumed that capital punishment deters crime. If it did, we would expect the abolition of capital punishment to be followed by an increase in homicide rates. But that does not seem to happen. A cross-national study indicated that the abolition of capital punishment tends to be followed by a decrease in homicide rates.[62]

NEGOTIATION AND MEDIATION   In many conflicts, the parties to a dispute may come to a settlement themselves by **negotiation.** There aren't necessarily any rules for how they will do so, but any solution is "good" if it restores peace.[63] Sometimes an outside or third party is used to help bring about a settlement between the disputants. We call it **mediation** when the outside party tries to help bring about a settlement, but that third party does not have the formal authority to force a settlement. Both negotiation and mediation are likely when the society is relatively egalitarian and it is important for people to get along.[64]

Among the Nuer of East Africa, a pastoral and horticultural people, disputes within the community can be settled with the help of an informal mediator called the "leopard-skin chief." This man is not a political chief but a mediator. His position is hereditary, has religious overtones, and makes its holder responsible for the social well-being of the district. Matters such as cattle stealing rarely come to the attention of the leopard-skin chief; the parties involved usually prefer to settle in their own private way. But if, for example, a murder has been committed, the culprit will go at once to the house of the leopard-skin chief. Immediately the chief cuts the culprit's arm so that blood flows; until the cut has been made the murderer may not eat or drink. If the murderer is afraid of vengeance by the slain man's family, he will remain at the house of the leopard-skin chief, which is considered sanctuary. Then, within the next few months, the chief attempts to mediate between the parties to the crime.

The chief elicits from the slayer's kin that they are prepared to pay compensation to avoid a feud, and he persuades the dead man's kin that they ought to accept compensation, usually in the form of cattle. During this period neither party may eat or drink from the same vessels as the other, and they may not, therefore, eat in the house of the same third person. The chief then collects the cattle—some 40 to 50 beasts—and takes them to the dead man's home, where he performs various sacrifices of cleansing and atonement.[65]

Throughout the process, the chief acts as a go-between. He has no authority to force either party to negotiate, and he has no power to enforce a solution once it has been arrived at. However, he is able to take advantage of the fact that because both disputants belong to the same community and are anxious to avoid a blood feud, they usually are willing to come to terms.

RITUAL RECONCILIATION—APOLOGY The desire to restore a harmonious relationship may also explain ceremonial apologies. An apology is based on deference—the guilty party shows obeisance and asks for forgiveness. Such ceremonies tend to occur in recent chiefdoms.[66] Among the Fijians of the South Pacific, there is a strong ethic of harmony and mutual assistance, particularly within a village. When a person offends someone of higher status, the offended person and other villagers begin to avoid, and gossip about, the offender. If offenders are sensitive to village opinion, they will perform a ceremony of apology called *i soro*. One of the meanings of *soro* is "surrender." In the ceremony the offender bows the head and remains silent while an intermediary speaks, presents a token gift, and asks the offended person for forgiveness. The apology is rarely rejected.[67]

OATHS AND ORDEALS Still another way of peacefully resolving disputes is through oaths and ordeals, both of which involve appeals to supernatural power. An **oath** is the act of calling upon a deity to bear witness to the truth of what one says. An **ordeal** is a means used to determine guilt or innocence by submitting the accused to dangerous or painful tests believed to be under supernatural control.[68]

Oaths, as one would expect, vary widely in content, according to the culture in which they are found. The Rwala Bedouin, for example, do the following:

> In serious disputes the judge requires the *msabba* oath, so called from the seven lines drawn with a saber on the ground. The judge first draws a circle with a saber, then its diameter; then he intersects with five vertical lines, inviting the witness to step inside and, facing south, to swear: "A false oath is the ruin of the descendants, for he who [swears falsely] is insatiable in his desire [of gain] and does not fear for his Lord."[69]

Scarcely is the oath finished when the witness jumps out of the circle and, full of rage, runs at his opponent, who has made him swear. The people at the trial have to hold him until he calms down.

A common kind of ordeal, found in almost every part of the world, is scalding. Among the Tanala of Madagascar, the accused person, having first had his hand carefully examined for protective covering, has to reach his hand into a cauldron of boiling water and grasp, from underneath, a rock suspended there. He then plunges his hand into cold water, has it bandaged, and is led off to spend the night under guard. In the morning his hand is unbandaged and examined. If there are blisters, he is guilty.

Oaths and ordeals have also been practiced in Western societies. Both were common in medieval Europe. Even today, in our own society, vestiges of oaths can be found. Children can be heard to say, "Cross my heart and hope to die," and witnesses in courts of law are obliged to swear to tell the truth.

Why do some societies use oaths and ordeals? John Roberts suggested that their use tends to be found in fairly complex societies in which political officials lack sufficient power to make and enforce judicial decisions or would make themselves unnecessarily vulnerable were they to attempt to do so. So the officials may use oaths and ordeals to let the gods decide guilt or innocence. When political officials gain more power, oaths and ordeals seem to decline or disappear.[70] In contrast, smaller and less complex societies probably have no need for elaborate mechanisms such as courts and oaths and ordeals to ascertain guilt. In such societies, everyone is aware of what crimes have been committed and who the guilty parties probably are.

ADJUDICATION, COURTS, AND CODIFIED LAW We call it **adjudication** when a third party acting as judge makes a decision that the disputing parties have to accept. Judgment may be rendered by one person (a judge), a panel of judges, a jury, or a political agent or agency (a chief, a royal personage, a council). Courts are often open to an audience, but they need not be. Judges and courts may rely on codified law and stipulated punishments, but codified law is not necessary for decisions to be made. Our own society relies heavily on codified law and courts to resolve disputes peacefully, but courts often, if not usually, rely on precedent—that is, the outcomes of previous, similar cases. Codified laws and courts

Many societies have adopted courts to resolve disputes, as here in Papua New Guinea.

are not limited to Western societies. From the late 17th to the early 20th centuries, for example, the Ashanti of West Africa had a complex political system with elaborate legal arrangements. The Ashanti state was a military-based empire possessing legal codes that resembled those of many ancient civilizations.[71]

The most effective sanction underpinning Ashanti law and its enforcement was the intense respect—almost religious deference—accorded the wishes of the ancestors and also the elders as custodians of the ancestral tradition. Ashanti law was based on a concept of natural law, a belief that there is an order of the universe whose principles lawmakers should follow in the decisions they make and in the regulations they design. Criminal and religious law were merged by the Ashanti. Crimes, especially homicide, cursing of a chief, cowardice, and sorcery, were regarded as sins against the ancestral spirits. In Ashanti court procedure, elders examined and cross-examined witnesses as well as parties to the dispute. There were also quasi-professional advocates, and appeals against a verdict could be made directly to a chief. Particularly noteworthy was the emphasis on intent when assessing guilt. Drunkenness constituted a valid defense for all crimes except murder and cursing a chief, and a plea of insanity, if proved, was upheld for all offenses.

Ashanti punishments could be severe. Physical mutilation, such as slicing off the nose or an ear—even castration in sexual offenses—was often employed. Fines were more frequent, however, and death sentences could often be commuted to banishment and confiscation of goods.

Why do some societies have codified systems and others do not? One explanation, advanced by E. Adamson Hoebel, A. R. Radcliffe-Brown, and others, is that in small, closely knit communities there is little need for formal legal guidelines because competing interests are minimal. Hence, simple societies need little codified law. There are relatively few matters to quarrel about, and the general will of the group is sufficiently well known and demonstrated frequently enough to deter transgressors.

This point of view is echoed in Richard Schwartz's study of two Israeli settlements. In one communal kibbutz, a young man aroused a good deal of community resentment because he had accepted an electric teakettle as a gift. It was the general opinion that he had overstepped the code about not having personal possessions, and he was so informed. Accordingly, he gave the kettle to the communal infirmary. Schwartz observed that "no organized enforcement of the decision was threatened, but had he disregarded the expressed will of the community, his life . . . would have been made intolerable by the antagonism of public opinion."[72]

In this community, where people worked and ate together, not only did everyone know about transgressions, but a wrongdoer could not escape public censure. Thus, public opinion was an effective sanction. In another Israeli community, however, where individuals lived in widely separated houses and worked and ate separately, public opinion did not work as well. Not only were community members less aware of problems, but they had no quick way of making their feelings known. As a result, they established a judicial body to handle trouble cases.

Larger, more heterogeneous and stratified societies are likely to have more frequent disputes, which at the same time are less visible to the public. Individuals in stratified societies are generally not so dependent on community members for their well-being and hence are less likely to know of, or care about, others' opinions. It is in such societies that codified laws and formal authorities for resolving disputes develop—in order, perhaps, that disputes may be settled impersonally enough so that the parties can accept the decision and social order can be restored.

A good example of how more formal systems of law develop is the experience of towns in the American West during the gold-rush period. These communities were literally swamped by total strangers. The townsfolk, having no control (authority) over these intruders because the strangers had no local ties, looked for ways to deal with the trouble cases that were continually flaring up. A first attempt at a

NEW PERSPECTIVES ON GENDER

New Courts Allow Women to Address Grievances in Papua New Guinea

In most societies in New Guinea, women did not traditionally participate in the resolution of disputes. And they could not bring actions against men. But when village courts were introduced, women began to go to court to redress offenses against them.

In colonial times, the introduced Western-style courts followed Western law, primarily Australian and British common law, not native customary law. After Papua New Guinea became an independent country, those courts remained in place. The lowest of the courts, called Local Courts, were located in town centers, often far from villages, so villagers rarely brought cases to them. But in 1973 a new kind of court was created. Called Village Courts, they were designed to settle local disputes in the villages, using a blend of customary law (relying on compromise) and Western law. In contrast to the Local Courts, magistrates in the Village Courts were not outsiders but were selected from the pool of traditional and local leaders who knew the local people.

When Richard Scaglion studied changes in Village Courts among the Abelam from 1977 to 1987, he noticed a shift toward the increased use of these courts by women. In 1977 most of the complainants were male, but by 1987 most of them were female. In a wider study of court cases over many regions of Papua New Guinea, Scaglion and Rose Whittingham found that most of the cases in which women were the plaintiffs were attempts to redress sex-related offenses (sexual jealousy, rape, incest, domestic disputes) committed by males. Most disputes in New Guinea villages are settled informally by self-help or by appeal to a "big man"; the courts are appealed to only as a last resort. Serious sex-related cases are unlikely to be settled informally but, rather, in the Village Court. Apparently women do not believe that they can get satisfaction informally. So they go to the Village Court, where they win some sort of punishment for the defendant in about 60 percent of the cases, just about the same rate that men achieve when they bring a case seeking punishment.

Culture change introduced from the outside often works against native peoples. But Papuan New Guinea women have benefited from the new Village Court system, particularly in redressing grievances against males. The traditional system for resolving disputes was largely male-dominated (women could not be plaintiffs) and so the possibility of taking disputes to the new courts has given women some measure of legal equality with men.

Sources: Richard Scaglion, "Legal Adaptation in a Papua New Guinea Village Court," *Ethnology,* 29 (1990): 17–33; Richard Scaglion and Rose Whittingham, "Female Plaintiffs and Sex-Related Disputes in Rural Papua New Guinea," in S. Toft, ed., *Domestic Violence in Papua New Guinea. Monograph No. 3* (Port Moresby, Papua New Guinea: Law Reform Commission, 1985), pp. 120–33.

solution was to hire gunslingers, who were also strangers, to act as peace officers or sheriffs, but this strategy usually failed. Eventually, towns succeeded in having federal authorities send in marshals backed by federal power.

Is there some evidence to support the theory that codified law is necessary only in larger, more complex societies? Data from a large, worldwide sample of societies suggest that codified law is associated with political integration beyond the local level. Murder cases, for example, are dealt with informally in societies that have only local political organization. In societies with multilocal political units, murder cases tend to be judged or adjudicated by specialized political authorities.[73] There is also some cross-cultural evidence that violence within a society tends to be less frequent when there are formal authorities (chiefs, courts) who have the power to punish murderers.[74] In general, adjudication or enforced decisions by outside authorities tend to occur in hierarchical societies with social classes and centralized power.[75]

Violent Resolution of Conflict

People are likely to resort to violence when regular, effective alternative means of resolving a conflict are not available. Some societies consider violence between individuals to be appropriate under certain circumstances; we generally do not, and call it **crime.** When violence occurs between political entities such as communities, districts, or nations, we call it **warfare.** The type of warfare, of course, varies in scope and complexity from society to society. Sometimes a distinction is made among feuding, raiding, and large-scale confrontations.

Some scholars talk about a cultural pattern of violence. But are some cultures more violent than others? The answer seems to be yes. More often than not, societies with one type of violence have others. Societies with more war tend to have warlike sports, malevolent magic, severe punishment for crimes, high murder rates, feuding, and family violence.

What might explain this tendency? One suggestion is that if war is frequent, the society may have to encourage boys to be aggressive, so that they can grow up to be effective warriors. But this socializing for aggression can spill over into other areas of life; high rates of crime and other violence may be inadvertent or unintended consequences of the encouragement of aggressiveness.[76]

INDIVIDUAL VIOLENCE   Although at first it may seem paradoxical, violent behavior itself is often used to try to control behavior. In some societies it is considered necessary for parents to beat children who misbehave. They don't consider this criminal behavior or child abuse; they consider it punishment (see the discussion of family violence in the chapter on global social problems). Similar views may attach to interpersonal behavior between adults. If a person trespasses on your property or hurts someone in your family, some societies consider it appropriate or justified to kill or maim the trespasser. Is this social control, or is it just lack of control? Most societies have norms about when such "punishment" is or is not appropriate, so the behavior of anyone who contemplates doing something wrong, as well as the behavior of the person wronged, is likely to be influenced by the "laws" of their society. For example, systems of individual self-help are characteristic of egalitarian societies.[77] How is this different from "community action," which earlier we classified under peaceful resolution of conflict? Because community action is explicitly based on obtaining a consensus, it is likely to lead to the ending of a particular dispute. Individual action, or self-help, particularly if it involves violence, is not.

FEUDING   Feuding is an example of how individual self-help may not lead to a peaceful resolution of conflict. **Feuding** is a state of recurring hostilities between families or groups of kin, usually motivated by a desire to avenge an offense—whether insult, injury, deprivation, or death—against a member of the group. The most common characteristic of the feud is that responsibility to avenge is carried by all members of the kin group. The killing of any member of the offender's group is considered appropriate revenge, because the kin group as a whole is regarded as responsible. Nicholas Gubser told of a feud within a Nunamiut Inuit community, caused by a husband's killing of his wife's lover, that lasted for decades. The Nunamiut take feuds seriously, as do many societies, especially when murder has been committed. Gubser described what happens when a man is killed:

> The closely related members of his kindred do not rest until complete revenge has been achieved. The immediate relatives of the deceased . . . recruit as much support from other relatives as they can. Their first action, if possible, is to kill the murderer, or maybe one of his closest kin. Then, of course, the members of the murderer's kindred are brought into the feud. These two kindreds may snipe at each other for years.[78]

Feuds are by no means limited to small-scale societies; they occur as frequently in societies with high levels of political organization.[79]

RAIDING   **Raiding** is a short-term use of force, planned and organized, to realize a limited objective. This objective is usually the acquisition of goods, animals, or other forms of wealth belonging to another, often neighboring community.

Raiding is especially prevalent in pastoral societies, in which cattle, horses, camels, or other animals are prized and an individual's own herd can be augmented by theft. Raids are often organized by temporary leaders or coordinators whose authority may not last beyond the planning and execution of the venture. Raiding may also be organized for the purpose of capturing people. Sometimes people are taken to marry—the capture of women to be wives or concubines is fairly common[80]—or to be slaves. Slavery has been practiced in about 33 percent of the world's known societies, and war has been one way of obtaining slaves either to keep or to trade for other goods.[81] Raiding, like feuding, is often self-perpetuating: the victim of a raid today becomes the raider tomorrow.[82]

LARGE-SCALE CONFRONTATIONS   Individual episodes of feuds and raids usually involve relatively small numbers of persons and almost always an element of surprise. Because they are generally attacked without warning, the victims are often unable to muster an immediate defense. Large-scale confrontations, in contrast, involve a large number of persons and planning by both sides of strategies of attack and defense. Large-scale warfare is usually practiced among societies with intensive agriculture or industrialization. Only these societies possess a technology sufficiently advanced to support specialized armies, military leaders, strategists, and so on. But large-scale confrontations are not limited to state societies; they occur, for example, among the horticultural Dugum Dani of central New Guinea.

The military history of the Dani, with its shifting alliances and confederations, is reminiscent of that of Europe, although Dani battles involve far fewer fighters and less sophisticated weaponry. Among the Dani, long periods of ritual warfare are characterized by formal battles announced through a challenge sent by one side to the opposing side. If the challenge is accepted, the protagonists meet at the agreed-upon battle site to set up their lines. Fighting with spears, sticks, and bows and arrows begins at midmorning and continues either until nightfall or until rain intervenes. There may also be a rest period during the midday heat during which the two sides shout insults at each other or talk and rest among themselves.

The front line of battle is composed of about a dozen active warriors and a few leaders. Behind them is a second line, still within arrow range, composed of those who have just left the forward line or are preparing to join it. The third line, outside arrow range, is composed of noncombatants—males too old or too young to participate and those recovering from wounds. This third line merely watches the battle taking place on the grassy plain. On the hillsides far back from the front line, some of the old men help to direct ancestral ghosts to the battle by gouging a line in the ground that points in the direction of the battlefield.[83]

Yet, as total as large-scale confrontations may be, even warfare has cultural rules. Among the Dani, for instance, no fighting occurs at night, and weapons are limited to simple spears and bows and arrows. Similarly, in state societies, governments will sign "self-denying" pacts restricting the use of poison gas, germ warfare, and so forth. Unofficially, private arrangements are common. One has only to glance through the memoirs of national leaders of the two world wars to become aware of locally arranged truces, visits to one another's front positions, exchanges of prisoners of war, and so on.

Explaining Warfare

Most societies anthropology knows about have had warfare between communities or larger territorial groups. The vast majority of the societies in a recent cross-cultural study had at least occasional wars when they were first described, unless they had been pacified or incorporated by more dominant societies.[84] Yet relatively little research has been done on the possible causes of war and why it varies in type and frequency. For instance, why have some people fought a great deal, and others only infrequently? Why in some societies does warfare occur internally, within the society or language group?

We have answers, based on cross-cultural studies, to some of those questions. There is evidence that people in preindustrial societies go to war mostly out of fear, particularly a fear of expectable but unpredictable natural disasters (e.g., droughts, floods, locust infestations) that will destroy food resources. People may think they can protect themselves against such disasters ahead of time by taking things from defeated enemies. In any case, preindustrial societies with higher frequencies of war are very likely to have had a history of expectable but unpredictable disasters. The fact that chronic (annually recurring and therefore predictable) food shortages do not predict higher frequencies of war suggests that people go to war in an attempt to cushion the impact of the disasters they expect to occur in the future but cannot predict. Consistent with this tentative conclusion is the fact that the victors in war almost always take land or other resources from the defeated. And this is true for simpler as well as more complex preindustrial societies.[85] Might similar motives affect decisions about war and peace in the modern world?

We know that complex or politically centralized societies are likely to have professional armies, hierarchies of military authority, and sophisticated weapons.[86] But surprisingly, the frequency of warfare seems to be not much greater in complex societies than in simple band or tribal societies.[87] We have some evidence that warfare is unlikely to occur internally (within a society) if it is small in population (21,000 or fewer people) or territory; in a larger society there is a high likelihood of warfare within the society, between communities or larger territorial divisions.[88] In fact, complex societies, even if they are politically unified, are not less likely than simpler societies to have internal warfare.[89]

What about the idea that men in band and tribal societies may mostly go to war over women?[90] If this were true, those band and tribal societies with the most frequent wars should have shortages of women, and those with little or no war—less often than once in 10 years—should have more equal numbers of women and men. But the cross-cultural evidence clearly contradicts this theory. Band and tribal societies with more wars do not have fewer women.[91]

What, if anything, do we know about recent warfare between nation-states? Although many people think that military alliances lessen the chance of war, it turns out that nations formally allied with other nations do not necessarily go to war less often than nations lacking formal alliances. Countries that are allies are, of course, less likely to go to war

Oil is a valuable resource in the world today. Iraq has more oil in the ground than most other countries.

with each other; however, alliances can drag dependent allies into wars they don't want.[91] Countries that are economically interdependent, that trade with each other for necessities, are less likely to go to war with each other.[92] Finally, military equality between nations, particularly when preceded by a rapid military buildup, seems to increase rather than lessen the chance of war between those nations.[93]

Clearly, these findings contradict some traditional beliefs about how to prevent war. Military buildups do not make war less likely, but trade does. What else may? We have already noted that participatory ("democratic") political systems are less likely to go to war with each other than are authoritarian political systems. Later, in the chapter on global social problems, we discuss how the results of cross-cultural and cross-national studies may translate into policies that could minimize the risk of war in the world.

⊚ Summary

1. All societies have customs or procedures that, organized on behalf of territorial groups, result in decision making and the resolution of disputes. These ways of creating and maintaining social order and coping with social disorder vary from society to society.

2. Societies with a band type of political organization are composed of fairly small, usually nomadic groups. Each of these bands is politically autonomous, the band being the largest group that acts as a political unit. Authority within the band is usually informal. Societies with band organization generally are egalitarian hunter-gatherers. But band organization may not have been typical of food collectors in the distant past.

3. Societies with tribal organization are similar to those with band organization in being egalitarian. But in contrast with band societies, they generally are food producers, have a higher population density, and are more sedentary. Tribal organization is defined by the presence of groupings, such as clans and age-sets, that can integrate more than one local group into a larger whole.

4. The personal qualities of leaders in tribal societies seem to be similar to the qualities of leaders in the United States, with one major difference: U.S. leaders are generally wealthier than others in their society.

5. Chiefdom organization differs from tribal organization in having formal authority structures that integrate multicommunity political units. Compared with societies with tribal organization, societies with chiefdoms are more densely populated and their communities are more permanent. In contrast to "big men" in tribal societies, who generally have to earn their privileges by their personal qualities, chiefs generally hold their positions permanently. Most chiefdom societies have social ranking.

6. A state has been defined as a political unit composed of many communities and having a centralized government with the authority to make and enforce laws, collect taxes, and draft men for military service. In state societies, the government tries to maintain a monopoly on the use of physical force. In addition, states are generally characterized by class stratification, intensive agriculture (the high productivity of which presumably allows the emergence of cities), commercial exchange, a high degree of economic and other specialization, and extensive foreign trade. The rulers of a state cannot depend forever on the use or threat of force to maintain their power; the people must believe that the rulers are legitimate or have the right to govern.

7. Degree of political participation varies in the societies studied by anthropologists, just as among modern nation-states. Degree of political participation seems to be high in small-scale societies, as well as in modern democratic nation-states, but not in those in between, such as feudal states and preindustrial empires.

8. Many societies lack specialized offices and institutions for dealing with conflict. Yet all societies have peaceful, regularized ways of handling at least certain disputes. Avoidance, community action, and negotiation and mediation are more common in simpler societies. Ritual apology occurs frequently in chiefdoms. Oaths and ordeals tend to occur in complex societies in which political officials lack power to enforce judicial decisions. Adjudication is more likely in stratified, more complex societies. Capital punishment seems to exist in nearly all societies, from the simplest to the most complex.

9. People are likely to resort to violence when regular, effective alternative means of resolving a conflict are not available. Violence can occur between individuals, within communities, and between communities. Violence that occurs between political entities such as communities, districts, or nations is generally referred to as warfare. The type of warfare varies in scope and complexity from society to society. Preindustrial societies with higher warfare frequencies are likely to have had a history of unpredictable disasters that destroyed food supplies. More often than not, societies with one type of violence have others.

⊚ Glossary Terms

adjudication	433	negotiation	432
band	420	oath	433
band organization	420	ordeal	433
chief	423	raiding	436
chiefdom	423	segmentary lineage system	422
codified laws	430	state	424
complementary opposition	423	state organization	424
crime	435	tribal organization	421
feuding	436	tribe	421
headman	421	warfare	435
mediation	432		

◎ Critical Questions

1. When, if ever, do you think the world will be politically unified? Why do you think so?
2. Why don't informal methods of social control work well in societies like our own? Why don't formal methods work better than they do?
3. What does research on war and violence suggest about how to minimize them?

◎ Research Navigator

1. Please go to www.researchnavigator.com and enter your Login Name and Password. For detailed instructions see Chapter 1.
2. Using ContentSelect search for two articles on one of the following topics: warfare, empires, or leadership. Try to find one article pertaining to the United States or another Western country and another article on another part of the world. Briefly summarize the contents.

◎ Discovering Anthropology: Researchers at Work

Read the chapter by Thomas Abler, "Iroquois: The Tree of Peace and the War Kettle" in the accompanying *Discovering Anthropology* reader and answer the following questions:

1. What was the Iroquois Confederacy? What kind of political organization was it?
2. What role did men and women play in making war and making peace?
3. What kinds of impacts did the Europeans have on the Iroquois?

CHAPTER TWENTY-FIVE

Psychology and Culture

Visitors to another society often come to feel that the people there think differently, or have different reactions to situations, that they seem to have different **personalities**—distinctive ways of thinking, feeling, and behaving—compared with people back home. Stereotypes are born from these casual observations. Certain peoples are thought to be reserved, others authoritarian, still others hot-tempered. Although anthropologists generally reject such stereotypes because they are often based on hasty, even ethnocentric judgments, they do not reject the idea that there may be differences from society to society in some aspects of thinking, feeling, and behaving.

Consider the contrast in feelings and behavior between the Semai of central Malaya and the Yanomamö of the Brazil–Venezuela border, a contrast that clearly expresses differences in personality. The Semai, as described by Robert Dentan, are famous in Malaya for their timidity and have never been described as hostile or surly. When asked about anger, the Semai say, "We do not get angry."[1] On the other hand, the Yanomamö, as described by Napoleon Chagnon, are known for their aggressiveness. They not only engage in chronic warfare between villages but frequently show aggression within a village. Shouting and threatening to obtain demands are frequent, as are wife beatings and bloody fights with clubs. Men are proud of their scars and sometimes shave their heads to display them.[2]

Even though there may be psychological differences between societies, there also are psychological similarities. After all, we are all human. People the world over cry or weep when a loved one dies, laugh or smile when something good happens, learn from mistakes, and have many of the same needs. Anthropologists who are interested in psychological differences between and within societies and in psychological similarities across the broad range of human societies call themselves *psychological anthropologists.* Psychologists who study people in two or more societies call themselves *cross-cultural psychologists.* Four main questions seem to characterize psychological anthropology: (1) To what extent do all human beings develop psychologically in the same ways? (2) If there are differences, what are they and what may account for them? (3) How do people in different societies conceive of personality and psychological development? and (4) What kinds of cultural variation might be explained by psychological factors? This chapter discusses some of the attempts made by researchers to answer these questions.

The Universality of Psychological Development

Anthropologists became interested in psychology in the early years of the 20th century partly because they did not believe that human nature was completely revealed in Western societies, as psychologists then generally assumed. Only recently have many psychologists joined anthropologists in questioning the assumption that humans are exactly the same psychologically in all societies. Psychologist Otto Klineberg, for example, scolded his colleagues in 1974: "My contact with anthropology affected me somewhat like a religious conversion. How could psychologists speak of *human* attributes and *human* behavior when they knew only one kind of human being?"[3]

How can we know what is universal about human behavior and what is variable until we study all kinds of humans? Because humans the world over are the same species and share a very large proportion of their genes, we might assume that there is a good deal of similarity across societies in the way people develop psychologically from birth to maturity or in the way people think, feel, and behave. We have already discussed many universals—culture, language, marriage, the incest taboo—but here we discuss some that are related more to psychology. Donald Brown compiled a list of probable human universals in the psychological realm.[4] They include the ability to create taxonomies, make binary contrasts, order phenomena, use logical operators (e.g., *and, not, equals*), plan for the future, and have an understanding of the world and what it is about.

With regard to ideas about people, it seems universal to have a concept of the self or person, to recognize individual faces, to try to discern other persons' intentions from observable clues in their faces, utterances, and actions, and to imagine what others are thinking. With regard to emotions, people seem universally to be able to empathize with the feelings of others; facially communicate and recognize, as well as hide or mimic, the emotions of happiness, sadness, anger, fear, surprise, disgust, and contempt (see the box "Do Masks Show Emotion in Universal Ways?" in the chapter on the arts); smile when friendly; cry when in pain or unhappy; play for fun; show and feel affection for others; feel sexual attraction, envy, and jealousy; and have similar childhood fears (e.g., fear of strangers). Indeed, it seems that people in different cultures even conceive of love in much the same ways, despite love's reputation as something mysterious and culturally variable.[5]

What about psychological development? We saw in the chapter on communication and language that certain aspects of language acquisition appear to be universal across cultures. In what respects is psychological development the same the world over? In what respects is it different?

Early Research on Emotional Development

When Margaret Mead went to American Samoa in the mid-1920s, psychologists believed that adolescence was universally a period of "storm and stress" because of the physiological changes that occur at puberty. Mead's observations of, and interviews with, Samoan adolescent girls led her to doubt the idea that adolescence was necessarily a time of turmoil. Samoan girls apparently showed little evidence of emotional upheaval and rebelliousness, and therefore it was questionable whether psychological development in adolescence was the same in all societies.[6]

Bronislaw Malinowski, another early anthropologist, questioned the universality of an assumption about emotional development, in this case Freud's assumption that young boys universally see themselves, unconsciously, as sexual rivals of their fathers for possession of their mothers. Freud called these feelings the *Oedipus complex*, after the character in Greek mythology who killed his father and married his mother without knowing that they were his parents. Freud thought that all boys before the age of 7 or so would show hostility toward their fathers, but Malinowski disagreed

Adolescence in many societies is a time for developing work skills. An Asmat boy in Indonesian New Guinea is learning to carve, and an adult is supervising.

on the basis of his fieldwork in the matrilineal Trobriand Islands.[7]

Malinowski suggested that young boys in nonmatrilineal societies may feel hostility toward the father not as a sexual rival but as the disciplinarian. Malinowski proposed this theory because he thought that the Oedipus complex works differently in matrilineal societies. Boys in matrilineal societies may feel more hostile toward their mother's brother—the main authority figure in the matrilineal kin group—than toward their father.

Derek Freeman criticized Mead's conclusions about Samoa,[8] and Melford Spiro challenged Malinowski's conclusions about the Trobriand Islanders.[9] Mead and Malinowski may or may not have been correct about the societies they studied, but the issues they raised remain crucial to the question of whether psychological development is similar across societies. To find out, we need research in many societies, not just a few. Only on the basis of extensive cross-cultural research will we be able to decide whether stages of emotional development can be affected by cultural differences.

For example, it is only recently that adolescence has been systematically studied cross-culturally. Alice Schlegel and Herbert Barry reported that adolescence is generally not a period of overt rebelliousness. The reason, they suggested, is related to the fact that most people in most societies live with or near (and depend on) close kin before and after they grow up. Only in societies like our own, where children leave home when they grow up, might adolescents be rebellious, possibly to prepare emotionally for going out on their own.[10] (See the box "Neolocality and Adolescent Rebellion: Are They Related?" in the chapter on marital residence and kinship.)

Research on Cognitive Development

One day the two of us went out for pizza. The pizza maker was laughing hilariously, and we asked what was so funny. He told us: "I just asked the guy ahead of you, 'How many slices do you want me to cut the pizza into, six or eight?' 'Six,' he said, 'I'm not very hungry.'" According to a theory of cognitive (intellectual) development suggested by Jean Piaget, the renowned Swiss psychologist, the "not very hungry" guy may not have acquired the concept of *conservation,* which characterizes a stage of thinking normally acquired by children between the ages of 7 and 11 in Western societies.[11] The pizza customer ahead of us, like many very young children, seemed not to understand that certain properties of an object, such as quantity, weight, and volume, remain constant even if the object is divided into small pieces or removed to a container of a different shape. They have not acquired the mental image of *reversibility,* the ability to imagine that if you put the pizza back together again it would be the same size whether you had cut it into eight or six slices. To the child or adult who has not acquired the ability to reverse actions mentally, eight slices may seem like more pizza than six slices, because eight is more than six.

Piaget's theory says that the development of thinking in humans involves a series of stages, each of which is characterized by different mental skills. To get to a higher stage of thinking, one has to pass through a lower stage. So Piaget's theory would predict that the pizza customer would not be able to think systematically about the possible outcomes of hypothetical situations, a defining feature of Piaget's *formal-operational* stage, because he had not acquired the notion of conservation and the other mental skills that characterize the previous, *concrete-operational* stage of cognitive development.

What does the evidence suggest about the universality of Piaget's supposed stages? And do people the world over get to each stage at the same age? The first stage of development, *sensorimotor,* has not been investigated in many societies, but the results of studies conducted so far are remarkably consistent. They support Piaget's notion that there is a predictable order in the sequence of stages.[12] And, on the basis of their reactions to the same conditions, babies in different places seem to think similarly. For example, a comparison of French babies and Baoulé babies in the Ivory Coast showed that the Baoulé babies, who had never seen objects such as red plastic tubes and paper clips, nevertheless tried to pass the clips through the tubes in the same way the French babies did. The two sets of babies even made the same kinds of errors.[13] And even though they had few toys, the Baoulé babies showed advances over French babies on such tasks as using instruments to increase the reach of the arm. But Baoulé babies are allowed to touch all kinds of objects, even things that Europeans consider dangerous.[14]

Most of the cross-cultural studies of Piaget's stages have focused on the transition between the second, *preoperational,* and third, *concrete-operational,* stages, particularly the attainment of the concept of conservation. The results of many of these studies are somewhat puzzling. Although older children are generally more likely to show conservation than younger children, it is not clear what to make of the apparent finding that the attainment of conservation is much delayed in many non-Western populations. Indeed, in some places most of the adults tested do not appear to understand one or more of the conservation properties.

Can this be true? Do people in different cultures differ that much in intellectual functioning, or is there some problem with the way conservation is measured? Is it possible that an adult who just brought water from the river in a large jug and poured it into five smaller containers does not know that the quantity of water is still the same? We may also be skeptical about the findings on the formal-operational stage. Most of the studies of formal-operational thinking have found little evidence of such thinking in non-Western populations. But people in nonliterate societies surely have formal-operational thinking if they can navigate using the stars, remember how to return to camp after a 15-mile trek, or identify how people are related to each other three and more generations back.

One reason to be skeptical about the apparent findings regarding delay of conservation and formal-operational thinking is that most of the cross-cultural psychologists have taken tests developed in our own and other Western countries to measure cognitive development elsewhere.[15] This procedure puts non-Westerners at a considerable disadvantage, because they are not as familiar as Westerners with the test materials and the whole testing situation. In tests of conservation, for example, researchers have often used strange-looking glass cylinders and beakers. Some researchers who have used natively familiar materials, however, have gotten different results. Douglass Price-Williams found no difference between Tiv, in West Africa, and European children in understanding the conservation of earth, nuts, and number.[16] Also, some researchers have retested children after brief training sessions and found that they improved substantially. It would seem, then, that children anywhere can acquire the concept of conservation if they have had preparatory life experiences or appropriate training.[17]

The results of tests elsewhere on formal-operational thinking may also be questionable. Such tests ask questions dealing with content that is taught in science and mathematics classes. It should not be surprising, then, that schooled individuals usually do better than the nonschooled on tests of formal-operational thinking. Where compulsory schooling is lacking, we should not expect people to do well on tests of such thinking.[18]

In trying to find out what may be universal in emotional and cognitive development, researchers have discovered some apparent differences between societies. These differences, to which we now turn, need to be explored and explained.

Cross-Cultural Variation in Psychological Characteristics

Thinking about personality differences seems to come easily to many North Americans. We like to talk about the psychology of those we know. We speculate why one friend is emotional, why another has a quick temper, why another is shy. We may also wonder why one friend is likely to remember faces and why another is a whiz at computers. We are interested in personality as an individual characteristic, and we emphasize the uniqueness of each individual. Indeed, because every person has a unique combination of genetic traits and life experiences, we can say that in some ways no person is like any other person. But anthropologists are interested in approaching personality from a different perspective. Instead of focusing on the uniqueness of an individual, psychological anthropologists are interested in those aspects of personality that may be common in a population.

Why should we expect different societies to differ in some personality characteristics? It is generally agreed that our personalities are the result of an interaction between genetic inheritance and life experiences. But a considerable portion of one's life experiences, as well as one's genes, is shared with others. Parents undoubtedly exert a major influence on the

way we grow up. Because family members share similar life experiences and genes, they may be somewhat similar in personality. But we have to consider why a particular family raises children the way it does. Much of the way parents rear children is influenced by their culture—by typical patterns of family life and by shared conceptions of the way to bring up children.

It is not easy to determine the extent to which members of a society share conceptions about childrearing. As we look at families in our own society, we see differences in upbringing that reflect different ideas about the "right" way to raise children. Indeed, some parents seem determined to bring up their children in unconventional ways in terms of our society. Still, in a study of unconventional California families, headed by single mothers, unmarried couples, or living in communes, researchers found that compared with parents in other societies, these so-called unconventional parents did not differ that much from conventional parents (married, living in nuclear families).[19] For example, even though unconventional California mothers breast-fed their children for a significantly longer period than conventional mothers did, both groups usually stopped breast-feeding after about a year, which is far below the worldwide average. In 70 percent of the world's societies, mothers typically breast-feed children for at least two years; last-born children may be weaned even later. In a few societies, such as the Chenchu of India, children typically were not weaned until they were 5 or 6 years old.[20] Both the unconventional and conventional California parents differed in other ways too, compared with parents in most other societies. In the California study, no parent, conventional or unconventional, was observed to carry a baby more than 25 percent of the time, but it is common in many preindustrial societies for babies to be held more than half the day.[21]

Our own cultural conceptions begin to become apparent only when we examine other societies and their patterns of childrearing. Consider how societies vary in how quickly parents respond to an infant's needs, in other words, the degree of "indulgence." In many aspects of indulgence—amount of time holding, feeding on demand, responding to crying—industrialized societies such as the United States tend to indulge babies less than do preindustrialized societies. In contrast to those preindustrial societies in which babies are held more than half the day, sometimes almost all day, consider the United States, England, and the Netherlands, where babies may spend most of the day in devices such as playpens, rockers, swings, or cribs. It is estimated that babies are held or touched only 12–20 percent of their daytime hours in these countries and in Japan. The same pattern continues at nighttime. In most preindustrial societies, babies are much more apt to be close to another person, usually sleeping with the mother in the same bed or, if not in the same bed, in the same room. During the day, babies are breast-fed in all preindustrial societies, usually on demand. In industrialized societies, bottle-feeding is common, and feeding is usually spaced out every few hours; in some preindustrial societies babies are fed 20–40 times a day. And in many

One major difference in childrearing between the West and other places is the degree to which an infant is held by a caretaker during the day. In the United States and other Western countries, an infant spends much of the day in a crib, playpen, or stroller. The Bai baby from Yunnan Province in China (on the right) spends a good deal of time in physical contact with the mother or other caretaker.

preindustrial societies people respond very quickly to an infant's crying. For example, among the Efe of the Ituri Forest in central Africa, a 3-month-old infant who cries gets a response within 10 seconds 75 percent of the time. In the United States, a caregiver deliberately *does not* respond at all about 45 percent of the time.[22]

The cross-cultural variation just described seems to reflect cultural attitudes toward childrearing. Parents in the United States say that they do not want their babies to be dependent and clingy; they want to produce independent and self-reliant children. Whether children become self-reliant because of our kind of childrearing is debatable,[23] but our attitudes about childrearing are certainly consistent with our practices.

Let us again consider the Yanomamö and the Semai. With respect to aggression, the two societies have very different ways of dealing with children. (The difference is not surprising, in view of the way adult behaviors and attitudes differ in the two societies.) Yanomamö boys are encouraged to be aggressive and are rarely punished for hitting either their parents or the girls in the village. One father, for example, lets his son Ariwari

> beat him on the face and head to express his anger and temper, laughing and commenting on his ferocity. Although Ariwari is only about four years old, he has already learned that the appropriate response to a flash of anger is to strike someone with his hand or with an object, and it is not uncommon for him to give his father a healthy smack in the face whenever something

displeases him. He is frequently goaded into hitting his father by teasing, being rewarded by gleeful cheers of assent from his mother and from the other adults in the household.[24]

Whereas the Yanomamö clearly and actively encourage aggression, the Semai communicate nonviolence in more subtle ways. They say, in fact, that they do not teach children. The Semai expect children to be nonviolent and are shocked when they are not. When a child loses his or her temper, an adult will simply cart the child off. The Semai do not physically punish a child's aggression, and this approach may be one of the most important teaching devices of all. With such teaching—by example—a child rarely sees an aggressive model and thus has no aggression to imitate.[25] In comparison with the ways Semai and Yanomamö parents treat their children, most North American parents are somewhere in the middle. Hardly any North American parents would encourage children to hit them in the face or encourage them to hit other children. Yet many probably use physical punishment sometimes, and many feel that boys especially should "stand up for themselves" if another child provokes a fight.

As these examples suggest, societies vary in how they raise children. We assume that the way children are reared partly determines the type of personality they will have in adulthood. In other words, different societies, with different customs of childrearing, will probably tend to produce different kinds of people. Other cultural differences also may produce differences in typical personality characteristics. As we will see, growing up in an extended family and going to school seem to affect personality development. We do not mean to suggest, however, that all personalities in a society are alike. An individual's uniqueness is derived from a distinctive genetic endowment and distinctive life experiences—and thus one personality will be at least somewhat different from another within the same culture or subculture.

Cultural anthropologists are interested in common or shared patterns of behavior, belief, feeling, and thinking. Psychological anthropologists are therefore often interested in those aspects of personality that are common or typically shared with others—other members of the society or other members of some subcultural group. Personality attributes are not all-or-nothing characteristics but usually need to be described or measured in terms of degree. So, for example, aggressiveness is not present or absent in a person but is found to a greater or lesser degree in some people than in others. Similarly, when we say that a great deal of physical or verbal aggression is a characteristic personality trait in a particular society, we are making a relative judgment. When we compare ethnographic descriptions of the Yanomamö and Semai, we can be fairly certain that the Yanomamö typically display much more aggression than the Semai. If fieldworkers based their judgments on systematic comparisons of behavior, we could say how often aggressive behavior is exhibited in a culture, and we could calculate the modal frequency of aggression among individuals within a given period of time. That modal frequency could then be compared with the modal frequencies of such behavior in other societies.

Just as culture is never fixed or static, so typical personality characteristics are never static. Individuals often alter their behavior in adapting to changing circumstances. When enough individuals in a society have altered their own behavior or the way they bring up their children, typical personality characteristics will also have changed.

Childrearing Explanations

Many researchers have tried to discover if variation in childrearing customs can account for observed psychological differences. **Socialization** is a term used by both anthropologists and psychologists to describe the development, through the influence of parents and other people, of patterns of behavior, and attitudes and values, in children that conform to cultural expectations. (The term **enculturation** has a similar meaning.) Parents and others often try to socialize children directly by rewarding certain behaviors and ignoring or punishing other behaviors. Socialization can be indirect or subtle as well as direct. In assigning tasks to children, parents are not only encouraging specific skills needed for adult life, but they may also be subtly communicating what kind of person they want their children to become. Going regularly to school may also affect the psychological, particularly cognitive, development of children. Finally, parents may affect the psychological development of their children by the way they generally feel about them.

PARENTAL ACCEPTANCE AND REJECTION   In a classic study of personality, Cora Du Bois spent almost 18 months on the island of Alor in eastern Indonesia studying the native Alorese. To understand the Alorese personality, she broke new ground by asking specialists in various fields to assess and interpret her field data independently. These authorities were given no background briefing on Alorese culture or attitudes, nor were they permitted to see Du Bois's general ethnographic notes or interpretations. To a remarkable degree, their findings concurred with hers.[26]

An unfavorable picture of the typical Alorese personality emerged from this many-sided investigation. Alorese of both sexes were described by Du Bois and her colleagues as suspicious and antagonistic, prone to violent, emotional, and often jealous outbursts. They tended to be uninterested in the world around them, slovenly in workmanship, and indifferent to goals. Turning to the possible causal influences, Du Bois and her co-researchers focused on the experiences of the Alorese infant, particularly time gaps between breastfeedings. At the root of much of Alorese personality development, they suggested, is the mother's long absence from the baby during the day; she returns to agricultural work about ten days to two weeks after the birth. Women are the major food suppliers, working daily in the family gardens; men occupy themselves with commercial affairs, usually the trading of pigs, gongs, and kettledrums. The infant is left in the care of the father, an older sibling, or a grandparent, but it is deprived of the breast as well as the mother for most of the day. Substitute foods are given, but infants often spit them out, suggesting that they are not satisfactory. In Freudian terms, the infant experiences oral frustration and resultant anxiety. At the same time, the baby suffers bewildering switches in attention, from loving and petting to neglect and bad-tempered rejection. Thus, maternal neglect in infancy is viewed as being largely responsible for Alorese personality.

But how do we know that maternal neglect is really responsible for the seeming suspiciousness and outbursts of jealousy among the Alorese? Perhaps maternal neglect is responsible, but the cause or causes could also be any number of other conditions of Alorese life. For example, some critics have suggested that the high prevalence of debilitating diseases in Alor may be responsible for much of the behavior of the Alorese.[27] To be more certain that a particular aspect of childrearing produces certain effects on Alorese personality, we must compare the people of Alor with people in other societies. Do other societies with this kind of maternal neglect show the same pattern of personality traits? If they do, then the presumed association becomes more plausible. If they do not, then the interpretation is questionable.

Although subsequent researchers have not specifically followed up on the possible effects of time gaps between breast-feedings, Ruth and Robert Munroe studied the effects of more versus less holding by the mother in infancy on Logoli children.[28] The Munroes had observational information on how often infants were held, and they were able to interview many of these individuals as children five years later. They were interested in seeing whether children who had been held more often by their mothers were more secure, trusting, and optimistic. So they designed a series of personality measures appropriate for young children. As a measure of optimism, they showed children smiling faces and nonsmiling faces and asked which they preferred. As measures of trust, they looked to see how long a child was willing to stay in a room with a stranger or play with new toys.

The results of the study suggest that children who were often held or carried by their mothers as infants are significantly more trusting and optimistic at age 5 than are other children. Somewhat to their surprise, the Munroes found that, although time held by other caregivers did not predict more trust and optimism, the sheer number of different people who had held the infant did predict more trust and optimism. Holding by the mother was important, but trust was even greater if the baby had been held by a large number of other persons. One possible explanation is that a highly trusting mother is likely to allow many others to hold the baby; by doing so she conveys trust to the baby.

What about the quality of parenting? Are there positive effects on personality when parents show love, warmth, and affection to their children and negative effects when parents are indifferent or hostile to their children? These questions are difficult to investigate cross-culturally because cultures vary in the ways feeling is expressed. If love and affection are not expressed in the same ways, outsiders may misinterpret parental behavior. Nevertheless, Ronald Rohner and his colleagues did extensive work on the effects of parental acceptance and rejection on children after infancy. In a cross-cultural comparison of 101 societies, using measures based on ethnographic materials, Rohner found that children tend to be hostile and aggressive when they are neglected and not treated affectionately by their parents. In societies in which children tend to be rejected, adults seem to view life and the world as unfriendly, uncertain, and hostile.[29] A large number of other studies have compared individuals in different cultures to see if the cross-cultural findings were supported. In general, they were. In addition to finding the world more unfriendly and hostile, individuals who think they were rejected are likely to be hostile and aggressive, emotionally unresponsive or unstable, and have negative evaluations of themselves.[30]

Under what conditions is parental rejection likely in childhood? The Rohner study suggests that rejection is likely where mothers get no relief from child care; when fathers and grandparents play a role in child care, rejection is less likely. Food-collecting societies (those dependent on wild food resources) tend to show warmth and affection to their children. More complex societies are less likely to be affectionate to their children.[31] It is not clear why this should be, but perhaps parental rejection is more likely where parents have less leisure time. Less leisure time may make parents more tired and irritable and therefore have less patience with their children. As we noted in the chapter on economic systems, leisure time probably decreases as cultural complexity increases. More complex societies, which rely on intensive agriculture, also tend to have more economic uncertainty, as we noted in the chapter on getting food. Not only do they tend to have more risk of famines and food shortages, but they also tend to have social inequality. In societies with social classes, many families may not have enough food and money to satisfy their needs, and this factor can also produce frustration in the parents. Whatever the reasons for parental rejection, it seems to perpetuate itself: Children who were rejected tend to reject their own children.

TASK ASSIGNMENT In our society, young children are not expected to help much with chores. If they do have chores, such as tidying up their rooms, they are not likely to affect the welfare of the family or its ability to survive. In contrast, in some societies known to anthropology young children, even 3- and 4-year-olds, are expected to help prepare food, care for animals, and carry water and firewood, as well as clean. A child between 5 and 8 years of age may even be given the responsibility of caring for an infant or toddler for much of the day while the mother works in the fields.[32] What are the effects of such task assignment on personality development?

We now have evidence from more than ten cultures that children who regularly baby-sit are more nurturant—that is, offer more help and support to others—than are other children, even when the children who baby-sit are not baby-sitting. Some of this evidence comes from a project known as the Six Cultures study, in which different research teams observed children's behavior in Kenya (Nyansongo), Mexico, India, the Philippines, Okinawa, and the United States (New England).[33] Ruth and Robert Munroe collected data on children's behavior in four other cultures that show the same relationship between baby-sitting and nurturant behavior; the Munroes' data come from Kenya (Logoli), Nepal, Belize, and American Samoa.[34] Clearly, children who baby-sit infrequently are less attuned to others' needs than are children who baby-sit often.

Why might task assignment affect the behaviors of children? One possibility is that children learn certain behaviors during performance of the task, and these behaviors become habitual. For example, a responsible baby-sitter is supposed to offer help. Mothers might directly instruct the baby-sitter to make sure that happens. But there is probably also an intrinsic satisfaction in doing a job well. For example, it is pleasurable to see an infant smile and laugh, but it is unpleasant to hear a baby cry. We might therefore expect that a child who is assigned baby-sitting would learn for him- or herself that comforting a baby brings its own rewards.[35]

CHILDREN'S SETTINGS Children who are assigned many tasks may spend their day in different kinds of settings, and these settings may indirectly influence behavior. For example, children who are asked to do many household chores are apt to be around both adults and younger children. Children who are assigned few or no tasks are freer to play with their age-mates. Beatrice Whiting suggests that one of the most powerful socializing influences on children is the type of setting they are placed in and the "cast of characters" there.[36] How does the setting influence a child's behavior? We have already noted that being around younger children may make

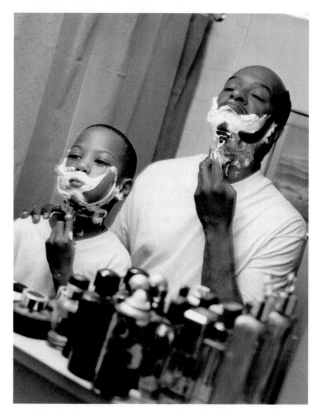

Children in many societies learn a lot by imitation as well as by instruction.

older children more nurturant. Aggressive behaviors also appear to be influenced by who is in the child's setting. Results from the Six Cultures project suggest that children tend to be more aggressive the more they are in the company of other children of roughly the same age. In contrast, children tend to inhibit aggression when adults are on the scene.[37] In the chapter on sex, gender, and culture we noted that boys usually exhibit more aggression than girls. Part of that difference may be due to the fact that girls are generally assigned more work in and around the home (where adults are), whereas boys are more often free to play with their peers. Parents may not be deliberately trying to inculcate certain behaviors, but they may produce certain behaviors by arranging the settings in which children spend their time.

Schooling　One of the most important settings for children in some societies is school. Most researchers focus on the parents when they investigate how children are brought up. But in our own and other societies, children may spend a substantial part of their time in school from the age of 3 or so. What influence does school have on children's social behavior and on how they think as measured by tests? To investigate the effect of schooling, researchers have compared children or adults who have not gone to school with those who have. All of this research has been done in societies that do not have compulsory schooling, otherwise we could not compare the schooled with the unschooled. We know relatively little about the influence of school on social behavior. In contrast, we know more about how schooling influences performance on cognitive tests.

Schooling clearly predicts "superior" performance on many cognitive tests, and within the same society schooled individuals will generally do better than the unschooled on those tests. So, for example, nonschooled individuals in non-Western societies are not as likely as schooled individuals to perceive depth in two-dimensional pictures, do not perform as well on tests of memory, are not as likely to classify items in certain ways, and do not display evidence of formal-operational thinking.[38] But schooling does not always produce superior performance on tests of inferential reasoning.[39]

Why does schooling have these effects? Although it is possible that something about schooling creates higher levels of cognitive thinking in some respects, there are other possible explanations. The observed differences may be due to the advantages that schoolchildren have because of their experiences in school, advantages that have nothing to do with general cognitive ability. For example, consider research that asks people to classify or group drawings of geometric shapes that belong together. Suppose a person is shown three cards—a red circle, a red triangle, and a white circle—and is asked which two are most alike. A person could choose to classify in terms of color or in terms of shape. In the United States, young children usually classify by color, and as they get older they classify more often by shape. Many psychologists assume that classification by color is more "concrete" and classification by shape or function is more "abstract." Unschooled adults in many parts of Africa sort by color, not by shape. Does this mean that they are classifying less abstractly? Not necessarily. It may just be that nonschooled Africans classify differently because they are likely to be unfamiliar with the test materials (drawings on paper, geometric shapes).

How can people classify "abstractly" (e.g., by shape) if they have never had the experience of handling or seeing shapes that are drawn in two dimensions? Is it likely that they would classify things as triangles if they had never seen a three-pointed figure with straight sides? In contrast, consider how much time teachers in the United States spend drilling children on various geometric shapes. People who are familiar with certain materials may for that reason alone do better on cognitive tests that use those materials.[40]

A comparative study of Liberian rice farmers in West Africa and U.S. undergraduates also illustrates the point that choice of materials may influence research results. The comparison involved a set of materials familiar to the rice farmers—bowls of rice—and a set of materials familiar to the undergraduates—geometric cards. Rice farmers appeared to classify more "abstractly" than undergraduates when they were asked to classify rice, and undergraduates seemed to classify more "abstractly" than rice farmers when they classified geometric cards.[41]

Schooled individuals may also enjoy an advantage on many cognitive tests just because they are familiar with tests and the way tests ask them to think of new situations. For example, consider the reaction of a nonschooled person in central Asia who was asked the following question by a Russian psychologist interested in measuring logical thinking:

"In the Far North where there is snow, all bears are white. Novaya Zemlya is in the Far North and there is always snow there. What color are the bears there?" The reply was, "We don't talk about what we haven't seen." Such a reply was typical of nonschooled individuals; they did not even try to answer the question because it was not part of their experience.[42] Clearly, we cannot judge whether people think logically if they do not want to play a cognitive game.

Much research needs to be done on exactly how and why schooling affects cognition. Is it important which specific things are taught? Is it important to be asked to attend to questions that are out of context? Is being literate a factor? This last question was the subject of research among the Vai of Liberia, who had a somewhat unusual situation in that schooling and literacy were not completely confounded. The Vai had an indigenous script learned outside of school. Thus, researchers Sylvia Scribner and Michael Cole were able to see how Vai individuals who were literate but not formally schooled compared with others who were formally schooled (and literate) and those who were unschooled (and illiterate). They found some, but relatively minor, effects of literacy itself; cognitive test performance was much more affected by the number of years of schooling. Similar results come from a study of the Cree of northern Ontario who have their own syllabic script learned outside of school.[43] These comparisons suggest that some other aspects of schooling are more important than literacy as determinants of cognitive performance.

Attending school has become customary in many parts of the world, as among the Baoulé of the Ivory Coast. Schooling seems to affect cognitive development, but we do not know exactly why or how.

console, and fought experimental procedures more. Chinese babies, on the other hand, seemed calmer and more adaptable. Navajo babies were similar to the Chinese, showing even more calmness.[68] Freedman also suggested that an infant's behavior can influence how the parents respond. A calm baby may encourage a calm parental response; a more active baby may encourage a more active response.[69] So, in Freedman's view, babies' genetically determined behavior can lead to ethnic differences in adult personality and caretaking styles.

But we cannot rule out nongenetic explanations of babies' behavior. For example, the mother's diet or her blood pressure could affect the baby's behavior. And it may be that the baby can learn even in the womb. After all, babies in the womb apparently can hear and respond to sounds and to other stimuli. Therefore, it is possible that in societies in which pregnant women are calm, their babies may have learned calmness even before they were born. Last, we still do not know if the initial differences observed in newborn babies persist to become personality differences in adulthood.

Just as the diet of the mother, including the intake of alcohol and drugs, may affect the developing fetus, the diet of infants and children may also affect their intellectual development and their behavior. Studies have shown that malnutrition is associated with lower levels of activity, less attentiveness, lack of initiative, and low tolerance of frustration. Behavior of children can change with short-term nutrition supplements. For example, Guatemalan children who were given nutritional supplements were observed to have less anxiety, more exploratoriness, and greater involvement in games than children who were not given supplements.[70] The problem of malnutrition is not just a matter of nutrition. Other kinds of care may also be reduced. For example, caretakers of malnourished children may interact with them less than do caretakers of healthy children. As a malnourished child shows reduced activity, caretakers tend to respond to the child with lower frequency and less enthusiasm. Then the child withdraws from interaction, creating a potentially serious vicious cycle.[71]

Physiological (not necessarily genetic) differences between populations may also be responsible for some personality differences in adulthood. Research by Ralph Bolton suggests that a physiological condition known as hypoglycemia may be responsible for the high levels of aggression recorded among the Qolla of Peru.[72] (People with hypoglycemia experience a big drop in their blood sugar level after they ingest food.) Bolton found that about 55 percent of the males he tested in a Qolla village had hypoglycemia. Moreover, those men with the most aggressive life histories tended to be hypoglycemic. Whether hypoglycemia is induced by genetic or environmental factors or both, the condition can be alleviated by a change in diet.

Abnormal Versus Normal Behavior

So far in this chapter we have discussed cross-cultural universals and societal differences in "normal" behavior, but anthropologists have also been intrigued by questions about

similarities and differences in *abnormal* behavior. Central to the study of abnormal behavior is how to define it. Is abnormality relative? That is, can what is normal in one society be abnormal in another? Or, alternatively, are there universals in abnormality cross-culturally?

In a very widely read book, Ruth Benedict suggested that abnormality was relative. In her view, behavior thought to be appropriate and normal in one society can be considered abnormal in another.[73] Many German officials, for instance, were regarded in every way as normal by their neighbors and co-workers during the period of Nazi control. Yet these officials committed acts of inhumanity so vicious that to many observers in other Western societies they appeared criminally insane. The Saora of Orissa, India, provide another example of behavior normal to one society that would be abnormal to another society. The Saora took for granted that certain of their womenfolk regularly were courted by lovers from the supernatural world, married them, and had children who were never seen, yet allegedly were suckled at night.[74] Behavior that is so alien to our own makes it no easy task for researchers to identify mental illness in other societies, let alone compare more complex and less complex societies on rates of mental disorder.

Although researchers disagree about the comparability of mental illnesses among cultures, most realize that effective treatment requires understanding a culture's ideas about a mental illness—why it occurs, what treatments are believed to be effective, and how families and others respond to those afflicted.[75] We discuss mental illness further in the chapter on medical anthropology.

Psychological Explanations of Cultural Variation

We have been talking only about societal variation in psychological characteristics and the possible causes of that variation. But psychological anthropologists, as well as other social scientists, have also investigated the possible *consequences* of psychological variation, particularly how psychological characteristics may help us understand certain aspects of cultural variation. For example, David McClelland's research suggests that societies that develop high levels of achievement motivation (a personality trait) in individuals will be likely to experience high rates of economic growth. Economic decline, McClelland suggested, will follow a decline in achievement motivation.[76] Differences in achievement motivation may even have political consequences. For example, Robert LeVine, who studied achievement motivation in three Nigerian ethnic groups, noted that the entry of one of them, the Ibo, into higher education and into many emerging professions may have been resented by the traditionally more influential groups.[77] Soon after LeVine's book was published, the friction between the rival groups escalated into rebellion by the Ibo and the defeat of a separatist Ibo state named Biafra.

Psychological factors may also help us explain why some aspects of culture are statistically associated with others. Abram Kardiner originally suggested that cultural patterns influence personality development through child training and that the resulting personality characteristics in turn influence the culture. He believed that **primary institutions,** such as family organization and subsistence techniques, give rise to certain personality characteristics. Once the personality is formed, though, it can have its own impact on culture. In Kardiner's view, the **secondary institutions** of society, such as religion and art, are shaped by common—he called them *basic*—personality characteristics. Presumably, these secondary institutions have little relation to the adaptive requirements of the society. But they may reflect and express the motives, conflicts, and anxieties of typical members of the society.[78] Thus, if we can understand why certain typical personality characteristics develop, we might, for example, be able to understand why certain kinds of art are associated with certain kinds of social systems (see the chapter on the arts).

Whiting and Child used the phrase **personality integration of culture** to refer to the possibility that an understanding of personality might help us explain connections between primary and secondary institutions.[79] As examples of how personality may integrate culture, we turn to some suggested explanations for cultural preferences in games and for the custom of male initiation ceremonies.

In a cross-cultural study conducted by John Roberts and Brian Sutton-Smith, cultural preferences for particular types of games were found to be related to certain aspects of child-

Games of strategy, such as this game played in Mali, tend to occur where societies are hierarchical and where obedience is stressed.

rearing. The researchers suggested that these associations are a consequence of conflict generated in many people in a society by particular types of childrearing pressures. Games of strategy, for example, are associated with child training that emphasizes obedience. Roberts and Sutton-Smith proposed that severe obedience training can create a conflict between the need to obey and the desire not to obey, a conflict that arouses anxiety. Such anxiety may or may not manifest itself against the person who instigates the anxiety. But the conflict and the aggression itself can be played out on the miniature battlefields of games of strategy such as chess or the Japanese game of *go*.[80] Politically complex and socially stratified societies are particularly likely to emphasize obedience, so it is not surprising that such societies are most likely to have games of strategy.[81] Similarly, games of chance may represent defiance of societal expectations of docility and responsibility. The general interpretation suggested by Roberts and Sutton-Smith is that players—and societies—initially become curious about games, learn them, and ultimately develop high involvement in them because of the particular kinds of psychological conflicts that are handled or expressed, but not necessarily resolved, by the games.

The possible role of psychological processes in connecting different aspects of culture is also illustrated in cross-cultural work on initiation ceremonies for boys at adolescence. In the ceremonies, boys are subjected to painful tests of manhood, usually including genital operations, which indicate the boys' transition to adulthood. Roger Burton and John Whiting found that initiation ceremonies tend to occur in patrilocal societies in which infant boys initially sleep exclusively with their mothers. They suggest that initiation rites in such societies are intended to break a conflict in sex identity. The conflict is believed to exist because boys in these societies would initially identify with their mothers, who exercise almost complete control over them in infancy. Later, when the boys discover that men dominate the society, they will identify secondarily with their fathers. This sex-role conflict is assumed to be resolved by the initiation ceremony, which demonstrates a boy's manhood, thus strengthening the secondary identification.[82]

In the next two chapters we discuss cultural variation in religion and the arts. In doing so we refer to some psychological explanations. Some researchers feel that such explanations may help us understand why gods in some societies are viewed as mean, why artists in some societies prefer repetitive designs, and why strangers in some societies tend to be the "bad ones" in folktales. It is often assumed by psychological anthropologists that conceptions of gods and artistic creations are not constrained by any objective realities, so people are free to create them as they wish. In other words, people may tend to project their personalities—their feelings, their conflicts, their concerns—into these areas. This idea of projection underlies what psychologists call **projective tests.** In such tests, which presumably reveal personality characteristics, subjects are given stimuli that are purposely ambiguous. So, for example, in the Thematic Apperception Test (TAT), subjects are shown vague drawings and asked what they think is going on in them, what happened before, and how they think things will turn out. Because the test materials give few instructions about what to say, it is assumed that subjects will interpret the materials by projecting their own personalities. As we will see in subsequent chapters, some aspects of religion and the arts may be similar to TAT stories and may express or reflect the common personality characteristics of a society.

⊚ Summary

1. Psychological anthropologists are interested in the psychological differences and similarities between societies. Their research has focused mainly on four questions: (1) Do all human beings develop psychologically in much the same ways? (2) What may explain the apparent differences in personality characteristics from one society to another? (3) How do people in different societies conceive of personality and psychological development? and (4) What kinds of cultural variation might be explained by psychological factors?

2. Early research in psychological anthropology was concerned mainly with how supposedly universal stages of emotional development seem to be affected by cultural differences. Some doubt has been cast on the idea that adolescence is necessarily a time of "storm and stress" and that the Oedipus complex, at least in the form stated by Freud, is universal.

3. Recent research on universals in psychological development has been concerned more with cognitive, or intellectual, development. In looking for universals, many researchers have discovered some apparent differences. But most of the tests used in research may favor people in Western cultures and those who attend formal schools.

4. To understand cross-cultural variation in psychological characteristics, many researchers have tried to discover if variation in childrearing customs can account for the observed psychological differences.

5. *Socialization* is a term used by anthropologists and psychologists to describe the development, through the influence of parents and others, of patterns of behavior in children that conform to cultural expectations.

6. Socialization can be direct or indirect. Indirectly, the degree to which parents like children, the kinds of work children are asked to do, and whether children go to school may at least partly influence how children develop psychologically.

7. Anthropologists seek not only to establish connections between childrearing customs and person-

ality traits but also to learn why those customs originated. Some anthropologists believe societies produce the kinds of personality best suited to performance of the activities necessary for the survival of the society.

8. Just as there are cross-cultural universals and societal differences in "normal" behavior, there are similarities and differences in "abnormal" behavior.

9. Psychological anthropologists are interested not only in the possible causes of psychological differences between societies but also in the possible consequences of psychological variation, particularly how psychological characteristics may help us understand statistical associations between various aspects of culture.

⊚ Glossary Terms

enculturation	446	projective tests	457
personality	441	secondary	
personality integration		institutions	457
of culture	457	socialization	446
primary institutions	457		

⊚ Critical Questions

1. Do you think indulging children makes them more or less self-reliant as adults? Why do you think so?

2. What may explain adolescent rebelliousness?

3. Agriculturalists and foragers seem to have somewhat different personalities, so method of food-getting may be related to personality. Do you think there is a similar relationship between occupation and personality? If so, why?

⊚ Research Navigator

1. Please go to www.researchnavigator.com and enter your LOGIN NAME and PASSWORD. For instructions on registering for the first time, please view the detailed instructions at the end of Chapter 1.

2. Using Link Library (Anthropology/Cultural Anthropology) find a Web site relevant to psychological anthropology. Describe something that is either different from what you read in this chapter or expand on some point made in this chapter.

◎ Discovering Anthropology: Researchers at Work

Read the chapter by Susan Schaefer Davis titled "Morocco: Adolescents in a Small Town" in the accompanying *Discovering Anthropology* reader, and answer the following questions:

1. Why do many (but not all) cultures have a stage of life called "adolescence"?

2. Do you think that rebelliousness is inevitable in adolescence?

3. Describe some of the aspects of adolescence that are different in Morocco from your own culture.

CHAPTER TWENTY-SIX

Religion and Magic

As far as we know, all societies have possessed beliefs that can be grouped under the term *religion*. These beliefs vary from culture to culture and from time to time. Yet, despite their variety, we shall define **religion** as any set of attitudes, beliefs, and practices pertaining to *supernatural power,* whether that power be forces, gods, spirits, ghosts, or demons.

In our society, we divide phenomena into the natural and the supernatural, but not all languages or cultures make such a neat distinction. Moreover, what is considered **supernatural**—powers believed to be not human or not subject to the laws of nature—varies from society to society. Some of the variation is determined by what a society regards as natural. For example, some illnesses commonly found in our society are believed to result from the natural action of bacteria and viruses. In other societies, and even among some people in our own society, illness is thought to result from supernatural forces, and thus it forms a part of religious belief.

Beliefs about what is, or is not, a supernatural occurrence also vary within a society at a given time or over time. In Judeo-Christian traditions, for example, floods, earthquakes, volcanic eruptions, comets, and epidemics were once considered evidence of supernatural powers intervening in human affairs. It is now generally agreed that they are simply natural occurrences—even though many still believe that supernatural forces may be involved. Thus, the line between the natural and the supernatural varies in a society according to what people believe about the causes of things and events in the observable world. Similarly, what is considered sacred in one society may not be so considered in another.

In many cultures, what we would consider religious is embedded in other aspects of everyday life. That is, it is often difficult to separate the religious, economic, or political from other aspects of the culture. Such cultures have little or no specialization of any kind; there are no full-time priests, no purely religious activities. So the various aspects of culture we distinguish (e.g., in the chapter titles of this book) are not separate and easily recognized in many societies, as they are in complex societies such as our own. However, it is sometimes difficult even for us to agree whether or not a particular custom of ours is religious. After all, the categorizing of beliefs as religious, political, or social is a relatively new custom. The ancient Greeks, for instance, did not have a word for religion, but they did have many concepts concerning the behavior of their gods and their own expected duties to the gods.

When people's duties to their gods are linked with duty to their princes, it is difficult to separate religious from political ideas. As an example of our own difficulty in labeling a particular class of actions or beliefs as religious or social, consider our attitudes about wearing clothes. Is our belief that it is necessary to wear clothing, at least in the company of nonlovers, a religious principle, or is it something else? Recall that in Genesis, the wearing of clothes, or fig leaves, is distinctly associated with the loss of innocence: Adam and Eve, after eating the apple, covered their nakedness. Accordingly, when Christian missionaries first visited islands in the Pacific in the 19th century, they forced the native women to wear more clothes, particularly to cover their sexual parts. Were the missionaries' ideas about sex religious or social, or perhaps both?

The Universality of Religion

Religious beliefs and practices are found in all known contemporary societies, and archaeologists think they have found signs of religious belief associated with *Homo sapiens* who lived at least 60,000 years ago. People then deliberately buried their dead, and many graves contain the remains of food, tools, and other objects that were probably thought to be needed in an afterlife. Some of the artistic productions of modern humans after about 30,000 years ago may have been used for religious purposes. For example, sculptures of females with ample secondary sex characteristics may have been fertility charms. Cave paintings in which the predominant images are animals of the hunt may reflect a belief that the image had some power over events. Perhaps early humans thought that their hunting would be more successful if they drew images depicting good fortune in hunting. The details of religions practiced in the distant past cannot be recovered. Yet evidence of ritual treatment of the dead suggests that early people believed in the existence of supernatural spirits and tried to communicate with, and perhaps influence, them.

We may reasonably assume the existence of prehistoric religion and we have evidence of the universality of religion in historic times, so we can understand why the subject of religion has been the focus of much speculation, research, and theorizing. As long ago as the 5th century B.C., Herodotus made fairly objective comparisons among the religions of the 50 or so societies he traveled to from his home in Greece. He noted many similarities among their gods and pointed out evidence of diffusion of religious worship. During the 2,500 years since Herodotus's time, scholars, theologians, historians, and philosophers have speculated about religion. Some have claimed superiority for their own forms of religion; others have derided the naive simplicity of others' beliefs; and some have expressed skepticism concerning all beliefs.

Speculation about which religion is superior is not an anthropological concern. What is of interest to anthropologists is why religion is found in all societies and how and why it varies from society to society. Many social scientists—particularly anthropologists, sociologists, and psychologists—have offered theories to account for the universality of religion. Most think that religions are created by humans in response to certain universal needs or conditions. We consider four such needs or conditions here: (1) a need for intellectual understanding, (2) reversion to childhood feelings, (3) anxiety and uncertainty, and (4) a need for community.

The Need to Understand

One of the earliest social scientists to propose a major theory of the origin of religion was Edward Tylor. In Tylor's view, religion originated in people's speculation about dreams, trances, and death. The dead, the distant, those in the next house, animals—all seem real in dreams and trances. Tylor thought that the lifelike appearances of these imagined persons and animals suggest a dual existence for all things—a physical, visible body and a psychic, invisible soul. In sleep, the soul can leave the body and appear to other people; at death, the soul permanently leaves the body. Because the dead appear in dreams, people come to believe that the souls of the dead are still around.

Tylor thought that the belief in souls was the earliest form of religion; **animism** is the term he used to refer to belief in souls.[1] But many scholars criticized Tylor's theory for being too intellectual and not dealing with the emotional component of religion. One of Tylor's students, R. R. Marett, felt that Tylor's animism was too sophisticated an idea to be the origin of religion. Marett suggested that **animatism**—a belief in impersonal supernatural forces (e.g., the power of a rabbit's foot)—preceded the creation of spirits.[2] A similar idea is that when people believe in gods, they are *anthropomorphizing*—attributing human characteristics and motivations to nonhuman, particularly supernatural, events.[3] Anthropomorphizing may be an attempt to understand what is otherwise incomprehensible and disturbing.

Reversion to Childhood Feelings

Sigmund Freud believed that early humans lived in groups each of which was dominated by a tyrannical man who kept all the women for himself.[4] Freud postulated that, on maturing, the sons were driven out of the group. Later they joined together to kill and eat the hated father. But then the sons felt enormous guilt and remorse, which they expressed (projected) by prohibiting the killing of a totem animal (the father-substitute). Subsequently, on ritual occasions, the cannibalistic scene was repeated in the form of a totem meal. Freud believed that these early practices gradually became transformed into the worship of deities or gods modeled after the father.

Freud's interpretation of the origin of religion is not accepted by most social scientists today. But there is widespread agreement with his idea that events in infancy can have long-lasting and powerful effects on beliefs and practices in adult life. Helpless and dependent on parents for many years, infants and children inevitably and unconsciously view their parents as all-knowing and all-powerful. When adults feel out of control or in need, they may unconsciously revert to their infantile and childhood feelings. They may then look to gods or magic to do what they cannot do for themselves, just as they looked to their parents to take care of their needs. As we shall see, there is evidence that feelings about the supernatural world parallel feelings in everyday life.

Anxiety and Uncertainty

Freud thought that humans would turn to religion during times of uncertainty, but he did not view religion positively, believing that humans would eventually outgrow the need for religion. Others viewed religion more positively. Bronislaw Malinowski noted that people in all societies are faced with anxiety and uncertainty. They may have skills and knowledge to take care of many of their needs, but knowledge is not sufficient to prevent illness, accidents, and natural disasters. The most frightening prospect is death itself. Consequently, there is an intense desire for immortality. As Malinowski saw it, religion is born from the universal need to find comfort in inevitable times of stress. Through religious belief, people affirm their convictions that death is neither real nor final, that people are endowed with a personality that persists even after death. In religious ceremony, humans can commemorate and communicate with those who have died, and in these ways achieve some measure of comfort.[5]

Theorists such as William James, Carl Jung, Erich Fromm, and Abraham Maslow have viewed religion even more positively: Religion is not just a way of relieving anxiety; it is thought to be therapeutic. James suggested that religion provides a feeling of union with something larger than oneself,[6] and Jung suggested that it helps people resolve their inner conflicts and attain maturity.[7] Fromm proposed that religion gives people a framework of values,[8] and Maslow argued that it provides a transcendental understanding of the world.[9]

The Need for Community

All those theories of religion agree on one thing: Whatever the beliefs or rituals, religion may satisfy psychological needs common to all people. But some social scientists believe that religion springs from society and serves social, rather than psychological, needs. Émile Durkheim, a French sociologist, pointed out that living in society makes humans feel pushed and pulled by powerful forces. These forces direct their behavior, pushing them to resist what is considered wrong, pulling them to do what is considered right. These are the forces of public opinion, custom, and law. Because they are largely invisible and unexplained, people would feel them as mysterious forces and therefore come to believe in gods and spirits. Durkheim suggested that religion arises out of the experience of living in social groups; religious belief and practice affirm a person's place in society, enhance feelings of community, and give people confidence. He proposed that society is really the object of worship in religion.

Consider how Durkheim explained totemism, so often discussed by early religious theorists. He thought that nothing inherent in a lizard, rat, or frog—animal totems for some Australian aboriginal groups—would be sufficient to make them *sacred*. The totem animal therefore must be a symbol. But a symbol of what? Durkheim noted that the people are organized into clans, and each clan has its own totem animal; the totem distinguishes one clan from another. So the totem is the focus of the clan's religious rituals and symbolizes both the clan and the clan's spirits. It is the clan with which people mostly identify, and it is the clan that is affirmed in ritual.[10]

Guy Swanson accepted Durkheim's belief that certain aspects or conditions of society generate the responses we call religious, but he thought that Durkheim was too vague about exactly what in society would generate the belief in spirits or gods. So what might? Swanson suggested that the belief in spirits derives from the existence of *sovereign groups* in a society. These are the groups that have independent jurisdiction (decision-making powers) over some sphere of life—the family, the clan, the village, the state. Such groups are not mortal; they persist beyond the lifetimes of their individual members. According to Swanson, then, the spirits or gods that people invent personify or represent the powerful decision-making groups in their society. Just like sovereign groups in a society, the spirits or gods are immortal and have purposes and goals that supersede those of an individual.[11]

Variation in Religious Beliefs

There is no general agreement among scholars as to why people need religion, or how spirits, gods, and other supernatural beings and forces come into existence. (Any or all of the needs we have discussed, psychological or social, may give rise to religious belief and practice.) Yet there is general recognition of the enormous variation in the details of religious beliefs and practices. Societies differ in the kinds of supernatural beings or forces they believe in and the character of those beings. They also differ in the structure or

CURRENT RESEARCH AND ISSUES

The Usefulness of Religion: Taboos among New England Fishermen

People who engage in risky activities may try to ensure their safety by carrying or wearing lucky charms. They believe the charms protect them by invoking the help of supernatural beings or forces. We might also believe we can protect ourselves by not doing some things. For example, baseball players on a hitting streak may choose not to change their socks or sweatshirt for the next game (to continue their luck). Or we obey a prohibition because we think that by doing so we can avoid supernatural punishment. For example, we may fast or give up certain foods for a period of time. Why? God knows!

Whether or not religious beliefs and practices can affect our success or reduce our risk, we may consider them useful or adaptive if they reduce our anxieties. And reducing anxiety might indirectly maximize our success. Doesn't an actor try to reduce his or her "stage fright" before a performance? Prohibitions (taboos) are perhaps particularly likely to be adaptive in this way. Consider some research on New England fishermen that suggests how their taboos, or "rituals of avoidance," may reduce anxiety.

John Poggie and Richard Pollnac interviewed a random sample of 108 commercial fishermen from three New England ports. They were trying to explain the number of taboos among the fishermen, as measured by asking them to describe all the superstitions related to fishing they could remember. The fishermen were often embarrassed when they talked about their ritual beliefs and practices. They would say they did not really believe in their taboos, but they admitted that they would not break them while fishing. The taboos prohibited saying or doing a certain thing, or something bad would happen. Most frequently mentioned were "Don't turn a

hatch cover upside down," "Don't whistle on a boat," and "Don't mention the word *pig* on board." When the fishermen were asked what these taboos meant, they talked about personal safety and preventing bad luck.

The results of the study suggest that anxiety about personal danger while fishing is the main stimulus for the taboo behavior observed among the fishermen. For example, there are more taboos reported when the duration of exposure to danger is longer. Fishermen who go out just for the day report significantly fewer taboos than fishermen who go out for longer periods of time. And longer trips are clearly more dangerous because they are farther from shore. If there is a storm, the farther out you are, the more risk of disaster because you are exposed longer to rough seas. And it is more difficult to deal with illness, injury, breakdowns, and damage to the boat far from shore. Also consistent with the conclusion that the fishermen's taboos reduce anxiety is the fact that inshore fishermen (those who are after shellfish close to shore) report a significantly smaller number of taboos than offshore fishermen (who go out farther in trawlers).

On shore, the fishermen express some disbelief in the effectiveness of their taboos. (They are called "superstitions," you know!) But at sea it seems that the omnipresence of danger raises anxiety levels and discourages the fishermen from testing their disbelief. It won't hurt to practice the taboo at sea, they say, but it might hurt not to!

Sources: John J. Poggie, Jr., and Richard B. Pollnac, "Danger and Rituals of Avoidance among New England Fishermen," *MAST: Maritime Anthropological Studies,* 1 (1988): 66–78; John J. Poggie, Jr., Richard B. Pollnac, and Carl Gersuny, "Risk as a Basis for Taboos among Fishermen in Southern New England," *Journal for the Scientific Study of Religion,* 15 (1976): 257–62.

hierarchy of those beings, in what the beings actually do, and in what happens to people after death. Variation exists also in the ways in which the supernatural is believed to interact with humans.

Types of Supernatural Forces and Beings

SUPERNATURAL FORCES Some supernatural forces have no personlike character. As we discussed earlier, Marett referred to such religious beliefs as animatism. For example, a supernatural, impersonal force called **mana,** after its Malayo-Polynesian name, is thought to inhabit some objects but not others, some people but not others. A farmer in Polynesia places stones around a field; the crops are bountiful; the stones have mana. During a subsequent year the

stones may lose their mana and the crops will be poor. People may also possess mana, as, for example, the chiefs in Polynesia were said to do. However, such power is not necessarily possessed permanently; chiefs who were unsuccessful in war or other activities were said to have lost their mana.

The word *mana* may be Malayo-Polynesian, but a similar concept is also found in our own society. We can compare mana to the power that golfers may attribute to some but, unhappily not all, of their clubs. A ballplayer might think a certain sweatshirt or pair of pants has supernatural power or force, and that more runs or points will be scored when they are worn. A four-leaf clover has mana; a three-leaf clover does not.

Objects, persons, or places can be considered **taboo.** Anthony Wallace distinguished mana from taboo by pointing

There's room in the world for all religions—those who believe in rocks, those who believe in trees, those who believe in clouds . . .

© 1984 by Sidney Harris

out that things containing mana are to be touched, whereas taboo things are not to be touched, for their power can cause harm.[12] Thus, those who touch them may themselves become taboo. Taboos surround food not to be eaten, places not to be entered, animals not to be killed, people not to be touched sexually, people not to be touched at all, and so on. An Australian aborigine could not normally kill and eat the animal that was his totem; Hebrew tribesmen were forbidden to touch a woman during menstruation or for seven days afterward.

SUPERNATURAL BEINGS Supernatural beings fall within two broad categories: those of nonhuman origin, such as gods and spirits, and those of human origin, such as ghosts and ancestral spirits. Chief among the beings of nonhuman origin, **gods** are named personalities. They are often *anthropomorphic*—that is, conceived in the image of a person—although they are sometimes given the shapes of other animals or of celestial bodies, such as the sun or moon. Essentially, the gods are believed to have created themselves, but some of them then created, or gave birth to, other gods. Although some are seen as creator gods, not all peoples include the creation of the world as one of the acts of gods.

After their efforts at creation, many creator gods retire. Having set the world in motion, they are not interested in its day-to-day operation. Other creator gods remain interested in the ordinary affairs of human beings, especially the affairs of one small, chosen segment of humanity. Whether or not a society has a creator god, the job of running the creation is often left to lesser gods. The Maori of New Zealand, for example, recognize three important gods: a god of the sea, a god of the forest, and a god of agriculture. They call upon each in turn for help and try to get all three to share their knowledge of how the universe runs. The gods of the ancient Romans, on the other hand, specialized to a high

degree. There were three gods of the plow, one god to help with the sowing, one for weeding, one for reaping, one for storing grain, one for manuring, and so on.[13]

Beneath the gods in prestige, and often closer to people, are multitudes of unnamed **spirits.** Some may be guardian spirits for people. Some, who become known for particularly efficacious work, may be promoted to the rank of named gods. Some spirits who are known to the people but are never invoked by them are of the hobgoblin type. Hobgoblins delight in mischief and can be blamed for any number of small mishaps; still other spirits take pleasure in deliberately working evil on behalf of people.

Many Native American groups believed in guardian spirits that had to be sought out, usually in childhood. For example, among the Sanpoil of northeastern Washington, boys and sometimes girls would be sent out on overnight vigils to acquire their guardians. Most commonly the spirits were animals, but they could also be uniquely shaped rocks, lakes, mountains, whirlwinds, or clouds. The vigil was not always successful. When it was, the guardian spirit appeared in a vision or dream, and always at first in human form. Conversation with the spirit would reveal its true identity.[14]

Ghosts are supernatural beings who were once human and **ancestor spirits** are ghosts of dead relatives. The belief that ghosts or their actions can be perceived by the living is almost universal.[15] The near-universality of the belief in ghosts may not be difficult to explain. There are many cues in everyday experience that are associated with a loved one, and even after the death those cues might arouse the feeling that the dead person is still somehow present. The opening of a door or the smell of tobacco or cologne in a room may evoke the idea that the person is still present, if only for a moment. Then, too, loved ones live on in dreams. Small wonder, then, that most societies believe in ghosts. If the idea of ghosts is generated by these familiar associations, we might expect that ghosts in most societies would be close relatives and friends, not strangers—and they are.[16]

Although the belief in ghosts is nearly universal, the spirits of the dead do not play an active role in the life of the living in all societies. In his cross-cultural study of 50 societies, Swanson found that people are likely to believe in active ancestral spirits where descent groups are important decision-making units. The descent group is an entity that exists over time, back into the past as well as forward into the future, despite the deaths of individual members.[17] The dead feel concern for the fortunes, the prestige, and the continuity of their descent group as strongly as the living. As a Lugbara elder (in northern Uganda in Africa) put it, "Are our ancestors not people of our lineage? They are our fathers and we are their children whom they have begotten. Those that have died stay near us in our homes and we feed and respect them. Does not a man help his father when he is old?"[18]

The Character of Supernatural Beings

Whatever type they may be, the gods or spirits venerated in a given culture tend to have certain personality or character traits. They may be unpredictable or predictable, aloof from or interested in human affairs, helpful or punishing. Why do the gods and spirits in a particular culture exhibit certain character traits rather than others?

We have some evidence from cross-cultural studies that the character of supernatural beings may be related to the nature of child training. Melford Spiro and Roy D'Andrade suggested that the god–human relationship is a projection of the parent–child relationship, in which case child-training practices might well be relived in dealings with the supernatural.[19] For example, if a child was nurtured immediately by her parents when she cried or waved her arms about or kicked, she might grow up expecting to be nurtured by the gods when she attracted their attention by performing a ritual. On the other hand, if her parents often punished her, she would grow up expecting the gods to punish her if she disobeyed them. William Lambert, Leigh Minturn Triandis, and Margery Wolf, in another cross-cultural study, found that societies with hurtful or punitive child-training practices are likely to believe that their gods are aggressive and malevolent; societies with less punitive child training are more likely to believe that the gods are benevolent.[20] These results are consistent with the Freudian notion that the supernatural world should parallel the natural. It is worth noting in this context that some peoples refer to the god as their father and to themselves as his children.

Structure or Hierarchy of Supernatural Beings

The range of social structures in human societies from egalitarian to highly stratified has its counterpart in the supernatural world. Some societies have gods or spirits that are not ranked; one god has about as much power as another. Other societies have gods or spirits that are ranked in prestige and power. For example, on the Pacific islands of Palau, which was a rank society, gods were ranked as people were. Each clan worshiped a god and a goddess that had names or titles similar to clan titles. Although a clan god was generally important only to the members of that clan, the gods of the various clans in a village were believed to be ranked in the same order that the clans were. Thus, the god of the highest-ranking clan was respected by all the clans of the village. Its shrine was given the place of honor in the center of the village and was larger and more elaborately decorated than other shrines.[21]

Although the Palauans did not believe in a high god or supreme being who outranked all the other gods, some societies do. Consider Judaism, Christianity, and Islam, which we call **monotheistic** religions. Although *monotheism* means "one god," most monotheistic religions actually include more than one supernatural being (e.g., demons, angels, the Devil). But the supreme being or high god, as the creator of the universe or the director of events (or both), is believed to be ultimately responsible for all events.[22] A **polytheistic** religion recognizes many important gods, no one of which is supreme.

Why do some societies have a belief in a high god and others do not? Recall Swanson's suggestion that people invent gods who personify the important decision-making groups in their society. He therefore hypothesized that societies with hierarchical political systems should be more likely to believe in a high god. In his cross-cultural study of 50 societies (none of which practiced any of the major world religions), he found that belief in a high god is strongly associated with three or more levels of "sovereign" (decision-making) groups. Of the 20 sample societies that had a hierarchy of three or more sovereign groups—for instance, family, clan, and chiefdom—17 possessed the idea of a high god. Of the 19 societies that had fewer than three levels of decision-making groups, only two had a high god.[23] Consistent with Swanson's findings, societies dependent on food production are more likely to have a belief in a high god than are food-collecting societies.[24] These results strongly suggest, then, that the realm of the gods parallels and may reflect the

A Guatemalan Maya family visits a cemetery on the Day of the Dead. It is believed that the spirits of the dead return for a visit on that day.

everyday social and political worlds. In the past many state societies had state religions in which the political officials were also the officials of the temples (e.g., the pharaohs in Egypt). In recent times most state societies have separated church and state, as in the United States and Canada.

Intervention of the Gods in Human Affairs

According to Clifford Geertz, it is when faced with ignorance, pain, and the unjustness of life that a person explains events by the intervention of the gods.[25] Thus, in Greek religion the direct intervention of Poseidon as ruler of the seas prevented Odysseus from getting home for ten years. In the Old Testament, the direct intervention of Yahweh caused the great flood that killed most of the people in the time of Noah. In other societies, people may search their memories for a violated taboo that has brought punishment through supernatural intervention.

In addition to unasked-for divine interference, there are numerous examples of requests for divine intervention, either for good for oneself and friends or for evil for others. Gods are asked to intervene in the weather and make the crops grow, to send fish to the fisherman and game to the hunter, to find lost things, and to accompany travelers and prevent accidents. They are asked to stop the flow of lava down the side of a volcano, to stop a war, or to cure an illness.

The gods do not intervene in all societies. In some, they intervene in human affairs; in others, they are not the slightest bit interested; and in still others, they interfere only occasionally. We have little research on why gods are believed to interfere in some societies and not in others. We do, however, have some evidence suggesting when the gods will take an interest in the morality or immorality of human behavior. Swanson's study suggests that the gods are likely to punish people for immoral behavior when there are considerable differences in wealth in the society.[26] His interpretation is that supernatural support of moral behavior is particularly useful where inequalities tax the ability of the political system to maintain social order and minimize social disorder. Envy of others' privileges may motivate some people to behave immorally; the belief that the gods will punish such behavior might deter it.

Life after Death

In many societies, ideas about an afterlife are vague and seemingly unimportant, but many other peoples have very definite and elaborate ideas of what happens after death. The Lugbara of Uganda see the dead as joining the ancestors of the living and staying near the family homesite. They retain an interest in the behavior of the living, both rewarding and punishing them. The Zuni of the southwestern United States think the dead join the past dead, known as the *katcinas,* in a katcina village at the bottom of a nearby lake. There they lead a life of singing and dancing and bring rain to the living Zuni. Just as they are swift to punish the priest who fails in his duty, they also punish the people in masks who ineffectively impersonate the katcinas during the dance ceremonies.[27]

The Chamulas have merged the ancient Mayan worship of the sun and moon with the Spanish conquerors' Jesus and Mary. Their vision of life after death contains a blending of the two cultures. All souls go to the underworld, where they live a humanlike life except that they are incapable of sexual intercourse. After the sun travels over the world, it travels under the underworld, so that the dead have sunlight. Only murderers and suicides are punished, being burned by the Christ-sun on their journey.[28]

Many Christians believe that the dead are divided into two groups: The unsaved are sent to everlasting punishment and the saved to everlasting reward. Accounts differ, but hell is often associated with torture by fire, heaven with mansions. Several societies see the dead as returning to earth to be reborn. The Hindus use this pattern of reincarnation to justify one's caste in this life and to promise eventual release from the pain of life through the attainment of *nirvana,* or inclusion into the One.

A recent cross-cultural study asks why some societies judge where you will go after death and others do not. Support was found for the idea that judgmental beliefs parallel the society's economic practices. Some societies have considerable delay between labor inputs and return of food. For example, intensive agriculturalists need considerable labor input to plow, fertilize, or create irrigation systems, and many months go by until crops can be harvested. Not planning ahead has dire long-term consequences. In contrast, mistakes by hunter-gatherers are realized more quickly and can be corrected more quickly. Religions that foster the idea that actions in the present will be judged after death reinforce the need for long-term planning. Consistent with this idea, societies with intensive agriculture are the most likely to believe that their actions in life affect where their souls will go after death.[29] This finding is consistent with Swanson's conclusion discussed above that the gods are generally likely to punish people for immoral behavior when there are considerable differences in wealth in the society. Intensive agricultural societies tend to have considerable differences in wealth.

In many respects, the afterworld in many religions may resemble the everyday world, but we still have only a few comparative studies that show exactly how.

◎ Variation in Religious Practices

Beliefs are not the only elements of religion that vary from society to society. There is also variation in how people interact with the supernatural. The manner of approach to the supernatural varies from supplication—requests, prayers, and so on—to manipulation. And societies vary in the kinds of religious practitioners they have.

Ways to Interact with the Supernatural

How to get in touch with the supernatural has proved to be a universal problem. Wallace identified a number of ways used by people the world over, though not necessarily all together, including, but not limited to, prayer (asking for

A worshipper making offerings at the feet of a statue in an Indian temple.

supernatural help), physiological experience (doing things to the body and mind), simulation (manipulating imitations of things), feasts, and sacrifices.[30] Prayer can be spontaneous or memorized, private or public, silent or spoken. The Lugbara do not say the words of a prayer aloud, for doing so would be too powerful; they simply think about the things that are bothering them. The gods know all languages.

Doing things to the body or mind may involve drugs (hallucinogenics such as peyote or opiates) or alcohol; social isolation or sensory deprivation; dancing or running until exhausted; being deprived of food, water, and sleep; and listening to repetitive sounds such as drumming. Such behaviors may induce trances or altered states of consciousness.[31] Erika Bourguignon found that achieving these altered states, which she generally referred to as *trances,* is part of religious practice in 90 percent of the world's societies.[32] In some societies, trances are thought to involve the presence of a spirit or power inside a person that changes or displaces that person's personality or soul. These types are referred to as possession trances. Other types of trances may involve the journey of a person's soul, experiencing visions, or transmitting messages from spirits. Possession trances are especially likely in societies that depend on agriculture and have social stratification, slavery, and more complex political hierarchies. Nonpossession trances are most likely to occur in food-collecting societies. Societies with moderate levels of social complexity have both possession and nonpossession trances.[33]

One puzzle is why there is a preponderance of women thought to be possessed. Alice Kehoe and Dody Giletti suggested that women are more likely than men to suffer from nutritional deficiencies because of pregnancy, lactation, and men's priority in gaining access to food. Calcium deficiency in particular can cause muscular spasms, convulsive seizures, and disorientation, all of which may foster the belief that an individual is possessed.[34] Douglas Raybeck and his colleagues suggest that women's physiology makes them more susceptible to calcium deficiency even with an equivalent diet. In addition, women are subject to more stress because they are usually less able to control their lives. Higher levels of stress, they suggest, lowers the body's reserves of calcium.[35] Erika Bourguignon suggests a more psychological explanation of women's preponderance in possession trances. In many societies, women are brought up to be submissive. But when possessed, women are taken over by spirits and they are not responsible for what they do or say—therefore they can unconsciously do what they are not able to do consciously.[36] Although intriguing, these suggestions need to be tested on individuals in field situations.

Voodoo employs simulation, or the imitation of things. Dolls are made in the likeness of an enemy and then are maltreated in hopes that the original enemy will experience pain and even death.

Divination seeks practical answers from the supernatural about anything that is troublesome—decisions to be made, interpersonal problems, or illness. (We discuss divination's role in curing illness in the chapter on medical anthropology.) Diviners use a variety of methods, including altered states of consciousness and simulation through the use of objects such as Ouija boards or tarot cards.[37]

Omar Moore suggested that among the Naskapi hunters of Labrador, divination is an adaptive strategy for successful hunting. The Naskapi consult the diviner every three or four days when they have no luck in hunting. The diviner holds a caribou bone over the fire, as if the bone were a map, and the burns and cracks that appear in it indicate where the group should hunt. Moore, unlike the Naskapi, did not believe that the diviner really can find out where the animals will be; the cracks in the bones merely provide a way of randomly choosing where to hunt. Because humans are likely to develop customary patterns of action, they might be likely to look for game according to some plan. But game might learn to avoid hunters who operate according to a plan. Thus, any method of ensuring against patterning or predictable plans—any random strategy—may be advantageous. Divination by "reading" the bones would seem to be a random strategy. It also relieves any individual of the responsibility of deciding where to hunt, a decision that might arouse anger if the hunt failed.[38]

The eating of a sacred meal is found in many religions. For instance, Holy Communion is a simulation of the Last Supper. Australian aborigines, normally forbidden to eat their totem animal, have one totem feast a year at which they eat the totem. Feasts are often part of marriage and funeral ceremonies, as well as a fringe benefit of the sacrifice of food to the gods.

Some societies make sacrifices to a god in order to influence the god's action, either to divert anger or to attract goodwill. Characteristic of all sacrifices is that something of value is given up to the gods, whether it be food, drink, sex, household goods, or the life of an animal or person. Some societies feel that the god is obligated to act on their behalf if they make the appropriate sacrifice. Others use the sacrifice in an attempt to persuade the god, realizing there is no guarantee that the attempt will be successful.

Of all types of sacrifice, we probably think that the taking of human life is the ultimate. Nevertheless, human sacrifice is not rare in the ethnographic and historical records. Why have some societies practiced it? One cross-cultural study found that among preindustrial societies, those with full-time craft specialists, slavery, and the corvée are most likely to practice human sacrifice. The suggested explanation is that the sacrifice mirrors what is socially important: Societies that depend mainly on human labor for energy (rather than animals or machines) may think of a human life as an appropriate offering to the gods when people want something very important.[39]

Magic

All these modes of interacting with the supernatural can be categorized in various ways. One dimension of variation is how much people in society rely on pleading or asking or trying to persuade the supernatural to act on their behalf, as opposed to whether they believe they can compel the supernatural to help by performing certain acts. For example, prayer is asking; performing voodoo is presumably compelling. When people believe their action can compel the supernatural to act in some particular and intended way, anthropologists often refer to the belief and related practice as **magic.**

Magic may involve manipulation of the supernatural for good or for evil. Many societies have magical rituals designed to ensure good crops, the replenishment of game, the fertility of domestic animals, and the avoidance and cure of illness in humans. We tend to associate the belief in magic with societies simpler than our own. But as many as 80,000 people in the United States take magic seriously.[40] Many claim to be witches. An understanding of why magic appeals to some individuals but not others in our own society may help us explain why magic is an important part of religious behavior in many societies.

As we will see, the witch doctor and the shaman often employ magic to effect a cure. But the use of magic to bring about harm has evoked perhaps the most interest.

SORCERY AND WITCHCRAFT Sorcery and witchcraft are attempts to invoke the spirits to work harm against people. Although the words *sorcery* and *witchcraft* are often used interchangeably, they are also often distinguished. **Sorcery** may include the use of materials, objects, and medicines to invoke supernatural malevolence. **Witchcraft** may be said to accomplish the same ills by means of thought and emotion alone. Evidence of witchcraft can never be found. This lack of visible evidence makes an accusation of witchcraft both harder to prove and harder to disprove.

To the Azande of Zaire, in central Africa, witchcraft was part of everyday living. It was not used to explain events for which the cause was known, such as carelessness or violation of a taboo, but to explain the otherwise unexplainable. A man is gored by an elephant. He must have been bewitched, because he had not been gored on other elephant hunts. A man goes to his beer hut at night, lights some straw, and holds it aloft to look at his beer. The thatch catches fire and the hut burns down. The man has been bewitched, for huts did not catch fire on hundreds of other nights when he and others did the same thing. Some of the pots of a skilled potter break; some of the bowls of a skilled carver crack. Witchcraft. Other pots, other bowls treated exactly the same have not broken.[41]

The witch craze in Europe during the 16th and 17th centuries and the witch trials in 1692 in Salem, Massachusetts, remind us that the fear of others, which the belief in witchcraft presumably represents, can increase and decrease in a society within a relatively short period of time. Many scholars have tried to explain these witch hunts. One factor often suggested is political turmoil, which may give rise to widespread distrust and a search for scapegoats. In the case of Europe during the 16th and 17th centuries, small regional political units were being incorporated into national states, and political allegiances were in flux. In addition, as Swanson noted, the commercial revolution and related changes were producing a new social class, the middle class, and "were promoting the growth of Protestantism and other heresies from Roman Catholicism."[42] In the case of Salem, the government of Massachusetts colony was unstable and there was much internal dissension. In 1692, the year of the witchcraft hysteria, Massachusetts was left without an English governor, and judicial practices broke down. These extraordinary conditions saw the accusation of a single person for witchcraft become the accusation of hundreds and the execution of 20 people. Swanson suggested that the undermining of legitimate political procedures may have generated the widespread fear of witches.[43]

It is also possible that epidemics of witchcraft accusation, as in Salem as well as other New England and European communities, may be the result of real epidemics—epidemics of disease. The disease implicated in Salem and elsewhere is the fungus disease called ergot, which can grow on rye plants. (The rye flour that went into the bread that the Salem people ate may have been contaminated by ergot.) It is now known that people who eat grain products contaminated by ergot suffer from convulsions, hallucinations, and other symptoms, such as crawling sensations in the skin. We also now know that ergot contains LSD, the drug that produces hallucinations and other delusions that resemble those occurring in severe mental disorders.

The presumed victims of bewitchment in Salem and other places had symptoms similar to victims of ergot poisoning today. They suffered from convulsions and the sensations of being pricked, pinched, or bitten. They had visions and felt as if they were flying through the air. We cannot know for sure that ergot poisoning occurred during those times when witchcraft accusations flourished. There is no direct evidence, of course, since the "bewitched" were not medically tested. But we do have some evidence that seems to be consistent with the ergot theory. Ergot is known to flourish on rye plants under certain climatic conditions—particularly a very cold winter followed by a cool, moist spring and summer. Tree-ring growth indicates that the early 1690s were particularly cold in eastern New England; and the outbreaks of witchcraft accusation in Europe seem to have peaked with colder winter temperatures.[44] Interestingly, too, when witchcraft hysteria was greatest in Europe, Europeans were using an ointment containing a skin-penetrating substance that we now know produces hallucinations and a vivid sensation of flying.[45] It may not be cause for wonder, then, that our popular image of witches is of people flying through the air on broomsticks.

But whether or not epidemics of witchcraft hysteria are due to epidemics of ergot poisoning or episodes of political turmoil or both, we still have to understand why so many societies in the ethnographic record believe in witchcraft and sorcery in the first place. Why do so many societies believe that there are ways to invoke the spirits to work harm against people? One possible explanation, suggested by Beatrice Whiting, is that sorcery or witchcraft will be found in societies that lack procedures or judicial authorities to deal with crime and other offenses. Her theory is that all societies need some form of social control—some way of deterring most would-be offenders and of dealing with actual offenders. In the absence of judicial officials who, if present, might deter and deal with antisocial behavior, sorcery may be a very effective social-control mechanism. If you misbehave, the person you mistreated might cause you to become ill or even die. The cross-cultural evidence seems to support this theory. Sorcery is more important in societies that lack judicial authorities than in those that have them.[46]

Types of Practitioners

Individuals may believe that they can directly contact the supernatural, but almost all societies also have part-time or full-time religious or magical practitioners. Research suggests there are four major types of practitioners: shamans, sorcerers or witches, mediums, and priests. As we shall see, the number of types of practitioners in a society seems to vary with degree of cultural complexity.[47]

THE SHAMAN   The word *shaman* may come from a language that was spoken in eastern Siberia. The **shaman** is usually a part-time male specialist who has fairly high status in his community and is often involved in healing.[48] We discuss the role of the shaman as healer in the chapter on medical anthropology. More generally the shaman deals with the spirit world to try to get their help or to keep them from causing harm.[49] Here we focus on the methods used by shamans to help others.

The shaman enters into a trance, or some other altered state of consciousness, and then journeys to other worlds in order to get help from guardians or other spirits. Dreams may be used to provide insight or as a way for shamans to commune with spirits. People may seek help for practical matters, such as where to get food resources or whether to relocate, but solving a health problem is most often the goal of the shaman.[50] Shamans may also bring news from spirits, such as a warning about an impending disaster.[51]

Someone may receive a "call" to the role of shaman in recovering from an illness, through a vision quest, or in a dream. Shamans-in-training may enhance the vividness of their imagery by using hallucinogens, sleep or food deprivation, or engaging in extensive physical activity such as dancing. An important part of the process of being a shaman is learning to control the imagery and the spirit powers. Shamanistic training can take several years under the guidance of a master shaman.[52]

SORCERERS AND WITCHES   In contrast with shamans, who have fairly high status, sorcerers and witches of both sexes tend to have very low social and economic status in their societies.[53] Suspected sorcerers and witches are usually feared because they are thought to know how to invoke the supernatural to cause illness, injury, and death. Because sorcerers use materials for their magic, evidence of sorcery can be found, and suspected sorcerers are often killed for their malevolent activities. Because witchcraft supposedly is accomplished by thought and emotion alone, it may be harder to prove that someone is a witch, but the difficulty of proving witchcraft has not prevented people from accusing and killing others for being witches.

MEDIUMS   Mediums tend to be females. These part-time practitioners are asked to heal and divine while in possession trances—that is, when they are thought to be possessed by spirits. Mediums are described as having tremors, convulsions, seizures, and temporary amnesia.

PRIESTS   Priests are generally full-time male specialists who officiate at public events. They have very high status and are thought to be able to relate to superior or high gods who are beyond the ordinary person's control. In most so-

Shamans are usually male. Here, female shamans in Korea perform a healing ritual.

MIGRANTS AND IMMIGRANTS

Colonialism and Religious Affiliation

Many of us might like to think that we belong to a particular religious group because we prefer its beliefs and practices. And that may be true for people who have chosen to switch their religious affiliation. But many religious people affiliate with the religion they grew up with, or one very much like it.

Clearly, religious affiliation is a complex issue. But one thing stands out. You are not likely to choose an affiliation you have never been exposed to. This goes for people who believe in religion and also for people who don't. Most North Americans say they are Christians. But how come?

Would so many in North America be Christians if Europeans (mostly Christian) hadn't established colonies here and elsewhere in the last 500 years? Would there be Muslims in Indonesia and the Philippines and North Africa if Arab kingdoms hadn't established colonies in those places after the 7th century? Would there have been Hindus in Sumatra if South Asians hadn't migrated and established the Srivijayan Kingdom in Sumatra before the time of Christ? Would there have been Jews in Yemen (until their emigration to Israel 50 years ago) if King Solomon's state had not colonized in the land of the Queen of Sheba more than 2,000 years ago? An expanding state society can directly or indirectly force a change in people's religious affiliation. It is not coincidental that the new religious affiliation usually matches the dominant society's.

Religion in some form may be a cultural universal. People may worship the supernatural, pray to it for help and guidance, and even try to control it (with "lucky charms" and other magic). But religion is not the same everywhere, as is evident in this chapter. Why people convert to a major religion carried by an expanding state society is still not completely understood. Sometimes the people do not convert, or do not convert right away. Anthropologist Elizabeth Brusco has written that one primary motivation for conversion, long recognized by scholars, is the desire to maximize advantages. In recent times, missionaries have offered new beliefs and practices that may be appealing, but they have also offered "protection, access to food and other desirable goods, medical care, literacy, technology, status, and, at times, political power." Was the same true, at least somewhat, in the past? Was adopting the new religion the best way to survive colonialism and its consequences?

Even if people adopt a religion, they often change important parts of it. For example, the Lahu of southwest China became Buddhist but the Buddha became a male–female couple rather than just a male. The Lahu were a stateless society (prior to the expansion of the Han Chinese) with a strong emphasis on gender equality. By identifying Buddha with their indigenous god, Xeul Sha, the image of the Buddha was changed. According to Lahu origin myths, Xeul Sha is a male–female pair of twins. They marry and propagate humanity. The identification of Xeul Sha with Buddha means that Buddha is considered a pair of male–female gods by most Lahu Buddhist villagers.

Sources: Elizabeth E. Brusco, "Religious Conversion," in David Levinson and Melvin Ember, eds., *Encyclopedia of Cultural Anthropology,* 4 vols. (New York: Henry Holt, 1996), vol. 3, pp. 1100–04; Phillips Stevens, Jr., "Religion," in David Levinson and Melvin Ember, eds., *Encyclopedia of Cultural Anthropology,* 4 vols. (New York: Henry Holt, 1996), vol. 3, pp. 1088–1100; Shanshan Du, "Is Buddha a Couple: Gender-Unitary Perspectives from the Lahu of Southwest China," *Ethnology,* 42 (2003): 253–71.

cieties with priests, the people who get to be priests obtain their offices through inheritance or political appointment.[54] Priests are sometimes distinguished from other people by special clothing or a different hairstyle. The training of a priest can be vigorous and long, including fasting, praying, and physical labor, as well as learning the dogma and the ritual of his religion. Priests in the United States complete four years of theological school and sometimes serve first as apprentices under established priests. The priest does not receive a fee for his services but is supported by donations from parishioners or followers. Priests often have some political power as a result of their office—the chief priest is sometimes also the head of state or is a close adviser to the chief of state—and their material well-being is a direct reflection of their position in the priestly hierarchy.

It is the dependence on memorized ritual that both marks and protects the priest. If a shaman repeatedly fails to effect a cure, he will probably lose his following, for he has obviously lost the support of the spirits. But if a priest performs his ritual perfectly and the gods choose not to respond, the priest will usually retain his position and the ritual will preserve its assumed effectiveness. The nonresponse of the gods will be explained in terms of the people's unworthiness of supernatural favor.

PRACTITIONERS AND SOCIAL COMPLEXITY More complex societies tend to have more types of religious or magical practitioners. If a society has only one type of practitioner, it is almost always a shaman; such societies tend to be nomadic or seminomadic food collectors. Societies with two types of practitioners (usually shaman-healers and priests) have agriculture. Those with three types of practitioners are agriculturalists or pastoralists with political integration beyond the community (the additional practitioner type tends to be either a sorcerer-witch or a medium). Finally, societies with all four types of practitioners have agriculture, political integration beyond the community, and social classes.[55]

Religion and Adaptation

Following Malinowski, many anthropologists take the view that religions are adaptive because they reduce the anxieties and uncertainties that afflict all peoples. We do not really know that religion is the only means of reducing anxiety and uncertainty, or even that individuals or societies *have* to reduce their anxiety and uncertainty. Still, it seems likely that certain religious beliefs and practices have directly adaptive consequences. For example, the Hindu belief in the sacred cow has seemed to many to be the very opposite of a useful or adaptive custom. Their religion does not permit Hindus to slaughter cows. Why do the Hindus retain such a belief? Why do they allow all those cows to wander around freely, defecating all over the place, and not slaughter any of them? The contrast with our own use of cows could hardly be greater.

Marvin Harris suggested that the Hindu use of cows may have beneficial consequences that some other use of cows would not have. Harris pointed out that there may be a sound economic reason for not slaughtering cattle in India. The cows, and the males they produce, provide resources that could not easily be gotten otherwise. At the same time, their wandering around to forage is no strain on the food-producing economy.

The resources provided by the cows are varied. First, a team of oxen and a plow are essential for the many small farms in India. The Indians could produce oxen with fewer cows, but to do so they would have to devote some of their food production to the feeding of those cows. In the present system, they do not feed the cows, and even though poor nutrition makes the cows relatively infertile, males, which are castrated to make oxen, are still produced at no cost to the economy. Second, cow dung is essential as a cooking fuel and fertilizer. The National Council of Applied Economic Research estimated that an amount of dung equivalent to 45 million tons of coal is burned annually. Moreover, it is delivered practically to the door each day at no cost. Alternative sources of fuel, such as wood, are scarce or costly. In addition, about 340 million tons of dung are used as manure—essential in a country obliged to derive three harvests a year from its intensively cultivated land. Third, although Hindus do not eat beef, cattle that die naturally or are butchered by non-Hindus are eaten by the lower castes, who, without the upper-caste taboo against eating beef, might not get this needed protein. Fourth, the hides and horns of the cattle that die are used in India's enormous leather industry. Therefore, because the cows do not themselves consume resources needed by people and it would be impossible to provide traction, fuel, and fertilizer as cheaply by other means, the taboo against slaughtering cattle may be very adaptive.[56]

Religious Change as Revitalization

The long history of religion includes periods of strong resistance to change as well as periods of radical change. Anthropologists have been especially interested in the founding of new religions or sects. The appearance of new religions is one of the things that may happen when cultures are disrupted by contact with dominant societies. Various terms have been suggested for these religious movements—cargo cults, nativistic movements, messianic movements, millenarian cults. Wallace suggested that they are all examples of **revitalization movements,** efforts to save a culture by infusing it with a new purpose and new life.[57] We turn to examples of such movements from North America and Melanesia.

THE SENECA AND THE RELIGION OF HANDSOME LAKE
The Seneca reservation of the Iroquois on the Allegheny River in New York State was a place of "poverty and humiliation" by 1799.[58] Demoralized by whiskey and dispossessed from their traditional lands, unable to compete with the new technology because of illiteracy and lack of training, the Seneca were at an impasse. In this setting, Handsome Lake, the 50-year-old brother of a chief, had the first of a number of visions. In them, he met with emissaries of the Creator who showed him heaven and hell and commissioned him to revitalize Seneca religion and society. This he set out to do for the next decade and a half. He used as his principal text the *Gaiwiio,* or "Good Word," a gospel that contains statements about the nature of religion and eternity and a code of conduct for the righteous. The *Gaiwiio* is interesting both for the influence of Quaker Christianity it clearly reveals[59] and for the way the new material was merged with traditional Iroquois religious concepts.

The first part of the "Good Word" has three main themes, one of which is the concept of an apocalypse. Handsome Lake offered many signs by which the faithful could recognize impending, cosmic doom. Great drops of fire would rain from the skies and a veil would be cast over the earth. False prophets would appear, witch women would openly cast spells, and poisonous creatures from the underworld would seize and kill those who had rejected the *Gaiwiio.* Second, the *Gaiwiio* emphasized sin. The great sins were disbelief in the "good way," drunkenness, witchcraft, and abortion. Sins had to be confessed and repented. Finally, the *Gaiwiio* offered salvation. Salvation could be won by following a code of conduct, attending certain important traditional rites, and performing public confession.

The second part of the *Gaiwiio* sets out the code of conduct. This code seems to orient the Seneca toward advantageous European-American practices without separating them from their culture. The code has five main sections:

1. **Temperance.** All Seneca leaders were fully aware of the social disorders arising out of abuse of liquor. Handsome Lake went to great lengths to illustrate and explain the harmfulness of alcohol.

2. **Peace and social unity.** Seneca leaders were to cease their futile bickering, and all were to be united in their approach to the larger society.

CURRENT RESEARCH AND ISSUES

One Appeal of Religion May Be the Wish for a Better World

There are many religions in the United States today, and new sects, often derisively called cults, emerge regularly. Few of us realize that nearly all of the major churches or religions in the world began as minority sects or cults. Indeed, some of the most established and prestigious Protestant churches were considered radical social movements at first. For example, what we now know as the United Church of Christ, which includes the Congregational Church, was founded by radicals in England who wanted church governance to be in the hands of the local congregation. Many of these radicals became the people we call Pilgrims, who had to flee to the New World. But they were very fundamentalist in their beliefs; for example, as late as the 1820s, Congregationalist-dominated towns in Connecticut prohibited celebrations of Christmas outside of church because such celebrations were not mentioned in the Bible. Nowadays, Congregationalists are among the most liberal Protestants.

We should not be surprised to learn that most of the various Protestant churches today, including some considered very conservative, began as militant sects that set out to achieve a better world. After all, that's why we call them "Protestant." At first, the rebellion was against Rome and the Catholic Church. Later, sects developed in opposition to church and government hierarchies. And remember that Christianity itself began as a radical group in the hinterland of the Roman Empire. So new sects or cults were probably always political and social,

as well as religious, movements. Recall that the word *millennium,* as used in discussions of religious movements, refers to a wished-for or expected future time when human life and society will be perfect and free of troubles; the world will then be prosperous, happy, and peaceful. Nowadays, the wish for a better world may or may not be religiously inspired. Some people who seek a more perfect world believe that humans alone must achieve it.

How should we categorize this wish for a better world? Should we call it "conservative" because the imagined world may have existed in the past? If the imagined world does not yet exist, is it "radical" to believe it can be achieved? Maybe the wish for a more perfect world is neither conservative nor radical. Maybe it is just that people who are not satisfied with the world as it is think that something can be done to improve things, with or without divine assistance. However it will come, the "millennium" will be different from now, and better.

Ideas about the millennium, and the origins of new cults and religions, might best be viewed then as human hopes: Which ones do people have? Do they vary from culture to culture, and why? Are some hopes universal? And how might they be achieved?

Sources: Rodney Stark, *The Future of Religion: Secularization, Revival and Cult Formation* (Berkeley: University of California Press, 1985); G. W. Trompf, ed., *Cargo Cults and Millenarian Movements: Transoceanic Comparisons of New Religious Movements* (Berlin: Mouton de Gruyter, 1990).

---

3. **Preservation of tribal lands.** Handsome Lake, fearing the piecemeal alienation of Seneca lands, was far ahead of his contemporaries in demanding a halt in land sales to non-Seneca.

4. **Proacculturation (favoring external culture traits).** Though individual property and trading for profit were prohibited, the acquisition of literacy in English was encouraged so that people would be able to read and understand treaties and to avoid being cheated.

5. **Domestic morality.** Sons were to obey their fathers, mothers should avoid interfering with daughters' marriages, and husbands and wives should respect the sanctity of their marriage vows.

Handsome Lake's teaching seems to have led to a renaissance among the Seneca. Temperance was widely accepted, as were schooling and new farming methods. By 1801, corn yields had been increased tenfold, new crops (oats, potatoes, flax) had been introduced, and public health and hygiene had improved considerably. Handsome Lake

himself acquired great power among his people. He spent the remainder of his life fulfilling administrative duties, acting as a representative of the Iroquois in Washington, and preaching his gospel to neighboring tribes. By the time of Handsome Lake's death in 1815, the Seneca clearly had undergone a dramatic rebirth, attributable at least in part to the new religion. Later in the century, some of Handsome Lake's disciples founded a church in his name that, despite occasional setbacks and political disputes, survives to this day.

Although many scholars believe cultural stress gives rise to these new religious movements, it is still important to understand exactly what the stresses are and how strong they have to become before a new movement emerges. Do different kinds of stresses produce different kinds of movements? And does the nature of the movement depend on the cultural elements already present? Let us consider some theory and research on the causes of the millenarian cargo cults that began to appear in Melanesia from about 1885 on.

A revitalization movement that became known as the Ghost Dance spread eastward from the Northwest from the 1870s to the 1890s. It was generally believed that if people did the dance correctly, ghosts would come to life with sufficient resources to allow the people to return to their old ways, and, as a result of some cataclysm, the whites would disappear.

Source: Ogallala Sioux performing the Ghost Dance at the Pine Ridge Indian Agency, South Dakota. Illustration by Frederic Remington, 1890.

CARGO CULTS   The *cargo cults* can be thought of as religious movements "in which there is an expectation of, and preparation for, the coming of a period of supernatural bliss."[60] Thus, an explicit belief of the cargo cults was the notion that some liberating power would bring all the Western goods (cargo in pidgin English) the people might want. For example, around 1932, on Buka in the Solomon Islands, the leaders of a cult prophesied that a tidal wave would sweep away the villages and a ship would arrive with iron, axes, food, tobacco, cars, and arms. Work in the gardens ceased, and wharves and docks were built for the expected cargo.[61]

What may explain such cults? Peter Worsley suggested that an important factor in the rise of cargo cults and millenarian movements in general is the existence of oppression—in the case of Melanesia, colonial oppression. He suggested that the reactions in Melanesia took religious rather than political forms because they were a way of pulling together people who previously had no political unity and who lived in small, isolated social groups.[62] Other scholars, such as David Aberle, suggested that *relative deprivation* is more important than oppression in explaining the origins of cults; when people feel that they could have more, and they have less than what they used to have or less than others, they may be attracted to new cults.[63] Consistent with Aberle's general interpretation, Bruce Knauft's comparative study of cargo cults found that such cults were more important in Melanesian societies that had had decreasing cultural contact with the West, and presumably *decreasing* contact with valued goods, within the year prior to the cult's emergence.[64]

If the recent as well as distant past is any guide, we can expect religious belief and practice to be revitalized periodically, particularly during times of stress. As we discuss in the chapter on culture change and globalization, change associated with globalization appears to be accompanied by the rise of fundamentalist religious movements. Paradoxically, globalization has increased the spread of world religions but it has also increased the worldwide interest in shamanism and other features of religion that are different from the dominant religions. Thus, we can expect the world to continue to have religious variation.

◎ Summary

1. Religion is any set of attitudes, beliefs, and practices pertaining to supernatural power. Such beliefs may vary within a culture as well as among societies, and they may change over time.

2. Religious beliefs are evident in all known cultures and are inferred from artifacts associated with *Homo sapiens* since at least 60,000 years ago.

3. Theories to account for the universality of religion suggest that humans create religion in response to certain universal needs or conditions, including a need for understanding, reversion to childhood feelings, anxiety or uncertainty, and a need for community.

4. There are wide variations in religious beliefs. Societies vary in the number and kinds of supernatural entities in which they believe. There may be impersonal supernatural forces (e.g., mana and taboo), supernatural beings of nonhuman origin (gods and spirits), and supernatural beings of human origin (ghosts and ancestor spirits). The religious belief system of a society may include any or all such entities.

5. Gods and spirits may be unpredictable or predictable, aloof from or interested in human affairs, helpful or punishing. In some societies, all gods are equal in rank; in others, there is a hierarchy of prestige and power among gods and spirits, just as among the humans in those societies.

6. A monotheistic religion is one in which there is one high god, as the creator of the universe or the director of events (or both); all other supernatural beings are either subordinate to, or function as alternative manifestations of, this god. A high god is generally found in societies with a high level of political development.

7. Faced with ignorance, pain, and injustice, people frequently explain events by claiming intervention by the gods. Such intervention has also been sought by people who hope it will help them achieve their own ends. The gods are likely to punish the immoral behavior of people in societies that have considerable differences in wealth.

8. Various methods have been used to attempt communication with the supernatural. Among them are prayer, taking drugs or otherwise affecting the body and mind, simulation, feasts, and sacrifices.

9. When people believe that their actions can compel the supernatural to act in a particular and intended way, anthropologists refer to the belief and related practice as magic. Sorcery and witchcraft are attempts to make the spirits work harm against people.

10. Almost all societies have part-time or full-time religious or magical practitioners. Recent cross-cultural research suggests that there are four major types of practitioners: shamans, sorcerers or witches, mediums, and priests. The number of types of practitioners seems to vary with degree of cultural complexity: the more complex the society, the more types of practitioners.

11. The history of religion includes periods of strong resistance to change and periods of radical change. One explanation for this cycle is that religious practices always originate during periods of stress. Religious movements have been called revitalization movements—efforts to save a culture by infusing it with a new purpose and new life.

⊚ Glossary Terms

ancestor spirits	465	priests	470
animatism	462	religion	461
animism	462	revitalization movements	472
divination	468		
ghosts	465	shaman	470
gods	465	sorcery	469
magic	469	spirits	465
mana	464	supernatural	461
mediums	470	taboo	464
monotheistic	466	witchcraft	469
polytheistic	466		

⊚ Critical Questions

1. How does your conception of God compare with beliefs about supernatural beings in other religious systems?

2. What do you think is the future of religion? Explain your answer.

3. Could any of the religious practices you know about be classified as magic? Are they associated with anxiety-arousing situations?

⊚ Research Navigator

1. Please go to www.researchnavigator.com and enter your LOGIN NAME and PASSWORD. For instructions on registering for the first time, please view the detailed instructions at the end of Chapter 1.

2. Using Link Library (Religion), search for a Web site or sites containing information about a religion that you are not familiar with. Compare some of the features to a religion with which you are more familiar. How are they similar and different?

⊚ Discovering Anthropology: Researchers at Work

Read the chapter by Debra Picchi titled "Bakairi: The Death of an Indian" in the accompanying *Discovering Anthropology* reader, and answer the following questions:

1. How come the Bakairi did not ask whether Western medicine works, but Westerners asked whether shamanism works?

2. Why would a shaman be able to settle disputes?

CHAPTER TWENTY-SEVEN

The Arts

Most societies do not have a word for art.[1] Perhaps that is because art, particularly in societies with relatively little specialization, is often an integral part of religious, social, and political life. Indeed, most of the aspects of culture we have already discussed—economics, kinship, politics, religion—are not easily separated from the rest of social life.[2]

The oldest art found so far comes from caves in South Africa. Pieces of red ochre were engraved there more than 77,000 years ago. In Australia, people painted on walls of rock shelters and on cliff faces between 70,000 and 60,000 years ago. And in southern Africa, Spain, and France, people painted slabs of rock 28,000 years ago. Art is clearly an old feature of human cultures. We say that those earliest paintings are art, but what do we mean by "art"? A stone spear point and a bone fish hook obviously require skill and creativity to make. But we do not call them art. Why do we feel that some things are art and others are not?

Some definitions of art emphasize its evocative quality. From the viewpoint of the person who creates it, art expresses feelings and ideas; from the viewpoint of the observer or participant, it evokes feelings and ideas. The feelings and ideas on each side may or may not be exactly the same. And they may be expressed in a variety of ways—drawing, painting, carving, weaving, body decoration, music, dance, story. An artistic work or performance is intended to excite the senses, to stir the emotions of the beholder or participant. It may produce feelings of pleasure, awe, repulsion, or fear, but usually not indifference.[3]

But emphasizing the evocative quality of art may make it difficult to compare the art of different cultures because what is evocative in one culture may not be evocative in another. For example, a humorous story in one culture may not be funny in another. Thus, most anthropologists agree that art is more than an attempt by an individual to express or communicate feelings and ideas. There is also some cultural patterning or meaning; societies vary in their characteristic kinds and styles of art.[4]

Artistic activities are always in part cultural, involving shared and learned patterns of behavior, belief, and feeling. What are some of the ideas about art in our own culture? We tend to think that anything useful is not art. If a basket has a design that is not necessary to its function, we may possibly consider it art, especially if we keep it on a shelf; but the basket with bread on the table would probably not be considered art. The fact that such a distinction is not made in other societies strongly suggests that our ideas about art are cultural. Among Native Americans in the Pacific Northwest, elaborately carved totem poles not only displayed the crests of the lineages of their occupants, they also supported the house.[5] The fact that artistic activities are partly cultural is evident when we compare how people in different societies treat the outsides of their houses. Most North Americans share the value of decorating the interiors of their homes with pictures—paintings, prints, or photographs hung on the walls. But they do not share the value of painting pictures on the outside walls of their houses, as Native Americans did in the Pacific Northwest.

In our society, we also insist that to be considered art, a work must be unique. This aspect is clearly consistent with our emphasis on the individual. However, even though we require that artists be unique and innovative, the art they produce must still fall within some range of acceptable variation. Artists must communicate to us in a way we can relate to, or at least learn to relate to. Often, they must follow certain current styles of expression that have been set by other artists or by critics, if they hope to have their art accepted by the public. The idea that an artist should be original is a cultural idea; in some societies the ability to replicate a traditional pattern is more valued than originality.

So art seems to have several qualities: It expresses as well as communicates. It stimulates the senses, affects emotions, and evokes ideas. It is produced in culturally patterned ways and styles. It has cultural meaning. In addition, some people are thought to be better at it than others.[6] Art does not require some people to be full-time artistic specialists; many societies in the ethnographic record had no full-time specialists of any kind. But, although everyone in some societies may participate in some arts (dancing, singing, body decoration), it is usually thought that certain individuals have superior artistic skill.

To illustrate the cross-cultural variation that exists in artistic expression, we will consider first the art of body decoration and adornment.

Body Decoration and Adornment

In all societies, people decorate or adorn their bodies. The decorations may be permanent—scars, tattoos, or changes in the shape of a body part. Or they may be temporary, in the form of paint or objects such as feathers, jewelry, skins, and clothing that are not strictly utilitarian. Much of this decoration seems to be motivated by aesthetic considerations, which, of course, vary from culture to culture. The actual form of the decoration depends on cultural traditions. Body

ornamentation includes the pierced noses of some women in India, the elongated necks of the Mangebetu of central Africa, the tattooing of North American males and females, the body painting of the Caduveo of South America, and the variety of ornaments found in almost every culture.

However, in addition to satisfying aesthetic needs, body decoration or adornment may be used to delineate social position, rank, sex, occupation, local and ethnic identity, or religion within a society. Along with social stratification come visual means of declaring status. The symbolic halo (the crown) on the king's head, the scarlet hunting jacket of the English gentleman, the eagle feathers of the Native American chief's bonnet, the gold-embroidered jacket of the Indian rajah—each mark of high status is recognized in its own society. Jewelry in the shape of a cross or the Star of David indicates Christian or Jewish inclinations. Clothes may set apart the priest or the nun or the member of a sect such as the Amish.

The erotic significance of some body decoration is also apparent. Women draw attention to erogenous zones of the body by painting, as on the lips, and by attaching some object—an earring, a flower behind the ear, a necklace, bracelet, brooch, anklet, or belt. Men draw attention, too, by beards, tattoos, and penis sheaths (in some otherwise naked societies) that point upward. We have only to follow the fashion trends for women of Europe and North America during the past 300 years, with their history of pinched waists, ballooned hips, bustled rumps, exaggerated breasts, painted faces, and exposed bosoms, to realize the significance of body adornment for sexual provocation. Why some societies emphasize the erotic adornment of women and others emphasize it in men is not yet understood.

In many societies the body is permanently marked or altered, often to indicate a change in status. For example, in the Poro initiation ceremony practiced by the Kpelle of Liberia, newly circumcised boys spent a period of seclusion in the forest with the older men. They returned with scars down their backs, symbolic tooth marks indicative of their close escape from *ngamu*, the Great Masked Figure, which ate the child but disgorged the young adult.[7]

A need to decorate the human body seems universal. We have noted some of the various methods people have used to adorn themselves in different societies. We are also aware of body-decoration practices that raise questions to which we have no ready answers. What explains adornment of the body by permanent marking such as scarification, bound feet, elongated ears and necks, shaped heads, pierced ears and septums, and filed teeth? (See the box "Politics and Art" for suggestions about the relationship between permanent body marking and politics.) Why do different societies adorn, paint, or otherwise decorate different parts of the body for sexual or other reasons? And what leads some members of our society to transfer body decoration to their animals? Why the shaped hair of the poodle, the braided manes of some horses, and diamond collars, painted toenails, coats, hats, and even boots for some pets?

Explaining Variation in the Arts

In our society we stress the freedom of the artist, so it may seem to us that art is completely free to vary. But our emphasis on uniqueness obscures the fact that different cultures not only use or emphasize different materials and have different ideas of beauty, but they also may have characteristic styles and themes. It is easy to see styles when we look at art that is different from our own; it is harder to see similarity when we look at the art of our own culture. If we look at dance styles, for example, we may think that the dance

style of the 1940s is completely different from the dance style of today. It might take an outsider to notice that in our culture we still generally see couples dancing as a pair rather than in a group line or circle, as in dances we call "folk dances." And, in our culture, females and males dance together rather than separately. Furthermore, our popular music still has a beat or combination of beats and is made by many of the same kinds of instruments as in the past.

But where do these similarities in form and style come from? Much of the recent research on variation in the arts supports the idea that form and style in visual art, music, dance, and folklore are very much influenced by other aspects of culture. Some psychological anthropologists, as we saw in the chapter on psychology and culture, would go even further, suggesting that art, like religion, expresses the typical feelings, anxieties, and experiences of people in a culture. And the typical feelings and anxieties in turn are influenced by basic institutions such as childrearing, economy, social organization, and politics.

Consider how the physical form of art preferred by a society may reflect its way of life. For example, Richard Anderson pointed out that the art of traditionally nomadic people such as the !Kung, Inuit, and Australian aborigines is mostly carryable.[8] Song, dance, and oral literature are very important in those societies and are as portable as they can be. Those societies decorate useful objects that they carry with them—harpoons for the Inuit, boomerangs for the Australian aborigines, ostrich egg "canteens" for the !Kung. But they don't have bulky things such as sculpture or elaborate costumes. And what about the presence of artists or art critics? Although some people in small-scale societies are more artistic than others, specialized artists, as well as critics or theoreticians of art, tend to be found only in societies with a complex, specialized division of labor.

Visual Art

Perhaps the most obvious way artistic creations reflect how we live is by mirroring the environment—the materials and technologies available to a culture. Stone, wood, bones, tree bark, clay, sand, charcoal, berries for staining, and a few mineral-derived ochers are generally available materials. In addition, depending on the locality, other resources are accessible: shells, horns, tusks, gold, copper, and silver. The different uses to which societies put these materials are of interest to anthropologists, who may ask, for example, why a people chooses to use clay and not copper when both items are available. Although we have no conclusive answers as yet, such questions have important ramifications. The way in which a society views its environment is sometimes apparent in its choice and use of artistic materials. Certain metals, for example, may be reserved for ceremonial objects of special importance. Or the belief in the supernatural powers of a stone or tree may cause a sculptor to be sensitive to that particular material.[9]

What is particularly meaningful to anthropologists is the realization that, although the materials available to a society may to some extent limit or influence what it can do artistically, the materials by no means determine what is done.

CURRENT RESEARCH AND ISSUES

Politics and Art

Art is exceedingly variable cross-culturally. But that does not mean that the variability is unexplainable, not linkable to other aspects of human existence. The various findings described in this chapter indicate that much of art is linkable to other aspects of culture. Here we consider the possibility that even politics, that messy and sometimes volatile arena of human social life, may have reflections in art. For example, Christopher Steiner's article, "Body Personal and Body Politic," focuses on four forms of self-decoration—body painting, tattooing, masking, and "crowning." (A mask conceals the face and head of the wearer; a crown or other headdress draws attention to, or identifies, the wearer.) Steiner first discusses how body decoration reflects politics on the islands of Melanesia and Polynesia (in the Pacific).

In Melanesia, political leadership is typically of the "big man" type. There is no fixed authority; big men gain influence by attracting followers, who may not follow for long. There are no political offices or permanent positions of authority. And of course there are no centralized chiefdoms and no hierarchy of influential or powerful people. The whole system is fragile and subject to change. In Polynesia, in contrast, there are permanent systems of authority, usually integrating large populations, with a chief or king at the top whose position is usually inherited. Leaders do not achieve their positions by personal action; rather, they succeed to their positions by genealogical right. The system is permanent or nonshifting as well as hierarchical.

Now consider how body adornment may reflect politics in the two areas. Melanesians paint their bodies, and the painting is ephemeral. It disappears within a short time, or after the first wash, just as a big man's status may go up or down quickly, depending on what he has done lately for his followers. Polynesians decorate their bodies with tattoos, which are permanent, as are their systems of leadership. Just as the chief retains his status over time, so, too, a tattoo does not wash away. In Samoa, for example, tattoos distinguished the chiefly class from commoners. Bands and stripes were restricted to persons of high status; low-status persons could have tattoos only of solid black and only from waist to knees. Within the ruling class, the number of tattooed triangles down a man's leg indicated his relative rank. Because tattooing is permanent, it is a form of body decoration well suited to a society with inherited social stratification.

The traditional political systems of Africa ranged from centralized kingdoms (on the complex end of the continuum) to village-based or segmentary lineage systems in which leadership was ephemeral or secret (tied to secret societies). Masks that conceal identity are often used in the uncentralized systems; crowns or other headdresses indicating high status are frequent in the kingdoms. Among the uncentralized Ibo of eastern Nigeria, masks are often worn by the young men of a village when they criticize the behavior of the village elders. In the kingdom of Ngoyo, in western Zaire, the king's status is indicated by his special cap as well as by his special three-legged stool.

If art may reflect politics on the cultural level, it may also do so on the psychological or individual level. Lewis Austin found that a person's preferences in visual (graphic) symbols can often be predicted from his or her political ideology. Experimental subjects from Japan and the United States were asked to locate themselves on a continuum from radical to conservative and to indicate their preferences in pairs of visual symbols—unbalanced versus balanced, uneven versus even, incomplete versus complete, varying versus uniform. So, for example, a set of bars, as in a bar graph, of the same height is even; bars of different heights are uneven. Conservatives preferred symbols that were orderly (bars side by side ordered from small to large vs. unequal-sized bars lying at angles to each other), passive (a flat line vs. a squiggle or sine wave), and uniform (four squares vs. three squares and a circle). In these terms, the Japanese subjects were generally more conservative than the American. But in each country artistic preferences varied in similar ways with political ideology.

If preferences in visual images have a metaphorical significance that is associated with political preferences, perhaps other style preferences—in clothing, furniture, architecture, and so on—also reflect political ideology. Only future research will tell.

Sources: Christopher B. Steiner, "Body Personal and Body Politic: Adornment and Leadership in Cross-Cultural Perspective," *Anthropos,* 85 (1990): 431–45; Lewis Austin, "Visual Symbols, Political Ideology, and Culture," *Ethos,* 5 (1977): 306–25.

The same materials may be used artistically in different ways. In Japan (on the left), sand is raked into patterns. In the Northern Territory of Australia (on the right), the Yuendumu paint the sand.

Why does the artist in Japanese society rake sand into patterns, the artist in Navajo society paint sand, and the artist in Roman society melt sand to form glass? Moreover, even when the same material is used in the same way in different societies, the form or style of the work varies enormously from culture to culture.

A society may choose to represent objects or phenomena that are especially important to the people or elite. An examination of the art of the Middle Ages tells us something about the medieval preoccupation with theological doctrine. In addition to revealing the primary concerns of a society, the content of that society's art may also reflect the culture's social stratification. Authority figures may be represented in obvious ways. In the art of ancient Sumerian society, the sovereign was portrayed as being much larger than his followers, and the most prestigious gods were given oversized eyes. Also, differences in clothing and jewelry styles within a society usually reflect social stratification.

Certain possible relationships between the art of a society and other aspects of its culture have always been recognized by art historians. Much of this attention has been concentrated on the content of art, since European art has been representational for such a long time. But the style of the art may reflect other aspects of culture. John Fischer, for example, examined the stylistic features of art with the aim of discovering "some sort of regular connection between some artistic feature and some social situation."[10] He argued that the artist expresses a form of social fantasy. In other words, in a stable society artists will respond to those conditions in the society that bring them, and the society, security or pleasure.

Assuming that "pictorial elements in design are, on one psychological level, abstract, mainly unconscious representations of persons in the society,"[11] Fischer reasoned that egalitarian societies would tend to have different stylistic elements in their art as compared with stratified societies. Egalitarian societies are generally composed of small, self-sufficient communities that are structurally similar and have little differentiation between persons. Stratified societies, on the other hand, generally have larger and more interdependent, and dissimilar, communities and great differences among persons in prestige, power, and access to economic resources. Fischer hypothesized, and found in a cross-cultural study, that certain elements of design were strongly related to the presence of social hierarchy. His findings are summarized in Table 27–1.

Repetition of a simple element, for example, tends to be found in the art of egalitarian societies, which have little political organization and few authority positions. If each element unconsciously represents individuals within the society, the relative sameness of people seems to be reflected

Table 27–1 Artistic Differences in Egalitarian and Stratified Societies

Egalitarian Society	Stratified Society
Repetition of simple elements	Integration of unlike elements
Much empty or irrelevant space	Little empty space
Symmetrical design	Asymmetrical design
Unenclosed figures	Enclosed figures

Source: Based on John Fischer, "Art Styles as Cultural Cognitive Maps," *American Anthropologist,* 63 (1961): 80–83.

A hand-woven Kalamkari cloth from Hyderabad, India (on left) and a 19th century Lakota skin bag decorated with beads from the plains of North America (above). The art of stratified societies like India has more unlike elements, asymmetry, and less open space.

in the repetitiveness of design elements. Conversely, the combinations of different design elements in complex patterns that tend to be found in the art of stratified societies seem to reflect the high degree of social differentiation that exists in such societies.

According to Fischer, the egalitarian society's empty space in a design represents the society's relative isolation. Because egalitarian societies are usually small and self-sufficient, they tend to shy away from outsiders, preferring to find security within their own group. In contrast, the art of stratified societies is generally crowded. The hierarchical society does not seek to isolate individuals or communities within the group because they must be interdependent, each social level ideally furnishing services for those above it and help for those beneath it. As Fischer suggested, we can, in general, discern a lack of empty space in the designs of societies in which security is not sought by avoiding strangers, but rather "security is produced by incorporating strangers into the hierarchy, through dominance or submission as the relative power indicates."[12]

Symmetry, the third stylistic feature related to type of society, is similar to the first. Symmetry may suggest likeness or an egalitarian society; asymmetry suggests difference and perhaps stratification. The fourth feature of interest here, the presence or absence of enclosures or boundaries—"frames" in our art—may indicate the presence or absence of hierarchically imposed rules circumscribing individual behavior. An unenclosed design may reflect free access to

most property; in egalitarian societies, the fencing off of a piece of property for the use of only one person is unknown. In the art of stratified societies, boundaries or enclosures may reflect the idea of private property. Or they may symbolically represent the real differences in dress, occupation, type of food allowed, and manners that separate the different classes of people.

Studies such as Fischer's offer anthropologists new tools with which to evaluate ancient societies that are known only by a few pieces of pottery or a few tools or paintings. If art reflects certain aspects of a culture, then the study of whatever art of a people has been preserved may provide a means of testing the accuracy of the guesses we make about their culture on the basis of more ordinary archaeological materials. For example, even if we did not know from classical Greek writings that Athens became more and more socially stratified between 1000 B.C. and 450 B.C., we might guess that such a transformation had occurred because of the changes we can see over time in the way the Athenians decorated vases. Consistent with Fischer's cross-cultural findings, as Athens became more stratified, its vase painting became more complex, more crowded, and more enclosed.[13]

Music

When we hear the music of another culture, we often don't know what to make of it. We may say it does not "mean" anything to us, not realizing that the "meaning" of music has been programmed into us by our culture. In music as well as in art, our culture largely determines what we consider acceptable variation, what we say has "meaning" to us. Even a trained musicologist, listening for the first time to music of a different culture, will not be able to hear the subtleties of tone and rhythm that members of the culture hear with ease. This predicament is similar to that of the linguist who, exposed to a foreign language, cannot at first distinguish phonemes, morphemes, and other regular patterns of speech.

Not only do instruments vary, but music itself varies widely in style from society to society. For example, in some societies people prefer music with a regularly recurring beat; in others, they prefer changes in rhythm. There are also variations in singing styles. In some places it is customary to have different vocal lines for different people; in other places people all sing together in the same way.

Is variation in music, as in the other arts, related to other aspects of culture? On the basis of a cross-cultural study of more than 3,500 folk songs from a sample of the world's societies, Alan Lomax and his co-researchers found that song style seems to vary with cultural complexity. As we will see, these findings about variation in song style are similar to Fischer's findings about variation in art.

Lomax and his co-researchers found some features of song style to be correlated with cultural complexity. (The societies classified as more complex tend to have higher levels of food-production technology, social stratification, and higher levels of political integration.) For example, wordiness and clearness of enunciation were found to be associated with cultural complexity. The association is a reasonable one: The more a society depends on verbal information, as in giving complex instructions for a job or explaining different points of law, the more strongly will clear enunciation in transmitting information be a mark of its culture. Thus, hunter-gatherer bands, in which people know their productive role and perform it without ever being given complex directions, are more likely than we are to base much of their singing on lines of nonwords, such as our refrain line "tra-la-la-la-la." Their songs are characterized by lack of explicit information, by sounds that give pleasure in themselves, by much repetition, and by relaxed, slurred enunciation.[14]

Examples of the progression from repetition or nonwords to wordy information are found within our society. The most obvious, and universal, example of a song made entirely of repetition is the relaxed lullaby of a mother repeating a comforting syllable to her baby while improvising her own tune. But this type of song is not characteristic of our society. Although our songs sometimes have single lines of nonwords, it is rare for an entire song to be made of them. Usually, the nonwords act as respites from information:

Zippity do dah
Zippety ay
My o my
What a wonderful day[15]

In associating variation in music with cultural complexity, Lomax found that elaboration of song parts also corresponds to the complexity of a society. Societies in which leadership is informal and temporary seem to symbolize their social equality by an *interlocked* style of singing. Each person sings independently but within the group, and no one singer is differentiated from the others. Rank societies, in which there is a leader with prestige but no real power, are characterized by a song style in which one "leader" may begin the song, but the others soon drown out his voice. In stratified societies, where leaders have the power of force, choral singing is generally marked by a clear-cut role for the leader and a secondary "answering" role for the others. Societies marked by elaborate stratification show singing parts that are differentiated and in which the soloist is deferred to by the other singers.

Lomax also found a relationship between **polyphony,** where two or more melodies are sung simultaneously, and a high degree of female participation in food-getting. In societies in which women's work is responsible for at least half of the food, songs are likely to contain more than one simultaneous melody, with the higher tunes usually sung by women. Moreover:

Counterpoint was once believed to be the invention of European high culture. In our sample it turns out to be most frequent among simple producers, especially gatherers, where women supply the bulk of the food. Counterpoint and perhaps even polyphony may then be very old feminine inventions. . . . Subsistence complementarity is at its maximum among gatherers, early gardeners, and horticulturalists. It is in such societies that we find the highest occurrence of polyphonic singing.[16]

In societies in which women do not contribute much to food production, the songs are more likely to have a single melody and to be sung by males.[17]

In some societies, survival and social welfare are based on a unified group effort; in those cultures, singing tends to be marked by cohesiveness. That is, cohesive work parties, teams of gatherers or harvesters, and kin groups, who work voluntarily for the good of the family or community, seem to express their interconnectedness in song by blending both tone and rhythm.

Some variations in music may be explained as a consequence of variation in childrearing practices. For example, researchers are beginning to explore childrearing as a way to explain why some societies respond to, and produce, regular rhythm in their music, whereas others enjoy free rhythm that has no regular beat. One hypothesis is that a regular beat in music is a simulation of the regular beat of the heart. For nine months in the womb, the fetus feels the mother's regular 80 or so heartbeats a minute. Moreover, mothers generally employ rhythmic tactics in quieting crying infants—patting their backs or rocking them. But the fact that children respond positively to an even tempo does not mean that the regular heartbeat is completely responsible for their sensitivity to rhythm. In fact, if the months in the womb were sufficient to establish a preference for rhythm, then every child would be affected in exactly the same manner

CURRENT RESEARCH AND ISSUES

Do Masks Show Emotion in Universal Ways?

Anthropologists have documented how forms and styles in art vary from culture to culture. But with all this variation, it seems that certain forms of art may show emotion in universally similar ways. For example, research on masks from different cultures supports the conclusion that masks, like faces, tend to represent certain emotions in the same ways. Face masks are commonly used in rituals and performances. They not only hide the real face of the mask wearer but they often evoke powerful emotions in the audience—anger, fear, sadness, joy. You might think, because so many things vary cross-culturally, that the ways in which emotion is displayed and recognized in the face vary too. But apparently they do not that much. We now have some evidence that the symbolism used in masks is often universal.

In this "Devil Dance" in Vare, Venezuela, males wearing masks try to get rid of the "devil" inside them. Like many masks around the world that are supposed to be frightening, these masks have sharp angular lines, such as in the large ears.

The research on masks builds on work done by Paul Ekman and Carroll Izard, who used photographs of individuals experiencing, or actors simulating, various emotions. Ekman and Izard showed photographs to members of different cultural groups and asked them to identify the emotions displayed in the photographs. A particular emotion was identified correctly by most viewers, whatever the viewer's native culture. The results for the viewers from less Westernized cultures paralleled the results for viewers from more Westernized cultures. Coding schemes were developed to enable researchers to compare the detailed facial positions of individual portions of the face (eyebrows, mouth, etc.) for different emotions. What exactly do we do when we scowl? We contract the eyebrows and lower the corners of the mouth; in geometric terms, we make

by a regular beat, and all societies would have the same rhythm in their music.

Barbara Ayres suggested that the importance of regular rhythm in the music of a culture is related to the rhythm's *acquired reward value*—that is, its associations with feelings of security or relaxation. In a cross-cultural study of this possibility, Ayres found a strong correlation between a society's method of carrying infants and the type of musical rhythm the society produced. In some societies, the mother or an older sister carries the child, sometimes for two or three years, in a sling, pouch, or shawl, so that the child is in bodily contact with her for much of the day and experiences the motion of her rhythmic walking. Ayres discovered that such societies tend to have a regularly recurring beat in their songs. Societies in which the child is put into a cradle or is strapped to a cradleboard tend to have music based either on irregular rhythm or on free rhythm.[18]

The question of why some societies have great tonal ranges in music whereas others do not was also studied by Ayres, who suggested that this difference, too, might be explained by certain childrearing practices. Ayres theorized that painful stimulation of infants before weaning might result in bolder, more exploratory behavior in adulthood, which would be apparent in the musical patterns of the culture. This hypothesis was suggested to her by laboratory experiments with animals. Contrary to expectations, those animals given electric shocks or handled before weaning showed greater than usual physical growth and more exploratory behavior when placed in new situations as adults. Ayres equated the range of musical notes (from low to high) with the exploratory range of animals and forcefulness of accent in music with boldness in animals.

The kinds of stress Ayres looked for in ethnographic reports were those that would be applied to all children or to

angles and diagonals on our faces. When we smile, we raise the corners of the mouth; we make it curved.

Psychologist Joel Aronoff and his colleagues compared two types of wooden face masks from many different societies—masks described as threatening (e.g., designed to frighten off evil spirits) versus masks associated with nonthreatening functions (a courtship dance). As suspected, the two sets of masks had significantly different proportions of certain facial elements. The threatening masks had eyebrows and eyes facing inward and downward and a downward-facing mouth. The threatening masks also were more likely to have pointed heads, chins, beards, and ears, as well as projections from the face such as horns. In more abstract or geometrical terms, threatening features generally tend to be angular or diagonal, and nonthreatening features tend to be curved or rounded. A face with a pointed beard is threatening; a baby's face is not. The theory—originally suggested by Charles Darwin, the evolutionist—is that humans express and recognize basic emotions in uniform ways because all human faces are quite similar, skeletally and muscularly.

But is it the facial features themselves that convey threat or is it the design elements of angularity and diagonality that convey threat? To help answer this question, students in the United States were asked to associate adjectives with drawings of abstract pairs of design features (e.g., a V shape and a U shape). Even with abstract shapes, the angular patterns were thought of as less "good," more "powerful," and "stronger" than the curved shapes.

We should not be surprised to discover that humans all over the world use their faces, and masks, to show emotions in the same ways. Aren't we all members of the same species? Our skin color may vary from dark to light. Our hair may be straight, wavy, or kinky—or skimpy. We vary in the percentages of a lot of characteristics. But those are the characteristics we see. We are not so likely to notice the things about us (by far most of the things about us) that don't vary, such as how we show emotion in our faces. That's why a movie made in Hollywood or Beijing may evoke the same feelings wherever people see it. The universality of human emotion as expressed in the face becomes obvious only when we see faces (and masks) from elsewhere, showing emotions in ways that are unmistakable to us.

Thus, we become aware of universality (in masks as well as other cultural things) in the same way we become aware of variation—by exposure through reading and direct experience to the ways cultures do and do not vary.

Sources: Joel Aronoff, Andrew M. Barclay, and Linda A. Stevenson, "The Recognition of Threatening Facial Stimuli," *Journal of Personality and Social Psychology,* 54 (1988): 647–55; Joel Aronoff, Barbara A. Woike, and Lester M. Hyman, "Which Are the Stimuli in Facial Displays of Anger and Happiness? Configurational Bases of Emotion Recognition," *Journal of Personality and Social Psychology,* 62 (1992): 1050–66.

all of one sex—for example, scarification; piercing of the nose, lips, or ears; binding, shaping, or stretching of feet, head, ears, or any limb; inoculation; circumcision; or cauterization. The results showed that in societies in which infants are stressed before the age of 2, music is marked by a wider tonal range than in societies in which children are not stressed or are stressed only at a later age. Also, a firm accent or beat is characteristic of music more often in societies that subject children to stress than in societies that do not.[19]

Cultural emphasis on obedience or independence in children is another variable that may explain some aspects of musical performance. In societies in which children are generally trained for compliance, cohesive singing predominates; where children are encouraged to be assertive, singing is mostly individualized. Moreover, assertive training of children is associated with a raspy voice or harsh

singing. A raspy voice seems to be an indication of assertiveness and is most often a male voice quality. Interestingly enough, in societies in which women's work predominates in subsistence production, the women sing with harsher voices.

Other voice characteristics may also be associated with elements of culture. For example, sexual restrictions in a society seem to be associated with voice restrictions, especially with a nasalized or narrow, squeezed tone. These voice qualities are associated with anxiety and are especially noticeable in sounds of pain, deprivation, or sorrow. Restrictive sexual practices may be a source of pain and anxiety, and the nasal tone in song may reflect such emotions.[20]

The cross-cultural results about music should be able to explain change over time as well as variation within a society. Future research in a variety of societies may help test the theories of Lomax and Ayres.[21]

Just as in art and song, dance style seems to reflect societal complexity. In less complex societies, everyone participates in dances in much the same way, as among the Huli of New Guinea. In more complex societies, there tend to be leading roles and minor roles, as in a Japanese Geisha show.

MIGRANTS AND IMMIGRANTS

The Spread of Popular Music

Music is a very visceral art. You feel it in your gut. Hearing a piece of music can make your belly vibrate and give you goosebumps. You don't forget that experience. The ideas expressed in a song can get to you, but you're mostly moved by the sound. You feel it. Music can lift you up or make you sad.

But we wouldn't know about lots of music if not for migration. Would there be "country music" radio stations in the United States if lots of people hadn't moved out of the South in the 20th century? Country music itself was an amalgam of Appalachian folk music heavily influenced by music from the British Isles and also by African music. The banjo, adapted by country musicians, was created by African Americans who modeled the banjo on the African stringed musical instrument called a banjar. Though the fiddle, an important instrument in country music, was European in origin, many of the fiddlers in the South were African American and country music incorporated African rhythmic styles and improvisation. There were other influences also—the guitar came from Spain, and yodeling from the Swiss. African American music also influenced much of popular American music—ragtime, the blues, jazz, rhythm and blues, rock and roll, disco and rap, to name just a few. African influences also came to the United States via the Caribbean and South America where people from different cultures created a creolized music. Would we like "salsa" dancing, a form of Afro-Cuban music, or reggae and hip-hop from Jamaica, if there were no immigration? The answer is probably not. If people didn't migrate, it is unlikely that we would know so many styles of music. To get to know music, you need personal contact with it through your own ears. Of course it is possible that you learn to like music from concerts, on CDs, the radio, or now on the Internet, without hearing it from migrants or immigrants. But most people don't listen to everything; they need to know something about the music before they listen to it further.

Probably no place imports or accepts all kinds of music. The movement of popular music is not guaranteed. For example, although there are many immigrants and migrants of Chinese or South Asian descent in the United States and Canada, Chinese or South Asian music has not become popular. Of course, it might in the future. Why the music of some immigrants and migrants is adopted or incorporated and other music is not is as yet not understood. The spread of music is quite different from the spread of technology. The computer and the automobile, like many technologies, can and do spread widely, as people earn more and can afford to buy them. In the case of technologies, there is an easy test of usefulness; a steel ax is better than a stone ax (which is why we don't see people making stone axes anymore). Music is not something that is or is not useful—the ideas and feelings communicated answer our needs. While young people, the most frequent consumers of popular music, are often looking for something "new," the latest style is probably not that different in some respects from the last style. Cultures have musical preferences, and musical styles that are very different are not readily accepted. And there are those who still like their "golden oldies."

With all the migration and immigration in the modern world, it is likely that the market demand for new popular music will continue to expand. In a few years we may have Internet-based radio for every demographic niche. Wouldn't that be a blast!

Sources: David Nicholls, ed., *The Cambridge History of American Music* (Cambridge, UK: Cambridge University Press, 1998); Donald R. Hill, "Music of the African Diaspora in the Americas," in Melvin Ember, Carol R. Ember, and Ian Skoggard, eds., *Encyclopedia of Diasporas: Immigrant and Refugee Cultures Around the World*, 2 vols. (New York: Kluwer Academic/Plenum, 2005), pp. 363–373.

Folklore

Folklore is a broad category comprising all the myths, legends, folktales, ballads, riddles, proverbs, and superstitions of a cultural group.[22] In general, folklore is transmitted orally, but it may also be written. Games are also sometimes considered folklore, although they may be learned by imitation as well as transmitted orally. All societies have a repertoire of stories that they tell to entertain each other and teach children. Examples of our folklore include fairy tales and the legends we tell about our folk heroes, such as George Washington's confessing that he chopped down the cherry tree. Folklore is not always clearly separable from the other arts, particularly music and dance; stories often are conveyed in those contexts.

Although some folklore scholars emphasize the traditional aspects of folklore and the continuity between the present and the past, more recently attention has been paid to the innovative and emergent aspects of folklore. In this view, folklore is constantly created by any social group that has shared experiences. So, for example, computer programmers may have their jokes and their own proverbs (e.g., "Garbage in, garbage out!").[23] Jan Brunvand compiled a set of recently arisen *urban legends.* One such legend is "The Hook." The story, which has many versions, is basically about a young couple parked on Lover's Lane with the radio on. There is an announcement that a killer with an artificial hand is loose, so the girl suggests that they leave. The boy starts the car and drives her home. When he walks around the car to open her door, he finds a bloody hook attached to the door handle.[24] There are even legends on college campuses. What is the answer to the question of how long students should wait for a tardy professor? Students have an answer, ranging from 10 to 20 minutes. Is this a rule, or only a legend? Brunvand reported that he never found a regulation about how long to wait for the professor on any campus that tells this story![25]

Some folklore scholars are interested in universal or recurrent themes. Clyde Kluckhohn suggested that five themes occur in the myths and folktales of all societies: catastrophe, generally through flood; the slaying of monsters; incest; sibling rivalry, generally between brothers; and castration, sometimes actual but more commonly symbolic.[26] Edward Tylor, who proposed that religion is born from the human need to explain dreams and death, suggested that hero myths follow a similar pattern the world over—the central character is exposed at birth, is subsequently saved by others (humans or animals), and grows up to become a hero.[27] Joseph Campbell argued that hero myths resemble initiations—the hero is separated from the ordinary world, ventures forth into a new world (in this case, the supernatural world) to triumph over powerful forces, and then returns to the ordinary world with special powers to help others.[28]

Myths may indeed have universal themes, but few scholars have looked at a representative sample of the world's societies, and therefore we cannot be sure that current conclusions about universality are correct. Indeed, most folklore researchers have not been interested in universal themes but in the particular folktales told in specific societies or regions. For example, some scholars have focused on the "Star Husband Tale," a common Native American story. Stith Thompson presented 84 versions of this tale; his goal was to reconstruct the original version and pinpoint its place of origin. By identifying the most common elements, Thompson suggested that the basic story (and probably the original) is the following:

> Two girls sleeping out of doors wish that stars would be their husbands. In their sleep the girls are taken to the sky where they find themselves married to stars, one of which is a young man and the other an old man. The women are warned not to dig, but they disregard the warning and accidentally open up a hole in the sky. Unaided they descend on a rope and arrive home safely.[29]

The tale, Thompson suggested, probably originated in the Plains and then spread to other regions of North America.

Alan Dundes has concentrated on the structure of folktales; he thinks that Native American folktales, including the "Star Husband Tale," have characteristic structures. One is a movement away from disequilibrium. Equilibrium is the desirable state; having too much or too little of anything is a condition that should be rectified as soon as possible. Disequilibrium, which Dundes calls *lack,* is indicated by the girls in the "Star Husband Tale" who do not have husbands. The lack is then corrected, in this case by marriage with the stars. This tale has another common Native American structure, says Dundes—a sequence of prohibition, interdiction, violation, and consequence. The women are warned not to dig, but they do—and as a consequence they escape for home.[30] It should be noted that the consequences in folktales are not always good. Recall the Garden of Eden tale. The couple are warned not to eat the fruit of a tree; they eat the fruit; they are cast out of their paradise. Similarly, Icarus in the Greek tale is warned not to fly too high or low. He flies too high; the sun melts the wax that holds his feathered wings, and he falls and drowns.

As useful as it might be to identify where certain tales originated, or what their common structures might be, many questions remain. What do the tales mean? Why did they arise in the first place? Why are certain structures common in Native American tales? We are still a long way from answering many of these questions, and trying to answer them is difficult. How does one try to understand the meaning of a tale?

It is easy for people to read different meanings into the same myth. For example, consider the myth the Hebrews told of a paradise in which only a man was present until Eve, the first woman, arrived and ate the forbidden fruit of knowledge. One might conclude that men in that society had some grudge against women. If the interpreter were a psychoanalyst, he, or especially she, might assume that the myth reflected the male's deeply hidden fears of female sexuality. A historian might believe that the myth reflected actual historical events and that men were living in blissful ignorance until women invented agriculture—the effect of Eve's "knowledge" led to a life of digging rather than gathering.

It is clearly not enough to suggest an interpretation. Why should we believe it? We should give it serious consideration only if some systematic test seems to support it. For example, Michael Carroll suggested a Freudian interpretation of the "Star Husband Tale"—that the story represents repressed sentiments in the society. Specifically, he suggested that incestuous intercourse is the underlying concern of this myth, particularly the desire of a daughter to have intercourse with her father. He assumed that the stars symbolize fathers. Fathers, like stars, are high above, in children's eyes. Carroll predicted that if the "Star Husband Tale" originated on the Plains, and if it symbolizes intercourse, then the Plains groups should be more likely than other societies to have intercourse imagery in their versions of the tale. That seems to be the case. Analyzing 84 versions of the tale, Carroll found that Plains societies are the Native American groups most likely to have imagery suggesting intercourse, including the lowering of a rope or ladder—symbolizing the penis—through a sky hole—symbolizing the vagina.[31]

Few studies have investigated why there is cross-cultural variation in the frequency of certain features in folktales. One feature of folktale variation that has been investigated cross-culturally is aggression. George Wright found that variation in childrearing patterns predicted some aspects of how aggression is exhibited in folktales. Where children are severely punished for aggression, more intense aggression appears in the folktales. And in such societies, strangers are more likely than the hero or friends of the hero to be the aggressors in the folktales. It seems that where children may be afraid to exhibit aggression toward their parents or those close to them because of fear of punishment, the hero or his or her close friends in folktales are also not likely to be aggressive.[32]

Other kinds of fears may be reflected in folktales. A cross-cultural study by Alex Cohen found that unprovoked aggression is likely in folktales of societies that are subject to unpredictable food shortages. Why? One possibility is that the folktales reflect reality; after all, a serious drought may seem capricious, not possibly provoked by any human activity, brought on by the gods or nature "out of the blue." Curiously, however, societies with a history of unpredictable food shortages hardly mention natural disasters in their folktales, perhaps because disasters are too frightening. In any case, the capriciousness of unpredictable disasters seems to be transformed into the capricious aggression of characters in the folktales.[33]

Folklore, just like other aspects of art, may at least partly reflect the feelings, needs, and conflicts that people acquire as a result of growing up in their culture.

Viewing the Art of Other Cultures

Sally Price raised some critical questions about how Western museums and art critics look at the visual art of less complex cultures. Why is it that when artworks from Western or Oriental civilizations are displayed in a museum here, they carry the artist's name? In contrast, art from less complex cultures, often labeled "primitive art," tends to be displayed without the name of the artist; instead, it often is accompanied by a description of where it came from, how it was constructed, and what it may be used for. More words of explanation seem to accompany displays of unfamiliar art. Price suggested that the art pieces that we consider the most worthy require the least labeling, subtly conveying that the viewer needs no help to judge a real work of art.[34] In addition, art acquired from less complex cultures tends to be labeled by the name of the Westerner who acquired it. It is almost as if the fame of the collector, not the art itself, sets the value of such art.[35]

Just as the art from less complex cultures tends to be nameless, it also tends to be treated as timeless. We recognize that Western art and the art from classical civilizations change over time, which is why it must be dated, but the art

from other places seems to be viewed as representing a timeless cultural tradition.[36] Do we know that the art of peoples with simpler technology changes less, or is this assumption a kind of ethnocentrism? Price, who has studied the art of the Saramakas of Suriname, points out that although Westerners think of Saramakan art as still representing its African ancestry, Saramakans themselves can identify shifts in their art styles over time. For example, they describe how calabashes used to be decorated on the outside, then the style changed to decorating the inside. They can also recognize the artist who made particular carved calabashes as well as identify those who were innovators of designs and techniques.[37]

When Westerners do notice changes over time in the art of less complex societies, it seems to be because they are concerned about whether the art represents traditional forms or is "tourist art." Tourist art is often evaluated negatively, perhaps because of its association with money. But famous Western artists often also worked for fees or were supported by elite patrons, and yet the fact that they were paid does not seem to interfere with our evaluation of their art.[38]

Although it seems that individual artists can usually be recognized in any community, some societies do appear to be more "communal" than others in their art style. For example, let us compare the Puebloan peoples of the Southwest with native peoples of the Great Plains. Traditionally, women Puebloan potters did not sign their pots, and they largely followed their pueblo's characteristic style. In contrast, each Plains warrior stressed his individual accomplishments by painting representations of those accomplishments on animal hides. Either the warrior would do it himself or he would ask someone else to do it for him. These hides were worn by the warrior or displayed outside his tipi.[39]

Artistic Change and Culture Contact

It is unquestionably true that contact with the West did alter some aspects of the art of other cultures, but that does not imply that their art was changeless before. What kinds of things changed with contact? In some places, artists began to represent European contact itself. For example, in Australia, numerous rock paintings by aborigines portray sailing ships, men on horseback carrying pistols, and even cattle brands. With encouragement from Europeans, indigenous artists also began drawing on tree bark, canvas, and masonite to sell to Europeans. Interestingly, the art for sale mostly emphasizes themes displayed before contact and does not include representations of ships and guns.[40] As aboriginal populations were decimated by European contact, a lot of their traditional art forms disappeared, particularly legends and rock paintings that were associated with the sacred sites of each clan. The legends described the creation of the sacred places, and art motifs with painted human or animal heroes marked the sites.[41]

In North America, contact between native groups produced changes in art even before the Europeans came.

Navajo rugs have changed over time. On the left are rugs from 1905; on the right, rugs from a modern trading post.

Copper, sharks' teeth, and marine shells were traded extensively in precontact times and were used in the artwork of people who did not have access to those materials locally. Ceremonies were borrowed among groups, and with the new ceremonies came changes in artistic traditions. Borrowing from other native groups continued after European contact. The Navajo, who are well known today for their rug weaving, were not weavers in the 17th century. They probably obtained their weaving technology from the Hopi and then began to weave wool and herd sheep. European contact also produced material changes in art; new materials, including beads, wool cloth, and silver, were introduced. Metal tools such as needles and scissors could now be used to make more tailored and more decorated skin clothing. In the Northwest, the greater availability of metal tools made it possible to make larger totem poles and house posts.[42]

After they were placed on reservations, virtually all Native Americans had to change their ways of making a living. Selling arts and crafts earned some of them supplementary income. Most of these crafts used traditional techniques and traditional designs, altered somewhat to suit European expectations. Outsiders played important roles in encouraging changes in arts and crafts. Some storekeepers became patrons to particular artists who were then able to devote themselves full time to their craft. Traders would often encourage changes, such as new objects—for example, ashtrays and cups made of pottery. Scholars have played a role too. Some have helped artisans learn about styles of the past that had disappeared. For example, with the encouragement of anthropologists and others in the Santa Fe area, Maria and Julian Martinez of San Ildefonso Pueblo brought back a polished black-on-black pottery style originally produced by nearby ancient peoples.[43]

Some of the artistic changes that have occurred after contact with the West are partly predictable from the results of cross-cultural research on artistic variation. Remember that Fischer found that egalitarian societies typically had less complex designs and more symmetry than did stratified societies. With the loss of traditional ways of making a living and with the increase in wage labor and commercial enterprises, many Native American groups have become more socially stratified. Extrapolating from Fischer's results, we would predict that designs on visual art should become more complex and asymmetrical as social stratification increases. Indeed, if early reservation art (1870–1901) among the Shoshone-Bannock of southeastern Idaho is compared with their recent art (1973–1983), it is clear that the art has become more complex as social stratification has increased.[44] It could also be true that the art changed because the artists came to realize that more asymmetry and complexity would sell better to people who collect art.

◎ Summary

1. Not all societies have a word for art, but art universally seems to have several qualities. It expresses as well as communicates. It stimulates the senses, affects emotions, and evokes ideas. It is produced in culturally patterned ways and styles. It has cultural meaning. And some people are thought to be better at it than others.

2. All societies decorate or adorn the body, temporarily or permanently. But there is enormous cultural variation in the parts decorated and how. Body decoration may be used to delineate social position, gender, or occupation.

It may also have an erotic significance, as, for example, in drawing attention to erogenous zones of the body.

3. The materials used to produce visual art, the way those materials are used, and the natural objects the artist may choose to represent all vary from society to society and reveal much about a particular society's relation to its environment. Some studies indicate a correlation between artistic design and social stratification.

4. Like the visual arts, music is subject to a remarkable amount of variation from society to society. Some studies suggest correlations between musical styles and cultural complexity. Other research shows links between childrearing practices and a society's preference for certain rhythmical patterns, tonal ranges, and voice quality.

5. Folklore is a broad category including all the myths, legends, folktales, ballads, riddles, proverbs, and superstitions of a cultural group. In general, folklore is transmitted orally, but it may also be written. Some anthropologists have identified basic themes in myths—catastrophe, slaying of monsters, incest, sibling rivalry, and castration. Myths may reflect a society's deepest preoccupations.

6. Art is always changing, but recent culture contact has had some profound effects on art in various parts of the world. With the decimation of many indigenous populations, many areas have lost some of their artistic traditions. But the art also changed as individuals began to sell arts and crafts.

⊚ Glossary Terms

folklore	487	polyphony	483

⊚ Critical Questions

1. How innovative or original can a successful artist be? Explain your answer.
2. What kind of art do you prefer, and why?
3. Do you think art made for tourists is inferior? Whatever you think, why do you think so?

⊚ Research Navigator

1. Please go to www.researchnavigator.com and enter your LOGIN NAME and PASSWORD. For instructions on registering for the first time, please view the detailed instructions at the end of Chapter 1.
2. Using Link Library (Art History or Anthropology), search for a Web site or sites containing information about art or folklore. Pick two different cultures and describe some of the similarities and differences. How does the art or folklore make you feel?

⊚ Discovering Anthropology: Researchers at Work

Read the chapter by Donald Mitchell titled "Nimpkish: Complex Foragers on the Northwest Coast of North America" in the accompanying *Discovering Anthropology* reader, and answer the following questions:

1. The art form of dance was important to the Nimpkish. Why do you think?
2. In what season were the dances held, and why do you think they occurred then?

CHAPTER TWENTY-EIGHT

Culture Change and Globalization

Most of us are aware that "times have changed," especially when we compare our lives with those of our parents. Witness the recent changes in attitudes about sex and marriage, as well as the changes in women's roles. But such culture change is not unusual. Throughout history humans have replaced or altered customary behaviors and attitudes as their needs have changed. Just as no individual is immortal, no particular cultural pattern is impervious to change. Anthropologists, therefore, want to understand how and why culture change occurs.

Three general questions can be asked about culture change: What is the source of a new trait? Why are people motivated, unconsciously as well as consciously, to adopt it? And is the new trait adaptive? The source of the change may be inside or outside the society. That is, a new idea or behavior may originate within the society, or it may come from another society. With regard to motivation, people may adopt the new idea or behavior voluntarily, even if unconsciously, or they may be forced to adopt it. Finally, the outcome of culture change may or may not be beneficial. In this chapter, we first discuss the various processes of culture change in terms of the three dimensions of source, motivation, and outcome. Then we discuss some of the major types of culture change in the modern world. As we will see, these changes are associated largely with the expansion of Western societies over the last 500 years. New cultures and new identities may arise, in a process called *ethnogenesis*. Finally, we discuss *globalization*—the ongoing spread of cultural features around the world—and what it portends for the future of cultural diversity.

How and Why Cultures Change

Discoveries and inventions, which may originate inside or outside a society, are ultimately the sources of all culture change. But they do not necessarily lead to change. If an invention or discovery is ignored, no change in culture results. It is only when society accepts an invention or discovery and uses it regularly that we can begin to speak of culture change.

Discovery and Invention

The new thing discovered or invented, the innovation, may be an object—the wheel, the plow, the computer—or it may involve behavior and ideas—buying and selling, democracy, monogamy. According to Ralph Linton, a discovery is any addition to knowledge and an invention is a new application of knowledge.[1] Thus, a person might discover that children can be persuaded to eat nourishing food if the food is associated with an imaginary character that appeals to them. And then someone might exploit that discovery by inventing a character named Popeye who appears in a series of animated cartoons, acquiring miraculous strength by devouring cans of spinach.

UNCONSCIOUS INVENTION   In discussing the process of invention, we should differentiate between various types of inventions. One type is the consequence of a society's setting itself a specific goal, such as eliminating tuberculosis or placing a person on the moon. Another type emerges less intentionally. This second process of invention is often referred to as *accidental juxtaposition* or *unconscious invention*. Linton suggested that some inventions, especially those of prehistoric days, were probably the consequences of literally dozens of tiny initiatives by "unconscious" inventors. These inventors made their small contributions, perhaps over many hundreds of years, without being aware of the part they were playing in bringing one invention, such as the wheel or a better form of hand ax, to completion.[2] Consider the example of children playing on a fallen log, which rolls as they walk and balance on it, coupled with the need at a given moment to move a slab of granite from a cave face. The children's play may have suggested the use of logs as rollers and thereby set in motion a series of developments that culminated in the wheel.

In reconstructing the process of invention in prehistoric times, however, we should be careful not to look back on our ancestors with a smugness generated by our more highly developed technology. We have become accustomed to turning to the science sections of our magazines and newspapers and finding, almost daily, reports of miraculous new discoveries and inventions. From our point of view, it is difficult to imagine such a simple invention as the wheel taking so many centuries to come into being. We are tempted to surmise that early humans were less intelligent than we are. But the capacity of the human brain has been the same for perhaps 100,000 years; there is no evidence that the inventors of the wheel were any less intelligent than we are.

INTENTIONAL INNOVATION   Some discoveries and inventions arise out of deliberate attempts to produce a new idea or object. It may seem that such innovations are obvious responses to perceived needs. For example, during the Industrial Revolution there was a great demand for inventions that would increase productivity. James Hargreaves, in 18th-century England, is an example of an inventor who responded to an existing demand. Textile manufacturers were clamoring for such large quantities of spun yarn that cottage laborers, working with foot-operated spinning wheels, could not meet the demand. Hargreaves, realizing that prestige and financial rewards would come to the person who invented a method of spinning large quantities of yarn in a short time, set about the task and developed the spinning jenny.

But perceived needs and the economic rewards that may be given to the innovator do not explain why only some people innovate. We know relatively little about why some people are more innovative than others. The ability to innovate may depend in part on individual characteristics such as high intelligence and creativity. And creativity may be influenced by social conditions.

A study of innovation among Ashanti artist-carvers in Ghana suggests that creativity is more likely in some socioeconomic groups than in others.[3] Some carvers produced only traditional designs; others departed from tradition and produced "new" styles of carving. Two groups were found to innovate the most—the wealthiest and the poorest carvers. These two groups of carvers may tolerate risk more than the middle socioeconomic group. Innovative carving entails some risk because it may take more time and it may not sell. Wealthy carvers can afford the risk, and they may gain some prestige as well as income if their innovation is appreciated. The poor are not doing well anyway, and they have little to lose by trying something new.

Some societies encourage innovativeness more than others and this can vary substantially over time. Patricia Greenfield and her colleagues describe the changes in weaving in a Mayan community in the Zinacantán region of Chiapas, Mexico.[4] In 1969 and 1970, innovation was not valued. Rather, tradition was; there was the old "true way" to do everything, including how one dressed. There were only four simple weaving patterns, and virtually all males wore ponchos with the same pattern. By 1991, virtually no poncho was the same and the villagers had developed elaborate brocaded and embroidered designs. In a period of 20 years, innovation had increased dramatically. Two other things had also changed. The economy was more commercialized; textiles as well as other items were now bought and sold. The other change was a shift to a much less directed teaching style. Earlier, mothers would give highly structured instruction to their daughters, often with "four hands" on the loom. Later, girls were allowed to learn more by themselves, by trial-and-error, and they produced more abstract and varied designs.

WHO ADOPTS INNOVATIONS?   Once someone discovers or invents something, there is still the question of whether the innovation will be adopted by others. Many researchers have studied the characteristics of "early adopters." Such individuals tend to be educated, high in social status, upwardly mobile, and, if they are property owners, have large farms and businesses. The individuals who most need technological improvements—those who are less well off—are generally the last to adopt innovations. The theory is that only the wealthy can afford to take the substantial risks associated with new ways of doing things. In periods of rapid technological change, therefore, the gap between rich and poor is likely to widen because the rich adopt innovations sooner, and benefit more from them, than the poor.[5]

Does this imply that the likelihood of adopting innovations is a simple function of how much wealth a possible adopter possesses? Not necessarily. Frank Cancian reviewed several studies and found that upper-middle-class individuals show more conservatism than lower-middle-class individuals. Cancian suggested that when the risks are unknown, the lower-middle-class individuals are more receptive to innovation because they have less to lose. Later on, when the risks are better known—that is, as more people adopt the innovation—the upper-middle class catches up to the lower-middle class.[6] So the readiness to accept innovation, like the likelihood of creativity among Ashanti carvers, may not be related to socioeconomic position in a linear way.

The speed of accepting an innovation may depend partly on how new behaviors and ideas are typically transmitted in a society. In particular, is a person exposed to many versus few "teachers"? If children learn most of what they know from their parents or from a relatively small number of elders, then innovation will be slow to spread throughout the society, and culture change is likely to be slow. Innovations may catch on more rapidly if individuals are exposed to various teachers and other "leaders" who can influence many in a relatively short time. And the more peers we have, the more we might learn from them.[7] Perhaps this is why the pace of change appears to be so quick today. In societies like our own, and increasingly in the industrializing world, it is likely that people learn in schools from teachers, from leaders in their specialties, and from peers.

COSTS AND BENEFITS An innovation that is technologically superior is not necessarily going to be adopted. There are costs as well as benefits for both individuals and large-scale industries. Take the computer keyboard. The keyboard used most often on computers today is called the QWERTY keyboard (named after the letters on the left side of the line of keys below the row of number keys). This keyboard was actually invented to slow typing speed down! Early typewriters had mechanical keys that jammed if the typist went too fast.[8] Computer keyboards don't have that problem, so an arrangement of keys that allowed faster typing would probably be better. Different keyboard configurations have been invented, but they haven't caught on. Most people probably would find it too hard or too time-consuming to learn a new style of typing, so the original style of keyboard persists.

In large-scale industries, technological innovations may be very costly to implement. A new product or process may require revamping a manufacturing or service facility and retraining workers. Before a decision is made to change, the costs of doing so are weighed against the potential benefits. If the market is expected to be large for a new product, the product is more likely to be produced. If the market is judged small, the benefits may not be sufficient inducement to change. Companies may also judge the value of an innovation by whether it could be copied by competitors. If the new innovation is easily copyable, the inventing company may not find the investment worthwhile. Although the market may be large, the inventing company may not be able to hold onto market share if other companies could produce the product quickly without having to invest in research and development.[9]

Diffusion

The source of new cultural elements in a society may also be another society. The process by which cultural elements are borrowed from another society and incorporated into the culture of the recipient group is called **diffusion.** Borrowing sometimes enables a group to bypass stages or mistakes in the development of a process or institution. For example, Germany was able to accelerate its program of industrialization in the 19th century because it was able to avoid some of the errors made by its English and Belgian competitors by taking advantage of technological borrowing. Japan did the same somewhat later. Indeed, in recent years some of the earliest industrialized countries have fallen behind their imitators in certain areas of production, such as automobiles, televisions, cameras, and computers.

In a well-known passage, Linton conveyed the far-reaching effects of diffusion by considering the first few hours in the day of an American man in the 1930s. This man

> . . .awakens in a bed built on a pattern which originated in the Near East but which was modified in northern Europe before it was transmitted to America. He throws back covers made from cotton, domesticated in India, or linen, domesticated in the Near East, or silk, the use of which was discovered in China. All of these materials have been spun and woven by processes invented in the Near East. . . . He takes off his pajamas, a garment invented in India, and washes with soap invented by the ancient Gauls. He then shaves, a masochistic rite which seems to have derived from either Sumer or ancient Egypt.

> Before going out for breakfast he glances through the window, made of glass invented in Egypt, and if it is raining puts on overshoes made of rubber discovered by the Central American Indians and takes an umbrella, invented in southeastern Asia. . . .

> On his way to breakfast he stops to buy a paper paying for it with coins, an ancient Lydian invention. . . . His plate is made of a form of pottery invented in China. His knife is of steel, an alloy first made in southern India, his fork a medieval Italian invention, and his spoon a derivative of a Roman original. . . . After his fruit (African watermelon) and first coffee (an Abyssinian plant) . . . he may have the egg of a species of bird domesticated in Indo-China, or thin strips of the flesh of an animal domesticated in Eastern Asia which have been salted and smoked by a process developed in northern Europe. . . .

> While smoking (an American Indian habit) he reads the news of the day, imprinted in characters invented by the ancient Semites upon a material invented in China by a process invented in Germany. As he absorbs the accounts of foreign troubles he will, if he is a good conservative citizen, thank a Hebrew deity in an Indo-European language that he is 100 percent American.[10]

Americans have not adopted most features of Japanese culture, but the interest in sushi is spreading.

PATTERNS OF DIFFUSION There are three basic patterns of diffusion: direct contact, intermediate contact, and stimulus diffusion.

1. **Direct contact.** Elements of a society's culture may first be taken up by neighboring societies and then gradually spread farther and farther afield. The spread of the use of paper (a sheet of interlaced fibers) is a good example of extensive diffusion by direct contact. The invention of paper is attributed to the Chinese Ts'ai Lun in A.D. 105. Within 50 years, paper was being made in many places in central China. While the art of papermaking was kept secret for about 500 years, paper was distributed as a commodity to much of the Arab world through the markets at Samarkand. But when Samarkand was attacked by the Chinese in 751, a Chinese prisoner was forced to set up a paper mill. Paper manufacture then spread to the rest of the Arab world; it was first manufactured in Baghdad in A.D. 793, Egypt about A.D. 900, and Morocco about A.D. 1100. Papermaking was introduced as a commodity in Europe by Arab trade through Italian ports in the 12th century. The Moors built the first European paper mill in Spain about 1150. The technical knowledge then spread throughout Europe with paper mills built in Italy in 1276, France 1348, Germany 1390, and England 1494.[11] In general, the pattern of accepting the borrowed invention was the same in all cases: Paper was first imported as a luxury, then in ever-expanding quantities as a staple product. Finally, and usually within one to three centuries, local manufacture began.

2. **Intermediate contact.** Diffusion by intermediate contact occurs through the agency of third parties. Frequently, traders carry a cultural trait from the society that originated it to another group. As an example of diffusion through intermediaries, Phoenician traders spread the alphabet, which may have been invented by another Semitic group, to Greece. At times, soldiers serve as intermediaries in spreading a culture trait. European crusaders, such as the Knights Templar and the Knights of St. John, acted as intermediaries in two ways: They carried Christian culture to Muslim societies of North Africa and brought Arab culture back to Europe. In the 19th century, Western missionaries in all parts of the world encouraged natives to wear Western clothing. The result is that in Africa, the Pacific Islands, and elsewhere, native peoples can be found wearing shorts, suit jackets, shirts, ties, and other typically Western articles of clothing.

3. **Stimulus diffusion.** In stimulus diffusion, knowledge of a trait belonging to another culture stimulates the invention or development of a local equivalent. A classic example of stimulus diffusion is the Cherokee syllabic writing system created by a Native American named Sequoya so that his people could write down their language. Sequoya got the idea from his contact with Europeans. Yet he did not adopt the English writing system; indeed, he did not even learn to write English. What he did was utilize some English alphabetic symbols, alter others, and invent new ones. All the symbols he used represented Cherokee syllables and in no way echoed English alphabetic usage. In other words, Sequoya took English alphabetic ideas and gave them a new, Cherokee form. The stimulus originated with Europeans; the result was peculiarly Cherokee.

THE SELECTIVE NATURE OF DIFFUSION Although there is a temptation to view the dynamics of diffusion as similar to a stone sending concentric ripples over still water, this would be an oversimplification of the way diffusion actually occurs. Not all cultural traits are borrowed as readily as the ones we have mentioned, nor do they usually expand in neat, ever-widening circles. Rather, diffusion is a selective process. The Japanese, for instance, accepted much from Chinese culture, but they also rejected many traits. Rhymed tonal poetry, civil service examinations, and foot binding, which were favored by the Chinese, were never adopted in Japan. The poetry form was unsuited to the structure of the Japanese language; the examinations were unnecessary in view of the entrenched power of the Japanese aristocracy; and foot binding was repugnant to a people who abhorred body mutilation of any sort.

Not only would we expect societies to reject items from other societies that are repugnant, we would also expect them to reject ideas and technology that do not satisfy some psychological, social, or cultural need. After all, people are not sponges; they don't automatically soak up the things around them. If they did, the amount of cultural variation in the world would be extremely small, which is clearly not the case. Diffusion is also selective because cultural traits differ in the extent to which they can be communicated. Elements of material culture, such as mechanical processes and techniques, and other traits, such as physical sports and the like, are not especially difficult to demonstrate. Consequently, they are accepted or rejected on their merits. But the moment we move out of the material context, we encounter real difficulties. Linton identified the problem in these words:

> Although it is quite possible to describe such an element of culture as the ideal pattern for marriage . . . it is much less complete than a description of basket-making. . . . The most thorough verbalization has difficulty in conveying the series of associations and conditioned emotional responses which are attached to this pattern [marriage] and which gave it meaning and vitality within our own society. . . . This is even more true of those concepts which . . . find no direct expression in behavior aside from verbalization. There is a story of an educated Japanese who after a long discussion on the nature of the Trinity with a European friend . . . burst out with: "Oh, I see now, it is a committee."[12]

Finally, diffusion is selective because the overt form of a particular trait, rather than its function or meaning, frequently seems to determine how the trait will be received. For example, the enthusiasm in women for bobbed hair (short haircuts) that swept through much of North America in the 1920s never caught on among the Native Americans of northwestern California. To many women of European ancestry, short hair was a symbolic statement of their freedom. To Native American women, who traditionally cut their hair short when in mourning, it was a reminder of death.[13]

In the process of diffusion, then, we can identify a number of different patterns. We know that cultural borrowing is selective rather than automatic, and we can describe how

a particular borrowed trait has been modified by the recipient culture. But our current knowledge does not allow us to specify when one or another of these outcomes will occur, under what conditions diffusion will occur, and why it occurs the way it does.

Acculturation

On the surface, the process of change called **acculturation** seems to include much of what we have discussed under the label of diffusion, since acculturation refers to the changes that occur when different cultural groups come into intensive contact. As in diffusion, the source of new cultural items is the other society. But more often than not, the term *acculturation* is used by anthropologists to describe a situation in which one of the societies in contact is much more powerful than the other. Thus, acculturation can be seen as a process of extensive cultural borrowing in the context of superordinate–subordinate relations between societies.[14] The borrowing may sometimes be a two-way process, but generally it is the subordinate or less powerful society that borrows the most. The concept of diffusion can then be reserved for the voluntary borrowing of cultural elements, in contrast with borrowing under external pressure, which characterizes acculturation.

External pressure for culture change can take various forms. In its most direct form—conquest or colonialization—the dominant group uses force or the threat of force to bring about culture change in the other group. For example, in the Spanish conquest of Mexico, the conquerors forced many of the native groups to accept Catholicism. Although such direct force is not always exerted in conquest situations, dominated peoples often have little choice but to change. Examples of such indirectly forced change abound in the history of Native Americans in the United States. Although the federal government made few direct attempts to force people to adopt American culture, it did drive many native groups from their lands, thereby obliging them to give

Students and teachers stand outside of the Lincoln Institution, an Indian girls' school in Delaware County, Pennsylvania. This picture was taken in October 1884.

up many aspects of their traditional ways of life. In order to survive, they had no choice but to adopt many of the dominant society's traits. When Native American children were required to go to schools, which taught the dominant society's values, the process was accelerated.

A subordinate society may acculturate to a dominant society even in the absence of direct or indirect force. The dominated people may elect to adopt cultural elements from the dominant society in order to survive in their changed world. Or, perceiving that members of the dominant society enjoy more secure living conditions, the dominated people may identify with the dominant culture in the hope that by doing so they will be able to share some of its benefits. For example, in Arctic areas many Inuit and Lapp groups seemed eager to replace dog sleds with snowmobiles without any coercion.[15]

But many millions of people never had a chance to acculturate after contact with Europeans. They simply died, sometimes directly at the hands of the conquerors, but probably more often as a result of the new diseases the Europeans inadvertently brought with them. Depopulation because of measles, smallpox, and tuberculosis was particularly common in North and South America and on the islands of the Pacific. Those areas had previously been isolated from contact with Europeans and from the diseases of that continuous landmass we call the Old World—Europe, Asia, and Africa.[16]

The story of Ishi, the last surviving member of a group of Native Americans in California called the Yahi, is a moving testimonial to the frequently tragic effect of contact with Europeans. In the space of 22 years, the Yahi population was reduced from several hundred to near zero. The historical record on this episode of depopulation suggests that European Americans murdered 30 to 50 Yahi for every European American murdered, but perhaps 60 percent of the Yahi died in the ten years following their initial exposure to European diseases.[17]

Nowadays, many powerful nations—and not just Western ones—may seem to be acting in more humanitarian ways to improve the life of previously subjugated as well as other "developing" peoples. For better or worse, these programs, however, are still forms of external pressure. The tactic used may be persuasion rather than force, but most of the programs are nonetheless designed to bring about acculturation in the direction of the dominant societies' cultures. For example, the introduction of formal schooling cannot help but instill new values that may contradict traditional cultural patterns. And even health-care programs may alter traditional ways of life by undermining the authority of shamans and other leaders and by increasing population beyond the number that can be supported in traditional ways. Confinement to "reservations" or other kinds of direct force are not the only ways a dominant society can bring about acculturation.

The process of acculturation also applies to immigrants, most of whom, at least nowadays, choose to leave one country for another. Immigrants are almost always a minority in the new country and therefore are in a subordinate position. If the immigrant's culture changes, it is almost always in the direction of the dominant culture. Immigrant groups vary considerably in the degree and speed with which they adopt the new culture and the social roles of the new society in which they live. An important area of research is explaining the variation in acculturation and assimilation. (*Assimilation* is a concept very similar to acculturation, but assimilation is a term more often used by sociologists to describe the process by which individuals acquire the social roles and culture of the dominant group.) Why do some immigrant groups acculturate or assimilate faster than others? Recall the comparative study by Robert Schrauf that assessed the degree to which immigrant groups coming to North America retained their native language over time. He looked at whether they lived in tightly knit communities, retained religious rituals, had separate schools and special festivals, visited their homeland, did not intermarry, or worked with others of their ethnic group. All of these factors might be expected to lead to retention of the native language (and presumably other cultural patterns), but only living in tightly knit communities and retaining religious rituals strongly predicted retaining the native language over a long period of time.[18]

Revolution

Certainly the most drastic and rapid way a culture can change is as a result of **revolution**—replacement, usually violent, of a country's rulers. Historical records, as well as our daily newspapers, indicate that people frequently rebel against established authority. Rebellions, if they occur, almost always occur in state societies, where there is a distinct ruling elite. They take the form of struggles between rulers and ruled, between conquerors and conquered, or between representatives of an external colonial power and segments of the native society. Rebels do not always succeed in overthrowing their rulers, so rebellions do not always result in revolutions. And even successful rebellions do not always result in culture change; the individual rulers may change, but customs or institutions may not. The sources of revolution may be mostly internal, as in the French Revolution, or partly external, as in the Russian-supported 1948 revolution in Czechoslovakia and the United States–supported 1973 revolution against President Allende in Chile.

The American War of Independence toward the end of the 18th century is a good example of a colonial rebellion, the success of which was at least partly a result of foreign intervention. The American rebellion was a war of neighboring colonies against the greatest imperial power of the time, Great Britain. In the 19th century and continuing into the middle and later years of the 20th century, there would be many other wars of independence, in Latin America, Europe, Asia, and Africa. We don't always remember that the American rebellion was the first of these anti-imperialist wars in modern times, and the model for many that followed. And just like many of the most recent liberation movements, the American rebellion was also part of a larger worldwide war, involving people from many rival nations. Thirty thousand German-speaking soldiers fought, for pay, on the British side; an army and navy from France fought on

Revolutionary leaders are often from high status backgrounds. Here we see a depiction of Patrick Henry giving his famous speech to the aristocratic landowners in the Virginia Assembly on March 23, 1775. Urging the Virginians to fight the British, Henry said that the choice was "liberty or death."

Source: Currier & Ives, "Give Me Liberty or Give Me Death!," 1775. Lithograph, 1876. © The Granger Collection, New York.

the American side. There were volunteers from other European countries, including Denmark, Holland, Poland, and Russia.

One of these volunteers was a man named Kosciusko from Poland, which at the time was being divided between Prussia and Russia. Kosciusko helped win a major victory for the Americans, and subsequently directed the fortification of what later became the American training school for army officers, West Point. After the war he returned to Poland and led a rebellion against the Russians, which was only briefly successful. In 1808 he published the *Manual on the Maneuvers of Horse Artillery,* which was used for many years by the American army. When he died he left money to buy freedom and education for American slaves. The executor of Kosciusko's will was Thomas Jefferson.

As in many revolutions, those who were urging revolution were considered "radicals." At a now famous debate in Virginia in 1775, delegates from each colony met at a Continental Congress. Patrick Henry put forward a resolution to prepare for defense against the British armed forces. The motion barely passed, by a vote of 65 to 60. Henry's speech is now a part of American folklore. He rose to declare that it was insane not to oppose the British and that he was not afraid to test the strength of the colonies against Great Britain. Others might hesitate, he said, but he would have "liberty or death." The "radicals" who supported Henry's resolution included many aristocratic landowners, two of whom, George Washington and Thomas Jefferson, became the first and third occupants of the highest political office in what became the United States of America.[19]

Not all peoples who are suppressed, conquered, or colonialized eventually rebel against established authority. Why this is so, and why rebellions and revolts are not always successful in bringing about culture change, are still open questions. But some possible answers have been investigated. One historian who examined the classic revolutions of the past, including the American, French, and Russian revolutions, suggested some conditions that may give rise to rebellion and revolution:

1. **Loss of prestige of established authority,** often as a result of the failure of foreign policy, financial difficulties, dismissals of popular ministers, or alteration of popular policies. France in the 18th century lost three major international conflicts, with disastrous results for its diplomatic standing and internal finances. Russian society was close to military and economic collapse in 1917, after three years of World War I.

2. **Threat to recent economic improvement.** In France, as in Russia, those sections of the population (professional classes and urban workers) whose economic fortunes had only shortly before taken an upward swing were "radicalized" by unexpected setbacks, such as steeply rising food prices and unemployment. The same may be said for the American colonies on the brink of their rebellion against Great Britain.

3. **Indecisiveness of government,** as exemplified by lack of consistent policy, which gives the impression of being controlled by, rather than in control of, events. The frivolous arrogance of Louis XVI's regime and the bungling of George III's prime minister, Lord North, with respect to the problems of the American colonies are examples.

4. **Loss of support of the intellectual class.** Such a loss deprived the prerevolutionary governments of France and Russia of any avowed philosophical support and led to their unpopularity with the literate public.[20]

The classic revolutions of the past occurred in countries that were industrialized only incipiently at best. For the most part, the same is true of the rebellions and revolutions in recent years; they have occurred mostly in countries we call "developing." The evidence from a worldwide survey of developing countries suggests that rebellions have tended to occur where the ruling classes depended mostly on the produce or income from land, and therefore were resistant to demands for reform from the rural classes that worked the land. In such agricultural economies, the rulers are not likely

reserve in Florida, and later, after the second Seminole war, removed most of them to Oklahoma.[52]

It would seem from this and other cases that cultural identities can be shaped and reshaped by political and economic processes.

◎ Globalization: Problems and Opportunities

Investment capital, people, and ideas are moving around the world at an ever faster rate.[53] Transportation now allows people and goods to circle the globe in days; telecommunications and the Internet make it possible to send a message around the world in seconds and minutes. Economic exchange is enormously more global and transnational. The word **globalization** is often used nowadays to refer to "the massive flow of goods, people, information, and capital across huge areas of the earth's surface."[54] The process of globalization has resulted in the worldwide spread of cultural features, particularly in the domain of economics and international trade. We buy from the same companies (that have factories all over the world), we sell our products and services for prices that are set by world market forces. We can eat pizza, hamburgers, curry, or sushi in most urban centers. In some ways, cultures are changing in similar directions. They have become more commercial, more urban, and more international. The job has become more important, and kinship less important, as people travel to and work in other countries, and return just periodically to their original homes. Ideas about democracy, the rights of the individual, alternative medical practices and religions, have become more widespread; people in many countries of the world watch the same TV shows, wear similar fashions, listen to the same or similar music. In short, people are increasingly sharing behaviors and beliefs with people in other cultures, and the cultures of the world are less and less things "with edges," as Paul Durrenberger says.[55]

But diffusion of a culture trait does not mean that it is incorporated in exactly the same way, and the spread of certain products and activities through globalization does not mean that change happens in the same way everywhere. For example, the spread of multinational fast-food restaurants like McDonald's or Kentucky Fried Chicken has come to symbolize globalization. But the behavior of the Japanese in such restaurants is quite different from behavior in the United States. Perhaps the most surprising difference is that the Japanese in McDonald's actually have more familial intimacy and sharing than in more traditional restaurants. We imagine that establishments like McDonald's promote fast eating. But Japan has long had fast food—noodle shops at train stations, street vendors, and boxed lunches. Sushi, which is usually ordered in the United States at a sit-down restaurant, is usually served in Japan at a bar with a conveyor belt—individuals only need to pluck off the wanted dish as it goes by. Observations at McDonald's in Japan suggest that mothers typically order food for the family while the father spends time with the children at a table, a rare event since fathers often work long hours and cannot get home for dinner often. Food, such as French fries, is typically shared by the family. Even burgers and drinks are passed around with many people taking a bite or a sip. Such patterns typify long-standing family practices. Japan has historically borrowed food, such as the Chinese noodle soup, now called ramen. Indeed, in a survey, ramen was listed as the most representative Japanese food. The burger was the second most-often listed. McDonald's has become Japanese—the younger generation does not even know that McDonald's is a foreign company—they think it is Japanese.[56]

Democracy—contested elections with widespread voting—is spreading around the world. In this rural area of South Africa, people line up to vote.

Globalization is not new. The world has been global and interdependent since the 16th century.[57] What we currently call "globalization" is a more widespread version of what we used to call by various other names—diffusion, acculturation, colonialism, imperialism, or commercialization. But globalization is now on a much grander scale; enormous amounts of international investment fuel world trade. Shifts in the world marketplace may drastically affect a country's well-being more than ever before. For example, 60 percent of Pakistan's industrial employment is in textile and apparel manufacturing, but serious unemployment resulted when that manufacturing was crippled by restrictive American import policies and fears about war between India and Afghanistan.[58]

As we have seen in this chapter, there are many negative effects of colonialism, imperialism, and globablization. Many native peoples in many places lost their land and have been forced to work for inadequate wages in mines and plantations and factories that are owned by foreign capitalists. Frequently, there is undernutrition if not starvation. But are there any positive consequences? As we discussed in the social stratification chapter, the "human development indicators" collected by the United Nations suggest an improvement in many respects, including increases in most countries in life expectancy and literacy. Much of the improvement in life expectancy is undoubtedly due to the spread of medicines developed in the advanced economies of the West. There is generally less warfare as colonial powers enforced pacification within the colonies that later became independent states. Most important, perhaps, has been the growth of middle classes all over the world, whose livelihoods depend on globalizing commerce. The middle classes in many countries have become strong and numerous enough to pressure governments for democratic reforms and the reduction of injustice.

World trade is the primary engine of economic development. Per capita income is increasing. Forty years ago, the countries of Asia were among the poorest countries in the world in terms of per capita income. Since then, because of their involvement in world trade, their incomes have risen enormously. In 1960, South Korea was as poor as India. Now its per capita income is 20 times higher than India's. Singapore is an even more dramatic example. In the late 1960s, its economy was a disaster. Today its per capita income is higher than Britain's.[59] Mexico used to be a place where North Americans built factories to produce garments for the North American market. Now its labor is no longer so cheap. But because it has easy access to the North American market and because its plentiful labor is acquiring the necessary skills, Mexico is now seeing the development of high-tech manufacturing with decent salaries.[60]

There is world trade also in people. Many countries of the world now export people to other countries. Mexico has done so for a long time. Virtually every family in a Bangladesh village depends on someone who works overseas and sends money home. Without those remittances, many would face starvation. The government encourages people to go abroad to work. Millions of people from Bangladesh are now overseas on government-sponsored work contracts.[61]

But does a higher per capita income mean that life has improved generally in a country? Not necessarily. As we saw in the chapter on social stratification, inequality within countries can increase with technological improvements because the rich often benefit the most. In addition, economic wealth is increasingly concentrated in a relatively small number of countries. Obviously, then, not everyone is better off even if on average most countries are doing better. Poverty has become more common as countries have become more unequal.

While many of the changes associated with globalization seem to be driven by the economic and political power of the richer countries, the movement of ideas, art, music, and food is more of a two-way process. A large part of that process involves the migration of people who bring their culture with them. As we have seen from the boxes on migrants and immigrants in previous chapters, movements of people have played a large role in the entry of food such as tortilla chips and salsa, sushi, and curries into the United States, music like reggae and many types of dance music from Latin America, and African carvings and jewelry such as beaded necklaces. Recently there has even been increased interest in acquiring indigenous knowledge of plants, the knowledge of indigenous healers, and learning about shamanistic trances. As indigenous knowledge comes to be viewed as potentially valuable, shamans have been able to speak out on national and international issues. In Brazil, shamans have organized to speak out against "biopiracy"—what is perceived as the unethical appropriation of biological knowledge for commercial purposes. In a more globalized world, shamans and other indigenous activists can be heard by more people than ever before. Despite the fact that indigenous people constitute less than one percent of the Brazilian population, some activist groups have been able to keep in touch with international environmentalists, using tape recorders and video cameras to convey information about their local situation.[62]

It is probably not possible to go back to a time when societies were not so dependent on each other, not so interconnected through world trade, not so dependent on commercial exchange. Even those who are most upset with globalization find it difficult to imagine that it is possible to return to a less connected world. For better or worse, the world is interconnected and will remain so. The question now is whether the average economic improvements in countries will eventually translate into economic improvements for most individuals.

⦾ Cultural Diversity in the Future

Measured in terms of travel time, the world today is much smaller than it has ever been. It is possible now to fly halfway around the globe in the time it took people less than a century ago to travel to the next state. In the realm of communication, the world is even smaller. We can talk to someone on the other side of the globe in a matter of minutes, we can send that person a message (by fax or Internet) in seconds, and through television we can see live coverage of events in that person's country. More and more people are drawn into the world market economy, buying and selling similar things and, as a consequence, altering the patterns of their lives in sometimes similar ways. Still, although modern transportation and communication facilitate the rapid spread of some cultural characteristics to all parts of the globe, it is highly unlikely that all parts of the world will end up the same culturally. Cultures are bound to retain some of their original characteristics or develop distinctive new adaptations. Even though television has diffused around the world, local people continue to prefer local programs when they are available. And even when people all over the world watch the same program, they may interpret it in very different ways. People are not just absorbing the messages they get; they often resist or revise them.[63]

Until recently, researchers studying culture change generally assumed that the differences between people of different cultures would become minimal. But in the last 30 years or so, it has become increasingly apparent that, although many differences disappear, many people are affirming ethnic identities in a process that often involves deliberately introducing cultural difference.[64] Eugeen Roosens describes the situation of the Huron of Quebec, who in the late 1960s seemed to have disappeared as a distinct culture. The Huron language had disappeared and the lives of the Huron were not obviously distinguishable from those of the French Canadians around them. The Huron then developed a new identity as they actively worked to promote the rights of indigenous peoples like themselves. That their new defining cultural symbols bore no resemblance to the past Huron culture is beside the point.

One fascinating possibility is that ethnic diversity and ethnogenesis may be a result of broader processes. Elizabeth Cashdan found that ethnic diversity appears to be related to environmental unpredictability, which is associated with greater distance from the equator.[65] There appear to be many more cultural groups nearer to the equator than in very northern and southern latitudes. Perhaps, Cashdan suggests, environmental unpredictability in the north and south necessitates wider ties between social groups to allow cooperation in case local resources fail. This may minimize the likelihood of cultural divergence, that is, ethnogenesis. Hence there will be fewer cultures further from the equator.

Future research on culture change should increase our understanding of how and why various types of change are occurring. If we can increase our understanding of culture change in the present, we should be better able to understand similar processes in the past. We may be guided in our efforts to understand culture change by the large number of cross-cultural correlations that have been discovered between a particular cultural variation and its presumed causes.[66] All cultures have changed over time; variation is the product of differential change. Thus, the variations we see are the products of change processes, and the discovered predictors of those variations may suggest how and why the changes occurred.

◎ Summary

1. Culture is always changing. Because culture consists of learned patterns of behavior and belief, cultural traits can be unlearned and learned anew as human needs change.

2. Discoveries and inventions, though ultimately the sources of all culture change, do not necessarily lead to change. Only when society accepts an invention or discovery and uses it regularly can culture change be said to have occurred. Some inventions are probably the result of dozens of tiny, perhaps accidental, initiatives over a period of many years. Other inventions are consciously intended. Why some people are more innovative than others is still only incompletely understood. There is some evidence that creativity and a readiness to adopt innovations may be related to socioeconomic position.

3. The process by which cultural elements are borrowed from another society and incorporated into the culture of the recipient group is called diffusion. Three patterns of diffusion may be identified: diffusion by direct contact, in which elements of a culture are first taken up by neighboring societies and then gradually spread farther and farther afield; diffusion by intermediate contact, in which third parties, frequently traders, carry a cultural trait from the originating society to another group; and stimulus diffusion, in which knowledge of a trait belonging to another culture stimulates the invention or development of a local equivalent.

4. Cultural traits do not necessarily diffuse; that is, diffusion is a selective, not automatic, process. A society accepting a foreign cultural trait is likely to adapt it in a way that effectively harmonizes it with the society's own traditions.

5. When a group or society is in contact with a more powerful society, the weaker group is often obliged to acquire cultural elements from the dominant group. This process of extensive borrowing in the context of superordinate–subordinate relations between societies is called acculturation. In contrast with diffusion, acculturation comes about as a result of some sort of external pressure.

6. Perhaps the most drastic and rapid way a culture can change is by revolution—a usually violent replacement of the society's rulers. Rebellions occur primarily in state societies, where there is a distinct ruling elite. However, not all peoples who are suppressed, conquered, or colonized eventually rebel or successfully revolt against established authority.

7. Even though customs are not genetically inherited, cultural adaptation may be somewhat similar to biological adaptation. Traits (cultural or genetic) that are more likely to be reproduced (learned or inherited) are likely to become more frequent in a population over time. And if culture is generally adapted to its environment, then culture change should also be generally adaptive.

8. Many of the cultural changes observed in the modern world have been generated, directly or indirectly, by the dominance and expansion of Western societies. One of the principal changes resulting from the expansion of Western culture is the increasing dependence of much of the world on commercial exchange—that is, the proliferation of buying and selling in markets, usually accompanied by the use of money as the medium of exchange. The borrowed custom of buying and selling may at first be supplementary to traditional means of distributing goods, but as the new commercial customs take hold, the economic base of the receiving society alters. Inevitably, this alteration is accompanied by other changes, which have broad social, political, and even biological and psychological ramifications.

9. One way commercialization can occur is for members of a community to become migratory workers, traveling to a place nearby that offers the possibility of working for wages. Commercialization can also occur when a simple, self-sufficient hunting or agricultural society comes to depend more and more on trading for its livelihood. A third way commercialization occurs is when those cultivating the soil produce more than they require for subsistence. The surplus is then sold for cash. In many instances, this cash income must be used to pay rent or taxes; under such circumstances, commercialization may be said to be associated with the formation of a peasantry. A fourth way in which commercialization can come about is through the introduction of commercial agriculture, in which all the cultivated commodities are produced for sale rather than for personal consumption. Along with this change, the system of agriculture may be industrialized, with some of the production processes being done by machine.

10. The growing influence of Western societies has also led to religious change in many parts of the world. In many societies, such change has been brought about intentionally through the efforts of missionaries.

11. One of the most striking types of culture change in the modern world is the spread of democracies. Participatory political institutions are now found in a majority of the world's countries.

12. Ethnogenesis is the process by which new cultures are created.

13. Globalization—the spread of cultural features around the world—is minimizing cultural diversity, but it is not eliminating it.

◎ Glossary Terms

acculturation	497	globalization	510
diffusion	495	peasants	503
ethnogenesis	508	revolution	498

◎ Critical Questions

1. What kinds of cultural items might most easily be borrowed by another culture? Why do you think so?

2. The expansion of the West has had terrible consequences for many peoples. Have there been any beneficial consequences?

3. Why might an increasing understanding of cultural variation also provide an increasing understanding of culture change?

◎ Research Navigator

1. Please go to www.researchnavigator.com and enter your LOGIN NAME and PASSWORD. For instructions on registering for the first time, please view the detailed instructions at the end of Chapter 1.

2. Using Link Library (Anthropology) look for a Web site dealing with acculturation, diffusion, migration, or globalization. Discuss some new aspect of culture change and globalization that was not covered in this chapter.

◎ Discovering Anthropology: Researchers at Work

Read the chapter by Ernest S. Burch, Jr., titled "North Alaskan Eskimos: A Changing Way of Life" in the accompanying *Discovering Anthropology* reader, and answer the following questions:

1. Why does Burch object to the notion that the Eskimos used to live in a state of "anarchy"?

2. How has their economy changed, and why?

population is aware of the benefits of the proposed change. Lack of awareness can be a temporary barrier to solving the problem at hand. For example, health workers have often had difficulty convincing people that they were becoming ill because something was wrong with their water supply. Many people do not believe that disease can be transmitted by water. At other times, the target population is perfectly aware of the problem. A case in point involved Taiwanese women who were introduced to family-planning methods beginning in the 1960s. The women knew they were having more children than they wanted or could easily afford, and they wanted to control their birth rate. They offered no resistance—they merely had to be given the proper devices and instructions, and the birth rate quickly fell to a more desirable, and more manageable, level.[21]

Resistance by the Target Population

Not all proposed change programs are beneficial to the target population. Sometimes resistance is rational. Applied anthropologists have pointed to cases where the judgment of the affected population has been better than that of the agents of change. One such example occurred during a Venezuelan government–sponsored program to give infants powdered milk. The mothers rejected the milk, even though it was free, on the grounds that it implied that the mothers' milk was no good.[22] But who is to say that the resistance was not in fact intuitively smart, reflecting an awareness that such a milk program would not benefit the children? Medical research now indicates quite clearly that mothers' milk is far superior to powdered milk or formula. First, human milk best supplies the nutrients needed for human development. Second, it is now known that the mother, through her milk, is able to transmit antibodies (disease resistances) to the baby. And third, nursing delays

Indians protest construction of a dam in their area.

ovulation and usually increases the spacing between births.[23]

The switchover to powdered milk and formula in many underdeveloped areas has been nothing short of a disaster, resulting in increased malnutrition and misery. For one thing, powdered milk must be mixed with water, but if the water and the bottles are not sterilized, more sickness is introduced. Then, too, if powdered milk has to be purchased, mothers without cash are forced to dilute the milk to stretch it. And if a mother feeds her baby formula or powder for even a short time, the process is tragically irreversible, for her own milk dries up and she cannot return to breast-feeding even if she wants to.

As the Venezuelan example suggests, individuals may be able to resist proposed medical or health projects because acceptance is ultimately a personal matter. Large development projects planned by powerful governments or agencies rarely are stoppable, but even they can be resisted successfully. The Kayapo of the Xingu River region of Brazil were able to cancel a plan by the Brazilian government to build dams along the river for hydroelectric power. The Kayapo gained international attention when some of their leaders appeared on North American and European television and then successfully organized a protest in 1989 by members of several tribal groups. Their success seemed to come in part from their ability to present themselves to the international community as guardians of the rain forest—an image that resonated with international environmental organizations that supported their cause. Although to outsiders it might seem that the Kayapo want their way of life to remain as it was, the Kayapo are not opposed to all change. In fact, they want greater access to medical care, other government services, and manufactured goods from outside.[24]

But even if a project is beneficial to a population, it may still meet with resistance. Factors that may hinder acceptance can be divided roughly into three, sometimes overlapping, categories: *cultural, social,* and *psychological* barriers.

Cultural barriers are shared behaviors, attitudes, and beliefs that tend to impede the acceptance of an innovation. For example, members of different societies may view gift giving in different ways. Particularly in commercialized societies, things received for nothing are often believed to be worthless. When the government of Colombia instituted a program of giving seedling orchard trees to farmers in order to increase fruit production, the farmers showed virtually no interest in the seedlings, many of which proceeded to die of neglect. When the government realized that the experiment had apparently failed, it began to charge each farmer a nominal fee for the seedlings. Soon the seedlings became immensely popular and fruit production increased.[25] The farmers' demand for the seedlings may have increased because they were charged a fee and therefore came to value the trees. The market demand for fruit may also have increased. Other examples of cultural resistance to change, which we discuss more in the next chapter, are beliefs about sex that make it difficult for people to follow medical guidelines for safer sex.

It is very important for agents of change to understand what the shared beliefs and attitudes are. First, indigenous cultural concepts or knowledge can sometimes be used effectively to enhance educational programs. For instance, in a program in Haiti to prevent child mortality from diarrhea, change agents used the terminology for traditional native herbal tea remedies (*rafrechi,* or cool refreshment) to identify the new oral rehydration therapy, which is a very successful medical treatment. In native belief, diarrhea is a "hot" illness and appropriate remedies have to have cooling properties.[26] Second, even if indigenous beliefs are not helpful to the campaign, not paying attention to contrary beliefs can undermine the campaign. But uncovering contrary beliefs is not easy, particularly when they do not emerge in ordinary conversation. In the next chapter, on medical anthropology, we discuss cultural theories about illness more extensively. The acceptance of planned change may also depend on social factors. Research suggests that acceptance is more likely if the change agent and the target or potential adopter are similar socially. But change agents may have higher social status and more education than the people they are trying to influence. So change agents may work more with higher-status individuals because they are more likely to accept new ideas. If lower-status individuals also have to be reached, change agents of lower status may have to be employed.[27]

Finally, acceptance may depend on psychological factors—that is, how the individuals perceive both the innovation and the agents of change. In the course of trying to encourage women in the southeastern United States to breast-feed rather than bottle-feed their infants, researchers discovered a number of reasons why women were reluctant to breast-feed their infants, even though they heard it was healthier. Many women did not have confidence that they would produce enough milk for their babies; they were embarrassed about breast-feeding in public; and their family and friends had negative attitudes.[28] In designing an educational program, change agents may have to address such psychological concerns directly.

Discovering and Utilizing Local Channels of Influence

In planning a project involving cultural change, the administrator of the project should find out what the normal channels of influence are in the population. In most communities, there are preestablished networks for communication, as well as persons of high prestige or influence who are looked to for guidance and direction. An understanding of such channels of influence is extremely valuable when deciding how to introduce a program of change. In addition, it is useful to know at what times, and in what sorts of situations, one channel is likely to be more effective in spreading information and approval than another.

An example of the effective use of local channels of influence occurred when an epidemic of smallpox broke out in the Kalahandi district of the state of Orissa in India. The efforts of health workers to vaccinate villagers against the disease were consistently resisted. The villagers, naturally suspicious and fearful of these strange men with their equally strange medical equipment, were unwilling to offer themselves, and particularly their babies, to the peculiar experiments the strangers wished to perform. Afraid of the epidemic, the villagers appealed for help to their local priest, whose opinions on such matters they trusted. The priest went into a trance, explaining that the illness was the result of the goddess Thalerani's anger with the people. She could be appeased, he continued, only by massive feasts, offerings, and other demonstrations of the villagers' worship of her. Realizing that the priest was the village's major opinion leader, at least in medical matters, the frustrated health workers tried to get the priest to convince his people to undergo vaccination. At first, the priest refused to cooperate with the strange men, but when his favorite nephew fell ill, he decided to try any means available to cure the boy. He thereupon went into another trance, telling the villagers that the goddess wished all her worshipers to be vaccinated. Fortunately, the people agreed, and the epidemic was largely controlled.[29]

If channels of influence are not stable, using influential persons in a campaign can sometimes backfire. In the educational campaign in Haiti to promote the use of oral rehydration therapy to treat diarrhea in children, Mme. Duvalier, the first lady of Haiti at the time, lent her name to the project. Because there were no serious social or cultural barriers to the treatment and mothers reported that children took to the solutions well, success was expected. But in the middle of the campaign, Haiti became embroiled in political turmoil and the first lady's husband was overthrown. Some of the public thought that the oral rehydration project was a plot by the Duvaliers to sterilize children, and this suspicion fueled resistance.[30] As the box on "Bringing the Trees Back to Haiti" shows, even after the Duvalier regime, people in Haiti were suspicious of any government-sponsored program.

Applied anthropologists often advocate integrating indigenous healers into medical change programs. This idea may encounter considerable resistance by the medical profession and by government officials who view such healers negatively. But this strategy may be quite effective in more isolated areas where indigenous healers are the only sources of health care. If they are involved in medical change programs, indigenous healers are likely to refer patients to hospitals when they feel unable to cope with an illness, and the hospitals choose sometimes to refer patients to the healers.[31]

Other social groups and their attitudes can play important roles in shaping the outcome of the change program. Most often the people who are being helped have few privileges, little political and economic power, and low prestige.[32] Change or development is often regarded as a threat to those with more privilege. If those who do have power object to the new program, they may effectively sabotage it. The development agent, then, not only has to reckon with the local community but may also have to persuade more powerful groups in the society that the new program should be introduced.

Need for More Collaborative Applied Anthropology

Most large-scale programs of planned change originate with governments, international aid organizations, or other agencies. Even if the programs are well intentioned and even if the appropriate evaluations are made to ensure that the population will not be harmed, the population targeted for the change is usually not involved in the decision making. Some anthropologists, like Wayne Warry, think that applied anthropology should be more collaborative. Warry explains that he was asked by a Native Canadian elder whether he (Warry) would tolerate his own methods and interpretations if he were the native.[33] This question prompted him to involve himself in a project with Native Canadian collaborators, directed by the Mamaweswen Tribal Council. The project assesses health-care needs and develops plans to improve local community health care. Funding is provided by the Canadian government as part of a program to transfer health care to the First Nations. Native researchers are conducting the surveys and workshops to keep the community informed about the project. The tribal council also reviews any publications and shares in any profits resulting from those publications.

Applied anthropologists may be increasingly asked to work on behalf of indigenous grassroots organizations. As we saw in the chapter on associations, the developing world has seen a proliferation of such groups. In some cases these small groups and networks of such groups are starting to hire their own technical assistance.[34] When such organizations do the hiring, they control the decision making. There is increasing evidence that grassroots organizations are the key to effective development. For example, Kenyan farmers who belong to grassroots organizations produce higher farm yields than those farmers who do not belong, even though the latter group is exposed to more agricultural extension agents.[35] Grassroots organizations can succeed where government or outside projects fail. We have plenty of instances of people effectively resisting projects. Their willingness to change, and their participation in crucial decision making, may be mostly responsible for the success of a change project.

Cultural Resource Management

Large-scale programs of planned change like those discussed earlier in this chapter have an impact not only on living people. They can also have an impact on the archaeological record left by the ancestors of living people. Recovering and preserving the archaeological record before programs of planned change disturb or destroy it is called **cultural resource management (CRM)**. CRM work is carried out by archaeologists who are often called "contract archaeologists" because they typically work under contract to a government agency, a private developer, or a native group.

What kinds of impact can programs of planned change have on the archaeological record? In the 1960s a large number of hydroelectric dam projects were initiated to provide flood control and to bring a stable source of electrical power to developing nations. In Egypt a dam was built on the Nile River at a site called Aswan. Archaeologists realized that once the dam was in place a huge lake would form behind it, submerging thousands of archaeological sites, including the massive temple of Rameses II. Something needed to be done; the archaeological record had to be salvaged or protected. In the language of CRM, there needed to be a *mitigation plan* put into action. And there was. As the Aswan dam was being built, archaeologists went to work excavating sites that would be flooded. Archaeologists and engineers designed a way to take apart the temple of Rameses II and rebuild it, piece by piece, on higher ground where it would not be flooded. By the time the dam was completed in 1965, hundreds of sites had been investigated and two entire temple complexes moved.

Large-scale development projects are not the only projects that involve CRM archaeologists. In many nations, including the United States and Canada, historic preservation laws require any project receiving federal funds to ensure that archaeological resources are protected or their damage mitigated. Highway construction projects in the United States are common places to find CRM archaeologists at work. Virtually all highway projects rely on federal funding, and before a highway can be built a complete archaeological survey of the proposed right-of-way has to be made. If archaeological sites are found, potential damage to them must be mitigated. A CRM archaeologist will work with the construction company, the state archaeologist, and perhaps a federal archaeologist to decide on the best course of action. In some cases the archaeological site will be excavated. In others, the right-of-way may be moved. In still others, the decision is to allow the archaeological site to be destroyed, because it would be too costly to excavate or the site may not be significant enough to warrant excavation. Regardless of the decision, the CRM archaeologist plays a crucial role in assessing and protecting the archaeological record.

CRM archaeologists do not work only for state or federal agencies. In many nations today CRM archaeologists are also working with native peoples to protect, preserve, and manage archaeological materials for them. Indeed, archaeologist John Ravesloot recently stated that "the future of American archaeology is with Indian communities functioning as active, not passive, participants in the interpretation, management, and preservation of their rich cultural heritage."[36] One example of such a working relationship is the Zuni Heritage and Historic Preservation Office. During the 1970s the Pueblo of Zuni decided it

Commuters look at 4th century ruins uncovered as part of a large scale CRM project associated with construction of the Athens metro system.

needed to train tribal members in archaeology in order to ensure that Zuni cultural resources and properties were managed properly. It hired three professional archaeologists and, with additional assistance from the National Park Service and the Arizona State Museum, initiated a program to train and employ tribal members in cultural resource management. Working with these non-Zuni archaeologists, the Pueblo of Zuni was able to establish its own historic preservation office that today manages and coordinates all historic preservation on the Zuni reservation, a task that was managed by the federal government until 1992. The Pueblo also established the Zuni Cultural Resource Enterprise, a Zuni-owned CRM business that employs both Zuni and non-Zuni archaeologists and carries out contract archaeology projects both on and off the Zuni reservation.[37]

Cultural resource management is a growing field. Indeed, a 1994 survey conducted by the Society for American Archaeology showed that more than 25 percent of archaeologists in the United States are now employed in private CRM firms working on federally funded contracts, and another 25 percent work directly for state and federal agencies. Thus 50 percent of all employed archaeologists in the United States have jobs directly related to CRM.[38] As development and construction projects continue to affect the archaeological record, the need for well-trained CRM archaeologists is not likely to decline.

 Forensic Anthropology

Many of us are fascinated by detective stories. We are interested in crimes and why they occur, and we like to read about them, fictional or not. Forensic anthropology is the specialty in anthropology that is devoted to solving crimes. It is attracting increasing attention by the public, and an increasing number of practitioners. One forensic anthro-

pologist says she is called "the bone lady" by law enforcement personnel.[39] Like others in her line of work, she is asked to dig up or examine human bones to help solve crimes. Often the task is simple: Are these the bones of a man or woman? How old was the person? Forensic anthropologists can answer such questions fairly easily, particularly if the remains include most bones of the skeleton. Other times the question may be more difficult to answer. For example, can the forensic anthropologist say that a skull is probably from an Asian male? (The police suspect that the skeletal remains they found are from an Asian man who disappeared under mysterious circumstances five years before.) But it is difficult enough to assign an unambiguous "racial" classification to living persons. Bones alone are even more ambiguous because different features in the skeleton do not all vary in correlated ways, as we noted in our earlier discussion of "race" in the chapter on social stratification. Still, the forensic anthropologist can suggest whether the skeletal remains show a constellation of features typically associated with a particular region of the world. Sometimes the forensic anthropologist can suggest the cause of death when the law enforcement people are stumped.

Some cultural anthropologists have also done forensic work, often in connection with legal cases involving Native Americans. For example, Barbara Joans was asked in 1978 to advise the defense in a trial of six older Bannock-Shoshoni women from the Fort Hall reservation who were accused of fraud. They had received "supplemental security income (SSI)," which the social service agency claimed they had no right to receive because they had not reported receiving rent money on land that they owned. Joans presented evidence that the women, although they spoke some English, did not have enough proficiency to understand the nuances of what the SSI people told them. The judge agreed with the defense and ruled that in the future the SSI would have to use a Bannock-Shoshoni interpreter when they went to the reservation to describe the requirements of the program.[40]

In recent years, Clyde Snow and other forensic anthropologists have been called on to confirm horrendous abuses of human rights. Governments have been responsible for the systematic killing of their citizens, and forensic anthropologists have helped to bring the perpetrators to justice. For example, Snow and other forensic anthropologists helped to confirm that the military dictatorship in Argentina in the 1980s was responsible for the deaths of many Argentine civilians who had "disappeared." The forensic anthropologists were also able to determine the location of mass graves and the identity of victims of state-organized brutality in Guatemala. In addition to bringing the perpetrators to justice, confirming the massacres and identifying the victims help the families of the "disappeared" put their anguish behind them. A special session (called "Uncovering the 'Disappeared': Clyde Snow and Forensic Anthropologists Work for Justice"[41]) at the annual meeting of the American Anthropological Association in November 2000 honored Snow and other forensic anthropologists.

◎ Summary

1. Applied anthropology in the United States developed out of anthropologists' personal experiences with disadvantaged peoples. Applied, or practicing, anthropologists may be involved in one or more phases of programs that are designed to change peoples' lives: assembling relevant knowledge, constructing alternative plans, assessing the likely social and environmental impact of particular plans, implementing the programs, and monitoring the programs and their effects.

2. Today many anthropologists are finding employment outside of anthropology departments—in medical schools, health centers, development agencies, urban-planning agencies, and other public and private organizations.

3. The code of ethics for those who work professionally as applied anthropologists specifies that the target population should be included as much as possible in the formulation of policy, so that people in the community may know in advance how the program may affect them. But perhaps the most important aspect of the code is the pledge not to be involved in any plan whose effect will not be beneficial. It is often difficult to evaluate the effects of planned changes. Long-term consequences may be detrimental even if the changes are beneficial in the short run.

4. Even if a planned change will prove beneficial to its target population, the people may not accept it. And if the proposed innovation is not utilized by the intended target, the project cannot be considered a success. Target populations may reject or resist a proposed innovation for various reasons: because they are unaware of the need for the change; because they misinterpret the symbols used to explain the change or fail to understand its real purpose; because their customs and institutions conflict with the change; or because they are afraid of it. The target population may also resist the proposed change because they unconsciously or consciously know it is not good for them.

5. To be effective, change agents may have to discover and use the traditional channels of influence in introducing their projects to the target population.

6. Cultural resource management usually takes the form of "contract archaeology" to record and/or conserve the archaeology of a building site.

7. Forensic anthropology is the use of anthropology to help solve crimes.

◎ Glossary Terms

applied or practicing
  anthropology   516

cultural resource
  management
  (CRM)   524

forensic
  anthropology   516

◎ Critical Questions

1. What particular advantages do anthropologists have in trying to solve practical problems?

2. Is it ethical to try to influence people's lives when they have not asked for help? Explain your answer.

3. If you were interested in solving a practical problem, would you do basic or applied research on the problem? Why?

◎ Research Navigator

1. Please go to www.researchnavigator.com and enter your LOGIN NAME and PASSWORD. For instructions on registering for the first time, please view the detailed instructions at the end of Chapter 1.

2. Using Link Library (Anthropology) find a Web site dealing with some aspect of applied anthropology such as cultural resource management or forensic anthropology. Summarize what you have learned.

◎ Discovering Anthropology: Researchers at Work

Read the chapter by Andrew W. Miracle titled "A Shaman for Organizations" in the accompanying *Discovering Anthropology* reader. Answer the following questions:

1. Why does Miracle call himself a "shaman"?
2. According to Miracle, what skills are useful to an applied anthropologist? Why does he think so?

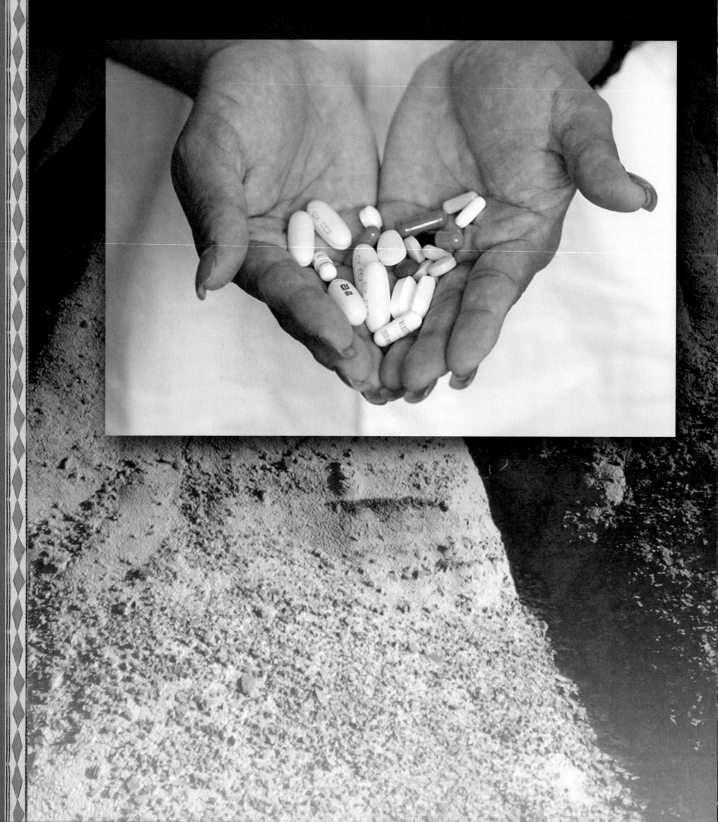

Medical Anthropology

Illness and death are significant events for people everywhere. No one is spared. So it should not be surprising that how people understand the causes of illness and death, how they behave, and what resources they marshal to cope with these events are extremely important parts of culture. Some argue that we will never completely understand how to treat illness effectively until we understand the cultural behaviors, attitudes, values, and the larger social and political milieux in which people live. Others argue that society and culture have little to do with the outcome of illness—the reason that people die needlessly is that they do not get the appropriate medical treatment.

But anthropologists, particularly medical anthropologists, who are actively engaged in studying health and illness, are increasingly realizing that biological *and* social factors need to be considered if we are to reduce human suffering. For instance, some populations have an appalling incidence of infant deaths due to diarrhea. The origin of this situation is mostly biological, in the sense that the deaths are caused by bacterial infection. But why are so many infants exposed to those bacteria? Usually, the main reason is social. The affected infants are likely to be poor. Because they are poor, they are likely to live with infected drinking water. Similarly, malnutrition may be the biological result of a diet poor in protein, but such a diet is usually also a cultural phenomenon, reflecting a society with classes of people with very unequal access to the necessities of life. In many ways, therefore, medical anthropology, and anthropology in general, are developing in the direction of a "biocultural synthesis."[1]

Medical anthropology is part of this developing synthesis. Indeed, the growth of jobs in medical anthropology is one of the more striking developments in contemporary anthropology. Medical anthropology has developed into a very popular specialty, and the Society for Medical Anthropology is now the second largest unit in the American Anthropological Association.[2]

The medical profession's ways of treating illness may be able to treat some conditions well, but by itself the medical profession cannot tell us why some groups are more affected than others, or why the effectiveness of treatment varies from group to group. This chapter discusses cultural variation in conceptions of health and illness, cultural universals and variables in how illness is treated, the political and social forces that affect health, and contributions of medical anthropology to the study and treatment of particular diseases and health conditions.

Cultural Understandings of Health and Illness

Medical researchers and medical practitioners in the United States and other Western societies do not exist in a social vacuum. Many of their ideas and practices are influenced by the culture in which they live. We may think of medicine as purely based on "fact," but on reflection it is clear that many ideas stem from the culture in which the researchers reside. Consider the recent shift in attitudes toward birth. It was not so long ago in the United States that fathers were excluded from the birth, hospitals whisked the baby away from the mother and only brought the baby to her infrequently, and visitors (but not attending nurses and doctors) had to wear masks when holding the baby. Rationalizations were given for those practices, but looking back at them, they do not appear to be based on scientific evidence. Many medical anthropologists now argue that the *biomedical paradigm* (the system in which physicians are trained) itself needs to be understood as part of the culture.

Discovering the health-related beliefs, knowledge, and practices of a cultural group—its **ethnomedicine**—is one of the goals of medical anthropology. How do cultures view health and illness? What are their theories about the causes of illness? Do those theories impact on how illnesses are treated? What is the therapeutic process? Are there specialized medical practitioners, and how do they heal? Are there special medicines, and how are they administered? These are just some of the questions asked by the anthropological study of ethnomedicine.

Concepts of Balance or Equilibrium

Many cultures have the view that the body should be kept in equilibrium or balance. The balance may be between hot and cold, or wet and dry, as in many cultures of Latin America and the Caribbean.[3] The notion of balance is not limited to opposites. For example, the ancient Greek system of medicine, stemming from Hippocrates, assumed that there were four "humors"—blood, phlegm, yellow bile, and black bile—that must be kept in balance. These humors have hot and cold and wet and dry properties. The Greek medical system was widely diffused in Europe and spread to parts of the Islamic world. In Europe, the humoral medical system was dominant until it was replaced by the germ theory in the 1900s.[4] In the Ayurvedic system, whose practice dates back 4,000 years in North India, Pakistan, Bangladesh, Sri Lanka, and in the Arab world, there are three humors (phlegm, bile, and flatulence), and a balance between hot and cold is also important.[5] The Chinese medical system, which dates back about 3,500 years, initially stressed the balance between the contrasting forces of *yin* and *yang* and later added the concept of humors, which were six in number in Chinese medicine.[6]

The concepts of hot and cold and *yin* and *yang* are illustrated in Emily Ahern's ethnographic description of the medical system of the Taiwanese Hokkien.[7] Both hot and cold substances are required by the body; when the body is out of balance, a lack of one substance can be restored by eating or drinking the missing substance. So, for example, when Ahern was faint with heat, she was told to drink some bamboo-shoot soup because it was "cold." In the winter, you need more hot substances; in the summer, you want fewer. Some people can tolerate more imbalance than others; the old, for instance, can tolerate less imbalance than the young. A loss of blood means a loss of heat. So, for a month after childbirth, women eat mostly a soup made of chicken, wine, and sesame oil—all "hot" ingredients. Hot things to eat are generally oily, sticky, or come from animals; cold things tend to be soupy, watery, or made from plants.

The body also has *yin* and *yang* parts. The *yang* part is visible to the living. The *yin* part exists in the underworld in the shape of a house and tree. The roof of the house corresponds to a person's head, the walls to the skin, a woman's reproductive organs correspond to the flowers on the woman's tree, the roots of the tree to the legs, and so on. A shaman can enable villagers to go into a trance to look around in the underworld where the dead live. If a person has a health problem, a traveler may be sent to the underworld to see what is wrong with the person's *yin* house or

In China and elsewhere, tai chi exercises are believed to bring harmony and balance.

tree. Fixing the *yin* house or tree should restore health to the *yang* part of the body. The *yin* world is also where ghosts reside; they sometimes may cause illness. In that case, people may ask for help from powerful gods who reside in the *yang* world.

Supernatural Forces

The Taiwanese Hokkien believe that most illnesses have natural or physiological causes, but around the world it is more common to believe that illnesses are caused by supernatural forces. In fact, in a cross-cultural study of 139 societies, George P. Murdock found that only two societies did not have the belief that gods or spirits could cause illness, making such a belief a near-universal. And 56 percent of those sample societies thought that gods or spirits were the major causes of illness.[8] As we discussed in the chapter on religion and magic, sorcery and witchcraft are common in the world's societies. Although both sorcery and witchcraft are practiced by humans and may be used for good or evil, making people ill is one of their major uses. Illness can also be thought of as caused by the loss of one's soul, fate, retribution for violation of a taboo, or contact with a polluting or tabooed substance or object. Sorcery is believed to be a cause of illness by most societies on all continents; retribution because of violation of a taboo is also very frequent in all but one region of the world. The belief that soul loss can cause illness is absent in the area around the Mediterranean, uncommon in Africa, infrequent in the New World and the Pacific, and has its highest frequency in Eurasia.[9]

On Chuuk (Truk), an atoll in the central Pacific, serious illnesses and death are mainly believed to be the work of spirits. Occasionally, the spirits of relatives are to blame, although they usually do not cause serious damage. More often, illness is caused by the spirit of a particular locality or a ghost on a path at night.[10] Nowadays, one of two therapeutic options or their combination is often chosen—hospital medicine or Chuuk medicine. Chuuk medical treatment requires a careful evaluation of symptoms by the patient and his or her relatives, because different spirits inflict different symptoms. If the symptom match is clear, the patient may choose an appropriate Chuuk medical formula to cure the illness. The patient may also ask whether he or she has done something wrong, and if so, what might point to the appropriate spirit and countervailing formula. For example, there is a taboo on having sexual relations before going to sea. If a person who violated this prohibition becomes ill, the reef spirits will be suspected. The Chuuk medical formula is supposed to cure illness quickly and dramatically. It is for this reason that Chuuk patients ask for a discharge from a hospital if their condition does not improve quickly. If treatment fails, the Chuukese believe that they need to reevaluate the diagnosis, sometimes with the aid of a diviner.[11] In contrasting their theories of illness to the American germ theory, the people of Chuuk point out that while they have seen ghosts, they have never seen the germs that Americans talk about. Using both methods, some people recover and some do not, so the ultimate cause is a matter of faith.[12]

Among the Ojibwa, the most serious illnesses, the ones resistant to ordinary treatment, are thought to be due to retribution for doing wrong to another person, an animal, or a spirit. To cure such an illness, to yourself or to your children, you must reflect on your own conduct to see what you did wrong. Bad conduct cannot be withheld from the doctor or from the other people in the *wigwam*. On the contrary, only after confessing can medicine help.[13] The Hopi similarly believed that a patient was responsible for his or her own illness, but the cause might be not just improper actions but also bad thoughts and anxiety. Witches could also cause illness, but the action of witches was most effective against people who were depressed or worried; so good thoughts ward off illness.[14]

People treat themselves with herbal medicines bought from an herbalist in Ghana.

The Biomedical Paradigm

In most societies, people simply think that their ideas about health and illness are true. Often it is not until they confront another medical system that people develop any awareness that there may be another way of viewing things. Western medical practice has spread widely. People with other medical systems have had to recognize that their ideas about health and illness may be considered deficient by Western practitioners, so it is often necessary to decide which course (Western or non-Western) to follow in dealing with illness. Change, however, is not entirely one-way. For example, for a long time the Chinese practice of acupuncture was disparaged by the Western medical profession, but now more medical practitioners are recognizing that acupuncture may provide effective treatment of certain conditions.

Most medical anthropologists use the term **biomedicine** to refer to the dominant medical paradigm in Western cultures today, with the *bio* part of the word emphasizing the biological emphasis of this medical system. As Robert Hahn points out, biomedicine appears to focus on specific diseases and cures for those diseases. Health is not the focus, as it is thought to be the *absence* of disease. Diseases are considered to be purely natural, and there is relatively little interest in the person or the larger social and cultural systems. Doctors generally do not treat the whole body but tend to specialize, with the human body partitioned into zones that belong to different specialties. Death is seen as a failure, and biomedical practitioners do everything they can to prolong life, regardless of the circumstances under which the patient would live his or her life.[15]

One of the most important discoveries that profoundly changed the course of Western medicine was Louis Pasteur's isolation of the organisms responsible for some major infectious diseases. Pasteur's discoveries stimulated the search for other disease-causing germs using scientific methods. But the *germ theory* of disease, although powerful, may have led researchers to pay less attention to the patient and the patient's social and cultural milieux.[16] For an example of how anthropologists try to redress the balance, see the box "Exploring Why an Applied Project Didn't Work."

 Treatment of Illness

Anthropologists who study diseases in this and other cultures can be roughly classified into two camps. First, there are those (the more relativistic) who think that the culture so influences disease symptoms, incidence, and treatment that there are few if any cultural universals about any illness. If each culture is unique, we should expect its conception and treatment of an illness to be unique too, not like beliefs and practices in other cultures. Second, there are those (the more universalistic) who see cross-cultural similarities in the conception and treatment of illness, despite the unique qualities (particularly in the belief system) of each culture. For example, native remedies may contain chemicals that are the same as, or similar in effect to, chemicals used in remedies by Western biomedicine.[17] The reader should note that our classification here of medical anthropologists is a crude one; many medical anthropologists do not fall unambiguously into one or the other group. And the reality might be that a given culture is very much like other cultures in some respects but unique in other respects.

In their extensive research on Maya ethnomedicine, Elois Ann Berlin and Brent Berlin make a strong case that although studies of the Maya have emphasized beliefs about illness that are based on supernatural causes, a good deal of Maya ethnomedicine is about natural conditions, their signs and symptoms, and the remedies used to deal with those conditions. In regard to gastrointestinal diseases, the Berlins found that the Maya have a wide-ranging and accurate understanding of anatomy, physiology, and symptoms. Furthermore, the remedies they use, including recommendations for food, drink, and herbal medicines, have properties that are not that different from those of the biomedical profession.[18]

Carole Browner also suggests that the emphasis on "hot–cold" theories of illness in Latin America has been overemphasized, to the neglect of other factors that influence choices about reproductive health and female health problems. In a study of the medical system in a highland Oaxacan community, Browner finds that certain plants are used to expel substances from the uterus—to facilitate labor at full term, to produce an abortion, or to induce menstrual flow. Other plants are used to retain things in the uterus—to prevent excess blood loss during menstruation, to help healing after delivery, and to prevent miscarriage. Most of these plant remedies appear to work.[19]

The biomedical establishment has become increasingly aware of the value of studying the "traditional" medicinal remedies discovered or invented by people around the world. In studying the indigenous medicines of the Hausa of Nigeria, Nina Etkin and Paul Ross asked individuals to describe the physical attributes of more than 600 plants and their possible medicinal uses, more than 800 diseases and symptoms, and more than 5,000 prepared medicines. While many medicines were used for treating sorcery, spirit aggression, or witchcraft, most medicines were used for illnesses regarded by the Hausa as having natural causes. Malaria is a serious endemic medical problem in the Hausa region, as in many areas of Africa. The Hausa use approximately 72 plant remedies for conditions connected with malaria—among them anemia, intermittent fever, and jaundice. Experimental treatment of malaria in laboratory animals supports the efficacy of many of the Hausa remedies. But perhaps the most important part of the Etkin and Ross findings is the role of diet. While most medical research does not consider the possible medical efficacy of the *foods* that people eat in combating illness, food is, of course, consumed in much larger quantities and more often than medicine. It is noteworthy, therefore, that the Hausa eat many plants with antimalarial properties; in fact, dietary consumption of these plants appears to be greatest during the time of year when the risk of malarial infection is at its highest. Recent research has also discovered that foods and spices like garlic, onions, cinnamon, ginger, and pepper have antiviral or antibacterial properties.[20]

APPLIED ANTHROPOLOGY

Exploring Why an Applied Project Didn't Work

When applied projects do not succeed, it is important for researchers to try to figure why. Part of the problem may be that the intended recipients' ideas about how things work may be very different from the researchers' ideas. Consider the following example.

In Guatemala, village health-care workers were not only testing people for malaria but they were also offering free antimalarial drugs. Yet, surprisingly, a community survey found that only 20 percent of people with malaria symptoms took advantage of the free treatment. More surprisingly, most people with symptoms spent the equivalent of a day's wages to buy an injection that was not strong enough to be effective! Why? What was going on?

Finding the answer was not easy. First, researchers designed interviews to elicit folk concepts about illness. What kinds of illnesses are there? What are their causes? What are their symptoms, and how are different illnesses to be treated? They conducted interviews with a random sample of households to find out what illnesses people had and what they did about them. Then they asked people to consider different hypothetical scenarios (vignettes), with different types of people and different degrees of severity of illness, to find out what treatment they would choose. All of these methods were well thought out, but the answers still did not predict what people actually did when they thought they had malaria. Finally, the researchers devised precise comparisons of the kinds of pills passed out by health-care workers and the pills and ampules for injections sold by the drugstore. They compared them two at a time, varying dosages and brands. People did think that more pills were more effective, as indeed they were. But they thought that the colorfully wrapped store-bought pill was more effective than the equivalent white unwrapped free pill, even though it was not. They also thought that one store-bought ampule used for injections, for which they would pay a day's wages, was more effective than four pills of any kind! In fact, one ampule was equivalent to only one pill.

Applied researchers often use such trial-and-error methods to find out how to get the information they need. Methods that work in one field setting don't always work in others. To get the information needed, researchers must sometimes let the subjects structure their own answers. At other times, as in this case, they may have to make very specific comparisons to get predictive answers. The people in the Guatemala study didn't believe that the free pills were strong enough to work, so they didn't use them. More research would be needed to uncover why they did not believe the free pills were effective. Was it because they were free? Was it because the store-bought drugs were attractively packaged? Or was there a belief that injections work better than pills? That's what the research process is like; it always leads to new questions, particularly more general questions requiring more extensive or more comparative research.

For example, the Guatemala project revealed why a particular program was not successful in a particular area. But how widespread are the interfering beliefs? Are they found throughout Guatemala? Do they interfere with the introduction of other medicines? Are we dealing with problems that exist in other areas of Central and South America? Although we don't yet have answers to these more extensive questions, anthropologists have developed efficient methods for assessing variation in beliefs within and between cultures.

We now know that if we ask one or two informants, we cannot assume that the answer is cultural. But that doesn't mean that we need to ask hundreds of people. If a belief is cultural and therefore commonly held, asking 10 to 20 individuals the same question is sufficient to provide the researcher with a high probability that an answer is correct. (The agreement among respondents is called *cultural consensus*.) So, for example, Guatemalan respondents mostly agreed about which illnesses were contagious. But they disagreed a lot about whether a particular disease should be treated with a "hot" or a "cold" remedy. Using cultural-consensus methods, researchers can compare rural and urban residents, and they can also compare informants in different cultures. When we have more of these systematic comparisons, medical anthropologists and health practitioners may have a better understanding of how to implement medical care.

Sources: Susan C. Weller, "The Research Process," in *Research Frontiers,* in Carol R. Ember, Melvin Ember, and Peter N. Peregrine, eds., *New Directions in Anthropology* (Upper Saddle River, NJ: Prentice Hall, CD-ROM, 2004), and the research referred to therein; A. Kimball Romney, Susan C. Weller, and William H. Batchelder, "Culture as Consensus: A Theory of Culture and Informant Accuracy," *American Anthropologist,* 88 (1986): 313–38.

Medical Practitioners

In our society we may be so used to consulting a full-time medical specialist (if we do not feel better quickly) that we tend to assume that biomedical treatment is the only effective medical treatment. If we are given a medicine, we expect it to have the appropriate medical effect and make us feel better. So, many in the biomedical system, practitioners and patients alike, are perplexed by the seeming effectiveness of other medical systems that are based in part on symbolic or ritual healing. As we noted earlier, many native plants have been shown to be medically effective, but their use is often accompanied by singing, dancing, noise-making, or rituals. Our difficulty in understanding the healing in such practices probably stems from the assumption in biomedicine that the mind is fundamentally different from the body. Yet, there is increasing evidence that the *form* of treatment may be just as important as the *content* of treatment.[21]

The practitioners who deal with more than the body are sometimes referred to as *personalistic* practitioners. In a personalistic view, illness may be viewed as being due to something in one's social life being out of order. The cause could be retribution for one's own bad behavior or thoughts, or the work of an angry individual practicing sorcery or witchcraft. Or a bad social situation or a bad relationship may be thought of as provoking physical symptoms because of anxiety or stress. In societies with occupational specialization, priests, who are formally trained full-time religious practitioners, may be asked to convey messages or requests for healing to higher powers.[22] Societies with beliefs in sorcery and witchcraft as causes of illness typically have practitioners who are believed to be able to use magic in reverse—that is, to undo the harm invoked by sorcerers and witches. Sometimes sorcerers or witches themselves may be asked to reverse illnesses caused by others. However, they may not be sought out because they are often feared and have relatively low status.[23] Shamans are perhaps the most important medical practitioners in societies lacking full-time occupational specialization.

THE SHAMAN   The *shaman,* usually a male part-time specialist, is often involved in healing.[24] Westerners often call shamans "witch doctors" because they don't believe that shamans can effectively cure people. Do shamans effectively cure people? Actually, Westerners are not the only skeptics. A Native American named Quesalid from the Kwakiutl of the Pacific Northwest didn't believe that shamanism was effective either. So he began to associate with the shamans in order to spy on them and was taken into their group. In his first lessons, he learned

> a curious mixture of pantomime, prestidigitation, and empirical knowledge, including the art of simulating fainting and nervous fits, . . . sacred song, the technique for inducing vomiting, rather precise notions of auscultation or listening to sounds within the body to detect disorders and obstetrics, and the use of "dreamers," that is, spies who listen to private conversations and secretly convey to the shaman bits of information concerning the origins and symptoms of

the ills suffered by different people. Above all, he learned the *ars magna.* . . . The shaman hides a little tuft of down in the corner of his mouth, and he throws it up, covered with blood at the proper moment—after having bitten his tongue or made his gums bleed—and solemnly presents it to his patient and the onlookers as the pathological foreign body extracted as a result of his sucking and manipulations.[25]

His suspicions were confirmed, but his first curing was a success. The patient had heard that Quesalid had joined the shamans and believed that only he could heal him. Quesalid remained with the shamans for the four-year apprenticeship, during which he could take no fee, and he became increasingly aware that his methods worked. He visited other villages, competed with other shamans in curing hopeless cases and won, and finally seemed convinced that his curing system was more valid than those of other shamans. Instead of denouncing the trickery of shamans, he continued to practice as a renowned shaman.[26]

After working with shamans in Africa, E. Fuller Torrey, a psychiatrist and anthropologist, concluded that they use the same mechanisms and techniques to cure patients as psychiatrists and achieve about the same results. He isolated four categories used by healers the world over:

1. **The naming process.** If a disease has a name—"neurasthenia" or "phobia" or "possession by an ancestral spirit" will do—then it is curable; the patient realizes that the doctor understands his case.

2. **The personality of the doctor.** Those who demonstrate some empathy, nonpossessive warmth, and genuine interest in the patient get results.

3. **The patient's expectations.** One way of raising the patient's expectations of being cured is the trip to the doctor; the longer the trip—to the Mayo Clinic, Menninger Clinic, Delphi, or Lourdes—the easier the cure. An impressive setting (the medical center) and impressive paraphernalia (the stethoscope, the couch, attendants in uniform, the rattle, the whistle, the drum, the mask) also raise the patient's expectations. The healer's training is important: The Ute has dreams analyzed; the Blackfoot has a seven-year training course; the American psychiatrist spends four years in medical school and three in hospital training and has diplomas on the wall. High fees also help to raise a patient's expectations. (The Paiute doctors always collect their fees before starting a cure; if they don't, it is believed that they will fall ill.)

4. **Curing techniques.** Drugs, shock treatment, conditioning techniques, and so on have long been used in many different parts of the world.[27]

Biomedical research is not unaware of the effect of the mind on healing. In fact, considerable evidence has accumulated that psychological factors can be very important in illness. Patients who believe that medicine will help them often recover quickly even if the medicine is only a sugar pill or a medicine not particularly relevant to their condition.

A Navajo medicine man performs a healing ceremony involving a snake painted on the ground.

Such effects are called *placebo* effects.[28] Placebos do not just have psychological effects. Although the mechanisms are not well understood, they may also alter body chemistry and bolster the immune system.[29]

Shamans may coexist with medical doctors. Don Antonio, a respected Otomi Indian shaman in central Mexico, has many patients, perhaps not as many as before modern medicine, but still plenty. In his view, when he was born God gave him his powers to cure, but his powers are reserved for removing "evil" illnesses (those caused by sorcerers). "Good" illnesses can be cured by herbs and medicine, and he refers patients with those illnesses to medical doctors; he believes that doctors are more effective than he could be in those cases. The doctors, however, do not seem to refer any patients to Don Antonio or other shamans![30]

PHYSICIANS The most important full-time medical practitioner in the biomedical system is the physician, and the patient–physican relationship is central. In the ideal scheme of things, the physician is viewed as having the ability, with some limits, of being able to treat illness, alleviate suffering, and prolong the life of the patient, as well as offering promises of patient confidentiality and privacy. The patient relies on the physician's knowledge, skill, and ethics. Consistent with the biomedical paradigm, doctors tend to treat patients as having "conditions" rather than as complete persons. Physicians presumably rely on science for authoritative knowledge, but they place a good deal of importance on the value of their own clinical experience. Often physicians con-

sider their own observations of the patient to be more valuable than the reports by the patient. Since patients commonly go to physicians to solve a particular condition or sickness, physicians tend to try to do something about it even in the face of uncertainty. Physicians tend to rely on technology for diagnoses and treatment and place relatively low value on talking with patients. In fact, physicians tend to give patients relatively little information, and they may not listen very well.[31]

Despite the importance of physicians in biomedicine, patients do not always seek physician care. In fact, one-third of the population of the United States regularly consults with alternative practitioners, such as acupuncturists or chiropractors, often unbeknown to the physician. Somewhat surprisingly, individuals with more education are more likely to seek alternative care.[32]

⊚ Political and Economic Influences on Health

People with more social, economic, and political power in a society are generally healthier.[33] Inequality in health in socially stratified societies is not surprising. The poor usually have more exposure to disease because they live in more crowded conditions. And the poor are more likely to lack the resources to get quality care. For many diseases, health problems, and death rates, incidence or relative frequency varies directly with social class. In the United Kingdom, for example, people in the higher social classes are less likely to have headaches, bronchitis, pneumonia, heart disease, arthritis, injuries, and mental disorders, to name just a few of the differences.[34] Ethnic differences also predict health inequities. In South Africa under apartheid, the 14 percent minority population, referred to as "white," controlled most of the income of the country and most of the high-quality land. "Blacks" were restricted to areas with shortages of housing, inadequate housing, and little employment. To get a job, families often had to be disrupted; usually the husband would have to migrate to find work. "Blacks" lived, on average, about nine years less than "whites" in 1985 and "black" infants died at about seven times the rate of "white" infants. In the United States recently, the differences between African Americans and European Americans in health are not as stark as in South Africa, but those favoring European Americans are still substantial. As of 1987, the difference in life expectancy was seven years, and African American infant mortality was about twice the rate for European American infants. Robert Hahn has estimated that poverty accounts for about 19 percent of the overall mortality in the United States.[35]

Inequities, because of class and ethnicity, are not limited to within-society differences. Power and economic differentials *between* societies also have profound health consequences. Over the course of European exploration and expansion, indigenous peoples died in enormous numbers from introduced diseases, wars, and conquests; they had their lands expropriated and diminished in size and quality. When incorporated into colonial territories or into

MIGRANTS AND IMMIGRANTS

The Spread of Leprosy

Leprosy is an ancient disease of humanity. The disease has existed in many places for more than 2,000 years. It seems to have followed people wherever they have gone. It is apparently caused by several related strains of bacteria, which people carry and transmit to others. The symptoms are horrific—damage to the skin and flesh, loss of the nose, and other disfiguring. The victim suffers for a long time. In the old days, lepers were quarantined in "leper colonies," in isolated places or on islands, to prevent the spread of the disease. New evidence suggests that the disease mainly spreads as a result of military and colonial activities, as people from expanding state societies sent out armies and others to colonize the world. They encountered the disease in many of these places, and they moved it to new places by moving carriers, particularly slaves.

Old texts refer to leprosy in China, India, and Egypt in about 600 B.C. Skeletal remains from Egypt show the effects of the disease. Leprosy may have originated in South Asia and been introduced into Europe by Greek soldiers returning from the military campaigns led by Alexander the Great. From Greece the disease spread around the Mediterranean Sea as the Greeks and others established colonies. The Romans in their own empire building may have introduced leprosy into the western parts of Europe. The disease existed in Africa prior to the movement of Europeans to establish colonies in Africa. The disease is believed to have spread from India to China and then to Japan, reaching Pacific islands such as New Caledonia as recently as the 19th century. Imperialism and colonialism seems to have driven the spread to many places.

Leprosy was most likely introduced into West Africa by infected explorers, traders, and colonialists of European and North African descent, rather than by migrants from East Africa. Scientists believe this because the bacterial causes of leprosy are different in East and West Africa. From the 18th century on, leprosy spread from West Africa with the slave trade to the Caribbean islands, Brazil, and probably other parts of South America. Soon after Scandinavians moved to the U.S. Midwest in the 18th and 19th centuries, many cases of leprosy occurred in the Midwest. Probably the disease came from Norway, where there was a major epidemic at the time. Leprosy is not the only human disease that spreads mostly because of what humans do. Malaria too spreads as a result of human activity. When early agriculturalists moved out of West Africa, they took the environment conducive to malaria with them. Clearing fields for their agriculture, they created habitats (reduced forest canopy, wet places exposed to sunlight) where the mosquitoes that transmit malaria could thrive.

Bites by insects, particularly aquatic ones, may also be involved in the spread of leprosy. But human migration has been the major driving force. Indeed, how the variant bacterial causes are distributed around the world provides information that helps us track human migrations: Where people came from is often revealed by the kind of leprosy bacteria they carry. So this terrible affliction of humanity can help us reconstruct human history. We are also fortunate now that medical science has found ways to limit and cure the disease. The "leper colony" is a thing of the past.

Sources: Marc Monot et al., "On the Origin of Leprosy," *Science* 308 (May 13, 2005), pp. 1040–1042; Paul E. Brodwin, "Disease and Culture," in David Levinson and Melvin Ember, eds. *Encyclopedia of Cultural Anthropology*, 4 vols., (New York: Henry Holt, 1996), vol. 1, pp. 355–359; Jeannine Coreil, "Malaria and Other Major Insect Vector Diseases, in Carol R. Ember and Melvin Ember, eds., *Encyclopedia of Medical Anthropology: Health and Illness in the World's Cultures*, 2 vols., (New York: Kluwer Academic/Plenum, 2004), vol. 1, pp. 479–485.

countries, indigenous people usually become minorities and they are almost always very poor. These conditions of life not only affect the incidence of disease, they also tend to lead to greater substance abuse, violence, depression, and other mental pathologies.[36]

Health Conditions and Diseases

Medical anthropologists have studied an enormous variety of conditions. What follows is only a small sampling.

AIDS

Epidemics of infectious disease have killed millions of people within short periods of time throughout recorded history. The Black Death—bubonic plague—killed between 25 and 50 percent of the population of Europe, perhaps 75 million people, during the 14th century; an epidemic during the 6th century killed an estimated 100 million people in the Middle East, Asia, and Europe. Less noted in our history books, but also devastating, was the enormous depopulation that accompanied the expansion of Europeans into the New World and the Pacific from the 1500s on. Not only were people killed directly by European conquerors, millions also died from introduced diseases to which the natives had little or no resistance, diseases such as smallpox and measles that the Europeans brought with them but were no longer dying from.

The current state of medical science and technology may lull us into thinking that epidemics are a thing of the past. But the recent and sudden emergence of the disease we call **AIDS (acquired immune deficiency syndrome)** reminds us that new diseases, or new varieties of old diseases, can appear at any time. Like all other organisms, disease-causing organisms also evolve. The human immunodeficiency virus (HIV) that causes AIDS emerged only recently. Viruses and bacteria are always mutating, and new strains emerge that are initially a plague on our genetic resistance and on medical efforts to contain them.

Millions of people around the world already have the symptoms of AIDS, and millions more are infected with HIV but do not know they are infected. The World Health Organization estimated a few years ago that about 40 million adults and children would be infected and 15 million people would have AIDS by the year 2000.[37] That prediction proved to be correct. As of December 2002, 42 million adults and children in the world were living with HIV/AIDS.[38] The death toll is enormous and growing. AIDS is now a leading cause of death of people between the ages of 25 and 44 in the United States and Western Europe. It is the leading cause of adult death in many countries as well.[39] AIDS is a frightening epidemic not only because of its death toll. It is also frightening because it takes a long time (on average, four years) after exposure for symptoms to appear. This means that many people who have been infected by HIV but do not know they are infected may continue, unknowingly, to transmit the virus to others.[40]

Transmission occurs mostly via sexual encounters, through semen and blood. Drug users may also transmit HIV by way of contaminated needles. Transmission by blood transfusion has been virtually eliminated in this and other societies by medical screening of blood supplies. In many countries, however, there is still no routine screening of blood prior to transfusions. HIV may be passed from a pregnant woman to her offspring through the placenta and after birth through her breast milk. The rate of transmission between a mother and her baby is 20 to 40 percent. Children are also at great risk because they are likely to be orphaned by a parent's death from AIDS. At the turn of the 21st century approximately 14 million children were parentless because of AIDS.[41]

Many people think of AIDS as only a medical problem that requires only a medical solution, without realizing that there are behavioral, cultural, and political issues that need to be addressed as well. It is true that developing a vaccine or a drug to prevent people from getting AIDS and finding a permanent cure for those who have it will finally solve the problem. But, for a variety of reasons, we can expect that the medical solution alone will not be sufficient, at least not for a while. First, to be effective worldwide, or even within a country, a vaccine has to be inexpensive and relatively easy to produce in large quantities; the same is true of any medical treatment. Second, governments around the world have to be willing and able to spend the money and hire the personnel necessary to manage an effective program.[42] Third, future vaccination and treatment will require the people at risk to be willing to get vaccinated and treated, which is not always the case. Witness the fact that the incidence of measles is on the rise in the United States because many people are not having their children vaccinated.

There are now expensive drug treatments that significantly reduce the degree of HIV infection, but we do not know if an effective and inexpensive vaccine or treatment will be developed soon. In the meantime, the risk of HIV infection can be reduced only by changes in social, particularly sexual, behavior. But to persuade people to change their sexual behavior, it is necessary to find out exactly what they do sexually, and why they do what they do.

Research so far suggests that different sexual patterns are responsible for HIV transmission in different parts of the

A neighborhood self-help group in Tamil Nadu, India, collects rice for people with HIV and AIDS. Each member of the group puts aside one handful of rice every time she cooks a meal. The group members also contribute money to pay for drugs to treat neighbors with HIV and AIDs.

world. In the United States, England, northern Europe, Australia, and Latin America, the recipients of anal intercourse, particularly men, are the most likely individuals to acquire HIV infection; vaginal intercourse can also transmit the infection, usually from the man to the woman. Needle sharing can transmit the infection, too. In Africa, the most common mode of transmission is vaginal intercourse, and so women get infected more commonly in Africa than elsewhere.[43] In fact, in Africa there are slightly more cases of HIV in women as compared with men.[44]

Some researchers are arguing that while the immediate cause of HIV infection may be mostly related to sexual practice, larger political and social issues, such as poverty and gender inequality, increase the likelihood of such infection. For example, sexually transmitted diseases increase the risk of HIV infection three to five times, but the poor are less likely to get adequate treatment. And, in the developing world, rural and poorer areas are also more likely to get tainted blood transfusions. Gender inequality is likely to increase the likelihood that women have to submit to unsafe sex and women are even less likely than men to have access to adequate medical care.[45]

As of now, there are only two known ways to reduce the likelihood of sexual HIV transmission. One way is to abstain from sexual intercourse; the other is to use condoms. Educational programs that teach how AIDS spreads and what one can do about it may reduce the spread somewhat, but such programs may fail where people have incompatible beliefs and attitudes about sexuality. For example, people in some central African societies believe that deposits of semen after conception are necessary for a successful pregnancy and generally enhance a woman's health and ability to reproduce. It might be expected then that people who have these beliefs about semen would choose not to use condoms; after all, condoms in their view are a threat to public health.[46] Educational programs may also emphasize the wrong message. Promiscuity may increase the risk of HIV transmission, so hardly anyone would question the wisdom of advertising to reduce the number of sexual partners. And, at least in the homosexual community in the United States, individuals report fewer sexual partners than in the past. What was not anticipated, however, was that individuals in monogamous relationships, who may feel safe, are less likely to use condoms or to avoid the riskiest sexual practices. Needless to say, sex with a regular partner who is infected is not safe![47] In what may seem like something of a paradox, the United Nations observed that for most women in the world today, the major risk factor for being infected with HIV is being married.[48] It is not marriage, *per se,* that causes the risk of HIV infection; rather, the proximate cause may be the lower likelihood of condom use or abstinence between a husband and wife.

The stigmas associated with AIDS also hinder efforts to reduce its spread. In some societies, there is the widespread belief that homosexual men are particularly likely to get infected.[49] In other societies, AIDS may be thought to be due to promiscuity. If a woman asks a man to use a condom, she may be assumed to be a prostitute. In addition, many people mistakenly fear even proximity to AIDS victims, as if any kind of contact could result in infection.

To solve the problem of AIDS, we may hope that medical science will develop an effective and inexpensive vaccination or treatment that can be afforded by all. There is a vaccine that seems to reduce HIV infection in monkeys to hardly detectable levels.[50] Perhaps soon there will be a similar vaccine for humans. In the meantime, we can try to understand why people engage in certain risky sexual practices. Such understanding may allow us to design educational and other programs that would help inhibit the spread of AIDS.

Mental and Emotional Disorders

Diagnosing mental or emotional disorders in one culture is difficult enough; diagnosing them in others poses much greater difficulty. Many researchers start with Western categories of mental illness and try to apply them elsewhere, without first trying to understand native conceptions of mental disorder. In addition, "mental" and "physical" disorders are rarely separate. For example, a host of illnesses can produce a loss of energy that some may see as depression; and fear or anger can produce physical symptoms such as a heart attack.[51]

When Western anthropologists first started describing mental illness in non-Western societies, there seemed to be unique illnesses in different cultures. These are referred to as *culture-bound syndromes.* For example, a mental disorder called *pibloktoq* occurred among some Eskimo adults of Greenland, usually women, who became oblivious to their surroundings and acted in agitated, eccentric ways. They might strip themselves naked and wander across the ice and over hills until they collapsed of exhaustion. Another disorder, *amok,* occurred in Malaya, Indonesia, and New Guinea, usually among males. It was characterized by John Honigmann as a "destructive maddened excitement . . . beginning with depression and followed by a period of brooding and withdrawal [culminating in] the final mobilization of tremendous energy during which the 'wild man' runs destructively berserk."[52] *Anorexia nervosa,* the disorder involving aversion to food, may be unique to the relatively few societies that idealize slimness.[53] (See the box "Eating Disorders, Biology, and the Cultural Construction of Beauty.")

Some scholars think that each society's views of personality and concepts of mental illness have to be understood in their own terms. Western understandings and concepts cannot be applied to other cultures. For example, Catherine Lutz suggested that the Western concept of depression cannot be applied to the Pacific island of Ifaluk. The people there have many words for thinking or feeling about "loss and helplessness," but all their words are related to a specific need for someone, such as when someone dies or leaves the island. Such thoughts and feelings of loss are considered perfectly normal, and there is no word in their language for general hopelessness or "depression."[54] Therefore Lutz questioned the applicability of the Western concept of depression as well as other Western psychiatric categories.

Other researchers are not so quick to dismiss the possible universality of psychiatric categories. Some think they have found a considerable degree of cross-cultural uniformity in conceptions of mental illness. Jane Murphy studied descriptions by the Inuit and the Yoruba, in Nigeria, of severely disturbed persons. She found that their descriptions not only were similar to each other but also corresponded to North American descriptions of schizophrenia. The Inuit word for "crazy" is *nuthkavihak*. They use this word when something inside a person seems to be out of order. *Nuthkavihak* people are described as talking to themselves, believing themselves to be animals, making strange faces, becoming violent, and so on. The Yoruba have a word, *were*, for people who are "insane." People described as *were* sometimes hear voices, laugh when there is nothing to laugh at, and take up weapons and suddenly hit people.[55]

Robert Edgerton found similarities in conceptions of mental illness in four East African societies. He noted not only that the four groups essentially agreed on the symptoms of psychosis but also that the symptoms they described were the same ones that are considered psychotic here.[56] Edgerton believed that the lack of exact translation in different cultures, such as the one pointed out by Lutz regarding Ifaluk, does not make comparison impossible. If researchers can come to understand another culture's views of personality and if the researchers can manage to communicate these views to people of other cultures, we can compare the described cases and try to discover what may be universal and what may be found only in some cultures.[57]

Some mental illnesses, such as schizophrenia and depression, seem so widespread that many researchers think they are probably universal. Consistent with this idea is the fact that schizophrenic individuals in different cultures seem to share the same patterns of distinctive eye movements.[58] Still, cultural factors may influence the risk of developing such diseases, the specific symptoms that are expressed, and the effectiveness of different kinds of treatment.[59] There may be some truly culture-bound (nearly unique) syndromes, but others thought at one time to be unique may be culturally varying expressions of conditions that occur widely. *Pibloktoq*, for example, may be a kind of hysteria.[60]

Biological but not necessarily genetic factors may be very important in the etiology of some of the widespread disorders such as schizophrenia.[61] With regard to hysteria, Anthony Wallace theorized that nutritional factors such as calcium deficiency may cause hysteria and that dietary improvement may account for the decline of this illness in the Western world since the 19th century.[62] By the early 20th century, the discovery of the value of good nutrition, coupled with changes in social conditions, had led many people to drink milk, eat vitamin-rich foods, and spend time in the sun (although spending a lot of time in the sun is no longer recommended because of the risk of skin cancer). These changes in diet and activity increased the intake of vitamin D and helped people to maintain a proper calcium level. Consequently, the number of cases of hysteria declined.

Regarding *pibloktoq*, Wallace suggested that a complex set of related variables may cause the disease. The Inuit live in an environment that supplies only a minimum amount of calcium. A diet low in calcium could result in two different conditions. One condition, rickets, would produce physical deformities potentially fatal in the Inuit hunting economy. Persons whose genetic makeup made them prone to rickets would be eliminated from the population through natural selection. A low level of calcium in the blood could also cause muscular spasms known as tetany. Tetany, in turn, may cause emotional and mental disorientation similar to the symptoms of *pibloktoq*. Such attacks last for only a relatively short time and are not fatal, so people who developed *pibloktoq* would have a far greater chance of surviving in the Arctic environment with a calcium-deficient diet than would people who had rickets.

Although researchers disagree about the comparability of mental illnesses among cultures, most agree that effective treatment requires understanding a culture's ideas about a mental illness—why people think it occurs, what treatments are believed to be effective, and how families and others respond to those afflicted.[63]

SUSTO *Susto* is often described as a "folk illness" or a culture-bound syndrome because there doesn't seem to be any direct counterpart in biomedical terms. In many areas of Latin America, it is believed that a person suffers susto, or becomes *astudado*, when a nonmaterial essence from the body becomes detached during sleep, or after suffering a fright. This essence is either held captive by supernatural forces or wanders freely outside the body.[64] Susto patients are described as restless during sleep, and listless, depressed, debilitated, and indifferent to food and hygiene during the day. Some researchers have suggested that people labeled as suffering from susto may in fact be suffering from mental illness. Believing that such conclusions were incomplete or premature, Arthur Rubel, Carl O'Nell, and Rolando Collado-Ardón designed a three-culture comparative study to evaluate whether susto victims were suffering from social, psychological, or organic problems. They compared individuals suffering from susto to other individuals matched by culture, age, and sex who defined themselves as "sick" when they came to health clinics (but who did not claim susto as their illness). The three cultures were Chichimec, Zapotec, and a Spanish-speaking mestizo community.[65]

From previous study of susto victims, Rubel and his colleagues hypothesized that susto was likely to strike people in socially stressful situations where they may think they are inadequate in required roles. For example, two cases of susto occurred among women who desperately wanted more children, but each had had a number of miscarriages (one had seven, the other two). In addition to measuring social stress, the researchers also had physicians evaluate organic problems with reference to the World Health Organization's *International Classification of Diseases*. Degree of psychiatric impairment was judged in an interview based on questions previously developed by other researchers. And seven years after the study, the researchers found out which, if any, of the studied individuals had died.

The research results supported the social stress hypothesis: Susto victims were significantly more likely to feel inadequate about social roles. The researchers did not expect to find evidence that susto victims had more psychiatric impairment or more organic disease. However, to their surprise,

APPLIED ANTHROPOLOGY

Eating Disorders, Biology, and the Cultural Construction of Beauty

Cultures differ about what they consider beautiful, including people. In many cultures, fat people are considered more beautiful than thin people. The second author of this book did fieldwork years ago on the islands of American Samoa. When he returned to the main island after three months on a distant island, he ran into a Samoan acquaintance, a prominent chief. The chief said: "You look good. You gained weight." In reality, the anthropologist had lost 30 pounds! The chief may not have remembered how heavy the anthropologist had been, but he clearly thought that fat was better than thin. Among the Azawagh Arabs of Niger, fatness was not merely valued and considered beautiful; great care was taken to ensure that young girls became fat by insisting and sometimes forcing them to drink large quantities of milk-based porridge.

Around the world, fatness is generally considered more desirable than thinness, particularly for women. Fatness is widely valued in these cultures not only because it is considered more beautiful, but also because it is thought to be a marker of health, fertility, and higher status in societies with social stratification. This view is in strong contrast to the ideal in the United States and many other Western societies, where fatness is thought to be unattractive, and to reflect laziness, a lack of self-control, and poor health. Thinness, partic-

ularly in the upper classes, is considered beautiful. How can we explain these differences in what is considered beautiful?

In an earlier box on obesity and modernization we discussed the idea that individuals who have very efficient metabolisms and who can store calories in fatty tissue are most apt to survive and reproduce in environments with frequent famines or chronic food shortages. If so, natural selection may have favored "thrifty genes" in such environments. Would such societies also be the most likely to idealize and value fatness? Recent cross-cultural research suggests that the picture is more complicated. It appears that societies with unpredictable resources actually value thinness, particularly in societies that have no way of storing food. At first glance, this seems puzzling. Shouldn't an individual who stores calories on the body be better off than an individual who is thin when facing starvation, particularly if there is no food storage? Perhaps. But 10 thin individuals will generally consume less than 10 heavier people, so perhaps there is a group advantage to being thin. Indeed, many societies with frequent episodes of famine encourage fasting or eating very light meals, as among the Gurage of Ethiopia. The strongest cross-cultural predictor of valuing fatness in women is what is often referred to as "machismo" or "protest masculinity." Societies with a

susto victims were also more likely to have had serious physical health problems. In fact, susto victims were more likely to have died in the seven years after the study. It is hard to say whether the susto victims had more disease because they were debilitated by susto or they were more prone to susto because they were physically sicker. The researchers guess that since many of the conditions that created social role impairment were of long duration (such as many miscarriages), it seemed likely that susto itself put its victims at risk for biological diseases.[66]

DEPRESSION Just as one kind of stress seems to be involved in the folk illness susto, researchers have considered the role of other kinds of stress in producing various other forms of mental illness. One of the most important stressors may be economic deprivation. Many studies have found that the lower classes in socially stratified societies have much higher proportions of all kinds of mental illness. Acute stressors like death of a loved one, divorce, loss of a job, or a natural disaster predict higher rates of mental illness for all

social classes; however, these events take more of a toll in lower-class families.[67]

In a study designed to evaluate the effect of these and other stressors on the prevalence of depression in an African American community in a southern city, William Dressler combined fieldwork methods and hypothesis testing to try to better understand depression.[68] While many studies rely on treatment or hospitalization rates, Dressler decided that such rates drastically underestimate the incidence of depression, inasmuch as many people do not seek treatment. He decided to rely on a symptom checklist, which asked such questions as how often in the last week a person felt like crying, felt lonely, or felt hopeless about the future. While such checklists do not provide clear divisions for characterizing someone as mildly depressed or seriously depressed, they do allow researchers to compare people along a continuum.

Dressler measured a variety of different possible stressors, including life crises, economic worries, perceived racial inequality, and problems in social roles, and found that some of the objective stressors, like life crises and unemployment,

strong emphasis on male aggression, strength, and sexuality are the most likely to value fatness in women; those with little machismo value thinness. Why machismo is associated with valuing fatness in women is far from clear. One suggestion is that machismo actually reflects male insecurity and fear of women. Such men may not be looking for closeness or intimacy with their wives, but they may want to show how potent they are by having lots of children. If fatness suggests fertility, men may look for wives who are fatter. Consistent with this idea, the ideal of thinness in women became more common in North America with the rise of women's movements in the 1920s and late 1960s. Consider that Marilyn Monroe epitomized beauty in the 1950s; she was well-rounded, not thin. Thin became more popular when women began to question early marriage and having many children. Behaviors associated with machismo became less acceptable at those times.

Cultural beliefs about what is considered a beautiful body can impose enormous pressures on females to achieve the ideal body type—whether it be fat or thin. In the United States and other Western countries, the effort to be thin can be carried to an extreme, resulting in the eating disorders anorexia and bulimia. If you suffer from these often fatal illnesses, you may regularly eat little and you may regularly force yourself to throw up, thus depriving your body of nutrients in your quest to be thinner and thinner. The irony of "thinness" being idealized in the United States and other Western countries is that obesity is becoming more and more common in those societies. In 2001 the incidence of obesity increased in the United States to 31% and medical researchers worried about the increase in heart disease and diabetes resulting from obesity. Whether or not obesity is a result of an eating disorder (in the psychological sense) is more debatable. Researchers are finding biological causes of obesity, such as resistance to the hormone leptin, which regulates appetite, suggesting that much of the obesity "epidemic" has biological causes. Still, fast food, increasing sedentariness, and extremely large portion sizes are probably contributing factors also.

Sources: Peter J. Brown, "Culture and the Evolution of Obesity," in Aaron Podolefsky and Peter J. Brown, eds., *Applying Cultural Anthropology: An Introductory Reader,* 4th ed. (Mountain View, CA: Mayfield, 1999), p. 100; Martha O. Loustaunau and Elisa J. Sobo, *The Cultural Context of Health, Illness, and Medicine* (Westport, CT: Bergin and Garvey, 1997), p. 85; Naomi Wolf, *The Beauty Myth: How Images of Beauty Are Used against Women* (New York: Morrow, 1991); Rebecca Popenoe, *Feeding Desire: Fatness, Beauty, and Sexuality Among a Saharan People* (London: Routledge, 2004); Carol R. Ember, Melvin Ember, Andrey Korotayev, and Victor de Munck, "Valuing Thinness or Fatness in Women: Reevaluating the Effect of Resource Scarcity," *Evolution and Human Behavior* 26 (2005): 257–270; J. L. Anderson, C. B. Crawford, J. Nadeau, and T. Lindberg, "Was the Dutchess of Windsor Right? A Cross-Cultural Review of the Socioecology of Ideal Female Body Shape," *Ethology and Sociobiology,* 13 (1992): 197–227; Jeffrey M. Friedman, "A War on Obesity, Not the Obese" *Science,* (February 7, 2003), pp. 856–858.

predict depression in the expected direction only in the lower classes. That is, for lower-class African Americans, unemployment and other life crises predicted more depression, but that result was not found among middle- and upper-class individuals. These results are consistent with previous findings that many stressors take more of a toll among poorer individuals. On the other hand, more subjective economic stressors, such as feeling you are not making enough money, predict depression across all class lines. So does "social role" stress, such as thinking you are missing promotions because you are African American or thinking that your spouse expects too much.[69]

Undernutrition

What people eat is intrinsically connected to their survival and the ability of a population to reproduce itself, so we would expect that the ways people obtain, distribute, and consume food have been generally adaptive.[70] For example, the human body cannot synthesize eight amino acids. Meat can provide all of these amino acids, and combinations of particular plants can also provide them for a complete complement of protein. The combination of maize and beans in many traditional Native American diets, or *tortillas* and *frijoles* in Mexico, can provide all the needed amino acids. In places where wheat (often made into bread) is the staple, dairy products combined with wheat also provide complete protein.[71] Even the way that people have prepared for scarcity, such as breaking up into mobile bands, cultivating crops that can better withstand drought, and preserving food in case of famine, are probably adaptive practices in unpredictable environments. As we saw in the box on obesity, hypertension, and diabetes in the chapter on culture change and globalization, geneticists have proposed that populations in famine-prone areas may have had genetic selection for "thrifty genes"—genes that allow individuals to need a minimum of food and store the extra in fatty tissue to get them past serious scarcity. Customary diets and genetic changes may have been selected over a long stretch of time, but many serious

A sisal plant in Bahia, Brazil. The switch to sisal production led to undernutrition in children.

nutritional problems observed today are due to rapid culture change.

Often the switch to commercial or cash crops has harmful effects on nutrition. As we noted in the chapter on culture change and globalization, when the farmer-herders of the arid region in northeastern Brazil started growing sisal, a drought-resistant plant used for making twine and rope, many of them abandoned subsistence agriculture. The small landholders used most of their land for sisal growing and when the price of sisal fell they had to work as laborers for others to try to make ends meet. Food then had to be mostly bought, but if a laborer or sisal grower didn't earn enough, there was not enough food for the whole family.

Analysis of allocation of food in some households by Daniel Gross and Barbara Underwood suggests that the laborer and his wife received adequate nutrition, but the children often received much less than required. Lack of adequate nutrition usually results in retarded weight and height in children. As is commonly the case when there is substantial social inequality, the children from lower-income groups weigh substantially less than those from higher-income groups. But even though there were some economic differences before sisal production, the effects on nutrition appeared negligible before, judging from the fact that there was little or no difference in weight among adults from higher and lower socioeconomic positions who grew up prior to sisal production. But more recently, 45 percent of the children from lower economic groups were undernourished as compared with 23 percent of those children from the higher economic groups.[72]

This is not to say that commercialization is always deleterious to adequate nutrition. For example, in the Highlands of New Guinea there is evidence that the nutrition of children improved when families started growing coffee for sale. However, in this case the families still had land to grow some crops for consumption. The extra money earned from coffee enabled them to buy canned fish and rice, which provided children with higher amounts of protein than the usual staple of sweet potatoes.[73]

Nutritional imbalances for females have a far-reaching impact on reproduction and the health of the infants they bear. In some cultures, the lower status of women has a direct bearing on their access to food. While the custom of feeding males first is well known, it is less often realized that females end up with less nutrient-dense food such as meat. Deprivation of food sometimes starts in infancy where girl babies, as in India, are weaned earlier than boy babies.[74] Parents may be unaware that their differential weaning practice has the effect of reducing the amount of high-quality protein that girl infants receive. Indeed, in Ecuador, Lauris McKee found that parents thought that earlier weaning of girls was helpful to them. They believed that mothers' milk transmitted sexuality and aggression, both ideal male traits, to their infants and so it was important that girl babies be weaned early. Mothers weaned their girls at about 11 months and their boys about 20 months, a 9-month difference. McKee found that girl infants had a significantly higher mortality than boy infants in their second year of life, suggesting that the earlier weaning time for girls and their probable undernutrition may have been responsible.[75]

Malnutrition and AIDS are biological and social problems. In the next chapter we turn to other global social problems and how anthropology and other social sciences may contribute to their solution.

◎ Summary

1. Medical anthropologists suggest that biological and social factors need to be considered if we are to understand how to treat illness effectively and reduce the suffering in human life.

2. Many of the ideas and practices of medical practitioners are influenced by the culture in which they reside. Understanding ethnomedicine—the medical beliefs and practices of a society or cultural group—is one of the goals of medical anthropology.

3. Many cultures have the view that the body should be kept in equilibrium or balance. The balance may be between hot and cold, or wet and dry, or there may be other properties that need to be balanced.

4. The belief that gods or spirits can cause illness is a near-universal. The belief in sorcery or witchcraft as a cause of illness is also very common.

5. Some anthropologists think that there are few cultural universals about conceptions of illness or its treatment, but some researchers are finding evidence that many of

the plant remedies used by indigenous peoples contain chemicals that are the same as, or similar in effect to, chemicals used in remedies by Western biomedicine.

6. In the biomedical system, medical practitioners emphasize disease and cures, focusing on the body of the patient, not the mind or the social circumstances of the patient. In some societies, healers are more "personalistic," and illness may be viewed as something out of order in one's social life. Shamans are perhaps the most important medical practitioners in societies lacking full-time specialization. Biomedical practitioners are becoming more aware of the psychological factors involved in healing.

7. People with more social, economic, and political power in a society are generally healthier. In socially stratified societies, the poor usually have increased exposure to disease because they are more likely to live in crowded and unsafe conditions and they are less likely to get access to quality care. Power and economic differentials between societies also have had profound health consequences.

8. The enormous death toll of AIDS, the leading cause of adult death in many countries today, will be reduced when medical science develops effective and inexpensive medicines to treat victims of HIV or AIDS and a vaccine to prevent individuals from getting HIV. In the meantime, if the death toll from AIDS is to be reduced, changes in attitudes, beliefs, and practices regarding sexual activity are needed.

9. Anthropologists debate the extent to which mental and emotional disorders are comparable across cultures. Some illnesses such as schizophrenia and depression seem so widespread as to be probably universal. Others, such as susto or anorexia nervosa, appear to be culture-bound syndromes.

10. The ways that people obtain, distribute, and consume food have been generally adaptive. Geneticists have proposed that populations in famine-prone areas may have had genetic selection for "thrifty genes." Many of the serious nutritional problems of today are due to rapid culture change, particularly those making for an increasing degree of social inequality.

⊚ Glossary Terms

AIDS (acquired immune deficiency syndrome) 537

biomedicine   532

ethnomedicine   530

⊚ Critical Questions

1. Do people get sick just because they are exposed to germs?

2. Why do native remedies often contain chemicals that are the same as, or similar in effect to, chemicals used in remedies by Western biomedicine?

3. Why might people engage in sexual practices that increase their likelihood of contracting AIDS?

⊚ Research Navigator

1. Please go to www.researchnavigator.com and enter your LOGIN NAME and PASSWORD. For instructions on registering for the first time, please view the detailed instructions at the end of Chapter 1.

2. Using Content Select or the *New York Times,* either find an article about HIV or AIDS in Africa or another continent or about shamanism. Summarize what you have learned.

⊚ Discovering Anthropology: Researchers at Work

Read the chapter by Ruthbeth Finerman titled "Saraguro: Medical Choices, Medical Changes" in the accompanying *Discovering Anthropology* reader. Answer the following questions:

1. Why do the Saraguros continue mostly to rely on mothers to treat illness in the household?

2. How are Saraguro herbal treatments like your use of medicines? How are they unlike your use of medicines?

Global Social Problems

The news on television and in the newspapers makes us aware every day that terrible social problems threaten people around the world. War, crime, family violence, natural disasters, poverty, famine—all these and more are the lot of millions of people in many places. And now there is an increasing threat of terrorism. Can anthropological and other research help us solve these global social problems? Many anthropologists and other social scientists think so.

High-tech communications have increased our awareness of problems all over the world, and we seem to be increasingly more aware of, and bothered by, problems in our own society. For these two reasons, and perhaps also because we know much more than we used to about human behavior, we may be more motivated now to try to solve those problems. We call them "social problems" not just because a lot of people worry about them but also because they have social causes and consequences, and treating or solving them requires changes in social behavior. Even AIDS, which we discussed in the previous chapter, is partly a social problem. It may be caused by a virus, but it is mostly transmitted by social (sexual) contact with another person. And the main ways to avoid it—abstinence and "safe" sex—require changes in social behavior.

The idea that we can solve social problems, even the enormous ones such as war and family violence, is based on two assumptions. First, we have to assume that it is possible to discover the causes of a problem. And two, we have to assume that we may be able to do something about the causes, once they are discovered, and thereby eliminate or reduce the problem. Not everyone would agree with these assumptions. Some would say that our understanding of a social problem cannot ever be sufficient to suggest a solution guaranteed to work. To be sure, no understanding in science is perfect or certain; there is always some probability that even a well-supported explanation is wrong or incomplete. But the uncertainty of knowledge does not rule out the possibility of application. With regard to social problems, the possible payoff from even incomplete understanding could be a better and safer world. This possibility is what motivates many researchers who investigate social problems. After all, the history of the various sciences strongly supports the belief that scientific understanding can often allow humans to control nature, not just predict and explain it. Why should human behavior be any different?

So what do we know about some of the global social problems, and what policies or solutions are suggested by what we know?

◐ Natural Disasters and Famine

Natural events such as floods, droughts, earthquakes, and insect infestations are usually but not always beyond human control, but their effects are not.[1] We call such events accidents or emergencies when only a few people are affected, but we call them disasters when large numbers of people or large areas are affected. The harm caused is not just a function of the magnitude of the natural event. Between 1960 and 1980, 43 natural disasters in Japan killed an average of 63 people per disaster. During the same period, 17 natural disasters in Nicaragua killed an average of 6,235 people per disaster. In the United States, between 1960 and 1976, the average flood or other environmental disturbance killed just one person, injured a dozen, and destroyed fewer than five buildings. These comparative figures demonstrate that climatic and other events in the physical environment become disasters because of events or conditions in the social environment.

If people live in houses that are designed to withstand earthquakes—if governing bodies require such construction and the economy is developed enough so that people can afford such construction—the effects of an earthquake will be minimized. If poor people are forced to live in deforested floodplains in order to be able to find land to farm (as in coastal Bangladesh), if the poor are forced to live in shanties built on precarious hillsides (like those of Rio de Janeiro), the floods and landslides that follow severe hurricanes and rainstorms can kill thousands and even hundreds of thousands.

Thus, natural disasters can have greater or lesser effects on human life, depending on social conditions. And therefore disasters are also social problems, problems that have social causes and possible social solutions. Legislating safe construction of a house is a social solution. The 1976 earthquake in Tangsham, China, killed 250,000 people, mostly because they lived in top-heavy adobe houses that could not withstand severe shaking, whereas the 1989 Loma Prieta earthquake in California, which was of comparable intensity, killed 65 people.

One might think that floods, of all disasters, are the least influenced by social factors. After all, without a huge runoff from heavy rains or snow melt, there cannot be a flood. But consider why so many people have died from Hwang River floods in China. (One such flood, in 1931, killed nearly 4 million people, making it the deadliest single disaster in history.) The floods in the Hwang River basin have occurred mostly because the clearing of nearby forests for fuel and farmland has allowed enormous quantities of silt to wash into the river, raising the riverbed and increasing the risk of floods that burst the dams that normally would contain them. The risk of disastrous flooding would be greatly reduced if different social conditions prevailed—if people were not so dependent on firewood for fuel, or if they did not have to farm close to the river, or if the dams were higher and more numerous.

Famines, episodes of severe starvation and death, often appear to be triggered by physical events such as a severe drought or a hurricane that kills or knocks down food trees and plants. But famines do not inevitably follow such an event. Social conditions can prevent a famine or increase the likelihood of one. Consider what is likely to happen in Samoa after a hurricane.[2] Whole villages that have lost their coconut and breadfruit trees, as well as their taro patches, pick up and move for a period of time to other villages where there are relatives and friends. The visitors stay and are fed until some of their cultivated trees and plants start to bear food again, at which point they return home. This kind of intervillage reciprocity probably could occur only in a society that has relatively little inequality in wealth. Nowadays, the central government or international agencies may also help out by providing food and other supplies.

Researchers point out that famine rarely results from just one bad food production season. During one bad season, people can usually cope by getting help from relatives,

The average flood in the United States does not kill that many people, but the storm surges from Hurricane Katrina and inadequate levees caused major flooding, massive homelessness, and hundreds of deaths in New Orleans (pictured here) and surrounding areas of the Gulf Coast in 2005.

friends, and neighbors or by switching to less desirable foods. The famine in the African Sahel in 1974 occurred after eight years of bad weather; a combination of drought, floods, and a civil war in 1983 to 1984 contributed to the subsequent famine in the Sahel, Ethiopia, and Sudan.[3] Famine almost always has some social causes. Who has rights to the available food, and do those who have more food distribute it to those who have less? Cross-cultural research suggests that societies with individual property rights rather than shared rights are more likely to suffer famine.[4] Nonetheless, government assistance can lessen the risk of famine in societies with individual property.

Relief provided by government may not always get to those who need it the most. In India, for example, the central government provides help in time of drought to minimize the risk of famine. But the food and other supplies provided to a village may end up being unequally distributed, following the rules of social and gender stratification. Members of the local elite arrange to function as distributors and find ways to manipulate the relief efforts to their advantage. Lower-class and lower-caste families still suffer the most. Within the family, biases against females, particularly young girls and elderly women, translate into their getting less food. It is no wonder, then, that in times of food shortage and famine, the poor and other socially disadvantaged persons are especially likely to die.[5]

Thus, the people of a society may not all be equally at risk in case of disaster. In socially stratified societies, the poor particularly suffer. It is they who are likely to be forced to overcultivate, overgraze, and deforest their land, making it more susceptible to degradation. A society most helps those it values the most.

People in the past, and even recently in some places, viewed disasters as divine retribution for human immorality. For example, the great Flood described in the Old Testament was understood to be God's doing. But scientific research increasingly allows us to understand the natural causes of disasters, and particularly the social conditions that magnify or minimize their effects. To reduce the impact of disasters, then, we need to reduce the social conditions that magnify the effects of disasters. If humans are responsible for those social conditions, humans can change them. If earthquakes destroy houses that are too flimsy, we can build stronger houses. If floods caused by overcultivation and overgrazing kill people directly (or indirectly by stripping their soils), we can grow new forest cover and provide new job opportunities to floodplain farmers. If prolonged natural disasters or wars threaten famine, social distribution systems can lessen the risk. In short, we may not be able to do much about the weather or other physical causes of disasters, but we can do a lot—if we want to—about the social factors that make disasters disastrous.

⊚ Inadequate Housing and Homelessness

In most nations, the poor typically live in inadequate housing, in areas we call *slums*. In many of the developing nations, where cities are growing very rapidly, squatter settlements emerge as people build dwellings (often makeshift) that are typically declared illegal, either because the land is illegally occupied or because the dwellings violate building codes. Squatter settlements are often located in degraded environments that are subject to flooding and mudslides or have inadequate or polluted water. The magnitude of the problem is made clear in some statistics. As of the 1980s, 40 percent of the population in Nairobi, Kenya, lived in unauthorized housing, and 67 percent of the people in five of El Salvador's major cities lived in illegal dwellings.[6]

But contrary to what some people have assumed, not all dwellers in illegal settlements are poor; all but the upper-income elite may be found in such settlements.[7] Moreover, although squatter settlements have problems, they are not chaotic and unorganized places that are full of crime. Most of the dwellers are employed, aspire to get ahead, live in intact nuclear families, and help each other.[8] People live in such settlements because they cannot find affordable housing and they house themselves as best they can. Many researchers think that such self-help tendencies should be assisted to improve housing, because governments in developing countries can seldom afford costly public housing projects. But they could invest somewhat in infrastructure—sewers, water supplies, roads—and provide construction materials to those who are willing to do the work required to improve their dwellings.[9]

Housing in slum areas or shantytowns does provide shelter, minimal though it may be. But many people in many areas of the world have no homes at all. Even in countries such as the United States, which are affluent by world standards, large numbers of people are homeless. They sleep in parks, over steam vents, in doorways, subways, and cardboard boxes. In 1987 it was estimated that there were more than 1 million homeless people in the United States.[10] Based on a survey conducted in 1996, the homeless in the United States have increased in number. Over 2 million people—almost one-third of them children—were estimated to be homeless for some period during 1996.[11]

Who are the homeless, and how did they get to be homeless? We have relatively little research on these questions, but what we do have suggests differences in the causes of homelessness in different parts of the world. In the United States, unemployment and the shortage of decent low-cost housing appear to be at least partly responsible for the large number of homeless persons.[12] But there is also another factor: the deliberate policy to reduce the number of people hospitalized for mental illness and other disabilities. For example, from the mid-1960s to the mid-1990s, New York State released thousands of patients from mental hospitals. Many of these ex-patients had to live in cheap hotels or poorly monitored facilities with virtually no support network. With very little income, they found it especially hard to cope with their circumstances. Ellen Baxter and Kim Hopper, who studied the homeless in New York City, suggest that one event is rarely sufficient to render a person homeless. Rather, poverty and disability (mental or physical) seem to lead to one calamity after another and, finally, homelessness.[13]

CURRENT RESEARCH AND ISSUES

Global Warming, Air Pollution, and Our Dependence on Oil

Scientists are increasingly sure that the world is heating up. And they are worried about the consequences. The more the temperature rises, the more the Greenland and Arctic ice will melt. The resulting higher sea level will flood many low-lying coastal areas, including many world cities. The weather in many places will also probably change, and not always for the better. For example, areas that now get enough rainfall to grow crops may turn into deserts.

The world is warming probably for several reasons. One of them is our increasing use of fossil fuels, particularly oil. We burn those fuels to make electricity, to power our cars (with the gasoline made from oil), to heat our homes, and to cook food. The emissions from all that burning may contribute to a "greenhouse effect": The atmosphere reflects the warmth produced on earth, and temperatures rise. And the air gets dirtier, resulting in other harmful consequences such as a higher incidence of breathing disorders.

Can people do anything about global warming and air pollution? Surely the answer is yes. If at least some of the problem is of human making, we could change our behavior and at least partly solve the problem. One way would be to reduce our use of oil as fuel. But how could we do that?

In the year 2000 the first hybrid cars were sold in the United States. These cars are powered by an electric motor and a small gasoline engine. The combination reduces the amount of fuel needed, because the electric motor moves the car much of the time. The battery that powers the electric motor is recharged by braking and when the gasoline engine is on, which is not much of the time. (For example, at a stop light, the gasoline engine turns off.) So a hybrid car allows a gallon of gasoline to go a lot farther. If most cars were hybrid cars, we would need much less oil to make the gasoline needed.

It is estimated that hybrid cars could cut greenhouse emissions by up to half, which would help alleviate or even reverse global warming and air pollution. So, given this rosy scenario, what is discouraging the world from switching to hybrid cars?

The answer is probably economics and politics. There is money to be made from the dependence on oil, particularly when supplies are short. The shorter the supplies, the more the oil producers abroad and the refiners at home can charge their customers. And the more the oil comes from abroad, the more the U.S. and other governments may feel that they have to keep the foreign producers happy. But this obligation runs counter to a foreign policy that would encourage democracy in the world; many of the countries that produce our oil are dictatorships. So the oil companies are dependent on those regimes to keep their refineries going, and they lobby governments (ours included) to maintain friendly relations with many of those regimes. Can we expect the oil companies to want to escape their dependence on foreign suppliers, if they are making a lot of money from that dependence? Hardly.

Our market economy does offer a way out of this dilemma. If hybrid cars and other ways to reduce the need for fossil fuels become more economical, the marketplace will turn the tide. Ironically, it will be the capitalist laws of supply and demand that may reduce the influence of oil companies on politics and help us solve the problems of global warming and air pollution. Even if the automobile manufacturers wanted to continue doing business as usual, they will not be able to resist making more fuel-efficient cars. Consumers will want to buy them to reduce their gasoline expenses. No car company will be able to ignore that kind of pressure from the marketplace. As of 2005, there seems to be more interest in making and buying hybrid vehicles, and there is the possibility of transforming organic garbage into oil.

Sources: J. Oerlemans, "Extracting a Climate Signal from 169 Glacial Records," *Science* 38 (April 28, 2005): 675–677; Matthew L. Wald, "Hybrid Cars Show Up in M.I.T.'s Crystal Ball," *New York Times,* November 3, 2000, p. F1; and the special advertisement produced by energy companies, "Energy: Investing for a New Century," *New York Times,* October 30, 2000, pp. EN1–EN8; Daniel Duane, "Turning Garbage Into Oil" *The New York Times Magazine,* December 14, 2003, p. 100.

Many people cannot understand why homeless individuals do not want to go to municipal shelters. But observations and interviews with the homeless suggest that violence pervades the municipal shelters, particularly the men's shelters. Many feel safer on the streets. Some private charities provide safe shelters and a caring environment. These shelters are filled, but the number of homeless they can accommodate is small.[14] Even single-room-occupancy hotels are hardly better. Many of them are infested with vermin, the common bathrooms are filthy, and they, like the shelters, are often dangerous.[15]

Some poor individuals may be socially isolated, with few or no friends and relatives and little or no social contact. But a society with many such individuals does not necessarily have much homelessness. Socially isolated individuals, even mentally ill individuals, could still have

A homeless boy in Calcutta, India with his belongings.

housing, or so the experience of Melbourne, Australia, suggests. Universal health insurance there pays for health care as well as medical practitioners' visits to isolated and ill individuals, wherever they live. Disabled individuals receive a pension or sickness benefits sufficient to allow them to live in a room or apartment. And there is still a considerable supply of cheap housing in Melbourne. Research in Melbourne suggests that a severe mental disorder often precedes living in marginal accommodations—city shelters, commercial shelters, and cheap single rooms. About 50 percent of the people living in such places were diagnosed as previously having some form of mental illness; this percentage is similar to what seems to be the case for homeless people and people living in marginal accommodations in the United States.

The contrast between the United States and Australia makes it clear that homelessness is caused by social and political policies. Individuals with similar characteristics live in both Australia and the United States, but in the United States a larger percentage of them are homeless.[16]

Because homelessness cannot occur if everybody can afford housing, some people would say that homelessness can happen only in a society with great extremes in income. Statistics on income distribution in the United States clearly show that since the 1970s the rich have gotten much richer and the poor have gotten much poorer. The United States now has more income inequality than other industrialized countries, such as Japan and the Netherlands. In fact, the profile of inequality in the United States more closely resembles that of developing countries, such as India and Mexico.[17]

In the United States, and many other countries, most homeless persons are adults. Whereas adults are "allowed" to be homeless, public sensibilities in the United States appear to be outraged by the sight of children living in the streets; when authorities discover homeless children, they try to find shelters or foster homes for them. But many countries have "street children." It has been estimated that 80 million of the world's children live in the streets. Forty million of them live in Latin America, 20 million in Asia, 10 million in Africa and the Middle East, and 10 million elsewhere.[18]

Lewis Aptekar, who studied street children in Cali, Colombia, reported some surprises.[19] Whereas many of the homeless in the United States and Australia are mentally disabled, the street children in Cali, ranging in age from 7 to 16, are mostly free of mental problems; by and large they also test normally on intelligence tests. In addition, even though many street children come from abusive homes or never had homes, they usually seem happy and enjoy the support and friendship of other street children. They cleverly and creatively look for ways to get money, frequently through entertaining passersby.

Although the observer might think that the street children must have been abandoned by their families, in actuality most of them have at least one parent they keep in touch with. Street life begins slowly, not abruptly; children usually do not stay on the streets full time until they are about 13 years old. Though street children in Cali seem to be in better physical and mental shape than their siblings who stay at home, they often are viewed as a "plague." The street children come from poor families and cope with their lives as best they can, so why are they not viewed with pity and compassion? Aptekar suggests that well-off families see the street children as a threat because a life independent of family may appeal to children, even those from well-off families, who wish to be free of parental constraint and authority.

Whether people become homeless, whether there are shantytowns, seems to depend on a society's willingness to share wealth and help those in need. The street children of Cali may remind us that children as well as adults need companionship and care. Addressing physical needs without responding to emotional needs may get people off the streets, but it won't get them a "home."

Family Violence and Abuse

In U.S. society we hear regularly about the abuse of spouses and children, which makes us think that such abuse is increasing—but is it? This seems to be a simple question, but it is not so simple to answer. We have to decide what we mean by *abuse*.

Is physical punishment of a child who does something wrong child abuse? Not so long ago, teachers in public schools in the United States were allowed to discipline children by hitting them with rulers or paddles, and many parents used switches or belts. Many would consider these practices to be child abuse, but were they abusive when they were generally accepted? Some would argue that abuse is going beyond what a culture considers appropriate behavior. Others would disagree and would focus on the violence and severity of parents' or teachers' behavior, not the cultural judgment of appropriateness. And abuse need not involve physical violence. It could be argued that verbal aggression and neglect may be just as harmful as physical aggression. Neglect presents its own problems of definition. People from other cultures might argue that we act abusively when we put an infant or child alone in a room to sleep.[20] Few would disagree about severe injuries that kill a child or spouse or require medical treatment, but other disciplinary behaviors are more difficult to judge.

To avoid having to decide what is or is not abuse, many researchers focus their studies on variation in the frequencies of specific behaviors. For example, one can ask which societies have physical punishment of children without calling physical punishment abusive.

According to three national interview surveys of married or cohabiting couples in the United States conducted in 1975, 1985, and 1992, physical violence against children appears to have decreased in frequency over time, as did serious assaults by husbands against wives. But serious assaults by wives on husbands did not decrease.[21] The decreasing rates of abuse may be mostly due to reporting differences: wife and child beating is less acceptable now. For example, men report dramatically fewer assaults on their wives, but wives report only slight declines.[22] However, the United States remains a society with a lot of physical violence in families. In 1992 alone, one out of ten couples had a violent assault episode and one out of ten children was severely assaulted by a parent.[23] A survey conducted in the mid-1990s found that about 75 percent of the violence against women comes from a male intimate partner, such as a husband. In contrast, most of the violence men experience comes from strangers and acquaintances. Just as women face more risk from those close to them, so do children. When a child is the target of violence, it usually comes from the birth mother.[24]

Cross-culturally, if one form of family violence occurs, others are also likely. So, for example, wife beating, husband beating, child punishment, and fighting among siblings are all significantly associated with each other. But the relationships between these types of family violence are not that strong, which means that they cannot be considered as different facets of the same phenomenon. Indeed, somewhat different factors seem to explain different forms of family violence.[25] We focus here on two forms of violence that are most prevalent cross-culturally: violence against children and violence against wives.

Violence against Children

Cross-culturally, many societies practice and allow infanticide. Frequent reasons for infanticide include illegitimacy, deformity of the infant, twins, too many children, or that the infant is unwanted. Infanticide is usually performed by the mother, but this does not mean that she is uncaring; it may mean that she cannot adequately feed or care for the infant or that it has a poor chance to survive. The reasons for infanticide are similar to those given for abortion. Therefore, it seems that infanticide may be performed when abortion does not work or when unexpected qualities of the infant (e.g., deformity) force the mother to reevaluate her ability to raise the child.[26]

Physical punishment of children occurs at least sometimes in over 70 percent of the world's societies.[27] And physical punishment is frequent or typical in 40 percent of the world's societies. Why? A recent cross-cultural study suggests that the major reason parents physically punish children is to prepare them for a life of power inequality, which will require them to fear those more powerful. Societies with class stratification and political hierarchy, either native or introduced (colonialism), are very likely to practice corporal punishment of children.[28] Research in the United States is consistent with the cross-cultural finding: those at the bottom of the socioeconomic hierarchy are more likely than those at the top to practice corporal punishment of children.[29]

Violence against Wives

Cross-culturally, wife beating is the most common form of family violence; it occurs at least occasionally in about 85 percent of the world's societies. In about half the societies, wife beating is sometimes serious enough to cause permanent injury or death.[30] It is often assumed that wife beating is common in societies in which males control economic and political resources. In a cross-cultural test of this assumption, David Levinson found that not all indicators of male dominance predict wife beating, but many do. Specifically, wife beating is most common when men control the products of family labor, when men have the final say in decision making in the home, when divorce is difficult for women, when remarriage for a widow is controlled by the husband's kin, and when women do not have any female work groups.[31] Similarly, in the United States, the more one spouse in the family makes the decisions and has the power, the more physical violence occurs in the family. Wife beating is even more likely when the husband controls the household and is out of work.[32]

Wife beating appears to be related to broader patterns of violence. Societies that have violent methods of conflict resolution within communities, physical punishment of criminals, high frequency of warfare, and cruelty toward enemies generally have more wife beating.[33] Corporal punishment of children may be related to wife beating. In the United States, many parents think that corporal punishment is necessary to teach children right and wrong. Corporal punishment of children may also teach that it is appropriate to hit people if you think they are misbehaving. As of 1995, one out of four parents hit children with objects.[34] Research in the United States supports the idea that individuals (males and females) who were punished corporally as adolescents are more likely to approve of marital violence and are more likely to commit it.[35]

Reducing the Risk

What can be done to minimize family violence? First, we have to recognize that probably nothing can be done as long as people in a society do not acknowledge that there is a problem. If severe child punishment and wife beating are perfectly acceptable by almost everyone in a society, they are unlikely to be considered social problems that need solutions. In our own society many programs are designed to take abused children or wives out of the family situation or to punish the abuser. (Of course, in these situations the violence has already occurred and was serious enough to have been noticed.) Cross-culturally, at least with respect to wife beating, intervention by others seems to be successful only if the intervention occurs before violence gets serious. As one would expect, however, those societies most prone to a high rate of wife beating are the least likely to practice immediate intervention. More helpful perhaps, but admittedly harder to arrange, is the promotion of conditions of life that are associated with low family violence. Research so far suggests that promoting the equality of men and women and the sharing of childrearing responsibilities may go a long way toward lessening incidents of family violence.[36] And reducing the risk of corporal punishment of children may reduce the risk of violence when they have families.

 Crime

What is a crime in one society is not necessarily a crime in another. Just as it is difficult to decide what constitutes abuse, it is difficult to define *crime*. In one society, it may be a crime to walk over someone's land without permission; in another, there might not be any concept of personal ownership, and therefore no concept of trespassing. In seeking to understand variation in crime, it is not surprising that many researchers have preferred to compare those behaviors that are more or less universally considered crimes and that are reliably reported. For example, in a large-scale comparison of crime in 110 nations over a span of 70 years, Dane Archer and Rosemary Gartner concentrated on homicide rates. They argued that homicide is harder for the public to hide and for officials to ignore than are other crimes. A comparison of interviews

about crime with police records suggests that homicide is the most reliably reported crime in official records.[37]

Nations not only have very different crime rates when we compare them at a given point in time; the rates also vary over time within a nation. In the last 600 years, homicide rates have generally declined in Western societies. In England, where homicide rates have been well documented for centuries, the chance of murder during the 13th and 14th centuries was 10 times higher than in England today. But beginning in the 1960s, homicide and other crime rates have surged upward in many Western countries.[38] Around 1970, some of the lowest homicide rates were found in Iran, Dahomey, Puerto Rico, New Zealand, Norway, England, and France. Some of the highest homicide rates were in Iraq, Colombia, Burma, Thailand, Swaziland, and Uganda. Compared with other countries, the United States had a fairly high homicide rate; approximately three-fourths of the countries surveyed had lower homicide rates than the United States.[39]

One of the clearest findings to emerge from comparative studies of crime is that war is associated with higher rates of homicide. Archer and Gartner compared changes in homicide rates of nations before and after major wars. Whether a nation is defeated or victorious, homicide rates tend to increase after a war. This result is consistent with the idea that a society or nation legitimizes violence during wartime. That is, during wartime, societies approve of killing the enemy; afterward, homicide rates may go up because inhibitions against killing have been relaxed.[40] Ted Gurr suggested that the long-term downtrend in crime in Western societies seems to be consistent with an increasing emphasis on humanistic values and nonviolent achievement of goals. But such goals may be temporarily suspended during wartime. In the United States, for example, surges in violent crime rates occurred during the 1860s and 1870s (during and after the Civil War), after World War I, after World War II, and during the Vietnam War.[41]

In the types of societies that anthropologists have typically studied, homicide statistics were not usually available; so cross-cultural studies of homicide usually measure homicide rates by comparing and rank-ordering ethnographers' statements about the frequency of homicide. For example, the statement that murder is "practically unheard of" is taken to mean that the murder rate is lower than where it is reported that "homicide is not uncommon." Despite the fact that the data on cultural homicide rates are not quantitative, the cross-cultural results are consistent with the cross-national results; more war is usually associated with more homicide and assault, as well as with socially approved aggressive behaviors (as in aggressive games) and severe physical punishment for wrongdoing.[42] A cross-cultural study suggests that the more war a society has, the more socialization or training of aggression in boys it will have, and such socialization strongly predicts higher rates of homicide and assault.[43]

Capital punishment—execution of criminals—is severe physical punishment for wrongdoing. It is commonly thought that would-be murderers are deterred by the prospect of capital punishment. Yet cross-national research suggests otherwise. More countries show murder rates going down rather than up after capital punishment was abolished.[44] Capital punishment may legitimize violence rather than deter it.

Research conducted in the United States suggests that juvenile delinquents (usually boys) are likely to come from broken homes, with the father absent for much of the time the boy is growing up. The conclusion often drawn is that father absence somehow increases the likelihood of delinquency and adult forms of physical violence. But other conditions that may cause delinquency are also associated with broken homes, conditions such as the stigma of not having a "regular" family and the generally low standard of living of such families. It is therefore important to conduct research in other societies, in which father absence does not occur in concert with these other factors, to see if father absence by itself is related to physical violence.

For example, in many polygynous societies, children grow up in a mother–child household; the father lives separately and is seldom around the child. Does the father-absence explanation of delinquency and violence fit such societies? The answer is apparently yes: Societies in which children are reared in mother-child households or the father spends little time caring for the child tend to have more physical violence by males than do societies in which fathers spend time with children.[45] The rate of violent crime is also more frequent in nations that have more women than men, which is consistent with the theory that father absence increases violence.[46]

More research is needed to discover exactly what accounts for these relationships. It is possible, as some suggest, that boys growing up without fathers are apt to act "supermasculine," to show how "male" they are. But it is also possible that mothers who rear children alone have more frustration and more anger, and therefore are likely to provide an aggressive role model for the child. In addition, high male mortality in war predicts polygyny, as we saw in the chapter on marriage and the family; therefore boys in polygynous societies are likely to be exposed to a warrior tradition.[47]

Trying to act supermasculine, however, may be likely to involve violence only if aggression is an important component of the male gender role in society. If men were expected by society to be sensitive, caring, and nonviolent, boys who grew up without fathers might try to be supersensitive and supercaring. So society's expectations for males probably shape how growing up in a mother–child household affects behavior in adolescence and later.[48] The expectations for males may also be influenced by the media. Numerous studies in the United States show that even controlling for other factors like parental neglect, family income, and mental illness, more television watching in childhood and adolescence predicts more overt aggression later. Estimates show that an hour of prime-time television depicts 3–5 violent acts, and an hour of children's television depicts 20–25 violent acts.[49]

One widely held idea is that poor economic conditions increase the likelihood of crime, but the relationship does not appear to be strong. Also, the findings are somewhat different for different types of crime. For example, hundreds of

Evidence indicates that violence on TV encourages violence in real life.

studies in this and other countries do not show a clear relationship between changes in economic well-being as measured by unemployment rates and changes in violent crime as measured by homicide. The rate of homicide does not appear to increase in bad times. Property crimes, however, do increase with increases in unemployment. Violent crime does appear to be associated with one economic characteristic: Homicide is usually highest in nations with high income inequality. Why income inequality predicts homicide but downturns in the economy do not is something of a puzzle.[50]

The fact that property crime is linked to unemployment is consistent with the cross-cultural finding that theft (but not violent crime) tends to occur less often in egalitarian societies than in stratified ones. Societies with equal access to resources usually have distribution mechanisms that offset any differences in wealth. Hence theft should be less of a temptation and therefore less likely in an egalitarian society. Theft rates are higher in socially stratified societies despite the fact that they are more likely than egalitarian societies to have police and courts to punish crime. Societies may try to deter property and other crimes when the rates of such are high, but we do not know that these efforts actually reduce the rates.

So what does the available research suggest about how we might be able to reduce crime? The results so far indicate that homicide rates are highest in societies that socialize their boys for aggression. Such socialization is linked to war and other forms of socially approved violence—capital punishment, television and movie violence by heroes, violence in sports. The statistical evidence suggests that war encourages socialization for aggression, which in turn results unintentionally in high rates of violence. The policy implication of these results is that if we can reduce socialization for aggression, by reducing the risk of war and therefore the necessity to produce effective warriors, and if we can reduce other forms of socially approved violence, we may thereby reduce the rates of violent crime. The reduction of inequalities in wealth may also help to reduce crime, particularly theft. And although it is not yet clear why, it appears that raising boys with a male role model around may reduce the likelihood of male violence in adulthood.

War

War is an unfortunate fact of life in most societies known to anthropology, judging by the cross-cultural research we referred to in the chapter on political life. Almost every society had at least occasional wars when it was first described, unless it had been pacified (usually by Western colonial powers).[51] Since the Civil War, the United States has not had any wars on its territory, but it is unusual in that respect. Before pacification, most societies had frequent armed combat between communities or larger units that spoke the same language. That is, most warfare was internal to the society or language group. Even some wars in modern times involved speakers of the same language; recall the wars between Italian states before the unification of Italy and many of the "civil" wars of the last two centuries. Although people in some societies might fight against people in other societies, such "external" wars were usually not organized on behalf of the entire society or even a major section of it.[52] That is, warfare in the ethnographic record did not usually involve politically unified societies. Finally, the absolute numbers of people killed may have been small, but this does not mean that warfare in nonindustrial societies was a trivial matter.

Indeed, it appears that nonindustrial warfare may have been even more lethal *proportionately* than modern warfare, judging by the fact that wars killed 25–30 percent of the males in some nonindustrial societies.[53]

In the chapter on political life, we discussed the possibility that people in nonindustrial societies go to war mostly out of fear, particularly a fear of expectable but unpredictable natural disasters (droughts, floods, hurricanes, among others) that destroy food supplies.[54] People with more of a history of such disasters have more war. It seems as if people go to war to protect themselves ahead of time from disasters, inasmuch as the victors in war almost always take resources (land, animals, other things) from the defeated, even when the victors have no current resource problems. Another factor apparently making for more war is teaching children to mistrust others. People who grow up to be mistrustful of others may be more likely to go to war than to negotiate or seek conciliation with "enemies." Mistrust or fear of others seems to be partly caused by threat or fear of disasters.[55]

Is warfare in and between modern state societies explainable in much the same way that nonindustrial warfare seems to be explainable? If the answer to that question turns out to be yes, it will certainly be a modified yes, because the realities of industrialized societies require an expanded conception of disasters. In the modern world, with its complex economic and political dependencies among nations, we may not be worried only about weather or pest disasters that could curtail food supplies. Possible curtailments of other resources, particularly oil, may also scare us into going to war. According to some commentators, the decision to go to war against Iraq after it invaded Kuwait in 1991 fits this theory of war.

But even if the "threat-to-resources" theory is true, we may be coming to realize (since the end of the Cold War) that war is not the only way to ensure access to resources. There may be a better way in the modern world, a way that is more cost-effective as well as more preserving of human life. If it is true that war is most likely when people fear unpredictable disasters of any kind, the risk of war should lessen

A society may encourage boys to play soldier, perhaps to prepare them to be courageous in combat later on. Cross-culturally, socialization for aggression strongly predicts homicide and assault.

CURRENT RESEARCH AND ISSUES

Ethnic Conflicts: Ancient Hatreds or Not?

Ethnic conflicts appear to be on the rise. In recent years, violent conflicts have erupted between ethnic groups in the former Yugoslavia, Russia, and Spain (in Europe), in Rwanda and Sierra Leone (in Africa), and in Sri Lanka and Indonesia (in Asia)—to name just a few of the many instances. Such conflicts are often thought to be intractable and inevitable because they are supposedly based on ancient hatreds. But is that true?

Social scientists are a long way from understanding the conditions that predict ethnic conflicts, but they do know that ethnic conflicts are not necessarily ancient or inevitable. For example, anthropologists who did fieldwork in the former Yugoslavia in the 1980s described villages where different ethnic groups had lived side by side for a long time without apparent difficulty. The differences between them were hardly emphasized. Mary Kay Gilliland worked in a midsize town (Slavonski Brod) in the Slavonian region of Croatia, which was part of Yugoslavia. The people in the town identified themselves as from Slavonia, rather than as Croats, Serbs, Hungarians, Czechs, Muslims (from Bosnia or from Albania), or Roma (Gypsies). Mixed marriages were not uncommon and people discussed differences in background without anger. But in 1991, when Gilliland returned to Croatia, people complained about Serb domination of the Yugoslav government and there was talk of Croatia seceding. Symbols of Croat nationalism had appeared—new place names, a new flag—and Croats were now said to speak Croatian, rather than the language they shared with the Serbs (Serbo-Croatian or Croato-Serbian). Later in 1991, violence broke out between Serbs and Croats, and atrocities were committed on both sides. Ethnicity became a matter of life or death and Croatia seceded from Yugoslavia. At the same time, Tone Bringa, a Norwegian anthropologist who worked in Bosnia (which was then still a region of Yugoslavia), reported that the people there also paid little attention to ethnicity. A few years later, however, ethnic violence erupted among Bosnian Serbs, Muslims, and Croats, and only the intervention of the United Nations established a precarious peace.

Ethnic conflict is frequently associated with secessionist movements. That is, secession often occurs after the eruption of ethnic conflict. Remember the American Revolution? The region that became the United States of America seceded from Great Britain and declared independence. To be sure, the ethnic differences between the Americans and the British were not great. After all, not too many years had passed since the first British colonizers had come to America. But there still was a secessionist movement, and there was violence. Ethnic differences do not always lead to violence. Sometimes, probably even most of the time, people of different ethnic backgrounds live in peace with each other. So the basic question is why do some places with ethnic differences erupt in violence, but not all? Why do different ethnic groups get along in some places?

We need research to answer this question. With all of the forced and voluntary immigration in the world, many countries are becoming more multiethnic or multicultural. The possibility of ethnic violence has become a global social problem. Gilliland suggests, among other things, that discontent over economic and political power (inequitable access to resources and opportunities) drove the Croatians to violence and secession. Other scholars have suggested other possible answers to the question of why ethnic relations do not always become ethnic conflict and violence. Violence may erupt in the absence of strong unifying interests (cross-cutting ties) between the parties. Another suggested factor is the absence of constitutional ways to resolve conflict. What we need now is cross-cultural, cross-national, and cross-historical studies to measure each of the possible explaining factors, so that we can compare how well (or poorly) they predict ethnic conflict throughout the world, controlling for the effects of the other factors. If we knew which factors generally give rise to ethnic violence, we might be able to think of ways to reduce or eliminate the causal conditions.

Sources: Mary Kay Gilliland, "Nationalism and Ethnogenesis in the Former Yugoslavia," in Lola Romanucci-Ross and George A. De Vos, eds., *Ethnic Identity: Creation, Conflict, and Accommodation*, 3rd ed. (Walnut Creek, CA: Alta Mira Press, 1995), pp. 197–221; Tone Bringa, *Being Muslim the Bosnian Way: Identity and Community in a Central Bosnian Village* (Princeton, NJ: Princeton University Press, 1995), as examined in the eHRAF Collection of Ethnography on the Web; Marc Howard Ross, "Ethnocentrism and Ethnic Conflict," in *Research Frontiers*, in Carol R. Ember, Melvin Ember, and Peter N. Peregrine, eds., *New Directions in Anthropology* (Upper Saddle River, NJ: Prentice Hall, CD-ROM, 2004).

Societies with participatory democracies are less likely to fight with other democracies. At a public meeting in Salina, New York, a town resident raises questions at a planning meeting.

when people realize that the harmful effects of disasters could be reduced or prevented by international cooperation. Just as we have the assurance of disaster relief within our country, we could have the assurance of disaster relief worldwide. That is, the fear of unpredictable disasters and the fear of others, and the consequent risk of war, could be reduced by the assurance ahead of time that the world would help those in need in case of disaster. Instead of going to war out of fear, we could go to peace by agreeing to share. The certainty of international cooperation could compensate for the uncertainty of resources.

Consider how Germany and Japan have fared in the years since their "unconditional surrender" in World War II. They were forbidden to participate in the international arms race and could rely on others, particularly the United States, to protect them. Without a huge burden of armaments, Germany and Japan thrived. But countries that competed militarily, particularly the United States and the Soviet Union at the height of the Cold War, experienced economic difficulties. Doesn't that scenario at least suggest the wisdom of international cooperation, particularly the need for international agreements to ensure worldwide disaster relief? Compared with going to war and its enormous costs, going to peace would be a bargain!

Recent research in political science and anthropology suggests an additional way to reduce the risk of war. Among the societies known to anthropology, studies indicate that people in more participatory—that is, more "democratic"—political systems rarely go to war with each other.[56] Thus, if authoritarian governments were to disappear from the world, because the powerful nations of the world stopped supporting them militarily and otherwise, the world could be more peaceful for this reason too.

Although democratically governed states rarely go to war with each other, it used to be thought that they are not necessarily more peaceful in general, that they are as likely to go to war as are other kinds of political systems, but not so much with each other. For example, the United States has gone to war with Grenada, Panama, and Iraq—all authoritarian states—but not with democratic Canada, with which the United States has also had disputes. But now a consensus is emerging among political scientists that democracies are not only unlikely to go to war with each other, they are also less warlike in general.[57] The theory suggested by the cross-national and cross-cultural results is that democratic conflict resolution within a political system generalizes to democratic conflict resolution between political systems, particularly if the systems are both democratic. If our participatory institutions and perceptions allow us to resolve our disputes peacefully, internally and externally, we may think that similarly governed people would also be disposed to settle things peacefully. Therefore, disputes between participatory political systems should be unlikely to result in war.

The understanding that participatory systems rarely fight each other, and knowing why they do not, would have important consequences for policy in the contemporary world. The kinds of military preparations believed necessary and the costs people would be willing to pay for them might be affected. On the one hand, understanding the relationship between democracy and peace might encourage war making against authoritarian regimes to overturn them—with enormous costs in human life and otherwise. On the other hand, understanding the consequences of democracy might encourage us to assist the emergence and consolidation of more participatory systems of government in the countries of eastern Europe, the former Soviet Union, and elsewhere. In any case, the relationship between democracy and peace strongly suggests that it is counterproductive to support any undemocratic regimes, even if they happen to be enemies of our enemies, if we want to minimize the risk of war in the world. The latest cross-national evidence suggests that extending democracy around the world would minimize the risk of war. Encouraging nations to be more interdependent

People light candles in memory of those killed by terrorist attacks on trains in Madrid, Spain in 2004.

economically, and encouraging the spread of international nongovernmental organizations (like professional societies and trade associations) to provide informal ways to resolve conflicts, would also minimize the risk of war, judging by results of recent research by political scientists.[58]

Terrorism

Ever since September 11, 2001, when terrorists crashed airliners into the World Trade Center towers in New York City and into the Pentagon in Arlington, Virginia, people all over the world realize that terrorism has become a social problem globally. It is now painfully clear that organized groups of terrorists can train their people to kill themselves and thousands of others half a world away, not only by hijacking airliners and flying them into skyscrapers, but also by using easily transported explosives and biological weapons. Social scientists are now actively trying to understand terrorism, in the hope that research may lead to ways to minimize the likelihood of future attacks. But there are lots of questions to answer. What is terrorism and how shall it be defined? How long has terrorist activity been around? What are the causes of terrorism? What kind of people are likely to become terrorists? And what are the consequences of terrorism?

Answering these questions is not so simple. Most people can point to instances that hardly anyone would have trouble calling terrorism—spraying nerve gas in a Japanese subway, Palestinian suicide bombers targeting Israeli civilians, Ku Klux Klan members lynching African Americans.[59] It is harder to identify the boundaries between terrorism, crime, political repression, and warfare.[60] Most researchers agree that terrorism involves the threat or use of violence against civilians. Terrorism is usually also politically or socially organized, in contrast to most crimes, which are usually perpetrated by individuals acting on their own. (To be sure,

crime can be socially organized too, as, for example, in what we call "organized crime.") One marker of the difference between most crime and terrorism is that criminals rarely take public credit for their activities, because they want to avoid being caught. In terrorism, the perpetrators usually proclaim their responsibility. In terrorism also, the violence is directed mostly at unarmed people, including women and children. It is intended to frighten the "enemy," to *terrorize* them, to scare them into doing something that the terrorists want to see happen. Generally, then, **terrorism** may be defined as the use or threat of violence to create terror in others, usually for political purposes.[61] Some define terrorism as perpetrated by groups that are not formal political entities. However, this criterion presents some difficulty. What are we to call it when governments support death squads and genocide against their own civilians? Some scholars call this "state terror."[62] And what are we to call the activities of some governments that support secret operations against other countries (often referred to as "state-sponsored terrorism")? Finally, while some nations conducting war explicitly try to avoid civilian casualties and focus primarily on combatants (armed soldiers), their weapons, and resources or "assets" such as factories, air strips, and fuel depots, many attacks in wartime throughout history have purposefully targeted civilians (e.g., the United States dropped atomic bombs on Hiroshima and Nagasaki to persuade the Japanese to end World War II).

One thing is certain about terrorism: It is not a new development. Some of the words we use for terrorists—for example, "zealots" and "assassins"—derive from terrorist movements in the past. The Zealots, Jewish nationalists who revolted against the Romans occupying Judea in the first century, would hide in crowds and stab officials and priests as well as soldiers. In the 11th and 12th centuries in southwest Asia, the Fedayeen (a group of Muslim Isma'ili Shi'ites) undertook to assassinate Sunni rulers despite the almost certainty of their own capture or death. The rulers said that the Fedayeen were under the influence of hashish and called

MIGRANTS AND IMMIGRANTS

Refugees Are a Global Social Problem

The continuing turmoil in many countries throughout the world has created a flow of refugees that is much larger than ever before in world history. Refugees have become a worldwide social problem; their numbers are so high. In the past, thousands of people might have had to flee persecution and war. Now the refugees number in the millions. They flee to other parts of the country, to neighboring countries, and to countries on the other side of the world. It has been estimated that as many as 140 million people became refugees in the 20th century. For example, the refugees from the civil wars in Somalia are not unusual; 10 percent of the Somali population is now living outside of Somalia, perhaps a million people altogether.

Conceivably, the problem could be handled with less suffering if countries were willing to accept any and all refugees. Shouldn't governments accept them for humanitarian reasons, just because the refugees could die otherwise? Or does there have to be an acknowledged or felt need in the accepting country for cheap labor? There is a fine line between people who want to migrate to have a better or safer life, and people who have to migrate because they would be killed if they don't flee. Refugees are a problem not just because they are suffering, and the world should do something. They are also a problem because countries may refuse to accept them, because their numbers are so large. Governments and charitable agencies have to provide support until the refugees acquire the skills for making a living on their own.

Compare how we think of refugees from different places. Some are accepted (however grudgingly), others are not. The U.S. only half-heartedly tries to prevent poor Mexicans from entering the country. But there is much more rejection of people from Africa who are threatened with genocide. Why? Is it because Mexicans and others from Latin America have skills that we need, and they are willing to take jobs that no one else wants because the pay is low and the benefits

nil? Who benefits from this state of affairs? Too many! Think of the employers who would otherwise have to pay their workers more or invest in labor-saving machinery. Think of the Chinese "coolies" who were brought in 150 years ago to build the railroads that linked east and west. And, of course, think of the refugee laborers. If they didn't "cross the border" looking for work, their children left at home would suffer or even die from malnutrition and other consequences of poverty.

So what are countries to do? Should they throw open their doors to everyone who wants to come in? Humanitarians might say yes. But this too would make for problems. Some would say that we should not accept and support refugees when we already have lots of poor people. Don't we owe them more than we owe poor people from somewhere else? Shouldn't our tax money go to improve the lives of people already here? What are taxes for, anyway?

How to help refugees is clearly a complex issue. But if we don't do anything to help them, is that ethical? Refugees are the consequences of social inequality and persecution. They are a global social problem that won't go away, as long as the world contains governments that persecute their own citizens, or allow some groups to persecute others. If the solution is not to rely on those governments, because they are not likely to change what they are doing, it would seem that we will have to rely for the near future on international organizations (like the United Nations and charitable foundations) if we want to reduce or eliminate the worldwide problem of refugees.

Sources: Barbara Harrell-Bond, "Refugees," in David Levinson and Melvin Ember, eds., *Encyclopedia of Cultural Anthropology,* 4 vols. (New York: Henry Holt, 1996), vol. 3, pp. 1076–81; Nicholas Van Hear, "Refugee Diasporas or Refugees in Diaspora," in Melvin Ember, Carol R. Ember, and Ian Skoggard, eds., *Encyclopedia of Diasporas: Immigrant and Refugee Cultures Around the World,* 2 vols. (New York: Kluwer Academic/Plenum, 2004), vol. 1, pp. 580–89.

them "Hashshashin," which is the root of the later term "assassin."[63] In the late 18th and early 19th centuries, the "reign of terror" occurred during and after the French Revolution. In the early and middle 20th century, the dictator Joseph Stalin ordered the execution of many millions of people who were considered enemies of the Soviet state. Six million Jews and millions of other innocents were exterminated by the

German Third Reich in the 1930s and 1940s.[64] And many Latin American regimes, such as that in Argentina, terrorized and killed dissidents in the 1970s and 1980s.[65] Now there is a heightened fear of terrorists who may have access to weapons of mass destruction. In a world made smaller by global transportation, cell phones, and the Internet, terrorism is a greater threat than ever before.

We still lack systematic research that explains why terrorism occurs and why people are motivated to become terrorists. But there is a good deal of research about state terrorism. Political scientist R. J. Rummel estimates that nearly 170 million people have been killed by governments in the 20th century (he calls this kind of terrorism "democide"). State terrorism has been responsible for four times more deaths than all the wars, civil and international, that occurred in the 20th century. Regimes in the Soviet Union (1917–1987), China (1923–1987), and Germany (1933–1945) were responsible for killing more than a total of 100 million civilians. Proportionately the Khmer Rouge regime in Cambodia topped them all, killing over 30 percent of its population from 1975 to 1978.[66] What predicts state terrorism against one's own people? Rummel finds one clear predictor—totalitarian governments. By far they have the highest frequencies of domestic state terrorism, controlling for factors such as economic wealth, type of religion, and population size. As Rummel puts it, "power kills; absolute power kills absolutely."[67] Democratic countries are less likely to practice state terrorism, but when they do it occurs during or after a rebellion or a war.[68]

We know relatively little so far about what predicts who will become a terrorist. We do know that terrorists often come from higher social statuses and generally have more education than the average person.[69] If state terrorism is more likely to occur in totalitarian regimes, terrorists and terrorist groups may be more likely to occur in such societies. If so, the spread of democracy may be our best hope of minimizing the risk of terrorism in the world, just as the spread of democracy seems to minimize the likelihood of war between countries.

Making the World Better

Many social problems afflict our world, not just the ones discussed in this chapter.[70] We don't have the space to discuss the international trade in drugs and how it plays out in violence, death, and corruption. We haven't talked about the negative effects of environmental degradations such as water pollution, ozone depletion, and destruction of forests and wetlands. We haven't said much, if anything, about overpopulation, the energy crisis, and a host of other problems we should care and do something about, if we hope to make this a safer world. But we have tried in this chapter to encourage positive thinking about global social problems; we have suggested how the results of past and future scientific research could be applied to solving some of those problems.

We may know enough now that we can do something about our problems, and we will discover more through future research. Social problems are mostly of human making and are therefore susceptible to human unmaking. There may be obstacles on the road to solutions, but we can overcome them if we want to. So let's go for it!

◎ Summary

1. We may be more motivated now to try to solve social problems because worldwide communication has increased our awareness of them elsewhere, because we seem to be increasingly bothered by problems in our own society, and because we know more than we used to about various social problems that afflict our world.

2. The idea that we can solve global social problems is based on two assumptions. We have to assume that it is possible to discover the causes of a problem, and we have to assume that we will be able to do something about the causes once they are discovered and thereby eliminate or reduce the problem.

3. Disasters such as earthquakes, floods, and droughts can have greater or lesser effects on human life, depending on social conditions. Therefore disasters are partly social problems, with partly social causes and solutions.

4. Whether people become homeless, whether there are shantytowns, seem to depend on a society's willingness to share wealth and to help those in need.

5. Promoting the equality of men and women and the sharing of childrearing responsibilities may reduce family violence.

6. We may be able to reduce rates of violent crime if we can reduce socialization and training for aggression. To do that we would have to reduce the likelihood of war, the high likelihood of which predicts more socialization for aggression and other forms of socially approved aggression. The reduction of inequalities in wealth may also help to reduce crime, particularly theft. And raising boys with a male role model around may reduce the likelihood of male violence in adulthood.

7. People seem to be most likely to go to war when they fear unpredictable disasters that destroy food supplies or curtail the supplies of other necessities. Disputes between more participatory (more "democratic") political systems are unlikely to result in war. Therefore, the more democracy spreads in the world, and the more people all over the world are assured of internationally organized disaster relief, the more they might go to peace rather than to war to solve their problems.

8. Terrorism has occurred throughout history. State terrorism has killed more than all wars in the 20th century and seems to be predicted mostly by totalitarianism.

◎ Glossary Term

terrorism   556

⊚ Critical Questions

1. What particular advantages do anthropologists have in trying to solve practical problems?
2. Select one of the social problems discussed in this chapter and suggest what you think could be done to reduce or eliminate it.
3. Do global problems require solutions by global agencies? If so, which?

⊚ Research Navigator

1. Please go to www.researchnavigator.com and enter your LOGIN NAME and PASSWORD. For instructions on registering for the first time, please view the detailed instructions at the end of Chapter 1.
2. Using the *New York Times,* find an article about homelessness, famine, global warming, or refugees. Describe the magnitude of the problem and what steps if any are taken to alleviate it.

⊚ Discovering Anthropology: Researchers at Work

Read the chapter by Paul C. Rosenblatt titled "Human Rights Violations" in the accompanying *Discovering Anthropology* reader. Answer the following questions:

1. Rosenblatt states that human rights may be enhanced by "promoting more respectful, peaceful, and nonexploitive relations among different groups within countries." Explain why he thinks so.
2. Why does he say that "saints can be sinners and sinners can be saints"?
3. Rosenblatt asks: "Is it moral for the United States and a handful of other powerful nations to impose their will on other nations?" What do you think, and why do you think so?

Glossary

Absolute dating   A method of dating fossils in which the actual age of a deposit or specimen is measured. Also known as chronometric dating.

Accent   Differences in pronunciation characteristic of a group.

Acclimatization   Impermanent physiological changes that people make when they encounter a new environment.

Acculturation   The process of extensive borrowing of aspects of culture in the context of superordinate-subordinate relations between societies; usually occurs as the result of external pressure.

Acheulian   A stone toolmaking tradition dating from 1.5 million years ago. Compared with the Oldowan tradition, Acheulian assemblages have more large tools created according to standardized designs or shapes. One of the most characteristic and prevalent tools in the Acheulian tool kit is the so-called hand axe, which is a teardrop-shaped bifacially flaked tool with a thinned sharp tip. Other large tools might have been cleavers and picks.

Achieved qualities   Those qualities a person acquires during her or his lifetime.

Adapid   A type of prosimian with many lemurlike features; appeared in the early Eocene.

Adaptation   Refers to genetic changes that allow an organism to survive and reproduce in a specific environment.

Adaptive customs   Customs that enhance survival and reproductive success in a particular environment. Usually applied to biological evolution, the term is also often used by cultural anthropologists to refer to cultural traits that enhance reproductive success.

Adjudication   The process by which a third party acting as judge makes a decision that the parties to a dispute have to accept.

Aegyptopithecus   An Oligocene anthropoid and probably the best-known propliopithecid.

Affinal kin   One's relatives by marriage.

Age-grade   A category of persons who happen to fall within a particular, culturally-distinguished age range.

Age-set   A group of persons of similar age and the same sex who move together through some or all of life's stages.

Agriculture   The practice of raising domesticated crops.

AIDS (Acquired Immune Deficiency Syndrome)   A disease caused by the HIV virus.

Allele   One member of a pair of genes.

Allen's rule   The rule that protruding body parts (particularly arms and legs) are relatively shorter in the cooler areas of a species' range than in the warmer areas.

Ambilineal descent   The rule of descent that affiliates an individual with groups of kin related to him or her through men or women.

Ancestor spirits   Supernatural beings who are the ghosts of dead relatives.

Animatism   A belief in supernatural forces.

Animism   A belief in a dual existence for all things—a physical, visible body and a psychic, invisible soul.

Anthropoids   One of the two suborders of primates; includes monkeys, apes, and humans.

Anthropological linguistics   The anthropological study of languages.

Anthropology   A discipline that studies humans, focusing on the study of differences and similarities, both biological and cultural, in human populations. Anthropology is concerned with typical biological and cultural characteristics of human populations in all periods and in all parts of the world.

Applied (practicing) anthropology   The branch of anthropology that concerns itself with applying anthropological knowledge to achieve practical goals, usually in the service of an agency outside the traditional academic setting.

^{40}Ar–^{39}Ar dating   Used in conjunction with potassium-argon dating, this method gets around the problem of needing different rock samples to estimate potassium and argon. A nuclear reactor is used to convert the ^{39}Ar to ^{39}K, on the basis of which the amount of ^{40}K can be estimated. In this way, both argon and potassium can be estimated from the same rock sample.

Arboreal   Adapted to living in trees.

Archaeology   The branch of anthropology that seeks to reconstruct the daily life and customs of peoples who lived in the past and to trace and explain cultural changes. Often lacking written records for study, archaeologists must try to reconstruct history from the material remains of human cultures. See also **Historical archaeology.**

Archaic   Time period in the New World during which food production first developed.

Ardipithecus ramidus   Perhaps the first hominid, dating to about 4.5 million years ago. Its dentition combines apelike and australopithecine-like features, and its skeleton suggests it was bipedal.

Artifact   Any object made by a human.

Ascribed qualities   Those qualities that are determined for a person at birth.

Association   An organized group not based exclusively on kinship or territory.

Atlatl   Aztec word for "spear-thrower."

Australopithecus   Genus of Pliocene and Pleistocene hominids.

Australopithecus aethiopicus   An early robust australopithecine.

Australopithecus afarensis   A species of *Australopithecus* that lived 4 million to 3 million years ago in East Africa and was definitely bipedal.

Australopithecus africanus   A species of *Australopithecus* that lived between about 3 million and 2 million years ago.

Australopithecus anamensis   A species of *Australopithecus* that lived perhaps 4.2 million years ago.

Australopithecus bahrelghazali   An early gracile australopithecine, dating to about 3 million years ago, and currently represented by only a single jaw. It is an interesting species because it is found in western Chad, distant from the East African Rift Valley where all other early australopithecines have been found.

Australopithecus boisei   An East African robust australopithecine species dating from 2.2 million to 1.3 million years ago with somewhat larger cranial capacity than *A. africanus*. No longer thought to be larger than other australopithecines, it is robust primarily in the skull and jaw, most strikingly in the teeth. Compared with *A. robustus*, *A. boisei* has even more features that reflect a huge chewing apparatus.

Australopithecus garhi   A gracile australopithecine, dating to about 2.5 million years ago.

Australopithecus robustus   A robust australopithecine species found in South African caves dating from about 1.8 million to 1 million years ago. Not as large in the teeth and jaws as *A. boisei.*

Avunculocal residence   A pattern of residence in which a married couple settles with or near the husband's mother's brother.

Balanced reciprocity   Giving with the expectation of a straightforward immediate or limited-time trade.

Balancing selection   A type of selection that occurs when a heterozygous combination of alleles is positively favored even though a homozygous combination is disfavored.

Band   A fairly small, usually nomadic local group that is politically autonomous.

Band organization   The kind of political organization where the local group or band is the largest territorial group in the society that acts as a unit. The local group in band societies is politically autonomous.

Behavioral ecology   The study of how all kinds of behavior may be related to the environment. The theoretical orientation involves the application of biological evolutionary principles to the behavior (including social behavior) of animals, including humans. Also called sociobiology, particularly when applied to social organization and social behavior.

Berdache   A male transvestite in some Native American societies.

Bergmann's rule   The rule that smaller-sized subpopulations of a species inhabit the warmer parts of its geographic range and larger-sized subpopulations the cooler areas.

Bifacial tool   A tool worked or flaked on two sides.

Bilateral kinship   The type of kinship system in which individuals affiliate more or less equally with their mother's and father's relatives; descent groups are absent.

Bilocal residence   A pattern of residence in which a married couple lives with or near either the husband's parents or the wife's parents.

Bilophodont   Having four cusps on the molars that form two parallel ridges. This is the common molar pattern of Old World monkeys.

Biological (physical) anthropology   The study of humans as biological organisms, dealing with the emergence and evolution of humans and with contemporary biological variations among human populations.

Biomedicine   The dominant medical paradigm in Western societies today.

Bipedalism   Locomotion in which an animal walks on its two hind legs.

Blade   A thin flake whose length is usually more than twice its width. In the blade technique of toolmaking, a core is prepared by shaping a piece of flint with hammerstones into a pyramidal or cylindrical form. Blades are then struck off until the core is used up.

Brachiators   Animals that move through the trees by swinging hand over hand from branch to branch. They usually have long arms and fingers.

Bride price or Bride wealth   A substantial gift of goods or money given to the bride's kin by the groom or his kin at or before the marriage.

Bride service   Work performed by the groom for his bride's family for a variable length of time either before or after the marriage.

Burin   A chisel-like stone tool used for carving and for making such artifacts as bone and antler needles, awls, and projectile points.

Canines   The cone-shaped teeth immediately behind the incisors; used by most primates to seize food and in fighting and display.

Carpolestes   A mouse-sized arboreal creature living about 56 million years ago; a strong candidate for the common primate ancestor.

Cash crop   A cultivated commodity raised for sale rather than for personal consumption by the cultivator.

Caste   A ranked group, often associated with a certain occupation, in which membership is determined at birth and marriage is restricted to members of one's own caste.

Catarrhines   The group of anthropoids with narrow noses and nostrils that face downward. Catarrhines include monkeys of the Old World (Africa, Asia, and Europe), as well as apes and humans.

Ceramics   Objects shaped from clay and baked at high temperature (fired) to make them hard. Containers such as pots and jars are typical ceramics, though they can take on many forms and uses.

Cercopithecoids   Old World monkeys.

Cerebral cortex   The "gray matter" of the brain; the center of speech and other higher mental activities.

Chief   A person who exercises authority, usually on behalf of a multicommunity political unit. This role is generally found in rank societies and is usually permanent and often hereditary.

Chiefdom   A political unit, with a chief at its head, integrating more than one community but not necessarily the whole society or language group.

Chromosomes   Paired rod-shaped structures within a cell nucleus containing the genes that transmit traits from one generation to the next.

Chronometric dating   See **Absolute dating.**

Civilization   Urban society, from the Latin word for "city-state."

Clan   A set of kin whose members believe themselves to be descended from a common ancestor or ancestress but cannot specify the links back to that founder; often designated by a totem. Also called a sib.

Class   A category of persons who have about the same opportunity to obtain economic resources, power, and prestige.

Classificatory terms   Kinship terms that merge or equate relatives who are genealogically distinct from one another; the same term is used for a number of different kin.

Class society   A society containing social groups that have unequal access to economic resources, power, and prestige.

Cline   The gradually increasing (or decreasing) frequency of a gene from one end of a region to another.

Codeswitching   Using more than one language in the course of conversing.

Codified laws   Formal principles for resolving disputes in heterogeneous and stratified societies.

Cognates   Words or morphs that belong to different languages but have similar sounds and meanings.

Commercial exchange   See **Market or commercial exchange.**

Commercialization   The increasing dependence on buying and selling, with money usually as the medium of exchange.

Compatibility-with-child-care theory   An explanation for the gender division of labor that suggests that women's work will typically involve tasks that do not take women far from home for long periods, do not place children in potential danger if they are taken along, and can be stopped and resumed if an infant needs care.

Complementary opposition   The occasional uniting of various segments of a segmentary lineage system in opposition to similar segments.

Consanguineal kin   One's biological relatives; relatives by birth.

Conservation   Techniques used on archaeological materials to stop or reverse the process of decay.

Context   The relationships between and among artifacts, ecofacts, fossils, and features.

Continental drift   The movement of the continents over the past 135 million years. In the early Cretaceous (ca. 135 million years ago) there were two "supercontinents": *Laurasia,* which included North America and Eurasia; and *Gondwanaland,* which included Africa, South America, India, Australia, and Antarctica. By the beginning of the Paleocene (ca. 65 million years ago), Gondwanaland had broken apart, with South America drifting west away from Africa, India drifting east, and Australia and Antarctica drifting south.

Core vocabulary   Nonspecialist vocabulary.

Corvée   A system of required labor.

Cretaceous   Geological epoch 135 million to 65 million years ago, during which dinosaurs and other reptiles ceased to be the dominant land vertebrates, and mammals and birds began to become important.

Crime   Violence not considered legitimate that occurs within a political unit.

Cro-magnons   Humans who lived in western Europe about 35,000 years ago. Once thought to be the earliest specimens of modern-looking humans, or *Homo sapiens sapiens.* But it is now known that modern-looking humans appeared earlier outside of Europe; the earliest so far found lived in Africa.

Cross-cousins   Children of siblings of the opposite sex. One's cross-cousins are father's sisters' children and mother's brothers' children.

Cross-cultural researcher   An ethnologist who uses ethnographic data about many societies to test possible explanations of cultural variation to discover general patterns about cultural traits—what is universal, what is variable, why traits vary, and what the consequences of the variability might be.

Crossing-over   Exchanges of sections of chromosomes from one chromosome to another.

Cultural anthropology   The study of cultural variation and universals in the past and present.

Cultural ecology   The analysis of the relationship between a culture and its environment.

Cultural relativism   The attitude that a society's customs and ideas should be viewed within the context of that society's problems and opportunities.

Cultural resource management (CRM)   The branch of applied anthropology that seeks to recover and preserve the archaeological record before programs of planned change disturb or destroy it.

Culture   The set of learned behaviors, beliefs, attitudes, values, and ideals that are characteristic of a particular society or other social group.

Culture history   A history of the cultures that lived in a given area over time. Until the 1950s, building such culture histories was a primary goal of archaeological research.

Cuneiform   Wedge-shaped writing invented by the Sumerians around 3000 B.C.

Descriptive or structural linguistics   The study of how languages are constructed.

Descriptive term   Kinship term used to refer to a genealogically distinct relative; a different term is used for each relative.

Dialect   A variety of a language spoken in a particular area or by a particular social group.

Diastema   A gap between the canine and first premolar found in apes.

Diffusion   The borrowing by one society of a cultural trait belonging to another society as the result of contact between the two societies.

Directional selection   A type of natural selection that increases the frequency of a trait (the trait is said to be positively favored, or adaptive).

Diurnal   Active during the day.

Divination   Getting the supernatural to provide guidance.

DNA   Deoxyribonucleic acid; a long, two-stranded molecule in the genes that directs the makeup of an organism according to the instructions in its genetic code.

Domestication   Modification or adaptation of plants and animals for use by humans. When people plant crops, we refer to the process as cultivation. It is only when the crops cultivated and the animals raised have been modified—are different from wild varieties—that we speak of plant and animal domestication.

Dominant   The allele of a gene pair that is always phenotypically expressed in the heterozygous form.

Double descent or double unilineal descent   A system that affiliates an individual with a group of matrilineal kin for some purposes and with a group of patrilineal kin for other purposes.

Dowry   A substantial transfer of goods or money from the bride's family to the bride.

Dryopithecus   Genus of ape from the later Miocene found primarily in Europe. It had thin tooth enamel and pointed molar-cusps very similar to those of the fruit-eating chimpanzees of today.

Early evolutionism   The view that culture develops in a uniform and progressive manner.

Ecofacts   Natural items that have been used by humans. Things such as the remains of animals eaten by humans or plant pollens found on archaeological sites are examples of ecofacts.

Economic resources   Things that have value in a culture, including land, tools and other technology, goods, as well as money.

Economy-of-effort theory   An explanation for the gender division of labor that suggests that it may be advantageous for a gender to do tasks that follow in a production sequence (e.g., those who cut lumber make wooden objects; those who quarry stone make stone objects); it may also be advantageous for one gender to perform tasks that are located near each other (e.g., child care and other chores done in or near the home).

Egalitarian society   A society in which all persons of a given age-sex category have equal access to economic resources, power, and prestige.

Ego   In the reckoning of kinship, the reference point or focal person.

Electron spin resonance dating   Like thermoluminescence dating, this technique measures trapped electrons from surrounding radioactive material. The material to be dated is exposed to varying magnetic fields in order to obtain a spectrum of the microwaves absorbed by the tested material. Because heat is not required for this technique, electron spin resonance is especially useful for dating organic materials, such as bone and shell, that decompose if heated.

Enculturation   See **Socialization.**

Endogamy   The rule specifying marriage to a person within one's own group (kin, caste, community).

Eocene   A geological epoch 55 million to 34 million years ago during which the first definite primates appeared.

Epipaleolithic   Time period during which food production first developed in the Near East.

Ethnicity   The process of defining ethnicity usually involves a group of people emphasizing common origins and language, shared history, and selected aspects of cultural difference such as a difference in religion. Since different groups are doing the perceiving, ethnic identities often vary with whether one is inside or outside the group.

Ethnocentric   Refers to judgment of other cultures solely in terms of one's own culture.

Ethnocentrism The attitude that other societies' customs and ideas can be judged in the context of one's own culture.

Ethnogenesis Creation of a new culture.

Ethnographer A person who spends some time living with, interviewing, and observing a group of people to describe their customs.

Ethnographic analogy Method of comparative cultural study that extrapolates to the past from recent or current societies.

Ethnography A description of a society's customary behaviors, and ideas.

Ethnohistorian An ethnologist who uses historical documents to study how a particular culture has changed over time.

Ethnology The study of how and why recent cultures differ and are similar.

Ethnomedicine The health-related beliefs, knowledge, and practices of a cultural group.

Ethnoscience An approach that attempts to derive rules of thought from the logical analysis of ethnographic data.

Evolutionary psychology The study of how evolution may have produced lasting variation in the way humans behave, interact, and perceive the world.

Exogamy The rule specifying marriage to a person from outside one's own group (kin or community).

Expendability theory An explanation for the gender division of labor that suggests that men, rather than women, will tend to do the dangerous work in a society because the loss of men is less disadvantageous reproductively than the loss of women.

Explanation An answer to a *why* question. In science, there are two kinds of explanation that researchers try to achieve: associations and theories.

Extensive cultivation A type of horticulture in which the land is worked for short periods and then left to regenerate for some years before being used again. Also called shifting cultivation.

Falsification Showing that a theory seems to be wrong by finding that implications or predictions derivable from it are not consistent with objectively collected data.

Family A social and economic unit consisting minimally of a parent and a child.

Fayum A site southwest of Cairo, Egypt, where the world's best record of Oligocene primate fossils has been found.

Features Artifacts of human manufacture that cannot be removed from an archaeological site. Hearths, storage pits, and buildings are examples of features.

Feuding A state of recurring hostility between families or groups of kin, usually motivated by a desire to avenge an offense against a member of the group.

Fieldwork Firsthand experience with the people being studied and the usual means by which anthropological information is obtained. Regardless of other methods (e.g., censuses, surveys) that anthropologists may use, fieldwork usually involves participant-observation for an extended period of time, often a year or more. See **Participant-observation.**

Fission-track dating A chronometric dating method used to date crystal, glass, and many uranium-rich materials contemporaneous with fossils or deposits that are from 20 billion to 5 billion years old. This dating method entails counting the tracks or paths of decaying uranium-isotope atoms in the sample and then comparing the number of tracks with the uranium content of the sample.

Folklore Includes all the myths, legends, folktales, ballads, riddles, proverbs, and superstitions of a cultural group. Generally, folklore is transmitted orally, but it may also be written.

Food collection All forms of subsistence technology in which food-getting is dependent on naturally occurring resources—wild plants and animals.

Food production The form of subsistence technology in which food-getting is dependent on the cultivation and domestication of plants and animals.

Foragers People who subsist on the collection of naturally occurring plants and animals. Also referred to as hunter-gatherers or food collectors.

Foramen magnum Opening in the base of the skull through which the spinal cord passes en route to the brain.

Forensic anthropology The use of anthropology to help solve crimes.

Fossils The hardened remains or impressions of plants and animals that lived in the past.

Fraternal polyandry The marriage of a woman to two or more brothers at the same time.

F-U-N trio Fluorine (F), uranium (U), and nitrogen (N) tests for relative dating. All three minerals are present in groundwater. The older a fossil is, the higher its fluorine or uranium content will be and the lower its nitrogen content.

Functionalism The theoretical orientation that looks for the part (function) some aspect of culture or social life plays in maintaining a cultural system.

Gender differences Differences between females and males that reflect cultural expectations and experiences.

Gender roles Roles that are culturally assigned to genders.

Gender stratification The degree of unequal access by the different genders to prestige, authority, power, rights, and economic resources.

Gene Chemical unit of heredity.

Gene flow The process by which genes pass from the gene pool of one population to that of another through mating and reproduction.

General evolution The notion that higher forms of culture arise from and generally supersede lower forms.

Generalized reciprocity Gift giving without any immediate or planned return.

General-purpose money A universally accepted medium of exchange.

Genetic drift The various random processes that affect gene frequencies in small, relatively isolated populations.

Genotype The total complement of inherited traits or genes of an organism.

Genus A group of related species; pl., genera.

Ghosts Supernatural beings who were once human; the souls of dead people.

Globalization The ongoing spread of goods, people, information, and capital around the world.

Gloger's rule The rule that populations of birds and mammals living in warm, humid climates have more melanin (and therefore darker skin, fur, or feathers) than populations of the same species living in cooler, drier areas.

Gods Supernatural beings of nonhuman origin who are named personalities; often anthropomorphic.

Gracile australopithecines The earliest group of australopithecines, usually differentiated from the robust australopithecines (see below) by their lighter dentition and smaller faces.

Group marriage Marriage in which more than one man is married to more than one woman at the same time; not customary in any known human society.

Group selection Natural selection of group characteristics.

Half-life The time it takes for half of the atoms of a radioactive substance to decay into atoms of a different substance.

Hand axe A teardrop-shaped stone tool characteristic of Acheulian assemblages.

Hard hammer A technique of stone tool manufacture where one stone is used to knock flakes from another stone. Flakes produced through hard hammer percussion are usually large and crude.

Headman   A person who holds a powerless but symbolically unifying position in a community within an egalitarian society; may exercise influence but has no power to impose sanctions.

Hermenutics   The study of meaning.

Heterozygous   Possessing differing genes or alleles in corresponding locations on a pair of chromosomes.

Hieroglyphics   "Picture writing," as in ancient Egypt and in Mayan sites in Mesoamerica (Mexico and Central America).

Historical archaeology   A specialty within archaeology that studies the material remains of recent peoples who left written records.

Historical linguistics   The study of how languages change over time.

Holistic   Refers to an approach that studies many aspects of a multifaceted system.

Hominids   The group of hominoids consisting of humans and their direct ancestors. It contains at least two genera: *Homo* and *Australopithecus*.

Hominoids   The group of catarrhines that includes both apes and humans.

Homo   Genus to which modern humans and their ancestors belong.

Homo Erectus   The first hominid species to be widely distributed in the Old World. The earliest finds are possibly 1.8 million years old. The brain (averaging 895–1,040 cc) was larger than that found in any of the australopithecines or *H. habilis* but smaller than the average brain of a modern human.

Homo Habilis   Early species belonging to our genus, *Homo*, with cranial capacities averaging about 630–640 cc, about 50 percent of the brain capacity of modern humans. Dating from about 2 million years ago.

Homo Heidelbergensis   A transitional species between *Homo Erectus* and *Homo Sapiens*.

Homo Neandertalensis   The technical name for the Neandertals, a group of robust and otherwise anatomically distinct hominids that are close relatives of modern humans—so close that some believe they should be classified as *Homo Sapiens Neandertalensis*.

Homo Rudolfensis   Early species belonging to our genus, *Homo*. Similar enough to *Homo habilis* that some paleoanthropologists make no distinction between the two.

Homo Sapiens   All living people belong to one biological species, *Homo Sapiens*, which means that all human populations on earth can successfully interbreed. The first *Homo Sapiens* may have emerged by 200,000 years ago.

Homo Sapiens Sapiens   Modern-looking humans, undisputed examples of which appeared about 50,000 years ago; may have appeared earlier.

Homozygous   Possessing two identical genes or alleles in corresponding locations on a pair of chromosomes.

Horticulture   Plant cultivation carried out with relatively simple tools and methods; nature is allowed to replace nutrients in the soil, in the absence of permanently cultivated fields.

Human paleontology   The study of the emergence of humans and their later physical evolution. Also called paleoanthropology.

Human variation   The study of how and why contemporary human populations vary biologically.

Hunter-gatherers   People who collect food from naturally occurring resources, that is, wild plants, animals, and fish. The phrase "hunter-gatherers" minimizes sometimes heavy dependence on fishing. Also referred to as foragers or food collectors.

Hybridization   The creation of a viable offspring from the mating of two different species.

Hylobates   The family of hominoids that includes gibbons and siamangs; often referred to as the lesser apes (as compared with the great apes such as gorillas and chimpanzees).

Hypotheses   Predictions, which may be derived from theories, about how variables are related.

Hypoxia   A condition of oxygen deficiency that often occurs at high altitudes. The percentage of oxygen in the air is the same as at lower altitudes, but because the barometric pressure is lower, less oxygen is taken in with each breath. Often, breathing becomes more rapid, the heart beats faster, and activity is more difficult.

Incest taboo   Prohibition of sexual intercourse or marriage between mother and son, father and daughter, and brother and sister.

Incisors   The front teeth; used for holding or seizing food and preparing it for chewing by the other teeth.

Indirect dowry   Goods given by the groom's kin to the bride (or her father, who passes most of them to her) at or before her marriage.

Indicator artifacts and ecofacts   Items that changed relatively rapidly and which, thus, can be used to indicate the relative age of associated items.

Indicator fossils   Well-known fossils used to assign dates to rock strata.

Indirect percussion   A toolmaking technique common in the Upper Paleolithic. After shaping a core into a pyramidal or cylindrical form, the toolmaker can put a punch of antler or wood or another hard material into position and strike it with a hammer. Using a hammer-struck punch enabled the toolmaker to strike off consistently shaped blades.

Individual selection   Natural selection of individual characteristics.

Insectivore   The order or major grouping of mammals, including modern shrews and moles, that is adapted to feeding on insects.

Intensive agriculture   Food production characterized by the permanent cultivation of fields and made possible by the use of the plow, draft animals or machines, fertilizers, irrigation, water-storage techniques, and other complex agricultural techniques.

Kenyanthropus platyops   A nearly complete 3.5 million year old skull found in western Kenya. It is thought by some scholars to be a species of gracile australopithecine (and hence should not be regarded as a separate genus).

Kenyapithecus   An apelike primate from the Middle Miocene found in East Africa. It had very thickly enameled teeth and robust jaws, suggesting a diet of hard, tough foods. Probably somewhat terrestrial.

Kindred   A bilateral set of close relatives.

Kinesics   The study of communication by nonvocal means, including posture, mannerisms, body movement, facial expressions, and signs and gestures.

Knuckle walking   A locomotor pattern of primates such as the chimpanzee and gorilla in which the weight of the upper part of the body is supported on the thickly padded knuckles of the hands.

Kula ring   A ceremonial exchange of valued shell ornaments in the Trobriand Islands, in which white shell armbands are traded around the islands in a counterclockwise direction and red shell necklaces are traded clockwise.

Laws (scientific)   Associations or relationships that are accepted by almost all scientists.

Levalloisian method   A method that allowed flake tools of a predetermined size to be produced from a shaped core. The toolmaker first shaped the core and prepared a "striking platform" at one end. Flakes of predetermined and standard sizes could then be knocked off. Although some Levallois flakes date from as far back as 400,000 years ago, they are found more frequently in Mousterian tool kits.

Levirate A custom whereby a man is obliged to marry his brother's widow.

Lexical content Vocabulary or lexicon.

Lexicon The words and morphs, and their meanings, of a language; approximated by a dictionary.

Lineage A set of kin whose members trace descent from a common ancestor through known links.

Lithics The technical name for tools made from stone.

Lower Paleolithic The period of the Oldowan and Acheulian stone tool traditions.

Magic The performance of certain rituals that are believed to compel the supernatural powers to act in particular ways.

Maladaptive customs Customs that diminish the chances of survival and reproduction in a particular environment. Usually applied to biological evolution, the term is often used by cultural anthropologists to refer to behavioral or cultural traits that are likely to disappear because they diminish reproductive success.

Mana A supernatural, impersonal force that inhabits certain objects or people and is believed to confer success and/or strength.

Manumission The granting of freedom to a slave.

Market or commercial exchange Transactions in which the "prices" are subject to supply and demand, whether or not the transactions occur in a marketplace.

Marriage A socially approved sexual and economic union, usually between a man and a woman, that is presumed, both by the couple and by others, to be more or less permanent, and that subsumes reciprocal rights and obligations between the two spouses and their future children.

Matriclan A clan tracing descent through the female line.

Matrifocal family A family consisting of a mother and her children.

Matrilineage A kin group whose members trace descent through known links in the female line from a common female ancestor.

Matrilineal descent The rule of descent that affiliates an individual with kin of both sexes related to him or her through women only.

Matrilocal residence A pattern of residence in which a married couple lives with or near the wife's parents.

Measure To describe how something compares with other things on some scale of variation.

Mediation The process by which a third party tries to bring about a settlement in the absence of formal authority to force a settlement.

Medium Part-time religious practitioner who is asked to heal and divine while in a trance.

Meiosis The process by which reproductive cells are formed. In this process of division, the number of chromosomes in the newly formed cells is reduced by half, so that when fertilization occurs the resulting organism has the normal number of chromosomes appropriate to its species, rather than double that number.

Mesolithic The archaeological period in the Old World beginning about 12,000 B.C. Humans were starting to settle down in semipermanent camps and villages, as people began to depend less on big game (which they used to have to follow over long distances) and more on relatively stationary food resources such as fish, shellfish, small game, and wild plants rich in carbohydrates, proteins, and oils.

Messenger RNA A type of ribonucleic acid that is used in the cell to copy the DNA code for use in protein synthesis.

Microlith A small, razorlike blade fragment that was probably attached in a series to a wooden or bone handle to form a cutting edge.

Middle Paleolithic The time period of the Mousterian stone tool tradition.

Miocene The geological epoch from 24 million to 5.2 million years ago.

Mitosis Cellular reproduction or growth involving the duplication of chromosome pairs.

Moiety A unilineal descent group in a society that is divided into two such maximal groups; there may be smaller unilineal descent groups as well.

Molars The large teeth behind the premolars at the back of the jaw; used for chewing and grinding food.

Monogamy Marriage between only one man and only one woman at a time.

Monotheistic Believing that there is only one high god and that all other supernatural beings are subordinate to, or are alternative manifestations of, this supreme being.

Morph The smallest unit of a language that has a meaning.

Morpheme One or more morphs with the same meaning.

Morphology The study of how sound sequences convey meaning.

Mousterian tool assemblage Named after the tool assemblage found in a rock shelter at Le Moustier in the Dordogne region of southwestern France. Compared with an Acheulian assemblage, the Middle Paleolithic (40,000–300,000 years ago) Mousterian has a smaller proportion of large core tools such as hand axes and cleavers and a bigger proportion of small flake tools such as scrapers. Flakes were often altered or "retouched" by striking small flakes or chips from one or more edges.

Mutation A change in the DNA sequence, producing an altered gene.

Natural selection The outcome of processes that affect the frequencies of traits in a particular environment. Traits that enhance survival and reproductive success increase in frequency over time.

Neandertal The common name for the species *Homo Neandertalensis.*

Negotiation The process by which the parties to a dispute try to resolve it themselves.

Neolithic Originally meaning "the new stone age," now meaning the presence of domesticated plants and animals. The earliest evidence of domestication comes from the Near East about 8000 B.C.

Neolocal residence A pattern of residence whereby a married couple lives separately, and usually at some distance, from the kin of both spouses.

Nocturnal Active during the night.

Nonfraternal polyandry Marriage of a woman to two or more men who are not brothers.

Nonsororal polygyny Marriage of a man to two or more women who are not sisters.

Normalizing selection The type of natural selection that removes harmful genes that arose by mutation.

Norms Standards or rules about acceptable behavior in a society. The importance of a norm usually can be judged by how members of a society respond when the norm is violated.

Nuclear family A family consisting of a married couple and their young children.

Oath The act of calling upon a deity to bear witness to the truth of what one says.

Obsidian A volcanic glass that can be used to make mirrors or sharp-edged tools.

Occipital torus A ridge of bone running horizontally across the back of the skull in apes and some hominids.

Oldowan The earliest stone toolmaking tradition, named after the tools found in Bed I at Olduvai Gorge, Tanzania; from about 2.5 million years ago. The stone artifacts include core tools and sharp-edged flakes made by striking one stone against another. Flake tools predominate. Among the core tools, so-called choppers are common.

Oligocene   The geological epoch 34 million to 24 million years ago during which definite anthropoids emerged.

Omnivorous   Eating both meat and vegetation.

Omomyid   A type of prosimian with many tarsierlike features that appeared in the early Eocene.

Operational definition   A description of the procedure that is followed in measuring a variable.

Opposable thumb   A thumb that can touch the tips of all the other fingers.

Optimal foraging theory   The theory that individuals seek to maximize the returns (in calories and nutrients) on their labor in deciding which animals and plants they will go after.

Ordeal   A means of determining guilt or innocence by submitting the accused to dangerous or painful tests believed to be under supernatural control.

Orrorin Tugenensis   An apparently bipedal primate dating to between 5.8 and 6 million years, making it possibly the earliest known hominid.

Paleoanthropologists   Anthropologists who work in the field of paleoanthropology or human paleontology.

Paleoanthropology   See **Human paleontology.**

Paleocene   The geological epoch 65 million to 55 million years ago.

Paleolithic   Period of the early Stone Age, when flint, stone, and bone tools were developed and hunting and gathering were the means of acquiring food.

Paleomagnetic dating   A method of dating archaeological and fossil deposits based on reversals and changes in the earth's magnetic field over time. By comparing the magnetic characteristics of a deposit to those known from the earth's past, a date when the deposit was formed can be determined.

Paralanguage   Refers to all the optional vocal features or silences apart from the language itself that communicate meaning.

Parallel cousins   Children of siblings of the same sex. One's parallel cousins are father's brothers' children and mother's sisters' children.

Parapithecids   Small monkeylike Oligocene primates found in the Fayum area of Egypt.

Participant-observation   Living among the people being studied—observing, questioning, and (when possible) taking part in the important events of the group. Writing or otherwise recording notes on observations, questions asked and answered, and things to check out later are parts of participant-observation.

Pastoralism   A form of subsistence technology in which food-getting is based directly or indirectly on the maintenance of domesticated animals.

Patriclan   A clan tracing descent through the male line.

Patrilineage   A kin group whose members trace descent through known links in the male line from a common male ancestor.

Patrilineal descent   The rule of descent that affiliates an individual with kin of both sexes related to him or her through men only.

Patrilocal residence   A pattern of residence in which a married couple lives with or near the husband's parents.

Peasants   Rural people who produce food for their own subsistence but who must also contribute or sell their surpluses to others (in towns and cities) who do not produce their own food.

Percussion flaking   A toolmaking technique in which one stone is struck with another to remove a flake.

Personality   The distinctive way an individual thinks, feels, and behaves.

Personality integration of culture   The theory that personality or psychological processes may account for connections between certain aspects of culture.

Pierolapithecus   A middle Miocene ape that has wrists and vertebrae that would have made it capable of brachiation, but also has relatively short fingers like modern monkeys.

Phenotype   The observable physical appearance of an organism, which may or may not reflect its genotype or total genetic constitution.

Phone   A speech sound in a language.

Phoneme   A sound or set of sounds that makes a difference in meaning to the speakers of the language.

Phonology   The study of the sounds in a language and how they are used.

Phratry   A unilineal descent group composed of a number of supposedly related clans (sibs).

Physical (biological) anthropology   See **Biological (physical) anthropology.**

Platyrrhines   The group of anthropoids that have broad, flat-bridged noses, with nostrils facing outward; these monkeys are currently found only in the New World (Central and South America).

Pleistocene   A geological epoch that started 1.6 million years ago and, according to some, continues into the present. During this period, glaciers have often covered much of the earth's surface and humans became the dominant life form.

Plesiadipis   The most well known of the plesiadipiforms, possibly an archaic primate.

Pliocene   The geological epoch 5.2 million to 1.6 million years ago during which the earliest definite hominids appeared.

Political economy   The study of how external forces, particularly powerful state societies, explain the way a society changes and adapts.

Polyandry   The marriage of one woman to more than one man at a time.

Polygamy   Plural marriage; marriage to more than one spouse simultaneously.

Polygyny   The marriage of one man to more than one woman at a time.

Polyphony   Two or more melodies sung simultaneously.

Polytheistic   Recognizing many gods, none of whom is believed to be superordinate.

Pongids   Hominoids whose members include both the living and extinct apes.

Potassium-argon (K-Ar) dating   A chronometric dating method that uses the rate of decay of a radioactive form of potassium (^{40}K) into argon (^{40}Ar) to date samples from 5,000 to 3 billion years old. The K-Ar method dates the minerals and rocks in a deposit, not the fossils themselves.

Postpartum sex taboo   Prohibition of sexual intercourse between a couple for a period of time after the birth of their child.

Potlatch   A feast among Pacific Northwest Native Americans at which great quantities of food and goods are given to the guests in order to gain prestige for the host(s).

Power   The ability to make others do what they do not want to do or influence based on the threat of force.

Practicing anthropology   See **Applied anthropology.**

Prairie   Grassland with a high grass cover.

Prehensile   Adapted for grasping objects.

Prehistory   The time before written records.

Premolars   The teeth immediately behind the canines; used in chewing, grinding, and shearing food.

Pressure flaking   Toolmaking technique whereby small flakes are struck off by pressing against the core with a bone, antler, or wooden tool.

Prestige   Being accorded particular respect or honor.

Priest   Generally a full-time specialist, with very high status, who is thought to be able to relate to superior or high gods beyond the ordinary person's access or control.

Primary institutions   The sources of early experiences, such as family organization and subsistence techniques, that presumably help form the basic, or typical, personality found in a society.

Primary subsistence activities   The food-getting activities: gathering, hunting, fishing, herding, and agriculture.

Primate   A member of the mammalian order Primates, divided into the two suborders of prosimians and anthropoids.

Primatologists   People who study primates.

Primatology   The study of primates.

Probability value (*p*-value)   The likelihood that an observed result could have occurred by chance.

Proconsul   The best-known genus of proto-apes from the Early Miocene.

Prognathic   A physical feature that is sticking out or pushed forward, such as the faces in apes and some hominid species.

Projective tests   Tests that utilize ambiguous stimuli; test subjects must project their own personality traits in order to structure the ambiguous stimuli.

Propliopithecids   Apelike anthropoids dating from the early Oligocene, found in the Fayum area of Egypt.

Prosimians   Literally "premonkeys," one of the two suborders of primates; includes lemurs, lorises, and tarsiers.

Protolanguage   A hypothesized ancestral language from which two or more languages seem to have derived.

Quadrupeds   Animals that walk on all fours.

Race   In biology, race refers to a subpopulation or variety of a species that differs somewhat in gene frequencies from other varieties of the species. All members of a species can interbreed and produce viable offspring. Many anthropologists do not think that the concept of race is usefully applied to humans because humans do not fall into geographic populations that can be easily distinguished in terms of different sets of biological or physical traits. Thus, race in humans is largely a culturally assigned category.

Rachis   The seed-bearing part of a plant. In the wild variety of grain, the rachis shatters easily, releasing the seeds. Domesticated grains have a tough rachis, which does not shatter easily.

Racism   The belief, without scientific basis, that one "race" is superior to others.

Radiocarbon (or carbon-14, ^{14}C) dating   A dating method uses the decay of carbon-14 to date organic remains. It is reliable for dating once-living matter up to 50,000 years old.

Raiding   A short-term use of force, generally planned and organized, to realize a limited objective.

Random sample   A sample in which all cases selected have had an equal chance to be included.

Rank society   A society that does not have any unequal access to economic resources or power, but with social groups that have unequal access to status positions and prestige.

Recessive   An allele phenotypically suppressed in the heterozygous form and expressed only in the homozygous form.

Reciprocity   Giving and taking (not politically arranged) without the use of money.

Redistribution   The accumulation of goods (or labor) by a particular person or in a particular place and their subsequent distribution.

Relative dating   A method of dating fossils that determines the age of a specimen or deposit relative to a known specimen or deposit.

Religion   Any set of attitudes, beliefs, and practices pertaining to supernatural power, whether that power rests in forces, gods, spirits, ghosts, or demons.

Revitalization movement   A new religious movement intended to save a culture by infusing it with a new purpose and life.

Revolution   A usually violent replacement of a society's rulers.

Ribosome   A structure in the cell used in making proteins.

Robust australopithecines   A later group of australopithecines usually differentiated from the gracile australopithecines (see above) by their heavier dentition and larger faces.

Rules of descent   Rules that connect individuals with particular sets of kin because of known or presumed common ancestry.

Sagittal crest   A ridge of bone running along the top of the skull in apes and early hominids.

Sagittal keel   An inverted V-shaped ridge running along the top of the skull in *Homo erectus*.

Sahelanthropus tchadensis   A hominoid found in Chad dating to around 7 million years ago.

Sampling universe   The list of cases to be sampled from.

Savanna   Tropical grassland.

Secondary institutions   Aspects of culture, such as religion, music, art, folklore, and games, which presumably reflect or are projections of the basic, or typical, personality in a society.

Secondary subsistence activities   Activities that involve the preparation and processing of food either to make it edible or to store it.

Sedentarism   Settled life.

Segmentary lineage system   A hierarchy of more and more inclusive lineages; usually functions only in conflict situations.

Segregation   The random sorting of chromosomes in meiosis.

Sex differences   The typical differences between females and males that are most likely due to biological differences.

Sexual dimorphism   A marked difference in size and appearance between males and females of a species.

Shaman   A religious intermediary, usually part time, whose primary function is to cure people through sacred songs, pantomime, and other means; sometimes called witch doctor by Westerners.

Shifting cultivation   See **Extensive cultivation.**

Sib   See **Clan.**

Siblings   A person's brothers and sisters.

Sickle-cell anemia (sicklemia)   A condition in which red blood cells assume a crescent (sickle) shape when deprived of oxygen, instead of the normal (disk) shape. The sickle-shaped red blood cells do not move through the body as readily as normal cells, and thus cause damage to the heart, lungs, brain, and other vital organs.

Sites   Locations where the material remains of human activity have been preserved in a way that archaeologists or paleoanthropologists can recover them.

Sivapithecus   A genus of ape from the later Miocene known for its thickly enameled teeth, suggesting a diet of hard, tough, or gritty items. Found primarily in western and southern Asia and now thought to be ancestral to orangutans.

Slash-and-burn   A form of shifting cultivation in which the natural vegetation is cut down and burned off. The cleared ground is used for a short time and then left to regenerate.

Slaves   A class of persons who do not own their own labor or the products thereof.

Socialization   A term used by anthropologists and psychologists to describe the development, through the direct and indirect influence of parents and others, of children's patterns of behavior (and attitudes and values) that conform to cultural expectations. Also called enculturation.

Society   A group of people who occupy a particular territory and speak a common language not generally understood by neighboring peoples. By this definition, societies do not necessarily correspond to nations.

Sociobiology   See **Behavioral ecology.**

Sociolinguistics The study of cultural and subcultural patterns of speaking in different social contexts.

Soft hammer A technique of stone tool manufacture in which a bone or wood hammer is used to strike flakes from a stone.

Sorcery The use of certain materials to invoke supernatural powers to harm people.

Sororal polygyny The marriage of a man to two or more sisters at the same time.

Sororate A custom whereby a woman is obliged to marry her deceased sister's husband.

Special-purpose money Objects of value for which only some goods and services can be exchanged.

Speciation The development of a new species.

Species A population that consists of organisms able to interbreed and produce viable and fertile offspring.

Specific evolution The particular sequence of change and adaptation of a society in a given environment.

Spirits Unnamed supernatural beings of nonhuman origin who are beneath the gods in prestige and often closer to the people; may be helpful, mischievous, or evil.

State A form of political organization that includes class stratification, three or more levels of hierarchy, and leaders with the power to govern by force.

State organization A society is described as having state organization when it includes one or more states.

Statistical association A relationship or correlation between two or more variables that is unlikely to be due to chance.

Statistically significant Refers to a result that would occur very rarely by chance. The result (and stronger ones) would occur fewer than 5 times out of 100 by chance.

Steppe Grassland with a dry, low grass cover.

Stratified An archaeological deposit that contains successive layers or strata.

Stratigraphy The study of how different rock formations and fossils are laid down in successive layers or strata. Older layers are generally deeper or lower than more recent layers.

Strength theory An explanation for the gender division of labor suggesting that men's work typically involves tasks (like hunting and lumbering) requiring greater strength and greater aerobic work capacity.

Structuralism The theoretical orientation that human culture is a surface representation of the underlying structure of the human mind.

Structural linguistics See **Descriptive linguistics.**

Subculture The shared customs of a subgroup within a society.

Subsistence economy Economies in which almost all able-bodied adults are largely engaged in getting food for themselves and their families.

Subsistence technology The methods humans use to procure food.

Supernatural Believed to be not human or not subject to the laws of nature.

Symbolic communication An arbitrary (not obviously meaningful) gesture, call, word or sentence that has meaning even when its *referent* is not present.

Syntax The ways in which words are arranged to form phrases and sentences.

Taboo A prohibition that, if violated, is believed to bring supernatural punishment.

Taphonomy The study of how natural processes form and disturb archaeological sites.

Taurodontism Having teeth with an enlarged pulp cavity.

Taxonomy The classification of extinct and living organisms.

Terrestrial Adapted to living on the ground.

Terrorism The use or threat of violence to create terror in others, usually for political purposes.

Theoretical construct Something that cannot be observed or verified directly.

Theoretical orientation A general attitude about how phenomena are to be explained.

Theories Explanations of associations or laws.

Thermoluminescence dating A dating technique that is well suited to samples of ancient pottery, brick, tile, or terra cotta, which (when they were made) were heated to a high temperature that released trapped electrons. Such an object continues over time to trap electrons from radioactive elements around it, and the electrons trapped after manufacture emit light when heated. Thus the age of the object can be estimated by measuring how much light is emitted when the object is heated.

Totem A plant or animal associated with a clan (sib) as a means of group identification; may have other special significance for the group.

Tribal organization The kind of political organization in which local communities mostly act autonomously but there are kin groups (such as clans) or associations (such as age-sets) that can temporarily integrate a number of local groups into a larger unit.

Tribe A territorial population in which there are kin or nonkin groups with representatives in a number of local groups.

Typology A way of organizing artifacts in categories based on their particular characteristics.

Unifacial tool A tool worked or flaked on one side only.

Unilineal descent Affiliation with a group of kin through descent links of one sex only.

Unilocal residence A pattern of residence (patrilocal, matrilocal, or avunculocal) that specifies just one set of relatives that the married couple lives with or near.

Unisex association An association that restricts its membership to one sex, usually male.

Universally ascribed qualities Those ascribed qualities (age, sex) that are found in all societies.

Upper Paleolithic The time period associated with the emergence of modern humans and their spread around the world.

Uranium-series dating A technique for dating fossil sites that uses the decay of two kinds of uranium (^{235}U and ^{238}U) into other isotopes (such as ^{230}Th, thorium). Particularly useful in cave sites. Different types of uranium-series dating use different isotope ratios.

Variable A thing or quantity that varies.

Variably ascribed qualities Those ascribed qualities (such as ethnic, religious, or social class differences) that are found only in some societies.

Vertical clinging and leaping A locomotor pattern characteristic of several primates, including tarsiers and galagos. The animal normally rests by clinging to a branch in a vertical position and uses its hind limbs alone to push off from one vertical position to another.

Warfare Violence between political entities such as communities, districts, or nations.

Witchcraft The practice of attempting to harm people by supernatural means, but through emotions and thought alone, not through the use of tangible objects.

"Y-5" pattern Refers to the pattern of cusps on human molars. When looked at from the top, the cusps of the molars form a Y opening toward the cheek.

Notes

Chapter 1

1. Harrison 1975; Durham 1991: 228–37.
2. Chen and Li 2001.
3. Chambers 1989, as referred to in Kushner 1991.
4. Miracle 2004; Kushner 1991.
5. L. A. White 1968.
6. E. T. Hall 1966: 144–53.

Chapter 2

1. R. Martin 1990: 42.
2. R. Etienne 1992.
3. Dibble, Chase, McPherron, and Tuffreau 1997.
4. Schiffer 1987.
5. Isaac 1997.
6. B. Fowler 2000.
7. A. Underhill 2002.
8. Michel, McGovern, and Badler 1993.
9. Sinopoli 2002.
10. Wynn 1979.
11. Keeley 1977.
12. Kay 2000a.
13. B. Wood 1994.
14. Conroy 1990.
15. Peregrine 1992.
16. Leakey 1965: 73–78.
17. F. H. Brown 1992.
18. Aitken 1985: 191–202.
19. Aitken 1985: 4, 211–13.
20. Kappelman 1993.
21. Gentner and Lippolt 1963.
22. F. H. Brown 2000: 225.
23. Schwarcz 1993.
24. Fleischer and Hart 1972: 474.
25. Fleischer, Price, Walker, and Leakey 1965: 72–74.
26. Trigger 1989.
27. Waldbaum 2005.

Chapter 3

1. Sagan 1975.
2. A. Lovejoy 1964: 58–63
3. A. Lovejoy 1964: 63.
4. Eiseley 1958: 17–26; Mayr 1982: 171–75, 340–41.
5. Mayr 1982: 339–60.
6. Wallace 1970 (1858).
7. Mayr 1982: 423.
8. Darwin had a still longer title. It continued, *Or the Preservation of the Favoured Races in the Struggle for Life.* Darwin's notion of "struggle for life" is often misinterpreted to refer to a war of all against all. Although animals may fight with each other at times over access to resources, Darwin was referring mainly to their metaphorical "struggle" with the environment, particularly to obtain food.
9. Darwin 1970 (1859).
10. Futuyma 1982 provides an overview of this long controversy.

11. Huxley 1970.
12. Brandon 1990: 6–7.
13. G. Williams 1992: 7.
14. J. M. Smith 1989: 42–45.
15. Hooper 2002.
16. Grant 2002.
17. Devillers and Chaline 1993: 22–23.
18. Beadle and Beadle 1966: 216.
19. Golden, Lemonick, and Thompson 2000; Hayden 2000; Marshall 2000; Pennisi, 2000; Travis 2000.
20. Daiger 2005.
21. Olsen 2002.
22. Dobzhansky 1962: 138–40.
23. Relethford 1990: 94.
24. G. A. Harrison et al. 1988: 198–200.
25. Brace 1996.
26. Grant and Grant 2002.
27. Rennie 2002: 83.
28. Chatterjee 1997.
29. Paley 1810.
30. Center for Renewal of Science and Culture, "The Wedge Strategy," cited in Forrest 2001: 16.
31. McMullin 2001: 174.
32. Rennie 2002.
33. Barash 1977.
34. Krebs and Davies 1984, 1987.
35. Badcock 2000.
36. Schaller 1972.
37. Hare, Brown, Williamson, and Tomasello 2002.
38. Wilson 1975.
39. B. Low 2004.
40. D. Campbell 1965.
41. Nissen 1958.
42. Boyd and Richerson 1985.
43. Durham 1991.

Chapter 4

1. The classic description of common primate traits is Napier and Napier 1967. For primate social organization see Smuts, Cheney, Seyfarth, Wrangham, and Struhsaker 1987.
2. Bearder 1987: 14.
3. Richard 1985: 22ff.
4. R. Martin 1975: 50. The opossum, which is not a primate but lives in trees and has many babies at one time, is a marsupial and has a pouch in which to keep the babies when they are very young.
5. Harlow et al. 1966.
6. Nicolson 1987: 339.
7. Gray 1985 (144–63) provides an overview of research that attempts to explain the variation among primates in the degree of male parental care.
8. Russon 1990: 379.
9. Dohlinow and Bishop 1972: 321–25.
10. Sade 1965; Hausfater, Altmann, and Altmann 1982.

11. Visaberghi and Fragaszy 1990: 265; Tomasello 1990: 304–305.
12. van Lawick-Goodall 1971: 242.
13. Visaberghi and Fragaszy 1990: 264–65.
14. R. Martin 1992: 17–19; Conroy 1990: 8–15.
15. This simplified chart of primate classification adapts information provided in R. Martin 1992 (21).
16. Doyle and Martin 1979; Tattersall 1982.
17. Richard 1987: 32.
18. Bearder 1987: 13.
19. Charles-Dominique 1977: 258; also R. Martin and Bearder 1979; Bearder 1987: 18–22.
20. MacKinnon and MacKinnon 1980.
21. Cartmill 1992a: 28; Fleagle 1999: 118–22.
22. Napier and Napier 1967: 32–33.
23. Richard 1985: 164–65.
24. Cartmill 1992a: 29; Goldizen 1987: 34; also Eisenberg 1977; Sussman and Kinzey 1984; Fleagle 1999: 168–174.
25. Eisenberg 1977: 15–17.
26. Robinson, Wright, and Kinzey 1987; Crockett and Eisenberg 1987; Robinson and Janson, 1987.
27. Hrdy 1977: 18.
28. Hrdy 1977: 18–19.
29. Napier 1970: 80–82.
30. Fedigan 1982: 11.
31. Fedigan 1982: 123–24.
32. P. Lee 1983: 231.
33. Fleagle 1999: 302.
34. LeGros Clark 1964: 184.
35. Preuschoft, Chivers, Brockelman, and Creel 1984.
36. Carpenter 1940; Chivers 1974, 1980.
37. Rijksen 1978: 22.
38. Normile 1998.
39. van Schaik, et al. 2003.
40. Galdikas 1979: 220–23.
41. Cheney and Wrangham 1987: 236.
42. Rijksen 1978: 321.
43. Fossey 1983: xvi.
44. Tuttle 1986: 99–114.
45. Schaller 1963; Schaller 1964.
46. Fossey 1983: 47.
47. Harcourt 1979: 187–92.
48. Susman 1984; White 1996.
49. Goodall 1963; van Lawick-Goodall 1971.
50. Teleki 1973.
51. Stanford 2002.
52. Stanford 2002: 35–41.
53. Normile 1998.
54. Tuttle 1986: 266–69.
55. Whiten et al. 1999.
56. M. Goodman 1992.
57. Falk 1987.
58. Female bonobos, or pygmy chimpanzees, engage in sexual intercourse nearly as often as human females—see Thompson-Handler, Malenky, and Badrian 1984.
59. By male–female bonding, we mean that at least one of the sexes is "faithful," that is, typically has intercourse with just one opposite-sex partner throughout at least one estrus or menstrual cycle or breeding season. Note that the bonding may not be monogamous; an individual may be bonded to more than one individual of the opposite sex. See M. Ember and C. R. Ember 1979.
60. M. Ember and C.R. Ember 1979: 43; also C.R. Ember and M. Ember 1984: 203–204.

61. C.R. Ember and M. Ember 1984: 207.
62. C.R. Ember and M. Ember 1984: 208–209.
63. de Waal and Lanting 1997.
64. Rumbaugh 1970: 52–58.
65. Boesche et al. 1994.
66. Observation by others cited by A. Jolly 1985 (53).
67. Hannah and McGrew 1987.
68. "The First Dentist," *Newsweek,* March 5, 1973, 73.
69. Seyfarth, Cheney, and Marler 1980.
70. Gardner and Gardner 1969.
71. Gardner and Gardner 1980.
72. Greenfield and Savage-Rumbaugh 1990.
73. Clutton-Brock and Harvey 1977: 8–9.
74. Aiello 1992; A. Jolly 1985: 53–54.
75. Aiello 1992.
76. A. Jolly 1985: 53–54.
77. Parker 1990: 130.
78. Milton 1981; Clutton-Brock and Harvey 1980.
79. Milton 1988.
80. A. Jolly 1985: 119.
81. Clutton-Brock and Harvey 1977: 9.
82. Terborgh 1983: 224–25.
83. A. Jolly 1985: 120.
84. A. Jolly 1985: 122.
85. Wrangham 1980.

Chapter 5

1. Ciochon and Etler 1994: 33, 37–67.
2. Gingerich 1986; Szalay 1972; Szalay, Tattersall, and Decker 1975.
3. Fleagle 1994; Ciochon and Etler 1994: 41; Cartmill 2002.
4. Block and Boyer 2002.
5. Conroy 1990: 49–53.
6. Conroy 1990: 53.
7. Habicht 1979.
8. Vrba 1995.
9. Sussman 1991.
10. Richard 1985: 31; Cartmill 1974.
11. Szalay 1968.
12. Cartmill 1974; for more recent statements see Cartmill 1992b; Cartmill 2002.
13. Sussman and Raven 1978.
14. Conroy 1990: 94–95; Bowen et al. 2002.
15. Conroy 1990: 99.
16. Fleagle 1994: 22–23.
17. Conroy 1990: 119.
18. Radinsky 1967.
19. Conroy 1990: 105; Fleagle 1994: 21.
20. Alexander 1992; Conroy 1990: 111.
21. Kay, Ross, and Williams 1997.
22. Martin 1990: 46; Conroy 1990: 46.
23. Kay, Ross, and Williams 1997; Fleagle and Kay 1985: 25.
24. Jaeger et al. 1999.
25. Simons 1995; Simons, and Rassmussen 1996.
26. Kay 2000b: 441.
27. Kay 2000b: 441–42; Conroy 1990: 156.
28. Fleagle 1999: 404–409.
29. Rosenberger 1979.
30. Fleagle and Kay 1987.
31. Aiello 1993; Hartwig 1994.
32. Andrews 2000a: 486.
33. Fleagle and Kay 1985: 25, 30; Conroy 1990: 160–61.
34. Fleagle 1999: 413–15; Fleagle and Kay 1983: 205.
35. Conroy 1990: 248–49.

36. Conroy 1990: 56.
37. R. Martin 1990: 56.
38. Begun 2002.
39. Conroy 1990: 206–11.
40. Begun 2002.
41. Andrews 2000b: 485.
42. Begun 2002.
43. Zimmer 1999; Ward, Brown, Hill, Kelley, and Downs 1999.
44. Begun 2002; Kelley 1992: 225.
45. Moyà-Solà et al. 2004.
46. Conroy 1990: 185, 255.
47. T. Harrison 1986; T. Harrison and Rook 1997.
48. Ward 1997.
49. Ciochon, Olsen, and James 1990: 99–102.
50. Begun 2002.
51. Begun 2002.
52. Fleagle 1999: 480–83.
53. Bilsborough 1992: 65.
54. Simons 1992: 207.
55. Sarich and Wilson 1966; Sarich 1968; Lewin 1983a.
56. Jones, Martin, and Pilbeam, 1992: 293; R. Martin 1990: 693–709.
57. Clark et al. 2003.
58. The material referred to in this paragraph is drawn from Jones, Martin, and Pilbeam 1992: 8, 293–321.

Chapter 6

1. Rose 1984.
2. Bilsborough 1992: 64–65.
3. Oakley 1964.
4. Kingston, Marino, and Hill 1994.
5. Hewes 1961.
6. Shipman 1986; Trinkaus 1987a.
7. Lovejoy 1981.
8. C. Jolly 1970.
9. Washburn 1960.
10. Pilbeam 1972: 153.
11. Wolpoff 1971.
12. Savage-Rumbaugh 1994
13. Wolpoff 1983.
14. Zimmer 2004.
15. Zihlman 1992.
16. Wheeler 1984, 1991.
17. Falk 1988.
18. Zihlman 1992: 414.
19. Lovejoy 1988.
20. Aiello and Dean 1990: 268–74.
21. Aiello and Dean 1990: 507–508.
22. Gibbons 2002.
23. Brunet, et al. 2002; Wong 2003.
24. Aiello and Collard 2001; Pickford, Senut, Gommercy and Treil 2002; Wong 2003.
25. White, Suwa, and Asfaw 1995.
26. White, Suwa, and Asfaw 1994.
27. Hailie-Selassie 2001.
28. Susman, Stern, and Jungers 1985; Rose 1984.
29. Conroy 1990: 274; Culotta 1995; Wilford 1995.
30. Asfaw et al. 1999.
31. Brunet et al. 1995.
32. Brunet et al. 1995.
33. Leakey et al. 2001.
34. Fleagle 1999: 511–515.
35. Fleagle 1999: 528.
36. White 2003.

37. Culotta 1995.
38. Leakey et al. 1995.
39. Tattersall and Schwartz 2000: 93.
40. Simpson 2002; White, Johanson, and Kimbel 1981; Johanson and White 1979.
41. Johanson and Edey 1981: 17–18.
42. Johanson and White 1979.
43. Lewin 1983b.
44. Conroy 1990: 291–292; Simpson 2002.
45. Fleagle 1999: 515–18.
46. Fleagle 1999: 515, 520.
47. Grine 1988a.
48. Kimbel, White, and Johansen 1984.
49. Jungers 1988a; Clarke and Tobias 1995.
50. Lovejoy 1988.
51. Tattersall and Schwartz 2000: 88–89; Clarke and Tobias 1995.
52. Dart 1925.
53. Bromage and Dean 1985; B. H. Smith 1986.
54. Eldredge and Tattersall 1982: 80–90.
55. Pilbeam 1972: 107.
56. Holloway 1974.
57. Szalay and Delson 1979: 504.
58. Conroy 1990: 280–282.
59. Conroy 1990: 294–303.
60. McHenry 2002.
61. Szalay and Delson 1979: 504; Wood 1992.
62. McHenry 1988; Jungers 1988b.
63. Fleagle 1999: 522.
64. Grine 1993; Walker and Leakey 1988.
65. Broom 1950.
66. Fleagle 1999: 522.
67. McHenry 2002.
68. McHenry 2002.
69. Grine 1988b.
70. Stringer 1985.
71. M. Leakey 1971, 1979.
72. McHenry 2002.
73. Fleagle 1999: 529.
74. Wood 1992.

Chapter 7

1. Susman 1994.
2. Susman 1994.
3. Holden 1997.
4. Leakey 1960.
5. Clark 1970: 68; Schick and Toth 1993: 97–99.
6. Schick and Toth 1993: 153–70.
7. Schick and Toth 1993: 129.
8. Schick and Toth 1993: 157–59.
9. Isaac 1984.
10. Whittaker 1994: 283–85.
11. Schick and Toth 1993: 175–76.
12. Speth 2002.
13. Shipman 1986. For the idea that scavenging may have been an important food-getting strategy even for protohominids, see Szalay 1975.
14. Speth and Davis 1976; Blumenschine et al. 2003.
15. Isaac 1971.
16. Leakey 1971.
17. Potts 1988: 253–58.
18. Potts 1984.
19. Potts 1988: 278–81.
20. Wolf 1984.

21. Boyd and Silk 2000: 249–50.
22. Dobzhansky 1962: 196.
23. Bromage and Dean 1985; B.H. Smith 1986.
24. McHenry 2002; Tobias 1994.
25. McHenry 1982.
26. McHenry 1982.
27. Pilbeam and Gould 1974.
28. Leonard 2002.
29. Stedman et al. 2004.
30. McHenry 2002; Tobias 1994.
31. Simpson 2002.
32. Rightmire 2000.
33. Swisher et al. 1994.
34. Balter and Gibbons 2000; Gabunia et al. 2000.
35. Vekua et al. 2002; Gore 2002.
36. Wolpoff and Nkini 1988. See also Rightmire 2000; Balter 2001.
37. Rightmire 1990: 12–14.
38. Swisher et al. 1994.
39. Rightmire 2000.
40. Fleagle 1999: 534–35; Day 1986: 409–12; Kramer 2002.
41. Rightmire 2000; Tobias 1994.
42. Franciscus and Trinkaus 1988.
43. Feibel and Brown 1993.
44. Ruff and Walker 1993.
45. Wolpoff, Thorne, Jelinek, and Yinyun 1993.
46. Morwood et al. 2004; Brown et al. 2004.
47. Falk et al. 2005
48. Diamond 2004
49. Wong 2005
50. Fleagle 1999: 306.
51. M. Ember and C. R. Ember 1979; cf. Lovejoy 1981.
52. Clayman 1989: 857–58.
53. Bordes 1968: 51–97.
54. Rogers, Iltis, & Wooding 2004.
55. Phillipson 1993: 57.
56. Schick and Toth 1993: 227, 233.
57. Schick and Toth 1993: 231–33; Whittaker 1994: 27.
58. Bordes 1968: 24–25; Whittaker 1994: 27.
59. Schick and Toth 1993: 258–60; Whittaker 1994: 27.
60. Lawrence Keeley's analysis reported in Schick and Toth 1993: 260; see that page for their analysis of tool use.
61. Calvin 1983.
62. Yamei et al. 2000.
63. Ciochon, Olsen, and James 1990: 178–83: Pope 1989.
64. Howell 1966
65. Klein 1987; Binford 1987.
66. L. G. Freeman 1994.
67. A good example of this problem is the ongoing debate about fire use at Zhoukoudian cave, as reported by Weiner et al. 1998.
68. Isaac 1984: 35–36. Other evidence for deliberate use of fire comes from the Swartkans cave in South Africa and is dated 1 million to 1.5 million years ago; see Brain and Sillen 1988.
69. Goren-Inbar et al. 2004.
70. Binford and Ho 1985.
71. Leonard 2002.
72. Clark 1970: 94–95.
73. Clark 1970: 96–97.
74. de Lumley 1969.
75. Dickson 1990: 42–44.
76. Dickson 1990: 45; Tattersall and Schwartz 2000: 155.

Chapter 8

1. Stringer 1985.
2. Stringer 1985.
3. Rightmire 1997.
4. Rightmire 1997; Fleagle 1999: 535–37.
5. Spencer 1984.
6. Trinkaus 1985.
7. Stringer 2000.
8. Trinkaus and Shipman 1993a, 1993b.
9. F. Smith 1984: 187.
10. Trinkaus 1984: 251–53.
11. Krings et al. 1997.
12. Cann 1988.
13. Cann 1988.
14. Vigilant et al. 1991.
15. Krings et al. 1997.
16. Ovchinnikov et al. 2000.
17. Tattersall 1999: 115–16; Gibbons 2001.
18. Mellars 1996: 405–19.
19. Mellars 1998.
20. Strauss 1989.
21. Schick and Toth 1993: 288–92.
22. Klein 1989: 291–96.
23. Schick and Toth 1993: 288–92; Whittaker 1994: 30–31.
24. Klein 1989: 421–22.
25. Binford and Binford 1969.
26. Fish 1981: 377.
27. Butzer 1982: 42.
28. Phillipson 1993: 63.
29. For the controversy about whether the inhabitants of the Dordogne Valley lived in their homesites year-round, see Binford 1973.
30. Schick and Toth 1993: 292.
31. Klein 1977.
32. Klein 1974.
33. Bordes 1961.
34. T. Patterson 1981.
35. Phillipson 1993: 64.
36. Klein 1983: 38–39.
37. Binford 1984: 195–97. To explain the lack of complete skeletons of large animals, Klein (1983) suggests that the hunters may have butchered the large animals elsewhere because they could carry home only small cuts.
38. Wilford 1997.
39. Pfeiffer 1978: 155.
40. Trinkaus 1984.
41. Chase and Dibble 1987.
42. Stringer, Hublin, and Vandermeersch 1984: 107.
43. Singer and Wymer 1982: 149.
44. Gibbons 2003.
45. Bräuer 1984: 387–89, 394; Rightmire 1984: 320.
46. Valladas et al. 1988.
47. Stringer, Hublin, and Vandermeersch 1984: 121.
48. For arguments supporting the single-origin theory, see the chapters by Günter Bräuer, F. Clark Howell, and C. B. Stringer et al., in F. Smith and Spencer 1984. For arguments supporting the multiregional theory, see the chapters by C. L. Brace et al., David W. Frayer, Fred H. Smith, and Milford H. Wolpoff et al. in the same volume.
49. Cann, Stoneking, and Wilson 1987.
50. Vigilant et al. 1991.
51. Stoneking 1997.
52. Hammer and Zegura 1996.
53. Hammer and Zegura 2002.

54. Cavalli-Sforza and Feldman 2003.
55. Stringer 2003.
56. Wolpoff 1999: 501–504, 727–31; Frayer et al. 1993.
57. Wolpoff 1999: 735–43; Frayer et al. 1993.
58. D. Lieberman 1995.
59. Templeton 1993.
60. Trinkaus 1986.
61. Eswaran 2002.
62. Templeton 1996. See also Ayala 1995, 1996.
63. Reed et al. 2004
64. Duarte et al. 1999.
65. Bahn 1998.
66. Tattersall 1999: 198–203.
67. Trinkaus 1986; see also Trinkaus and Howells 1979.
68. Culotta 2005.
69. Klein 2003.

Chapter 9

1. R. White 1982.
2. Strauss 1982.
3. Dawson 1992: 24–71.
4. COHMAP 1988.
5. Martin and Wright 1967.
6. Mellars 1994.
7. L. Patterson 1981.
8. Klima 1962.
9. Whittaker 1994: 33; Schick and Toth 1993: 293–99.
10. Whittaker 1994: 31.
11. Bordaz 1970: 68.
12. Whittaker 1994: 33.
13. Phillipson 1993: 60.
14. Bordaz 1970: 68.
15. We thank Robert L. Kelly (personal communication) for bringing this possibility to our attention. See also J.D. Clark 1977: 136.
16. Ascher 1961.
17. Semenov 1970: 103. For a more recent discussion of research following this strategy, see Keeley 1980.
18. Klein 1994: 508.
19. Soffer 1993: 38–40.
20. Phillipson 1993: 74.
21. Morell 1995.
22. Henshilwood et al. 2002.
23. Ucko and Rosenfeld 1967.
24. Rice and Paterson 1985, 1986.
25. Rice and Paterson 1985: 98.
26. Marshack 1972.
27. McDermott 1996.
28. For a review, see Dobres 1998.
29. Hawkins and Kleindienst 2001.
30. Peregrine 2001a.
31. Jayaswal 2002.
32. Peregrine and Bellwood 2001.
33. McDonald 1998.
34. Hoffecker, Powers, and Goebel 1993.
35. Gibbons 1995; Roosevelt et al. 1996.
36. Dillehay 2000.
37. Parry 2002.
38. Greenberg and Ruhlen 1992: 94–99.
39. Turner 1989.
40. Szathmary 1993.
41. McDonald 1998.
42. Wheat 1967.
43. Fagan 1991: 79.
44. Hoffecker, Powers, and Goebel 1993.
45. Jennings 1968: 72–88.
46. Judge and Dawson 1972.
47. Wheat 1967.
48. Fagan 1989: 221.
49. Wheat 1967.
50. Wheat 1967.
51. Fagan 1989: 227.
52. Fagan 1991: 192.
53. Fagan 1989: 227.
54. Collins 1975: 88–125.
55. Chard 1969: 171.
56. G. Clark 1975: 101–61.
57. Petersen 1973: 94–96.
58. Daniel 2001.
59. Sassaman 1996: 58–83.
60. Sassaman 1996: 58–83.
61. J. Brown 1983: 5–10.

Chapter 10

1. Miller 1992.
2. Crawford 1992; Phillipson 1993: 118; MacNeish 1991: 256, 268.
3. Flannery 1986: 6–8; Pearsall 1992; B. Smith 1992a.
4. Hole 1992.
5. Binford 1971.
6. Flannery 1973a.
7. Simcha et al. 2000.
8. Harlan 1967.
9. Flannery 1971.
10. Mellaart 1961.
11. Henry 1989: 214–15.
12. Brown and Price 1985.
13. Henry 1989: 38–39, 209–10; 1991. See Olszewski 1991 for some questions about the degree of social complexity in Natufian sites.
14. Martin and Wright 1967.
15. A recent analysis of these changes is Kuehn 1998; see also J. Brown 1985.
16. Marcus and Flannery 1996: 49–50.
17. Marcus and Flannery 1996: 50–53.
18. Gorman 1970.
19. Chang 1970; Gorman 1970.
20. J. Clark 1970: 171–72.
21. Phillipson 1993: 111–12.
22. Alroy 2001.
23. Martin 1973.
24. Grayson 1977, 1984. See also L. G. Marshall 1984; Guthrie 1984; Barnosky et al. 2004.
25. Holdaway and Jacomb 2000.
26. Cohen 1977b: 12, 85.
27. Cohen 1977b: 85; Hassan 1981: 207. For the view that hunter-gatherers were very unlikely to have lived in tropical forests before agriculture developed, see Bailey et al. 1989.
28. Cohen 1989: 112–13.
29. Frayer 1981.
30. Cohen 1989: 113–15.
31. Flannery 1973b.
32. Patterson 1971.
33. G. Johnson 1977; D. Harris 1977.
34. Sussman 1972; Lee 1972.
35. For some examples of societies that have practiced infanticide, D. Harris 1977.
36. Howell 1979; Lee 1979.

37. Frisch 1980; Howell 1979.

38. Phillipson 1993: 60–61.

39. Semenov 1970: 63, 203–204; Whittaker 1994: 36–37.

40. Zohary 1969.

41. Flannery 1965.

42. Flannery 1965. For the view that a high proportion of immature animals does not necessarily indicate domestication, see Collier and White 1976.

43. Hole 1992; MacNeish 1991: 127–28.

44. Clutton-Brock 1992.

45. Hole, Flannery, and Neely 1969.

46. Simmons et al. 1988.

47. Mellaart 1964.

48. Flannery 1986: 3–5; Pringle 1998.

49. Marcus and Flannery 1996: 64–66.

50. Flannery 1986: 6–8.

51. Fedoroff 2003.

52. Flannery 1986: 8–9; Marcus and Flannery 1996: 66–67.

53. Marcus and Flannery 1996: 65–66.

54. Marcus and Flannery 1996: 66–68.

55. Flannery 1986: 31–42.

56. Flannery 1986: 502.

57. Piperno and Stothert 2003.

58. MacNeish 1991: 37, 47; Hole 1992.

59. B. Smith 1992b: 163, 287.

60. Asch and Asch 1978.

61. B. Smith 1992a, 1992b: 39, 274–75, 292.

62. B. Smith 1992b: 6.

63. B. Smith 1992b: 180.

64. Savolainen, et al. 2002.

65. Clutton-Brock 1992.

66. Crawford 1984.

67. Clutton-Brock 1992.

68. Müller-Haye 1984.

69. Wenke 1984: 350, 397–98.

70. Chang 1981; MacNeish 1991: 159–63.

71. MacNeish 1991: 267–68.

72. Neumann 2003; Denham et al. 2003.

73. Hole 1992.

74. Phillipson 1993: 118.

75. MacNeish 1991: 314.

76. Hanotte, et al. 2002; Clutton-Brock 1992.

77. Diamond 1997a, 1997b.

78. Cited in MacNeish 1991: 6.

79. Braidwood 1960.

80. Braidwood and Willey 1962.

81. Binford 1971; Flannery 1973a.

82. Wright 1971.

83. Flannery 1986: 10–11.

84. Cohen 1977a, 1977b:279.

85. Byrne 1987, referred to in Blumler and Byrne 1991; see also Henry 1989: 30–38; McCorriston and Hole 1991.

86. Henry 1989: 41.

87. McCorriston and Hole 1991.

88. Henry 1989: 54.

89. Speth and Spielmann 1983.

90. B. White 1973; see also Kasarda 1971.

91. C. R. Ember 1983.

92. Konner and Worthman 1980.

93. Roosevelt 1984; see also M. N. Cohen and Armelagos 1984b:585–602; Cohen 1987, 2002. For evidence suggesting that the transition to food production was not generally associated with declining health, see Wood et al. 1992.

94. Roosevelt 1984

95. Goodman and Armelagos 1985; see also A. H. Goodman et al. 1984; Cohen 2002.

96. Clark and Piggott 1965: 240–42.

97. Clark and Piggott 1965: 235.

98. Renfrew 1969.

Chapter 11

1. Wenke 1990; Connah 1987; Service 1975.

2. Flannery 1972.

3. Flannery 1972; Redman 1978: 215–16.

4. Wright and Johnson 1975.

5. The discussion in the remainder of this section draws from Wright and Johnson 1975; see also G. Johnson 1987.

6. Wright and Johnson 1975.

7. Flannery 1972.

8. Service 1975: 207.

9. Service 1975; Flannery 1972.

10. This description of Sumerian civilization is based on Kramer 1963.

11. Diamond 1989.

12. Helms 1975: 34–36, 54–55; Sanders, Parsons, and Santley 1979.

13. Millon 1967.

14. Millon 1976.

15. Millon, 1967.

16. Helms 1975: 61–63; Weaver 1993.

17. Blanton 1981; J. Marcus 1983.

18. Blanton 1976, 1978.

19. B. Turner 1970; Harrison and Turner 1978.

20. Houston 1988.

21. Wenke 1984: 289.

22. Connah 1987: 67.

23. Fagan 1989: 428–30.

24. Connah 1987: 216–17.

25. Vogel 2002.

26. Wenke 1984: 305–20.

27. Chang 1981.

28. Chang 1968: 235–55.

29. Solis, Haas, and Creamer 2001; Haas, Creamer, and Ruiz 2004.

30. For an overview, see Lumbreras 1974.

31. M. Fowler 1975.

32. For a more complete review of the available theories, see various chapters in Cohen and Service 1978; see also Chapter 1 in Zeder 1991.

33. Wittfogel 1957.

34. Adams 1960; H. T. Wright 1986.

35. Wheatley 1971: 291.

36. Adams, 1960.

37. Adams 1981: 244.

38. Adams 1981: 243; Service 1975: 274–75.

39. Carneiro 1970; Sanders and Price 1968: 230–32.

40. M. Harris 1979: 101–102.

41. T. C. Young 1972.

42. Sanders and Price 1968: 141.

43. Blanton et al. 1981: 224. For the apparent absence of population pressure in the Teotihuacán Valley, see Brumfiel 1976. For the Oaxaca Valley, see Feinman et al. 1985.

44. Wright and Johnson 1975. Carneiro 1988, however, argued the opposite: that the population grew just before the states emerged in southwestern Iran. Whether or not population declined, Frank Hole 1994 has suggested that climate change around that time may have forced local populations to relocate, some to centers that became cities.

45. Polanyi, Arensberg, and Pearson 1957: 257–62; Sanders 1968.
46. Wright and Johnson 1975.
47. Rathje 1971.
48. Chang 1986: 234–94.
49. For a discussion of how political dynamics may play an important role in state formation, see Brumfiel 1983.
50. Johnson and Earle 1987: 324–26.
51. Childe 1950.
52. Service 1975: 12–15, 89–90.
53. J. Diamond 1997a:205–207.
54. Dirks 1993.
55. Johnson and Earle 1987: 243–48; 304–306.
56. C. R. Ember and M. Ember 1992.
57. Ferguson and Whitehead 1992.
58. Weiss et al. 1993.
59. Kerr 1998; Grossman 2002.
60. Haug et al. 2003.
61. deMenocal 2001; Haug et al. 2003; Hodell et al. 2001.
62. Holden 1996.
63. Wilkinson 1995.
64. Tainter 1988: 128–52.
65. Charnais 1953.

Chapter 12

1. See Durham 1991: 154–225 for an extensive discussion of the relationship between genes and culture.
2. Steward 1950.
3. *Genesis* 17: 9–15.
4. Hanna, Little, and Austin 1989: 133–36; G. A. Harrison et al. 1988: 504–507.
5. Roberts 1953. Cited in Garn 1971: 73. See also Roberts 1978.
6. Roberts 1953.
7. Harrison et al. 1988: 505.
8. Riesenfeld 1973: 427–59.
9. Riesenfeld 1973: 452–53.
10. Weiner 1954: 615–18; Steegman 1975. See also Larsen 2002.
11. Harrison et al. 1988: 308–10.
12. Polednak 1974: 49–57. See also Branda and Eaton 1978.
13. Loomis 1967.
14. Post, Daniels, and Binford 1975: 65–80.
15. Holden 2000; Jablonski and Chaplin 2000.
16. Stini 1975: 53.
17. Mazess 1975.
18. Greksa and Beall 1989: 223.
19. Greksa and Beall 1989: 226.
20. Frisancho and Greksa 1989: 204.
21. Eveleth and Tanner 1990: 176–79.
22. Eveleth and Tanner 1990: 205–206.
23. Bogin 1988: 105–106.
24. Harrison et al. 1988: 300.
25. Harrison et al. 1988: 198.
26. Huss-Ashmore and Johnston 1985: 482–83.
27. Harrison et al. 1988: 385–86.
28. Martorell 1980: 81–106.
29. Martorell et al. 1991.
30. Landauer and Whiting 1964, 1981; Gunders and Whiting 1968; Gray and Wolfe 1980.
31. Landauer and Whiting, 1964, 1981; Gunders and Whiting 1968.
32. Gray and Wolfe 2002.
33. Landauer and Whiting 1981.
34. Eveleth and Tanner 1990: 205.
35. Landauer 1973.
36. Motulsky 1971: 223.
37. Motulsky 1971: 226.
38. Motulsky 1971: 229.
39. Motulsky 1971: 230.
40. Motulsky 1971: 233.
41. Motulsky 1971: 233.
42. Black 1992.
43. An examination of the epidemic diseases spread by Europeans can be found in Chapter 11 of J. Diamond 1997a.
44. Neel et al. 1970; Patrick Tierney in his *Darkness in El Dorado* (New York: Norton, 2000) accused the Neel research team of fueling a measles outbreak among the Yanomamö by administering a harmful measles vaccine. But the scientific evidence indicates that Tierney is wrong. The vaccine used by Neel and associates was widely pretested and there was no way that the vaccine could have caused the epidemic. Measles was already spreading in the Amazon, which was why the vaccination program was initiated. See Gregor and Gross 2004.
45. Relethford 1990: 425–27.
46. Merbs 1992.
47. Durham 1991: 105–107.
48. Durham 1991: 105–107.
49. Durham 1991: 107.
50. Harrison et al. 1988: 231.
51. For a review of the early research, see Durham 1991: 123–27. The particular form of malaria that is discussed is caused by the species *Plasmodium falciparum*.
52. See Madigral 1989 for a report of her own research and a review of earlier studies.
53. Pennisi 2001a.
54. Durham 1991: 124–45.
55. Motulsky 1971: 238.
56. Diamond 1993.
57. Molnar 1998: 158; Pennisi 2001b.
58. Durham 1991: 230.
59. Brodey 1971.
60. Durham 1991: 233–35.
61. Relethford 1990: 127.
62. McCracken 1971; see also references to the work of F. J. Simoons as referred to in Durham 1991: 240–41.
63. McCracken 1971; Huang 2002.
64. Durham 1991: 263–69.
65. Marks 1994; Shanklin 1994: 15–17.
66. Molnar 1998: 19.
67. Brace et al. 1993.
68. Brooks et al. 1993.
69. Brace et al. 1993.
70. Brooks et al. 1993.
71. King and Motulsky 2002.
72. Goodrich 1959: 7–15.
73. Coe 1966: 74–76.
74. Thompson 1966: 89.
75. McNeill 1976.
76. Motulsky 1971: 232.
77. Motulsky 1971: 232.
78. MacArthur and Wilson 1967.
79. Johansen and Edey 1981.
80. Peregrine, Ember, and Ember 2000, 2003.
81. Lieberman 1999.
82. Klineberg 1935, 1944.
83. Jensen 1969.
84. M. W. Smith 1974.

85. Dobzhansky 1973: 11.
86. Dobzhansky 1973: 14–15.
87. Research by Sandra Scarr and others reported in Boyd and Richerson 1985: 56.
88. Dobzhansky 1962: 243.
89. Haldane 1963.
90. Simpson 1971: 297–308.

Chapter 13

1. Linton 1945: 30.
2. See, for example, Holland and Quinn 1987: 4.
3. Sapir 1938, cited by Pelto and Pelto 1975: 1.
4. Pelto and Pelto 1975: 14–15.
5. de Waal 2001: 269.
6. Hewlett 2003.
7. Miner 1956: 504–505, reproduced by permission of the American Anthropological Association. Although Miner was not a foreign visitor, he wrote this description in a way that shows how these behaviors might be seen from an outside perspective.
8. R. B. Lee 1972.
9. Hatch 1997.
10. Durkheim 1938 [originally published 1895]: 3.
11. Asch 1956: 1–70.
12. Hall 1966: 159–60.
13. Ibid., p. 120.
14. J. W. M. Whiting 1964: 511–44.
15. Wagley 1974: 377–84.
16. R. Brown 1965: 549–609.
17. Chibnik 1981: 256–68.

Chapter 14

1. Tylor 1958 [1871].
2. Morgan 1964 [1877].
3. Engels, 1972 [1884].
4. Harris 1968: 380–84; Langness 1974: 50–53.
5. Ibid.
6. Ibid.
7. Langness 1974: 53–58; Harris 1968: 304–77.
8. Langness 1974: 50.
9. Boas 1940: 270–80.
10. Langness 1974: 85–93; Bock 1980: 57–82.
11. Kardiner, with Linton 1946 [1939]: 471–87.
12. Benedict 1946; Gorer 1943; LaBarre 1945.
13. Gorer and Rickman 1950.
14. Barry, Child, and Bacon 1959.
15. J. Whiting and Child 1953.
16. Malinowski 1939.
17. Radcliffe-Brown 1952.
18. Ibid.
19. L. White 1949: 368–69.
20. Steward 1955b.
21. Sahlins and Service 1960.
22. Lévi-Strauss 1969a: 75.
23. Lévi-Strauss 1966; Lévi-Strauss 1969b.
24. Ortner 1984.
25. Douglas 1975.
26. Colby 1996.
27. Steward 1955a: 30–42.
28. Vayda and Rappaport 1968. For a selection of recent studies in human ecology, see. Bates and Lees, eds., 1996.
29. Vayda and Rappaport 1968: 493.
30. Rappaport 1967.
31. Kottak 1999.

32. Ortner 1984: 141–42.
33. Sanderson 1995.
34. Roseberry 1988: 163; see also E. R. Wolf 1956 and Mintz 1956.
35. Roseberry 1988: 164; see also Leacock 1954.
36. Roseberry 1988: 166; see also Frank 1967.
37. Roseberry 1988: 166–67; see also Wallerstein 1974.
38. Irons 1979: 10–12. For a mathematical model and a computer simulation suggesting that group selection is likely in cultural evolution, see Boyd and Richerson 1990.
39. Irons 1979.
40. Low 2004.
41. Ibid.
42. Weiner 1987.
43. Slocum 1975.
44. Behar and Gordon 1995.
45. Clifford 1986: 3.
46. Geertz 1973c: 3–30, 412–53; see also Marcus and Fischer 1986: 26–29.
47. Geertz 1973a.
48. Sperber 1985: 34.
49. Foucault 1970.
50. Salzman 2001: 135.

Chapter 15

1. Hempel 1965: 139.
2. J. W. M. Whiting 1964.
3. Nagel 1961: 88–89.
4. Ibid., pp. 83–90.
5. Ibid., p. 85. See also McCain and Segal 1988: 75–79.
6. McCain and Segal 1988: 62–64.
7. Caws 1969: 1378.
8. McCain and Segal 1988: 114.
9. Ibid: 56–57, 131–32.
10. J. W. M. Whiting 1964: 519–20.
11. McCain and Segal 1988: 67–69.
12. Blalock 1972: 15–20 and Thomas 1986: 18–28. See also M. Ember 1970: 701–703.
13. For examples, see Murdock 1967 and Murdock and White 1969: 329–69.
14. Sets of the HRAF in paper or microfiche format, and now on the Web, are found in almost 300 universities and research institutions around the world. See the HRAF Web site: http://www.yale.edu/hraf.
15. Ogburn 1922: 200–80.
16. Bernard 2001: 323.
17. Peacock 1986: 54.
18. Lawless et al. 1983: xi–xxi; Peacock 1986: 54–65.
19. Romney et al. 1986.
20. Bernard 2001: 190.
21. American Anthropological Association 1991.
22. Szklut and Reed 1991.
23. K. Hill and Hurtado 2004.
24. See Murdock and White 1969 for a description of the SCCS sample; the HRAF Collection of Ethnography is described at http://www.yale.edu/hraf; for a description of many different cross-cultural samples see C.R. Ember and M. Ember 2001: 76–88.
25. Helms 2004.

Chapter 16

1. Keller 1974 [originally published 1902], p. 34.
2. Wilden 1987: 124, referred to in Christensen, Hockey, and James 2001.

3. Lambert 2001.
4. Ekman and Keltner 1997: 32.
5. Poyatos 2002: 103–5, 114–8.
6. von Frisch 1962.
7. King 1999a; Gibson and Jessee 1999: 189–190.
8. Seyfarth and Cheney 1982: 242, 246.
9. Hockett and Ascher 1964.
10. T. S. Eliot 1963.
11. Snowdon 1999: 81.
12. Pepperberg 1999.
13. Mukerjee 1996: 28.
14. Savage-Rumbaugh 1992: 138–41.
15. J. H. Hill 1978: 94; J. H. Hill 2004.
16. Ibid.
17. Senner 1989b.
18. See Snowdon 1999; Gibson and Jessee 1999; Burling 1999; Wilcox 1999.
19. Chomsky 1975.
20. Southworth and Daswani 1974: 312. See also Boas 1964: 121–23.
21. Bickerton 1983.
22. Ibid., p. 122.
23. B. Berlin 1992; Hays 1994.
24. G. Miller 2004.
25. Gleitman and Wanner 1982; Blount 1981.
26. R. Brown 1980: 93–94.
27. de Villiers and de Villiers 1979: 48; see also Wanner and Gleitman 1982.
28. Bickerton 1983: 122.
29. E. Bates and Marchman 1988 as referred to by Snowdon 1999: 88–91.
30. Crystal 1971: 168.
31. Ibid., pp. 100–1.
32. Barinaga 1992: 535.
33. Akmajian, Demers, and Harnish 1984: 136.
34. R. L. Munroe, R. H. Munroe, and Winters 1996; M. Ember and C. R. Ember 1999. The theory about the effect of baby-holding on consonant–vowel alternation is an extension of the theory that regular baby-holding encourages a preference for regular rhythm in music; see Ayres 1973.
35. Sapir and Swadesh 1964: 103.
36. Akmajian, Demers, and Harnish 1984: 164–66.
37. Chaucer 1926: 8. Our modern English translation is based on the glossary in this book.
38. Akmajian, Demers, and Harnish 1984: 356.
39. Baldi 1983: 3.
40. Ibid., p. 12.
41. Friedrich 1970: 168.
42. Ibid., p. 166.
43. Gimbutas 1974: 293–95. See Skomal and Polomé 1987.
44. Anthony, Telegin, and Brown 1991.
45. Renfrew 1987.
46. Greenberg 1972; see also Phillipson 1976: 71.
47. Phillipson 1976: 79.
48. Trudgill 1983: 34.
49. Gumperz 1961: 976–88.
50. Trudgill 1983: 35.
51. Gumperz 1971: 45.
52. Weinreich 1968: 31.
53. But see Thomason and Kaufman 1988 for a discussion of how grammatical changes due to contact may be more important than was previously assumed.
54. Berlin and Kay 1969.
55. Ibid.
56. Ibid., pp. 5–6.
57. Ibid., p. 104; Witkowski and Brown 1978: 427–51.
58. Bornstein 1973: 41–101.
59. M. Ember 1978: 364–67.
60. Ibid.
61. C. H. Brown 1977.
62. C. H. Brown 1979.
63. Witkowski and Burris 1981.
64. Ibid.
65. C. H. Brown and Witkowski 1980: 379.
66. C. H. Brown 1984: 106.
67. Hoijer 1964: 146.
68. Webb 1977: 42–49; see also Rudmin 1988.
69. Sapir 1931: 578; see also J. B. Carroll 1956.
70. Wardhaugh 2002: 222.
71. Denny 1979: 97.
72. Friedrich 1986.
73. Guiora et al. 1982.
74. Lucy 1992: 46.
75. Ibid., pp. 85–148.
76. Hymes 1974: 83–117.
77. Fischer 1958; Wardhaugh 2002: 160–88.
78. Trudgill 1983: 41–42.
79. Geertz 1960: 248–60; see also Errington 1985.
80. R. Brown and Ford 1961.
81. Wardhaugh 2002: 315.
82. Shibamoto 1987: 28.
83. Holmes 2001: 153.
84. Lakoff 1973: 45–80; Lakoff 1990.
85. Wardhaugh 2002: 328; Holmes 2001: 158–59; Trudgill 1983: 87–8.
86. M. R. Haas 1944: 142–49.
87. Keenan 1989.
88. Holmes 2001: 289.
89. Tannen 1990: 49–83.
90. Wardhaugh 2002: 100.
91. Heller 1988: 1.
92. Pfaff 1979.
93. Wardhaugh 2002: 108.
94. Gal 1988: 249–55.
95. Collins and Blot 2003: 1–3.

Chapter 17

1. Hitchcock and Beisele 2000: 5.
2. C.. R. Ember 1978b.
3. Kent 1996.
4. Schrire 1984; Myers 1988.
5. The discussion of the Australian aborigines is based on R. A. Gould 1969.
6. Burbank 1994: 23; Burbank 2004b.
7. Burch 2004; 1988.
8. Data from Textor 1967 and Service 1979.
9. Murdock and Provost 1973: 207.
10. Palsson 1988; Roscoe 2002.
11. Keeley 1991.
12. R. L. Kelly 1995: 293–315.
13. Mitchell 2004; Tollefson 2004.
14. R. B. Lee 1968; DeVore and Konner 1974.
15. C. R. Ember 1978b.
16. McCarthy and McArthur 1960.
17. R B. Lee 1979: 256–58, 278–80.
18. D. Werner 1978.
19. Textor 1967.
20. Hames 2004.

21. Chagnon 1987: 60.
22. This section is based mostly on Melvin Ember's fieldwork on the islands of American Samoa in 1955 to 1956.
23. Oliver 1974: 252–53.
24. S. S. King 1979.
25. Friedl 1962.
26. Hickey 1964: 135–65.
27. C. R. Ember 1983: 289.
28. Textor 1967; Dirks 2004; Messer 1996: 244.
29. Barlett 1989: 253–91.
30. U.S. Bureau of the Census 1993.
31. Salzman 1996.
32. Lees and Bates 1974; A. L. Johnson 2002.
33. Barth 1968.
34. Whitaker 1955; Itkonen 1951.
35. Paine 1994.
36. Textor 1967.
37. Dirks 2004.
38. Data from Textor 1967.
39. L. R. Binford 1990; see also Low 1990a: 242–43.
40. The few food collectors in cold areas relying primarily on hunting have animals (dogs, horses, reindeer) that can carry transportable housing; see L. R. Binford 1990.
41. Bailey et al. 1989.
42. Data from Textor 1967.
43. Janzen 1973. For an argument supporting the "weeding" explanation, see Carneiro 1968.
44. L. R. Binford 1971; Flannery 1971.
45. G. A. Wright 1971: 470.
46. Flannery 1986: 10–11.
47. M. N. Cohen, 1977b: 138–41; see also M. N. Cohen 1977a: 279.
48. Byrne 1987: 21–34, referred to in Blumler and Byrne 1991; D. O. Henry 1989; McCorriston and Hole 1991.
49. Henry 1989: 41.
50. McCorriston and Hole 1991.
51. Weiss and Bradley 2001.
52. Speth and Spielmann 1983.
53. Boserup 1993 [1965].
54. R. C. Hunt 2000.
55. Janzen 1973.
56. Roosevelt 1992.

Chapter 18

1. Hoebel 1968: 46–63.
2. Woodburn 1968.
3. Pryor 2005: 36.
4. Leacock and Lee 1982: 8.
5. R. Dyson-Hudson and Smith 1978; E. Andrews 1994.
6. R. Murphy 1960: 69, 142–43.
7. Salzman 1996.
8. Not all pastoralists have individual ownership. For example, the Tungus of northern Siberia have kin group ownership of reindeer. See Dowling 1975: 422.
9. Barth 1961: 124.
10. Dowling 1975.
11. Salzman 2002.
12. Creed 2004.
13. Bodley 1990: 77–93; Wilmsen 1989: 1–14.
14. Bodley 1990: 79–81.
15. Ibid., pp. 86–89.
16. Salzman 1996: 904–5.
17. Service 1979: 10.
18. E. M. Thomas 1959: 22.

19. Groger 1981.
20. Plattner 1989b: 379–96.
21. Hage and Powers 1992.
22. Carneiro 1968 cited in Sahlins 1972: 68.
23. Harris 1975: 127–28.
24. Sahlins 1972: 87 introduced North American anthropology to Alexander Chayanov and coined the phrase *Chayanov's rule.* See discussion in Durrenberger and Tannenbaum 2002.
25. Chayanov 1966: 78; for a discussion of Chayanov's analysis, see Durrenberger 1980.
26. Durrenberger and Tannenbaum. 2002.
27. Chibnik 1987.
28. Durrenberger and Tannenbaum. 2002.
29. Sahlins 1972: 101–48.
30. McClelland 1961.
31. Steward and Faron 1959: 122–25.
32. B. B. Whiting and Edwards 1988: 164.
33. Nag, White, and Peet 1978: 295–96.
34. B. B. Whiting and Edwards 1988: 97–107.
35. Draper and Cashdan 1988: 348.
36. N. B. Jones, Hawkes, and O'Connell 1996: 166–69.
37. Nag, White, and Peet 1978: 293; see also Bradley 1984–1985: 160–64.
38. C. R. Ember 1983: 291–97.
39. M. Wilson 1963.
40. Udy 1970: 35–37.
41. Sahlins 1962: 50–52.
42. Pospisil 1963: 43.
43. Udy 1970: 35–39.
44. E. A. Smith 1983: 626.
45. K. Hill et al. 1987: 17–18.
46. Sih and Milton 1985.
47. Sosis 2002.
48. Gladwin 1980: 45–85.
49. Chibnik 1980.
50. Polanyi 1957.
51. Sahlins 1972: 188–96.
52. L. Marshall 1961: 239–41.
53. The // sign in the name for the G//ana people symbolizes a click sound not unlike the sound we make when we want a horse to move faster.
54. Cashdan 1980: 116–20.
55. H. Kaplan and Hill 1985; H. Kaplan, Hill, and Hurtado 1990; Gurven, Hill, and Kaplan 2002: 114.
56. Hames 1990.
57. Gurven, Hill, and Kaplan 2002: 114.
58. H. Kaplan, Hill, and Hurtado 1990.
59. Winterhalder 1990.
60. Mooney 1978.
61. Balikci 1970 quoted in Mooney 1978: 392.
62. Mooney 1978: 392.
63. Fehr and Fischbacher 2002, Ensminger 2002; Henrich et al. 2004, as cited by Ensminger 2002.
64. Angier 2002: F1, F8.
65. Marshall 1961: 242.
66. Abler 2004.
67. N. Peacock and Bailey 2004.
68. Gibbs 1965: 223.
69. Humphrey and Hugh-Jones 1992b.
70. Blanton 2004; Gregory 1982.
71. Uberoi 1962.
72. Malinowski 1920; Uberoi 1962.
73. J. Leach 1983a: 12, 16.

74. Weiner 1976: 77–117.
75. Sahlins 1972: 196–204.
76. Pryor 1977: 204, 276.
77. Vayda, Leeds, and Smith 1962.
78. Drucker 1967.
79. M. Harris 1975: 120.
80. Tollefson 2004.
81. Vayda 1967.
82. Beattie 1960.
83. Thurnwald 1934: 125.
84. Pryor 1977: 284–86.
85. Service 1962: 145–46.
86. M. Harris 1975: 118–21.
87. Plattner 1985: viii.
88. Pryor 1977: 31–33.
89. Thurnwald 1934: 122.
90. Plattner 1985: xii.
91. Pryor 1977: 153–83; Stodder (1995: 205) finds that monetary trade is more likely with capital-intensive agriculture.
92. Pryor 1977: 109–11.
93. B. Foster 1974.
94. Pryor 1977: 125–48.
95. E. Wolf 1955: 452–71; Carrasco 1961.
96. W. R. Smith 1977; M. Harris 1964.
97. Ibid.

Chapter 19

1. In an analysis of many native societies in the New World, Gary Feinman and Jill Neitzel argue that egalitarian and rank societies ("tribes" and "chiefdoms," respectively) are not systematically distinguishable. See their "Too Many Types: An Overview of Sedentary Prestate Societies in the Americas," in Michael B. Schiffer, ed., *Advances in Archaeological Method and Theory* Vol. 7 (Orlando, FL: Academic Press, 1984), p. 57.
2. Fried 1967: 33.
3. Boehm 1993: 230–31; Boehm 1999.
4. M. G. Smith 1966: 152.
5. Salzman 1999.
6. D. Mitchell 2004.
7. Drucker 1965: 56–64.
8. Service 1978: 249.
9. Sahlins 1958: 80–81.
10. Betzig 1988.
11. W. L. Warner and Lunt 1941.
12. Lynd and Lynd 1929; and Lynd and Lynd 1937.
13. Brittain 1978.
14. Higley 1995: 1–47.
15. Argyle 1994.
16. S. R. Barrett 1994: 17–19, 34–35.
17. Ibid., p. 155.
18. Stille 2001: A17, A19.
19. Treiman and Ganzeboom 1990: 117; Featherman and Hauser 1978: 4, 481.
20. Argyle 1994: 36–37, 178.
21. S. R. Barrett 1994: 17, 41.
22. K. Phillips 1990; U.S. Bureau of the Census 1993; *New York Times* International 1997: A26; Johnston 1999: 16.
23. Durrenberger 2001b, who refers to Goldschmidt 1999 and Newman 1988, 1993.
24. Scott and Leonhardt 2005.
25. S. R. Barrett 1994: 17, 41.
26. Klass 2004.
27. Ruskin 1963: 296–314.

28. O. Lewis 1958.
29. Kristof 1995: A18.
30. For more information about caste in Japan, see Berreman 1973 and 1972: 403–14.
31. Kristof 1995; Kristof 1997.
32. For more information about caste in Rwanda, see Berreman 1973, and 1972.
33. "Book of the Year (1995): World Affairs: RWANDA," and "Book of the Year (1995): Race and Ethnic Relations.
34. Berreman 1960: 120–27.
35. O. Patterson 1982: vii–xiii, 105.
36. Pryor 1977: 219.
37. Euripides 1937: 52.
38. Nadel 1942.
39. Lassiter et al. 2004: 49–50.
40. Ibid: 59–67.
41. Pryor 1977: 217–47.
42. Marks 1994, 33; Shanklin 1993: 15–17.
43. Molnar 1998: 19.
44. Brace et al. 1993: 17–19.
45. Brooks, Jackson, and Grinker 1993: 11.
46. Brace et al. 1993: 19.
47. M. D. Williams 2004.
48. S. S. Friedman 1980: 206.
49. M. H. Ross 2004a.
50. Marks 1994: 32.
51. Armelagos and Goodman 1998: 365.
52. O. Patterson 2000.
53. M. Nash 1989: 2.
54. Ibid., p. 10.
55. Barth 1994: 27.
56. Yinger 1994: 169.
57. Ibid., pp. 169–71.
58. Ibid., pp. 216–17.
59. Benjamin 1991; see also M. D. Williams 2004.
60. Flannery 1972.
61. Data from Textor 1967.
62. Ibid.
63. Lenski 1984: 308–18.
64. Treiman and Ganzeboom 1990: 117; Cutright 1967: 564.
65. Sahlins 1958.
66. Ibid., p. 4.
67. Sahlins 1972.
68. Lenski 1984.
69. Gilman 1990.
70. Fried 1967: 201ff; and Harner 1975.
71. Meek 1940: 149–50.

Chapter 20

1. Leibowitz 1978: 43–44.
2. Schlegel 1989: 266; Epstein 1988: 5–6; Chafetz 1990: 28.
3. Jacobs and Roberts 1989.
4. Segal 2004; Segal also cites the work of W. Williams 1992.
5. Lang 1999: 93–94; Blackwood 1984b.
6. Wikan 1982: 168–186.
7. Stini 1971.
8. Frayer and Wolpoff 1985.
9. For reviews of theories and research on sexual dimorphism and possible genetic and cultural determinants of variation in degree of dimorphism over time and place, see Frayer and Wolpoff 1985 and Gray 1985: 201–209, 217–25.
10. J. K. Brown 1970b: 1074.

11. Among the Aché hunter-gatheres of Paraguay, women collect the type of honey produced by stingless bees (men collect other honey); this division of labor is consistent with the compatibility theory. See Hurtado et al. 1985: 23.
12. Murdock and Provost 1973: 213; Byrne 1994.
13. R. O'Brian 1999: 30–42.
14. D. R. White, Burton, and Brudner 1977: 1–24.
15. Mukhopadhyay and Higgins 1988: 473.
16. J. K. Brown 1970b: 1073–78; and D. R. White, Burton, and Brudner 1977.
17. Nerlove 1974.
18. N. E. Levine 1988.
19. M. J. Goodman et al. 1985.
20. Noss and Hewlett 2001.
21. C.R. Ember 1983: 288–89.
22. Mead 1950 [originally published 1935]: 180–84.
23. Rivers 1967 [originally published 1906]: 567.
24. M. Ember and Ember 1971: 573, table 1.
25. Schlegel and Barry 1986.
26. Boserup 1970: 22–25; see also Schlegel and Barry 1986: 144–45.
27. Boserup 1970: 22–25.
28. Ibid., pp. 31–34.
29. C. R. Ember 1983: 286–87; data from Murdock and Provost 1973: 212; Bradley 1995.
30. C. R. Ember 1983.
31. Ibid.
32. Ibid., pp. 287–93.
33. M. Ember and Ember 1971: 579–80.
34. Ibid., p. 581; see also Sanday 1973: 1684.
35. Nerlove 1974.
36. Schlegel and Barry 1986.
37. Whyte 1978a: 217.
38. Nussbaum 1995: 2, based on data from Human Development Report 1993.
39. Whyte 1978a, D. B. Adams 1983: 196–212.
40. J. K. Brown 1970a: 151–67.
41. Sanday 1974; and Divale and Harris 1976.
42. Quinn 1977: 189–90.
43. Graham 1979.
44. D. Werner 1982; and Stogdill 1974 cited in ibid.; see also Handwerker and Crosbie 1982.
45. Draper 1975: 103.
46. D. Werner 1984.
47. M. H. Ross 1986.
48. This description is based on the fieldwork of Elizabeth and Robert Fearnea (1956–1958), as reported in M. K. Martin and Voorhies 1975: 304–31.
49. Begler 1978.
50. Ibid. See also Whyte 1978a: 229–32.
51. Whyte 1978b: 95–120; see also Quinn 1977.
52. Whyte 1978b: 124–29, 145; see also Sanday 1973.
53. Whyte 1978b: 129–30.
54. J. K. Brown 1970a.
55. Whyte 1978b: 135–36.
56. Ibid., p. 135.
57. Doyle 2005.
58. Quinn 1977: 85; see also Etienne and Leacock 1980: 19–20.
59. Chafetz 1990: 11–19.
60. B. B. Whiting and Edwards 1973: 171–88.
61. R. L. Munroe et al. 2000: 8–9.
62. Maccoby and Jacklin 1974.
63. For a more extensive discussion of behavior differences and possible explanations of them, see C. R. Ember 1981: 531–80.
64. B. B. Whiting and Edwards 1973.
65. For references to this research, see C. R. Ember 1981: 559.
66. Rubin, Provenzano, and Haskett 1974: 512–19.
67. For a discussion of this evidence, see Ellis 1986: 525–27; C. R. Ember 1981: 531–80.
68. For example, Ellis 1986 considers the evidence for the biological view of aggression "beyond reasonable dispute."
69. For a discussion of other possibilities, see C. R. Ember 1981.
70. Rohner 1976: 57–72.
71. B. B. Whiting and Whiting 1975; see also B. B. Whiting and Edwards 1988: 273.
72. C. R. Ember 1973: 424–39.
73. B. B. Whiting and Edwards 1973: 175–79; see also Maccoby and Jacklin 1974.
74. Burbank 1994.
75. Heise 1967: 726–39.
76. C. S. Ford and Beach 1951: 191.
77. O. Lewis 1951: 397.
78. Farley 1996: 60.
79. C. S. Ford and Beach 1951: 23–25, 68–71.
80. Ibid., pp. 40–41, 73.
81. Broude 2004b.
82. C. S. Ford and Beach 1951: 82–83.
83. Broude and Greene 1976: 409–29.
84. Kluckhohn 1948: 101.
85. M. Hunt 1974: 254–57; Lewin 1994.
86. Broude 1980: 184.
87. C. S. Ford and Beach 1951: 114.
88. Jankowiak, Nell and Buckmaster 2002.
89. Lang 1999: 97 citing Thomas 1993.
90. J. Morris 1938: 191.
91. Underhill 1938: 117, 186.
92. 'Abd Allah 1917: 7, 20.
93. Cardoso and Werner 2004.
94. R. C. Kelly 1974.
95. Cardoso and Werner 2004.
96. Blackwood and Wieringa 1999: 49; Blackwood 1984a.
97. Cardoso and Werner 2004: 207.
98. Data from Textor 1967.
99. W. N. Stephens 1972: 1–28.
100. Broude 1976: 243.
101. D. Werner 1979; D. Werner 1975.
102. D. Werner 1979: 345–62; see also D. Werner 1975, p. 36.
103. D. Werner 1979: 358.
104. Data from Textor 1967.
105. Schlegel 1991: 719–34.

Chapter 21

1. W. N. Stephens 1963: 5.
2. Murdock 1949: 8.
3. Stephens 1963, 170–71.
4. Hoebel 1960: 77.
5. Evans-Pritchard 1970: 1428–34.
6. O'Brien 1977; Oboler 1980.
7. Oboler 2004. p. 104
8. Murdock 1949: 7–8.
9. Ibid., pp. 9–10.
10. See, for example, Linton, 1936: 135–36.
11. M. Ember and C. R. Ember 1979.
12. Ibid.
13. Marlowe 2003: 221–223.

14. M. Ember and C. R. Ember 1979.
15. Graburn 1969: 188–200.
16. Malinowski 1932: 77.
17. Ibid., p. 88.
18. J. W. M. Whiting 1941: 125.
19. Doyle 2004.
20. Service 1978.
21. LeVine and LeVine 1963: 65. p. 84
22. Ibid.
23. For an extensive discussion of the symbolism of Rotuman weddings, see A. Howard and Rensel 2004. p. 69
24. Schlegel and Eloul 1987: 119.
25. Schlegel and Eloul 1988: 295, table 1. We used the data to calculate the frequency of various types of economic transaction in a worldwide sample of 186 societies.
26. Oboler 2004. p. 104
27. Frake 1960.
28. Mead 1931: 206–208.
29. Borgerhoff Mulder, George-Cramer, Eshleman, and Ortolani 2001.
30. Schlegel and Eloul 1988: 298–99.
31. Pryor 1977: 363–64.
32. Ibid.
33. R. F. Spencer 1968: 136.
34. Schlegel and Eloul 1988: 296–97.
35. Ibid.
36. Ibid.
37. Radcliffe-Brown 1922: 73.
38. Murdock 1967; Goody 1973: 17–21.
39. Pryor 1977: 363–65; Schlegel and Eloul 1988: 296–99.
40. Research is reported in Gaulin and Boster 1990: 994–1005. The first theory discussed herein is associated with Boserup 1970. The second is put forward by Gaulin and Boster.
41. Schlegel and Eloul 1988 following Goody 1973: 20.
42. Barth 1961: 18–19; as reported in (and coded as indirect dowry by) Schlegel and Eloul 1987: 131. p. 8
43. Middleton 1962: 606.
44. Durham 1991: 293–94; citing research by Hopkins 1980.
45. Westermarck 1894.
46. Talmon 1964: 492.
47. Ibid., p. 504.
48. A. Wolf 1968: 864.
49. Wolf and Chieh-shan Huang 1980: 159, 170, 185.
50. H. Parker and S. Parker 1986: 531–49.
51. M. Ember 1975; Durham 1991: 341–57.
52. For a discussion of mechanisms that might lead to sexual aversion, see S. Parker 1976, 1984.
53. Freud 1943.
54. Malinowski 1927.
55. Quoted in L. A. White 1949: 313.
56. Kang 1979: 85–99.
57. Stern 1973: 494–95, as cited in M. Ember 1975: 256. For a review of the theory and evidence, see Durham 1991.
58. Seemanova 1971: 108–28, as cited in Durham 1991: 305–309.
59. Durham 1991: 305–309.
60. Ibid., pp. 346–52.
61. Firth 1957: 287–88, cited (somewhat differently) in Durham 1991: 349–50.
62. A mathematical model of early mating systems suggests that people may have noticed the harmful effects of inbreeding once populations began to expand as a result of agriculture; people therefore may have deliberately adopted the incest taboo to solve the problem of inbreeding. See

M. Ember 1975. For a similar subsequent suggestion, see Durham 1991: 331–39.
63. Goode 1982: 61–62.
64. C. S. Ford 1941: 149.
65. A. Howard and Rensel 2004.
66. S. S. Davis 2004.
67. Goode 1970: 210.
68. Lingenfelter 2004.
69. MacDonald and Hewlett 1999: 504–506.
70. M. Ember 1975: 262, table 3.
71. Busby 2004.
72. M. Ember 1975: 260–69; see also Durham 1991: 341–57.
73. Murdock 1949: 29.
74. Bogoras 1909, cited in W. Stephens 1963: 195.
75. Oliver 1955: 352–53.
76. Ibid., pp. 223–24, quoted in W. Stephens 1963: 58.
77. Mead 1950: 101.
78. The discussion of these customs is based on W. Stephens 1963: 63–67.
79. Kilbride and Kilbride 1990: 202–206.
80. C. Anderson 2000: 102–103.
81. Linton 1936: 183.
82. J. W. M. Whiting 1964.
83. Ibid., p. 518.
84. Ibid., pp. 516–17.
85. M. Ember 1974b.
86. M. Ember 1984–1985. The statistical relationship between late age of marriage for men and polygyny was first reported by Witkowski 1975.
87. M. Ember 1974b: 202–205.
88. M. Ember 1984–1985. For other predictors of polygyny, see D. R. White and Burton 1988.
89. Sellen and Hruschka 2004.
90. Low 1990b: 325–39.
91. Coult and Habenstein 1965; Murdock 1957.
92. M. C. Goldstein 1987: 39.
93. Stephens 1963: 45.
94. Hiatt 1980.
95. M. Goldstein 1987. Formerly, in feudal Tibet, a class of serfs who owned small parcels of land also practiced polyandry. Goldstein suggested that a shortage of land would explain their polyandry too. See M. C. Goldstein 1971.
96. For example, see M. L. Cohen 1976.
97. Pasternak 1976: 96.
98. Coult and Habenstein 1965.
99. Mead 1928, quoted in Stephens 1963: 134–35.
100. Ibid., p. 135.
101. Nimkoff and Middleton 1960.
102. Pasternak, Ember, and Ember 1976: 109–23.
103. Block 1983.

Chapter 22
1. Coult and Habenstein 1965; Murdock 1957.
2. Percentages calculated from Coult and Habenstein 1965
3. L. Bohannan and P. Bohannan 1953.
4. J. H. Moore and Campbell 2002; Ensor 2003.
5. Lowe 2002.
6. J. D. Freeman 1961.
7. Jarvenpa 2004.
8. Murdock 1949: 49–50.
9. C. R. Ember, M. Ember, and Pasternak 1974: 84–89.
10. Pospisil 1963.
11. Schneider 1961a.
12. M. Ember and Ember 1971: 581.

13. Schneider 1961b.
14. Goodenough 1951: 145.
15. Coult and Habenstein 1965.
16. Data from Textor 1967.
17. Fortes 1949.
18. Davenport 1959.
19. The description of the Samoan descent system is based on M. Ember's 1955 to 1956 fieldwork. See also M. Ember 1959: 573–77; and Davenport 1959.
20. M. Ember 1967.
21. M. Ember and C. R. Ember. 1971. See also Divale 1974.
22. M. Ember and Ember 1971: 583–85; and Divale 1974.
23. M. Ember and Ember 1971. For a different theory—that matrilocal residence precedes, rather than follows, the development of purely external warfare—see Divale 1974.
24. Helms 2004; see also M. Ember and Ember 1971.
25. Service 1962: 137.
26. C. R. Ember and M. Ember 1972.
27. C. R. Ember 1975.
28. M. Ember 1974a: 203–209.
29. Data from Textor 1967.
30. C. R. Ember, Ember, and Pasternak 1974.
31. The importance of warfare and competition as factors in the formation of unilineal descent groups is also suggested by Service 1962 and Sahlins 1961: 332–45.
32. C. R. Ember and Ember 1972.
33. C. R. Ember and Ember 1997.
34. See, for example, Murdock 1949: 199–222.
35. Reported in Textor 1967.
36. Textor 1967.
37. Murdock 1949: 125.
38. Textor 1967.
39. L. A. White 1939.
40. Goody 1970.
41. Pasternak 1976: 142.
42. Textor 1967.
43. Ibid.
44. This conjecture is based on unpublished cross-cultural research by the Embers.

Chapter 23

1. N. Dyson-Hudson 1966: 155. This section draws from this source.
2. This section is based on Maybury-Lewis 1967.
3. Leis 1974. p. 83
4. Meggitt 1964.
5. Ibid., p. 207. For why men in some societies may fear sex with women, see C. R. Ember 1978a.
6. Meggitt 1964: 218.
7. Bellman 1984: 8, 25–28, 33.
8. Ibid., p. 8.
9. Ibid., pp. 8, 80–88.
10. Ibid., pp. 33, 80; also Bledsoe 1980: 67.
11. K. Little 1965/1966: 349–65; and 1966: 62–71; Bledsoe 1980: 68–70.
12. Ericksen 1989.
13. Leis 1974.
14. Hoebel 1960.
15. W. K. Powers and Powers 2004. p. 112
16. R. H. Thompson 2004.
17. Mangin 1965: 311–23. p. 89.
18. Okamura 1983.
19. R. H. Thompson 2004. p. 139
20. K. Little 1965; and Meillassoux 1968.

21. K. Little 1957: 582.
22. Ibid., p. 583.
23. Ardener 1995b: 1.
24. Ardener 1995a: appendix.
25. See the many chapters in Ardener and Burman 1995 for examples.
26. Fessler 2002.
27. N. Nelson 1995. Quote on page 58.
28. Bortei-Doku and Ernest Aryeetey 1995.
29. Fessler 2002.
30. Light and Deng 1995.
31. Warry 1986.
32. Ervin 1987.
33. Caulkins 2004.
34. Naroll 1983: 74–75.
35. Eisenstadt 1954: 102.
36. Bernardi 1952.
37. Ritter 1980.
38. Ibid.
39. For an explanation of age-sets among North American Plains Indians, see Hanson 1988.

Chapter 24

1. Service 1962.
2. Schrive 1984b; see also Leacock and Lee 1982: 8.
3. Service 1962: 109.
4. Briggs 1974.
5. Mathiassen 1928: 213, as seen in Weyer 1932.
6. Service 1962: 114–15.
7. Bohannan 1954: 3.
8. Sahlins 1961: 342.
9. R. C. Kelly 1985: 1.
10. Sahlins 1961: 345.
11. N. Dyson-Hudson 1966: chapters 5 and 6.
12. Ibid.
13. Sahlins 1962: 293–94.
14. Sahlins 1963: 295.
15. Sahlins 1983: 519.
16. Sahlins 1963: 297.
17. Carneiro 1970: 733.
18. Weber 1947: 154.
19. Lightfoot 2005.
20. Ferguson 2004.
21. Wiberg 1983: 43–65. p. 153
22. For an extensive review of the various theories about legitimacy, see R. Cohen 1988: 1–3.
23. Finley 1983.
24. Carcopino 1940: 18–20.
25. Our discussion of Nupe is based on S. F. Nadel 1935: 257–303.
26. M. Ember 1963: 228–48.
27. Textor 1967.
28. M. Ember 1963.
29. Textor 1967.
30. Naroll 1961: 15–39. See also Ross 1981.
31. M. Ember 1963: 244–46.
32. Service 1962; see also Braun and Plog 1982: 504–25; Haas 1990a: 171–89.
33. A. Johnson and Earle 1987: 158; Carneiro 1990.
34. Service 1962: 112, 145.
35. Feinman and Nietzel 1984: 39–102.
36. For more details, see Chapter 11.
37. McNeill 1976.
38. Carneiro 1978: 215. p. 23

39. Textor 1967.
40. Carneiro 1978; Hart 1948; Naroll 1967; Marano 1973: 35–40. (cf. Peregrine, Ember, and Ember 2004 and other article in Graber 2004.)
41. For a review of the descriptive literature until the late 1970s, see Vincent 1978.
42. D. Werner 1982.
43. Kracke 1979: 232.
44. D. Werner 1982.
45. Sahlins 1963.
46. Kracke 1979: 41.
47. Lederman 1990.
48. Brandewie 1991.
49. Lepowsky 1990.
50. Ross 1988: 73. The discussion in this section draws mostly from Ibid., pp. 73–89, and from Ross 2004b. p. 119
51. Bondarenko and Korotayev 2000; Korotayev and Bondarenko 2000.
52. For studies of international relations that support these conclusions, see footnotes 2 and 3 in C. R. Ember, Ember, and Russett 1992; see also chapter 3 in Russett and Oneal 2001.
53. C. R. Ember, Ember, and Russett 1992.
54. Rummel 2002b.
55. Scaglion 2004b. p. 123
56. Hoebel 1968: 4, quoting S. P. Simpson and Field 1946: 858.
57. Fry and Björkqvist 1997.
58. D. Black 1993: 79–83.
59. Ross 1988.
60. Boas 1888: 668.
61. Otterbein 1986: 107.
62. Archer and Gartner 1984: 118–39.
63. Scaglion 2004b, Black 1993 83–86.
64. Ibid.
65. Evans-Pritchard 1940: 291. The discussion of the Nuer follows this source. p. 44
66. Hickson 1986: 283–94.
67. Ibid.; and Koch et al. 1977: 279.
68. J. M. Roberts 1967: 169. p. 116
69. Musil 1928: 430, as cited in Roberts 1967: 169–70. p. 116
70. Roberts 1967: 192.
71. Hoebel 1968: chapter 9.
72. Schwartz 1954: 475.
73. Textor 1967.
74. Masumura 1977: 388–99. p. 123
75. Scaglion 2004b; Black 1993; Newman 1983: 131.
76. C. R. Ember and Ember 1994.
77. Newman 1983: 131.
78. Gubser 1965: 151.
79. Otterbein and Otterbein 1965: 1476.
80. D. R. White 1988: 529–58.
81. Patterson 1982: 345–52.
82. Gat 1999; 373, as referred to in Wadley 2003.
83. Heider 1970: 105–11; Heider 1979: 88–99.
84. M. Ember and Ember 1992: 188–89.
85. C. R. Ember and Ember 1992; M. Ember 1982. For a discussion of how Dani warfare seems to be motivated mainly by economic considerations, see Shankman 1991. B. W. Kang 2000: 878–79, finds a strong correlation between environmental stress and warfare frequency in Korean history.
86. Otterbein 1970.
87. C. R. Ember and Ember 1992; see also Otterbein 1970 and Loftin 1971.
88. C. R. Ember 1974: 135–49.
89. Otterbein 1968: 283; Ross 1985.
90. Divale and Harris 1976: 521–38; see also Gibbons 1993.
91. C. R. Ember and Ember 1992: 251–52.
92. Russett and Oneal 2001: 89.
93. Ibid.; pp. 145–48.
94. Singer 1980: 349–67.

Chapter 25

1. Dentan 1968: 55–56.
2. Chagnon 1987.
3. Quoted in Otto Klineberg, "Foreword," in Segall 1979: v.
4. Donald E. Brown 1991.
5. C. C. Moore 1997, pp. 8–9; see also C. C. Moore et al. 1999: 529–46.
6. M. Mead 1961.
7. Mahnowski 1927.
8. D. Freeman 1983. For reasons to be skeptical about Freeman's criticism, see M. Ember 1985: 906–909.
9. Spiro 1982.
10. Schlegel and Barry 1991: 44.
11. Piaget 1970: 703–32. p. 110.
12. Berry et al. 1992: 40.
13. Ibid., pp. 40–41.
14. Dasen and Heron 1981: 305–306.
15. C. R. Ember 1977; and Rogoff 1981.
16. Price-Williams 1961.
17. Segall et al. 1990: 149.
18. Rogoff 1981: 264–67.
19. Weisner, Bausano, and Kornfein 1983.
20. J. W. M. Whiting and Child 1953: 69–71.
21. Weisner, Bausano, and Kornfein 1983: 291; Hewlett 2004.
22. See the research cited in Hewlett 2004; See also Small 1997.
23. Ibid.
24. Chagnon 1983: 115.
25. Dentan 1968: 61.
26. Du Bois 1944.
27. Barnouw 1985: 118.
28. R. H. Munroe and Robert L. Munroe 1980: 295–315.
29. Rohner 1975: 97–105.
30. See research reported in Rohner and Britner 2002: 16–47.
31. Rohner 1975: 112–16.
32. B. B. Whiting and Whiting 1975: 94. See also R. H. Munroe, Munroe, and Shimmin 1984.
33. B. B. Whiting and Edwards 1988: 265.
34. R. L. Munroe, Munroe, and Shimmin 1984: 374–76; see also C. R. Ember 1973.
35. B. B. Whiting and Whiting 1975: 179.
36. B. B. Whiting 1988: 35.
37. Ibid., pp. 152–63; and C. R. Ember 1981: 560.
38. C. R. Ember 1977; Rogoff 1981.
39. Rogoff 1981: 285.
40. For how school experiences may improve particular cognitive skills, rather than higher levels of cognitive development in general, see Rogoff 1990: 46–49.
41. Irwin, Schafer, and Feiden 1974: 407–23.
42. Luria 1976: 108; quoted in Rogoff 1981: 254.
43. Scribner and Cole 1981; Berry and Bennett 1989: 429–50, as reported in Berry et al. 1992: 123–24.
44. Godoy et al. 2004; Bowles, Gintis, and Osborne 2001.
45. Geertz 1984: 123–36.
46. Although Melford Spiro does not believe that this Western/non-Western pattern exists, the reader is referred to his article for the many references to the works of those who do (Spiro 1993).

47. For a review of the literature on "individualism" versus "collectivism," which is mostly based on studies of educated individuals from industrialized cultures, see Triandis 1995. Using data collected by anthropologists on mostly preindustrial cultures, Carpenter (2000: 38–56) finds support for the idea that the concept of self differs in individualist as compared with collectivist cultures.
48. Bachnik 1992.
49. Stairs 1992.
50. Spiro 1993.
51. Research reported in Hollan 1992: 289–90.
52. For a review of the concept of ethnotheories about parenting, see Super and Harkness 1997.
53. Harkness and Super 1997 in Small 1997: 45.
54. Weisner 2004.
55. Straus 2001.
56. J. W. M. Whiting and Child 1953: 310.
57. Edgerton 1992: 206.
58. R. A. LeVine 1988: 4–6; see also discussion in Hewlett 2004.
59. Barry, Child, and Bacon 1959: 51–63. For a somewhat different analysis of the data used in ibid. see Hendrix 1985.
60. Hoffman 1988: 101–103.
61. Minturn and Lambert 1964: 289.
62. J. W. M. Whiting 1959: 5–9.
63. Edgerton 1971.
64. Berry 1976.
65. Witkin 1967.
66. Dawson 1967; and Berry 1971.
67. C. R. Ember 2004; Halpern 2000: 110–112.
68. D. G. Freedman 1979.
69. Ibid., pp. 40–41. For a discussion of possible genetic influences on the social environment, see Scarr and McCartney 1983.
70. See Dasen, Berry, and Sartorius 1988 for references to research, particularly by Barrett 1984.
71. Dasen, Berry, and Sartorius 1988: 117–18, 126–28.
72. Bolton 1973.
73. Benedict 1959.
74. Elwin 1955; cited in Barnouw 1985: 356.
75. Kleinman 1988: 167–85.
76. McClelland 1961.
77. LeVine 1966: 2.
78. Kardiner 1946: 471.
79. J. W. M. Whiting and Child 1953: 32–38.
80. J. M. Roberts and Sutton-Smith 1962: 178.
81. J. M. Roberts Arth, and Bush (1959) first established the relationship between games of strategy and social stratification and political complexity. Chick (1998) has replicated those findings.
82. R. V. Burton and Whiting 1961. See also R. L. Munroe, Munroe, and Whiting 1981. For a review of cross-cultural research on initiation, see Burbank 2004a.

Chapter 26

1. Tylor 1979.
2. Marett 1909.
3. Guthrie 1993.
4. Freud 1967; Badcook 1988: 126–27, 133–36.
5. Malinowski 1939: 959; Malinowski 1948: 50–51.
6. W. James 1902.
7. Jung 1938.
8. Fromm 1950.
9. Maslow 1964.
10. Durkheim 1961.
11. Swanson 1969: 1–31.
12. A. Wallace 1966: 60–61.
13. Malefijt 1968: 153.
14. Ray 1954: 172–89.
15. Rosenblatt, Walsh, and Jackson 1976: 51.
16. Ibid., p. 55.
17. Swanson 1969: 97–108; see also Sheils 1975: 427–40.
18. Middleton 1971: 488.
19. Spiro and D'Andrade 1958: 456–66.
20. Lambert, Triandis, and Wolf 1959: 162–69; Rohner 1975: 108.
21. H. G. Barnett 1960: 79–85.
22. Swanson 1969: 56.
23. Ibid., pp. 55–81; see also W. D. Davis 1971. Peregrine (1996: 84–112) replicated Swanson's finding for North American societies.
24. Textor 1967; R. Underhill 1975.
25. Geertz 1966.
26. Swanson 1969: 153–74.
27. Bunzel 1971: 493–95.
28. Gossen 1979: 116–28.
29. Dickson et al. 2005.
30. A. Wallace 1966: 52–67.
31. Winkelman 1986: 178–83.
32. Bourguignon 1973a.
33. Bourguignon and Evascu 1977; Winkelman 1986: 196–98.
34. Kehoe and Giletti 1981.
35. Raybeck 1998, referring to Raybeck, Shoobe, and Grauberger 1989: 139–61.
36. Bourguignon 2004: 572.
37. Winkleman and Peck 2004.
38. O. K. Moore 1957.
39. Sheils 1980.
40. M. Adler 1986: 4–5.
41. Evans-Pritchard 1979: 362–66.
42. Swanson 1969: 150; see also H. R. Trevor-Roper 1971: 444–49.
43. Swanson 1969: 150–51.
44. Caporael: 1976; Matossian 1982; and Matossian 1989: 70–80. For possible reasons to dismiss the ergot theory, see Spanos 1983.
45. Harner 1972b: 127–50.
46. B. B. Whiting 1950: 36–37; see also Swanson 1969: pp. 137–52, 240–41.
47. Winkelman 1986a.
48. Ibid., pp. 28–29.
49. Kriecht 2003: 11.
50. Harner and Doore 1987: 3, 8–9; Noll 1987: 49; Krippner 1987: 128.
51. de Laguna 1972: 701C.
52. See Krippner 1987: 126–27; Noll 1987: 49–50.
53. Winkelman 1986: 27–28.
54. Ibid., p. 27.
55. Ibid., pp. 35–37.
56. M. Harris 1966: 51–63.
57. A. Wallace 1966: 30.
58. A. Wallace 1970: 239.
59. The Quakers, long-time neighbors and trusted advisers of the Seneca, took pains not to interfere with Seneca religion, principles, and attitudes.
60. Worsley 1957: 12.
61. Ibid., pp. 11, 115.
62. Ibid., p. 122.

63. Aberle 1971.
64. Knauft 1978.

Chapter 27

1. Maquet 1986: 9.
2. R. L. Anderson 1989: 21.
3. R. P. Armstrong 1989: 11.
4. R. L. Anderson 1990: 278; R. L. Anderson 1992.
5. Malin 1986: 27.
6. Anderson 1989: 11.
7. Gibbs 1965: 222.
8. Anderson 1990: 225–26.
9. Sweeney 1952: 335.
10. Fischer 1961: 80.
11. Ibid., p. 81.
12. Ibid., p. 83.
13. Dressler and Robbins 1975.
14. Lomax 1968: 117–28.
15. © 1945 Walt Disney Music Company; words by Ray Gilbert, music by Allie Wrubel.
16. Lomax 1968: 166–67.
17. Ibid., pp. 167–69.
18. Ayres 1973.
19. Ayres 1968.
20. E. Erickson 1968.
21. For a study of variation in music within India that does not support some of Lomax's findings, see E. O. Henry 1976.
22. Dundes 1989: viii.
23. Bauman 1992a.
24. Brunvand 1993: 14.
25. Ibid., p. 296.
26. Kluckhohn 1965.
27. As discussed R. A. Segal 1987: 1–2.
28. J. Campbell 1949: 30, as quoted in R. A. Segal 1987: 4.
29. S. Thompson 1965: 449.
30. Dundes 1965a: 206–15 reported in F. W. Young 1970.
31. Carroll 1979.
32. G. O. Wright 1954.
33. A. Cohen 1990.
34. S. Price 1989: 82–85.
35. Ibid., pp. 102–103.
36. Ibid., pp. 56–67.
37. Ibid., p. 112.
38. J. A. Warner 1986: 172–75.
39. Price 1989: 77–81.
40. Layton 1992: 93–94.
41. Ibid., pp. 31, 109.
42. J. C. H. King 1986.
43. J. A. Warner 1986: 178–86.
44. Merrill 1987.

Chapter 28

1. Linton 1936: 306.
2. Ibid., pp. 310–11.
3. Silver 1981.
4. Greenfield, Maynard, and Childs 2000.
5. Rogers 1983: 263–69.
6. Cancian 1980.
7. Hewlett and Cavalli-Sforza 1986; Cavalli-Sforza and Feldman 1981.
8. Valente 1995: 21.
9. W. Cohen 1995.
10. Linton 1936: 326–27.
11. Printing, Typography, and Photoengraving 1998; "Paper," 1980.
12. Linton 1936: 338–39.
13. G. M. Foster 1962: 26.
14. Bodley 1990: 7.
15. Pelto and Müller-Wille 1987: 207–43.
16. Bodley 1990: 38–41.
17. T. Kroeber 1967: 45–47.
18. Schrauf 1999.
19. The historical information we refer to comes from a book by Nevins 1927. For how radical the American Revolution was, see G. S. Wood 1992.
20. Brinton 1938.
21. Paige 1975.
22. Roth 2001.
23. Boyd and Richerson 1985: 106.
24. Ibid., p. 135.
25. D. T. Campbell 1965: 19–49. See also Boyd and Richerson 1985 and Dunham 1991. p. 22.
26. McNeill 1967: 283–87.
27. See e.g., Gross et al. 1979.
28. The description of Tikopia is based on Firth 1959: Chapters 5, 6, 7, and 9, passim.
29. Most of this discussion is based on R. F. Murphy and Steward 1956.
30. Burkhalter and Murphy 1989.
31. E. Wolf 1966: 3–4.
32. Hobsbawm 1970.
33. Gross and Underwood 1971.
34. D. O. Larson, Johnson, and Michaelsen 1994.
35. Discussion is based on Firth 1970.
36. Ibid., p. 387.
37. Ibid., p. 418.
38. Mason 1962.
39. Antoun 2001.
40. Nagata 2001.
41. Antoun 2001: 17–18.
42. Ibid., p. 45.
43. Russett 1993: 10–11, 14, 138.
44. Bernard and Pelto 1987a: 367.
45. Pelto and Müller-Wille 1987: 237.
46. J. D. Hill 1996: 1.
47. Bilby 1996: 127–28, referring to Hoogbergen 1990: 23–51.
48. Bilby 1996: 128–37.
49. Sattler 1996: 42.
50. Ibid., pp. 50–51.
51. Ibid., p. 54.
52. Ibid., pp. 58–59.
53. Bestor 2001: 76.
54. Trouillot 2001: 128.
55. Durrenberger 2001a; see also Hannerz 1996.
56. Traphagan and Brown 2002.
57. Trouillot 2001: 128.
58. Bradsher 2002: 3.
59. Yergin 2002: A29.
60. G. Thompson 2002: A3.
61. Sengupta 2002: A3.
62. Conklin 2002.
63. Kottak 1996: 136, 153. p. 79.
64. Roosens 1989: 9.

65. Cashdan 2001: 968–91. p. 24.
66. C. R. Ember and Levinson 1991.

Chapter 29

1. Kushner 1991.
2. Mead 1978: 426–29.
3. Frankel and Trend 1991: 177.
4. Hackenberg 1988: 172.
5. Kushner 1991.
6. Partridge and Eddy 1987: 25–26.
7. Ibid., pp. 31–40.
8. Mead 1977: 149.
9. Partridge and Eddy 1987: 31–40.
10. G. M. Foster 1969: 200.
11. Partridge and Eddy 1987: 52.
12. "Appendix C: Statements on Ethics. . ." 2002 and "Appendix I: Revised Principles. . ." 2002.
13. "Appendix A: Report of the Committee on Ethics. . ." 2002 and "Appendix F: Professional and Ethical Responsibilities. . ." 2002.
14. "Appendix H: National Association of Practicing Anthropologists' Ethical Guidelines. . ." 2002.
15. Scudder 1978.
16. Ibid., p. 204ff.
17. A good summary of this extraordinary case was put together by Slayman, 1997.
18. Public Law 101–601 (25 U.S.C. 3001–3013).
19. Picchi 1991: 26–38; for a more general description of the Bakairi, see Picchi 2004.
20. Murray 1997: 131.
21. Niehoff 1966: 255–67.
22. G. M. Foster 1969: 8–9.
23. Jelliffe and Jelliffe 1975.
24. W. H. Fisher 1994.
25. G. M. Foster 1969: 122–23.
26. Coreil 1989: 149–50.
27. Rogers 1983: 321–31.
28. Bryant and Bailey 1990.
29. Niehoff 1966: 219–24.
30. Coreil 1989: 155.
31. Warren 1989.
32. Goodenough 1963: 416.
33. Warry 1990: 61–62.
34. J. Fisher 1996: 57.
35. Ibid., p. 91; data from Kenya referred to in Oxby 1983.
36. Ravesloot 1997: 174.
37. Anyon and Ferguson 1995.
38. Zeder 1997.
39. Manhein 1999.
40. Joans 1997.
41. "Association Business: Clyde Snow. . ." 2000.

Chapter 30

1. A. H. Goodman and Leatherman 1998; Kleinman, Das, and Lock 1997.
2. Baer, Singer, and Susser 1997: viii.
3. Rubel and Haas 1996: 120; Loustaunau and Sobo 1997: 80–81.
4. Loustaunau and Sobo 1997: 82–83, referring to Magner 1992: 93.
5. Loustaunau and Sobo 1997, referring to Gesler 1991: 16.
6. Loustaunau and Sobo 1997, referring to C. Leslie 1976: 4; and G. Foster 1994: 11.
7. Ahern 1975: 92–97, as appearing in the eHRAF Collection of Ethnography on the Web, 2000.
8. Murdock 1980: 20.
9. C. C. Moore 1988.
10. T. Gladwin and Sarason 1953: 64–66.
11. Mahony 1971: 34–38, as seen in the eHRAF Collection of Ethnography on the Web, 2000.
12. Gladwin and Sarason 1953: 65.
13. Hallowell 1976.
14. J. E. Levy 1994: 318.
15. Hahn 1995: 133–39.
16. Loustaunau and Sobo 1997: 115.
17. For an exhaustively documented presentation of the more universalistic approach, see E. A. Berlin and Berlin 1996; see also Browner 1985: 13–32; and Rubel, O'Nell, and Collado-Ardón 1984.
18. E. A. Berlin 1996.
19. Browner 1985; Ortiz de Montellano and Browner 1985.
20. Etkin and Ross 1997.
21. Moerman 1997: 240–41.
22. Loustaunau and Sobo 1997: 98–101.
23. Winkelman 1986a.
24. Ibid., pp. 28–29.
25. Levi-Strauss 1963a: 169.
26. Boas 1930: 1–41, reported in Lévi-Strauss 1963b: 169–73.
27. Torrey n.d.
28. Loustaunau and Sobo 1997: 101–102; and Moerman 1997.
29. Loustaunau and Sobo 1997: 102.
30. Dow 1986: 6–9, 125.
31. Hahn 1995: 131–72.
32. Ibid., p. 165.
33. For a discussion of some of the relevant research, see Ibid., pp. 80–82.
34. Mascie-Taylor 1990: 118–21.
35. See references in Hahn 1995: 82–87.
36. A. Cohen 1999.
37. As reported in S. Jones, Martin, and Pilbeam 1992: 420.
38. Reported in Carey et al. 2004: 462.
39. Herdt 1997: 3–22.
40. Bolton 1989.
41. Reported in Carey et al. 2004: 462.
42. Bolton 1989.
43. Carrier and Bolton 1991; Schoepf 1988: 625, cited in Carrier and Bolton 1991.
44. Simmons, Farmer, and Schoepf 1996: 64.
45. Ibid., pp. 39–57.
46. Schoepf 1988: 637–38.
47. Bolton 1992.
48. Farmer 1997: 414. Married men in Thailand are gradually turning away from commercial sex and having affairs with married women who are believed to be safe; see Lyttleton 2000: 299.
49. Feldman and Johnson 1986a: 2.
50. Shen and Siliciano 2000.
51. A. Cohen 2004.
52. Honigmann 1967: 406.
53. Kleinman 1988: 3.
54. Lutz 1985: 63–100.

55. J. Murphy 1981: 813.
56. Edgerton 1966.
57. Edgerton 1992: 16–45.
58. J. S. Allen et al. 1996.
59. Kleinman 1988: 34–52; Berry et al, 1992: 357–64.
60. Honigmann 1967: 401.
61. Kleinman 1988: 19.
62. A. F. C. Wallace 1972.
63. Kleinman 1988: pp. 167–85.
64. Rubel, Nell, and Collado-Ardón 1984: 8–9.
65. Ibid., pp. 15–29, 49–69.
66. Ibid., pp. 71–111.
67. Dressler 1991: 11–16.
68. Ibid., pp. 66–94.
69. Ibid., pp. 165–208.
70. Quandt 1996: 272–89.
71. McElroy and Townsend 2002.
72. Gross and Underwood 1971.
73. McElroy and Townsend 2002: 187, referring to Harvey and Heywood 1983: 27–35.
74. Quandt 1996: 277.
75. McKee 1984: 96.

Chapter 31

1. The discussion in this section draws extensively from Aptekar 1994.
2. Information collected during Melvin Ember's fieldwork in American Samoa, 1955–1956.
3. Mellor and Gavian 1987: 539–44.
4. Dirks 1993.
5. Torry 1986: 125–60.
6. Hardoy and Satterthwaite 1987.
7. Rodwin and Sanyal 1987.
8. Mangin 1967.
9. Rodwin and Sanyal 1987; for a critique of self-help programs, see Ward 1982a.
10. A. Cohen and Paul Koegel 2004.
11. Urban Institute 2000.
12. A. Cohen and Koegel 2004.
13. Baxter and Hopper 1981: 30–33, 50–74.
14. Ibid.
15. A. Cohen and Koegel 2004. p. 29.
16. Herrman 1990.
17. Barak 1991: 63–65.
18. Aptekar 1991: 326.
19. Ibid., pp. 326–49; Aptekar 1988.
20. Korbin 1981b: 4.
21. Straus 2001: 195–96.
22. Straus and Kantor 1994.
23. Straus 1995: 30–33; Straus and Kantor 1995.
24. "Children as Victims," 2000; "Violent Crime" 1994; "Prevalence, Incidence, and Consequences of Violence Against Women," 1998; and Straus 1991.
25. Levinson 1989: 11–12, 44.
26. Minturn and Stashak 1982. Using a sociobiological orientation, a study by Daly and Wilson (1988: 43–59) also suggests that infanticide is largely due to the difficulty of raising the infant successfully.
27. Levinson 1989: 26–28.
28. C. R. Ember and Ember 2005; see also Petersen, Lee, and Ellis 1982, as cited in Levinson 1989: 63.
29. Lareau 2003: 230.
30. Levinson 1989: 31.
31. Ibid., p. 71.
32. Gelles and Straus 1988: 78–88.
33. Erchak 2004; Levinson 1989: 44–45.
34. Straus 2001: 187.
35. Straus and Yodanis 1996: 825–41.
36. Levinson 1989: 104–107.
37. Archer and Gartner 1984: 35.
38. Gurr 1989b: 11–12.
39. The comparison described here is based on data we retrieved from the extensive appendix in Archer and Gartner 1984.
40. Archer and Gartner 1984: 63–97.
41. Gurr 1989a: 47–48.
42. Russell 1972; Eckhardt 1975; Sipes 1973.
43. C. R. Ember and Ember 1994.
44. Archer and Gartner 1984: 118–39.
45. Bacon, Child, and Barry 1963; B. B. Whiting 1965.
46. Barber 2000.
47. C. R. Ember and Ember 1994: 625.
48. C. R. Ember and Ember 1993: 227.
49. C. A. Anderson and Bushman 2002: 2377; J. G. Johnson et al. 2002.
50. Loftin, McDowall, and Boudouris 1989: 163–77; Krahn, Hartnagel, and Gartrell 1986: 269–95, as referred to in Daly and Wilson 1988: 287–88; Gartner 2004.
51. C. R. Ember and Ember 1997.
52. Most of the discussion in this section comes from M. Ember and Ember 1992: 204–206.
53. Meggitt 1977: 201; Gat 1999.
54. Data from Korea is consistent with this explanation of war: More environmental stress strongly predicts higher frequencies of warfare in Korea between the 1st century B.C. and the 8th century A.D. B. W. Kang 2000: 878.
55. For the cross-cultural results suggesting the theory of war described here, see C. R. Ember and Melvin Ember 1992.
56. For the results on political participation and peace in the ethnographic record, see C. R. Ember, Ember, and Russett 1992. For the results on political participation and peace in the modern world, see the references in that essay.
57. Russett and Oneal 2001: 49.
58. Ibid., pp. 125ff.
59. Some of these examples are from Henderson 2001.
60. See the discussions in Ibid., pp. 3–9, and S. K. Anderson and Sloan 2002: 1–5.
61. S. K. Anderson and Sloan 2002: 465.
62. This definition is adapted from Chomsky, who is quoted in Henderson 2001: 5.
63. S. K. Anderson and Sloan 2002: 6–7.
64. Ibid., pp. 6–8.
65. Suárez-Orozco 1992.
66. Rummel 2002a.
67. R. J. Rummel 2002c.
68. R. J. Rummel 2002d.
69. S. K. Anderson and Sloan 2002: 422.
70. "Crossroads for Planet Earth" 2005.

Bibliography

'Abd Allah, Mahmud M. 1917. "Siwan Customs." *Harvard African Studies,* 1: 1–28.

Aberle, David. 1971. "A Note on Relative Deprivation Theory as Applied to Millenarian and Other Cult Movements." In W. A. Lessa and E. Z. Vogt, eds., *Reader in Comparative Religion,* 3rd ed. New York: Harper & Row.

Abler, Thomas S. 2004. "Iroquois: The Tree of Peace and the War Kettle." In *Portraits of Culture,* in C. R. Ember, M. Ember, and P. N. Peregrine, *New Directions in Anthropology.* Upper Saddle River, NJ: Prentice Hall, CD-ROM.

Adams, David B. 1983. "Why There Are So Few Women Warriors." *Behavior Science Research,* 18: 196–212.

Adams, Robert McC. 1960. "The Origin of Cities." *Scientific American* (September): 153–68.

Adams, Robert McC. 1981. *Heartland of Cities: Surveys of Ancient Settlement and Land Use on the Central Floodplain of the Euphrates.* Chicago: University of Chicago Press.

Adler, Mortimer. 1986. *Drawing Down the Moon.* Boston: Beacon.

Adovasio, J., and Page, J. 2002. *The First Americans: In Pursuit of Archaeology's Greatest Mystery.* New York: Random House.

Ahern, Emily M. 1975. "Sacred and Secular Medicine in a Taiwan Village: A Study of Cosmological Disorders." In A. Kleinman et al., eds., *Medicine in Chinese Cultures: Comparative Studies of Health Care in Chinese and Other Societies.* Washington, DC: U.S. Department of Health, Education, and Welfare, National Institutes of Health.

Aiello, Leslie C. 1992. "Body Size and Energy Requirements." In S. Jones, R. Martin, and D. Pilbeam, eds., *The Cambridge Encyclopedia of Human Evolution.* New York: Cambridge University Press.

Aiello, Leslie C. 1993. "The Origin of the New World Monkeys." In W. George and R. Lavocat, eds., *The Africa-South America Connection.* Oxford: Clarendon Press, 100–18.

Aiello, Leslie C, and Mark Collard, 2001. "Our Newest Oldest Ancestor?" *Nature* 410 (November 29): 526–27.

Aiello, Leslie C. and Christopher Dean. 1990. *An Introduction to Human Evolutionary Anatomy.* London: Academic Press, 268–74.

Aitken, M. J. 1985. *Thermoluminescence Dating.* London: Academic Press.

Akmajian, Adrian, Richard A. Demers, and Robert M. Harnish. 1984. *Linguistics: An Introduction to Language and Communication.* 2nd ed. Cambridge, MA: MIT Press.

Albert, Steven M., and Maria G. Cattell. 1994. *Old Age in Global Perspective: Cross-Cultural and Cross-National Views.* New York: G. K. Hall/Macmillan.

Alberts, Bruce, president of the National Academy of Sciences, November 9, 2000. "Setting the Record Straight Regarding Darkness in El Dorado," which can be found at the Web address: http://www4.nationalacademies.org/nas/nashome.nsf.

Alberts, Bruce, Dennis Bray, Julian Lewis, Martin Raff, Keith Roberts, and James D. Watson. 1983. *Molecular Biology of the Cell.* New York: Garland.

Alexander, John P. 1992. "Alas, Poor *Notharctus.*" *Natural History* (August): 55–59.

Algaze, Guillermo. 1993. *The Uruk World System: The Dynamics of Expansion of Early Mesopotamian Civilization.* Chicago: University of Chicago Press.

Allen, John S., and Susan M. Cheer. 1996. "The Non-Thrifty Genotype." *Current Anthropology,* 37: 831–42.

Allen, John S., A. J. Lambert, F. Y. Attah Johnson, K. Schmidt, and K. L. Nero. 1996. "Antisaccadic Eye Movements and Attentional Asymmetry in Schizophrenia in Three Pacific Populations." *Acta Psychiatrica Scandinavia,* 94: 258–65.

Alroy, John. 2001. "A Multispecies Overkill Simulation of the End-Pleistocene Megafaunal Mass Extinction." *Science* 292 (June 8): 1893–96.

Alvarez, Lizette. 2003. "Arranged Marriages Get a Little Rearranging," *The New York Times,* June 22, p 1.3.

American Anthropological Association 1991. "Revised Principles of Professional Responsibility, 1990." In Carolyn Fluehr-Lobban, ed. *Ethics and the Profession of Anthropology: Dialogue for a New Era.* Philadelphia: University of Pennsylvania Press, 274–79.

Anderson, Connie M. 2000. "The Persistence of Polygyny as an Adaptive Response to Poverty and Oppression in Apartheid South Africa." *Cross-Cultural Research* 34: 99–112.

Anderson, Craig A. 2002. "The Effects of Media Violence on Society." *Science,* 295, (March 29): 2377–79.

Anderson, J. L., C. B. Crawford, J. Nadeau, and T. Lindberg. 1992. "Was the Dutchess of Windsor Right? A Cross-Cultural Review of the Socioecology of Ideal Female Body Shape. *Ethnology and Sociobiology,* 13: 197–227.

Anderson, Richard L. 1989. *Art in Small-Scale Societies.* 2nd ed. Englewood Cliffs, NJ: Prentice Hall.

Anderson, Richard L. 1990. *Calliope's Sisters: A Comparative Study of Philosophies of Art.* Upper Saddle River, NJ: Prentice Hall.

Anderson, Richard L. 1992. "Do Other Cultures Have 'Art'?" *American Anthropologist,* 94: 926–29.

Anderson, Sean K., and Stephen Sloan. 2002. *Historical Dictionary of Terrorism.* 2nd ed. Lanham, MD: Scarecrow Press.

Anderson, William L. "Cherokee: The European Impact on the Cherokee Culture," in *Portraits of Culture,* in C. R. Ember, M. Ember, and P. N. Peregrine, eds., *New Directions in Anthropology.* Upper Saddle River, NJ: Prentice Hall, CD-ROM.

Andrews, Elizabeth. 1994. "Territoriality and Land Use among the Akulmiut of Western Alaska." In E. S. Burch, Jr., and L. J. Ellanna, *Key Issues in Hunter-Gatherer Research.* Oxford: Berg.

Andrews, Peter. "Propliopithecidae." 2000a. In I. Tattersall, E. Delson, and J. van Couvering, eds., *Encyclopedia of Human Evolution and Prehistory.* New York, Garland.

Andrews, Peter. "Proconsul." 2001b. In I. Tattersall, E. Delson, and J. van Couvering, eds., *Encyclopedia of Human Evolution and Prehistory.* New York: Garland.

Andrews, Peter, and Christopher Stringer. 1989. *Human Evolution: An Illustrated Guide.* London: British Museum.

Angier, Natalie. 2002. "Why We're So Nice: We're Wired to Cooperate." Science Times in the *New York Times,* July 23, pp. F1, F8.

Anthony, David, Dimitri Y. Telegin, and Dorcas Brown. 1991. "The Origin of Horseback Riding." *Scientific American* (December): 94–100.

Antoun, Richard T. 2001. *Understanding Fundamentalism: Christian, Islamic, and Jewish Movements.* Walnut Creek, CA: AltaMira Press.

Anyon, Roger, and T. J. Ferguson. 1995. "Cultural Resources Management at the Pueblo of Zuni, New Mexico, USA." *Antiquity,* 69: 913–30.

"Appendix A: Report of the Committee on Ethics, Society for Applied Anthropology." 2002. In C. Fluehr-Lobban, ed., *Ethics and the Profession of Anthropology.* Philadelphia: University of Pennsylvania Press.

"Appendix C: Statements on Ethics: Principles of Professional Responsibility, Adopted by the Council of the American Anthropological Association, May 1971." 1991. In C. Fluehr-Lobban, ed., *Ethics and the Profession of Anthropology.* Philadelphia: University of Pennsylvania Press.

"Appendix F: Professional and Ethical Responsibilities, SfAA." 2002. In C. Fluehr-Lobban, ed., *Ethics and the Profession of Anthropology.* Philadelphia: University of Pennsylvania Press.

"Appendix H: National Association of Practicing Anthropologists' Ethical Guidelines for Practitioners, 1988." 1991. In C. Fluehr-Lobban, ed., *Ethics and the Profession of Anthropology.* Philadelphia: University of Pennsylvania Press.

"Appendix I: Revised Principles of Professional Responsibility, 1990." 1991. In C. Fluehr-Lobban, ed., *Ethics and the Profession of Anthropology.* Philadelphia: University of Pennsylvania Press.

Aptekar, Lewis. 1988. *Street Children of Cali.* Durham, NC: Duke University Press.

Aptekar, Lewis. 1991. "Are Colombian Street Children Neglected? The Contributions of Ethnographic and Ethnohistorical Approaches to the Study of Children."*Anthropology and Education Quarterly,* 22: 326–49.

Aptekar, Lewis. 1994. *Environmental Disasters in Global Perspective.* New York: G. K. Hall/Macmillan.

Archer, Dane, and Rosemary Gartner. 1984. *Violence and Crime in Cross-National Perspective.* New Haven, CT: Yale University Press.

Ardener, Shirley. 1995a [1964]. "The Comparative Study of Rotating Credit Associations." In S. Ardener and S. Burman, *Money-Go-Rounds.* Oxford: Berg.

Ardener, Shirley. 1995b [1964]. "Women Making Money Go Round: ROSCAs Revisited." In S. Ardener and S. Burman, *Money-Go-Rounds.* Oxford: Berg.

Ardener, Shirley, and Sandra Burman. 1995 [1964]. *Money-Go-Rounds: The Importance of Rotating Savings and Credit Associations for Women.* Oxford: Berg.

Argyle, Michael. 1994. *The Psychology of Social Class.* New York: Routledge.

Armelagos, George J., and Alan H. Goodman. 1998. "Race, Racism, and Anthropology." In A. H. Goodman and T. L. Leatherman, eds., *Building a New Biocultural Synthesis: Political-Economic Perspectives on Human Biology.* Ann Arbor: University of Michigan Press.

Armstrong, Robert P. 1981. *The Powers of Presence.* Philadelphia: University of Pennsylvania Press.

Aronoff, Joel, Andrew M. Barclay, and Linda A. Stevenson. 1988. "The Recognition of Threatening Facial Stimuli." *Journal of Personality and Social Psychology,* 54: 647–55.

Aronoff, Joel, Barbara A. Woike, and Lester M. Hyman. 1992. "Which Are the Stimuli in Facial Displays of Anger and Happiness? Configurational Bases of Emotion Recognition." *Journal of Personality and Social Psychology,* 62: 1050–66.

Asch, Nancy B., and David L. Asch. 1978. "The Economic Potential of *Iva annua* and Its Prehistoric Importance in the Lower Illinois Valley." In R. Ford, ed., *The Nature and Status of Ethnobotany.* Anthropological Papers No 67, Museum of Anthropology. Ann Arbor: University of Michigan.

Asch, Solomon. 1956. "Studies of Independence and Conformity: A Minority of One against a Unanimous Majority." *Psychological Monographs,* 70: 1–70.

Ascher, Robert. 1961. "Analogy in Archaeological Interpretation." *Southwestern Journal of Anthropology,* 17: 317–25.

Asfaw, Berhane, Tim White, Owen Lovejoy, Bruce Latimer, Scott Simpson, and Glen Suwa. 1999. "*Australopithecus garhi:* A New Species of Early Hominid from Ethiopia." *Science,* 284 (April 23): 629–36.

Ashton, Hugh. 1967. *The Basuto.* 2nd ed. London: Oxford University Press.

"Association Business: Clyde Snow, Forensic Anthropologist, Works for Justice." *Anthropology News* (October 2000): 12.

Austin, Lewis. 1977. "Visual Symbols, Political Ideology, and Culture." *Ethos,* 5: 306–25.

Ayala, Francisco J. 1995. "The Myth of Eve: Molecular Biology and Human Origins." *Science,* 270 (December 22): 1930–936.

Ayala, Francisco J. 1996. "Communication" in *Science,* 274 (November 29): 1354.

Ayres, Barbara C. 1968. "Effects of Infantile Stimulation on Musical Behavior." In A. Lomax, ed., *Folk Song Style and Culture.* Washington, D.C.

Ayres, Barbara C. 1973. "Effects of Infant Carrying Practices on Rhythm in Music." *Ethos,* 1: 387–404.

Bachnik, Jane M. 1992. "The Two 'Faces' of Self and Society in Japan." *Ethos,* 20: 3–32.

Bacon, Margaret, Irvin L. Child, and Herbert Barry III. 1963. "A Cross-Cultural Study of Correlates of Crime." *Journal of Abnormal and Social Psychology,* 66: 291–300.

Badcock, C. R. 2000. *Evolutionary Psychology: A Critical Introduction.* Cambridge: Blackwell.

Badcock, Christopher. 1988. *Essential Freud.* Oxford: Blackwell.

Baer, Hans A., Merrill Singer, and Ida Susser. 1997. *Medical Anthropology and the World System: A Critical Perspective.* Westport, CT: Bergin & Garvey.

Bahn, Paul. 1996. *Archaeology: A Very Short Introduction.* New York: Oxford University Press.

Bahn, Paul. 1998. "Neanderthals Emancipated." *Nature,* 394 (August 20): 719–20.

Bahn, Paul, and J. Vertut. 1988. *Images of the Ice Age.* New York: Facts on File.

Bailey, Robert C., Genevieve Head, Mark Jenike, Bruce Owen, Robert Rectman, and Elzbieta Zechenter. 1989. "Hunting and Gathering in Tropical Rain Forest: Is It Possible?" *American Anthropologist,* 91: 59–82.

Baldi, Philip. 1983. *An Introduction to the Indo-European Languages.* Carbondale: Southern Illinois University Press.

Balikci, Asen. 1970. *The Netsilik Eskimo.* Garden City, NY: Natural History Press.

Balter, Michael. 2001. "In Search of the First Europeans," *Science,* 291 (March 2): 1722–25.

Balter, Michael, and Ann Gibbons. 2000. "A Glimpse of Humans' First Journey Out of Africa." *Science,* 288 (May 12): 948–50.

Banton, Michael, ed. 1966. *Anthropological Approaches to the Study of Religion.* Association of Social Anthropologists of the Commonwealth, Monograph No. 3. New York: Praeger.

Barak, Gregg. 1991. *Gimme Shelter: A Social History of Homelessness in Contemporary America.* New York: Praeger.

Barash, David P. 1977. *Sociobiology and Behavior.* New York: Elsevier.

Barber, Nigel. 2000. "The Sex Ratio as a Predictor of Cross-National Variation in Violent Crime," *Cross-Cultural Research,* 34: 264–82.

Barber, Nigel. 2003. "Paternal Investment Prospects and Cross-National Differences in Single Parenthood." *Cross-Cultural Research,* 37: 163–77.

Barinaga, Maria. 1992. "Priming the Brain's Language Pump." *Science,* 255 (January 31): 535.

Barlett, Peggy F., ed 1980. *Agricultural Decision Making: Anthropological Contributions to Rural Development.* New York: Academic Press.

Barlett, Peggy F. 1989. "Industrial Agriculture." In S. Plattner, ed., *Economic Anthropology.* Stanford, CA: Stanford University Press.

Barnard, Alan. 2000. *History and Theory in Anthropology.* Cambridge, UK: Cambridge University Press.

Barnett, H. G. 1960. *Being a Palauan.* New York: Holt, Rinehart & Winston.

Barnosky, Anthony, Paul Koch, Robert Feranec, Scott Wing, and Alan Shabel. 2004. "Assessing the Causes of Late Pleistocene Extinctions on the Continents." *Science*, 306 (October 1): 70–75.

Barnouw, Victor. 1985. *Culture and Personality.* 4th ed. Homewood, IL: Dorsey Press.

Barrett, D. E. 1984. "Malnutrition and Child Behavior: Conceptualization, Assessment and an Empirical Study of Social-Emotional Functioning." In J. Brozek and B. Schürch, eds., *Malnutrition and Behavior: Critical Assessment of Key Issues.* Lausanne, Switzerland: Nestlé Foundation, 280–306.

Barrett, Stanley R. 1994. *Paradise: Class, Commuters, and Ethnicity in Rural Ontario.* Toronto: University of Toronto Press.

Barringer, Herbert, George Blankstein, and Raymond Mack, eds. 1965. *Social Change in Developing Areas: A Re-Interpretation of Evolutionary Theory.* Cambridge, MA: Schenkman.

Barry, Herbert III, Irvin L. Child, and Margaret K. Bacon. 1959. "Relation of Child Training to Subsistence Economy." *American Anthropologist*, 61: 51–63.

Barth, Fredrik. 1961. *Nomads of South Persia.* Boston: Little, Brown.

Barth, Fredrik. 1994. "Enduring and Emerging Issues in the Analysis of Ethnicity." In H. Vermeulen and C. Govers, eds., *The Anthropology of Ethnicity.* Amsterdam: Het Spinhuis.

Bates, Daniel G., and Susan H. Lees, Eds. 1996. *Case Studies in Human Ecology.* New York: Plenum Press.

Bates, E. and V. A. Marchman, 1988. "What Is and Is Not Universal in Language Acquisition." In F. Plum, ed., *Language, Communication, and the Brain.* New York: Raven Press, 19–38.

Bauman, Richard. 1992a. "Folklore." In Bauman, ed., *Folklore, Cultural Performances, and Popular Entertainments.* New York: Oxford University Press.

Bauman, Richard, ed. 1992b. *Folklore, Cultural Performances, and Popular Entertainments: A Communications-Centered Handbook.* New York: Oxford University Press.

Bauman, Richard, and Joel Sherzer. 1989. *Explorations in the Ethnography of Speaking.* 2nd ed. New York: Cambridge University Press.

Baxter, Ellen, and Kim Hopper. 1981. *Private Lives/Public Spaces: Homeless Adults on the Streets of New York City.* New York: Community Service Society of New York.

Beadle, George, and Muriel Beadle. 1966. *The Language of Life.* Garden City, NY: Doubleday.

Bearder, Simon K. 1987. "Lorises, Bushbabies, and Tarsiers: Diverse Societies in Solitary Foragers." In B. Smuts et al., eds., *Primate Societies.* Chicago: University of Chicago Press.

Beattie, John. 1960. *Bunyoro: An African Kingdom.* New York: Holt, Rinehart & Winston.

Begler, Elsie B. 1978. "Sex, Status, and Authority in Egalitarian Society." *American Anthropologist*, 80: 571–88.

Begun, David. 2002. "Miocene Apes." In P. N. Peregrine, C. R. Ember, and M. Ember, eds., *Physical Anthropology: Original Readings in Method and Practice.* Upper Saddle River, NJ: Prentice Hall.

Behar, Ruth and Deborah Gordon, eds. 1995. *Women Writing Culture.* Berkeley: University of California Press.

Bellman, Beryl L. 1984. *The Language of Secrecy: Symbols and Metaphors in Poro Ritual.* New Brunswick, NJ: Rutgers University Press.

Benedict, Ruth. 1946. *Chrysanthemum and the Sword.* Boston: Houghton Mifflin.

Benedict, Ruth. 1959 [1934]. *Patterns of Culture.* New York: Mentor.

Benjamin, Lois. 1991. *The Black Elite: Facing the Color Line in the Twilight of the Twentieth Century.* Chicago: Nelson-Hall.

Berg, Paul, and Maxine Singer. 1992. *Dealing with Genes: The Language of Heredity.* Mill Valley, CA: University Science Books.

Berggren, William A., Dennis V. Kent, John D. Obradovich, and Carl C. Swisher III. 1992. "Toward a Revised Paleogene Geochronology." In D. R. Prothero and W. A. Berggren, eds., *Eocene-Oliocene*

Climatic and Biotic Evolution. Princeton, NJ: Princeton University Press.

Berlin, Brent. 1992. *Ethnobiological Classification: Principles of Categorization of Plants and Animals in Traditional Societies.* Princeton, NJ: Princeton University Press.

Berlin, Brent, and Paul Kay. 1969. *Basic Color Terms: Their Universality and Evolution.* Berkeley: University of California Press.

Berlin, E. A. "General Overview of Maya Ethnomedicine." 1996. In E. A. Berlin and B. Berlin, *Medical Ethnobiology of the Highland Maya of Chiapas, Mexico.* Princeton, NJ: Princeton University Press, 52–53.

Berlin, Elois Ann, and Brent Berlin. 1996. *Medical Ethnobiology of the Highland Maya of Chiapas, Mexico: The Gastrointestinal Diseases.* Princeton, NJ: Princeton University Press.

Bernard, H. Russell. 2001. *Research Methods in Cultural Anthropology: Qualitative and Quantitative Approaches.* 3rd ed. Walnut Creek, CA: AltaMira Press.

Bernard, H. Russell, and Pertti J. Pelto. 1987. "Technology and Anthropological Theory: Conclusions." In H. R. Bernard and P. J. Pelto, eds., *Technology and Social Change,* 2nd ed. Prospect Heights, IL: Waveland.

Bernard, H. Russell, and Pertti J. Pelto, eds. 1987. *Technology and Social Change.* 2nd ed. Prospect Heights, IL: Waveland.

Bernardi, B. 1952. "The Age-System of the Nilo-Hamitic Peoples." *Africa*, 22: 316–32.

Berreman, Gerald D. 1960. "Caste in India and the United States." *American Journal of Sociology*, 66: 120–27.

Berreman, Gerald D. 1972. "Race, Caste and Other Invidious Distinctions in Social Stratification." *Race*, 13: 403–14.

Berreman, Gerald D. 1973. *Caste in the Modern World.* Morristown, NJ: General Learning Press.

Berry, John W. 1971. "Ecological and Cultural Factors in Spatial Perceptual Development." *Canadian Journal of Behavioural Science*, 3: 324–36.

Berry, John W. 1976. *Human Ecology and Cognitive Style.* New York: Wiley.

Berry, John W., and J. Bennett. 1989. "Syllabic Literacy and Cognitive Performance among the Cree." *International Journal of Psychology*, 24: 429–50.

Berry, John W., Ype H. Poortinga, Marshall H. Segall, and Pierre R. Dasen. 1992. *Cross-Cultural Psychology: Research and Applications.* New York: Cambridge University Press.

Bestor, Theodore C. 2001. "Supply-Side Sushi: Commodity, Market, and the Global City." *American Anthropologist*, 103: 76–95.

Betzig, Laura. 1988. "Redistribution: Equity or Exploitation?" In Laura Betzig, Monique Borgerhoff Mulder, and Paul Turke, eds., *Human Reproductive Behavior.* Cambridge: Cambridge University Press, 49–63.

Betzig, Laura. 1989. "Causes of Conjugal Dissolution: A Cross-Cultural Study." *Current Anthropology*, 30: 654–676.

Bickerton, Derek. 1983. "Creole Languages." *Scientific American* (July): 116–22.

Bilby, Kenneth. 1996. "Ethnogenesis in the Guianas and Jamaica: Two Maroon Cases." In J. D. Hill, ed., *Ethnogenesis in the Americas.* Iowa City: University of Iowa Press, 119–41.

Bilsborough, Alan. 1992. *Human Evolution.* New York: Blackie Academic & Professional.

Bindon, James R., and Douglas E. Crews. 1993. "Changes in Some Health Status Characteristics of American Samoan Men: Preliminary Observations from a 12-Year Follow-up Study." *American Journal of Human Biology*, 5: 31–37.

Bindon, James R., Amy Knight, William W. Dressler, and Douglas E. Crews. 1997. "Social Context and Psychosocial Influences on Blood Pressure among American Samoans." *American Journal of Physical Anthropology*, 103: 7–18.

Binford, Lewis R. 1971. "Post-Pleistocene Adaptations." In S. Struever, ed., *Prehistoric Agriculture.* Garden City, NY: Natural History Press.

Binford, Lewis R. 1973. "Interassemblage Variability: The Mousterian and the 'Functional' Argument." In C. Renfrew, ed., *The Explanation of Culture Change.* Pittsburgh: University of Pittsburgh Press.

Binford, Lewis R. 1984. *Faunal Remains from Klasies River Mouth.* Orlando, FL: Academic Press.

Binford, Lewis R. 1987. "Were There Elephant Hunters at Torralba?" In M. Nitecki and D. Nitecki, eds., *The Evolution of Human Hunting.* New York: Plenum.

Binford, Lewis R. 1990. "Mobility, Housing, and Environment: A Comparative Study." *Journal of Anthropological Research,* 46: 119–52.

Binford, Lewis R., and Chuan Kun Ho. 1985. "Taphonomy at a Distance: Zhoukoudian, 'The Cave Home of Beijing Man'?" *Current Anthropology,* 26: 413–42.

Binford, Sally R., and Lewis R. Binford. 1969. "Stone Tools and Human Behavior." *Scientific American* (April): 70–84.

Bishop, W. A., and J. A. Miller, eds. 1972. *Calibration of Hominid Evolution.* Toronto: University of Toronto Press.

Black, Donald. 1993. *The Social Structure of Right and Wrong.* San Diego: Academic Press.

Black, Francis L. 1992. "Why Did They Die?" *Science,* 258 (December 11): 1739–40.

Blackwood, Evelyn. 1984a. Cross-Cultural Dimensions of Lesbian Relations. Master's Thesis. San Francisco State University. As referred to in Blackwood and Wieringa 1999.

Blackwood, Evelyn. 1984b. "Sexuality and Gender in Certain Native American Tribes: The Case of Cross-Gender Females." *Signs,* 10: 27–42.

Blackwood, Evelyn and Saskia E. Wieringa. 1999. "Sapphic Shadows: Challenging the Silence in the Study of Sexuality." In Evelyn Blackwood and Saskia E. Weiringa, eds. *Female Desires: Same-Sex Relations and Transgender Practices Across Cultures.* New York: Columbia University Press, pp. 39–63.

Blalock, Hubert M., 1972. *Social Statistics.* 2nd ed. New York: McGraw-Hill.

Blanton, Richard E. 1976. "The Origins of Monte Albán." In Cleland, ed., *Cultural Continuity and Change.* New York: Academic Press.

Blanton, Richard E. 1978. *Monte Albán: Settlement Patterns at the Ancient Zapotec Capital.* New York: Academic Press.

Blanton, Richard E. 1981. "The Rise of Cities." In J. Sabloff, ed., *Supplement to the Handbook of Middle American Indians,* Vol. 1. Austin: University of Texas Press.

Blanton, Richard E. 2004. "Variation in Economy." In *Cross-Cultural Research for Social Science,* in C. R. Ember, M. Ember, and P. N. Peregrine, eds., *New Directions in Anthropology.* Upper Saddle River, NJ: Prentice Hall, CD-ROM.

Blanton, Richard E., Stephen A. Kowalewski, Gary Feinman, and Jill Appel. 1981. *Ancient Mesoamerica: A Comparison of Change in Three Regions.* New York: Cambridge University Press.

Blanton, Richard E., Stephen A. Kowalewski, Gary M. Feinman, and Laura M. Finsten. 1993. *Ancient Mesoamerica: A Comparison of Change in Three Regions.* 2nd ed. Cambridge: Cambridge University Press.

Blanton, Richard E., Peter N. Peregrine, Deborah Winslow, and Thomas D. Hall, eds. 1997. *Economic Analysis beyond the Local System.* Lanham, MD: University Press of America.

Bledsoe, Caroline H. 1980. *Women and Marriage in Kpelle Society.* Stanford, CA: Stanford University Press.

Block, Jean L. 1983. "Help! They've All Moved Back Home!" *Woman's Day* (April 26): 72–76.

Block, Jonathan I. and Doug M. Boyer. 2002. "Grasping Primate Origins," *Science,* 298 (November 22): 1606–10.

Blount, Ben G. 1981. "The Development of Language in Children." In R. H. Munroe, R. L. Munroe, and B. B. Whiting, eds., *Handbook of Cross-Cultural Human Development.* New York: Garland.

Blount, Ben G., ed. 1995. *Language, Culture, and Society; A Book of Readings.* 2nd ed. Prospect Heights, IL: Waveland.

Blumenschine, Robert J. et al., 2003. "Late Pliocene Homo and Hominid Land Use from Western Olduvai Gorge, Tanzania," *Science,* 299 (February 21): 1217–21.

Blumler, Mark A., and Roger Byrne. 1991. "The Ecological Genetics of Domestication and the Origins of Agriculture." *Current Anthropology,* 32: 23–35.

Boas, Franz. 1888. *Central Eskimos.* Bureau of American Ethnology Annual Report No. 6. Washington, DC.

Boas, Franz. 1930. "The Religion of the Kwakiutl." *Columbia University Contributions to Anthropology,* Vol. 10, pt. 2. New York: Columbia University.

Boas, Franz. 1940. *Race, Language, and Culture.* New York: Macmillan.

Boas, Franz. 1964 [1911]. "On Grammatical Categories." In D. Hymes, ed., *Language in Culture and Society.* New York: Harper & Row.

Boaz, Noel T., and Alan J. Almquist. 1997. *Biological Anthropology: A Synthetic Approach to Human Evolution.* Upper Saddle River, NJ: Prentice Hall.

Boaz, Noel T., and Alan J. Almquist. 1999. *Essentials of Biological Anthropology.* Upper Saddle River, NJ: Prentice Hall.

Boaz, Noel T., and Alan J. Almquist. 2001. *Biological Anthropology: A Synthetic Approach to Human Evolution.* 2nd ed. Upper Saddle River, NJ: Prentice Hall.

Bock, Philip K. 1980. *Continuities in Psychological Anthropology: A Historical Introduction.* San Francisco: W. H. Freeman and Company.

Bodine, John J. 2004. "Taos Pueblo: Maintaining Tradition." In *Portraits of Culture.* In C. R. Ember, M. Ember, and P. N. Peregrine, eds., *New Directions in Anthropology.* Upper Saddle River, NJ: Prentice Hall, CD-ROM.

Bodley, John H. 1990. *Victims of Progress.* 3rd ed. Mountain View, CA: Mayfield.

Bodley, John H. 1998. *Victims of Progress.* 4th ed. Mountain View, CA: Mayfield.

Bodley, John H. 2000. *Anthropology and Contemporary Human Problems.* 4th ed. New York: McGraw Hill.

Boehm, Christopher. 1993. "Egalitarian Behavior and Reverse Dominance Hierarchy." *Current Anthropology,* 34: 230–31.

Boehm, Christopher. 1999. *Hierarchy in the Forest: The Evolution of Egalitarian Behavior.* Cambridge, MA: Harvard University Press.

Boesche, C. et al. 1994. "Is Nut Cracking in Wild Chimpanzees a Cultural Behavior?" *Journal of Human Evolution,* 26: 325–38.

Bogin, Barry. 1988. *Patterns of Human Growth.* Cambridge: Cambridge University Press.

Bogoras, Waldemar. 1909. "The Chukchee." Pt. 3. *Memoirs of the American Museum of Natural History,* 2.

Bohannan, Laura, and Paul Bohannan. 1953. *The Tiv of Central Nigeria.* London: International African Institute.

Bohannan, Paul. 1954. "The Migration and Expansion of the Tiv." *Africa,* 24: 2–16.

Bohannan, Paul, and John Middleton, eds. 1968. *Marriage, Family and Residence.* Garden City, NY: Natural History Press.

Bollen, Kenneth A. 1993. "Liberal Democracy: Validity and Method Factors in Cross-National Measures." *American Journal of Political Science,* 37: 1207–30.

Bolton, Ralph. 1973. "Aggression and Hypoglycemia among the Qolla: A Study in Psychobiological Anthropology." *Ethnology,* 12: 227–57.

Bolton, Ralph. 1989. "Introduction: The AIDS Pandemic, a Global Emergency." *Medical Anthropology,* 10: 93–104.

Bolton, Ralph. 1992. "AIDS and Promiscuity: Muddled in the Models of HIV Prevention." *Medical Anthropology,* 14: 145–223.

Bondarenko, Dmitri and Andrey Korotayev. 2000. "Family Size and Community Organization: A Cross-Cultural Comparison." *Cross-Cultural Research,* 34: 152–89.

"Book of the Year (1995): World Affairs: RWANDA," and "Book of the Year (1995): Race and Ethnic Relations: Rwanda's Complex Ethnic History," *Britannica Online,* December.

Borchert, Catherine, and Adrienne Zihlman. 1990. "The Ontogeny and Phylogeny of Symbolizing." In M. LeC. Foster and L. J. Botsharow, *The Life of Symbols.* Boulder, CO: Westview, 15–44.

Bordaz, Jacques. 1970. *Tools of the Old and New Stone Age.* Garden City, NY: Natural History Press.

Bordes, François. 1961. "Mousterian Cultures in France." *Science,* 134 (September 22): 803–10.

Bordes, François. 1968. *The Old Stone Age.* New York: McGraw-Hill, 51–97.

Borgerhoff Mulder, Monique, Margaret George-Cramer, Jason Eshleman, and Alessia Ortolani, 2001. "A Study of East African Kinship and Marriage Using a Phylogenetically Based Comparative Method," *American Anthropologist,* 103: 1059–82.

Bornstein, Marc H. 1973. "The Psychophysiological Component of Cultural Difference in Color Naming and Illusion Susceptibility." *Behavior Science Notes,* 8: 41–101.

Bortei-Doku, Ellen, and Ernest Aryeetey. 1995 [1964]. "Mobilizing Cash for Business: Women in Rotating Susu Clubs in Ghana." In S. Ardener and S. Burman, *Money-Go-Rounds.* Oxford: Berg, 77–94.

Boserup, Ester. 1970. *Woman's Role in Economic Development.* New York: St. Martin's Press.

Boserup, Ester. 1993 [1965]. *The Conditions of Agricultural Growth: The Economics of Agrarian Change under Population Pressure.* Toronto: Earthscan Publishers.

Bourguignon, Erika. 1973a. "Introduction: A Framework for the Comparative Study of Altered States of Consciousness." In E. Bourguignon, ed. *Religion, Altered States of Consciousness, and Social Change.* Columbus: Ohio State University Press.

Bourguignon, Erika, ed. 1973b. *Religion, Altered States of Consciousness, and Social Change.* Columbus: Ohio State University Press.

Bourguignon, Erika. 2004. "Suffering and Healing, Subordination and Power: Women and Possession Trance." *Ethos,* 32: 557–74.

Bourguignon, Erika, and Thomas L. Evascu. 1977. "Altered States of Consciousness within a General Evolutionary Perspective: A Holocultural Analysis." *Behavior Science Research,* 12: 197–216.

Bowen, Gabriel J. et al. 2002. "Mammalian Dispersal at the Paleocene/Eocene Boundary," *Science,* 295 (March 15): 2062–64.

Bowles, S., H. Gintis, and M. Osborne. 2001. "The Determinants of Earnings: A Behavioral Approach." *Journal of Economic Literature* 39: 1137–76, as referred to in Godoy et al. 2004.

Boyd, Robert, and Peter J. Richerson. 1990. "Group Selection among Alternative Evolutionarily Stable Strategies." *Journal of Theoretical Biology,* 145: 331–42.

Boyd, Robert, and Peter J. Richerson. 1996 [1985]. *Culture and the Evolutionary Process.* Chicago: University of Chicago Press.

Boyd, Robert, and Joan Silk. 2000. *How Humans Evolved.* 2nd ed. New York: Norton.

Brace, C. Loring. 1996. "A Four-Letter Word Called Race." In Larry T. Reynolds and Leonard Leiberman, eds., *Race and Other Misadventures: Essays in Honor of Ashley Montague in His Ninetieth Year.* New York: General Hall.

Brace, C. Loring, David P. Tracer, Lucia Allen Yaroch, John Robb, Kari Brandt, and A. Russell Nelson. 1993. "Clines and Clusters versus 'Race': A Test in Ancient Egypt and the Case of a Death on the Nile." *Yearbook of Physical Anthropology,* 36: 1–31.

Bradley, Candice. 1984–1985. "The Sexual Division of Labor and the Value of Children." *Behavior Science Research,* 19: 159–85.

Bradley, Candice. 1995. "Keeping the Soil in Good Heart: Weeding, Women and Ecofeminism." In K. Warren, ed., *Ecofeminism.* Bloomington: Indiana University Press.

Bradsher, Keith. 2002. "Pakistanis Fume as Clothing Sales to U.S. Tumble." *New York Times,* June 23, p. 3.

Braidwood, Robert J. 1960. "The Agricultural Revolution." *Scientific American,* (September): 130–48.

Braidwood, Robert J., and Gordon R. Willey. 1962. "Conclusions and Afterthoughts." In Braidwood and Willey, eds., *Courses Toward Urban Life.* Chicago: Aldine.

Braidwood, Robert J., and Gordon R. Willey, eds. 1962b. *Courses Toward Urban Life: Archaeological Considerations of Some Cultural Alternatives.* Viking Fund Publications in Anthropology No. 32. Chicago: Aldine.

Brain, C. K., and A. Sillen. 1988. "Evidence from the Swartkrans Cave for the Earliest Use of Fire." *Nature,* 336 December 1: 464–66.

Branda, Richard F., and John W. Eaton. 1978. "Skin Color and Nutrient Photolysis: An Evolutionary Hypothesis." *Science,* 201 (August 18): 625–26.

Brandewie, Ernest. 1991. "The Place of the Big Man in Traditional Hagen Society in the Central Highlands of New Guinea." In F. McGlynn and A. Tuden, eds., *Anthropological Approaches to Political Behavior.* Pittsburgh, PA: University of Pittsburg Press.

Brandon, George. 2004. "African-Americans: Getting into the Spirit." In *Portraits of Culture,* in C. R. Ember, M. Ember, and P. N. Peregrine, eds. *New Directions in Anthropology.* Upper Saddle River, NJ: Prentice Hall, CD-ROM.

Brandon, Robert N. 1990. *Adaptation and Environment.* Princeton, NJ: Princeton University Press.

Bräuer, Günter. 1984. "A Craniological Approach to the Origin of Anatomically Modern *Homo Sapiens* in Africa and Implications for the Appearance of Modern Europeans." In F. Smith and F Spencer, eds., *The Origins of Modern Humans.* New York: Alan R. Liss.

Braun, David P., and Stephen Plog. 1982. "Evolution of 'Tribal' Social Networks: Theory and Prehistoric North American Evidence." *American Antiquity,* 47: 504–25.

Brettell, Caroline B. 1996. "Migration." In D. Levinson and M. Ember, eds. *Encyclopedia of Cultural Anthropology,* 4 vols., New York: Henry Holt, vol. 3, pp. 793–97.

Brettell, Caroline and Robert V. Kemper. 2002. "Migration and Cities." In M. Ember and C. R. Ember, eds. *Encyclopedia of Urban Cultures: Cities and Cultures Around the World,* 4 vols., Danbury, CT: Grolier/Scholastic, vol. 1, pp. 30–38.

Brettell, Caroline B., and Carolyn F. Sargent, eds. 2000. *Gender in Cross-Cultural Perspective,* 3rd ed. Upper Saddle River, NJ: Prentice Hall.

Briggs, Jean L. 1974. "Eskimo Women: Makers of Men." In C. J. Matthiasson, *Many Sisters: Women in Cross-Cultural Perspective.* New York: Free Press.

Bringa, Tone. 1995. *Being Muslim the Bosnian Way: Identity and Community in a Central Bosnian Village.* Princeton, NJ: Princeton University Press, as examined in the eHRAF Collection of Ethnography on the Web.

Brinton, Crane. 1938. *The Anatomy of Revolution.* Upper Saddle River, NJ: Prentice Hall.

Brittain, John A. 1978. *Inheritance and the Inequality of Material Wealth.* Washington, DC: Brookings Institution.

Brodwin, Paul E. 1996. "Disease and Culture." In D. Levinson and M. Ember, eds. *Encyclopedia of Cultural Anthropology,* New York: Henry Holt, vol. 1, pp. 355–59.

Brodey, Jane E. 1971. "Effects of Milk on Blacks Noted." *New York Times,* October 15, p. 15.

Bromage, Timothy G. 2002 "Paleoanthropology and Life History, and Life History of a Paleoanthropologist." In P. N. Peregrine, C. R. Ember, and M. Ember eds., *Physical Anthropology: Original*

Readings in Method and Practice. Upper Saddle River, NJ: Prentice Hall.

Bromage, Timothy G., and M. Christopher Dean. 1985. "Reevaluation of the Age at Death of Immature Fossil Hominids." *Nature,* 317 (October 10): 525–27.

Brooks, Alison S., Fatimah Linda Collier Jackson, and R. Richard Grinker. 1993. "Race and Ethnicity in America." *Anthro Notes* (National Museum of Natural History Bulletin for Teachers), 15, no. 3 (Fall): 1–3, 11–15.

Broom, Robert. 1950. *Finding the Missing Link.* London: Watts.

Brothwell, Don, and Eric Higgs, eds. 1963. *Science in Archaeology.* New York: Basic Books.

Broude, Gwen J. 1976. "Cross-Cultural Patterning of Some Sexual Attitudes and Practices." *Behavior Science Research,* 11: 227–62.

Broude, Gwen J. 1980. "Extramarital Sex Norms in Cross-Cultural Perspective." *Behavior Science Research,* 15: 181–218.

Broude, Gwen J. 2004a. "Sexual Attitudes and Practices." In C. Ember and M. Ember, eds., *Encyclopedia of Sex and Gender: Men and Women in the World's Cultures.* New York: Kluwer Academic/ Plenum Publishers, vol. 1, pp. 177–86.

Broude, Gwen J. 2004b. "Variations in Sexual Attitudes, Norms, and Practices." In *Cross-Cultural Research for Social Science,* in C. R. Ember, M. Ember, and P. N. Peregrine eds., *New Directions in Anthropology.* Upper Saddle River, NJ: Prentice Hall, CD-ROM.

Broude, Gwen J., and Sarah J. Greene. 1976. "Cross-Cultural Codes on Twenty Sexual Attitudes and Practices." *Ethnology,* 15: 409–29.

Brown, Cecil H. 1977. "Folk Botanical Life-Forms: Their Universality and Growth." *American Anthropologist,* 79: 317–42.

Brown, Cecil H. 1979. "Folk Zoological Life-Forms: Their Universality and Growth." *American Anthropologist,* 81: 791–817.

Brown, Cecil H. 1984. "World View and Lexical Uniformities." *Reviews in Anthropology,* 11: 99–112.

Brown, Cecil H., and Stanley R. Witkowski. 1980. "Language Universals." Appendix B in D. Levinson and M. J. Malone, eds., *Toward Explaining Human Culture.* New Haven, CT: HRAF Press.

Brown, Donald E. 1991. *Human Universals.* Philadelphia: Temple University Press.

Brown, Frank H. 1992. "Methods of Dating." In S. Jones, R. Martin, and D. Pilbeam, eds., *The Cambridge Encyclopedia of Human Evolution.* New York: Cambridge University Press.

Brown, Frank H. 2000. "Geochronometry." In I. Tattersall, G. Delson, and J. van Couvering, eds., *Encyclopedia of Human Evolution and Prehistory.* New York: Garland.

Brown, James A. 1983. "Summary." In J. L. Phillips and J. A. Brown, eds., *Archaic Hunters and Gatherers in the American Midwest.* New York: Academic Press, 5–10.

Brown, James A. 1985. "Long-Term Trends to Sedentism and the Emergence of Complexity in the American Midwest." In T. Price and J. Brown, eds., *Prehistoric Hunter-Gatherers,* Orlando, FL: Academic Press, 201–31.

Brown, James A., and T. Douglas Price. 1985. "Complex Hunter-Gatherers: Retrospect and Prospect." In T. Price and J. Brown, eds., *Prehistoric Hunter-Gatherers.* Orlando, FL: Academic Press.

Brown, Judith K. 1970a. "Economic Organization and the Position of Women among the Iroquois." *Ethnohistory,* 17: 151–67.

Brown, Judith K. 1970b. "A Note on the Division of Labor by Sex." *American Anthropologist,* 72: 1073–78.

Brown, Peter J. 1997. "Culture and the Evolution of Obesity." In A. Podolefsky and P. J. Brown, eds., *Applying Cultural Anthropology.* Mountain View, CA: Mayfield.

Brown, Roger. 1965. *Social Psychology.* New York: Free Press.

Brown, Roger. 1980. "The First Sentence of Child and Chimpanzee." In T. A. Sebeok and J. Umiker-Sebeok, eds., *Speaking of Apes.* New York: Plenum Press.

Brown, Roger, and Marguerite Ford. 1961. "Address in American English." *Journal of Abnormal and Social Psychology,* 62: 375–85.

Browner, C. H. 1985. "Criteria for Selecting Herbal Remedies." *Ethnology,* 24: 13–32.

Brumfiel, Elizabeth M. 1976. "Regional Growth in the Eastern Valley of Mexico: A Test of the 'Population Pressure' Hypothesis." In K. Flannery, ed., *The Early Mesoamerican Village.* New York: Academic Press.

Brumfiel, Elizabeth M. 1983. "Aztec State Making: Ecology, Structure, and the Origin of the State." *American Anthropologist,* 85: 261–84.

Brumfiel, Elizabeth M. 1992. "Distinguished Lecture in Archeology: Breaking and Entering the Ecosystem—Gender, Class, and Faction Steal the Show." *American Anthropologist,* 94: 551–67.

Brumfiel, Elizabeth M., ed. 1994. *The Economic Anthropology of the State.* Lanham, MD: University Press of America.

Brumfiel, Elizabeth M. 2002. "Origins of Social Inequality." In P. N. Peregrine, C. R. Ember, and M Ember, eds., *Archaeology.* Upper Saddle River, NJ: Prentice Hall.

Brumfiel, Elizabeth M. 2004. "Origins of Social Inequality," in *Research Frontiers in Anthropology,* in C. R. Ember, M. Ember, and P. N. Peregrine, eds., *New Directions in Anthropology.* Upper Saddle River, NJ: Prentice Hall, CD-ROM.

Brunet, Michel, et al. 2002. "A New Hominid from the Upper Miocene of Chad, Central Africa," *Nature,* 418 (July 11): 145–51.

Brunvand, Jan Harold. 1993. *The Baby Train: And Other Lusty Urban Legends.* New York: Norton.

Brusco, Elizabeth E. 1996. "Religious Conversion." In D. Levinson and M. Ember, eds., *Encyclopedia of Cultural Anthropology,* New York: Henry Holt, vol. 3, pp. 1100–04.

Bryant, Carol A., and Doraine F. C. Bailey. 1990. "The Use of Focus Group Research in Program Development." In J. van Willigen and T. L. Finan, eds., *Soundings.* NAPA Bulletin No. 10. Washington, DC: American Anthropological Association.

Bryne, Richard, and Andrew Whiten, eds. 1988. *Machiavellian Intelligence: Social Expertise and the Evolution of Intellect in Monkeys, Apes, and Humans.* Oxford: Clarendon Press.

Budiansky, Stephen. 1992. *The Covenant of the Wild: Why Animals Chose Domestication.* New York: Morrow.

Buettner-Janusch, John. 1973. *Physical Anthropology: A Perspective.* New York: Wiley.

Bunzel, Ruth. 1971. "The Nature of Katcinas." In W. A. Lessa and E. Z. Vogt, eds., *Reader in Comparative Religion.* 3rd ed. New York: Harper & Row.

Burbank, Victoria K. 1994. *Fighting Women: Anger and Aggression in Aboriginal Australia.* Berkeley: University of California Press.

Burbank, Victoria K. 2004a. "Adolescent Socialization and Initiation Ceremonies." In *Cross-Cultural Research for Social Science,* in C. R. Ember, M. Ember, and P. N. Peregrine, eds., *New Directions in Anthology.* Upper Saddle River, NJ: Prentice Hall CD-ROM.

Burbank, Victoria K. 2004b. "Australian Aborigines: An Adolescent Mother and Her Family." In *Portraits of Culture,* in C. R. Ember, M. Ember, and P. N. Peregrine, eds., *New Directions in Anthropology.* Upper Saddle River, NJ: Prentice Hall CD-ROM.

Burch, Ernest S., Jr. 1988. *The Eskimos.* Norman: University of Oklahoma Press.

Burch, Ernest S., Jr. 2004. "North Alaskan Eskimos: A Changing Way of Life." In *Portraits of Culture,* in C. R. Ember, M. Ember, and P. N. Peregrine, eds., *New Directions in Anthropology.* Upper Saddle River, NJ: Prentice Hall, CD-ROM.

Burch, Ernest S., Jr., and Linda J. Ellanna. 1994. *Key Issues in Hunter-Gatherer Research.* Oxford: Berg.

Burenhult, G., ed. 1994. *Old World Civilizations: The Rise of Cities and States.* St. Lucia, Queensland, Australia: University of Queensland Press.

Burkhalter, S. Brian, and Robert F. Murphy. 1989. "Tappers and Sappers: Rubber, Gold and Money among the Mundurucú." *American Ethnologist,* 16: 100–16.

Burling, Robbins. 1999. "Motivation, Conventionalization, and Arbitrariness in the Origin of Language." In B. J. King, ed., *The Origins of Language*. Santa Fe, NM: School of American Research Press, 307–50.

Burns, Alisa, and Cath Scott. 1994. *Mother-Headed Families and Why They Have Increased*. Hillsdale, NJ: Lawrence Erlbaum Associates.

Burton, Roger V., and John W. M. Whiting. 1961. "The Absent Father and Cross-Sex Identity." *Merrill-Palmer Quarterly of Behavior and Development*, 7, no. 2: 85–95.

Busby, Annette. 2004. "Kurds: A Culture Straddling National Borders." In *Portraits of Culture*, in C. R. Ember, M. Ember, and P. N. Peregrine, eds., *New Directions in Anthropology*. Upper Saddle River, NJ: Prentice Hall, CD-ROM.

Butzer, Karl W. 1982. "Geomorphology and Sediment Stratigraphy." In R. Singer and J. Wymer, *The Middle Stone Age at Klasies River Mouth in South Africa*. Chicago: University of Chicago Press.

Byrne, Bryan. 1994. "Access to Subsistence Resources and the Sexual Division of Labor among Potters." *Cross-Cultural Research*, 28: 225–50.

Byrne, Roger. 1987. "Climatic Change and the Origins of Agriculture." In L. Manzanilla, ed., *Studies in the Neolithic and Urban Revolutions*. British Archaeological Reports International Series 349. Oxford.

Calvin, William H. 1983. *The Throwing Madonna: Essays on the Brain*. New York: McGraw-Hill.

Campbell, Allan M. 1991. "Microbes: The Laboratory and the Field." In B. Davis, ed., *The Genetic Revolution*. Baltimore: Johns Hopkins University Press.

Campbell, Bernard G. 1985. *Humankind Emerging*. 4th ed. Boston: Little, Brown.

Campbell, Donald T. 1965. "Variation and Selective Retention in Socio-Cultural Evolution." In H. Barringer, G. Blankstein, and R. Mack, eds., *Social Change in Developing Areas*. Cambridge, MA: Schenkman.

Campbell, Joseph. 1949. *The Hero with a Thousand Faces*. New York: Pantheon.

Cancian, Frank. 1980. "Risk and Uncertainty in Agricultural Decision Making." In P. F. Barlett, ed., *Agricultural Decision Making*. New York: Academic Press.

Cann, Rebecca. 1988. "DNA and Human Origins." *Annual Review of Anthropology*, 17: 127–43.

Cann, Rebecca, M. Stoneking, and A. C. Wilson. 1987. "Mitochondrial DNA and Human Evolution." *Nature*, 325 (January 1): 31–36.

Caporael, Linnda R. 1976. "Ergotism: The Satan Loosed in Salem?" *Science*, (April 2): 21–26.

Cardoso, Fernando Luis and Dennis Werner. 2004. "Homosexuality." In C. Ember and M. Ember, eds. *Encyclopedia of Sex and Gender: Men and Women in the World's Cultures*. Vol 1. New York: Kluwer Academic/Plenum Publishers, pp. 204–15.

Carey, James W., Erin Picone-DeCaro, Mary Spink Neumann, Devorah Schwartz, Delia Easton, and Daphne Cobb St. John. 2004. "HIV/AIDS Research and Prevention." In C. R. Ember and M. Ember, eds. *Encyclopedia of Medical Anthropology: Health and Illness in the World's Cultures*. New York: Kluwer Academic/Plenum, vol. 1, pp. 462–79.

Carcopino, Jerome. 1940. *Daily Life in Ancient Rome: The People and the City at the Height of the Empire*. Edited with bibliography and notes by Henry T. Rowell. Translated from the French by E. O. Lorimer. New Haven, CT: Yale University Press.

Carneiro, Robert L. 1968. "Slash-and-Burn Cultivation among the Kuikuru and Its Implications for Settlement Patterns." In Y. Cohen, ed., *Man in Adaptation*. Chicago, Aldine.

Carneiro, Robert L. 1970. "A Theory of the Origin of the State." *Science*, 169 (August 21): 733–38.

Carneiro, Robert L. 1978. "Political Expansion as an Expression of the Principle of Competitive Exclusion." In R. Cohen and E. R. Service, eds., *Origins of the State*. Philadelphia: Institute for the Study of Human Issues.

Carneiro, Robert L. 1988. "The Circumscription Theory: Challenge and Response." *American Behavioral Scientist*, 31: 497–511.

Carneiro, Robert L. 1990. "Chiefdom-Level Warfare as Exemplified in Fiji and the Cauca Valley." In J. Haas, ed., *The Anthropology of War*. New York: Cambridge University Press.

Carpenter, C. R. 1940. "A Field Study in Siam of the Behavior and Social Relations of the Gibbon (*Hylobates lar*)." *Comparative Psychology Monographs*, 16, no. 5: 1–212.

Carpenter, Sandra. 2000. "Effects of Cultural Tightness and Collectivism on Self-Concept and Causal Attributions." *Cross-Cultural Research*, 34: 38–56.

Carrasco, Pedro. 1961. "The Civil-Religious Hierarchy in Mesoamerican Communities: Pre-Spanish Background and Colonial Development." *American Anthropologist*, 63: 483–97.

Carrier, James G. 1987. "Marine Tenure and Conservation in Papua New Guinea." In B. M. McCay and J. M. Acheson, eds., *The Question of the Commons*. Tucson: University of Arizona Press.

Carrier, Joseph, and Ralph Bolton. 1991. "Anthropological Perspectives on Sexuality and HIV Prevention." *Annual Review of Sex Research*, 2: 49–75.

Carroll, John B., ed. 1956. *Language, Thought, and Reality: Selected Writings of Benjamin Lee Whorf*. New York: Wiley.

Carroll, Michael. 1979. "A New Look at Freud on Myth." *Ethos*, 7: 189–205.

Cartmill, Matt. 1974. "Rethinking Primate Origins," *Science*, (April 26): 436–37.

Cartmill, Matt. 1992a. "New Views on Primate Origins." *Evolutionary Anthropology*, 1: 105–11.

Cartmill, Matt. 1992b. "Non-Human Primates." In S. Jones, R. Martin, and D. Pilbeam, eds., *The Cambridge Encyclopedia of Human Evolution*. New York: Cambridge University Press.

Cartmill, Matt. 2002. "Explaining Primate Origins." In P. N. Peregrine, C. R. Ember, and M. Ember, eds., *Physical Anthropology: Original Readings in Method and Practice*. Upper Saddle River, NJ: Prentice Hall.

Cashdan, Elizabeth A. 1980. "Egalitarianism among Hunters and Gatherers." *American Anthropologist*, 82: 116–20.

Cashdan, Elizabeth, ed. 1990. *Risk and Uncertainty in Tribal and Peasant Economies*. Boulder, CO: Westview.

Cashdan, Elizabeth. 2001. "Ethnic Diversity and Its Environmental Determinants: Effects of Climate, Pathogens, and Habitat Diversity." *American Anthropologist*, 103: 968–91.

Cattell, Maria G., And Steven M. Albert. 2004. "Caring for the Elderly." In *Research Frontiers*, in C. R. Ember, M. Ember and P. N. Peregrine, eds., *New Directions in Anthropology*. Upper Saddle River, NJ: Prentice Hall, CD-ROM.

Caulkins, D. Douglas. 1997. "Welsh." In D. Levinson and M. Ember, eds., *American Immigrant Cultures: Builders of a Nation*. New York: Macmillan Reference, vol. 2, pp. 935–41.

Caulkins, D. Douglas. 2004. "Norwegians: Cooperative Individualists." In *Portraits of Culture*, in C. R. Ember, M. Ember, and P. N. Peregrine, eds, *New Directions in Anthropology*. Upper Saddle River, NJ: Prentice Hall, CD-ROM.

Cavalli-Sforza, L. L., and M. W. Feldman. 1981. *Cultural Transmission and Evolution: A Quantitative Approach*. Princeton, NJ: Princeton University Press.

Cavalli-Sforza, L. Luca, and Marcus W. Feldman. 2003. "The Application of Molecular Genetic Approaches to the Study of Human Evolution." *Nature Genetics Supplement* 33: 266–75.

Caws, Peter. 1969. "The Structure of Discovery." *Science*, 166 (December 12): 1375–80.

Center for Renewal of Science and Culture. 2001. "The Wedge Strategy," cited in Barbara Forrest, "The Wedge at Work," in Robert Pennock, ed., *Intelligent Design Creationism and its Critics*. Boston, IT Press, p. 16.

Cernea, Michael M., ed. 1991. *Putting People First: Sociological Variables in Development.* 2nd ed. New York: Oxford University Press.

Chafetz, Janet Saltzman. 1990. *Gender Equity: An Integrated Theory of Stability and Change.* Sage Library of Social Research No. 176. Newbury Park, CA: Sage.

Chagnon, Napoleon. 1987. *Yanomamö: The Fierce People.* 3rd ed. New York: Holt, Rinehardt, and Winston.

Chagnon, Napoleon, and William Irons, eds. 1979. *Evolutionary Biology and Human Social Behavior: An Anthropological Perspective.* North Scituate, MA: Duxbury.

Chambers, Erve. 1989. *Applied Anthropology: A Practical Guide.* Rev. ed. Prospect Heights, IL: Waveland.

Chang, Kwang-Chih. 1968. *The Archaeology of Ancient China.* New Haven, CT: Yale University Press.

Chang, Kwang-Chih. 1970. "The Beginnings of Agriculture in the Far East." *Antiquity,* 44: 175–85.

Chang, Kwang-Chih. 1981. "In Search of China's Beginnings: New Light on an Old Civilization." *American Scientist,* 69: 148–60.

Chang, Kwang-Chih. 1986. *Archaeology of Ancient China.* 4th ed. New Haven, CT: Yale University Press: 234–94.

Chapman, Jefferson. 1985. *Tellico Archaeology.* Knoxville: Tennessee Valley Authority.

Chard, Chester S. 1969. *Man in Prehistory.* New York: McGraw-Hill.

Charles-Dominique, Pierre. 1977. *Ecology and Behaviour of Nocturnal Primates.* Trans. R. D. Martin. New York: Columbia University Press.

Charnais, Peter. 1953. "Economic Factors in the Decline of the Roman Empire." *Journal of Economic History,* 13: 412–24.

Chase, Philip and Harold Dibble. 1987. "Middle Paleolithic Symbolism: A Review of Current Evidence and Interpretations." *Journal of Anthropological Archaeology,* 6: 263–69.

Chatterjee, Sankar, 1997. *The Rise of Birds: 225 Million Years of Evolution.* Baltimore: Johns Hopkins.

Chatty, Dawn. 1996. *Mobile Pastoralists: Development Planning and Social Change in Oman.* New York: Columbia University Press.

Chaucer, Geoffrey. 1926. *The Prologue to the Canterbury Tales, the Knights Tale, the Nonnes Prestes Tale.* Ed. Mark H. Liddell. New York: Macmillan.

Chayanov, Alexander V. 1966. *The Theory of Peasant Economy,* Eds. Daniel Thorner, Basile Kerblay, and R. E. F. Smith. Homewood, IL: Richard D. Irwin.

Chen, F. C., and W. H. LI. 2001. "Genomic Divergences between Humans and Other Hominoids and the Effective Population Size of the Common Ancestor of Humans and Chimpanzees." *American Journal of Human Genetics,* 68: 445–56.

Cheney, Dorothy, and Robert Seyfarth. 1990. *How Monkeys See the World.* Chicago: University of Chicago Press.

Cheney, Dorothy, L., and Richard W. Wrangham. 1987. "Predation." In B. Smuts et al., eds., *Primate Societies.* Chicago: University of Chicago Press.

Chia, L. 1990. *The Story of Peking Man: From Archaeology to Mystery.* Oxford: Oxford University Press.

Chibnik, Michael. 1980. "The Statistical Behavior Approach: The Choice between Wage Labor and Cash Cropping in Rural Belize." In P. F. Barlett, ed., *Agricultural Decision Making.* New York: Academic Press.

Chibnik, Michael. 1981. "The Evolution of Cultural Rules." *Journal of Anthropological Research,* 37: 256–68.

Chibnik, Michael. 1987. "The Economic Effects of Household Demography: A Cross-Cultural Assessment of Chayanov's Theory." In M. D. MacLachlan, ed., *Household Economies and Their Transformations.* Monographs in Economic Anthropology No 3. Lanham, MD: University Press of America.

Chick, Garry. 1998. "Games in Culture Revisited: A Replication and Extension of Roberts, Arth, and Bush [1959]." *Cross-Cultural Research,* 32: 185–206.

Child, Alice B., and Irvin L. Child. 1993. *Religion and Magic in the Life of Traditional Peoples.* Upper Saddle River NJ: Prentice Hall.

Childe, V. Gordon. 1950. "The Urban Revolution." *Town Planning Review,* 21: 3–17.

"Children as Victims." 2000. *Juvenile Justice Bulletin 1999.* National Report Series. Washington, DC: U.S. Department of Justice.

Chiras, D. D. 2002. *Human Biology: Health, Homeostasis, and the Environment,* 4th ed. Boston: Jones and Bartlett.

Chivers, David J. 1974. *The Siamang in Malaya.* Basel, Switzerland: Karger.

Chivers, David J., ed. 1980. *Malayan Forest Primates: Ten Years' Study in Tropical Rain Forest.* New York: Plenum.

Chivers, David J., Bernard A. Wood, and Alan Bilsborough, eds. 1984. *Food Acquisition and Processing in Primates.* New York: Plenum.

Chomsky, Noam. 1975. *Reflections on Language.* New York: Pantheon.

Christensen, Pia, Jenny Hockey, and Allison James, 2001. "Talk, Silence and the Material World: Patterns of Indirect Communication among Agricultural Farmers in Northern England." In J. Hendry and C. W. Watson, eds., *An Anthropology of Indirect Communication.* London: Routledge, 68–82.

Ciochon, Russell L., and Robert S. Corruccini, eds. 1983. *New Interpretations of Ape and Human Ancestry.* New York: Plenum.

Ciochon, Russell L., and Dennis A. Etler. 1994. "Reinterpreting Past Primate Diversity." In R. Corruccini and R. Ciochon, eds., *Integrative Paths to the Past.* Upper Saddle River, NJ: Prentice Hall.

Ciochon, Russell L., and John G. Fleagle, eds. 1993. *The Human Evolution Source Book.* Upper Saddle River, NJ: Prentice Hall.

Ciochon, Russell, John Olsen, and Jamie James. 1990. *Other Origins: The Search for the Giant Ape in Human Prehistory.* New York: Bantam.

Claassen, Cheryl. 1991. "Gender, Shellfishing, and the Shell Mound Archaic." In J. Gero and M. Conkey, eds., *Engendering Archaeology.* Oxford: Blackwell.

Claassen, Cheryl. 2002. "Gender and Archaeology." In P. N. Peregrine, C. R. Ember, and M. Ember, eds., *Archaeology: Original Readings in Method and Practice.* Upper Saddle River, NJ: Prentice Hall.

Clark, Andrew et al., 2003. "Inferring Nonneutral Evolution from Human-Chimp-Mouse Orthologous Gene Trios," *Science,* 302 (December 12): 1960–63.

Clark, Geoffrey A., ed. 1991. *Perspectives on the Past: Theoretical Biases in Mediterranean Hunter-Gatherer Research.* Philadelphia: University of Pennsylvania Press.

Clark, Grahame. 1975. *The Earlier Stone Age Settlement of Scandinavia.* Cambridge: Cambridge University Press.

Clark, Grahame, and Stuart Piggott. 1965. *Prehistoric Societies.* New York: Knopf.

Clark, J. Desmond. 1970. *The Prehistory of Africa.* New York: Praeger.

Clark, J. Desmond. 1977. "Interpretations of Prehistoric Technology from Ancient Egyptian and Other Sources. Pt. II: Prehistoric Arrow Forms in Africa as Shown by Surviving Examples of the Traditional Arrows of the San Bushmen." *Paleorient,* 3: 127–50.

Clark, W. E. Le Gros. 1964. *The Fossil Evidence for Human Evolution.* Chicago: University of Chicago Press, p. 184.

Clarke, Ronald J., and P. V. Tobias. 1995. "Sterkfontein Member 2 Foot Bones of the Oldest South African Hominid." *Science,* 269 (July 28): 521–24.

Clayman, Charles B., ed. 1989. *American Medical Association Encyclopedia of Medicine.* New York: Random House: 857–58.

Cleland, C., ed. 1976. *Cultural Continuity and Change.* New York: Academic Press.

Clifford, James. 1986. "Introduction: Partial Truths." In J. Clifford and G. E. Marcus, eds. *Writing Culture: The Poetics and Politics of Ethnography.* Berkeley: University of California Press.

Clifton, James H., ed. 1968. *Introduction to Cultural Anthropology.* Boston: Houghton Mifflin.

Clutton-Brock, Juliet. 1984. "Dog." In I. Mason, *Evolution of Domesticated Animals.* New York: Longman.

Clutton-Brock, Juliet. 1992. "Domestication of Animals." In S. Jones, R. Martin, and D. Pilbeam, eds., *The Cambridge Encyclopedia of Human Evolution.* New York: Cambridge University Press.

Clutton-Brock, Juliet. 1995. "Origins of the Dog: Domestication and Early History." In James Serpell, ed., *The Domestic Dog: Its Evolution, Behaviour, and Interactions with People.* Cambridge: Cambridge University Press, 8–20.

Clutton-Brock, T. H., and Paul H. Harvey. 1977. "Primate Ecology and Social Organization." *Journal of Zoology,* London, 183: 1–39.

Clutton-Brock, T. H., and Paul H. Harvey. 1980. "Primates, Brains and Ecology." *Journal of Zoology,* London, 190: 309–23.

Coale, Ansley J. 1974. "The History of the Human Population." *Scientific American* (September): 41–51.

Coe, Michael D. 1966. *The Maya.* New York: Praeger.

Cohen, Alex. 1990. "A Cross-Cultural Study of the Effects of Environmental Unpredictability on Aggression in Folktales." *American Anthropologist,* 92: 474–79.

Cohen, Alex. 1999. *The Mental Health of Indigenous Peoples: An International Overview.* Geneva: Department of Mental Health, World Health Organization.

Cohen, Alex. 2004. "Mental Disorders." In C. R. Ember and M. Ember, eds. *Encyclopedia of Medical Anthropology: Health and Illness in the World's Cultures.* New York: Kluwer Academic/Plenum, vol. 1, 486–93.

Cohen, Alex, and Paul Koegel. 2004. "Homelessness." In *Research Frontiers,* in C. R. Ember, M. Ember, and P. N. Peregrine, eds. *New Directions in Anthropology.* Upper Saddle River, NJ: Prentice Hall, CD-ROM.

Cohen, Mark N. 1977a. *The Food Crisis in Prehistory: Overpopulation and the Origins of Agriculture.* New Haven, CT: Yale University Press.

Cohen, Mark N. 1977b. "Population Pressure and the Origins of Agriculture." In C. A. Reed, ed., *Origins of Agriculture.* The Hague: Monton.

Cohen, Mark N. 1987. "The Significance of Long-Term Changes in Human Diet and Food Economy." In M. Harris and E Ross, eds., *Food and Evolution.* Philadelphia: Temple University Press.

Cohen, Mark. 1989. *Health and the Rise of Civilization.* New Haven, CT: Yale University Press.

Cohen, Mark. 1998. *Culture of Intolerance: Chauvinism, Class, and Racism in the United States.* New Haven, CT: Yale University Press.

Cohen, Mark N. 2002. "Were Early Agriculturalists Less Healthy Than Food Collectors?" In P. N. Peregrine, C. R. Ember, and M. Ember, eds., *Archaeology: Original Readings in Method and Practice.* Upper Saddle River, NJ: Prentice Hall.

Cohen, Mark Nathan, and George J. Armelagos, eds. 1984a. *Paleopathology at the Origins of Agriculture.* Orlando, FL: Academic Press.

Cohen, Mark Nathan, and George J. Armelagos. 1984b. "Paleopathology at the Origins of Agriculture: Editors' Summation." In M. N. Cohen and G. J. Armelagos, eds., *Paleopathology at the Origins of Agriculture.* Orlando, FL: Academic Press.

Cohen, Myron. 1970. "Developmental Process in the Chinese Domestic Group." In M. Freedman, ed., *Family and Kinship in Chinese Society.* Stanford, CA: Stanford University Press.

Cohen, Myron L. 1976. *House United, House Divided: The Chinese Family in Taiwan.* New York: Columbia University Press.

Cohen, Ronald. 1988. "Introduction." In R. Cohen and J. D. Toland, eds., *State Formation and Political Legitimacy.* Vol. 6: *Political Anthropology.* New Brunswick, NJ: Transaction Books.

Cohen, Ronald, and Elman R. Service, eds. 1978. *Origins of the State: The Anthropology of Political Evolution.* Philadelphia: Institute for the Study of Human Issues.

Cohen, Ronald, and Judith D. Toland, eds. 1988. *State Formation and Political Legitimacy.* Vol. 1: *Political Anthropology.* New Brunswick, NJ: Transaction Books.

Cohen, Ronald, and Judith D. Toland, eds. 1988. *State Formation and Political Legitimacy.* Vol. 6: *Political Anthropology.* New Brunswick, NJ: Transaction Books.

Cohen, Wesley. 1995. "Empirical Studies of Innovative Activity." In P. Stoneman, ed., *Handbook of the Economics of Innovation and Technological Change.* Oxford: Blackwell.

Cohen, Yehudi, ed. 1968. *Man in Adaptation: The Cultural Present.* Chicago: Aldine.

COHMAP Personnel. 1988. "Climatic Changes of the Last 18,000 Years." *Science,* 241 (August 26): 1043–52.

Colby, Benjamin N. 1996. "Cognitive Anthropology." In D. Levinson and M. Ember, eds. *Encyclopedia of Cultural Anthropology,* 4 vols. New York: Henry Holt, vol. 1, pp. 209–15.

Collier, Stephen, and J. Peter White. 1976. "Get Them Young? Age and Sex Inferences on Animal Domestication in Archaeology." *American Antiquity,* 41: 96–102.

Collins, Desmond. 1976. "Later Hunters in Europe." In D. Collins, ed., *The Origins of Europe.* New York: Thomas Y. Crowell.

Collins, James and Richard Blot. 2003. *Literacy and Literacies.* Cambridge: Cambridge University Press.

Conklin, Beth A. 2002. "Shamans versus Pirates in the Amazonian Treasure Chest." *American Anthropologist,* 104: 1050–61.

Connah, Graham. 1987. *African Civilizations: Precolonial Cities and States in Tropical Africa.* Cambridge: Cambridge University Press.

Conroy, Glenn C. 1990. *Primate Evolution.* New York: Norton.

Conroy, Glenn C. 1997. *Reconstructing Human Origins: A Modern Synthesis.* New York: W. W. Norton.

Cooper, Richard S., Charles N. Rotimi, and Ryk Ward. 1999. "The Puzzle of Hypertension in African-Americans." *Scientific American* (February): 56–63.

Coreil, Jeannine. 1989. "Lessons from a Community Study of Oral Rehydration Therapy in Haiti." In J. van Willigen, B. Rylko-Bauer, and A. McElroy, eds., *Making Our Research Useful.* Boulder, CO: Westview.

Coreil, Jeannine. 2004. "Malaria and other Major Insect Vector Diseases." In C. R. Ember and M. Ember, eds. *Encyclopedia of Medical Anthropology: Health and Illness in the World's Cultures.* New York: Kluwer Academic/Plenum, vol. 1, 479–85.

Corruccini, Robert S., and Russell L. Ciochon, eds. 1994. *Integrative Paths to the Past: Paleoanthropological Advances in Honor of F. Clark Howell.* Upper Saddle River, NJ: Prentice Hall.

Costin, Cathy Lynne. 2002. "Cloth Production and Gender Relations in the Inka Empire." In P. N. Peregrine, C. R. Ember, and M. Ember, eds., *Archaeology: Original Readings in Method and Practice.* Upper Saddle River, NJ: Prentice Hall.

Coult, Allan D., and Robert W. Habenstein. 1965. *Cross Tabulations of Murdock's World Ethnographic Sample.* Columbia: University of Missouri Press.

Cowan, C. Wesley, and Patty Jo Watson, eds. 1992. *The Origins of Agriculture.* Washington, DC: Smithsonian Institution Press.

Crawford, Gary W. 1992. "Prehistoric Plant Domestication in East Asia." In C. Cowan and P. Watson, eds., *The Origins of Agriculture.* Washington, DC: Smithsonian Institution Press.

Crawford, R. D. 1984. "Turkey." In I. Mason, ed., *Evolution of Domesticated Animals.* New York: Longman.

Creed, Gerald W. 2004. "Bulgaria: Anthropological Corrections to Cold War Stereotypes." In *Portraits of Culture,* in C. R. Ember, M. Ember, and P. N. Peregrine, eds., *New Directions in Anthropology.* Upper Saddle River, NJ: Prentice Hall, CD-ROM.

Crockett, Carolyn, and John F. Eisenberg. 1987. "Howlers: Variations in Group Size and Demography." In B. Smuts et al., eds., *Primate Societies*. Chicago: University of Chicago Press.

"Cross-Cultural and Comparative Research: Theory and Method." 1991. *Behavior Science Research*, 25: 1–270.

"Crossroads for Planet Earth." 2005. *Scientific American*. Special Issue, September.

Crystal, David. 1971. *Linguistics*. Middlesex, UK: Penguin.

Culotta, Elizabeth. 1995. "New Hominid Crowds the Field." *Science*, 269 (August 18): 918.

Culotta, Elizabeth. 2005. "Calorie Count Reveals Neandertals Out-Ate Hardiest Modern Humans." *Science*, 307 (February 11): 840.

Curtin, Philip D. 1984. *Cross-Cultural Trade in World History*. Cambridge: Cambridge University Press.

Cutright, Phillips. 1967. "Inequality: A Cross-National Analysis." *American Sociological Review*, 32: 562–78.

Dahlberg, Frances, ed. 1981. *Woman the Gatherer*. New Haven, CT: Yale University Press.

Daiger, Stephen. 2005. "Was the Human Genome Project Worth the Effort?" *Science*, 308 (April 15): 362–64.

Dalton, George, ed. 1967. *Tribal and Peasant Economies: Readings in Economic Anthropology*. Garden City, NY: Natural History Press.

Daly, Martin, and Margo Wilson. 1988. *Homicide*. New York: Aldine.

Damon, Albert, ed. 1975. *Physiological Anthropology*. New York: Oxford University Press.

Daniel, I. Randolph. 2001. "Early Eastern Archaic." In P. N. Peregrine and M. Ember, eds., *Encyclopedia of Prehistory*. Vol. 6: North America. Kluwer: Academic/Plenum.

Dart, Raymond. 1925. "*Australopithecus africanus*: The Man-Ape of South Africa." *Nature*, 115: 195.

Darwin, Charles. [1859]. "The Origin of Species." In L. B. Young, ed., *Evolution of Man*. New York: Oxford University Press.

Dasen, Pierre R., John W. Berry, and N. Sartorius, eds. 1988. *Health and Cross-Cultural Psychology: Toward Applications*. Newbury Park, CA: Sage.

Dasen, Pierre R., and Alastair Heron. 1981. "Cross-Cultural Tests of Piaget's Theory." In H. C. Triandis and A. Heron, eds., *Handbook of Cross-Cultural Psychology*. Vol. 4: *Developmental Psychology*. Boston: Allyn & Bacon.

Davenport, William. 1959. "Nonunilinear Descent and Descent Groups." *American Anthropologist*, 61: 557–72.

Davis, Bernard D. 1991a. "The Issues: Prospects versus Perceptions." In Davis, ed., *The Genetic Revolution*. Baltimore: Johns Hopkins University Press.

Davis, Bernard D. 1991b. "Summary and Comments: The Scientific Chapters." In Davis, ed., *The Genetic Revolution*. Baltimore: Johns Hopkins University Press.

Davis, Bernard D., ed. 1991. *The Genetic Revolution: Scientific Prospects and Public Perceptions*. Baltimore: Johns Hopkins University Press.

Davis, Deborah, and Stevan Harrell, eds. 1993. *Chinese Families in the Post-Mao Era*. Berkeley: University of California Press.

Davis, Susan Schaefer. 1993. "Rebellious Teens? A Moroccan Instance." Paper presented at MESA, November.

Davis, Susan Schaefer. 2004. "Morocco: Adolescents in a Small Town." In *Portraits of Culture*, in C. R. Ember, M. Ember, and P. N. Peregrine, eds., *New Directions in Anthropology*. Upper Saddle River, NJ: Prentice Hall, CD-ROM.

Davis, William D. 1971. "Societal Complexity and the Nature of Primitive Man's Conception of the Supernatural." Ph.D. dissertation; University of North Carolina, Chapel Hill.

Dawson, Alistair. 1992. *Ice Age Earth*. London: Routledge: 24–71.

Dawson, J. L. M. 1967. "Cultural and Physiological Influences upon Spatial-Perceptual Processes in West Africa." *International Journal of Psychology*, 2: 115–28, 171–85.

Day, Michael. 1986. *Guide to Fossil Man*. 4th ed. Chicago: University of Chicago Press.

De Laguna, Frederica. 1972. *Under Mount Saint Elias: The History and Culture of the Yakutat Tlingit*. Washington, DC: Smithsonian Institution Press, as seen in the eHRAF Collection of Ethnography on the Web, 2000.

De Lumley, Henry. 1969. "A Paleolithic Camp at Nice." *Scientific American* (May): 42–50.

DeMenocal, Peter. 2001. "Cultural Responses to Climate Change During the Late Holocene." *Science*, 292 (April 27): 667–673.

De Munck, Victor C., and Andrey Korotayev. 1999. "Sexual Equality and Romantic Love: A Reanalysis of Rosenblatt's Study on the Function of Romantic Love." *Cross-Cultural Research*, 33: 265–273.

De Munck, Victor C., and Elisa J. Sobo, eds. 1998. *Using Methods in the Field: A Practical Introduction and Casebook*. Walnut Creek, CA: AltaMira Press.

De Villiers, Peter A., and Jill G. De Villiers. 1979. *Early Language*. Cambridge, MA: Harvard University Press.

De Vita, Philip, and James D. Armstrong. 2001. *Distant Mirrors: America as a Foreign Culture*, 3rd ed. Belmont, CA: Wadsworth.

De Waal, Frans. 2001. *The Ape and the Sushi Master: Cultural Reflections of a Primatologist*. New York: Basic Books.

De Waal, Frans, and Frans Lanting. 1997. *Bonobo: The Forgotten Ape*. Berkeley: University of California Press.

Deacon, Terrence. 1992. "Primate Brains and Senses." In S. Jones, R. Martin, and D. Pilbeam, eds., *The Cambridge Encyclopedia of Human Evolution*. New York: Cambridge University Press.

Deacon, Terrence. 1997. *The Symbolic Species: The Co-Evolution of Language and the Brain*. New York: Norton.

Delson, Eric, ed. 1985. *Ancestors: The Hard Evidence*. New York: Alan R. Liss.

Denham, T. P., S. G. Haberle, C. Lentfer, R. Fullagar, J. Field, M. Therin, N. Porch, and B. Winsborough. 2003. "Origins of Agriculture at Kuk Swamp in the Highlands of New Guinea." *Science*, 301 (July 11): 189–93.

Denny, J. Peter. 1979. "The 'Extendedness' Variable in Classifier Semantics: Universal Features and Cultural Variation." In M. Mathiot, ed., *Ethnolinguistics*. The Hague: Mouton.

Dentan, Robert K. 1968. *The Semai: A Nonviolent People of Malaya*. New York: Holt, Rinehart & Winston.

Deutsch, A., ed. 1948. *Sex Habits of American Men*. Upper Saddle River, NJ: Prentice Hall.

Devillers, Charles, and Jean Chaline. 1993. *Evolution: An Evolving Theory*. New York: Springer Verlag.

DeVore, Irven, and Melvin J. Konner. 1974. "Infancy in Hunter-Gatherer Life: An Ethological Perspective." In N. F. White, ed., *Ethology and Psychiatry*. Toronto: Ontario Mental Health Foundation and University of Toronto Press.

Diament, Michelle. 2005. "Diversifying Their Crops: Agriculture Schools, Focusing on Job Prospects, Reach out to Potential Students from Cities and Suburbs," *The Chronicle of Higher Education*, pp. A32–34.

Diamond, Jared. 1989. "The Accidental Conqueror." *Discover* (December): 71–76.

Diamond, Jared. 1991. "The Saltshaker's Curse—Physiological Adaptations That Helped American Blacks Survive Slavery May Now Be Predisposing Their Descendants to Hypertension." *Natural History* (October): 20–27.

Diamond, Jared. 1993. "Who Are the Jews?" *Natural History* (November): 12–19.

Diamond, Jared. 1997a. *Guns, Germs, and Steel*. New York: Norton: 205–207.

Diamond, Jared. 1997b. "Location, Location, Location: The First Farmers." *Science*, 278 (November 14): 1243–44.

Diamond, Jared. 2004. "The Astonishing Micropygmies." *Science*, 306 (December 17): 2047–48.

Diamond, Norma. 1975. "Collectivization, Kinship, and the Status of Women in Rural China." In R. R. Reiter, *Toward an Anthropology of Women.* New York: Monthly Review Press.

Diamond, Stanley. 1974. *In Search of the Primitive: A Critique of Civilization.* New Brunswick, NJ: Transaction Books.

Dibble, Harold, and P. Mellars, eds. 1992. *The Middle Paleolithic: Adaptation, Behavior, and Variability.* Philadelphia: University Museum.

Dibble, Harold P. Chase, S. McPherron, and A. Tuffreau. 1997. "Testing the Reality of a 'Living Floor' with Archaeological Data." *American Antiquity,* 62: 629–51.

Dickson, D. Bruce. 1990. *The Dawn of Belief.* Tucson: University of Arizona Press, 42–44.

Dickson, D. Bruce, Jeffrey Olsen, P. Fred Dahm, and Mitchell S. Wachtel. 2005. "Where Do You Go When You Die? A Cross-Cultural Test of the Hypothesis That Infrastructure Predicts Individual Eschatology." *Journal of Anthropological Research,* 1: 53–79.

Dillehay, Thomas. 2000. *The Settlement of the Americas.* New York: Basic Books.

Dirks, Robert. 1993. "Starvation and Famine." *Cross-Cultural Research,* 27: 28–69.

Dirks, Robert. 2004. "Hunger and Famine." In *Research Frontiers* in C. R. Ember, M. Ember, and P. N. Peregrine, eds., *New Directions in Anthropology.* Upper Saddle River, NJ: Prentice Hall, CD-ROM.

Divale, William T. 1974. "Migration, External Warfare, and Matrilocal Residence." *Behavior Science Research,* 9: 75–133.

Divale, William T., and Marvin Harris. 1976. "Population, Warfare, and the Male Supremacist Complex." *American Anthropologist,* 78: 521–38.

Divale, William, and Clifford Zipin. 1977. "Hunting and the Development of Sign Language: A Cross-Cultural Test." *Journal of Anthropological Research,* 33: 185–201.

Dobres, Marcia-Anne. 1998. "Venus Figurines." In B. Fagan, ed., *Oxford Companion to Archaeology.* Oxford: Oxford University Press, 740–41.

Dobzhansky, Theodosius. 1962. *Mankind Evolving: The Evolution of the Human Species.* New Haven, CT: Yale University Press.

Dohlinow, Phyllis Jay, ed. 1972. *Primate Patterns.* New York: Holt, Rinehart & Winston.

Dohlinow, Phyllis Jay, and Naomi Bishop. 1972. "The Development of Motor Skills and Social Relationships among Primates through Play." In Phyllis Jay Dohlinow, ed., *Primate Patterns.* New York: Holt, Rinehart & Winston.

Donaldson, Peter. 1971. *Worlds Apart: The Economic Gulf between Nations.* London: British Broadcasting Corporation.

Douglas, Mary. 1975. *Implicit Meanings: Essays in Anthropology.* London: Rontledge and Kegan Paul.

Dow, James. 1986. *The Shaman's Touch: Otomi Indian Symbolic Healing.* Salt Lake City: University of Utah Press.

Dow, James W. 2004. "Sierra Otomi: People of the Mexican Mountains." In *Portraits of Culture,* in C. R. Ember, M. Ember, and P. N. Peregrine, *New Directions in Anthropology.* Upper Saddle River, NJ: Prentice Hall, CD-ROM.

Dowling, John H. 1975. "Property Relations and Productive Strategies in Pastoral Societies." *American Ethnologist,* 2: 419–26.

Doyle, G. A., and R. D. Martin, eds. 1979. *The Study of Prosimian Behavior.* New York: Academic Press.

Doyle, Rodger. 2004. "Living Together: In the U.S. Cohabitation is Here to Stay." *Scientific American* (January): 28.

Doyle, Rodger. 2005. "Leveling the Playing Field: Economic Development Helps Women Pull Even with Men." *Scientific American* (June): 32.

Draper, Patricia. 1975. "!Kung Women: Contrasts in Sexual Egalitarianism in Foraging and Sedentary Contexts." In R. R. Reiter, ed., *Toward an Anthropology of Women.* New York: Monthly Review Press.

Dobzhansky, Theodosius, 1973. *Genetic Diversity and Human Equality.* New York: Basic Books.

Draper, Patricia, and Elizabeth Cashdan. 1988. "Technological Change and Child Behavior among the !Kung." *Ethnology,* 27: 339–65.

Dressler, William W. 1991. *Stress and Adaptation in the Context of Culture.* Albany: State University of New York Press.

Dressler, William W. 1993. "Health in the African American Community: Accounting for Health Inequalities." *Medical Anthropology Quarterly,* 7: 325–45.

Dressler, William W., and Michael C. Robbins. 1975. "Art Styles, Social Stratification, and Cognition: An Analysis of Greek Vase Painting." *American Ethnologist,* 2: 427–34.

Drucker, Philip. 1965. *Cultures of the North Pacific Coast.* San Francisco: Chandler.

Drucker, Philip. 1967. "The Potlatch." In G. Dalton, ed., *Tribal and Peasant Economies.* Garden City, NY: Natural History Press.

Du Bois, Cora. 1944. *The People of Alor: A Social-Psychological Study of an East Indian Island.* Minneapolis: University of Minnesota Press.

Du, Shanshan. 2003. "Is Buddha a Couple: Gender-Unitary Perspectives from the Lahu of Southwest China." *Ethnology,* 42: 253–71.

Duarte, Cidalia, J. Mauricio, P. B. Pettitt, P. Souto, E. Trinkaus, H. van der Plicht, and J. Zilhao. 1999. "The Early Upper Paleolithic Human Skeleton from the Abrigo do Lagar Velho (Portugal) and Modern Human Emergence in Iberia." *Proceedings of the National Academy of Sciences of the United States,* 96: 7604–09.

Duhard, Jean-Pierre. 1993. "Upper Paleolithic Figures as a Reflection of Human Morphology and Social Organization." *Antiquity,* 67: 83–91.

Dunbar, Robin. 1988. *Primate Social Systems.* Ithaca, NY: Comstock, 107–10.

Dundes, Alan. 1965a. "Structural Typology in North American Indian Folktales." In A. Dundes, ed., *The Study of Folklore.* Upper Saddle River, NJ: Prentice Hall.

Dundes, Alan, ed. 1965b. *The Study of Folklore.* Upper Saddle River, NJ: Prentice Hall.

Dundes, Alan. 1989. *Folklore Matters.* Knoxville: University of Tennessee Press.

Durham, William H. 1991. *Coevolution: Genes, Culture and Human Diversity.* Stanford, CA: Stanford University Press.

Durkheim, Émile. 1938 [1895]. *The Rules of Sociological Method.* 8th ed. Trans. Sarah A. Soloway and John H. Mueller. Ed. George E. Catlin. New York: Free Press.

Durkheim, Émile. 1961 [1912]. *The Elementary Forms of the Religious Life.* Trans. Joseph W. Swain. New York: Collier Books.

Durrenberger, E. Paul. 1980. "Chayanov's Economic Analysis in Anthropology." *Journal of Anthropological Research,* 36: 133–48.

Durrenberger, E. Paul. 2001a. "Anthropology and Globalization." *American Anthropologist,* 103: 531–35.

Durrenberger, E. Paul. 2001b. "Explorations of Class and Consciousness in the U.S." *Journal of Anthropological Research,* 57: 41–60.

Durrenberger, E. Paul and Nicola Tannenbaum. 2002. "Chayanov and Theory in Economic Anthropology." In Jean Ensminger, ed. *Theory in Economic Anthropology.* Walnut Creek, CA: AltaMira Press, pp. 137–53.

Dyson-Hudson, Neville. 1966. *Karimojong Politics.* Oxford: Clarendon Press.

Dyson-Hudson, Rada, and Eric Alden Smith. 1978. "Human Territoriality: An Ecological Reassessment." *American Anthropologist,* 80: 21–41.

Eckhardt, William. 1975. "Primitive Militarism." *Journal of Peace Research,* 12: 55–62.

Eddy, Elizabeth M., and William L. Partridge, eds. 1978. *Applied Anthropology in America.* New York: Columbia University Press.

Eddy, Elizabeth M., and William L. Partridge, eds. 1987. *Applied Anthropology in America.* 2nd ed. New York: Columbia University Press.

Edgerton, Robert B. 1966. "Conceptions of Psychosis in Four East African Societies." *American Anthropologist,* 68: 408–25.

Edgerton, Robert B. 1971. *The Individual in Cultural Adaptation: A Study of Four East African Peoples.* Berkeley: University of California Press.

Edgerton, Robert B. 1992. *Sick Societies: Challenging the Myth of Primitive Harmony.* New York: Free Press.

Eiseley, Loren C. 1958. "The Dawn of Evolutionary Theory." In Loren C. Eiseley, *Darwin's Century: Evolution and the Men Who Discovered It.* Garden City, NY: Doubleday.

Eisenberg, John F. 1977. "Comparative Ecology and Reproduction of New World Monkeys." In Devra Kleinman, ed., *The Biology and Conservation of the Callitrichidae.* Washington, DC: Smithsonian Institution.

Eisenstadt, S. N. 1954. "African Age Groups." *Africa,* 24: 100–111.

Eisenstadt, S. N. 1956. *From Generation to Generation: Age Groups and Social Structure.* New York: Free Press.

Ekman, Paul, and Dachner Keltner. 1997. "Universal Facial Expressions of Emotion: An Old Controversy and New Findings." In U. Segerstrale and P. Molnar, eds., *Nonverbal Communication: Where Nature Meets Culture.* Mahwah, NJ: Lawrence Erlbaum.

Eldredge, Niles, and Ian Tattersall. 1982. *The Myths of Human Evolution.* New York: Columbia University Press.

Eliot, T. S. 1963. "The Love Song of J. Alfred Prufrock." In *Collected Poems, 1909–1962.* New York: Harcourt, Brace & World.

Ellis, Lee. 1986. "Evidence of Neuroandrogenic Etiology of Sex Roles from a Combined Analysis of Human, Nonhuman Primate and Nonprimate Mammalian Studies." *Personality and Individual Differences,* 7: 519–52.

Ellison, Peter T. 2001. *On Fertile Ground: A Natural History of Human Reproduction.* Cambridge, MA: Harvard.

Ellison, Peter T. 2002. "Natural Variation in Human Fecundity." In P. N. Peregrine, C. R. Ember, and M. Ember, eds., *Physical Anthropology: Original Readings in Method and Practice.* Upper Saddle River, NJ: Prentice Hall.

Elwin, Verrier. 1955. *The Religion of an Indian Tribe.* London: Oxford University Press.

Ember, Carol R. 1973. "Feminine Task Assignment and the Social Behavior of Boys." *Ethos,* 1: 424–39.

Ember, Carol R. 1974. "An Evaluation of Alternative Theories of Matrilocal versus Patrilocal Residence." *Behavior Science Research,* 9: 135–49.

Ember, Carol R. 1975. "Residential Variation among Hunter-Gatherers." *Behavior Science Research,* 9: 135–49.

Ember, Carol R. 1977. "Cross-Cultural Cognitive Studies." *Annual Review of Anthropology,* 6: 33–56.

Ember, Carol R. 1978a. "Men's Fear of Sex with Women: A Cross-Cultural Study." *Sex Roles,* 4: 657–78.

Ember, Carol R. 1978b. "Myths about Hunter-Gatherers." *Ethnology,* 17: 439–48.

Ember, Carol R. 1981. "A Cross-Cultural Perspective on Sex Differences." In R. H. Munroe, R. L. Munroe, and B. B. Whiting, eds., *Handbook of Cross-Cultural Human Development.* New York, Garland.

Ember, Carol R. 1983. "The Relative Decline in Women's Contribution to Agriculture with Intensification." *American Anthropologist,* 85: 285–304.

Ember, Carol R. 2004. "Universal and Variable Patterns of Gender Difference." In *Cross-Cultural Research for Social Science,* in C. R. Ember, M. Ember, and P. N. Peregrine, eds. *New Directions in Anthropology.* Upper Saddle River, NJ: Prentice Hall, CD-ROM.

Ember, Carol R., and Melvin Ember. 1972. "The Conditions Favoring Multilocal Residence." *Southwestern Journal of Anthropology,* 28: 382–400.

Ember, Carol R., and Melvin Ember. 1984. "The Evolution of Human Female Sexuality: A Cross-Species Perspective." *Journal of Anthropological Research,* 40: 202–10.

Ember, Carol R., and Melvin Ember. 1992. "Resource Unpredictability, Mistrust, and War: A Cross-Cultural Study." *Journal of Conflict Resolution,* 36: 242–62.

Ember, Carol R., and Melvin Ember. 1993. "Issues in Cross-Cultural Studies of Interpersonal Violence." *Violence and Victims,* 8: 217–33.

Ember, Carol R., and Melvin Ember. 1994. "War, Socialization, and Interpersonal Violence: A Cross-Cultural Study." *Journal of Conflict Resolution,* 38: 620–46.

Ember, Carol R., and Melvin Ember. 1997. "Violence in the Ethnographic Record: Results of Cross-Cultural Research on War and Aggression." In D. Martin and D. Frayer, eds., *Troubled Times.* Langhorn, PA: Gordon and Breach.

Ember, Carol R., and Melvin Ember. 2001. *Cross-Cultural Research Methods.* Walnut Creek, CA: AltaMira Press.

Ember, Carol R., and Melvin Ember. 2004. "On Cross-Cultural Research." In *Cross-Cultural Research for Social Science,* in C. R. Ember, M. Ember, and P. N. Peregrine, eds., *New Directions in Anthropology.* Upper Saddle River, NJ: Prentice Hall, CD-ROM.

Ember, Carol R. and Melvin Ember. 2005. "Explaining Corporal Punishment of Children: A Cross-Cultural Study." *American Anthropologist,* 107: 609–619.

Ember, Carol R., Melvin Ember, Andrey Korotayev, Victor de Munck. 2005. "Valuing Thinness or Fatness in Women: Reevaluating the Effect of Resource Scarcity. *Evolution and Human Behavior,* 26: 257–70.

Ember, Carol R., Melvin Ember, and Burton Pasternak. 1974. "On the Development of Unilineal Descent." *Journal of Anthropological Research,* 30: 69–94.

Ember, Carol R., Melvin Ember, and Peter N. Peregrine, eds. 2004. *Research Frontiers in Anthropology,* in C. R. Ember, M. Ember, and P. N. Peregrine, eds., *New Directions in Anthropology.* Upper Saddle River, NJ: Prentice Hall, CD-ROM.

Ember, Carol R., Melvin Ember, and Bruce Russett. 1992. "Peace between Participatory Polities: A Cross-Cultural Test of the 'Democracies Rarely Fight Each Other' Hypothesis." *World Politics,* 44: 573–99.

Ember, Carol R., and David Levinson. 1991. "The Substantive Contributions of Worldwide Cross-Cultural Studies Using Secondary Data." *Behavior Science Research* (special issue, "Cross-Cultural and Comparative Research: Theory and Method"), 25: 79–140.

Ember, Melvin. 1959. "The Nonunilinear Descent Groups of Samoa." *American Anthropologist,* 61: 573–77.

Ember, Melvin. 1963. "The Relationship between Economic and Political Development in Nonindustrialized Societies." *Ethnology,* 2: 228–48.

Ember, Melvin. 1967. "The Emergence of Neolocal Residence." *Transactions of the New York Academy of Sciences,* 30: 291–302.

Ember, Melvin. 1970. "Taxonomy in Comparative Studies." In R. Naroll and R. Cohen, eds., *A Handbook of Method in Cultural Anthropology.* Garden City, NY: Natural History Press.

Ember, Melvin. 1974a. "The Conditions That May Favor Avunculocal Residence." *Behavior Science Research,* 9: 203–9.

Ember, Melvin. 1974b. "Warfare, Sex Ratio, and Polygyny." *Ethnology,* 13: 197–206.

Ember, Melvin. 1975. "On the Origin and Extension of the Incest Taboo." *Behavior Science Research,* 10: 249–81.

Ember, Melvin. 1978. "Size of Color Lexicon: Interaction of Cultural and Biological Factors." *American Anthropologist,* 80: 364–67.

Ember, Melvin. 1982. "Statistical Evidence for an Ecological Explanation of Warfare." *American Anthropologist,* 84: 645–49.

Ember, Melvin. 1984–1985. "Alternative Predictors of Polygyny." *Behavior Science Research,* 19: 1–23.

Ember, Melvin. 1985. "Evidence and Science in Ethnography: Reflections on the Freeman-Mead Controversy." *American Anthropologist*, 87: 906–9.

Ember, Melvin, and Carol R. Ember. 1971. "The Conditions Favoring Matrilocal versus Patrilocal Residence." *American Anthropologist*, 73: 571–94.

Ember, Melvin, and Carol R. Ember. 1979. "Male–Female Bonding: A Cross-Species Study of Mammals and Birds." *Behavior Science Research*, 14: 37–56.

Ember, Melvin, and Carol R. Ember. 1983. *Marriage, Family, and Kinship: Comparative Studies of Social Organization.* New Haven, CT: HRAF Press.

Ember, Melvin, and Carol R. Ember. 1992. "Cross-Cultural Studies of War and Peace: Recent Achievements and Future Possibilities." In S. P. Reyna and R. E. Downs, eds., *Studying War.* New York: Gordon and Breach.

Ember, Melvin, and Carol R. Ember. 1999. "Cross-Language Predictors of Consonant-Vowel Syllables." *American Anthropologist*, 101: 730–42.

Ember, Melvin, Carol R. Ember, and Bruce Russett. 1997. "Inequality and Democracy in the Anthropological Record." In M. I. Midlarsky, ed., *Inequality, Democracy, and Economic Development.* Cambridge: Cambridge University Press.

Ember, Melvin, Carol R. Ember, and Ian Skoggard, eds. 2005. *Encyclopedia of Diasporas: Immigrant and Refugee Cultures Around the World,* 2 vols. New York: Kluwer Academic/Plenum.

Emener, William G., and Margaret Darrow, eds. 1991. *Career Explorations in Human Services.* Springfield, IL: Charles C Thomas.

"Energy: Investing for a New Century." 2000. *New York Times,* (October 30): EN1–EN8.

Engels, Frederick, 1972 [1884]. *The Origin of the Family, Private Property, and the State.* New York: International Publishers.

Ensminger, Jean. 2002. "Experimental Economics: A Powerful New Method for Theory Testing in Anthropology." In J. Ensminger, ed., *Theory in Economic Anthropology.* Walnut Creek, CA: AltaMira Press, pp. 59–78.

Ensor, Bradley E. 2003. "Kinship and Marriage Among the Omaha, 1886–1902." *Ethnology* 42: 1–14.

Epstein, Cynthia Fuchs. 1988. *Deceptive Distinctions: Sex, Gender, and the Social Order.* New York: Russell Sage Foundation.

Erchak, Gerald M. 2004. "Family Violence." In *Research Frontiers*, in C. R. Ember, M. Ember, and P. N. Peregrine, eds., *New Directions in Anthropology.* Upper Saddle River, NJ: Prentice Hall, CD-ROM.

Ericksen, Karen Paige. 1989. "Male and Female Age Organizations and Secret Societies in Africa." *Behavior Science Research*, 23: 234–64.

Erickson, Edwin. 1968. "Self-Assertion, Sex Role, and Vocal Rasp." In A. Lomax, ed., *Folk Song Style and Culture.* Washington, DC.

Errington, J. Joseph. 1985. "On the Nature of the Sociolinguistic Sign: Describing the Javanese Speech Levels." In E. Mertz and R. J. Parmentier, eds., *Semiotic Mediation.* Orlando, FL: Academic Press.

Ervin, Alexander M. 1987. "Styles and Strategies of Leadership during the Alaskan Native Land Claims Movement: 1959–71." *Anthropologica*, 29: 21–38.

Eswaran, Vinayak. 2002. "A Diffusion Wave Out of Africa." *Current Anthropology*, 43: 749–74.

Etienne, Mona, and Eleanor Leacock, eds. 1980. *Women and Colonization: Anthropological Perspectives.* New York: Praeger.

Etienne, Robert. 1992. *Pompeii: The Day a City Died.* New York: Abrams.

Etkin, Nina L., and Paul J. Ross. 1997. "Malaria, Medicine, and Meals: A Biobehavioral Perspective." In L. Romanucci-Ross, D. E. Moerman, and L. R. Tancredi, eds., *The Anthropology of Medicine.* Westport, CT: Bergin & Garvey, 169–209.

Euripides. 1937. "The Trojan Women." In E. Hamilton, trans., *Three Greek Plays.* New York: Norton, 52.

Evans-Pritchard, E. E. 1940. "The Nuer of the Southern Sudan." In M. Fortes and E. E. Evans-Pritchard, eds., *African Political Systems.* New York: Oxford University Press.

Evans-Pritchard, E. E. 1970. "Sexual Inversion among the Azande." *American Anthropologist*, 72: 1428–34.

Evans-Pritchard, E. E. 1979. "Witchcraft Explains Unfortunate Events." In W. A. Lessa and E. Z. Vogt, eds., *Reader in Comparative Religion,* 3rd ed. New York: Harper & Row.

Eveleth, Phyllis B., and James M. Tanner. 1990. *Worldwide Variation in Human Growth.* 2nd ed. Cambridge: Cambridge University Press.

Ezzell, Carol. 2002. "Hope in a Vial: Will There Be An AIDS Vaccine Anytime Soon? *Scientific American* (June): 36–45.

Fagan, Brian M. 1972. *In the Beginning.* Boston: Little, Brown.

Fagan, Brian M. 1989. *People of the Earth: An Introduction to World Prehistory,* 6th ed. Glenview, IL: Scott, Foresman.

Fagan, Brian M. 1991. *Ancient North America: The Archaeology of a Continent.* London: Thames and Hudson.

Fagan, Brian M. 1992. *People of the Earth: An Introduction to World Prehistory.* 7th ed. New York: HarperCollins.

Fagan, Brian M. 1997. *People of the Earth: An Introduction to World Prehistory.* 9th ed. New York: HarperCollins.

Fagan, Brian. M. 2001. *People of the Earth: An Introduction to World Prehistory,* 10th ed. Upper Saddle River, NJ: Prentice Hall.

Falk, Dean. 1983. "Cerebral Cortices of East African Early Hominids." *Science*, 221 (September 9): 1072–74.

Falk, Dean. 1987. "Hominid Paleoneurology." *Annual Review of Anthropology*, 16: 13–30.

Falk, Dean. 1988. "Enlarged Occipital/Marginal Sinuses and Emissary Foramina: Their Significance in Hominid Evolution." In F. E. Grine, ed., *Evolutionary History of the "Robust" Australopithecines.* New York: Aldine.

Falk, Dean. 1992. *Brain Dance.* New York: Henry Holt.

Falk, Dean. 1993. "A Good Brain Is Hard to Cool." *Natural History* (August): 65–66.

Falk, Dean, C. Hildebolt, K. Smith, M. J. Morwood, T. Sutikna, P. Brown, Jatmiko, E. W. Saptomo, B. Brunsden, F. Prior. 2005. "The Brain of LBI, *Homo floresiensis.*" *Science*, 308 (April 8): 242–245.

Farley, Reynolds. 1996. *The New American Reality: Who We Are, How We Got Here, Where We Are Going.* New York: Russell Sage Foundation.

Farmer, Paul. 1997. "Ethnography, Social Analysis, and the Prevention of Sexually Transmitted HIV Infection among Poor Women in Haiti." In M. C. Inhorn and P. J. Brown, eds., *The Anthropology of Infectious Disease.* Amsterdam: Gordon and Breach, 413–38.

Featherman, David L., and Robert M. Hauser. 1978. *Opportunity and Change.* New York: Academic Press.

Feder, Kenneth. 1996. *Past in Perspective.* Mountain View, CA: Mayfield.

Feder, Kenneth. 2000. *Past in Perspective.* 2d ed. Mountain View, CA: Mayfield Publishing Company.

Fedigan, Linda Marie. 1982. *Primate Paradigms: Sex Roles and Social Bonds.* Montreal: Eden Press.

Fedoroff, Nina. 2003. "Prehistoric GM Corn." *Science*, 302 (November 14): 1158–1159.

Fehr, Ernst and Urs Fischbacher. 2003. "The Nature of Human Altruism." *Nature*, (October 23): pp. 785–791.

Feibel, Craig S., and Francis H. Brown. 1993. "Microstratigraphy and Paleoenvironments." In A. Walker and R. Leakey, eds., *The Nariokotome* Homo erectus *Skeleton.* Cambridge, MA: Harvard University Press.

Feinman, Gary M., and J. Marcus, eds. 1998. *Archaic States.* Santa Fe, NM: School of American Research Press.

Feinman, Gary, and Jill Neitzel. 1984. "Too Many Types: An Overview of Sedentary Prestate Societies in the Americas." In

M. B. Schiffer, ed., *Advances in Archaeological Methods and Theory.* Vol. 7. Orlando, FL: Academic Press.

Feinman, Gary M., Stephen A. Kowalewski, Laura Finsten, Richard E. Blanton, and Linda Nicholas. 1985. "Long-Term Demographic Change: A Perspective from the Valley of Oaxaca, Mexico." *Journal of Field Archaeology,* 12: 333–62.

Feldman, Douglas A., and Thomas M. Johnson. 1986a "Introduction." In D. A. Feldman and T. M. Johnson, eds., *The Social Dimensions of AIDS.* New York: Praeger.

Feldman, Douglas A., and Thomas M. Johnson, eds. 1986b. *The Social Dimensions of AIDS: Method and Theory.* New York: Praeger.

Feldman, Douglas A., and Julia W. Miller. 1998. *The AIDS Crisis: A Documentary History.* Westport, CT: Greenwood Press.

Ferguson, Niall. 2004. *Colossus: The Price of America's Empire.* New York: Penguin Press.

Ferguson, R. Brian., ed. 1984. *Warfare, Culture, and Environment.* Orlando, FL: Academic Press.

Ferguson, R. Brian, and Neil L. Whitehead. 1992. Violent Edge of Empire." In R. B. Ferguson and N. Whitehead, eds., *War in the Tribal Zone.* Santa Fe, NM: School of American Research Press, 1–30.

Fernea, Elizabeth, and Robert Fernea, as reported in M. Kay Martin and Barbara Voorhies, 1975. *Female of the Species.* New York: Columbia University Press.

Ferraro, Gary P. 2002. *The Cultural Dimension of International Business.* 4th ed. Upper Saddle River, NJ: Prentice Hall.

Fessler, Daniel M. T. 2002. "Windfall and Socially Distributed Willpower: The Psychocultural Dynamics of Rotating Savings and Credit Associations in a Bengkulu Village." *Ethos,* 30: 25–48.

Finerman, Ruthbeth. 2002. "Saraguro: Medical Choices, Medical Changes." In *Portraits of Culture,* in C. R. Ember, M. Ember, and P. N. Peregrine, eds., *New Directions in Anthropology.* Upper Saddle River, NJ: Prentice-Hall, CD-ROM.

Finley, M. I. 1983. *Politics in the Ancient World.* Cambridge: Cambridge University Press.

"The First Dentist." 1973. *Newsweek* (March 5): 73.

"The First Tool Kit." 1997. *Science,* 275 (January 31): 623.

Firth, Raymond. 1957. *We, the Tikopia.* Boston: Beacon Press.

Firth, Raymond. 1959. *Social Change in Tikopia.* New York: Macmillan.

Firth, Raymond. 1970. *Rank and Religion in Tikopia.* Boston: Beacon Press.

Fischer, John L. 1958. "Social Influences on the Choice of a Linguistic Variant." *Word,* 14: 47–56.

Fischer, John. 1961. "Art Styles as Cultural Cognitive Maps." *American Anthropologist,* 63: 80–83.

Fish, Paul R. 1981. "Beyond Tools: Middle Paleolithic Debitage Analysis and Cultural Inference." *Journal of Anthropological Research,* 37: 374–86.

Fisher, Julie. 1996. "Grassroots Organizations and Grassroots Support Organizations: Patterns of Interaction." In E. F. Moran, ed., *Transforming Societies, Transforming Anthropology.* Ann Arbor: University of Michigan Press.

Fisher, William H. 1994. "Megadevelopment, Environmentalism, and Resistance: The Institutional Context of Kayapo Indigenous Politics in Central Brazil." *Human Organization,* 53: 220–32.

Flannery, Kent V. 1965. "The Ecology of Early Food Production in Mesopotamia." *Science,* 147 (March 12): 1247–56.

Flannery, Kent V. 1971. "The Origins and Ecological Effects of Early Domestication in Iran and the Near East." In S. Struever, ed., *Prehistoric Agriculture.* Garden City, NY: Natural History Press.

Flannery, Kent V. 1972. "The Cultural Evolution of Civilizations." *Annual Review of Ecology and Systematics,* 3: 399–426.

Flannery, Kent V. 1973a. "The Origins of Agriculture." *Annual Review of Anthropology,* 2: 271–310.

Flannery, Kent V. 1973b. "The Origins of the Village as a Settlement Type in Mesoamerica and the Near East: A Comparative Study."

In R. Tringham, ed., *Territoriality and Proxemics.* Andover, MA: Warner.

Flannery, Kent V., ed. 1976. *The Early Mesoamerican Village.* New York: Academic Press.

Flannery, Kent V., ed. 1986. *Guila Naquitz: Archaic Foraging and Early Agriculture in Oaxaca, Mexico.* Orlando, FL: Academic Press.

Fleagle, John G. 1988. *Primate Adaptation and Evolution.* San Diego: Academic Press.

Fleagle, John G. 1994. "Anthropoid Origins." In R. Corruccini and R. Ciochon, eds., *Integrative Paths to the Past.* Upper Saddle River, NJ: Prentice Hall.

Fleagle, John G. 1999. *Primate Adaptation and Evolution,* 2nd ed. San Diego: Academic Press.

Fleagle, John G., and Richard F. Kay. 1983. "New Interpretations of the Phyletic Position of Oligocene Hominoids." In R. Ciochon and R. Corruccini, eds., *New Interpretations of Ape and Human Ancestry.* New York: Plenum

Fleagle, John G., and Richard F. Kay. 1985. "The Paleobiology of Catarrhines." In E. Delson, ed., *Ancestors.* New York: Alan R. Liss.

Fleagle, John G., and Richard F. Kay, 1987. "The Phyletic Position of the *Parapithecidae.*" *Journal of Human Evolution,* 16: 483–531.

Fleagle, John G., and Richard F. Kay, eds. 1994. *Anthropoid Origins.* New York: Plenum.

Fleagle, John G., Charles H. Janson, and Kaye E. Reed, eds. 1999. *Primate Communities.* Cambridge: Cambridge University Press.

Fleischer, Robert L., and Howard R. Hart, Jr. 1972. "Fission-Track Dating: Techniques and Problems." In W. Bishop and J. Miller, eds., *Calibration of Hominid Evolution.* Toronto: University of Toronto Press.

Fleischer, Robert L., P. B. Price, R. M. Walker, and L. S. B. Leakey. 1965. "Fission-Track Dating of Bed I, Olduvai Gorge." *Science,* 148 (April 2): 72–74.

Fluehr-Lobban, Carolyn, ed. 1991. *Ethics and the Profession of Anthropology: Dialogue for a New Era.* Philadelphia: University of Pennsylvania Press.

Fluehr-Lobban, Carolyn, ed. 2002. *Ethics and the Profession of Anthropology: Dialogue for a New Era.* 2nd ed. Philadelphia: University of Pennsylvania Press.

Foley, W. A. 1997. *Anthropological Linguistics: An Introduction.* Malden, MA: Blackwell.

Ford, Clellan S. 1941. *Smoke from Their Fires.* New Haven, CT: Yale University Press.

Ford, Clellan S., ed. 1967. *Cross-Cultural Approaches: Readings in Comparative Research.* New Haven, CT: HRAF Press.

Ford, Clellan S., and Frank A. Beach. 1951. *Patterns of Sexual Behavior.* New York: Harper.

Ford, Richard I., ed. 1978. *The Nature and Status of Ethnobotany.* Anthropological Papers No. 67, Museum of Anthropology. Ann Arbor: University of Michigan.

Forrest, Barbara, 2001. "The Wedge at Work." In Robert Pennock, ed., *Intelligent Design Creationism and its Critics.* Boston: MIT Press.

Fortes, Meyer. 1949. *The Web of Kinship among the Tallensi.* New York: Oxford University Press.

Fortes, Meyer, and E. E. Evans-Pritchard, eds. 1940. *African Political Systems.* New York: Oxford University Press.

Fossey, Dian. 1983. *Gorillas in the Mist.* Boston: Houghton Mifflin.

Foster, Brian L. 1974. "Ethnicity and Commerce." *American Ethnologist,* 1:437–47.

Foster, George M. 1962. *Traditional Cultures and the Impact of Technological Change.* New York: Harper & Row.

Foster, George M. 1969. *Applied Anthropology.* Boston: Little, Brown.

Foster, George M. 1994. *Hippocrates' Latin American Legacy: Humoral Medicine in the New World.* Amsterdam: Gordon and Breach.

Foster, Philips. 1992. *The World Food Problem: Tackling the Causes of Undernutrition in the Third World.* Boulder, CO: Lynne Rienner.

Foucault, Michel. 1970. *The Order of Things: An Archaeology of the Human Sciences.* New York: Random House.

Fowler, Brenda. 2000. *Iceman: Uncovering the Life and Times of a Prehistoric Man Found in an Alpine Glacier.* New York: Random House.

Fowler, Melvin L. 1975. "A Pre-Columbian Urban Center on the Mississippi." *Scientific American* (August): 92–101.

Frake, Charles O. 1960. "The Eastern Subanun of Mindanao." In G. P. Murdock, ed., *Social Structure in Southeast Asia.* Chicago: Quadrangle.

Franciscus, Robert G., and Erik Trinkaus. 1988. "Nasal Morphology and the Emergence of *Homo erectus.*" *American Journal of Physical Anthropology,* 75: 517–27.

Frank, André Gunder. 1967. *Capitalism and Underdevelopment in Latin America: Historical Studies of Chile and Brazil.* New York: Monthly Review Press.

Frankel, Barbara, and M. G. Trend. 1991. "Principles, Pressures and Paychecks: The Anthropologist as Employee." In C. Fluehr-Lobban, ed., *Ethics and the Profession of Anthropology.* Philadelphia: University of Pennsylvania Press.

Frayer, David W. 1981. "Body Size, Weapon Use, and Natural Selection in the European Upper Paleolithic and Mesolithic." *American Anthropologist,* 83: 57–73.

Frayer, David W. 2002. "Testing Theories and Hypotheses about Human Origins." In P. N. Peregrine, C. R. Ember, and M. Ember, eds., *Physical Anthropology: Original Readings in Method and Practice.* Upper Saddle River, NJ: Prentice Hall.

Frayer, David W., and Milford H. Wolpoff. 1985. "Sexual Dimorphism." *Annual Review of Anthropology,* 14: 429–73.

Frayer, David W., M. Wolpoff, A. Thorne, F. Smith, and G. Pope. 1993. "Theories of Modern Human Origins: The Paleontological Test." *American Anthropologist,* 95: 24–27.

Frayser, Suzanne G. 1985. *Varieties of Sexual Experience.* New Haven, CT: HRAF Press.

Freedman, Daniel G. 1979. "Ethnic Differences in Babies." *Human Nature* (January): 36–43.

Freeman, Derek. 1983. *Margaret Mead and Samoa: The Making and Unmaking of an Anthropological Myth.* Cambridge, MA: Harvard University Press.

Freeman, J. D. 1961. "On the Concept of the Kindred." *Journal of the Royal Anthropological Institute,* 91: 192–220.

Freeman, Leslie G. 1994 "Torralba and Ambrona: A Review of Discoveries." In R. Corruccini and R. Ciochon, eds., *Integrative Paths to the Past.* Upper Saddle River, NJ: Prentice Hall.

Freud, Sigmund. 1943 [1917]. *A General Introduction to Psychoanalysis.* Garden City, NY: Garden City Publishing. (Originally published in German)

Freud, Sigmund. 1967 [1939]. *Moses and Monotheism.* Katherine Jones, trans. New York: Vintage Books.

Freyman, R. 1987. "The First Technology." *Scientific American* (April): 112.

Fried, Morton H. 1967. *The Evolution of Political Society: An Essay in Political Anthropology.* New York: Random House.

Fried, Morton H., ed. 1968. *Readings in Anthropology.* vol. 1, 2nd ed. New York: Thomas Y. Crowell.

Friedl, Ernestine. 1962. *Vasilika: A Village in Modern Greece.* New York: Holt, Rinehart & Winston.

Friedman, J., and M. J. Rowlands, eds. 1977. *The Evolution of Social Systems.* London: Duckworth.

Friedman, Jeffrey M. 2003. "A War on Obesity, Not the Obese." *Science,* 299 (February 7): 856–58.

Friedman, Saul S. 1980. "Holocaust." In *Academic American* [now Grolier] *Encyclopedia.* vol. 10. Princeton, NJ: Areté.

Friedrich, Paul. 1970. *Proto-Indo-European Trees: The Arboreal System of a Prehistoric People.* Chicago: University of Chicago Press.

Friedrich, Paul. 1986. *The Language Parallax.* Austin: University of Texas Press.

Frisancho, A. Roberto, and Lawrence P. Greksa. 1989. "Development Responses in the Acquisition of Functional Adaptation to High Altitude." In M. Little and J. Haas, eds., *Human Population Biology.* New York: Oxford University Press.

Frisch, John. 1968. "Individual Behavior and Intergroup Variability in Japanese Macaques." In P. C. Jay, ed., *Primates: Studies in Adaptation and Variability.* New York: Holt, Rinehart & Winston, 243–52.

Frisch, Rose. E. 1980. "Fatness, Puberty, and Fertility." *Natural History* (October): 16–27.

Fromm, Erich. 1950. *Psychoanalysis and Religion.* New Haven, CT: Yale University Press.

Frunet, Michel, Alain Beauvilain, Yves Coppens, Elile Heintz, Aladji H. E. Moutaye, and David Pilbeam. 1995. "The First Australopithecine 2500 Kilometers West of the Rift Valley (Chad)." *Nature,* 378: 273–75.

Fry, Douglas P., and Kaj Björkqvist, eds. 1997. *Cultural Variation in Conflict Resolution: Alternatives to Violence.* Mahwah, NJ: Lawrence Erlbaum Associates.

Futuyma, Douglas. 1982. *Science on Trial.* New York: Pantheon.

Gabunia, Leo, A. Vekua, D. Lordkipanidze, et al. 2000. "Earliest Pleistocene Hominid Cranial Remains from Dmanisi, Republic of Georgia: Taxonomy, Geological Setting, and Age." *Science,* 288 (May 12): 1019–25.

Gal, Susan. 1988. "The Political Economy of Code Choice." In M. Heller, ed., *Codeswitching.* Berlin: Mouton de Gruyter, 245–64.

Galdikas, Biruté M. F. 1979. "Orangutan Adaptation at Tanjung Puting Reserve: Mating and Ecology." In D. Hamburg and E. McCown, eds., *The Great Apes.* Menlo Park, CA: Benjamin/Cummings.

Garb, Paula. 2004. "Abkhazians: Growing in Age and Wisdom." In *Portraits of Culture,* in C. R. Ember, M. Ember, and P. N. Peregrine, eds., *New Directions in Anthropology.* Upper Saddle River, NJ: Prentice Hall, CD-ROM.

Gardner, Beatrice T., and R. Allen Gardner. 1980. "Two Comparative Psychologists Look at Language Acquisition." In K. Nelson, ed., *Children's Language,* Vol. 2. New York: Halsted Press.

Gardner, R. Allen, and Beatrice T. Gardner. 1969. "Teaching Sign Language to a Chimpanzee." *Science,* 165 (August 15): 664–72.

Garfield, Viola E., ed. 1962. *Symposium: Patterns of Land Utilization, and Other Papers.* Proceedings of the Annual Spring Meeting of American Ethnological Society, 1961. Seattle: University of Washington Press.

Garn, Stanley M. 1971. *Human Races.* 3rd ed. Springfield, IL: Charles C Thomas.

Gartner, Rosemary. 2004. "Crime Variations across Cultures and Nations." In *Cross-Cultural Research for Social Science,* in C. R. Ember, M. Ember, and P. N. Peregrine, eds., *New Directions in Anthropology.* Upper Saddle River, NJ: Prentice Hall, CD-ROM.

Gat, Azar. 1999. "The Pattern of Fighting in Simple, Small-Scale, Prestate Societies." *Journal of Anthropological Research,* 55: 563–83.

Gaulin, Steven J. C., and James S. Boster. 1990. "Dowry as Female Competition." *American Anthropologist,* 92: 994–1005.

Geertz, Clifford. 1960. *The Religion of Java.* New York: Free Press.

Geertz, Clifford. 1966. "Religion as a Cultural System." In M. Banton, ed., *Anthropological Approaches to the Study of Religion.* New York: Praeger.

Geertz, Clifford. 1973a. "Deep Play: Notes on the Balinese Cockfight." In C. Geertz, *The Interpretation of Cultures.* New York: Basic Books.

Geertz, Clifford. 1973b. *The Interpretation of Cultures: Selected Essays.* New York: Basic Books.

Geertz, Clifford. 1973c. "Thick Description: Toward an Interpretative Theory of Culture." In C. Geertz, *The Interpretation of Cultures*. New York: Basic Books.

Geertz, Clifford. 1984. " 'From the Native's Point of View': On the Nature of Anthropological Understanding." In R. A. Shweder and R. A. LeVine, eds., *Culture Theory*. New York: Cambridge University Press.

Gelles, Richard J., and Murray A. Straus. 1988. *Intimate Violence*. New York: Simon & Schuster.

Gentner, W., and H. J. Lippolt. 1963. "The Potassium-Argon Dating of Upper Tertiary and Pleistocene Deposits." In D. Brothwell and E. Higgs, eds., *Science in Archaeology*. New York: Basic Books.

Gero, Joan M., and Margaret W. Conkey, eds. 1991. *Engendering Archaeology: An Introduction to Women and Prehistory*. Oxford: Blackwell.

Gesler, W. 1991. *The Cultural Geography of Health Care*. Pittsburgh, PA: University of Pittsburgh Press.

Gibbon, G. 1984. *Anthropological Archaeology*. New York: Columbia University Press.

Gibbons, Ann. 1993. "Warring over Women." *Science*, 261 (August 20): 987–88.

Gibbons, Ann. 1995. "First Americans: Not Mammoth Hunters, but Forest Dwellers?" *Science*, 268 (April 19): 346–47.

Gibbons, Ann. 2001. "The Riddle of Co-Existence." *Science*, 291 (March 2): 1725–29.

Gibbons, Ann. 2002. "One Scientist's Quest for the Origin of Our Species." *Science*, 298 (November 29): 1708–11.

Gibbons, Ann. 2003. "Oldest Members of *Homo sapiens* Discovered in Africa." *Science*, 300 (June 13): 1641.

Gibbs, James L., Jr. 1965. "The Kpelle of Liberia." In J. L. Gibbs, Jr., ed., *Peoples of Africa*. New York: Holt, Rinehart & Wintson.

Gibson, Kathleen R. and Stephen Jessee. 1999. "Language Evolution and Expansions of Multiple Neurological Processing Areas." In B. J. King, ed. *The Origins of Language*. Santa Fe, NM: School of American Research Press, 189–227.

Gilligan, Carol. 1982. *In a Different Voice: Psychological Theory and Women's Development*. Cambridge, MA: Harvard University Press.

Gilligan, Carol, and Jane Attanucci. 1988. "Two Moral Orientations." In C. Gilligan, J. V. Ward, and J. M. Taylor, eds., *Mapping the Moral Domain*. Cambridge, MA: Harvard University Press.

Gilligan, Carol, Janie Victoria Ward, and Jill McLean Taylor, eds. 1988. *Mapping the Moral Domain: A Contribution of Women's Thinking to Psychological Theory and Education*. Cambridge, MA: Harvard University Press.

Gilliland, Mary Kay. 1995. "Nationalism and Ethnogenesis in the Former Yugoslavia." In L. Romanucci-Ross and G. A. De Vos, eds., *Ethnic Identity: Creation, Conflict, and Accommodation*. 3rd ed. Walnut Creek, CA: Alta Mira Press, 197–221.

Gilman, Antonio. 1990. "The Development of Social Stratification in Bronze Age Europe." *Current Anthropology*, 22: 1–23.

Gimbutas, Marija. 1974. "An Archaeologist's View of PIE* in 1975." *Journal of Indo-European Studies*, 2: 289–307.

Gingerich, P. D. 1986. "*Pleisiadipis* and the Delineation of the Order Primates." In B. Wood, L. Martin, and P. Andrews, eds., *Major Topics in Primate Evolution*. Cambridge: Cambridge University Press, 32–46.

Gladwin, Christina H. 1980. "A Theory of Real-Life Choice: Applications to Agricultural Decisions." In P. F. Barlett, ed., *Agricultural Decision Making*. New York: Academic Press.

Gladwin, Thomas, and Seymour B. Sarason. 1953. *Truk: Man in Paradise*. New York: Wenner-Gren Foundation for Anthropological Research.

Glass, H. Bentley. 1953. "The Genetics of the Dunkers." *Scientific American* (August): 76–81.

Glasser, Irene. 1994. *Homelessness in Cross-Cultural Perspective*. New York: G. K. Hall/Macmillan.

Gleitman, Lila R., and Eric Wanner. 1982. "Language Acquisition: The State of the State of the Art." In E. Wanner and L. R. Gleitman, eds., *Language Acquisition*. Cambridge: Cambridge University Press.

Godoy, Ricardo, Elizabeth Byron, Victoria Reyes-Garcia, William R. Leonard, Karishma Patel, Lilian Apaza, Eddy Pérez, Vincent Vadez, and David Wilke. 2004. "Patience in a Foraging-Horticultural Society: A Test of Competing Hypotheses." *Journal of Anthropological Research*, 60: 179–202.

Golden, Frederic, Michael Lemonick, and Dick Thompson. 2000. "The Race Is Over." *Time* (July 3): 18–23.

Goldizen, Anne Wilson. 1987. "Tamarins and Marmosets: Communal Care of Offspring." In B. Smuts et al., eds., *Primate Societies*. Chicago: University of Chicago Press.

Goldschmidt, Walter. 1999. "Dynamics and Status in America." *Anthropology Newsletter* 40(5): 62, 64.

Goldstein, Joshua S. 2001. *War and Gender: How Gender Shapes the War System and Vice Versa*. New York: Cambridge University Press.

Goldstein, Joshua S. 2004. "War and Gender." In C. R. Ember and M. Ember, eds. *Encyclopedia of Sex and Gender: Men and Women in the World's Cultures*, Vol. 1. New York: Kluwer Academic/Plenum Publishers, 107–116.

Goldstein, Melvyn C. 1971. "Stratification, Polyandry, and Family Structure in Central Tibet." *Southwestern Journal of Anthropology*, 27: 65–74.

Goldstein, Melvyn C. 1987. "When Brothers Share a Wife." *Natural History* (March): 39–48.

Goldstone, J. A. 1982. "The Comparative and Historical Study of Revolutions." *Annual Review of Sociology*, 8: 187–207.

Goodall, Jane. 1963. "My Life among Wild Chimpanzees." *National Geographic* (August): 272–308.

Goodall, Jane. 1990. *Through a Window*. Boston: Houghton Mifflin.

Goode, William J. 1970. *World Revolution and Family Patterns*. New York: Free Press.

Goode, William J. 1982. *The Family*. 2nd ed. Upper Saddle River, NJ: Prentice Hall.

Goodenough, Ward H. 1951. *Property, Kin, and Community on Truk*. New Haven, CT: Yale University Press.

Goodenough, Ward H. 1963. *Cooperation in Change*. New York: Russell Sage Foundation.

Goodenough, Ward H., ed. 1964. *Explorations in Cultural Anthropology*. New York: McGraw-Hill.

Goodman, Alan H., and George J. Armelagos. 1985. "Disease and Death at Dr. Dickson's Mounds." *Natural History* (September): 12–19.

Goodman, Alan H., and Thomas L. Leatherman, eds. 1998. *Building a New Biocultural Synthesis: Political-Economic Perspectives on Human Biology*. Ann Arbor: University of Michigan Press.

Goodman, Alan H., John Lallo, George J. Armelagos, and Jerome C. Rose. 1984. "Health Changes at Dickson Mounds, Illinois (A.D. 950–1300)." In M. N. Cohen and G. J. Armelagos, eds., *Paleopathology at the Origins of Agriculture*. Orlando, FL: Academic Press.

Goodman, Madeleine J., P. Bion Griffin, Agnes A. Estioko-Griffin, and John S. Grove. 1985. "The Compatibility of Hunting and Mothering among the Agta Hunter-Gatherers of the Philippines." *Sex Roles*, 12: 1199–209.

Goodman, Morris. 1992. "Reconstructing Human Evolution from Proteins." In S. Jones, R. Martin, and D. Pilbeam, eds., *The Cambridge Encyclopedia of Human Evolution*. New York: Cambridge University Press.

Goodrich, L. Carrington. 1959. *A Short History of the Chinese People*. 3rd ed. New York: Harper & Row.

Goody, Jack. 1970. "Cousin Terms." *Southwestern Journal of Anthropology*, 26: 125–42.

Goody, Jack. 1973. "Bridewealth and Dowry in Africa and Eurasia." In J. Goody and S. H. Tambiah, eds., *Bridewealth and Dowry*. Cambridge: Cambridge University Press.

Goody, Jack, and S. H. Tambiah, eds. 1973. *Bridewealth and Dowry*. Cambridge: Cambridge University Press.

Gore, Rick. 2002. "The First Pioneer?" *National Geographic* (August), Departments.

Goren-Inbar, Naama, N. Alperson, M. Kislev, O. Simchoni, Y. Melamed, A. Ben-Nun, and E. Werker. "Evidence of Hominin Control of Fire at Gesher Benot Ya'aqov, Israel." *Science*, 304 (April 30): 725–27.

Gorer, Geoffrey. 1943. "Themes in Japanese Culture." *Transactions of the New York Academy of Sciences*, 5: 106–24.

Gorer, Geoffrey and John Rickman. 1950. *The People of Great Russia: A Psychological Study*. New York: Chanticleer.

Gorman, Chester. 1970. "The Hoabinhian and After: Subsistence Patterns in Southeast Asia during the Late Pleistocene and Early Recent Periods." *World Archaeology*, 2: 315–19.

Gossen, Gary H. 1979. "Temporal and Spatial Equivalents in Chamula Ritual Symbolism." In W. A. Lessa and E. Z. Vogt, eds., *Reader in Comparative Religion*. 4th ed. New York: Harper & Row.

Gough, Kathleen. 1959. "The Nayars and the Definition of Marriage." *Journal of the Royal Anthropological Institute*, 89: 23–34.

Gould, Richard A. 1969. *Yiwara: Foragers of the Australian Desert*. New York: Scribner's.

Gould, S. J. 1996. *The Mismeasure of Man*. New York: W. W. Norton.

Graburn, Nelson H. 1969. *Eskimos without Igloos*. Boston: Little, Brown.

Graham, Susan Brandt. 1979. "Biology and Human Social Behavior: A Response to van den Berghe and Barash." *American Anthropologist*, 81: 357–60.

Grant, Bruce S. 2002. "Sour Grapes of Wrath." *Science*, 297 (August 9): 940–41.

Grant, Peter R. 1991. "Natural Selection and Darwin's Finches." *Scientific American* (October): 82–87.

Grant, Peter R., and Rosemary Grant. 2002. "Unpredictable Evolution in a 30-Year Study of Darwin's Finches," *Science*, 296 (April 26): 707–11.

Gray, J. Patrick. 1985. *Primate Sociobiology*. New Haven, CT: HRAF Press.

Gray, J. Patrick, and Linda D. Wolfe. 1980. "Height and Sexual Dimorphism of Stature among Human Societies." *American Journal of Physical Anthropology*, 53: 446–52.

Gray, J. Patrick, and Linda Wolfe. 2002. "What Accounts for Population Variation in Height?" In P. N. Peregrine, C. R. Ember, and M. Ember, eds., *Physical Anthropology: Original Readings in Method and Practice*. Upper Saddle River, NJ: Prentice Hall.

Grayson, Donald K. 1977. "Pleistocene Avifaunas and the Overkill Hypothesis." *Science*, 195 (February 18): 691–92.

Grayson, Donald K. 1984. "Explaining Pleistocene Extinctions: Thoughts on the Structure of a Debate." In P. S. Martin and R. Klein, eds., *Quaternary Extinctions*. Tucson: University of Arizona Press.

Greenberg, Joseph H. 1972. "Linguistic Evidence Regarding Bantu Origins." *Journal of African History*, 13: 189–216.

Greenberg, Joseph H., and Merritt Ruhlen. 1992. "Linguistic Origins of Native Americans." *Scientific American* (November): 94–99.

Greene, L., and F. E. Johnston, eds. 1980. *Social and Biological Predictors of Nutritional Status, Physical Growth, and Neurological Development*. New York: Academic Press.

Greenfield, Patricia M., Ashley E. Maynard, and Carla P. Childs. 2000. "History, Culture, Learning, and Development." *Cross-Cultural Research*, 34: 351–74.

Greenfield, Patricia Marks, and E. Sue Savage-Rumbaugh. 1990. "Grammatical Combination in *Pan paniscus*: Processes of Learning and Invention in the Evolution and Development of Language." In S. Parker and K. Gibson, eds., *"Language" and Intelligence in Monkeys and Apes*. New York: Cambridge University Press.

Gregor, Thomas A., Daniel R. Gross., 2004. "Guilt by Association: The Culture of Accusation and the American Anthropological Association's Investigation of Darkness in El Dorado." *American Anthropologist*, 106: 687–698.

Gregory, C. A. 1982. *Gifts and Commodities*. New York: Academic Press.

Greksa, Lawrence P., and Cynthia M. Beall. 1989. "Development of Chest Size and Lung Function at High Altitude." In M. Little and J. Haas, eds., *Human Population Biology*. New York: Oxford University Press.

Grine, Frederick E. 1986. "Dental Evidence for Dietary Differences in *Australopithecus* and *Paranthropus*: A Quantitative Analysis of Permanent Molar Microwear." *Journal of Human Evolution*, 15: 783–822.

Grine, Frederick E. 1988a. "Evolutionary History of the 'Robust' Australopithecines: A Summary and Historical Perspective." In F. E. Grine, ed., *Evolutionary History of the "Robust" Australopithecines*. New York: Aldine.

Grine, Frederick E., ed. 1988b. *Evolutionary History of the "Robust" Australopithecines*. New York: Aldine.

Grine, Frederick E. 1993. "Australopithecine Taxonomy and Phylogeny: Historical Background and Recent Interpretation." In R. Ciochon and J. Fleagle, eds., *The Human Evolution Source Book*. Upper Saddle River, NJ: Prentice Hall.

Gröger, B. Lisa. 1981. "Of Men and Machines: Cooperation among French Family Farmers." *Ethnology*, 20: 163–75.

Gross, Daniel R., and Barbara A. Underwood. 1971. "Technological Change and Caloric Costs: Sisal Agriculture in Northeastern Brazil." *American Anthropologist*, 73: 725–40.

Gross, Daniel R., George Eiten, Nancy M. Flowers, Francisca M. Leoi, Madeline Latiman Ritter, and Dennis W. Werner. 1979. "Ecology and Acculturation among Native Peoples of Central Brazil." *Science*, 206 (November 30): 1043–50.

Grossman, Daniel. 2002. "Parched Turf Battle." *Scientific American* (December): 32–33.

Grubb, Henry J. 1987. "Intelligence at the Low End of the Curve: Where Are the Racial Differences?" *Journal of Black Psychology*, 14: 25–34.

Grubb, Henry J., and Andrea G. Barthwell. 1996. "Superior Intelligence and Racial Equivalence: A Look at Mensa." Paper presented at the 1996 annual meeting of the Society for Cross-Cultural Research.

Gubser, Nicholas J. 1965. *The Nunamiut Eskimos: Hunters of Caribou*. New Haven, CT: Yale University Press.

Guiora, Alexander Z., Benjamin Beit-Hallahmi, Risto Fried, and Cecelia Yoder. 1982. "Language Environment and Gender Identity Attainment." *Language Learning*, 32: 289–304.

Gumperz, John J. 1961. "Speech Variation and the Study of Indian Civilization." *American Anthropologist*, 63: 976–88.

Gumperz, John J. 1971. "Dialect Differences and Social Stratification in a North Indian Village." In *Language in Social Groups: Essays by John J. Gumperz*, selected and introduced by Anwar S. Dil. Stanford, CA: Stanford University Press.

Gunders, S., and J. W. M. Whiting. 1968. "Mother-Infant Separation and Physical Growth." *Ethnology*, 7: 196–206.

Gurr, Ted Robert. 1989a. "Historical Trends in Violent Crime: Europe and the United States." In T. R. Gurr, ed., *Violence in America*. Vol. 1: *The History of Crime*. Newbury Park, CA: Sage.

Gurr, Ted Robert, 1989b. "The History of Violent Crime in America: An Overview." In T. R. Gurr, ed., *Violence in America*. Vol. 1: *The History of Crime*. Newbury Park, CA: Sage.

Gurr, Ted Robert, ed. 1989c. *Violence in America.* Vol. 1: *The History of Crime.* Newbury Park, CA: Sage.

Gurven, Michael, Kim Hill, and Hillard Kaplan. 2002. "From Forest to Reservation: Transitions in Food-sharing Behavior among the Ache of Paraguay." *Journal of Anthropological Research,* 58: 93–120.

Guthrie, Dale R., 1984. "Mosaics, Allelochemics, and Nutrients: An Ecological Theory of Late Pleistocene Megafaunal Extinctions." In P. S. Martin and R. Klein, eds., *Quaternary Extinctions.* Tucson: University of Arizona Press.

Guthrie, Stewart Elliott. 1993. *Faces in the Clouds: A New Theory of Religion.* New York: Oxford University Press.

Haas, Jonathan. 1990. "Warfare and the Evolution of Tribal Polities in the Prehistoric Southwest." In J. Haas, ed., *The Anthropology of War.* New York: Cambridge University Press.

Haas, Jonathan, Winifred Creamer, and Alvaro Ruiz. 2004. "Dating the Late Archaic Occupation of the Norte Chico Region in Peru." *Nature,* 432 (December 23): 1020–23.

Haas, Mary R. 1944. "Men's and Women's Speech in Koasati." *Language,* 20: 142–49.

Habicht, J. K. A. 1979. *Paleoclimate, Paleomagnetism, and Continental Drift.* Tulsa, OK: American Association of Petroleum Geologists.

Hackenberg, Robert A. 1988. "Scientists or Survivors? The Future of Applied Anthropology under Maximum Uncertainty." In R. T. Trotter, II, ed., *Anthropology for Tomorrow.* Washington, DC: American Anthropological Association.

Hage, Jerald, and Charles H. Powers. 1992. *Post-Industrial Lives: Roles and Relationships in the 21st Century.* Newbury Park, CA: Sage.

Hahn, Robert A. 1995. *Sickness and Healing: An Anthropological Perspective.* New Haven, CT: Yale University Press.

Hailie-Selassie, Yohannes. 2001. "Late Miocene Hominids from the Middle Awash, Ethiopia." *Nature,* 412 (July 12): 178–81.

Haldane, J. B. S. 1963. "Human Evolution: Past and Future." In G. Jepsen, E. Mayr, and G. Simpson, eds., *Genetics, Paleontology, and Evolution.* New York: Atheneum.

Hall, Edward T. 1966. *The Hidden Dimension.* Garden City, NY: Doubleday.

Hall, Edward T., and Mildred R. Hall. 1990. *Hidden Differences: Doing Business with the Japanese.* New York: Doubleday.

Hall, K. L. R. 1968. "Social Learning in Monkeys." In P. C. Jay, ed., *Primates: Studies in Adaptation and Variability.* New York: Holt, Rinehart & Winston, 383–97.

Hallowell, A. Irving. 1976. "Ojibwa World View and Disease." In *Contributions to Anthropology: Selected Papers of A. Irving Hallowell.* Chicago: University of Chicago Press, 410–13.

Halpern, Diane F. 2000. *Sex Differences in Cognitive Abilities,* 3rd ed. Mahwah, NJ: Lawrence Erlbaum Associates.

Hamburg, David A., and Elizabeth R. McCown, eds. 1979. *The Great Apes.* Menlo Park, CA: Benjamin/Cummings.

Hames, Raymond. 1990. "Sharing among the Yanomamö. Pt. I. The Effects of Risk." In E. Cashdan, ed., *Risk and Uncertainty in Tribal and Peasant Economies.* Boulder, CO: Westview.

Hames, Raymond. 2004. "Yanomamö: Varying Adaptations of Foraging Horticulturalists." In *Portraits of Culture,* in C. R. Ember, M. Ember, and P. N. Peregrine, eds., *New Directions in Anthropology.* Upper Saddle River, NJ: Prentice Hall.

Hamilton, Edith, trans. 1937. *Three Greek Plays.* New York: Norton.

Hammer, Michael F., and Stephen L. Zegura. 1996. "The Role of the Y Chromosome in Human Evolutionary Studies." *Evolutionary Anthropology,* 5: 116–34.

Hammer, Michael F., and Stephen L. Zegura. 2002. "The Human Y Chromosome Haplogroup Tree," *Annual Review of Anthropology,* 31: 303–21.

Handwerker, W. Penn, and Paul V. Crosbie. 1982. "Sex and Dominance." *American Anthropologist,* 84: 97–104.

Hanna, Joel M., Michael A. Little, and Donald M. Austin. 1989. "Climatic Physiology." In M. Little and J. Haas, eds., *Human Population Biology.* New York: Oxford University Press.

Hannah, Alison C., and W. C. McGrew. 1987. "Chimpanzees Using Stones to Crack Open Oil Palm Nuts in Liberia." *Primates,* 28: 31–46.

Hannerz, Ulf. 1996. *Transnational Connections: Culture, People, Places.* London: Routledge.

Hanotte, Olivier, et al. 2002. "African Pastoralism: Genetic Imprints of Origins and Migrations." *Science,* 296 (April 12): 336–43.

Hanson, Jeffery R. 1988. "Age-Set Theory and Plains Indian Age-Grading: A Critical Review and Revision." *American Ethnologist,* 15: 349–64.

Harcourt, A. H. 1979. "The Social Relations and Group Structure of Wild Mountain Gorillas." In D. Hamburg and E. McCown, eds., *The Great Apes.* Menlo Park, CA: Benjamin/Cummings.

Hardin, Garrett. 1968. "The Tragedy of the Commons." *Science,* 162 (December 13): 1243–48.

Hardoy, Jorge, and David Satterthwaite. 1987. "The Legal and the Illegal City." In L. Rodwin, ed., *Shelter, Settlement, and Development.* Boston: Allen & Unwin.

Hare, Brian, Michelle Brown, Christina Williamson, and Michael Tomasello. 2002. "The Domestication of Social Cognition in Dogs." *Science,* 298 (November, 22): 1634–36.

Harkness, Sara, and Charles. M. Super, eds. 1996. *Parents' Cultural Belief Systems: Their Origins, Expressions, and Consequences.* New York: Guilford Press.

Harkness, Sara and Charles M. Super. 1997 "An Infant's Three Rs." A box in M. Small, "Our Babies, Ourselves," *Natural History* (October): 45.

Harlan, Jack R. 1967. "A Wild Wheat Harvest in Turkey." *Archaeology,* 20: 197–201.

Harlow, Harry F., et al. 1966. "Maternal Behavior of Rhesus Monkeys Deprived of Mothering and Peer Association in Infancy." *Proceedings of the American Philosophical Society,* 110: 58–66.

Harner, Michael, ed. 1972a. *Hallucinogens and Shamanism.* New York: Oxford University Press.

Harner, Michael. 1972b. "The Role of Hallucinogenic Plants in European Witchcraft." In M. Harner, ed., *Hallucinogens and Shamanism.* New York: Oxford University Press.

Harner, Michael J. 1975. "Scarcity, the Factors of Production, and Social Evolution." In S. Polgar, ed., *Population, Ecology, and Social Evolution.* The Hague: Mouton.

Harner, Michael, and Gary Doore. 1987. "The Ancient Wisdom in Shamanic Cultures." In S. Nicholson, comp., *Shamanism.* Wheaton, IL: Theosophical Publishing House.

Harrell-Bond, Barbara. 1996. "Refugees," in D. Levinson and M. Ember, eds., *Encyclopedia of Cultural Anthropology,* New York: Henry Holt, vol. 3, 1076–81.

Harris, David R. 1977. "Settling Down: An Evolutionary Model for the Transformation of Mobile Bands into Sedentary Communities." In J. Friedman and M. Rowlands, eds., *The Evolution of Social Systems.* London: Duckworth.

Harris, Marvin. 1964. *Patterns of Race in the Americas.* New York: Walker.

Harris, Marvin. 1966. "The Cultural Ecology of India's Sacred Cattle." *Current Anthropology,* 7: 51–63.

Harris, Marvin. 1968. *The Rise of Anthropological Theory: A History of Theories of Culture.* New York: Thomas Y. Crowell.

Harris, Marvin. 1975. *Cows, Pigs, Wars and Witches: The Riddles of Culture.* New York: Random House, Vintage.

Harris, Marvin. 1979. *Cultural Materialism: The Struggle for a Science of Culture.* New York: Random House.

Harris, Marvin, and Eric B. Ross. 1987. *Food and Evolution: Toward a Theory of Human Food Habits.* Philadelphia: Temple University Press.

Harrison, G. A., James M. Tanner, David R. Pilbeam, and P. T. Baker. 1988. *Human Biology: An Introduction to Human Evolution, Variation, Growth, and Adaptability.* 3rd ed. Oxford: Oxford University Press.

Harrison, Gail G. 1975. "Primary Adult Lactase Deficiency: A Problem in Anthropological Genetics." *American Anthropologist,* 77: 812–35.

Harrison, Peter D., and B. L. Turner, II, eds. 1978. *Pre-Hispanic Maya Agriculture.* Albuquerque: University of New Mexico Press.

Harrison, T. 1986. "A Reassessment of the Phylogenetic Relationships of *Oreopithecus bamboli.*" *Journal of Human Evolution,* 15: 541–84.

Harrison, T., and L. Rook. 1997. "Enigmatic Anthropoid or Misunderstood Ape? The Phylogenetic Status of *Oreopithecus bamboli* Reconsidered." In D. R. Begun, C. V. Ward, and M. D. Rose, eds., *Function, Phylogeny and Fossils: Miocene Hominoid Evolution and Adaptation.* New York: Plenum, 327–62.

Hart, Hornell. 1948. "The Logistic Growth of Political Areas." *Social Forces,* 26: 396–408.

Hartwig, W. C. 1994. "Pattern, Puzzles and Perspectives on Platyrrhine Origins." In R. Corruccini and R. Ciochon, eds., *Integrative Paths to the Past,* Upper Saddle River, NJ: Prentice Hall. 69–93.

Hartwig, W. C., ed. 2002. *The Primate Fossil Record.* Cambridge: Cambridge University Press.

Harvey, Philip W., and Peter F. Heywood. 1983. "Twenty-five Years of Dietary Change in Simbu Province, Papua New Guinea." *Ecology of Food and Nutrition,* 13: 27–35.

Hassan, Fekri A. 1981. *Demographic Archaeology.* New York: Academic Press.

Hastorf, Christine. 1991. "Gender, Space, and Food Prehistory." In J. Gero and M. Conkey, eds., *Engendering Archaeology.* Oxford: Blackwell.

Hatch, Elvin. 1997. "The Good Side of Relativism." *Journal of Anthropological Research,* 53: 371–81.

Hatcher, Evelyn Payne. 1999. *Art as Culture: An Introduction to the Anthropology of Art.* 2nd ed. Westport, CT: Bergin & Garvey.

Haug, Gerald et al. 2003. "Climate and the Collapse of Maya Civilization," *Science,* 299 (March 14): 1731–35.

Hausfater, Glenn, Jeanne Altmann, and Stuart Altmann. 1982. "Long-Term Consistency of Dominance Relations among Female Baboons." *Science,* 217 (August 20): 752–54.

Hawkins, Alicia, and M. Kleindienst. 2001. "Aterian." In P. N. Peregrine and M. Ember, eds., *Encyclopedia of Prehistory.* Vol. 1: *Africa.* New York: Kluwer Academic/Plenum, 23–45.

Hayden, Thomas. 2000. "A Genome Milestone." *Newsweek* (July 3): 51–52.

Haynes, Vance. 1973. "The Calico Site: Artifacts or Geofacts?" *Science,* 181 (July 27): 305–10.

Hays, Terence E. 1994. "Sound Symbolism, Onomatopoeia, and New Guinea Frog Names." *Journal of Linguistic Anthropology,* 4: 153–74.

Hays, Terence E. 2004. "From Ethnographer to Comparativist and Back Again." In *Research Frontiers,* in C. R. Ember, M. Ember and P. N. Peregrine, eds., *New Directions in Anthropology.* Upper Saddle River, NS: Prentice Hall, CD-ROM.

Heath, Dwight B., and Richard N. Adams, eds. 1965. *Contemporary Cultures and Societies of Latin America.* New York: Random House.

Heider, Karl. 1970. *The Dugum Dani.* Chicago: Aldine.

Heider, Karl. 1979. *Grand Valley Dani: Peaceful Warriors.* New York: Holt, Rinehart & Winston.

Heise, David R. 1967. "Cultural Patterning of Sexual Socialization." *American Sociological Review,* 32: 726–39.

Heller, Monica, ed. 1988. *Codeswitching: Anthropological and Sociolinguistic Perspectives.* Berlin: Mouton de Gruyter.

Helms, Mary W. 1975. *Middle America.* Upper Saddle River, NJ: Prentice Hall.

Helms, Mary W. 2004. "Miskito: Adaptations to Colonial Empires, Past and Present." In *Portraits of Culture,* in C. R. Ember, M. Ember, and P. N. Peregrine, eds., *New Directions in Anthropology.* Upper Saddle River, NJ: Prentice Hall, CD-ROM.

Hempel, Carl G. 1965. *Aspects of Scientific Explanation.* New York: Free Press.

Henderson, A. M., and Talcott Parsons, trans. 1947. *The Theory of Social and Economic Organization.* New York: Oxford University Press.

Henderson, Harry. 2001. *Global Terrorism: The Complete Reference Guide.* New York: Checkmark Books.

Henderson, Stephen. 2002. "Weddings: Vows; Rakhi Dhanoa and Ranjeet Purewal," *The New York Times,* August 18, p. 9.2.

Hendrix, Llewellyn. 1985. "Economy and Child Training Reexamined." *Ethos,* 13: 246–61.

Hendrix, Llewellyn. 2004. "Courtship and Marriage." In C. R. Ember and M. Ember, eds., *Encyclopedia of Sex and Gender: Men and Women in the World's Cultures,* New York: Kluwer Academic/Plenum Publishers, vol 1, 71–77.

Hendrix, Llewellyn. 2004. "Varieties of Marital Relationships." In *Cross-Cultural Research for Social Science,* in C. R. Ember, M. Ember, and P. N. Peregrine, eds., *New Directions in Anthropology.* Upper Saddle River, NJ: Prentice Hall, CD-ROM.

Hendry, Joy and C. W. Watson, eds. 2001. *An Anthropology of Indirect Communication.* London: Routledge.

Hennig, Willi. 1966. *Phylogenetic Systematics.* Urbana: University of Illinois Press.

Henrich, Joseph, Robert Boyd, Samuel Bowles, Colin Camerer, Ernst Fehr, and Herbert Gintis, eds. 2004. *Foundations of Human Sociality: Economic Experiments and Ethnographic Evidence from Fifteen Small-Scale Societies.* Oxford: Oxford University Press.

Henry, Donald O. 1989. *From Foraging to Agriculture: The Levant at the End of the Ice Age.* Philadelphia: University of Pennsylvania Press.

Henry, Donald O. 1991. "Foraging, Sedentism, and Adaptive Vigor in the Natufian: Rethinking the Linkages." In G. A. Clark, ed., *Perspectives on the Past.* Philadelphia: University of Pennsylvania Press.

Henry, Edward O. 1976. "The Variety of Music in a North Indian Village: Reassessing Cantometrics." *Ethnomusicology,* 20: 49–66.

Henshilwood, Christopher, et al., 2002. "Emergence of Modern Human Behavior: Middle Stone Age Engravings from South Africa," *Science,* 295 (February 15): 1278–80.

Herbig, Paul A. 1994. *The Innovation Matrix: Culture and Structure Prerequisites to Innovation.* Westport, CT: Quorum Books.

Herdt, Gilbert. 1997. "Sexual Cultures and Population Movement: Implications for AIDS/STDs." In G. Herdt, ed., *Sexual Cultures and Migration in the Era of AIDS: Anthropological and Demographic Perspectives.* Oxford: Oxford University Press, 3–22.

Herrman, Helen. 1990. "A Survey of Homeless Mentally Ill People in Melbourne, Australia." *Hospital and Community Psychiatry,* 41: 1291–92.

Herrnstein, Richard J., and Charles Murray. 1994. *The Bell Curve: Intelligence and Class Structure in American Life.* New York: Free Press.

Hewes, Gordon W. 1961. "Food Transport and the Origin of Hominid Bipedalism." *American Anthropologist,* 63: 687–710.

Hewlett, Barry. 2004. "Diverse Contexts of Human Infancy." In *Cross-Cultural Research for Social Science,* in C. R. Ember, M. Ember, and P. N. Peregrine, eds., *New Directions in Anthropology.* Upper Saddle River, NJ: Prentice Hall, CD-ROM.

Hewlett, Barry S., and L. L. Cavalli-Sforza. 1986. "Cultural Transmission among Aka Pygmies." *American Anthropologist,* 88: 922–34.

Hiatt, L. R. 1980. "Polyandry in Sri Lanka: A Test Case for Parental Investment Theory." *Man,* 15: 583–98.

Hickey, Gerald Cannon. 1964. *Village in Vietnam*. New Haven, CT: Yale University Press.

Hickson, Letitia. 1986. "The Social Contexts of Apology in Dispute Settlement: A Cross-Cultural Study." *Ethnology*, 25: 283–94.

Higgins, Patricia J., and J. Anthony Paredes, eds. 2000. *Classics of Practicing Anthropology: 1978–1998*. Oklahoma City, OK: Society for Applied Anthropology.

Higley, Stephen Richard. 1995. *Privilege, Power, and Place: The Geography of the American Upper Class*. Lanham, MD: Rowman & Littlefield, 1–47.

Hill, Donald R. 2005. "Music of the African Diaspora in the Americas." In M. Ember, C. R. Ember, and I. Skoggard, eds., *Encyclopedia of Diasporas: Immigrant and Refugee Cultures Around the World*, New York: Kluwer Academic/Plenum, 363–73.

Hill, Jane H. 1978. "Apes and Language." *Annual Review of Anthropology*, 7: 89–112.

Hill, Jane H. 2004. "Do Apes Have Language?" In *Research Frontiers* in C. R. Ember, M. Ember, and P. N. Peregrine, eds., *New Directions in Anthropology*. Upper Saddle River, NJ: Prentice Hall, CD-ROM.

Hill, Jonathan D. 1996. "Introduction: Ethnogenesis in the Americas. 1492–1992." In J. D. Hill, ed., *Ethnogenesis in the Americas*. Iowa City: University of Iowa Press, 1–19.

Hill, Kim and A. Magdalena Hurtado. 2004. "The Ethics of Anthropological Research with Remote Tribal Populations." In F. M. Salzano and A. M. Hurtado, eds. *Lost Paradises and the Ethics of Research and Publication*. Oxford: Oxford University Press, 193–210.

Hill, Kim, Hillard Kaplan, Kristen Hawkes, and A. Magdalena Hurtado. 1987. "Foraging Decisions among Aché Hunter-Gatherers: New Data and Implications for Optimal Foraging Models." *Ethology and Sociobiology*, 8: 1–36.

Hitchcock, Robert K. and Megan Biesele. 2000. "Introduction." In P. P. Schweitzer, M. Biesele, and R. K. Hitchcock, eds. *Hunters and Gatherers in the Modern World: Conflict, Resistance, and Self-Determinations*. New York: Berghahn Books, 1–27.

Hobsbawm, E. J. 1970. *Age of Revolution*. New York: Praeger.

Hockett, C. F., and R. Ascher. 1964. "The Human Revolution." *Current Anthropology*, 5: 135–68.

Hodder, I. 1990. *The Domestication of Europe: Structure and Contingency in Neolithic Societies*. Oxford: Blackwell.

Hoebel, E. Adamson. 1960. *The Cheyennes: Indians of the Great Plains*. New York: Holt, Rinehart & Winston.

Hoebel, E. Adamson. 1968 [1954]. *The Law of Primitive Man*. New York: Atheneum.

Hoffecker, John F., W. Roger Powers, and Ted Goebel. 1993. "The Colonization of Beringia and the Peopling of the New World." *Science*, 259 (January 1): 46–53.

Hoffman, Lois Wladis. 1988. "Cross-Cultural Differences in Child-Rearing Goals." In R. A. LeVine, P. M. Miller, and M. M. West, eds., *Parental Behavior in Diverse Societies*. San Francisco: Jossey-Bass.

Hoijer, Harry. 1964. "Cultural Implications of Some Navaho Linguistic Categories." In D. Hymes, ed., *Language in Culture and Society*. New York: Harper & Row.

Holdaway, R. N., and C. Jacomb. 2000. "Rapid Extinction of the Moas (Aves: Dinornithiformes): Model, Test, and Implications." *Science*, 287 (March 24): 2250–57.

Holden, Constance. 2000. "Selective Power of UV." *Science*, 289 (September 1): 1461.

Hole, Frank, ed. 1987. *Archaeology of Western Iran*. Washington, DC: Smithsonian Institution Press.

Hole, Frank. 1992. "Origins of Agriculture." In S. Jones, R. Martin, and D. Pilbeam, eds., *The Cambridge Encyclopedia of Human Evolution*. New York: Cambridge University Press.

Hole, Frank. 1994. "Environmental Shock and Urban Origins." In G. Stein and M. Rothman, eds., *Chiefdoms and Early States in the Near East*. Madison, WI: Prehistory Press.

Hole, Frank, and Robert F. Heizer. 1973. *An Introduction to Prehistoric Archeology*. 3rd ed. New York: Holt, Rinehart & Winston.

Hole, Frank, Kent V. Flannery, and James A. Neely. 1969. *Prehistory and Human Ecology of the Deh Luran Plain*. Memoirs of the Museum of Anthropology, No. 1. Ann Arbor: University of Michigan.

Hollan, Douglas. 1992. "Cross-Cultural Differences in the Self." *Journal of Anthropological Research*, 48: 289–90.

Holland, Dorothy, and Naomi Quinn, eds. 1987. *Cultural Models in Language and Thought*. Cambridge: Cambridge University Press.

Holloway, Marguerite. 1993. "Sustaining the Amazon." *Scientific American* (July): 91–99.

Holloway, Ralph L. 1974. "The Casts of Fossil Hominid Brains." *Scientific American* (July): 106–15.

Holmes, Janet. 2001. *An Introduction to Sociolinguistics*. 2nd ed. London: Longman.

Honigmann, John J. 1967. *Personality in Culture*. New York: Harper & Row.

Hoogbergen, Wim. 1990. *The Boni Maroon Wars in Suriname*. Leiden: E. J. Brill.

Hooper, Judith. 2002. *Of Moths and Men: The Untold Story of Science and the Peppered Moth*. New York: W. W. Norton.

Hopkins, K. 1980. "Brother–Sister Marriage in Roman Egypt." *Comparative Studies in Society and History*, 22: 303–54.

Horowitz, Michael M. 1990. "Donors and Deserts: The Political Ecology of Destructive Development in the Sahel." In R. Huss-Ashmore and S. H. Katz, eds., *African Food Systems in Crisis, Part Two: Contending with Change*. New York: Gordon and Breach.

Houston, Stephen D. 1988. "The Phonetic Decipherment of Mayan Glyphs." *Antiquity*, 62: 126–35.

Howard, Alan, and Jan Rensel. 2004. "Rotuma: Interpreting a Wedding." In *Portraits of Culture*, in C. R. Ember, M. Ember, and P. N. Peregrine, eds., *New Directions in Anthropology*. Upper Saddle River, NJ: Prentice Hall, CD-ROM.

Howell, F. Clark. 1966. "Observations on the Earlier Phases of the European Lower Paleolithic." In *Recent Studies in Paleoanthropology. American Anthropologist*, special publication, April, 88–200.

Howell, Nancy. 1979. *Demography of the Dobe !Kung*. New York: Academic Press.

Howells, W. 1997. *Getting Here: The Story of Human Evolution*. 2nd ed. Washington, DC: Compass Press.

Hrdy, Sarah Blaffer. 1977. *The Langurs of Abu: Female and Male Strategies of Reproduction*. Cambridge, MA: Harvard University Press.

Hsu, Francis L. K. ed. 1972. *Psychological Anthropology*. 2nd ed. Cambridge, MA: Schenkman.

Huang, H. T. 2002. "Hypolactasia and the Chinese Diet." *Current Anthropology*, 43: 809–19.

Human Development Report 2001, published for the United Nations Development Programme. New York: Oxford University Press, 2001, 9–25.

Humphrey, Caroline, and Stephen Hugh-Jones. 1992. "Introduction: Barter, Exchange and Value." In C. Humphrey and S. Hugh-Jones, eds., *Barter, Exchange and Value*. New York: Cambridge University Press.

Hunt, Morton. 1974. *Sexual Behavior in the 1970s*. Chicago: Playboy Press.

Hunt, Robert C. 2000. "Labor Productivity and Agricultural Development: Boserup Revisited." *Human Ecology*, 28: 251–77.

Hunt, Robert C., and Antonio Gilman, eds. 1998. *Property in Economic Context*. Lanham, MD: University Press of America.

Hurtado, Ana M., Kristen Hawkes, Kim Hill, and Hillard Kaplan. 1985. "Female Subsistence Strategies among the Aché Hunter-Gatherers of Eastern Paraguay." *Human Ecology*, 13: 1–28.

Huss-Ashmore, Rebecca, and Francis E. Johnston. 1985. "Bioanthropological Research in Developing Countries." *Annual Review of Anthropology,* 14: 475–527.

Huss-Ashmore, Rebecca, and Solomon H. Katz, eds. 1990. *African Food Systems in Crisis. Part Two: Contending with Change.* New York: Gordon and Breach.

Huxley, Thomas H. 1970. "Man's Place in Nature." In Young, ed., *Evolution of Man.* New York: Oxford University Press.

Hymes, Dell, ed. 1964. *Language in Culture and Society: A Reader in Linguistics and Anthropology.* New York: Harper & Row.

Hymes, Dell. 1974. *Foundations in Sociolinguistics: An Ethnographic Approach.* Philadelphia: University of Pennsylvania Press.

Ingold, Tim, David Riches, and James Woodburn, eds. 1988. *Hunters and Gatherers. 1: History, Evolution and Social Change.* New York: St. Martin's Press.

Inhorn, Marcia C., and Peter J. Brown, eds. 1997. *The Anthropology of Infectious Disease: International Health Perspectives.* Amsterdam: Gordon and Breach.

Irons, William. 1979. "Natural Selection, Adaptation, and Human Social Behavior." In N. Chagnon and W. Irons, eds., *Evolutionary Biology and Human Social Behavior.* North Scituate, MA: Duxbury.

Irwin, Marc H., Gary N. Schafer, and Cynthia P. Feiden. 1974. "Emic and Unfamiliar Category Sorting of Mano Farmers and U.S. Undergraduates." *Journal of Cross-Cultural Psychology,* 5: 407–23.

Isaac, Glynn. 1971. "The Diet of Early Man: Aspects of Archaeological Evidence from Lower and Middle Pleistocene Sites in Africa." *World Archaeology,* 2: 277–99.

Isaac, Glynn. 1984. "The Archaeology of Human Origins: Studies of the Lower Pleistocene in East Africa, 1971–1981." In F. Wendorf and A. Close, eds., *Advances in World Archaeology.* Orlando, FL: Academic Press.

Isaac, Glynn, ed., assisted by Barbara Isaac. 1997. *Plio-Pleistocene Archaeology.* Oxford: Clarendon Press.

Itkonen, T. I. 1951. "The Lapps of Finland." *Southwestern Journal of Anthropology,* 7: 32–68.

Itoigawa, Naosuke, Yukimaru Sugiyama, Gene P. Sackett, and Roger K. R. Thompson, eds. 1992. *Topics in Primatology,* vol. 2. Tokyo: University of Tokyo Press.

Jablonski, Nina G., and George Chaplin. 2000. "The Evolution of Human Skin Color." *Journal of Human Evolution,* 39: 57–106.

Jablonsky, Nina G., and George Chaplin. 2002. "Skin Deep." *Scientific American* (October): 74–81.

Jacobs, Sue-Ellen, and Christine Roberts. 1989. "Sex, Sexuality, Gender and Gender Variance." In S. Morgen, ed., *Gender and Anthropology.* Washington, DC: American Anthropological Association.

Jaeger, J., T. Thein, M. Benammi, Y. Chaimanee, A. N. Soe, T. Lwin, T. Tun, S. Wai, and S. Ducrocq. 1999. "A New Primate from the Middle Eocene of Myanmar and the Asian Early Origins of Anthropoids." *Science,* 286 (October 15): 528–30.

James, William. 1902. *The Varieties of Religious Experience: A Study in Human Nature.* New York: Modern Library.

Jankowiak, William R. 2004. "Urban Mongols: Ethnicity in Communist China." In *Portraits of Culture,* in C. R. Ember, M. Ember, and P. N. Peregrine, eds., *New Directions in Anthropology.* Upper Saddle River, NJ: Prentice Hall, CD-ROM.

Jankowiak, William R., and Edward F. Fischer. 1992. "A Cross-Cultural Perspective on Romantic Love." *Ethnology,* 31: 149–55.

Jankowiak, William, M. Diane Nell, and Ann Buckmaster. 2002. "Managing Infidelity: A Cross-Cultural Perspective." *Ethnology,* 41: 85–101.

Janzen, Daniel H. 1973. "Tropical Agroecosystems." *Science,* 182 (December 21): 1212–19.

Jarvenpa, Robert. 2004. "*Silot'ine:* An Insurance Perspective on Northern Dene Kinship Networks in Recent History." *Journal of Anthropological Research* 60: 153–78.

Jayaswal, Vidula. 2002. "South Asian Upper Paleolithic." In P. N. Peregrine and M. Ember, eds., *Encyclopedia of Prehistory.* Vol. 8: *South and Southwest Asia.* New York: Kluwer Academic/Plenum.

Jelliffe, Derrick B., and E. F. Patrice Jelliffe. 1975. "Human Milk, Nutrition, and the World Resource Crisis." *Science,* 188 (May 9): 557–61.

Jennings, J. D. 1968. *Prehistory of North America.* New York: McGraw-Hill.

Jensen, Arthur. 1969. "How Much Can We Boost IQ and Scholastic Achievement?" *Harvard Educational Review,* 29: 1–123.

Jepsen, Glenn L., Ernst Mayr, and George Gaylord Simpson, eds. 1963. *Genetics, Paleontology, and Evolution.* New York: Atheneum.

Joachim, Michael. 1996. "Hunting and Gathering Societies." In D. Levinson and M. Ember, eds., *Encyclopedia of Cultural Anthropology.* New York: Henry Holt.

Joans, Barbara. 1997. "Problems in Pocatello: A Study in Linguistic Misunderstanding." In A. Podolefsky and P. J. Brown, eds., 1997. *Applying Cultural Anthropology: An Introductory Reader,* 3rd ed. Mountain View: CA: Mayfield, 51–54.

Johannes, R. E. 1981. *Words of the Lagoon: Fishing and Marine Lore in the Palau District of Micronesia.* Berkeley: University of California Press.

Johanson, Donald C., and Maitland Edey. 1981. *Lucy: The Beginnings of Humankind.* New York: Simon & Schuster.

Johanson, Donald C., and Tim D. White. 1979. "A Systematic Assessment of Early African Hominids." *Science,* 203 (January 26): 321–30.

Johnson, Allen, and Timothy Earle. 1987. *The Evolution of Human Societies: From Foraging Group to Agrarian State.* Stanford, CA: Stanford University Press.

Johnson, Amber Lynn. 2002. "Cross-Cultural Analysis of Pastoral Adaptations and Organizational States: A Preliminary Study." *Cross-Cultural Research,* 36: 151–80.

Johnson, Gregory A. 1977. "Aspects of Regional Analysis in Archaeology." *Annual Review of Anthropology,* 6: 479–508.

Johnson, Gregory A. 1987. "The Changing Organization of Uruk Administration on the Susiana Plain." In F. Hole, ed., *Archaeology of Western Iran.* Washington, DC: Smithsonian Institution Press.

Johnson, Jeffrey G., Patricia Cohen, Elizabeth M. Smailies, Stephanie Kasen, and Judith S. Brook. 2002. "Television Viewing and Aggressive Behavior During Adolescence and Adulthood." *Science,* 295 (March 29): 2468–70.

Johnson, Thomas M., and Carolyn F. Sargent, eds. 1990. *Medical Anthropology: Contemporary Theory and Method.* Westport, CT: Praeger.

Johnston, David Cay. 1999. "Gap Between Rich and Poor Found Substantially Wider." *New York Times National,* (September 5): p. 16.

Jolly, Alison. 1985. *The Evolution of Primate Behavior.* 2nd ed. New York: Macmillan.

Jolly, Clifford. 1970. "The Seed-Eaters: A New Model of Hominid Differentiation Based on a Baboon Analogy." *Man,* 5: 5–28.

Jones, Nicholas Blurton, Kristen Hawkes, and James F. O'Connell. 1996. "The Global Process and Local Ecology: How Should We Explain Differences between the Hadza and the !Kung?" In S. Kent, *Cultural Diversity among Twentieth-Century Foragers.* Cambridge: Cambridge University Press.

Jones, Steve, Robert Martin, and David Pilbeam, eds. 1992. *The Cambridge Encyclopedia of Human Evolution.* New York: Cambridge University Press.

Jordan, Ann T., ed. 1994. *Practicing Anthropology in Corporate America: Consulting on Organizational Culture.* NAPA Bulletin No. 14. Arlington, VA: American Anthropological Association.

Judge, W. James, and Jerry Dawson. 1972. "Paleo-Indian Settlement Technology in New Mexico." *Science,* 176 (June 16): 1210–16.

Jung, Carl G. 1938. *Psychology and Religion.* New Haven, CT: Yale University Press.

Jungers, William L. 1988a. "Relative Joint Size and Hominoid Locomotor Adaptations with Implications for the Evolution of Hominid Bipedalism." *Journal of Human Evolution,* 17: 247–65.

Jungers, William L. 1988b. "New Estimates of Body Size in Australopithecines." In F. Grine, ed., *Evolutionary History of the "Robust" Australopithecines.* New York: Aldine.

Kamin, Leon J. 1995. "Behind the Curve." *Scientific American* (February): 99–103.

Kang, Bong W. 2000. "A Reconsideration of Population Pressure and Warfare: A Protohistoric Korean Case." *Current Anthropology,* 41: 873–81.

Kang, Gay Elizabeth. 1979. "Exogamy and Peace Relations of Social Units: A Cross-Cultural Test." *Ethnology,* 18: 85–99.

Kaplan, Hillard, and Kim Hill. 1985. "Food Sharing among Aché Foragers: Tests of Explanatory Hypotheses." *Current Anthropology,* 26: 223–46.

Kaplan, Hillard, Kim Hill, and A. Magdalena Hurtado. 1990. "Risk, Foraging and Food Sharing among the Aché." In E. Cashdan, ed., *Risk and Uncertainty in Tribal and Peasant Economies.* Boulder, CO: Westview.

Kappelman, John. 1993. "The Attraction of Paleomagnetism." *Evolutionary Anthropology,* 2: 89–99.

Kardiner, Abram, with Ralph Linton. 1946 [1939]. *The Individual and His Society.* New York: Golden Press. (Originally published 1939 by Columbia University Press.)

Kasarda, John D. 1971. "Economic Structure and Fertility: A Comparative Analysis." *Demography,* 8, no. 3 (August): 307–18.

Kay, Richard F. 2000a. "*Parapithecidae.*" In I. Tattersall, E. Delson, and J. van Couvering, eds., *Encyclopedia of Human Evolution and Prehistory.* New York: Garland.

Kay, Richard F. 2000b. "Teeth." In I. Tattersall, E. Delson, and J. van Couvering, eds., *Encyclopedia of Human Evolution and Prehistory.* New York: Garland.

Kay, Richard F., C. Ross, and B. A. Williams. 1997. "Anthropoid Origins." *Science,* 275 (February 7): 797–804.

Keeley, Lawrence H. 1977. "The Functions of Paleolithic Flint Tools." *Scientific American* (November): 108–26.

Keeley, Lawrence H. 1980. *Experimental Determination of Stone Tool Uses: A Microwear Analysis.* Chicago: University of Chicago Press.

Keeley, Lawrence H. 1991. "Ethnographic Models for Late Glacial Hunter-Gatherers." In N. Barton, A. J. Roberts, and D. A. Roe, eds., *The Late Glacial in North-West Europe: Human Adaptation and Environmental Change at the End of the Pleistocene.* London: Council for British Archaeology. CBA Research Report 77, 179–190.

Keenan, Elinor. 1989. "Norm-Makers, Norm-Breakers: Uses of Speech by Men and Women in a Malagasy Community." In R. Bauman and J. Sherzer, *Explorations in the Ethnography of Speaking.* 2nd ed. New York: Cambridge University Press.

Kehoe, Alice B., and Dody H. Giletti. 1981. "Women's Preponderance in Possession Cults: The Calcium-Deficiency Hypothesis Extended." *American Anthropologist,* 83: 549–61.

Keller, Helen. 1974 [1902]. *The Story of My Life.* New York: Dell.

Kelley, Jay. 1992. "The Evolution of Apes." In S. Jones, R. Martin, and D. Pilbeam, eds., *The Cambridge Encyclopedia of Human Evolution.* New York: Cambridge University Press.

Kelly, Raymond C. 1974. "Witchcraft and Sexual Relations: An Exploration in the Social and Semantic Implications of the Structure of Belief." Paper presented at the annual meeting of the American Anthropological Association, Mexico City.

Kelly, Raymond C. 1985. *The Nuer Conquest: The Structure and Development of an Expansionist System.* Ann Arbor: University of Michigan Press.

Kelly, Robert L. 1995. *The Foraging Spectrum: Diversity in Hunter-Gatherer Lifeways.* Washington, DC: Smithsonian Institution Press.

Kelly, Robert L. 2002. "Lithic Analysis: Chipped Stone Tools and Waste Flakes in Archaeology." In P. N. Peregrine, C. R. Ember, and M. Ember, *Archaeology: Original Readings in Method and Practice.* Upper Saddle River, NJ: Prentice Hall.

Kent, Susan, ed. 1996. *Cultural Diversity among Twentieth-Century Foragers: An African Perspective.* Cambridge: Cambridge University Press.

Kerr, Richard A. 1998. "Sea-Floor Dust shows Drought Felled Akkadian Empire." *Science,* 299 (January 16): 325–26.

Khosroshashi, Fatemeh. 1989. "Penguins Don't Care, but Women Do: A Social Identity Analysis of a Whorfian Problem." *Language in Society,* 18: 505–25.

Kilbride, Philip L., and Janet C. Kilbride. 1990. "Polygyny: A Modern Contradiction?" In P. L. Kilbride and J. C. Kilbride, *Changing Family Life in East Africa.* University Park: Pennsylvania State University Press.

Kimbel, William H., T. D. White, and D. C. Johansen. 1984. "Cranial Morphology of *Australopithecus afarensis*: A Comparative Study Based on Composite Reconstruction of the Adult Skull." *American Journal of Physical Anthropology,* 64: 337–88.

King, Barbara J. 1999. "Introduction." In B. J. King, ed., *The Origins of Language.* Santa Fe, NM: School of American Research Press. 3–19.

King, Barbara. 1999. *The Origins of Language: What Nonhuman Primates Can Tell Us.* Santa Fe: School of American Research Press.

King, J. C. H. 1986. "Tradition in Native American Art." In E. L. Wade, ed., *The Arts of the North American Indian.* New York: Hudson Hills Press.

King, Marie-Claire, and Arno Motulsky. 2002. "Mapping Human History," *Science,* 298 (December 20): 2342–43.

King, Seth S. 1979. "Some Farm Machinery Seems Less Than Human." *New York Times,* (April 8): p. E9.

Kingston, John D., Bruno D. Marino, and Andrew Hill. 1994. "Isotopic Evidence for Neogene Hominid Paleoenvironments in the Kenya Rift Valley." *Science,* 264 (May 13): 955–59.

Klass, Morton. 2004. "Is There 'Caste' Outside of India?" In *Cross-Cultural Research for Social Science.* In C. R. Ember, M. Ember, and P. N. Peregrine, eds., *New Directions in Anthropology.* Upper Saddle River, NJ: Prentice Hall, CD-ROM.

Klein, J, and Takahata, N. 2002. *Where Do We Come From?: The Molecular Evidence for Human Descent.* New York: Springer Verlag.

Klein, Richard G. 1974. "Ice-Age Hunters of the Ukraine." *Scientific American* (June): 96–105.

Klein, Richard G. 1977. "The Ecology of Early Man in Southern Africa." *Science,* 197 (July 8): 115–26.

Klein, Richard G. 1983. "The Stone Age Prehistory of Southern Africa." *Annual Review of Anthropology,* 12: 25–48.

Klein, Richard G. 1987. "Reconstructing How Early People Exploited Animals: Problems and Prospects." In M. Nitecki and D. Nitecki, eds., *The Evolution of Human Hunting.* New York: Plenum.

Klein, Richard G. 1989. *The Human Career: Human Biological and Cultural Origins.* Chicago: University of Chicago Press.

Klein, Richard G. 1994. "Southern Africa before the Ice Age." In R. Corruccini and R. Ciochon, eds., *Integrative Paths to the Past.* Upper Saddle River, NJ: Prentice Hall.

Klein, Richard G. 2003. "Whither the Neanderthals" *Science,* 299 (March 7): 1525–28.

Kleinberg, Jill. 1994. "Practical Implications of Organizational Culture Where Americans and Japanese Work Together." In A. T. Jordan, ed., *Practicing Anthropology in Corporate America.* Arlington, VA: American Anthropological Association.

Kleinman, Arthur. 1988. *Rethinking Psychiatry: From Cultural Category to Personal Experience.* New York: Macmillan.

Kleinman, Arthur, and Byron Good, eds. 1985. *Culture and Depression: Studies in the Anthropology and Cross-Cultural Psychiatry of Affect and Disorder.* Berkeley: University of California Press.

Kleinman, Arthur, Veena Das, and Margaret Lock, eds. 1997. *Social Suffering.* Berkeley: University of California Press.

Kleinman, Devra, ed., 1977. *The Biology and Conservation of the Callitrichidae.* Washington, DC: Smithsonian Institution.

Klima, Bohuslav. 1962. "The First Ground-Plan of an Upper Paleolithic Loess Settlement in Middle Europe and Its Meaning," In R. Braidwood and G. Willey, eds., *Courses Toward Urban Life.* Chicago: Aldine.

Klineberg, Otto. 1935. *Negro Intelligence and Selective Migration.* New York: Columbia University Press.

Klineberg, Otto, ed. 1944. *Characteristics of the American Negro.* New York: Harper & Brothers.

Klineberg, Otto. 1979. "Foreword." In M. H. Segall, *Cross-Cultural Psychology.* Monterey, CA: Brooks/Cole.

Kluckhohn, Clyde. 1948. "As an Anthropologist Views It." In A. Deutsch, ed., *Sex Habits of American Men.* Upper Saddle River, NJ: Prentice Hall.

Kluckhohn, Clyde. 1965. "Recurrent Themes in Myths and Mythmaking." In A. Dundes, ed., *The Study of Folklore.* Upper Saddle River, NJ: Prentice Hall.

Knauft, Bruce M. 1978. "Cargo Cults and Relational Separation." *Behavior Science Research,* 13: 185–240.

Knecht, Peter. 2003. "Aspects of Shamanism: An Introduction." In C. Chilson and P. Knecht, eds. *Shamans in Asia.* London: RoutledgeCurzon, 1–30.

Knudsen, Dean D., and Joann L. Miller, eds. 1991. *Abused and Battered: Social and Legal Responses to Family Violence.* New York: Aldine.

Koch, Klaus-Friedrich, Soraya Altorki, Andrew Arno, and Letitia Hickson. 1977. "Ritual Reconciliation and the Obviation of Grievances: A Comparative Study in the Ethnography of Law." *Ethnology,* 16: 269–84.

Konner, Melvin, and Carol Worthman. 1980. "Nursing Frequency, Gonadal Function, and Birth Spacing among !Kung Hunter-Gatherers." *Science,* 267 (February 15): 788–91.

Korbin, Jill E. 1981. "Introduction." In J. E. Korbin, ed., *Child Abuse and Neglect.* Berkeley: University of California Press.

Korotayev, Andrey and Dmitri Bondarenko. 2000. "Polygyny and Democracy: A Cross-Cultural Comparison." *Cross-Cultural Research,* 34: 190–208.

Kottak, Conrad P. 1983. *Assault on Paradise: Social Change in a Brazilian Village.* New York: Random House.

Kottak, Conrad P. 1999. "The New Ecological Anthropology." *Current Anthropology,* 101: 23–35.

Kottak, Conrad Phillip. 1996. "The Media, Development, and Social Change." In E. F. Moran, *Transforming Societies, Transforming Anthropology.* Ann Arbor: University of Michigan Press.

Kozlowski, S. K., ed. 1973. *The Mesolithic in Europe.* Warsaw: Warsaw University Press.

Kracke, Waud H. 1979. *Force and Persuasion: Leadership in an Amazonian Society.* Chicago: University of Chicago Press.

Krahn, H., T. F. Hartnagel, and J. W. Gartrell. 1986. "Income Inequality and Homicide Rates: Cross-National Data and Criminological Theories." *Criminology,* 24: 269–95.

Kramer, Andrew. 2002. "The Natural History and Evolutionary Fate of *Homo erectus.*" In P. N. Peregrine, C. R. Ember, and M. Ember, eds., *Physical Anthropology: Original Readings in Method and Practice.* Upper Saddle River, NJ: Prentice Hall.

Kramer, Samuel Noel. 1963. *The Sumerians: Their History, Culture, and Character.* Chicago: University of Chicago Press.

Krebs, J. R., and N. B. Davies, eds. 1984. *Behavioural Ecology: An Evolutionary Approach.* 2nd ed. Sunderland, MA: Sinauer.

Krebs, J. R., and N. B. Davies. 1987. *An Introduction to Behavioural Ecology.* 2nd ed. Sunderland, MA: Sinauer.

Krings, Matthias, A. Stone, R. W. Schmitz, H. Krainitzki, M. Stoneking, and S. Paabo. 1997. "Neandertal DNA Sequences and the Origin of Modern Humans." *Cell,* 90: 19–30.

Krippner, Stanley. 1987. "Dreams and Shamanism." In S. Nicholson, Comp., *Shamanism.* Wheaton, IL: Theosophical Publishing House, 125–32.

Kristof, Nicholas D. 1995. "Japan's Invisible Minority: Better Off Than in Past, but Still Outcasts." *New York Times International* (November 30): A18.

Kristof, Nicholas D. 1997. "Japan's Invisible Minority: Burakumin," *Britannica Online.* December.

Kroeber, Alfred L. 1952. *The Nature of Culture.* Chicago: University of Chicago Press.

Kroeber, Theodora. 1967. *Ishi in Two Worlds.* Berkeley: University of California Press.

Kuehn, Steven. 1998. "New Evidence for Late Paleoindian–Early Archaic Subsistence Behavior in the Western Great Lakes." *American Antiquity,* 63: 457–76.

Kushner, Gilbert. 1991. "Applied Anthropology." In W. G. Emener and M. Darrow, eds., *Career Explorations in Human Services.* Springfield, IL: Charles C Thomas.

Kuznar, Lawrence A. 1997. *Reclaiming a Scientific Anthropology.* Walnut Creek, CA: AltaMira Press.

Lakoff, Robin. 1973. "Language and Woman's Place." *Language in Society,* 2: 45–80.

Lakoff, Robin. 1990. "Why Can't a Woman Be Less Like a Man?" In R. Lakoff, *Talking Power.* New York: Basic Books.

Lambert, Helen. "Not Talking About Sex in India: Indirection and the Communication of Bodily Intention." In J. Hendry and C. W. Watson, eds. *An Anthropology of Indirect Communication.* London: Routledge, 51–67.

Lambert, William W., Leigh Minturn Triandis, and Margery Wolf. 1959. "Some Correlates of Beliefs in the Malevolence and Benevolence of Supernatural Beings: A Cross-Societal Study." *Journal of Abnormal and Social Psychology,* 58: 162–69.

Landauer, Thomas K. 1973. "Infantile Vaccination and the Secular Trend in Stature." *Ethos,* 1: 499–503.

Landauer, Thomas K., and John W. M. Whiting. 1964. "Infantile Stimulation and Adult Stature of Human Males." *American Anthropologist,* 66: 1007–28.

Landauer, Thomas K., and John W. M. Whiting. 1981. "Correlates and Consequences of Stress in Infancy." In R. H. Munroe, R. Munroe, and B. Whiting, eds., *Handbook of Cross-Cultural Human Development.* New York: Garland.

Lang, Sabine. 1999. "Lesbians, Men-Women and Two-Spirits: Homosexuality and Gender in Native American Cultures." In Evelyn Blackwood and Saskia E. Weiringa, eds. *Female Desires: Same-Sex Relations and Transgender Practices Across Cultures.* New York: Columbia University Press, 91–116.

Langness, Lewis L. 1974. *The Study of Culture.* San Francisco: Chandler and Sharp.

Lareau, Annette. 2003. *Unequal Childhoods: Class, Race, and Family Life.* Berkeley, CA: University of California Press.

Larsen, Clark Spenser. 2002. "Bare Bones Anthropology: The Bioarchaeology of Human Remains." In P. N. Peregrine, C. R. Ember, and M. Ember, eds., *Archaeology: Original Readings in Method and Practice.* Upper Saddle River, NJ: Prentice Hall.

Larson, Daniel O., John R. Johnson, and Joel C. Michaelsen. 1994. "Missionization among the Coastal Chumash of Central California: A Study of Risk Minimization Strategies." *American Anthropologist,* 96: 263–99.

Lassiter, Luke Eric, Hurley Goodall, Elizabeth Campbell, and Michelle Natasya Johnson, eds., 2004. *The Other Side of Middletown: Exploring Muncie's African American Community.* Walnut Creek, CA: AltaMira Press.

Lasswell, Harold. 1936. *Politics: Who Gets What, When, How.* New York: McGraw-Hill.

Lawless, Robert. 2004. "Haitians: From Political Repression to Chaos." In *Portraits of Culture,* in C. R. Ember, M. Ember, and

P. N. Peregrine, eds., *New Directions in Anthropology.* Upper Saddle River, NJ: Prentice Hall, CD-ROM.

Lawless, Robert, Vinson H. Sutlive, Jr., and Mario D. Zamora, eds. 1983. *Fieldwork: The Human Experience.* New York: Gordon and Breach.

Layton, Robert. 1992. *Australian Rock Art: A New Synthesis.* Cambridge: Cambridge University Press.

Leach, Jerry W. 1983. "Introduction." In J. W. Leach and E. Leach, eds., *The Kula.* Cambridge: Cambridge University Press.

Leach, Jerry W., and Edmund Leach, eds. 1983. *The Kula: New Perspectives on Massim Exchange.* Cambridge: Cambridge University Press.

Leacock, Eleanor. 1954. "The Montagnais 'Hunting Territory' and the Fur Trade." *American Anthropological Association Memoir, 78:* 1–59.

Leacock, Eleanor, and Richard Lee. 1982. "Introduction." In E. Leacock and R. Lee, eds., *Politics and History in Band Societies.* Cambridge: Cambridge University Press.

Leakey, Louis S. B. 1960. "Finding the World's Earliest Man." *National Geographic* (September): 420–35.

Leakey, Louis S. B. 1965. *Olduvai Gorge, 1951–1961,* Vol. I: *A Preliminary Report on the Geology and Fauna.* Cambridge: Cambridge University Press.

Leakey, Maeve, C. S. Feibel, I. McDougall, and A. Walker. 1995. "New Four-Million-Year-Old Hominid Species from Kanapoi and Allia Bay, Kenya." *Nature,* 376 (August 17): 565–71.

Leakey, Maeve, Ian Tattersall, 1995. *The Fossil Trail.* Adapted from *New York Times* (September 5): C9.

Leakey, Maeve, Fred Spoor, Frank Brown, Patrick Gathogo, Christopher Kiarie, Louise Leakey, Ian McDougall. 2001. "New Hominin Genus from Eastern Africa Shows Diverse Middle Pliocene Lineages." *Nature,* 410 (March 22): 433–51.

Leakey, Mary. 1971. *Olduvai Gorge: Excavations in Beds I and II.* Cambridge: Cambridge University Press.

Leakey, Mary. 1979. *Olduvai Gorge: My Search for Early Man.* London: Collins.

Leakey, Richard E. 1981. *The Making of Mankind.* New York: Dutton.

Lederman, Rena. 1990. "Big Men, Large and Small? Towards a Comparative Perspective." *Ethnology,* 29: 3–15.

Lee, Phyllis C. 1983. "Home Range, Territory and Intergroup Encounters." In R. A. Hinde, ed., *Primate Social Relationship: An Integrated Approach.* Sunderland, MA: Sinauer.

Lee, Phyllis C. 1999. *Comparative Primate Socioecology.* New York: Cambridge University Press.

Lee, Richard B. 1968. "What Hunters Do for a Living, or, How to Make Out on Scarce Resources." In R. B. Lee and I. DeVore, eds., *Man the Hunter.* Chicago: Aldine.

Lee, Richard B. 1972. "Population Growth and the Beginnings of Sedentary Life among the !Kung Bushmen." In B. Spooner, ed., *Population Growth.* Cambridge, MA: MIT Press.

Lee, Richard B. 1979. *The !Kung San: Men, Women, and Work in a Foraging Society.* Cambridge: Cambridge University Press.

Lee, Richard B., and Irven DeVore, eds. 1968. *Man the Hunter.* Chicago: Aldine.

Lees, Susan H., and Daniel G. Bates. 1974. "The Origins of Specialized Nomadic Pastoralism: A Systemic Model." *American Antiquity,* 39: 187–93.

Leibowitz, Lila. 1978. *Females, Males, Families: A Biosocial Approach.* North Scituate, MA: Duxbury.

Leis, Nancy B. 1974. "Women in Groups: Ijaw Women's Associations." In M. Z. Rosaldo and L. Lamphere, eds., *Woman, Culture, and Society.* Stanford, CA: Stanford University Press.

Lenski, Gerhard. 1984 [1966]. *Power and Privilege: A Theory of Social Stratification.* Chapel Hill: University of North Carolina Press.

Leonard, William R. 2002. "Food for Thought: Dietary Change Was a Driving Force in Human Evolution." *Scientific American* (December): 108–15.

Lepowsky, Maria. 1990. "Big Men, Big Women and Cultural Autonomy." *Ethnology,* 29: 35–50.

Leslie, C. 1976. "Introduction." In C. Leslie, ed., *Asian Medical Systems: A Comparative Study.* Los Angeles: University of California Press.

Lett, James. 1996. "Scientific Anthropology." In D. Levinson and M. Ember, eds., *Encyclopedia of Cultural Anthropology.* New York: Henry Holt.

Lett, James 1997. *Science, Reason, and Anthropology: The Principles of Rational Inquiry.* Lanham, MD: Rowman & Littlefield.

Levine, James A., Robert Weisell, Simon Chevassus, Claudio D. Martinez, and Barbara Burlingame. 2002. "The Distribution of Work Tasks for Male and Female Children and Adults Separated by Gender" in "Looking at Child Labor." *Science,* 296 (May 10): 1025.

Levine, Nancy E. 1988. "Women's Work and Infant Feeding: A Case from Rural Nepal." *Ethnology,* 27: 231–51.

LeVine, Robert A. 1966. *Dreams and Deeds: Achievement Motivation in Nigeria.* Chicago: University of Chicago Press.

LeVine, Robert A. 1988. "Human Parental Care: Universal Goals, Cultural Strategies, Individual Behavior." In R. A. LeVine, P. M. Miller, and M. M. West, eds., *Parental Behavior in Diverse Societies.* San Francisco: Jossey-Bass.

LeVine, Robert A., and Barbara B. LeVine. 1963. "Nyansongo: A Gusii Community in Kenya." In B. B. Whiting, ed., *Six Cultures.* New York: Wiley.

LeVine, Robert A., Patrice M. Miller, and Mary Maxwell West, eds. 1988. *Parental Behavior in Diverse Societies.* San Francisco: Jossey-Bass.

Levinson, David. 1989. *Family Violence in Cross-Cultural Perspective.* Newbury Park, CA: Sage.

Levinson, David, and Martin J. Malone, eds. 1980. *Toward Explaining Human Culture: A Critical Review of the Findings of Worldwide Cross-Cultural Research.* New Haven, CT: HRAF Press.

Levinson, David, and Melvin Ember, eds. 1996. *Encyclopedia of Cultural Anthropology.* 4 vols. New York: Henry Holt.

Levinson, David and Melvin Ember, eds., 1997. *American Immigrant Cultures: Builders of a Nation,* 2 vol. New York: Macmillan Reference.

Lévi-Strauss, Claude. 1963a. "The Sorcerer and His Magic." In C. Lévi-Strauss, *Structural Anthropology.* New York: Basic Books.

Lévi-Strauss, Claude. 1963b. *Structural Anthropology.* Trans. Claire Jacobson and Brooke Grundfest Schoepf. New York: Basic Books.

Lévi-Strauss, Claude. 1966. *The Savage Mind,* trans. George Weidenfeld and Nicolson, Ltd. Chicago: University of Chicago Press. [First published in French 1962.]

Lévi-Strauss, Claude. 1969a. *The Elementary Structures of Kinship,* rev. ed., trans. James H. Bell and J. R. von Sturmer, ed. Rodney Needham. Boston: Beacon Press. [First published in French 1949.]

Lévi-Strauss, Claude. 1969b. *The Raw and the Cooked,* trans. John Weightman and Doreen Weightman. New York: Harper & Row [First published in French 1964.]

Levy, Jerrold E. 1994. "Hopi Shamanism: A Reappraisal." In R. J. DeMallie and A. Ortiz, eds., *North American Indian Anthropology: Essays on Society and Culture.* Norman: University of Oklahoma Press, 307–27.

Lev-Yadun, Simcha, Avi Gopher, and Shahal Abbo, 2000. "The Cradle of Agriculture," *Science,* 288 (June 2): 1602–03.

Lewin, Roger. 1983a. "Is the Orangutan a Living Fossil?" *Science,* 222 (December 16): 1222–23.

Lewin, Roger. 1983b. "Fossil Lucy Grows Younger, Again." *Science,* 219 (January 7): 43–44.

Lewin, Tamar. 1994. "Sex in America: Faithfulness in Marriage Is Overwhelming." *New York Times National,* October 7: A1, A18.

Lewis, I. M., ed. 1983. *Nationalism and Self-Determination in the Horn of Africa.* London: Ithaca Press.

Lewis, I. M. 2003. *Ecstatic Religion: A Study of Shamanism and Spirit Possession.* London: Routledge.

Lewis, Oscar. 1951. *Life in a Mexican Village: Tepoztlan Revisited.* Urbana: University of Illinois Press.

Lewis, Oscar (with the assistance of Victor Barnouw). 1958. *Village Life in Northern India.* Urbana: University of Illinois Press.

Lichter, Daniel T., Diane K. McLaughlin, George Kephart, and David J. Landry. 1992. "Race and the Retreat from Marriage: A Shortage of Marriageable Men?" *American Sociological Review,* 57: 781–99.

Lieberman, Daniel E. 1995. "Testing Hypotheses about Recent Human Evolution from Skulls: Integrating Morphology, Function, Development, and Phylogeny." *Current Anthropology,* 36: 159–97.

Lieberman, Leonard. 1999. "Scientific Insignificance." *Anthropology Newsletter,* 40: 11–12.

Lieberman, Philip. 1991. *Uniquely Human: The Evolution of Speech, Thought, and Selfless Behavior.* Cambridge, MA: Harvard University Press.

Light, Ivan, and Zhong Deng. 1995 [1964]. "Gender Differences in ROSCA Participation within Korean Business Households in Los Angeles." In S. Ardener and S. Burman, *Money-Go-Rounds: The Importance of Rotating Savings and Credit Associations for Women.* Oxford: Berg, 217–40.

Lightfoot, Kent G. 2005. "The Archaeology of Colonialism: California in Cross-Cultural Perspective," in G. J. Stein, ed., *The Archaeology of Colonial Encounters: Comparative Perspectives,* Santa Fe, NM: School of American Research, pp. 207–35.

Lingenfelter, Sherwood G. 2004. "Yap: Changing Roles of Men and Women." In *Portraits of Culture,* in C. R. Ember, M. Ember, and P. N. Peregrine, eds., *New Directions in Anthropology.* Upper Saddle River, NJ: Prentice Hall, CD-ROM.

Linton, Ralph. 1936. *The Study of Man.* New York: Appleton-Century-Crofts.

Linton, Ralph. 1945. *The Cultural Background of Personality.* New York: Appleton-Century-Crofts.

Little, Kenneth. 1957. "The Role of Voluntary Associations in West African Urbanization." *American Anthropologist,* 59: 582–93.

Little, Kenneth. 1965. *West African Urbanization.* New York: Cambridge University Press.

Little, Kenneth. 1965–1966. "The Political Function of the Poro." *Africa,* 35: 349–65; 36: 62–71.

Little, Michael A. 2002. "Growth and Development of Turkana Pastoralists." In P. N. Peregrine, C. R. Ember, and M. Ember, *Physical Anthropology: Original Readings in Method and Practice.* Upper Saddle River, NJ: Prentice Hall.

Little, Michael A., and Jere D. Haas, eds. 1989. *Human Population Biology: A Transdisciplinary Science.* New York: Oxford University Press.

Lock, Margaret. 2004. "Japan: Glimpses of Everyday Life." In *Portraits of Culture,* in C. R. Ember, M. Ember, and P. N. Peregrine, eds., *New Directions in Anthropology.* Upper Saddle River, NJ: Prentice Hall, CD-ROM.

Loftin, Colin K. 1971. "Warfare and Societal Complexity: A Cross-Cultural Study of Organized Fighting in Preindustrial Societies." Ph.D. dissertation, University of North Carolina at Chapel Hill.

Loftin, Colin, David McDowall, and James Boudouris. 1989. "Economic Change and Homicide in Detroit, 1926–1979." In T. R. Gurr, ed., *Violence in America.* Vol. 1: *The History of Crime.* Newbury Park, CA: Sage.

Lomax, Alan, ed. 1968. *Folk Song Style and Culture.* American Association for the Advancement of Science Publication No. 88. Washington, DC.

Loomis, W. Farnsworth. 1967. "Skin-Pigment Regulation of Vitamin-D Biosynthesis in Man." *Science,* 157 (August 4): 501–06.

Loustaunau, Martha O., and Elisa J. Sobo. 1997. *The Cultural Context of Health, Illness, and Medicine.* Westport, CT: Bergin & Garvey.

Lovejoy, Arthur O. 1964. *The Great Chain of Being: A Study of the History of an Idea.* Cambridge, MA: Harvard University Press.

Lovejoy, C. Owen. 1981. "The Origin of Man." *Science,* 211 (January 23): 341–50.

Lovejoy, C. Owen. 1988. "Evolution of Human Walking." *Scientific American* (November): 118–25.

Lovejoy, C. Owen, Kingsbury Heiple, and Albert Bernstein. 1973. "The Gait of *Australopithecus.*" *American Journal of Physical Anthropology,* 38: 757–79.

Low, Bobbi. 1990a. "Human Responses to Environmental Extremeness and Uncertainty." In E. Cashdan, ed., *Risk and Uncertainty in Tribal and Peasant Economies.* Boulder, CO: Westview.

Low, Bobbi. 1990b. "Marriage Systems and Pathogen Stress in Human Societies." *American Zoologist,* 30: 325–39.

Low, Bobbi S. 2004. "Behavioral Ecology, 'Sociobiology' and Human Behavior." In *Research Frontiers,* in C. R. Ember, M. Ember, and P. N. Peregrine, eds., *New Directions in Anthropology.* Upper Saddle River, NJ: Prentice Hall, CD-ROM.

Lowe, Edward D. 2002. "A Widow, a Child, and Two Lineages: Exploring Kinship and Attachment in Chuuk." *American Anthropologist,* 104: 123–37.

Lucy, John A. 1992. *Grammatical Categories and Cognition: A Case Study of the Linguistic Relativity Hypothesis.* Cambridge: Cambridge University Press.

Luhrmann, Tanya M., 1989. *Persuasions of the Witch's Craft: Ritual Magic and Witchcraft in Present-Day England.* Oxford: Blackwell.

Lumbreras, Luis. 1974. *The Peoples and Cultures of Ancient Peru.* Washington, DC: Smithsonian Institution Press.

Luria, A. R. 1976. *Cognitive Development: Its Cultural and Social Foundations.* Cambridge, MA: Harvard University Press.

Lutz, Catherine. 1985. "Depression and the Translations of Emotional Worlds." In A. Kleinman and B. Good, eds., *Culture and Depression.* Berkeley: University of California Press.

Lynd, Robert S., and Helen Merrell Lynd. 1929. *Middletown.* New York: Harcourt, Brace.

Lynd, Robert S., and Helen Merrell Lynd. 1937. *Middletown in Transition.* New York: Harcourt, Brace.

Lyon, Patricia J., ed. 1974. *Native South Americans: Ethnology of the Least Known Continent.* Boston: Little, Brown.

Lyons, Nona Plessner. 1988. "Two Perspectives: On Self, Relationships, and Morality." In C. Gilligan, J. V. Ward, and J. M. Taylor, eds., *Mapping the Moral Domain.* Cambridge, MA: Harvard University Press.

Lyttleton, Chris. 2000. *Endangered Relations: Negotiating Sex and AIDS in Thailand.* Bangkok: White Lotus Press.

MacArthur, R. H., and E. O. Wilson. 1967. *Theory of Island Biogeography.* Princeton, NJ: Princeton University Press.

Maccoby, Eleanor E. 1998. *The Two Sexes: Growing Up Apart, Coming Together.* Cambridge, MA: Belknap Press of Harvard University Press.

Maccoby, Eleanor E., and Carol N. Jacklin. 1974. *The Psychology of Sex Differences.* Stanford, CA: Stanford University Press.

Macdonald, Douglas H. and Barry S. Hewlett. 1999. "Reproductive Interests and Forager Mobility." *Current Anthropology,* 40: 501–23.

Macionis, John J. 1993. *Sociology.* 4th ed. Upper Saddle River, NJ: Prentice Hall.

MacKinnon, John, and Kathy MacKinnon. 1980. "The Behavior of Wild Spectral Tarsiers." *International Journal of Primatology,* 1: 361–79.

MacKintosh, N. J. 1998. *IQ and Human Intelligence.* Oxford: Oxford University Press.

MacLachlan, Morgan D., ed. 1987. *Household Economies and Their Transformations.* Monographs in Economic Anthropology No. 3. Lanham, MD: University Press of America.

MacNeish, Richard S. 1973. "The Evaluation of Community Patterns in the Tehuacán Valley of Mexico and Speculations about the Cultural Processes." In R. Tringham, ed., *Ecology and Agricultural Settlements.* Andover, MA: Warner Modular.

MacNeish, Richard S. 1991. *The Origins of Agriculture and Settled Life.* Norman: University of Oklahoma Press.

Madigral, Lorena. 1989. "Hemoglobin Genotype, Fertility, and the Malaria Hypothesis." *Human Biology,* 61: 311–25.

Magner, L. 1992. *A History of Medicine.* New York: Marcel Dekker.

Mahony, Frank Joseph. 1971. *A Trukese Theory of Medicine.* Ann Arbor, MI: University Microfilms.

Malefijt, Annemarie De Waal. 1968. *Religion and Culture: An Introduction to Anthropology of Religion.* New York: Macmillan.

Malin, Edward. 1986. *Totem Poles of the Pacific Northwest Coast.* Portland, OR: Timber Press.

Malinowski, Bronislaw. 1920. "Kula: The Circulating Exchange of Valuables in the Archipelagoes of Eastern New Guinea." *Man,* 51, no. 2: 97–105.

Malinowski, Bronislaw. 1927. *Sex and Repression in Savage Society.* London: Kegan Paul, Trench, Trubner.

Malinowski, Bronislaw. 1932. *The Sexual Life of Savages in Northwestern Melanesia.* New York: Halcyon House.

Malinowski, Bronislaw. 1939. "The Group and the Individual in Functional Analysis." *American Journal of Sociology,* 44: 938–64.

Malinowski, Bronislaw. 1954a. "Magic, Science, and Religion." In B. Malinowski, *Magic, Science, and Religion and Other Essays.* Garden City, NY: Doubleday.

Malinowski, Bronislaw. 1954b. *Magic, Science and Religion and Other Essays.* Garden City, NY: Doubleday.

Mangin, William. 1967. "Latin American Squatter Settlements: A Problem and a Solution." *Latin American Research Review,* 2: 65–98.

Mangin, William P. 1965. "The Role of Regional Associations in the Adaptation of Rural Migrants to Cities in Peru." In D. B. Health and R. N. Adams, eds., *Contemporary Cultures and Societies of Latin America.* New York: Random House.

Manhein, Mary H. 1999. *The Bone Lady: Life as a Forensic Anthropologist.* Baton Rouge: Louisiana State University Press.

Manzanilla, Linda, ed. 1987. *Studies in the Neolithic and Urban Revolutions.* British Archaeological Reports International Series 349. Oxford.

Maquet, Jacques. 1986. *The Aesthetic Experience: An Anthropologist Looks at the Visual Arts.* New Haven, CT: Yale University Press.

Marano, Louis A. 1973. "A Macrohistoric Trend toward World Government." *Behavior Science Notes,* 8: 35–40.

Marcus, George E., and Michael M. J. Fischer. 1986. *Anthropology as Cultural Critique: An Experimental Moment in the Human Sciences.* Chicago: University of Chicago Press.

Marcus, Joyce. 1983. "On the Nature of the Mesoamerican City." In E. Vogt and R. Leventhal, eds., *Prehistoric Settlement Patterns.* Albuquerque: University of New Mexico Press.

Marcus, Joyce. 2002. "Maya Hieroglyphs: History or Propaganda?" In P. N. Peregrine, C. R. Ember, and M. Ember, eds., *Archaeology: Original Readings in Method and Practice.* Upper Saddle River, NJ: Prentice Hall.

Marcus, Joyce, and Kent V. Flannery. 1996. *Zapotec Civilization.* London: Thames and Hudson.

Marett, R. R. 1909. *The Thresholds of Religion.* London: Methuen.

Marks, Jonathan. 1994. "Black, White, Other: Racial Categories Are Cultural Constructs Masquerading as Biology." *Natural History* (December): 32–35.

Marks, Jonathan. 2002. "Genes, Bodies, and Species," in P. N. Peregrine, C. R. Ember, and M. Ember, eds., *Physical Anthropology: Original Reading in Method and Practice.* Upper Saddle River, NJ: Prentice Hall.

Marshack, Alexander. 1972. *The Roots of Civilization.* New York: McGraw-Hill.

Marshall, Eliot. 2000. "Rival Genome Sequencers Celebrate a Milestone Together." *Science,* 288 (June 30): 2294–95.

Marshall, Eliot. 2001. "Pre-Clovis Sites Fight for Acceptance," *Science,* 291: 1730–32.

Marshall, Larry G. 1984. "Who Killed Cock Robin? An Investigation of the Extinction Controversy." In P. Martin and R. Klein, eds., *Quaternary Extinctions.* Tucson: University of Arizona Press.

Marshall, Lorna. 1961. "Sharing, Talking and Giving: Relief of Social Tensions among !Kung Bushmen." *Africa,* 31: 239–42.

Martin, M. Kay, and Barbara Voorhies. 1975. *Female of the Species.* New York: Columbia University Press.

Martin, Paul S. 1973. "The Discovery of America." *Science,* 179 (March 9): 969–74.

Martin, Paul S., and Richard Klein, eds. 1984. *Quaternary Extinctions: A Prehistoric Revolution.* Tucson: University of Arizona Press.

Martin, Paul S., and H. E. Wright, eds. 1967. *Pleistocene Extinctions: The Search for a Cause.* New Haven, CT: Yale University Press.

Martin, Robert D. 1975. "Strategies of Reproduction." *Natural History* (November): 48–57.

Martin, Robert D. 1990. *Primate Origins and Evolution: A Phylogenetic Reconstruction.* Princeton, NJ: Princeton University Press.

Martin, Robert D. 1992. "Classification and Evolutionary Relationships." In S. Jones, R. Martin, and D. Pilbeam, eds., *The Cambridge Encyclopedia of Human Evolution.* New York: Cambridge University Press.

Martin, Robert D., and Simon K. Bearder. 1979. "Radio Bush Baby." *Natural History* (October): 77–81.

Martorell, Reynaldo. 1980. "Interrelationships between Diet, Infectious Disease and Nutritional Status." In L. Greene and F. Johnston, eds., *Social and Biological Predictors of Nutritional Status, Physical Growth and Neurological Development.* New York: Academic Press.

Martorell, Reynaldo, Juan Rivera, Haley Kaplowitz, and Ernesto Pollitt. 1991. "Long-Term Consequences of Growth Retardation during Early Childhood." Paper presented at the Sixth International Congress of Auxology, September 15–19, Madrid.

Mascie-Taylor, C. G. Nicholas. 1990. "The Biology of Social Class," in C. G. N. Mascie-Taylor, ed., *Biosocial Aspects of Social Class.* Oxford: Oxford University Press, 117–42.

Mascie-Taylor, C. G. N., and G. W. Lasker. 1991. *Applications of Biological Anthropology to Human Affairs.* New York: Cambridge University Press.

Maslow, Abraham H. 1964. *Religions, Values, and Peak-Experiences.* Columbus: Ohio State University Press.

Mason, Ian L. 1984. *Evolution of Domesticated Animals.* New York: Longman.

Mason, Philip. 1962. *Prospero's Magic.* London: Oxford University Press.

Masumura, Wilfred T. 1977. "Law and Violence: A Cross-Cultural Study." *Journal of Anthropological Research,* 33: 388–99.

Matejcek, Zdenek. 1983. "Perceived Parental Acceptance-Rejection and Personality Organization among Czech Elementary School Children." *Behavior Science Research,* 18: 259–68.

Mathiassen, Therkel. 1928. *Material Culture of Iglulik Eskimos.* Copenhagen: Glydendalske.

Mathiot, Madeleine, ed. 1979. *Ethnolinguistics: Boas, Sapir and Whorf Revisited.* The Hague: Mouton.

Matlock, James G. 2004. "Universals and Variation in Religious Belief and Practice." In *Cross-Cultural Research for Social Science,* in C. R. Ember, M. Ember, and P. N. Peregrine, eds., *New Directions in Anthropology.* Upper Saddle River, NJ: Prentice Hall, CD-ROM.

Matossian, Mary K. 1982. "Ergot and the Salem Witchcraft Affair." *American Scientist,* 70: 355–57.

Matossian, Mary K. 1989. *Poisons of the Past: Molds, Epidemics, and History.* New Haven, CT: Yale University Press.

Matthiasson, Carolyn J. 1974. *Many Sisters: Women in Cross-Cultural Perspective.* New York: Free Press.

Maybury-Lewis, David. 1967. *Akwe-Shavante Society.* Oxford: Clarendon Press.

Mayr, Ernst. 1972. "The Nature of the Darwinian Revolution." *Science,* 176 (June 2): 981–89.

Mayr, Ernst. 1982. *The Growth of Biological Thought: Diversity, Evolution, and Inheritance.* Cambridge, MA: Belknap Press of Harvard University Press.

Mayr, Ernst. 1993. *One Long Argument: Charles Darwin and the Genesis of Modern Evolutionary Thought.* Cambridge, MA: Harvard University Press.

Mayr, Ernst. 2002. *What Evolution Is.* New York: Basic Books.

Mazess, Richard B. 1975. "Human Adaptation to High Altitude." In A. Damon, ed., *Physiological Anthropology.* New York: Oxford University Press.

McAnany, Patricia. 2002. "Ancestor Veneration in Lowland Maya Society: A Case Study from K'axob, Belize." In P. N. Peregrine, C. R. Ember, and M. Ember, eds., *Archaeology: Original Readings in Method and Practice.* Upper Saddle River, NJ: Prentice Hall.

McCain, Garvin, and Erwin M. Segal. 1988. *The Game of Science.* 5th ed. Monterey, CA: Brooks/Cole.

McCarthy, Frederick D., and Margaret McArthur. 1960. "The Food Quest and the Time Factor in Aboriginal Economic Life." In C. P. Mountford, ed., *Records of the Australian-American Scientific Expedition to Arnhem Land.* Vol. 2: *Anthropology and Nutrition.* Melbourne: Melbourne University Press.

McCay, Bonnie M, and James M. Acheson. 1987. "Introduction." In B. M. McCay and J. M. Acheson, eds., *The Question of the Commons.* Tucson: University of Arizona Press.

McCay, Bonnie M, and James M. Acheson, eds. 1987. *The Question of the Commons: The Culture and Ecology of Communal Resources.* Tucson: University of Arizona Press.

McClelland, David C. 1961 *The Achieving Society.* New York: Van Nostrand.

McCorriston, Joy, and Frank Hole. 1991. "The Ecology of Seasonal Stress and the Origins of Agriculture in the Near East." *American Anthropologist,* 93: 46–69.

McCracken, Robert D. 1971. "Lactase Deficiency: An Example of Dietary Evolution." *Current Anthropology,* 12: 479–500.

McDermott, LeRoy. 1996. "Self-Representation in Female Figurines." *Current Anthropology,* 37: 227–75.

McDonald, Kim A. 1998. "New Evidence Challenges Traditional Model of How the New World Was Settled." *Chronicle of Higher Education* (March 13): A22.

McDowell, Nancy. 2004. "Mundugumor: Sex and Temperament Revisited." In *Portraits of Culture,* in C. R. Ember, M. Ember, and P. N. Peregrine, eds., *New Directions in Anthropology.* Upper Saddle River, NJ: Prentice Hall, CD-ROM.

McElroy, Ann, and Patricia R. Townsend. 1996. *Medical Anthropology.* Boulder, CO: Westview.

McElroy, Ann, and Patricia Townsend. 2002. *Medical Anthropology in Ecological Perspective.* 3rd ed. Boulder, CO: Westview.

McGarvey, Stephen T. 1994. "The Thrifty Gene Concept and Adiposity Studies in Biological Anthropology." *Journal of the Polynesian Society,* 103: 29–42.

McGlynn, Frank, and Arthur Tuden, eds. 1991. *Anthropological Approaches to Political Behavior.* Pittsburgh, PA: University of Pittsburgh Press.

McGrew, W. 1992. *Chimpanzee Material Culture: Implications for Human Evolution.* Cambridge: Cambridge University Press.

McHenry, Henry M. 1982. "The Pattern of Human Evolution: Studies on Bipedalism, Mastication, and Encephalization." *Annual Review of Anthropology,* 11: 151–73.

McHenry, Henry M. 1988. "New Estimates of Body Weight in Early Hominids and Their Significance to Encephalization and Megadontia in 'Robust' Australopithecines." In F. E. Grine, ed., *Evolutionary History of the "Robust" Australopithecines.* New York: Aldine.

McHenry, Henry M. 2002. " 'Robust' Australopithecines. Our Family Tree, and Homoplasy." In P. N. Peregrine, C. R. Ember, and M.

Ember, eds., *Physical Anthropology: Original Readings in Method and Practice.* Upper Saddle River, NJ: Prentice Hall.

McKee, Lauris. 1984. "Sex Differentials in Survivorship and the Customary Treatment of Infants and Children." *Medical Anthropology,* 8: 91–108.

McKee, Lauris A. 2004. "Andean Mestizos: Growing Up Female and Male." In *Portraits of Culture,* in C. R. Ember, M. Ember, and P. N. Peregrine, eds., *New Directions in Anthropology.* Upper Saddle River, NJ: Prentice Hall, CD-ROM.

McKeown, Adam. 2004. "Chinese Diaspora." In M. Ember, C. R. Ember, and I. Skoggard, eds. *Encyclopedia of Diasporas: Immigrant and Refugee Cultures Around the World.* (New York: Kluwer Academic/Plenum, vol. 1, pp. 65–76.

McMullin, Ernan. 2001. "Plantinga's Defense of Special Creation." In R. Pennock, ed., *Intelligent Design Creationism and its Critics.* Boston: MIT Press, 174.

McNeill, William H. 1967. *A World History.* New York: Oxford University Press.

McNeill, William H. 1976. *Plagues and Peoples.* Garden City, NY: Doubleday/Anchor.

McNeill, William H. 1998. *Plagues and Peoples.* New York: Anchor Books/Doubleday.

Mead, Margaret. 1931. *Growing Up in New Guinea.* London: Routledge & Kegan Paul.

Mead, Margaret. 1950 [1935]. *Sex and Temperament in Three Primitive Societies.* New York: Mentor.

Mead, Margaret. 1961 [1928]. *Coming of Age in Samoa.* 3rd ed. New York: Morrow.

Mead, Margaret. 1977. "Applied Anthropology: The State of the Art." In A. Wallace et al., eds., *Perspectives on Anthropology 1976.* Washington, DC: American Anthropological Association.

Mead, Margaret. 1978. "The Evolving Ethics of Applied Anthropology." In E. M. Eddy and W. L. Partridge, eds., *Applied Anthropology in America.* New York: Columbia University Press.

Meek, C. K. 1940. *Land Law and Custom in the Colonies.* London: Oxford University Press.

Meggers, Betty J., ed. 1968. *Anthropological Archaeology in the Americas.* Washington, DC: Anthropological Society of Washington.

Meggitt, Mervyn J. 1964. "Male–Female Relationships in the Highlands of Australian New Guinea." *American Anthropologist,* 66: 204–24.

Meggitt, Mervyn J. 1977. *Blood Is Their Argument: Warfare among the Mae Enga Tribesmen of the New Guinea Highlands.* Palo Alto, CA: Mayfield.

Meillassoux, Claude. 1968. *Urbanization of an African Community.* Seattle: University of Washington Press.

Mellaart, James. 1961. "Roots in the Soil." In S. Piggott, ed., *The Dawn of Civilization.* London: Thomas & Hudson.

Mellaart, James. 1964. "A Neolithic City in Turkey." *Scientific American* (April): 94–104.

Mellars, Paul. 1994. "The Upper Paleolithic Revolution." In B. Cunliffe, ed., *The Oxford Illustrated Prehistory of Europe.* Oxford: Oxford University Press, 42–78.

Mellars, Paul. 1996. *The Neanderthal Legacy.* Princeton, NJ: Princeton University Press, 405–19.

Mellars, Paul. 1998. "The Fate of the Neanderthals." *Nature,* 395 (October 8): 539–40.

Mellor, John W., and Sarah Gavian. 1987. "Famine: Causes, Prevention, and Relief." *Science,* 235 (January 30): 539–44.

Meltzer, David J. 1993. "Pleistocene Peopling of the Americas." *Evolutionary Anthropology,* 1, 1, pp. 157–169.

Meltzer, David J., Don D. Fowler, and Jeremy A. Sabloff, eds. 1986. *American Archaeology Past and Future.* Washington, DC: Smithsonian Institution Press.

Merbs, Charles F. 1992. "A New World of Infectious Disease." *Yearbook of Physical Anthropology,* 35: 3–42.

Merrill, Elizabeth Bryant. 1987. "Art Styles as Reflections of Sociopolitical Complexity." *Ethnology,* 26: 221–30.

Mertz, Elizabeth, and Richard J. Parmentier, eds. 1985. *Semiotic Mediation: Sociocultural and Psychological Perspectives.* Orlando, FL: Academic Press.

Messer, Ellen. 1996. "Hunger Vulnerability from an Anthropologist's Food System Perspective." In E. F. Moran, ed., *Transforming Societies, Transforming Anthropology.* Ann Arbor: University of Michigan Press.

Michel, R. H., McGovern, P. E., and Badler, V. R. 1993. "The First Wine and Beer: Chemical Detection of Ancient Fermented Beverages." *Analytical Chemistry,* 65: 408A–13A.

Middleton, John. 1971. "The Cult of the Dead: Ancestors and Ghosts." In W. A. Lessa and E. Z. Vogt, eds., *Reader in Comparative Religion,* 3rd ed. New York: Harper & Row.

Middleton, Russell. 1962. "Brother–Sister and Father–Daughter Marriage in Ancient Egypt." *American Sociological Review,* 27: 603–11.

Midlarsky, Manus I., ed., 1997. *Inequality, Democracy, and Economic Development.* Cambridge: Cambridge University Press.

Milanovic, Branko. 2002. "True World Income Distribution, 1988 and 1993: First Calculation Based on Household Surveys Alone." *The Economic Journal,* 112: 51–92.

Miller, Bruce G. 1992. "Women and Politics: Comparative Evidence from the Northwest Coast." *Ethnology,* 31: 367–82.

Miller, Greg. 2004. "Listen, Baby." *Science,* 306 (November 12): 1127.

Miller, Henry I. 1991. "Regulation." In B. Davis, ed., *The Genetic Revolution.* Baltimore: Johns Hopkins University Press.

Miller, Joan G. 1994. "Cultural Diversity in the Morality of Caring: Individually Oriented versus Duty-Based Interpersonal Moral Codes." *Cross-Cultural Research,* 28: 3–39.

Miller, Naomi F. 1992. "The Origins of Plant Cultivation in the Near East." In C. W. Cowan and P. J. Watson, eds., *The Origins of Agriculture.* Washington, DC: Smithsonian Institution Press.

Millon, René. 1967. "Teotihuacán." *Scientific American* (June): 38–48.

Millon, René. 1976. "Social Relations in Ancient Teotihuacán." In E. Wolf, ed., *The Valley of Mexico.* Albuquerque: University of New Mexico Press.

Milton, Katharine. 1981. "Distribution Patterns of Tropical Plant Foods as an Evolutionary Stimulus to Primate Mental Development." *American Anthropologist,* 83: 534–48.

Milton, Katharine. 1988. "Foraging Behaviour and the Evolution of Primate Intelligence." In R. Byrne and A. Whiten, eds., *Machiavellian Intelligence: Social Expertise and the Evolution of Intellect in Monkeys, Apes, and Humans.* Oxford: Clarendon Press.

Milton, Katharine. 2002. "The Evolution of a Physical Anthropologist." In P. N. Peregrine, C. R. Ember, and M. Ember, eds., *Physical Anthropology: Original Readings in Method and Practice.* Upper Saddle River, NJ: Prentice Hall.

Miner, Horace. 1956. "Body Rituals among the Nacirema." *American Anthropologist,* 58: 504–05.

Minturn, Leigh. 1993. *Sita's Daughters: Coming Out of Purdah: The Rajput Women of Khalapur Revisited.* New York: Oxford University Press.

Minturn, Leigh, and William W. Lambert. 1964. *Mothers of Six Cultures: Antecedents of Child Rearing.* New York: Wiley.

Minturn, Leigh, and Jerry Stashak. 1982. "Infanticide as a Terminal Abortion Procedure." *Behavior Science Research,* 17: 70–85.

Mintz, Sidney W. 1956. "Canamelar: The Subculture of a Rural Sugar Plantation Proletariat." In J. H. Steward et al., *The People of Puerto Rico.* Urbana: University of Illinois Press.

Minugh-Purvis, Nancy. 2002. "Neandertal Growth: Examining Developmental Adaptations in Earlier *Homo sapiens.*" In P. N. Peregrine, C. R. Ember, and M. Ember, eds., *Physical Anthropology: Original Readings in Method and Practice.* Upper Saddle River, NJ: Prentice Hall.

Miracle, Andrew W. 2004. "A Shaman to Organizations." In *Research Frontiers,* in C. R. Ember, M. Ember, and P. N. Peregrine, eds., *New Directions in Anthropology.* Upper Saddle River, NJ: Prentice Hall, CD-ROM.

Mitchell, Donald. 2004. "Nimpkish: Complex Foragers on the Northwest Coast of North America." In *Portraits of Culture,* in C. R. Ember, M. Ember, and P. N. Peregrine, eds., *New Directions in Anthropology.* Upper Saddle River, NJ: Prentice Hall, CD-ROM.

Mittermeier, Russell A., and Eleanor J. Sterling. 1992. "Conservation of Primates." In S. Jones, R. Martin, and D. Pilbeam, eds., *The Cambridge Encyclopedia of Human Evolution.* New York: Cambridge University Press.

Moerman, Daniel E. 1997. "Physiology and Symbols: The Anthropological Implications of the Placebo Effect." In L. Romanucci-Ross, D. E. Moerman, and L. R. Tancredi, eds., *The Anthropology of Medicine.* 3rd ed. Westport, CT: Bergin & Garvey, 240–53.

Molnar, Stephen. 1998. *Human Variation: Races, Types, and Ethnic Groups.* 4th ed. Upper Saddle River, NJ: Prentice Hall.

Monot, Marc, et al. 2005. "On the Origin of Leprosy," *Science,* 308 (May 13): 1040–42.

Montagu, A. 1997. *A Man's Most Dangerous Myth: The Fallacy of Race.* 6th ed. Walnut Creek, CA: AltaMira Press.

Mooney, Kathleen A. 1978. "The Effects of Rank and Wealth on Exchange among the Coast Salish." *Ethnology,* 17: 391–406.

Moore, Carmella C. 1997. "Is Love Always Love?" *Anthropology Newsletter* (November): 8–9.

Moore, Carmella C., A. Kimball Romney, Ti-Lien Hsia, Craig D. Rusch. 1999. "The Universality of the Semantic Structure of Emotion Terms: Methods for the Study of Inter- and Intra-Cultural Variability." *American Anthropologist,* 101: 529–46.

Moore, Carmella Caracci. 1988. "An Optimal Scaling of Murdock's Theories of Illness Data—An Approach to the Problem of Interdependence." *Behavior Science Research,* 22: 161–79.

Moore, John H. and Janis E. Campbell. 2002. "Confirming Unilocal Residence in Native North America." *Ethnology* 41: 175–88.

Moore, Omar Khayyam. 1957. "Divination: A New Perspective." *American Anthropologist,* 59: 69–74.

Moran, Emilio F. 1993. *Through Amazon Eyes: The Human Ecology of Amazonian Populations.* Iowa City: University of Iowa Press.

Moran, Emilio F., ed. 1996. *Transforming Societies, Transforming Anthropology.* Ann Arbor: University of Michigan Press.

Moran, Emilio F. 2000. *Human Adaptability: An Introduction to Ecological Anthropology.* 2nd ed. Boulder, CO: Westview.

Morell, Virginia. 1995. "The Earliest Art Becomes Older—And More Common." *Science,* 267 (March 31): 1908–09.

Morgan, Lewis H. 1964 [1877]. *Ancient Society.* Cambridge, MA: Harvard University Press.

Morgen, Sandra, ed. 1989. *Gender and Anthropology: Critical Reviews for Research and Teaching.* Washington, DC: American Anthropological Association.

Morris, B. 1987. *Anthropological Studies of Religion: An Introductory Text.* Cambridge: Cambridge University Press.

Morris, John. 1938. *Living with Lepchas: A Book about the Sikkim Himalayas.* London: Heinemann.

Morris, Laura Newell, ed. 1971. *Human Populations, Genetic Variation, and Evolution.* San Francisco: Chandler.

Morwood, M. J., R. Soejono, R. Roberts, T. Sutikna, C. Turney, K. Westaway, W. Rink, J. Zhao, G. van den Bergh, R. Due, D. Hobbs, M. Moore, M. Bird, and L. Fifeld. 2004. "Archaeology and Age of a New Hominin from Flores in Eastern Indonesia." *Nature,* 431 (October 28): 1087–91.

Moser, Stephanie. 1998. *Ancestral Images: The Iconography of Human Origins.* Ithaca, NY: Cornell University Press.

Motulsky, Arno. 1971. "Metabolic Polymorphisms and the Role of Infectious Diseases in Human Evolution." In L. N. Morris, ed., *Human Populations, Genetic Variation, and Evolution.* San Francisco: Chandler.

Mountford, C. P., ed. 1960. *Records of the Australian-American Scientific Expedition to Arnhem Land.* Vol. 2: *Anthropology and Nutrition.* Melbourne: Melbourne University Press.

Moyà-solà, Salvador, et al. 2004. "*Pierolapithecus catalaunicus.* A New Middle Miocene Great Ape from Spain." *Science,* 306 (November 19): 1339–44.

Mukerjee, Madhusree. 1996. "Field Notes: Interview with a Parrot." *Scientific American* (April): 28.

Mukhopadhyay, Carol C., and Patricia J. Higgins. 1988. "Anthropological Studies of Women's Status Revisited: 1977–1987." *Annual Review of Anthropology,* 17: 461–95.

Muller, Edward N. 1994. "Economic Determinants of Democracy." Paper presented at a conference on Inequality and Democracy, Rutgers University, February.

Müller-Haye, B. 1984. "Guinea Pig or Cuy." In I. Mason, *Evolution of Domesticated Animals.* New York: Longman.

Munroe, Robert L., Robert Hulefeld, James M. Rodgers, Damon L. Tomeo, Steven K. Yamazaki. 2000. "Aggression Among Children in Four Cultures." *Cross-Cultural Research,* 34: 3–25.

Munroe, Robert L., and Ruth H. Munroe. 1969. "A Cross-Cultural Study of Sex, Gender, and Social Structure." *Ethnology,* 8: 206–11.

Munroe, Robert L., Ruth H. Munroe, and John W. M. Whiting. 1981. "Male Sex-Role Resolutions." In R. H. Munroe, R. L. Munroe, and B. B. Whiting, eds., *Handbook of Cross-Cultural Human Development.* New York: Garland.

Munroe, Robert L., Ruth H. Munroe, and Stephen Winters. 1996. "Cross-Cultural Correlates of the Consonant-Vowel (CV) Syllable." *Cross-Cultural Research,* 30: 60–83.

Munroe, Ruth H., and Robert L. Munroe. 1980a. "Household Structure and Socialization Practices." *Journal of Social Psychology,* 111: 293–94.

Munroe, Ruth H., and Robert L. Munroe. 1980b. "Infant Experience and Childhood Affect among the Logoli: A Longitudinal Study." *Ethos,* 8: 295–315.

Munroe, Ruth H., Robert L. Munroe, and Harold S. Shimmin. 1984. "Children's Work in Four Cultures: Determinants and Consequences." *American Anthropologist,* 86: 369–79.

Munroe, Ruth H., Robert L. Munroe, and Beatrice B. Whiting, eds. 1981. *Handbook of Cross-Cultural Human Development.* New York: Garland.

Murdock, George P. 1949. *Social Structure.* New York: Macmillan.

Murdock, George P. 1957. "World Ethnographic Sample." *American Anthropologist,* 59: 664–87.

Murdock, George P., ed. 1960. *Social Structure in Southeast Asia.* Viking Fund Publications in Anthropology No. 29. Chicago: Quadrangle.

Murdock, George P. 1967. "Ethnographic Atlas: A Summary." *Ethnology,* 6: 109–236.

Murdock, George P., and Caterina Provost. 1973. "Factors in the Division of Labor by Sex: A Cross-Cultural Analysis." *Ethnology,* 12: 203–25.

Murdock, George Peter. 1980. *Theories of Illness: A World Survey.* Pittsburgh: University of Pittsburgh Press.

Murdock, George Peter, and Douglas R. White. 1969. "Standard Cross-Cultural Sample." *Ethnology,* 8: 329–69.

Murphy, Jane. 1981. "Abnormal Behavior in Traditional Societies: Labels, Explanations, and Social Reactions." In R. H. Munroe, R. L. Munroe, and B. B. Whiting, eds., *Handbook of Cross-Cultural Human Development.* New York: Garland.

Murphy, Robert F. 1960. *Headhunter's Heritage: Social and Economic Change among the Mundurucú.* Berkeley: University of California Press.

Murphy, Robert F., and Julian H. Steward. 1956. "Tappers and Trappers: Parallel Process in Acculturation." *Economic Development and Cultural Change,* 4 (July): 335–55.

Murray, Gerald F. 1997. "The Domestication of Wood in Haiti: A Case Study in Applied Evolution." In A. Podolefsky and P. J.

Brown, eds., *Applying Cultural Anthropology: An Introductory Reader,* Mountain View CA: Mayfield.

Musil, Alois. 1928. *The Manners and Customs of the Rwala Bedouins.* American Geographical Society, Oriental Exploration Studies No. 6. New York.

Mussen, Paul, ed. 1970. *Carmichael's Manual of Child Psychology.* Vol. 1, 3rd ed. New York: Wiley.

Myers, Fred R. 1988. "Critical Trends in the Study of Hunter-Gatherers." *Annual Review of Anthropology,* 17: 261–82.

Nadel, S. F. 1935. "Nupe State and Community." *Africa,* 8: 257–303.

Nadel, S. F. 1942. *A Black Byzantium: The Kingdom of Nupe in Nigeria.* London: Oxford University Press.

Nag, Moni, Benjamin N. F. White, and R. Creighton Peet. 1978. "An Anthropological Approach to the Study of the Economic Value of Children in Java and Nepal." *Current Anthropology,* 19: 293–301.

Nagata, Judith. 2001. "Beyond Theology: Toward an Anthropology of 'Fundamentalism'." *American Anthropologist,* 103: 481–98.

Nagel, Ernest. 1961. *The Structure of Science: Problems in the Logic of Scientific Explanation.* New York: Harcourt, Brace & World.

Napier, J. R. 1970. "Paleoecology and Catarrhine Evolution." In J. R. Napier and P. H. Napier, eds., *Old World Monkeys: Evolution, Systematics, and Behavior.* New York: Academic Press.

Napier, J. R., and P. H. Napier. 1967. *A Handbook of Living Primates.* New York: Academic Press.

Naroll, Raoul. 1961. "Two Solutions to Galton's Problem." *Philosophy of Science,* 28 (January): 15–39.

Naroll, Raoul. 1967. "Imperial Cycles and World Order." *Peace Research Society: Papers,* 7: 83–101.

Naroll, Raoul. 1983. *The Moral Order: An Introduction to the Human Situation.* Beverly Hills, CA: Sage.

Naroll, Raoul, and Ronald Cohen, eds. 1970. *A Handbook of Method in Cultural Anthropology.* Garden City, NY: Natural History Press.

Nash, Manning. 1989. *The Cauldron of Ethnicity in the Modern World.* Chicago: University of Chicago Press.

Neel, James V., Willard R. Centerwall, Napoleon A. Chagnon, and Helen L. Casey. 1970. "Notes on the Effect of Measles and Measles Vaccine in a Virgin-Soil Population of South American Indians." *American Journal of Epidemiology,* 91: 418–29.

Nelson, K. E., ed. 1980. *Children's Language.* Vol. 2. New York: Halsted Press.

Nelson, Nici. 1995 [1964]. "The Kiambu Group: A Successful Women's ROSCA in Mathare Valley, Nairobi (1971 to 1990)." In S. Ardener and S. Burman, *Money-Go-Rounds: The Importance of Rotating Savings and Credit Associations for Women.* Oxford: Berg, 49–69.

Nerlove, Sara B. 1974. "Women's Workload and Infant Feeding Practices: A Relationship with Demographic Implications." *Ethnology,* 13: 207–14.

Neumann, Katharina. 2003. "New Guinea: A Cradle of Agriculture." *Science,* 301 (July 11): 180–81.

Nevins, Allan. 1927. *The American States during and after the Revolution.* New York: Macmillan.

Newman, K. S. 1988. *Falling From Grace: The Experience of Downward Mobility in the American Middle Class.* New York: The Free Press.

Newman K. S. 1999. *Declining Fortunes: The Withering of the American Dream.* New York: Basic Books.

Newman, Katherine S. 1983. *Law and Economic Organization: A Comparative Study of Preindustrial Societies.* Cambridge, MA: Cambridge University Press.

Nicholls, David, ed. 1998. *The Cambridge History of American Music.* Cambridge. Cambridge University Press.

Nicholson, Shirley, comp. 1987. *Shamanism: An Expanded View of Reality.* Wheaton, IL: Theosophical Publishing House.

Nicolson, Nancy A. 1987. "Infants, Mothers, and Other Females." In B. Smuts et al., eds., *Primate Societies.* Chicago: University of Chicago Press.

Niederberger, Christine. 1979. "Early Sedentary Economy in the Basin of Mexico." *Science,* 203 (January 12): 131–42.

Niehoff, Arthur H. 1966. *A Casebook of Social Change.* Chicago: Aldine.

Nimkoff, M. F., and Russell Middleton. 1960. "Types of Family and Types of Economy." *American Journal of Sociology,* 66: 215–25.

Nishida, Toshisada. 1992. "Introduction to the Conservation Symposium." In Naosuke Itoigawa, Yukimaru Sugiyama, Gene P. Sackett, and Roger K. R. Thompson, *Topics in Primatology.* Vol. 2. Tokyo: University of Tokyo Press.

Nishida, Toshisada, William C. McGrew, Peter Marler, Martin Pickford, and Frans B. M. de Waal, eds. 1992. *Topics in Primatology.* Vol. 1: *Human Origins.* Tokyo: University of Tokyo Press.

Nissen, Henry W. 1958. "Axes of Behavioral Comparison." In A. Roe and G. G. Simpson, eds., *Behavior and Evolution.* New Haven, CT: Yale University Press.

Nitecki, Matthew H., and Doris V. Nitecki, eds. 1987. *The Evolution of Human Hunting.* New York: Plenum.

Noble, William, and Ian Davidson. 1996. *Human Evolution, Language, and Mind.* Cambridge: Cambridge University Press, 162–214.

Noll, Richard. 1987. "The Presence of Spirits in Magic and Madness." In S. Nicholson, comp., *Shamanism.* Wheaton, IL: Theosophical Publishing House, 47–61.

Normile, Dennis. 1998. "Habitat Seen Playing Larger Role in Shaping Behavior." *Science,* 279 (March 6): 1454–55.

Noss, Andrew J., and Barry S. Hewlett. 2001. "The Contexts of Female Hunting in Central Africa." *American Anthropologist,* 103: 1024–40.

Nussbaum, Martha C. 1995. "Introduction." In M. C. Nussbaum and J. Glover, *Women, Culture, and Development: A Study of Human Capabilities.* Oxford: Clarendon Press.

Oakley, Kenneth. 1964. "On Man's Use of Fire, with Comments on Tool-Making and Hunting." In S. L. Washburn, ed., *Social Life of Early Man.* Chicago: Aldine.

Oakley, Kenneth P. 1963. "Analytical Methods of Dating Bones." In D. Brothwell and E. Higgs, eds., *Science in Archaeology.* New York: Basic Books.

Oboler, Regina Smith. 1980. "Is the Female Husband a Man? Woman/Woman Marriage among the Nandi of Kenya." *Ethnology,* 19: 69–88.

Oboler, Regina Smith. 2004. "Nandi: From Cattle-Keepers to Cash-Crop Farmers." In *Portraits of Culture,* in C. R. Ember, M. Ember, and P. N. Peregrine, eds., *New Directions in Anthropology.* Upper Saddle River, NJ: Prentice Hall, CD-ROM.

O'Brian, Robin. 1999. "Who Weaves and Why? Weaving, Loom Complexity, and Trade." *Cross-Cultural Research,* 33: 30–42.

O'Brien, Denise. 1977. "Female Husbands in Southern Bantu Societies." In A. Schlegel, ed., *Sexual Stratification.* New York: Columbia University Press.

Ogburn, William F. 1922. *Social Change.* New York: Huebsch.

Okamura, Jonathan Y. 1983. "Filipino Hometown Associations in Hawaii." *Ethnology,* 22: 341–53.

Oliver, Douglas L. 1955. *A Solomon Island Society.* Cambridge, MA: Harvard University Press.

Oliver, Douglas L. 1974. *Ancient Tahitian Society.* Vol. 1: *Ethnography.* Honolulu: University of Hawaii Press.

Olsen, Steve. 2002. "Seeking the Signs of Selection." *Science,* 298 (November 15): 1324–25.

Olszewski, Deborah I. 1991. "Social Complexity in the Natufian? Assessing the Relationship of Ideas and Data." In G. Clark, ed., *Perspectives on the Past.* Philadelphia: University of Pennsylvania Press.

Ortiz de Montellano, B. R., and C. H. Browner. 1985. "Chemical Bases for Medicinal Plant Use in Oaxaca, Mexico." *Journal of Ethnopharmacology,* 13: 57–88.

Ortner, Sherry B. 1984. "Theory in Anthropology since the Sixties." *Comparative Studies in Society and History,* 26: 126–66.

Osti, Roberto. 1994. "The Eloquent Bones of Abu Hureyra." *Scientific American* (August): 1.

Ostrom, Elinor, Joanna Burger, Christopher B. Field, Richard B. Norgaard, and David Policansky. 1999. "Revisiting the Commons: Local Lessons, Global Challenges." *Science* (April 9): 278–82.

Otterbein, Keith. 1968. "Internal War: A Cross-Cultural Study." *American Anthropologist,* 70: 277–89.

Otterbein, Keith. 1970. *The Evolution of War.* New Haven, CT: HRAF Press.

Otterbein, Keith. 1986. *The Ultimate Coercive Sanction: A Cross-Cultural Study of Capital Punishment.* New Haven, CT: HRAF Press.

Otterbein, Keith, and Charlotte Swanson Otterbein. 1965. "An Eye for an Eye, a Tooth for a Tooth: A Cross-Cultural Study of Feuding." *American Anthropologist,* 67: 1470–82.

Ovchinnikov, Igor V. et al. 2000. "Molecular Analysis of Neanderthal DNA from the Northern Caucasus." *Nature,* 404 (March 30): 490–94.

Oxby, Clare. 1983. "Farmer Groups in Rural Areas of the Third World." *Community Development Journal,* 18: 50–59.

Paige, Jeffery M. 1975. *Agrarian Revolution: Social Movements and Export Agriculture in the Underdeveloped World.* New York: Free Press.

Paine, Robert. 1994. *Herds of the Tundra.* Washington, DC: Smithsonian Institution Press.

Paley, William. 1810. *Natural Theology.* Boston: Joshua Belcher.

Palsson, Gisli. 1988. "Hunters and Gatherers of the Sea." In T. Ingold, D. Riches, and J. Woodburn, eds., *Hunters and Gatherers. 1. History, Evolution and Social Change.* New York: St. Martin's Press.

Panter-Brick, Catherine, Deborah S. Lotstein, and Peter T. Ellison. 1993. "Seasonality of Reproductive Function and Weight Loss in Rural Nepali Women." *Human Reproduction,* 8: 684–90.

"Paper." 1980. *Academic American Encyclopedia.* Princeton, NJ: Areté.

Parfit, Michael. 2000. "Who Were the First Americans?" *National Geographic* (December): 41–67.

Parker, Hilda, and Seymour Parker. 1986. "Father–Daughter Sexual Abuse: An Emerging Perspective." *American Journal of Orthopsychiatry,* 56: 531–49.

Parker, Seymour. 1976. "The Precultural Basis of the Incest Taboo: Toward a Biosocial Theory." *American Anthropologist,* 78: 285–305.

Parker, Seymour. 1984. "Cultural Rules, Rituals, and Behavior Regulation." *American Anthropologist,* 86: 584–600.

Parker, Sue Taylor. 1990. "Why Big Brains Are So Rare." In S. Parker and K. Gibson, eds., *"Language" and Intelligence in Monkeys and Apes.* New York: Cambridge University Press.

Parker, Sue Taylor, and Kathleen Rita Gibson, eds. 1990. *"Language" and Intelligence in Monkeys and Apes: Comparative Developmental Perspectives.* New York: Cambridge University Press.

Parry, William J. 2002. "When and How Did Humans Populate the New World?" In P. N. Peregrine, C. R. Ember, and M. Ember, eds., *Archaeology: Original Readings in Method and Practice.* Upper Saddle River, NJ: Prentice Hall.

Partridge, William L., and Elizabeth M. Eddy. 1987. "The Development of Applied Anthropology in America." In E. M. Eddy and W. L. Partridge, eds., *Applied Anthropology in America,* 2nd ed. New York: Columbia University Press.

Pasternak, Burton. 1976. *Introduction to Kinship and Social Organization.* Upper Saddle River, NJ: Prentice Hall.

Pasternak, Burton. 2004a. "Family and Household: Who Lives Where, Why Does It Vary, and Why Is It Important?" In *Cross-Cultural Research for Social Science,* in C. R. Ember, M. Ember, and P. N. Peregrine, eds., *New Directions in Anthropology.* Upper Saddle River, NJ: Prentice Hall, CD-ROM.

Pasternak, Burton. 2004b. "Han: Pastoralists and Farmers on a Chinese Frontier." In *Portraits of Culture*, in C. R. Ember, M. Ember, and P. N. Peregrine, eds., *New Directions in Anthropology*. Upper Saddle River, NJ: Prentice Hall, CD-ROM.

Pasternak, Burton, Carol R. Ember, and Melvin Ember. 1976. "On the Conditions Favoring Extended Family Households." *Journal of Anthropological Research*, 32: 109–23.

Pasternak, Burton, Carol R. Ember, and Melvin Ember. 1997. *Sex, Gender, and Kinship: A Cross-Cultural Perspective*. Upper Saddle River, NJ: Prentice Hall.

Patterson, Leland. 1983. "Criteria for Determining the Attributes of Man-Made Lithics." *Journal of Field Archaeology*, 10: 297–307.

Patterson, Orlando. 1982. *Slavery and Social Death: A Comparative Study*. Cambridge, MA: Harvard University Press.

Patterson, Orlando. 2000. Review of *One Drop of Blood: The American Misadventure of Race* by Scott L. Malcomson. *New York Times Book Review*, October 22, pp. 15–16.

Patterson, Thomas C. 1971. "Central Peru: Its Population and Economy." *Archaeology*, 24: 316–21.

Patterson, Thomas C. 1981. *The Evolution of Ancient Societies: A World Archaeology*. Upper Saddle River, NJ: Prentice Hall.

Peacock, James L. 1986. *The Anthropological Lens: Harsh Light, Soft Focus*. Cambridge: Cambridge University Press.

Peacock, Nadine, and Robert Bailey. 2004. "Efe: Investigating Food and Fertility in the Ituri Rain Forest." In *Portraits of Culture*, in C. R. Ember, M. Ember, and P. N. Peregrine, eds., *New Directions in Anthropology*. Upper Saddle River, NJ: Prentice Hall, CD-ROM.

Peak, Lois. 1991. *Learning to Go to School in Japan: The Transition from Home to Preschool*. Berkeley: University of California Press.

Pearsall, Deborah. 1992. "The Origins of Plant Cultivation in South America." In C. Cowan and P. Watson, eds., *The Origins of Agriculture*. Washington, DC: Smithsonian Institution Press.

Pearson, J. D., Gary D. James, and Daniel E. Brown. 1993. "Stress and Changing Lifestyles in the Pacific: Physiological Stress Responses of Samoans in Rural and Urban Settings." *American Journal of Human Biology*, 5: 49–60.

Pelto, Pertti J., and Ludger Müller-Wille. 1987. "Snowmobiles: Technological Revolution in the Arctic." In H. R. Bernard and P. J. Pelto, eds., *Technology and Social Change*, 2nd ed. Prospect Heights, IL: Waveland Press.

Pelto, Pertti J., and Gretel H. Pelto. 1975. "Intra-Cultural Diversity: Some Theoretical Issues." *American Ethnologist*, 2: 1–18.

Pennisi, Elizabeth. 2000. "Finally, the Book of Life and Instructions for Navigating It." *Science*, 288 (June 30): 2304–07.

Pennisi, Elizabeth. 2001a. "Malaria's Beginnings: On the Heels of Hoes?" *Science*, 293 (July 20): 416–17.

Pennisi, Elizabeth. 2001b. "Genetic Change Wards Off Malaria." *Science*, 294 (November 16): 1439.

Pepperberg, Irene Maxine. 1999. *The Alex Studies: Cognitive and Communicative Abilities of Grey Parrots*. Cambridge, MA: Harvard University Press.

Peregrine, Peter N. 1992. "Social Change in the Woodland-Mississippian Transition: A Study of Household and Community Patterns in the American Bottom." *North American Archaeologist*, 13: 131–47.

Peregrine, Peter N. 1996. "The Birth of the Gods Revisited: A Partial Replication of Guy Swanson's (1960) Cross-Cultural Study of Religion." *Cross-Cultural Research*, 30: 84–112.

Peregrine, Peter N. 2001a. "Southern and Eastern Africa Later Stone Age." In P. N. Peregrine and M. Ember, eds., *Encyclopedia of Prehistory*. Vol. 1, *Africa*, New York: Kluwer Academic/Plenum, 272–73.

Peregrine, Peter N. 2001b. "Cross-Cultural Approaches in Archaeology." *Annual Review of Anthropology*, 30: 1–18.

Peregrine, Peter N. 2002. *World Prehistory: Two Million Years of Human Life*. Upper Saddle River, NJ: Prentice Hall.

Peregrine, Peter N. 2004. "Variation in Stratification." In *Cross-Cultural Research for Social Science*, in C. R. Ember, M. Ember, and P. N. Peregrine, eds., *New Directions in Anthropology*. Upper Saddle River, NJ: Prentice Hall, CD-ROM.

Peregrine, Peter N. 2006. *Outline of Archaeological Traditions*. New Haven, CT: HRAF.

Peregrine, Peter N., and Peter Bellwood. 2001. "Southeast Asia Upper Paleolithic." In P. N. Peregrine and M. Ember, eds., *Encyclopedia of Prehistory*. Vol. 3: *East Asia and Oceania*. New York: Kluwer Academic/Plenum, 307–09.

Peregrine, Peter. N. and M. Ember, eds. 2001–2002. *Encyclopedia of Prehistory*, 9 vols. New York: Kluwer Academic/Plenum.

Peregrine, Peter N., Carol R. Ember, and Melvin Ember. 2000. "Teaching Critical Evaluation of Rushton." *Anthropology Newsletter*, 41 (February): 29–30.

Peregrine, Peter N., Carol R. Ember, and Melvin Ember, eds. 2002a. *Archaeology: Original Readings in Method and Practice*. Upper Saddle River, NJ: Prentice Hall.

Peregrine, Peter N., Carol R. Ember, and Melvin Ember, eds. 2002b. *Physical Anthropology: Original Readings in Method and Practice*. Upper Saddle River, NJ: Prentice Hall.

Peregrine, Peter N., Carol R. Ember, and Melvin Ember. 2003. "Cross-Cultural Evaluation of Predicted Associations between Race and Behavior." *Evolution and Human Behavior* 24: 357–64.

Petersen, Erik B. 1973. "A Survey of the Late Paleolithic and the Mesolithic of Denmark." In S. K. Kozlowski, ed., *The Mesolithic in Europe*. Warsaw: Warsaw University Press.

Petersen, L. R., G. R. Lee, and G. J. Ellis. 1982. "Social Structure, Socialization Values, and Disciplinary Techniques: A Cross-Cultural Analysis." *Journal of Marriage and the Family*, 44: 131–42.

Pfaff, C. 1979. "Constraints on Language Mixing." *Language*, 55: 291–318, as cited in Wardhaugh, *An Introduction to Sociolinguistics*, 2nd ed. Oxford: Blackwell.

Pfeiffer, John E. 1978. *The Emergence of Man*. 3rd ed. New York: Harper & Row.

Philips, Susan U., Susan Steele, and Christine Tanz, eds. 1987. *Language, Gender, and Sex in Comparative Perspective*. Cambridge: Cambridge University Press.

Phillips, Kevin. 1990. *The Politics of Rich and Poor: Wealth and the American Electorate in the Reagan Aftermath*. New York: Random House.

Phillipson, D. W. 1976. "Archaeology and Bantu Linguistics." *World Archaeology*, 8: 65–82.

Phillipson, David W. 1993. *African Archaeology*. 2nd ed. New York: Cambridge University Press.

Piaget, Jean. 1970. "Piaget's Theory." In P. Mussen, ed., *Carmichael's Manual of Child Psychology*. Vol. 1, 3rd ed. New York: Wiley.

Picchi, Debra. 1991. "The Impact of an Industrial Agricultural Project on the Bakairí Indians of Central Brazil." *Human Organization*, 50: 26–38.

Picchi, Debra. 2004. "Bakairí: The Death of an Indian." In *Portraits of Culture*, in C. R. Ember, M. Ember, and P. N. Peregrine, eds., *New Directions in Anthropology*. Upper Saddle River, NJ: Prentice Hall, CD-ROM.

Pickford, Martin, Brigette Senut, Dominique Gommercy, and Jacques Treil. 2002. "Bipedalism in *Orrorin tugenensis* Revealed by its Femora," *Comptes Rendu de l'Académie de Science des Paris: Palevol 1*, 1–13.

Piggot, Stuart, 1961. *The Dawn of Civilization*. London: Thames & Hudson.

Pilbeam, David. 1972. *The Ascent of Man*. New York: Macmillan.

Pilbeam, David, and Stephen Jay Gould. 1974. "Size and Scaling in Human Evolution." *Science*, 186 (December 6): 892–900.

Piperno, Dolores, and Karen Stothert. 2003. "Phytolith Evidence for Early Holocene *Cucurbita* Domestication in Southwest Ecuador." *Science*, 299 (February, 14): 1054–57.

Plattner, Stuart, ed. 1985. *Markets and Marketing.* Monographs in Economic Anthropology No. 4. Lanham, MD: University Press of America.

Plattner, Stuart, ed. 1989a. *Economic Anthropology.* Stanford, CA: Stanford University Press.

Plattner, Stuart. 1989b. "Marxism." In S. Plattner, ed., *Economic Anthropology.* Stanford, CA: Stanford University Press. "Plundering Earth Is Nothing New". 1994. *Los Angeles Times* News Service, as reported in the *New Haven Register,* June 12, pp. A18–A19.

Poggie, John J., Jr., and Richard B. Pollnac. 1988. "Danger and Rituals of Avoidance among New England Fishermen." *MAST: Maritime Anthropological Studies,* 1: 66–78.

Poggie, John J., Jr., Richard B. Pollnac, and Carl Gersuny. 1976. "Risk as a Basis for Taboos among Fishermen in Southern New England." *Journal for the Scientific Study of Religion,* 15: 257–62.

Polanyi, Karl. 1957. "The Economy as Instituted Process." In K. Polanyi, C. M. Arensberg, and H. W. Pearson, eds., *Trade and Market in the Early Empires.* New York: Free Press.

Polanyi, Karl, Conrad M. Arensberg, and Harry W. Pearson, eds. 1957. *Trade and Market in the Early Empires.* New York: Free Press.

Polednak, Anthony P. 1974. "Connective Tissue Responses in Negroes in Relation to Disease." *American Journal of Physical Anthropology,* 41: 49–57.

Polgar, Steven, ed. 1975. *Population, Ecology, and Social Evolution.* The Hague: Mouton.

Pope, Geoffrey G. 1989. "Bamboo and Human Evolution." *Natural History* (October): 49–57.

Popenoe, David. 1988. *Disturbing the Nest: Family Change and Decline in Modern Societies.* New York: Aldine.

Popenoe, Rebecca. 2004. *Feeding Desire: Fatness, Beauty, and Sexuality Among a Saharan People.* London: Routledge.

Pospisil, Leopold. 1963. *The Kapauku Papuans of West New Guinea.* New York: Holt, Rinehart & Winston.

Post, Peter W., Farrington Daniels, Jr., and Robert T. Binford, Jr. 1975. "Cold Injury and the Evolution of 'White' Skin." *Human Biology,* 47: 65–80.

Potts, Richard. 1984. "Home Bases and Early Hominids." *American Scientist,* 72: 338–47.

Potts, Richard. 1988. *Early Hominid Activities at Olduvai.* New York: Aldine.

Powers, William K., and Marla N. Powers. 2004. "Lakota: A Study in Cultural Continuity." In *Portraits of Culture,* in C. R. Ember, M. Ember, and P. N. Peregrine, eds., *New Directions in Anthropology.* Upper Saddle River, NJ: Prentice Hall, CD-ROM.

Poyatos, Fernando. 2002. *Nonverbal Communication across Disciplines.* Vol. 1. Philadelphia: John Benjamins Publishing Company.

Prag, John, and Richard Neave. 1997. *Making Faces: Using Forensic and Archaeological Evidence.* College Station: Texas A&M University Press.

Preuschoft, Holger, David J. Chivers, Warren Y. Brockelman, and Norman Creel, eds. 1984. *The Lesser Apes: Evolutionary and Behavioural Biology.* Edinburgh: Edinburgh University Press.

"Prevalence, Incidence, and Consequences of Violence against Women: Findings from the National Violence against Women Survey." 1988. Washington, DC: U.S. Department of Justice, November.

Price, Sally. 1989. *Primitive Art in Civilized Places.* Chicago: University of Chicago Press.

Price, T. Douglas, and James A. Brown. 1985. *Prehistoric Hunter-Gatherers: The Emergence of Cultural Complexity.* Orlando, FL: Academic Press.

Price, T. Douglas, and A. B. Gebauer, eds. 1995. *Last Hunters, First Farmers: New Perspectives on the Prehistoric Transition to Agriculture.* Santa Fe, NM: School of American Research Press.

Price-Williams, Douglass. 1961. "A Study Concerning Concepts of Conservation of Quantities among Primitive Children." *Acta Psychologica,* 18: 297–305.

Pringle, Heather. 1998. "The Slow Birth of Agriculture." *Science,* 282 (November 20): 1446–50.

"Printing, Typography, and Photoengraving"; History of Prints: Origins in China: Transmission of Paper to Europe (12th Century)." 1998. *Britannica Online.* February.

Prothero, Donald R., and William A. Berggren, eds. 1992. *Eocene-Oligocene Climatic and Biotic Evolution.* Princeton, NJ: Princeton University Press.

Pryor, Frederic L. 1977. *The Origins of the Economy: A Comparative Study of Distribution in Primitive and Peasant Economies.* New York: Academic Press.

Pryor, Frederic L. 2005. *Economic Systems of Foraging, Agricultural, and Industrial Societies.* Cambridge: Cambridge University Press.

Public Law 101-601 (25 U.S.C. 3001-3013).

Puntenney, Pamela J. ed. 1995. *Global Ecosystems: Creating Options through Anthropological Perspectives,* NAPA Bulletin. 15: 60–70.

Purdy, B. 1996. *How to Do Archaeology the Right Way.* Gainesville: University Press of Florida.

Quandt, Sara A. 1996. "Nutrition in Anthropology." In C. F. Sargent and T. M. Johnson, eds., *Handbook of Medical Anthropology.* Rev. ed. Westport, CT: Greenwood Press, 272–89.

Quinn, Naomi. 1977. "Anthropological Studies on Women's Status." *Annual Review of Anthropology,* 6: 181–225.

Radcliffe-Brown, A. R. 1922. *The Andaman Islanders: A Study in Social Anthropology.* Cambridge: Cambridge University Press.

Radcliffe-Brown, A. R. 1952. *Structure and Function in Primitive Society.* London: Cohen & West.

Radin, Paul, ed. 1952. *African Folktales and Sculpture.* New York: Pantheon.

Radinsky, Leonard. 1967. "The Oldest Primate Endocast." *American Journal of Physical Anthropology,* 27: 358–88.

Rappaport, Roy A. 1967. "Ritual Regulation of Environmental Relations among a New Guinea People." *Ethnology,* 6: 17–30.

Rasmussen, D. Tab. 1990. "Primate Origins: Lessons from a Neotropical Marsupial." *American Journal of Primatology,* 22: 263–77.

Rasmussen, T., ed. 1993. *The Origin and Evolution of Humans and Humanness.* Boston: Jones and Bartlett.

Rathje, William L. 1971. "The Origin and Development of Lowland Classic Maya Civilization." *American Antiquity,* 36: 275–85.

Ravesloot, John. 1997. "Changing Native American Perceptions of Archaeology and Archaeologists." In N. Swidler et al., eds., *Native Americans and Archaeologists.* Walnut Creek, CA: AltaMira Press.

Ray, Verne F. 1954. *The Sanpoil and Nespelem: Salishan Peoples of Northeastern Washington.* New Haven, CT: Human Relations Area Files.

Raybeck, Douglas. 1998. "Toward More Holistic Explanations: Cross-Cultural Research and Cross-Level Analysis." *Cross-Cultural Research,* 32: 123–42.

Raybeck, Douglas, J. Shoobe, and J. Grauberger. 1989. "Women, Stress and Participation in Possession Cults: A Reexamination of the Calcium Deficiency Hypothesis." *Medical Anthropology Quarterly,* 3: 139–61.

Redman, Charles L. 1978. *The Rise of Civilization: From Early Farmers to Urban Society in the Ancient Near East.* San Francisco: W. H. Freeman.

Reed, Charles A., ed. 1977. *Origins of Agriculture.* The Hague: Mouton.

Reed, David, V. Smith, S. Hammond, A. Rogers, and D. Clayton. 2004. "Genetic Analysis of Lice Supports Direct Contact between Modern and Archaic Humans." *PLoS Biology,* 2 (November): 1972–1983.

Reisner, Marc. 1993. *Cadillac Desert: The American West and Its Disappearing Water.* Rev. ed. New York: Penguin.

Reiter, Rayna R., ed. 1975. *Toward an Anthropology of Women.* New York: Monthly Review Press.

Relethford, John. 1990. *The Human Species: An Introduction to Biological Anthropology.* Mountain View, CA: Mayfield.

Renfrew, Colin. 1969. "Trade and Culture Process in European History." *Current Anthropology,* 10: 156–69.

Renfrew, Colin, ed. 1973. *The Explanation of Culture Change: Models in Prehistory.* Pittsburgh: University of Pittsburgh Press.

Renfrew, Colin. 1987. *Archaeology and Language: The Puzzle of Indo-European Origins.* London: Jonathan Cape.

Renfrew, Colin, 1994. "World Linguistic Diversity." *Scientific American* (January): 116–23.

Renfrew, Colin, and P. Bahn. 1996. *Archaeology; Theories, Methods, and Practice.* New York: Thames and Hudson.

Rennie, John. 2002. "15 Answers to Creationist Nonsense." *Scientific American* (July): 78–85.

Revkin, Andrew C. 2005. "Tracking the Imperiled Bluefin From Ocean to Sushi Platter." *The New York Times,* May 3, pp. F1, F4.

Reyna, S. P., and R. E. Downs, eds. 1992. *Studying War: Anthropological Perspectives.* New York: Gordon and Breach.

Rhine, Stanley. 1998. *Bone Voyage: A Journey in Forensic Anthropology.* Albuquerque: University of New Mexico Press.

Rice, Patricia C. 1981. "Prehistoric Venuses: Symbols of Motherhood or Womanhood?" *Journal of Anthropological Research,* 37: 402–14.

Rice, Patricia C., and Ann L. Paterson. 1985. "Cave Art and Bones: Exploring the Interrelationships." *American Anthropologist,* 87: 94–100.

Rice, Patricia C., and Ann L. Paterson. 1986. "Validating the Cave Art—Archeofaunal Relationship in Cantabrian Spain." *American Anthropologist,* 88: 658–67.

Richard, Alison F. 1985. *Primates in Nature.* New York: W. H. Freeman.

Richard, Alison F. 1987. "Malagasy Prosimians: Female Dominance." In B. Smuts et al., eds., *Primate Societies.* Chicago: University of Chicago Press.

Riesenfeld, Alphonse. 1973. "The Effect of Extreme Temperatures and Starvation on the Body Proportions of the Rat." *American Journal of Physical Anthropology,* 39: 427–59.

Rightmire, G. Philip. 1984. "*Homo sapiens* in Sub-Saharan Africa." In F. H. Smith and F. Spencer, eds., *The Origins of Modern Humans.* New York: Alan R. Liss.

Rightmire, G. Philip. 1985. "The Tempo of Change in the Evolution of Mid-Pleistocene *Homo.*" In E. Delson, ed., *Ancestors.* New York: Alan R. Liss.

Rightmire, G. Philip. 1990. *The Evolution of* Homo erectus: *Comparative Anatomical Studies of an Extinct Human Species.* Cambridge: Cambridge University Press.

Rightmire, G. Philip. 1997. "Human Evolution in the Middle Pleistocene: The Role of *Homo heidelbergensis.*" *Evolutionary Anthropology,* 6: 218–27.

Rightmire, G. Philip. 2000. "*Homo erectus.*" In I. Tattersall, E. Delson, and J. van Couvering, eds., *Encyclopedia of Human Evolution and Prehistory.* New York: Garland.

Rijksen, H. D. 1978. *A Fieldstudy on Sumatran Orang Utans* (Pongo Pygmaeus Abelii Lesson 1827): *Ecology, Behaviour and Conservation.* Wageningen, The Netherlands: H. Veenman and Zonen.

Ritter, Madeline Lattman. 1980. "The Conditions Favoring Age-Set Organization." *Journal of Anthropological Research,* 36: 87–104.

Rivers, W. H. R. 1967 [1906]. *The Todas.* Oosterhout, N.B., The Netherlands: Anthropological Publications.

Roberts, D. F. 1953. "Body Weight, Race, and Climate." *American Journal of Physical Anthropology,* 533–58.

Roberts, D. F. 1978. *Climate and Human Variability.* 2nd ed. Menlo Park, CA: Cummings.

Roberts, John M. 1967. "Oaths, Autonomic Ordeals, and Power." In C. S. Ford, ed., *Cross-Cultural Approaches.* New Haven, CT: HRAF Press.

Roberts, John M., and Brian Sutton-Smith. 1962. "Child Training and Game Involvement." *Ethnology,* 1: 166–85.

Roberts, John M., Malcolm J. Arth, and Robert R. Bush. 1959. "Games in Culture." *American Anthropologist,* 61: 597–605.

Robins, Ashley H. *Biological Perspectives on Human Pigmentation.* Cambridge University Press.

Robinson, John G., and Charles H. Janson. 1987. "Capuchins, Squirrel Monkeys, and Atelines: Socioecological Convergence with Old World Primates." In B. Smuts et al., eds., *Primate Societies.* Chicago: University of Chicago Press.

Robinson, John G., Patricia C. Wright, and Warren G. Kinzey. 1987. "Monogamous Cebids and Their Relatives: Intergroup Calls and Spacing." In B. Smuts et al., eds., *Primate Societies.* Chicago: University of Chicago Press.

Robinson, Roy. 1984. "Cat." In I. Mason, *Evolution of Domesticated Animals.* New York: Longman.

Rodwin, Lloyd, ed. 1987. *Shelter, Settlement, and Development.* Boston: Allen & Unwin.

Rodwin, Lloyd, and Bishwapriya Sanyal. 1987. "Shelter, Settlement, and Development: An Overview." In L. Rodwin, ed., *Shelter, Settlement, and Development.* Boston: Allen & Unwin.

Rogers, Alan, D. Iltis, and S. Wooding. 2004. "Genetic Variation at the MC1R Locus and the Time since Loss of Human Body Hair." *Current Anthropology,* 45: 105–08.

Rogers, Everett M. 1983. *Diffusion of Innovations.* 3rd ed. New York: Free Press.

Rogoff, Barbara. 1981. "Schooling and the Development of Cognitive Skills." In H. C. Triandis and A. Heron, eds., *Handbook of Cross-Cultural Psychology,* Vol. 4: *Developmental Psychology.* Boston: Allyn & Bacon.

Rogoff, Barbara. 1990. *Apprenticeship in Thinking: Cognitive Development in Social Context.* New York: Oxford University Press.

Rohner, Ronald P. 1975. *They Love Me, They Love Me Not: A Worldwide Study of the Effects of Parental Acceptance and Rejection.* New Haven, CT: HRAF Press.

Rohner, Ronald P. 1976. "Sex Differences in Aggression: Phylogenetic and Enculturation Perspectives." *Ethos,* 4: 57–72.

Rohner, Ronald P. 1986. *The Warmth Dimension.* Beverly Hills, CA: Sage.

Rohner, Ronald P., and Preston A. Britner. 2002. "Worldwide Mental Health Correlates of Parental Acceptance-Rejection: Review of Cross-Cultural Research and Intracultural Evidence." *Cross-Cultural Research,* 36: 16–47.

Rohner, Ronald P., and Evelyn Rohner, eds. 1980. "Special Issue on Worldwide Tests of Parental Acceptance-Rejection Theory: An Overview." *Behavior Science Research,* 15: v–88.

Romaine, Suzanne. 1994. *Language in Society: An Introduction to Sociolinguistics.* Oxford: Oxford University Press.

Romanucci-Ross, Lola, and George A. De Vos, eds. 1995. *Ethnic Identity: Creation, Conflict, and Accommodation.* 3rd ed. Walnut Creek, CA: AltaMira Press.

Romanucci-Ross, Lola, Daniel E. Moerman, and Laurence R. Tancredi, eds. 1997. *The Anthropology of Medicine: From Culture to Method.* 3rd ed. Westport, CT: Bergin & Garvey.

Romney, A. Kimball, Carmella C. Moore, and Craig D. Rusch. 1997. "Cultural Universals: Measuring the Semantic Structure of Emotion Terms in English and Japanese." *Proceedings of the National Academy of Sciences, U.S.A.,* 94: 5489–94.

Romney, A. Kimball, Susan C. Weller, and William H. Batchelder. 1986. "Culture as Consensus: A Theory of Culture and Informant Accuracy." *American Anthropologist,* 88: 313–38.

Roosens, Eugeen E. 1989. *Creating Ethnicity: The Process of Ethnogenesis.* Newbury Park, CA: Sage Publications.

Roosevelt, Anna Curtenius. 1984. "Population, Health, and the Evolution of Subsistence: Conclusions from the Conference." In M. Cohen and G. Armelagos, eds., *Paleopathology at the Origins of Agriculture.* Orlando, FL: Academic Press.

Roosevelt, Anna Curtenius. 1992. "Secrets of the Forest." *The Sciences* (November/December), 22–28.

Roosevelt, Anna Curtenius, et al. 1996. "Paleoindian Cave Dwellers in the Amazon: The Peopling of the Americas." *Science,* 272 (April 19): 373–84.

Roscoe, Paul. 2002. "The Hunters and Gatherers of New Guinea." *Current Anthropology,* 43: 153–62.

Rose, M. D. 1984. "Food Acquisition and the Evolution of Positional Behaviour: The Case of Bipedalism." In D. Chivers, B. Wood, and A. Bilsborough, eds., *Food Acquisition and Processing in Primates.* New York: Plenum.

Roseberry, William. 1988. "Political Economy." *Annual Review of Anthropology,* 17: 161–259.

Rosenberg, John D., ed. 1963. *The Genius of John Ruskin: Selection from His Writings.* New York: Braziller.

Rosenberger, A. L. 1979. "Cranial Anatomy and Implications of *Dolichocebus,* a Late Oligocene Ceboid Primate." *Nature,* 279 (May 31): 416–18.

Rosenblatt, Paul C. 2004. "Human Rights Violations." In *Research Frontiers,* in C. R. Ember, M. Ember, and P. N. Peregrine, eds., *New Directions in Anthropology.* Upper Saddle River, NJ: Prentice Hall, CD-ROM.

Rosenblatt, Paul C., R. Patricia Walsh, and Douglas A. Jackson. 1976. *Grief and Mourning in Cross-Cultural Perspective.* New Haven, CT: HRAF Press.

Rosenblum, L. A., ed. 1970. *Primate Behavior.* Vol. 1. New York: Academic Press.

Ross, Marc Howard. 1981. "Socioeconomic Complexity, Socialization, and Political Differentiation: A Cross-Cultural Study." *Ethos,* 9: 217–47.

Ross, Marc Howard. 1985. "Internal and External Conflict and Violence." *Journal of Conflict Resolution,* 29: 547–79.

Ross, Marc Howard. 1986. "Female Political Participation: A Cross-Cultural Explanation." *American Anthropologist,* 88: 843–58.

Ross, Marc Howard. 1988. "Political Organization and Political Participation: Exit, Voice, and Loyalty in Preindustrial Societies." *Comparative Politics,* 21: 73–89.

Ross, Marc Howard. 2004a. "Ethnocentrism and Ethnic Conflict." In *Research Frontiers,* in C. R. Ember, M. Ember, and P. N. Peregrine, eds., *New Directions in Anthropology.* Upper Saddle River, NJ: Prentice Hall, CD-ROM.

Ross, Marc Howard. 2004b. "Political Participation." In *Cross-Cultural Research for Social Science,* in C. R. Ember, M. Ember, and P. N. Peregrine, eds., *New Directions in Anthropology.* Upper Saddle River, NJ: Prentice Hall, CD-ROM.

Roth, Eric Abella. 2001. "Demise of the Sepaade Tradition: Cultural and Biological Explanations." *American Anthropologist,* 103: 1014–23.

Rowe, N. 1996. *The Pictorial Guide to the Living Primates.* East Hampton, NY: Pogonias Press.

Rubel, Arthur J., and Michael R. Hass. 1996. "Ethnomedicine." In C. F. Sargent and T. M. Johnson, *Medical Anthropology.* Rev. ed. Westport, CT: Praeger.

Rubel, Arthur J., Carl O. Nell, and Rolando Collado-Ardón (with the assistance of John Krejci and Jean Krejci). 1984. *Susto: A Folk Illness.* Berkeley: University of California Press.

Rubin, J. Z., F. J. Provenzano, and R. F. Haskett. 1974. "The Eye of the Beholder: Parents' Views on the Sex of New Borns." *American Journal of Orthopsychiatry,* 44: 512–19.

Rudmin, Floyd Webster. 1988. "Dominance, Social Control, and Ownership: A History and a Cross-Cultural Study of Motivations for Private Property." *Behavior Science Research,* 22: 130–60.

Ruff, Christopher B., and Alan Walker. 1993. "Body Size and Body Shape." In A. Walker and R. Leakey, eds., *The Nariokotome* Homo erectus *Skeleton.* Cambridge, MA: Harvard University Press.

Rumbaugh, Duane M. 1970. "Learning Skills of Anthropoids." In L. Rosenblum, ed., *Primate Behavior,* Vol. 1. New York: Academic Press.

Rummel, R. J. 2002a. "Death by Government." Chapter 1. Accessed at http://www.hawaii.edu/powerkills/DBG.CHAP1.HTM.

Rummel, R. J. 2002b. "Democracies Are Less Warlike Than Other Regimes." Accessed at http://www.hawaii.edu/powerkills/DP95.HTM.

Rummel, R. J. 2002c. "Statistics of Democide." Chapter 17. Accessed at http://www.hawaii.edu/powerkills/SOD.CHAP17.HTM.

Rummel, R. J. 2002d. "Statistics of Democide." Chapter 21. Accessed at http://www.hawaii.edu/powerkills/SOD.CHAP21.HTM.

Ruskin, John. 1963. "Of King's Treasures." In J. D. Rosenberg, ed., *The Genius of John Ruskin.* New York: Braziller.

Russell, Elbert W. 1972. "Factors of Human Aggression." *Behavior Science Notes,* 7: 275–312.

Russett, Bruce (with the collaboration of William Antholis, Carol R. Ember, Melvin Ember, and Zeev Maoz). 1993. *Grasping the Democratic Peace: Principles for a Post–Cold War World.* Princeton, NJ: Princeton University Press.

Russett, Bruce, and John R. Oneal. 2001. *Triangulating Peace: Democracy, Interdependence, and International Organizations.* New York: Norton.

Russon, Anne E. 1990. "The Development of Peer Social Interaction in Infant Chimpanzees: Comparative Social, Piagetian, and Brain Perspectives." In S. Parker and K. Gibson, eds., *"Language" and Intelligence in Monkeys and Apes.* New York: Cambridge University Press.

Sabloff, Jeremy A., ed. 1981. *Supplement to the Handbook of Middle American Indians.* Vol. 1. Austin: University of Texas Press.

Sade, D. S. 1965. "Some Aspects of Parent-Offspring and Sibling Relationships in a Group of Rhesus Monkeys, with a Discussion of Grooming." *American Journal of Physical Anthropology,* 23: 1–17.

Sagan, Carl. 1975. "A Cosmic Calendar." *Natural History* (December): 70–73.

Sahlins, Marshall. 1983. "Other Times, Other Customs: The Anthropology of History." *American Anthropologist,* 85: 517–44.

Sahlins, Marshall D. 1958. *Social Stratification in Polynesia.* Seattle: University of Washington Press.

Sahlins, Marshall D. 1961. "The Segmentary Lineage: An Organization of Predatory Expansion." *American Anthropologist,* 63: 332–45.

Sahlins, Marshall D. 1962. *Moala: Culture and Nature on a Fijian Island.* Ann Arbor: University of Michigan Press.

Sahlins, Marshall D. 1963. "Poor Man, Rich Man, Big-Man, Chief: Political Types in Melanesia and Polynesia." *Comparative Studies in Society and History,* 5: 285–303.

Sahlins, Marshall D. 1972. *Stone Age Economics.* Chicago: Aldine.

Sahlins, Marshall and Elman Service. 1960. *Evolution and Culture.* Ann Arbor: University of Michigan Press.

Salzman, Philip Carl. 1996. "Pastoralism." In D. Levinson and M. Ember, eds., *Encyclopedia of Cultural Anthropology,* vol. 3. New York: Henry Holt, 899–905.

Salzman, Philip Carl. 1999. "Is Inequality Universal?" *Current Anthropology,* 40: 31–61.

Salzman, Philip Carl. 2001. *Understanding Culture: An Introduction to Anthropological Theory.* Long Grove, IL: Waveland, p.135.

Salzman, Philip Carl. 2002. "Pastoral Nomads: Some General Observations Based on Research in Iran." *Journal of Anthropological Research,* 58: 245–64.

Sanday, Peggy R. 1973. "Toward a Theory of the Status of Women." *American Anthropologist,* 75: 1682–700.

Sanday, Peggy R. 1974. "Female Status in the Public Domain." In M. Z. Rosaldo and L. Lamphere, eds., *Woman, Culture, and Society.* Stanford, CA: Stanford University Press.

Sanders, William T. 1968. "Hydraulic Agriculture, Economic Symbiosis, and the Evolution of States in Central Mexico." In B. Meggers, ed., *Anthropological Archaeology in the Americas.* Washington, DC: Anthropological Society of Washington.

Sanders, William T., and Barbara J. Price. 1968. *Mesoamerica.* New York: Random House.

Sanders, William T., Jeffrey R. Parsons, and Robert S. Santley. 1979. *The Basin of Mexico: Ecological Processes in the Evolution of a Civilization.* New York: Academic Press.

Sanderson, Stephen K. 1995. "Expanding World Commercialization: The Link between World-Systems and Civilizations." In S. K. Sanderson, ed., *Civilizations and World Systems: Studying World-Historical Change.* Walnut Creek, CA: AltaMira Press.

Sapir, Edward. 1931. "Conceptual Categories in Primitive Languages." Paper presented at the autumn meeting of the National Academy of Sciences, New Haven, CT. Published in *Science,* 74.

Sapir, Edward. 1938. "Why Cultural Anthropology Needs the Psychiatrist." *Psychiatry,* 1: 7–12.

Sapir, Edward. 1949 [1921]. *Language: An Introduction to the Study of Speech.* New York: Harcourt Brace Jovanovich.

Sapir, Edward, and M. Swadesh. 1964. "American Indian Grammatical Categories." In D. Hymes, ed., *Language in Culture and Society.* New York: Harper & Row.

Sarich, Vincent M. 1968. "The Origin of Hominids: An Immunological Approach." In S. L. Washburn and P. C. Jay, eds., *Perspectives on Human Evolution,* Vol. 1. New York: Holt, Rinehart & Winston.

Sarich, Vincent M., and Allan C. Wilson. 1966. "Quantitative Immunochemistry and the Evolution of Primate Albumins: Micro-Component Fixations." *Science,* 154 (December 23): 1563–66.

Sassaman, Kenneth. 1996. "Early Archaic Settlement in the South Carolina Coastal Plain." In D. G. Anderson and K. E. Sassaman, eds., *The Paleoindian and Early Archaic Southeast.* Tuscaloosa: University of Alabama Press, 58–83.

Sattler, Richard A. 1996. "Remnants, Renegades, and Runaways: Seminole Ethnogenesis Reconsidered." In J. D. Hill, *Ethnogenesis in the Americas.* Iowa City: University of Iowa Press, 36–69.

Saul, Mahir. 1983. "Work Parties, Wages, and Accumulation in a Voltaic Village." *American Ethnologist,* 10: 77–96.

Savage-Rumbaugh, E. S. 1992. "Language Training of Apes." In S. Jones, R. Martin, and D. Pilbeam, eds., *The Cambridge Encyclopedia of Human Evolution.* New York: Cambridge University Press.

Savage-Rumbaugh, E. S. 1994. "Hominid Evolution: Looking to Modern Apes for Clues." In D. Quiatt and J. Itani, eds., *Hominid Culture in Primate Perspective.* Niwot: University Press of Colorado.

Savolainen, Peter, J. Luo, J. Lunderberg, and T. Leitner. 2002. "Genetic Evidence for an East Asian Origin of Domestic Dogs." *Science,* 296 (November 22): 1610–1614.

Scaglion, Richard. 1990. "Legal Adaptation in a Papua New Guinea Village Court." *Ethnology,* 29: 17–33.

Scaglion, Richard. 2004a. "Abelam: Giant Yams and Cycles of Sex, Warfare and Ritual." In *Portraits of Culture,* in C. R. Ember, M. Ember, and P. N. Peregrine, eds., *New Directions in Anthropology.* Upper Saddle River, NJ: Prentice Hall, CD-ROM.

Scaglion, Richard. 2004b. "Law and Society." In *Cross-Cultural Research for Social Science,* in C. R. Ember, M. Ember, and P. N. Peregrine, eds., *New Directions in Anthropology.* Upper Saddle River, NJ: Prentice Hall, CD-ROM.

Scaglion, Richard, and Rose Whittingham. 1985. "Female Plaintiffs and Sex-Related Disputes in Rural Papua New Guinea." In S. Toft, ed., *Domestic Violence in Papua New Guinea.* New Guinea; Law Reform Commission.

Scarr, Sandra, and Kathleen McCartney. 1983. "How People Make Their Own Environments: A Theory of Genotype—Environment Effects." *Child Development,* 54: 424–35.

Schaefer, Stacy B. 2004. "Huichol: Becoming a Godmother." In *Portraits of Culture,* in C. R. Ember, M. Ember, and P. N. Peregrine, eds., *New Directions in Anthropology.* Upper Saddle River, NJ: Prentice Hall, CD-ROM.

Schaller, George. 1963. *The Mountain Gorilla: Ecology and Behavior.* Chicago: University of Chicago Press.

Schaller, George. 1964. *The Year of the Gorilla.* Chicago: University of Chicago Press.

Schaller, George. 1972. *The Serengeti Lion: A Study of Predator-Prey Relations.* Chicago: University of Chicago Press.

Schick, Kathy D., and Nicholas Toth. 1993. *Making Silent Stones Speak.* New York: Simon & Schuster.

Schiffer, Michael B., ed. 1984. *Advances in Archaeological Method and Theory.* Vol. 7. Orlando, FL: Academic Press.

Schiffer, Michael B. 1987. *Formation Processes of the Archaeological Record.* Albuquerque: University of New Mexico Press.

Schlegel, Alice. 1972. *Male Dominance and Female Autonomy.* New Haven, CT: HRAF Press.

Schlegel, Alice, ed. 1977. *Sexual Stratification: A Cross-Cultural View.* New York: Columbia University Press.

Schlegel, Alice. 1989. "Gender Issues and Cross-Cultural Research." *Behavior Science Research,* 23: 265–80.

Schlegel, Alice. 1991. "Status, Property, and the Value on Virginity." *American Ethnologist,* 18: 719–34.

Schlegel, Alice. 2003. "The Status of Women." In *Cross-Cultural Research for Social Science,* in C. R. Ember, M. Ember, and P. N. Peregrine, eds., *New Directions in Anthropology.* Upper Saddle River, NJ: Prentice Hall, CD-ROM.

Schlegel, Alice, and Herbert Barry, III. 1986. "The Cultural Consequences of Female Contribution to Subsistence." *American Anthropologist,* 88: 142–50.

Schlegel, Alice, and Herbert Barry III. 1991. *Adolescence: An Anthropological Inquiry.* New York: Free Press.

Schlegel, Alice, and Rohn Eloul. 1987. "A New Coding of Marriage Transactions." *Behavior Science Research,* 21: 118–40.

Schlegel, Alice, and Rohn Eloul. 1988. "Marriage Transactions: Labor, Property, and Status." *American Anthropologist,* 90: 291–309.

Schneider, David M. 1961a. "Introduction: The Distinctive Features of Matrilineal Descent Groups." In D. M. Schneider and K. Gough, eds., *Matrilineal Kinship.* Berkeley: University of California Press, 1–29.

Schneider, David M. 1961b. "Truk." In D. M. Schneider and K. Gough, eds., *Matrilineal Kinship.* Berkeley: University of California Press, 202–33.

Schoepf, B. 1988. "Women, AIDS and Economic Crisis in Central Africa." *Canadian Journal of African Studies,* 22: 625–44.

Schrauf, Robert W. 1999. "Mother Tongue Maintenance Among North American Ethnic Groups." *Cross-Cultural Research,* 33: 175–92.

Schrire, Carmel. 1980. "An Inquiry into the Evolutionary Status and Apparent Identity of San Hunter-Gatherers." *Human Ecology,* 8: 9–32.

Schrire, Carmel, ed. 1984a. *Past and Present in Hunter-Gatherer Studies.* Orlando, FL: Academic Press.

Schrire, Carmel. 1984b. "Wild Surmises on Savage Thoughts." In C. Schrire, ed., *Past and Present in Hunter-Gatherer Studies.* Orlando, FL: Academic Press.

Schwarcz, Henry P. 1993. "Uranium-Series Dating and the Origin of Modern Man." In H. P. Schwarcz, *The Origin of Modern Humans and the Impact of Chronometric Dating.* Princeton, NJ: Princeton University Press.

Schwarcz, Henry P. ed. 1993. *The Origin of Modern Humans and the Impact of Chronometric Dating.* Princeton, NJ: Princeton University Press.

Schwartz, J. 1999. *Sudden Origins: Fossils, Genes, and the Emergence of Species.* New York: John Wiley.

Schwartz, Richard D. 1954. "Social Factors in the Development of Legal Control: A Case Study of Two Israeli Settlements." *Yale Law Journal*, 63 (February): 471–91.

Scollon, Ron, and Susan Wong Scollon. 2001. *Intercultural Communication: A Discourse Approach.* 2nd ed. Malden, MA.: Blackwell.

Scollon, Ron, and Suzanne B. K. Scollon. 1981. *Narrative, Literacy and Face in Interethnic Communication.* Norwood, NJ: Ablex.

Scott, Janny, and David Leonhardt. 2005. "Class in America: Shadowy Lines That Still Divide." *The New York Times National,* May 15: 1, 26.

Scribner, Sylvia, and Michael Cole. 1981. *The Psychology of Literacy.* Cambridge, MA: Harvard University Press.

Scudder, Thayer. 1978. "Opportunities, Issues and Achievements in Development Anthropology since the Mid-1960s: A Personal View." In E. M. Eddy and W. L. Partridge, eds., *Applied Anthropology in America,* 2nd ed. New York: Columbia University Press.

Sebeok, Thomas A., and Jean Umiker-Sebeok, eds. 1980. *Speaking of Apes: A Critical Anthology of Two-Way Communication with Man.* New York: Plenum Press.

Seemanová, Eva. 1971. "A Study of Children of Incestuous Matings." *Human Heredity,* 21: 108–28.

Segal, Edwin S. 2004. "Cultural Constructions of Gender." In C. Ember and M. Ember, eds. *Encyclopedia of Sex and Gender: Men and Women in the World's Cultures.* Vol 1, New York: Kluwer Academic/Plenum Publishers, 3–10.

Segal, Robert A. 1987. *Joseph Campbell: An Introduction.* New York: Garland.

Segall, Marshall H. 1979. *Cross-Cultural Psychology: Human Behavior in Global Perspective.* Monterey, CA: Brooks/Cole.

Segall, Marshall, Pierre R. Dasen, John W. Berry, and Ype H. Poortinga. 1990. *Human Behavior in Global Perspective: An Introduction to Cross-Cultural Psychology.* New York: Pergamon.

Segerstrále, Ullica, and Peter Molnar, eds. 1997. *Nonverbal Communication: Where Nature Meets Culture.* Mahwah, NJ: Lawrence Erlbaum.

Sellen, Daniel W. and Daniel J. Hruschka. 2004. "Extracted-Food Resource-Defense Polygyny in Native Western North American Societies at Contact." *Current Anthropology,* 45: 707–14.

Selig, Ruth Osterweis, and Marilyn R. London, eds. 1998. *Anthropology Explored: The Best of Smithsonian AnthroNotes.* Washington, DC: Smithsonian Institution Press. Also in E-book format. 2000.

Semenov, S. A. 1970. *Prehistoric Technology.* Trans. M. W. Thompson. Bath, England: Adams & Dart.

Sengupta, Somini. 2002. "Money From Kin Abroad Helps Bengalis Get By." *New York Times* (June 24): A3.

Senner, Wayne M., ed. 1989a. *The Origins of Writing.* Lincoln: University of Nebraska Press.

Senner, Wayne M. 1989b. "Theories and Myths on the Origins of Writing: A Historical Overview." In W. M. Senner, ed., *The Origins of Writing.* Lincoln: University of Nebraska Press.

Sered, Susan S. 1994. *Priestess, Mother, Sacred Sister.* New York: Oxford University Press.

Service, Elman R. 1962. *Primitive Social Organization: An Evolutionary Perspective.* New York: Random House.

Service, Elman R. 1975. *Origins of the State and Civilization: The Process of Cultural Evolution.* New York: Norton.

Service, Elman R. 1978. *Profiles in Ethnology.* 3rd ed. New York: Harper & Row.

Service, Elman R. 1979. *The Hunters.* 2nd ed. Upper Saddle River, NJ: Prentice Hall.

Seyfarth, Robert M., and Dorothy L. Cheney., 1982. "How Monkeys See the World: A Review of Recent Research on East African Vervet Monkeys." In C. T. Snowdon, C. H. Brown, and M. R. Petersen, eds., *Primate Communication.* New York: Cambridge University Press.

Seyfarth, Robert M., Dorothy L. Cheney, and Peter Marler. 1980. "Monkey Response to Three Different Alarm Calls: Evidence of Predator Classification and Semantic Communication." *Science,* 210 (November 14): 801–03.

Shanklin, Eugenia. 1993. *Anthropology and Race.* Belmont, CA: Wadsworth.

Shankman, Paul. 1991. "Culture Contact, Cultural Ecology, and Dani Warfare." *Man,* 26: 299–321.

Shankman, Paul. 2004. "Sex, Lies, and Anthropologists: Margaret Mead, Derek Freeman, and Samoa." In *Research Frontiers,* in C. R. Ember, M. Ember, and P. N. Peregrine, eds., *New Directions in Anthropology.* Upper Saddle River, NJ: Prentice Hall, CD-ROM.

Sheils, Dean. 1975. "Toward a Unified Theory of Ancestor Worship: A Cross-Cultural Study." *Social Forces,* 54: 427–40.

Sheils, Dean. 1980. "A Comparative Study of Human Sacrifice." *Behavior Science Research,* 15: 245–62.

Shen, Xuefei, and Robert F. Siliciano. 2000. "Preventing AIDS but Not HIV-1 Infection with a DNA Vaccine." *Science,* 290 (October 20): 463–65.

Shibamoto, Janet S. 1987. "The Womanly Woman: Japanese Female Speech." In S. U. Philips, S. Steele, and C. Tanz, eds., *Language, Gender, and Sex in Comparative Perspective.* Cambridge: Cambridge University Press.

Shipman, Pat. 1986. "Scavenging or Hunting in Early Hominids: Theoretical Framework and Tests." *American Anthropologist,* 88: 27–43.

Shipman, Pat. 1994. *The Evolution of Racism: Human Differences and the Use and Abuse of Science.* New York: Simon & Schuster.

Shipman, Pat. 2001. *The Man Who Found the Missing Link: Eugene Dubois and His Lifelong Quest to Prove Darwin Right.* New York: Simon & Schuster.

Shulman, Seth. 1993. "Nurturing Native Tongues." *Technology Review* (May/June): 16.

Shweder, Richard A., and Robert A. LeVine, eds. 1984. *Culture Theory: Essays on Mind, Self, and Emotion.* New York: Cambridge University Press.

Sih, Andrew, and Katharine A. Milton. 1985. "Optimal Diet Theory: Should the !Kung Eat Mongongos?" *American Anthropologist,* 87: 395–401.

Silk, Joan B., and Robert Boyd. 2002. "Why Are Primates So Smart?" In P. N. Peregrine, C. R. Ember, and M. Ember, eds., *Physical Anthropology: Original Readings in Method and Practice.* Upper Saddle River, NJ: Prentice Hall, 53–67. Also in C. R. Ember, M. Ember, and P. N. Peregrine eds., *New Directions in Anthropology.* Upper Saddle River, NJ: Prentice Hall, CD-ROM, 2004.

Silver, Harry R. 1981. "Calculating Risks: The Socioeconomic Foundations of Aesthetic Innovation in an Ashanti Carving Community." *Ethnology,* 20: 101–14.

Simcha Lev-Yadun, Avi Gopher, and Shahal Abbo, 2000. "The Cradle of Agriculture." *Science,* 288 (June 2): 1602–03.

Simmons, Alan H., Ilse Köhler-Rollefson, Gary O. Rollefson, Rolfe Mandel, and Zeidan Kafafi. 1988. "Ain Ghazal: A Major Neolithic Settlement in Central Jordan." *Science,* 240 (April 1): 35–39.

Simmons, Janie, Paul Farmer, and Brooke G. Schoepf. 1996. "A Global Perspective." In P. Farmer, M. Connors, and J. Simmons, eds., *Women, Poverty, and AIDS: Sex, Drugs, and Structural Violence.* Monroe, ME: Common Courage Press, 39–90.

Simons, Elwyn L. 1992. "The Primate Fossil Record." In S. Jones, R. Martin, and D. Pilbeam, eds., *The Cambridge Encyclopedia of Human Evolution.* New York: Cambridge University Press.

Simons, Elwyn L. 1995. "Skulls and Anterior Teeth of *Catopithecus* (Primates: Anthropoidea) from the Eocene Shed Light on Anthropoidean Origins." *Science,* 268 (June 30): 1885–88.

Simons, Elwyn L., and D. T. Rassmussen. 1996. "Skull of *Catopithecus browni*, an Early Tertiary Catarrhine." *American Journal of Physical Anthropology,* 100: 261–92.

Simpson, George Gaylord. 1971. *The Meaning of Evolution.* New York: Bantam.

Simpson, S. P., and Ruth Field. 1946. "Law and the Social Sciences." *Virginia Law Review,* 32: 858.

Simpson, Scott W. 2002. "*Australopithecus afarensis* and Human Evolution." In P. N. Peregrine, C. R. Ember, and M. Ember, eds., *Physical Anthropology: Original Readings in Method and Practice.* Upper Saddle River, NJ: Prentice Hall.

Singer, J. David. 1980. "Accounting for International War: The State of the Discipline." *Annual Review of Sociology,* 6: 349–67.

Singer, Ronald, and John Wymer. 1982. *The Middle Stone Age at Klasies River Mouth in South Africa.* Chicago: University of Chicago Press.

Sinopoli, Carla. 2002. "Learning about the Past through Archaeological Ceramics: An Example from Yijayanagara, India." In P. N. Peregrine, C. R. Ember, and M. Ember, eds., *Archaeology: Original Readings in Method and Practice.* Upper Saddle River, NJ: Prentice Hall.

Sipes, Richard G. 1973. "War, Sports, and Aggression: An Empirical Test of Two Rival Theories." *American Anthropologist,* 75: 64–86.

Sivard, Ruth Leger. 1993. *World Military and Social Expenditures 1993.* 15th ed. Washington, DC: World Priorities.

Skomal, Susan N., and Edgar C. Polomé, eds. 1987. *Proto-Indo-European: The Archaeology of a Linguistic Problem.* Washington, DC: Washington Institute for the Study of Man.

Slayman, Andrew. 1997. "A Battle over Old Bones," *Archaeology,* 50: 16–23.

Slocum, Sally. 1975. "Woman the Gatherer: Male Bias in Anthropology," in Rayna Reiter, ed, *Toward an Anthropology of Women.* New York: Monthly Review Press.

Small, David B., and Nicola B. Tannenbaum, eds. 1999. *At the Interface: The Household and Beyond.* Lanham, MD: University Press of America.

Small, Meredith. 1997. "Our Babies, Ourselves." *Natural History* (October): 42–51.

Smith, B. Holly. 1986. "Dental Development in *Australopithecus* and Early *Homo.*" *Nature,* 323 (September 25): 327–30.

Smith, Bruce D. 1992a. "Prehistoric Plant Husbandry in Eastern North America." In C. Cowan and P. Watson, eds., *The Origins of Agriculture.* Washington, DC: Smithsonian Institution Press.

Smith, Bruce D. 1992b. *Rivers of Change.* Washington, DC: Smithsonian Institution Press.

Smith, Bruce D. 1995. *The Emergence of Agriculture.* New York: Scientific American Library.

Smith, Eric A. 1983. "Anthropological Applications of Optimal Foraging Theory: A Critical Review." *Current Anthropology,* 24: 625–40.

Smith, Fred H. 1984. "Fossil Hominids from the Upper Pleistocene of Central Europe and the Origin of Modern Humans." In F. H. Smith and F. Spencer, eds., *The Origins of Modern Humans.* New York: Alan R. Liss.

Smith, Fred H., and Frank Spencer, eds. 1984. *The Origins of Modern Humans: A World Survey of the Fossil Evidence.* New York: Alan R. Liss.

Smith, John Maynard. 1989. *Evolutionary Genetics.* New York: Oxford University Press.

Smith, M. W. 1974. "Alfred Binet's Remarkable Questions: A Cross-National and Cross-Temporal Analysis of the Cultural Biases Built into the Stanford-Binet Intelligence Scale and Other Binet Tests." *Genetic Psychology Monographs,* 89: 307–34.

Smith, Michael G. 1966. "Pre-Industrial Stratification Systems." In N. J. Smelser and S. M. Lipset, eds., *Social Structure and Mobility in Economic Development.* Chicago: Aldine.

Smith, Waldemar R. 1977. *The Fiesta System and Economic Change.* New York: Columbia University Press.

Smuts, Barbara B., Dorothy L. Cheney, Robert M. Seyfarth, Richard W. Wrangham, and Thomas T. Struhsaker, eds. 1987. *Primate Societies.* Chicago: University of Chicago Press.

Snowdon, Charles T. 1999. "An Empiricist View of Language Evolution and Development." In B. J. King, *The Origins of Language.* Santa Fe, NM: School of American Research Press, 79–114.

Snowdon, Charles T., Charles H. Brown, and Michael R. Petersen, eds. 1982. *Primate Communication.* New York: Cambridge University Press.

Soffer, Olga. 1985. *The Upper Paleolithic of the Central Russian Plain.* Orlando, FL: Academic Press.

Soffer, Olga. 1993. "Upper Paleolithic Adaptations in Central and Eastern Europe and Man-Mammoth Interactions." In O. Soffer and N. D. Praslov, eds., *From Kostenki to Clovis.* New York: Plenum.

Soffer, Olga, and N. D. Praslov, eds. 1993. *From Kostenki to Clovis: Upper Paleolithic–Paleo-Indian Adaptations.* New York: Plenum.

Soffer, Olga, J. M. Adovasio, and D. C. Hyland. 2000. "The 'Venus' Figurines: Textiles, Basketry, Gender, and Status in the Upper Paleolithic." *Current Anthropology,* 41: 511–37.

Solis, Ruth Shady, Jonathan Haas, and Winifred Creamer. 2001. "Dating Caral, A Preceramic Site in the Supe Valley of the Central Coast of Peru." *Science,* 292 (April 27): 723–726.

Sosa, John R. 2004. "Maya: The Sacred in Everyday Life." In *Portraits of Culture,* in C. R. Ember, M. Ember, and P. N. Peregrine, eds., *New Directions in Anthropology.* Upper Saddle River, NJ: Prentice Hall, CD-ROM.

Sosis, Richard 2002. "Patch Choice Decisions among Ifaluk Fishers." *American Anthropologist,* 104: 583–598.

Southworth, Franklin C., and Chandler J. Daswani. 1974. *Foundations of Linguistics.* New York: Free Press.

Spanos, Nicholas P. 1983. "Ergotism and the Salem Witch Panic: A Critical Analysis and an Alternative Conceptualization." *Journal of the History of the Behavioral Sciences,* 19: 358–69.

Spencer, Frank. 1984. "The Neandertals and Their Evolutionary Significance: A Brief Historical Survey." In F. H. Smith and F. Spencer, eds., *The Origins of Modern Humans.* New York: Alan R. Liss.

Spencer, Robert F. 1968. "Spouse-Exchange among the North Alaskan Eskimo." In P. Bohannan and J. Middleton, eds., *Marriage, Family and Residence.* Garden City, NY: Natural History Press.

Sperber, Dan. 1985. *On Anthropological Knowledge: Three Essays.* Cambridge: Cambridge University Press.

Speth, John D. 2002. "Were Our Ancestors Hunters or Scavengers?" In P. N. Peregrine, C. R. Ember, and M. Ember, eds., *Physical Anthropology: Original Readings in Method and Practice.* Upper Saddle River, NJ: Prentice Hall.

Speth, John D., and Dave D. Davis. 1976. "Seasonal Variability in Early Hominid Predation." *Science,* 192 (April 30): 441–45.

Speth, John D., and Katherine A. Spielmann. 1983. "Energy Source, Protein Metabolism, and Hunter-Gatherer Subsistence Strategies." *Journal of Anthropological Archaeology,* 2: 1–31.

Spiro, Melford. 1993. "Is the Western Conception of the Self 'Peculiar' within the Context of the World Cultures?" *Ethos,* 21: 107–53.

Spiro, Melford. 2004. "On the Strange and the Familiar in Recent Anthropological Thought." In *Research Frontiers,* in C. R. Ember, M. Ember, and P. N. Peregrine, eds., *New Directions in Anthropology.* Upper Saddle River, NJ: Prentice Hall, CD-ROM.

Spiro, Melford E. 1982. *Oedipus in the Trobriands.* Chicago: University of Chicago Press.

Spiro, Melford E., and Roy G. D'Andrade. 1958. "A Cross-Cultural Study of Some Supernatural Beliefs." *American Anthropologist,* 60: 456–66.

Spooner, Brian, ed. 1972. *Population Growth: Anthropological Implications*. Cambridge, MA: MIT Press.

Spring, Anita. 1995. *Agricultural Development and Gender Issues in Malawi*. Lanham, MD: University Press of America.

Stairs, Arlene. 1992. "Self-Image, World-Image: Speculations on Identity from Experiences with Inuit." *Ethos*, 20: 116–26.

Stanford, Craig. 2002. "Chimpanzee Hunting Behavior and Human Evolution." In P. N. Peregrine, C. R. Ember, and M. Ember, eds., *Physical Anthropology: Original Readings in Method and Practice*. Upper Saddle River, NJ: Prentice Hall.

Stanford, Craig B. 1998. "The Social Behavior of Chimpanzees and Bonobos: Empirical Evidence and Shifting Assumptions." *Current Anthropology*, 39: 399–420.

Stanford, Craig B., Janette Wallis, Hilali Matama, and Jane Goodall. 1994. "Patterns of Predation by Chimpanzees on Red Colobus Monkeys in Gombe National Park, Tanzania, 1982–1991." *American Journal of Physical Anthropology*, 94: 213–29.

Stark, Rodney. 1985. *The Future of Religion: Secularization, Revival and Cult Formation*. Berkeley: University of California Press.

State of the World 1994: A Worldwatch Institute Report on Progress toward a Sustainable Society. 1994. New York: Norton.

Stedman, Hansell, B. Kozyak, A. Nelson, D. Thesier, L. Su, D. Low, C. Bridges, J. Shrager, N. Minugh-Purvis, and M. Mitchell. 2004. "Myosin Gene Mutation Correlates with Anatomical Changes in the Human Lineage." *Nature*, 428 (March 25): 415–418.

Steegman, A. T., Jr. 1975. "Human Adaptation to Cold." In A. Damon, ed., *Physiological Anthropology*. New York: Oxford University Press.

Stein, Gil, and Mitchell Rothman, eds. 1994. *Chiefdoms and Early States in the Near East: The Organizational Dynamics of Complexity*. Madison, WI: Prehistory Press.

Stein, P., and B. Rowe. 2000. *Physical Anthropology*, 7th ed. Boston: McGraw Hill.

Steiner, Christopher B. 1990. "Body Personal and Body Politic: Adornment and Leadership in Cross-Cultural Perspective." *Anthropos*, 85: 431–45.

Stephens, William N. 1963. *The Family in Cross-Cultural Perspective*. New York: Holt, Rinehart & Winston.

Stephens, William N. 1972. "A Cross-Cultural Study of Modesty." *Behavior Science Research*, 7: 1–28.

Stern, Curt. 1973. *Principles of Human Genetics*. 3rd ed. San Francisco: W. H. Freeman.

Stevens, Phillips, Jr. 1996. "Religion." In D. Levinson and M. Ember, eds., *Encyclopedia of Cultural Anthropology*. New York: Henry Holt, vol. 3, 1088–100.

Steward, Julian H. 1955a. "The Concept and Method of Cultural Ecology." In J. H. Steward, *Theory of Culture Change*. Urbana: University of Illinois Press.

Steward, Julian H. 1955b. *Theory of Culture Change*. Urbana: University of Illinois Press.

Steward, Julian H., and Louis C. Faron. 1959. *Native Peoples of South America*. New York: McGraw-Hill.

Steward, Julian H., Robert A. Manners, Eric R. Wolf, Elena Padilla Seda, Sidney W. Mintz, and Raymond L. Scheele. 1956. *The People of Puerto Rico*. Urbana: University of Illinois Press.

Stewart, T. D. 1950. "Deformity, Trephanating, and Mutilation in South American Indian Skeletal Remains." In J. A. Steward, ed., *Handbook of South American Indians*. Vol. 6: *Physical Anthropology, Linguistics, and Cultural Geography*. Bureau of American Ethnology Bulletin 143. Washington, DC: Smithsonian Institution.

Stille, Alexander. 2001. "Grounded by an Income Gap." *New York Times*, Arts & Ideas, December 15.

Stimpson, David, Larry Jensen, and Wayne Neff. 1992. "Cross-Cultural Gender Differences in Preference for a Caring Morality." *Journal of Social Psychology*, 132: 317–22.

Stini, William A. 1971. "Evolutionary Implications of Changing Nutritional Patterns in Human Populations." *American Anthropologist*, 73: 1019–30.

Stini, William A. 1975. *Ecology and Human Adaptation*. Dubuque, IA: Wm. C. Brown.

Stocking, George W., Jr., ed. 1983–1989. *History of Anthropology*. Vols. 1–6. Madison: University of Wisconsin Press.

Stodder, James. 1995. "The Evolution of Complexity in Primitive Exchange." *Journal of Comparative Economics*, 20: 205.

Stogdill, Ralph M. 1974. *Handbook of Leadership: A Survey of Theory and Research*. New York: Macmillan.

Stoneking, Mark. 1997. "Recent African Origin of Human Mitochondrial DNA." In P. Donnelly and S. Tavaré, eds., *Progress in Population Genetics and Human Evolution*. New York: Springer, 1–13.

Straus, Murray A. 1991. "Physical Violence in American Families: Incidence Rates, Causes, and Trends." In D. D. Knudsen and J. L. Miller, eds., *Abused and Battered*. New York: Aldine.

Straus, Murray A. 1995. "Trends in Cultural Norms and Rates of Partner Violence: An Update to 1992." In S. M. Stith and M. A. Straus, eds. *Understanding Partner Violence: Prevalence, Causes, Consequences, and Solutions*. Minneapolis, MN: National Council on Family Relations, 30–33, accessed at http://pubpages.unh.edu/~mas2/v56.pdf/, August 2002.

Straus, Murray A. 2001. "Physical Aggression in the Family: Prevalence Rates, Links to Non-Family Violence, and Implications for Primary Prevention of Societal Violence." In M. Martinez, ed., *Prevention and Control of Aggression and the Impact on Its Victims*. New York: Kluwer Academic/Plenum, 181–200.

Straus, Murray A., and Glenda Kaufman Kantor. 1994. "Change in Spouse Assault Rates from 1975 to 1992: A Comparison of Three National Surveys in the United States." Paper presented at the 13th World Congress of Sociology, Bielefeld, Germany, July, as seen at http://pubpages.unh.edu/~mas2/v55.pdf/, August 2002.

Straus, Murray A., and Glenda Kaufman Kantor. 1995. "Trends in Physical Abuse by Parents From 1975 to 1992: A Comparison of Three National Surveys." Paper presented at the annual meeting of the American Society of Criminology, Boston, November 18, accessed at http://pubpages.unh.edu/~mas2/V57.pdf/, August 2002.

Straus, Murray A., and Glenda Kaufman Kantor. 2002. "Change in Spouse Assault Rates from 1975 to 1992: A Comparison of Three National Surveys in the United States." Paper presented at the 13th World Congress of Sociology, Bielefeld, Germany, July 1994. Accessed at http://pubpages.unh.edu/~mas2/v55.pdf/.

Straus, Murray A., and Carrie L. Yodanis. 1996. "Corporal Punishment in Adolescence and Physical Assaults on Spouses in Later Life: What Accounts for the Link?" *Journal of Marriage and the Family*, 58: 825–41.

Strauss, Lawrence Guy. 1982. "Comment on White." *Current Anthropology*, 23: 185–86.

Strauss, Lawrence Guy. 1989. "On Early Hominid Use of Fire." *Current Anthropology*, 30: 488–91.

Strauss, Lawrence Guy. 2000. "Solutrean Settlement of North America? A View of Reality." *American Antiquity*, 65: 219–26.

Stringer, Christopher B. 1985. "Evolution of a Species." *Geographical Magazine*, 57: 601–07.

Stringer, Christopher B. 2000. "Neandertals." In I. Tattersall, E. Delson, and J. van Couvering, eds., *Encyclopedia of Human Evolution and Prehistory*. New York: Garland.

Stringer, Christopher. B. 2003. "Out of Ethiopia." *Nature*, 423 (June 12) 692–95.

Stringer, Christopher B, and Clive Gamble. 1993. *In Search of the Neandertals*. New York: Thames and Hudson.

Stringer, Christopher B., J. J. Hublin, and B. Vandermeersch. 1984. "The Origin of Anatomically Modern Humans in Western Europe." In F. H. Smith and F. Spencer, eds., *The Origins of Modern Humans.* New York: Alan R. Liss.

Strouthes, Daniel P. 1995. *Law and Politics: A Cross-Cultural Encyclopedia.* Santa Barbara, CA: ABC-CLIO.

Struever, Stuart, ed. 1971. *Prehistoric Agriculture.* Garden City, NY: Natural History Press.

Stutley, Margaret. 2003. *Shamanism: A Concise Introduction.* London: Routledge.

Suárez-Orozco, Marcelo. 1992. "A Grammar of Terror: Psychocultural Responses to State Terrorism in Dirty War and Post-Dirty War Argentina." In C. Nordstrom and J. Martin, eds. *The Paths to Domination, Resistance, and Terror.* Berkeley, CA: University of California Press, 219–59.

Super, Charles M., and Sara Harkness. 1997. "The Cultural Structuring of Child Development." In J. W. Berry, P. R. Dasen, and T. S. Saraswathi, eds. *Handbook of Cross-Cultural Psychology,* Vol. 2, 2nd ed. Boston: Allyn & Bacon, 1–39.

Susman, Randall L., ed. 1984. *The Pygmy Chimpanzee: Evolutionary Biology and Behavior.* New York: Plenum.

Susman, Randall L. 1994. "Fossil Evidence for Early Hominid Tool Use." *Science,* 265 (September 9): 1570–73.

Susman, Randall L., Jack T. Stern, Jr., and William L. Jungers. 1985. "Locomotor Adaptations in the Hadar Hominids." In E. Delson, ed., *Ancestors: The Hard Evidence.* New York: Alan R. Liss, 184–92.

Sussman, Robert W. 1972. "Child Transport, Family Size, and the Increase in Human Population Size during the Neolithic." *Current Anthropology,* 13: 258–67.

Sussman, Robert W. 1991. "Primate Origins and the Evolution of Angiosperms." *American Journal of Primatology,* 23: 209–23.

Sussman, Robert W. 1999. *Primate Ecology and Social Structure.* Needham Heights, MA: Pearson Custom Publishing.

Sussman, Robert W., and W. G. Kinzey. 1984. "The Ecological Role of the Callitrichidae: A Review." *American Journal of Physical Anthropology,* 64: 419–49.

Sussman, Robert W., and Peter H. Raven. 1978. "Pollination by Lemurs and Marsupials: An Archaic Coevolutionary System." *Science,* 200 (May 19): 734–35.

Swanson, Guy E. 1969. *The Birth of the Gods: The Origin of Primitive Beliefs.* Ann Arbor: University of Michigan Press.

Sweeney, James J. 1952. "African Negro Culture." In P. Radin, ed., *African Folktales and Sculpture.* New York: Pantheon.

Swisher, C. C., III, G. H. Curtis, T. Jacob, A. G. Getty, A. Suprijo, and Widiasmoro. 1994. "Age of the Earliest Known Hominids in Java, Indonesia." *Science,* 263 (February 25): 1118–21.

Szalay, Frederick S. 1968. "The Beginnings of Primates." *Evolution* 22: 32–33.

Szalay, Frederick S. 1972. "Paleobiology of the Earliest Primates." In R. Tuttle, ed., *The Functional and Evolutionary Biology of the Primates.* Chicago: University of Chicago Press, 3–35.

Szalay, Frederick S. 1975. "Hunting-Scavenging Protohominids: A Model for Hominid Origins." *Man,* 10: 420–29.

Szalay, Frederick S., and Eric Delson. 1979. *Evolutionary History of the Primates.* New York: Academic Press.

Szalay, Frederick S., I. Tattersall, and R. Decker. 1975. "Phylogenetic Relationships of *Plesiadipis*—Postcranial Evidence." *Contributions to Primatology,* 5: 136–66.

Szathmary, Emöke J. E. 1993. "Genetics of Aboriginal North Americans." *Evolutionary Anthropology,* 1: 202–20.

Szklut, Jay, and Reed, Robert Roy. 1991. "Community Anonymity in Anthropological Research: A Reassessment." In Carolyn Fluehr-Lobban, ed., *Ethics and the Profession of Anthropology: Dialogue for a New Era.* Philadelphia: University of Pennsylvania Press, 97–116.

Tainter, Joseph. 1988. *The Collapse of Complex Societies.* Cambridge: Cambridge University Press, 128–52.

Talmon, Yonina. 1964. "Mate Selection in Collective Settlements." *American Sociological Review,* 29: 491–508.

Tannenbaum, Nicola. 1984. "The Misuse of Chayanov: 'Chayanov's Rule' and Empiricist Bias in Anthropology." *American Anthropologist,* 86: 927–42.

Tannen, Deborah. 1990. *You Just Don't Understand: Women and Men in Conversation.* New York: William Morrow and Company.

Tattersall, Ian. 1982. *The Primates of Madagascar.* New York: Columbia University Press.

Tattersall, Ian. 1993. *The Human Odyssey.* Upper Saddle River, NJ: Prentice Hall.

Tattersall, Ian. 1995. *The Fossil Trail: How We Know What We Think We Know about Human Evolution.* New York: Oxford University Press.

Tattersall, Ian. 1999. *The Last Neanderthal.* Boulder, CO: Westview, 115–16.

Tattersall, Ian. 2002. "Paleoanthropology and Evolutionary Theory." In P. N. Peregrine, C. R. Ember, and M. Ember, eds., *Physical Anthropology: Original Readings in Method and Practice.* Upper Saddle River, NJ: Prentice Hall.

Tattersall, Ian, and Jeffrey Schwartz. 2000. *Extinct Humans.* Boulder, CO: Westview, 93.

Tattersall, Ian, Eric Delson, and John Van Couvering, eds. 2000. *Encyclopedia of Human Evolution and Prehistory.* New York: Garland.

Taylor, R. E., and M. J. Aitken, eds. 1997. *Chronometric Dating in Archaeology.* New York: Plenum.

Teleki, Geza. 1973. "The Omnivorous Chimpanzee." *Scientific American* (January): 32–42.

Templeton, Alan R. 1993. "The 'Eve' Hypotheses: A Genetic Critique and Reanalysis." *American Anthropologist,* 95: 51–72.

Templeton, Alan R. 1996. "Gene Lineages and Human Evolution." *Science,* 272 (May 31): 1363.

Terborgh, John. 1983. *Five New World Primates: A Study in Comparative Ecology.* Princeton, NJ: Princeton University Press.

Textor, Robert B., comp. 1967. *A Cross-Cultural Summary.* New Haven, CT: HRAF Press.

Thomas, David H. 1986. *Refiguring Anthropology: First Principles of Probability and Statistics.* Prospect Heights, IL: Waveland.

Thomas, Elizabeth Marshall. 1959. *The Harmless People.* New York: Knopf.

Thomas, Wesley. 1993. "A Traditional Navajo's Perspectives on the Cultural Construction of Gender in the Navajo World." Paper presented at the University of Frankfurt, Germany. As referred to in Lang 1999.

Thomason, Sarah Grey, and Terrence Kaufman. 1988. *Language Contact, Creolization, and Genetic Linguistics.* Berkeley: University of California Press.

Thompson, Elizabeth Bartlett. 1966. *Africa, Past and Present.* Boston: Houghton Mifflin.

Thompson, Ginger. 2002. "Mexico Is Attracting a Better Class of Factory in Its South." *New York Times,* June 29, p. A3.

Thompson, Richard H. 1996. "Assimilation." In D. Levinson and M. Ember, eds. *Encyclopedia of Cultural Anthropology,* 4 vols., New York: Henry Holt, vol. 1, pp. 112–16.

Thompson, Richard H. 2004. "Chinatowns: Immigrant Communities in Transition." In *Portraits of Culture,* in C. R. Ember, M. Ember, and P. N. Peregrine, eds., *New Directions in Anthropology.* Upper Saddle River, NJ: Prentice Hall, CD-ROM.

Thompson, Stith. 1965. "Star Husband Tale." In A. Dundes, ed., *The Study of Folklore.* Upper Saddle River, NJ: Prentice Hall.

Thompson-Handler, Nancy, Richard K. Malenky, and Noel Badrian. 1984. "Sexual Behavior of *Pan paniscus* under Natural Conditions in the Lomako Forest, Equateur, Zaire." In R. Susman, ed., *The Pygmy Chimpanzee.* New York: Plenum.

Thorne, Alan G., and Milford H. Wolpoff. 1992. "The Multiregional Evolution of Humans." *Scientific American* (April): 76–83.

Thurnwald, R. C. 1934. "Pigs and Currency in Buin: Observations about Primitive Standards of Value and Economics." *Oceania*, 5: 119–41.

Tierney, Patrick. 2000. *Darkness in El Dorado.* New York: Norton.

Timpane, John. 1991. "Essay: The Poetry of Science." *Scientific American* (July): 128.

Tobias, Philip V. 1987. "The Brain of *Homo habilis:* A New Level of Organization in Cerebral Evolution." *Journal of Human Evolution*, 16: 741–61.

Tobias, Philip V. 1994. "The Craniocerebral Interface in Early Hominids: Cerebral Impressions, Cranial Thickening, Paleoneurobiology, and a New Hypothesis on Encephalization." In R. Corruccini and R. Ciochon, eds., *Integrative Paths to the Past.* Upper Saddle River, NJ: Prentice Hall.

Tobin, Joseph J., David Y. H. Wu, and Dana H. Davidson. 1989. *Preschool in Three Cultures: Japan, China, and the United States.* New Haven, CT: Yale University Press.

Toft, S., ed. 1985. *Domestic Violence in Papua New Guinea.* Monograph No. 3. Port Moresby, Papua New Guinea: Law Reform Commission.

Tollefson, Kenneth D. 2004. "Tlingit: Chiefs Past and Present." In *Portraits of Culture*, in C. R. Ember, M. Ember, and P. N. Peregrine, eds., *New Directions in Anthropology.* Upper Saddle River, NJ: Prentice Hall, CD-ROM.

Tomasello, Michael. 1990. "Cultural Transmission in the Tool Use and Communicatory Signaling of Chimpanzees." In S. Parker and K. Gibson, eds., *"Language" and Intelligence in Monkeys and Apes.* New York: Cambridge University Press.

Torrey, E. Fuller. 1972. *The Mind Game: Witchdoctors and Psychiatrists.* New York: Emerson Hall.

Torry, William I. 1986. "Morality and Harm: Hindu Peasant Adjustments to Famines." *Social Science Information*, 25: 125–60.

Traphagan, John W., and L. Keith Brown. 2002. "Fast Food and Intergenerational Commensality in Japan: New Styles and Old Patterns." *Ethnology*, 41: 119–34.

Travis, John. 2000. "Human Genome Work Reaches Milestone." *Science News* (July 1): 4–5.

Treiman, Donald J., and Harry B. G. Ganzeboom. 1990. "Cross-National Comparative Status-Attainment Research." *Research in Social Stratification and Mobility*, 9: 117.

Trevor-Roper, H. R. 1971. "The European Witch-Craze of the Sixteenth and Seventeenth Centuries." In W. A. Lessa and E. Z. Vogt, eds., *Reader in Comparative Religion*, 3rd ed. New York: Harper & Row.

Triandis, Harry C. 1995. *Individualism and Collectivism.* Boulder, CO: Westview.

Triandis, Harry C., and Alastair Heron, eds. 1981. *Handbook of Cross-Cultural Psychology.* Vol. 4: *Developmental Psychology.* Boston: Allyn & Bacon.

Trigger, Bruce G. 1989. *A History of Archaeological Thought.* Cambridge: Cambridge University Press.

Trigger, Bruce G. 2003. *Understanding Early Civilizations: A Comparative Study.* Cambridge: Cambridge University Press.

Trinkaus, Erik. 1983. *The Shanidar Neandertals.* New York: Academic.

Trinkaus, Erik. 1984. "Western Asia." In F. H. Smith and F. Spencer, eds., *The Origins of Modern Humans.* New York: Alan R. Liss.

Trinkaus, Erik. 1985. "Pathology and the Posture of the La Chapelle-aux-Saints Neandertal." *American Journal of Physical Anthropology*, 67: 19–41.

Trinkaus, Erik. 1986. "The Neandertals and Modern Human Origins." *Annual Review of Anthropology*, 15: 193–218.

Trinkaus, Erik. 1987a. "Bodies, Brawn, Brains and Noses: Human Ancestors and Human Predation." In M. Nitecki and D. Nitecki, eds., *The Evolution of Human Hunting.* New York: Plenum.

Trinkaus, Erik. 1987b. "The Neandertal Face: Evolutionary and Functional Perspectives on a Recent Hominid Face." *Journal of Human Evolution*, 16: 429–43.

Trinkaus, Erik., ed. 1989. *The Emergence of Modern Humans: Biocultural Adaptations in the Later Pleistocene.* Cambridge: Cambridge University Press.

Trinkaus, Erik, and William W. Howells. 1979. "The Neanderthals." *Scientific American* (December): 118–33.

Trinkaus, Erik, and Pat Shipman. 1993a. *The Neandertals: Changing the Image of Mankind.* New York: Knopf.

Trinkaus, Erik, and Pat Shipman. 1993b. "Neandertals: Images of Ourselves." *Evolutionary Anthropology*, 1: 194–201.

Trompf, G. W., ed. 1990. *Cargo Cults and Millenarian Movements: Transoceanic Comparisons of New Religious Movements.* Berlin: Mouton de Gruyter.

Trotter, Robert T., II, ed. 1988. *Anthropology for Tomorrow: Creating Practitioner-Oriented Applied Anthropology Programs.* Washington, DC: American Anthropological Association.

Trouillot, Michel-Rolph. 2001. "The Anthropology of the State in the Age of Globalization: Close Encounters of the Deceptive Kind." *Current Anthropology*, 42: 125–38.

Trudgill, Peter. 1983. *Sociolinguistics: An Introduction to Language and Society.* Rev. ed. New York: Penguin.

Turner, B. L. 1970. "Population Density in the Classic Maya Lowlands: New Evidence for Old Approaches." *Geographical Review*, 66 (January): 72–82.

Turner, B. L., and Steven B. Brush. 1987. *Comparative Farming Systems.* New York: Guilford.

Turner, Christy G., II. 1987. "Telltale Teeth." *Natural History* (January): 6–9.

Turner, Christy G., II. 1989. "Teeth and Prehistory in Asia." *Scientific American* (February): 88–95.

Turner, Terence, and Carole Nagengast, eds. 1997. "Universal Human Rights versus Cultural Relativity." *Journal of Anthropological Research*, 53, no. 3: 267–381.

Tutin, Caroline, and L. White. 1999. "The Recent Evolutionary Past of Primate Communities: Likely Environmental Impacts during the Past Three Millennia." In J. G. Fleagle, C. Janson, and K. E. Reed, eds., *Primate Communities.* Cambridge: Cambridge University Press, 230–31.

Tuttle, Russell H. 1986. *Apes of the World: Their Social Behavior, Communication, Mentality, and Ecology.* Park Ridge, NJ: Noyes.

Tylor, Edward B. 1958 [1971]. *Primitive Culture.* New York: Harper Torchbooks.

Tylor, Edward B. 1979. "Animism." In W. A. Lessa and E. Z. Vogt, eds., *Reader in Comparative Religion*, 4th ed. New York: Harper & Row.

Uberoi, J. P. Singh. 1962. *The Politics of the Kula Ring: An Analysis of the Findings of Bronislaw Malinowski.* Manchester, UK: University of Manchester Press.

Ucko, Peter J., and Andrée Rosenfeld. 1967. *Paleolithic Cave Art.* New York: McGraw-Hill.

Ucko, Peter J., and G. W. Dimbleby, eds. 1969. *The Domestication and Exploitation of Plants and Animals.* Chicago: Aldine.

Ucko, Peter J., Ruth Tringham, and G. W. Dimbleby, eds. 1972. *Man, Settlement, and Urbanism.* Cambridge, MA: Schenkman.

Udy, Stanley H., Jr. 1970. *Work in Traditional and Modern Society.* Upper Saddle River, NJ: Prentice Hall.

Underhill, Anne. 2002. "Investigating Craft Specialization during the Longshan Period of China." In P. N. Peregrine, C. R. Ember, and M. Ember, eds., *Archaeology: Original Readings in Method and Practice.* Upper Saddle River, NJ: Prentice Hall.

Underhill, Ralph. 1975. "Economic and Political Antecedents of Monotheism: A Cross-Cultural Study." *American Journal of Sociology*, 80: 841–61.

Underhill, Ruth M. 1938. *Social Organization of the Papago Indians.* New York: Columbia University Press.

United Nations Development Programme. 2001. *Human Development Report 2001*. New York: Oxford University Press.

Unnithan, N. Prabha. 2004. "Nayars: Tradition and Change in Marriage and Family." In *Portraits of Culture*, in C. R. Ember, M. Ember, and P. N. Peregrine, eds., *New Directions in Anthropology*. Upper Saddle River, NJ: Prentice Hall, CD-ROM.

Upham, Steadman, ed. 1990. *The Evolution of Political Systems: Sociopolitics in Small-Scale Sedentary Societies*. Cambridge: Cambridge University Press.

Urban Institute. 2000. "America's Homeless II: Populations and Services." Washington, DC: Urban Institute, February 1. Accessed at http://www.urban.org/housing/homeless/numbers/index .htm.

U.S. Bureau of the Census. 1993. *Statistical Abstract of the United States: 1993*. 113th ed. Washington, DC: U.S. Government Printing Office.

Valente, Thomas W. 1995. *Network Models of the Diffusion of Innovations*. Cresskill, NJ: Hampton Press.

Valladas, H., J. L. Joron, G. Valladas, O. Bar-Yosef, and B. Vandermeersch. 1988. "Thermoluminescence Dating of Mousterian 'Proto-Cro-Magnon' Remains from Israel and the Origin of Modern Man." *Nature*, 337 (February 18): 614–16.

Van der Merwe, N. J. 1992. "Reconstructing Prehistoric Diet." In S. Jones, R. Martin, and D. Pilbeam, eds., *The Cambridge Encyclopedia of Human Evolution*. New York: Cambridge University Press.

Van Hear, Nicholas. 2004. "Refugee Diasporas or Refugees in Diaspora," in M. Ember, C. R. Ember, and I. Skoggard, eds., *Encyclopedia of Diasporas: Immigrant and Refugee Cultures Around the World*. New York: Kluwer Academic/Plenum, vol. 1, 580–89.

Van Lawick-Goodall, Jane. 1971. *In the Shadow of Man*. Boston: Houghton Mifflin.

Van Schaik, C. P. et al. 2003. "Orangutan Cultures and the Evolution of Material Culture." *Science*, 299 (January 3): 102–05.

Van Willigen, John. 2002. *Applied Anthropology: An Introduction*, 3rd ed. Westport, CT: Bergin and Garvey.

Vanneman, Reeve, and Lynn Weber Cannon. 1987. *The American Perception of Class*. Philadelphia: Temple University Press.

Vayda, Andrew P. 1967. "Pomo Trade Feasts." In G. Dalton, ed., *Tribal and Peasant Economies*. Garden City, NY: Natural History Press.

Vayda, Andrew P., and Roy A. Rappaport. 1968. "Ecology: Cultural and Noncultural." In J. H. Clifton, ed., *Introduction to Cultural Anthropology*. Boston: Houghton Mifflin.

Vayda, Andrew P., Anthony Leeds, and David B. Smith. 1962. "The Place of Pigs in Melanesian Subsistence." In V. E. Garfield, ed., *Symposium*. Seattle: University of Washington Press.

Vekua, Abesalom, et al. 2002. "A New Skull of Early *Homo* from Dmanisi, Georgia." *Science*, 297 (July 5): pp. 85–89.

Vermeulen, Hans, and Govers, Cora, eds. 1994. *The Anthropology of Ethnicity*. Amsterdam: Het Spinhuis.

Vigil, James Diego. 1988. "Group Processes and Street Identity: Adolescent Chicano Gang Members." *Ethos*, 16: 421–45.

Vigil, James Diego. 2004. "Mexican Americans: Growing Up on the Streets of Los Angeles." In *Portraits of Culture*, in C. R. Ember, M. Ember, and P. N. Peregrine, eds., *New Directions in Anthropology*. Upper Saddle River, NJ: Prentice Hall, CD-ROM.

Vigilant, Linda, Mark Stoneking, Henry Harpending, Kristen Hawkes, and Allan C. Wilson. 1991. "African Populations and the Evolution of Human Mitochrondrial DNA." *Science*, 253 (September 27): 1503–07.

Vincent, Joan. 1978. "Political Anthropology: Manipulative Strategies." *Annual Review of Anthropology*, 7: 175–94.

"Violent Crime." NCJ-147486. Washington, DC: U.S. Department of Justice, April 1994.

Visaberghi, Elisabetta, and Dorothy Munkenbeck Fragaszy. 1990. "Do Monkeys Ape?" In S. Parker and K. Gibson, eds., *"Language"*

and Intelligence in Monkeys and Apes. New York: Cambridge University Press.

Vogel, Gretchen. 1999. "Chimps in the Wild Show Stirrings of Culture." *Science*, 284 (June 25): 2070–73.

Vogel, Joseph O. 2002. "De-Mystifying the Past: Great Zimbabwe, King Solomon's Mines, and Other Tales of Old Africa." In P. N. Peregrine, C. R. Ember, and M. Ember, eds., *Archaeology: Original Readings in Method and Practice*. Upper Saddle River, NJ: Prentice Hall.

Vogt, Evon Z., and Richard M. Levanthal, eds. 1983. *Prehistoric Settlement Patterns: Essays in Honor of Gordon R. Willey*. Albuquerque: University of New Mexico Press.

von Frisch, Karl. 1962. "Dialects in the Language of the Bees." *Scientific American* (August): 78–87.

Vrba, Elizabeth S. 1995. "On the Connection between Paleoclimate and Evolution." In E. S. Vrba, G. H. Denton, T. C. Partridge, and L. H. Burckle, eds., *Paleoclimate and Evolution*. New Haven, CT: Yale University Press, 24–45.

Wade, Edwin L., ed. 1986. *The Arts of the North American Indian: Native Traditions in Evolution*. New York: Hudson Hills Press.

Wagley, Charles. 1974. "Cultural Influences on Population: A Comparison of Two Tupi Tribes." In P. J. Lyon, ed., *Native South Americans*. Boston: Little, Brown.

Wald, Matthew L. 2000. "Hybrid Cars Show Up in M.I.T.'s Crystal Ball." *New York Times*, November 3, F1; and the special advertisement produced by energy companies, "Energy: Investing for a New Century," *New York Times*, October 30, EN1–EN8.

Waldbaum, Jane C. 2005. "Helping Hand for China." *Archaeology*, 58:6.

Waldman, Amy. 2005. "Sri Lankan Maids' High Price for Foreign Jobs." *The New York Times*, May 8, pp. 1, 20.

Walker, Alan, and R. Leakey. 1988. "The Evolution of *Australopithecus boisei*," in F. Grine, ed., *Evolutionary History of the "Robust" Australopithecines*. New York: Aldine, 247–58.

Walker, Alan, and Richard Leakey, eds. 1993. *The Nariokotome* Homo erectus *Skeleton*. Cambridge, MA: Harvard University Press.

Walker, Alan, and M. Pickford. 1983. "New Postcranial Fossils of *Proconsul Africanus* and *Proconsul Nyananzae*." In R. Ciochon and R. Corruccini, eds., *New Interpretation of Ape and Human Ancestry*. New York: Plenum.

Walker, Alan, and Pat Shipman. 1996. *The Wisdom of the Bones: In Search of Human Origins*. New York: Knopf.

Wallace, Alfred Russell. 1970. "On the Tendency of Varieties to Depart Indefinitely from the Original Type." (Originally published in 1858.) In L. B. Young, ed., *Evolution of Man*. New York: Oxford University Press.

Wallace, Anthony. 1966. *Religion: An Anthropological View*. New York: Random House.

Wallace, Anthony. 1970. *The Death and Rebirth of the Seneca*. New York: Knopf.

Wallace, Anthony. 1972. "Mental Illness, Biology and Culture." In F. L. K. Hsu, ed., *Psychological Anthropology*. 2nd ed. Cambridge, MA: Schenkman.

Wallace, Anthony, J. Lawrence Angel, Richard Fox, Sally McLendon, Rachel Sady, and Robert Sharer, eds. 1977. *Perspectives on Anthropology 1976*. American Anthropological Association Special Publication No. 10. Washington, DC: American Anthropological Association.

Wallerstein, Immanuel. 1974. *The Modern World-System*. New York: Academic Press.

Wanner, Eric, and Lila R. Gleitman, eds. 1982. *Language Acquisition: The State of the Art*. Cambridge: Cambridge University Press.

Ward, Peter M. 1982. "Introduction and Purpose." In P. M. Ward, ed., *Self-Help Housing*. London: Mansell.

Ward, Peter M., ed. 1982. *Self-Help Housing: A Critique*. London: Mansell.

Ward, Steve. 1997. "The Taxonomy and Phylogenetic Relationships of *Sivapithecus* Revisited." In D. R. Begun, C. V. Ward, and M. D. Rose, eds. *Function, Phylogeny and Fossils: Miocene Hominoid Evolution and Adaptation.* New York: Plenum, 269–90.

Ward, Steve, B. Brown, A. Hill, J. Kelley, and W. Downs. 1999. "*Equatorius:* A New Hominoid Genus from the Middle Miocene of Kenya." *Science,* 285 (August 27): 1382–86.

Wardhaugh, Ronald. 2002. *An Introduction to Sociolinguistics,* 4th ed. Oxford: Blackwell.

Warner, John Anson. 1986. "The Individual in Native American Art: A Sociological View." In E. L. Wade, ed., *The Arts of the North American Indian.* New York: Hudson Hills Press.

Warner, W. Lloyd. 1937. *A Black Civilization: A Social Study of an Australian Tribe.* New York: Harper.

Warner, W. Lloyd and Paul S. Lunt. 1941. *The Social Life of a Modern Community.* New Haven, CT: Yale University Press.

Warren, Dennis M. 1989. "Utilizing Indigenous Healers in National Health Delivery Systems: The Ghanaian Experiment." In J. van Willigen, B. Rylko-Bauer, and A. McElroy, eds., *Making Our Research Useful.* Boulder, CO: Westview.

Warren, Karen, ed. 1995. *Ecofeminism: Multidisciplinary Perspectives.* Bloomington: Indiana University Press.

Warry, Wayne. 1986. "Kafaina: Female Wealth and Power in Chuave, Papua New Guinea." *Oceania,* 57: 4–21.

Warry, Wayne. 1990. "Doing unto Others: Applied Anthropology, Collaborative Research and Native Self-Determination." *Culture,* 10: 61–62.

Washburn, Dorothy K., ed. 1983. *Structure and Cognition in Art.* Cambridge: Cambridge University Press.

Washburn, S. L., ed. 1964. *Social Life of Early Man.* Chicago: Aldine.

Washburn, Sherwood. 1960. "Tools and Human Evolution." *Scientific American* (September): 62–75.

Washburn, S. L., and Phyllis C. Jay, eds. 1968. *Perspectives on Human Evolution.* Vol. 1. New York: Holt, Rinehart & Winston.

Watson, James L. 2004. "Presidential Address: Virtual Kinship, Real Estate, and Diaspora Formation—the Man Lineage Revisited," *Journal of Asian Studies,* 63: 893–910.

Weaver, Muriel Porter. 1993. *The Aztecs, Maya, and Their Predecessors.* 3rd ed. San Diego: Academic Press.

Webb, Karen E. 1977. "An Evolutionary Aspect of Social Structure and a Verb 'Have.'" *American Anthropologist,* 79: 42–49.

Weber, Max. 1947. *The Theory of Social and Economic Organization.* Trans. A. M. Henderson and Talcott Parsons. New York: Oxford University Press.

Webster's New World Dictionary, Third College Edition. New York: Webster's New World, 1988.

Weiner, Annette B. 1976. *Women of Value, Men of Renown: New Perspectives in Trobriand Exchange.* Austin: University of Texas Press.

Weiner, Annette B. 1987. *The Trobrianders of Papua New Guinea.* New York: Holt, Rinehart and Winston.

Weiner, J. S. 1954. "Nose Shape and Climate." *Journal of Physical Anthropology,* 4: 615–18.

Weiner, Jonathan. 1994. *Beak of the Finch.* New York: Vintage.

Weiner, Steve, Q. Xi, P. Goldberg, J. Liu, and O. Bar-Yousef. 1998. "Evidence for the Use of Fire at Zhoukoudian, China." *Science,* 281 (July 10): 251–53.

Weinreich, Uriel. 1968. *Languages in Contact.* The Hague: Mouton.

Weisner, Thomas S. 2004. "The American Dependency Conflict." *Ethos,* 29: 271–95.

Weisner, Thomas S., and Ronald Gallimore. 1977. "My Brother's Keeper: Child and Sibling Caretaking." *Current Anthropology,* 18: 169–90.

Weisner, Thomas S., Mary Bausano, and Madeleine Kornfein. 1983. "Putting Family Ideals into Practice: Pronaturalism in Conventional and Nonconventional California Families." *Ethos,* 11: 278–304.

Weiss, Harvey and Raymond S. Bradley. 2001. "What Drives Societal Collapse?" *Science,* 291 (January 26): 609–10.

Weiss, Harvey, M. A. Courty, W. Wetterstrom, F. Guichard, L. Senior, R. Meadow, and A. Curnow. 1993. "The Genesis and Collapse of Third Millennium North Mesopotamian Civilization." *Science,* 261 (August 20): 995–1004.

Weller, Susan C. 2004. "The Research Process." In *Research Frontiers,* in C. R. Ember, M. Ember, and P. N. Peregrine, eds., *New Directions in Anthropology.* Upper Saddle River, NJ: Prentice Hall, CD-ROM.

Wells, Spencer. 2002. *The Journey of Man: A Genetic Odyssey.* Princeton, NJ: Princeton University Press.

Wendorf, Fred, and Angela E. Close, eds. 1984. *Advances in World Archaeology.* Vol. 3. Orlando, FL: Academic Press.

Wenke, Robert J. 1984. *Patterns in Prehistory: Humankind's First Three Million Years.* 2nd ed. New York: Oxford University Press.

Wenke, Robert. 1990. *Patterns in Prehistory: Humankind's First Three Million Years.* 3rd ed. New York: Oxford University Press.

Werner, Dennis. 1975. "On the Societal Acceptance or Rejection of Male Homosexuality." M. A. thesis, Hunter College of the City University of New York.

Werner, Dennis. 1978. "Trekking in the Amazon Forest." *Natural History* (November): 42–54.

Werner, Dennis. 1979. "A Cross-Cultural Perspective on Theory and Research on Male Homosexuality." *Journal of Homosexuality,* 4: 345–62.

Werner, Dennis. 1982. "Chiefs and Presidents: A Comparison of Leadership Traits in the United States and among the Mekranoti-Kayapo of Central Brazil." *Ethos,* 10: 136–48.

Werner, Dennis. 1984. "Child Care and Influence among the Mekranoti of Central Brazil." *Sex Roles,* 10: 395–404.

Werner, Oswald, and G. Mark Schoepfle. 1987. *Systematic Fieldwork.* Vol. 1: *Foundations of Ethnography and Interviewing.* Newbury Park, CA: Sage.

Westermarck, Edward. 1894. *The History of Human Marriage.* London: Macmillan.

Weyer, E. M. 1932. *The Eskimos: Their Environment and Folkways.* New Haven, CT: Yale University Press.

Wheat, Joe B. 1967. "A Paleo-Indian Bison Kill." *Scientific American* (January): 44–52.

Wheatley, Paul. 1971. *The Pivot of the Four Quarters.* Chicago: Aldine.

Wheeler, Peter. 1984. "The Evolution of Bipedality and Loss of Functional Body Hair in Hominids." *Journal of Human Evolution,* 13: 91–98.

Wheeler, Peter. 1991. "The Influence of Bipedalism in the Energy and Water Budgets of Early Hominids." *Journal of Human Evolution,* 23: 379–88.

Whitaker, Ian. 1955. *Social Relations in a Nomadic Lappish Community.* Oslo: Utgitt av Norsk Folksmuseum.

White, Benjamin. 1973. "Demand for Labor and Population Growth in Colonial Java." *Human Ecology,* 1, no. 3 (March): 217–36.

White, Douglas R. 1988. "Rethinking Polygyny: Co-Wives, Codes, and Cultural Systems." *Current Anthropology,* 29: 529–88.

White, Douglas R., and Michael L. Burton. 1988. "Causes of Polygyny: Ecology, Economy, Kinship, and Warfare." *American Anthropologist,* 90: 871–87.

White, Douglas R., Michael L. Burton, and Lilyan A. Brudner. 1977. "Entailment Theory and Method: A Cross-Cultural Analysis of the Sexual Division of Labor." *Behavior Science Research,* 12: 1–24.

White, Frances. J. 1996. "*Pan paniscus* 1973 to 1996: Twenty-three Years of Field Research." *Evolutionary Anthropology,* 5: 11–17.

White, Leslie A. 1939. "A Problem in Kinship Terminology." *American Anthropologist,* 41: 569–70.

White, Leslie A. 1949. *The Science of Culture: A Study of Man and Civilization.* New York: Farrar, Straus & Cudahy.

White, Leslie A. 1968. "The Expansion of the Scope of Science." In M. H. Fried, ed., *Readings in Anthropology.* Vol. 1, 2nd ed. New York: Thomas Y. Crowell.

White, N. F., ed. 1974. *Ethology and Psychiatry.* Toronto: Ontario Mental Health Foundation and University of Toronto Press.

White, Randall. 1982. "Rethinking the Middle/Upper Paleolithic Transition." *Current Anthropology,* 23: 169–75.

White, Tim D. 2003. "Early Hominids—Diversity or Distortion?" *Science,* 299 (March 28): 1994–97.

White, Tim D., Donald C. Johanson, and William H. Kimbel. 1981. "*Australopithecus africanus:* Its Phyletic Position Reconsidered." *South African Journal of Science,* 77: 445–70.

White, Timothy D., G. Suwa, and B. Asfaw. 1994. "*Australopithecus ramidus,* a New Species of Early Hominid from Aramis, Ethiopia." *Nature,* 371 (September 22): 306–33.

White, Timothy D., G. Suwa, and B. Asfaw. 1995. "Corrigendum: *Australopithecus ramidus,* a New Species of Early Hominid from Aramis, Ethiopia." *Nature,* 375 (May 4): 88.

Whiten, A., et al. 1999. "Cultures in Chimpanzees," *Nature* 399 (June 17): 682–85.

Whiting, Beatrice Blyth. 1950. *Paiute Sorcery.* Viking Fund Publications in Anthropology No. 15. New York: Wenner-Gren Foundation.

Whiting, Beatrice B. 1965. "Sex Identity Conflict and Physical Violence." *American Anthropologist,* 67: 123–40.

Whiting, Beatrice B., ed. 1963. *Six Cultures.* New York: Wiley.

Whiting, Beatrice B., and Carolyn Pope Edwards. 1973. "A Cross-Cultural Analysis of Sex Differences in the Behavior of Children Aged Three through Eleven." *Journal of Social Psychology,* 91: 171–88.

Whiting, Beatrice B., and John W. M. Whiting (in collaboration with Richard Longabaugh). 1975. *Children of Six Cultures: A Psycho-Cultural Analysis.* Cambridge, MA: Harvard University Press.

Whiting, Beatrice Blyth. 1980. "Culture and Social Behavior: A Model for the Development of Social Behavior." *Ethos,* 8: 95–116.

Whiting, Beatrice Blyth, and Carolyn Pope Edwards (in collaboration with Carol R. Ember, Gerald M. Erchak, Sara Harkness, Robert L. Munroe, Ruth H. Munroe, Sara B. Nerlove, Susan Seymour, Charles M. Super, Thomas S. Weisner, and Martha Wenger). 1988. *Children of Different Worlds: The Formation of Social Behavior.* Cambridge, MA: Harvard University Press.

Whiting, John W. M. 1941. *Becoming a Kwoma.* New Haven, CT: Yale University Press.

Whiting, John W. M. 1959. "Cultural and Sociological Influences on Development." In *Maryland Child Growth and Development Institute: Growth and Development of the Child in His Setting.* Baltimore: Maryland State Department of Health.

Whiting, John W. M. 1964. "Effects of Climate on Certain Cultural Practices." In W. Goodenough, ed., *Explorations in Cultural Anthropology.* New York: McGraw-Hill.

Whiting, John W. M., and Irvin L. Child. 1953. *Child Training and Personality: A Cross-Cultural Study.* New Haven, CT: Yale University Press.

Whittaker, John C. 1994. *Flintknapping: Making and Understanding Stone Tools.* Austin: University of Texas Press.

Whyte, Martin K. 1978a. "Cross-Cultural Codes Dealing with the Relative Status of Women." *Ethnology,* 17: 211–37.

Whyte, Martin K. 1978b. *The Status of Women in Preindustrial Societies.* Princeton, NJ: Princeton University Press.

Wiberg, Hakan. 1983. "Self-Determination as an International Issue." In I. M. Lewis, ed., *Nationalism and Self-Determination in the Horn of Africa.* London: Ithaca Press.

Wilcox, Sherman. 1999. "The Invention and Ritualization of Language." In B. J. King, ed. *The Origins of Language.* Santa Fe, NM: School of American Research Press. 351–84.

Wilden, Anthony. 1987. *The Rules are No Game: The Strategy of Communication.* London: Routledge and Kegan Paul.

Wikan, Unni. 1982. *Beyond the Veil in Arabia.* Baltimore: The Johns Hopkins University Press.

Wilford, John Noble. 1995. "The Transforming Leap, from 4 Legs to 2." *New York Times,* September 5, p. C1ff.

Wilford, John Noble. 1997. "Ancient German Spears Tell of Mighty Hunters of Stone Age." *New York Times,* March 4, p. C6.

Wilkinson, Robert L. 1995. "Yellow Fever: Ecology, Epidemiology, and Role in the Collapse of the Classic Lowland Maya Civilization." *Medical Anthropology,* 16: 269–94.

Williams, George C. 1992. *Natural Selection: Domains, Levels, and Challenges.* New York: Oxford University Press.

Williams, Melvin D. 2004. "Racism: The Production, Reproduction, and Obsolescence of Social Inferiority." In *Research Frontiers,* in C. R. Ember, M. Ember, and P. N. Peregrine, eds., *New Directions in Anthropology.* Upper Saddle River, NJ: Prentice Hall, CD-ROM.

Williams, Walter L. 1992. *The Spirit and the Flesh.* Boston: Beacon Press.

Wilmsen, Edwin N., ed. 1989. *We Are Here: Politics of Aboriginal Land Tenure.* Berkeley: University of California Press.

Wilson, Allan C., and Rebecca L. Cann. 1992. "The Recent African Genesis of Humans." *Scientific American* (April): 68–73.

Wilson, Edward O. 1975. *Sociobiology: The New Synthesis.* Cambridge, MA: Belknap Press of Harvard University Press.

Wilson, Monica. 1963 [1951]. *Good Company: A Study of Nyakyusa Age Villages.* Boston: Beacon Press.

Winkelman, Michael 1986a. "Magico-Religious Practitioner Types and Socioeconomic Conditions." *Behavior Science Research,* 20: 17–46.

Winkelman, Michael. 1986b. "Trance States: A Theoretical Model and Cross-Cultural Analysis." *Ethos,* 14: 174–203.

Winkleman, Michael, and Philip M. Peck, eds. 2004. *Divination and Healing: Potent Vision.* Tucson: University of Arizona Press.

Winterbottom, Robert. 1995. "The Tropical Forestry Plan: Is It Working?" In P. J. Puntenney, ed., *Global Ecosystems: Creating Options through Anthropological Perspectives,* NAPA Bulletin 15.

Winterhalder, Bruce. 1990. "Open Field, Common Pot: Harvest Variability and Risk Avoidance in Agricultural and Foraging Societies." In E. Cashdan, ed., *Risk and Uncertainty in Tribal and Peasant Economies.* Boulder, CO: Westview.

Witkin, Herman A. 1967. "A Cognitive Style Approach to Cross-Cultural Research." *International Journal of Psychology,* 2: 233–50.

Witkowski, Stanley R. 1975. "Polygyny, Age of Marriage, and Female Status." Paper presented at the annual meeting of the American Anthropological Association, San Francisco.

Witkowski, Stanley R., and Cecil H. Brown. 1978. "Lexical Universals." *Annual Review of Anthropology,* 7: 427–51.

Witkowski, Stanley R., and Harold W. Burris. 1981. "Societal Complexity and Lexical Growth." *Behavior Science Research,* 16: 143–59.

Wittfogel, Karl. 1957. *Oriental Despotism: A Comparative Study of Total Power.* New Haven, CT: Yale University Press.

Wolf, Arthur. 1968. "Adopt a Daughter-in-Law, Marry a Sister: A Chinese Solution to the Problem of the Incest Taboo." *American Anthropologist,* 70: 864–74.

Wolf, Arthur P., and Chieh-Shan Huang. 1980. *Marriage and Adoption in China, 1845–1945.* Stanford, CA: Stanford University Press.

Wolf, Eric. 1955. "Types of Latin American Peasantry: A Preliminary Discussion." *American Anthropologist,* 57: 452–71.

Wolf, Eric R. 1956. "San José: Subcultures of a 'Traditional' Coffee Municipality." In J. H. Steward et al., *The People of Puerto Rico.* Urbana: University of Illinois Press.

Wolf, Eric. 1966. *Peasants.* Upper Saddle River, NJ: Prentice Hall.

Wolf, Eric R., ed. 1976. *The Valley of Mexico: Studies in Pre-Hispanic Ecology and Society.* Albuquerque: University of New Mexico Press.

Wolf, Eric. 1984. "Culture: Panacea or Problem." *American Antiquity,* 49: 393–400.

Wolf, Naomi. 1991. *The Beauty Myth: How Images of Beauty Are Used against Women.* New York: Morrow.

Wolff, Ronald G. 1991. *Functional Chordate Anatomy.* Lexington, MA: D. C. Heath.

Wolpoff, Milford H. 1971. "Competitive Exclusion among Lower Pleistocene Hominids: The Single Species Hypothesis." *Man,* 6: 601–13.

Wolpoff, Milford H. 1983. "*Ramapithecus* and Human Origins: An Anthropologist's Perspective of Changing Interpretations." In R. Ciochon and R. Corruccini, eds., *New Interpretations of Ape and Human Ancestry.* New York: Plenum.

Wolpoff, Milford H. 1999. *Paleoanthropology.* 2nd ed. Boston: McGraw-Hill, 501–04, 727–31.

Wolpoff, Milford H., and Abel Nikini. 1985. "Early and Early Middle Pleistocene Hominids from Asia and Africa." In E. Delson, ed., *Ancestors.* New York: Alan R. Liss.

Wolpoff, Milford H. A. G. Thorne, J. Jelinek, and Zhang Yinyun. 1993. "The Case for Sinking *Homo erectus*: 100 years of *Pithecanthropus* Is Enough!" In J. L. Franzen, ed., *100 Years of* Pithecanthropus: *The* Homo Erectus *Problem. Courier Forshungsinstitut Senckenberg,* 171: 341–61.

Womack, Mari, and Judith Marti. 1993. *The Other Fifty Percent: Multicultural Perspectives on Gender Relations.* Prospect Heights, IL: Waveland.

"Women in Science '93: Gender and the Culture of Science." 1993. *Science,* 260 (April 16): 383–430.

Wong, Kate. 2003. "An Ancestor to Call Our Own." *Scientific American* (January): 54–63.

Wong, Kate, 2005. "The Littlest Human." *Scientific American* (February): 56–65.

Wood, Bernard A. 1992. "Evolution of Australopithecines." In S. Jones, R. Martin, and D. Pilbeam, eds., *The Cambridge Encyclopedia of Human Evolution.* New York: Cambridge University Press.

Wood, Bernard A. 1994. "Hominid Paleobiology: Recent Achievements and Challenges." In R. Corruccini and R. Ciochon, eds., *Integrative Paths to the Past.* Upper Saddle River, NJ: Prentice Hall.

Wood, Gordon S. 1992. *The Radicalism of the American Revolution.* New York: Knopf.

Wood, James W., George R. Milner, Henry C. Harpending, and Kenneth M. Weiss, "The Osteological Paradox: Problems of Inferring Prehistoric Health from Skeletal Samples," *Current Anthropology,* 33 (1992): 343–70.

Woodburn, James. 1968. "An Introduction to Hadza Ecology." In R. B. Lee and I. DeVore, eds., *Man the Hunter.* Chicago: Aldine.

World Bank. 1995. *World Development Report 1995. Workers in an Integrating World.* Oxford: Oxford University Press.

Worsley, Peter. 1957. *The Trumpet Shall Sound: A Study of "Cargo" Cults in Melanesia.* London: MacGibbon & Kee,

Wrangham, Richard W. 1980. "An Ecological Model of Female-Bonded Primate Groups." *Behaviour,* 75: 262–300.

Wright, Gary A. 1971. "Origins of Food Production in Southwestern Asia: A Survey of Ideas." *Current Anthropology,* 12: 447–78.

Wright, George O. 1954. "Projection and Displacement: A Cross-Cultural Study of Folktale Aggression." *Journal of Abnormal and Social Psychology,* 49: 523–28.

Wright, Henry T. 1986. "The Evolution of Civilizations." In D. Meltzer, D. Fowler, and J. Sabloff, eds., *American Archaeology Past and Future.* Washington, DC: Smithsonian Institution Press.

Wright, Henry T., and Gregory A. Johnson. 1975. "Population, Exchange, and Early State Formation in Southwestern Iran." *American Anthropologist,* 77: 267–77.

Wulff, Robert and Shirley Fiste. 1987. "The Domestication of Wood in Haiti." In R. M. Wulff and S. J. Fiste, *Anthropological Praxis.* Boulder, CO: Westview.

Wynn, Thomas. 1979. "The Intelligence of Later Acheulean Hominids." *Man,* 14: 371–91.

Yamei, Hou, R. Potts, Y. Baoyin, et al. 2000. "Mid-Pleistocene Acheulean-like Stone Technology of the Bose Basin, South China." *Science,* 287 (March 3): 1622–26.

Yergin, Daniel. 2002. "Giving Aid to World Trade," *New York Times,* June 27, p. A29.

Yinger, J. Milton. 1994. "*Ethnicity: Source of Strength? Source of Conflict?*" Albany: State University Press.

Young, Frank W. 1970. "A Fifth Analysis of the Star Husband Tale." *Ethnology,* 9: 389–413.

Young, Louise B., ed. 1970. *Evolution of Man.* New York: Oxford University Press.

Young, T. Cuyler, Jr. 1972. "Population Densities and Early Mesopotamian Urbanism." In Ucko, Tringham, and Dimbleby, eds., *Man, Settlement and Urbanism.* Cambridge, MA: Scherkman.

Zechenter, Elizabeth M. 1997. "In the Name of Culture: Cultural Relativism and the Abuse of the Individual." *Journal of Anthropological Research,* 53: 319–47.

Zeder, Melinda A. 1991. *Feeding Cities: Specialized Animal Economy in the Ancient Near East.* Washington, DC: Smithsonian Institution Press.

Zeder, Melinda A. 1994. "After the Revolution: Post-Neolithic Subsistence in Northern Mesopotamia." *American Anthropologist,* 96: 97–126.

Zeder, Melinda A. 1997. *The American Archaeologist: A Profile.* Walnut Creek, CA: AltaMira Press.

Zenner, Walter P., and George Gmelch. 2004. "Urbanism and Urbanization." In *Cross-Cultural Research for Social Science,* in C. R. Ember, M. Ember, and P. N. Peregrine, eds., *New Directions in Anthropology.* Upper Saddle River, NJ: Prentice Hall. CD-ROM.

Zihlman, Adrienne L. 1992. "The Emergence of Human Locomotion: The Evolutionary Background and Environmental Context." In T. Nishida et al., eds., *Topics in Primatology,* Vol. 1.

Zihlman, Adrienne L. 1997. "Women's Bodies, Women's Lives: An Evolutionary Perspective." In M.E. Morbeck, A. Galloway, and A. Zihlman, eds., *The Evolving Female: A Life-History Perspective.* Princeton, NJ: Princeton University Press, 185–97.

Zimmer, Carl. 1999. "Kenyan Skeleton Shakes Ape Family Tree." *Science,* 285 (August 27): 1335–37.

Zimmer, Carl. 2004. "Faster Than a Hyena? Running May Make Humans Special." *Science,* 306 (November 19): 1283.

Zohary, Daniel. 1969. "The Progenitors of Wheat and Barley in Relation to Domestication and Agriculture Dispersal in the Old World." In P. J. Ucko and G. W. Dimbleby, eds., *The Domestication and Exploitation of Plants and Animals.* Chicago: Aldine.

Photo Credits

Cover: Photo Researchers, Inc. © John Reader/Photo Researchers Inc.

Chapter 1. Page 2: Doranne Jacobson/International Images; page 6: Spooner/Redmond-Callow/Gamma Press USA, Inc.—Liaison; page 8: Mary G. Hodge; page 10: Terence Hays; page 12 (top): Robert Brenner/PhotoEdit; page 12 (bottom): © Mark Peterson/Corbis SABA.

Chapter 2. Page 16: Jonathan Blair/Corbis/Bettmann; page 18: Andy Crawford © Dorling Kindersley, Courtesy of the Royal Tyrrell Museum of Palaeontology, Alberta, Canada; page 19: Richard Vogel/AP Wide World Photos; page 21: © John Reader/Photo Researchers, Inc; page 22: Greenberg, Jeff/Omni-Photo Communications, Inc.; page 23: Asian Art & Archaeology, Inc./Corbis/Bettmann; page 24: Colin Keates © Dorling Kindersley, Courtesy of the Natural History Museum, London; page 26: George Gerster/Photo Researchers, Inc.

Chapter 3. Page 34: Tek Image/Photo Researchers, Inc.; page 40: Peter Arnold/Peter Arnold, Inc.; page 41: M.W. Tweedie/Photo Researchers, Inc.; page 41: Archiv/Photo Researchers, Inc.; page 42: © Clare A. Hasenkampf/Biological Photo Service; page 42: © Clare A. Hasenkampf/Biological Photo Service; page 50: Peter Oxford/Nature Picture Library; page 51: EyeWire Collection/Getty Images–Photodisc.

Chapter 4. Page 54: Karen Huntt Mason/Corbis/Bettmann; page 58: Martin Rogers/Woodfin Camp & Associates; page 59: Schafer, Kevin/Getty Images Inc.–Image Bank; page 60: © Clem Haagner, Gallo Images/CORBIS; page 60: Michael Dick/Animals Animals/Earth Scenes; page 62: Shane Moore/Animals Animals/Earth Scenes; page 62: Santokh Kocher/Getty Images, Inc.–Photodisc; page 62: Nature Picture Library; page 64: Anup Shah/Nature Picture Library; page 65: Peter Oxford/Nature Picture Library; page 66: © Kennan Ward/CORBIS; page 66: Karen Bass/Nature Picture Library; page 67: © Renee Lynn/CORBIS All Rights Reserved; page 68: Charles Krebs/Corbis/Bettmann; page 69: C. Bromhall/Animals Animals/Earth Scenes.

Chapter 5. Page 74: Christopher R. DeCorse; page 78: Dorothy Norton/Pearson Education/PH College; page 78: Corbis/Bettmann; page 81: Illustration Courtesy P. Wynne, Ian Tattersall & American Museum of Natural History; page 82: Harry Taylor © Dorling Kindersley, Courtesy of the Natural History Museum, London; page 83: Dorothy Norton/Pearson Education/PH College; page 85: ©2001 The Natural History Museum, London; page 85: E.R. Degginger/Photo Researchers, Inc.; page 86: Russell L. Ciochon, University of Iowa.

Chapter 6. Page 90: John Reader/Science Photo Library/Photo Researchers, Inc.; page 95: Patrick Robert/Corbis/Bettmann; page 97: Original housed in National Museum of Ethiopia, Addis Ababa. ©1999 David L. Brill Atlanta; page 98: John Reader/Science Photo Library/Photo Researchers, Inc.; page 98: Dr. Owen Lovejoy and students, Kent State University. © 1985 David L. Brill; page 99: © John Reader/Photo Researchers, Inc; page 99: © Christian Jegou/Photo Researchers, Inc; page 104: National Museum of Tanzania, Dar es Salaam/© 1985 David L. Brill.

Chapter 7. Page 106: Harry Taylor ©Dorling Kindersley, Courtesy of the Hunterian Museum (University of Glasgow); Page 109: George Gerster/Photo Researchers, Inc.; page 110: © Pictures of Record, Inc.; page 115: Original housed in National Museum of Kenya, Nairobi. ©1994 David L. Brill; page 119: Brill Atlanta; page 119: Dr. Peter Brown; page 120: Anup Shah/Nature Picture Library; page 122: © Christian Jegou/Photo Researchers, Inc.

Chapter 8. Page 126; Volker Steger/Nordstar/Photo Researchers, Inc.; page 129 (left): ©E.R. Degginger/Photo Researchers, Inc.; page 129 (right): © E. R. Degginger/Photo Researchers, Inc.; page 130: © Bettmann/Corbis; page 136: Dallas and John Heaton/The Stock Connection; page 137: © 2001 David L. Brill/Atlanta.

Chapter 9. Page 142: Corbis/Sygma; page 147: © Gianni Dagli Orti/Corbis; page 148: National Geographic Image Collection; page 150: © Archivo Iconografico, S.A./Corbis; page 151: ©Warren Morgan/Corbis; page 154: University of Colorado Museum, Joe Ben Wheat Photo; page 155: Michel Zabe ©CONACULTA-INAH-MEX. Authorized reproduction by the Instituto Nacional de Antropologia e Historia.

Chapter 10. Page 157: Pete Oxford/Nature Picture Library; page 158: Joe Raedie/Getty Images, Inc.; page 162: ©Kenneth Garrett. All Rights Reserved; page 163: Frank Kroenke/Das Fotoarchiv/ Peter Arnold, Inc.; page 165 (top): Peter Johnson/ Corbis/Bettmann; page 165 (bottom): The Art Archive / Egyptian Museum Turin / Dagli Orti ; page 170: Catalhoyuk Research Project; page 173 (top): Gavin Hellier/ Robert Harding World Imagery; page 173 (bottom): Mark Edwards/Still Pictures/ Peter Arnold, Inc.; page 176: "The Eloquent Bones of Abu Hureyras," Roberto Osti. Courtesy of Scientific American, Aug. 1994, p.73; page 178: Dagli Orti/ Picture Desk, Inc./Kobal Collection.

Chapter 11. Page 180: Dallas and John Heaton/The Stock Connection; page 183: Alan Hills © The British Museum; page 184 (bottom, left): © Gianni Dagli Orti/Corbis; page 184 (bottom, right): © Brian Brake/Photo Researchers, Inc.; page 185: Neil Beer/Getty Images, Inc.–Photodisc; page 188 (top): Randy Olson/NGS Image Collection; page 188 (bottom): ©The British Museum; page 189: Cahokia Mounds State Historic Site, painting by Michael Hampshire; page 191: Paul Harris/Getty Images Inc.-Stone Allstock; page 194: Wolfgang Kaehler/Corbis/Bettmann.

Chapter 12. Page 196: Photolibrary.Com; page 198: San Diego Museum of Man, photograph by (unknown); page 199: Tim Davis/Davis/Lynn Images; page 200: David Hiser/Getty Images Inc.–Stone Allstock; page 202: Glen Allison/Getty Images Inc.–Stone Allstock; page 203: Ken Huang/Getty Images Inc.–Image Bank; page 205: Reuters NewMedia Inc./Corbis/Bettmann; page 207: S.D. Halperin/Animals Animals/Earth Scenes; page 207: Irven DeVore/Anthro-Photo File; page 209: Geoff Dann ©Wallace Collection, London; page 212: Don Hamerman/Folio, Inc.

Chapter 13. Page 214: © Mark A. Johnson/Corbis, All Rights Reserved; page 217: © Cameron/Corbis—All Rights Reserved; page 218 (left): N. Martin Haudrich/Photo Researchers, Inc.; page 218 (right): James L. Stanfield/National Geographic Society; page 222 (left): © Ariel Skelley/Corbis—All Rights Reserved; page 222 (right): © Rolf Bruderer/Corbis—All Rights Reserved; page 224 (left): Jeremy Horner/Corbis; page 224 (right): Jonathan Blair/Corbis; page 227: © Christel Gerstenberg/Corbis—All Rights Reserved.

Chapter 14. Page 230: Spencer Grant/PhotoEdit Inc.; page 232: © Bettmann/Corbis—All Rights Reserved; page 233: ALBERT EINSTEIN and related rights TM/© of The Hebrew University of Jerusalem, used under license. Represented exclusively by Corbis Corporation; page 234: © Neil Rabinowitz/ Corbis—All Rights Reserved; page 238: Kal Muller/ Woodfin Camp & Associates; page 239: © Andrew Holbrooke/ Corbis—All Rights Reserved; page 240: © Caroline Penn /Corbis—All Rights Reserved.

Index

A

Abelam, and yams, 241
Aberle, David, 474
Abnormal behavior, 456
Absolute dating, 27, 29
Abuse, 550–51
Acceleration mass spectrometry (AMS), 27
Accent, 262
Accidental juxtaposition, 494
Acclimatization, and human variation, 198
Acculturation, 497–98
Aché, and food collection, 311
Acheulian tools, 24, 121, 122, 124
Achieved qualities, 404
Acquired reward value, 484
Actual cultural patterns, *versus* ideal, 222–23
Adams, David, 348
Adams, Robert, 188
Adapids, 77, 81–82
Adaptation
   and human variation, 195–96
   and religion, 472–74
Adaptive, culture as, 224–26, 240
Adaptive radiation, 97
Adaptive traits, 39
Adjudication, 433–36
Adolescents
   rebellion and neolocality, 384–85
   sexual freedom, Samoa, 256
Aegyptopithecus, 83
Affiliation
   ambilineal descent, 385–86
   double descent, 386
   double unilineal descent, 386
   matrilineal descent, 384–85
   patrilineal descent, 383
   unilocal descent, 383
Affinal kin, 397
Africa
   domestication in, 173
   preagriculture in, 163
   race in, 209
   skin color of population, 201
   Upper Paleolithic culture in, 150
African Americans
   cause of death of, 336
   health issues for, 535
   intelligence of, 210–12
   lactase deficiency in, 4, 207–8
   sickle-cell anemia in, 205–7
   slavery, 333

spread of popular music from, 487
   terrorism against, 556
Agassiz, Louis, 204
Age-grade, 406
Age-sets, 404–6
   Karimojong, 405, 423
   Shavante, 405–6
   systems, 423
Aggression, gender differences, 352
Agribusiness, 291
Agriculture
   commercialization of, 291
   definition of, 159
   industrial, introduction of, 503, 505
   mechanization of, 291
   and state formation, 191
   women in, 11, 291, 351
Ahern, Emily, 530
AIDS (acquired immune deficiency syndrome), 536–38, 545
Aid to Families with Dependent Children, 377
'Ain Ghazal, population growth, 169
Air pollution, 548
Akkadian empire, fall of, 192–93
Aleut, language family, 153
Algaze, Guillermo, 192, 193
Ali Kosh, domestication, 167–69
Alleles, 41, 42
Allen's rule, 199, 200
Allman, J., 80
Altitude
   adaptations to high, 202
   food collection and, 162
Altruism, 240
Alvarez, Louis, 39
Amazon, deforestation of, 319
Amazon Development Agency, 319
Ambilineal descent, 385–86
Ambilineal systems, 393
   explanation for, 396–97
Ambrona, Spain, tool and bone finds, 124
American Anthropological Association, 529
American Legion, 410
American Sign Language
   and chimpanzees, 70
   and primate learning, 264
Ancestor spirits, 465
Ancient Society, 232
Andeans, adaptation to high altitude, 202
Angiosperms, 78
Animals

communication, 262–64
   tending, 310
Animatism, 462
Animism, 462
Anomalies, 20
Anorexia nervosa, 538
Anthropoid evolution, 67, 82–83
   Aegyptopithecus, 83
   Catopithecus, 82
   Dryopithecus, 86–87
   Gigantopithecus, 86
   Kenyapithecus, 84
   Oligocene epoch, 82–83
   parapithecids, 82–83
   Pierolapithecus, 84–85
   Proconsul, 84
   propliopithecids, 83
   proto-apes, 84
   Sivapithecus, 85–86
Anthropoids, 58, 61–63
   catarrhines, 61
   New World monkeys, 61–62
   Old World monkeys, 62–63
   place of origin issue, 82–83
   platyrrhines, 61
Anthropological linguistics, scope of study, 6, 7
Anthropology
   applied, 9, 516–26
   biological, 5–6
   and business, 516–17
   cultural, 6–9
   defined, 3
   fields of, 4–9
   forensic, 516, 525–26
   holistic approach to, 4
   medical, 529–42
   practicing, 516–26
   rationale for study of, 4
   relevance of, 11–13
   scope of, 3–4
   specialized areas, 9–10
Anthropomorphization, of Gods, 462
Antoun, Richard, 506
Apache language, 153
Apes, evolution of, 84–87
Apidium, 82
Applied anthropology, 5, 9, 516–26
   collaborative, 524
   cultural resource management (CRM), 524–25
   ethics of, 519–20
   history and types of, 518–19